FEDERAL COURTS

FEDERAL COURTS

Second Edition

Larry W. Yackle
Professor of Law
Boston University

Carolina Academic Press
Durham, North Carolina

ISBN 0-89089-200-8
LCCN 2002116045

Carolina Academic Press
700 Kent Street
Durham, North Carolina 27701
Telephone (919) 489-7486
Fax (919) 493-5668
Email: cap@cap-press.com
www.cap-press.com

Printed in the United States of America

Dedication for the Second Edition

For Clark Byse

Dedication for the First Edition

For Jeanette

Contents

Foreword

I mean in this book to offer a concise introductory account of the constitutional, statutory, and judge-made law governing federal courts—the tribunals that exercise the judicial power of the United States. I will chiefly be concerned with the federal courts' authority to adjudicate questions of federal law, especially questions touching individual constitutional rights. I will guide readers along the path a litigant must follow, and over the hurdles a litigant must clear, to obtain a federal court decision on the merits of a federal claim. In that sense, I will investigate and explicate matters of genuine operational meaning in the world. Still, my goal is not to brief students and lawyers on the procedures that govern federal legal practice. I want to examine the federal courts as institutions, functioning alongside other centers of governmental power within an overarching constitutional framework.

I lean heavily and shamelessly on the prodigious research and insightful analysis that others have displayed in course materials prepared for law school classes. Inasmuch as those materials form the basis of university education regarding the federal courts, they have *become*, in effect, the corpus of this field. I mean this book to be a supplemental text that helps students work their way through the course books they are asked to master. Accordingly, I often track the subject headings, principal decisions, and commentaries that the authors of law school course books employ.[1]

I do not promise to answer all the questions that may arise. Neither my own discussion nor my references to the work of others can hope to be exhaustive or anything like it. I do believe, however, that what I have to say about the federal courts will be of help to readers who wish to consult a text that organizes and elucidates basic ideas. In aid of brevity and coherence, I will deliberately sacrifice some scope. I will give only piecemeal attention to the federal courts' jurisdiction in "diversity" cases to enforce state law claims in disputes between citizens of different states and very little attention to the

1. The first great course book, The Federal Courts and the Federal System, is about to appear in its fifth edition. Previous editors (Henry M. Hart, Jr., Herbert Wechsler, Paul J. Mishkin, and Paul M. Bator) set a standard of excellence that the current editors (Richard H. Fallon, Jr., Daniel J. Meltzer, and David L. Shapiro) have somehow managed to maintain. Other excellent course books also organize and analyze masses of materials: Federal Courts: Theory and Practice (Robert N. Clinton, Richard A. Matasar & Michael G. Collins eds.); Federal Jurisdiction: Policy and Practice (Howard P. Fink, Linda S. Mullenix, Thomas D. Rowe, Jr. & Mark V. Tushnet eds.); Federal Courts: Cases, Comments, and Questions (Martin H. Redish & Susanna Sherry eds.); Federal Courts and the Law of Federal-State Relations (Peter W. Low & John C. Jeffries, Jr. eds.); Federal Courts, Federalism and Separation of Powers: Cases and Materials (Donald L. Doernberg & C. Keith Wingate eds.); Federal Courts: Cases and Comments on Judicial Federalism and Judicial Power (Louise Weinberg ed.); and Federal Courts: Cases and Materials (Charles A. Wright & John B. Oakley eds.). Professor Baker has prepared an exhaustive collection of other books and articles. Thomas E. Baker, Federal Court Practice and Procedure: A Third Branch Bibliography, 30 Tex. Tech. L. Rev. 909 (1999).

rules under which cases are processed. I will address state courts only insofar as they relate to questions touching federal courts, and, I am sorry to say, I will neglect tribal courts entirely. I will tailor my account to the typical academic course on the subject, which shares little in common with civil procedure and often spills over into constitutional law and theory.

Federal courts are the product of history, politics, and shifting and developing theoretical understandings of law and legal institutions in the modern world. Small wonder they defy easy description and may at first appear curious, even incomprehensible. To understand them, it is essential to appreciate both their relationship to the legislative and executive branches of the national government and their intercourse with the states and state courts. Accordingly, I will devote substantial space to the authority that Congress enjoys to establish federal courts in the first instance and to prescribe their purview, to the authority that state courts retain to adjudicate federal questions, and to the structural arrangements the resulting allocation of power both reflects and fortifies. I will dedicate even more space to the role federal courts play in protecting individual federal rights against encroachments by the states. The operative constitutional themes are everywhere apparent: the separation of powers, federalism, individual liberty, and the unique form of democracy that has developed in this country.

My approach is descriptive, not prescriptive.[2] That will be apparent from the manner in which I try to weave materials together in pursuit of a coherent whole. I scarcely expect many readers to devour this book from start to finish. Some will take it a chapter at a time, perhaps with some backing and filling. Others will dip into it for guidance on particular points. Yet over the years, I have become convinced that these ideas can best be digested in the order I adopt here. I mean, then, to offer a linear treatment, which builds on itself as the manuscript progresses. The law in this field is not a seamless web. I will do my best to present an organized treatment without imposing discipline where the materials themselves resist.

Having stated my expository objectives, I hasten to say that the really important and interesting aspects of this subject invariably lurk beneath the surface. Decision-makers commonly wrestle with delicate questions of substance indirectly, by contesting what appears to be only the procedural question whether an issue is subject to judicial resolution and, if so, whether a federal court or some alternative tribunal (typically a state court) should bear the adjudicatory responsibility.

To put the point bluntly, the doctrines I will examine in this book are not always the value-neutral administrative devices they seem to be. They often reflect ideological perspectives on what the American governmental structure should be and how it should function. And in some instances at least, they are instruments for advancing or discouraging the claims in issue. When, for example, a citizen asks a federal court for help regarding a federal claim, the judge charged to say whether the court's doors are open

---

2. I collected my personal views on selected issues in Reclaiming the Federal Courts (1994). Readers should be aware that I served as counsel in two of the cases I discuss in this book: *Rodriguez v. Mitchell* and *Triestman v. United States*. In fourteen other cases, I filed *amicus curiae* briefs in the Supreme Court on behalf of the American Civil Liberties Union: *Bell v. Cone*, *Bousley v. United States*, *Brecht v. Abrahamson*, *Gilmore v. Taylor*, *Hohn v. United States*, *McFarland v. Scott*, *Miller v. Fenton*, *Murray v. Carrier*, *O'Neal v. McAninch*, *Sawyer v. Whitley*, *Stewart v. Martinez-Villareal*, *Michael Williams v. Taylor*, *Terry Williams v. Taylor*, and *Withrow v. Williams*. In *Wright v. West*, I filed an *amicus curiae* brief on behalf of an *ad hoc* group of law teachers. I consulted with the attorneys in many other cases.

cannot be (and in the real world is not) indifferent to the possibility that the answer may determine whether the claim is vindicated at all.

The law touching federal courts bears profound significance for the very nature and character of the American order of things. Certainly, this body of law adjusts the distribution of power within the national government and between the national government and the states. Behind those structural arrangements lie other delicate questions—about governmental incursions on individual liberty, governmental laxity in the enforcement of federal law, and private indifference to the public interest. I will not attempt to resolve the ideological controversies these materials evoke. Yet I will certainly identify and explore them. To do otherwise would be to miss half the picture (and nearly all the fun).

Acknowledgments

As I prepared the first edition, I received help, advice, and constructive criticism from Susan A. Bandes, Jack M. Beermann, Robert G. Bone, Clark Byse, Ronald A. Cass, Michael G. Collins, Donald L. Doernberg, Frederick M. Lawrence, Evan Tsen Lee, James S. Liebman, Daniel G. MacLeod, Daniel J. Meltzer, William E. Ryckman, Jr., Lawrence G. Sager, David J. Seipp, Aviam Soifer, Michael Wells, and Jeanette F. Yackle. I had excellent research assistance from Richard Bowman, Stuart S. Koonce, Melissa Mandroc, Joshua Perlman, and Alfred Saikali. I had equally fine administrative help from Sebastian Bach, Mark Barrasso, Sara Cunningham-Cooper, Charlotte Gliksman, Linda Skinner, Edith Solomon, and Elizabeth Teixeira. And I enjoyed extremely valuable library support from Marlene Alderman, Terri Geiger, Dan J. Freehling, Joshua Kantor, and Russell Sweet.

As I prepared the second edition, I received help from many of the same people and additional assistance from Sean Bennett, Karen M. Blum, John Blume, April Breck, Edwin Caldie, Holly Escott, Barry Friedman, Berit Huseby, William Kaleva, George Kendall, Allan Macurdy, Thomas D. Rowe, Jr., David L. Shapiro, Suzanna Sherry, Zachary Smith, Max D. Stern, Ronald Tabak, Kenneth Westhassel, and Keir Weyble.

FEDERAL COURTS

Chapter I

Methodology

The law governing federal courts is largely concerned with allocating power among the three branches of the national government and between the national government and the states. To understand the way in which allocations are made, it is essential to master the methodology the Supreme Court employs in resolving actual cases as they arise. Specifically, it is vital to develop a facility for using the sources the Court regards as authoritative and the policy arguments the Court finds persuasive.

A. Constitutional Interpretation

The Court invariably begins with the relevant constitutional provisions. Of course, the Constitution rarely commands any particular answer to a close question. The judicial article, Article III, is notoriously opaque. Justices who hope to read that Article according to its "original understanding" usually find the relevant historical materials obscure and scarcely dispositive. If they purport to derive constitutional meaning from those sources, they invite telling methodological criticism.[1] The fact of the matter is that the Court's constitutional decisions with respect to the purview of the federal courts depend in the main on the Court's best judgment in the circumstances and thus are neither more nor less manageable and predictable than its constitutional decisions in other contexts. The Court relies primarily on inferences it draws from the constitutional structure as a whole and on interpretive techniques the Court finds especially helpful. Two structural ideas predominate: the separation of powers and federalism. One interpretive technique is extremely common: the syllogism that the "greater" power ineluctably includes any "lesser" power subsumed within it.

1. Separation of Powers

The Constitution does not distribute authority and responsibility among the legislative, executive, and judicial branches of the national government in so many words.[2] Yet

---

1. See Chapter II, notes 11–53 and accompanying text (sketching the backdrop behind Article III); Chapter X, notes 193–95 and accompanying text (discussing criticisms of the Court's originalist methodology in sovereign immunity cases).

2. In response to Anti-Federalist demands that the Constitution should state the separation idea expressly, James Madison prepared an amendment that would have articulated the principle as tautology: "The powers delegated by the Constitution to the government of the United States shall be exercised as therein appropriated, so that the Legislative shall never exercise the powers vested in the Executive or Judicial; nor the Executive the powers vested in the Legislative or Judicial; nor the Judicial the powers vested in the Legislative or Executive." IV Documentary History of the First Federal

the theme of separation is everywhere apparent. The organizing articles differentiate both the three powers and the institutions in which those powers "shall be vested."[3] There is, then, a federal judicial power (of some character) that is distinguishable (in some fashion) from the legislative and executive powers. Courts established under Article III (not Congress or the President) are supposed to exercise that judicial power. And those courts are not supposed to be doing the jobs assigned to the other two branches. These premises in place, the interpretive difficulties are only beginning.

The existence of a power identified as judicial begs for some definition. That definition demands, in turn, some conceptual understanding of the way the three species of power fit together. History provides no answer. The rough idea of separation was popular in the founding period, but there was no genuine consensus on what it really meant to the public men who promoted it. They probably drew no clear distinction between distributing legislative, executive, and judicial power within the new national government and allocating any kind of authority among other groups—social and economic classes, for example.[4] Logic, too, is inadequate. It is unrealistic to think that each of the three national powers occupies its own distinctive turf and that any incursion is an offense to the separation principle. The separation of powers is tempered by "checks and balances," according to which each department routinely exercises significant authority with respect to affairs primarily assigned to the others.[5] If the judicial power had absolute boundary lines with the legislative and executive powers, those lines would have to be specified, so that decision-makers (namely, courts) might know a trespass when they see one. Any attempt to do that would be futile.

Justice Holmes once explained that a judicial proceeding "investigates, declares and enforces liabilities as they stand on present or past facts and under laws supposed already to exist." Legislative action, by contrast, "looks to the future and changes existing conditions by making a new rule to be applied thereafter to all or some part of those subject to its power."[6] The Court often relies on Holmes' explanation.[7] Yet it scarcely distinguishes judicial from legislative action in a definitive way. Consistent with Holmes, the judicial function embraces three tasks: (1) ascertaining the facts; (2) identifying the applicable legal standard; and (3) applying that standard to the facts. In the performance of those duties, courts necessarily "make law" for the future, if only by shaping preexisting legal standards to the needs of new cases and by contributing new prece-

---

Congress of the United States of America, 1789–1791, 45–48 (Bickford & Veit eds. 1986). That amendment was not adopted. See Chapter II, text accompanying note 35.

3. U.S. Const. art. I, §1 (stating that "[a]ll legislative Powers herein granted shall be vested in a Congress"); U.S. Const. art. II, §1 (stating that "[t]he executive Power shall be vested in a President"); U.S. Const. art. III, §1 (stating that "[t]he judicial Power of the United States, shall be vested in one supreme Court, and in such inferior Courts as the Congress may from time to time ordain and establish").

4. See generally Gerhard Casper, Separating Power: Essays on the Founding Period 7–22 (1997).

5. See Alan L. Feld, *Separation of Political Powers: Boundaries or Balance?*, 21 Ga. L. Rev. 171 (1986).

6. *Prentis v. Atlantic Coast Line Co.*, 211 U.S. 210, 226 (1908). In *Prentis*, the Virginia Supreme Court exercised final authority over railroad freight rates. Holmes explained that rate-making was a legislative function. Accordingly, if a railroad challenged rates established by the Virginia Supreme Court in a lawsuit filed in a federal trial-level court, the railroad would not be asking the inferior federal court to exercise appellate jurisdiction. See Chapter XI, notes 39–43 and accompanying text (providing a more complete discussion).

7. The need to distinguish (however roughly) between judicial and legislative action appears at numerous junctures in the law of federal courts. See, e.g., Chapter VI, notes 188–89, 205–08 and accompanying text (discussing the problem with respect to the *Rooker/Feldman* and preclusion doctrines).

dents to the body of legal materials that will form the baseline for later decisions.[8] Nor does Holmes' account distinguish cleanly between judicial and legislative action, on the one hand, and executive action, on the other. Executive officers routinely identify the law they are charged to enforce, ascertain the factual circumstances in which they must act, and apply the law they have identified to the facts before them. Thus the conventional, three-step understanding of the judicial function collapses into routine executive activity. In reality, our notions about what counts as adjudication (as opposed to legislation and execution) rest on experience and pragmatic judgment. They are not logically preordained.[9]

Even if an abstract definition of judicial power could be formulated, it would defy practical implementation. If we had a system in which the legislative, executive, and judicial powers were relentlessly isolated and we permitted none of the three to rub shoulders with the others, then we would have a recipe for "*impasse* reminiscent of the Nebraska statute which decreed that when two trains met at a crossing, neither could start until the other had moved on."[10] In fact, the three branches must cooperate in order to get anything accomplished. There are modern decisions in which the Supreme Court has attempted to define and enforce separate conceptual spheres for Congress and the President.[11] And some of the justices would plainly prefer an even more rule-oriented approach.[12] On the whole, though, the Court is more flexible. The idea of separated powers is not so much a hard "rule of decision"[13] as it is an extremely influential consideration in cases in which the Court must strike a sensible balance within the national government.

This certainly is true with respect to the Court's treatment of judicial power. The Court recognizes a significant role for Congress with respect to the judicial function. The cases permitting Congress to restrict the federal courts' jurisdiction illustrate the point,[14] as do less celebrated decisions allowing Congress to assign adjudicative functions to agencies other than Article III courts.[15] In other instances, the Court allows fed-

---

8. See notes 61–72 and accompanying text (describing the traditional private rights model of adjudication).

9. Paul M. Bator, *The Constitution as Architecture: Legislative and Administrative Courts Under Article III*, 65 Ind. L.J. 233, 264 (1990). See text accompanying notes 63–64 (explaining that this same three-step conception of adjudication also involves policy-making—a function typically regarded as legislative in character).

10. Edward S. Corwin, *Tenure of Office and the Removal Power Under the Constitution*, 27 Colum. L. Rev. 353, 385 (1927) (dismissing "the notion—or superstition—that the Constitution effects such a nice apportionment of the total field of governmental activity among the three departments").

11. E.g., *INS v. Chadha*, 462 U.S. 919 (1983) (invalidating a legislative encroachment on the executive branch); *Bowsher v. Synar*, 478 U.S. 714 (1986) (invalidating an executive encroachment on the legislative branch). Many of these decisions have been criticized for being overly formalistic and for claiming support in historical materials that is not there to be found. E.g., Jack M. Beermann, *"Bad" Judicial Activism and Liberal Federal-Courts Doctrine: A Comment on Professor Doernberg and Professor Redish*, 40 Case W. Res. L. Rev. 1053 (1990); Erwin Chemerinsky, *A Paradox Without A Principle: A Comment on the Burger Court's Jurisprudence in Separation of Powers Cases*, 60 So. Calif. L. Rev. 1083 (1987).

12. Justice Scalia in particular has rather firm views regarding the powers that each branch enjoys. E.g., *Morrison v. Olson*, 487 U.S. 654, 697 (1988) (dissenting opinion).

13. Philip B. Kurland, *The Rise and Fall of the "Doctrine" of Separation of Powers*, 85 Mich. L. Rev. 592, 603 (1986).

14. See Chapter IV, notes 10–25, 62–71 and accompanying text.

15. See Chapter V; Harold J. Krent, *Separating the Strands in Separation of Powers Controversies*, 74 Va. L. Rev. 1253 (1988); Peter L. Strauss, *Formal and Functional Approaches to Separation-of-Powers Questions—A Foolish Inconsistency?*, 72 Cornell L. Rev. 488 (1987).

eral courts to fashion common law, which provides rules of decision when Congress has enacted no controlling rules by statute. In those cases, the courts plainly perform a legislative function.[16] The decisions on litigant "standing" to appear in federal court explicitly rest on the separation theme. By restricting Article III courts to the adjudication of disputes that demand and justify judicial settlement, standing doctrine keeps those courts from establishing legal rules and principles in the abstract, thus interfering with the legislative function assigned to Congress. At the same time, Congress retains some authority to confer standing on litigants, thus permitting private citizens to invoke judicial power in circumstances in which the Court, acting alone, would turn them away.[17]

It is not enough simply to mouth the separation principle and insist that it *means* that an action by one of the branches has unconstitutionally trespassed on another's preserve. It is essential to dig beneath the rhetoric of separation and to ask precisely *how* the other branch is affected. That is the level at which an argument either has genuine substance or, instead, merely offers an apparently neutral excuse for siding with one party or claim over another. There is, of course, the danger that the effect of individual actions in isolation may seem negligible, but that over time one branch may achieve hegemony over another incrementally. But the possibility that any of the branches is suffering death by a thousand pin pricks is itself a factor to be considered.[18]

2. Federalism

The Constitution nowhere mentions federalism, but nonetheless clearly contemplates an important role for the states. The system thus demands some distribution of authority and responsibility between the central government and autonomous states. As a matter of fact, the lion's share of the law associated with federal courts is concerned with reconciling two parallel sets of courts, one federal and the other state, coexisting in a single political framework.[19]

Here, too, definitional problems abound, and abstract reasoning from formal conceptual premises produces irreconcilable conflict. The Supreme Court's allocations of authority between the federal and state courts may perhaps be explained by the general perspective on federal-state relations that the Court brings to bear. In some periods, and in some individual cases, the Court adopts a decidedly "nationalist" perspective and regards federal courts as the tribunals of choice. In other periods and cases, the Court is comparatively "federalist" in its approach and tends to prefer the state courts. It is hardly surprising, then, that the precedents appear to be inconsistent and federal courts doctrine unstable.[20]

---

16. See Chapter VIII, notes 47–119 and accompanying text.

17. See Chapter IX, notes 295–380 and accompanying text.

18. 18See Chapter V, notes 120–43 and accompanying text (noting the way the Court attempts to handle this problem when Congress confers judicial authority on "legislative" courts).

19. But see Edward L. Rubin & Malcolm Feeley, *Federalism: Some Notes on a National Neurosis*, 41 U.C.L.A. L. Rev. 903 (1994) (offering an engaging *refutation* of federalism as an important American theme).

20. This is Professor Fallon's assessment. He elaborates and defends it in Richard H. Fallon, Jr., *The Ideologies of Federal Courts Law*, 74 Va. L. Rev. 1141 (1988). Fallon's nomenclature can be confusing. The perspective he calls "federalist" does not necessarily correspond to the attitudes typically ascribed to Federalists in the early years of the Republic and may, in fact, more closely approach the views associated with the Anti-Federalists in that era. See Chapter II, note 30 and accompanying text. Fallon makes it clear that his "nationalist" and "federalist" models are "ideal types" that may be helpful in analyzing the Court's decisions, but do not track the precedents. As a matter of fact, nei-

Decisions that reflect a more nationalist perspective take the view that state prerogatives are, or should be, subordinate to the vindication of federal rights, especially individual constitutional rights against state power established by the fourteenth amendment. The working idea is that the national government bears primary responsibility for enforcing federal rights and that litigants' desire to be in federal court should be respected. By contrast, decisions that reflect a federalist perspective regard the states as the sovereign units of government at the system's core and the state courts as the presumptive tribunals for adjudication, *ceteris paribus*. Federalist decisions thus deny that federal courts have a special purchase on the vindication of federal rights and insist that there must be some particularized justification for allowing litigants to escape or bypass state courts. In close cases, the Supreme Court needs and employs a default position, which prevails in the absence of a good reason to choose an alternative state of affairs. The Court's currently ascendant (nationalist or federalist) perspective may account for the default position the Court selects.

Many of the Supreme Court's decisions regarding federalism do not appear to serve any functional purpose, but rather to demonstrate respect for the dignity of individual states within the constitutional structure.[21] Justice Thomas has explained those decisions as efforts to ensure that the states retain a status that enables them to monitor and check the federal government's exercise of power. In that way, state sovereignty ultimately safeguards individual liberty from untoward governmental action.[22] Not everyone is convinced.[23] The task, here again, is to cut through the rhetoric down to underly-

---

ther comes even close—which tends to prove, in Fallon's view, that the Court has lurched back and forth between extremes that resist reconciliation. Professor Redish thinks Fallon's two categories are insufficient and that as many as seven considerations together are needed to explain the Court's decisions: "cross-pollenization, systemic representativeness, litigant choice, litigation efficiency, fundamental fairness, institutionalism, and logical consistency." Martin H. Redish, *Reassessing the Allocation of Judicial Business Between State and Federal Courts: Federal Jurisdiction and "The Martian Chronicles,"* 78 Va. L. Rev. 1769, 1770–71 (1992). Professor Solimine and Professor Walker have organized academic approaches into five rough categories, distinguished by the way (and the extent to which) academicians consider and value the same or similar factors. See Michael E. Solimine & James L. Walker, Respecting State Courts: The Inevitably of Judicial Federalism (1999). Professor Wells argues that the Court's results, if not its stated explanations, probably turn on the justices' desire to channel litigation to the courts likely to reach judgments the justices themselves think are correct. In Wells' view, the Warren Court typically routed cases to federal courts in hopes those courts would favor civil rights and civil liberties claims, while the current Court more often sends cases to state courts in the expectation that those courts will side with the government in individual liberty cases. See, e.g., Michael Wells, *Naked Politics, Federal Courts Law, and the Canon of Acceptable Arguments*, 47 Emory L.J. 89 (1998); Michael Wells, *Rhetoric and Reality in the Law of Federal Courts: Professor Fallon's Faulty Premise*, 6 Const. Comm. 367 (1989).

21. See Chapter X, note 227 and accompanying text (discussing decisions regarding state sovereign immunity).

22. Clarence Thomas, *Why Federalism Matters*, 48 Drake L. Rev. 231, 235–36 (2000). Relatedly, the Court and some academics promote federalism as a device for maintaining the lines of accountability in a democracy. Congress can obscure those lines by commandeering the states to act as its agents and making it appear to the public that the states are responsible for policies that Congress, in fact, has established. See Chapter VI, notes 84–92 and accompanying text; Chapter X, notes 170–74 and accompanying text; see generally Vicki C. Jackson, *Federalism and the Uses and Limits of Law: Printz and Principle?*, 111 Harv. L. Rev. 2181 (1998) (collecting authorities).

23. See, e.g., Susan Bandes, *Erie and the History of One True Federalism*, 110 Yale L.J. 829, 871 (2001) (contending that recent federalism decisions in the Supreme Court "overstate the determinacy" of federalism as a basis of decision and fail to explain the "choices" the Court inevitably makes about the proper balance between federal and state authority); Frank B. Cross, *Realism About Federalism*, 74 N.Y.U. L. Rev. 1305, 1306 (1999) (arguing that federalism has no principled content and

ing values. To argue for federalism is not invariably to insist on a generalized devolution of power to the states. In any particular instance, judicial business should be placed in one system or the other according to a careful appraisal of the interests conventionally associated with federalism in this context—namely, the extent to which state court adjudication promotes diversity, self-determination, efficiency, and, to be sure, civil liberties.[24] The Court wrestles with federalism in a host of circumstances, but particularly in cases involving the federal courts' authority (and obligation) to abstain from exercising jurisdiction in deference to state court litigation.[25]

3. The "Greater Power" Syllogism

In coming to terms with constitutional questions touching federal courts, the Court routinely employs a range of familiar interpretive techniques. For example, the Court commonly invokes the prudential considerations that Justice Brandeis identified in the *Ashwander* case: Upon the whole, the Court hesitates to address a constitutional question unless and until it appears necessary to do so. To that end, the Court will prefer a non-constitutional ground of decision when it is available, it will construe statutes in a way that avoids constitutional questions, and, when it does decide a constitutional issue, it will not formulate a rule of decision that is broader than needed to dispose of the matter immediately at hand.[26]

One other device in particular is ubiquitous in the law of federal courts: the proposition that if a unit of government (typically Congress) enjoys a "greater" (encompassing) power to take or forbear some significant action, it follows as a logical imperative that it also enjoys a "lesser" (subset) power to take or forbear some less sweeping action. The "greater power" syllogism is appealing inasmuch as it promises an irrefutable, deductive answer to a legal problem and thus makes it unnecessary to offer additional persuasive reasoning. Despite its allure, however, the syllogism almost always constitutes a mistake in legal analysis.

In some contexts, the "greater power" proposition is perfectly logical. If the Mighty Casey has the physical strength to smack a baseball over the left field wall at Fenway Park, it follows that he also has the physical strength to slap a ball onto the grass in front of the wall. Legal power is not physical strength. In federal courts cases, "greater power" argu-

---

that courts invoke it only when it serves their "ideological agendas"); Sylvia A. Law, *In the Name of Federalism: The Supreme Court's Assault on Democracy and Civil Rights*, 70 U. Cin. L. Rev. 367, 372 (2002) (contending that the Supreme Court's current federalism cases reflect the "aggrandizement of the power of the federal judiciary" and the "evisceration of the civil rights of workers, women, people with disabilities, and others").

24. See generally Ann Althouse, *Variations on a Theory of Normative Federalism: A Supreme Court Dialogue*, 42 Duke L.J. 979 (1993); Deborah Jones Merritt, *The Guarantee Clause and State Autonomy: Federalism for a Third Century*, 88 Colum. L. Rev. 1, 3–10 (1988); Michael W. McConnell, *Federalism: Evaluating the Founders' Design*, 54 U. Chi. L. Rev. 1484, 1491–1511 (1987). See generally Robert F. Nagel, The Implosion of American Federalism (2001); David L. Shapiro, Federalism: A Dialogue (1995); Barry Friedman, *Valuing Federalism*, 82 Minn. L. Rev. 317 (1997).

25. See Chapter XI. Professor Wells proposes that in the interests of candor and clear thinking, the Court should entertain express arguments that sending a case to federal or state court is likely to affect the result that will be reached. Wells, *Naked Politics*, note 20, at 92.

26. *Ashwander v. TVA*, 297 U.S. 288, 346 (1936) (concurring opinion). See Lisa A. Kloppenberg, *Avoiding Constitutional Questions*, 35 B.C. L. Rev. 1003 (1994). These are not rigid rules, of course, but persuasive considerations that are given significant weight, if sometimes in the breach.

ments often rest on an invalid premise. Typically, the power said to be the "greater" does exist, but the power said to be the "lesser" is not (as a logical matter) a subset power at all. Instead, it is a different (though related) power. Illustrations are obvious: If Congress forbids interstate shipments of widgets in trucks operated by female drivers, it is no answer that Congress might have barred shipments of widgets altogether. The power to prohibit all widget shipments is easy enough to establish, but the power to forbid only some shipments (identified by a gender discriminatory rule) is another thing entirely.[27]

This is not to suggest that the "greater power" syllogism routinely raises constitutional difficulties. It does not. The point is only that the existence of one power (however capacious) typically does *not* establish the existence of another power (however the two powers may appear to be related). The second power may well exist, but it *does* require additional justification. The Supreme Court often relies on the "greater power" syllogism to reach perfectly sound results despite its flawed reasoning. The classic illustrations are the Court's decisions on the power of Congress to prescribe the jurisdiction of inferior federal courts.[28]

B. Statutory Construction

Statutes are typically more definitive than the Constitution. Yet the enactments in this field are often vague and ambiguous. They, too, require exegesis. In some important instances, the Supreme Court self-consciously takes it upon itself to elaborate statutes according to its own sense of proper policy. The best illustrations are the Court's decisions regarding 28 U.S.C. §1331 (the basic statute conferring jurisdiction on federal district courts to entertain federal question cases) and the decisions regarding 42 U.S.C. §1983 (the general statute authorizing private litigants to sue state officials for violations of federal rights).[29] In other instances, the Court invokes the usual canons of statutory construction, coupled with two techniques: (1) special attention to the text of enacted statutes; and (2) the doctrine of "clear statement."

1. Textualism

Traditional statutory construction draws on numerous sources. In recent years, however, and particularly in cases in this field, the Supreme Court has focused primarily

---

27. See Chapter IV, note 131 and accompanying text (discussing "external" restraints on congressional authority).

28. See Chapter IV, notes 67–71 and accompanying text. There are many other illustrations. See, e.g., Chapter V, text accompanying note 9 (describing this kind of argument with respect to Congress' power to create "legislative" courts); Chapter VI, text accompanying notes 140–43 (describing a similar argument on behalf of Congress' power to confer "protective" jurisdiction on federal courts). For a discussion of the "greater power" proposition in constitutional law generally, see Michael Herz, *Justice Byron White and the Argument That the Greater Includes the Lesser*, 1994 B.Y.U. L. Rev. 227.

29. See Chapter VIII, text accompanying notes 234–37 (§1331); Chapter VIII, text accompanying notes 132–36 (§1983). See also Chapter XII (describing the Court's interpretations of the habeas corpus statutes).

(though not exclusively) on the text of the statutes that Congress actually places in the United States Code.[30] Occasionally, the Court expresses its emphasis on a statute's text in the familiar language of the "plain meaning" rule: "[W]here language is plain and admits of no more than one meaning, the duty of interpretation does not arise."[31] That is misleading. Individual statutory terms and provisions *have* no meaning in isolation.[32] The Court's textualism is more sophisticated. It begins with particular terms and their accepted dictionary definitions, but also takes account of the context in which terms appear in a statute, as well as the statute's fit with other related statutes and judicially fashioned doctrines.[33] Nevertheless, the Court sometimes portrays its focus on the letter of enacted statutes as a fairly extreme kind of legal formalism.[34]

One practical implication of textualism is that the Court attaches little or no value to "legislative history" (background materials like committee reports and floor speeches) that might illuminate a statute's meaning. Even when the Court insists it is interested in Congress' "intentions," the Court regards the language actually used in a statute as the best evidence of those intentions.[35] Better said, the Court looks not for the intentions of

---

30. For discussions of the relationship between literary theory and the interpretive function in law, see Richard A. Posner, Law and Literature: A Misunderstood Relation (1988); Robert M. Cover, *Foreword: Nomos and Narrative*, 97 Harv. L. Rev. 4 (1983); *Symposium, Interpretation*, 58 So. Calif. L. Rev. 1 (1985).

31. *Caminetti v. United States*, 242 U.S. 470, 485 (1917).

32. Cass R. Sunstein, The Partial Constitution 8 (1993) (explaining that there is no such thing as "preinterpretive meaning"); Frank H. Easterbrook, *Statutes' Domains*, 50 U. Chi. L. Rev. 533, 536 (1983) (crediting Wittgenstein with the insight that isolated words do not have "intrinsic meanings"). Professor Schauer does not disagree, but contends that people who share a common language can communicate with one another in an ordinary vocabulary, which can be the starting point for further interpretive work. Frederick Schauer, *Statutory Construction and the Coordinating Function of Plain Meaning*, 1990 Sup. Ct. Rev. 231.

33. E.g., *Textron Lycoming Reciprocating Engine Div. v. UAW*, 523 U.S. 653, 656–58 (1998) (moving quickly from dictionary definitions to context); *King v. St. Vincent's Hosp.*, 502 U.S. 215, 221 (1991) (explaining that the meaning of statutory language "plain or not" depends on the context in which the language is used); *United States Savings Ass'n v. Timbers of Inwood Forest Ass'n*, 484 U.S. 365, 371 (1988) (explaining that a statutory provision "that may seem ambiguous in isolation is often clarified by the remainder of the statutory scheme"); *West Va. Univ. Hosp. v. Casey*, 499 U.S. 83, 100–01 (1991) (explaining that the Court will construe ambiguous statutory terms "to contain that permissible meaning which fits most logically and comfortably into the body of both previously and subsequently enacted law... [in order to] make sense rather than nonsense out of the *corpus juris*"). See generally *Symposium: Textualism and the Constitution*, 66 Geo. Wash. L. Rev. 1081 (1998); George H. Taylor, *Structural Textualism*, 75 B.U. L. Rev. 321 (1995). Professor Schacter reports a decline in citations to the dictionary. Jane S. Schacter, *The Confounding Common Law Originalism in Recent Supreme Court Statutory Interpretation: Implications for the Legislative History Debate and Beyond*, 51 Stan. L. Rev. 1, 5 (1998).

34. E.g., *Great-West Life & Annuity Ins. v. Knudson*, 534 U.S. 204 (2002) (explaining that it is not the Court's "job" to "find reasons for what Congress has plainly done" and that it "*is*" the Court's job to "avoid rendering what Congress has plainly done... devoid of reason and effect") (emphasis in original).

35. See generally William N. Eskridge, Jr., *The New Textualism*, 37 U.C.L.A. L. Rev. 621 (1990). Justice Scalia, the Court's chief exponent of textualism, would discard all talk of legislative "intent" and focus, instead, on legislative "meaning." Antonin Scalia, *Common-Law Courts in a Civil-Law System: The Role of United States Federal Courts in Interpreting the Constitution and Laws* 22–23, in A Matter of Interpretation (Gutmann ed. 1997). Justice Scalia quotes Holmes approvingly: "We do not inquire what the legislature *meant*; we ask only what the statute *means*." Oliver Wendell Holmes, Collected Legal Papers 207 (1920) (emphasis added). According to Justice Scalia, if a court attempts to discover what the legislature "*meant*" (rather than what it said), the court is likely to end up with what a "wise and intelligent" person "*should* have meant," which will turn out to be what the court itself thinks is a good idea. Scalia, at 18. Other justices continue to refer to legislative "intent," even

the people who drafted or voted for a bill, but for the intentions of the enacted statute itself. Legislators who propose or oppose public policies typically come to naught if they merely record their views in reports and speeches, but lack the political muscle it takes to put hard language in the text of an enacted statute.[36] What matters is the point of the text, derived from the text.[37]

By some accounts, the Court's textualism reflects democratic values. Congress is empowered to make public policy jointly with the President. Proponents of a bill must marshal majority votes in both the House and the Senate, present their product to the President, and achieve at least his acquiescence.[38] In a formal sense, only a statute enacted in that way qualifies as law. Background materials have no such status. They have not survived the crucible of the actual law-making process, but may, instead, be manipulated by individual members of Congress and their staffs,[39] as well as courts seeking

---

as they increasingly rely primarily on statutory text. E.g., *Thompson v. Thompson*, 484 U.S. 174, 179 (1988) (professing to be investigating legislative "intent" but explicitly declining to ask what members of Congress "actually had in mind"). For evidence of the divisions on the Court regarding the uses of legislative history (especially floor speeches), compare the views expressed by Justice Thomas and Justice Stevens in *Barnhart v. Sigmon Coal Co.*, 534 U.S. 438 (2002).

36. See *Morse v. Republican Party*, 517 U.S. 186, 276 n.18 (1996) (Thomas, J., dissenting) (explaining that there are "myriad reasons" why a majority of the members of Congress might have "wanted" to enact a bill that never became law but that the Court "must look to the extant text of the statute and see what Congress has in fact...enacted"). Justice Breyer insists that courts should not abandon legislative history entirely. Stephen Breyer, *On the Uses of Legislative History in Interpreting Statutes*, 65 So. Calif. L. Rev. 845 (1992). By one account, both justices who examine legislative history and those who ignore it actually share a single interpretive methodology, which regards courts as "agents" of the legislature, obliged to be guided *by* the legislature in some way or other. The Federal Courts and the Federal System 758 (Fallon, Meltzer & Shapiro eds. 1996). This "agency theory" of statutory interpretation probably does not help to analyze the differences between the justices over the value of legislative history. Yet it may help to distinguish the text-based interpretive methodology most of the justices employ from other approaches suggested in the academic literature—approaches that deny that courts are agents of the enacting legislature and argue for a more "dynamic" and "creative" role for the judiciary in the elaboration of policy. Id. at 760–61. See note 42. Professor Schacter reports that Justice Scalia has not won the day. By her account, the Court often relies both on legislative history and on judicially crafted canons and policy considerations—not just the text. So the Court takes into account the policy implications of its interpretations and does not simply and reflexively give statutes a literalist construction without concern for the consequences. See Schacter note 33.

37. See Taylor, note 33, at 338. The extent to which this kind of textualism departs significantly from classic accounts of statutory interpretation can be debated. When Justices Jackson and Frankfurter called on courts to identify a statute's "purpose," they contemplated that the text of the statute under review would provide the guide (as opposed to background materials). E.g., *D'Oench, Duhme & Co. v. FDIC*, 315 U.S. 447, 465 (1942) (Jackson, J., concurring); Felix Frankfurter, *Some Reflections on the Reading of Statutes*, 47 Colum. L. Rev. 527, 538 (1947). The Legal Process school, too, eschewed any search for the subjective desires of a statute's authors and also regarded courts' function as identifying a more objective "purpose" for a statute. Henry M. Hart, Jr. & Albert M. Sacks, The Legal Process: Basic Problems in the Making and Application of Law 1378 (Eskridge & Frickey eds. 1994).

38. *Landgraf v. USI Film Products*, 511 U.S. 244, 263 (1994).

39. Professor Manning contends that the Court's textualism is best understood as a refusal to permit Congress essentially to delegate legislative power to the professional staff who prepare background materials. John F. Manning, *Textualism as a Non-delegation Doctrine*, 97 Colum. L. Rev. 673 (1997). See also John F. Manning, *Textualism and the Equity of the Statute*, 101 Colum. L. Rev. 1 (2001) (elaborating the argument that strict textualism is a feature of the separation of powers). Cf. Victoria F. Nourse & Jane S. Schacter, *The Politics of Legislative Drafting: A Congressional Case Study*, 77 N.Y.U. L. Rev. 575 (2002) (offering empirical evidence regarding the work of staff lawyers serving the Senate Judiciary Committee).

some basis for setting aside the text actually enacted.[40] Strict textualism can thus be defended for respecting only the formal law that Congress and the President forge in the constitutionally prescribed manner.[41]

By other accounts, the Court's exclusive focus on the literal text of statutes is an undemocratic manner in which to proceed. The Court facetiously assumes an omniscient legislature whose every utterance constitutes a rigorous linguistic specification of a policy best known by (and left to) Congress itself. Often, however, Congress may simply have used inartful language in an effort to advance objectives that would be easy enough to identify if the Court were to make the effort. The Court thus plays the "gotcha" game with Congress—insisting that it is willing to vindicate whatever policies Congress chooses to adopt, but actually frustrating those very policies by reading the syntax of enacted statutes to do something else. By deliberately blinding itself to any evidence or considerations not captured in the text, the Court assumes for itself the task of fastening meaning on the text. The meaning the Court chooses is likely to reflect what the justices themselves believe to be good policy.[42]

---

40. Committee reports and floor speeches can be voluminous and internally inconsistent, tempting courts to select what they like and leave the rest. Judge Harold Leventhal once described the use of legislative history as "the equivalent of entering a crowded cocktail party and looking over the heads of the guests for one's friends." See *Conroy v. Aniskoff*, 507 U.S. 511, 519 (1993) (Scalia, J., concurring).

41. Scalia, note 35, at 22 (explaining that "[t]he text is the law...and it is the text that must be observed"). See *Musick, Peeler & Garrett v. Employ. Ins.*, 508 U.S. 286, 305–06 (1993) (Thomas, J., dissenting) (insisting that "[c]ourts should not treat legislative...silence as a tacit license to accomplish what Congress...[is] unable or unwilling to do"). In some instances, the Supreme Court acknowledges that statutory construction must take account of the complex way in which public policy is fashioned by and through administrative agencies. In *Chevron v. Natural Resources Defense Council*, 467 U.S. 837 (1984), the Court held that courts should ordinarily accept "reasonable" agency interpretations of the statutes the agencies are charged to implement—on the theory that Congress has delegated legislative authority to the agencies concerned. Thomas W. Merrill & Kristin E. Hickman, *Chevron's Domain*, 89 Gtn. L.J. 833 (2001); Henry P. Monaghan, *Marbury and the Administrative State*, 83 Colum. L. Rev. 1, 27–28 (1983). Courts can avoid *Chevron* by finding statutes to be clear. See, e.g., *Ragsdale v. Wolverine World Wide*, 122 S.Ct. 1155 (2002). Cf. Antonin Scalia, *Judicial Deference to Administrative Interpretations of Law*, 1989 Duke L.J. 511, 521 (explaining that judges who rely on the "plain meaning rule" are less constrained by *Chevron* than are judges who typically find statutes less clear). Professor Pierce argues that the Court often undermines *Chevron* by concluding that a statute's meaning is plain from its text and, accordingly, that an administrative agency's interpretation is entitled to no special consideration. See Richard J. Pierce, Jr., *The Supreme Court's New Hypertextualism: An Invitation to Cacophony and Incoherence in the Administrative State*, 95 Colum. L. Rev. 749 (1995).

42. See *Circuit City Stores v. Adams*, 532 U.S. 105, 133 (2001) (Stevens, J., dissenting) (ascribing this general point to Justice Aharon Barak of the Supreme Court of Israel). See also Peter L. Strauss, *The Common Law and Statutes*, 70 U. Colo. L.Rev. 225 (1999). Commentators offer a variety of answers to the resulting dilemma. Professor Eskridge proposes that courts should decide close cases by reading statutes to comport with courts' best understanding of the public good. William N. Eskridge, Jr., Dynamic Statutory Interpretation (1994); William N. Eskridge, Jr., *Public Values in Statutory Interpretation*, 137 U. Pa. L. Rev. 1007 (1989). Professor Sunstein argues that courts should construe statutes in a way that reflects the needs and requirements of the modern administrative state. Cass R. Sunstein, *Interpreting Statutes in the Regulatory State*, 103 Harv. L. Rev. 405 (1989). Public choice adherents debate the way in which courts should contend with statutes that, in their view, merely reflect the bargained-for results of legislative deals. Compare Posner, note 30, at 245 (arguing that courts should explore the intentions of "those who wrote the provision that is being interpreted"), with Easterbrook, note 32, at 539 (insisting that only the text of a statute should ordinarily be consulted). See William N. Eskridge, Jr. & Philip P. Frickey, *Legislative Intent and Public Choice*, 74 Va. L. Rev. 423 (1988). Cf. Nicholas Q. Rosenkranz, *Federal Rules of Statutory*

Textualism as a statutory construction methodology does not, in itself, entail any particular allocation of power among the three departments of the national government or between the central government and the states. The results the Court reaches depend on the values and policies that textualism allows the Court to introduce when statutes are susceptible to more than one interpretation. The Court does not always specify what those extra-text considerations may be, but buries them beneath intricate arguments about what the text alone truly means. This is the pattern, for example, in cases in which the justices debate the meaning to be assigned to the statutes governing federal habeas corpus.[43]

2. The Doctrine of Clear Statement

In many cases touching federal courts, the Supreme Court resolves statutory construction questions by insisting that a statute must spell out a policy in particularly clear language, else the Court will assign it a different (specified) meaning.[44] On occasion, the Court explains that a clear statement requirement is constitutionally compelled.[45] More often, the Court demands unambiguous language when Congress operates near the perimeter of its constitutional power.[46] In many instances, the Court requires explicit statutory text simply as a matter of policy.[47] The idea of demanding a clear statement from Congress in some circumstances is attractive. Precise language demonstrates awareness, confidence, and resolve. So when the Court demands clarity from a statute and finds it, the Court has every justification for accepting the policy that Congress has so plainly demonstrated it wants to promote. In practice, however, the Court typically finds statutes insufficiently clear. When that happens, the Court itself takes responsibility for making policy choices.

This is the way it works: The doctrine of clear statement is distinct from textualism in two respects. First, where a clear statement is required, the Court not only insists that the text of a statute alone is the source of its meaning, but also demands that the text must speak in especially exacting terms. Second, where a clear statement is necessary, the Court selects a default position: the construction the Court will place on a statute in the absence of clarity. If, for example, the Court announces that federal courts can entertain a class of cases if Congress is clear (but only if Congress is clear), it follows that if Congress is not clear (enough), state courts will handle those cases. The choice of a default position is not self-evident, and it is not value-neutral. When the Court makes such a choice, it selects the allocation of judicial power it thinks best. If, then, the Court demands a clear statement from Congress before permitting federal courts to handle

---

Interpretation, 115 Harv. L. Rev. 2085 (2002) (arguing that Congress can affect the judiciary's interpretative function by enacting statutes mandating rules of construction for courts to follow).

43. See Chapter XII, text accompanying notes 178, 188, 533; Chapter VIII, note 118.

44. The doctrine of clear statement is not reserved for legislation affecting federal courts. Yet it is deployed routinely in this field, typically to divert judicial business *away* from federal courts. William N. Eskridge, Jr. & Philip P. Frickey, *Quasi-Constitutional Law: Clear Statement Rules as Constitutional Lawmaking*, 45 Vand. L. Rev. 593 (1992).

45. E.g., Chapter X, notes 233–35 and accompanying text (discussing the clear statement requirement for federal legislation overriding state sovereign immunity).

46. E.g., Chapter IV, notes 114–17 and accompanying text (discussing the clear statement requirement for statutes that preclude all judicial consideration of federal claims).

47. E.g., Chapter IV, notes 26–48, 72–76 and accompanying text (discussing the clear statement requirement for legislation that arguably repeals federal jurisdiction previously granted).

lawsuits, it is because the Court has decided, as an antecedent matter, that those suits should not be heard in federal court. Otherwise, the Court would have chosen the opposite baseline and allowed the federal courts to proceed in the absence of a clear statute stating that they cannot.[48]

In practice, the default position the Court chooses is likely to prevail, because Congress is so rarely perfectly clear. The legislative process runs on compromise. When a power-allocation question excites controversy, Congress typically submerges disagreement in statutory language that is deliberately inexact. If, then, the Court wants to achieve a particular distribution of power, the Court need only invoke a clear statement rule, which establishes the state of affairs the Court prefers as the default position and challenges anyone who disagrees to get Congress clearly to insist on a different policy—the very thing Congress is unlikely to do.[49]

The Court employs the doctrine of clear statement in a variety of contexts. The Court insists, for example, that if Congress wishes to give federal courts exclusive jurisdiction over a class of cases, carving state courts out of the picture entirely, only a clear statement will do.[50] The default position in that context, accordingly, is that state courts enjoy concurrent jurisdiction. That is the state of affairs the Court thinks is preferable, and in most quarters the Court's attitude is non-controversial.[51] In other circumstances, however, the Court insists on express language in federal statutes when the consequences are politically explosive. In some cases in which plaintiffs hope to enforce federal statutes by means of private suits under the authority of the Ku Klux Klan Act, for example, the Court demands clear statutory text establishing the statutory rights to be vindicated.[52] The clear statement doctrine in that context determines whether private litigants are able to implement federal civil rights statutes.

C. Conceptual Perspectives

Usually, the Supreme Court finds itself unable to anchor decisions in preexisting authority alone and therefore must exercise even more judgment. The literature in point suggests several models that help to explain both the way in which the Court sets about its task and its results.

---

48. Justice Scalia acknowledges that a clear statement requirement "load[s] the dice" and thus requires independent justification. Scalia, note 35, at 28–29.

49. Professor Shapiro regards this effect as typically conservative inasmuch as it makes "radical change less likely by raising interpretive barriers to such a change." David L. Shapiro, *Continuity and Change in Statutory Interpretation*, 67 N.Y.U. L. Rev. 921, 941 (1992). Professor Bandes argues that the Court's insistence on clear legislative language "ratifies the choices of the powerful and relegates the powerless to explicit legislative remedies they are unlikely to secure." Susan Bandes, *Reinventing Bivens: The Self-Executing Constitution*, 68 So. Calif. L. Rev. 289, 314 (1995).

50. See Chapter VI, notes 34–38 and accompanying text.

51. See also Chapter VI, text accompanying note 1 (explaining the significance of state court availability).

52. See Chapter VIII, notes 176–87 and accompanying text.

1. The Hart and Wechsler Paradigm

A particular set of underlying assumptions supplies the paradigm within which thinking about federal courts occurs and on which, in many instances, Supreme Court analysis proceeds.[53] Those assumptions are ascribable to Professor Henry Hart and Professor Herbert Wechsler, who built them into the original edition of their great course book.[54] In a real sense, Hart and Wechsler *defined* the federal courts field by focusing their work (and the work of everyone else to follow) on allocations of power within the federal system and, concomitantly, by contending that power distributions are defensible only if they conform to presuppositions that Hart and Wechsler themselves viewed as proper.[55] In the main, Hart and Wechsler argued that power should *not* be allocated with a self-conscious purpose to ensure that federal claims receive a generous interpretation. Instead, power should be distributed (both among the branches of the national government and between the national government and the states) according to policies that are neutral with respect to the issues to be decided and the results to be reached. The law should assign a matter to the branch of government, or the body of courts, that is institutionally most competent to address it.[56]

In the Hart and Wechsler view, legislatures are chiefly competent to make substantive value choices, while courts are competent to resolve disputes. Accordingly, the law should leave it to Congress to define national public policies and should prevent the federal courts from adjusting those policies by means of creative interpretation. Equally, the law should ensure that federal courts can adjudicate disputes independently and should prevent Congress from interfering with the courts' adjudicative function. The law should also assign judicial business to federal or state courts in light of neutral administrative policies: the extent to which one set of courts or the other can offer special expertise regarding the questions presented, protect individual and societal interests in finality and repose, operate with a minimum of friction, ensure the uniformity of federal law, and dispose of a legal dispute more efficiently. Typically, by this account, state courts offer an adequate opportunity for "full and fair" adjudication, even in cases implicating questions of federal law.[57]

---

53. Professor Fallon initially offered this characterization. Richard H. Fallon, Jr., *Reflections on the Hart and Wechsler Paradigm*, 47 Vand. L. Rev. 953 (1994).

54. The Federal Courts and the Federal System (Hart & Wechsler eds. 1953).

55. Fallon, note 53, at 961–63.

56. Hart and Wechsler's commitment to neutrality was not complete, but it was certainly characteristic of their work. Their particular aim to achieve a body of consistent, neutral policies to control adjudication was a product of the Legal Process movement in the 1940s and 1950s, to which both Hart and Wechsler contributed. For an account of the jurisprudential background, see William N. Eskridge, Jr. & Gary Peller, *The New Public Law Movement: Moderation as a Postmodern Cultural Form*, 89 Mich. L. Rev. 707 (1991). Professor Fallon argues that Hart and Wechsler did not celebrate neutrality to a fault, but offered an approach whose very strength lay in its sensitivity to the interactions between substantive and procedural values. Richard H. Fallon, Jr., *Comparing Federal Courts "Paradigms,"* 12 Const. Comm. 3, 6 (1995). Professor Pfander contends that Hart and Wechsler individually took different routes to roughly the same ends. Hart typically concentrated on explaining and reconciling judicial precedents on the basis of overarching principles, while Wechsler often focused more closely on history and on relevant textual materials, especially the text of the Constitution. James E. Pfander, *Fifty Years (More or Less) of "Federal Courts": An Anniversary Review*, 77 Notre Dame L. Rev. 1083 (2002).

57. See also text accompanying note 73 (discussing this proposition as the key feature of the process model).

According to the Hart and Wechsler paradigm, the law of federal courts is and should be indifferent to the result that a court reaches in a case. Once the proper court has been given authority to adjudicate a matter, that court's judgment on the merits is entitled to be accepted. This is so not because that outcome *is* right in an absolute sense, but rather because a result that has been generated by a court with properly assigned authority to make a decision should be *taken* as right—for the necessary and sufficient reason that we have no better measure of the way things *should* turn out.[58] Importantly, according to the paradigm, there is no reason to think that the judgment a federal court reaches on an issue, even an issue of federal law, is any better than the judgment a state court produces. Both are subject to appellate review. But until an appellate court finds a decision to be erroneous, it should be respected.

According to the paradigm, the Constitution itself recognizes the primacy of state law. The states preexisted the Constitution and the new central government it created. They were previously entitled to fashion public policy on the basis of their police power, and they retain that general law-making power today. State law, in turn, forms the general background web of standards to which society looks, as an initial matter, to test the legal effects of human behavior. Federal law, on the other hand, is by nature "interstitial," consisting of fragments sprinkled over the corpus of state law in places where national standards are needed.[59] By this account, the complex modern judicial system is nonetheless basically the decentralized common law regime that has always prevailed. The task at hand is to adjust that common law framework to accommodate a body of legislative and administrative activity, particularly at the federal level, which brings new centripetal pressure to bear on the traditional order. Positing the primacy of state law (and the contingent, supplemental nature of federal law), it follows naturally enough, according to the paradigm, that state courts (exercising judicial authority given them by state law) constitute our first-line adjudicative mechanisms when disputes arise. Federal courts (exercising a much more limited jurisdiction) are summoned to service only in exceptional circumstances.[60]

2. The Private Rights Model

Power allocations in this field also reflect the "private rights" or "dispute resolution" model of adjudication, which posits that the role of courts, as opposed to legislatures and executive officers, is to resolve actual disputes between contending parties. By this

58. Professor Fallon explains that the paradigm's "single, controlling insight" is that "authority to decide must... include authority to decide wrongly." Fallon, note 53, at 962.

59. The Federal Courts and the Federal System, note 54, at 435.

60. Professor Hart reached the same conclusion by another route in a famous law review article in which he produced a lively dialog between fictional antagonists, one (a student or colleague) pressing the other (Hart's alter ego) on whether a citizen with a federal claim is entitled to proceed in a federal court rather than a state court. That question quickly reduced to whether Congress can constitutionally deny such a litigant a federal forum. Given the explicit text of Article III, Hart found it inescapable that no litigant can claim a federal forum if Congress does not provide one. See Chapter IV, text accompanying notes 133–35. Hart was equally sure, however, that no litigant can be denied access to *all* courts to press a federal claim. Consequently, if Congress withholds a federal forum, the state courts must be open. "In the scheme of the Constitution," Hart's alter ego declared, state courts are "the primary guarantors of constitutional rights, and in many cases they may be the ultimate ones." Henry M. Hart, Jr., *The Power of Congress to Limit the Jurisdiction of the Federal Courts: An Exercise in Dialectic*, 66 Harv. L. Rev. 1362, 1401 (1953).

account, the parties come to a court for help not when they want to change the law, but when they have a quarrel over existing law. When asked to decide who has the better legal position, a court undertakes the familiar duties of adjudication.[61] Initially, the court determines the material facts. The court examines any evidence the parties offer, decides who is telling the truth, and ascertains the state of affairs on which the law must be brought to bear. Next, the court identifies the controlling legal standard: the substantive law that establishes rights, duties, and prescriptions for behavior in circumstances of the relevant kind. Finally, the court applies that legal standard to the facts of the particular case at hand.[62]

Conventionally, when a court decides what has transpired to give rise to the parties' dispute, the court is said to be determining basic, primary, historical facts—this is to say, describing historical events.[63] When the court articulates the controlling legal standard, it is said to be deciding an abstract or pure question of law. And when the court applies that legal standard to the facts of a particular case, the court is said to be deciding a "mixed" question of law and fact—that is, determining the legal significance of the basic, primary, historical facts. These duties entail judicial law-making. When courts ascertain applicable legal standards, they necessarily elucidate preexisting authorities of various kinds, assigning meaning to those sources of law. And when courts apply abstract legal standards to the facts of particular cases, they necessarily elaborate and enrich the law, adding to its corpus an additional precedent on which future courts will rely. According to the private rights model, this much judicial law-making is appropriate and legitimate inasmuch as it is essential to the resolution of disputes for which courts exist and to which their authority is limited.[64]

The most famous illustration of the private rights model is *Marbury v. Madison*.[65] In that case, John Marshall held that the Supreme Court had authority to invalidate a federal statute the Court found to conflict with the Constitution. He gave as his chief reason that it was essential for the Court to elaborate the Constitution's meaning in order

---

61. See text accompanying notes 6–8. The "private rights" nomenclature in this context can be misleading. In some circumstances, the Supreme Court uses this same label to identify legal claims that one "private" (i.e., non-governmental) party has against another. See, e.g., Chapter V, text accompanying note 47. Here, by contrast, the label is meant only to denote the traditional function of courts to adjudicate legal issues for the purpose of resolving actual disputes between the immediate parties (sometimes including representatives of government), and not for the purpose of elaborating law more abstractly in the interests of the public at large. See notes 78–91 and accompanying text (describing the "public rights" model).

62. Obviously, a court cannot isolate these steps from each other and take them one at a time in this order. When, for example, a court sets about to find the basic facts, it must already have in mind the legal standard that is applicable. Otherwise, the court can have no idea what facts are legally relevant and thus need finding. Moreover, all three steps run together at the fringes. In particular, one must understand that the difference between a legal standard and its application in particular instances is elusive. A legal rule, articulated in the abstract, is only a generalized account of the way a series of cases should be resolved.

63. Professor Monaghan describes this fact-finding step as a "case-specific inquiry into *what happened here*." Henry P. Monaghan, *Constitutional Fact Review*, 85 Colum. L. Rev. 229, 235 (1985) (emphasis in original).

64. The classic explanation of the categories is Justice Frankfurter's opinion in *Brown v. Allen*, 344 U.S. 443, 506 (1953) (concurring opinion). The classic statement of the private rights model is Lon Fuller, *The Forms and Limits of Adjudication*, 92 Harv. L. Rev. 353 (1978). Professor Bone contends that Fuller's theory was more fluid than others have suggested. See Robert G. Bone, *Lon Fuller's Theory of Adjudication and the False Dichotomy Between Dispute Resolution and Public Law Models of Litigation*, 75 B.U. L. Rev. 1273 (1995).

65. 5 U.S. (1 Cranch) 137 (1803).

to resolve an actual dispute between two litigants. On one side, William Marbury claimed he had been named a justice of the peace in the District of Columbia and had a right to his commission. On the other, James Madison (the Secretary of State) had refused to give Marbury the commission and thus, by Marbury's account, had violated Marbury's legal right to it. According to Marbury, §13 of the Judiciary Act of 1789 established the Supreme Court's jurisdiction to adjudicate his dispute with Madison as an "original" matter (not on appeal from some inferior court), because he was pursuing a writ of mandamus instructing Madison to deliver the commission.[66]

Chief Justice Marshall held, first, that Marbury had a legal right to the commission, and, second, that a writ of mandamus was an appropriate judicial remedy for a violation of that right. As a general rule, according to Marshall, "where there is a legal right, there is also a legal remedy by suit or action at law."[67] A federal court of proper jurisdiction, accordingly, might have issued the writ and thus ordered Madison to do his duty by delivering the commission to Marbury.[68] Marshall concluded, however, that §13 failed to supply the needed jurisdiction, because that provision of the 1789 Act was unconstitutional: It purported to grant the Court original jurisdiction of a case that was not among those that Article III authorized the Court to consider as an original matter.[69] In the end, accordingly, Marshall interpreted the Constitution in *Marbury* only because it was necessary to do so to resolve the dispute at hand. Unfortunately for Marbury himself, when Marshall turned to the Constitution for that reason, he decided that the Court had no jurisdiction to give Marbury what he wanted after all and thus was obliged to dismiss his complaint.[70]

The private rights model corresponds to the separation of national powers. It contemplates a role for federal courts that is analytically distinct from the functions left to the other two branches of the national government. Modern cases on "standing" provide the best illustrations.[71] In those cases, the Supreme Court insists that federal judges are not elected and thus should not develop substantive law to promote their own notions of good public policy in an affirmative, freewheeling way. They can elaborate the law only when they adjudicate actual "cases" and "controversies" involving adverse parties whose personal interests in the results establish their standing to appear in an Article III court. Then (and only then) is the federal courts' authority to create law both justified and limited by the necessity of resolving disputes. By this account, judicial law-making is contingent and incidental; it is a by-product of courts' primary adjudicative responsibility.

The private rights model also corresponds to the role the Hart and Wechsler paradigm contemplates for federal courts. According to the paradigm, courts are not suited

---

66. See Chapter IV, text accompanying note 5 (identifying the elements of the Court's original jurisdiction); Chapter VII, notes 1–40 and accompanying text (offering a more complete account).

67. 5 U.S. at 163, quoting Blackstone, III Commentaries, at 23.

68. See Chapter X, note 24 and accompanying text. On the other hand, the statutes in place at the time did not clearly confer jurisdiction on any inferior federal court, either. See *McIntire v. Wood*, 11 U.S. (7 Cranch) 504 (1813) (holding that the original circuit courts created in 1789 had no jurisdiction to issue the writ of mandamus); cf. *McClung v. Silliman*, 19 U.S. (6 Wheat.) 598 (1821) (holding that a state court had no power to issue the writ to a federal officer). See generally Akhil R. Amar, *Marbury, Section 13, and the Original Jurisdiction of the Supreme Court*, 56 U. Chi. L. Rev. 443, 461 & n.90 (1989).

69. See Chapter VII, notes 13–15 and accompanying text (elaborating this point).

70. But see notes 85–89 and accompanying text (discussing an alternative perspective on *Marbury*).

71. See Chapter IX.

to making public policy for the future, but are competent to settle disputes that have already arisen regarding the law as it is. Courts are not good at assessing the popular will and identifying the public interest. Courts are good at marshaling evidence, making credibility choices, analyzing precedents, and elaborating legal rules and principles in particular circumstances. It follows that courts should confine their policy-making to what is necessary to settle actual disputes.

Inasmuch as the private rights model regards dispute resolution as the only judicial function to be performed, this model, like the Hart and Wechsler paradigm to which it is so closely linked, contemplates that state courts can and will shoulder responsibility for most judicial business, irrespective of subject matter. State courts of general jurisdiction are typically open to adjudicate any cases that come through the door. Federal courts, by contrast, are reserved for special circumstances in which they, rather than the state courts, are suited to provide the adjudication required.[72]

3. The Process Model

Both the private rights model of adjudication and the Hart and Wechsler paradigm contemplate occasions on which federal courts are needed. Certain subjects plainly invite national tribunals: cases involving foreign affairs, for example. And in some instances, the policy considerations the paradigm invokes will select federal courts. This will be true, in the main, when the premise on which the Hart and Wechsler paradigm ordinarily proceeds does not obtain—namely, when state courts fail to provide the kind of process that is needed to reach an acceptable result.

Recall that the working idea in the paradigm is that jurisdictional power should be allocated on the basis of outcome-neutral criteria in the expectation that the results on the merits will be unaffected. Then, when any court (but often a state court) produces a result, that decision is entitled to respect *because* it is the product of an appropriate decision-making process. If, however, state court process is flawed, so that the matter is denied "full and fair" adjudication, the situation is altered.[73] A state court judgment cannot be *taken* to be right on the ground that it was generated in a procedurally proper way, if it is clear in the circumstances of a case that the state court has not delivered the caliber of process on which its claim to adjudicate depends.

Herein the "process model" in the law of federal courts, which supplies what the private rights model and the Hart and Wechsler paradigm plainly require: a subordinate model for deciding when the ordinary expectation of state court adjudication should give way to adjudication in federal court. The process model answers that federal courts may properly be called to duty when the procedural machinery in state court breaks down. Like the private rights model and the Hart and Wechsler paradigm, the process model attends exclusively to *process*. It summons the federal courts not because those courts are thought to be superior to state courts, nor because they are more likely to

---

72. Academics debate the extent to which the Hart and Wechsler paradigm tends to prefer state courts over federal courts. Professor Wells contends that the paradigm is systematically biased in favor of state court adjudication. Wells, *Rhetoric and Reality*, note 20. Professor Fallon contends that the paradigm is neutral in this respect, but that the great capacity of state courts understandably attracts considerable business. Fallon, note 53.

73. See Paul M. Bator, *Finality in Criminal Law and Federal Habeas Corpus for State Prisoners*, 76 Harv. L. Rev. 441, 462 (1963).

reach objectively correct decisions, nor, certainly, because they are more likely to render judgments more favorable to federal claims. The process model engages federal courts not when state court *results* are unpalatable, but rather when the *processes of adjudication* in state court are inadequate. Outcomes the state courts reach by procedurally irregular means are not, by hypothesis, entitled to the respect that outcomes reached via procedurally sound adjudication routinely receive.[74]

The Supreme Court employs the process model in a variety of contexts. In "abstention" cases, for example, the Court allows federal courts to enjoin state proceedings if it appears that state courts have denied a litigant an opportunity for "full and fair" adjudication of a federal claim.[75] The process model also figures in the Court's decisions on whether federal courts can examine federal claims that were, or might have been, determined previously in state court,[76] as well as in decisions on whether the Supreme Court can review state court judgments that purport to rest on adequate state grounds of decision.[77]

4. The Public Rights Model

Together, the Hart and Wechsler paradigm, the private rights model, and the process model undoubtedly help to explain a large measure of federal courts law. Yet they do not capture everything federal courts do. Moreover, they have come under attack for failing to appreciate fundamental changes that have occurred in the American legal culture since Hart and Wechsler fashioned their understanding of legal institutions a half century ago.[78] By some accounts, a competing "public rights" model offers both a better explanation of the federal courts' work in some instances and a better normative vision of what the federal courts *should* be about.

The idea of "public rights" is elusive. In a line of decisions stretching back to the Nineteenth Century, the Supreme Court has used the public rights label to refer to claims involving the federal government as a party. Historically, matters of that nature had negligible significance for the federal legal system as a whole. According to some authorities, Congress was free to dispose of them without involving the courts at all.[79] In the modern era, however, courts and commentators use the same public rights designation to identify extremely important cases that can have profound implications for the body of federal law and the framework for its enforcement. Some of the new public rights cases are the very disputes with the federal government that previously were thought to be *de minimis* but have taken on new meaning in light of expansive modern

---

74. Professor Bator explained that the idea is to set aside any debate over the substantive accuracy of outcomes and to focus, instead, on "arrangements and procedures which provide a reasoned and acceptable probability that justice will be done." Id. at 448. The process model's insistence on "full and fair" adjudication does not address the general question whether state courts are fungible with federal courts, but only tests whether, in some case or class of cases, state courts do not or cannot offer the process required. Paul M. Bator, *The State Courts and Federal Constitutional Litigation*, 22 Wm. & Mary L. Rev. 605, 626–27 (1981).

75. See Chapter XI, notes 183–203 and accompanying text.

76. See Chapter VI, notes 181–85 and accompanying text.

77. See Chapter VII, notes 167–68 and accompanying text.

78. Professor Amar contends that the assumptions associated with Hart and Wechsler were out of date even in 1953, when their case book was published. Akhil R. Amar, *Law Story*, 102 Harv. L. Rev. 688, 710 (1989).

79. See Chapter V, notes 96–108 and accompanying text.

governmental regulation. Some have an entirely different shape and scope. At all events, the public rights label in this context is meant to identify suits in which federal courts elaborate federal law not merely as the by-product of isolated dispute-resolution, but for its own sake, or better said, for the sake of the public at large.

When the Court first described claims against the federal government as public rights cases, the private rights model captured the really important function that federal courts performed. Superintending the conduct of government agents was no essential part of that work. Today, by contrast, the public rights model depicts the legal system in a quite different way. Federal courts are not limited to settling quarrels between individual litigants, and they do not merely fill gaps that state courts leave open. Rather, federal courts have a special office within the American political structure. They are in place to enforce federal statutes and the Constitution and thus to hold governmental power in check in a wide range of circumstances.

The Hart and Wechsler paradigm and the private rights model respond to the separation of powers, federalism, and efficient judicial methodology. They contemplate that power should be distributed with those structural and functional values in mind. By contrast, the public rights model celebrates access to the federal judiciary for the vindication of federal claims.[80] Two related developments suggest that the public rights model helps to explain the role federal courts play in the modern American legal system.

First, the rise of the "administrative state" since the 1930s has transformed the very nature and character of American law. In many contexts, the law is no longer largely comprised of the individual rights and duties that common law courts enforced. Instead, much of the substantive law in place today is federal constitutional law (which has exploded in the wake of *Brown v. Board of Education*) and federal regulatory law (which often creates no individual rights and typically is administered in the first instance by federal administrative agencies). Different forms of law and legal institutions place novel demands on federal courts to perform in ways that would have been alien to the common law.[81]

Second, many of the disputes with which federal courts contend are not between private litigants at all, but between private citizens, groups, and corporations, on the one hand, and governmental officers, on the other. In many instances, private litigants continue to advance particularized individual claims that fit the private rights model. Yet when the substance of their complaints is that governmental officers have acted arbitrarily or abusively, the adjudicative function of courts is especially sensitive (and important). Increasingly, federal courts have assumed responsibility for checking the excesses of executive officers (like police officers and low-level bureaucrats).[82] In addition, litigants in the modern age often insist more generally that governmental

80. Professor Bandes contends that by adopting a public rights model of this kind, the Court could rationalize the very idea of a constitutional "case" for resolution in federal court. See Susan Bandes, *The Idea of a Case*, 42 Stan. L. Rev. 227 (1990).

81. For an account of these developments, see Eskridge & Peller, note 56. For an argument that federal courts have necessarily come to forge public policy straightforwardly, see Malcolm M. Feeley & Edward L. Rubin, Judicial Policymaking and the Modern State: How the Courts Reformed America's Prisons (1998). Professor Resnik adds that federal courts law today must take greater account of the judicial work performed by magistrate judges, bankruptcy judges, administrative law judges, and tribal courts. Judith Resnik, *Rereading "The Federal Courts": Revising the Domain of Federal Courts Jurisprudence at the End of the Twentieth Century*, 47 Vand. L. Rev. 1021 (1994).

82. Seth F. Kreimer, *Exploring the Dark Matter of Judicial Review: A Constitutional Census of the 1990s*, 5 Wm. & Mary Bill of Rts. J. 427 (1997).

officers should simply comply with the law. Class actions challenge governmental activities on a wide scale and demand broad-gauged equitable relief that can affect millions of lives. The claims in those cases are less personal than the private rights recognized at common law. They may better be understood as public rights claims inasmuch as they are in service of the public interest in seeing that the law is enforced.[83]

According to the public rights model, federal law is no longer typically the exception, but is now very often the rule. Superintending the conduct of government officials is no longer a minor matter, but has become the central function that federal courts perform. Federal injunctive relief no longer demands special justification, but is typically necessary to force government officials to conform their behavior to law. The task at hand now is not to teach a basically common law system to accommodate new developments. It is to understand and nourish the new federal public law system in light of its stubborn common law past.[84]

There is a way in which the public rights model arguably has figured in a variety of traditional cases, even *Marbury v. Madison*.[85] After all, John Marshall was scarcely dragged kicking and screaming through his analysis in that case. He might have made quick work of Marbury's claim, simply by holding that Marbury had no right to the commission until it was delivered or that mandamus was not an appropriate remedy.

---

83. Here, too, conventional jargon can be confusing. The new public rights cases are "public" not only because they turn on federal law and often involve government officials as defendants, but also because they are pursued in the general public interest. American jurisprudence distinguishes between an *interest* and a *right*, the one being a human concern or desire of any kind, the other capturing only an entitlement, guaranteed by law, to demand a particular form of treatment by another. Mutt has an *interest* in attending a Red Sox game with Jeff, an interest that will be injured if Jeff decides (inexplicably) to go to the ballet, instead. But, *ceteris paribus*, Mutt has no *right* to demand that Jeff keep their date at Fenway Park. Nevertheless, when courts and commentators use the phrase "public rights," they typically do not mean the public equivalent of private individual *rights*, but rather the public *interest*. Likewise, when courts and commentators refer to litigation in the "public interest," they typically have in mind litigation conforming at least roughly to the model of public *rights*. But see Chapter IX, notes 374–77 and accompanying text (discussing the way in which law may affect what society considers to *be* a *de facto* interest).

84. The idea of "public law" litigation is also elusive. In the main, plaintiffs in public rights lawsuits attempt to force government officials to comply with federal law (the Constitution or a federal statute) and do not attempt to force other private actors to do so. That is an important sense in which both the litigation and the law to be enforced are *public*. Nevertheless, courts and commentators may well place some suits against private actors in the public law category (e.g., suits to force corporations to comply with federal civil rights and environmental legislation). The more fundamental point of the label "public rights" is to distinguish these policy-oriented suits, which typically are in the class action form and invariably seek injunctive or declaratory relief, from the comparatively simple suits envisioned by the model of private rights, which are discrete disputes between self-interested litigants that can be resolved without implicating the public at large in any self-conscious way and in which compensatory damages ordinarily supply a sufficient remedy. Judge Oakes has explained it this way: "[W]e no longer think in simple terms of adjudication based on retrospective, self-contained, party-initiated and controlled bipolar lawsuits seeking to constrain power. We now recognize a form of public law litigation which enforces affirmative values running to groups and which needs prospective judicial enforcement." James L. Oakes, *The Proper Role of the Federal Courts in Enforcing the Bill of Rights*, 54 N.Y.U. L. Rev. 911, 918 (1979). For good sources, see Bruce A. Ackerman, Reconstructing American Law (1984); Owen M. Fiss, The Civil Rights Injunction (1978); Abram Chayes, *The Role of the Judge in Public Law Litigation*, 89 Harv. L. Rev. 1281 (1976).

85. See notes 65–70 and accompanying text.

Certainly, Marshall might have construed § 13 of the Judiciary Act to authorize the Court to issue the writ of mandamus only in appellate cases, thus reaching the same result (that the Court had no original jurisdiction to entertain Marbury's application) on a statutory ground.[86] Instead, Marshall wrote a lengthy opinion in which he not only *exercised* judicial power to give the Constitution its authoritative meaning, but also *asserted* judicial power (in a case of proper jurisdiction) to issue orders to a member of the President's cabinet.[87] In those early years, that was judicial muscle-flexing of an extraordinary order.[88] Accordingly, even as Marshall insisted that his task was only to settle the dispute at bar, he seized the opportunity to project judicial power a good deal further: "It is emphatically the province and duty of the judicial department to say what the law is."[89]

The modern Supreme Court's decisions allocating judicial power often defy explanation as the product of outcome-neutral policies of the kind that the Hart and Wechsler paradigm and the private rights model make central. By all accounts, the Warren Court of the 1950s and 1960s encouraged citizens to go to federal court seeking injunctive orders that would desegregate the public schools, restructure the administration of prisons and mental hospitals, and enforce federal civil rights and environmental legislation. If the liberal justices then sitting did not always endorse the ends that the plaintiffs in those cases hoped to achieve, they plainly thought it was appropriate that the federal courts should be open to litigation with public objectives in view. By most accounts, the Court became uncomfortable with suits of that nature in the 1970s. If the more conservative justices then sitting did not always disapprove of the goals the plaintiffs in public rights suits were seeking, they thought it was inappropriate that those plaintiffs should

86. Marshall thus reached out to decide constitutional questions that might easily have been avoided. Cf. text accompanying note 26 (discussing the Court's usual caution). See generally William W. Van Alstyne, *A Critical Guide to Marbury v. Madison*, 1969 Duke L.J. 1, 16. Professor Amar argues that §13 was not a jurisdictional provision at all, but only authorized the Court to issue the writ of mandamus as a remedy. Amar, note 68, at 456.

87. According to Professor McCloskey, Marshall's opinion was a "masterwork of indirection, a brilliant example of Marshall's capacity to sidestep danger while seeming to court it, to advance in one direction while his opponents [were] looking in another." Robert G. McCloskey, The American Supreme Court 40 (1960).

88. At the time *Marbury* was decided, Jefferson had just become President and Republicans had gained control of Congress. The outgoing Federalists were attempting to retain (and expand) their power in the judicial branch. When the Court first took up the case, it issued a "show cause" order to Madison, instructing him to appear and explain why a writ of mandamus should not issue. Madison ignored that order and gave every appearance that he would also ignore an actual writ if the Court should send him one. The really contentious issue in the case, then, may not have been the Court's power to interpret the Constitution, but its power to demand that the executive branch carry out judicial orders. Given that Madison (and Jefferson) were poised to rebuff any order the Court might issue, Marshall may have thought it prudent (and politically expedient) merely to *say* that the Court might have issued a writ of mandamus in a proper jurisdictional posture, but to find an excuse for withholding an order that Madison would disregard. The *Marbury* decision thus may have been an attempt to strengthen and protect the federal judiciary at one and the same time. See James O'Fallon, *Marbury*, 44 Stan. L. Rev. 219 (1992). These points granted, Professor Alfange argues that *Marbury* is still best understood as the classic precedent on the power of judicial review. Dean Alfange, Jr., *Marbury v. Madison and Original Understandings of Judicial Review: In Defense of Traditional Wisdom*, 1993 Sup. Ct. Rev. 329. See also John Harrison, *The Constitutional Origins and Implications of Judicial Review*, 84 Va. L. Rev. 333 (1998) (contending that Article V and the Supremacy Clause justify *Marbury's* conclusion that the Court need not defer to a congressional interpretation of the Constitution).

89. *Marbury*, 5 U.S. at 177.

advance their contentions in federal court, instead of pressing them on Congress or state legislatures.[90]

Today, by most accounts, the Court is divided over the legitimacy and advisability of public rights litigation. Individual justices undoubtedly attach different significance and weight to the outcome-neutral concerns they debate with such vigor. Yet there is no escaping the suspicion that they are also moved by deeper attitudes regarding both the substantive goals and values at stake in litigation and the role of federal courts in the system. In many minds, then, the law of federal courts is more result-oriented than the Hart and Wechsler paradigm and the private rights model can readily explain. The genuine explanation for the justices' performance may lie in their attempts, individually and collectively, to wrestle with the implications of the public rights model and its distinctive vision for the Article III judiciary. The very decisions that illustrate the current Court's commitment to the private rights model reflect these divisions inasmuch as the justices in the majority typically take pains to explain why they reject the competing public rights model.[91]

5. The Parity Debate

When arguments about power allocations become more ideological, they commonly take the form of a candid debate over whether federal and state courts are likely to reach the same judgments in federal question cases. If federal and state courts do tend to agree, then, by hypothesis, channeling jurisdictional power in one direction or the other will have no appreciable effect on outcomes. The Supreme Court can sensibly distribute power exclusively on the basis of the considerations captured in the Hart and Wechsler paradigm. To put the point the other way, the paradigm rests on the premise that federal and state courts are interchangeable. That is *why* the paradigm conceives that jurisdiction can be allocated on outcome-neutral grounds without concern that federal law will suffer.[92] If, however, there is no parity between federal and state courts, then the premise of the Hart and Wechsler paradigm is unsound, and allocations of power without consideration of the effect on results make little sense.

Obviously, a great deal turns on the question of parity. Many observers are convinced that federal and state courts are not fungible at all and that, with few exceptions, federal courts are better adjudicators—in general and especially in cases involving federal claims. The question does not lend itself to empirical testing.[93] Arguments

---

90. For an account of the Warren Court's ideological orientation, see Morton J. Horwitz, The Warren Court and the Pursuit of Justice (1998). For a discussion of the Burger Court, see The Burger Court: The Counter-Revolution That Wasn't (Blasi ed. 1983).

91. See text accompanying note 71 (citing the Court's decisions on "standing" as illustrations). Professor Wells insists that the jurisdictional policies that the Hart and Wechsler paradigm embraces do not account for the Court's results and that a more pragmatic perspective is required to get at the "real differences between jurisdictional law and the law of primary rights and obligations." Michael Wells, *Busting the Hart & Wechsler Paradigm*, 11 Const. Comm. 557, 586 (1995).

92. See text accompanying note 57.

93. Efforts have been made to test the parity thesis empirically. E.g., Michael E. Solimine & James L. Walker, *Constitutional Litigation in Federal and State Courts: An Empirical Analysis of Judicial Parity*, 10 Hastings Const. L.Q. 213 (1983) (reporting no pattern of state court hostility to federal rights); Brett C. Gerry, *Parity Revisited: An Empirical Comparison of State and Lower Federal Court Interpretations of Nollan v. California Coastal Commission*, 23 Harv. J. L. & Pub. Policy 233 (1999) (reviewing numerous state and federal court decisions implementing the Supreme Court's decision in *Nollan* and concluding that there was no systematic difference between the performance of state and federal courts). But methodological difficulties render the results unreliable. Erwin

for and against parity rest on formal arrangements, experience, and intuition. The Hart and Wechsler paradigm takes parity as a given.[94] Yet there are reasoned arguments on both sides.

The case *against* parity goes this way: Initially, it is said that the Constitution deliberately makes federal courts more independent than state courts.[95] Article III judges are appointed (not elected). They serve (in effect) for life and thus need not answer for their decisions either in Congress or at the polls. Their salaries cannot be diminished while they are in office. These structural devices insulate federal courts from political accountability and thus enable them to vindicate unpopular civil rights and civil liberties claims without fear that they will suffer repercussions. State court judges are typically elected. They rarely enjoy the same safeguards once they are on the bench. And they thus labor under the threat of reprisals if their judgments displease politicians or the public at large.[96]

In addition, and on a different level, it is said that in a host of other ways federal courts are superior institutions. The federal judiciary is small, making it comparatively easy to achieve a high level of quality among individual members; the ranks of state judges are legion, making quality control comparatively difficult. Federal judges are underpaid, but still receive significant salaries; state judges are typically less handsomely compensated. Federal court appointments are enormously prestigious; state court positions, at least at the trial level, enjoy less public repute. Federal judges are appointed under a scheme that, for all its faults, takes some account of professional qualifications; state judges often are selected under systems heavily influenced by political patronage. Federal judges are assisted by excellent young law clerks; state judges typically are served by career staff with less rigorous training. Federal judges face a large but tolerable case load; state judges are swamped with work. Federal judges are generally able to prepare reasoned opinions to guide the public and to explain results to higher courts; state judges are, on the whole, less proficient. In all these ways, federal judges are said to be more capable of interpreting federal law generously, provided they choose to do so.[97]

Many observers are convinced that federal judges *do* choose to be more hospitable to federal claims. They succeed to a unique perspective on the federal system, which generates an expansive understanding of federal law. Federal judges operate within a grand tradition as an elite core of jurists with the duty and responsibility to implement federal

---

Chemerinsky, *Parity Reconsidered: Defining a Role for the Federal Judiciary*, 36 U.C.L.A. L. Rev. 233 (1988) (identifying flaws in the Solimine/Walker study).

94. See text accompanying note 57.

95. Geoffrey C. Hazard, Jr., *Reflections on the Substance of Finality*, 70 Cornell L. Rev. 642, 646–47 (1985); see Chapter III, text accompanying note 3.

96. See Stephen B. Bright, *Can Judicial Independence Be Attained in the South? Overcoming History, Elections, and Misperceptions About the Role of the Judiciary*, 14 Ga. St. L. Rev. 817 (1998); Chapter III, text accompanying notes 1–2 (describing the benefits of federal judicial independence). Electoral schemes for selecting state judges are arguably problematic on various practical grounds. For example, judges who run for office must raise the capital essential to an effective campaign in the first instance, and, once in office, they must continue to invest time and effort in preparation for the next election. The practical requirement of campaigning obviously does not discourage all good candidates from seeking state judicial office. But it may discourage some.

97. See generally Burt Neuborne, *The Myth of Parity*, 90 Harv. L. Rev. 1105 (1977) (making these points). Professor Lee has developed an argument that individuals behind a Rawlsian veil would choose a system that guarantees litigants with federal claims an opportunity to press those claims in a federal court. Evan Tsen Lee, *On the Received Wisdom in Federal Courts*, 147 U. Penn. L. Rev. 1111 (1999).

law; state judges lack the same tradition and sense of responsibility. By this account, the federal courts' tradition supersedes even the personal ideological inclinations that judges exhibited before they were appointed to the federal bench—arousing men and women who, as lawyers, represented the haves of society to champion, as judges, the interests of society's have-nots. Acting on these presuppositions, lawyers advancing civil rights and civil liberties claims often prefer to be in federal court, simply to gain a "litigating edge."[98]

Defenders of parity insist, by contrast, that there are valid reasons for treating federal and state courts as fungible—if not as extant reality, then at least as a worthy objective.[99] It is said that a gross comparison of *all* state judges with *all* federal judges ignores variations in quality from state to state and within individual state court hierarchies. Moreover, even if state trial judges do not compare well with federal district judges, the same cannot be said (so easily) about the judges who sit on state appellate courts. It is said that the quality of state judges has improved over time. So the case against parity, whatever its strength, is now presumably weaker than at any time in the past. If, indeed, state courts are getting better, there is all the more reason to set aside previous doubts about them and to establish incentives for continued improvement.

Defenders of parity contend that if civil rights and civil liberties plaintiffs prefer to be in federal court, it is because they are understandably concerned only with vindicating their own claims *against* governmental power. They thus neglect other constitutional values that state courts, operating from a different perspective, are peculiarly positioned to appreciate: values like federalism and state sovereignty. It is said, accordingly, that the case against parity suffers from a normative bias *in favor* of individual federal claims to be free of governmental coercion and *against* countervailing (but equally constitutional) values served by (or at least reflected in) the exercise of governmental authority.[100]

The parity debate provides the backdrop for many of the Supreme Court's decisions allocating judicial authority. Until recently, the Court declined to discuss the parity question openly in its opinions. Yet it is frankly hard to account for many of the Warren Court's decisions, except as a reflection of that Court's sense that federal claims were best addressed in federal court.[101] Today, the Court often declares its conviction that state courts are perfectly willing to vindicate federal claims.[102] Accordingly, the current Court typically explains its judgments on the basis of the outcome-neutral policies associated with the Hart and Wechsler paradigm—which, again, rests on the premise that parity does, indeed, exist. In all candor, however, many observers question whether those considerations genuinely explain the Court's decisions in politically sensitive

98. Michael Wells, *Behind the Parity Debate: The Decline of the Legal Process Tradition in the Law of Federal Courts*, 71 B.U. L. Rev. 609, 611 (1991). For differing accounts of the implications of allowing litigants to choose where they will press their claims, compare Martin H. Redish, *Judicial Parity, Litigant Choice, and Democratic Theory: A Comment on Federal Jurisdiction and Constitutional Rights*, 36 U.C.L.A. L. Rev. 329 (1988), with Erwin Chemerinsky, *Federal Courts, State Courts, and the Constitution: A Rejoinder to Professor Redish*, 36 U.C.L.A. L. Rev. 369 (1988).

99. Bator, note 74, at 623–35.

100. Id. at 631–35.

101. See *Dombrowski v. Pfister*, 380 U.S. 479, 498 (1965) (Harlan, J., dissenting) (expressing this assessment); accord Owen M. Fiss, *Dombrowski*, 86 Yale L.J. 1103 (1977).

102. See, e.g., *Stone v. Powell*, 428 U.S. 465, 494 n.35 (1976) (insisting that there is no reason to think that a federal court is a more competent or conscientious adjudicator in federal question cases than a state court).

cases.[103] The best critiques and defenses of the Court's work question what normative, ideological influences lie muted just beneath the surface.[104]

103. Professor Nichol laments "how little honest, straightforward, old-fashioned, explanation-giving is ever attempted." Gene R. Nichol, *Is There a Law of Federal Courts?*, 96 W. Va. L. Rev. 147, 166 (1993). Professor McManamon argues that "[w]hen one looks beyond the so-called neutral Federal Courts principles... one sees that the Supreme Court's choices are value-laden." Mary Brigid McManamon, *Challenging the Hart and Wechsler Paradigm*, 27 Conn. L. Rev. 833, 839 (1995). Professor Little's empirical research indicates that the Supreme Court's language in opinions on federal courts issues is, to a statistically significant degree, more "obfuscatory" than its grammar in opinions regarding other subjects. Laura E. Little, *Hiding with Words: Obfuscation, Avoidance, and Federal Jurisdiction Opinions*, 46 U.C.L.A. L. Rev. 75 (1998).

104. Professor Wells and Professor Matasar call for more explicit attention to the likelihood that the Court distributes jurisdictional power on the basis of unstated predictions that state and federal courts will *not* reach the same outcomes. Michael Wells, *Who's Afraid of Henry Hart?*, 14 Const. Comm. 175 (1997); Wells, *Naked Politics*, note 20; Richard A. Matasar, *Treatise Writing and Federal Jurisdiction: Does Doctrine Matter When Law is Politics?*, 89 Mich. L. Rev. 1449 (1991). Professor Althouse promotes doctrinal devices that draw out the best in state courts, but she laments the harsh consequences that often befall litigants who are denied access to a federal tribunal. Ann Althouse, *Late Night Confessions in the Hart and Wechsler Hotel*, 47 Vand. L. Rev. 993, 1003–04 (1994).

Chapter II

History and Modern Structure

The extent to which history affects (or should affect) modern thinking about federal courts is debatable. Originalists insist on beginning with historical materials as the anchor for analysis. Yet few observers believe the founding generation had any definite vision for federal courts. Fewer still believe that, if such a vision existed then, it is retrievable now. Historians do agree, however, on some important features of the historical backdrop. And it is *de rigueur* to take stock of what little we know, or think we know, of the relevant history.

A. The Colonial Period

The early colonists probably had no developed conception of the judicial function. They only dimly perceived the difference between the King's executive power and any separate legislative authority that the emerging Parliament presumed to exercise. To the extent they grasped the idea of judicial power at all, they probably regarded adjudication as a species of administration.[1] The judges the colonists knew were the socially connected landowners whom the Crown commissioned to serve in the American provinces. They were "not highly regarded," but rather were typically distrusted as "appendages... of royal authority."[2] Those magistrates superintended public affairs in an informal way. They imposed taxes, supervised public works projects, and generally presided over their communities.[3]

The royal judges did settle disputes, and the colonists recognized that they might abuse that authority. The colonists thus insisted that judges were empowered only to apply irrefutable legal rules to undisputed facts. If any serious question arose, regarding either the law or the facts, a jury made the necessary judgment. It may be, then, that the colonists either considered juries actually to *be* the courts on which they might rely or saw themselves as participating in judicial decisions by means of jury service. In any

---

1. Jack N. Rakove, Original Meanings: Politics and Ideas in the Making of the Constitution 297–300 (1996).

2. Gordon S. Wood, *The Origins of Judicial Review Revisited, Or How the Marshall Court Made More Out of Less*, 56 Wash. & Lee L. Rev. 787, 789 (1999).

3. Gordon S. Wood, The Radicalism of the American Revolution 71–72, 82 (1992). Nor did colonial assemblies behave in anything like the way modern legislatures operate. They rarely enacted broadly applicable regulatory statutes. Instead, they typically received and addressed petitions and grievances from private individuals and groups seeking favors. Thus the ordinances they enacted were, by modern standards, more adjudicative than legislative. Gordon S. Wood, *The Origins of American Democracy or How the People Became Judges in Their Own Causes*, 47 Clev. St. L. Rev. 309, 315–18 (1999).

case, they regarded judges not as professionals who would protect them and their rights, but rather as instruments of the ruling class—against which ordinary citizens needed protection.[4]

In England, the King surrendered absolute power to name and remove judges fairly early. Pursuant to the Act of Settlement in 1701, English judges held office during "good behaviour."[5] In the colonies, however, the King insisted on appointing judges to serve at his pleasure (or that of his royal governors) and gave colonial assemblies no say in the matter.[6] It is hardly surprising, then, that the Declaration of Independence condemned George III for naming judges "dependent on his will alone, for the tenure of their offices, and the amount & paiment of their salaries." Some early state constitutions adopted the "good behavior" standard for judges. Most gave state legislatures authority both to select and to remove judges, typically by means of impeachment.[7]

B. The Articles of Confederation

After the Revolution, the states established the semblance of unified government under the Articles of Confederation. The Articles made no provision for national courts. They routed border disputes between states to a complicated arbitration scheme and relied on state courts for any adjudicative functions required in other situations. In maritime cases, state court judgments were subject to review by a special Court of Appeals for Cases of Capture (staffed by judges but answerable to Congress). State courts entertained any legal actions the central government brought to enforce its laws and claims.[8] The experience under the Articles was not good, and part of the reason may have been the absence of national courts. Chiefly, however, the Articles failed because the member states refused to cooperate with the weak national legislature.[9] Virginia ultimately lost patience and invited the other states to a convention that would explore ways to reform the Articles. That meeting in Annapolis in 1786 produced a call for the Constitutional Convention, which convened the following year in Philadelphia.

The chief task was to devise some means to discipline the states, whose divisive activities frustrated common interests. At the time, even the most insightful of future "framers," James Madison, had no expectation that national courts would be of much

4. Rakove, note 1, at 300–02, 305–06; William E. Nelson, Americanization of the Common Law: The Impact of Legal Change on Massachusetts Society, 1760–1830, 18–35 (1994). The procedural arrangements under which early courts operated were quite different from anything we would recognize today. Professor Bilder illustrates that general point in her history of the idea of "appeal" in early American jurisprudence. Mary S. Bilder, *The Origins of Appeal in America*, 48 Hastings L. Rev. 913 (1997).

5. Joseph H. Smith, *An Independent Judiciary: The Colonial Background*, 124 U. Pa. L. Rev. 1104–12 (1976).

6. Martha Andes Ziskind, *Judicial Tenure in the American Constitution: English and American Precedents*, 1969 Sup. Ct. Rev. 135.

7. Gerhard Casper, *The Judiciary Act of 1789 and Judicial Independence*, in Origins of the Federal Judiciary: Essays on the Judiciary Act of 1789, at 281–84 (Marcus ed. 1992).

8. Hampton L. Carson, The Supreme Court of the United States 44–64 (1891).

9. The Continental Congress lacked sufficient power to enforce the Treaty of Paris, to raise the revenues needed for westward expansion, and to regulate commerce with other nations and among the states. The Articles required a vote of nine states to take significant action and unanimity for amendments. See Rakove, note 1, at 25–28.

help in that effort. Madison, for his part, hoped to fashion a viable union by means of a strong central political structure that could bypass the states and address the people directly. He doubted that courts could curb state abuses and envisioned, instead, a congressional veto over ill-advised state legislation. Madison anticipated using Supreme Court justices only as members of a council of revision, which would review statutes the new Congress enacted before they became effective.[10]

C. The Constitutional Convention

The delegates to the Convention in Philadelphia focused on the powers that would be given to Congress and on the creation of a national executive. Yet both Randolph's Virginia plan and Patterson's New Jersey plan proposed to establish a federal judiciary as well. The delegates accepted the idea of at least a single Supreme Court. They debated whether other federal tribunals, inferior to the Supreme Court, should also be established.

Nationally inclined delegates, whom we now (oddly) call "Federalists,"[11] argued that the Constitution should mandate a full complement of inferior federal courts. Delegates more concerned with preserving state prerogatives insisted that the state courts already in existence would suffice. In the debate that ensued, Madison and other Federalists contended that state courts could not be relied upon to protect federal interests when those interests conflicted with the concerns of individual states.[12] According to conventional wisdom, the *impasse* was broken by the "Madisonian Compromise," under which the delegates agreed that the Constitution would permit, but would not require, the new Congress to create inferior federal courts.[13] The implication is that, even today, the

10. Id. at 51–54.

11. It is conventional to refer to the more nationally oriented delegates in Philadelphia as Federalists but unconventional to label their adversaries Anti-Federalists. Only three delegates present at the final meeting refused to sign the new Constitution. The "Anti-Federalist" designation is typically reserved for delegates to the state ratifying conventions, who openly opposed the Constitution. See note 30 and accompanying text.

12. Max Farrand, The Framing of the Constitution 80 (1913). By some accounts, Madison meant that state courts could not be trusted to enforce federal *law*, including the new Constitution, and that the Supreme Court alone would be unable to bring them to heel. E.g., Casper, note 7, at 286. Accordingly, Madison anticipated that inferior federal courts would be important to the development of the national framework the Federalists envisioned. By other accounts, he had no expectation that a significant body of federal law, as distinguished from the common law or state law, would be developed—by any court. Instead, he was concerned that state courts would not protect federal *interests*. They might fail to appreciate the unity of the nation under the new Constitution and thus might favor their own citizens in disputes with citizens of other states. That was the kind of provincialism that had made the Articles of Confederation unworkable, and Madison hoped to avert it by the introduction of new federal courts that would be free of local bias. See Carl McGowan, The Organization of Judicial Power in the United States 26–28 (1967) (making this point with respect to Madison's similarly ambiguous argument during the debate on the Judiciary Act of 1789). If Madison was worried about substantive law at all, he anticipated that state legislatures would enact statutes in violation of vaguely defined natural rights that Americans had always claimed (entitlements reflected in the rights of Englishmen that colonists insisted were theirs) and that state courts would be unable to stand in their way. Even as to those rights, Madison put his trust primarily in structural limitations on power rather than on federal courts simply enforcing rights in the teeth of political opposition. Rakove, note 1, at 290, 314–16.

13. Rakove, note 1, at 172. Accord Farrand, note 12, at 155. Some delegates may have hoped that new federal courts would not be created, but that state courts would be commissioned to act as

very existence of lower federal courts may not be constitutionally guaranteed, but may be contingent on Congress' policy predilections.[14]

Inasmuch as the Supreme Court itself was sure to be created, the Convention took responsibility for specifying its purview, at least in broad outline. The delegates agreed that the Court should function in the main as an appellate body, correcting the mistakes made by state courts and inferior federal courts (if the latter were created). In some narrow circumstances, however, they concluded that the Court should have original jurisdiction to determine matters not previously examined elsewhere. Those instances were unremarkable: disputes involving states as parties or implicating representatives of foreign governments.[15] The delegates left the shape of the Supreme Court largely undefined. For example, nothing in Article III specified the size of the Court or so much as mentioned its presiding officer.[16]

The delegates argued at some length about the means by which Supreme Court justices would be chosen. There was no suggestion that the justices might be *elected*; the question was how they would be *appointed*—and by whom.[17] The original Virginia Plan contemplated that the full Congress would make selections. Madison preferred the Senate, perhaps because the smaller body might be less inclined to name justices on the basis of personal friendship or talents for legislative, as opposed to judicial, service. His view prevailed on the whole. Yet in the end, after the Convention decided that Senate membership would be apportioned by states rather than by population, Madison and others evidently concluded that a nationally elected officer, namely the President, should share the responsibility. That is the implication typically drawn from the scheme established by the Appointments Clause.[18]

The means by which justices would be held accountable also excited attention. On that point, the colonies' history with King George was paramount. The delegates agreed that Supreme Court justices (as well as any inferior court judges who were ultimately appointed) would not be subject to removal at will (by either the President or Con-

---

federal tribunals. Federalists almost certainly would have opposed a scheme of that kind and may have thwarted the idea by dropping early language indicating that federal courts would be "appointed" and substituting the language ultimately adopted—by which Congress was given authority to "ordain and establish" inferior federal tribunals. That language arguably connotes new federally chartered institutions, not new authority for existing state judges. See Michael G. Collins, *Article III Cases, State Court Duties, and the Madisonian Compromise*, 1995 Wis. L. Rev. 39, 112–26. Nevertheless, Madison evidently suggested to the Virginia ratifying convention that at least some state courts might be recruited for federal duty. Of course, Madison might have been willing to stretch the truth a bit in aid of getting Virginia into line behind the new Constitution. See McGowan, note 12, at 21–22.

14. See Chapter IV, notes 49–61 and accompanying text (elaborating this point).

15. U.S. Const. art. III, §2, cl.2. Professor Collins speculates that the Convention may have circumscribed the Supreme Court's original jurisdiction in order to reinforce the Madisonian Compromise. If original jurisdiction had been more expansive, the Court might itself have functioned in the manner of a full body of federal tribunals—by dividing itself into numerous panels for conducting trials. Collins, note 13, at 107–10.

16. Article I designates the chief justice to preside at any Senate impeachment trial of the President. U.S. Const. art. I, §3, cl.6. See John Niven, Salmon P. Chase: A Biography 415–32 (1995) (describing Chief Justice Chase in the trial of Andrew Johnson); Richard A. Posner, An Affair of State 168–69 (1999) (describing Chief Justice Rehnquist in the trial of Bill Clinton).

17. The election of judges in this country was a Nineteenth Century idea, the product of Jacksonian populism. See Mary Volcansek & Jacqueline Lafon, Judicial Selection: The Cross-Evolution of French and American Practices 75–98 (1988).

18. U.S. Const. art. II, §2, cl.2. See Chapter III, notes 7–21 and accompanying text (describing the appointment of Supreme Court justices today).

gress). Instead, adopting language directly from the English Act of Settlement, the delegates proposed that judges would serve "during good Behaviour" and would receive salaries that could not be reduced during their tenure.[19] Both justices and judges would be removable, but only for misconduct and then only by impeachment.

Some points of vital conceptual importance apparently aroused no substantial controversy. The delegates readily agreed, for example, that the Supreme Court would have authority to review state court decisions. Perhaps in light of that authority, they rejected Madison's idea for a congressional veto over errant state statutes. Instead, the delegates adopted the Supremacy Clause, which contemplated that the Supreme Court would review state court judgments to ensure that state judges respected federal law, anything to the contrary in state law notwithstanding.[20] By some accounts, it was the delegates who most feared the expansion of federal power in general who least resisted that innovation in particular. To them, it was easier to accept that state courts would be subject to the Supreme Court's appellate supervision than it was to tolerate the obvious alternative: a constitutionally mandated body of inferior federal courts. The thinking leading to the Supremacy Clause was thus linked with the Madisonian Compromise.[21]

The delegates also agreed that the Supreme Court would have authority to determine the Constitution's meaning. It was for that reason, perhaps, that they rejected Madison's idea for a council of revision (whose membership would have included sitting members of the Court) to pass on federal legislation. The justices scarcely needed to examine legislation as soon as it was enacted if they would have ample opportunity to determine its validity later.[22] Moreover, the delegates may have thought that involving federal judges in the legislative process was inconsistent with the developing (though as yet still primitive) sense that governmental power in the new framework should not be concentrated in any one place.[23] The Convention's answer to ill-considered federal legislation was, instead, the President's veto power.[24]

The delegates expressed no clear view regarding the conditions under which the Supreme Court, or any inferior courts Congress created, would exercise judicial power. At one point, Madison said that the federal judiciary should be limited to cases of a "Judiciary Nature."[25] Yet it is unclear what he meant by that characterization. Certainly, it is unclear what anyone else understood him to mean. Recall in this vein that the preexisting royal courts had routinely performed duties that today would be regarded as legislative or executive in nature.[26]

---

19. U.S. Const. art. III, §1. See Chapter III, notes 29–49 and accompanying text (describing impeachment and alternative means of discipline now in place).

20. U.S. Const. art. VI, cl.2.

21. Rakove, note 1, at 171–77.

22. This is not to say that the delegates regarded the Supreme Court's power of judicial review as particularly important or that they anticipated that the Court's unifying force would hold the country together. It is more likely that the delegates put their faith in various structural devices built into the constitutional scheme, which constantly divided and subdivided power in an apparent attempt to achieve a shifting yet viable balance. See Robert A. Burt, The Constitution in Conflict 46, 56–72 (1992); Gordon S. Wood, The Creation of the American Republic, 1776–1787, 549–50 (1969). See Chapter I, note 2 and accompanying text (noting the early appreciation for the separation principle).

23. Casper, note 7, at 286. See James T. Barry, *The Council of Revision and the Limits of Judicial Power*, 56 U. Chi. L. Rev. 235, 253–54 (1989).

24. U.S. Const. art. I, §7.

25. Max Farrand, II The Records of the Federal Constitution of 1787, 430 (1937).

26. See notes 2–4 and accompanying text.

The Committee on Detail produced a draft, under which federal judicial power might be exercised in nine overlapping categories of "cases" and "controversies." By most accounts, the draft (and ultimately Article III) used the terms "cases" and "controversies" interchangeably.[27] In some instances, Article III defined "cases" or "controversies" according to their subject matter. That was true, for example, with respect to "cases arising under this Constitution, the Laws of the United States, and Treaties made, or which shall be made, under their Authority."[28] In other instances, Article III defined "cases" or "controversies" according to the identity or alignment of the parties. That was true with respect to what we now call "diversity" jurisdiction over "Controversies ... between Citizens of different States."

Once the delegates approved a final document, they asked the Continental Congress to transmit it to specially formed state ratifying conventions. Importantly, they insisted that the Constitution must be presented as an indivisible whole, not subject to amendment. That take-it-or-leave-it strategy evoked significant opposition. But it worked. Ultimately, all the states accepted the full document without insisting on changes as a condition of ratification.[29]

D. Ratification and the Federalist Papers

At some of the state ratifying conventions, the Constitution encountered opposition from detractors, grouped under the label "Anti-Federalists." Roughly speaking, the Anti-Federalists were the conservatives of their day. They were suspicious of change, insistent upon stability, and fearful that the new Constitution would subvert state autonomy.[30] Where the delegates in Philadelphia had focused no great attention on the judicial

27. Alternatively, it has been suggested that a "case" could be a criminal proceeding, but a "controversy" was necessarily civil. See William A. Fletcher, *Exchange on the Eleventh Amendment*, 57 U. Chi. L. Rev. 131, 133 (1990); Daniel J. Meltzer, *The History and Structure of Article III*, 138 U. Pa. L. Rev. 1569, 1575–76 & nn. 18 & 22 (1990). Professor Pushaw argues that the founding generation regarded a "case" as an occasion for resolving important public questions, but regarded a "controversy" as an occasion for resolving a private dispute between self-interested adversaries. Robert J. Pushaw, Jr., *Article III's Case/Controversy Distinction and the Dual Functions of Federal Courts*, 69 Notre Dame L. Rev. 447 (1994); see Chapter IX, note 13 (discussing the implications of Pushaw's research for the modern justiciability doctrines). Professor Pfander argues that the distinction between "cases" and "controversies" fortifies his (revisionist) account of the Supreme Court's original jurisdiction. See Chapter VII, note 10.

28. See Chapter IV, text accompanying note 3; Chapter VIII (elaborating the federal courts' jurisdiction to decide federal question cases).

29. Rakove, note 1, at 100–16.

30. The "Anti-Federalist" label has always been confusing. Professor Storing explains that delegates to whom it was applied "usually denied, in fact, that the name was either apt or just, and seldom used it." According to Storing, the Anti-Federalists "often claimed" they were "the true federalists." Yet the "pro-Constitution party" saw "the advantage of a label that would suggest that those who opposed the Constitution also opposed such a manifestly good thing as federalism.... But what has not been sufficiently understood is that the term 'federal' had acquired a specific ambiguity that enabled [pro-Constitution delegates] not merely to take but to keep the name." Herbert J. Storing, What the Anti-Federalists Were For: The Political Thought of the Opponents of the Constitution 7–9 (1981). For other discussions of the Anti-Federalists, see Saul Cornell, The Other Founders: Anti-Federalism and the Dissenting Tradition in America, 1788–1828 (1999); Paul Finkelman, *Turning Losers into Winners: What Can We Learn, If Anything, From the Antifederalists?*, 79 Tex. L. Rev. 849 (2001).

branch, Anti-Federalist delegates to the state ratifying conventions made the prospect of a powerful federal judiciary a major focus of their attack. They charged that the Supreme Court and any inferior courts that might be established would be insulated from political constraints. Courts with that kind of independence would know no other authority but themselves.[31] Recall that the colonial courts had exercised broad governmental power and that one of the chief objections to that regime had always been that those courts were free from any legislative check.[32] Moreover, the new Constitution did not clearly preserve the right to jury trial and thus threatened to discard the only safeguard against judicial power with which the colonists were familiar.[33]

The Anti-Federalists obviously did not defeat the Constitution. But they did persuade many ratifying conventions to urge the new Congress to give early consideration to several amendments regarding the federal judiciary. There were proposals, for example, to specify the separation-of-powers principle more explicitly, to delimit the federal courts' purview, to eliminate the Supreme Court's authority to review determinations of *fact* as well as *law*, and to confirm the right to trial by jury expressly. Several conventions also offered amendments that would have immunized the states from suit in federal court.[34]

Madison collected the proposals advanced by the ratifying conventions, sifted them into categories, and developed a list of amendments for submission to Congress. Ten were adopted in 1791. The first eight formed the Bill of Rights. In some instances, those early amendments addressed the ratifying conventions' concerns about the federal judicial branch. The provisions for trial by jury in the sixth and seventh amendments fit that description. In other instances, state concerns were overlooked or deliberately neglected. Madison himself almost certainly thought that no explicit acknowledgment of the separation principle was needed or desirable. He nonetheless drafted an innocuous amendment to satisfy others' concerns. The House accepted it, but the Senate did not.[35] Madison declined to prepare an amendment regarding state sovereign immunity—an issue that was revisited when the eleventh amendment was promulgated.[36]

The ratification debates produced more than formal adoption of the Constitution. They also generated the Federalist Papers: thoughtful and illuminating essays about the Constitution by Madison, Alexander Hamilton, and John Jay. The Federalist Papers were neither disinterested appraisals of the new Constitution's meaning nor neutral recollections of the actual deliberations in Philadelphia. They were works of advocacy—political tracts meant to dispel Anti-Federalist objections. Nevertheless, they are typically cited in modern arguments about constitutional interpretation. For as Madison, Hamilton, and Jay responded to the concerns raised by their Anti-Federalist adversaries, they developed what many now regard as the United States' unique contribution to political theory.[37]

Most of the Federalist Papers explored structural themes in the Constitution: the separation of powers, as well as federalism and the idea of republicanism.[38] Some ad-

---

31. See Casper, note 7, at 288–89 (collecting relevant primary materials).
32. See notes 2–7 and accompanying text.
33. See note 4 and accompanying text.
34. See Rakove, note 1, at 318–21.
35. See Chapter I, note 2 and accompanying text.
36. See text accompanying note 69; see Chapter X, notes 98–111 and accompanying text (discussing the later adoption of the eleventh amendment).
37. See generally Bernard Bailyn, The Ideological Origins of the American Revolution (1977).
38. E.g., Federalist 10, 51 (Madison).

dressed questions raised at the state conventions about the new federal judiciary. Hamilton in particular made a series of related points about the judicial branch.

The status of the federal courts. By Hamilton's account, it would be "essential to the idea of law" in the new constitutional system "that it be attended by a sanction, or, in other words, a penalty or punishment for disobedience."[39] Adjudication in the courts would provide the only available vehicle for ensuring that law was respected. Hamilton recognized that courts would have no physical power to force the states and the other two branches of the national government to cooperate, but would have to depend on Congress (which would control the public purse) and the President (who would control the sword). Thus the judiciary must always be, in Hamilton's memorable description, the "least dangerous" feature of the new framework.[40]

The independence of federal courts. By Hamilton's account, an independent federal judiciary would not be a vice, but a virtue. He insisted that the country could not depend entirely on state courts, but would need national tribunals that would be insulated from parochial interests. In the same vein, he argued that federal courts must be free from manipulation by the elected branches of the national government. It was to ensure judicial independence that the new Constitution guaranteed that federal judges would serve for life (given good behavior) and would receive irreducible salaries. Hamilton insisted that "a power over a man's subsistence amounts to a power over his will."[41] Without personal protections for individual judges, federal courts would be forced to "consult popularity" as well as "the constitution and the laws" in reaching judicial decisions.[42] They would be at the mercy of the President and Congress and would be unable to enforce checks on governmental power.[43]

The removal of federal judges. Hamilton acknowledged that federal judges could be forced from office. But he contended that the only means available would be formal impeachment (as prescribed in Article I of the Constitution) and that the only permissible basis would be "mal-conduct"[44]—by which he probably meant "Treason, Bribery, or other high Crimes and Misdemeanors" (as prescribed in Article II).[45] Hamilton justified severe limits on removal as a further safeguard for judicial independence. So intent was he on protecting the judiciary from the other branches that he resisted even the possibility that Article III judges should be unseated for "inability." A standard of that kind might tempt the President or Congress to declare unpopular judges incompetent and thus to deprive them of their offices by indirection. For Hamilton, only "insanity" could be "safely pronounced a virtual disqualification."[46]

The supremacy of federal law. In Hamilton's view, the federal courts would certainly have jurisdiction to adjudicate cases implicating the new Constitution. That power would be especially important to ensure that the federal judiciary could force state legis-

39. Federalist 15.

40. Federalist 78.

41. Federalist 79.

42. Federalist 78.

43. Federalist 78, 79. Hamilton added that federal judges would need an extended tenure in order to gain and retain command of the precedents that would develop as the nation grew. Good candidates might be discouraged from accepting federal appointments and achieving expertise in federal materials, if they risked losing their positions after an ordinary term of office. Federalist 78.

44. Federalist 79; U.S. Const. art I, §3.

45. U.S. Const. art. II, §4. See Chapter III, notes 32–36 and accompanying text (discussing the grounds for impeachment today).

46. Federalist 79.

latures and state courts to conform to the Constitution as the supreme law of the land. Otherwise, the states might continue to obstruct national unity as they had under the Articles of Confederation.[47]

The uniformity of federal law. By Hamilton's account, federal judicial power must be co-extensive with federal legislative power. This is to say, the federal courts must be able to handle the judicial business generated when Congress enacted federal statutes. Otherwise, state courts would have to do service, and it would be difficult to obtain consistent interpretations of federal law in all the states.[48]

Cases in which the United States is a party. Under the Articles of Confederation, attorneys representing the national government had been forced to sue in state court. That, in Hamilton's view, not only jeopardized the supremacy and uniformity of federal law, but also offended proper "decorum."[49] Under the new Constitution, it would be vital that federal courts have jurisdiction in cases in which the United States itself was a party.

Diversity jurisdiction. According to Hamilton, federal courts must have authority to adjudicate disputes that cut across state boundary lines, especially disputes between two states as parties, as well as cases involving foreign nations and their citizens. There, too, Hamilton thought state courts would be incapable of providing the necessary independence, national perspective, and respect for the status and dignity of other states and nations. Hamilton referred to suits against *unconsenting* states, but only elliptically. He may have meant to paper over the controversial question of sovereign immunity.[50]

The state courts. Hamilton recognized that state courts had jurisdiction, grounded in state law, to handle a wide range of cases having nothing to do with the new national framework. Article III authorized Congress to establish federal tribunals to adjudicate some of those same cases—for example, disputes between citizens of different states. But Article III did not purport to make federal jurisdiction of those cases exclusive and thus to divest state courts of the power they previously had under state law. Hamilton acknowledged that the Constitution might be read to preclude state court jurisdiction implicitly inasmuch as Article III declared that the federal judicial power "shall" be vested in Article III courts. Yet he insisted that Article III should not be construed to alienate the state courts' prior jurisdiction by implication. In this, Hamilton stated the general proposition that, *ceteris paribus*, the state courts and any new federal courts would function side-by-side, typically with concurrent jurisdiction over the same subject matter and parties.[51]

Exclusive federal jurisdiction. By Hamilton's account, Congress would have authority to make the federal courts' jurisdiction exclusive (and thus to foreclose the state courts from acting) in cases or controversies arising entirely from the new federal framework. But he insisted that state courts would have concurrent jurisdiction, unless and until Congress "expressly" barred them from entertaining specified business. He thus carved

---

47. Federalist 80.

48. In this, Hamilton embraced the understanding, common in the period, that a government's legislative and judicial powers must be coterminous. That may have suggested to Anti-Federalists that the more expansive the power Hamilton contemplated for the judicial branch, the more expansive, in turn, the power he must contemplate for Congress. See G. Edward White, *Recovering Coterminous Power Theory: The Lost Dimension of Marshall Court Sovereignty Cases*, in Origins, note 7, at 66, 93–94.

49. Federalist 80.

50. Id. See also Federalist 81.

51. Federalist 82.

out a significant measure of congressional power, but at the same time also conditioned that power on Congress' willingness (and ability) to satisfy a clear statement rule.[52]

Supreme Court jurisdiction to review state judgments. Again to ensure the supremacy and uniformity of federal law, Hamilton explained that the Supreme Court would have appellate jurisdiction to review state court judgments regarding cases and controversies subject to federal judicial power. He insisted that Article III's express reference to the Court's appellate jurisdiction plainly contemplated that appeals from state courts might be heard. Moreover, it was implicit in the underlying plan that state courts, as well as any inferior federal courts that might be created, were elements of a single judicial system and thus were naturally subject to the final discipline that a single Supreme Court would provide.[53]

E. The Judiciary Acts of 1789–1793

After the new government was assembled, Congress made the creation of the judicial branch a priority. The Judiciary Act of 1789 established both the Supreme Court and a body of inferior federal courts: district courts (with only original jurisdiction) and circuit courts (with both original and appellate jurisdiction). The circuit courts were assigned no judges of their own and had to be staffed by district judges and Supreme Court justices, who, in turn, traveled very significant distances to sit periodically on the circuit bench.[54] The particulars of the jurisdictional grants to the early district and circuit courts are unimportant today.[55] But some general points are of some conceptual significance.

The Judiciary Act of 1789 conferred substantial jurisdictional power on the federal judicial branch, covering most of the categories that Hamilton had identified as crucial.[56] Most of the jurisdictional assignments depended on the status or alignment of the

---

52. Id. See Chapter I, notes 44–52 and accompanying text (discussing the clear statement doctrine and its function).

53. Federalist 82. Elaborating this point, Hamilton conceded that Article III left it to Congress to decide whether to create inferior federal courts with appellate jurisdiction to review state court judgments.

54. Itinerant judges had been common in England, and Congress may have chosen the same pattern without considering the burdens on justices in a much larger country. Historians report that some candidates for the Court declined to be considered rather than face "riding circuit." Those who served complained bitterly. The notorious "Midnight Judges Act" of 1801 assigned the old circuit courts their own judges and eliminated circuit-riding for a brief period. But that action by the outgoing Federalists was immediately reversed by the incoming Jeffersonians, who jettisoned the 1801 Act (and circuit judgeships with it) in 1802—as part of the episode that produced *Marbury v. Madison*. See Chapter I, notes 65–70 and accompanying text. Circuit-riding survived (at least formally) until 1891. Professor Amar suggests that the circuit-riding idea may have had conceptual significance as an indication that Supreme Court justices were not on a different hierarchical plane from district court judges. That, he thinks, is why justices could be expected to staff lower court positions routinely. Akhil R. Amar, *Jurisdiction Stripping and the Judiciary Act of 1789*, in Origins, note 7, at 40, 58–60.

55. For a more detailed summary, see Wilfred J. Ritz, Rewriting the History of the Judiciary Act of 1789, 63–70 (Holt & LaRue eds. 1990).

56. See text accompanying notes 39–53. Typically, the Act restricted jurisdiction to cases involving specified monetary amounts in controversy. For example, the circuit courts could review district court judgments only if the amount in controversy exceeded $50.

parties. For example, the Act gave the Supreme Court original jurisdiction over civil controversies in which a state was a party. And it gave district and circuit courts authority (concurrent with state courts) to entertain cases involving parties of diverse citizenship and, as well, cases in which the United States was the plaintiff. The Act also extended federal judicial power to cases identified by subject matter. For example, the Act granted the district and circuit courts jurisdiction over admiralty cases and federal criminal prosecutions. And it gave both those inferior courts and the Supreme Court authority to entertain petitions for the writ of habeas corpus filed by prisoners who claimed that federal officials were detaining them in violation of federal law.[57] Jurisdiction in habeas corpus cases ensured that the federal judiciary would have a significant role to play in protecting individual liberty.[58]

The Act nevertheless stopped short of conferring on federal courts the full measure of judicial power specified in Article III. Academicians have identified numerous instances in which the Act might have extended the federal courts' authority further than it did. Congress evidently understood that it had discretion to create courts, but at the same time to withhold from the courts it created at least some parts of (indeed, large chunks of) the business that Article III potentially made available as a constitutional matter.[59]

The gaps between the jurisdiction that Article III would have allowed Congress to assign and the jurisdiction that Congress actually conferred were extremely significant. The chief example is the Judiciary Act's failure to give the district and circuit courts a general jurisdiction to entertain cases "arising under" federal law. That is the one basis of jurisdiction one might have expected the Act to recognize—for the reasons that Hamilton and others had articulated. In 1789, there was no substantial body of federal law (as distinct from state law or English common law) to enforce in any court. Moreover, the district and circuit courts were positioned to address issues of federal law that appeared in cases within their party-based jurisdiction.[60] Nevertheless, the Act's omission of a general jurisdiction in federal question cases appears to be important.[61]

---

57. The Constitution bars the suspension of the "privilege" of the writ of habeas corpus, "unless when in Cases of Rebellion or Invasion the public Safety may require it." U.S. Const. art. I, §9, cl.2. Nevertheless, John Marshall suggested in *Ex parte Bollman*, 8 U.S. (4 Cranch) 75 (1807), that the statutory provision in the Judiciary Act was necessary to confer jurisdiction on federal courts to issue the writ. See Chapter IV, note 36. For a discussion of the Suspension Clause generally, see Chapter XII, notes 15–37.

58. The 1789 Act also introduced the idea of removal jurisdiction—by which lawsuits initiated in state court can sometimes be transferred (removed) to federal court. See Chapter VI, notes 125–35 and accompanying text (discussing modern removal statutes and describing the relationship between removal and original jurisdiction in federal question cases). In addition, the 1789 Act contained the precursors of the All-Writs Act, now codified in 28 U.S.C. §1651. The All-Writs Act authorizes both the Supreme Court and inferior federal courts to issue common law writs (like certiorari, prohibition, and coram nobis) when writs of that kind are "necessary or appropriate in aid of their respective jurisdictions and agreeable to the usages and principles of law." See Chapter VI, notes 130, 203; Chapter VII, notes 59, 218, 222; Chapter X, note 26; Chapter XI, note 13, text accompanying notes 20–21; Chapter XII, note 78.

59. See Chapter IV, notes 62–64 and accompanying text (elaborating this point).

60. See Akhil R. Amar, *A Neo-Federalist View of Article III: Separating the Two Tiers of Federal Jurisdiction*, 65 B.U. L. Rev. 205 (1985).

61. See Meltzer, note 27, at 1585; Chapter IV, notes 123–25 and accompanying text (discussing the implications of congressional power to withhold jurisdiction in civil liberties cases). Professor Holt argues that some members of Congress hesitated to give inferior federal courts a general jurisdiction in federal question cases, in fear that those courts would serve as collection agencies for Revolutionary War debts based on treaties. Wythe Holt, *To Establish Justice: Politics, the Judiciary Act of*

The 1789 Act gave the Supreme Court jurisdiction (via the writ of error) to review civil judgments rendered either in the lower federal courts or in the highest state courts.[62] There, too, however, the Act withheld the full appellate power that Article III would have permitted. The Act pointedly restricted the Court's purview to judgments in which a party had advanced a federal claim below and *lost*. If, instead, the lower court had sustained a federal claim (over, for example, an opponent's state law defense), the Act made no provision for Supreme Court review. The implication was that the Court had appellate jurisdiction to ensure that federal law was held *supreme*, but not to ensure that federal law was interpreted *uniformly*.

In addition to creating new federal tribunals and prescribing their jurisdiction, the Judiciary Act of 1789 attended to various other organizational and logistical matters. Inasmuch as the Constitution prescribed no set number of justices for the Supreme Court, Congress necessarily exercised its own judgment regarding that practical problem. The 1789 Act fixed the number at six. In 1801, Congress (then controlled by Federalists) reduced the Court to five seats, apparently to prevent the newly elected Jefferson from naming a replacement for Justice Cushing, who was ill at the time. Thereafter, Congress increased the number of justices—to seven, to nine, and to a high of ten during Lincoln's tenure. After the Civil War, Congress reduced the Court back to seven seats, apparently to keep Andrew Johnson from advancing any nominations at all. The number returned to nine with Grant's election and has remained there ever since.[63]

The 1789 Act left other important matters to be resolved by custom and practice. Like the Constitution itself, the Act largely neglected the Supreme Court's presiding officer, acknowledging only that one of its members would be chief justice.[64] From there,

---

1789, and the Invention of the Federal Courts, 1989 Duke L.J. 1421. See Chapter X, notes 128–29 and accompanying text (discussing the relationship between the war debt cases and the eleventh amendment). Because the Judiciary Act of 1789 came so early, and because so many members of Congress at the time had also been delegates to the Constitutional Convention, the state ratifying conventions, or both, the Act is often cited as evidence of what the founding generation thought the Constitution itself contemplated. E.g., *Wisconsin v. Pelican Ins. Co.*, 127 U.S. 265, 297 (1888). Maeva Marcus and Natalie Wexler have discovered evidence that many members neglected the text of Article III and, instead, made pragmatic judgments about the jurisdiction the federal courts needed to safeguard federal interests. Maeva Marcus & Natalie Wexler, *The Judiciary Act of 1789: Political Compromise or Constitutional Interpretation?*, in Origins, note 7, at 24. It appears, then, that the Act may not have simply embodied what Congress took to be the meaning of the cases and controversies to which Article III referred. It does seem clear that Congress read the Constitution to leave the particulars of the federal courts' purview to legislation—within the outer limits established by Article III. Perhaps relatedly, the Act *did* contain what we now call the Rules of Decision Act, which specifies that "the laws of the several states" typically provide the "rules of decision" in "civil actions in the courts of the United States." See Chapter VIII, notes 57, 92 and accompanying text (discussing the Rules of Decision Act in connection with the federal courts' authority to create federal common law).

62. The Act conferred no appellate jurisdiction on the Court in federal criminal cases. *United States v. More*, 7 U.S. (3 Cranch) 159 (1805); see Marc M. Arkin, *Rethinking the Constitutional Right to a Criminal Appeal*, 39 U.C.L.A. L. Rev. 503, 521–22 (1992). Professor Liebman has shown that the Court was able to exercise review by means of its jurisdiction to issue writs of habeas corpus. James S. Liebman, *Apocalypse Next Time? The Anachronistic Attack on Habeas Corpus/Direct Review Parity*, 92 Colum. L. Rev. 1997, 2058–59 (1992).

63. Franklin Roosevelt asked Congress to increase the number of justices, ostensibly to ensure that elderly members were not overworked but, by all accounts, actually to achieve a majority to sustain the New Deal. That effort failed and is now widely regarded as an attempt to undermine the Court's independence. See Chapter III, note 2.

64. See note 16 and accompanying text.

things might have developed in any number of directions.[65] In the event, President Washington specifically identified his choice for chief justice (John Jay). Since then, the custom has been that candidates are nominated, confirmed, and appointed to that particular office and then hold it for life (barring impeachment).[66]

After affirmatively establishing the federal judiciary and prescribing its many authorities in 1789, Congress turned to housekeeping amendments and a series of restrictive measures. The Judiciary Acts of 1790 and 1793 contained both a version of what is now the Anti-Injunction Act, 28 U.S.C. §2283,[67] and the Full Faith and Credit Statute, 28 U.S.C. §1738.[68] Concomitantly in 1793, Congress took the initial steps toward the eleventh amendment, which was formally proposed in 1794 and ultimately ratified in 1798.[69]

While the Capitol was under construction in Washington, the new national government established itself in New York City, where the Continental Congress had been located. The Supreme Court met for the first time in 1790 in a room in the Royal Exchange Building on Broad Street. There were no cases, and the Court summarily adjourned. There were still no cases the following year, when the government moved to Philadelphia. Over the next ten years, the justices routinely surrendered their quarters to city and state courts, which had comparatively heavy caseloads to manage. It was well into the Nineteenth Century before either the Supreme Court or the lower federal courts handled a significant body of judicial business beyond maritime and real property disputes.[70]

When the Capitol was completed in 1800, Congress had a home, but the Supreme Court still did not. The justices took a spare room on the first floor of the Capitol building, but often found that space intolerably dry and preferred to conduct what little business they had across the road at Long's Tavern, where the Library of Congress now stands. Later, the Court used another room just beneath the Senate chamber. Legend has it that when British troops burned the Capitol in 1814, they used some of the Court's official documents as tinder. There is no commonly accepted account of whether the papers were missed. The Court moved to the building it now occupies in 1935.

The federal judiciary's structure and jurisdiction changed comparatively little, and then only incrementally, for three quarters of a century. On a number of occasions, for example, Congress extended federal court authority to issue the writ of habeas corpus. During Reconstruction, however, the federal courts' place in the system was altered in ways that can only be regarded as revolutionary.

---

65. To name only a few, the President might have named six justices and left them to choose their own presiding officer, perhaps according to seniority or by election. The chief judges of the modern district courts and circuit courts of appeals are determined by seniority. 28 U.S.C. §§45(a)(1), 136(a)(1). Alternatively, the President might have named one of the six as chief justice, but with the understanding that the justice selected would preside for a fixed term or, perhaps, during the President's own term of office. The Lord Chancellor of England is obliged to surrender his office with a change in the British government. Henry Cecil, The English Judge 19–20 (1970).

66. The current statute only identifies the chief justice as a distinct member of the Court. 28 U.S.C. §1. See Chapter III, notes 7–21 and accompanying text (discussing the appointment process).

67. See Chapter XI, notes 7–29 and accompanying text.

68. See Chapter VI, notes 161–95 and accompanying text.

69. See Chapter X, notes 88–137 and accompanying text.

70. John P. Frank, *Historical Bases of the Federal Judicial System*, 13 Law & Contemp. Prob. 3, 15–18 (1948). Early on, the Supreme Court's station was such that John Rutledge, named as one of the first associate justices, promptly resigned to become chief justice of the Supreme Court of South Carolina. Henry J. Abraham, Justices and Presidents: A Political History of Appointments to the Supreme Court 65, 71 (3d ed. 1992).

F. Reconstruction

The Reconstruction period is aptly named. That brief span of years, 1865–1876, produced a fundamental transformation of the relations between the central government and the states. The post-Civil War constitutional amendments, particularly the fourteenth, together with a host of civil rights statutes, established crucial new federal restraints on state power. Simultaneously, numerous new statutes extended the jurisdiction and the remedial authority of the federal courts in order that they might provide the adjudicative machinery needed to enforce the new federal rights. The Reconstruction Congress enacted the Habeas Corpus Act of 1867, 28 U.S.C. §2241, *et seq.* (which authorized the federal courts to entertain petitions from prisoners held in *state*, as well as federal, custody in violation of federal law);[71] the Civil Rights Removal Statute, 28 U.S.C. §1443 (which allowed defendants sued in state court to remove the actions against them to federal court on a showing that they would be denied their federally protected civil rights in state court);[72] and the Judiciary Act of 1875, containing 28 U.S.C. §1331 (which finally assigned the federal courts a general jurisdiction in civil actions "arising under" federal law).[73] In 1871, Congress enacted the Ku Klux Klan Act, 42 U.S.C. §1983, which (fortified by an accompanying jurisdictional statute)[74] authorized federal courts to entertain civil actions on behalf of anyone claiming to be deprived of federal rights by a person acting under color of state law.[75] By means of that Act and others, the Reconstruction Congress charged the federal courts to shoulder new and enormously important authority and responsibility for securing individuals' civil rights against state power.[76]

G. The Modern Structure

In the wake of Reconstruction, the federal courts' role in American public life became ever more significant. At the end of the Nineteenth Century, Congress finally discarded much of the framework erected in 1789 in favor of a more rational and coherent structure. Statutes enacted between 1887 and 1925, particularly the Evarts Act in 1891

71. See Chapter IV, notes 12–25 and accompanying text (discussing the classic habeas corpus cases that soon followed); Chapter XII (discussing modern habeas corpus).

72. See Chapter VI, notes 144–60 and accompanying text.

73. See Chapter VIII, notes 231–387 and accompanying text.

74. E.g., 28 U.S.C. §1343. See Chapter VIII, note 136 (discussing the interplay between §1343 and §1331 in §1983 cases).

75. See Chapter VI, notes 39, 50–56 and accompanying text (discussing the argument that state courts are obligated to entertain §1983 actions); Chapter VIII, notes 132–36, 165–91, 200 and accompanying text (discussing §1983 as an authorization to enforce federal rights in *some* court); Chapter X, notes 367–423 and accompanying text (discussing §1983 as a vehicle for suing state officers); Chapter XI, notes 16–19 and accompanying text (discussing §1983's exemption from the Anti-Injunction Act); Chapter XII, notes 553–73 and accompanying text (discussing the relationship between §1983 and habeas corpus).

76. Robert J. Kaczorowski, The Politics of Judicial Interpretation: The Federal Courts, Department of Justice and Civil Rights, 1866–1876 (1985). Professor Gressman contends that Congress actually enacted only a "pitiful handful" of measures that, in turn, were narrowly construed by the unsympathetic justices who sat on the Supreme Court in the post-War period. Eugene Gressman, *The Unhappy History of Civil Rights Legislation*, 50 Mich. L. Rev. 1323, 1357 (1952).

and the Judges Bill in 1925, established the basic elements of the modern scheme. During the same period, Congress extended the federal courts' purview in extremely important ways. In 1934, Congress enacted the Declaratory Judgment Act, 28 U.S.C. §2201,[77] and in 1946 the judicial review provision of the Administrative Procedure Act, 5 U.S.C. §702.[78]

Today, five kinds of federal courts are organized under the authority of Article III to exercise the federal judicial power: (1) district courts (which handle most trial-level work); (2) courts of appeals for each of the twelve regional circuits (which have appellate jurisdiction to review district court judgments and some orders issued by federal administrative agencies); (3) the Court of Appeals for the Federal Circuit (which has responsibility for appeals in cases involving claims against the United States, customs matters, and patent and trademark disputes); (4) the Court of International Trade (which handles matters touching customs duties, import quotas, and international trade agreements); and (5) the Supreme Court itself (which now has a largely discretionary appellate jurisdiction to review most federal question judgments from most courts, irrespective of whether the party claiming under federal law won or lost below).[79]

The district courts enjoy the services of adjunct officers who perform judicial functions under the auspices of, and subject to control by, the Article III judges they attend. Magistrate judges fit that description, as do bankruptcy judges.[80] In addition, Congress has created other institutions that exercise judicial authority but are not Article III courts inasmuch as their decision-making officers are appointed for limited terms and receive salaries that are subject to diminution. Those so-called "legislative" courts include territorial courts, military courts, local courts in the District of Columbia, the Court of Federal Claims, and the Tax Court.[81]

Where once the federal courts functioned as autonomous entities, today they are linked in an integrated system. This structural reformation is in major part due to the creation of several administrative institutions that have unified the federal judicial branch more, perhaps, than anyone might have envisioned. In 1922, Congress established the Conference of Senior Circuit Judges to serve as a governing body for the federal judiciary as a whole. Since renamed the Judicial Conference of the United States, that body not only establishes policy within the judicial branch, but also speaks for the judiciary in Congress. In 1939, Congress established the Administrative Office of United States Courts to provide the judiciary with administrative support, and in 1967 the Federal Judicial Center to conduct research and educational programs. Those insti-

77. See Chapter VIII, notes 134, 140–47, 332–87 and accompanying text (discussing §2201's effect on jurisdiction pursuant to 28 U.S.C. §1331); Chapter IX, notes 17–24, 416–20 and accompanying text (discussing the relationship between declaratory judgment actions and the advisory opinion and ripeness doctrines).

78. See Chapter VIII, notes 133, 137–39 and accompanying text (discussing §702 as an authorization to sue); Chapter IX, notes 107–20 and accompanying text (discussing §702 as a congressional grant of standing).

79. See Chapter VII, notes 41–57 and accompanying text (discussing the Court's authority to review state court judgments); Chapter VII, notes 211–18 and accompanying text (discussing the Court's authority to review inferior federal court judgments).

80. See Chapter V, notes 52–54. The current arrangement for bankruptcy cases is a product of the Supreme Court's decision invalidating the previous scheme on Article III grounds. See Chapter V, notes 55–65 and accompanying text.

81. See Chapter V (providing a general discussion of non-Article III federal adjudicative officers and bodies).

tutions bring federal judges together on a regular basis to discuss common problems and formulate recommendations for reform.[82]

H. Modern Federal Caseloads

In recent years, the common problem the federal courts have emphasized is the volume of business they are asked to do. Well over ninety percent of the litigation in the United States occurs in state, not federal, court.[83] Nevertheless, by some accounts, federal dockets have expanded to crisis proportions.[84] The reasons are clear enough: population growth, the rise of the federal administrative state, and the "federalization" of American law.[85] The national government now routinely assumes responsibility for matters that historically were left to the states (and the state courts). In particular, federal criminal jurisdiction is much more extensive than it was in the past.[86] Concerns about caseload may be inflated.[87] Yet they must be taken seriously.

Remedies for the caseload problem fall into four broad categories: (1) more judges to do the work assigned to the federal judiciary; (2) better case management to improve the productivity of the judges already in place; (3) structural reforms to distribute business more efficiently within the federal judicial branch; and (4) reductions in the federal courts' jurisdiction.

Additional judges. Congress has steadily increased the number of Article III judgeships. The Judiciary Act of 1789 provided for only 19, with 6 of those set aside for the Supreme Court. By 1970, there were 500, and today the number of authorized positions is about 1,000. The number will almost certainly go higher. There is strong sentiment, however, for keeping the size of the federal judiciary small—both to maintain the quality of the federal bench and to avoid creating even more work simply by introducing

---

82. Professor Resnik contends that these bureaucratic developments have made the federal judiciary a genuine third branch of the national government in a way it never was before. Judith Resnik, *Trial as Error, Jurisdiction as Injury: Transforming the Meaning of Article III*, 113 Harv. L. Rev. 924, 997 (2000). Concomitantly, she argues that the evolution of Article III and non-Article III judicial functions has fundamentally altered the nature of "federal courts" within their sphere. Judith Resnik, *"Uncle Sam Modernizes His Justice": Inventing the Federal District Courts of the Twentieth Century for the District of Columbia and the Nation*, 90 Gtn. L.J. 607 (2002) (offering an extremely thorough appraisal of the federal judiciary's structure and behavior). For a description of the Judicial Conference, the Administrative Office, and the Judicial Center and their (sometimes fractious) relations with Congress, see Charles G. Geyh, *Paradise Lost, Paradigm Found: Redefining the Judiciary's Imperiled Role in Congress*, 71 N.Y.U. L. Rev. 1165 (1996).

83. Professor Baker explains that "[w]hile state courts of general jurisdiction have 15 times as many judges as the U.S. district courts, state trial judges handle 83 times as many criminal cases and 41 times as many civil cases as their federal colleagues." Thomas E. Baker, *A View to the Future of Judicial Federalism: "Neither Out Far Nor In Deep,"* 45 Case Western Res. L. Rev. 705, 716 (1995).

84. E.g., Report of the Federal Courts Study Committee 109 (1990).

85. See William W. Schwarzer & Russell R. Wheeler, On the Federalization of the Administration of Civil and Criminal Justice (1994).

86. Baker, note 83, at 752.

87. Jack M. Beermann, *Crisis? What Crisis?*, 80 Nw. U. L. Rev. 1383 (1986). Judge Posner subtitled the original edition of his book "Crisis and Reform." He now believes that by various means the "crisis" has been averted, justifying a change in title: Richard A. Posner, The Federal Courts: Challenge and Reform xiii (1996). By contrast, Professor Baker predicts an increase in federal litigation of various kinds. Baker, note 83.

more opportunities for disagreement.[88] Not everyone shares these concerns in equal measure.[89] Nevertheless, respected observers warn that simply increasing the number of judges will not answer.[90]

Improved productivity. District courts have become "managerial" in an attempt to streamline litigation and encourage settlement.[91] They now make extensive use of magistrate judges and staff lawyers, alternative dispute-resolution devices, mediation conferences, and various other mechanisms for conserving the judicial effort required to dispose of cases.[92] Pursuant to the Civil Justice Reform Act of 1990, the district courts rely on local advisory groups to formulate case management programs.[93] If anything, the courts of appeals are even more creative. All the circuits have local rules and plans for resolving appeals via truncated process. Most appeals are now considered without benefit of oral argument and, more importantly, are decided without published opinion.[94] The Supreme Court has relied upon its discretion to reduce the sheer number of cases to which it gives full dress review.[95] Many of these developments are controversial.

---

88. Study Committee, note 84, at 7.

89. The risk that digging deeper into the talent pool would compromise quality is debatable. Professor Wells argues that the country would not have to settle for lesser lights if federal judgeships lost their "snob appeal." Michael Wells, *Against an Elite Judiciary: Comments on the Federal Courts Study Committee*, 1991 B.Y.U. L. Rev. 923, 937.

90. See, e.g., Jon O. Newman, *Restructuring Federal Jurisdiction: Proposals to Preserve the Federal Judicial System*, 56 U. Chi. L. Rev. 761 (1989); Jon O. Newman, *1,000 Judges—The Limit for an Effective Federal Judiciary*, 76 Judicature 187 (1993).

91. See Judith Resnik, *Managerial Judges*, 96 Harv. L. Rev. 374 (1982). Compare Robert F. Peckham, *The Federal Judge as a Case Manager: The New Role in Guiding a Case from Filing to Disposition*, 69 Calif. L. Rev. 770 (1981) (offering a favorable appraisal), with Owen M. Fiss, *Against Settlement*, 93 Yale L.J. 1073 (1984) (responding in the negative).

92. See Owen M. Fiss, *The Bureaucratization of the Federal Judiciary*, 92 Yale L.J. 1442 (1983). Professor Resnik argues that it "may be time to leave behind [the] romance" that federal courts are committed to "guarding rights" and recognize that they have now adopted an "anti-adjudication and pro-settlement agenda." Resnik, *Trial as Error*, note 82, at 995.

93. By most accounts, the procedural reforms adopted pursuant to the Act have not significantly improved efficiency. See Rand Corporation, Just, Speedy, and Inexpensive? An Evaluation of Judicial Case Management Under the Civil Justice Reform Act (1996); John B. McArthur, *Inter-Branch Politics and Judicial Resistance to Federal Civil Justice Reform*, 33 U. S.F. L. Rev. 551 (1999) (exploring the reasons why reform efforts have been unsuccessful). For an appraisal of the ways that Congress and the courts can best pool their efforts and talents in the development of rules, see Robert G. Bone, *The Process of Making Process: Court Rulemaking, Democratic Legitimacy, and Procedural Efficacy*, 87 Gtn. L.J. 887 (1999).

94. Thomas E. Baker, Rationing Justice on Appeal: The Problems of the U.S. Courts of Appeals 105–139 (1994) (offering an examination of these and other management tools). It is important to distinguish between failing to publish an opinion and failing to issue one at all. Circuit courts almost always provide some explanation of their results to the parties. Moreover, to say that an opinion is "unpublished" is only to say that it does not appear in the Federal Reporters. Nearly all opinions issued by circuit courts appear on line, via the court's web page, Westlaw, and LEXIS. Most circuits have rules, however, prohibiting lawyers from citing "unpublished" opinions. See Boyce F. Martin, Jr., *In Defense of Unpublished Opinions*, 60 Ohio St. L.J. 177, 185–86 (1999) (arguing that publishing all opinions would be impractical in an era in which appellate courts are asked to decide so many cases). Yet another commission suggests that circuit court time might be saved by assigning some cases to two-judge circuit panels and others to special panels of district judges. Report of the Commission on Structural Alternatives for the Federal Courts of Appeals 62–66 (1998); see also id. at 70–74 (discussing the possibility of making at least some of the circuit courts' appellate jurisdiction discretionary).

95. In recent years, the Court has received more and more petitions for review, but has actually accepted fewer and fewer. By limiting the number of cases it decides, the Court may concomitantly limit its capacity to referee the justice system. Professor Hellman reports that during the year ending

By some accounts, the resolution of disputes by some means other than district court trials is best understood as the regrettable consequence of impatience with federal judicial machinery. Private disputants simply contract out of the traditional adjudicatory responsibilities of federal trial courts and, in the process, both diminish the significance of the federal judiciary and compromise the quality of justice that federal courts have traditionally offered.[96]

Structural reform. Specialized Article III courts might bring experience and expertise to certain technical fields. Yet many observers insist that the federal courts' tradition as generalists is extremely valuable and should not be compromised.[97] Chief Justice Burger's idea for a unique Article III court of appeals for the resolution of intercircuit conflicts won only limited academic support.[98] The Freund Committee's proposal for a "National Court of Appeals" to screen cases for the Supreme Court evoked arguments that it might be unconstitutional.[99] Current initiatives concentrate on modest adjustments in the way the district and circuit courts address classes of cases that may be especially suited for streamlined adjudication.[100]

Reductions in jurisdiction. Forthright reductions in jurisdiction may be the most controversial remedies for the workload problem. All the plans in this vein share a common theme: Federal courts should be reserved for those matters in which there is suffi-

---

in June of 1996, the Court considered only half the number of cases it reviewed in a single year during the 1970s and 1980s. Arthur D. Hellman, *The Shrunken Docket of the Rehnquist Court*, 1996 Sup. Ct. Rev. 403. See Chapter VII, notes 219–45 (discussing the discretionary nature of the Court's appellate jurisdiction).

96. Judge Patrick Higginbotham registered this concern at a workshop sponsored by the Federal Courts Section of the Association of American Law Schools, held in Washington, D.C. in May, 2002. There are other criticisms. The Civil Justice Reform Act decentralizes federal rule-making and thus compromises the uniformity of federal law. See Linda S. Mullenix, *The Counter-Reformation in Procedural Justice*, 77 Minn. L. Rev. 375, 379 (1992); Lauren Robel, *Fractured Procedure: The Civil Justice Reform Act of 1990*, 46 Stan. L. Rev. 1447 (1994). The practice of deciding cases without signed published opinions has deeper significance. The public depends on the courts' published explanations for their actions as a check on federal judicial power, and lawyers and courts rely on reported cases as the material for *stare decisis* arguments. See Baker, note 94, at 130; William L. Reynolds & William M. Richman, *An Evaluation of Limited Publication in the United States Courts of Appeals: The Price of Reform*, 48 U. Chi. L. Rev. 573 (1981).

97. See, e.g., Judicial Conference of the United States, Long Range Plan for the Federal Courts 43 (1995) (recommending the preservation of "generalist" courts of appeals—apart from the Court of Appeals for the Federal Circuit already in place). On specialized Article III courts, see Posner, note 87, at 244–70; Paul M. Bator, *The Judicial Universe of Judge Posner*, 52 U. Chi. L. Rev. 1146 (1985); Judith Resnik, *History, Jurisdiction, and the Federal Courts: Changing Contexts, Selective Memories, and Limited Imagination*, 98 W. Va. L. Rev. 171 (1995); Richard L. Revesz, *Specialized Courts and the Administrative Lawmaking System*, 138 U. Pa. L. Rev. 1111 (1990).

98. Warren Burger, *Annual Report on the State of the Judiciary*, 69 A.B.A. J. 442 (1983); see Thomas E. Baker & Douglas D. McFarland, *The Need for a New National Court*, 100 Harv. L. Rev. 1400 (1987).

99. Report of the Study Group on the Caseload of the Supreme Court (1972). See Charles L. Black, Jr., *The National Court of Appeals: An Unwise Proposal*, 83 Yale L.J. 883, 885–87 (1974) (insisting that such a court would violate the Article III mandate that there shall be "one" Supreme Court). Numerous other ideas have been advanced. Note, *Of High Designs: A Compendium of Proposals to Reduce the Workload of the Supreme Court*, 97 Harv. L. Rev. 307 (1983). See also Commission on Structural Alternatives for the Federal Courts of Appeals, Final Report (1998). Professor Tobias has critiqued this last commission's recommendations. Carl Tobias, *The Federal Appeals Courts at Century's End*, 34 U.C. Davis. L. Rev. 549 (2000) (discussing the commission's report); Carl Tobias, *A Divisional Arrangement for the Federal Appeals Courts*, 43 Ariz. L. Rev. 633 (2001).

100. The Federal Courts Study Committee recommends changes in the way certain Social Security, taxation, and employment cases are handled. Study Committee, note 84.

cient federal interest to justify the deployment of Article III resources. Other business should be channeled either to alternative federal tribunals and agencies or to state courts.[101] The Judicial Conference has adopted that theme as its primary policy recommendation.[102] The implications are both conceptual and practical. Decisions must be made regarding what matters *are* of such national interest to warrant federal jurisdiction. And alternative tribunals, typically state courts, must accept responsibility for the overflow.

Many observers have attempted to identify the ideal allocation of jurisdiction between the federal and state courts.[103] Yet no plan is value-neutral. At some point, everyone makes a normative judgment about what the federal courts *ought* to do and what, in consequence, *ought* to be left to other institutions.[104] Agreement on matters of that kind does not come easily.[105] The Judicial Conference has targeted two categories of cases to be shifted in whole or in part to state court: criminal prosecutions having no peculiar national character and civil cases in which federal jurisdiction is based on the parties' diverse citizenship.[106] Congress, for its part, has steadily *expanded* the federal courts' criminal docket and has been willing to adjust the workload in diversity cases only by raising the required amount that must be in controversy to invoke a district court's jurisdiction.[107]

The federal courts are acutely aware that the decisions they make with respect to their jurisdiction inevitably have implications for their crowded dockets. There is a way, then, in which questions regarding resources can influence the substantive and procedural law the federal courts are constantly developing and applying in the cases that come before them.[108]

---

101. E.g., American Law Institute, Study of the Division of Jurisdiction Between State and Federal Courts 1–6 (1969).

102. Long Range Plan, note 97, at 23 (encouraging Congress to "conserve the federal courts as a distinctive federal forum of limited jurisdiction" and to assign civil and criminal jurisdiction to the federal courts "only to further clearly defined and justified national interests").

103. E.g., Henry J. Friendly, Federal Jurisdiction: A General View (1973).

104. See Erwin Chemerinsky & Larry Kramer, *Defining the Role of the Federal Courts*, 1990 B.Y.U. L. Rev. 67, 76–77; Martin H. Redish, *Reassessing the Allocation of Judicial Business Between State and Federal Courts: Federal Jurisdiction and "The Martian Chronicles,"* 78 Va. L. Rev. 1769 (1992).

105. Diverting judicial business to other federal bodies raises a host of vexing constitutional problems. See Chapter V, notes 1–32 and accompanying text. State courts of general jurisdiction are formally open to receive any business that is channeled their way. See Chapter VI, notes 3–38 and accompanying text. By most accounts, however, state courts face an even more serious workload crisis than the federal courts.

106. Long Range Plan, note 97, at 24–33. Accord Study Committee, note 84, at 14–17, 35–42.

107. See 110 Stat. 3850 (1996) (raising the amount to $75,000).

108. See Judith Resnik, *The Programmatic Judiciary: Lobbying, Judging, and Invalidating the Violence Against Women Act*, 74 So. Calif. L. Rev. 269 (2000) (describing judicial efforts to discourage Congress from enacting the VAWA prior to the Supreme Court's decision finding it unconstitutional). For a general appraisal of current thinking within the federal judiciary, see Judith Resnik, *The Federal Courts and Congress: Additional Sources, Alternative Texts, and Altered Aspirations*, 86 Gtn. L.J. 2589 (1998).

Chapter III

Judicial Independence

The Anti-Federalists may have been troubled by the idea that federal judges should be free of political influence.[1] Yet today that idea is received wisdom. Judicial independence: (1) ensures that federal courts can check the excesses of the President and Congress (as well as the states); (2) insulates the courts from public pressure to reach popular judgments (particularly in civil rights and civil liberties cases involving *un*popular claims and individuals); (3) promotes confidence in federal courts and enhances their prestige (which, in turn, makes judicial service attractive to qualified candidates for federal judgeships); and (4) protects individual judges from their colleagues on the bench (and thus promotes honesty and creativity).[2]

The Constitution itself establishes structural safeguards for judicial independence. Article III judges are neither elected in the first instance nor answerable at the polls thereafter. They are appointed pursuant to a scheme that captures and channels political and ideological considerations. Once seated, they serve, effectively, for life. Their salaries, once fixed, cannot be diminished.[3] Federal judges can be disciplined within the judicial branch, but they are not subject to penalties imposed unilaterally by the Presi-

---

1. See Chapter II, notes 30–34 and accompanying text.

2. This fourth virtue has implications for modern disciplinary procedures. See note 47 and accompanying text; see generally Irving R. Kaufman, *The Essence of Judicial Independence*, 80 Colum. L. Rev. 671 (1980). Professor Redish explains that federal judges have "institutional" independence in order that they can have "decisional" independence. Martin H. Redish, *Federal Judicial Independence: Constitutional and Political Perspectives*, 46 Mercer L. Rev. 697, 698–99 (1995). The classic illustration of the nation's commitment to judicial independence is Franklin Roosevelt's failure to win support for his plan to "pack" the Supreme Court. The President presented his proposal (to add as many as seven justices to the Court) as a means of helping elderly justices stay abreast of their workload. Yet the practical effect would have been to give FDR a large number of places to fill with nominees likely to validate his New Deal programs. See William E. Leuchtenberg, The Supreme Court Reborn: The Constitutional Revolution in the Age of Roosevelt 82–162 (1995); Frank Freidel, Franklin D. Roosevelt: A Rendezvous with Destiny 226–39 (1990). There is an enormous and always expanding literature on judicial independence. E.g., *Symposium, Judicial Independence and Accountability*, 72 So. Calif. L. Rev. 1 (1999).

3. This does not mean that Congress is constitutionally obligated to adjust judicial salaries periodically to account for inflation. See *Williams v. United States*, 122 S.Ct. 1221, 1227 (2002) (Breyer, J., dissenting from the denial of *certiorari*) (noting that plaintiff judges had conceded that Congress has no such duty). Legislation regarding salaries sometimes raises constitutional questions. Occasionally, for example, Congress enacts legislation promising judges a raise, but then changes its mind and blocks the increase. In *United States v. Will*, 449 U.S. 200 (1980), the Supreme Court held that Congress can renege, so long as it does so before higher salaries formally take effect. But see *Williams*, at 1221 (Breyer, J., dissenting) (urging the Court to consider the validity of an arguably distinguishable congressional change of heart). Congress may tax judicial income in the same way other income is taxed, but cannot single judges out for unfavorable tax treatment. *United States v. Hatter*, 532 U.S. 557 (2001).

dent or Congress.[4] They enjoy a range of "implied" or "inherent" powers that enable them to perform their judicial duties effectively. For example, they can manage the processing of cases (within limits), punish disruptive behavior by holding lawyers or parties in contempt, and superintend the administration of criminal justice (again, within limits).[5] They are subject to removal (as individuals) only by means of impeachment.[6]

A. Selection of Supreme Court Justices

The Supreme Court is the only federal tribunal that Article III makes mandatory.[7] Apparently for that reason, the Appointments Clause speaks expressly only to the selection of justices who serve the Supreme Court itself. The President "shall *nominate*, and by and *with the advice and consent of the Senate*, shall *appoint* Ambassadors, other public Ministers and Consuls, *Judges of the supreme Court*, and all other Officers of the United States, whose Appointments are not herein otherwise provided for, and which shall be established by Law."[8] That language distributes authority for selecting justices in a complex way that reflects important structural themes.

On one level, the Appointments Clause incorporates the separation principle, tempered by checks and balances. Both the President and the Senate have their own roles in

---

4. In what may be a telling recent incident, members of Congress urged President Clinton to ask Judge Harold Baer for his resignation after Baer rendered an unpopular decision in a search and seizure case. Initially, the White House press secretary suggested that the President might well do so. The President's counsel soon explained, however, that while Clinton thought Baer's decision was erroneous, he supported "the independence of the federal judiciary" and would simply instruct the prosecutors to appeal if Baer declined to change his position. Meanwhile, Senator Dole, then campaigning against Clinton for the presidency, declared that if Baer did not resign, he should be impeached. When other federal judges asked Clinton and Dole to reconsider their "rhetoric," both responded with assurances that they thought it inappropriate for elected officials to coerce a judge into changing a ruling. Judge Baer ultimately withdrew his order, ostensibly on the basis of new evidence. The episode received widespread publicity. The correspondence is reproduced in Jon O. Newman, *The Judge Baer Controversy*, 80 Judicature 156 (1997).

5. The formal limits of these powers have never been established. For a good discussion, see Robert J. Pushaw, Jr., *The Inherent Powers of Federal Courts and the Structural Constitution*, 86 Iowa L. Rev. 735 (2001).

6. See notes 29–43 and accompanying text. The so-called midnight judges lost their judgeships *en masse* by dint of the elimination of the circuit courts on which they were appointed to serve. See Chapter II, note 54 (describing the Judiciary Act of 1801). That action was sustained in *Stuart v. Laird*, 5 U.S. (1 Cranch) 299 (1803), in a brief opinion that entirely failed to explain the Court's rationale. See Charles G. Geyh & Emily Van Tassel, *The Independence of the Judicial Branch in the New Republic*, 74 Chi. Kent L. Rev. 31, 81–85 (1998). Short of abolishing courts wholesale, Congress can apply pressure to the federal judiciary by manipulating the power of the purse. Professor Resnik reports that the Supreme Court and the federal judiciary occasionally "seem anxious" about the way that Congress may use its authority regarding the budget. Judith Resnik, *The Federal Courts and Congress: Additional Sources, Alternative Texts, and Altered Aspirations*, 86 Gtn. L.J. 2589, 2596, 2602–03 (1998). Professor Peterson describes instances in which some members of Congress have arguably attempted to use Congress' power over the judiciary's funds to affect internal court operations. Todd D. Peterson, *Controlling the Federal Courts Through the Appropriation Process*, 1998 Wis. L. Rev. 993, 998–1003 (describing floor speeches indicating that a provision in an appropriations bill was meant to disallow expenditures on studies of race and gender bias in the courts).

7. See Chapter II, notes 11–14 and accompanying text (explaining that the debate was over the creation of inferior courts).

8. U.S. Const. art. II, §2, cl.2 (emphasis added).

the selection of justices, but they ultimately share responsibility for the candidates who actually obtain seats on the Court—the one branch balancing (and checking) the other. The result is that the players must cooperate. Neither can unilaterally appropriate the Court to its own agenda.[9] On another level, the Appointments Clause acknowledges the balance between popular democracy and federation. The President's role reflects the former, the Senate's the latter. Since the Senate's membership is apportioned by state, rather than by population, the Senate's authority in this instance (to the exclusion of the House of Representatives) ensures that the states as corporate entities can influence the selection of Supreme Court justices.[10]

The Appointments Clause specifies no eligibility standards for Court membership. There is no age limit, nor any requirement that justices have professional credentials of any kind. In the absence of constitutional guidance, the "qualifications" that the President and the Senate can or should seek in candidates are endlessly debated. Most authorities converge on the same list of desirable attributes: integrity, intelligence, education, experience, temperament, technical competence, and physical stamina.[11] Yet the really crucial question is intensely controversial: whether, or the extent to which, a candidate's ideological views may properly be considered.

Some observers argue that ideological considerations should be ruled out of order.[12] That view has appeal for at least two related reasons. First, it seems to promote the impartiality expected of judges. It would not do to appoint zealots who are predisposed to favor some litigants or claims over others and thus to undermine the judiciary's neutrality and integrity. Second, the view that ideology should not be considered seems consistent with a commonly held conception of the judicial function. Adjudication, by that account, is an exercise of disinterested judgment in light of preexisting legal standards as distinguished from the exertion of political will. Accordingly, candidates for the Court should not be chosen because their philosophical views are in harmony with those of the President or the Senate, but rather because they have talents that will enable them to perform distinctly judicial duties. The President and the Senate corrupt the judicial branch if they treat judicial candidates as potential policy-makers in robes.[13]

Other observers dismiss that kind of thinking as either hopelessly naive or dangerously duplicitous. Some critics argue that judicial impartiality is a myth, that the justices make policy with no more constraint than the President or Congress, and that any argument for banishing ideological considerations from judicial selection is mere pretense. Thus the system should frankly recognize that candidates' values matter, the better to identify those values before justices are seated (for life).[14]

---

9. See Chapter I, notes 2–18 and accompanying text (discussing the separation principle).

10. David Strauss & Cass R. Sunstein, *The Senate, the Constitution and the Confirmation Process*, 101 Yale L.J. 1491 (1992).

11. See Larry W. Yackle, *Choosing Judges the Democratic Way*, 69 B.U. L. Rev. 273, 307–10 (1989).

12. E.g., Bruce Fein, *A Circumscribed Senate Confirmation Role*, 102 Harv. L. Rev. 672 (1989).

13. Professor Carter acknowledges that this conception of the judicial function may be aspirational. But he insists that the Senate should not "surrender the myth." Stephen Carter, *The Confirmation Mess*, 101 Harv. L. Rev. 1185, 1201 (1988). Carter argues that the Senate should eschew an exploration of candidates' ideological views and concentrate, instead, on their capacity for "moral reflection." Id. at 1199.

14. Professor Nagel argues that the Senate should use the confirmation process to exert "overt pressure" on the Court to chart a course the Senate finds politically satisfying. Robert F. Nagel, *Advice, Consent, and Influence*, 84 Nw. U. L. Rev. 858, 874 (1990).

Most observers settle into a comfortable middle ground, nodding respectfully in each direction. No one really thinks that human beings can set aside their personal predilections entirely. Everyone, including a Supreme Court justice, brings a certain amount of ideological baggage to every task. Yet American society routinely depends on professional jurists to discipline themselves against bias and prejudice, to restrict attention to the evidence presented, and to respect authoritative legal materials. Accordingly, the President and the Senate can select justices on the basis of ideology without undermining the Court's integrity in the adjudication of individual cases.

It may be that some ideologies are so alien to the adjudicatory function as to be disabling. But a candidate's political allegiances are not typically of that caliber, or anything like it. Similarly, a candidate's generalized views about an issue do not necessarily command a foreseeable result in some identifiable case in which that issue may arise. It is one thing, then, to consider a candidate's general respect for individual liberty as a selection criterion and quite another to condition confirmation on the candidate's promise to sustain (or reject) a particular kind of claim in some hypothetical case.[15]

Adjudication *is* different from legislation in a variety of ways. But in no sense is it a logical or mechanical function, devoid of any need to bring values into play. At the Supreme Court level in particular, justices face extraordinarily difficult issues that demand sound human judgment to resolve. By taking account of candidates' views in the selection process, the President and the Senate may improve the chances of selecting men and women with a sufficient grip on moral and social reality to make those decisions responsibly.[16]

Positing that justices of the Supreme Court will inevitably fashion public policy from the bench, it still is incorrect to regard them as of a piece with ordinary public officials who (properly) must stand for election. The justices' policy-making authority only warrants the President and the Senate to subject candidates to some form of political screening to ensure, at least, that the justices who are selected begin on the same page with the executive and one house of Congress. That measure of electoral control, albeit at several steps removed, may even mitigate the counter-majoritarian difficulty that attends the very existence of unelected, life-tenured justices.[17]

---

15. By convention, the Senate Judiciary Committee leaves it to its members to decide what questions they will ask and to nominees to decide which, if any, questions they will answer. Still, it is bad form for a senator to ask flatly how a nominee would vote on some controversial matter, and when any question comes at all close to that description, candidates routinely respond that they will not prejudge issues that are likely to reach the Court. In a celebrated incident in 1985, Senator Denton sent a candidate for a circuit judgeship, Andrew Frey, a lengthy questionnaire meant to pin Frey down on the abortion issue. That action was widely regarded as an inappropriate effort to manipulate the judicial branch through the confirmation process. See 131 Cong. Rec. S21662–63 (July 31, 1985). Professor Lubet contends that it may be unethical for candidates to "evince a settled intention to decide certain cases in a certain manner." Steven Lubet, *Advice and Consent: Questions and Answers*, 84 Nw. U. L. Rev. 879, 882 (1990). But see *Republican Party of Minnesota v. White*, 122 S.Ct. 2528 (2002) (invalidating a state rule of judicial conduct barring candidates for elective judgeships from announcing their views on legal or political issues).

16. But see Carter, note 13 (contending that the Senate should concern itself only with candidates' moral fitness for judicial judgment).

17. Henry P. Monaghan, *The Confirmation Process: Law or Politics?*, 101 Harv. L. Rev. 1202, 1203 (1988). Chief Justice Rehnquist takes the view that "a president who sets out to pack the Court does nothing more than... appoint people... who are sympathetic to his... principles"—which allows "public opinion" to have "some say in who shall become judges of the Supreme Court." William H. Rehnquist, The Supreme Court 235–36 (1987).

Finally, the Constitution's silence with respect to qualifications may actually speak volumes. Since the Appointments Clause prescribes no value-neutral criteria for selecting justices, and since it assigns the nomination and approval of candidates to demonstrably political entities, it invites the inference that justices are supposed to be selected with politics and ideology in view. At the same time, however, the Appointments Clause forces the President and the Senate to share in the ultimate decision and thus disciplines their ability to bring political influence to bear. Candidates can win seats on the Court only if they demonstrate the attributes and talents that everyone agrees are needed to perform the judicial function.[18]

As a practical matter, candidates' views have always figured in the selection of Supreme Court justices.[19] Presidents have routinely exercised ideological judgment in naming nominees in the first instance, and the Senate has often countered the President's strategy with its own. This is not to suggest, of course, that the selection of Supreme Court justices is merely a matter of patronage. Men and women whose views make them appealing also may offer other talents that excellent jurists need. Moreover, the mortality of justices and the general vagaries of life make it virtually impossible to manipulate the Court's decisions over time simply by choosing new members with particular points of view.[20]

Proceeding from the skeletal baseline fixed by the Appointments Clause, the President and the Senate have developed the modern selection process by custom. When an opening appears on the Court, the President chooses a nominee to fill the position, typically relying on the advice he receives from legal advisors like the Attorney General. The President submits the nominee to the Senate Judiciary Committee, which screens the candidate on behalf of the Senate as a whole. The committee conducts an investigation which, in modern times, invariably includes public hearings at which the nominee is asked to respond to questions.[21]

---

18. Professor Monaghan thinks that the founding generation may have regarded the President's power to nominate candidates as tantamount to an authority actually to make appointments. Yet he explains that in modern times the absence of constitutional criteria for the Senate's confirmation decision leads ineluctably (and properly) to a much more active (and political) role for the Senate. Monaghan, note 17, at 1204–08.

19. When John Jay resigned, President Washington recalled John Rutledge to succeed him as chief justice. Rutledge had been intimately involved in the formulation of the judicial branch and, indeed, had chaired the Committee on Detail in Philadelphia. Moreover, he had been confirmed as one of the original associate justices (albeit he had not actually served in that capacity). See Chapter II, note 70. Nevertheless, the Senate refused to confirm him as chief justice, primarily because he had opposed the Jay Treaty. Henry J. Abraham, Justices and Presidents: A Political History of Appointments to the Supreme Court 73 (3d ed. 1992). Two recent nominees, Robert Bork and Clarence Thomas, faced fierce opposition on ideological grounds. Bork and Thomas were regarded as "conservative" and were opposed by more "liberal" critics. See *Symposium*, *Confirmation Controversy: The Selection of a Supreme Court Justice*, 84 Nw. U. L. Rev. 832 (1990); *Symposium*, *Gender, Race and the Politics of Supreme Court Appointments: The Impact of the Anita Hill/Clarence Thomas Hearings*, 65 So. Calif. L. Rev. 1279 (1992). In previous episodes, "liberal" or "progressive" nominees provoked a similar reaction, albeit from "conservative" quarters. Louis Brandeis and Felix Frankfurter are the classic illustrations. See Abraham, at 180–84, 220–25; see generally Charles L. Black, Jr., *A Note On Senatorial Consideration of Supreme Court Nominees*, 79 Yale L.J. 657 (1970); Paul A. Freund, *Appointments to the Supreme Court: Some Historical Perspectives*, 101 Harv. L. Rev. 1146 (1988).

20. See Bruce A. Ackerman, *Transformative Appointments*, 101 Harv. L. Rev. 1164, 1183 (1988); Richard D. Friedman, *Tribal Myths: Ideology and the Confirmation of Supreme Court Nominations*, 95 Yale L.J. 1283, 1291 (1986).

21. Nominees did not appear at confirmation hearings in person until Frankfurter broke from tradition in 1939. The absence of candidates did not keep the proceedings calm, however. The hear-

B. Selection of Inferior Court Judges

The Appointments Clause does not establish that judges assigned to inferior Article III courts must be selected by the mechanism prescribed for Supreme Court justices. By some accounts, an affirmative answer has been assumed.[22] Yet presidential nomination coupled with senatorial advice and consent is explicitly mandated only for "principal" officers: Supreme Court justices, ambassadors, and "other public Ministers and Consuls."[23] Federal judges serving lower federal courts fit none of those categories.[24] The presidential nomination/senatorial consent scheme *may* also be employed in the selection of "all other Officers of the United States, whose Appointments are not herein otherwise provided for." But according to a further proviso in the Appointments Clause, Congress may "by Law vest the Appointment of such inferior Officers, as they think proper, in the President alone, in the Courts of Law, or in the Heads of Departments." The "Appointments" of inferior court judges are "not herein otherwise provided for."[25] Lower court judges may be "inferior Officers" who can be chosen by some alternative means.[26]

Whatever alternatives the Constitution may permit, Congress has in fact specified that judges serving the district courts and the courts of appeals are to be selected in the same way that Supreme Court justices are chosen.[27] The selection process at this different level is more bureaucratic. The President typically depends on political relationships in individual states to generate nominees. Senators of the President's party have histori-

---

ings on Brandeis' nomination resembled a trial *in abstentia*. Brandeis himself was not there, but he was formally represented by counsel—as was the organized opposition. See Leonard S. Baker, Brandeis and Frankfurter: A Dual Biography 103–11 (1984).

22. E.g., Richard A. Posner, The Federal Courts: Challenge and Reform 16 n.17 (1996) (citing no authority).

23. *Buckley v. Valeo*, 424 U.S. 1, 132 (1976). See John M. Burkoff, *Appointment and Removal Under the Federal Constitution: The Impact of Buckley v. Valeo*, 22 Wayne L. Rev. 1335 (1976).

24. The possibility that judges in the lower courts are "other public Ministers" is foreclosed by the very next subdivision of Article II, which specifies that the President is to "receive Ambassadors and other public Ministers." U.S. Const. art. II, §3. That provision refers to "public Ministers" as representatives of foreign nations. It seems to follow that when the Appointments Clause uses the same label, it contemplates similar officers of the United States—i.e., officers with authority for foreign affairs.

25. The officers whose appointments *are* "herein otherwise provided for" include the President himself and the Vice President, as well as the members of the House and Senate and the constitutionally prescribed officers in each—all of whom are selected by means specified elsewhere in the Constitution. The Constitution also prescribes the way in which officers of the state militia and the members of the electoral college are to be chosen. But since those authorities are selected by the states concerned, they are not officers "of" the United States at all. *Fitzgerald v. Green*, 134 U.S. 377 (1890) (holding as much with respect to electoral college members).

26. Congress might turn the duty over to the President alone or allow the judicial branch to fill openings in its own ranks. See Burke Shartel, *Federal Judges—Appointment, Supervision, and Removal—Some Possibilities Under the Constitution*, 28 Mich. L. Rev. 485, 488–92 (1930). Or Congress might recruit the "Head" of some "Department" to duty. The Attorney General presides over the Department of Justice and thus might be available. Or Congress might establish a new department to assume this responsibility. Whether Congress might mix and match selection schemes is problematic. Consider, for example, the possibility that Congress might give the Supreme Court authority to fill vacancies in the lower courts, but only subject to the Senate's "advice and consent." See Yackle, note 11, at 322–26 (offering wild speculation).

27. 28 U.S.C. §133(a) (district judges); 28 U.S.C. §44(a) (circuit judges).

cally exercised significant influence. The American Bar Association Standing Committee on the Federal Judiciary also appraises nominees' qualifications and offers recommendations both to the President and to the Senate.[28]

C. Removal by Impeachment

Since the Constitution empowers the President to appoint confirmed candidates, it might have been expected that it would equally empower the President to remove them—the one power implying the other.[29] Instead, Article III states that all judges appointed under its authority hold office "during good Behaviour" and, in addition, are entitled to an irreducible salary while they are on the bench. Plainly, then, the Constitution separates the appointment and removal powers where Article III judges are concerned.[30] In this way, too, federal judges enjoy independence from the political branches.

The Constitution does not squarely address judicial removal or discipline in so many words. But the last section in Article II provides for impeaching "the President, Vice President, and *all civil Officers of the United States.*" Article III judges have always been understood to be "civil Officers" within the meaning of that provision.[31] Three further questions are controversial: (1) the grounds that warrant impeachment; (2) the process that impeachment cases must follow; and (3) the extent to which removal can be based on prior criminal proceedings.

Grounds for impeachment. Article II specifies that "civil Officers" can be removed if the House of Representatives impeaches them for, and the Senate convicts them of,

---

28. See Laura E. Little, *The ABA's Role in Prescreening Federal Judicial Candidates: Are We Ready to Give Up on the Lawyers?*, 10 Wm. & Mary Bill of Rts. J. 37 (2001). The formal procedural mechanisms for identifying and screening candidates for inferior court judgeships are anything but constant. Most modern Presidents have established special offices in the Justice Department for the purpose. President Carter supplemented that model with nominating commissions, charged to seek out qualified women and members of minority groups as potential nominees. During the Carter years, the number of women and African Americans on the federal bench increased dramatically. President Reagan rescinded Carter's executive orders in favor of an advisory group located in the Justice Department's Office of Legal Policy. President George Herbert Bush used a similar Justice Department division, but also relied on a deputy attorney general and the Office of White House Counsel. President Clinton employed the Office of Policy Development at the Justice Department, working jointly with the Office of White House Counsel. Clinton, too, substantially increased the number of women and minorities on federal courts. Carl Tobias, *Leaving Legacy on the Federal Courts*, 53 U. Miami L. Rev. 315 (1999). President George W. Bush has not made his selection system public. For an account of the judicial selection process and its results in the modern era, see Sheldon Goldman, Picking Federal Judges (1997). For proposals for improving the process by which federal judges are selected, see Robert A. Katzmann, Courts and Congress (1997); Miller Center of Public Affairs, Improving the Process of Appointing Federal Judges (1996); Charles G. Geyh, *Courts, Congress, and the Constitutional Politics of Interbranch Restraint*, 87 Gtn. L.J. 243 (1998) (reviewing the Katzmann book). For a discussion of the federal appointments process generally, see Michael J. Gerhardt, The Appointments Process: A Constitutional and Historical Analysis (2000).

29. See *Myers v. United States*, 272 U.S. 52, 122 (1926) (stating in connection with the removal of an executive officer that "[t]he power of removal is incident to the power of appointment"—even if the appointive power is conditioned on the Senate's "advice and consent").

30. See Edward S. Corwin, *Tenure of Office and the Removal Power Under the Constitution*, 27 Colum. L. Rev. 353, 379 n.69 (1927).

31. U.S. Const. art. II, §4. See Chapter II, notes 44–46 and accompanying text (discussing Hamilton's views in Federalist 79).

"Treason, Bribery, or other high Crimes and Misdemeanors." By negative inference, it appears that judges cannot be forced from office on some other basis.[32] Yet the phrase "high Crimes and Misdemeanors" is ambiguous. The definition of "impeachable" offenses has been debated in cases involving executive officers, and the answer in that context may ultimately be that anything will do if it wins sufficient votes in the House of Representatives. Equally in the context of judicial officers, it has been said that an "impeachable" offense is "whatever a majority of the House... considers [it] to be at a given moment in history."[33]

That assessment may reflect political reality, but not history. The first federal judge to be impeached, John Pickering, was by all accounts mentally disturbed and thus unable to perform judicial duties. Pickering was ultimately convicted, but only after a lengthy (and inconclusive) debate over whether incompetence alone was a sufficient basis for his removal.[34] The only Supreme Court justice ever to be impeached, Samuel Chase, was charged both with criminal conduct and for unprofessional behavior in James Callender's celebrated sedition trial. In truth, Chase had made himself a target by attacking Republican policies from the bench. He was acquitted in the Senate, and his case is now regarded as having settled, in American culture if not formally in American law, that federal judges are not subject to removal on the basis of their decisions.[35] All the lower court judges impeached in recent years were charged with personal misconduct (usually criminal offenses) said to undermine their integrity and impartiality.[36]

The impeachment process. The Constitution prescribes the general process for impeachment cases in bare outline. The House of Representatives has "the sole Power of impeachment" and thus lays formal charges.[37] The Senate has "the sole Power to try all Impeachments" and thus determines whether a judge should actually be removed from office.[38] The Supreme Court held in *Nixon v. United States*[39] that the Senate can determine for itself whether to delegate responsibility for holding hearings to a committee.[40]

Reliance on criminal prosecutions. The Constitution neither insulates federal judges from criminal charges nor specifies that they must be impeached before, rather than

---

32. Peter M. Shane, *Who May Discipline or Remove Federal Judges? A Constitutional Analysis*, 142 U. Pa. L. Rev. 209, 218–19 (1993).

33. This was Gerald Ford's famous statement during the debates on whether Justice William O. Douglas should be impeached because of his personal lifestyle. 116 Cong. Rec. H11913 (April 15, 1970). See Robert Kramer & Jerome A. Barron, *The Constitutionality of Removal and Mandatory Retirement Procedures for the Federal Judiciary: The Meaning of "During Good Behaviour,"* 35 Geo. Wash. L. Rev. 455 (1967); Paul S. Fenton, *The Scope of the Impeachment Power*, 65 Nw. U. L. Rev. 719 (1970).

34. Richard Ellis reports that Pickering's opponents doubted that he could be impeached for insanity and thus were forced into the awkward posture of insisting that he was lucid and thus able to commit "high Crimes and Misdemeanors." See Richard E. Ellis, The Jeffersonian Crisis: Courts and Politics in the Young Republic 69–75 (1971).

35. Report of the National Commission on Judicial Discipline and Removal 11 (1993). See William H. Rehnquist, Grand Inquests: The Historic Impeachments of Justice Samuel Chase and President Andrew Johnson (1992); Suzanna Sherry, *Judicial Independence: Playing Politics With the Constitution*, 14 Ga. St. L. Rev. 795 (1998).

36. National Commission, note 35, at 44–45.

37. U.S. Const. art. I, §2, cl.5.

38. U.S. Const. art. I, §3, cl.6.

39. 506 U.S. 224 (1993); see Chapter IX, notes 62–69 and accompanying text.

40. See National Commission, note 35, at 27–82 (reviewing existing House and Senate rules and offering modest recommendations for reform).

after, prosecution.[41] If a judge has already been found guilty of serious crime, but nonetheless declines to resign, the House and Senate are likely to impeach and convict in short order. It is debatable whether the prior judicial determination of guilt can be given preclusive effect in impeachment proceedings, such that the House and Senate have nothing independently to decide.[42] Yet by extension, the Court's decision in *Nixon* may leave the resolution of that issue to the Senate.[43]

D. Alternative Means of Discipline

The Judicial Councils Reform Act charges judicial councils in all circuits to investigate both complaints that judges are unable to discharge their duties because of mental or physical disability and allegations that judges have engaged in conduct "prejudicial" to the administration of justice.[44] Those judicial councils cannot *remove* judges in the constitutional sense of depriving them of their offices and salaries. But they can reprimand judges found to have misbehaved and, perhaps more importantly, they can temporarily reassign a judge's official duties to others while investigations are under way.[45]

---

41. *United States v. Claiborne*, 727 F.2d 842, 846 (9th Cir.), *cert. denied*, 469 U.S. 829 (1984); *United States v. Hastings*, 681 F.2d 706, 709 (11th Cir. 1982). See Shane, note 32, at 223–32.

42. See National Commission, note 35, at 45–47 (recommending that some form of preclusion be accepted). An obstreperous judge can remain in office while impeachment proceedings are under way. That is possible even if the judge is first convicted and sent to prison. Yet experience shows that judges under fire almost always resign. Emily Field Van Tassel, *Resignations and Removals: A History of Federal Judicial Service—and Disservice—1789–1992*, 142 U. Pa. L. Rev. 333, 337–38 (1993). Any practical difficulties in this vein can probably be resolved by reassigning cases to others. See National Commission, note 35, at 15–16; notes 45–49 and accompanying text.

43. It has been suggested that Congress might short circuit the impeachment process entirely by making forfeiture of a judge's office part of the penalty for a serious crime. That would involve Congress in the removal of a judge without benefit of impeachment, but it would be neutral with respect to the judge's exercise of judicial power and thus would not present the risks of legislative overreaching that the (deliberately difficult) impeachment process presumably hopes to forestall. Moreover, the courts superintend criminal prosecutions. If Congress achieves removal by means of judicial action, the concerns that unilateral congressional steps evoke are, once again, defused. There is already a statute that disqualifies a judge who is convicted of bribery from holding office. See 18 U.S.C. §201. But see Raoul Berger, Impeachment: The Constitutional Problems 141–53 (1973) (explaining that §201 has never been utilized). All this said, the fact remains that the Constitution clearly separates impeachment from criminal prosecutions. That suggests that the one cannot do service for the other. And by most accounts, impeachment is the only valid means by which the legislative branch can drive an Article III judge from office. See National Commission, note 35, at 23; Philip B. Kurland, *The Constitution and the Tenure of Federal Judges: Some Notes from History*, 36 U. Chi. L. Rev. 665 (1969).

44. 28 U.S.C. §372(b)–(c). Judge Edwards has criticized the Act as a misuse of judicial resources. He would prefer informal means of persuading judges to behave properly. Harry T. Edwards, *Regulating Judicial Misconduct and Divining 'Good Behavior' for Federal Judges*, 87 Mich. L. Rev. 765 (1989).

45. 28 U.S.C. §372(c)(6)(B). In *Chandler v. Judicial Council*, 398 U.S. 74 (1970), the Supreme Court bypassed an opportunity to decide whether reassigning a judge's cases constitutes removal in substance and whether, accordingly, removal at the hands of other judges (rather than via impeachment) is valid. Dissenting in that case, Justices Douglas and Black reached the merits of those questions and insisted that depriving judges of their caseloads in the absence of impeachment is unconstitutional. Id. at 136–37. In a concurring opinion, Justice Harlan concluded that a judicial council's reassignment of a case constitutes part of the adjudicative process in that case, so that such an order is reviewable as judicial action by an Article III court. Id. at 110. See Chapter IV, notes 108–11 and

This system of legislatively prescribed, but judicially administered, discipline is far less cumbersome than the impeachment process, but still minimizes the concerns about legislative overreaching.

Nonetheless, objections can be raised. Depriving judges of case assignments may amount to removal—in fact, if not in form. If Congress truly is restricted to impeachment as a means of discharging miscreants, a statute authorizing judicial councils to achieve the same end in a different way may be invalid.[46] Leaving it to other judges to decide whether to reassign a judge's cases responds to most of the values associated with judicial independence. Yet it arguably neglects one important item on that list: the idea that individual judges have tenure and salary protections to insulate them from overbearing colleagues, as well as from the legislative and executive branches.[47] Despite these theoretical difficulties, the Act is probably valid—provided, of course, that judicial councils do not abuse their authority in an effort to affect the outcomes that Article III judges can reach.[48] There is no definitive Supreme Court authority on the constitutionality of the judicial disciplinary scheme the Act establishes.[49]

---

accompanying text (discussing the constitutional questions raised when Article III courts undertake administrative functions apart from their judicial duties).

46. See Lynn A. Baker, *Unnecessary and Improper: The Judicial Councils Reform and Judicial Conduct and Disability Act of 1980*, 94 Yale L.J. 1117 (1985).

47. See text accompanying note 2; Michael J. Gerhardt, The Federal Impeachment Process: A Constitutional and Historical Analysis 101 (1996). See also Shane, note 32, at 235 n.104 (collecting authorities contending that judicial branch discipline jeopardizes individual judges' independence). But see National Commission, note 35, at 15–16 (acknowledging but rejecting those arguments).

48. Appellate court judges have a more appropriate remedy for what they regard as an erroneous judicial decision. They can reverse.

49. But see note 45 (noting the positions that Justices Douglas and Black took in the *Chandler* case).

Chapter IV

Article III Courts

The Constitution establishes only the bare outlines of the federal judiciary's structure and purview. Article III states that "the judicial Power" of the United States "*shall* be vested" in "one supreme Court" and in "such inferior Courts as the Congress *may* from time to time ordain and establish."[1] The federal judicial power "*shall* extend" to "*all* Cases"[2] in three categories (most of them defined by subject matter): (1) "all Cases, in Law and Equity, arising under this Constitution, the Laws of the United States, and Treaties made, or which shall be made, under their Authority;" (2) "all Cases affecting Ambassadors, other public Ministers and Consuls;" and (3) "all Cases of admiralty and maritime Jurisdiction."[3]

In addition, the judicial power extends to "controversies" in six other categories (all of them defined by the identity or alignment of the parties): (1) "Controversies to which the United States shall be a Party;" (2) "Controversies between two or more States;" (3) "[Controversies] between a State and Citizens of another State;" (4) "[Controversies] between Citizens of different States;" (5) "[Controversies] between Citizens of the same State claiming Lands under the Grants of different States;" and (6) "[Controversies] between a State, or the Citizens thereof, and foreign States, Citizens or Subjects."[4]

The Supreme Court may have original jurisdiction over only a very few matters: "all Cases affecting Ambassadors, other public Ministers and Consuls, and those in which a State shall be a Party."[5] With respect to "the other Cases before mentioned," the Court's jurisdiction is appellate, "with such *Exceptions*, and under such *Regulations*, as the Congress shall make."[6] Operating within this general framework, Congress fills in the details by statute. Questions regarding congressional power fall under three headings: (1) Congress' authority to prescribe the Supreme Court's jurisdiction; (2) Congress' discretion to create (or to eschew) federal courts inferior to the Supreme Court; and (3) Congress' authority to fix the jurisdiction of any inferior courts it chooses to establish.

A. Supreme Court Jurisdiction

By common account, the Constitution gives Congress no choice but to create "one supreme Court." The jurisdiction the Supreme Court can or must exercise is another

1. U.S. Const. art. III, §1 (emphasis added).
2. U.S. Const. art. III, §2 (emphasis added).
3. See Chapter VIII, notes 5–46 and accompanying text (discussing cases "arising under" federal law).
4. See notes 63–66 and accompanying text (discussing diversity jurisdiction).
5. See Chapter VII, notes 1–40 and accompanying text.
6. U.S. Const. art. III, §2, cl.2 (emphasis added).

matter. Article III fixes the Court's original jurisdiction and gives Congress no power either to add to that jurisdiction or to detract from it.[7] That much was decided in *Marbury v. Madison*.[8] By contrast, the Court's appellate jurisdiction is subject to the "Exceptions Clause," which authorizes Congress to make "Exceptions" and "Regulations" that limit the Court's ability to reach all the cases and controversies on the Article III menu.[9]

1. The Exceptions Clause

With respect to the Exceptions Clause, the Supreme Court has generally indulged Congress. In *Durousseau v. United States*,[10] the Court explained that Article III itself establishes the Court's appellate jurisdiction and that the authority assigned to Congress is only to make "Exceptions" from that constitutionally derived judicial power. The Court acknowledged, however, that Congress typically enacts legislation that appears to grant jurisdiction to the Court affirmatively—as though Congress had authority to determine the Court's appellate jurisdiction in the first instance. Deferring to Congress' preferred style, the Court said that it would not insist that jurisdictional statutes be stated as negative "Exceptions" to Article III power, but would read affirmative statutory grants of jurisdiction to make "Exceptions" for any jurisdiction omitted. As a practical matter, then, the Court's appellate jurisdiction is "wholly the creature of legislation."[11]

Coming to the "Exceptions" that Congress is entitled to make, the Court has again deferred to Congress. The classic precedent in point, *Ex parte McCardle*,[12] is widely cited for the proposition that Congress has plenary authority under the Exceptions Clause to withhold appellate jurisdiction as Congress sees fit. No doubt there are *some* limits on that authority, not implicated in *McCardle*. Yet in light of *McCardle*, those limits appear to be narrow and often contestable.[13] The story behind *McCardle* is complicated, but roughly it goes this way.

Recall that the Judiciary Act of 1789 gave both the lower federal courts and the Supreme Court jurisdiction to entertain habeas corpus petitions filed by prisoners claiming to be held in the custody of federal officers in violation of federal law.[14] After the Civil War, the Reconstruction Congress enacted the Habeas Corpus Act of 1867, which extended the federal courts' jurisdiction in habeas corpus cases by removing the requirement that petitioners be in the custody of federal authorities. Under the 1867 Act, federal courts could entertain petitions from prisoners held by either federal or state officers, so long as the prisoners alleged that they were deprived of their freedom in violation of federal law. The Act explicitly provided that prisoners who failed to win their freedom in the lower courts could appeal to the Supreme Court.[15] The point of the

---

7. See Chapter VII, notes 36–40 and accompanying text (discussing modern decisions on original jurisdiction).

8. See Chapter I, text accompanying notes 65–70.

9. See notes 10–25 and accompanying text.

10. 10 U.S. (6 Cranch) 307 (1810).

11. *Daniels v. R.R. Co.* 70 US. (3 Wall.) 250, 254 (1866), citing *Durousseau*, 10 U.S. at 314.

12. 74 U.S. (7 Wall.) 506 (1869).

13. See notes 131–49 and accompanying text (discussing non-controversial external limits on congressional power and more debatable internal restrictions).

14. See Chapter II, text accompanying note 57.

15. See Chapter II, text accompanying note 71. Specifically, the 1867 Act gave the federal courts, including the Supreme Court, jurisdiction "in addition to the authority already conferred by law," to

1867 Act was to make federal courts, including the Supreme Court, accessible to African Americans in the South, who were often deprived of their liberty despite formal emancipation. Simultaneously, Congress enacted the Military Reconstruction Act, which installed martial law in the states of the former Confederacy. Those statutes and other measures evoked passionate resentment in the South. President Andrew Johnson sympathized with southerners and resisted significant aspects of the Reconstruction program. Ultimately, he was impeached in the House and brought to stand trial in the Senate. Meanwhile, the Supreme Court, too, expressed doubts about Congress' actions and let it be known that the Military Reconstruction Act might be held unconstitutional.[16]

McCardle wrote newspaper editorials condemning martial law in Mississippi.[17] Federal military authorities arrested him and charged him with inciting insurrection. Today, McCardle's case would present a straightforward first amendment issue; then, it supplied a vehicle for challenging the law under which the military purported to act. Awaiting trial in a military brig, McCardle filed a habeas corpus petition in federal circuit court, complaining that the military commander who held him in custody lacked authority to do so and relying on the newly enacted 1867 Habeas Corpus Act to invoke the federal court's jurisdiction. The circuit court denied his petition, and McCardle appealed to the Supreme Court—now relying on the specific provision of the 1867 Act granting the Court appellate jurisdiction in habeas corpus cases.

When the case was initially argued, Lyman Trumball contended on the government's behalf that McCardle's petition was not covered by the 1867 Act. Trumball, a sitting senator who had himself largely written that Act, explained that it was meant not for white southerners contesting the actions of *federal* officials, but rather for recently freed slaves seeking the federal courts' protection from *state* authorities. The Court rejected that argument: By its terms, the Act empowered the federal courts to entertain petitions from prisoners challenging any kind of custody (state or federal), provided the basis of the challenge was an alleged violation of federal law.[18] At that point, it appeared that the Court would reach the merits of McCardle's claims against the Military Reconstruction Act and, in all probability, would strike that Act down.

Trumball promptly went back to Congress and ushered through yet another statute in 1868, this one expressly repealing that part of the 1867 Habeas Corpus Act giving the Supreme Court appellate jurisdiction in cases arising under that Act. Then, when the Court reconvened, Trumball argued that Congress had exercised its power under the Exceptions Clause to withdraw the Court's jurisdiction in the *McCardle* case itself. The circumstances were extraordinary. On at least one occasion, Chief Justice Chase had to excuse himself in order to preside in President Johnson's impeachment trial, then under way in the Senate. No one could have failed to comprehend Congress' determination to have its way.[19] In the end, Chase wrote a brief opinion for a unanimous Court, deferring to Congress' power under the Exceptions Clause and dismissing McCardle's appeal for want of jurisdiction to consider it further.

---

grant writs of habeas corpus in "all cases where any person may be restrained of his or her liberty in violation of the Constitution, or of any treaty or law of the United States." 15 Stat. 44.

16. *Ex parte Milligan*, 71 U.S. (4 Wall.) 2 (1867).

17. See generally William W. Van Alstyne, *A Critical Guide to Ex parte McCardle*, 15 Ariz. L. Rev. 229 (1973).

18. *Ex parte McCardle*, 73 U.S. (6 Wall.) 318 (1868).

19. One of the counts in the President's indictment was his unsuccessful veto of the 1868 repealer.

Taken literally, the *McCardle* decision appears to recognize extensive congressional power to deny or withdraw appellate jurisdiction from the Supreme Court. After all, in that case the Court approved an "Exception" in a case implicating free speech, after the case had been argued and it appeared the Court would reach a decision that Congress wanted to avoid. The repealer was outcome-neutral on its face, but it clearly was enacted to forestall a decision declaring martial law in the South unconstitutional. If Congress was successful in *McCardle*, it seems that Congress should be equally successful in most other instances *a fortiori*.[20] Nevertheless, there are two reasons to doubt that *McCardle* actually stands for such a broad proposition. One, of course, is the politically charged context in which the decision was rendered. That special historical context arguably makes *McCardle* an unreliable precedent for ordinary modern cases in which the Court is under less pressure to pacify Congress.[21]

The other reason for pause is the Court's own warning that the *McCardle* decision was less sweeping than it appeared to be. Near the end of his opinion, Chief Justice Chase said that the parties apparently assumed that the provision in the 1867 Act giving the Supreme Court appellate jurisdiction over cases filed under that Act was the only jurisdictional basis available, so that if the repealer was valid there was no other jurisdictional ground on which the Court could rely. That, he said, was untrue. The repealer in 1868 had no effect on "the jurisdiction which was previously exercised."[22] Chase meant, of course, the jurisdiction the Court had always had pursuant to the Judiciary Act of 1789. In *McCardle*, where the custody complained of was federal, the petitioner might have proceeded under the earlier statute—without relying on the 1867 Act and thus without running into the 1868 repealer of the Supreme Court's appellate jurisdiction under that Act.[23]

The Court thus hinted in *McCardle* itself that, in another case, it might read the 1868 repealer to leave the Court's jurisdiction under the 1789 Act in place—so that, by switching jurisdictional statutes, the Court might yet exercise appellate jurisdiction in the same kind of situation. In *Ex parte Yerger*,[24] decided shortly thereafter, the Court did precisely that.[25] It appears, then, that the Court in *McCardle* did not actually face the constitutional question whether Congress has power to withdraw every basis of appellate jurisdiction in a case. Instead, the Court may only have addressed a far less significant issue: whether Congress can change the jurisdictional ground on which the Court can proceed by eliminating the jurisdictional statute that initially authorized the Court to hear a case and leaving the Court to act on the basis of another, unaffected jurisdictional statute. A statute that simply shifts pending cases from one jurisdictional anchorage to another presents no obvious constitutional difficulty.

---

20. But see note 82 and accompanying text (discussing the *Klein* case).

21. Justice Douglas once suggested that *McCardle's* conclusion would not be accepted today. *Glidden Co. v. Zdanok*, 370 U.S. 530, 606 (1962) (dissenting opinion).

22. *McCardle*, 74 U.S. at 515.

23. The 1867 Act arguably supported this thesis inasmuch as it conferred new jurisdiction on the federal courts "in addition to the authority already conferred by law." See note 15. And Chase was surely right that the repealer in 1868 expressly eliminated only "so much [of the 1867 Act] as authorized an appeal from the judgment of the Circuit Court to the Supreme Court of the United States." 74 U.S. at 508.

24. 75 U.S. (8 Wall.) 85 (1869).

25. The Court still did not determine the constitutionality of the Military Reconstruction Act in *Yerger*, because the authorities released the prisoner before the Court could reach a decision.

2. The Doctrine of Clear Statement

If Congress once grants the Supreme Court some species of appellate jurisdiction and then wishes to withdraw that jurisdiction, Congress can do so.[26] Yet to accomplish a repeal, Congress must enact a new statute making it "explicit" and "unambiguous" that the relevant jurisdiction is to be eliminated.[27] A statute will be unsuccessful if it merely appears to jettison some form of jurisdiction without expressly referring to it by name. Judicial authority once established cannot be repealed by implication.[28] This is one of many "sensitive"[29] contexts in which the Court employs a doctrine of clear statement.[30] The Court traces this particular clear statement rule to *Yerger*, which, in turn, built upon the Court's suggestion in *McCardle*.

The Court has invoked this doctrine of clear statement in two additional, and much more recent, habeas corpus cases: *Felker v. Turpin*[31] and *INS v. St. Cyr*.[32] The *Felker* case was the Court's first encounter with the Antiterrorism and Effective Death Penalty Act of 1996 (AEDPA).[33] Under a provision of that Act, state prisoners who wished to file more than one habeas corpus petition attacking their criminal convictions were required to obtain permission to do so from a panel of three circuit judges.[34] AEDPA explicitly stated that if the panel refused, the disappointed prisoner could not seek review of the panel's decision in the Supreme Court in the customary way by filing a petition for *certiorari*.[35] In *Felker*, however, Chief Justice Rehnquist explained that the Act did not mention the Court's jurisdiction to entertain habeas corpus petitions "as an original matter." That independent basis of jurisdiction survived (to be used by prisoners like Felker who could not invoke the Court's ordinary *certiorari* jurisdiction).[36]

---

26. This is to say, Supreme Court appellate jurisdiction is not a ratchet permitting movement only in a forward direction and never allowing for adjustment backward.

27. *INS v. St. Cyr*, 533 U.S. 289, 299 (2001).

28. See note 72 and accompanying text (explaining that this same canon of statutory construction applies to statutes regarding the jurisdiction of inferior federal courts).

29. *St. Cyr*, 533 U.S. at 299 n.10, quoting *Gregory v. Ashcroft*, 501 U.S. 452, 461 (1991).

30. See Chapter I, notes 44–52 and accompanying text.

31. 518 U.S. 651 (1996).

32. 533 U.S. 289 (2001).

33. See Chapter XII (discussing other decisions regarding AEDPA).

34. 28 U.S.C. §2244(b)(3).

35. 28 U.S.C. §2244(b)(3)(E). See Chapter VII, text accompanying notes 211–18 (discussing the Supreme Court's jurisdiction to review lower federal court decisions under 28 U.S.C. §1254); Chapter XII, notes 508–52 and accompanying text (discussing other issues touching multiple habeas corpus petitions from a single prisoner).

36. The prisoner in *Felker* was held in state custody. Accordingly, the Court could not reach back to the 1789 Act for its authority to entertain his petition, but had to rely on the 1867 Act. See Chapter II, text accompanying note 57 (explaining that the 1789 Act conferred jurisdiction only to grant habeas corpus relief to prisoners in federal custody). That presented no difficulty, however, since AEDPA was silent with respect to the Court's "original" jurisdiction under the 1867 statute. For a discussion of *Felker*, see Mark V. Tushnet, *The King of France With Forty Thousand Men: Felker v. Turpin and the Supreme Court's Deliberative Processes*, 1996 Sup. Ct. Rev. 163. The Court's jurisdiction to entertain a habeas corpus petition "as an original matter" (i.e., without taking the case on appellate review from a lower court) is problematic. Recall that the Court held in *Marbury* that Congress cannot confer original jurisdiction outside the narrow limits prescribed in Article III. A petition for a writ of habeas corpus is no more one of the cases that Article III assigns to the Court's original jurisdiction than is a petition for a writ of mandamus. See Chapter I, text accompanying

The *St. Cyr* case involved another provision in AEDPA, as well as related sections of the Illegal Immigration Reform and Immigrant Responsibility Act of 1996 (IIRIRA). Under prior law, resident aliens who committed certain criminal offenses were deportable, but could escape actual deportation by obtaining a waiver from the Attorney General. IIRIRA eliminated the Attorney General's authority to grant waivers. In addition, both AEDPA and IIRIRA contained provisions purporting to foreclose judicial consideration of any claims that convicts might advance regarding their treatment. For example, one provision in IIRIRA stated: "Notwithstanding any other provision of law, no court shall have jurisdiction to review any final order of removal against an alien who is removable by reason of having committed" any of certain designated offenses.[37] That language appeared to bar access to any court at all—including the Supreme Court or even a state court.[38]

The petitioner in *St. Cyr* conceded that he had committed one of the designated offenses and was therefore removable. Yet he contended that IIRIRA eliminated the Attorney General's discretion to waive deportation only for cases in which aliens committed offenses after the date on which that Act was signed into law. Since his offense had occurred earlier, he argued that the Attorney General retained capacity to waive deportation in his case. The Attorney General read IIRIRA to abolish the authority to grant waivers in any case, irrespective of the date of any applicant's criminal offense. Accordingly, the Attorney General declined to consider the petitioner's request. The petitioner then argued that neither AEDPA nor IIRIRA barred him from challenging the Attorney General's interpretation in *some* federal court.

In the Supreme Court, Justice Stevens explained that the petitioner was not pressing a constitutional claim. The government conceded that neither AEDPA nor IIRIRA should be read to foreclose federal jurisdiction regarding constitutional arguments.[39] Nor was the petitioner arguing that he was entitled to judicial review of a decision by the Attorney General to deny a waiver in his particular case. Instead, the petitioner contended that some federal court retained jurisdiction to examine the Attorney General's determination of a "pure" question of federal statutory law—namely, the Attorney General's position that IIRIRA eliminated even the authority to consider whether a waiver was appropriate.[40] Turning to the specific provisions of AEDPA and IIRIRA pertaining to jurisdiction, Justice Stevens found none of them explicit enough to satisfy the

---

note 69. John Marshall defused the tension with *Marbury* in *Ex parte Bollman*, 8 U.S. (4 Cranch) 75 (1807), where he said that when a prisoner files a petition for a writ of habeas corpus in the Supreme Court without first applying to a lower court, the Court's jurisdiction is nonetheless appellate in nature—because somewhere along the line some lower court, state or federal, has typically had a hand in the prisoner's detention and the Supreme Court is now being asked to review that court's action, at least indirectly. Professor Paschal speculates that Marshall overlooked the Court's "original" habeas corpus jurisdiction when he wrote the *Marbury* opinion and then, in *Bollman*, contrived a way to accommodate habeas corpus to his analysis in *Marbury*. Francis Paschal, *The Constitution and Habeas Corpus*, 1970 Duke L.J. 605, 651.

37. 8 U.S.C. §1252(a)(2)(C).

38. See notes 112–21 and accompanying text (discussing the absolute preclusion of jurisdiction in federal question cases). The Act did establish a limited form of jurisdiction for some immigration issues in the circuit courts of appeals. But that jurisdiction did not include authority to entertain the kind of claim the petitioner in *St. Cyr* wished to advance.

39. Nothing in the Act explicitly reserved constitutional issues. The government may have anticipated that the Court would nonetheless balk at the absolute preclusion of constitutional claims. See note 117 and accompanying text.

40. 533 U.S. at 298.

clear statement rule. None of those provisions referred to the basic jurisdictional statute for habeas corpus cases, 28 U.S.C. §2241, so none of them repealed that basis of federal adjudication. Accordingly, a district court had jurisdiction to entertain the petitioner's claim, and the Supreme Court itself retained appellate jurisdiction to review a lower federal court judgment for error.[41]

The clear statement rule is sufficient in itself to determine whether a statute effectuates a repeal of preexisting appellate jurisdiction. In *St. Cyr*, however, Justice Stevens explained that two other canons of statutory construction provided "additional reinforcement."[42] Those canons were: (1) the rule that Congress must speak clearly when it operates near the "outer limits" of its constitutional power; and (2) the rule that a statute will ordinarily be construed in a way that avoids constitutional questions.[43] In *Felker* and *St. Cyr*, the Court may have invoked the clear statement rule, coupled with these additional canons, to avoid the Article III question in *McCardle*—namely, the question whether the Exceptions Clause authorizes Congress to manipulate the Court's appellate jurisdiction as it pleases.[44] In *St. Cyr*, however, Justice Stevens did not suggest that AEDPA and IIRIRA would raise constitutional questions under Article III if they were read to foreclose habeas jurisdiction pursuant to § 2241. Instead, he said that they would present constitutional questions under the Suspension Clause, which arguably limits Congress' capacity to deny the writ of habeas corpus to prisoners in some circumstances.[45] All the leading decisions under this heading, *McCardle*, *Yerger*, *Felker*, and *St. Cyr*, were habeas cases. It may be, then, that the constitutional questions about which the Court is concerned arise only from the special status that the Constitution accords to the Great Writ.[46] By most accounts, however, the Court is moved not only by the Suspension Clause, but also by Article III (and due process).[47] At any rate, the Court plainly relies on the doctrine of clear statement and related rules of construction to keep Congress at bay without formally coming to grips with the constitutional scope of Congress' authority to adjust the Court's appellate jurisdiction.[48]

---

41. In dissent, Justice Scalia criticized the majority for finding ambiguity in "utterly clear language." 533 U.S. at 326–27 (dissenting opinion) (joined by Rehnquist, C.J., O'Connor, J. & Thomas, J.).

42. Id. at 289 (majority opinion).

43. Id. at 289–90. See Chapter I, note 26 and accompanying text. Justice Stevens also referred to the "strong presumption in favor of judicial review of administrative action." 535 U.S. at 298. See Chapter V, notes 141–43 and accompanying text.

44. The Court did not mention the doctrine of constitutional doubt in *Felker*. But Professor Young has suggested that the invocation of the no-repeal-by-implication rule may have been "motivated—at least in part—by constitutional concerns." Ernest A. Young, *Constitutional Avoidance, Resistance Norms, and the Preservation of Judicial Review*, 78 Tex. L. Rev. 1549, 1561–62 (2000).

45. See Chapter II, note 57; Chapter XII, notes 15–37 and accompanying text.

46. It is hard to think that *St. Cyr* is limited to immigration cases. Generally, the Court is more (not less) solicitous of Congress in that context. If anything, *St. Cyr* illustrates that immigration cases do not occupy an entirely separate jurisprudential universe, but share at least some common doctrines with the wider body of federal courts law. See Gerald L. Neuman, *Federal Courts Issues in Immigration Law*, 78 Tex. L. Rev. 1661 (2000).

47. See notes 122–49 and accompanying text; Chapter XII, notes 40–43 and accompanying text.

48. Professor Friedman understands this pattern to reflect a "dialogic" approach to congressional and judicial power, under which both Congress and the Court contribute to the development of the law and neither ultimately asserts dominance over the other. Barry Friedman, *A Different Dialogue: The Supreme Court, Congress and Federal Jurisdiction*, 85 Nw. U. L. Rev. 1 (1990). For criticism, see Michael Wells, *Congress's Paramount Role in Setting the Scope of Federal Jurisdiction*, 85 Nw. U. L. Rev. 465 (1990).

B. Inferior Article III Courts

Article III contemplates that Congress may "ordain and establish" other federal courts beyond the Supreme Court itself, and Article I explicitly grants Congress authority "[t]o constitute Tribunals inferior to the supreme Court."[49] Congress' authority to decide *in favor* of creating inferior federal courts is therefore perfectly clear.[50] Congress' authority to decide *against* creating inferior courts is more problematic. If the federal judiciary were limited to the Supreme Court alone, the significance of the judicial branch would be seriously diminished. Congress established inferior federal courts in 1789 and has maintained them ever since. So any question about whether Congress might have left them out of the mix arouses only academic interest today.[51] Still, by most accounts, Congress was initially obliged only to create the Supreme Court itself and might have chosen to forgo lower federal courts entirely, at least so long as state courts were able to take up the slack. That, after all, was the point of the Madisonian Compromise.[52]

History aside, the proposition that Congress can choose whether or not to create inferior federal courts is neither surprising nor (necessarily) troubling. In a democracy, controversial issues are usually left to politically accountable institutions. Congress' power with respect to the courts may be regarded as no more than another legislative check on the judicial branch—the kind of device that does not undercut, but only further defines, the separation principle.[53] Federal courts are not subservient to Congress after they are in place, but are structurally insulated from politics in order that they can exercise independent judgment in the cases that come before them.[54] It may be sensible, then, that Congress should exercise political judgment at a prior stage, when the question is whether the country should have inferior federal courts to conduct its judicial business (independently).[55] Moreover, Congress is unlikely to use its discretion regarding inferior courts to undermine the judicial branch. Congress often needs those courts to implement its legislative policies.[56]

There is an argument that Congress was required to create inferior courts, the Madisonian Compromise notwithstanding. Justice Story made the case for mandatory inferior courts in his opinion for the Court in *Martin v. Hunter's Lessee*.[57] The judgment

---

49. U.S. Const. art. I, §8, cl.9.

50. Moreover, the power to create inferior courts implies the power to establish the procedural rules and arrangements under which they operate. *Budinich v. Becton Dickinson & Co.*, 486 U.S. 196, 199 (1998) (also invoking the Necessary and Proper Clause).

51. See Chapter II, text accompanying notes 56–66 (discussing the Judiciary Act of 1789).

52. See Chapter II, notes 11–14 and accompanying text (discussing the Compromise).

53. See Chapter I, text accompanying note 5 (discussing the "checks and balances" idea).

54. See Chapter III, notes 1–2 and accompanying text (describing the values associated with judicial independence).

55. Professor Black argued that Congress' authority with respect to the courts mitigates the "counter-majoritarian difficulty" attending judicial decisions that override legislation. If the courts are in a position to invalidate statutes only because Congress has created them and given them the necessary jurisdiction, there is a way in which Congress bears indirect responsibility for what the courts do with the power they are assigned. Charles L. Black, Jr., Decision According to Law 18 (1981).

56. In many instances, however, Congress may rely on non-Article III tribunals to dispose of disputes arising from the implementation of legislative programs. When Congress chooses that course, the point of guaranteeing that Article III courts are independent may be threatened. See Chapter V.

57. 14 U.S. (1 Wheat.) 304 (1816).

in that case touched only the Supreme Court's jurisdiction to review state court judgments. Story's discussion of the lower federal courts was dicta. Nevertheless, the points he made retain significance for modern analysis.

Story began with the first line of Article III, which states that the judicial power of the United States "shall be vested" in the Supreme Court and any inferior courts that Congress creates.[58] He took "shall" in that line to establish a constitutional mandate that the entire judicial power must be "vested" in some federal court or courts—either in the Supreme Court alone or in the Supreme Court supplemented by inferior federal courts. Turning to the content of the judicial power to be vested, Story focused on the adjective "all," which appears before the items identified in Article III as "cases," but not before the entries identified as "controversies."[59] Taking that modifier to heart, Story interpreted the judicial power of the United States to include "all" the *cases* on the list, but not to "all" the *controversies*. Returning to his initial premise, he said that Congress could satisfy the command that the entire judicial power "shall be vested" by conferring jurisdiction on the Supreme Court (and any inferior courts) to determine "all" the cases, but not (necessarily) "all" the controversies described in Article III.

Next, Story considered whether responsibility for "all" those cases could be given to the Supreme Court alone, so that Congress need not create any lower federal courts to share the load. He recognized that the Court could entertain some cases as an original matter. But most would have to reach the Court on appeal from some other court. Story conceded that the state courts could do service in most instances. In his view, however, some of the cases on the Article III menu could not be adjudicated originally in state court and therefore could not reach the Supreme Court on appeal from those courts. Those cases would be left out entirely, unless Congress established inferior federal courts to consider them in the first instance. The cases Justice Story had in mind were federal criminal prosecutions. He argued that state courts could not enforce another system's penal laws and that inferior federal courts were constitutionally mandated at least to deal with those cases. On that point, Story was wrong. State and federal courts operate together in a single judicial system. There is no *constitutional* reason why state courts cannot handle federal criminal prosecutions.[60] Neat and tidy as Story's deductive logic may have seemed to him, it collapsed in the end and is now generally rejected.[61]

---

58. See text accompanying note 1.

59. See text accompanying note 2.

60. Recall that under the Articles of Confederation the central government was forced to take its lawsuits to state court. See Chapter II, text accompanying note 8. Early statutes under the new Constitution contemplated that certain federal criminal offenses would be prosecuted in state court. Even today, it is occasionally proposed to revive that idea in the interest of solving the caseload crisis in the federal courts. See Chapter II, notes 101–02 and accompanying text; Chapter VI, note 13 and accompanying text.

61. Professor Goebel argued that the forceful "ordain and establish" language in Article III connotes obligation rather than discretion. Julius Goebel, History of the Supreme Court of the United States: Antecedents and Beginnings to 1801, 247 (1971). Professor Collins contends that, at the time Story wrote, many people took the view that state courts were unable to adjudicate all the cases identified in Article III—thus making inferior federal courts essential. Michael G. Collins, *Article III Cases, State Court Duties, and the Madisonian Compromise*, 1995 Wis. L. Rev. 39, 58–78. Professor Eisenberg argues that if inferior federal courts were not constitutionally obligatory in 1789, they nonetheless are today inasmuch as the country has grown so large and diverse that the Supreme Court cannot manage the judicial branch alone. Theodore Eisenberg, *Congressional Authority to Restrict Lower Federal Court Jurisdiction*, 83 Yale L.J. 498 (1974).

C. Inferior Court Jurisdiction

Congress' authority to prescribe the jurisdiction of inferior courts poses different questions: (1) whether Congress can give the courts it creates only part of the jurisdiction that Article III permits; (2) whether Congress can apportion jurisdiction for Article III business between different inferior courts; and (3) whether Congress can assign inferior courts jurisdiction over matters that are not mentioned in Article III.

1. Jurisdiction Within Article III Limits

Congress can decide to give inferior federal courts jurisdiction in only some of the cases and controversies listed in Article III. Recall that the Judiciary Act of 1789 left a number of matters out in the very beginning.[62] That has always been the pattern. The opposite proposition (that federal courts must have authority to determine all the various cases and controversies on the Article III menu) would have implausible implications. Notice, for example, that Article III places a controversy between citizens of different states within the federal judicial power.[63] If federal courts were constitutionally obligated to entertain all diversity matters that fit that description, they would have jurisdiction in any lawsuits in which only two of what may be dozens of parties reside in different states. It would make little sense to saddle the federal courts with "minimal diversity" jurisdiction as a matter of policy, far less as an interpretation of Article III.[64]

The leading precedent in point is *Sheldon v. Sill*.[65] A bank in Michigan assigned a bond to a New York citizen, who filed suit to recover the amount of the bond in a federal court in Michigan, naming a Michigan citizen as the defendant and invoking the court's diversity jurisdiction (now prescribed by 28 U.S.C. §1332). The defendant objected to the federal court's jurisdiction on the ground that a related statute barred a litigant like the bank from assigning an instrument for the sole purpose of manufacturing diversity.[66] In response, the New York plaintiff insisted that Article III contemplated diversity jurisdiction in such a case and that Congress had no power to define the court's power more narrowly. The Supreme Court rejected that argument.

Unfortunately, the Court explained its result in *Sill* at least in part on the basis of the "greater power" syllogism.[67] Positing that Congress had the "greater" power to decide in the first instance whether to create lower federal courts at all, the Court said it followed "as a necessary consequence" that Congress had power to establish such courts, but to give them only part of the authority the Constitution allowed. Of course, that was not a "necessary consequence" at all. The authority to decide whether to establish courts is certainly a significant (settled) power. But the power to prescribe jurisdiction is not a subset power at all. It is a different power. It would have been perfectly *logical* in *Sill* to interpret Congress' power in another way. Article III might give

62. See Chapter II, text accompanying notes 56–66.

63. See text accompanying note 4.

64. See *Strawbridge v. Curtis*, 7 U.S. (3 Cranch) 267 (1806) (reading *statutory* diversity jurisdiction to require "complete" diversity).

65. 49 U.S. (8 How.) 441 (1850).

66. For the current provision, see 28 U.S.C. §1359 (barring district court jurisdiction if a party is joined by assignment for the purpose of "improperly or collusively" invoking §1332 jurisdiction).

67. See Chapter I, text accompanying notes 27–28.

Congress a choice—either to create federal courts with jurisdiction over all the cases and controversies the Constitution allows, or to establish no inferior federal courts at all and to rely entirely on state courts. That interpretation would actually flow more easily from the text of Article I, which refers expressly only to Congress' power to "constitute" inferior courts and says nothing about power to prescribe their jurisdiction.[68] Moreover, this alternative interpretation would be consistent with the "checks and balances" motif. It would give Congress a check on the courts at one level (the power to decide whether to create inferior federal courts at all). But it would balance that check at another level (by insisting that the courts Congress creates have more jurisdiction than Congress might like to assign to them—thus preventing Congress from having its cake and eating it, too).

This is not to say that *Sill* was wrongly decided. Nobody seriously takes that position.[69] It makes sense that Congress should have authority to adjust the federal courts' jurisdiction to ensure that their resources are not squandered on matters that can be left to state courts without jeopardizing federal interests. Moreover, it makes sense to say that the power to create inferior courts *implies* the power to prescribe their jurisdiction.[70] The problem with *Sill* is that the Court did not simply draw a rational inference, but purported to identify a logical imperative. That analysis was unsound. By common account, the Court reached the right outcome for the wrong reason and thus failed to grapple with the serious interpretive question presented.[71]

Poorly reasoned cases like *Sill* beg the question whether there are constitutional limits on Congress' power to circumscribe inferior court jurisdiction. Yet the Court has recognized two important limiting propositions: (1) the doctrine of clear statement regarding statutes said to repeal jurisdiction by implication; and (2) a constitutional prohibition on statutes that purport to tell an Article III court what result to reach in a case.

The doctrine of clear statement revisited. If Congress once confers jurisdiction on an inferior federal court, Congress can withdraw that jurisdiction only by employing explicit, unambiguous language. The same clear statement rule that operates with respect to statutes touching the Supreme Court's appellate jurisdiction also operates with respect to statutes affecting inferior federal court jurisdiction.[72] Repeals of jurisdiction must be explicit; they cannot be implicit. In *Utah v. Evans*,[73] for example, the state of Utah sued federal officials responsible for conducting the census, claiming that their use of "hot-deck imputation" methodology violated both federal statutes and the constitutional requirement that the census must be an "actual Enumeration."[74] The Court had

68. See text accompanying note 49.

69. Professor Bator insisted that it would make "nonsense" of the Madisonian Compromise to read Article III to give Congress an "all-or-nothing" power to decide whether "*none* or *all*" the cases and controversies listed warrant a federal forum. Paul M. Bator, *Congressional Power Over the Jurisdiction of the Federal Courts*, 27 Vill. L. Rev. 1030, 1031 (1982) (emphasis in original).

70. See *United States v. Hudson*, 11 U.S. (7 Cranch) 32, 33 (1812).

71. The Court so committed itself to the "greater power" syllogism that it declared at one point that a jurisdictional statute written by Congress could be unconstitutional only if it purported to assign the federal courts jurisdiction beyond the boundaries fixed by Article III. 49 U.S. at 449. That neglected the possibility that a jurisdictional statute might run afoul of an external restraint on congressional power—for example, due process. See text accompanying note 131.

72. See notes 26–48 and accompanying text.

73. 122 S.Ct. 2191 (2002); see also Chapter IX, notes 230–38 and accompanying text (discussing other aspects of *Evans*).

74. U.S. Const. art. I, §2, cl.3.

previously entertained a similar lawsuit in another case. In *Evans*, however, an intervenor argued that a recently enacted statute had repealed the jurisdictional statute on which the prior litigation proceeded. Previously, litigants like Utah had been able to sue after a census was completed, but the new statute authorized only suits before a census was concluded. Writing for the Court, Justice Breyer refused to read the new statute to repeal federal court jurisdiction by negative implication.

The *St. Cyr* decision made this same point. In that case, Justice Stevens focused primarily on the possibility that AEDPA and IIRIRA might be read to repeal district court jurisdiction to entertain the petitioner's habeas corpus application. The Court's own appellate jurisdiction to review district court judgments on habeas petitions was also at stake. But Justice Stevens plainly engaged the doctrine of clear statement, as well as other supporting canons of construction, to justify a construction of those statutes that preserved inferior court jurisdiction in the first instance. In *St. Cyr* itself, Justice Stevens explained that a contrary construction would force the Court to deal with difficult constitutional questions under the Suspension Clause.[75] He indicated, however, that the basic clear statement rule regarding jurisdictional statutes established an independent, and sufficient, basis for the Court's decision.[76]

Legislated judicial decisions. Congress cannot tell an inferior federal court what result to reach in a case properly within the court's jurisdiction. This proposition, accurate in itself, is nonetheless ambiguous. The idea can best be explained by illustration via the classic precedent in point, *United States v. Klein*.[77] That was another Reconstruction Era decision concerning the Supreme Court's jurisdiction. It's historical context no doubt colors its full precedential value today. Yet the basic lesson to be drawn from *Klein* is sound, both with respect to Congress' power to make "Exceptions" from the Supreme Court's appellate jurisdiction and with respect to Congress' power to prescribe the jurisdiction of inferior Article III courts. The story in *Klein* goes this way.

As Union troops advanced into the Confederacy during the last years of the Civil War, they confiscated valuable property. The Abandoned Property and Collection Act of 1863 authorized federal agents to sell that property and deposit the proceeds in the United States Treasury. The Act allowed for compensation claims to be filed in the Court of Claims, but conditioned all claims on loyalty to the Union. Claimants were out of luck if they had given aid or comfort to the Confederacy. John Klein filed a claim on behalf of Victor Wilson, whose cotton had been seized and sold pursuant to the Act. The government resisted payment on the ground that Wilson had signed a surety bond for two Confederate officers, thus demonstrating that he was disloyal to the Union. Klein produced a presidential pardon, issued to Wilson after the date on which he had

75. See text accompanying note 45.

76. In *Zadvydas v. Davis*, 533 U.S. 678 (2001), Justice Breyer held for the Court that none of the jurisdictional provisions in IIRIRA deprived federal district courts of habeas jurisdiction to entertain claims by aliens that they were being held "indefinitely" after their deportation orders were final. Accordingly, jurisdiction under §2241 was available. There were dissents in *Zadvydas*, but they went to the merits. No one contested Justice Breyer's holding that federal jurisdiction existed. In *Verizon v. Pub. Svc. Comm'n*, 122 S.Ct. 1753 (2002), the Court unanimously held that a provision of the Telecommunications Act of 1996 did not repeal the federal district courts' ordinary jurisdiction pursuant to 28 U.S.C. §1331. Justice Scalia's opinion for the Court did not invoke the doctrine of constitutional doubt.

77. 80 U.S. (13 Wall.) 128 (1871).

signed the bonds. According to the Supreme Court's then-recent decision in *United States v. Padleford*,[78] that pardon rendered Wilson loyal in law, if not in fact, inasmuch as it forgave any allegiance he had shown the rebel cause. The Court of Claims accepted the pardon as a legal basis for Klein's loyalty claim and ordered compensation to be paid. The government sought appellate review in the Supreme Court.

While the *Klein* case was working its way to the Court, Senator Trumball sponsored new legislation plainly meant to thwart the claim in that case. Having just succeeded in withdrawing the Court's jurisdiction in *McCardle*,[79] Trumball tried the same strategy with respect to *Klein*. This time, however, Congress went much further. The new law, enacted in 1870, was not merely a facially outcome-neutral repealer of the statute on which the Court's jurisdiction depended. It declared that an individual could not rely on a pardon to demonstrate loyalty under the 1863 Act, that the existence of a pardon actually proved disloyalty, and that in any case in which an individual had won compensation in the Court of Claims on the basis of a pardon, the Supreme Court was obliged to dismiss the petitioner's original claim so that the petitioner would take nothing.[80] When the Supreme Court turned to the *Klein* case some time later, Chief Justice Chase held the 1870 Act unconstitutional and affirmed the lower court's judgment in Klein's favor.

The opinion Chase wrote for the Court is impenetrable and appears to stand for a variety of questionable propositions. Chase said, for example, that jurisdictional legislation cannot be "a means to an end."[81] That suggests that even outcome-neutral limits on jurisdiction are invalid if they are motivated by a desire to affect judicial results. Given the difficulties of any search for congressional motives, it is hard to think that a proposition like that can be sustained.[82] In addition, Chase faulted the 1870 Act for attempting to "prescribe rules of decision" for the courts to follow.[83] That idea is also hard to take seriously. Congress certainly can establish substantive legal rules to govern cases, even cases already under way.[84] That, after all, is the principal (and legitimate) function performed by the legislative branch.

Looking back at *Klein* more recently, the Court has read that case to stand for three propositions. First, at a minimum, Congress cannot employ its authority over jurisdiction to undermine the effect of a presidential pardon. The Court had decided in *Padleford* that a pardon rendered a claimant eligible for compensation under the 1863 Act. But the 1870 repealer proposed to defeat that interpretation of the President's power. This understanding seems artificial inasmuch as it turns on the peculiar subject matter

78. 76 U.S. (9 Wall.) 531 (1869).

79. See notes 12–23 and accompanying text.

80. See Gordon G. Young, *Congressional Regulation of Federal Courts' Jurisdiction and Processes: United States v. Klein Revisited*, 1981 Wis. L. Rev. 1189.

81. 80 U.S. at 145–46.

82. If a purpose to affect the Court's results were sufficient to invalidate otherwise neutral jurisdictional legislation, then presumably *McCardle* was wrongly decided. See text accompanying note 19. But see Eugene Gressman & Eric K. Gressman, *Necessary and Proper Roots of Exceptions to Federal Jurisdiction*, 51 Geo. Wash. L. Rev. 495, 520–23 (1983) (arguing that *McCardle* did not address an exception meant to weaken the Court and that *Klein* did establish that congressional motivation is "relevant to the inquiry" whether an exception is valid).

83. 80 U.S. at 146.

84. Federal courts routinely apply the law in place at the time of decision, even if it is changed while a case is pending. See *Landgraf v. USI Film Products*, 511 U.S. 244 (1994).

in *Klein*. Yet it illustrates a more general idea: Jurisdictional statutes, like all other enactments, are subject to restraints located elsewhere in the Constitution.[85] Second, Congress cannot manipulate jurisdiction to ensure that the government wins.This proposition is more significant inasmuch as it bars Congress from enacting self-serving jurisdictional limits that skew judicial results in the government's favor.[86]

Third, and most important, Congress cannot use its authority regarding jurisdiction to tell an Article III court what decision to reach in a case. This is by far the most powerful lesson to be drawn from *Klein*. Congress may have authority to limit a federal court's jurisdiction at the outset in an outcome-neutral way, provided that the statute enacted is sufficiently clear. Congress may change the substantive law governing a case and, in that way, affect the judgment a court will reach. But Congress cannot allow an Article III court to exercise jurisdiction, leave the controlling law unchanged, and simply tell the court what judgment to render.[87]

This last understanding of *Klein*, solid as it is, nonetheless entails a distinction that can be extremely hard to draw—namely, the familiar distinction between legislation and adjudication.[88] Ordinarily, Congress enacts general legal standards to govern a field of play and leaves it to the courts to decide how those standards work in particular instances. That pattern comports with conventional understandings of the differences between legislative power to prescribe substantive law and judicial power to adjudicate disputes over how that law applies in individual cases.[89] Congress may choose, however,

---

85. See text accompanying note 131. Professor Sager sees deeper meaning in the Court's objection in *Klein* to being made a party to Congress' scheme to defeat the proper effect of a pardon. The Court had previously held that a pardon rendered a claimant loyal as a matter of federal constitutional law, but the 1870 Act instructed the Court to deny that very interpretation of the Constitution. It called on the Court to receive evidence that a pardon existed and then, because of its existence, to wash its hands of a case and thus to deny the very relief that the pardon, were it given its rightful effect, would command. According to Sager, the principal import of *Klein* is that the Court refused to participate in a process in which it would be called upon to speak and act in conflict with its own understanding of the Constitution. Lawrence G. Sager, *Klein's First Principle: A Proposed Solution*, 86 Gtn. L.J. 2525 (1998). See also Christopher L. Eisgruber & Lawrence G. Sager, *Why the Religious Freedom Restoration Act is Unconstitutional*, 69 N.Y.U. L. Rev. 437 (1994) (offering a similar reading of *Klein*). Professor Meltzer agrees that Congress cannot force the Court to "speak a constitutional untruth." But he thinks that Sager's interpretation of *Klein* is unsound (and dangerous) in that it draws into question congressional enactments that achieve results by statute that could not be reached in reliance on the Constitution alone. Meltzer cites, for example, the Voting Rights Act of 1992, which outlaws voting rules having a discriminatory *effect* on minority voters, while the fifteenth amendment itself condemns only voting rules having a discriminatory *purpose*. Daniel J. Meltzer, *Congress, Courts, and Constitutional Remedies*, 86 Gtn. L.J. 2537, 2538–49 (1998).

86. E.g., *United States v. Sioux Nation of Indians*, 448 U.S. 371, 405 (1980). Recall that in *Klein* the individual had won in the lower court, and it was the government that appealed. Ordinarily, a statute depriving the Supreme Court of jurisdiction would preserve the lower court judgment. That is what happened in *McCardle*. In *Klein*, however, the 1870 repealer did not merely withdraw the Court's jurisdiction of the government's appeal, but reached back to the judgment below in Klein's favor and instructed the Court to dismiss the original claim. In that way, then, Congress attempted to manipulate things in its own favor. See Gordon G. Young, *A Critical Reassessment of the Case Law Bearing on Congress's Power to Restrict the Jurisdiction of the Lower Federal Courts*, 54 Md. L. Rev. 132, 158–59 (1995).

87. See *Plaut v. Spendthrift Farm*, 514 U.S. 211, 226–27 (1995) (explaining that Congress cannot wait until Article III courts have reached final judgments and *then* attempt to alter their results by retroactively changing the applicable law).

88. See Chapter I, notes 6–9 and accompanying text.

89. See Martin H. Redish, *Federal Judicial Independence: Constitutional and Political Perspectives*, 46 Mercer L. Rev. 697, 718–21 (1995).

to enact much more detailed statutes that are so finely tuned to a particular set of circumstances that they effectively prescribe their own effect, leaving little for a court to decide. When that happens, the courts must determine whether Congress has been uncharacteristically (but legitimately) particular in specifying the controlling law or has (illegitimately) pushed beyond its legislative function and presumed to adjudicate disputes as well.

In *Robertson v. Seattle Audubon Society*,[90] environmental groups filed lawsuits contesting the manner in which lumber was to be harvested from federal lands in the Pacific Northwest. While those suits were pending, Congress enacted legislation prescribing new policies, explicitly identifying the suits by name, and stating that the new policies would bring the lumbering activities involved in the suits into conformity with federal law. In the Supreme Court, Justice Thomas explained that Congress had altered the substantive law governing the pending cases and thus legitimately affected their results. Accordingly, there was no concern that Congress had run afoul of *Klein*.[91] In this same vein, Congress can also amend the federal courts' authority with respect to certain remedies and, in that way, adjust preexisting injunctive decrees that assume a wider remedial power. That is what Congress did in the Prison Litigation Reform Act when it declared that extant consent decrees must be withdrawn unless district courts make certain determinations.[92]

2. Apportionment of Article III Jurisdiction

Congress can allocate Article III cases and controversies among different inferior federal courts. In *Lockerty v. Phillips*[93] and *Yakus v. United States*,[94] the Supreme Court upheld the Emergency Price Control Act of 1942, which established a system for controlling inflation during World War II. That Act authorized a federal administrative agency to issue regulations fixing the maximum prices that manufacturers could charge for their goods. It was a criminal offense to violate a price regulation, and anyone who did so could be prosecuted in a district court. Nevertheless, the Act explicitly denied the district courts any authority to determine the validity of price regulations. Instead, the Act granted a special Article III court (the Emergency Court of Appeals) exclusive jurisdiction to decide whether regulations were lawful, subject to appellate review in the Supreme Court.

In *Lockerty*, meat packers filed a civil action in a district court, seeking an injunction against a United States attorney who threatened to prosecute them for violating price

---

90. 503 U.S. 429 (1992).

91. It is in part because Congress can alter the substantive law applicable to a case that Professor Sager contends that *Klein*'s principal point is not that Congress must couch legislation in that form, but rather that the Court will not be placed in a position in which it cannot keep faith with its own interpretation of the Constitution. Sager, note 85, at 2527–28. Professor Meltzer finds more significance in the formal difference between statutes that purport merely to make public policy legislatively, on the one hand, and statutes that purport to interpret the Constitution, on the other. Meltzer, note 85, at 2549.

92. *Miller v. French*, 530 U.S. 327 (2000). See generally Brian M. Hoffstadt, *Retaking the Field: The Constitutional Constraints on Federal Legislation that Displaces Consent Decrees*, 77 Wash. U. L.Q. 53 (1999).

93. 319 U.S. 182 (1943).

94. 321 U.S. 414 (1944).

regulations they contended were unconstitutional. The Court held that the district court lacked jurisdiction, because Congress had chosen, in its discretion, to channel attacks on price regulations to the Emergency Court.[95] In *Yakus*, a manufacturer charged with violating a price regulation built its defense on an argument that the regulation was invalid. The Court held that, under the Act, the district court handling the criminal prosecution had no jurisdiction to inquire into the lawfulness of the regulation—so long as the defendant had received an "adequate" opportunity to raise that question in a prior civil action in the Emergency Court. Between them, *Lockerty* and *Yakus* held that Congress could apportion jurisdiction between the two tribunals—giving the Emergency Court exclusive authority to determine the *validity* of regulations and giving the district courts authority to determine whether particular manufacturers had *violated* regulations.[96]

In at least one instance, *Lauf v. Shinner*,[97] the Supreme Court arguably approved a federal scheme depriving *all* inferior federal courts of jurisdiction over certain constitutional claims and leaving those claims exclusively to state courts, subject to appellate review in the Supreme Court. Previously, the Court had held that state statutes prohibiting state courts from enjoining unlawful labor union activities violated the fourteenth amendment.[98] In *Lauf*, however, the Court held that the Norris-LaGuardia Act validly barred the federal courts from issuing injunctions in the very same circumstances.

---

95. The meat packers argued that a suit in the Emergency Court would not protect their constitutional rights, because that court had no authority to insulate them from prosecution while it considered their claims. The Supreme Court responded that the Act's prohibition on interlocutory relief did not condemn the basic allocation of jurisdiction between the Emergency Court and the district courts. Even if that feature of the scheme was problematic, it was separable from the rest. The Court hinted that the meat packers might be able to contest the Act's prohibition on interlocutory relief in some other court. Professor Hart suggested that an action of that kind might have been filed in state court, notwithstanding that the Act equally purported to deprive state courts of any jurisdiction to entertain lawsuits attacking price regulations. In his view, it would have been unconstitutional for Congress to foreclose all judicial avenues for advancing a constitutional claim. Henry M. Hart, Jr., *The Power of Congress to Limit the Jurisdiction of Federal Courts: An Exercise in Dialectic*, 66 Harv. L. Rev. 1362, 1401 (1953). See notes 133–35 and accompanying text. It is hard to think that the statute in *Lockerty* could plausibly be read to route interlocutory relief questions to state courts rather than to some federal tribunal—if not the Emergency Court, then a federal district court. Nevertheless, *Lockerty* suggests that neither the Emergency Court nor a district court had jurisdiction to consider the meat packers' argument that they were entitled to protection while their lawsuit was pending.

96. Of these two cases, *Yakus* was the more significant inasmuch as the Court held in that case that Congress could subject a defendant to criminal liability in a federal district court while withholding from that court any ability to determine the validity of the regulation the defendant was charged with violating. More recently, the Court has said that *Yakus* presupposed a "meaningful" previous opportunity to test the validity of a regulation in some other court. *United States v. Mendoza-Lopez*, 481 U.S. 828, 837–38 (1987). In *Mendoza-Lopez*, the Court concluded that an alien who claimed that a deportation order was invalid had not had such an opportunity and therefore could attack the order as a defense to the criminal charge of re-entering the country after deportation. In two World War II conscription cases, *Falbo v. United States*, 320 U.S. 549 (1944), and *Estep v. United States*, 327 U.S. 114 (1944), the Court wrestled with a similar attempt by Congress to keep the district courts from considering the validity of induction orders that defendants were charged with violating. In *Estep*, the Court said that Congress could insist that defendants exhaust administrative remedies before attacking induction notices as defendants in criminal prosecutions, but that anyone who did that could argue that a draft board had acted beyond its jurisdiction in ordering a defendant to report for military duty. It is hard to say what light those war-time cases throw on the current Court's thinking.

97. 303 U.S. 323 (1938).

98. *Truax v. Corrigan*, 257 U.S. 312 (1921).

The implications of *Lauf* are debatable. By some accounts, that case is authority for the proposition that Congress can absolutely deny the federal courts jurisdiction in a class of constitutional cases, provided state courts remain open for that business.[99] By other accounts, *Lauf* merely recognized that Congress can adjust the *remedies* that federal courts provide to successful plaintiffs.[100] By still other accounts, *Lauf* is best understood as an illustration of the Court's developing acceptance of regulatory legislation in the 1930s. The previous cases holding that state courts could not refuse to enjoin unlawful strikes were part of the Court's economic due process excesses in the 1920s, while *Lauf*, decided in 1938, formed part of the Court's post-New Deal jurisprudence. By this last account, *Lauf* is more significant for what it implied about Congress' power to regulate national economic affairs than for what it said about Congress' power to prescribe the federal courts' jurisdiction.[101]

3. Jurisdiction Outside Article III Limits

Congress (probably) cannot give inferior Article III courts (or the Supreme Court) jurisdiction to entertain matters that are not on the Article III menu. Chief Justice Marshall virtually said as much in *Hodgson v. Bowerbank*,[102] when he disapproved a provision in the Judiciary Act of 1789 purporting to give lower federal courts jurisdiction over state law disputes between two aliens.[103] Moreover, the modern Court insists that Congress can confer "standing" on litigants to press their claims in an Article III court only if the actions affected are "cases" or "controversies" within the meaning of Article III.[104] Those decisions proceed from the premise that it would be unconstitutional for Congress to assign Article III courts jurisdiction to adjudicate disputes that Article III does not mention.[105]

The leading case in point, *Nat'l Mutual Ins. Co. v. Tidewater Transfer Co.*,[106] honored this proposition, albeit in the breach. In a prior decision, the Court had held that the District of Columbia was not a "State" within the meaning of the provision in Article III providing for federal jurisdiction between citizens of different "States." In 1940, Congress nonetheless enacted a jurisdictional statute authorizing federal district courts to entertain suits between citizens of the District and citizens of ordinary states. In *Tidewater*, a citizen of the District relied on that statute to sue a Maryland citizen in a district court in Maryland. The Supreme Court sustained the district court's jurisdiction, but without a majority opinion.

Justice Jackson announced the Court's judgment in an opinion joined by two other justices. He acknowledged that the suit was not a diversity action within the contempla-

---

99. Hart, note 95 at 1363. See Chapter VI, notes 80–96 and accompanying text (providing a more complete account of the argument that Congress can impose jurisdiction on state courts).

100. See Chapter VI, note 61 (discussing various meanings for the term "remedy"); Chapter VIII, note 121 (noting further complications).

101. See Young, note 86, at 176–78.

102. 9 U.S. (5 Cranch) 303 (1809).

103. Professor Mahoney contends that Marshall actually construed the Judiciary Act not to extend the courts' jurisdiction that far. Dennis J. Mahoney, *A Historical Note on Hodgson v. Bowerbank*, 49 U. Chi. L. Rev. 725 (1982).

104. See Chapter IX, notes 70–75 and accompanying text.

105. *Hayburn's Case*, 2 U.S. (2 Dall.) 408 (1792), also stands for this proposition—to the extent the judges in that case said that Article III courts could be assigned only "judicial" duties. See Chapter IX, notes 37–40 and accompanying text.

106. 337 U.S. 582 (1949).

tion of Article III. Nevertheless, he said that Congress could confer extra-Article III jurisdiction on Article III courts as an exercise of other congressional powers collected in Article I. In *Tidewater*, then, three justices said that Article III does *not* fix the outer boundaries of the work that Congress can assign to Article III courts. Four other members of the Court dissented, both from the Court's judgment and from Justice Jackson's view that Article III courts can be given non-Article III business. The decisive votes rested with the two remaining justices. They concurred in Jackson's result, but dissented from his analysis.[107] In the end, accordingly, six members of the Court explicitly disclaimed the proposition that Congress can assign Article III courts jurisdiction of matters not on the Article III menu.

The dangers that would be presented if Congress could routinely channel non-Article III business to Article III courts are obvious enough. Just as Congress might upset the balance between the legislative and judicial branches by depriving the courts of jurisdiction in important cases, Congress might equally upset the balance by swamping the courts with extraneous work. As a matter of experience, however, Congress has never attempted to do any such thing, and the system has operated since *Tidewater* without serious difficulty, despite the Court's failure to revisit the issue in that case and spell out the controlling principle.

A few precedents suggest that Congress *can* give Article III courts assignments beyond Article III. But they are confined to narrow circumstances. In *O'Donoghue v. United States*,[108] for example, the Court held that Congress could give the local courts in the District of Columbia (then understood to be Article III courts) certain administrative tasks falling outside Article III. Congress' special relationship to the District may cabin that precedent. Today, the local courts in the District are legislative tribunals that can be given non-Article III duties without raising the same questions.[109] By some accounts, federal courts breach Article III boundaries when they engage in rule-making or other ostensibly legislative activities. The Court has not found arguments of that kind persuasive. In *Mistretta v. United States*,[110] the Court held that individual federal judges can be appointed to the United States Sentencing Commission. As commissioners, those individuals perform non-judicial functions. But they do so as presidential appointees, not as Article III judges.[111]

D. Preclusion of Jurisdiction

It is established beyond argument that some legal disputes can constitutionally go without judicial resolution. Cases in which a governmental defendant successfully asserts sovereign immunity provide familiar illustrations.[112] Nevertheless, most justiciable

107. Justices Rutledge and Murphy argued that the precedents were wrong, that the District of Columbia *was* a "State" within the meaning of Article III, and that the new statute giving the district courts jurisdiction of disputes between citizens of the District and citizens of other "States" did not attempt to give the district courts jurisdiction of matters outside Article III's limits.

108. 289 U.S. 516 (1933).

109. See Chapter V, text accompanying notes 73–75.

110. 488 U.S. 361 (1989).

111. See Chapter III, note 45 (noting Justice Harlan's discussion of these problems in the *Chandler* case).

112. See Chapter X, notes 9–13, 53–55 and accompanying text.

cases can reach courts of some ilk. And the question whether Congress can absolutely foreclose all judicial consideration of federal questions has always excited controversy. That question remains open. In some instances, the Court has apparently held that due process requires the states (and presumably the federal government) to offer litigants some access to courts to vindicate certain federal constitutional claims.[113] And in a host of other cases, the Court has gone to great lengths to read statutes to contemplate some form of judicial review for other constitutional questions. In this context, too, the Court applies a clear statement rule that preserves federal jurisdiction in the absence of exacting language to the contrary.[114] In the *St. Cyr* case, the Court refused to read provisions in AEDPA and IIRIRA absolutely to disable all courts from adjudicating the petitioner's statutory claim. Instead, the Court insisted that a district court retained jurisdiction to entertain the petitioner's habeas corpus application. That, in turn, meant that the Supreme Court, too, would have jurisdiction at the appellate stage.[115] Still, if Congress were to *be* sufficiently clear in a particular instance, some justices plainly would permit Congress to insulate even constitutional issues from judicial examination entirely.[116] Others are doubtful.[117]

---

113. See Chapter VI, notes 57–79 and accompanying text.

114. E.g., *Webster v. Doe*, 486 U.S. 592 (1988) (reading a statute not to preclude judicial review of a constitutional challenge to the decision of the Director of the CIA to dismiss an employee); *Franklin v. Massachusetts*, 505 U.S. 788 (1992) (allowing Massachusetts to press constitutional claims regarding the way in which federal officers conduct the census); *Dalton v. Specter*, 511 U.S. 462 (1994) (construing the Defense Base Closure Act to preclude judicial review only of statutory claims against actions taken by the Secretary of Defense).

115. In dissent, Justice Scalia pointed out that the only jurisdiction that IIRIRA explicitly allowed was initially at the circuit court level, with further appellate review in the Supreme Court thereafter. See note 38. By the Court's account, however, the district courts retained initial jurisdiction to entertain habeas corpus petitions. In Justice Scalia's view, that construction of IIRIRA created an anomaly: a continuation of district court jurisdiction within a new system that plainly meant to channel immigration cases directly to the circuit courts (when it allowed judicial review at all). *INS v. St. Cyr*, 533 U.S. at 334–35 (Scalia, J., dissenting). To the extent the Court's interpretation was at odds with that "channeling" objective, the decision in *St. Cyr* may illustrate that the Court will choose even an awkward construction of a jurisdictional statute rather than an interpretation that deprives all courts of power to hear a federal claim.

116. See, e.g., *Webster*, 486 U.S. at 612 (Scalia, J., dissenting) (contending that Congress can put some constitutional questions "beyond judicial review"). Cf. *Bartlett v. Bowen*, 816 F.2d 695, 719–20 (D.C. Cir. 1987) (Bork, J., dissenting) (arguing that Congress can foreclose judicial review in reliance on sovereign immunity). Cf. Chapter V (discussing congressional power to send federal question cases to non-Article III tribunals). Professor Tribe notes in this connection that the Court has often sustained sharp limits on judicial review in administrative law cases implicating non-constitutional issues. Laurence H. Tribe, American Constitutional Law 289 (3d ed. 2000).

117. E.g., *Webster*, 486 U.S. at 603 (Rehnquist, C.J.) (stating that an attempt by Congress to bar all judicial review of a constitutional question would itself "raise a serious constitutional question"). In *Reno v. American-Arab Anti-Discrimination Committee*, 525 U.S. 471 (1999), Justice Scalia held that IIRIRA foreclosed resident aliens from invoking immediate federal court jurisdiction to determine whether the Attorney General was pressing for their deportation because of their political views and activities. He rejected the aliens' argument that their free speech claim commanded prompt adjudication. On that point, he held that aliens who are unlawfully in this country (typically) *have* no constitutional right to resist deportation on the ground that they have been selected because of their politics. Accordingly, the Act created no constitutional difficulty by eliminating federal court jurisdiction to entertain such a claim. The aliens in *American-Arab* were entitled to seek judicial review of any final orders for their deportation in an appropriate circuit court. Yet they could not press their selective enforcement claim in that setting. Professor Weinberg cites *American-Arab* as an illustration of an absolute elimination of judicial review. Louise Weinberg, *The Article III Box: The Power of Congress to Attack the Jurisdiction of Federal Courts*, 78 Tex. L. Rev. 1405, 1417 (2000).

In one famous lower court case, *Battaglia v. General Motors*,[118] the Second Circuit grappled with the problem, but ultimately rested its decision on a distinction that is difficult to credit. In previous decisions, the Supreme Court had held that the Fair Labor Standards Act entitled workers to be paid while they traveled through underground mines to the place where they would actually set to work.[119] Those decisions made both private employers and the federal government liable for billions of dollars in back wages. To avert that liability, Congress enacted the Portal-to-Portal Act of 1947. That Act purported not only to abrogate any claims that workers had, but also to withdraw the jurisdiction of *any* court to entertain suits by workers seeking any kind of relief.

The court in *Battaglia* nonetheless entertained a suit by workers claiming back wages. Without mentioning Article III, the court reasoned that a withdrawal of jurisdiction having the effect of depriving workers of their property without due process of law would itself violate due process. Turning to the merits, the court held that the abrogation of the workers' claims did *not* violate due process. Then, in an ironic twist, the court said that it was unnecessary to decide whether the Act's attempt to withdraw jurisdiction from the courts would have been successful if the workers' underlying due process claims had been meritorious.

The principal holding in *Battaglia* is compelling. Jurisdictional statutes, like any other form of legislation, must conform to the Constitution. And the courts must be institutionally capable of ensuring that they do. Accordingly, courts must have threshold jurisdiction to decide whether any particular jurisdictional statute confers on them all the jurisdiction the Constitution requires.[120] The court's discussion, however, is problematic in two respects. First, inasmuch as the court relied exclusively on the fifth amendment, it implied that Article III poses no bar to federal statutes that bar all courts from adjudicating constitutional claims. Second, inasmuch as the court suggested that it might have lacked jurisdiction if the workers' claims had been good, it implied that the question whether Congress can withhold jurisdiction may be contingent on the validity of the governmental action that a withdrawal of jurisdiction attempts to shield. It is hard to think that Congress can carve all courts, federal and state, out of the picture—but only when those courts would disapprove the activity under attack if they had jurisdiction to consider it. That would be circular.

By common account, the preclusion of judicial review in cases implicating constitutional interpretation is more problematic than the preclusion of judicial review in cases involving the interpretation of federal non-constitutional law. The Constitution establishes the bedrock on which government operates, and it is especially important that the courts retain adequate power to ensure the preservation of that foundation. In addition, the preclusion of judicial review in cases involving the construction of federal statutes is comparatively democratic. If Congress bars the courts from deciding disputes over the meaning of statutes that Congress itself has enacted, the country at least has the assurance that Congress brought some roughly democratic judgment to bear both on the wisdom of the statute and on the means of enforcing it. If, however, Congress purports

118. 169 F.2d 254 (2d Cir. 1948).

119. E.g., *Tennessee Coal, Iron & R. Co. v. Muscoda Local No. 123*, 321 U.S. 590 (1944).

120. See Richard H. Fallon, Jr., *Some Confusions About Due Process, Judicial Review, and Constitutional Remedies*, 93 Colum. L. Rev. 309, 368 (1993) (crediting Professor Hart with this insight).

to deprive the courts of power to decide disputes involving the meaning of Constitution, the same assurance of politically accountable judgment does not obtain.[121]

E. Academic Theories

The Supreme Court's failure to elaborate clear limits on Congress' power invites academicians to fill the vacuum with theoretical constructions of their own. The possibility of identifying constitutional constraints is attractive, because congressional authority to allocate and adjust jurisdiction threatens the system's balance. The problems presented are immense. Consider that the policy Congress adopts in one context typically has implications for the policies it simultaneously adopts in others. It is one thing, for example, for Congress to deny inferior federal courts jurisdiction regarding some category of Article III business (even cases involving federal constitutional rights)—so long as Congress permits the Supreme Court to consider cases of that kind on appeal from state courts. Even then, the formal availability of Supreme Court review is of only theoretical significance.[122] It is another thing for Congress to withhold jurisdiction from both lower federal courts and the Supreme Court, thus leaving federal question cases entirely to state courts. It is still another thing for Congress to strip all courts, federal and state, of jurisdiction to adjudicate federal claims.

Moreover, Congress' manipulation of jurisdiction may have implications for the vindication of federal legal claims that Article III courts ordinarily enforce.[123] When Congress closes federal courts, state courts typically remain open. If, however, there is no parity between federal courts and state courts, the substantive claims that federal courts would otherwise enforce may suffer for being channeled into a less inviting forum.[124] Over the years, Congress has considered (but never enacted) measures that would withdraw the federal courts' jurisdiction to address controversial questions (like

121. See Note, *The Doctrine of Political Accountability and Supreme Court Jurisdiction: Applying a New External Constraint to Congress's Exceptions Clause Power*, 106 Yale L.J. 197 (1996) (arguing that for this reason it is less troubling for Congress to preclude judicial review regarding the interpretation of federal statutes than it is for Congress to preclude judicial review regarding constitutional attacks on state statutes).

122. See Chapter VII, notes 224–27 and accompanying text (explaining that the Supreme Court does not sit to correct errors in state court proceedings). Congress routinely closes the inferior federal courts in circumstances in which Supreme Court may have appellate jurisdiction to review state court judgments. For example, the basic statute on which district courts rely for jurisdiction in federal question cases, 28 U.S.C. §1331, demands that a federal issue appear on the face of the plaintiff's properly pleaded complaint. Yet Article III allows Congress to give district courts a more extensive jurisdiction. See Chapter VIII, notes 5–46 and accompanying text. Ordinarily, when a case is not within the district courts' jurisdiction pursuant to §1331 and thus is heard in state court, the Supreme Court has appellate jurisdiction to review any decisive state court judgment on a federal question. See Chapter VII, notes 41–57 and accompanying text.

123. See Chapter VIII (describing federal court jurisdiction to vindicate federal claims).

124. See Chapter I, text accompanying notes 92–104 (discussing the parity debate). Proposals to withdraw federal court jurisdiction in controversial cases usually made no attempt to affect state court jurisdiction to decide those same cases. Proponents may have hesitated to restrict state court capacity, either in deference to state prerogatives or in (unstated) recognition that depriving *all* courts of jurisdiction would trigger independent constitutional questions. See note 117 and accompanying text.

organized prayer in public schools, the apportionment of state legislatures, desegregation, and abortion).[125] Proponents of those initiatives meant to attack judicial treatments of those matters indirectly by depriving federal courts of jurisdiction and routing cases to state courts, where proponents hoped different results would be forthcoming.

Some observers insist that the genuine risks are modest.[126] For example, it is often argued that Congress cannot easily thwart unpopular Supreme Court decisions by making exceptions to the Court's appellate jurisdiction.[127] If the Court's own power were withdrawn, state courts (and perhaps inferior federal courts, as well) would arguably be duty-bound to follow the very Supreme Court precedents to which Congress objects.[128] Those precedents would effectively be frozen in place. Even if the Court itself were inclined to reconsider them, it would be unable to do so. Congress' refusal to enact restrictive bills in the past may be evidence that Congress sees this point. Other observers are less sanguine.[129] And many regard congressional power with respect to jurisdiction as a serious, looming threat. The resulting literature is rich in detail, typically combining intricate analysis of historical materials with explicit normative arguments about the way the legislative and judicial branches can best function together.[130]

Academics identify two kinds of limits the Constitution places on congressional power: "external" limits and "internal" limits. External limits typically rest on rights-bearing provisions of the Constitution that Congress must respect when it enacts any kind of legislation. The fifth amendment's Due Process Clause and the first amendment's Free Exercise Clause are common examples. Obviously, a statute depriving district courts of jurisdiction in cases in which the plaintiff is African-American would violate due process. Equally, a statute making an "Exception" to the Supreme Court's

---

125. See Ronald D. Rotunda, *Congressional Power to Restrict the Jurisdiction of the Lower Federal Courts and the Problem of School Busing*, 64 Gtn. L.J. 839 (1976); Robert B. McKay, *Courts, Congress, and Reapportionment*, 63 Mich. L. Rev. 255 (1964).

126. Professor Gunther argued that Congress is in the driver's seat, but that the dangers are not grave. Gerald Gunther, *Congressional Power to Curtail Federal Court Jurisdiction: An Opinionated Guide to the Ongoing Debate*, 36 Stan. L. Rev. 895 (1984).

127. See notes 10–25 and accompanying text.

128. See Herbert Wechsler, *The Courts and the Constitution*, 65 Colum. L. Rev. 1001, 1006–07 (1965).

129. Professor Caminker argues that if Congress withdrew appellate jurisdiction from the Supreme Court, state courts would be free to depart from existing Supreme Court precedents to the extent state courts are convinced that the Court itself would—if it had jurisdiction to revisit earlier decisions. Evan H. Caminker, *Why Must Inferior Courts Obey Superior Court Precedents?*, 46 Stan. L. Rev. 817, 837–38, 868–69 (1994). Professor Sager acknowledges that state courts might be tempted to ignore existing precedents with which they disagree—knowing that the Supreme Court is no longer in a position to reverse them. Congress may anticipate that response and thus withdraw jurisdiction from the Court with a "lewd wink" at the state courts waiting in the wings. Lawrence G. Sager, *Foreword: Constitutional Limitations on Congress' Authority to Regulate the Jurisdiction of the Federal Courts*, 95 Harv. L. Rev. 17, 41 (1981). Professor Weinberg has argued that the serious risk is that Congress might use jurisdictional legislation to prevent the enforcement of individual federal rights. In her view, that risk "cannot have much bite" as long as state courts are available. So the important question is whether Congress can close both federal and state courts. That, in turn, makes the question one of due process rather than Article III or the separation of powers. Louise Weinberg, note 117 at 1416.

130. Professor Wells and Professor Larson criticize the "originalist premises" of much of this literature. They argue that commentators would do better to fashion principles that take greater account of modern circumstances. Michael Wells & Edward J. Larson, *Original Intent and Article III*, 70 Tulane L. Rev. 75 (1995).

appellate jurisdiction for cases involving Jews would violate free exercise. The jurisdictional character of a statute does not shield it from external restraints of that kind.[131]

Internal limits flow from the scope of the legislative authority Congress purports to exercise; they are tied up in the very definition of that power and limit Congress even when no external restraint is implicated. Congress has explicit power to create tribunals inferior to the Supreme Court and implicit power to prescribe the jurisdiction those courts will enjoy within the boundaries established by Article III. Congress also has explicit power to make "Exceptions" from the Supreme Court's appellate jurisdiction. Those powers have not only an affirmative side (what they allow Congress to do), but also a negative side (what they do not authorize Congress to do). Any interpretation of them must therefore contemplate that some congressional actions will reach beyond the scope of the power Congress purports to be exercising and thus exceed the limits "internal" to that power.[132]

Of the two kinds of constitutional limits, internal limits are the more difficult to elaborate. The most influential academic accounts of internal restraints fall under three headings: (1) essential function theories; (2) zero-sum theories; and (3) judicial independence theories.

Essential function theories. Many academicians are content with a large measure of congressional control over lower federal courts, but insist that Congress' ability to make "Exceptions" from the Supreme Court's appellate jurisdiction is subject to significant restraints. As a matter of grammar alone, an *exception* presupposes a body of jurisdiction from which Congress removes some piece. Accordingly, Congress cannot make "Exceptions" for the entirety of the appellate jurisdiction that Article III prescribes, leaving nothing behind.[133] Congress cannot meet this grammatical objection simply by allowing the Court some trifle of jurisdiction while making "Exceptions" for everything else. Congress' power under the Exceptions Clause must be reconciled with the constitutional framework within which it is located and therefore must respect the Supreme Court's role in the tripartite system. Congress' power must therefore be limited to adjustments that are not disabling, but rather preserve the Court's ability to perform its "essential functions."[134] What counts as an essential function can be contro-

---

131. See Richard H. Fallon, Jr., *The Ideologies of Federal Courts Law*, 74 Va. L. Rev. 1141, 1221 (1988). Professor Tribe once argued that foreclosing federal jurisdiction of cases involving a specified individual right and thus shifting adjudication of that right to state court imposes a "burden" that violates the right itself. Laurence H. Tribe, *Jurisdictional Gerrymandering: Zoning Disfavored Rights Out of the Federal Courts*, 16 Harv. C.R.—C.L. L. Rev. 129 (1981). That argument is attractive, particularly if it is true (as it invariably is) that proponents of the limitation on federal jurisdiction hope the state courts will be less generous to the federal right in issue. If, however, federal and state courts are fungible in constitutional cases, Professor Tribe's argument is less compelling. See Tribe, note 116, at 274 n.28 (indicating that for this reason the thesis "seems in retrospect to have been misguided").

132. Professor Engdahl critiques the Court's account of congressional power for relying too heavily on external restraints and neglecting internal restraints that promise more significant checks on the legislative branch. In his view, the Court makes a threshold mistake by locating Congress' power to prescribe the jurisdiction of Article III courts in Article I, §8, cl. 9, together with Article III. See text accompanying notes 49, 62–71. Those bases of power offer few, if any, serious internal limits. Engdahl proposes, instead, that Congress' power regarding federal court jurisdiction must depend on the Necessary and Proper Clause in Article I, §8, cl.18. That clause, in his view, establishes numerous internal checks. See David E. Engdahl, *Intrinsic Limits of Congress' Power Regarding the Judicial Branch*, 1999 B.Y.U. L. Rev. 75 (presenting an originalist argument in defense of this thesis). Needless to say, Engdahl's approach is unconventional.

133. This was Professor Hart's approach to the problem. Hart, note 95, at 1365.

134. Id.

versial. It seems clear, however, that the Court's crucial role concerns matters of federal law, particularly constitutional law. The Court must serve as the judicial system's ultimate referee, ensuring that federal law is accurately elaborated, that it is held supreme over state law, and that it is uniformly understood and enforced throughout the country.[135]

The essential functions thesis has the virtue of being consistent with the Supreme Court's precedents. Then again, Congress has not (yet) enacted jurisdictional legislation that genuinely threatens the Court's capacity to referee the system in federal question cases. Most observers endorse this theory as a minimalist account of the constitutional limits on congressional power. Yet many doubt its sufficiency without more. As a practical matter, the essential functions limit may be unenforceable. It would be hard to say that any particular, isolated restriction on the Supreme Court's jurisdiction is in itself disabling. The essential functions limiting principle may thus be evaded if Congress enacts a series of modest restrictions that are devastating only in cumulative effect.

Academics are divided over one (possible) feature of the Court's essential role, which, if recognized, would be comparatively easy to identify and preserve. That is the Court's arguable constitutional power and duty to superintend "inferior" federal tribunals. By some accounts, the federal judiciary exists as a unit with its own hierarchical structure. This means that the Supreme Court, the one "superior" court at the top of the hierarchy, must necessarily have authority and responsibility to superintend "inferior" courts further down. It would be unconstitutional, then, for Congress to deny the Supreme Court sufficient jurisdiction to supervise inferior federal tribunals.[136] Equally, it would be unconstitutional for Congress to confer jurisdiction on inferior federal courts in a way that would have those courts defy Supreme Court precedent.[137]

By other accounts, the federal judiciary is more fragmented—composed of many discrete Article III tribunals (including the Supreme Court), each with its own independent constitutional and statutory mandates. Observers in this general camp contend that when Congress confers jurisdiction on any particular federal tribunal, it speaks to that court alone. It follows that the tribunal concerned exercises judicial power (subject to its jurisdictional limits) without any necessary regard for other courts, including the Supreme Court. Thus an inferior federal court is duty-bound to proceed independently, interpreting federal law as it thinks proper, even though the Supreme Court may take a different view.[138] The "inferior" label that attaches to federal courts other than the Supreme Court means only that, if Congress decides to give one federal tribunal appellate authority to superintend another, it must accord the "superior" position to the

135. See Leonard Ratner, *Congressional Power Over the Appellate Jurisdiction of the Supreme Court*, 109 U. Pa. L. Rev. 157, 161 (1960).

136. See James E. Pfander, *Jurisdiction-Stripping and the Supreme Court's Power to Supervise Inferior Tribunals*, 78 Tex. L. Rev. 1433 (2000). According to Pfander, Congress may be able to make healthy exceptions to the Court's ordinary appellate jurisdiction to review lower federal court judgments. But Congress cannot dislodge the Court's authority to supervise lower federal courts by means of prerogative writs: (mandamus, habeas corpus, prohibition, certiorari, and quo warranto).

137. See Evan H. Caminker, *Allocating the Judicial Power in a Unified Judiciary*, 78 Tex. L. Rev. 1513, 1515–17 (2000).

138. See Gary Lawson, *The Constitutional Case Against Precedent*, 17 Harv. J.L. & Pub. Pol'y 23 (1994) (arguing that inferior federal courts cannot take Supreme Court precedents to be authoritative). Recall that the Article III judges who sit on inferior federal courts are entitled to the same tenure and salary protections that Supreme Court justices enjoy. Those safeguards for independence are generally thought to rest, in part, on the need to protect individual judges from over-reaching by their colleagues on the federal bench. Chapter III, text accompanying note 2.

Supreme Court.[139] Congress is free, however, to confer jurisdiction on inferior federal courts without prescribing any corresponding appellate role for the Supreme Court.[140]

Zero-sum theories. Other academics advance alternative theories, which attempt to delineate both Congress' authority to make "Exceptions" from the Supreme Court's appellate jurisdiction and Congress' authority to prescribe the jurisdiction of inferior federal courts. Zero-sum theories proceed from Justice Story's premise that the term "shall" in the first section of Article III establishes a constitutional mandate that the judicial power of the United States *must* be vested in Article III courts.[141]

By one account, Congress must give Article III courts jurisdiction in all the (nontrivial) cases and controversies listed in Article III. If Congress creates only the Supreme Court, that single tribunal must be able to reach everything, either by exercising original jurisdiction or by taking appeals from state courts. In that instance, Congress' power to make "Exceptions" from the Court's appellate jurisdiction is limited to allocating business between the Court's original and appellate dockets. It is a zero-sum game. Everything must be in one place or the other, with nothing (or almost nothing) entirely omitted. If, on the other hand, Congress creates inferior federal courts, then by this account Congress can deny the Supreme Court either original or appellate jurisdiction of some case or controversy and channel that business to those inferior courts. The constitutional mandate is satisfied so long as everything can reach *some* Article III court in *some* way.[142]

Another zero-sum account builds on Story's observation that only the "cases" on the Article III menu are preceded by the modifier "all."[143] By this second account, Congress is obliged only to allow the Supreme Court (together with inferior federal courts if they are created) jurisdiction in those *cases*—and not the *controversies* on the Article III list. Article III thus establishes two "tiers" of matters over which federal courts *can* exercise jurisdiction. The cases in the one tier (preceded by "all") are especially important. Jurisdiction to entertain them must be vested. The controversies listed further down are of another order and need not have access to an Article III forum.[144]

---

139. See Akhil R. Amar, *A Neo-Federalist View of Article III: Separating the Two Tiers of Federal Jurisdiction*, 65 B.U. L. Rev. 205, 221 n.60 (1985).

140. See Chapter VII, notes 211–18 and accompanying text (discussing the Supreme Court's actual role with respect to inferior federal tribunals).

141. See text accompanying note 58.

142. This is the understanding that Professor Clinton ascribes to the founding generation. Of course, he explains and defends it in much finer detail. Robert N. Clinton, *A Mandatory View of Federal Court Jurisdiction: A Guided Quest for the Original Understanding of Article III*, 132 U. Pa. L. Rev. 741 (1984). See also Robert N. Clinton, *A Mandatory View of Federal Court Jurisdiction: Early Implementation of and Departures from the Constitutional Plan*, 86 Colum. L. Rev. 1515 (1986).

143. See text accompanying note 59.

144. This is a nutshell of Professor Amar's thesis. He, too, elaborates his argument in much greater depth. See Amar, note 139. Amar fortifies his theory of Article III with a related argument that it conforms (in most respects) to the Judiciary Act of 1789. Akhil R. Amar, *The Two-Tiered Structure of the Judiciary Act of 1789*, 138 U. Pa. L. Rev. 1499 (1990). See Chapter II, notes 56–62 and accompanying text. For criticism, see John Harrison, *The Power of Congress to Limit the Jurisdiction of Federal Courts and the Text of Article III*, 64 U. Chi. L. Rev. 203 (1997); Martin H. Redish, *Text, Structure, and Common Sense in the Interpretation of Article III*, 138 U. Pa. L. Rev. 1633 (1990); Daniel J. Meltzer, *The History and Structure of Article III*, 138 U. Pa. L. Rev. 1569 (1990); Robert J. Pushaw, Jr., *Congressional Power Over Federal Court Jurisdiction: A Defense of the Neo-Federalist Interpretation of Article III*, 1997 B.Y.U. L. Rev. 847. For Professor Amar's response, see Akhil R. Amar, *Reports of My Death Are Greatly Exaggerated: A Reply*, 138 U. Pa. L. Rev. 1651 (1990).

These theories have appeal, but they are also open to criticism. By contrast to the essential functions thesis, they plainly depart from established precedent. The Supreme Court has often permitted Congress to make net withdrawals of Article III jurisdiction from federal courts and thus has implicitly rejected the zero-sum baseline. The first zero-sum account has it that the federal courts must constitutionally be given much more jurisdiction than they have ever had. If Congress were to place the entirety of that business in the Supreme Court itself, the burden would be enormous—and extremely difficult to justify.[145] The second zero-sum account would be easier to implement. But that approach, too, insists that Article III courts must shoulder much more responsibility than may be either wise or practical.[146]

Judicial independence theories. Still other academics insist that Congress' power to prescribe the jurisdiction of federal courts must be reconciled with constitutional safeguards for the independence of those courts: Congress cannot have such plenary authority to withhold jurisdiction that it can defeat Article III's tenure and salary protections by indirection, simply by channeling judicial business to state judges who stand for popular election.[147] According to this last theory, Congress can deny federal courts significant portions of the power that Article III would allow. But Congress cannot deprive the federal judiciary of the capacity to handle critical constitutional cases. This theory also conflicts with established precedent. Observers who are comfortable with the Hart and Wechsler paradigm and the private rights model will find it unattractive, as will observers who accept the parity of state and federal courts.[148] Observers who embrace the public rights model may find it appealing.[149]

---

145. If Congress creates no inferior federal courts and, under Clinton's theory, must confer "minimal" diversity jurisdiction on the Supreme Court, then the Court would have jurisdiction to accept appeals from the state courts in a wide range of cases controlled by state law. See text accompanying notes 63–64; Chapter VII, notes 104–11 (discussing the understanding that state courts are authoritative with respect to state law). Professor Harrison contends that Clinton's theory would "fill the federal courts with diversity cases." Harrison, note 144, at 207.

146. Professor Amar has it that federal question cases are among those that must be vested in some Article III court. That seems attractive. Yet under the precedents a case "arises under" federal law not only when it actually implicates a federal issue, but also when a federal question may potentially appear. That, suffice it to say, is a lot of cases. Professor Harrison contends that Amar reads too much into the term "all." See Harrison, note 144, at 233.

147. Professor Sager is the principal proponent of this position. Sager, note 129. He, too, explains his approach in much more detail. For criticism, see Martin H. Redish, *Constitutional Limitations on Congressional Power to Control Federal Jurisdiction: A Reaction to Professor Sager*, 77 Nw. U. L. Rev. 143 (1982).

148. See Chapter I, text accompanying notes 53–72.

149. See Chapter I, text accompanying notes 78–91.

Chapter V

Legislative Courts

The Supreme Court and the inferior federal tribunals organized under Article III are the "constitutional" or "Article III" courts in which "[t]he judicial Power of the United States... shall be vested." Congress often creates other federal officers, agencies, and tribunals and gives them authority to perform adjudicative functions. Those entities differ from Article III courts in one crucial respect: Their decision-makers do not enjoy the life tenure and salary protections that the Constitution guarantees to Article III judges. Instead, they serve for a term of years, and their compensation can be reduced.

Some of the bodies in question are units or officers operating within Article III courts. Others form the legions of federal administrative agencies located within the executive branch, but performing legislative and judicial functions as well. Agencies forge federal policy to govern their respective fields, both when they promulgate formal rules (in proceedings that look and feel legislative) and when they apply statutes and rules in particular instances (in proceedings that look and feel adjudicative). Agencies do not exercise "the judicial Power" of the United States specified in the Constitution. Only Article III courts do that. Nevertheless, whenever agencies determine facts and apply the law to those facts, they engage in adjudication.[1]

Early in this century, federal agencies were thought to be constitutionally troubling, both because they combine executive, legislative, and judicial functions under one roof and because, with respect to adjudication, they trespass into territory occupied by the Article III judiciary. The Supreme Court defused those concerns in the 1930s, and for many years thereafter agency adjudication was rarely questioned. The great mass of modern administrative law developed to assimilate agencies into the constitutional framework.[2] Recently, however, the Supreme Court has revisited the tension between the judicial work that agencies do and the Constitution's contemplation that judicial power lies with Article III courts.

The occasion for this reassessment is Congress' increasing reliance on non-Article III adjudicators called "legislative" or "Article I" courts. Labels can be confusing. These entities are not called "legislative" courts because they perform legislative functions (any more than do Article III courts), but rather because Congress creates them in ser-

1. See Chapter I, text accompanying notes 6–9. In *Fed. Maritime Comm'n v. South Carolina Ports Authority*, 122 S.Ct. 1864 (2002), the Court held that an agency's adjudicative functions closely resemble the functions of a court. Accordingly, a state may assert sovereign immunity to defeat a complaint by a private citizen before an agency, just as the state might assert immunity as a defense to a private citizen's lawsuit brought in a federal court. See Chapter X, notes 197–210 and accompanying text.

2. See notes 43–51 and accompanying text (discussing *Crowell v. Benson*). For a discussion of the development and significance of administrative agencies, see Chapter VIII, notes 124, 137–39, 182 and accompanying text; Chapter IX, notes 79–120 and accompanying text.

vice of its legislative programs. Nor are legislative courts called "Article I" courts because they are created pursuant to Congress' Article I power to "constitute Tribunals inferior to the supreme Court."[3] That clause authorizes Congress to create Article III courts.[4] Legislative courts are called "Article I" courts because Congress claims power to create them as an exercise of various other legislative powers, typically (though not always) enumerated in Article I—for example, the commerce power.[5] Legislative courts cannot easily be justified as auxiliary staff. They occupy their own precincts and resolve legal disputes independently, without any expectation that Article III courts need be involved prior to an appellate stage. In most respects, legislative courts are conceptually indistinguishable from administrative agencies performing adjudicative functions. Yet the Supreme Court has worried at length over whether they can be squared with Article III. The Court's concerns about legislative courts, in turn, rekindle similar concerns about agencies.

One might have expected the Court to be especially suspicious of Congress' use of non-Article III tribunals in cases in which the federal government is a party and may wish to appear before judges more susceptible to influence.[6] As a matter of fact, the Court indulges Congress' use of legislative courts in cases of that kind with equanimity and reserves its concern for cases in which Congress employs legislative courts to resolve disputes between private litigants. It is in those cases, perhaps, that legislative courts seem most clearly to be doing the work historically regarded as judicial—thus poaching on Article III courts' preserve.[7]

A. Theoretical Models

Analysis of non-Article III tribunals is both energized and handicapped by three competing models: (1) the simple Article I model; (2) the simple Article III model; and (3) the executive policy model. No one offers any of these models as a single, comprehensive basis for deciding whether any particular assignment of jurisdiction is valid. Yet all three plainly animate the arguments that are advanced in the cases and in the accompanying academic literature.

The simple Article I model. According to the simple Article I model, legislative courts present no great constitutional difficulty. Since Article I gives Congress power to make

3. U.S. Const. art. I, §8, cl.9; see Chapter IV, note 49 and accompanying text.

4. *Glidden Co. v. Zdanok*, 370 U.S. 530, 543 (1962).

5. Legislative courts are nonetheless "Courts of Law" within the meaning of the Appointments Clause, U.S. Const. art. II, §2, cl.2, and therefore can be assigned the authority to appoint inferior legislative court judges. *Freytag v. Commissioner*, 501 U.S. 868 (1991).

6. See Chapter III, text accompanying note 2 (identifying the values associated with the independence of Article III courts); Chapter IV, notes 122–30 and accompanying text (describing the implications of congressional power to withhold jurisdiction from federal courts in sensitive cases).

7. Professor Resnik has noted the "irony" of reading the Constitution to give litigation between private citizens the strongest claim to an Article III tribunal. Judith Resnik, *The Mythic Meaning of Article III Courts*, 56 U. Colo. L. Rev. 581, 600 (1985). Professor Redish finds it "bizarre" that the Court overlooks cases in which the threat of congressional overreaching is greatest and focuses, instead, on cases that are "barely within any of the... categories" of cases and controversies that Article III includes in the federal judicial power. Martin H. Redish, *Legislative Courts, Administrative Agencies, and the Northern Pipeline Decision*, 1983 Duke L.J. 197, 208–09.

substantive law in a variety of fields, Congress must also have the implied power to choose the means by which its regulatory mandates will be carried out. Under the simple Article I model, Congress need not rely on Article III courts to elaborate the meaning of federal legislation and to settle any disputes. Instead, Congress can choose to implement statutes by other means—namely, by channeling disputes to non-Article III adjudicative bodies created for the purpose.[8]

The simple Article I model is a classic illustration of a "greater power" mistake.[9] It posits that Congress' power to establish a regulatory scheme under Article I constitutes a "greater" power, which necessarily includes as a "lesser" power the authority to create and use a legislative court. That rationale is unsound. It may be perfectly sensible to interpret a legislative power to include the power to create a legislative court. But it is not logically imperative that Article I powers must be interpreted that way. The Constitution might also be read to authorize Congress to fashion substantive policies to govern a field, but to specify that if Congress wants federal tribunals to resolve any disputes that arise in connection with its regulation, Congress must rely on independent Article III courts. A requirement that Congress use Article III courts exclusively might be a check that balances Congress' power to make and implement policy in the first instance. In any case, the simple Article I model fixes no apparent limits and thus ignores the separation principle altogether. There must be some check on non-Article III adjudicators. Otherwise, Congress would be able to carve Article III courts out of the picture entirely.

The simple Article III model. According to the simple Article III model, legislative courts conflict with fundamental constitutional principles. The Constitution unmistakably places the federal judicial power in the hands of Article III courts alone, and Congress must make do with those courts or none at all. To allow Congress to create other tribunals and to route federal judicial business to them is to invite Congress to bypass independent Article III courts at will, to ignore the federal judicial branch that Article III envisions, and thus to dismantle the fundamental tripartite framework of the national government.[10]

The simple Article III model is an example of separation-of-powers formalism run amok. It proceeds from a contestable interpretation of Article III's text and an equally contestable inference from the constitutional structure. Recall that what qualifies as adjudication is not logically determinable, but turns on conventional practices and pragmatic judgment.[11] If there is no principled line between adjudication and everything else, it is useless to insist that only Article III judges can perform judicial functions. Moreover, the simple Article III model is infeasible. Federal agencies with adjudicative authority are vital to the modern administrative state—a complex political and economic order unknown to the common law and unmanageable by common law courts.[12]

---

8. This model is sometimes associated with Justice White's dissent in *Northern Pipeline Constr. Co. v. Marathon Pipe Line Co.*, 458 U.S. 50, 92–118 (1982). But Justice White's position was not nearly so extreme. See note 119 and accompanying text.

9. See Chapter I, notes 27–28 and accompanying text.

10. Professor Fallon calls this point of view "Article III literalism." Richard H. Fallon, Jr., *Of Legislative Courts, Administrative Agencies, and Article III*, 101 Harv. L. Rev. 915, 918 (1988). Professor Bator called it the "Simple Model." Paul M. Bator, *The Constitution as Architecture: Legislative and Administrative Courts Under Article III*, 65 Ind. L.J. 233, 235 (1990).

11. See Chapter I, note 9 and accompanying text.

12. Agencies might still perform legislative functions by formal rule-making. But they would lose the flexibility to fashion policy via adjudicative proceedings and the ability to resolve problems *ad hoc* at the implementation stage.

The country might get along without so many agencies doing judicial work. And Congress might meet the constitutional difficulties with some agencies simply by making their decision-making officers Article III judges. Yet the charge the simple Article III model lays against agencies runs deep. It condemns all adjudicative action by non-Article III bodies and thus could presumably be answered only if all federal officers performing judicial functions were given Article III judgeships.

The point is not that federal officers other than Article III judges must be employed at will. Most already enjoy a large measure of job security under the civil service system. The point is not even (entirely) that the application of the various trappings attending federal judgeships to officers in the executive branch would rework well-established schemes for the appointment, retention, compensation, and dismissal of federal employees—from desk clerks to FBI agents. The real point is that making federal executive officers Article III judges would fundamentally transmute the nature of their offices. They would no longer serve within an ordinary hierarchical system, taking orders from their superiors, but would occupy their own comparatively independent preserves and would be answerable in the much different manner of inferior Article III judges. They would be obliged to follow Supreme Court precedent, and their judicial actions would be subject to reversal on appeal to a higher court—but only for *error*.[13] Any attempt by superiors within an executive department or agency to reexamine the *wisdom* of their decisions would presumably constitute interference with the judicial function in violation of Article III.[14]

The executive policy model. According to the executive policy model, at least some federal agencies properly undertake adjudicative functions strictly for the purpose of determining what, if any, action the federal government should take with respect to a controversy. Agencies frequently entertain complaints from private citizens who charge some party with violating federal law. To determine whether a complaint is valid, the agency may institute proceedings at which an agency officer considers both the complainant's evidence and arguments and any counters that the alleged violator may offer. The hearing officer (typically an administrative law judge) certainly performs an adjudicative function. Yet, according to this third model, the point of that adjudication is only to build a record on which the agency can rely in formulating the position it will adopt on behalf of the executive branch. Accordingly, the adjudication that occurs within the agency does not place the agency in competition with the federal courts for the responsibility of actually determining a dispute and bringing coercive power to bear on a party who has violated federal law.[15]

---

13. See Chapter IV, notes 137–40 (discussing the relationship between inferior federal courts and the Supreme Court); Chapter VII, note 211 (noting the same arguments).

14. See Chapter IX, notes 35–44 and accompanying text. Professor Stern insists that Article III can be read literally without such dire consequences merely by defining the exercise of federal judicial power according to the identity of the officer concerned (rather than the function the officer performs). By his account, executive officers may routinely perform adjudicative functions without implicating Article III, because they (not being Article III judges) do not exercise federal judicial authority. Craig A. Stern, *What's a Constitution Among Friends?—Unbalancing Article III*, 146 U. Pa. L. Rev. 1043 (1998). Stern claims that Justice Scalia essentially adopted that position in his concurring opinion in *Freytag*. 501 U.S. at 911.

15. Justice Breyer sketched this general conceptual understanding of agency behavior in his dissent in *Ports Authority*. 122 S.Ct. at 1881 (joined by Stevens, Souter & Ginsburg, J.J.). See Chapter X, text accompanying note 209.

The executive policy model is sound so far as it goes. There is no obvious constitutional objection if the executive branch, for its own internal purposes, chooses to employ procedural machinery that resembles judicial proceedings. After all, we should hope that the government tries to get the facts straight before it adopts an official position. Yet it is unrealistic to portray the operations of non-Article III adjudicators as so many instances of executive officers trying to make up their minds about the merits of a complaint. Parties accused of violating federal law may not be formally obliged to cooperate with agencies. But if they refuse, they invariably limit their options. Typically, parties may not blithely ignore agency adjudicative proceedings and then expect to offer arguments and evidence to the courts, if and when an agency files a lawsuit. At that point, parties usually forfeit defenses that they failed to present to the agency. Moreover, federal courts typically are not free simply to substitute their own judgment for that of an agency regarding disputed facts and legal issues. Instead, courts review agency findings and conclusions on a standard that necessarily gives some preliminary effect to what the agency determined previously. For these reasons, agency adjudicative proceedings do substitute for original jurisdiction in an Article III court and thus require some constitutional justification.[16]

Struck by the obvious deficiencies in these three models, many academics urge the Court to hold that non-Article III adjudicators can validly exercise *original* responsibility for resolving disputes, so long as Article III courts can reexamine their decisions in some kind of *appellate* capacity.[17] Congress typically makes judgments by legislative courts final (if unchallenged), but subject to review in an Article III court. Parties who are displeased by what legislative courts decide thus bear the burden of pressing on to the Article III judiciary. Consistent with the executive policy model, Congress usually specifies that administrative agency judgments are *not* immediately effective. Agencies must ordinarily file independent lawsuits in the Article III courts, seeking judicial orders enforcing their decisions. Article III courts must therefore participate if agencies are to bring coercive power to bear on individuals. The form that Article III court review takes may have practical significance for the litigants involved. Yet by most accounts, the *constitutional* point is that Article III courts perform a serious supervisory

16. Writing for the Court in *Ports Authority*, Justice Thomas explained that the agency in that case, the Federal Maritime Commission, operated very much like an ordinary court, even to the point of following most of the Federal Rules of Civil Procedure. An enterprise accused of violating the Shipping Act failed to appear and answer a complaint at its peril. If an alleged violator offered no defense before the administrative law judge, it could not do so later before a federal district court. By the terms of the controlling statute, moreover, the district court's purview was limited to reviewing the agency's order to determine whether it was "regularly made and duly issued." 122 S.Ct. at 1876. Justice Thomas acknowledged that the alleged violator in the case at bar (an arm of the state of South Carolina) nevertheless could choose to disregard the agency's proceedings. Yet the price of a failure to cooperate was too high to justify a holding that South Carolina was not subject to a form of judicial power at the agency itself. For that and other reasons, South Carolina was entitled to defeat the agency proceeding by asserting sovereign immunity. See Chapter X, notes 197–210 and accompanying text.

17. Professor Fallon, for example, contends that Article III court review is not only a necessary, but a sufficient, response to Article III difficulties generally. Fallon, note 10. Professor Stern disparages the appellate review approach, but nonetheless appears to be content that Article III is satisfied so long as the "ultimate" decision-maker is an Article III judge. Stern, note 14, at 1047, 1073–74. Justice Thomas explained in *Ports Authority* that he had no occasion to decide whether a state would be entitled to assert sovereign immunity before an agency under a regime that guaranteed "*de novo*" review of all issues in an Article III court. 122 S.Ct. at 1876 n.15; see Chapter X, note 205.

function—whoever has the burden of bringing them into play.[18] The real question is the *scope* of Article III court review. Asking Article III courts essentially to rubberstamp the work of non-Article III bodies would make the courts superfluous. Asking them to review all issues *de novo* would defeat the point of introducing non-Article III adjudicators in the first place.[19]

The Supreme Court plainly finds Article III court involvement critical. If the courts serve in an appellate capacity, the Court is ambivalent about whether it is preferable that individuals or non-Article III bodies have the burden of seeking judicial review. The Court is not convinced, however, that *any* form of after-the-fact review is sufficient in itself. By contrast, the Court insists that the Constitution imposes limits of some kind on *original* adjudication by non-Article III entities.[20] Accordingly, the Court has set about the task of finding its own middle passage between the simple Article I and Article III models. The first order of business is to look behind the models themselves and to identify and evaluate the reasons for employing legislative courts, on the one hand, and the genuine problems and hazards they present, on the other.

In many instances, legislative courts have obvious advantages and pose very few risks. Some of them are nothing new at all, but are quite old and familiar.[21] They operate in fields in which Congress has special constitutional authority and responsibility.[22] Many serve temporary purposes for which Article III courts are not needed. It makes sense, then, to allow Congress to employ decision-makers for fixed terms and thus to avoid building up a battery of life-tenured Article III judges whose services may not always be required.[23] Some legislative courts have jurisdiction over a limited geographic area and thus have little capacity to extend their influence beyond fixed borders. While they may handle cases implicating legal standards of wider applicability, they rarely affect the national adjudicative system as a whole.[24] Most legislative courts have jurisdiction over a limited subject matter;[25] many offer special expertise with respect to the jurisdiction they exercise.[26] Legislative courts sometimes dispose of comparatively

18. See Redish, note 7, at 216–17. Professor Meltzer also doubts that the constitutionality of non-Article III adjudication should turn on "which party has the burden of seeking judicial review." Daniel J. Meltzer, *Legislative Courts, Legislative Power, and the Constitution*, 65 Ind. L.J. 291, 303 n.61 (1990). Cases involving states as parties are exceptions to this generalization. A state typically may assert sovereign immunity to defeat an attempt by a private citizen to seek judicial enforcement of an agency judgment in court. Yet a state has no similar immunity regarding a suit instituted by a federal agency (an arm of the United States) to enforce its own order. See Chapter X, notes 63–66 and accompanying text.

19. See note 143 (elaborating this point of view).

20. See text accompanying note 141.

21. Territorial courts may be the best example under this heading, but military courts martial, too, are typically explained in this way. See notes 66–72, 76–81 and accompanying text.

22. Once again, territorial and military courts are illustrations.

23. Early territorial courts met this description, though the territorial courts we now have may not. See note 68 and accompanying text. Temporary tribunals established *ad hoc* to handle cases in other nations may be the best illustrations. But see Maryellen Fullerton, *Hijacking Trials Overseas: The Need for an Article III Court*, 28 Wm. & Mary L. Rev. 1 (1986).

24. Territorial courts and the courts of the District of Columbia share this feature. See notes 73–75 and accompanying text.

25. Military courts martial are restricted to armed forces personnel, for example, and the Tax Court of the United States is limited to taxation cases. See note 77 and accompanying text.

26. Numerous modern tribunals fit under this heading. By contrast, there is strong sentiment that Article III judges should be generalists. See Chapter II, note 97 and accompanying text.

routine, fact-sensitive matters expeditiously, without the expenditures and delays that often accompany ordinary litigation.[27] Finally, legislative courts can mitigate the caseload crisis simply by assuming adjudicative responsibility that Article III courts would otherwise have to shoulder.[28]

Legislative courts nonetheless entail problems and potential perils. Since their decision-makers lack the salary and tenure protections enjoyed by Article III judges, their independence from political pressure is less secure. That, in turn, threatens both structural arrangements on which society as a whole depends and the personal interests of individuals in appearing before independent federal judges—if they appear before federal adjudicators at all. The Constitution does not systematically guarantee anyone a right to litigate in an Article III court.[29] Nevertheless, if Congress chooses to provide a federal forum, the independence of the judge who sits is Article III-sensitive.[30] Legislative courts' vulnerability to political pressure may rob their proceedings of fairness and thus violate due process.[31] Finally, legislative courts typically rely exclusively on professional decision-makers and therefore may compromise litigants' independent seventh amendment right to trial by jury.[32]

To accommodate these competing interests and concerns, the Supreme Court has relied on two distinct theories of its own creation: (1) the "adjunct" theory, which justifies certain non-Article III adjudicators as arms of the Article III judiciary; and (2) a much

27. Classic examples include federal pension cases, customs disputes, and some immigration cases—in which truncated procedures are thought to be expedient. See Bator, note 10, at 261–62; but see note 101 (regarding immigration cases). The Court of Federal Claims and the Benefits Review Board illustrate the specialized tribunals that may be established to hear claims against the federal government.

28. See Chapter II, notes 101–02 and accompanying text. This justification for legislative courts is open to debate. Professor Meltzer argues that if Congress is unprepared to increase the number of Article III judgeships, judicial independence might better be served by diverting the overflow into state court. Meltzer, note 18, at 293–94.

29. In many instances, individuals must proceed in state court. Few state judges have tenure and salary safeguards, and it would be extravagant to argue that, for that reason, their adjudicative functions violate Article III. See Chapter IV, text accompanying notes 62–64 (explaining that Congress routinely gives federal courts less jurisdiction than Article III would allow); Chapter VI, notes 23–26 and accompanying text (discussing the presumptive authority of state courts to entertain federal question cases).

30. State judges may have no structural safeguards to ensure their independence, but they do not depend on Congress for their maintenance, either. Larry Kramer, *The Constitution as Architecture: A Charette*, 65 Ind. L.J. 283, 286 (1990).

31. This point draws on the same theme as the previous point. Yet the argument from fairness is more conventional inasmuch as it rests on a principle of individual liberty (due process) rather than on a structural theme (the separation of powers reflected in Article III). Justice Brandeis contended that if an individual litigant has any constitutional complaint about the status of the judge assigned to determine a case, that complaint must be anchored in due process rather than in Article III. *Crowell v. Benson*, 285 U.S. 22, 87–88 (1932) (dissenting opinion). Yet the modern Court has acknowledged that an individual has a (waivable) Article III right to appear before a judge who is protected from the influences of other branches. See note 122.

32. See note 41 (discussing the authority of magistrate judges to conduct jury trials); notes 144–68 and accompanying text (discussing the tension between the constitutional right to trial by jury and non-Article III adjudication in which juries are not available). This point, too, can be debated. Recall that trial by jury was understood historically as a democratic safeguard against powerful judges, answerable to the Crown or, after 1787, only to themselves. See Chapter II, notes 31–33 and accompanying text. There is an argument, then, that the seventh amendment right to jury trial is chiefly at risk when cases are adjudicated by life-tenured Article III judges.

more complex theory, which justifies legislative courts and agencies as autonomous entities, though typically subject to appellate supervision by Article III courts.[33]

B. Adjuncts to Article III Courts

Under the adjunct theory, the Supreme Court finds that non-Article III adjudication is essentially consistent with the simple Article III model. The officers and bodies concerned are conceptualized as auxiliary elements of Article III courts. If adjunct officers or bodies perform adjudicative duties *for* Article III courts, there is no serious conflict with Article III, and the separation of powers is preserved.[34]

Magistrate judges. The best illustrations of adjunct officers are magistrate judges. They have been in place since the Judiciary Act of 1789, albeit traveling under different names.[35] Magistrate judges handle misdemeanor criminal trials, preliminary proceedings in serious criminal cases, habeas corpus hearings, a wide range of civil matters, and any "additional duties as are not inconsistent with the Constitution and laws of the United States."[36] They prepare reports setting forth proposed findings of fact and recommendations for disposition. If parties object, district judges make *de novo* determinations. When the parties consent (and a district court directs), magistrate judges can fully dispose of any civil case. In that instance, any appeal lies not to a judge of the district court, but directly to the appropriate circuit court of appeals.[37] In *United States v. Raddatz*,[38] the Supreme Court held that a district judge could rule on a criminal defendant's motion to suppress incriminating evidence on the basis of a magistrate's report, without independently seeing the witnesses. Neither the Due Process Clause nor Article III required the district judge to hold another hearing, even though the defendant's constitutional rights were at stake. It was enough that the district judge was empowered to "accept or reject" the magistrate's recommendations and might have *chosen* to "hear the evidence *de novo*." Since the magistrate judge acted under the district court's "total control," all constitutional requirements were satisfied.[39]

---

33. Professor Strauss explains that "the whole point" is that "*no judicial involvement at all*" is required before a legislative court can coerce a litigant to conform to its orders. Peter L. Strauss, *The Place of Agencies in Government: Separation of Powers and the Fourth Branch*, 84 Colum. L. Rev. 573, 632 (1984) (emphasis in original).

34. Professor Bator acknowledged (but derided) the adjunct theory as a device for finding non-Article III bodies to be "in harmony with the fundamentals of the Simple Model." Bator, note 10, at 253.

35. See Linda J. Silberman, *Masters and Magistrates, Part II: The American Analogue*, 50 N.Y.U. L. Rev. 1297 (1975). Under current law, magistrate judges are appointed for eight-year terms by the Article III district court judges whose courts they serve. 28 U.S.C. §631(a). Those same district judges may remove them for "incompetency, misconduct, neglect of duty, or physical or mental disability." 28 U.S.C. §631(e), (i).

36. 28 U.S.C. §636(b)(3). The Court held in *Wingo v. Wedding*, 418 U.S. 461 (1974), that previous law did not permit magistrates to conduct evidentiary hearings in habeas corpus cases. Thereafter, Congress expanded their authority to handle a host of proceedings—subject to reconsideration by district judges if it is "shown" that a magistrate's order is "clearly erroneous or contrary to law." 28 U.S.C. §636(b)(1)(A).

37. 28 U.S.C. §636(b)–(c). The lower courts have upheld these provisions against constitutional attack, albeit frequently citing the parties' consent. E.g., *Pacemaker Diagnostic Clinic of Amer. v. Instromedix*, 725 F.2d 537 (9th Cir. 1984), *cert. denied*, 469 U.S. 824 (1985).

38. 447 U.S. 667 (1980).

39. Id. at 681.

The Court has never specified the nature and scope of the review that district courts must give, or be empowered to give, to the original judgments that magistrate judges reach.[40] And the Court has yet to explain fully the effect the parties' consent to magistrate judge activities may have on the validity of those actions under Article III.[41] In light of the caseload crisis, it is likely that the tasks assigned to magistrate judges will continue to grow and that the Supreme Court will approve so long as Article III judges retain theoretical control and responsibility.[42]

Administrative agencies. In some instances, administrative agencies are understood to perform adjudicative functions as adjuncts of Article III courts. In *Crowell v. Benson*,[43] the Supreme Court held that when agencies determine facts related to "private rights," they, like magistrate judges, may do so as instruments of Article III courts—performing judicial duties, but leaving "the essential attributes of...judicial power" to the courts.[44] Knudsen claimed he had been injured in a maritime accident while employed by Benson. He filed a complaint with the Employees Compensation Commission, seeking compensation from Benson. Crowell, a deputy commissioner, heard the evidence and concluded that Knudsen was entitled to recover. Benson then sued Crowell in federal district court, seeking an injunction against enforcement of the judgment in Knudsen's favor.[45] Benson contended, first, that Crowell had acted beyond his jurisdiction (because Knudsen had not been in Benson's employ at the time of the accident)

---

40. Since district judges now have authority to reexamine magistrate judge actions top to bottom, the Court has had no occasion to decide whether some lesser measure of district court supervision would satisfy the Constitution. The Court has equally failed to specify minimal standards of judicial review in other contexts, in which Article III courts have less sweeping supervisory authority and in which, accordingly, the need for greater clarity is more urgent. See notes 141–43 and accompanying text. For an argument that magistrate judges receive too little Article III oversight, see J. Anthony Downs, *The Boundaries of Article III: Delegation of Final Decisionmaking Authority to Magistrates*, 52 U. Chi. L. Rev. 1032 (1985).

41. In *Peretz v. United States*, 501 U.S. 923 (1991), the Court held that district courts can allow magistrate judges to conduct jury selection hearings in criminal cases in which defendants consent. By giving consent, defendants waive any personal Article III or due process claim they have to an Article III judge. The Court had no occasion in *Peretz* to decide whether Article III allows magistrate judges to select juries in criminal cases when defendants refuse to consent. Nor has the Court decided whether, under current statutes, magistrate judges can conduct jury trials (in either criminal or civil cases) without the parties' consent. The Court expressly bypassed that question in *McCarthy v. Bronson*, 500 U.S. 136 (1991), where the parties had waived jury trial. The Federal Courts Improvement Act of 1996 authorizes magistrate judges to conduct trials in petty criminal cases without the defendant's consent. 28 U.S.C. §636(a)(3). The Court has elaborated the role that consent plays in Article III cases in other contexts. See note 122.

42. The Administrative Office of United States Courts reports that the magistrate system is operating well. Report, *A Constitutional Analysis of Magistrate Judge Authority*, 150 F.R.D. 247 (1993). By some accounts, however, the district courts' increasing reliance on magistrate judges threatens to relegate vulnerable litigants (e.g., prison inmates) to non-Article III judges. Reinier H. Kraakman, *Article III Constraints and the Expanding Civil Jurisdiction of Federal Magistrates: A Dissenting View*, 88 Yale L.J. 1023 (1979). Professor Resnik argues that magistrate judges offer a "neat solution" to political battles in Congress over presidential nominees for Article III judgeships. Yet as the work performed by magistrate judges expands, the practical significance of designating district judges as Article III jurists with salary and tenure safeguards may shrink in direct proportion. Resnik, *Trial as Error, Jurisdiction as Injury: Transforming the Meaning of Article III*, 113 Harv. L. Rev. 924, 1016 (2000).

43. 285 U.S. 22 (1932).

44. Id. at 51.

45. The deputy's award was not immediately effective, but had to be enforced in a separate lawsuit in the appropriate district court. See text accompanying notes 17–19 (discussing the form that Article III court involvement typically takes in cases in which agencies make original determina-

and, second, that Crowell's actions on behalf of the Commission violated both due process and Article III. The district court held a *de novo* hearing, concluded that Knudsen had not been employed by Benson at the time of the accident, and on that basis enjoined enforcement of the Commission's order.

The Supreme Court sustained the district court in a famous opinion by Chief Justice Hughes. Initially, Hughes distinguished between questions of law, on the one hand, and questions of fact, on the other. Regarding questions of law, he said that the district court was entitled and obligated to exercise its own independent judgment. The statute in *Crowell* was clear (enough) on that point, and Hughes hinted that the Constitution would have called for independent judicial judgment on legal questions in any event.[46] The decisive issue in *Crowell*, then, was whether Congress could give the Commission authority to determine the underlying facts.

Chief Justice Hughes took it to be significant that the case was "one of private right, that is, of the liability of one individual to another."[47] In private rights cases, he said, the Constitution places limits on Congress' power to assign adjudicative power to a non-Article III adjudicator. Otherwise, Congress might "oust the courts of all determinations of fact by vesting the authority to make them with finality in its own instrumentalities or in the executive department." Those limits, however, leave agencies with a good deal of work to do. Chief Justice Hughes recognized that the very point of the scheme in *Crowell* was to provide workers like Knudsen with a streamlined administrative procedure for determining their claims and, concomitantly, to relieve Article III courts of the responsibility to handle such routine matters. To make that plan work, it was essential that the courts should treat Commission findings of fact as final, provided they were supported by substantial evidence. Hughes therefore allowed Congress to give the Commission authority for ordinary fact-finding, subject to judicial review in an Article III court.[48]

Chief Justice Hughes used the *Crowell* case to fashion a pragmatic compromise of enormous power and influence. To protect the independent role of the federal judiciary, he insisted that agency declarations of *law* must be open to *de novo* judicial examination. Yet to reap the advantages of administrative adjudication, he characterized agencies as adjuncts of the courts—able to find the *facts* in particular cases, subject to judicial review and ultimate responsibility.[49] It is debatable whether administrative agencies

---

tions). Either the Commission itself or the beneficiary of an award could sue to enforce it. Anyone found liable could sue to enjoin it. That is what Benson did in *Crowell*.

46. This feature of *Crowell* survives today, but in an altered form. See Chapter I, note 41 (noting the *Chevron* doctrine).

47. *Crowell*, 285 U.S. at 51.

48. Id. at 51, 64.

49. The compromise in *Crowell* was actually more complex. The Court said that an Article III court must exercise independent judgment on "jurisdictional" facts (the facts on which the Commission's jurisdiction depended) and on "constitutional" facts (the facts related to constitutional claims). Since the question whether Knudsen had been in Benson's employ at the time of the accident went to the Commission's authority to entertain Knudsen's claim, it was one of "jurisdictional" fact. Accordingly, the Court approved the district court's *de novo* assessment of that question. 285 U.S. at 65. In dissent, Justice Brandeis dismissed the distinction between ordinary facts and "constitutional" facts as inconsequential and insisted that if the "jurisdictional" fact category was important in some cases, it was not so in *Crowell* itself because Knudsen's employment status went only to the applicability of federal substantive law, not to the Commission's authority to entertain his claim. More recently, the Court has largely abandoned any requirement that the courts always make independent judgments regarding "jurisdictional" or "constitutional" facts. See Henry P. Monaghan, *Constitutional Fact Review*, 85 Colum. L. Rev. 229 (1985); Chapter VII, text accompanying note

operating in their own regulatory environment can persuasively be analogized to auxiliary officers acting under the watchful eye of a district court.[50] Nevertheless, the adjunct theory on which Chief Justice Hughes relied in *Crowell* has shown genuine staying power.[51]

Bankruptcy judges. Under current statutory arrangements, enacted in 1984, bankruptcy judges also appear to fit the adjunct model. The basic jurisdiction in bankruptcy cases rests with federal district courts. District courts, in turn, must decline to exercise jurisdiction over state law claims that would not otherwise be within the jurisdiction of a federal court, provided an action is commenced and can be "timely adjudicated" in state court.[52] With respect to claims and issues properly before them, district courts are not obliged themselves to take up the merits. They can (and invariably do) refer bankruptcy matters to bankruptcy judges for disposition. Bankruptcy judges are "units" or "officers" of the district courts in which they serve.[53] Their actions are reviewable in the ordinary course, first by the district courts and then by the circuit courts of appeals.[54] Congress fashioned this structure for handling bankruptcy cases in response to the Supreme Court's decision in *Northern Pipeline Constr. Co. v. Marathon Pipe Line Co.*,[55] which invalidated the configuration that Congress had previously established in 1978. The Court has acknowledged the current statutory scheme,[56] but has had no occasion to consider whether current arrangements cure all the constitutional difficulties that attended the earlier scheme.[57]

The decision in *Northern Pipeline* remains important for analytic purposes, despite the restructuring of bankruptcy courts by Congress and, indeed, despite the Supreme

---

202. Administrative agencies now routinely determine all the facts necessary to resolve civil disputes—the very result that Brandeis and other progressives hoped to achieve.

50. Professor Bator thought it was "ludicrously inapt" and "patronizing" to conceive of administrative agencies as "adjuncts" of "some article III court," simply because that court might later review their judgments. Bator, note 10, at 252.

51. The *Crowell* decision endorsed Congress' ability to depart from the common law tradition of relying exclusively on courts to perform adjudicative functions and, instead, to create administrative agencies to superintend the public law system just beginning to take shape in 1932. Even so, Justice Brandeis contended that the Court did not open its arms to agencies widely enough. Professor Young has traced the emerging appreciation for administrative process during the period when *Crowell* was decided. Despite Brandeis' disappointment at the time, *Crowell* ultimately promoted the development of the modern administrative state. Gordon G. Young, *Public Rights and the Federal Judicial Power: From Murray's Lessee Through Crowell to Schor*, 35 Buffalo L. Rev. 765 (1986).

52. 28 U.S.C. §1334(b)–(c). See generally Lawrence K. Snider, et al., *The Bankruptcy Amendments and Federal Judgeship Act of 1984*, 63 Mich. B.J. 775 (1984).

53. 28 U.S.C. §151. Bankruptcy judges are appointed by circuit judges. 28 U.S.C. §152(a). They can be removed by a circuit judicial council for "incompetence, misconduct, neglect of duty, or physical or mental disability." 28 U.S.C. §152(e). See Chapter III, notes 44–49 and accompanying text (describing circuit judicial councils). Professor Resnik has pointed out that the appointment of judges by other judges may undermine the independence of the appointees. Judith Resnik, *"Uncle Sam Modernizes His Justice": Inventing the Federal District Courts of the Twentieth Century for the District of Columbia and the Nation*, 90 Gtn. L.J. 607, 668–84 (2002).

54. 28 U.S.C. §158. Pursuant to §158(b), the parties may consent to appellate review by special panels of bankruptcy judges. The judgments of panels of that sort are nonetheless reviewable in the circuit courts.

55. 458 U.S. 50 (1982).

56. See *Celotex Corp. v. Edwards*, 514 U.S. 300 (1995) (employing a generous estimate of the jurisdiction delegated to bankruptcy judges).

57. One controversial constitutional question is whether even Article III courts can be given jurisdiction to determine state law claims advanced by or against non-diverse parties other than the bankruptcy estate. See Chapter VIII, notes 36–37 and accompanying text.

Court's own departure from the analysis that *Northern Pipeline* employed.[58] The Bankruptcy Act of 1978 established relatively independent bankruptcy courts in each federal district and gave those courts jurisdiction not only over bankruptcy proceedings, but also over other civil proceedings "arising in or related to" bankruptcies.[59] Bankruptcy court judgments were final when issued and required no further enforcement actions in an Article III court. A disappointed party could appeal a bankruptcy court order to a panel of three other bankruptcy judges—and then, if necessary, to a court of appeals. That court, however, could review bankruptcy court judgments only to decide whether they were "clearly erroneous." Northern initially filed a petition for reorganization in one of the new bankruptcy courts and then, three months later, added to that proceeding a lawsuit against Marathon, seeking damages for breach of a previous contract between the two companies. That contract action was governed by state law and might have been brought in state court.[60] Yet Northern contended that the bankruptcy court could entertain it as an action "related to" the pending petition for reorganization. Marathon responded that if the 1978 Act extended the bankruptcy court's jurisdiction that far, it violated Article III. The Supreme Court sustained Marathon's position in a plurality opinion by Justice Brennan.

Justice Brennan explained that the bankruptcy court's jurisdiction of the contract claim could not be sustained under the adjunct theory. That claim turned on state (not federal) law and, in any event, the bankruptcy court had too much authority and did not leave "the essential attributes" of judicial power with the district court.[61] Brennan distinguished both *Crowell* and *Raddatz*. In *Crowell*, the Court had allowed Congress to employ an agency as a fact-finding adjunct to an Article III court, but only with respect to a *federal* statutory claim.[62] In *Raddatz*, the Court had permitted Congress to employ a magistrate judge to determine a constitutional issue, but only where the supervising

---

58. See notes 109–28 and accompanying text.

59. The judges who staffed the bankruptcy courts under the 1978 Act were appointed by the President after confirmation by the Senate, but they held office for fourteen-year terms and were removable by the relevant circuit judicial council for "incompetency, misconduct, neglect of duty or physical or mental disability." Previously, district courts were themselves courts of bankruptcy, albeit they employed referees to handle most of the work. The district courts had "summary" jurisdiction to dispose of property actually or constructively in their possession, but they needed the parties' consent to exercise "plenary" jurisdiction to deal with property in the hands of a third party. See Maryellen Fullerton, *No Light at the End of the Pipeline: Confusion Surrounds Legislative Courts*, 49 Brooklyn L. Rev. 207, 216–19 (1983).

60. Actually, Northern had previously advanced the same state law claim in an independent lawsuit in a federal district court with diversity jurisdiction over the claim.

61. 458 U.S. at 87. Justice Brennan relied on both those grounds and thus suggested that they must be considered together and not as alternatives. Professor Redish has pointed out that if Congress is entitled to rely on non-Article III adjudicators as a means of carrying out its policies, it is unclear why an Article III court must be involved at all, let alone that such a court must retain the "essential attributes" of judicial power. And if an Article III court does make the ultimate decision, it is unclear why it makes any difference whether a case involves the implementation of a congressional regulatory scheme. Redish, note 7, at 215–16.

62. In this, Brennan appeared to rely on the "greater power" syllogism. See Chapter I, notes 27–28 and accompanying text. In dissent, Justice White said that Brennan conceded "that Congress may provide for initial adjudications by Art. I courts or administrative judges of all rights and duties arising under otherwise valid laws." 458 U.S. at 94. Justice Brennan denied any such concession, explained that he meant only to confirm *Crowell's* holding that Congress can assign "some" adjudicatory functions to non-Article III bodies, and said it was unnecessary to "specify further any limitations that may exist with respect to Congress' power to create adjuncts to assist in the adjudication of federal statutory rights." Id. at 81 n.32 (plurality opinion).

district judge made the ultimate decision. In *Northern Pipeline*, by contrast, Congress purported to give a bankruptcy court authority to determine a state law contract action and to render a judgment that would almost certainly be decisive.[63] Justice Brennan contrasted the many powers the 1978 Act assigned to bankruptcy judges with the more limited authorities exercised by the agency and the magistrate judge in *Crowell* and *Raddatz*.[64] In particular, he noted that, by contrast to *Crowell*, the bankruptcy court's order was final when issued. There was no need to file an enforcement action in an Article III court. Brennan acknowledged that the bankruptcy court's decision was subject to review at the instance of the losing party. But he found the scope of that review too limited to satisfy Article III in itself.[65]

C. Legislative Courts

Many non-Article III adjudicative bodies resist conceptualization as adjuncts of Article III courts. They are sustained on the different theory that Congress can forthrightly assign judicial duties to legislative courts and agencies. Precisely what a given body must be or do to win approval under this second theory can be maddeningly obscure. Having set the simple Article III model to one side, the Court finds itself floating toward the simple Article I model, but laboring heroically to articulate limiting principles and considerations that keep Congress within bounds.

1. Familiar Illustrations

Some legislative courts are solidly in place. Their existence (and the justifications that fortify them) provide the analytic backdrop for more recent (and more controversial) cases.

Territorial courts. The Constitution gives Congress plenary power to provide for the territories, and it has always been thought that in the exercise of that power Congress may act for the territories in the way that state legislatures act for the states. In that capacity, Congress has authority to establish non-Article III tribunals to manage local ju-

63. Justice Brennan acknowledged that many of the issues to be determined by bankruptcy courts under the 1978 Act were matters of federal law. But he distinguished Northern's state law contract action, over which the bankruptcy court had jurisdiction only because it was "related to" the pending reorganization. Id. at 84 n.36. He explained that a contract action on a "state-created right" did not become "a matter between the Government and the petitioner" [Northern] merely because Congress gave the bankruptcy court jurisdiction to hear it. In dissent, Justice White argued that most of the claims considered in a bankruptcy proceeding under the Act had previously "accrued under state law" and that it was misleading to distinguish so cleanly between federal and state issues. Id. at 96. See Chapter VIII, notes 33–37 and accompanying text (discussing federal and state issues in bankruptcy cases).

64. 458 U.S. at 84–86.

65. In a concurring opinion, then-Justice Rehnquist (joined by Justice O'Connor) agreed that the bankruptcy courts could not be justified as adjuncts when they took such extensive responsibility for deciding "[a]ll matters of fact and law" with respect to a state law contract action, "with only traditional appellate review by Article III courts apparently contemplated." 458 U.S. at 91.

dicial business that state courts would ordinarily do. John Marshall coined the term "legislative court" in the classic case on territorial courts, *Amer. Ins. Co. v. 356 Bales of Cotton (Canter)*.[66] The validity of those courts has been settled ever since.[67] They are familiar features of the landscape, they serve important functions in a field for which Congress has special responsibility, they have historically existed only temporarily,[68] they operate within geographic limits, and they handle many matters that are not among the cases and controversies listed in Article III.

It was open in *Canter* to hold that Congress can create legislative courts to determine local matters for the territories, but must rely on Article III courts to adjudicate cases and controversies listed in Article III. Marshall chose instead to analogize territorial courts to state courts and thus to allow them to do both kinds of judicial business. That approach has survived. Still, Marshall's analysis in *Canter* has drawn considerable criticism. The question in that case was whether a territorial court could entertain a dispute in admiralty—that is, a matter admittedly within the federal judicial power established by Article III. Marshall responded that the territorial court could adjudicate such a case, but he insisted that, in doing so, it would not exercise "the judicial power conferred by the Constitution." That power, he insisted, was reserved for Article III courts, and legislative courts were "incapable of receiving it."[69]

Some critics understand Marshall to have meant that Article III comes into play only when Congress uses Article III courts forthrightly to exercise "the judicial power conferred by the Constitution" and not when Congress chooses, instead, to create non-Article III tribunals to do the same judicial business.[70] That is circular. To be sure, a legislative court is not an Article III court. Yet it hardly follows that Article III has nothing to say about whether Congress may grant such a court authority to adjudicate cases and controversies that Article III courts, too, might decide. Legislative courts obviously exercise federal judicial power given them by Congress. And when they decide cases and controversies listed in Article III, their judgments may be reviewed by Article III courts, provided Congress establishes such an appellate jurisdiction. So either Marshall was wrong, or he meant only to make the (admittedly formal) point that legislative courts, like state courts, handle cases and controversies listed in Article III on the basis of judicial power they derive from independent sources.[71] Today, the court systems in the territories are structured in a variety of ways. Puerto Rico has an Article III district court. Other territories have non-Article III courts whose judgments regarding Article III matters are typically subject to appellate review in a designated circuit court of appeals.[72]

---

66. 26 U.S. (1 Pet.) 511 (1828).

67. The validity of state courts staffed by judges who lack tenure and salary protections does not, in itself, equally establish the validity of territorial courts, staffed by similarly unprotected federal judges. State courts rely on their own state law status for independence from Congress.

68. The temporary nature of territorial courts was once a more significant factor in this mix than it is now. Early on, many territories were predictably on a course to statehood, and it would have been "doctrinaire in the extreme" to insist that their territorial courts must be Article III tribunals when state courts would soon be installed in their place. *Glidden Co. v. Zdanok*, 370 U.S. 530, 544–46 (1962). The territories that exist today (e.g., American Samoa, the Virgin Islands, and Guam) are not plainly on the same path.

69. *Canter*, 26 U.S. at 546.

70. E.g., Stern, note 14, at 1068.

71. See *Glidden*, 370 U.S. at 544–45. Professor Bator dismissed even this point as "theological." Bator, note 10, at 240–43.

72. E.g., 48 U.S.C. §1424 (Guam); 48 U.S.C. §§1611–13 (Virgin Islands). See 28 U.S.C. §1291. Judgments rendered by the territorial court in American Samoa are not appealable in the ordinary

The courts of the District of Columbia. The Constitution gives Congress general responsibility for the District of Columbia. There, too, Congress acts in the place of a state legislature. Since 1970, Congress has chosen to employ legislative courts in the District, staffed by judges serving fixed terms.[73] It cannot be said that the District's courts have always been non-Article III tribunals or that they are needed only temporarily pending the District's statehood. Yet the geographic limits are self-evident, the analogy to state courts palpable. In the leading modern case, *Palmore v. United States*,[74] Justice White wrote a sweeping opinion for the Court, holding that the legislative courts in the District can handle cases and controversies listed on the Article III menu, including felony criminal prosecutions in which constitutional issues are implicated. By analogy to decisions by state courts, judgments rendered by the highest court in the District system are reviewable in the Supreme Court itself.[75]

Military courts. The Constitution also confers power on Congress to provide for the military services. Historically, the special sensitivities that attach to military discipline have been thought to warrant Congress' use of tribunals staffed by judges who lack tenure and salary safeguards.[76] Of course, all military courts are not temporary, and their jurisdictional reach is geographically restricted only in the practical sense that most service-related matters arise on military reservations. Article III judges might be employed in many cases that implicate military personnel and interests.[77] At least at the highest levels, that might be in order today.[78] At present, however, the Court of Appeals for the Armed Services remains a legislative court, whose judgments are usually (but not always) reviewable in the Supreme Court by *certiorari*.[79] Inferior federal courts have no routine authority to superintend military courts martial. They can entertain habeas corpus petitions from prisoners held in military custody either before or following con-

---

fashion. For a description of the peculiar scheme for Samoa, see *Church of Latter Day Saints v. Hodel*, 830 F.2d 374 (D.C. Cir. 1987), *cert. denied*, 486 U.S. 1015 (1988).

73. The judges in the District of Columbia courts are appointed by the President with the advice and consent of the Senate. They serve fifteen-year terms and are removable by order of the District of Columbia Commission on Judicial Disabilities and Tenure for criminal activities, willful misconduct, or "any other conduct which is prejudicial to the administration of justice or which brings the judicial office into disrepute." D.C. Code Ann. §§11-1501–02, 1526.

74. 411 U.S. 389 (1973).

75. 28 U.S.C. §1257(b).

76. See *Weiss v. United States*, 510 U.S. 163 (1994) (holding that military judges may be employed at the will of the commanding general). Professor Stern contends that military courts do not exercise federal judicial power at all, but serve only as "in-house—almost advisory—committees" that determine the way in which military commanders "take care of their own." Stern, note 14, at 1058. Recall that Professor Stern rejects the conventional (functional) definition of judicial power and reads Article III to exclude from its purview any adjudicative functions performed by federal officers other than Article III judges themselves.

77. Ordinary military courts martial can try only military personnel. *Toth v. Quarles*, 350 U.S. 11 (1955). In *O'Callahan v. Parker*, 395 U.S. 258 (1969), the Court held that a serviceman could not be tried by court martial for an offense that was not "service-connected." The Court soon thought better of that position, however, and overruled *O'Callahan* in *Solorio v. United States*, 483 U.S. 435 (1987).

78. Professor Fallon proposes that military courts martial should be retained in their conventional non-Article III form, but that their judgments in serious cases should be subject to appellate review in an Article III court. Fallon, note 10, at 973–74.

79. 10 U.S.C. §942 (prescribing fifteen-year terms for the three judges on the court); 28 U.S.C. §1259 (prescribing the kinds of cases in which *certiorari* review is available in the Supreme Court). The Court's appellate jurisdiction is comparatively new and, at that, is quite narrow. For details, see Bennett Boskey & Eugene Gressman, *The Supreme Court's New Certiorari Jurisdiction Over Military Appeals*, 102 F.R.D. 329 (1984).

viction.[80] Yet when they operate on the basis of their authority in habeas corpus proceedings, federal courts are limited to questions going to the jurisdiction of the military courts concerned.[81]

There is authority for the use of *ad hoc* military tribunals or commissions to try civilians and members of the armed services of other nations either for ordinary criminal offenses or for violations of the "laws of war."[82] The principal practical significance of *ad hoc* tribunals is that they deny suspects the full panoply of procedural rights to which defendants tried in Article III courts and ordinary courts martial are routinely entitled.[83] The use of military tribunals in war zones or occupied territories abroad is typically justified both by the executive's authority for the conduct of war and diplomacy and by the military's responsibility to maintain order in the absence of ordinary civil authority.[84] The use of military tribunals in this country is more problematic. In *Ex parte Milligan*,[85] the Court held that a non-combatant civilian who held American citizenship could not be tried in a military tribunal on charges that he violated the "laws of war." But in *Ex parte Quirin*,[86] the Court held that German servicemen who had allegedly entered the United States to commit sabotage could be tried by military authorities, notwithstanding that ordinary Article III courts were available.[87] By some accounts, certain circumstances in *Quirin* may limit the scope of the Court's decision in that case: (1) Congress had declared war on Germany; (2) Congress had also explicitly authorized the use of military tribunals for trying foreign servicemen for violations of the "laws of war;" (3) most of the defendants were citizens of Germany;[88] (4) all of them were combat soldiers in service of a foreign nation with which this country was at war; and (5) the usual (though limited) capacity of Article III courts to entertain their habeas corpus petitions remained intact.[89]

Soon after two commercial airliners crashed into the World Trade Center on September 11, 2001, President Bush issued an executive order providing for the trial of suspected "terrorists" in special military tribunals or commissions.[90] At the time of the President's order, Congress had not formally declared war on any other nation or group. But Congress had enacted legislation contemplating military tribunals apart from

---

80. E.g., *Noyd v. Bond*, 395 U.S. 683 (1969) (explaining that applicants for the writ must typically exhaust the avenues available to them in military courts); see Chapter XII (discussing federal habeas corpus jurisdiction).

81. E.g., *Toth*, 350 U.S. at 13 n.3 & 15.

82. See generally David J. Bederman, *Article II Courts*, 44 Mercer L. Rev. 825 (1993); Jordan J. Paust, *Antiterrorism Military Commissions: Courting Illegality*, 23 Mich. J. Intnat'l L. 1 (2001).

83. Then again, the very *ad hoc* character of special military tribunals contemplates that the procedural safeguards available may vary according to the executive's judgment. Of course, if the executive is content with all the procedures that ordinary courts martial entail, there is presumably no reason to employ special tribunals in the first place.

84. *See Johnson v. Eisentrager*, 339 U.S. 763 (1950) (involving German nationals tried in China); *Application of Yamashita*, 327 U.S. 1 (1946) (involving a Japanese general tried in the Philippines); *Madsen v. Kinsella*, 343 U.S. 341 (1952) (involving an American citizen tried in Germany).

85. 72 U.S. (4 Wall.) 2 (1866).

86. 317 U.S. 1 (1942).

87. Cf. *Ex parte Mudd*, 17 F. Cas. 954 (S.D. Fla. 1868) (approving the military trial of Dr. Samuel A. Mudd for allegedly helping John Wilkes Booth escape after Lincoln's assassination).

88. One of the German soldiers contended that he had been born in this country and was therefore an American citizen. The Court responded that American citizenship, if it existed, did not absolve the prisoner of the consequences of his "belligerency." *Quirin*, 317 U.S. at 37.

89. But see *Mudd v. Caldera*, 134 F.Supp.2d 138, 145–46 (D.D.C. 2001) (holding that *Quirin* can be read to approve military trials of non-combatant citizens accused of violating the "laws of war").

90. 66 Fed. Reg. 57,833 (Nov. 16, 2000).

courts martial.[91] And Congress had adopted a joint resolution authorizing the President to use "all necessary and appropriate force" against those responsible for "the September 11 attacks" and anyone who "harbored" them.[92] The President's order explicitly restricted its reach to suspects who are not citizens of the United States, but it did not specify that they must be combatants. Nor did it explain whether any Article III judicial review would be available. Some months later, the Department of Defense promulgated procedures for use in the tribunals. Those procedures stated that tribunal judgments would be reviewable by a military review panel and ultimately by the President. They did not specify whether Article III courts would have jurisdiction to examine tribunal proceedings or judgments, either by appeal or via petitions for the writ of habeas corpus. Nor did they describe the scope of any judicial review that might be available.[93]

The validity of the tribunals authorized by the President's order is unclear. Violent acts committed by individuals and private groups are usually matters for the ordinary processes of law enforcement, irrespective of the political motivations behind them. Accordingly, anyone who is suspected of violating a federal criminal statute in connection with the September 11 tragedy is subject to arrest, prosecution, and trial (in a federal district court) in the ordinary course.[94] Yet the "War on Terrorism" metaphor and the invasion of Afghanistan arguably transform this particular episode into an occasion for exercising the military authority available to the President and Congress. It seems unlikely that the special military tribunals contemplated by the President's order can be sustained so easily as can ordinary courts martial. But that premise only sets up the hard constitutional problems the tribunals present. The ultimate resolution of those problems will almost certainly turn on the significance and weight the current Supreme Court assigns to the factors that potentially limit the precedent set in *Quirin*.[95]

2. Public Rights

Other legislative courts depend in some measure on the doctrine of "public rights." Recall that in *Crowell* the Court relied on the adjunct theory to approve agency adjudi-

91. 10 U.S.C. §821.

92. 10 U.S.C. §836.

93. Department of Defense, Military Commission Order No. 1, March 21, 2002.

94. In one instance, this is precisely what happened. Zacarias Moussaoui was indicted by a federal grand jury and held for trial in the United States District Court for the Northern District of Virginia. U.S.D.C. Crim. No. 01-455-A.

95. Chief Justice Rehnquist has recalled that *Quirin* was decided in "the dark days of the summer of 1942" when the nation's "fortunes of war" were only "beginning to recover from their lowest ebb." Japan had just attacked Pearl Harbor, the Bataan death march was under way in the Phillippines, and the German Army had captured Tobruck. According to the Chief Justice, "[c]ivil liberties were not high on anyone's agenda, including the judges." William H. Rehnquist, *Remarks of the Chief Justice*, 47 Drake L. Rev. 201, 206 (1999). See Neal K. Katyal & Laurence H. Tribe, *Waging War, Deciding Guilt: Trying the Military Tribunals*, 111 Yale L.J. 1259 (2002) (arguing that the President's unilateral executive order is unconstitutional in the absence of a more explicit congressional endorsement and that Congress may override it by statute); David B. Rivkin, Jr., Lee A. Casey & Darin R. Bartram, *Bringing Al-Qaeda to Justice: The Constitutionality of Trying Al-Qaeda Terrorists in the Military Justice System*, The Heritage Foundation Legal Memorandum, Nov. 5, 2001, at 10 (suggesting that the telling issue is whether Congress formally declares war on "the Taliban/al-Qaeda regime in Afghanistan"); see also Paust, note 82, at 28 (contending that the President's order is illegal and that military officers may have a duty to disobey it).

cation of facts in a "private rights" setting.[96] In passing, Chief Justice Hughes said that public rights cases are different. He offered no definitive account of what public rights might be, but quoted a passage from *Murray's Lessee v. Hoboken Land & Improv. Co.*,[97] which today has come to play an important, if controversial, role in the analysis of legislative courts. In that famous passage, Justice Curtis distinguished three kinds of questions that Congress might think to assign to courts of some ilk: (1) a "matter which, from its nature, is the subject of a suit at the common law, or in equity, or admiralty;" (2) a matter "which, from its nature, is not a subject for judicial determination;" and (3) "matters, involving public rights, which may be presented in such form that the judicial power is capable of acting on them, and which are susceptible of judicial determination, but which congress may or may not bring within the cognizance of the courts of the United States, as it may deem proper."[98] Congress is obliged to allow traditional courts to adjudicate cases in the first category. Congress is forbidden to ask those courts to determine cases in the second category. As to the third (public rights) category, Congress is free to choose whether to employ traditional courts or to adopt some other means of resolution.

The *Murray's Lessee* case itself involved not agency adjudication, but unilateral executive action. The Treasury Department discovered that the tax collector for the Port of New York, one Swarthout, had absconded with more than a million dollars. Pursuant to statute, Treasury issued a warrant authorizing a federal marshal to confiscate any personal property that Swarthout had left behind to offset the loss. The principal question in the Supreme Court was whether Swarthout had been denied due process, because he had been deprived of his property by executive action rather than through a judicial proceeding. After rejecting that due process claim, Justice Curtis turned to a different question implicating Article III and the separation of powers.[99] Under the statute, Swarthout was entitled to attack Treasury's action in an Article III court after the fact. Positing that Congress could involve the courts (at any stage) only if the case was "judicial" in character, the plaintiff insisted that Treasury had violated Article III when it seized Swarthout's property without proceeding in an Article III court in the first instance.[100]

Justice Curtis responded that the plaintiff's Article III argument proceeded from an erroneous premise. While some matters (the subjects of suits at common law, or in equity, or admiralty) were intrinsically judicial and must be tried in court, other matters were not of that order. Some subjects were not susceptible to judicial determination at all (and thus could not be assigned to a court), while others (like the seizure of Swarthout's property) could be handled at Congress' option either by executive or judicial means. It made no difference, then, that Congress had decided as a matter of grace that a citizen in Swarthout's position could seek judicial review of a seizure at some later time. That did not mean that the seizure was an inherently "judicial controversy," such that an Article III court had to be involved when Treasury initially took action. The seizure was not by its *nature* judicial, because it was not the sort of thing that had tradi-

---

96. See text accompanying note 47.

97. 59 U.S. (18 How.) 272 (1855).

98. Id. at 284.

99. See Chapter VI, notes 57–79 and accompanying text (discussing the argument that due process requires a judicial forum in some circumstances).

100. The plaintiff in *Murray's Lessee* had acquired land previously owned by Swarthout. When the marshal seized that land and sold it to the defendant, the plaintiff filed an ejectment action to try the title—contending in that suit (between private parties) that the defendant's claim was invalid inasmuch as it rested on Treasury's violation of Swarthout's rights.

tionally been the basis of suits at common law, in equity, or in admiralty. It was something that Congress might have asked the courts to address. Yet it fell in that category of judicially cognizable subjects that Congress could give to Article III courts (or not) as a matter of discretion—namely, the category of public rights.

Classic illustrations of public rights matters are easy enough to name: claims against the federal government for money or land, for example, as well as disputes over customs duties and some immigration matters.[101] Theoretical explanations are more difficult to supply. In truth, the public rights idea took shape in an age when conflicts with government were not generally conceived as matters for the courts to resolve. The federal government's affirmative regulatory role had not yet emerged. There were comparatively few occasions for citizens or companies to contest the validity of governmental behavior. Suits in the courts over disputes involving the government (or any special governmental interest) were of marginal significance at best.[102] Recreating the past today, Academicians identify three intellectual foundations on which the public rights doctrine rested in its formative period, each with its troubling features: (1) history; (2) legislative authority; and (3) sovereign immunity.

History. Congress may have been free to employ non-Article III adjudicators in any circumstances in which English law permitted non-judicial dispute resolution in 1787.[103] This answer is problematic. It makes the content of public rights turn on historical understandings and practices that are difficult to retrieve today. It also makes the public rights category extremely expansive. At the dawn of the Republic, independent courts were a novel phenomenon.[104] Where they existed, they *were* concerned with classic common law, equity, and maritime disputes. Yet that left a great deal of adjudicative business for executive officers to discharge.

Legislative authority. Congress may have been able to employ non-Article III bodies to settle disputes over the largesse that Congress chose to dispense.[105] This answer is also problematic. It relies on another version of the "greater power" syllogism.[106] Positing that Congress has the "greater" power to withhold a benefit entirely, it is said that Congress must have the "lesser" power to extend the benefit on condition that any disputes that arise will be resolved outside Article III courts. That does not follow logically. The power to employ a legislative court is not (necessarily) a subset power within the power to withhold a benefit in the first instance.[107]

---

101. See generally *Ex parte Bakelite Corp.*, 279 U.S. 438, 452–58 (1929). The notion that immigration cases can be resolved administratively without involving courts is problematic. Since individual liberty is at stake in those cases, they implicate more than the usual measure of Article III sensitivity. Moreover, the Suspension Clause may place limits on congressional power to deny courts (federal or state) the authority to entertain habeas corpus petitions from would-be immigrants. See Chapter II, note 57; Chapter IV, text accompanying notes 45–46. For a discussion of the Suspension Clause and habeas corpus jurisdiction generally, see Chapter XII, notes 15–37 and accompanying text.

102. See Chapter IX, notes 80–83 (explaining that complaints about government had to be repackaged as disputes with individual government officers having the look and feel of the common law actions with which courts were familiar).

103. This was Professor Jaffe's understanding. Louis Jaffe, Judicial Control of Administrative Action 87–90 (1965).

104. See Chapter II, notes 1–4 and accompanying text.

105. This was Professor Hart's view. Henry M. Hart, Jr., *The Power of Congress to Limit the Jurisdiction of Federal Courts: An Exercise in Dialectic*, 66 Harv. L. Rev. 1362, 1365 (1953).

106. See Chapter I, notes 27–28 and accompanying text.

107. See Kramer, note 30, at 284. This account of the public rights doctrine reflects the discredited right/privilege distinction, which had it that government had no duty to respect procedural norms so long as it dealt with benefits it had no obligation to provide in the first place. Today, of

Sovereign immunity. Congress may have been entitled to employ non-Article III adjudicators in cases involving the federal government as a party on the theory that the government was free to assert sovereign immunity to defeat liability. If the government was not obliged to submit to the jurisdiction of Article III courts, Congress could provide for the settlement of legal disputes without involving those courts.[108] This last answer rests on yet another "greater power" mistake. Positing Congress' power to withhold consent to suit, it does not follow logically that Congress can agree to be sued only in the non-Article III tribunal of its choice. Here again, the two powers may go hand-in-hand, but there is no logical imperative that they do so.

The public rights doctrine has resurfaced more recently in cases concerning legislative courts. The initial occasion was *Northern Pipeline*, where the bankrupt company, Northern, argued that if the bankruptcy court could not adjudicate Northern's contract action as an adjunct of the district court, it could do so as an independent legislative court. Justice Brennan addressed that alternative theory, but rejected it in partial reliance on the public rights idea.

Justice Brennan denied that the Court's precedents supported a "broad departure from the constitutional command that the judicial power of the United States must be vested in Art. III courts." Instead, he said, the precedents in place reduced to "three narrow" exceptions to that command: territorial courts, military courts, and courts and agencies adjudicating public rights cases. Brennan explained the first two exceptions in the familiar way.[109] Turning to the public rights exception, he acknowledged the ambiguities of *Murray's Lessee*, but insisted that one thing is clear: "At a minimum," public rights cases arise "between the government and others" and do not implicate "the liabil-

---

course, the Supreme Court recognizes that the right to due process attaches to entitlements that government creates as a matter of policy. E.g., *Cleveland Bd. of Ed. v. Loudermill*, 470 U.S. 532 (1985). See William W. Van Alstyne, *The Demise of the Right-Privilege Distinction in Constitutional Law*, 81 Harv. L. Rev. 1439 (1968). Professor Woolhandler contends that it is a mistake to regard *Murray's Lessee* itself as a right/privilege doctrine case. The assets the government seized in that case can be considered largesse only because the embezzler was a government employee. Ann Woolhandler, *Judicial Deference to Administrative Action—A Revisionist History*, 43 Admin. L. Rev. 197, 231 (1991). A congressional decision to place a dispute in a non-Article III court is not, in itself, an attempt to deprive an individual of the process that is due. Agencies and legislative courts can provide due process even though their decision-making officers lack tenure and salary protections. State courts, whose judges are typically elected, can do so as well. But see Chapter IV, notes 147–49 and accompanying text (discussing the argument that Congress undermines the independence provisions in Article III if it shifts significant *constitutional* business to state judges who must stand for election).

108. This is Justice Scalia's view. *Granfinanciera, S.A. v. Nordberg*, 492 U.S. 33, 65–66 (1989) (Scalia, J., concurring); see text accompanying note 165. See also Chapter X, notes 8–16 and accompanying text (discussing the federal government's immunity from suit). The Court said in *Bakelite* that Congress can route public rights cases to non-Article III bodies as a "condition" attached to its "consent" to be sued at all. 279 U.S. at 452. Redish and LaFave have pointed out that the sovereign immunity explanation works only in cases in which the government is a defendant, not when the government is a plaintiff. Yet Justice Scalia understands that it captures all cases in which the government is a party. Martin H. Redish & Daniel J. LaFave, *Seventh Amendment Right to Jury Trial in Non-Article III Proceedings: A Study in Dysfunctional Constitutional Theory*, 4 Wm. & Mary Bill of Rts. J. 407, 438–39 (1995). Professor Stern cites Justice Scalia's opinion in *Granfinanciera* with apparent approval. Yet Stern argues that a public rights matter (within Scalia's terms) must be determined by an Article III court when (and if) it leaves the executive branch. Stern, note 14, at 1063–64.

109. See notes 66–72, 76–81 and accompanying text. Justice Brennan placed the courts in the District of Columbia in the category with territorial courts.

ity of one individual to another under the law as defined."[110] On that ground alone, Northern's contract action against Marathon could not fit the public rights category.[111]

Justice Brennan explained that the Constitution gives Congress special authority for the territories and the military services and insisted that, if bankruptcy were added to the list, there would be no stopping place.[112] He accepted the validity of the non-Article III tribunals the Court had approved in the past, but in an apparent concern that Congress might continue on the same path, he called a halt—even in a context in which it was unlikely that Congress was using legislative courts in order to exercise influence it could not bring to bear on the Article III judiciary.[113] Brennan took what he needed from the public rights doctrine, but failed to elaborate that doctrine more fully.[114] He identified the government's party status as a necessary, but not a sufficient, basis for concluding that a case fits the public rights category.[115] He explained that a criminal prosecution is not a public rights matter.[116] And he only suggested, but did not decide, that subsequent review in an Article III court is always constitutionally required.[117]

Then-Justice Rehnquist and Justice O'Connor concurred only in the judgment in *Northern Pipeline.* They declined to discuss all the powers the 1978 Act conferred on bankruptcy courts and, instead, said only that giving a bankruptcy court jurisdiction to determine Northern's traditional contract action against Marathon (without Marathon's consent) violated Article III. The claim in that lawsuit was the "stuff of the traditional actions at common law tried by the courts at Westminster in 1789" and was governed by state, not federal, law. Accordingly, that claim must be heard either in a state court or in an Article III court. It could not be heard in a bankruptcy court merely because Northern happened to be involved in a reorganization.[118]

In dissent, Justice White insisted that it was "too late" to take Article III so literally. Unless the Court meant to overrule a host of decisions approving legislative courts and agencies, White said it was "inevitable" to conclude that there is "no difference in principle" between the work that Congress can assign to legislative courts and the business the

110. 458 U.S. at 69, quoting *Bakelite*, 279 U.S. at 451, and *Crowell*, 285 U.S. at 50. But see text accompanying notes 121–28 (explaining that the Supreme Court has since disavowed this definition of public rights cases).

111. Despite his insistence that public rights cases must involve the government as a party, Justice Brennan conceded that the restructuring of a private bankrupt's debts and its ultimate discharge may constitute a public rights matter. 458 U.S. at 71–72. Of course, the federal government is not typically a party of record when a bankruptcy court enters a discharge order.

112. Professor Redish points out that the Constitution also gives Congress explicit power with respect to bankruptcy. U.S. Const. art. I, §8, cl.3. Redish contends that Brennan might have approved bankruptcy courts on that basis without opening the floodgates to other legislative courts. Redish, note 7, at 218.

113. Professor Resnik has suggested that Brennan's opinion was a lengthy elaboration of a simple point: "hold that line." Resnik, note 7, at 598–99.

114. With respect to the public rights doctrine's conceptual origins, Brennan said only that the doctrine "may be explained in part by reference to the traditional principle of sovereign immunity," but that it also "draws upon the principle of separation of powers" and a "historical understanding that certain prerogatives were reserved" to the political branches. 458 U.S. at 67.

115. Id. at 70 n.23.

116. Id. at 70 n.24. Compare *Toth*, note 77, with *Palmore*, text accompanying note 74.

117. 458 U.S. at 70 n.23.

118. Id. at 91 (concurring opinion). Rehnquist and O'Connor thought it was unnecessary to decide whether the Court's precedents supported a general rule against legislative courts "with three tidy exceptions," or whether the public rights doctrine might justify the various other powers that Congress had bestowed on the bankruptcy courts.

Constitution itself assigns to Article III courts. White urged the Court to discard Brennan's framework entirely and deal with legislative court cases *ad hoc*, balancing the "values Congress hopes to serve" by employing legislative courts against the consequent "burdens" on Article III "values." According to Justice White, the Court should *require* only that Congress make "ample provision" for subsequent review of a legislative court's work in an Article III court.[119]

3. Current Doctrine

In subsequent cases, the Court largely abandoned Justice Brennan's account of legislative courts in *Northern Pipeline* in favor of the balancing approach that Justice White advocated in dissent in that case.

In *Thomas v. Union Carbide*,[120] the Court approved non-Article III adjudication of claims under recent amendments to the Federal Insecticide, Fungicide, and Rodenticide Act. Pesticide manufacturers needed the Environmental Protection Agency's approval before they could market their products. Companies typically invested large sums in the research necessary to convince the EPA that their chemicals were safe. Research results with respect to one product could often be useful in determining the reliability of another. When one company filed results that could bear on another company's product, the Act authorized the EPA to use the first company's data rather than wasting money on redundant studies. The Act specified, however, that the second company must agree to compensate the first company for free-riding on its research. If the two companies could not settle on an appropriate sum, the Act required them to submit the issue to an arbitrator. The arbitrator's decision was final when rendered. If a company failed to comply with it, the EPA was obliged to cancel registration of the company's product. A party could seek judicial review in an Article III court, but only for "fraud, misrepresentation, or other misconduct."

The plaintiffs in *Union Carbide* were chemical companies complaining that if their claims to compensation were handled in that way, the arbitrator would undertake judicial functions that only an Article III court could perform. In light of *Northern Pipeline*, that argument had some force. The arbitrator plainly had adjudicative duties and was to

---

119. Id. at 115 (dissenting opinion). In particular, Justice White objected to the suggestion that the precedents approving the courts in the District of Columbia rested on the geographic limits on those courts' jurisdiction. Id. at 104–05. He himself had authored the Court's opinion in *Palmore*, which, in his view, stood for a much more sweeping explanation of congressional power. See text accompanying note 74. The concurring justices, Rehnquist and O'Connor, characterized White's view of the precedents as "landmarks on a judicial 'darkling plain' where ignorant armies have clashed by night." 458 U.S. at 91 (concurring opinion). Chief Justice Burger dissented separately to say that the Article III difficulties in the case, if they existed at all, could be remedied by channeling "related" state law actions like Northern's to the district court, while leaving other issues to the bankruptcy court. Id. at 92 (dissenting opinion). Burger had long opposed giving Article III judgeships to bankruptcy judges and may have worried that Congress would see that as the only course open after the *Northern Pipeline* decision. See Vern Countryman, *Scrambling to Define Bankruptcy Jurisdiction: The Chief Justice, the Judicial Conference, and the Legislative Process*, 22 Harv. J. Legis. 1 (1985). In fact, the Court stayed its order to give Congress time to enact new legislation. Congress ultimately produced a revised scheme that preserves the non-Article III status of bankruptcy judges, but hopes to ensure that their duties can be justified under the adjunct theory. See notes 52–57 and accompanying text.

120. 473 U.S. 568 (1985).

discharge those duties independently (not as an adjunct of any Article III court). The arbitrator was not a territorial or military court. And the dispute in question involved only private companies (not the federal government). Nevertheless, the Supreme Court sustained the arbitration scheme in an opinion by Justice O'Connor.

Justice O'Connor limited the holding in *Northern Pipeline* to what she and Justice Rehnquist had agreed to in their concurring opinion in that case: "Congress may not vest in a non-Article III court the power to adjudicate, render final judgment, and issue binding orders in a traditional contract action arising under state law, without consent of the litigants, and subject only to ordinary appellate review."[121] Importantly, she rejected Justice Brennan's account of the public rights doctrine. Brennan had said that public rights cases form a category of judicial business (all of it involving the federal government as a party) that Congress can channel to non-Article III adjudicators. In *Union Carbide*, by contrast, Justice O'Connor reconceptualized the public rights doctrine as "a pragmatic understanding that when Congress selects a quasi-judicial method of resolving matters that 'could be conclusively determined by the Executive and Legislative Branches,' the danger of encroaching on the judicial powers is reduced."[122]

Justice Brennan concurred in the judgment in *Union Carbide*, but he offered an alternative analysis that retained the idea that public rights cases form a category of judicial business that, once identified, can be assigned to non-Article III decision-makers. Brennan acknowledged that the definition of public rights matters must be flexible enough to accommodate numerous familiar administrative schemes. He agreed, accordingly, that the appearance of the government as a party is not the *sine qua non* of a public rights case. In his view, the arbitration in the case at hand could qualify as a matter of public rights because it arose "in the context of a federal regulatory scheme that virtually occupie[d] the field" and involved "not only the congressional prescription of a federal rule of decision to govern [the] private dispute but also the active participation of a federal regulatory agency."[123] Since the Act allowed for review in an Article III court,

121. Id. at 584.

122. Id. at 589, quoting *Northern Pipeline*, 458 U.S. at 68 (plurality opinion). Justice O'Connor acknowledged that a party has an "independent right to adjudication in a constitutionally proper forum." Id. at 579. Accordingly, she recognized that a participating company might object to a scheme by which compensation awards were determined by a non-Article III federal adjudicator. She explained however, that a company could waive that right and pointed out that at least the follow-on company at bar had consented to the arbitration arrangement as a condition for participating in the EPA registration program. Id. at 592. It is questionable whether the Court should credit individual constitutional rights in this context. The primary values at work are structural: the maintenance of three basic spheres of federal power and the independence of the Article III judiciary. Moreover, an individual's consent to an arrangement for non-Article III adjudication cannot defuse independent constitutional questions regarding those structural values. Justice O'Connor subsequently explained in *Commodity Futures Trading Comm'n v. Schor*, 478 U.S. 833 (1986), that individuals "cannot be expected to protect" the "institutional interests" that judicial independence serves and thus "cannot by consent cure" any "difficulty" with those interests. Id. at 848. The practical answer is that in the absence of some individual interest in a validly organized federal tribunal, a private party would have no standing to advance a claim that the assignment of jurisdiction to a non-Article III adjudicator violates structural constitutional principles. An individual is not obviously injured simply because his or her dispute is resolved by one federal tribunal rather than another, provided that the process accorded is the process that is "due" under the fifth amendment. See note 31. If, however, the Court acknowledges that an individual has a separate interest in appearing before a federal adjudicator of a particular character (as a formal hedge against unfair treatment), an injury to that interest establishes the constitutional standing requirement of injury in fact. See Chapter IX (discussing standing generally).

123. *Union Carbide*, 473 U.S. at 600.

Justice Brennan found it unnecessary to consider whether Congress is "always free to cut off all judicial review of decisions respecting such exercises of Art. I authority."[124]

In the wake of *Union Carbide*, the public rights doctrine no longer distinguishes categorically between cases that can be routed to non-Article III adjudicators and those that cannot. This is true, at least, in cases in which the seventh amendment right to jury trial does not figure.[125] The "public rights" label has been transmuted into a description of the "*public purpose*" for which Congress fashions a regulatory scheme contemplating non-Article III adjudication.[126] In *Union Carbide*, Justice O'Connor insisted that this different approach is in keeping with the "enduring lesson" of *Crowell*: Article III cases call for "practical attention to substance rather than doctrinaire reliance on formal categories."[127] Accordingly, the Court must attend to the reasons why tenure and salary protections are accorded to Article III judges. To decide concrete cases, the Court must marshal the values and interests at stake and strike a balance.[128]

Justice O'Connor solidified the balancing approach in *Commodity Futures Trading Comm'n v. Schor*.[129] Schor, an investor, filed a complaint against his brokerage house, Conti-Commodity Services, with the Commodity Futures Trading Commission. He alleged that Conti had violated the federal Commodity Exchange Act with respect to his account and that, as a result, he had lost money and was entitled to reparations under that Act. Meanwhile, Conti sued Schor in a federal district court in Illinois, invoking that court's diversity jurisdiction to determine a state law claim: Schor's account was in arrears and he had failed to make up the loss. Schor filed a counterclaim in that district court lawsuit, alleging that his losses were due to Conti's practices in violation of the federal Act. At that point, the parties' state and federal claims were properly before an Article III court for decision.

Next, however, Schor moved the district court to stay or dismiss Conti's diversity action in order that the CFTC could determine any and all claims the two parties had against each other. The district court refused either to stay or to dismiss the pending diversity action. Nevertheless, Conti withdrew its action from the district court and filed its state law claim against Schor with the CFTC as a counterclaim to Schor's federal claim for reparations. An administrative law judge at the CFTC determined both claims in Conti's favor. Schor then filed an objection to the CFTC's jurisdiction to determine Conti's state claim. In the Supreme Court, Justice O'Connor balanced a range of considerations and ultimately affirmed the CFTC's jurisdiction to determine Conti's state

---

124. Id. at 601.

125. See notes 144–68 and accompanying text.

126. 473 U.S. at 589 (emphasis added). Justice O'Connor noted a number of precedents in which the Court had treated disputes between private parties as public rights cases and on that basis allowed Congress to commit them to non-Article III bodies. In *Switchmen v. Nat'l Med. Bd.*, 320 U.S. 297 (1943), for example, the Court upheld a scheme by which workers' disputes over the choice of their bargaining representatives were determined by the Mediation Board.

127. 473 U.S. at 587.

128. Justice O'Connor did not explicitly endorse the approach that Justice White had suggested in his *Northern Pipeline* dissent, but she did cite that dissent approvingly in several places. White joined O'Connor's opinion. Professor Sward distinguishes between "pure" public rights cases and "quasi-public" rights cases. The former fit the categorical definition at work in *Northern Pipeline* in that they "concern regulatory or public benefit adjudications between the government and a private party." That's the kind of public rights case with a strong historical pedigree. Ellen E. Sward, *Legislative Courts, Article III, and the Seventh Amendment*, 77 N. Car. L. Rev. 1037, 1073 (1999). The latter concern adjudications of "new regulatory right[s]" involving only private parties. Id. at 1077.

129. 478 U.S. 833 (1986).

claim against Schor in connection with its determination of Schor's federal claim against Conti.[130] Justice Brennan dissented in *Schor*, insisting that the Court's *ad hoc* balancing approach had started down a slippery slope and threatened to "dilute" the independence of the Article III judiciary, if not immediately then incrementally.[131]

The Supreme Court's emergent approach to legislative courts issues can be questioned. Balancing a number of factors *ad hoc* is not the most intellectually satisfying analysis of constitutional questions. In this instance, however, balancing reflects an honest attempt to find a middle ground between untenable polar extremes. In light of *Union Carbide* and *Schor*, everyone understands that the Court will rarely find reliance on non-Article III adjudicators invalid. The strategy is only to preserve the formal idea that there are constitutional limits in hopes that Congress will take the traditional constitutional structure into account when it decides whether and how to allocate jurisdiction between non-Article III officers and entities, on the one hand, and the Article III judiciary, on the other.

Between them, *Union Carbide* and *Schor* identify four factors bearing on Congress' ability to assign adjudicative authority to a legislative court or agency: (1) the source of the claim to be determined; (2) the federal government's involvement or interest; (3) the reasons for employing a non-Article III adjudicator; and (4) the form and scope of subsequent Article III court involvement. Justice O'Connor explained that "none" of the factors is "determinative."[132] Each is entitled to weight, and in the end the Court makes a reasoned judgment about whether, in cumulative effect, the circumstances of a particular assignment satisfy constitutional standards.

The source of the claim. In *Northern Pipeline*, the claim in issue was a matter of state contract law.[133] That certainly cut against the validity of legislative court adjudication. By contrast, the issue in *Union Carbide* was a matter of federal statute law. Apart from the entitlement to compensation established by the Act, the plaintiff companies would have had no right to reimbursement from other companies using their data.[134] That cut in favor of the validity of legislative court action. Justice O'Connor acknowledged that

---

130. Justice O'Connor again recognized that if private parties are subject to adjudication in a federal tribunal, they have a "primarily personal" constitutional right to "have" their claims "decided before judges who are free from potential domination by other branches of government." Id. at 848. See note 122. Yet she again explained that parties can forgo that right. Inasmuch as Schor had known that the district court in Illinois was poised to determine Conti's state claim when he insisted that the CFTC was a better forum for resolving all the parties' differences, he consented to the jurisdiction of the non-Article III body. That consent only defused any claim that Schor might advance that his personal rights were violated. It did not resolve the structural Article III issue in *Schor*, which then turned on balancing relevant factors. See *Schor*, 478 U.S. at 848–51.

131. *Schor*, 478 U.S. at 866–67 (dissenting opinion). Brennan dismissed Schor's consent as superfluous inasmuch as a party could not surrender the institutional interests served by judicial independence.

132. Id. at 851 (majority opinion).

133. Recall that in *Northern Pipeline*, Justice Brennan cited the state law nature of Northern's contract claim as a basis for distinguishing *Crowell*, which, by Brennan's account, involved a question of federal statutory law. See text accompanying note 62. In *Union Carbide*, however, Justice O'-Connor added that the federal right in *Crowell* was not entirely new with Congress, but replaced the action that Knudsen might have had against his employer under the common law of contracts for hire. In that sense, the source of the right to compensation in *Crowell* was not so exclusively "federal" as was the source of the right to compensation in *Union Carbide*. 473 U.S. at 584.

134. Justice O'Connor explained that under state law a company that disclosed its research findings to the EPA would have placed them in the public domain and thus would have had no action against another company's use of the data for its own purposes. It was only the federal statute that gave a company submitting data a right to compensation from a follow-on user.

in this respect *Schor* was more like *Northern Pipeline* than *Union Carbide*. Yet that was not enough to render the CFTC's jurisdiction invalid. In *Northern Pipeline*, the bankruptcy court had authority to determine a state contract claim that was "related to" the bankruptcy proceeding only because one of the parties happened to be involved in a reorganization proceeding. In *Schor*, however, Conti's state claim was, in effect, a counterclaim to Schor's federal claim for reparations.[135]

The federal government's involvement or interest. The federal government was not party to any of the three cases, *Northern Pipeline*, *Union Carbide*, or *Schor*. That cut against the validity of legislative court adjudication, but only mildly. The rights the private parties cases advanced in *Union Carbide* and *Schor* were not "purely private," but bore "many of the characteristics of a public right."[136] In both instances, the federal government's interest was substantial. In *Union Carbide*, the government had an interest in encouraging companies to share their research results as an "integral part of a program safeguarding the public health."[137] In *Schor*, the government had an interest in seeing that federal reparations claims were considered in context, along with state law counterclaims "incidental to, and completely dependent upon, adjudication of reparations claims created by federal law."[138]

The reasons for employing a non-Article III tribunal. In all three cases, Congress had neutral reasons for employing legislative courts. Congress was not attempting to manipulate the adjudicatory process by banishing independent judges and substituting tribunals on which Congress could exercise pressure. That cut in favor of approving legislative court adjudication. In *Union Carbide* and *Schor*, the reasons for introducing non-Article III adjudicators were especially obvious and powerful. The arbitration scheme in *Union Carbide* exploited the arbitrator's expertise for making technical determinations of the appropriate size of compensation awards. That promoted Congress'

135. Essentially, then, Congress had given the CFTC supplemental jurisdiction of the state law claim. Since the federal nature of Schor's reparations claim was clear, there was no question that the district court in Illinois might have entertained both that claim and Conti's state law claim, even in the absence of diversity. See Chapter VIII, notes 402–22 and accompanying text (discussing supplemental jurisdiction under 28 U.S.C. §1367). In *Schor*, then, the Court did not have to face the question noted in *Northern Pipeline* regarding even an Article III court's ability to adjudicate an exclusively state law dispute between non-diverse parties. See note 63; Chapter VIII, notes 36–37 and accompanying text. In *Coit Indep. Joint Venture v. Federal Savings & Loan Ins. Corp.*, 489 U.S. 561 (1989), the Court construed the statutes regarding the FSLIC not to confer jurisdiction on that agency to determine state law claims pressed by creditors of failed savings and loan associations under FSLIC receivership. Justice O'Connor explained the Court's result in part on the ground that an alternative construction would raise the constitutional question whether Congress could authorize the FSLIC to adjudicate "private rights" at the "core" of "matters normally reserved to Article III courts." Id. at 578–79. O'Connor's explicit reference to "private rights" was arguably in some tension with her reconceptualization of the "public rights" doctrine in *Union Carbide* and *Schor*. But Justice O'Connor was probably only being sloppy. She cited not only *Northern Pipeline*, but also *Schor*—where she had referred to "private rights" in a discussion of *Crowell v. Benson*. On that same page in *Schor*, Justice O'Connor disclaimed the idea that a categorical distinction between "private" and "public" rights is any longer viable. *Schor*, 478 U.S. at 853.

136. *Union Carbide*, 473 U.S. at 589.

137. Id. Justice O'Connor recalled that Justice Brennan himself had conceded in *Northern Pipeline* that a bankrupt's discharge might implicate a public right even though the bankruptcy proceeding plainly would not involve the federal government as a party of record. 473 U.S. at 586; see note 111. In that small way, Brennan himself signaled that some cases fit the public rights category not because the government is a party, but because the government has an interest—namely, a public purpose to advance.

138. *Schor*, 478 U.S. at 856.

overarching purpose to ensure that only safe products reached the market.[139] The supplemental jurisdiction of state law claims in *Schor* allowed litigants to resolve all their related claims in a single place. That promoted Congress' objective to create incentives for settling federal reparations claims in a prompt and inexpensive manner.[140]

The form and scope of Article III court involvement. Justice O'Connor said in *Union Carbide* that "judicial review" does not in itself meet "minimal" constitutional requirements and that it is always necessary to take other considerations into account. She thus rejected the arguments in academic circles that the Constitution permits non-Article III bodies to make original judgments, as long as there is a serious brand of after-the-fact review in an Article III court.[141] O'Connor nonetheless focused on the way in which Article III courts figured in each of the three cases. In all three, litigants disappointed with the decision rendered by a non-Article III adjudicator could complain to an Article III court. According to Justice O'Connor, the *existence* of Article III court involvement after-the-fact cut in favor of upholding legislative court adjudication, the *modest character* of that involvement against it.

In *Northern Pipeline*, the bankruptcy court's judgment was final, and appellate review in an Article III court was closely circumscribed. In *Union Carbide*, the arbitrator's award was equally final, subject to equally truncated Article III court review. Nevertheless, Justice O'Connor applauded the scheme in *Union Carbide*, because it did not contemplate that the EPA would seek an enforcement order from an Article III court in the conventional manner associated with administrative agencies. Instead, the Act required the EPA itself to enforce an arbitrator's award administratively, without involving a federal court. The Article III judiciary was implicated only if private companies sought judicial review on the extremely limited grounds available. O'Connor thus made a virtue of what she might have regarded as a vice. She found it reassuring that the scheme in

139. Justice O'Connor said that Congress might have fashioned a different means of allocating the costs of pesticide research and avoided "implicating Article III." For example, Congress might have authorized the EPA simply to charge follow-on companies for permission to rely on research results generated by others and used the money to subsidize the companies that furnished the data. By establishing the arbitration framework, Congress merely collapsed those two steps into one and saved the EPA the time and trouble of determining the amount of compensation into the bargain. O'Connor thus invoked another "greater power" argument—namely, that Congress' power to fix fees and subsidies was a "greater" power that subsumed a "lesser" power to force unwilling companies into an adjudicative proceeding before a non-Article III officer. In addition, O'Connor suggested that Congress might have avoided Article III by conditioning a company's ability to apply for a permit on "compliance with agency procedures." *Union Carbide*, 473 U.S. at 589. That suggested that any Article III difficulties in *Union Carbide* might have been defused by gaining party consent to the arbitration scheme. See note 122.

140. *Schor*, 478 U.S. at 855. Justice O'Connor recognized that the parties might have taken their claims to an Article III court and they had chosen to use the CFTC, instead. She explained that Congress was entitled to encourage them to resolve their dispute in a non-Article III process, just as it would have been entitled to encourage them to settle their differences by agreement without invoking any formal dispute-resolution mechanism at all. That point overlapped with O'Connor's reliance on consent to defeat any personal claim Schor had to appear before a properly constructed tribunal. Yet she offered it as evidence that Congress had not attempted to banish Article III courts altogether. If Conti's counterclaim had been compulsory rather than permissive, it would have been more closely linked to Schor's federal reparations claim, thus fortifying the conclusion that Congress had given the CFTC jurisdiction of the former in service of its scheme to ensure efficient and speedy resolution of typical cases. In that event, however, Justice O'Connor would have been unable to make the different point that Congress had allowed parties the option of remaining in an Article III court.

141. *Union Carbide*, 473 U.S. at 587. See text accompanying notes 17–19.

Union Carbide did not contemplate that an unwilling private party would be subjected to an Article III court order enforcing an arbitrator's decision. Alternatively, she might have said that Congress would have preserved judicial independence better by requiring the EPA to obtain Article III court approval for its actions in the ordinary manner rather than mandating that the agency take unilateral action on its own and placing the burden of seeking judicial review on the companies concerned.

Justice O'Connor was also persuaded that the scheme in *Schor* left the "essential attributes of judicial power" with Article III courts. The CFTC's adjudicative duties tracked those of the agency in *Crowell* and thus nearly met the "agency" (i.e., adjunct) model approved in that case. Like the agency in *Crowell*, but unlike the bankruptcy court in *Northern Pipeline*, the CFTC was limited to a "particularized area of law."[142] Justice O'Connor acknowledged that the CFTC in *Schor*, unlike the EPA in *Union Carbide*, was empowered (and required) to seek an enforcement order in an Article III court. Shifting ground, she found that feature of the scheme in *Schor* not at all troubling, but actually satisfying. In the end, then, she said in *Union Carbide* that Congress was on safer ground for *not* sending the EPA to an Article III court for an enforcement order. But in *Schor* she found it reassuring that Congress required the CFTC to go to an Article III court for just such an order.[143]

D. Trial by Jury

After *Union Carbide* and *Schor*, it appeared that the Court was committed to *ad hoc* balancing in this field and that in future it would treat the categorical features of the analysis it had employed in *Northern Pipeline* simply as factors for consideration. Certainly, that seemed to be true of the public rights doctrine. In *Union Carbide*, the Court stripped that doctrine of its analytical content and historical underpinnings. And in *Schor*, the Court failed even to refer to any useful distinction between public and private rights cases. Nevertheless, when Justice Brennan again wrote for the Court in *Granfinanciera, S.A. v. Nordberg*,[144] he explained that the category of public rights cases retains decision-making bite, at least in some instances. The category of public rights matters bears both on Congress' power to confer jurisdiction on non-Article III adjudicators and on litigants' ability to invoke their right to trial by jury in "Suits at common law," guaranteed by the seventh amendment.[145]

Nordberg was a bankruptcy trustee appointed to superintend the reorganization of the Chase & Sanborn company. He sued Granfinanciera, a Columbian company, in a

---

142. Justice O'Connor mentioned that the CFTC could not conduct jury trials. *Schor*, 478 U.S. at 853.

143. Cf. note 16 (discussing the *Ports Authority* case). The Court's ambivalence regarding the form of Article III court involvement suggests that the real issue is the scope of Article III court review. In that vein, Professor Fallon argues that *Northern Pipeline* was wrongly decided (because the bankruptcy court's judgment in that case was subject to sufficient review at the circuit level), that *Union Carbide*, too, was wrongly decided (because the arbitrator's judgment was reviewable only for fraud and misconduct), and that *Schor* was correctly decided (because the CFTC's determinations of legal questions were subject to *de novo* review in an Article III court). Fallon, note 10, at 991.

144. 492 U.S. 33 (1989).

145. See Chapter II, text accompanying notes 34–36. See generally Ann Woolhandler & Michael G. Collins, *The Article III Jury*, 87 Va. L. Rev. 587 (2001) (tracing the conceptual history of federal juries from the earliest days to modern times).

federal district court in Florida. He alleged that Granfinanciera had received in excess of a million dollars from Chase & Sanborn within one year prior to bankruptcy, that the deal had been actually or constructively fraudulent, and that Granfinanciera, accordingly, should repay the money so that it could be placed in the pool of assets to be divided among all the creditors. The district court referred the matter to a bankruptcy judge.[146] Granfinanciera did not object to that, but did assert its right to trial by jury. The bankruptcy judge found the seventh amendment inapplicable, tried the issues without a jury, and entered judgment for Nordberg. In the Supreme Court, Justice Brennan said that Granfinanciera was entitled to trial by jury—if not before the bankruptcy judge, then in the district court.[147]

Initially, Justice Brennan explained that the seventh amendment guarantees trial by jury only in cases that, by their nature, would have been triable in the law courts in 1791, prior to the merger of law and equity. A claim was usually tried in the law courts if the plaintiff sought money damages. If a modern plaintiff advances a statutory claim that did not exist in 1791, the Court determines whether it *would* have been tried at law if it *had* existed at that time.[148] He concluded that Nordberg's fraudulent conveyance claim against Granfinanciera would have been tried at law. That claim rested on federal bankruptcy law, but it was not formally a part of the (equitable) bankruptcy proceeding. Instead, it had to do with identifying and collecting assets to be distributed rather than with distributing assets properly in hand.[149]

Next, Justice Brennan acknowledged that Congress can sometimes deny trial by jury even in a case in which the seventh amendment would otherwise guarantee one—by channeling the claim to a non-Article III adjudicator "with which the jury would be incompatible."[150] He explained, however, that Congress' ability to dispense with jury trial has limits.[151] Otherwise, the seventh amendment would cease to check congressional power at all when Congress chooses to employ non-Article III bodies. Those limits are captured by the public rights doctrine: Congress can deny trial by jury even when the

---

146. See notes 52–57 and accompanying text (discussing the Bankruptcy Act of 1984).

147. Granfinanciera conceded that it had no statutory right to jury trial under the Bankruptcy Act of 1984, but only because Nordberg had filed his action prior to the effective date of that Act. Justice Brennan accepted that concession and moved to the seventh amendment question without (expressly) deciding whether, apart from the seventh amendment, the 1984 Act either authorized the bankruptcy court to conduct a jury trial or entitled Granfinanciera to such a jury trial on a fraudulent conveyance claim. 492 U.S. at 39 n.2; see notes 155–56 and accompanying text.

148. *Feltner v. Columbia Pictures*, 523 U.S. 340 (1998); *Parsons v. Bedford*, 28 U.S. (3 Pet.) 433 (1830). The precedents do not always line up neatly. In *NLRB v. Jones & Laughlin Steel Corp.*, 301 U.S. 1 (1937), for example, the Court allowed Congress to deny trial by jury to a claim for damages, because it was "incident" to a claim for equitable relief pending before an agency that could not offer jury trial. The Court has never held that the seventh amendment right to trial by jury in common law cases is "incorporated" into the fourteenth amendment so as to be applicable in state court.

149. Justice Brennan found *Schoenthal v. Irving Trust Co.*, 287 U.S. 92 (1932), to control the historical characterization of Nordberg's fraudulent transfer claim. He acknowledged that the 1984 Act placed fraudulent conveyance actions within the "core proceedings" in which a bankruptcy judge could render final judgment (subject to review in the district and circuit courts). He also recognized Justice White's concomitant argument that the Court should defer to Congress' apparent judgment that such an action was part of the equitable bankruptcy proceeding itself. Yet Brennan insisted that Congress had no power to "re-classif[y]" a common law action and, on that basis, to evade the seventh amendment. 492 U.S. at 60.

150. 492 U.S. at 61, quoting *Atlas Roofing Co. v. Occup. Safety and Health Review Comm'n*, 430 U.S. 442, 455 (1977).

151. Id. at 50.

seventh amendment would ordinarily demand a jury. But Congress can do that only when Congress can validly route the case to a non-Article III adjudicator. Congress can do *that*, in turn, only when the case is a matter of public rights.[152]

Justice Brennan recognized, of course, that this analysis demands a definition of public rights cases different from the definition he himself employed in *Northern Pipeline*. It is no longer tenable to insist on the old categorical rule that a case is one of public rights only if the federal government is a party. Instead, Justice Brennan relied on the new definition that he articulated in his concurring opinion in *Union Carbide*: A case can involve public rights even though the federal government is not a party, provided that Congress, "acting for a valid legislative purpose," creates "a seemingly 'private' right that is so closely integrated into a public regulatory scheme as to be a matter appropriate for agency resolution with limited involvement by the Article III judiciary."[153] Since Nordberg's fraudulent transfer claim was not a public rights matter under that new definition, Congress could not deprive Granfinanciera of the right to jury trial by assigning that claim to a non-Article III court.[154]

The analysis in *Granfinanciera* is controversial. Yet the square holding is fairly clear. When a litigant complains that non-jury adjudication by a non-Article III entity violates the seventh amendment, the first order of business is to decide whether the claim at stake triggers the seventh amendment because it at least resembles a claim that historically would have been handled in the law courts. Some claims resting on modern federal statutes fit that model; others do not. If the claim at hand does ordinarily invoke the seventh amendment, the next question is whether it also fits the new definition of public rights matters identified in *Granfinanciera* and Justice Brennan's concurrence in *Union Carbide*. If the claim does fit that definition, Congress can send it to a non-Article III adjudicator to be tried without a jury. If the claim does not, Congress cannot dispense with jury trial by that means. A litigant who insists on jury trial is entitled to one—in some forum.

Justice Brennan declined to decide in *Granfinanciera* whether the Bankruptcy Act authorizes a bankruptcy judge to conduct a jury trial or, if it does, whether a jury trial before a non-Article III judge would satisfy the seventh amendment.[155] It is questionable,

---

152. Id. at 51. In putting the point in such an uncompromising way, Justice Brennan overlooked territorial and military courts. The Court has never decided whether Congress can deny trial by jury in those courts despite the seventh amendment. In *Pernell v. Southall Realty*, 416 U.S. 363 (1974), the Court held that the seventh amendment establishes a litigant's right to jury trial in a court in the District of Columbia.

153. 492 U.S. at 54, quoting *Union Carbide*, 473 U.S. at 586 (concurring opinion); see text accompanying note 123. Given this definition of public rights cases, it seems clear that litigants advancing constitutional claims against government remain entitled to jury trial in cases in which the seventh amendment operates. See Eric Grant, *A Revolutionary View of the Seventh Amendment and the Just Compensation Clause*, 91 Nw. U. L. Rev. 144, 207–08 (1996) (referring particularly to "takings" claims for just compensation).

154. In a previous case, *Katchen v. Landy*, 382 U.S. 323 (1966), the Court had rejected a creditor's seventh amendment claim to a jury trial on a similar fraudulent transfer claim. In that case, however, the creditor voluntarily entered the bankruptcy proceeding by filing a claim against the asset pool and thus placed the value of the previous transfer within the bankruptcy court's constructive possession. On that basis, *Katchen* was distinguishable. Accord *Langenkamp v. Culp*, 498 U.S. 42 (1990). Cf. *McCarthy v. Bronson*, 500 U.S. 136, 138 (1991) (confirming that individuals are free to waive seventh amendment rights). It may be that most creditors in Granfinanciera's position make claims against the bankrupt's estate. If so, the practical significance of the *Granfinanciera* decision is substantially diminished.

155. See note 147.

however, whether Brennan could leave the authority of the bankruptcy judge untouched. He explained that a litigant's seventh amendment right to jury trial and Congress' ability to use a non-Article III adjudicator go hand-in-hand, both governed by the public rights doctrine. If that is true, then the holding that Nordberg's claim was not one of public rights would seem to preclude adjudication by the bankruptcy judge in the first place, wholly apart from the method of trial available in that forum. Then again, bankruptcy judges operating pursuant to the 1984 Act may be justified as adjuncts of district courts. If that foundation is sound, it would follow that they can do any work that district courts themselves might perform.[156]

Justice Brennan recognized that a judgment reached by a bankruptcy judge is reviewable by the district court. Yet he explained that Article III oversight after trial cannot substitute for the actual conduct of a jury trial in the first instance.[157] There is, moreover, another problem. If Article III courts second-guess jury verdicts in trials conducted by bankruptcy judges, they may themselves violate the seventh amendment—which states that "no fact tried by jury, shall be otherwise re-examined in any Court of the United States." That provision, in turn, responds to Anti-Federalist concerns that Article III courts would not respect the only device citizens then had to hold judges in check: juries drawn from the citizenry.[158] It may be that the Court can square all this up by allowing district courts to review legal decisions by bankruptcy judges (which may satisfy Article III), while disallowing them to review jury verdicts after trials that bankruptcy judges conduct (which may avoid any conflict with the seventh amendment).[159] Since *Granfinanciera*, Congress has enacted another amendment to the Bankruptcy Act, which authorizes bankruptcy judges to conduct jury trials with the express consent of the parties.[160] Given that the seventh amendment establishes a waivable personal right, the consent condition in the new statute arguably robs it of any substantive significance.[161]

The *Granfinanciera* decision appears to reinvigorate a more categorical conception of public rights. Justice Brennan accommodated the balancing approach reflected in *Union Carbide* and *Schor* only insofar as he had in his concurring opinion in *Union Carbide*. He mentioned *Schor* only in passing as a case in which the Court relied on the complaining party's consent.[162] It seems plain that Justice Brennan (and the five justices who joined his opinion) hesitated to surrender the seventh amendment to the *ad hoc* balancing approach that *Union Carbide* and *Schor* apply to Article III cases in which the seventh amendment is not implicated. That impulse where a provision of the Bill of Rights is at stake may be entirely understandable.[163] Yet by connecting public rights not only to the seventh amendment, but also to Article III, *Granfinanciera* reintroduced an obscure, outmoded, and intellectually dissatisfying doctrine to the body of case law on legislative

---

156. See notes 52–57 and accompanying text.

157. *Granfinanciera*, 492 U.S. at 64. Justice Brennan had no occasion in *Granfinanciera* to decide whether Congress can mix and match—sending public rights cases to Article III courts, but barring trial by jury there. Given the historical backdrop of the jury trial provision, it is unlikely that the Court would approve a scheme of that kind.

158. See Chapter II, text accompanying notes 34–36.

159. See Douglas G. Baird, *The Seventh Amendment and Jury Trials in Bankruptcy*, 1989 Sup. Ct. Rev. 261, 280–82 (cautiously noting this possible resolution).

160. 28 U.S.C. §157.

161. See note 122.

162. 492 U.S. at 59 n.14. See note 130. Recall that Justice Brennan dissented in *Schor*, insisting that the consent theory could not justify the Court's judgment in that case. See note 131.

163. See Redish & LaFave, note 108, at 408–11.

courts. In dissent, Justice White warned that Brennan's analysis would prevent Congress from establishing effective non-Article III machinery in a variety of contexts.[164] Justice Scalia agreed, but drew a different conclusion. Concurring in *Granfinanciera*, he insisted that public rights cases necessarily involve the government as a party and, therefore, that both *Union Carbide* and *Schor* were wrongly decided.[165]

It is difficult to measure the precedential value of yet another complicated decision, generated by a divided vote of justices some of whom are no longer on the Court, which not only fails to continue on a linear path of doctrinal development, but actually doubles back to ideas previously discarded.[166] Certainly, it is hard to conclude that the Court has abandoned the general balancing approach illustrated by *Schor*, albeit that approach is obviously distasteful to Justice Scalia (and perhaps to other justices now sitting) for the very reason that it is less manageable and predictable than categorical doctrinal rules.[167] Plainly, the Court rejects Scalia's position regarding the content of public rights cases—for the obvious reason that Scalia's view would invalidate the entire body of federal arrangements contemplating non-Article III adjudication of disputes between private parties. Finally, it may be important that *Granfinanciera* arguably left room for further developments. Justice Brennan said that the seventh amendment would give way in a case in which jury trial would be totally "incompatible" with Congress' purpose in using a non-Article III adjudicator.[168]

---

164. Justice White argued that both Article III and seventh amendment issues should be addressed via *ad hoc* balancing. 492 U.S. at 77–78. Justice O'Connor joined Justice Blackmun's separate dissent, which expressed agreement with White "generally" but plainly found the particular case at bar a closer call. Id. at 91.

165. 492 U.S. at 65; see note 108 and accompanying text.

166. See text accompanying notes 121–28.

167. See *Granfinanciera*, 492 U.S. at 70 (Scalia, J., concurring).

168. *Id.* at 61 (majority opinion). In a subsequent case, Justice Brennan said that the right to trial by jury is unavailable where "Congress has permissibly delegated the particular dispute to a non-Article III decisionmaker and jury trials would frustrate Congress' purposes in enacting a particular statutory scheme." *Chauffeurs, Teamsters & Helpers Local No. 391 v. Terry*, 494 U.S. 558, 574 (1990) (Brennan, J., concurring). Professor Sward insists that the seventh amendment will not permit Congress to withhold jury trial in every case in which Article III permits Congress to employ a non-Article III adjudicator. In her view, the constitutional right to trial by jury turns only on the conventional analysis in the seventh amendment cases—namely, on what counted as a suit at common law. If litigants advance claims that are analogous to legal claims at common law, they are entitled to jury trial—wherever Congress places the case. Sward, note 128, at 1105–06. Professor Sward acknowledges, however, that her position would entail a radical change in existing arrangements and might be impractical. Id. at 1108.

Chapter VI

Federal Questions in State Court

State courts routinely entertain the kinds of cases and controversies that Article III permits federal courts to adjudicate. In most instances, state courts of general jurisdiction are constitutionally obligated to provide a forum for federal claims. State courts may lack the remedial authority that federal courts can bring to bear on officers of the federal government. But for the most part, state courts constitute an alternative judicial forum for federal question lawsuits. The omnipresence of state courts informs the statutes and doctrines that govern access to federal courts. If state courts were not routinely available, much less practical significance would attach to the Supreme Court's acceptance of the parity premise and its consequent inclination to foster federal question litigation in state tribunals.[1] As it is, the Court is free to reinforce state court authority and responsibility for conducting federal question business as co-equals with the lower federal courts.

Subject to important exceptions,[2] civil litigants who find themselves in state court with a federal claim or defense will almost certainly have to be satisfied with the determination the state courts provide. They will rarely be able to escape state court and reach a federal court for an adjudication in the first instance. And after the state courts have arrived at a decision, they will rarely be able to challenge that judgment in a federal forum. The state court judgment will almost certainly be final, even though it determines the federal rights and duties of the parties. This fact of life establishes the stakes for battles over access to the federal courts as an original matter. Litigants who wish to advance a federal claim in federal court must get to a federal district court with that claim *first*, in advance of any proceedings in state court that, once begun, will almost certainly produce a decision that will conclude the matter.

A. State Court Authority

The basic proposition that state courts can handle Article III business is scarcely controversial. State courts do not exercise "the judicial Power" of the United States pre-

1. See Chapter I, notes 92–104 and accompanying text.

2. See notes 125–60 and accompanying text (discussing the possibility of removal to a federal district court); notes 161–95 and accompanying text (discussing the possibility of attacking a state court judgment collaterally in federal court); Chapter VII (discussing the possibility of appellate review in the Supreme Court of the United States); Chapter XII (discussing the availability of federal habeas corpus as a sequel to state court litigation).

scribed for the federal courts by Article III.[3] Instead, state courts of general jurisdiction are empowered by state law to adjudicate matters on the Article III menu, subject only to federal constitutional limitations.[4] Nothing in the Constitution expressly bars those courts from proceeding in the ordinary course simply because a case might also have been taken to a federal tribunal. Following Hamilton, the Supreme Court has declined to interpret Article III to divest state courts of any authority they previously enjoyed to decide the kinds of cases and controversies that Article III brings within the federal judicial power.[5] Moreover, again following Hamilton, the Court has held that even with respect to cases and controversies that are peculiar to the federal constitutional system (for example, federal question cases), Article III allows state courts to act, subject to any limits that Congress may establish by statute.[6]

This construction of Article III is fortified by the Constitution's history, text, and structure. State courts' ability to do Article III business formed the premise of the Madisonian Compromise.[7] Recall the conventional understanding that federal courts inferior to the Supreme Court need never have been created. If there were no such lower federal courts, state courts would have to adjudicate Article III cases and controversies in the first instance in order to establish judgments on which the Supreme Court could exercise appellate jurisdiction. By the same token, if the cases and controversies that state courts adjudicate were not matters to which Article III extends, the Supreme Court would be unable to review the judgments the state courts reach.[8] The Supremacy Clause, which flowed naturally from the Compromise, states explicitly that state judges are bound by the Constitution and other "Laws of the United States" and thus plainly contemplates that state courts will adjudicate cases in which federal questions must be considered.[9] Inasmuch as the states are united in a single national structure, federal law is as much a part of their law as is local state law.[10] It only makes sense, accordingly, that the courts the states commission share responsibility for federal question litigation with the courts established by Congress under Article III.[11] Finally, it is more practical to adjust the distribution of jurisdiction between federal and state courts by statutes (which

---

3. See Chapter IV, text accompanying notes 1–4.

4. *Minnespolis & St. Louis R.R. v. Bombolis*, 241 U.S. 211, 222–23 (1916). See Chapter V, text accompanying note 1 (discussing a similar point regarding federal legislative courts).

5. See Chapter II, text accompanying note 51.

6. See Chapter II, text accompanying note 52.

7. See Chapter II, note 13 and accompanying text.

8. See Chapter V, text accompanying notes 69–71.

9. U.S. Const. art VI, cl.2. See note 89 (discussing the two parts of the Supremacy Clause); Chapter II, text accompanying notes 20–21. Professor Collins contends that some members of the founding generation agreed with Justice Story that state courts would be unable to handle all the business included in Article III and that inferior federal courts would be necessary. Michael G. Collins, *Article III Cases, State Court Duties, and the Madisonian Compromise*, 1995 Wis. L. Rev. 39; see Chapter IV, notes 57–61 and accompanying text. Collins acknowledges, however, that it is "difficult if not impossible to argue today that there are areas of Article III jurisdiction within the Supreme Court's appellate jurisdiction that could not be heard in the first instance by the state courts if they were so inclined and if Congress were agreeable." Collins, at 46.

10. *Claflin v. Houseman*, 93 U.S. 130, 136 (1876).

11. Not all the constitutional values typically associated with federalism are served by state court jurisdiction in federal question cases. There is no argument, for example, that state courts should participate in the resolution of federal questions in order to foster experimentation and diversity or to accommodate local sentiments not shared in other regions. By contrast, state courts, if they decide federal questions at all, must decide them in conformity to a uniform body of federal law. Paul M. Bator, *The State Courts and Federal Constitutional Litigation*, 22 Wm. & Mary L. Rev. 605, 608 (1981).

can themselves be adjusted from time to time) than through judicial elaboration of the Constitution itself.[12]

The federal statutes in point, as well as tradition and practice, also support the understanding that state court jurisdiction is presumptively concurrent with that of federal courts. Recall that the Judiciary Act of 1789 left considerable Article III business to state courts by default and that Congress did not grant inferior federal courts a general jurisdiction in federal question cases until Reconstruction.[13] Experience shows, accordingly, that the system has often depended on state court adjudication of a significant body of federal question cases—including some federal criminal prosecutions.[14] The states typically choose local courts when they enforce local policies in litigation with individual citizens. Federal issues often arise in that context, and, when they do, state courts are positioned to address them. Any other scheme would be difficult to orchestrate. Either state officials would have to proceed in federal court in the first place, or litigation initiated in state court would have to be shifted to a federal tribunal later. At the least, significant institutional costs would accompany both possibilities.[15]

Congress has power to preempt state courts. In *The Moses Taylor*,[16] the Court said that Congress can give federal courts exclusive jurisdiction to determine "all cases to which the judicial power of the United States extends."[17] That may be an overstatement. Taken literally, it would mean that if the Constitution does not itself divest state courts of jurisdiction they had before 1787, Congress can do so by statute.[18] It would also revive the vexing constitutional questions implicated when Congress curbs the jurisdiction of the federal courts. Consider the implications, for example, if Congress were to deny state courts jurisdiction to determine any of the cases and controversies listed in Article III and, at the same time, were to dismantle the lower federal courts—thus leaving the Supreme Court to manage what Article III business it could as an original matter.[19] At the very least, Congress would find it infeasible to paint state courts out of the picture. It would be needlessly and hopelessly disruptive if, for example, Congress were to assign federal courts exclusive jurisdiction over all cases involving citizens of different states—cases in which federal courts would apply *state* law.[20]

By some accounts, Congress should decline to make federal jurisdiction exclusive in any case, but should always provide for concurrent jurisdiction in both federal and state court. The parties presumably make rational choices about the best forum in which to litigate, and it may be that a loose "market" for selecting courts will produce good results in most instances, without any attempt to control forum selection by law. In some contexts, however, special expertise or uniformity may be needed, and Congress may

---

12. See Chapter IV, text accompanying notes 69–71.

13. See Chapter II, notes 60–61, 73 and accompanying text.

14. See *Testa v. Katt*, 330 U.S. 386, 390 (1947); Chapter IV, note 60 and accompanying text. Today, a federal statute places federal criminal prosecutions exclusively within the federal courts' jurisdiction. 18 U.S.C. §3231. But a move is afoot to amend that statute and channel some classes of federal prosecutions into state court for trial in order to conserve federal judicial resources. See Chapter II, note 106 and accompanying text.

15. Bator, note 11, at 608–09, 621.

16. 71 U.S. (4 Wall.) 411 (1867).

17. Id. at 429.

18. See text accompanying note 5.

19. See Chapter IV, notes 122–49 and accompanying text (discussing manipulations of federal jurisdiction generally); Chapter VII, notes 1–40 and accompanying text (discussing the Court's original jurisdiction).

20. See Chapter VIII, text accompanying note 57.

sensibly respond by foreclosing state court jurisdiction and forcing litigants into the federal forum.[21] The federal courts' exclusive jurisdiction in patent cases is controversial in some quarters inasmuch as the Supreme Court's precedents often allow for state court treatment of the same issues.[22]

As a practical matter, Congress rarely makes federal jurisdiction exclusive. Some statutes explicitly indicate that state courts, too, have jurisdiction to proceed. Others refer only to the federal courts, and still others ambiguously refer to courts of "competent jurisdiction." In most contexts, it does not matter. State courts are understood to have any jurisdiction that is not explicitly disclaimed—either by an express statement that federal jurisdiction is exclusive or by a statement that state court jurisdiction is foreclosed. Litigants therefore have the dominant role in deciding where a case will be resolved. When the two sides agree on the appropriate forum, there is typically no difficulty getting the case into that tribunal. When the parties disagree, various statutes and doctrines determine whose preference prevails.

The leading case is *Claflin v. Houseman*,[23] in which the Supreme Court held that state courts could entertain contract and real property suits initiated by an assignee in bankruptcy. Justice Bradley rejected the argument that state courts were deprived of jurisdiction merely because the assignee derived his procedural right to sue from the federal bankruptcy statute. That statute said nothing about state court jurisdiction. Accordingly, the occasion called for judgment regarding the proper inference to be drawn from legislative silence. Justice Bradley adopted a presumption in favor of concurrent state court jurisdiction: A federal statute should be read to allow for state court jurisdiction, unless the statute precludes that jurisdiction either "by express provision" or by "incompatibility in its exercise arising from the nature of the particular case."[24] The claims in *Claflin* were traditional common law claims over which state courts enjoyed jurisdiction prior to the Constitution. Accordingly, *Claflin* may itself be authority only for a presumption in favor of state court jurisdiction in cases of that kind. Again following Hamilton,[25] however, more recent decisions have clarified the picture: State courts presumptively have concurrent jurisdiction in all cases, irrespective of subject matter.[26]

In *Gulf Offshore Co. v. Mobil Oil Corp.*,[27] the Supreme Court restated the *Claflin* doctrine as a default position, subject to three exceptions. State court concurrent jurisdiction will be found, unless it is foreclosed by: (1) "explicit statutory" language; (2) "unmistakable implication" from legislative history; or (3) "clear incompatibility" with "federal interests."[28] The leading case on the *Gulf Offshore* formulation is *Tafflin v.*

---

21. Conventional examples include: 28 U.S.C. §1334 (bankruptcy proceedings); 28 U.S.C. §1355 (actions to recover fines under federal statutes); and 28 U.S.C. §1364 (actions against insurers of foreign governments).

22. See 28 U.S.C. §1338. E.g., *Lear v. Adkins*, 395 U.S. 653 (1969); see generally *T.B. Harms v. Eliscu*, 339 F.2d 823 (2d Cir. 1964), *cert. denied*, 381 U.S. 915 (1965) (providing a good discussion); see also Donald S. Chisum, *The Allocation of Jurisdiction Between State and Federal Courts in Patent Litigation*, 46 Wash. L. Rev. 633 (1971).

23. 93 U.S. 130 (1876).

24. Id. at 136.

25. See Chapter II, text accompanying notes 51–52.

26. E.g., *Charles Dowd Box Co. v. Courtney*, 368 U.S. 502 (1962) (holding that state courts have concurrent jurisdiction to entertain federal labor relations cases in which federal common law controls); *Garrett v. Moore-McCormack Co.*, 317 U.S. 239 (1942) (holding that state courts can handle claims under federal maritime statutes).

27. 453 U.S. 473 (1981).

28. Id. at 478.

Levitt.[29] The Court held in *Tafflin* that state courts have concurrent jurisdiction to entertain civil actions under the federal Racketeering Influenced and Corrupt Organizations Act.[30] Justice O'Connor initially found no express language in RICO purporting to deny state court jurisdiction.[31] Turning to the legislative history, she said that "the question is not whether any intent at all may be divined from legislative *silence* on the issue, but whether Congress in its deliberations may be said to have *affirmatively* or *unmistakably* intended jurisdiction to be exclusively federal."[32] Coming to the "incompatibility" exception, O'Connor acknowledged that state jurisdiction of RICO cases would lead to state court interpretations of federal criminal offenses (which often form part of civil RICO violations). Yet she found no sufficient conflict with federal interests.[33]

Inasmuch as *Tafflin* considered all three *Gulf Offshore* exceptions, it is hard to say that any of the three can be dismissed. Nevertheless, Justice O'Connor's treatment of the latter two suggests that the first (an express statement in the text of a statute that state courts have no jurisdiction) is now predominant. Certainly, the second exception appears anomalous. Concurring in *Tafflin*, Justice Scalia urged the Court to abandon that exception entirely. In his view, Congress can deprive state courts of jurisdiction only by means of an enacted statute, not committee reports and similar background materials.[34] Justice Scalia conceded that the third exception may be acceptable, provided that "incompatibility" is found only when a statute "expressly mentions only the federal courts" and state court jurisdiction would "plainly disrupt" the federal statutory scheme.[35]

Justice Scalia's position reflects the kind of statutory construction analysis that now pervades Supreme Court decisions in this field: strict attention to the text of enacted statutes, disregard for legislative history, and a tendency to choose a baseline default po-

29. 493 U.S. 455 (1990).

30. The suit in *Tafflin* was initiated in a federal district court, but that court abstained in favor of pending litigation in state court. See Chapter XI (discussing the abstention doctrines). The validity of that action turned on the existence of state court jurisdiction over the plaintiff's RICO claims.

31. The relevant provision in RICO states that a plaintiff "may" sue "in any appropriate United States district court" but does not explicitly state either that federal jurisdiction is exclusive or that a plaintiff may not sue in state court. 493 U.S. at 460.

32. Id. at 462 (emphasis added). Justice O'Connor found no hard evidence in the legislative history to suggest that Congress so much as considered whether state courts would handle RICO cases. She might have taken the absence of any mention of state courts to imply that only federal district courts would do so. Moreover, Congress borrowed statutory language from the Clayton Act for use in RICO. Since Clayton Act cases had previously been held to be exclusively within the federal courts' jurisdiction, Justice O'Connor might have drawn the inference, again by implication, that the same would be true of RICO lawsuits. In the event, she declined to assign any meaning to silence in the legislative record.

33. Justice O'Connor explained that state courts handling civil RICO cases do not enforce federal criminal law directly. They are guided by the precedents set by federal courts, and, in any event, they have sufficient expertise in criminal law matters to manage RICO litigation—particularly in situations in which violations of state (as well as federal) criminal law figure in a defendant's civil liability.

34. 493 U.S. at 472. Justice Scalia recognized that the Court had previously found state court jurisdiction to be foreclosed by implication in Clayton and Sherman Act cases. Yet he criticized the reasoning in those cases and insisted that if "exclusion by implication is possible" at all, it should be possible only on the basis of what can be found implicit in the text of the statute itself, not in legislative history. Id. at 471.

35. Id. at 472. But see Chapter VIII, notes 102–03, 117–19 and accompanying text (discussing Justice Scalia's controversial opinion for the Court in the *Boyle* case).

sition from which Congress can depart only by making a clear statement.[36] If the full Court did not adopt that approach in *Tafflin*, it did so in the very next case, *Yellow Freight System v. Donnelly*.[37] In *Yellow Freight*, the Court unanimously held that state courts have concurrent jurisdiction to entertain private civil actions under Title VII of the 1964 Civil Rights Act. Justice Stevens discussed the possibility that state court jurisdiction might be implicitly disclaimed by legislative history or incompatible with federal interests—but only briefly. In the main, he said that the absence of an explicit disclaimer of state court jurisdiction in the Act itself was "strong *and arguably sufficient*" evidence that state courts can entertain Title VII suits.[38]

B. State Court Obligation

The question whether state courts *must* entertain federal question lawsuits is problematic. As a practical matter, state courts of general jurisdiction are not free to turn away federal business. This is true for a host of reasons elaborated in the precedents. Still, it would be incorrect to say flatly either that the Constitution of its own force always commands state courts to handle federal question cases or that Congress can routinely force them to do so by legislation.[39] Those ultimate questions implicate a variety of ideas: (1) the principle of national unity; (2) the principle of non-discrimination; (3) the demands of due process; (4) the scope of congressional power; (5) valid excuses for declining federal business; and (6) the place of local procedural rules.

National unity. In expansive moments, the Supreme Court is wont to conflate the state courts' constitutional *authority* to adjudicate federal question cases with a constitutional *obligation* to undertake the task. The classic illustration is Justice Harlan's statement in *Robb v. Connolly*: "Upon the State courts, equally with the courts of the Union, rests the *obligation* to guard, enforce, and protect every right granted or secured by the Constitution of the United States."[40] And in the leading case, *Testa v. Katt*,[41] the Court said that the precedents on state court power, particularly *Claflin*,[42] equally answer "most" of the questions regarding state courts' "duty" to enforce federal law.[43] The vi-

36. See Michael E. Solimine, *Rethinking Federal Jurisdiction*, 52 U. Pitt. L. Rev. 383, 385 (1991); Chapter I, notes 44–52 and accompanying text. Cf. *Village of Bolingbrook v. Citizens Utilities Co.*, 864 F.2d 481, 485 (7th Cir. 1988) (opinion of Easterbrook, J.) (proposing that the precedents holding that the anti-trust laws implicitly foreclose state court jurisdiction are now open to question). Redish and Muench argue that the Court should take greater responsibility for determining whether state court jurisdiction will satisfactorily protect federal interests. Martin H. Redish & John E. Muench, *Adjudication of Federal Causes of Action in State Courts*, 75 Mich. L. Rev. 311 (1976).

37. 494 U.S. 820 (1990).

38. Id. at 823 (emphasis added).

39. In *Nat'l Private Truck Council v. Oklahoma Tax Comm'n*, 515 U.S. 582 (1995), the Court explicitly stated that it is an open question whether state courts "generally must hear" federal question cases pursuant to the Ku Klux Klan Act, 42 U.S.C. §1983. Id. at 587 n.4. See notes 50–56 and accompanying text (discussing the *Howlett* case). In *Alden v. Maine*, 527 U.S. 706 (1999), the Court held that Congress cannot subject the states themselves to suits by private litigants advancing federal statutory claims in state court. See Chapter X, notes 150–51 and accompanying text.

40. 111 U.S. 624, 637 (1884) (emphasis added).

41. 330 U.S. 386 (1947).

42. See notes 23–26 and accompanying text.

43. 330 U.S. at 391.

sion of national unity has considerable force. If the states are units of an indivisible whole, if they do not and cannot function as independent nations, and if federal law is part of their law (and, indeed, a superior form of it), it is hard to think that state courts can blithely refuse to adjudicate claims that depend on that law.

In *Testa*, a consumer alleged that an automobile dealer had exacted a selling price that exceeded the war-time ceiling established by the federal Emergency Price Control Act. Under the provisions of that Act, the consumer was entitled to sue in "any court of competent jurisdiction" and, if successful, to obtain treble damages. The consumer chose to sue in the state courts of Rhode Island. The Rhode Island Supreme Court held that the treble damages provision was penal in character and, accordingly, that the courts of Rhode Island had no obligation to enforce it. The court relied by analogy on the settled understanding that an individual state need not give "full faith and credit" to the penal actions and judgments of another state or nation—if to do so would conflict with the forum state's public policy.[44]

In the Supreme Court, Justice Black assumed that the treble damages provision was penal in nature and that the Rhode Island courts might have declined to enforce it if it had been enacted by another state or a foreign nation. But he rejected the state court's premise that it could equally refuse to enforce a federal statute. Black relied on two theories, though he failed to distinguish them one from the other. First, he implied that the Constitution of its own force obligated the Rhode Island courts to entertain the plaintiff's federal claim. Congress, he said, acted for "all the people and all the states" when it established the treble damages provision as policy for the country as a whole.[45] A state court was not free to treat a federal statute as though it were a law "emanating from a foreign sovereign," but must, instead, accept it as the supreme law of the single American nation. Second, Justice Black suggested that the Emergency Price Control Act required the state courts to entertain the plaintiff's action even if the Constitution, standing alone, did not. On this second point, Black said that the 1789 Judiciary Act and a variety of later statutes "conferred jurisdiction upon state courts to enforce" federal law and that this new statute did the same. By his account, challenges to Congress' power to "require" the state courts to entertain federal claims were essentially rejected in *Claflin*.[46]

Justice Black overlooked one alternative understanding of the Supremacy Clause and slighted (but ultimately relied on) yet another. Initially, he failed to consider whether the Supremacy Clause might demand only that state courts enforce federal law in cases the state courts voluntarily accept for consideration. If a state court chooses not to entertain a suit at all, it avoids putting itself in a position to decide whether a proposition of federal law preempts some feature of state law. Once a state court accepts a case, however, it is necessarily in such a position. At that point, it is inescapable that the

---

44. The Full Faith and Credit Clause, U.S. Const. art. IV, §1, generally instructs the states to give "Full Faith and Credit" to the "public Acts, Records, and judicial Proceedings of every other State." See note 161. Yet states may decline to credit "penalties." E.g., *Wisconsin v. Pelican Ins. Co.*, 127 U.S. 265, 291 (1888).

45. 330 U.S. at 392, citing *Mondou v. New York R.R.*, 223 U.S. 1, 57 (1912), for the proposition that the policy reflected in a federal statute is "as much the policy of [an individual state] as if the act had emanated from its own legislature." Accord *Claflin*, 93 U.S. at 137 (explaining that state and federal law "form one system of jurisprudence"). This point is not inconsistent with the rule that a state can object to policies adopted by other states. That idea reflects a kind of horizontal federalism. It recognizes a baseline responsibility in the states to cooperate with each other, but still accommodates occasional differences in the interests of autonomy and diversity.

46. 330 U.S. at 389, 391.

court must give proper effect to federal law. Both *Testa* and subsequent precedents read the Supremacy Clause to address both a state court's decision to entertain a case in the first instance and its adjudication of a case after it has been accepted. Yet the supremacy of federal law is clearly less at risk in the former instance than it is in the latter.[47]

The Supremacy Clause might also be read to permit a state court to refuse a federal question lawsuit in the first instance, provided the court equally refuses similar cases arising under state law. Justice Black stated the question presented in *Testa* in a sweeping manner: "whether state courts may decline to enforce federal laws" on the grounds cited by the Rhode Island Supreme Court.[48] And his elaboration of the national unity principle suggested that he meant to decide the ultimate question whether the state courts must generally be open for federal question business. In the end, however, he appeared to rest the decision in *Testa* on a narrow basis—namely, that a state court cannot discriminate against federal claims.

Non-discrimination. It was conceded in *Testa* that the state courts would enforce a treble damages statute if it were enacted by the Rhode Island legislature. By refusing to enforce such a statute enacted by Congress, the Rhode Island Supreme Court engaged in discrimination between state and federal law—disfavoring the latter. That is what Justice Black condemned. Accordingly, *Testa* may stand only for a non-discrimination principle: State courts cannot refuse to entertain a *federal* claim on the ground that it offends local policy if they are willing to enforce a similar policy when it is advanced by means of state law.[49]

The Court confirmed the non-discrimination principle in *Howlett v. Rose*.[50] A public school student sued a local school board in a Florida state court, alleging that an assistant principal had searched his car in violation of state tort law and the fourth amendment. With respect to the latter claim, the student relied on the federal Ku Klux Klan Act, 42 U.S.C. §1983, which authorizes a plaintiff to sue any "person" for violating the plaintiff's federal rights while acting "under color of state law."[51] In defense, the school board set up sovereign immunity (as a matter of Florida state law). The state courts held that a state statute waived any state-law immunity the board might otherwise have with respect to state tort claims, but not with respect to federal constitutional claims. Accordingly, the state courts considered the student's state claim against the school board on the merits, but dismissed his federal claim on the theory that it was barred by state-law sovereign immunity. In the Supreme Court, Justice Stevens reversed on the ground that discrimination against federal law violates the Supremacy Clause.[52]

Justice Stevens (like Justice Black before him) suggested both that the Constitution always requires state courts to entertain federal claims and that Congress can by statute

47. But see text accompanying note 52 (noting the non-discrimination principle's basis in the Supremacy Clause).

48. 330 U.S. at 388.

49. Id. at 394. Professor Collins contends that this reading of *Testa* conforms to historical understandings of the state courts' role in the federal system. Collins, note 9, at 166–77.

50. 496 U.S. 356 (1990).

51. See Chapter II, notes 74–75 and accompanying text (noting the history behind §1983 and the many places in modern practice in which §1983 plays a role).

52. 496 U.S. at 383. The state's federal constitutional immunity from suit in its own courts was not implicated in *Howlett*. The school board was a local entity and thus was not entitled to assert the state's federal immunity. In any event, the board purported to defend only on the basis of state-law sovereign immunity. See Chapter X, notes 164–65 and accompanying text (discussing these points as the basis for distinguishing *Howlett* in *Alden v. Maine*).

command state courts to accept federal question cases. On the first point, he said that the existence of jurisdiction "creates an implication of duty to exercise it."[53] On the second, he said that §1983 authorizes litigants to press federal claims in *either* federal or state court and, into the bargain, abolishes any sovereign immunity that state officials might otherwise enjoy under state law.[54] Nevertheless, Justice Stevens set those lines of argument to one side when he explained the result in *Howlett.* He cited *Testa* and other precedents as illustrations of the non-discrimination principle.[55] And he squarely held only that the Florida courts were obligated to entertain the student's federal claim, if, at the same time, those courts were willing to consider his parallel state tort claim. Consequently, *Howlett,* too, rests on the (comparatively narrow) principle of non-discrimination.[56]

Due process. In some circumstances, the Due Process Clause of the fourteenth amendment requires the states to provide some means for redressing violations of federal law.[57] But, here again, it is risky to generalize. Recall that litigants who wish to press

---

53. 496 U.S. at 370, quoting *Mondou,* 223 U.S. at 58. Justice Stevens explained that state courts in Florida concededly had subject matter jurisdiction of the plaintiff's federal claim and that the only "jurisdictional" problem in the case resided with the sovereign immunity defense. Accordingly, he had no occasion to decide whether a state must in the first instance "establish courts competent to entertain §1983 claims"—namely, federal claims advanced via the procedural vehicle that §1983 provides. 496 U.S. at 378 n.20. See Chapter VIII, note 136 and accompanying text (explaining that §1983 establishes no substantive rights and thus cannot itself be violated).

54. Justice Stevens cited *Martinez v. California,* 444 U.S. 277 (1980), for this point. There is solid supporting language in that case: "Conduct by persons acting under color of state law which is wrongful under 42 U.S.C. §1983...cannot be immunized by state law." Id. at 284 n.8. Yet in *Martinez* the state courts willingly entertained a §1983 suit, and it was in that posture that Justice Stevens (who also wrote for the Court in *Martinez*) said that state sovereign immunity did not control. Stevens intimated that the state courts in *Martinez* might have (correctly) understood that they were under an obligation to hear the §1983 suit in order to avoid discrimination against the plaintiffs' federal claim. Id. at 283 n.7 (citing the language from *Testa* regarding discrimination). He also noted that the Court had never considered the question whether state courts must generally entertain §1983 actions, discrimination to one side. That question remains open today. See note 39. For a discussion of §1983 litigation in state court, see Steven H. Steinglass, *The Emerging State Court §1983 Action: A Procedural Review,* 38 U. Miami L. Rev. 381 (1984).

55. In *McKnett v. St. Louis Ry.,* 292 U.S. 230 (1934), the Court found it discriminatory for a state court to reject a Federal Employers Liability Act claim filed by a non-resident when it would have accepted a similar claim if it had rested on another state's law. In *Felder v. Casey,* 487 U.S. 131 (1988), the Court found it discriminatory for a state to invoke a 120-day filing deadline to cut off a federal claim pressed in a §1983 action, even though the same deadline applied to state law claims. The deadline frustrated federal civil rights policy.

56. In *Alden v. Maine,* 527 U.S. 706 (1999), the state of Maine waived its sovereign immunity under state law but refused to waive its immunity under the federal Constitution. Distinguishing both *Testa* and *Howlett,* the Court said that Maine's assertion of its federal immunity was an exercise of a constitutional privilege that Maine was not obliged to forgo in the interests of non-discrimination. *Alden,* 527 U.S. at 757–58 (also noting that there was "no evidence" that Maine had "manipulated its immunity in a systematic fashion to discriminate against federal" claims). See Chapter X, notes 150–96 and accompanying text (discussing *Alden*). For a critique of this feature of *Alden,* see Vicki C. Jackson, *Principle and Compromise in Constitutional Adjudication: The Eleventh Amendment and State Sovereign Immunity,* 75 Notre Dame L. Rev. 953, 1003 (2000).

57. The states must engage some kind of process if they deprive an individual of life, liberty, or property. States typically do so by providing a mix of administrative and judicial proceedings. In at least some instances (e.g., criminal prosecutions) the process that is "due" surely includes judicial process. In others, it is not entirely clear whether court proceedings of some kind are constitutionally required. See Chapter IV, text accompanying notes 113–14; cf. Chapter V, text accompanying note 99 (describing the Court's treatment of the issue in connection with adjudication by federal agencies). In an ordinary due process case, the triggering event is a deprivation of a liberty or property interest, not a violation of a federal right independent of due process. Accordingly, the familiar

federal claims in state court are often also entitled to go to federal court, instead. If the federal courts are not available, it is typically because of some statute enacted by Congress.[58] It is not obvious that state courts should be constitutionally obliged to conduct federal business simply because Congress withholds jurisdiction from federal courts. If the federal government wishes federal law to be enforced, it can supply federal tribunals for the purpose. Then again, state courts can hardly play a serious role in the larger national system if they ignore federal claims. At the least, state courts may have a general duty to adjudicate *constitutional* claims, if not federal *statutory* claims created by Congress as a matter of federal legislative policy.[59]

Justice Holmes said in the *Atchison Railroad* case that due process requires states to offer citizens a "clear and certain remedy" for taxes collected in violation of federal law.[60] That seems easy enough. Yet a "remedy" is one thing. A procedural mechanism for seeking a remedy is another.[61] If some procedural avenue for pursuing a remedy is required, it might be administrative rather than judicial.[62] And even if litigation in state court is mandated, there still may be circumstances in which some form of immunity can thwart recovery.[63] In some taxation cases, the Court has squarely held that states are

---

precedents regarding procedural due process do not establish that state courts have a threshold constitutional responsibility to adjudicate federal claims. Of course, if a state court once accepts a federal question case, it is bound to adjudicate that case consistent with due process.

58. See Chapter IV, notes 62–101 and accompanying text (discussing Congress' authority to prescribe the federal courts' jurisdiction legislatively).

59. Recall that the influential Hart and Wechsler paradigm contemplates that federal statute law is interstitial by nature. See Chapter I, note 59 and accompanying text.

60. *Atchison, T. & S.F.R. Co. v. O'Connor*, 223 U.S. 280, 285 (1912). If a state collects taxes that violate federal law "by coercive means," due process establishes a duty to reimburse the taxpayers concerned. *Ward v. Bd. of County Comm. of Love County*, 253 U.S. 17, 24 (1920). See Chapter VII, notes 126–27 and accompanying text (discussing the Supreme Court's jurisdiction to review the state court's decision in *Ward* notwithstanding the argument that it rested on an adequate state ground).

61. Courts sometimes use the term "remedy" to mean a right of action—a procedural right to pursue a judicial remedy in court. That is the sense in which §1983 is sometimes said to provide a "remedy" for federal rights. E.g., *Monroe v. Pape*, 365 U.S. 167, 172 (1961). Conventionally, however, a remedy is a form of relief granted to a party whose claim is judged to be meritorious. Illustrations include compensatory damages, injunctions, and declaratory judgments. See Chapter VIII, notes 120–21 and accompanying text.

62. See Chapter V, text accompanying note 1 (discussing adjudication in administrative agencies).

63. Note in this vein that the fourteenth amendment incorporates the fifth amendment principle that a state cannot "take" private property without giving just compensation in return. In "takings" cases, accordingly, the states are obliged to reimburse citizens whose property is seized by eminent domain. States routinely establish administrative and judicial mechanisms for handling "takings" cases and determining the compensation that is just. So it has not been necessary for the Supreme Court actually to decide whether states can deploy sovereign immunity to avoid meeting their admitted constitutional obligations. But cf. *First English Church v. County of Los Angeles*, 482 U.S. 304, 316 n.9 (1987) (coming close to saying that the fifth amendment overrides state immunity). If the question were squarely presented, it is by no means clear how the Court would answer it. See Chapter X, notes 150–96 and accompanying text (discussing the holding in *Alden v. Maine* that a state can evade liability under most federal statutes). Professor Seamon thinks that existing case law (especially *Alden v. Maine*) suggests that a state can set up sovereign immunity. Richard H. Seamon, *The Asymmetry of State Sovereign Immunity*, 76 Wash. L. Rev. 1067, 1112 (2001). Seamon argues, however, that due process should override state immunity in genuine "takings" cases filed in state court. Id. at 1069. What counts as a "taking" can be controversial—and certainly was in *First English* (an inverse condemnation case). Professor Beermann argues that states are constitutionally required to compensate the victims of the torts that state officers commit. He contemplates, how-

obliged by due process to make some kind of procedural mechanism available to citizens seeking tax refunds on federal grounds. But on examination, the scope of those precedents is quite narrow.

In *McKesson Corp. v. Div. of Alcoholic Beverages & Tobacco*[64] and *Reich v. Collins*,[65] the Court recognized that a state can force taxpayers to pay taxes on the condition that they will have an opportunity to raise their legal objections later in suits for reimbursement. If a state does that, however, the state must deliver on the promise of a post-payment process.[66] Even at that, however, neither *McKesson* nor *Reich* held squarely that state *courts* must have *jurisdiction* to entertain tax refund claims resting on federal law. It just happened that in both cases, the states employed state courts for the determination of tax reimbursement claims. The possibility that exclusively administrative schemes might suffice was not at issue. Nor did *McKesson* and *Reich* squarely grapple with sovereign immunity. Justice O'Connor said in *Reich* that a state's failure to return money exacted by unlawful taxation violates due process, "the sovereign immunity States traditionally enjoy in their own courts notwithstanding."[67] But that was *dicta*.[68] Neither the state of Georgia in *Reich* nor the state of Florida in *McKesson* attempted to shield itself from a monetary award by setting up sovereign immunity. In both cases, the states offered other legal and equitable justifications for refusing to reimburse taxpayers.[69]

All this said, there remains a certain suspicion that due process reaches further and, in the end, when all other arguments fail and there is nowhere else to turn, will require the states to open their courts to hear at least federal claims.[70] Once it is posited that the

---

ever, that claims of that kind should be vindicated in §1983 actions in federal court. Jack M. Beermann, *Government Official Torts and the Takings Clause: Federalism and State Sovereign Immunity*, 68 B.U. L. Rev. 277 (1988).

64. 496 U.S. 18 (1990).

65. 513 U.S. 106 (1994).

66. See also *Newsweek v. Florida Dep't of Revenue*, 522 U.S. 442 (1998) (*per curiam*) (following *McKesson* and *Reich*).

67. 513 U.S. at 110.

68. Daniel J. Meltzer, *The Seminole Decision and State Sovereign Immunity*, 1996 Sup. Ct. Rev. 1, 58.

69. See Vicki C. Jackson, *Seminole Tribe, the Eleventh Amendment and the Potential Evisceration of Ex parte Young*, 72 N.Y.U. L. Rev. 495, 504–05 n.40 (1997). The state did rely on (state-law) sovereign immunity in *Howlett v. Rose*, 496 U.S. 356 (1990); see notes 50–56 and accompanying text. Professor Woolhandler concedes that *Reich* is "arguably" a case in which a state's consent to suit was beside the point. Yet she contends that there is also a way to read *Reich* to depend on state consent. The Georgia legislature established a statutory scheme by which taxpayers could sue the state itself for tax refunds. That scheme substituted for an older system in which taxpayers sued state officers on common law theories. Woolhandler contends that Georgia was constitutionally obligated to allow taxpayers to sue state officers in the traditional form. Accordingly, when the state established an alternative system, it must have implicitly agreed to forgo sovereign immunity in the reimbursement actions the new scheme contemplated. Otherwise, the shift to suits against the state itself would have unilaterally eliminated a constitutional guarantee. Ann Woolhandler, *The Common Law Origins of Constitutionally Compelled Remedies*, 107 Yale L.J. 77, 150–51 (1997). In the main, Professor Woolhandler thinks that in the late Nineteenth Century state courts had a constitutional obligation to entertain tort actions against state officers. The best citation for that proposition may be *Poindexter v. Greenhow*, 114 U.S. 270 (1884), one of the Virginia cases. Professor Wolcher agrees, though he concentrates on a wide range of modern decisions (prior to *McKesson* and *Reich*). See Louis E. Wolcher, *Sovereign Immunity and the Supremacy Clause: Damages Against States in Their Own Courts for Constitutional Violations*, 69 Calif. L. Rev. 189 (1981).

70. With the exception of cases in which states or the federal government can assert sovereign immunity. See Chapter X. In *Daniels v. United States*, 532 U.S. 374 (2001), Justice Scalia suggested that a prisoner serving a sentence that was enhanced on the basis of a prior conviction may be con-

Constitution demands a remedy, it would seem to follow that some procedural mechanism must be available to secure that remedy and that state courts must have jurisdiction either to dispense the remedy to deserving litigants in the first instance or to review the remedial actions of state administrative officers.[71] If state courts must be open for at least some federal claims touching taxes, it may be a short step to the proposition that they must be open for other federal claims as well. The classic case on this general problem is *General Oil Co. v. Crain*.[72] A taxpayer sued a state officer in state court, seeking to enjoin a state tax on the theory that it violated the (dormant) Commerce Clause. The state officer in *Crain*, like the school board in *Howlett v. Rose*, set up state sovereign immunity (apparently as a matter of state law). The state courts dismissed the claim on that basis. In the Supreme Court, Justice McKenna explained that if the plaintiff's claim could be barred from state court on the basis of the state's sovereign immunity under state law, and if it could equally be barred from federal court on the basis of the state's federal constitutional immunity, then it would go without any judicial forum at all. McKenna refused to accept the state court's determination of state sovereign immunity law as dispositive. He reached the taxpayer's federal constitutional claim and, finding it wanting, affirmed the state court's judgment on the merits.

Justice Souter once cited *Crain* for the general proposition that state sovereign immunity cannot "constitutionally excuse a state court of general jurisdiction from an obligation to hear a suit brought to enjoin a state official's action" on federal constitutional grounds.[73] That is an overstatement. For one thing, *Crain* was a suit for injunctive relief only and therefore may be distinguishable in cases (like *McKesson* and *Reich*) in which plaintiffs seek monetary relief to compensate for violations of federal law in the past.[74] For another, Justice McKenna's emphasis on the risk that a federal claim might be barred from *both* state and federal court suggests that any due process obligation state courts may have is triggered only if the federal courts' doors are closed. That under-

---

stitutionally entitled to an opportunity to attack the enhanced sentence if he had no previous chance to challenge the underlying conviction. Id. at 386. Typically, claims of that kind are procedurally barred in federal habeas corpus. See Chapter XII, notes 243–57 and accompanying text. Justice Scalia suggested, however, that "the precepts of fundamental fairness inherent in 'due process'" may require the jurisdiction that rendered the prior judgment to accord the prisoner the opportunity he was denied earlier. 532 U.S. at 387. Cf. *Christopher v. Harbury*, 122 S.Ct. 2179 (2002) (discussing decisions recognizing a due process right of access to the courts).

71. See Richard H. Fallon, Jr., *The Ideologies of Federal Courts Law*, 74 Va. L. Rev. 1141, 1209 (1988); Henry P. Monaghan, *Third Party Standing*, 84 Colum. L. Rev. 277, 294 (1984). The converse is not true. Courts may have jurisdiction to adjudicate claims, but still lack authority to award prevailing litigants the remedies they seek. See Chapter XI, text accompanying notes 65–66 (discussing the prerequisites for equitable relief); see also Richard H. Fallon, Jr., *Some Confusions About Due Process, Judicial Review, and Constitutional Remedies*, 93 Colum. L. Rev. 309, 339, 370–71 (1993).

72. 209 U.S. 211 (1908).

73. *Idaho v. Coeur d'Alene Tribe*, 521 U.S. 261, 316 (1997) (dissenting opinion) (joined by Stevens, Ginsburg & Breyer, J.J.). See Chapter X, notes 303–09 and accompanying text (discussing the *Coeur d'Alene* case). In *Georgia R.R. & Banking Co. v. Musgrove*, 335 U.S. 900 (1949), the Court dismissed an appeal from a state court judgment that appeared to rest on state sovereign immunity to defeat liability for a constitutional violation. In that case, the losing party below was entitled to invoke the Court's appellate jurisdiction (under a statute since repealed). Accordingly, *Musgrove* was not a denial of *certiorari*. See Chapter VII, text accompanying notes 219–22 (explaining that the Court now can decline appellate review at its discretion). In *Coeur d'Alene*, Justice Souter said that *Musgrove* probably found a different state law ground to preclude review. See Fallon, *Ideologies*, note 71, at 1211 n.317.

74. See Chapter X, notes 340–49 and accompanying text.

standing is also problematic, however. On the day the Court decided *Crain*, it also held (in *Ex parte Young*) that the state's federal constitutional immunity did not bar a suit in federal court seeking to enjoin a state officer from enforcing an unconstitutional state statute.[75] Accordingly, *Crain* itself was not driven by the need to find some tribunal for the plaintiff's claim apart from a federal trial-level court.[76]

Justice Kennedy said in *Alden v. Maine*[77] that *Crain* actually proceeded from the premise that the plaintiff's suit was barred by the state's federal constitutional immunity from suit in *state* court. And it was because the state courts were closed that the Court found it so important, in *Ex parte Young*, to let a similar suit go forward in federal court. That reading of *Crain* is hard to take seriously. With respect to sovereign immunity, the state court lawsuit in *Crain* was indistinguishable from the federal court lawsuit in *Ex parte Young*. So even if the state was entitled to the same federal constitutional immunity in both places, it would seem that neither suit should have been barred. The theory that eluded the state's federal immunity in *Ex parte Young* should equally have eluded the same kind of state immunity in *Crain*. Moreover, the plaintiff in *Crain* sued in state court and was nonetheless able to get to the Supreme Court on direct review. That is proof enough that the Court did not think that the state court suit was barred by state immunity resting on the Constitution. Instead, it seems clear enough that the sovereign immunity defense to the state court suit in *Crain* rested on state law. That understanding, however, suggests yet another account of *Crain*. Perhaps Justice McKenna meant to say only that state-law sovereign immunity could not establish an adequate state ground of decision foreclosing direct review in the Supreme Court.[78] McKenna did not squarely reverse on the ground that it was constitutional error for the state court below to invoke sovereign immunity. He said that since the state court had given effect to a state tax that the plaintiff contended was unconstitutional, the state court's judgment was "reviewable."[79]

Congressional power. If the Constitution itself imposes an obligation on state courts *ceteris paribus*, the only role for Congress is to decide whether to foreclose state court actions by making federal court jurisdiction exclusive.[80] If, by contrast, the Constitution only permits Congress to create an obligation by statute, Congress must exercise some enumerated power—subject to the internal restraints that attend that power.[81] Article

---

75. *Ex parte Young*, 209 U.S. 123 (1908). See Chapter X, notes 283–88 and accompanying text. At that time, moreover, Congress had not yet enacted the Tax Injunction Act, 28 U.S.C. §1341, which now bars federal district courts from restraining the assessment of state taxes if state courts are available to consider taxpayer claims. See Chapter XI, note 35 and accompanying text.

76. The state argued in *McKesson* that its federal constitutional sovereign immunity should bar the Supreme Court from considering a suit for monetary relief on appeal from state court. The Court rejected that idea out of hand in light of settled precedent. *McKesson*, 496 U.S. at 26; see Chapter VII, notes 52–57 and accompanying text (discussing *Cohens v. Virginia*); Chapter X, notes 112–13 and accompanying text (also discussing *Cohens*). It is hard to think that *Crain* was itself a sovereign immunity decision, holding only that the state's federal constitutional immunity did not bar the Supreme Court from accepting appellate jurisdiction in that case.

77. *Alden*, 527 U.S. at 747–48; see Chapter X, notes 166–67 and accompanying text.

78. See Chapter VII, notes 116–99 and accompanying text (discussing the adequate state ground doctrine).

79. Writing for the Court in *McKesson*, Justice Brennan mentioned that the Court's appellate jurisdiction is subject to the adequate state ground doctrine. He did not link that doctrine to *Crain*. *McKesson*, 496 U.S. at 29 n.12.

80. See notes 16–17 and accompanying text.

81. See Chapter IV, text accompanying notes 131–32 (explaining internal and external restraints on congressional power).

III presumably establishes no congressional authority to confer jurisdiction on *state* courts. Statutes like the Emergency Price Control Act in *Testa* rest on one or more of the legislative powers listed in Article I and the Civil War amendments—for example, the power to regulate interstate commerce. It is typically easy enough to show that enactments of that kind are within the internal restraints fixed by the authority Congress invokes. Yet statutes that prescribe jurisdictional work for state courts may touch other limitations on Congress' ability to regulate state institutions—namely, state sovereignty implied in the overarching constitutional structure (and reflected in the tenth amendment).[82] Federal statutes authorizing suits against the states themselves are especially problematic.[83] But statutes authorizing ordinary suits against private defendants may also raise constitutional concerns.

The Supreme Court has held that Congress cannot "commandeer" state legislative and executive authorities as instruments for the enactment and administration of federal programs.[84] In those cases, however, the Court has distinguished *Testa* by name. It appears, then, that Congress can usually compel state courts to entertain federal claims, at least when failure to do so would constitute discrimination against federal law.[85] In *Printz v. United States*,[86] Justice Scalia offered three justifications for the distinction between state legislative and executive authorities, on the one hand, and state courts, on the other: (1) Early federal statutes routinely recruited state courts to service in the implementation of federal programs; (2) the Madisonian Compromise contemplated that state courts would be available if and when inferior federal courts were not; and (3) the Supremacy Clause imposes obligations on state judges that no comparable constitutional provision imposes on local legislative and executive officers.[87] Those explanations can be questioned.[88] Consider, in particular, that the Supremacy Clause is not itself a source of congressional power.[89] Then again, Justice Scalia did not rely on the Su-

---

82. U.S. Const. amend. X: "The powers not delegated to the United States by the Constitution, nor prohibited by it to the States, are reserved to the States respectively, or to the people."

83. See Chapter X (discussing state sovereign immunity).

84. *New York v. United States*, 505 U.S. 144 (1992); *Printz v. United States*, 521 U.S. 898 (1997). See generally Evan H. Caminker, *State Sovereignty and Subordinacy: May Congress Commandeer State Officers to Implement Federal Law?*, 95 Colum. L. Rev. 1001 (1995).

85. See *Alden*, 527 U.S. at 752; see also *Palmore v. United States*, 411 U.S. 389, 402 (1973) (ascribing this proposition to *Testa* itself). Justice Peters has pointed out that it would be difficult for state courts to insist that they are capable of enforcing federal law but at the same time to contend that they cannot be required to exercise that capability. Ellen A. Peters, *Capacity and Respect: A Perspective on the Historic Role of the State Courts in the Federal System*, 73 N.Y.U. L. Rev. 1065 (1998).

86. 521 U.S. 898 (1997).

87. Id. at 928–29. See U.S. Const. art. VI, cl.2 (the Supremacy Clause); Chapter II, note 13 and accompanying text (discussing the Madisonian Compromise).

88. Justice Frankfurter once declared that state court authority to handle federal question cases rests on state, not federal, law and that only state law can "create" state courts and "confer jurisdiction upon them." *Brown v. Gerdes*, 321 U.S. 178, 188 (1944) (concurring opinion). Professor Collins argues that the Court's attempt to distinguish *Testa* is unsuccessful and that cases like *New York* and *Printz* create a solid foundation for an argument that Congress cannot force the states to provide state courts with the jurisdiction necessary to enforce congressional programs. Collins, note 9, at 192.

89. The Supremacy Clause is actually two clauses. The first clause states the proposition for which the Supremacy Clause is typically cited: "This Constitution, and the Laws of the United States which shall be made in Pursuance thereof...shall be the supreme Law of the Land." In *Printz*, Justice Scalia said that clause establishes that valid federal statutes form part of the supreme law of the land, but does not independently ensure that any particular statute is constitutionally sound. 521 U.S. at 924–25. See *Alden*, 527 U.S. at 731 (making the same point). The second clause contains what is often called the State Judges Clause: "[T]he Judges in every State

premacy Clause to establish affirmative congressional authority to act in the first instance. He assumed that Congress could draw upon one of its familiar enumerated powers. He relied on the Supremacy Clause only to rebut any argument that state sovereignty is offended when Congress exercises one of those powers both to enact a federal statute and also to require state courts to entertain lawsuits to enforce it.[90]

Federal law does not affect the activities of state judicial authorities in the way it affects the activities of legislative and executive officers. State courts are not told that they must comply with federal law and that they will be held to account if they fail to do so. They are told, instead, that they must embrace federal law as a rule of decision in cases that come before them. They must enforce that federal law as part of the common system of jurisprudence for which all courts, federal and state, are responsible. This is in keeping with the national unity principle, which has it that state courts are co-equal partners with federal courts. State court judgments on federal questions are subject to appellate (and sometimes collateral) review and may be overturned if found to be erroneous. But disappointed state court litigants cannot simply file federal lawsuits attacking state court decisions in the way they file suits challenging state statutes or the actions of state executive officers. If litigants could do that, state courts would cease to be co-equal judicial tribunals at all, but would instead be additional governmental units whose activities are subject to attack in real courts—namely, federal courts.[91] There is, moreover, a practical explanation for exempting state courts from the anti-commandeering principle. In a variety of contexts, the Court itself channels business into state courts in the name of federalism. It might appear inconsistent, then, to hold that Congress offends federalism when it does essentially the same thing by statute.[92]

If Congress has power to impose jurisdiction on state courts, it follows that the construction the Court places on any particular statute touches delicate federalism concerns. The occasion is ripe for the application of a doctrine of clear statement, which demands clarity regarding Congress' wishes from the text of the enacted statute.[93] As

---

shall be bound thereby, any Thing in the Constitution or Laws of any State to the Contrary notwithstanding." Justice Scalia relied on that clause to support the conclusion that Congress can recruit state courts to service. *Printz*, 521 U.S. at 928–29. The State Judges Clause does not appear to delegate power to Congress, either. It addresses only the duty of state judges to enforce federal statutes whose validity is determined independently. Redish and Sklaver understand Justice Scalia to read the State Judges Clause as a source of congressional power. Martin H. Redish & Steven G. Sklaver, *Federal Power to Commandeer State Courts: Implications for the Theory of Judicial Federalism*, 32 Ind. L. Rev. 71, 82–83 (1998). But that understanding is almost certainly wrong.

90. See Anthony J. Bellia, Jr., *Federal Regulation of State Court Procedures*, 110 Yale L.J. 947, 973–74 (2001).

91. See *Howlett*, 496 U.S. at 369 n.16 (sketching this understanding).

92. See, e.g., Chapter XI, notes 144–295 and accompanying text (discussing the *Younger v. Harris* abstention doctrine). Redish and Sklaver argue that once the Court has recognized congressional power to draft the state courts, the Court must concede that state courts generally adjudicate federal claims not because they are assumed to be the equal of federal courts, but because their availability serves the federal government's purposes. If that is true, according to Redish and Sklaver, then the Court is obliged to rethink an array of doctrines (including *Younger* abstention) that now are said to depend on the parity of state courts. Redish and Sklaver, note 89, at 91–99. See Chapter I, notes 92–104 and accompanying text (discussing the parity debate).

93. See Chapter I, notes 44–52 and accompanying text (discussing the clear statement doctrine); Chapter X, note 233 and accompanying text (discussing the requirement that Congress must satisfy a clear statement rule in order to abrogate a state's federal constitutional immunity from suit). Some *amici* in the *Howlett* case asked the Court to hold that, to the extent the state courts' obligation to entertain §1983 actions rests on §1983 itself (rather than on the Supremacy Clause), the Court

usual, the crucial policy question is the direction in which the clear statement rule should cut. Here again, the Court may be pulled in both directions. Recall that the Court already insists that Congress must specify that state court jurisdiction is *foreclosed* in favor of exclusive federal jurisdiction.[94] That understanding preserves state courts as active participants in the enforcement of federal law. By demanding a clear statement from Congress to impose an *obligation* on state courts, the Court would forgo state court participation in the resolution of cases that state courts, for their own reasons, decline to entertain.[95] At the very least, a doctrine of clear statement working against mandatory state jurisdiction would produce a body of judicial business regarding which state court jurisdiction exists in a purely voluntary form, neither clearly precluded nor clearly demanded by the relevant federal statute.[96]

Valid excuses. Any duty that state courts may have to entertain federal business is subject to exceptions. The Court captures that idea in the valid excuse doctrine, which

---

should require a clear statement from Congress (not found in §1983). See notes 50–56 and accompanying text (discussing *Howlett*). Justice Stevens dismissed that invitation on the ground that the state courts in *Howlett* drew their subject matter jurisdiction from state law. 496 U.S. at 370 n.17. That response was incomplete. Since §1983 is not by nature a jurisdictional statute, it could have imposed no jurisdictional duty on the state courts in any event. See Chapter VIII, note 136 and accompanying text. The basis of the decision in *Howlett* was not that Congress had abrogated the school board's sovereign immunity (as a matter of state law). Nor was it that Congress had itself created state court subject matter jurisdiction. It was that the state of Florida had discriminated to the disadvantage of federal law by insisting on state-law immunity with respect to a federal claim even though it had waived that very state-law immunity with respect to a similar state law claim. Still, Justice Stevens apparently found it important that §1983 authorized the plaintiff in *Howlett* to invoke the state courts' subject matter jurisdiction (grounded in state law) to advance his federal fourth amendment claim.

94. See notes 37–38 and accompanying text.

95. Cf. *Gregory v. Ashcroft*, 501 U.S. 452 (1991) (acknowledging that Congress has power to establish a mandatory retirement age for state employees and to apply it to state judges—but declining to read the ADEA that way in the absence of "unmistakably clear" text). Professor Sandalow contends that the allocation of jurisdiction between federal and state courts is a legislative function and, accordingly, that the Supreme Court should not hold state courts to an obligation to entertain federal business unless Congress clearly establishes such a duty by statute. Terrance Sandalow, *Henry v. Mississippi and the Adequate State Ground: Proposals for a Revised Doctrine*, 1965 Sup. Ct. Rev. 187, 207.

96. Here, too, the Court typically takes account of the availability (or not) of jurisdiction in federal court. In most instances, Congress can and does ensure some forum by opening the federal courts. But see *Intnat'l Science & Tech. Inst. v. Inacom*, 106 F.3d 1146 (4th Cir. 1997) (reading the Telephone Consumer Protection Act to establish exclusive jurisdiction of some actions in state court). In *Hilton v. South Carolina Pub. Ry. Comm'n*, 502 U.S. 197 (1991), the Court declined to invoke a doctrine of clear statement regarding the question whether the Federal Employers Liability Act authorizes private suits for damages against the states in state court. The question in *Hilton* was not (formally) whether Congress had enacted legislation requiring state courts to entertain FELA claims. The state did not set up sovereign immunity to defeat the claim in that case; the state courts dismissed the plaintiff's action on the (mistaken) theory that the FELA gave the plaintiff no right of action to sue (in any court). Moreover, Justice Kennedy explained the result primarily on the ground of *stare decisis*. The Court had previously held that the FELA does establish a private right of action. *Parden v. Terminal Ry.*, 377 U.S. 184 (1964). Finally, Kennedy expressly stated that, apart from the special circumstances in *Hilton*, a doctrine of clear statement would make sense—bringing symmetry and predictability to the law. Nevertheless, the risk that claims might have no judicial home at all plainly affected Kennedy's conclusion that the FELA authorizes private plaintiffs to sue in state court. See Chapter X, note 161 and accompanying text (discussing the Court's treatment of *Hilton* in *Alden v. Maine*); Chapter X, note 256 (noting that the Court has since overruled *Parden*).

figures in all the decisions in this context. Arguments against a state court obligation to adjudicate invariably are couched as arguments that state courts have a valid excuse for declining. To qualify as valid, an excuse must be neutral with respect to the content and character of federal law. When the Court held in *Testa* that Rhode Island courts could not refuse to enforce a federal claim because it reflected an objectionable policy, and equally when the Court held in *Howlett* that Florida courts could not turn a claim away simply because it was federal in nature, the Court stated its conclusion as a determination that the excuses the state courts offered for their actions were invalid.[97] In other instances, the Court has found genuinely neutral excuses to be sufficient. The Court has explained, for example, that the baseline requirement that state courts must treat federal statutes as the supreme law of the land does not require states to create courts competent to entertain a lawsuit in which a claim under federal statute law is presented.[98] Any obligation state courts may have to entertain federal question cases attaches to state courts of general jurisdiction and does not require the states to abandon jurisdictional limitations designed to allocate business among state courts in aid of efficiency.[99]

State procedures. When state courts entertain federal question cases, they must apply the federal law that those cases necessarily entail.[100] Ordinarily, state courts are entitled to employ local procedural rules that differ from the rules that would be followed in the federal courts or in the courts in other states.[101] In keeping with the principle of nondiscrimination, however, there are two conditions: (1) any rules the state courts employ must be the same rules they would apply in cases involving similar state law claims;[102] and (2) the procedural rules state courts use must not undermine the purposes fur-

---

97. *Testa*, 330 U.S. at 392; *Howlett*, 496 U.S. at 371. The valid excuse doctrine resembles the adequate state ground doctrine in the context of Supreme Court appellate jurisdiction. See text accompanying notes 78–79 (discussing that doctrine in connection with the *Crain* case); Chapter VII, notes 116–99 and accompanying text (providing a general discussion). Yet there is an important difference. If a state court's excuse for declining to entertain a federal claim is invalid, the state court has committed error and can be reversed. If, by contrast, a state court's state ground of decision is inadequate, the court has not (necessarily) committed reversible error. It is just that the inadequacy of the state ground permits the Supreme Court to exercise appellate jurisdiction regarding otherwise dispositive federal issues.

98. *Howlett*, 496 U.S. at 372.

99. In *Herb v. Pitcairn*, 324 U.S. 117 (1945), the Court held that a municipal court of limited jurisdiction had a valid excuse for declining to consider a federal FELA claim. In *Missouri ex rel. Southern Ry. Co. v. Mayfield*, 340 U.S. 1 (1950), the Court held that even a state court of general jurisdiction had a valid excuse for declining FELA claims on the theory of *forum non conveniens*, so long as the state court administered that doctrine without disfavoring federal question cases. In the *Inacom* case, the circuit court read the TCPA to allow state courts to decline jurisdiction. *Inacom*, 106 F.3d at 1157–58. According to the circuit court, that defused any constitutional difficulty that might otherwise have attended the Act's assignment of exclusive jurisdiction to those courts. See note 96.

100. *Dice v. Akron, Canton & Youngstown R.R.*, 342 U.S. 359 (1952) (holding that federal law controlled a state court's determination whether a worker had released an employer from liability under FELA).

101. E.g., *Minneapolis & St. Louis R.R. v. Bombolis*, 241 U.S. 211 (1916) (allowing a state court handling a FELA case to follow its usual practice of concluding civil cases on the verdict of a nonunanimous jury even though a unanimous jury would have been necessary if the case had been tried in federal court); see *Central Vermont Ry. Co. v. White*, 238 U.S. 507 (1915) (explaining that state courts can typically apply local rules governing pleading and the admissibility of evidence to FELA cases).

102. E.g., *Felder v. Casey*, 487 U.S. 131 (1988) (perceiving discrimination to the detriment of federal claims where a state court invoked a local notice rule to cut off a §1983 suit).

thered by the substantive federal law the state courts are enforcing.[103] Both those conditions are anchored in constitutional obligation.[104]

In most circumstances, "federal law takes the state courts as it finds them."[105] The Court might have held, on that basis, that state courts can employ any ordinary rules in federal question cases and that if disuniformity ensues Congress is free to shift all such cases to the federal courts. The Supreme Court takes a different view, because the Court plainly *wants* to channel federal question litigation into state court—particularly litigation under the Federal Employers Liability Act (which generates much of the case law in this context). The Court thus finds it essential to keep the state courts from employing procedural rules that discourage litigants from filing suit in the state forum.[106]

C. State Courts and Federal Officials

State courts typically have jurisdiction (granted to them by state law) to adjudicate lawsuits in which federal officers are named as defendants. If the state courts determine that a litigant's claim is meritorious, they equally have power (from the same source) to award appropriate compensatory relief.[107] Nevertheless, in a line of cases stretching back to the Nineteenth Century, the Supreme Court has held that state courts have limited authority to issue coercive orders requiring federal officers to take prescribed action.[108] In two famous instances, the Court reversed state court decisions granting habeas corpus relief to prisoners in the custody of federal officers. The prisoner in *Ableman v. Booth*[109] was an antislavery activist who had been convicted in federal court for a violation of the Fugitive Slave Act. In that case, accordingly, the state court interfered with federal judicial authority. The prisoner in *Tarble's Case*[110] was a soldier who had been re-

---

103. E.g., *Brown v. Western Ry. of Alabama*, 338 U.S. 294 (1949) (holding that strict state pleading requirements imposed "unnecessary burdens" on workers' right to recovery on a FELA claim).

104. The Court appeared to rest its decision in *Felder* at least in part on the Supremacy Clause. *Felder*, 487 U.S. at 150–51. Some academics have suggested that there are limits to Congress' power to prescribe procedural rules for state courts to follow. Here again, those limits may be derived from state sovereignty. See, e.g., Bellia, note 90. Professor Parmet has explored potential constitutional objections to congressionally prescribed rules for state court proceedings on state law claims. Wendy E. Parmet, *Stealth Preemption: The Proposed Federalization of State Court Procedures*, 44 Vill. L. Rev. 1 (1999); see also Louise Weinberg, *The Power of Congress Over Courts in Nonfederal Cases*, 1995 B.Y.U. L. Rev. 731.

105. Henry M. Hart, Jr., *The Relations Between State and Federal Law*, 54 Colum. L. Rev. 489, 508 (1954).

106. Professor Herman's account is exhaustive. Susan N. Herman, *Beyond Parity: Section 1983 and the State Courts*, 54 Brooklyn L. Rev. 1057 (1989). Redish and Sklaver would have the Court go further and (usually) require state courts to employ federal procedural rules when they adjudicate federal claims. Redish & Sklaver, note 89, at 99–110. For a critique, see Vicki C. Jackson, *Printz and Testa: The Infrastructure of Federal Supremacy*, 32 Ind. L. Rev. 111 (1998).

107. E.g., *Teal v. Felton*, 53 U.S. (12 How.) 284 (1852); *Buck v. Colbath*, 70 U.S. (3 Wall.) 334 (1866). Federal officials may, however, avoid liability on the basis of official immunity. See Chapter X, notes 424–94 and accompanying text.

108. See Richard S. Arnold, *The Power of State Courts to Enjoin Federal Officers*, 73 Yale L.J. 1385 (1964); see also Chapter X, notes 21–40 and accompanying text (discussing the ability of federal officers to assert the federal government's sovereign immunity).

109. 62 U.S. (21 How.) 506 (1859).

110. 80 U.S. (13 Wall.) 397 (1872).

cruited when he was too young to serve. There, the state court interfered with federal executive authority.[111]

Justice Field's opinion for the Court in *Tarble's Case* is a classic. Field understood the question to be of fundamental importance: whether "any judicial officer of a State" had "jurisdiction to issue a writ of habeas corpus" or "to continue proceedings under the writ when issued" where the prisoner was held under a claim of federal authority by an officer of the United States.[112] Field answered that question in the negative and gave both constitutional and statutory rationales for his judgment. Initially, he relied on the Constitution of its own force. He said that the state's ability to confer jurisdiction on its courts was "restricted by the Constitution," which established a "sphere of action" for the federal government that was "far beyond the reach of the judicial process issued by a State judge." Wisconsin was "sovereign" within its own borders "to a certain extent," but could not authorize its courts to interfere with the affairs of another "sovereign"—namely, the nation as a whole.[113] In addition, Field insisted that Congress "certainly" had not conferred jurisdiction on state courts to entertain habeas corpus petitions from prisoners challenging the actions of federal officers. Instead, Congress had given that jurisdiction to federal courts (and thus implicitly withheld it from state courts).[114]

The result in *Tarble's Case* can readily be explained. Justice Field was plainly concerned that state courts might disrupt the federal military services by calling federal commanders to account for their recruits.[115] Yet both his rationales have been questioned. By insisting that state courts are constitutionally disabled from checking excesses of federal power, Field neglected the conventional understanding that Congress might never have created the lower federal courts and might have relied, instead, on

111. Ordinarily, prisoners use habeas corpus to challenge unlawful detention in connection with criminal prosecutions. See Chapter XII.

112. 80 U.S. at 402. Justice Field used the term "jurisdiction" in a special way. He did not mean to suggest that the Constitution absolutely bars the states from granting their courts subject matter jurisdiction to adjudicate cases in which federal officers are named as defendants. If that were true, the federal statute giving federal officers the option of removing state court suits against them to federal court would be unintelligible. See text accompanying notes 136–38. Field had in mind the special circumstances of a habeas corpus action, in which a court's authority to act (in the subject matter jurisdiction sense) is inextricably linked to its authority to issue a special kind of remedy. Under common law procedure, a court issued the writ of habeas corpus immediately upon receiving a petition. The writ's function was to require the custodian to justify a prisoner's detention. It thus immediately purported to coerce the custodian into action. If the court concluded that the custodian's explanation was inadequate, the court issued a further order actually requiring the custodian to release the prisoner. This is why Justice Field's statement of the question in *Tarble's Case* covered both the state court's issuance of the writ in the first instance and subsequent proceedings "under the writ"—including, of course, the state court's ultimate order that the soldier must be discharged. It is common to refer to a court's "jurisdiction" to issue both common law writs like habeas corpus and equitable remedies like injunctions. In the case of injunctions, use of the "jurisdiction" label can be traced back to the time in this country and in England when only courts of equity had power to issue equitable relief. See *Steel Co. v. Citizens for a Better Environment*, 523 U.S. 83, 90 (1998) (noting that it is "commonplace" even today to use the term "jurisdiction" to mean the authority to issue a particular form of relief).

113. 80 U.S. at 405–06.

114. Id. See Chapter II, note 57 and accompanying text (discussing the provision in the Judiciary Act of 1789 granting the federal courts jurisdiction to entertain habeas corpus petitions from federal prisoners).

115. The case was decided immediately following the Civil War, and the Court explicitly recognized that "in times of great popular excitement" opponents might use state courts to "embarrass the operations of the government." 80 U.S. at 408.

state courts to police the system, subject to appellate review by the Supreme Court.[116] By depicting separate sovereign spheres for the states and the federal government, Field dismissed the vision of national unity that typically animates the modern Court's discussions of state court jurisdiction.[117] And by drawing a negative inference from congressional silence, he overlooked the more conventional default position: state court jurisdiction is concurrent, unless Congress specifies that federal jurisdiction is exclusive.[118] Moreover, if Field meant to acknowledge that Congress might have conferred jurisdiction on the courts of Wisconsin, it is hard to understand how he could also propose that the Constitution of its own force barred that very jurisdiction. In the end, Justice Field presumably meant to hold that state court authority in *Tarble's Case* was simply incompatible with the federal interests at stake.[119]

It is unclear whether *Ableman* and *Tarble's Case* reach far beyond their particular context.[120] The Court held in *Donovan v. City of Dallas*[121] that a state court cannot enjoin a private litigant from filing a lawsuit in federal court. In that case, Justice Black (like Justice Field before him) relied both on an apparent constitutional ground and on congressional silence. He explained that Congress had "in no way relaxed the old and well-established judicially declared rule that state courts are completely without power to restrain federal-court proceedings."[122] The Court has refused to allow a state court to direct a writ of mandamus to a federal officer, but has permitted state courts to entertain other kinds of actions in which federal officers may be given orders with which they must comply.[123] The uncertainties that attend the decisions from *Ableman* and

---

116. See Chapter II, notes 13–14 and accompanying text; Chapter IV, notes 51–52 and accompanying text; Chapter XII, notes 15–37 and accompanying text (discussing the Suspension Clause).

117. See text accompanying notes 3–15, 40–48.

118. See notes 37–38 and accompanying text.

119. See text accompanying note 28.

120. Professor Collins cites *Tarble's Case* as evidence that state courts were not always thought to have capacity to adjudicate all the cases to which Article III extends. Collins, note 9, at 103. Redish and Woods once argued that the tension between *Tarble's Case* and the Madisonian Compromise demonstrates that Congress has a constitutional duty to establish inferior federal courts, after all—to shoulder responsibility in cases in which state courts cannot act. Martin H. Redish & Curtis E. Woods, *Congressional Power to Control the Jurisdiction of Lower-Federal Courts: A Critical Review and a New Synthesis*, 124 U. Pa. L. Rev. 45 (1975). More recently, Professor Redish has advanced the view that Congress can divest state courts of jurisdiction, if the federal courts are open. Martin H. Redish, *Constitutional Limitations on Congressional Power to Control Federal Jurisdiction: A Reply to Professor Sager*, 77 Nw. U. L. Rev. 143, 159 (1982). Professor Amar insists that *Tarble's Case* cannot be understood to deny state court jurisdiction as a constitutional matter, but can only be read to mean that Congress can make jurisdiction in that kind of case exclusive in the federal courts. Amar laments, however, any sentiment that only federal courts are suitable to check abuses by federal officers. He proposes, instead, that state courts should routinely do so on the basis of their own independent jurisdiction under state law. Akhil R. Amar, *Of Sovereignty and Federalism*, 96 Yale L.J. 1425, 1428 & 1510 (1987). Professor Fallon and Professor Meltzer understand this line of cases to represent the Court's effort to develop a federal common law of remedies that orchestrates delicate relations between the federal government and the states. See Richard H. Fallon, Jr. & Daniel J. Meltzer, *New Law, Non-Retroactivity, and Constitutional Remedies*, 104 Harv. L. Rev. 1731 (1991); Daniel J. Meltzer, *State Court Forfeitures of Federal Rights*, 99 Harv. L. Rev. 1128 (1986).

121. 377 U.S. 408 (1964).

122. Id. at 413; see Chapter XI, notes 7–29, 144–295 and accompanying text (discussing federal court injunctions that interfere with state court proceedings).

123. E.g., *Slocum v. Mayberry*, 15 U.S. (2 Wheat.) 1 (1817) (holding that a state court could issue a writ of replevin requiring federal customs officials to return property they had seized). See Arnold, note 108, at 1397 (expressing confidence that state courts can award specific relief in cases involving the possession of property).

Tarble's Case through *Donovan* may explain why the Court has never squarely decided whether state courts can issue injunctions directing federal officers to take specified action.[124]

D. Protections for State Court Jurisdiction

In most instances, then, state courts have both the authority and the obligation to adjudicate federal questions, and when they conclude that a federal claim is meritorious, they typically can award the winning party an appropriate remedy. The exceptions to these generalizations are important, but they are nonetheless exceptions. In keeping with this pattern, state jurisdiction, once invoked, is largely insulated from interference by the federal courts. There are three reasons why litigants who choose to sue in state court in the first instance can typically expect that their cases will proceed to judgment there and that the decisions the state courts render will be effectively final: (1) the removal of lawsuits to federal court for trial is tightly guarded; (2) state judgments are usually entitled to preclusive effect in later federal court actions; and (3) appellate review in federal court is limited to the Supreme Court.

1. Limited Removal

A few federal statutes authorize suits that begin in state court to be "removed" to federal court. Historically, some statutes authorized either the plaintiff or the defendant to seek removal, even after judgment in state court.[125] The statutes in place today permit only the defendant to remove, and then only before trial.[126] Removal is available in diversity cases, but typically bears more theoretical significance in federal question cases—where its limited scope underscores the general understanding that state court adjudication of federal claims will usually proceed undisturbed.[127]

Federal removal jurisdiction is a cousin of federal exclusive jurisdiction. The difference is that when federal jurisdiction is exclusive, Congress forecloses litigation in state court altogether and gives litigants no say in the matter. In the case of removal, state courts have jurisdiction in the first instance, but the defendant can force them to surrender that jurisdiction to federal courts. The rationale for removal jurisdiction is sometimes quite clear, sometimes obscure. Removal is ostensibly permitted when state proceedings threaten federal interests enough to warrant an exception to the

124. Cf. *Brooks v. Dewar*, 313 U.S. 354, 360 (1941) (declining to decide the question).

125. See Michael G. Collins, *The Unhappy History of Federal Question Removal*, 71 Iowa L. Rev. 717, 720 (1986).

126. The Court held in *Shamrock Oil & Gas Corp. v. Sheets*, 313 U.S. 100 (1941), that a plaintiff cannot remove on the basis of a defendant's counterclaim.

127. Under 28 U.S.C. §1441(c), if a "separate and independent" federal claim over which a federal court would have jurisdiction is joined in state court with a claim that would not be removable, the "entire case" can be removed. For a discussion of that provision and its controversial history, see Edward A. Hartnett, *A New Trick from an Old and Abused Dog: Section 1441(c) Lives and Now Permits the Remand of Federal Question Cases*, 63 Fordham L. Rev. 1099 (1995). The procedures for removal are prescribed by 28 U.S.C. §§1446–48.

usual pattern, but not enough to warrant a blanket prohibition on state court adjudication.

Removal in ordinary civil cases. The principal modern removal statute, 28 U.S.C. §1441, is derived from the Judiciary Act of 1875 and important amendments adopted in 1887.[128] It authorizes a defendant in a civil lawsuit initiated in state court to transfer the case to a federal district court, but only if the federal court would have had jurisdiction to entertain the case if the plaintiff had chosen to go there originally.[129] This means that in federal question cases the plaintiff's claim, initially advanced in state court, must "arise under" federal law within the meaning of 28 U.S.C. §1331, which governs the federal district courts' original jurisdiction in federal question cases.[130]

One might have expected §1441 to allow removal at the defendant's behest if the *defendant* offers a federal theory in response to the plaintiff's allegations. A rule of that kind would ensure that litigants with affirmative federal claims can gain access to federal court. It would initially allow a plaintiff who has a federal claim the option of suing either in state or federal court, but would allow a defendant who has a federal defense or counterclaim to override the plaintiff's choice of the state forum. Instead, §1441 makes a defendant's ability to trump the plaintiff's decision to sue in state court contingent on the nature of the *plaintiff's* claim. It thus vindicates a defendant's desire to be in federal court in hopes of *defeating* a federal theory advanced by the plaintiff, but forces a defendant who has a federal theory to raise as a defense to submit that theory to the state courts.[131] The practical implication of pegging removal to the plaintiff's claim is clear. Litigants typically must advance any federal theories they wish to present in federal court as original actions filed in a district court pursuant to §1331. If they wait to advance federal theories as defendants in state court, §1441 will be unavailing. The idea may be to prevent defendants from injecting minor federal issues into cases in order to

---

128. See Chapter II, text accompanying notes 58, 72. Professor Collins has explored the 1887 legislation. Collins, note 125, at 735.

129. Federal jurisdiction pursuant to §1441 is constitutionally valid. The presence of the plaintiff's federal claim renders a removable lawsuit a case "arising under" federal law within the meaning of Article III. See Chapter VIII, notes 5–17 and accompanying text.

130. See Chapter VIII, notes 231–90 and accompanying text (discussing the prerequisites for original §1331 jurisdiction); Chapter XI, text accompanying note 167 (discussing the relationship between this feature of removal under §1441 and the federal-question abstention doctrine). In some instances, a lawsuit in state court is little more than a rehash of previous litigation in federal court. Yet the defendant may be unable to remove under §1441 because the plaintiff in state court could not have begun in federal court pursuant to §1331. Nor can the defendant in state court obtain a writ from a federal court, issued pursuant to the All-Writs Act, 28 U.S.C. §1651, which has the effect of moving matters to the federal forum. *Syngenta Crop Prot. v. Henson*, 2002 WL 31453983 (U.S. Sup. Ct. 2002). See Chapter II, note 58 (quoting the All-Writs Act); Chapter VIII, notes 402–22 and accompanying text (discussing federal supplemental jurisdiction). Recall that the All-Writs Act does not itself establish federal court jurisdiction, but can only piggyback on some other basis of judicial power to act in a case. Moreover, the defendant's proper remedy is not a federal writ that operates as a *de facto* removal order, but rather one that serves as an injunction that prohibits the plaintiff in state court from proceeding further. See Chapter XI, notes 7–29 and accompanying text (discussing the Anti-Injunction Act). For academic commentaries anticipating the decision in *Henson*, see, e.g., Lonny S. Hoffman, *Removal Jurisdiction and the All Writs Act*, 148 U. Pa. L. Rev. 401 (1999); Joan Steinman, *The Newest Frontier of Judicial Activism: Removal Under the All Writs Act*, 80 B.U. L. Rev. 773 (2000).

131. Professor Wechsler explained that §1441 permits a litigant to invoke federal jurisdiction as a "sword" but not as a "shield." Herbert Wechsler, *Federal Jurisdiction and the Revision of the Judicial Code*, 13 Law & Contemp. Prob. 216, 234 (1948).

obtain removal, thus transferring lawsuits to federal court even when state issues predominate. Nevertheless, this feature of §1441 has often been criticized.[132]

The link between removal jurisdiction under §1441 and original jurisdiction under §1331 leads to curiosities in the law of federal courts: Questions regarding the original jurisdiction of federal district courts pursuant to §1331 are often raised not in cases in which plaintiffs genuinely seek access to federal court, but in cases in which they, instead, choose to proceed in state court and defendants wish to transfer the litigation to the federal forum.[133] Moreover, in some instances, plaintiffs characterize their claims as matters of state law, and defendants attempt to recharacterize those claims as federal in nature in order to obtain removal under §1441. On the whole, litigants are masters of the theories they wish to advance.[134] Yet there are limits. Some complaints necessarily press federal claims, because federal law preempts any state law that would otherwise control. Where that is true, defendants may remove, even if plaintiffs themselves regard their claims as matters of state law.[135]

Removal by federal officers. Another statute, 28 U.S.C. §1442, allows removal of either civil or criminal actions initiated in state court against the federal government itself or one of its agencies or officers. That removal provision dates from 1815.[136] It plainly reflects concern that federal interests might be compromised if federal officials were forced to defend themselves against claims and charges in state court. In *Tennessee v. Davis*,[137] for example, a federal revenue officer was indicted for murder after a shoot-out with moonshiners in the hills of Tennessee. The Supreme Court sustained the officer's ability to remove the case to federal court.[138]

The constitutional basis of removal under §1442 has excited theoretical interest. If the officer concerned raises an explicit federal defense, there is no difficulty. That defense supplies a federal issue on which the federal court can exercise Article III power, once the prosecution (itself anchored in state law) is removed to the federal forum. If the officer advances only a state law defense, the case is altered. In that event, the federal court's constitutional authority to adjudicate only state law issues is open to question. By some accounts, the district court can exercise "protective jurisdiction." The idea is that Congress might have enacted a body of federal substantive law to govern all aspects of a federal officer's field of operations, displacing state law and transforming all issues into federal questions. That would be extreme, however, and unwarranted as a matter

132. E.g., Herman L. Trautman, *Federal Right Jurisdiction and the Declaratory Remedy*, 7 Vand. L. Rev. 445, 471 (1954); Wechsler, note 131, at 224. The American Law Institute has recommended that removal be made available in most instances on the basis of a dispositive federal defense or counterclaim. ALI, Study of the Division of Jurisdiction Between State and Federal Courts 25 (1969). Meanwhile, the precedents relentlessly deny removal in the most compelling circumstances.

133. See Chapter VIII, text accompanying notes 250–51 (explaining that the removal posture in which cases are presented can complicate the elaboration of §1331).

134. See Chapter VIII, note 261 and accompanying text (noting the Court's classic precedents in point).

135. See Chapter VIII, notes 388–401 and accompanying text.

136. Today, most tort claims in state court against federal officers operating in the course of their official duties are handled under 28 U.S.C. §2679, which substitutes the United States as the formal defendant and requires removal to federal court.

137. 100 U.S. (10 Otto) 257 (1879).

138. The Court rejected the contention that removal invaded state sovereignty. In this context, of course, there is no argument that Congress has "commandeered" the state courts. See notes 84–90 and accompanying text. Instead, Congress has made federal jurisdiction available for suits initiated in state court.

of policy. Accordingly, Congress should be entitled to take the modest step of providing for federal court adjudication of any disputes that arise, even though the only issues to be decided are matters of state law.[139]

The protective jurisdiction idea has considerable appeal. In *Davis*, for example, federal interests were at risk if local authorities pursued a federal revenue officer with questionable criminal charges, irrespective of the precise defense the officer raised. Local hostility to federal policies of all kinds might play itself out in a pattern of harassing state court lawsuits instituted to frustrate federal officers' enforcement efforts. Nevertheless, protective jurisdiction theory has been questioned. It reflects the "greater power" syllogism, and to that extent it is analytically troubling.[140] Moreover, it invites expansive application and ultimately threatens the body of case law regarding the prerequisites for federal question jurisdiction in the federal courts.[141] In *Mesa v. California*,[142] the Supreme Court disposed of the protective jurisdiction idea in this context by reading §1442 to authorize removal only when a federal officer actually asserts a "colorable" federal defense.[143]

Civil rights removal. One final statute, 28 U.S.C. §1443(1), permits private litigants to remove if they are "denied or cannot enforce" a "right under any law providing for the equal civil rights of citizens of the United States."[144] That provision was originally enacted during Reconstruction, but saw little use or attention until the desegregation movement.[145] In the 1960s, civil rights workers routinely invoked §1443(1) to extricate themselves from prosecutions in state court arising from their participation in protest demonstrations. They insisted (with some justice) that they were being harassed for activities that were protected by the Constitution and federal civil rights laws and that state courts would not respect their federal defenses. Accordingly, they argued that they

---

139. See Wechsler, note 131, at 224–25; Carole Goldberg-Ambrose, *The Protective Jurisdiction of the Federal Courts*, 30 U.C.L.A. L. Rev. 542 (1983). Professor Mishkin advances the more cautious argument that protective jurisdiction can safely be acknowledged, but only if Congress gives the federal courts jurisdiction to consider state law claims in a field in which Congress has previously deployed a "developed" and "active" federal regulatory policy. Paul J. Mishkin, *The Federal Question in the District Courts*, 53 Colum. L. Rev. 157, 195 (1953). For another discussion of protective jurisdiction, see Chapter VIII, notes 21–24 and accompanying text.

140. See Chapter I, notes 26–28 and accompanying text.

141. See Chapter VIII, notes 252–90 and accompanying text (describing the relevant precedents).

142. 489 U.S. 121 (1989).

143. Id. at 139. On examination, Justice O'Connor said that the defense in *Davis* (self-defense) was essentially federal in nature inasmuch as the officer contended that he had a federal duty to respond to hostile gunfire while he was investigating an unlawful distillery. O'Connor invoked the prudential rule that statutes should be construed to avoid constitutional questions whenever possible, see Chapter I, text accompanying note 26, and said that the protective jurisdiction theory would raise a "grave constitutional problem." 489 U.S. at 137. The Court has explained that an officer advances a "colorable" federal defense if there is a causal connection between the conduct over which the officer is sued and a plausible claim of official duty. *Jefferson County v. Acker*, 527 U.S. 423 (1999) (finding it sufficient that federal judges contended that they had a federal defense against a state court suit to force them to pay a local license tax).

144. Subsection (2) of §1443 allows removal if defendants are prosecuted for "any act under color of authority derived from any law providing for equal rights, or for refusing to do any act on the ground that it would be inconsistent with such law." That provision is available only to federal or state officers, or to private citizens acting in concert with them. *City of Greenwood v. Peacock*, 384 U.S. 808 (1966). Accordingly, it overlaps significantly with §1442. See notes 136–43 and accompanying text.

145. See Robert D. Goldstein, *Blyew: Variations on a Jurisdictional Theme*, 41 Stan. L. Rev. 469 (1989).

were entitled to remove the actions against them to federal court in order that the federal courts could enforce their federal rights.[146] Ultimately, the Supreme Court construed §1443(1) so narrowly that removal under that statute became virtually impossible.

In *Georgia v. Rachel*,[147] Justice Stewart explained that it is not enough for a defendant to show, on the basis of evidence in a particular case, that federal rights will not be respected in state court. Removal is available under §1443(1) only if some state "law of general application" demonstrates that "specific" federal rights "stated in terms of racial equality" will be denied if the state prosecution is allowed to proceed.[148] In the typical case, a defendant must show that a particular federal anti-discrimination rule will not be respected in state court, because the state courts will follow a state statute or demonstrable state policy that frustrates that rule. Stewart found it insufficient that the civil rights workers in *Rachel* alleged that the state courts would not enforce their federal rights to free speech and due process. Those rights were implicated in *Rachel*, but they were not "stated in terms of racial equality" within the meaning of §1443(1).[149] Nor did it appear that a state statute or policy would prevent the state courts from giving those rights their proper scope.

Justice Stewart insisted that his interpretation of §1443(1) would not deprive it of all meaning and that some defendants would be able to meet the admittedly stringent standards that *Rachel* put in place. To illustrate, he cited *Strauder v. West Virginia*,[150] where the Court had allowed removal to protect a criminal defendant's right to a jury chosen without discrimination on the basis of race, guaranteed by the Civil Rights Act of 1866. In that case, a West Virginia statute flatly barred African Americans from serving on juries. In *Virginia v. Rives*,[151] by contrast, the Court had denied removal where, in the absence of a similar statute, defendants could allege only that the authorities in Virginia would, in fact, select a jury in a discriminatory way. According to Justice Stewart, the difference between *Strauder* and *Rives* is crucial to removal under §1443(1). In the one case, a state statute required the state courts to conduct a trial in violation of a federal right "stated in terms of racial equality." In the other, state law did not mandate disrespect for federal rights of that kind.

There was a plausible argument that *Rachel* itself was attracted by *Strauder* rather than *Rives*. The defendants in *Rachel* contended that the Civil Rights Act of 1964 established their right to use places of public accommodation and thus qualified as a federal anti-discrimination rule. Moreover, they were charged under a state statute making it a criminal offense to refuse to leave a restaurant on request. By their account, that statute authorized criminal prosecution for the mere exercise of rights protected by the 1964 Act. Accordingly, they argued that they were entitled to removal even under Stewart's

146. Professor Amsterdam devised the strategy of using §1443 in the cause of the civil rights movement. See Anthony G. Amsterdam, *Criminal Prosecutions Affecting Federally Guaranteed Rights: Federal Removal and Habeas Corpus Jurisdiction to Abort State Court Trial*, 113 U. Pa. L. Rev. 793 (1965).

147. 384 U.S. 780 (1966).

148. Id. at 800.

149. Justice Stewart did not say, nor has the Court since decided, whether the Equal Protection Clause provides a sufficiently "specific" federal anti-discrimination rule for purposes of §1443(1). The Court has held that 18 U.S.C. §245 does not support removal under §1443(1). *Johnson v. Mississippi*, 421 U.S. 213 (1975). That statute bars interference with federal rights, but only "by force or threat of violence." Thus it does not immunize defendants from prosecution in state court.

150. 100 U.S. 303 (1879).

151. 100 U.S. 313 (1879).

grudging construction of §1443(1). Stewart acknowledged that argument and remanded the case for a hearing on whether the defendants had been asked to leave "solely for racial reasons" and therefore could argue that the very initiation of state criminal proceedings violated the 1964 Act. In a companion case, however, Justice Stewart made it clear that §1443(1) will not allow removal in more routine cases. The civil rights workers in *City of Greenwood v. Peacock*[152] were charged with a range of state offenses, including obstructing public streets and driving without a valid operator's permit. Neither the 1964 Act nor the Equal Protection Clause insulated them from prosecution for those offenses. They were able to contend only that they were being harassed by local authorities because of their political activities and that they were likely to be convicted after a racially charged trial. Given *Rachel*, that was insufficient.

The distinction Justice Stewart drew between *Strauder* and *Rives* and, in turn, between *Rachel* and *Peacock* is problematic. The rationale is that state courts cannot be expected to defy a state statute of general application, but *can* be expected to prevent state officials from violating federal rights *ad hoc.* Yet if a state statute conflicts with federal law, the state courts may be *more* likely (not less) to recognize and enforce defendants' federal rights. Accordingly, there may be *less* (not more) reason to allow removal. If, then, the idea is to avoid disparaging state courts' ability and inclination to respect federal rights, the Court's construction of §1443(1) is counterproductive. Consider, however, that the facial validity of a statute is a legal matter that can be determined without exploring case-specific factual allegations. Accordingly, removal in that instance can be accomplished quickly and efficiently.[153]

The Court might have brought the process model to bear in *Rachel* and *Peacock.*[154] The Court might have read §1443(1) to deny removal in routine cases in which defendants insist that they will be treated unfairly in state court, but to allow removal in extraordinary cases in which defendants demonstrate that state court proceedings will not provide an opportunity for "full and fair" adjudication of a federal defense.[155] Yet it is hardly surprising that the Court declined to adopt that approach. The civil rights workers in *Rachel* and *Peacock* presented a sympathetic case for removal. Yet their arguments for wider removal authority could not easily be limited to the civil rights context and threatened to reach ordinary criminal prosecutions in which defendants assert that state courts will not properly adjudicate federal defenses.[156] The states have a powerful inter-

152. 384 U.S. 808 (1966).

153. The state statute in *Rachel* itself was not unconstitutional on its face, but was only susceptible to unconstitutional application if invoked against customers asked to leave the premises solely because of race. Justice Stewart explained, however, that if, on remand, the plaintiffs proved that they had been asked to leave only because they were African Americans, the very initiation of any criminal charges against them would frustrate their federal rights. So a federal district court would find it easy to decide, on the basis of a pending state prosecution, that the plaintiffs were denied a fair opportunity to enforce those rights in state court.

154. See Chapter I, notes 73–77 and accompanying text.

155. Martin H. Redish, *Revitalizing Civil Rights Removal Jurisdiction*, 64 Minn. L. Rev. 523 (1980).

156. Recall in this vein that defendants may often have fourteenth amendment arguments to advance, at least with respect to state court procedures. Justice Stewart was acutely aware of the risk that a more generous interpretation of §1443(1) might open the floodgates. He noted in a footnote that the rate of removal petitions under that statute had risen dramatically in recent years—particularly in the South (where Professor Amsterdam's strategy was pursued routinely on behalf of civil rights workers). 384 U.S. at 788 n.8. See note 146.

est in vindicating local criminal law policy in their own courts. It would be disruptive to require state authorities to respond to allegations that state processes are flawed. Certainly, it would be revolutionary to allow defendants actually to remove ordinary prosecutions to federal court for trial.[157]

Justice Stewart explained in *Peacock* that state criminal defendants may have recourse to federal district courts by other means. In some circumstances, defendants may file suit in a federal district court pursuant to the Ku Klux Klan Act (42 U.S.C. §1983), seeking an injunction against a state prosecution.[158] And, under some conditions, defendants who are in some form of custody may be entitled to petition a federal court for a writ of habeas corpus.[159] Those alternatives threaten the states' ability to enforce local policy in state court in much the same manner as would removal. Yet they, too, are restricted in ways that mitigate the effect on state court jurisdiction. In some respects, the process model *does* help to explain the doctrines that attend §1983 actions and habeas corpus petitions.[160]

In the end, the Court's general acceptance of state court authority and responsibility for federal question litigation explains why removal is not routinely available. Once it is posited (as it conventionally is) that state courts are routinely open for federal question cases, and it is assumed (as it usually is) that those courts are the equal of federal courts for these purposes, then it is unremarkable that defendants in state court should typically be unable to remove litigation to federal court. Removal jurisdiction by its nature connotes some concern that state court proceedings will put federal interests at risk. If the Court perceives no such risks, the Court will find no justification for reading an ambiguous statute to upset conventional arrangements.

2. Preclusion

When litigation on a federal question proceeds to judgment in state court, a party who is disappointed in the outcome usually cannot try again in federal court. The opposing party can typically defeat a later federal lawsuit that attempts to address issues the state courts treated (or might have treated) previously. In subsequent suits of that kind, the Full Faith and Credit Statute, 28 U.S.C. §1738, instructs the federal courts to give previous state court judgments the preclusive effect that state law would accord

157. The Court's attention to federalism, not to mention the federal caseload crisis, counsels against such a significant departure. See Chapter I, notes 19–25 and accompanying text (discussing federalism); Chapter II, notes 83–108 and accompanying text (discussing docket congestion in the federal courts). See also Chapter XI, text accompanying note 167 (discussing the relationship between removal in criminal cases and the federal-question abstention doctrine). Alternatively, the Court might have read §1443(1) to authorize removal for want of exacting language to the contrary. See Chapter I, notes 44–52 and accompanying text. Yet when the doctrine of clear statement appears in this context, it typically cuts in favor of state court jurisdiction. E.g., notes 37–38 and accompanying text.

158. See text accompanying note 51; Chapter II, notes 74–75 and accompanying text (noting the history behind §1983 and the many places in modern practice in which §1983 plays a role).

159. See Chapter XII, notes 75–88 and accompanying text.

160. See Chapter XI, notes 195–203 and accompanying text (discussing the role the process model plays in conditioning federal injunctions against pending state court proceedings); Chapter XII, notes 89–131, 299–302 and accompanying text (discussing the exhaustion doctrine and the process model in connection with the availability of federal habeas corpus).

them.[161] Preclusion is not a jurisdictional bar to federal court action.[162] Yet if it is asserted in a timely fashion, it is devastating.[163]

In effect, §1738 incorporates state preclusion law for application in federal court. That local law can vary in its details from state to state, but typically respects central propositions. In the main, a final judgment cannot be reopened in subsequent litigation between the same parties or their privies. Along one branch of conventional doctrine, denominated "collateral estoppel" or "issue preclusion," issues of fact or law that were actually determined in an initial action typically may not be relitigated. Along a second branch, denominated "res judicata" or "claim preclusion," issues of fact or law that might have been (but were not) raised and determined in initial proceedings regarding the same transaction typically cannot be revived in a later action. Of the two kinds of preclusion, claim preclusion is plainly the more powerful. Where it operates, a question may receive no judicial attention at all.[164]

Within a single jurisdiction, preclusion makes a great deal of sense. It protects the parties' reliance interests and conserves judicial resources. Any attendant unfairness can be handled by recognizing appropriate exceptions. Typically, an initial judgment is entitled to preclusive effect only if the party affected is accorded an opportunity for "full and fair" adjudication.[165] In this, state preclusion law reflects the process model, albeit in a different context and for a different purpose.[166] Across jurisdictional lines, however, the unexamined application of a particular state's preclusion doctrine can be questioned. The Full Faith and Credit Statute employs state preclusion law to adjust the relations between state and federal courts. In issue preclusion cases, it fortifies state court decisions regarding federal questions by preventing relitigation in federal court. In claim preclusion cases, it forecloses the adjudication of federal questions in any forum.

The Supreme Court has not always been clear that §1738 (and thus state preclusion law) controls cases in which federal courts are asked to adjudicate issues that were or

161. The Full Faith and Credit Clause, U.S. Const. art. IV, §1, provides: "Full Faith and Credit shall be given in each State to the public Acts, Records, and judicial Proceedings of every other State." It also empowers Congress to "prescribe" the manner in which such judgments are proved "and the Effect thereof." Pursuant to that authority, Congress enacted §1738 in 1790 as one of its first statutes touching the federal courts. Modern amendments to §1738 specify the full faith and credit that a state owes to child support orders entered in a sister state (a good deal) and to marriages between "persons of the same sex" (none). The Full Faith and Credit Statute does not address the preclusive effects of federal court judgments. If a judgment by a federal court is challenged subsequently either in another federal court or in a state court, the follow-on court will give the previous judgment preclusive effect, relying on federal common law both for the initial proposition that the previous judgment is entitled to preclusive effect and for the content of the preclusion rules to be applied. E.g., *Federated Dep't Stores v. Moitie*, 452 U.S. 394 (1981); *Blonder-Tongue Labs. v. University of Illinois Found.*, 402 U.S. 313 (1971). Then again, the Court sometimes borrows state law as the content of that federal common law. E.g., *Semtek v. Lockheed*, 531 U.S. 497 (2001). For a discussion, see Stephen B. Burbank, *Interjurisdictional Preclusion, Full Faith and Credit and Federal Common Law: A General Approach*, 71 Cornell L. Rev. 733 (1986). See Chapter VIII, notes 47–119 and accompanying text (discussing federal common law).

162. Fed. R. Civ. P. 8(c) (identifying preclusion as an "affirmative defense"); see *Arizona v. California*, 530 U.S. 392, 410 (2000) (explaining that litigants cannot "wake up" and assert preclusion after the time for raising that defense has expired).

163. Preclusion must be compared and contrasted with the *Rooker/Feldman* doctrine. See notes 196–225 and accompanying text.

164. By hypothesis, the first court to consider the parties' dispute did not address the question, and the second court deliberately declines to consider it.

165. See *Richards v. Jefferson County*, 517 U.S. 793, 801 (1996).

166. See Chapter I, notes 73–77 and accompanying text.

might have been addressed in previous state court judgments. In *Allen v. McCurry*,[167] Justice Stewart suggested that a general body of preclusion law might be in play. More recently, however, the Court has insisted that state preclusion law is the first, and typically the last, authority to be consulted. In *Marrese v. Amer. Academy of Orth. Surgeons*,[168] for example, a physician initially sued in state court, contending that the Academy's refusal to admit him to membership violated state law. When that lawsuit failed, he filed a new action in federal court, contending that the Academy had violated federal anti-trust laws. The state courts would have had no authority to consider the anti-trust claim if it had been advanced in the first suit. Accordingly, it was unlikely that state preclusion law would have anything to say about the effects of failing to press such a claim. Nevertheless, Justice O'Connor explained that §1738 required the federal court to "look first to state preclusion law" in hopes that its treatment of analogous issues should throw some light on the problem.[169]

Other federal statutes can trump §1738 and thus allow federal courts to entertain new federal actions, despite previous state court judgments. The statute conferring jurisdiction on federal courts to hear habeas corpus petitions, 28 U.S.C. §2241, has that effect.[170] But neither the Ku Klux Klan Act (§1983) nor Title VII of the Civil Rights Act of 1964 exempts lawsuits filed under their authority from §1738 and state preclusion rules.[171] In *McCurry*, a prisoner was charged with a criminal offense in state court. He moved to suppress evidence allegedly obtained by an unconstitutional search. The state courts denied the motion, and the prisoner was convicted. Ordinarily, a prisoner in custody pur-

---

167. 449 U.S. 90 (1980).

168. 470 U.S. 373 (1985).

169. If state preclusion law turns out to be silent on the matter, a federal court presumably must look elsewhere. Justice O'Connor suggested in *Marrese* that if the policies furthered by the federal courts' exclusive jurisdiction of a class of claims warrants it, courts may read the statutes conferring that exclusive jurisdiction to constitute an "implied repeal" of §1738. 470 U.S. at 381. Suspending preclusion might be sensible in many contexts, but not necessarily in all. Typically, a litigant who possesses a claim over which the federal courts have exclusive jurisdiction is in a position to file a federal court suit advancing that claim in the first instance, invoking the federal court's supplemental jurisdiction of related state law claims. See Chapter VIII, notes 402–22 and accompanying text. If, then, a litigant goes first to state court, it is not always unjust to preclude resort to federal court later (and thus to foreclose the federal claim altogether). In *Matsushita Elec. Indus. Co. v. Epstein*, 516 U.S. 367 (1996), a state court approved a settlement in a class action case, which appeared to preclude members of the class from pressing federal claims against the defendant in independent litigation—including federal claims that were within the exclusive jurisdiction of the federal courts. The Supreme Court held that the preclusive effects of the state court's ruling must be determined according to the preclusion rules the state would apply to the settlement. For commentary, see Marcel Kahan & Linda Silberman, *Matsushita and Beyond: The Role of State Courts in Class Actions Involving Exclusive Federal Claims*, 1996 Sup. Ct. Rev. 219.

170. *Kremer v. Chem. Constr. Corp.*, 456 U.S. 461, 485 n.27 (1982); see Chapter XII, note 4 and accompanying text.

171. *McCurry*, 449 U.S. at 104–05 (§1983); *Kremer*, 456 U.S. at 467–76 (Title VII). In *Kremer*, a worker filed an employment discrimination claim with the appropriate state agency and, when his claim was rejected, a lawsuit in state court. When the state courts, too, denied relief, he filed a Title VII action in federal court, arguing that Title VII entitled him to *de novo* federal court consideration of his claim, despite the previous state court judgment. Justice White refused to read Title VII to "repeal" §1738 by implication and thus instructed the district court below to consult state preclusion law. The worker would have been entitled to federal court adjudication if he had gone to federal court rather than state court to attack the state agency's unfavorable decision. When he chose the state forum at that juncture, however, he committed his claim to the state courts and could reopen the state court judgment against him in federal court only if state preclusion law would permit him to do so.

suant to a state criminal conviction would have been able to petition a federal district court for a writ of habeas corpus and to revisit his federal claim in that posture. In *McCurry*, however, habeas corpus was not available.[172] Accordingly, the prisoner attempted to take his fourth amendment claim to federal court by means of a §1983 action against the offending police officers, contending that §1983 actions were exempt from §1738. Justice Stewart rejected that argument on the basis of a clear statement rule: "Repeals by implication are disfavored."[173] In the absence of greater clarity in the text of §1983 itself or its history, Stewart would not conclude that Congress "intended" §1983 "to overrule §1738 or the common-law rules of collateral estoppel and res judicata."[174]

The Court held in *Migra v. Warren City School Dist.*[175] that §1738 also makes at least one kind of claim preclusion available in §1983 actions. A public school principal initially sued school officials in an Ohio state court, contending that she had been discharged in violation of state law. After obtaining a favorable judgment and compensatory damages from the state courts, she filed a §1983 suit in federal court, contending that her dismissal also violated the first and fourteenth amendments and that, on that basis, she was entitled to punitive damages. She maintained that the prior state judgment did not preclude her from litigating federal claims that might have been raised and considered in state court, but in fact had been omitted from the earlier suit.[176] Justice Blackmun responded, however, that *Migra* was controlled by *McCurry*. He saw no reason to distinguish claim preclusion from issue preclusion and thus held that, pursuant to §1738, the plaintiff's §1983 action was subject to both kinds of state preclusion rules.[177]

The plaintiff in *Migra* was in a weak position. She herself had chosen to go to state court in the first instance, and she herself was responsible for failing to press her federal claims at that time and, instead, waiting to do so in a subsequent lawsuit in federal court. Justice Blackmun declined to say whether the Court's result would have been different if the party seeking to avoid claim preclusion in federal court had been an unwilling defendant in state court, unable to remove the matter to federal court.[178] Still, it is hard to think that Blackmun would have reached a different result in that kind of case. Recall that the reason defendants are unable to escape state court is that removal is typically unavailable on the basis of a federal defense or counterclaim. The point of §1441 must be that defendants are expected to submit any federal theories they have to the state courts. That arrangement would be defeated if defendants were able to withhold

---

172. The Court had previously held that federal district courts ordinarily should not enforce the fourth amendment exclusionary rule in federal habeas corpus proceedings. *Stone v. Powell*, 428 U.S. 465 (1976); see Chapter XII, notes 298–302 and accompanying text.

173. See Chapter I, notes 44–52 (discussing the doctrine of clear statement).

174. 449 U.S. at 99. Justice Stewart distinguished *Mitchum v. Foster*, 407 U.S. 225 (1972) (holding that §1983 is an express statutory exception to the Anti-Injunction Act). See Chapter XI, notes 16–19 (discussing *Mitchum*).

175. 465 U.S. 75 (1984).

176. The plaintiff in *Migra* did not argue that the Ohio courts would have declined to consider her federal claims if she had included them with her state claims in the previous lawsuit in state court. Nor did she deny that she might have sued originally in federal court rather than state court.

177. 465 U.S. at 82. There is a reason to distinguish claim preclusion from issue preclusion as a matter of policy, the one idea being so much more powerful than the other. Yet Justice Blackmun found nothing in §1983 that draws that distinction.

178. Id. at 83. Blackmun had dissented in *McCurry* in part on the ground that the prisoner in that case had been an unwilling defendant in the previous state court action. Id. at 85 n.7

federal defenses from state proceedings and reserve them for subsequent litigation in federal court.[179]

The decisions in *McCurry* and *Migra* establish only that §1738 requires federal district courts to invoke state preclusion law. In any particular case, however, questions can arise about "how" that law applies and whether "any exceptions or qualifications" nonetheless defeat a preclusion argument.[180] Justice Stewart explained in *McCurry*, moreover, that one exception *must* be recognized: Preclusion rules "cannot apply when the party against whom the earlier decision is asserted did not have a 'full and fair opportunity' to litigate that issue in the earlier case."[181] That idea reflects the process model in a more familiar role—namely, as a means of respecting state court adjudication in the main, but making federal courts available when the processes of adjudication in state court break down and the outcomes reached in state court are, for that reason, unreliable.[182] Nevertheless, the Court's basis for introducing the process model here is unclear.

There are three apparent possibilities. First, the requirement that a litigant must have a fair opportunity to litigate a claim in state court may be a feature of state preclusion law. If that is the answer, then by noting that requirement explicitly, Justice Stewart did not invoke a federal limitation on preclusion in §1738 cases, but only predicted what state law is likely to entail. Second, the requirement of full and fair process in state court may mean only that state courts must accord litigants the process that is "due" in the constitutional sense. In *Kremer v. Chem. Constr. Corp.*,[183] Justice White said that, where the Court is "bound by the statutory directive of §1738, state proceedings need do no more than satisfy the minimum procedural requirements of the Fourteenth Amendment's Due Process Clause in order to qualify for the full faith and credit guaranteed by federal law."[184] Third, if *Kremer* does not conclude the matter, the requirement of full and fair process in state court may rest independently on federal judge-made law. This

---

179. Professor Atwood generally defends preclusion in these circumstances. But she argues that federal courts should not be barred from considering issues and claims in circumstances in which subsequent federal litigation does not attempt to nullify a previous state court judgment. In cases of that kind, according to Atwood, a litigant should be able to withhold a claim from state court proceedings and assert it later as an affirmative claim in federal court. Barbara A. Atwood, *State Court Judgments in Federal Litigation: Mapping the Contours of Full Faith and Credit*, 58 Ind. L.J. 59, 62–63, 88–90, 98–100 (1982). The Court embraced something of that view in *Haring v. Prosise*, 462 U.S. 306 (1983), when it held that a litigant's previous plea of guilty to a state criminal charge did not prevent him from suing the police in federal court for conducting an unlawful search to obtain evidence against him. Professor Shapiro has endorsed *Haring*. See David L. Shapiro, *Should a Guilty Plea Have Preclusive Effect?*, 70 Iowa L. Rev. 27 (1984). But see *Tower v. Glover*, 467 U.S. 914, 923 (1984) (suggesting that a prisoner who expressly raised the same claims in previous state proceedings may be precluded from pressing them again in a federal §1983 action).

180. *McCurry*, 449 U.S. at 105 n.25, 95 n.7.

181. Id. at 95, quoting *Montana v. United States*, 440 U.S. 147, 153 (1979). Inasmuch as *McCurry* itself concerned issue preclusion, Justice Stewart referred only to that. There is no reason to doubt that the "full and fair opportunity" exception is equally available in claim preclusion cases. If anything, claim preclusion presents a more compelling occasion for making an exception in the interest of fairness.

182. See Chapter I, notes 73–77 and accompanying text.

183. 456 U.S. 461 (1982).

184. Id. at 481. Justice White explained that a federal constitutional definition of "full and fair" adjudication is consistent with the premise that §1738 makes state law controlling. The fourteenth amendment is equally a part of state law. See note 10 and accompanying text. Accordingly, the state preclusion law that §1738 brings into play cannot contemplate giving a state court judgment any preclusive effect that the fourteenth amendment does not permit. 456 U.S. at 482.

is the most interesting of the three possibilities inasmuch as it leaves room in §1738 cases for the operation of a generally useful device for adjusting the relations between state and federal courts.[185]

By its terms, §1738 instructs federal courts to apply state preclusion law only with respect to judgments rendered in prior proceedings in state court. Nevertheless, the Court has held that federal courts should also consult state preclusion rules with respect to the adjudicative actions of state administrative bodies. In *University of Tennessee v. Elliott*,[186] an employee filed a race discrimination claim before the appropriate state agency, but was denied full relief after a hearing. He then filed a §1983 action in federal court, arguing that his federal constitutional rights had been violated. In the Supreme Court, Justice White said that the findings of fact in the state administrative proceeding were entitled to the preclusive effect they would receive in a state court. At the outset, White held that the agency's proceedings were sufficiently "judicial" in character to warrant preclusive effect.[187] He did not rehearse the essentials of proceedings that are characteristically judicial. Yet it is a safe bet that he meant to incorporate Justice Holmes' account in *Prentis v. Atlantic Coast Line Co.*[188] Extrapolating from *Prentis*, agency fact-finding proceedings are judicial in the necessary sense if the agency takes evidence and testimony, makes credibility choices, and then determines the primary facts.[189] Next, Justice White turned to the preclusive effect that agency findings should receive. He explained that in the absence of a controlling statute, the Court typically develops federal common law for preclusion issues.[190] In *Elliott*, however, he thought it best to borrow state law as the content of that federal common law.[191] In the end, then, Justice White had it that when state agencies reach determinations of fact via conventional adjudicative process, the preclusive effect prescribed by state law is appropriate.[192]

It seems clear that the Court hopes to reduce the traffic into the district courts by insulating state adjudicative activities from federal court oversight.[193] Yet giving preclusive

---

185. But see notes 219–25 and accompanying text (noting the potential conflict with the *Rooker/Feldman* doctrine).

186. 478 U.S. 788 (1986).

187. See Chapter I, notes 6–9 and accompanying text (discussing the character of adjudicative as opposed to legislative action).

188. 211 U.S. 210 (1908); see Chapter I, note 6 and accompanying text; Chapter XI, notes 39–43 and accompanying text.

189. *Prentis*, 211 U.S. at 226.

190. For example, the Court typically gives preclusive effect to the findings of federal administrative agencies. E.g., *United States v. Utah Construction & Mining Co.*, 384 U.S. 394, 422 (1966).

191. See Chapter VIII, notes 104–16 and accompanying text (discussing the practice of borrowing state law).

192. The employee in *Elliott* had made no attempt to press his claims in state court and thus had done nothing to implicate §1738. To the extent he relied on Title VII in federal court, preclusion was unavailable in light of Title VII's explicit guarantee that federal court adjudication would be *de novo*. Even though the Court itself usually gives preclusive effect to both state and federal administrative findings, Congress can always prescribe otherwise. See, e.g., *Astoria Fed. Savings & Loan Ass'n v. Solimino*, 501 U.S. 104 (1991) (holding that Congress had trumped the usual presumption in favor of preclusion). Arbitration judgments are not entitled to preclusive effect, because they depend on the "law of the shop" pertaining to labor contracts and therefore do not represent a reliable determination of factual issues touching a worker's Title VII race discrimination claim. *McDonald v. City of West Branch*, 466 U.S. 284 (1984).

193. Justice White once suggested that federal courts should give state court judgments more preclusive effect than they would enjoy under state law. *Migra*, 465 U.S. at 88 (concurring opinion). The full Court has rejected that view. See, e.g., *Johnson v. DeGrandy*, 512 U.S. 997, 1005 (1994) (explaining that §1738 contemplates that federal courts give state court judgments precisely the preclu-

effect to state administrative findings may have just the opposite effect. It discourages litigants from taking their claims to state agencies established for the very purpose of handling complaints without resort to the courts and encourages them to regard immediate §1983 actions in federal court as the primary means of vindicating their rights. There is no requirement that litigants exhaust state administrative procedures before filing §1983 actions. So litigants in cases like *Elliott* are free to leapfrog over state administrative authorities into federal court.[194] Then again, the consequences of *Elliott* in the run of actual cases can only be determined empirically.[195]

3. Limited Appellate Review

Preclusion is not the only barrier facing litigants who file lawsuits in federal court hoping to revisit issues that were or might have been determined in previous state court proceedings. In addition, the Supreme Court has established an independent doctrine to implement the understanding that federal district courts have no appellate jurisdiction to review state court judgments for error. Two famous cases, *Rooker v. Fidelity Trust Co.*[196] and *District of Columbia Court of Appeals v. Feldman,*[197] give this second doctrine its name. Like preclusion, the *Rooker/Feldman* doctrine reinforces the general expectation that litigants who find themselves in state court with federal question cases typically must be satisfied with the decisions the state courts reach.

The Court derives *Rooker/Feldman* from a construction of the relevant jurisdictional statutes. Pursuant to 28 U.S.C. §1331, district courts have original jurisdiction in civil actions arising under federal law.[198] That explicit grant of original jurisdiction forecloses, by negative implication, any appellate jurisdiction to second-guess state courts. Pursuant to 28 U.S.C. §1257, the Supreme Court may review final judgments rendered by a state's highest court.[199] That explicit grant (or acknowledgment[200]) of appellate jurisdiction in the Supreme Court also forecloses, by negative implication, any such appellate jurisdiction in district courts.[201] Since *Rooker/Feldman* rests on these mutually

---

sive effect they would enjoy in another state court). Professor Shreve argues that §1738 allows federal courts to give state judgments greater effect, but only if state interests are not compromised. Gene R. Shreve, *Preclusion and Federal Choice of Law*, 64 Tex. L. Rev. 1209 (1986).

194. *Patsy v. Bd. of Regents*, 457 U.S. 496 (1982); see Chapter XI, notes 47–51 and accompanying text.

195. In many instances, state administrative processes may be attractive on various other counts, such that litigants may choose to employ them despite the risk that they will produce unfavorable findings entitled to preclusive effect in federal court. Professor Ryckman explains, for example, that only "idealism or despair" would drive real estate developers to bypass local zoning boards and planning commissions in favor of litigation in federal court. William E. Ryckman, Jr., *Land Use Litigation, Federal Jurisdiction, and the Abstention Doctrines*, 69 Calif. L. Rev. 377 (1981).

196. 263 U.S. 413 (1923).

197. 460 U.S. 462 (1983).

198. See Chapter VIII, text accompanying notes 234–37.

199. See Chapter VII, text accompanying note 59.

200. See Chapter IV, text accompanying notes 10–11 (explaining that Article III formally establishes the Court's appellate jurisdiction and that statutes purporting to grant jurisdiction to the Court only negate constitutionally permissible jurisdiction that is not specified).

201. *Rooker*, 263 U.S. at 416 (explaining that the jurisdiction of the district courts is "strictly original"). When a district court dismisses a suit on the basis of *Rooker/Feldman*, it does so because it lacks subject matter jurisdiction. Justice Souter's reference to the "Rooker/Feldman abstention doctrine" cannot be taken seriously. *DeGrandy*, 512 U.S. at 1005.

reinforcing statutory grounds, it is a creature of congressional policy and requires no independent justification.[202] By most accounts, however, *Rooker/Feldman* reflects a well-established vision of the federal structure: State courts and inferior federal courts have co-equal status. Neither set of courts is responsible to the other for its decisions. Both are answerable only to the Supreme Court, which sits astride the unified judicial system as the final referee regarding questions of federal law.[203]

No knowledgeable plaintiff formally styles a complaint in a federal district court as an appeal from a previous state court judgment. The trick in *Rooker/Feldman* cases is to determine whether a complaint purporting to invoke a district court's *original* jurisdiction is actually an invalid invitation to exercise *appellate* jurisdiction. The plaintiffs in *Rooker* filed suit in a federal district court, seeking a declaration that a state court judgment was null and void. In the Supreme Court, Justive Van Devanter viewed that lawsuit as a request for appellate review in the district court. The plaintiffs in *Feldman* initially asked the District of Columbia Court of Appeals (the local court for the District) for waivers of its general rule that only graduates of accredited law schools could become members of the District bar. When that court refused, they filed suit in a federal district court, contending that the general rule was invalid both as written and as applied to them. In the Supreme Court, Justice Brennan held that the district court had no jurisdiction to entertain the second of those two claims: the claim that the rule requiring bar applicants to be graduates of accredited schools could not constitutionally be applied in the plaintiffs' particular cases. By contrast, Brennan explained that the district court *did* have jurisdiction to address the first claim: the claim that the general rule was unconstitutional on its face.[204]

The elements of the *Rooker/Feldman* doctrine are simple to state, though they can be unruly in operation. Initially, a district court must decide whether a previous proceeding in state court was truly adjudicative in nature so that a subsequent suit in federal court should be treated as an unwarranted appeal from a judicial judgment. Not every action taken by state courts is judicial in the necessary sense. State courts sometimes perform legislative and executive duties. When state courts act in those

---

202. For critiques of the Court's statutory construction analysis, see Susan Bandes, *The Rooker-Feldman Doctrine: Evaluating its Jurisdictional Status*, 74 Notre Dame L. Rev. 1175, 1187–93 (1999); Jack M. Beermann, *Comments on Rooker-Feldman or Let State Law Be Our Guide*, 74 Notre Dame L. Rev. 1209, 1227–33 (1999).

203. See notes 1–12 and accompanying text. The Constitution would probably tolerate a different structure. For example, Congress may have power to grant inferior federal courts appellate jurisdiction to review state court judgments for federal error. Hamilton thought Congress might do that, but he discouraged the prospect. See Chapter II, note 53. See also James E. Pfander, *An Intermediate Solution to State Sovereign Immunity: Federal Appellate Court Review of State-Court judgments After Seminole Tribe*, 46 U.C.L.A. L. Rev. 161, 213–22 (1998) (arguing that Article III permits Congress to make the judgment as a matter of policy). Nonetheless, Congress has always kept state and inferior federal courts on an equal footing. Professor Sherry has suggested that *Rooker/Feldman* neatly complements other doctrines and statutes reflecting that conception. The All-Writs Act authorizes inferior federal courts to issue injunctions in aid of their own jurisdiction, and the Anti-Injunction Act permits federal courts to enjoin state court proceedings to protect or effectuate their judgments. See Chapter XI, notes 20–26 and accompanying text. Yet state courts are forbidden to enjoin federal court proceedings for any reason. See *Donovan v. City of Dallas*, 377 U.S. 408 (1964); text accompanying notes 121–22. By Sherry's account, *Rooker/Feldman* forces federal district courts to do for state courts what state courts are unable to do for themselves. Federal district courts stay their own hand when necessary to avoid revisiting matters the state courts have already resolved. Suzanna Sherry, *Judicial Federalism in the Trenches: The Rooker-Feldman Doctrine in Action*, 74 Notre Dame L. Rev. 1085, 1105 (1999).

204. See note 218 and accompanying text.

different capacities, disappointed parties can file original lawsuits attacking the product of their actions in federal court. The label a state attaches either to a state institution or to its behavior is not controlling.[205] All that matters is the function the state body performs in a particular instance. The proper characterization of a state court proceeding for *Rooker/Feldman* purposes is a question of federal law for the district court to determine.[206] In this context, the Court relies explicitly on Justice Holmes' formulation of adjudicative action in the *Prentis* case. A state court performed a judicial function if it undertook to "investigate, declare, and enforce 'liabilities as they [stood] on present or past facts and under laws supposed already to exist.'"[207] If, however, the state court established a "new rule" that changed the law for cases in the future, it performed a legislative function (not subject to *Rooker/Feldman*).[208]

In the *Rooker* case, there was no serious doubt that the prior state court proceeding was adjudicative. In *Feldman*, the situation was more complicated. The District of Columbia Court of Appeals not only applied the rule limiting bar admission to graduates of accredited schools to the plaintiffs, but had itself promulgated that general rule in the first instance. Justice Brennan explained that the D.C. court's handling of the plaintiffs' individual cases involved sufficient attention to the facts alleged in their petitions to count as adjudication.[209] Accordingly, the federal district court had no jurisdiction to entertain any federal claim questioning the D.C. court's refusal to grant the plaintiffs a waiver from the general rule. Brennan held, however, that the D.C. court's antecedent adoption of the general bar admission rule was an exercise of legislative power. Accordingly, *ceteris paribus*, the federal district court *did* have jurisdiction to entertain an original lawsuit challenging the validity of that legislative act. If, then, the plaintiffs in *Feldman* had never appeared before the D.C. court, but had simply filed suit in federal district court challenging the bar admission rule on its face, they could not have been accused of attempting to appeal from a judicial decision by the D.C. court.[210]

Once a district court concludes that a previous state proceeding was judicial in nature, the next question is whether the claim the plaintiff seeks to litigate in federal court "arose" in that state proceeding.[211] If so, the federal district court has no jurisdiction to

---

205. *Public Svc. Co. v. Corboy*, 250 U.S. 153, 161–62 (1919).

206. *Feldman*, 460 U.S. at 476–77 & n.13.

207. Id. at 477, quoting *Prentis*, 211 U.S. at 226.

208. Id.

209. *Feldman*, 460 U.S. at 479. The circuit court below considered the D.C. court's administration of bar admissions to be a ministerial function and therefore held that decisions in particular cases were not judicial in the necessary sense. Justice Brennan explicitly rejected that characterization. State administrative agencies as well as state courts can perform adjudicative work. See notes 186–95 and accompanying text (discussing this point in the preclusion context); Chapter I, text accompanying note 9; see also Chapter XI, notes 279–87 (discussing the same point in the context of federal-question abstention).

210. In fact, the plaintiffs in *Feldman* went first to the D.C. court. If they had raised their facial challenge to the rule in that setting, the D.C. court would have determined that claim in its judicial capacity, and the plaintiffs would have been barred from advancing the same claim later in federal district court. See Bandes, note 202, at 1183 (making this point). As it was, the plaintiffs did not raise the facial validity claim in the D.C court, that court addressed only questions related to the fairness of applying the rule in the plaintiffs' personal circumstances, and, in the end, the Supreme Court concluded that the facial validity claim was not jurisdictionally barred in the district court because it was not "inextricably intertwined" with the D.C. court's judgment on the issues that court actually decided. See note 218 and accompanying text.

211. *Rooker*, 263 U.S. at 415.

reverse or modify the resulting state judgment.[212] A claim "arose" for *Rooker/Feldman* purposes if one of two things is true: (1) the claim was raised and actually adjudicated in state court; or (2) the claim was "inextricably intertwined" with the judgment the state court reached on the issues it considered.[213] If a claim was actually raised and determined in state court, it follows naturally enough that a federal district court cannot address the same claim without reviewing the state court judgment, in effect if not in form.[214] If a claim was *not* raised and determined, it still may have been "inextricably intertwined" with the state court's disposition of other issues that *were*. In that event, too, the district court can entertain the claim only by effectively reviewing the state court's prior work. Justice Marshall once explained that a claim is "inextricably intertwined" with a state court judgment if the claim "succeeds only to the extent that the state court wrongly decided the issues before it."[215] If that formulation is reliable, the analysis is straightforward: If, in order to address a claim that the state court did not actually decide, a federal district court must necessarily second-guess the state court's determination of the issues the state court *did* decide, then the federal court is being asked to exercise appellate jurisdiction it does not possess.

In this respect, too, *Rooker* was easy, at least as the Court conceived the facts in that case to be. The Court assumed that the claims the plaintiffs wished to advance in federal court had been tied up in the previous judgment in state court.[216] Accordingly, the federal court had no jurisdiction to consider those claims. In *Feldman*, the situation was again more complicated. Neither of the claims the plaintiffs in that case pressed in federal district court had been raised in the D.C. Court of Appeals. In that court, the plaintiffs had asserted only non-constitutional arguments that it was arbitrary, discriminatory, and unfair to refuse them a waiver. Justice Brennan held that the plaintiffs' claim that the *application* of the general bar admission rule *to them* violated due process was "inextricably intertwined" with the judgment the D.C. court rendered on those non-constitutional arguments.[217] Accordingly, the district court had no jurisdiction to con-

---

212. Id.

213. *Feldman*, 460 U.S. at 482–83 n.16, 486. Justice Scalia has explained that *Rooker/Feldman* does not bar an original action in a federal district court if the district court "need not decide any issue either actually litigated in [state court] or inextricably intertwined with issues so litigated." *Pennzoil Co. v. Texaco*, 481 U.S. 1, 18 (1987) (concurring opinion). That formulation is probably reliable. Yet it departs from the Court's precise language. Justice Scalia refers to a claim that was intertwined with *issues* that were actually litigated in state court. Writing for the full Court in *Feldman*, Justice Brennan referred to a claim that was intertwined with the state court's *decision* regarding other issues. *Feldman*, 460 U.S. at 486–87.

214. Federal district courts entertaining habeas corpus petitions from state prisoners frequently examine claims that state courts previously considered and rejected. Yet that form of federal court jurisdiction is not conceived to be appellate in nature for reasons peculiar to the writ of habeas corpus. See Chapter XII, notes 44–46 and accompanying text.

215. *Pennzoil*, 481 U.S. at 25 (Marshall, J., concurring in the judgment).

216. In fact, the plaintiffs in *Rooker* did not advance their federal claim in the state trial court or in their initial appeal to the state supreme court. Neither of those courts considered any such claim. The plaintiffs did raise federal constitutional claims in a petition for rehearing in the state supreme court. But that petition was summarily denied. See Note, *The Rooker-Feldman Doctrine: Toward a Workable Rule*, 149 U. Penn. L. Rev. 1555, 1563 (2001) (pointing out that the Court's apparent assumptions about the state court proceedings in *Rooker* were mistaken).

217. *Feldman*, 460 U.S. at 486–87. Professor Sherry reports that some lower courts erroneously assume that if a claim could have been raised in state court, but was not, it follows that the claim was "inextricably intertwined" with the state court's judgment. Sherry, note 203, at 1097–1100. The correct understanding is that a claim that could have been raised, but was not, *may* have been "intertwined" with the state court judgment in a way that bars a district court from considering the

sider that "as applied" constitutional claim. By contrast, Brennan held that the plaintiffs' challenge to the *facial validity* of the bar admission rule was not "inextricably intertwined" with the D. C. court's judgment on the non-constitutional issues it considered. Accordingly, the federal district court had jurisdiction to entertain that claim.[218]

The *Rooker/Feldman* doctrine operates in the same channel with the law of preclusion, which also restricts a federal district court's ability to adjudicate in the wake of a state court judgment.[219] Yet there are important differences. Preclusion is not a jurisdictional doctrine in service of federalism, but a non-jurisdictional doctrine in service of efficiency. The Full Faith and Credit Statute, §1738, presupposes that federal courts have *power* and only orchestrates the way they must exercise that power. The *Rooker/Feldman* denies the district courts any power at all to entertain lawsuits that seek appellate review. Preclusion establishes a *defense* that defendants may advance at their option. By contrast, *Rooker/Feldman* recognizes a jurisdictional prohibition that operates irrespective of the parties' desires and presumably must be addressed *sua sponte*.[220]

Preclusion doctrine and *Rooker/Feldman* typically produce the same practical results. Ordinarily, state issue preclusion rules (applicable via §1738) bar litigants from revisiting the very issues that *Rooker/Feldman* insulates from federal district court adjudication—namely, issues that actually were determined previously in state court. Questions that might have been, but were not, adjudicated in state court also typically meet the same fate under either preclusion or *Rooker/Feldman* principles. State claim preclusion rules typically bar litigants from pressing issues of that kind, and the *Rooker/Feldman* doctrine does so as well to the extent the issues at stake were "inextricably intertwined" with issues that were actually determined in state court. A significant overlap between preclusion and *Rooker/Feldman* is not necessarily worrisome. It is not always a serious condemnation of legal doctrine that it contemplates alternative means by which matters

---

claim later. If anything, a litigant's failure to raise a claim in state court may make it less, not more, likely that a federal court will be jurisdictionally barred from entertaining it. But see note 164 and accompanying text (explaining that preclusion rules typically defeat claims that might have been vindicated in previous state court proceedings). In any event, in order to decide whether a claim was "inextricably intertwined" with a prior state court judgment on other issues, a district court must engage an independent analysis of the relationship between the claim and the state court's decision on those issues. Cf. Bandes, note 202, at 1196–1204 (describing cases in which the lower federal courts have had difficulty making the necessary judgments).

218. *Feldman*, 460 U.S. at 487. Justice Brennan did not suggest that *Rooker/Feldman* will typically permit a litigant who attacks the facial validity of a legislative rule to advance that claim in a federal district court as a sequel to state court litigation. A facial challenge claim is not, by nature, exempted from *Rooker/Feldman* analysis. Again, that kind of claim will be jurisdictionally barred in federal district court if it was raised and decided in a state court. And, in some cases at least, a claim of that order may be regarded as "inextricably intertwined" with a previous state court judgment in a way that the facial validity claim in *Feldman* was not. Cf. Barry Friedman & James E. Gaylord, *Rooker-Feldman, From the Ground Up*, 74 Notre Dame L. Rev. 1129, 1172 (1999) (contending that facial attacks on general rules are typically intertwined with prior state court applications of those rules to particular cases and that the contrary decision in *Feldman* "makes no sense").

219. The *Rooker/Feldman* doctrine also responds to themes that underlie statutes and judicially crafted doctrines that mediate between federal and state courts while state court proceedings are under way: removal statutes, the Anti-Injunction Act, and various abstention doctrines. See notes 125–35 and accompanying text (covering removal); Chapter XI (covering the Anti-Injunction Act and the abstention doctrines). *Rooker/Feldman* differs from those statutes and doctrines inasmuch as it presupposes an extant state court judgment (and thus no "pending" proceedings in state court with which a federal court may interfere).

220. See David P. Currie, *Res Judicata: The Neglected Defense*, 45 U. Chi. L. Rev. 317, 324 (1978).

of a feline character can be relieved of their epidermal layer. Then again, as an aesthetic matter, the overlap in this instance may be so complete that there is little point to maintaining *Rooker/Feldman* as an independent basis for barring federal court action.[221]

There are, however, instances in which results under the two headings are not the same. Note, for example, that the category of issues that might have been adjudicated in previous state court proceedings is larger than the category of claims that *both* might have been addressed in state court and *also* were intertwined with the issues actually considered. There will be cases, then, in which preclusion cuts off issues that *Rooker/Feldman* would not. By most accounts, it is not especially troubling if preclusion bars federal court adjudication of matters that *Rooker/Feldman* allows. The very existence of §1738 suggests that the problems in this field are generally to be resolved by reference to state preclusion law. In *Feldman* itself, Justice Brennan acknowledged that the very claim that *Rooker/Feldman* allowed the district court to consider (the claim that the bar admission rule was unconstitutional on its face) might nonetheless be precluded.[222]

Instances in which *Rooker/Feldman* forecloses federal court adjudication that state preclusion law would permit are more controversial. Recall, for example, that defendants in federal court may forgo their ability to assert preclusion as a defense and that, in any event, some peculiarity in state preclusion rules may allow litigants a chance to revisit issues that *Rooker/Feldman* bars in a more sweeping manner. When *Rooker/Feldman* forecloses federal court action that §1738 and state preclusion law would not, there is a serious argument that *Rooker/Feldman* undermines the policies embedded in preclusion and thus *is* problematic, after all. Moreover, there is evidence that lower federal courts often misuse *Rooker/Feldman* to rid their dockets of unwanted cases.[223] By some accounts, then, *Rooker/Feldman* may actually do more harm than good.[224] Never-

---

221. See, e.g., Beermann, note 202; Friedman & Gaylord, note 218.

222. *Feldman*, 460 U.S. at 487–88 (explicitly leaving the preclusion question to the district court on remand). If the plaintiffs had raised the facial validity claim in the D.C. court, that court would have determined it in the exercise of judicial power. Id. at 473 n.9. Accordingly, the district court might have dismissed that claim on the basis of claim preclusion. See text accompanying note 164.

223. Professor Sherry reports cases in which lower federal courts have relied on *Rooker/Feldman* to dismiss complaints in light of previous state trial court proceedings. Sherry, note 203, at 1092–93. Yet if there was no appeal within the state court system, one of the statutory rationales for *Rooker/Feldman* is undermined. The United States Supreme Court's appellate jurisdiction under § 1257 is restricted to judgments rendered by a state's highest court. See Chapter VII, notes 60–63 and accompanying text. That assignment of jurisdiction to the Supreme Court does not necessarily imply that district courts have no jurisdiction to review state trial court decisions. See Friedman & Gaylord, note 218, at 1137. Professor Sherry also reports cases in which lower federal courts have invoked *Rooker/Feldman* to bar district court jurisdiction to entertain claims pressed by litigants who were not parties in prior state court proceedings. Sherry, note 203, at 1112–23. Sherry contends that litigants who might have intervened in previous state proceedings and had reason to do so should be jurisdictionally barred from federal district court. Id. at 1123. Yet that result may raise constitutional difficulties. See Friedman & Gaylord, note 218, at 1141–47.

224. Professor Bandes contends that lower federal courts invoke *Rooker/Feldman* reflexively as a jurisdictional bar and thus shirk responsibility for explaining the policies that may justify refusing litigants a federal forum. Bandes, note 202, at 1176. Professor Beermann suspects that lower federal courts use *Rooker/Feldman* as a means of giving prior state court judgments greater preclusive effect than the Full Faith and Credit Statute allows. Beermann, note 202, at 1212. See note 193 (explaining that §1738 prevents federal courts from according state court judgments more preclusive effect than state law prescribes).

theless, the *Rooker/Feldman* doctrine is alive and well and can occasionally affect cases in the federal district courts in ways that preclusion law does not.[225]

225. Professor Sherry identifies cases in which preclusion sometimes leaves "gaps" that she thinks *Rooker/Feldman* can legitimately fill. Sherry, note 203, at 1089–90.

Chapter VII

The Supreme Court

The Supreme Court of the United States resolves very few cases on the merits. Yet the opinions the Court generates establish the baseline from which much of the law governing American public institutions proceeds. The Supreme Court thus demands attention for the systemic functions it performs, even if there is very little chance that any particular case will reach the justices for decision. The Court does the lion's share of its work as the ultimate appellate tribunal for the resolution of federal questions. In some respects, the Court's jurisdiction is governed by statutes and doctrines that bear serious study. In the main, however, the Court has discretion to set its own agenda. When the Court accepts cases for review, they become vehicles for articulating an accurate, uniform, and supreme body of federal law.

A. Original Jurisdiction

Article III establishes the menu of "cases" and "controversies" that comprise the judicial business that federal courts can handle. Article III also distributes that business between the Supreme Court's original jurisdiction, on the one hand, and its appellate jurisdiction, on the other.[1] Insofar as the *Constitution* is concerned, the Court *can* exercise jurisdiction in every "case" or "controversy" on the list, either by entertaining a suit that originates in the Court itself or, when a suit is initially filed in an inferior federal court or a state court, by reviewing the judgment reached at that level.[2] Article III specifies that the Court *can* entertain some cases as an original matter: "all Cases affecting Ambassadors, other public Ministers and Consuls, and those in which a State shall be a Party." Yet Article III does not make that original jurisdiction exclusive.[3] Nor does it bar the Court from handling those same cases, as well as the other matters on the general menu, in an appellate posture. Thus when a case that might have begun in the Supreme Court as an original matter actually begins in an inferior federal court or in a state court, Article III permits the Supreme Court to consider the lower court's judgment on appeal.[4]

Taken literally, Article III appears to say that the Supreme Court can exercise original jurisdiction of any suit on the menu, provided that a foreign emissary is involved or one

1. See Chapter IV, text accompanying notes 5–6.
2. But see Chapter X (treating sovereign immunity).
3. *Bors v. Preston*, 111 U.S. 252 (1884) (holding that inferior federal courts may be given concurrent jurisdiction over cases involving foreign ambassadors and consuls); *Ames v. Kansas*, 111 U.S. 449 (1884) (holding that inferior federal courts and state courts may handle cases in which the Supreme Court also has original jurisdiction).
4. *Cohens v. Virginia*, 19 U.S. (6 Wheat.) 264, 392–403 (1821).

of the states is a party.[5] That understanding would have provocative implications. The state is a party in an ordinary state criminal prosecution of one of its citizens. It would be extraordinary if, for that reason, local criminal cases could routinely be tried in the Supreme Court of the United States. Accordingly, the Court has chosen a different interpretation: Article III establishes jurisdiction only when it identifies the nine overlapping matters that form the federal judicial power, not when it later allocates that power between the two modes of Supreme Court jurisdiction. Accordingly, the statement that the Supreme Court "shall have original Jurisdiction" in cases "in which a State shall be a Party" does not create jurisdictional power independently of the cases and controversies listed in the previous paragraph.[6] It follows that original jurisdiction extends not to every case on the Article III menu in which a foreign officer happens to be involved or a state happens to be a party, but only to cases that are on the menu *because* a foreign representative is concerned or a state is a party.[7] The result is that original jurisdiction is limited to suits that are on the list because they are "Cases affecting Ambassadors, other public Ministers and Consuls" or "Controversies between two or more States," between "a State and Citizens of another State," or between "a State...and foreign states, Citizens, or Subjects."[8]

Original jurisdiction in the Supreme Court is a special form of diversity jurisdiction, depending not on the nature of the issues at stake, but rather on the identity and alignment of litigants who command the Court's attention either because they represent foreign sovereigns or because they are sovereign American states themselves. The scope of original jurisdiction is negligible, its purpose largely symbolic. The explanations for its existence bear this out. Historically, original jurisdiction promised superior procedures, geographic convenience, and greater assurances of neutrality. Prior to the development of long-arm statutes, the states were unable to sue citizens of other states in their own courts, because they had no means of obtaining *in personam* jurisdiction. States and representatives of foreign nations may have found it most convenient to proceed in Washington, where their lawyers typically resided. Foreign representatives may also have preferred to appear in the Supreme Court rather than trust their fortunes to the provincialism of a state court. All these explanations have weaknesses, but they probably account for the way Article III was written.[9] Today, original jurisdiction offers only the formal dignity of litigation in our most prestigious tribunal.[10]

---

5. The Court held in *Ex parte Gruber*, 269 U.S. 302 (1925), that "Ambassadors, or other public Ministers and Consuls" are representatives of foreign governments, not representatives of this country serving abroad.

6. *Pennsylvania v. Quicksilver Co.*, 77 U.S. (10 Wall.) 553, 556 (1870).

7. *California v. Southern Pac. Co.*, 157 U.S. 229, 257–58 (1895).

8. When, for example, Oregon challenged the validity of the eighteen-year-old vote statute on constitutional grounds, the state invoked the Supreme Court's original jurisdiction on the theory that the defendant, Attorney General Mitchell, was a citizen of Virginia—*not* on the theory that the suit arose under federal law. *Oregon v. Mitchell*, 400 U.S. 112 (1970).

9. See Akhil R. Amar, *Marbury, Section 13, and the Original Jurisdiction of the Supreme Court*, 56 U. Chi. L. Rev. 443, 469–78 (1989) (attributing original jurisdiction largely to geography); James E. Pfander, *Marbury, Original Jurisdiction, and the Supreme Court's Supervisory Powers*, 101 Colum. L. Rev. 1515 (2001) (amassing additional historical support for the geographic explanation).

10. *California v. Arizona*, 440 U.S. 59, 65–66 (1979). Recall that Alexander Hamilton took the view that only federal courts could accord other nations the respect they were due. See Chapter II, text accompanying note 50. Professor Pfander disputes the "dignified tribunal" thesis, as well as other explanations for the conventional understanding of original jurisdiction. James E. Pfander, *Rethinking the Supreme Court's Original Jurisdiction in State-Party Cases*, 82 Calif. L. Rev. 555, 562–72 (1994). Pfander offers, instead, a revisionist account of the history behind Article III and an

With respect to original jurisdiction, Article III is self-executing. The Court is free to exercise the power that Article III makes available, whether or not Congress enacts a statute purporting to confer original jurisdiction on the Court as a matter of legislative policy.[11] Nevertheless, Congress has enacted legislation touching the Court's original jurisdiction and thus has purported to have something to say about it.[12] There are three possibilities. Congress might wish: (1) to confer original jurisdiction that Article III does not contemplate; (2) to withhold some or all the original jurisdiction that Article III prescribes; or (3) to make some or all the Court's original jurisdiction concurrent with the jurisdiction of other courts. The first and second of these tactics are apparently foreclosed by precedent; the third is available and routinely employed.

The Court held in *Marbury v. Madison*[13] that Congress cannot *add* to the original jurisdiction fixed by Article III. That decision has often been questioned.[14] Yet it has a plausible rationale. If Congress could expand the Court's original jurisdiction, it might compromise the Court's effectiveness by swamping the justices with work.[15] It is "extremely doubtful" that Congress can *deny* the Court original jurisdiction established by Article III.[16] To avoid that "grave" constitutional question, the Court reads ambiguous statutes to make no attempt to withhold any part of it.[17] The rationale for resisting reductions in original jurisdiction is not immediately apparent. Since the scope of original jurisdiction is so narrow in the first instance, it is hard to think that the Court's ability to perform its core functions would be impaired if some of it were lost. The Court cannot rely on original jurisdiction as a vehicle for deciding federal questions.[18] Moreover, the justices plainly do not relish original jurisdiction and exercise it only sparingly.[19] It may be, then, that the inviolate character of original jurisdiction rests largely on symbolic grounds.[20]

---

argument that *any* case in which a state is a party is within the Supreme Court's original jurisdiction, if the case appears on the Article III menu for *any* reason. He draws support from the text of Article III, which refers to "cases" when it describes the Supreme Court's original jurisdiction, but to "controversies" when it describes the diversity suits to which the conventional interpretation limits that jurisdiction. Pfander counters that when Article III refers to "cases," it means to capture matters that appear on the Article III list for different reasons—in particular, "cases" arising under federal law in which a state is a party. Id. at 600. See Chapter II, note 27 (discussing other accounts of "cases" and "controversies").

11. *Arizona v. California*, 373 U.S. 546, 564 (1963).

12. The Court insists that its appellate jurisdiction, too, is formally conferred by Article III rather than by statute. Yet the Court typically accepts the jurisdictional legislation that Congress writes in that context as authoritative. See Chapter IV, notes 10–11 and accompanying text.

13. 5 U.S. (1 Cranch) 137 (1803); see Chapter I, notes 65–70 and accompanying text.

14. E.g., William W. Van Alstyne, *A Critical Guide to Marbury v. Madison*, 1969 Duke L.J. 1. Professor Pfander has developed historical evidence suggesting that the statute invalidated in *Marbury* (§13 of the Judiciary Act of 1789) was meant to effectuate a then-familiar authority in "supreme courts" to issue prerogative writs (like mandamus) as a means of superintending other courts and executive officers. Pfander, note 9, 1561.

15. But see note 34 and accompanying text (explaining that litigants must have the Court's leave before filing an original action).

16. *California v. Arizona*, 440 U.S. at 66.

17. *South Carolina v. Regan*, 465 U.S. 367, 395 (1984) (O'Connor, J., concurring); see Chapter I, text accompanying note 26 (discussing the practice of avoiding constitutional questions when possible).

18. See notes 5–8 and accompanying text.

19. See notes 34–40 and accompanying text

20. Professor Amar argues that (subject to other constitutional restraints) Congress *can* withhold original jurisdiction from the Court in cases in which that jurisdiction must rest on the party status of a state. He relies on the precise text of Article III, which refers to "all" cases affecting for-

The Court can allow inferior federal courts and state courts to entertain the kinds of cases that Article III prescribes for the Supreme Court's original jurisdiction.[21] The current statute in point, 28 U.S.C. §1251, contemplates that the Court will have "exclusive" jurisdiction only with respect to "controversies between two or more states" and that the rest of its original jurisdiction will "not" be exclusive, but rather may be concurrent with that of other courts.[22] When Congress wishes to confer jurisdiction on inferior federal courts to entertain matters in the latter category, it is free to do so.[23] And when state courts exercise their own jurisdictional power arising from state law to adjudicate those cases, they, too, are on solid ground.[24] Inferior federal courts and state courts often enjoy the concurrent jurisdiction required. Accordingly, most cases that might have been filed originally in the Supreme Court are now filed elsewhere and reach the Court, if at all, only on appellate review.[25]

The Court occasionally makes adjustments to these basic arrangements. In *United States v. Texas*,[26] the Court upheld original jurisdiction to entertain a suit by the federal government against a state. Suits in which the United States is a party are on the Article III menu, but *not* because a state is invariably a party. Accordingly, the Court was forced to carve out an exception to the usual understanding of original jurisdiction. That was not difficult to do. In the *Texas* case, the government sued to determine the boundary between Texas and the territory of Oklahoma.[27] No inferior court had jurisdiction to entertain that action, and if the Supreme Court itself was constitutionally foreclosed, the only alternative was a Texas state court. The Court found it implausible that the Constitution should force the government to submit a suit against a state to the courts of that very state. It was more sensible to infer that the national sovereign could sue in its own courts (namely, the Supreme Court itself) to settle its differences with a member state—the usual limitation of original jurisdiction to three kinds of diversity actions notwithstanding.[28]

---

eign envoys but does not equally refer to "all" cases in which a state is a party. Amar, note 9, at 480–81. See also Chapter IV, notes 143–46 and accompanying text.

21. *Ames v. Kansas*, 111 U.S. 449 (1884).

22. The remaining matters to which §1251 refers do not reach all the cases that Article III places within the Supreme Court's original jurisdiction. For example, while Article III extends original jurisdiction to all cases "affecting" foreign envoys, §1251 acknowledges jurisdiction only in actions in which foreign representatives are "parties." If cases can *affect* foreign officers even though they are not parties, then §1251 presents the "grave" question whether Congress can deprive the Supreme Court of original jurisdiction by statute or, better said, by negative implication from statute. See notes 16–17 and accompanying text.

23. Since §1251 merely establishes that the Supreme Court's jurisdiction is not exclusive in most instances, that statute does not itself confer concurrent jurisdiction on any other court. Independent jurisdictional statutes are required to do that additional work. They exist in abundance. E.g., 28 U.S.C. §1351 (conferring jurisdiction on district courts to adjudicate suits against representatives of foreign governments). District courts have jurisdiction in federal question cases in which a state is a party, albeit state immunity from suit may be asserted. 28 U.S.C. §1331; see Chapter X.

24. See Chapter VI, note 4 and accompanying text.

25. But cf. Chapter IV, note 36 and accompanying text (describing the Court's peculiar "original" jurisdiction in habeas corpus cases).

26. 143 U.S. 621 (1892).

27. The law governing the boundary was federal common law. Accordingly, the suit in *United States v. Texas* was within the federal judicial power both because the United States was a party and because the suit arose under federal law. See Chapter VIII, notes 47, 68–70 and accompanying text (explaining that a case can "arise under" federal common law).

28. See text accompanying note 8. Recall that Hamilton took a similar view. See Chapter II, note 49 and accompanying text. The Court has made other adjustments that appear to conflict with one

Cases in which two states oppose each other are governed by federal common law.[29] Yet in fashioning federal law for particular occasions the Court often draws on the law of the states concerned. When local law predominates, disputes have no national consequence and thus have little purchase on original disposition.[30] They typically involve state interests in land or water,[31] or some species of contract obligation.[32] On the whole, original jurisdiction cases are notoriously dull or, if not dull, then trivial.[33] A party seeking to invoke original jurisdiction must first obtain leave to file the action.[34] The Court denies most motions without opinion. The Court has decided no cases involving foreign envoys in years and only two in its entire history.[35] In *Ohio v. Wyandotte Chem. Co.*,[36] Justice Harlan explained that the Court can best meet its responsibilities as the system's ultimate referee by reviewing cases in an appellate posture. Moreover, as the nation has matured the historical justifications for original jurisdiction have collapsed. In most instances today, an inferior federal court or a state court offers states a perfectly good forum in which to litigate.[37] Even in cases involving two disputing states (in which original jurisdiction is exclusive), the Court may force the states concerned to find another way to settle their differences.[38] In the rare cases in which the Court grants leave to

---

another, but probably rest on expediency. In *United States v. Wyoming*, 331 U.S. 440 (1947), the Court permitted the federal government to join private defendants to a suit against a state, even though the government plainly would not have been able to invoke the Court's original jurisdiction if it had sued those defendants alone. In *Louisiana v. Cummins*, 314 U.S. 577 (1941), however, the Court refused to allow a state to join its own citizens as defendants (thus insisting on complete diversity in original jurisdiction cases of that kind). The difference is probably that in the *Wyoming* case the Court fortified the government's ability to keep its disputes with a state in the federal forum, while in *Cummins* the Court followed its typical policy of discouraging original jurisdiction. Expediency plainly explains a third famous case, *Wisconsin v. Pelican Ins. Co.*, 127 U.S. 265 (1888), in which the Court insisted that original jurisdiction lies only for civil cases and disclaimed jurisdiction of a state's suit against a citizen of another state, seeking to impose a "penalty" for the violation of a state statute. That action may have looked too much like a local criminal prosecution, filed in the Supreme Court merely because the defendant resided in another state. Certainly, it was not the kind of matter the Court finds suitable for its own original jurisdiction. See text accompanying notes 5–8.

29. See *Connecticut v. Massachusetts*, 282 U.S. 660, 670 (1931).

30. *Kentucky v. Indiana*, 281 U.S. 163 (1930) (involving local contract law); *Texas v. New Jersey*, 379 U.S. 674 (1965) (involving the local law of escheat).

31. See, e.g., *Rhode Island v. Massachusetts*, 37 U.S. (12 Pet.) 657 (1838) (an early boundary dispute case); *Kansas v. Colorado*, 185 U.S. 125 (1902) (a classic western water rights case).

32. See, e.g., *Texas v. New Mexico*, 462 U.S. 554 (1983) (a suit to enforce an interstate compact).

33. In *California v. West Virginia*, 454 U.S. 1027 (1981), California asked the Court to decide whether West Virginia had breached a contract providing for football games between San Jose State and the University of West Virginia.

34. Sup. Ct. R. 17. The Court's discretion may be justified by the equitable character of most original jurisdiction cases, or simply on an analogy to the discretion that Congress has formally allowed the Court with respect to its appellate jurisdiction. See notes 219–20 and accompanying text.

35. Vincent L. McKusick, *Discretionary Gatekeeping: The Supreme Court's Management of Its Original Jurisdiction Docket Since 1961*, 45 Me. L. Rev. 185, 187 (1993).

36. 401 U.S. 493, 497–98 (1971).

37. This is especially true when a state or the federal government sues in *parens partriae*, advancing the interests of its citizens as well as its own quasi-sovereign interests. E.g., *Alfred L. Snapp & Son v. Puerto Rico*, 458 U.S. 592 (1982) (a suit by Puerto Rico on behalf of its farm workers); *Pasadena City Bd. of Ed. v. Spangler*, 427 U.S. 424 (1976) (a school desegregation suit prosecuted by the federal government).

38. See *Wyoming v. Oklahoma*, 502 U.S. 437 (1992) (defending the Court's exercise of *ad hoc* judgment on whether to accept cases within exclusive original jurisdiction). In *Louisiana v. Mississippi*, 488 U.S. 990 (1988), the Court denied Louisiana's motion for leave to file a boundary dispute

file an original action, the Court invariably appoints a special master to marshal the facts and offer a recommended disposition.[39] The Court eschews any *de novo* consideration of reports by masters and typically gives them an "appellate" examination.[40]

B. Appellate Review of State Judgments

By conventional account, the Supreme Court's appellate jurisdiction to review state court judgments formed the key feature of the Madisonian Compromise.[41] Article III contemplates that the Court will have appellate jurisdiction, but does not tie that jurisdiction to the kind of court that decided a matter below. Instead, Article III specifies only the "cases" or "controversies" on which the Court can rule. Since state courts, as well as inferior federal courts, may initially decide many of those matters, Article III permits the Court to review both state and federal court decisions. Recall that Congress might never have created inferior federal courts and thus might have left state courts alone to handle all the trial-level work in cases in which Article III envisioned the Supreme Court would have appellate jurisdiction. The Supremacy Clause binds "the Judges in every State" to respect federal law as the supreme Law of the Land." That clause does not obligate state courts to bow to the Supreme Court in so many words. Yet by common account it does contemplate both that state courts will have occasion to pass on federal questions and that their decisions will be subject to the discipline of a hierarchical appellate authority located in the "one supreme Court" the Constitution makes mandatory.[42]

Congress provided for the Court's review of state court judgments in §25 of the Judiciary Act of 1789.[43] The Court, for its part, quickly shouldered responsibility for superintending state courts and laid any constitutional objections to rest in three great cases from Virginia. The treaties that concluded the Revolutionary War guaranteed that land in America held by British loyalists would not be confiscated. Nevertheless, Vir-

---

action against Mississippi. Justice White's dissent revealed that the Court probably hoped that the dispute between the two states would be resolved in a pending district court action involving private parties, in which Louisiana had already filed a third-party complaint against Mississippi. Later, however, the Court held that, in light of §1251, the district court lacked jurisdiction to determine that third–party claim. *Mississippi v. Louisiana*, 506 U.S. 73 (1992). For a time, it appeared that Louisiana would have no forum at all for its claim against Mississippi. But in the end the Court relented and granted a second motion for leave to file an original action. *Louisiana v. Mississippi*, 510 U.S. 941 (1993).

39. E.g., *New Jersey v. New York*, 523 U.S. 767 (1998) (reviewing a master's absurd and unnatural conclusion that most of Ellis Island is in Jersey).

40. See *Maryland v. Louisiana*, 451 U.S. 725, 765 (1981) (Rehnquist, J., dissenting).

41. See Chapter II, notes 13–14, 20–21 and accompanying text.

42. See Chapter IV, text accompanying note 1; Chapter II, text accompanying notes 47–48, 51 (discussing Hamilton's explanation in the Federalist Papers). Professor Caminker agrees that state courts must follow Supreme Court precedent. But he insists that the literal text of the Supremacy Clause does not conclude the matter. Evan H. Caminker, *Why Must Inferior Courts Obey Superior Court Precedents?*, 46 Stan. L. Rev. 817, 837–38 (1994). See Chapter IV, notes 136–40 and accompanying text (discussing the different questions whether and why inferior federal courts are obliged to accept Supreme Court judgments as inviolate).

43. See Chapter II, text accompanying note 62.

ginia enacted a statute specifying that British land in the rich Northern Neck region should be seized and sold. In *Fairfax's Devisee v. Hunter's Lessee*,[44] the plaintiff, Hunter, claimed to have purchased some of that land from the state of Virginia. The defendant, Martin, claimed that he had inherited the same land from his uncle, Lord Fairfax, and that, in light of the treaties, Virginia could not lawfully sell it to Hunter.[45] The Virginia Court of Appeals upheld Hunter's claim on the theory that, as a matter of state law, he had obtained title to the parcel before the treaties became effective.[46] The Supreme Court reversed that judgment in an opinion by Justice Story, who concluded that Hunter's title had not been established before the treaties took effect and that Martin's federal claim under the treaties must therefore prevail.[47]

On remand, the Virginia Court of Appeals issued an order denying that the Supreme Court had appellate jurisdiction to review Virginia court judgments and declaring that the provision in the Judiciary Act of 1789 authorizing that jurisdiction was unconstitutional. In a famous separate opinion, Judge Cabell insisted that the Constitution recognized that both state and federal courts would handle federal question cases, but had "provided no umpire" if the two sets of courts should disagree. According to Cabell, the Supremacy Clause did not require state courts to accept judgments from the Supreme Court. By contrast, it instructed them to enforce federal law as they themselves understood it and thus *barred* them from bowing to a Supreme Court decision with which they disagreed.[48] In his view, the Supreme Court had direct appellate jurisdiction only

---

44. 11 U.S. (7 Cranch) 603 (1812).

45. The odd style of the case derived from the common law procedure in ejectment. In order to test his title to the land, Hunter formally alleged that he had leased the property to a fictitious person, that the person had entered the land, and that he had been ousted by Martin. That allowed Hunter's fictitious lessee to sue Martin for interference with the lease, which, in turn, put Hunter's original authority to lease the property in issue. Martin was allowed to defend his own claim only if he first admitted the fictitious lease, entry, and ouster. Actually, the case was even more fictitious than the ejectment action required it to be. Hunter was only nominally involved. The true moving party was the state of Virginia, which wanted to confirm its authority to seize land held by British loyalists. Martin's role was also marginal. He had contracted to sell the land to a group of Virginians that included John Marshall. That group actually pressed the federal treaty claim against the opposing state claim that Virginia had sold the land pursuant to state statute. Marshall represented his group in some early proceedings in state court. His personal involvement probably explains why he did not participate in the Supreme Court's ultimate disposition.

46. Spencer Roane, John Marshall's rival in Virginia, wrote the state court's opinion.

47. The Supreme Court apparently understood that it had appellate jurisdiction to consider the case pursuant to the Judiciary Act of 1789, because the Virginia Court of Appeals had rejected Martin's federal treaty claim in favor of Hunter's state law claim. See Chapter II, text accompanying note 62. In order to reach the federal claim that Martin advanced, however, Justice Story first had to reject the state court's determination that, as a matter of state property law, Hunter had obtained title to the land before the treaties took effect. Story expressly reexamined the state court's treatment of that question and reached the opposite conclusion. *Fairfax's Devisee*, 11 U.S. at 622. Matasar and Bruch contend that *Fairfax's Devisee* proceeded from a premise that would not hold today—namely, that the Court had jurisdiction to second-guess the state court regarding an issue of state law. Richard A. Matasar & Gregory S. Bruch, *Procedural Common Law, Federal Jurisdictional Policy, and Abandonment of the Adequate and Independent State Grounds Doctrine*, 86 Colum. L. Rev. 1291, 1297–98 (1986); see notes 104–06 and accompanying text. It is more likely that Justice Story found it necessary to review the state court's treatment of the state law issue to prevent the state court from frustrating Martin's federal claim by manipulating an antecedent matter of local law. See text accompanying note 123.

48. *Hunter v. Martin*, 18 Va. 1, 9–11 (1815).

over inferior federal courts. If a single referee was essential to achieve uniformity, Congress could provide for the removal of federal question litigation to those courts and, ultimately, to the Supreme Court.[49]

The *Fairfax* litigation then went back to the Supreme Court. Again writing for the Court in *Martin v. Hunter's Lessee*,[50] Justice Story rejected the arguments advanced by Judge Cabell and confirmed that state court judgments *are* subject to Supreme Court review. Perhaps to avoid further conflict with the Virginia Court of Appeals, however, Story declined to issue another order to that court, but, instead, simply entered judgment for Martin.[51] Thereafter, the Court equally dismissed objections to its appellate jurisdiction in state criminal cases. In *Cohens v. Virginia*,[52] Chief Justice Marshall recognized that a criminal appeal is arguably different from a civil appeal inasmuch as the state is a formal party and, at that, a party *defendant* when a convict seeks review of a conviction. The presence of the state as a party, in turn, invites the argument that the Court's jurisdiction can only be original rather than appellate,[53] as well as the argument that review may be barred if a state asserts sovereign immunity.[54] Marshall rejected both contentions—the first on the ground that original jurisdiction need not be exclusive, the second on the theory that a criminal action is originally initiated *by* the state in state court.[55]

The Virginia cases were essential to the constitutional framework that is now so familiar. State courts act on the basis of the power they are granted by state law, and they enjoy equal and parallel status with the inferior federal courts. They are nonetheless part of a single national juridical system and must conform their judgments to the Supreme Court's ultimate authority for that system.[56] The Court's modern functions are clear enough: to maintain the accuracy, uniformity, and supremacy of federal law. The Court can be successful in those responsibilities only if it can subject state courts to a hierarchical discipline.[57]

---

49. See Chapter VI, notes 125–35 and accompanying text (discussing the removal mechanism).

50. 14 U.S. (1 Wheat.) 304 (1816).

51. Id. at 362. When the Court reverses state court judgments today, it invariably remands for proceedings "not inconsistent" with its opinion. That disposition not only avoids the indelicacy of ordering state courts to take action, but also allows state courts the flexibility to reach other issues that may still control the result—for example, some previously unexamined state law question. See text accompanying note 151 (explaining that state courts may resolve cases on state law grounds in the wake of Supreme Court decisions on federal issues).

52. 19 U.S. (6 Wheat.) 264 (1821).

53. See Chapter IV, text accompanying note 5.

54. See Chapter X.

55. See Chapter X, notes 112–13 and accompanying text.

56. Liebman and Ryan find it important that Justice Story explicitly rejected a further argument—that the Judiciary Act authorized the Supreme Court only to determine the meaning of the treaties in the abstract, but not to reexamine the state court's application of those treaties (properly understood) to the facts of the particular case. That understanding would have reduced the Court's effective appellate jurisdiction to rare cases that can be resolved by determining "pure" legal questions alone and would have deprived the Court of the ability to ensure that state court judgments in actual cases are correct. James S. Liebman & William F. Ryan, *"Some Effectual Power": The Quantity and Quality of Decisionmaking Required of Article III Courts*, 98 Colum. L. Rev. 696, 798 (1998). See text accompanying notes 207–08.

57. See Chapter IV, notes 133–40 and accompanying text (discussing Professor Hart's "essential function" thesis).

C. Federal Questions

Just as the Supreme Court's constitutional decisions confirm and sustain a unitary federal system, modern statutes regarding the Court's jurisdiction equally support that same framework. The Judiciary of 1789 conferred appellate jurisdiction on the Court to review "final" judgments by a state's "highest" court, but only if the party advancing a federal theory *lost* below.[58] That arrangement allowed the Court to insist that federal law was held supreme, but it denied the Court authority to ensure as well that federal law was accurately and uniformly interpreted. Beginning in 1914, Congress eliminated those older features of appellate jurisdiction. Today, pursuant to 28 U.S.C. §1257, the Supreme Court has appellate jurisdiction to review a state court judgment irrespective of the outcome below, if: (1) a substantial federal question was presented to the highest state court that could determine that question; and (2) the state court issued a final judgment.[59]

1. The Preservation Requirement

Litigants who wish to invoke the Supreme Court's appellate jurisdiction must first present a federal question to the highest state court with jurisdiction to consider it. In so doing, they must make the state court aware of the federal character of the question.[60] The Court has explained this requirement both as a construction of §1257 and as a sound rule of judicial policy.[61] If parties were free to withhold a federal claim from the state courts and press it for the first time at the Supreme Court level, familiar structural arrangements would be compromised. State courts would have no opportunity to fulfill their duty and responsibility to address federal issues, and the Supreme Court would be unable to exercise genuine *appellate* review of the state courts' work. The highest state court is typically the tribunal of last resort in the relevant state, even if that court has discretion to decline jurisdiction (tracking in that respect the Supreme Court's own discretionary control of its docket).[62] The rationale is that there is no final state judgment to which the Supreme Court's appellate jurisdiction can properly attach until the state court of last resort has had an opportunity to rule on a question. The highest state court can be an inferior state tribunal, even a trial-level court, if in the particular circum-

58. For a discussion, see Daniel J. Meltzer, *The History and Structure of Article III*, 138 U. Pa. L. Rev. 1569, 1585–92 (1990).

59. But see notes 114–15 and accompanying text (explaining that state courts can insulate their judgments by resting them on adequate state grounds of decision). The Supreme Court can protect its ability to exercise jurisdiction by issuing any "necessary" or "appropriate" writs. See 28 U.S.C. §1651; *Ex parte Republic of Peru*, 318 U.S. 578 (1943); Chapter II, note 58.

60. *Adams v. Robertson*, 520 U.S. 83 (1997) (*per curiam*); *New York Central & H.R. Co. v. New York*, 186 U.S. 269 (1902).

61. E.g., *Cardinale v. Louisiana*, 394 U.S. 437 (1969). The "highest state court" requirement is specified by §1257, but the Supreme Court would undoubtedly have adopted it in the absence of statute.

62. E.g., *Gotthilf v. Sills*, 375 U.S. 79 (1963); see notes 219–23 and accompanying text; Chapter XII, notes 108–09 and accompanying text (explaining that the exhaustion doctrine in federal habeas corpus also typically demands that litigants seek discretionary review in the highest state court).

stances there is no further avenue for appellate review.[63] If a party does not raise a question in the highest state court, but that court nonetheless addresses the question on its own, the preservation requirement does not bar Supreme Court review. In that event, there is an authoritative state court judgment for the Court to examine, and the party's procedural default is inconsequential.[64] The Court occasionally entertains issues that were not preserved in state court, perhaps on the theory that it is appropriate to overlook a party's default in order to correct "plain error."[65] Yet in the main, the Court adheres to the preservation requirement.

2. The Final Judgment Requirement

The Supreme Court's appellate jurisdiction equally depends on a final judgment by the highest state court below. For more than a century following the 1789 Act, the Court took the term "final" literally and thus disclaimed appellate jurisdiction if anything remained to be decided by the state courts in order to conclude the parties' dispute. Today, the Court construes §1257 to allow considerable room for judgment. The shift undoubtedly reflects the Court's attempt to police state court determinations of federal law in an effective way. If the finality rule were more rigid, the Court might have no jurisdiction to examine federal claims at the time and in the posture best suited to maintaining the accuracy, uniformity, and supremacy of federal law.

Flexibility comes at a price. Chief Justice Rehnquist has argued that a more rigid finality rule would serve structural values.[66] When the Court adheres to the finality requirement and disclaims jurisdiction to review a state court judgment, the Court avoids confronting the state court unnecessarily and thus threatening harmonious relations within the federal system. In other contexts, the Court insists that inferior federal courts should avoid unnecessary interference with state courts.[67] Chief Justice Rehnquist contends that the Court itself should show similar restraint and thus should not reach out to decide federal questions that might be left for the time being, or indefinitely, with the state courts.[68]

The full Court resists Chief Justice Rehnquist's invitation to borrow from doctrines and practices designed to mitigate the lower federal courts' conflicts with state courts. Inferior federal courts are the co-equals of state courts. The Supreme Court's relationship to state courts stands on a different footing. The Court's appellate jurisdiction to review state judgments for error must be exercised efficiently (to conserve the Court's scarce resources), and also in a timely way (to ensure that the Court performs its func-

63. E.g., *Thompson v. Louisville*, 362 U.S. 199 (1960).

64. *Adams*, 520 U.S. at 86 (explaining that the Court has jurisdiction if a federal question was "*either* addressed by" or was "properly presented" to the court below) (emphasis added).

65. Professor Spann argues that the Court has at least that much jurisdiction. Girardeau Spann, *Functional Analysis of the Plain-Error Rule*, 71 Gtn. L.J. 945 (1983).

66. *Cox Broadcasting Corp. v. Cohn*, 420 U.S. 469, 503–05 (1975) (Rehnquist, J., dissenting). See also *Radio Station WOW v. Johnson*, 326 U.S. 120, 123 (1945) (opinion of Frankfurter, J.); *Hudson Dist. v. Eli Lilly*, 377 U.S. 386, 397 (1964) (Harlan, J., dissenting).

67. In *Cohn*, Rehnquist referred explicitly to the abstention doctrine associated with *Younger v. Harris*, 401 U.S. 37 (1971); see Chapter XI, notes 144–295 and accompanying text.

68. The Chief Justice also contends that a flexible rule is administratively burdensome in that it requires the Court to anticipate the way it is likely to decide a federal question on the merits and to take that potential decision into account when it determines whether to address the issue in the current posture of a case. *Cohn*, 420 U.S. at 501–08 (dissenting opinion). See note 78.

tions as the system's ultimate referee). Moreover, the Court must reconcile the final judgment requirement with the adequate state ground doctrine, which typically bars the Court from examining state court decisions that rest exclusively on state law grounds.[69] If the Court concludes that it has no current appellate jurisdiction to review a state court determination of a federal question (because the state court judgment is not yet final), it may happen that later, after pending state court proceedings have been completed, the Court will equally have no appellate jurisdiction (because the state courts ultimately resolve the parties' dispute on state law grounds alone). The Court can easily be caught in the middle between the final judgment requirement, on the one side, and the adequate state ground doctrine, on the other.

The Court responds to these difficulties by striking a balance. The Court retains and respects the final judgment requirement in the run of cases, but recognizes a variety of exceptions. In the leading case, *Cox Broadcasting Corp. v. Cohn*,[70] Justice White organized those exceptions under four headings: (1) cases in which the state proceedings yet to be undertaken are so *contingent* on an existing decision regarding a federal question that the result of those proceedings is preordained and it would be wasteful to delay Supreme Court review; (2) cases in which the state proceedings yet to be undertaken are so *independent* of an existing decision regarding a federal question that the federal question will survive for Supreme Court consideration, irrespective of the outcome of the further proceedings in state court; (3) cases in which the state proceedings yet to be undertaken will *insulate* a federal question from the Supreme Court's jurisdiction; and (4) cases in which further proceedings in state court *may* shield a federal question from Supreme Court review, depending on the outcome, and in which an immediate decision by the Supreme Court may both preclude those proceedings and avoid the erosion of important federal policies.

State proceedings that are contingent on a state court decision regarding a federal question. In some cases, the highest state court decides a federal question, and the only remaining issues are so dependent on that disposition that it is wasteful for the Supreme Court to postpone consideration of the federal question until the state court proceedings are complete. Justice White cited as illustrations cases in which criminal defendants lose on federal issues in the state appellate courts and then are scheduled for trials they cannot possibly win. In *Mills v. Alabama*,[71] for example, the Alabama Supreme Court rejected a criminal defendant's argument that an indictment violated the first amendment and remanded the case for trial. The Supreme Court assumed immediate jurisdiction to examine the state supreme court's decision. The defendant had no other defense and would plainly be convicted. At that point, he would appeal again, presenting the same federal question for the Court's attention. If, however, the Court sustained his first amendment claim with the case in its current posture, there would be no need to conduct a state trial.[72]

---

69. See notes 114–15 and accompanying text.

70. 420 U.S. 469 (1975).

71. 384 U.S. 214 (1966).

72. See also *Duquesne Light Co. v. Barasch*, 488 U.S. 299 (1989). In *Barasch*, the Pennsylvania Supreme Court rejected a power company's claim that its property would be taken unconstitutionally if it were not allowed to raise rates to recoup losses on a nuclear power plant. The state court remanded the matter to the public utilities commission, which had yet to compute the rates the company would be permitted to charge (without consideration of the losses the company insisted must constitutionally be taken into account). The Supreme Court held that the state court's decision on the federal "takings" claim was immediately reviewable. Nothing the public utility commission had yet to do could affect that decision. If the state supreme court was wrong, the commission was

State proceedings that are independent of a state court decision on a federal question. In some instances, the highest state court renders a decision on a federal question and orders a trial on other issues that are so separate from the federal question that they cannot affect the state court's disposition of that issue. It will remain for review by the Supreme Court, no matter what happens in further state proceedings. Justice White offered as illustrations cases in which criminal defendants prevail on some grounds, but not on others. In *Brady v. Maryland*,[73] the Maryland Court of Appeals sustained a criminal defendant's claim that the prosecution had withheld exculpatory evidence in violation of due process and remanded the case for an adjustment in his sentence. The Supreme Court assumed immediate jurisdiction to consider the state court's decision. The sentencing adjustment still to come in state court could have no effect on that judgment, and there was no point in postponing review of the federal issue.[74]

State proceedings that will insulate a federal question from Supreme Court jurisdiction. In some cases, the highest state court renders a decision on a federal question that will elude review in the Supreme Court if state proceedings yet to be undertaken proceed, irrespective of the outcome. Justice White gave as illustrations criminal cases in which the highest state court initially decides a federal question in the defendant's favor and remands for trial on that basis. In that kind of case, the dispute will ultimately be resolved exclusively on state law grounds, foreclosing the Supreme Court's appellate jurisdiction later. Ordinarily, the Court regards the prospect of avoiding federal questions as a good thing and thus cause for deferring any action. Yet in cases in this third category, the Court's failure to act in the current posture of a case cannot avoid a federal question entirely. The Supreme Court itself will not pass on it, but the state court below already has. In *California v. Stewart*,[75] the California Supreme Court reversed a criminal defendant's conviction on the ground that his confession had been obtained in violation of the fourteenth amendment. The state court then remanded for a new trial. The Supreme Court accepted appellate jurisdiction immediately. If the defendant was convicted in the second trial, he might appeal on some other ground (but not the ground on which he had already succeeded); if he was acquitted, the prosecution would be unable to appeal. Either way, the previous state court decision regarding the admissibility of the confession under federal law would escape the Supreme Court's appellate jurisdiction.

State proceedings that may insulate a federal question from Supreme Court review. In a final set of cases, the highest state court reaches a decision on a federal question that *may* be insulated from the Supreme Court's review, depending on the outcome of further state proceedings. Justice White offered as illustrations cases in which the highest state court decides a first amendment question against the party asserting the federal claim. In that kind of case, it is not certain that the dispute will be resolved on state law grounds, eliminating the Court's opportunity to examine the state court's existing deci-

---

about to undertake an expensive and time-consuming computation that would have to be revisited later.

73. 373 U.S. 83 (1963).

74. In *Radio Station WOW*, the Nebraska Supreme Court rejected a radio station's claim that its federal license would be impaired if it were required to transfer assets and remanded the case for computation of those assets with the expectation that they would be assigned to another company. The Supreme Court assumed immediate jurisdiction to examine the state supreme court's decision on the federal license issue. The outcome of the proceedings still planned in state court was not controlled by the state supreme court's decision on the station's federal claim. But nothing the state courts might decide regarding the value of the assets could affect that decision. Accordingly, the Court found it appropriate to consider it immediately. 326 U.S. at 127.

75. 384 U.S. 436 (1966) (consolidated with *Miranda v. Arizona*).

sion on the federal question. The party advancing the free speech claim *may* yet prevail in state court on other grounds, but then again may not. The risk of losing jurisdiction to review a state court decision on the meaning of the first amendment is too great. If the Supreme Court postpones review in the expectation that it will be able to reach the federal issue after state court proceedings are complete, the state court's determination will remain in place to frustrate first amendment rights during the interim. In some circumstances, delay itself violates free speech.[76]

According to Justice White, the *Cohn* case itself fell into this last category. In that case, a state statute in Georgia made it a criminal offense to publish a rape victim's name. In apparent violation of that statute, a television station identified the victim in a celebrated local case. Her father sued the station in state court, contending that the station's violation of the statute could be the basis for liability in damages. The station responded that it was entitled under the first amendment to identify the victim and that the statute was unconstitutional. The Georgia Supreme Court rejected the station's first amendment defense, but held that a violation of the statute did not alone establish the plaintiff's right to compensation under state law. The court thus remanded the case for trial to determine whether the plaintiff could recover for an invasion of privacy under general state tort law. The station sought review in the Supreme Court. Justice White acknowledged that the state courts had more work to do in order to resolve the dispute: The trial on the plaintiff's state claim lay ahead. Yet since the state supreme court had said all it would ever say about the station's constitutional claim, that court's judgment on that issue was immediately reviewable.

To justify an exception from the final judgment rule, Justice White anticipated three scenarios. First, the station might be held liable under state tort law and might, then, appeal again. In that event, the state supreme court would only reaffirm its decision that a television station could be forced to pay damages for broadcasting a rape victim's name, the first amendment notwithstanding. At that point, the station might again seek review in the Supreme Court. But the federal issue would be in no better position for the Court's attention then than it was already. Second, the station might elude liability under state law. If that happened, the federal question would fall out of the case. The disappointed plaintiff might appeal, but not on a federal theory. In that event, the state supreme court's unreviewed decision sustaining the statute against constitutional attack would remain in place, indicating (perhaps erroneously) that a television station had no first amendment right to identify a rape victim.

Justice White found both those scenarios unacceptable. Under the one, the Court would only postpone an important first amendment question that it would decide later, anyway. Under the other, the Court would allow that question to escape review altogether and thereby leave an important free press question in "an uneasy and unsettled constitutional posture."[77] Accordingly, White preferred a third scenario. If the Court examined the station's first amendment claim immediately and sustained the station's position, the litigation would be at an end. That would not only vindicate the first amendment claim advanced by the television station in the instant case, but would also avoid

---

76. See *Nat'l Socialist Party v. Skokie*, 432 U.S. 43, 44 (1977) (explaining that a restraint on expression is problematic even if it continues only until the merits of a first amendment question can be resolved); *Org. for a Better Austin v. Keefe*, 402 U.S. 415, 418 (1971) (concluding that a preliminary injunction was sufficiently final because it had been in effect for three years and plainly restricted expression).

77. *Cohn*, 420 U.S. at 485–86.

leaving other stations in Georgia to operate in the "shadow" of the statute even though its validity was in "serious doubt."[78]

The Court has not limited cases in this last category to disputes over the first amendment.[79] Nor has the Court fully rebutted Chief Justice Rehnquist's contention that this last category of exceptions from the finality rule (if not the first three) is entirely "formless" and thus threatens to swallow the rule itself.[80] By some accounts, the decisions under this heading reflect a prudential sense that the final judgment rule can and should be relaxed on an *ad hoc* basis when immediate appellate jurisdiction is appropriate to ensure the accuracy, uniformity, and supremacy of federal law.[81] The Court formally disclaims any "expansion of the exceptions stated in" *Cohn*.[82] Yet the Court's actual decisions continue to suggest that the final order rule allows a lot of play in the joints.

In *Florida v. Thomas*,[83] the Court unanimously concluded that it lacked jurisdiction to consider the question it had granted review to settle. The Court had previously held in *New York v. Belton*[84] that when a police officer arrests the occupant of a car, the officer automatically is entitled to search the passenger compartment. In *Thomas*, the Court was poised to decide whether that "bright-line" rule applies to a case in which a suspect is arrested outside his vehicle. Neither party challenged the Court's jurisdiction, but Chief Justice Rehnquist raised the jurisdictional issue *sua sponte*.[85] He explained that the Florida Supreme Court below had considered the issue pursuant to an interlocutory appeal prior to the suspect's trial, decided that the *Belton* "bright-line" rule was inapplicable, and remanded the case with instructions that the state trial court should determine the validity of the search under another Supreme Court decision, *Chimel v. California*.[86] That order was not final. Numerous state court proceedings and the trial itself lay ahead. Nor did the case fit under any of the first three exceptions identified in *Cohn*. The choice between the *Belton* and the *Chimel* rules would not necessarily determine the result of the state prosecution, the state trial court might yet conclude that the search was valid under *Chimel*, and if the trial court decided that the search was unconstitutional the prosecution might seek appellate review of that decision.[87] Coming to the

78. Id. at 486. Justice White conceded that, in this, he necessarily anticipated the Court's view of the merits of the station's first amendment claim. See note 68. In *Cohn*, as in many other cases like it, the Court reserved judgment on the finality issue until it heard the parties' arguments on the merits and was in a position to know the result it would reach if it had jurisdiction. There may be a lesson in that familiar practice. Once the justices have invested time and resources in a case and are poised to render a decision on the merits, they are unlikely to withhold judgment for want of a final order below. If, at that point, the justices *do* wash their hands of a case, it is probably for another reason (stated or unstated).

79. See, e.g., *Goodyear Atomic Corp. v. Miller*, 486 U.S. 174 (1988) (exercising jurisdiction to protect the federal interest in safety standards at nuclear power plants); *Southland Corp. v. Keating*, 465 U.S. 1 (1984) (exercising jurisdiction to avoid interference with the arbitration of labor disputes).

80. *Cohn*, 420 U.S. at 505–08 (dissenting opinion).

81. See Matasar & Bruch, note 47, at 1355.

82. *Jefferson v. City of Tarrant*, 522 U.S. 75 (1997). See text accompanying notes 213–14 (discussing the parallel final judgment rule attending appellate review of federal court judgments).

83. 532 U.S. 774 (2001).

84. 453 U.S. 454 (1981).

85. See Chapter VIII, notes 238–46 and accompanying text (explaining that Article III courts are obliged to determine their subject matter jurisdiction at the outset of every case whether or not a party raises the issue).

86. 395 U.S. 752 (1969).

87. Florida law allowed the prosecution to seek pre-trial appellate review of a trial court order excluding evidence.

last category in *Cohn*, Chief Justice Rehnquist found no credible argument that immediate Supreme Court review was justified to forestall a "serious erosion of federal policy" that would not equally be available in any "run-of-the-mine" case involving the suppression of evidence in criminal prosecutions.[88]

In *Bush v. Gore*,[89] by contrast, the Court reached and decided the merits of a federal claim without pausing to discuss the final judgment rule. The Florida Elections Canvassing Commission certified that George W. Bush had won the presidential election in Florida. His opponent, Al Gore, contested that action in state court. The state trial court denied relief, and Mr. Gore appealed. The Florida Supreme Court held that some 9,000 contested ballots might contain "legal votes" sufficient to change the result of the election. Accordingly, that court remanded the case to the trial court with instructions to superintend a manual count of those ballots. Mr. Bush then sought review in the United States Supreme Court. At that point, the Florida Supreme Court's judgment was not final. The case would not be settled in state court until the trial court finished with the manual count it was under an order to conduct. Mr. Bush argued that the Court could exercise appellate jurisdiction nonetheless, because the case fell within the last exception in *Cohn*: If the Court postponed the exercise of appellate jurisdiction, the dispute between the parties might be resolved on a non-federal basis, and the Court would lose the opportunity to address Mr. Bush's federal claim. After the contested ballots were counted, Mr. Bush might still be the winner. It was a bit awkward for Mr. Bush to make that particular argument. To do so, he had to contend that it was so important that the Court consider his federal claim that the Court should not wait to see whether he might win the election simply by getting a majority of the votes cast by the people of Florida. Mr. Gore did not address the finality issue, and the Supreme Court took jurisdiction without discussing it. The justices may have been convinced that immediate review was warranted to avoid the "serious erosion of national policy" that would follow postponement of the federal (equal protection) claim that Mr. Bush advanced. Yet that same claim would presumably be presented in any state-wide election case from Florida. If the Court acted in service of a different national interest (perhaps the interest in settling the presidential election as quickly as possible), then *Bush v. Gore* suggests, again, that the final order rule is more flexible than the Court formally admits.[90]

D. State Questions

The Supreme Court has jurisdiction to review state court judgments for mistakes of federal (not state) law. This has been the pattern from the outset. Section 25 of the Judiciary Act of 1789 specified that the Court could exercise appellate jurisdiction only if a state court first decided a federal question and could reverse only for error with respect to that federal question.[91] The Reconstruction Congress introduced doubts in 1867

88. 532 U.S. at 780.

89. 531 U.S. 98 (2000) (*per curiam*).

90. See notes 213–14 and accompanying text (noting a similar final order rule with respect to inferior federal court decisions).

91. See Chapter II, text accompanying note 62. Recall that Congress has considerable authority with respect to the Court's appellate jurisdiction. See Chapter IV, notes 10–48 and accompanying text.

when it enacted new legislation retaining the requirement that the Court could consider only cases in which a state court had ruled on a federal claim, but deleting the follow-on requirement that only an error touching the federal question could be the basis for reversal. That change suggested that Congress had altered the scope of the Court's work in a fundamental way. Where previously the Court had been limited to dispositive questions of *federal* law, it appeared that under the 1867 Act the Court would also consider *state* law issues. In *Murdock v. City of Memphis*,[92] however, the Court rejected that construction of the 1867 legislation.

Murdock's ancestors entered an agreement with Memphis, under which they conveyed a parcel of waterfront property to the city with the understanding that it would be used by the United States Navy. The agreement specified that if the Navy failed to establish a depot on the site, the land would be held in trust for the grantors and their heirs. The city sold the land to the Navy, and the Navy, in turn, began constructing a depot as planned. Ten years later, however, the Navy abandoned the project. By act of Congress, the federal government conveyed the parcel back to the city for the city's "use and benefit." Murdock filed suit in state court, claiming that as a beneficiary of the trust he was entitled to the land under the terms of the original agreement. The city responded that, as a matter of state property law, the ten-year attempt to establish the depot satisfied the original agreement and defeated the trust, that the suit was barred by the state statute of limitations, and that, in any event, the statute under which the city had received the land back from the government independently cleared the city's title as a matter of federal law. The state's highest court ruled for the city on all counts.

On appellate review in the Supreme Court, Murdock insisted that he, too, claimed the land under federal law on the theory that the statute conveying the land to the city actually confirmed the trust created by the original agreement. Justice Miller doubted the merit of that theory, but agreed that it was sufficiently federal in character to invoke the Court's appellate jurisdiction.[93] Miller focused, then, on Murdock's further argument that, pursuant to the 1867 Act, the Court should consider not only that federal question, but also the state law questions on which he had lost in state court. Justice Miller acknowledged the difficulty that the 1867 Act had introduced by dropping the provision in the 1789 Act restricting the Court to federal issues. But he refused to read the 1867 Act actually to discard that requirement and, instead, effectively read it back into the statute governing the Court's appellate jurisdiction.

Murdock contended that the Court's constitutional jurisdiction extended to "cases" and "controversies," which necessarily included both federal and state issues.[94] If, then, the Court was restricted to considering only federal questions *within* cases, it must be because Congress had established that limit by statute. The 1789 Act might well have done so, but the superseding 1867 Act did not. That argument had force. Yet it proved too much. Justice Miller declined to infer such a "radical and hazardous" change from legislative silence. Invoking a clear statement rule, he insisted that if Congress had "intended" to alter something that had been policy since the central government's "foundation," it would have done so explicitly. Miller inferred just the opposite from the 1867 Act's express preservation of the baseline requirement that the state court must have decided a federal question in order to trigger the Court's jurisdiction. If, on considering a

92. 87 U.S. (20 Wall.) 590 (1874).

93. Recall that, at the time, only a party who had lost below on a federal claim could invoke the Supreme Court's appellate jurisdiction. See text accompanying note 62.

94. See Chapter VIII, text accompanying note 6 (discussing this point).

case, the Court was to examine all manner of state issues, Miller found it implausible that Congress would have made the existence of a federal question crucial in the first place.[95]

Justice Miller added that general policy fortified his conclusion that the Court's jurisdiction was limited to federal issues. In the past, when Congress had thought that federal rights could be protected only by giving a federal court jurisdiction to decide related state law issues, Congress had conferred that kind of jurisdiction on the inferior federal courts.[96] Moreover, an expanded scope for the Court's appellate jurisdiction would be subject to abuse. Unscrupulous litigants might inject marginal federal issues into cases for the purpose of obtaining Supreme Court consideration of state law questions.[97] Finally, Justice Miller said it was not entirely clear, after all, that the Court had previously restricted itself to federal issues only because of the limitation in the 1789 Act and not on the basis of "general principles." By that, Miller plainly meant the Constitution. He explained in the end that by reading the 1867 Act still to restrict the Court's purview to federal issues, he avoided any need to decide whether the Act would have been constitutional if it had extended the Court's reach to state law issues as well.[98]

It is possible (though by no means clear) that the Reconstruction Congress meant the 1867 Act to reshape the Court's appellate jurisdiction in the radical manner that Justice Miller disclaimed. Miller's opinion in *Murdock*, like his opinion for the Court in the *Slaughterhouse Cases*[99] and other notorious decisions in the period, may have been part of a general effort on the part of a conservative Supreme Court to circumscribe, if not to frustrate entirely, the nationalist agenda then ascendant in Congress.[100] Nevertheless, Miller's result was pragmatic and, in retrospect, essential to foundational understandings of American constitutional law.

Justice Miller recognized that the decision in *Murdock* had important implications both for the Supreme Court's relationship to state courts and for the practical conduct of appeals. By his account, the Court had appellate jurisdiction to determine any federal issue that had been decided by the state court below and to affirm the state court judgment if it was correct. If, however, the Court concluded that the state court had reached an erroneous decision on a federal issue, the Court must determine whether there was a separate state law ground on which the state court's judgment could properly rest. If so, the Court still must affirm, notwithstanding the state court's error with respect to the federal question that triggered appellate jurisdiction in the first instance. The Court

95. 87 U.S. at 619, 626, 630.

96. See Chapter VIII, notes 402–22 and accompanying text (discussing the district courts' supplemental jurisdiction pursuant to 28 U.S.C. §1367).

97. 87 U.S. at 629. None of Justice Miller's points was unanswerable. For example, he insisted that if Congress had meant the Court to consider state law issues, it would not have made a federal issue the trigger for appellate jurisdiction. Yet Congress might well have required the presence of at least one federal question to ensure that an appellate case arose under federal law for purposes of Article III. Still, Miller's arguments were powerful in cumulative effect. Congress made no effort in the wake of *Murdock* to enact clear language calling on the Court to second-guess state courts on state law issues.

98. 87 U.S. at 632–33.

99. 83 U.S. (16 Wall.) 36 (1872).

100. See William M. Wiecek, *Murdock v. Memphis: Section 25 of the 1789 Judiciary Act and Judicial Federalism*, in Origins of the Federal Judiciary: Essays on the Judiciary Act of 1789, at 223, 238–39 (Marcus ed. 1992); Chapter II, notes 71–76 and accompanying text (discussing Reconstruction).

could reverse a state court only if it both *found* federal error and *failed to find* an alternative state law ground for the state court's judgment.[101]

Subsequently, the Court went a significant step further. In *Eustis v. Bolles*,[102] Justice Shiras explained that if a state court judgment rests independently on a determination of state law, the Court must decline jurisdiction altogether, disclaiming authority to examine even the state court's decision on a federal question. The proper disposition is neither to affirm nor to reverse on any basis, but to *dismiss* for want of power to consider either federal or state law issues.[103] Together, *Murdock* and *Eustis* entail three ideas that play crucial roles in the modern framework: (1) the state courts' authority to determine questions of state law; (2) the Supreme Court's inability to exercise supplemental jurisdiction over state law claims; and (3) the adequate state ground limit on the Supreme Court's appellate jurisdiction.

State court authority. State courts are authoritative with respect to state law. This follows from the absence of any federal court with jurisdiction to review state interpretations of state law for error.[104] More fundamentally, state court authority with respect to state issues almost certainly has substantive footing in constitutional law.[105] Justice Miller found it unnecessary to hold in *Murdock* that the Constitution leaves state questions to state courts. Yet if the Supreme Court *had* authority to reject state courts' views of local law (and thus to substitute its own ideas of better policy), the very existence of autonomous state law (as distinct from federal law) would be unintelligible.[106] In this respect, Miller was surely right in *Murdock*. A change from the traditional understanding on this point would have revolutionized the system, top to bottom.

Exceptional cases occasionally arise. In *Bush v. Gore*,[107] the Florida Supreme Court identified an apparent conflict between two provisions of the state statutes governing elections. One provision appeared to require the Secretary of State to certify the winner of an election by a date certain; the other provision appeared to authorize manual re-

---

101. *Murdock*, 87 U.S. at 635 (majority opinion).

102. 150 U.S. 361 (1893).

103. Matasar and Bruch contend that *Murdock* unjustifiably refused to accept jurisdiction to decide state law issues conferred by the 1867 Act and that *Eustis* unjustifiably refused to accept even the jurisdiction to decide federal issues that *Murdock*, for its part, recognized. Matasar & Bruch, note 47, at 1319–20.

104. *Dorchy v. Kansas*, 264 U.S. 286, 291 (1924). Federal courts *do* determine state law questions in a variety of contexts. But they do their best to anticipate the decisions that the state's highest court would reach. See *Salve Regina College v. Russell*, 499 U.S. 225, 241 (1991) (Rehnquist, C.J., dissenting). Federal courts do not have authority actually to second-guess state courts with respect to their own local law and to override state court decisions they regard as erroneous. See also Chapter VI, notes 198–201 and accompanying text (explaining that inferior federal courts have no appellate jurisdiction to review state judgments for error even with respect to *federal* law). A federal court can sometimes obtain an answer to a state law question from the state's highest court. Thereafter, with an authoritative account of state law in hand, the federal court can proceed to federal questions. See Chapter XI, notes 92–94 and accompanying text (describing the use of certification schemes).

105. In *Johnson v. Frankell*, 520 U.S. 911 (1977), the Court explained: "Neither this Court nor any other federal tribunal has any authority to place a construction on a state statute different from the one rendered by the highest court of the state.... This proposition, fundamental to our system of federalism, is applicable to procedural as well as to substantive rules." Id. at 916. See also *Fay v. Noia*, 372 U.S. 391, 466–67 (1963) (Harlan, J., dissenting) (explicitly contending that state court authority regarding state law issues is a constitutional mandate).

106. See Martha A. Field, *Sources of Law: The Scope of Federal Common Law*, 99 Harv. L. Rev. 881, 921 (1986).

107. 531 U.S. 98 (2000) (*per curiam*); see notes 89–90 and accompanying text.

counts of contested ballots, which could not be completed by that date. The state supreme court resolved the conflict by construing state law to permit an extension that would make it possible to conduct recounts. In the Supreme Court, Chief Justice Rehnquist filed a concurring opinion in which he declared that in his view the Florida Supreme Court was under a special *federal* obligation to respect the state legislature's wishes. As he read it, Article II of the federal Constitution gave the legislature exclusive authority to define the way in which presidential electors were chosen.[108] It followed, according to the Chief Justice, that the Court was obliged to review the state supreme court's interpretation of the state election law statutes in order to ensure that the state court did not thwart the state legislature's federal constitutional function by placing its own gloss on the legislature's enactments. Undertaking that review, the Chief Justice concluded that the state supreme court's construction of the two provisions conflicted with the scheme the Florida Legislature had established and thus could not stand.[109] The full Court disposed of the case in a *per curiam* that did not address Chief Justice Rehnquist's argument. In dissent, Justice Souter credited Rehnquist's understanding of Article II (apparently for purposes of argument) and, on that basis, examined the Florida Supreme Court's construction of the relevant statutes. Souter concluded that the state supreme court's interpretation did not transcend "the limits of reasonable statutory interpretation to the point of supplanting the statute enacted by the 'legislature' within the meaning of Article II."[110] In a separate dissent, Justice Ginsburg criticized the Chief Justice for failing to accord the Florida Supreme Court's decision the "full measure of respect" owed to "an interpretation of state law by a State's highest court."[111]

Supplemental jurisdiction. The inferior federal courts have jurisdiction to determine both federal and related state law questions in order to adjudicate cases within their original jurisdiction.[112] When, by contrast, the Supreme Court reviews state court judgments, the Court is limited to federal issues, even though state law issues, too, must be determined before disputes can be finally settled. This proposition can rest on the Court's interpretation of the 1867 Act and its modern iteration in §1257. By statute, then, the Court is limited to federal issues and has no authority to determine state questions, however important they may be to the just and proper resolution of an entire dispute. Any constitutional basis for the Supreme Court's inability to exercise supplemental jurisdiction is problematic. If the Constitution *does* make the state courts authoritative with respect to state law, it surely must follow that the Supreme Court has no power to review state court decisions for "error" that, by hypothesis, cannot exist. Yet if a federal question "case" within the meaning of Article III encompasses both federal and state law issues, then it seems to follow that the Supreme Court, like the inferior federal courts, should be able to determine whatever state law issues demand resolution in order to dispose of the entire "case."[113]

The answer lies in the different structural arrangements under which inferior federal courts and the Supreme Court operate. When a federal district court entertains an ac-

---

108. U.S. Const. art. II, §1, cl.2.

109. 531 U.S. at 118 (Rehnquist, C.J., concurring) (joined by Scalia & Thomas, J.J.).

110. Id. at 133 (Souter, J., dissenting) (joined by Stevens, Ginsburg & Breyer, J.J.). But see id. at 148–49 (Breyer, J., dissenting) (joined by Stevens, Souter & Ginsburg, J.J.) (rejecting Chief Justice Rehnquist's understanding of Article II).

111. Id. at 137 (Ginsburg, J., dissenting) (joined by Stevens, Souter & Breyer, J.J.).

112. See Chapter VIII, notes 6, 402–22 and accompanying text.

113. In a famous *amicus curiae* brief in *Murdock*, Benjamin Curtis, himself a former associate justice, argued that an Article III "case" cannot mean one thing when a district court exercises original jurisdiction and something else when the Supreme Court entertains an appeal.

tion as an original matter, there is typically no previous state court decision on any state law issues in the case. It makes sense, then, that the district court should have jurisdiction to give those issues an initial determination—hoping that its decision matches what a state court would have done in its place. When the Supreme Court entertains a case on appellate review from a state court, however, there *is* a previous state court judgment already in place. It makes little sense, then, that the Supreme Court should have jurisdiction either to second-guess the state courts regarding their own law or simply to rubberstamp a state decision the Supreme Court has jurisdiction to *consider*, but not to *change*. This is why Congress has never enacted a statute contemplating that the Supreme Court should exercise appellate jurisdiction in diversity cases initially adjudicated in state court. Given that state law controls in cases of that kind, the only "error" the Supreme Court might detect would be state court mistakes regarding state law.

Independent and adequate state grounds. As a general matter, the Supreme Court cannot upset state court judgments that rest on independent and adequate state grounds. The Court's appellate jurisdiction hinges on a state court's resolution of a case on a federal basis. The Court can affirm or reverse only with respect to a decision of that kind. If, then, a state court judgment is based independently on a separate state law ground, the Supreme Court has no jurisdiction in the matter at all—not to reexamine the state court's decision regarding state law, no more to reexamine the state court's decision regarding a question of federal law. This is *Eustis*' extension beyond *Murdock*. The great flexibility of modern practice in the Supreme Court permits the Court to manipulate the issues presented for decision and, in that way, to elude some of the rigidity of the *Eustis* doctrine.[114] In the main, however, that doctrine holds: A state ground of decision, both independent and adequate, defeats the Supreme Court's appellate jurisdiction.

Once again, the explanation for this understanding may be simply that the Court has construed the statutes governing its jurisdiction this way. Yet there is also a constitutional argument. If a state court has properly disposed of a case by means of an interpretation of state law that the Supreme Court has no authority to question, the constitutional framework may contemplate that the Court should not presume to interfere, even to address a federal question. The Court itself occasionally suggests that if it were to reexamine a state court's judgment on a federal question in those circumstances, it would act in an improper advisory capacity: If the state judgment will remain in place (resting as it does on state law), the Supreme Court's review of the federal issue can make no difference in the outcome.[115]

---

114. See notes 224–31 and accompanying text.

115. See, e.g., *Herb v. Pitcairn*, 324 U.S. 117, 125–26 (1945); *Noia*, 372 U.S. at 466–67 (Harlan, J., dissenting). See Chapter IX, notes 11–34 and accompanying text (discussing the ban on advisory opinions). Professor Fountaine contends that the adequate state ground doctrine is constitutionally grounded. Cynthia L. Fountaine, *Article III and the Adequate and Independent State Grounds Doctrine*, 48 Am. U. L. Rev. 1053 (1999). Matasar and Bruch argue that if the parties continue to dispute a federal question, there is still a case or controversy sufficient to support the exercise of Article III judicial power. Matasar & Bruch, note 47, at 1301–05. By some accounts, *Eustis* is best understood as a matter of pragmatic judgment. By disclaiming appellate jurisdiction, the Court avoids grappling with difficult federal questions, eschews unnecessary confrontations with state courts, and reserves its time and resources for other matters. Thomas E. Baker, *The Ambiguous Independent and Adequate State Ground in Criminal Cases: Federalism Along a Mobius Strip*, 19 Ga. L. Rev. 799 (1985). That explanation is probably correct, but incomplete. The Court needs no hard jurisdictional bar to achieve those ends, but can recognize formal jurisdiction and simply decline to exercise it. See notes 219–22 and accompanying text.

E. Independent State Grounds

Within its field of operation, the doctrine of independent and adequate state grounds insulates state court determinations of federal law from Supreme Court oversight. Accordingly, the administration of the doctrine bears implications for the Court's function as the system's ultimate referee.[116] Upon the whole, the Court retains ample appellate jurisdiction to maintain the accuracy, uniformity, and supremacy of federal law. There are exceptions, but they tend to prove this general rule.

1. Parallel State and Federal Issues

When a litigant in state court advances parallel state and federal claims in the alternative, he or she can succeed on *either* theory. In that kind of case, the effect of the adequate state ground doctrine on the Court's core functions depends on which party prevails in state court and the claim that proves successful there. If the party advancing a federal claim wins on both federal and state theories, the Supreme Court has no jurisdiction to review the judgment. The state court decision on the state claim is authoritative and decisive. The judgment can rest on that ground alone, and it will make no difference if the Supreme Court finds fault with the state court's treatment of the federal issue. The Court's ability to ensure the accuracy and uniformity of federal law is compromised. Yet, by hypothesis, the state court has either construed federal law correctly or given it an overly generous interpretation. Accordingly, the Court's capacity to ensure the supremacy of federal law is unaffected.

A famous old case, *Fox Film Corp. v. Muller*,[117] is the most commonly cited illustration of this point. Fox sued Muller in state court to recover damages for breach of two contracts. Muller answered that the contracts were unenforceable, because they contained an arbitration clause that had previously been held invalid under federal antitrust law. Fox countered that the offending arbitration clause was severable and that the remaining portions of the contracts could be enforced. The state supreme court held for Muller. When Fox sought appellate review, Muller argued that the state court had decided only that the arbitration clause was inseverable and that, since severability was a matter of state law, the state court had decided no federal issue to which the Supreme Court's jurisdiction could attach. Fox argued, by contrast, that the state court had decided both that the arbitration clause was inseverable (as a matter of state law) and that the contracts were invalid (as a matter of federal law). Justice Sutherland assumed that the state court had decided both issues, but then disclaimed Supreme Court appellate jurisdiction. Since the contracts were unenforceable on the state ground alone, nothing the Court said about any federal issues in the case would change the result below. As Sutherland saw the matter, the Supreme Court lacked jurisdiction in light of the "settled rule" that when a state court judgment "rests upon

116. This said, it must also be said that the inquiries that this doctrine entails regarding the interplay of federal and state law issues are equally contemplated in cases on abstention at the district court level. See Chapter XI, notes 80–90 and accompanying text. Note, too, that the adequate state ground doctrine is also applicable (by analogy) to cases in which federal court jurisdiction rests on the federal courts' authority to entertain habeas corpus petitions from state prisoners. See Chapter XII, notes 209–10 and accompanying text.

117. 296 U.S. 207 (1935).

two grounds, one of which is federal and the other nonfederal," the Court's appellate jurisdiction "fails" if the state ground is "independent of the federal ground and adequate to support the judgment."[118]

If, by contrast, the party advancing a federal claim *loses* on both federal and state theories, the Supreme Court *does* have appellate jurisdiction to review the state court's decision on the federal issue. The state court's unfavorable determination of the state question counts as an authoritative interpretation of state law, immune from Supreme Court review. But the state court's judgment cannot rest on that ground alone. Now it *does* make a difference if the Supreme Court takes a different view of the federal claim. The Court can reverse the state court's failure to give that claim its rightful scope. Accordingly, the Court's ability to ensure the accuracy, uniformity, and supremacy of federal law is preserved intact. In *Hurley v. Irish-American Gay, Lesbian and Bisexual Group of Boston*,[119] for example, GLIB sued the organizers of the St. Patrick's Day Parade in state court, contending that the organizers had violated the Massachusetts public accommodations statute by refusing to allow GLIB to participate. The organizers responded on both state and federal grounds: By their account, the parade was not a public accommodation within the meaning of the state statute, and, if it was, they were nonetheless entitled under the first amendment to exclude GLIB in order to avoid association with GLIB's message. The state supreme court ruled against the organizers on both issues. Writing for the Supreme Court, Justice Souter reached the first amendment claim and reversed.

If a litigant advancing a federal claim loses on that claim, but wins on a parallel state claim, the Supreme Court has no appellate jurisdiction. The state court's decision on the state issue is decisive. The judgment will not change, irrespective of what the Court might say regarding the state court's treatment of the federal claim. The state court's favorable judgment on the state law claim may insulate a mistaken interpretation of federal law from Supreme Court review. Yet the harm is comparatively modest. By hypothesis, the party who might have won on the basis of a federal claim succeeds on an alternative state law basis. The Court's capacity to ensure the accuracy, uniformity, and supremacy of federal law is affected only moderately. If, by contrast, a litigant advancing parallel federal and state claims wins on the federal theory, but loses on the state theory, the Supreme Court has jurisdiction to examine the state court's decision on the federal issue (at the behest of the opposing party). The state court's decision on the state issue is authoritative as always, but it is not independently decisive. The moving party's victory depends, instead, on the state court's determination of the federal claim. If that determination is erroneous, the Supreme Court can correct it and thus make a difference in the way the dispute is settled—namely, by overturning the state court's unduly expansive interpretation of federal law. Once again, then, the Court has appellate jurisdiction to ensure accuracy and uniformity, though that jurisdiction is unnecessary to ensure the supremacy of federal law.

In *Michigan v. Long*,[120] for example, a state criminal defendant asked the state courts to suppress evidence that he contended had been obtained in a search that violated both

118. Id. at 210. Justice Sutherland recognized that the severability issue arose only because the arbitration clause had previously been invalidated on federal grounds and, accordingly, that there was a formal federal issue at the bottom of the case. Yet since Fox conceded that the arbitration clause violated federal law, Sutherland found that question "foreclosed" and no longer a "subject of controversy" for the state courts. Id. See note 127 (discussing an alternative analysis of *Fox*).

119. 515 U.S. 557 (1995).

120. 463 U.S. 1032 (1983).

the fourth amendment and the corresponding provision of the state constitution. The state supreme court ruled in the defendant's favor. In the Supreme Court, Justice O'-Connor recognized that if that judgment rested exclusively on the state constitutional provision, the Court had no jurisdiction to address either that issue or the fourth amendment question. If, however, the state court judgment rested on the defendant's fourth amendment claim, the Court *did* have jurisdiction. In *Long*, Justice O'Connor resolved the ambiguity in favor of the Court's jurisdiction, reexamined the state court's treatment of the fourth amendment issue, and reversed.[121]

2. State and Federal Issues in Tandem

The analysis is different if state and federal issues are linked sequentially, so that a litigant must prevail on both state and federal questions in order to succeed. If the state court holds against such a party on a threshold question of state law, that determination is authoritative. And, *ceteris paribus*, it is decisive. The state court will typically decline even to consider the further federal issue. In this situation, however, the Supreme Court has jurisdiction to look beneath the state court's resolution of the state law issue and may, in the end, examine the federal question even though the state court declined (for state law reasons) to reach it. Since the state court's decision regarding the antecedent state issue forecloses consideration of the follow-on federal question, it is not entirely independent. It must be tested to ensure that it is not an insubstantial (or even manipulative or duplicitous) excuse for refusing to enforce federal law.

In some instances, the Supreme Court treats an antecedent state law issue as part of a party's ultimate federal claim and, on that basis, assumes jurisdiction to determine whether the state court's decision on the state question enjoys "fair support."[122] In the *Fairfax* litigation, for example, the state law question whether Hunter had obtained title to the contested parcel before the treaties took effect was antecedent to the federal ques-

121. See notes 141–55 and accompanying text. Dissenting in *Long*, Justice Stevens argued that the Court should reserve its appellate jurisdiction for cases in which Supreme Court action is needed to "*vindicate*" federal law and should not review state court judgments that over-protect federal rights. Id. at 1068 (emphasis in original). Yet the Court does have jurisdiction to correct state court judgments that read federal rights too generously—and uses that jurisdiction to maintain accuracy and uniformity. When it is advisable to bypass a case in which a party prevailed below on the basis of an erroneously expansive interpretation of federal law, the Court need not rely on the adequate state ground doctrine, but can simply decline review in its discretion. See notes 219–22 and accompanying text. Justice Stevens has also argued (consistently) that to forestall needless Supreme Court consideration of federal claims, state courts should address state law issues first and resolve cases on that basis when possible. In that way, too, litigants advancing federal claims in state court may prevail (on state law grounds), even though the Supreme Court, were it to consider the merits of their federal claims on direct review, would find them wanting. *Massachusetts v. Upton*, 466 U.S. 727, 735 (1984) (concurring opinion).

122. Professor Wechsler called this an exercise of "ancillary" jurisdiction. Herbert Wechsler, *The Appellate Jurisdiction of the Supreme Court: Reflections on the Law and Logistics of Direct Review*, 34 Wash. & Lee L. Rev. 1043, 1052 (1977). But see notes 112–13 and accompanying text. The Court also safeguards federal claims from ill-advised determinations of threshold state law issues by insisting that state grounds must be *adequate* to support the state court's judgment. The cases on adequate state grounds typically involve litigants who fail to comply with state procedural rules and, for that reason, forfeit the opportunity to press federal claims in state court. See note 163 and accompanying text. If a state court's jurisdictional explanation for failing to consider a federal claim is found to be *inadequate*, it does not count as a "valid excuse." See Chapter VI, notes 97–99 and accompanying text.

tion whether the treaties, if they were in force, defeated Hunter's claim.[123] To succeed, the party claiming under the treaties (Martin) had to prevail both on the issue of state property law and on the further theory that the treaties established his title. The Virginia Court of Appeals resolved the threshold state law issue against Martin, and ordinarily that decision would have foreclosed Supreme Court appellate jurisdiction. Nevertheless, Justice Story reviewed the state court's determination of the state law issue, evidently to ensure that Martin's federal claim was not prejudiced by means of a manipulative decision on an analytically prior question of state law.

Similarly, in *Creswill v. Grand Lodge Knights of Pythias*,[124] the Court reviewed the Georgia Supreme Court's findings of fact underlying its determination of an antecedent question of state law. The plaintiffs in *Creswill* operated a whites-only Knights of Pythias lodge in Georgia. They sued a competing lodge (said to be operated for the "negro" and "Asiatic races") in state court, seeking an injunction preventing that lodge from incorporating in Georgia under the "Knights of Pythias" name. The African Americans who operated the second lodge countered that they were entitled to use that title under an act of Congress, which had authorized the original formation of their group in the District of Columbia. The state court rested judgment for the segregationist lodge on the theory that the African American defendants had waited too long to incorporate in Georgia and thus were guilty of *laches* within the meaning of state law. In the Supreme Court, Chief Justice White explained that since the state court's decision on the *laches* issue threatened to defeat a claim of federal right, the Court had appellate jurisdiction to determine whether that decision had "fair support" in the factual record. Finding that the evidence actually showed that the African American lodge had *not* withheld its claim to use the "Knights of Pythias" name, White reversed the state court decision.[125]

In *Ward v. Bd. of County Comm. of Love County*,[126] local authorities contended that members of an Indian tribe had paid state taxes voluntarily and thus could not sue for a refund on the theory that the taxes violated federal law. The Supreme Court acknowledged that if the Indians had actually paid the taxes without objection, there was an independent state law basis on which the state court judgment against them could rest—namely, the absence of a state statute authorizing reimbursement for unlawful taxes willingly paid. The Court explained, however, that it would be unconstitutional for the state to deny a refund if the Indians had been coerced. To ensure that the state's asserted state ground was genuine, the Court conducted its own examination of the question. Finding no "fair or substantial" support for the state court judgment that the Indians had paid voluntarily, the Court concluded that they had, in fact, paid under compulsion. Accordingly, there was no state law ground that could insulate the state court judgment from review.[127]

---

123. *Fairfax's Devisee v. Hunter's Lessee*, 11 U.S. (7 Cranch) 603 (1812); see note 47.

124. 225 U.S. 246 (1912).

125. Id. at 261.

126. 253 U.S. 17 (1920).

127. Id. at 22–24. The *Fox* case may also fit under this heading. Justice Sutherland acknowledged the argument that the state law severability question was analytically prior to the question whether the remaining provisions of the contract violated federal antitrust law, even with the admittedly invalid arbitration clause stripped out. In that vein, he explained that the state court's decision on severability was "not without fair support." Accordingly, he may have been satisfied that, if the state and federal issues *were* linked sequentially, the state's disposition of the state issue was not duplicitous. Id. at 209. Formally, however, Sutherland insisted that he did not see the case that way and, in fact, said explicitly that state and federal issues were *not* arranged in tandem. Id. at 211.

3. Hybrid Cases

The independence requirement can be difficult to administer when state and federal issues are not arranged neatly either in parallel or in sequence, but are entangled with each other. Decisions in hard cases are not always anchored in clear and predictable rules, but typically turn on pragmatic judgment about the needs of the federal system.[128] Illustrations fall into three groups: (1) cases in which state and federal issues are so intertwined that they defy separation; (2) cases in which state law incorporates federal law; and (3) cases in which federal law incorporates state law.

State and federal law interwoven. In some instances, state and federal issues are so entangled that they resist the very delineation that the requirement of independence demands. If the Court were to disclaim appellate jurisdiction, federal claims would suffer for their close association with state issues over which state courts have plenary authority. Accordingly, the Court has consistently insisted that its jurisdiction is *not* defeated. In *Enterprise Irrigation Dist. v. Farmers Mutual Canal Co.*,[129] the Court said that its appellate jurisdiction is "plain" in any case in which a state court rests judgment on a state ground that is "so interwoven" with federal law that it is not "an independent matter."[130] These cases overlap with the cases on state and federal issues arranged sequentially. Here, too, the Court typically focuses on an issue the state court considered to be a matter of state law and determines whether the state court decision on that question has "fair support." The overlap is not surprising. In both instances, the practical question is whether the state court's treatment of local law enjoys enough support to defuse concerns that the state court has only concocted an ostensible state law excuse for frustrating the enforcement of federal law.[131]

In *Enterprise Irrigation* itself, the Court concluded that the Supreme Court of Nebraska had fairly applied the state law of estoppel to foreclose a federal due process claim. The Canal Company obtained permission from a state administrative agency to develop a waterway. After the Company completed the project, competitors for the water sued in state court, claiming that they had been given no opportunity to be heard in the administrative proceeding in which the Canal Company had been authorized to proceed. Justice Van Devanter said that the state court's decision on the state law estoppel theory was perfectly sound. The plaintiffs had stood idly by while the Canal Company invested resources in the project and only then had asserted their claims.

State law incorporation of federal law. Cases in which state law incorporates federal law are prime candidates for Supreme Court appellate jurisdiction.[132] Even though a state court's analysis is formally a matter of state law, the state court purports to elaborate federal law as the content of state law and, on that basis, reaches a judgment that implicates federal interests. In the classic case, *State Tax Comm'n v. Van Cott*,[133] Van Cott filed suit in state court contending that the salary he earned as a federal employee was

128. See Ronald J. Greene, *Hybrid State Law in the Federal Courts*, 83 Harv. L. Rev. 289 (1969).

129. 243 U.S. 157 (1917).

130. Id. at 164.

131. Justice Sutherland essentially made this point in *Fox* when he said that the rule in *Enterprise Irrigation* (regarding "interwoven" issues) did not "apply" *because* the issues did not appear in tandem. Id. at 210–11.

132. See Chapter VIII, notes 252–53, 276–82, 300–31 and accompanying text (discussing original district court jurisdiction in similar circumstances).

133. 306 U.S. 511 (1939).

exempt from state income tax, both because income from federal sources was immune under federal law and because the state income tax statute recognized a similar exemption. The Utah Supreme Court held for Van Cott, and the Tax Commission sought review. The Commission conceded that the judgment rested formally on the state court's interpretation of the state statute. But the Commission insisted that the state court had not exercised independent judgment, but rather had thought that it was compelled to read the statute to exempt Van Cott's income in light of prior Supreme Court precedents (upholding exemptions in similar cases on federal constitutional grounds). In the Supreme Court, Justice Black agreed. In effect, state law incorporated federal law. The state court's judgment, then, was sufficiently federal in nature to warrant appellate review.

Justice Black explained in *Van Cott* that the Court had just upset the precedents on which the Utah court had relied and wanted to give the state court the opportunity to reexamine its construction of state law, free of the weight those precedents had previously carried.[134] A similar theme operated in *Ohio v. Reiner.*[135] In that case, the state trial court granted immunity to a key prosecution witness who would have asserted her fifth amendment privilege against self-incrimination. On the strength of that immunized testimony, the defendant was convicted. The Ohio Supreme Court reversed the conviction on the ground that the witness was ineligible for immunity. The witness had denied any involvement in the crime. The state court held that she therefore had no fifth amendment privilege to assert and, as a matter of state law, could not be given immunity to induce her to talk. The Supreme Court exercised appellate jurisdiction and reversed, *per curiam*. The Court acknowledged that the formal issue in the case was the witness' entitlement to immunity under local law. Yet the state supreme court had based its determination of that state law question on its understanding of the fifth amendment privilege. That threshold federal issue was inseparable from the state question for jurisdictional purposes. The Court then addressed the constitutional issue, explained that the fifth amendment privilege is available to a witness despite a disclaimer of criminal responsibility, and remanded the case so that the state supreme court could decide whether state law still made the witness ineligible for immunity.

The Court also exercises appellate jurisdiction when state law is not compelled to incorporate federal law, but does so nonetheless. In *Delaware v. Prouse,*[136] the Court reviewed a state court decision on a question of state constitutional law, because it appeared that the state court essentially equated the rights-bearing provisions of the state constitution with the federal Bill of Rights. In cases like *Prouse*, the Court asserts appellate jurisdiction to prevent state courts from either deflating or inflating federal constitutional rights behind the cover of interpreting their own local constitutions.[137]

---

134. Id. at 515. No matter. The Utah Supreme Court ultimately reaffirmed its decision in Van Cott's favor.

135. 532 U.S. 17 (2001) (*per curiam*).

136. 440 U.S. 648 (1979).

137. In *Moore v. Chesapeake & Ohio Ry.*, 291 U.S. 205 (1934), the Court said it would have appellate jurisdiction to review a state court determination of state tort law, if that local tort law incorporated federal safety regulations. In both *Prouse* and *Moore*, the Court preserved its ability to superintend the state courts regarding federal issues, even when only state law questions were formally on the table. In *Moore*, moreover, the Court's assertion that it would have appellate jurisdiction if federal law ultimately figured in the resolution of the dispute made it easier for the Court to hold that the case, as it stood, did not "arise under" federal law for purposes of original jurisdiction in a federal district court. See Chapter VIII, notes 272–75 and accompanying text.

Federal law incorporation of state law. The Court equally asserts appellate jurisdiction to supervise the state courts in cases in which federal law embraces state law. Cases under this heading also implicate the risks associated with state and federal issues arranged in tandem: State courts may resolve issues that are formally matters of state law in a way that frustrates federal law. In *Indiana ex rel. Anderson v. Brand*,[138] a tenured teacher sued school authorities in state court, contending that they had breached her employment contract. The authorities answered that the state legislature had repealed the tenure statute on which her contract was based. The state courts held for the school officials. In the Supreme Court, Justice Roberts explained that while the state court's interpretation of state contract law was entitled to "great weight," the Supreme Court must necessarily decide independently whether the state had violated the Contracts Clause. Otherwise, that clause would merge with state law entirely and become a "dead letter."[139] There are other instances in which state law concepts are essential ingredients of federal claims. The obvious illustrations are cases under the Due Process Clause in which some substantive interest created by state law forms the property interest that, in turn, triggers constitutional protections. In those cases, too, the Supreme Court has jurisdiction to reexamine state court judgments regarding issues that are formally matters of state law, but plainly figure in the analysis of related federal claims.[140]

4. Ambiguous State Court Decisions

The independence requirement is all the more difficult to administer when state courts fail to explain the grounds of their decisions. Over its history, the Court has dealt with ambiguous state court opinions in a variety of ways.[141] In *Michigan v. Long*,[142] however, the Court adopted a single approach. Justice O'Connor explained that when a state court judgment "fairly appears" to "rest primarily on federal law" or to be "interwoven" with federal law, "and when the adequacy and independence of any possible state law ground is not clear from the face of the opinion," the Court will "accept as the most reasonable explanation" that the state court "decided the case the way it did because it believed that federal law required it to do so."[143]

This formulation has two elements: (1) a default position; and (2) a means of defeating that default position. The default position is *not* that the Court will always presume

138. 303 U.S. 95 (1938).

139. Id. at 100; see U.S. Const. art. I, §10, cl.1.

140. See *Phillips v. Washington Legal Found.*, 524 U.S. 156, 167 (1998) (explaining that the Constitution "protects rather than creates property interests" but nonetheless insisting that a state cannot "sidestep" a "takings" claim by "disavowing traditional property interests long recognized under state law"); *Webb's Fabulous Pharmacies v. Beckwith*, 449 U.S. 155 (1980) (rejecting a state court's determination that funds deposited in a state bank account were the "property" of the county rather than the individuals who had contributed to the account). Professor Merrill argues that the Court's decisions on the meaning of "property" are inconsistent. Thomas W. Merrill, *The Landscape of Constitutional Property*, 85 Va. L. Rev. 885, 889 (2000).

141. E.g., *Philadelphia Newspapers v. Jerome*, 434 U.S. 241 (1978) (asking a state court for clarification); *South Dakota v. Neville*, 459 U.S. 553 (1983) (making the determination itself); *Durley v. Mayo*, 351 U.S. 277 (1956) (dismissing on the theory that the Court's jurisdiction could not be established because the basis of the decision below was unclear).

142. 463 U.S. 1032 (1983); see notes 120–21 and accompanying text.

143. 463 U.S. at 1040–41.

a federal ground in any case of uncertainty. It first must "fairly appear" that a state court decision rests either on a federal ground or on a ground that is "interwoven" with federal law in the sense of the rule articulated in the hybrid cases.[144] In *Long* itself, the Michigan Supreme Court cited the state constitution twice, but otherwise relied entirely on federal decisions elaborating federal search and seizure principles. Accordingly, Justice O'Connor concluded that the state decision "fairly appear[ed]" to depend "primarily" on federal law.[145]

The means by which the default position can be defeated is a clear statement rule: A state court can specify the basis of its own decision. If it wishes to rely entirely on state law, it need only make that intention "clear" by inserting a "plain statement" in its opinion that precedents regarding federal law are being used only for "guidance" and "do not themselves compel" the result.[146] If the state court "indicates clearly and expressly" that its decision "is alternatively based on bona fide separate, adequate, and independent grounds," the Supreme Court will "not undertake to review the decision." Justice O'-Connor explained in *Long* that, in this, the Court means both to respect state court autonomy and to avoid rendering "advisory" opinions on federal law.[147]

The approach announced in *Long* has been questioned in academic circles.[148] If the point is to demonstrate respect for state courts, a rule that tells those courts that their decisions will be reviewed unless they write clear opinions scarcely seems apposite. If the point is actually to discover whether state court decisions depend on federal law, a rule that invites disclaimers of federal grounds may be ineffective. State judges may not satisfy the Court's desire for clarity, especially when so few parties seek Supreme Court review in any event. Instead, they may "dismiss" or "deny" claims without relying "primarily" on federal law (thus failing to trigger the presumption) and may often decline to offer any explanation at all for their judgments.[149] Moreover, the Court's effort to distin-

---

144. Id. at 1038 n.4, citing *Enterprise Irrigation*, 243 U.S. at 164; see notes 129–31 and accompanying text. See, e.g., *Pennsylvania v. Labron*, 518 U.S. 938 (1996) (*per curiam*) (asserting appellate jurisdiction because a state supreme court's application of state law precedents was "interwoven" with reliance on federal law).

145. The Court underscored this important limitation on the default position in three subsequent cases: *Harris v. Reed*, 489 U.S. 255 (1989), *Coleman v. Thompson*, 501 U.S. 722 (1991), and *Ylst v. Nunnemaker*, 501 U.S. 797 (1991). In those cases, the question was not whether state courts had decided federal questions in a prisoner's favor, so that the Supreme Court could exercise appellate jurisdiction at the behest of the prosecution (and thus be in a position to reverse the state courts and *sustain* a criminal conviction). Instead, the question in *Harris*, *Coleman*, and *Ylst* was whether state courts had decided federal claims *against* a prisoner, so that the prisoner could petition a federal district court for a writ of habeas corpus (in hopes of *defeating* a criminal conviction as the justification for detention). See Chapter XII, note 210 and accompanying text. The Court was comfortable with invoking a default position favoring access to federal court in a case like *Long*, where the effect was to ensure its own jurisdiction. The Court was plainly less enthusiastic about doing the same thing in cases like *Harris*, *Coleman*, and *Ylst*, where the effect was to allow convicts access to the inferior federal courts. Thus when the Court *did* extend the default rule to the habeas context, the justices may have taken special care to limits its operation to cases in which state court opinions chiefly rely on federal law and federal courts therefore have "good reason to question whether there is an independent and adequate state ground" for the results in state court. *Coleman*, 501 U.S. at 739.

146. 463 U.S. at 1041.

147. Id. See note 115 and accompanying text.

148. E.g., Matasar & Bruch, note 47, at 1368–69.

149. At least in habeas corpus cases, the Court has employed additional canons and "presumptions" in an effort to contend with opaque state court orders and opinions. Writing for the Court in *Coleman*, for example, Justice O'Connor declared that an unexplained summary order *dismissing* a

guish federal and state grounds more accurately may backfire: State courts may routinely drop boilerplate disclaimers of federal grounds into every opinion and thus formally rest all their decisions on state law—whether or not federal principles play a significant role.[150] If the Court presumes that a state court has rested its decision on a federal ground, accepts jurisdiction, and reverses, the state court is free on remand to reinstate its earlier judgment by clarifying that it actually was based on state law. The result is arguably an unseemly pattern of Supreme Court decisions that are not ultimately dispositive.[151]

The chief criticism of *Long* is that it places the Court in a position to correct state court errors of federal law primarily when the state courts have given federal rights an overly generous interpretation. On the whole, the default position controls in cases like *Long* itself, in which litigants advance parallel state and federal claims and obtain a favorable judgment in state court.[152] In cases of that kind, the only way in which the Supreme Court can alter the resolution is to take appellate jurisdiction of the federal claim and reverse. That is what happened in *Long*. A federal claim that had been upheld in state court was ultimately defeated. Supreme Court appellate jurisdiction in a case like *Long* serves the accuracy and uniformity of federal law, but it is unnecessary to guard its supremacy.[153] When the Court overturns a state judgment that sustained a federal claim, the Court not only respects countervailing state interests, but also vindicates

---

claim in response to a motion to dismiss on procedural grounds is very likely to rest on the procedural ground asserted. *Coleman*, 501 U.S. at 740. In *Ylst*, Justice Scalia suggested that a state order *denying* a claim may be more likely to rest on the federal merits. *Ylst*, 501 U.S. at 802. Justice Scalia recognized in *Ylst* that higher level state appellate courts commonly give no explanation at all for their rulings against convicts in cases in which lower state courts *did* explain negative decisions on either state or federal grounds. Where that is the case, Justice Scalia said that a federal habeas court should "presume" that the highest state court embraced the rationale of the last "reasoned" decision below. If an intermediate state appellate court rested on a state procedural ground, that rationale should be ascribed to an otherwise unexplained order issued by a higher state court. And if a lower state court relied primarily on federal grounds, that basis of decision should equally be ascribed to an unexplained order by a higher court, thus engaging the default position from *Long*. Justice Scalia explained that litigants are entitled to rebut this presumption in the circumstances of individual cases. Yet he insisted that, when unrebutted, a presumption that takes the last reasoned state court opinion to be authoritative produces both an administrable scheme and one that is likely to identify state court rationales accurately. 501 U.S. at 803.

150. See James A. Gardner, *The Failed Discourse of State Constitutionalism*, 90 Mich. L. Rev. 761, 803–04 (1992) (reporting that the New Hampshire Supreme Court has adopted this very practice).

151. See *Arizona v. Evans*, 514 U.S. 1, 31–33 (1995) (Ginsburg, J., dissenting).

152. The Court did not employ the *Long* approach in *Capital Cities Media v. Toole*, 466 U.S. 378 (1984). Broadcasting companies sued in state court, seeking access to state criminal proceedings. The Pennsylvania Supreme Court refused to issue a writ of prohibition that would have forced a trial court to open the proceedings more fully. It was unclear whether the state supreme court rejected the broadcasters' first amendment claims or, instead, merely found a writ of prohibition unavailable as a matter of state law. Since the state court wrote no opinion at all, its decision could not "fairly appear" to be based on the federal ground. See note 149 (discussing the Court's subsequent discussion of this problem in *Ylst*). The Court might have been expected to dismiss for want of jurisdiction. Instead, the Court vacated the state judgment and remanded for clarification. The disposition in *Capital Cities* may represent a departure from *Long* in a case in which the Court was particularly concerned that a federal right might otherwise be violated. It seems more likely, however, that the Court regarded *Capital Cities* as a case in which state and federal issues were arranged in tandem. The Court therefore assumed responsibility to test the independence and sufficiency of any supposed threshold state ground, lest it frustrate a federal claim that depended upon it. See notes 122–27 and accompanying text.

153. See text accompanying note 121.

values that have their own constitutional footing in federalism, state autonomy, and democratic decision-making.[154] That insight, however, may only underscore the ideological implications of the approach the Supreme Court takes to its own jurisdiction in *Long* and similar cases.[155]

The Court did not invoke the *Long* presumption in the *Bush v. Gore* litigation. But it is hard to think that, in that respect, the Court was playing politics. Recall that the Florida Supreme Court initially decided that the state statutes governing elections permitted an extension of time to allow for manual recounts.[156] On the surface, the state court had simply given those statutes an authoritative construction. That, in turn, suggested a state ground of decision. Yet the state supreme court appeared to rely on the Florida Constitution to provide context for its interpretation of the statutes. In the minds of at least some justices of the United States Supreme Court, the invocation of the state constitution injected *federal* constitutional issues into the case. Recall that some justices understood Article II to give the state legislature exclusive authority for establishing the means for choosing presidential electors.[157] To the extent the state supreme court relied on the state constitution as an independent source of state election law, the state court arguably overstepped its Article II bounds. In *Bush v. Palm Beach County Canvassing Bd.*,[158] the Court vacated the state court's judgment and remanded for clarification. In doing so, however, the Court did not depart from *Long*. The uncertainty was not over whether the state court had relied on federal or state grounds, but whether the state ground on which the state court had plainly relied was a matter of state statutory construction alone or, as well, state constitutional interpretation. Predictably, the Florida Supreme Court responded with a new opinion purporting to rest judgment entirely on the court's construction of the statutes enacted by the Florida Legislature.[159]

F. Adequate State Grounds

State law grounds of decision can foreclose Supreme Court appellate jurisdiction only if they are both independent and adequate. The adequacy of a state law ground is a question of federal law for the Court to determine.[160] Both state substantive and procedural grounds can qualify.[161] State substantive grounds tend to be tested for ade-

154. Professor Bator often made this point. See Paul M. Bator, *The State Courts and Federal Constitutional Litigation*, 22 Wm. & Mary L. Rev. 605, 633 (1981).

155. Professor Glennon argues that *Long* allows the Court "to rein in liberal state judges." Robert J. Glennon, *The Jurisdictional Legacy of the Civil Rights Movement*, 61 Tenn. L. Rev. 869, 902 (1994). Professor Wells sees *Long* as one of many instances in which procedural rules are employed to promote substantive values. Michael Wells, *The Impact of Substantive Interests on the Law of Federal Courts*, 30 Wm. & Mary L. Rev. 499, 523–530 (1989). Professor Solimine agrees that *Long* limits the Court's capacity to superintend state courts. But he thinks that state courts faithfully apply federal law and may need no routine surveillance. Michael E. Solimine, *Supreme Court Monitoring of State Courts in the Twenty-First Century*, 35 Ind. L. Rev. 335 (2002).

156. See notes 89–90 and accompanying text.

157. See text accompanying notes 108–09.

158. 531 U.S. 70 (2000) (*per curiam*).

159. *Palm Beach Canvassing Bd. v. Harris*, 772 So.2d 1273 (2000).

160. *Street v. New York*, 394 U.S. 576, 583 (1969).

161. The *Murdock* case illustrates a state substantive ground of decision. The state court's judgment in that case rested on a matter of local real property law. See notes 92–98 and accompanying text.

quacy when state and federal issues are linked sequentially.[162] Most of the cases in which the Supreme Court finds state law grounds inadequate involve procedural grounds.[163]

1. Illustrations

State procedural grounds typically promote efficiency. For example, a state "contemporaneous objection" rule requires litigants to object to the admissibility of evidence at the time the evidence is offered on pain of forfeiting any later opportunity to complain either to the trial court or to the state appellate courts.[164] A rule of that kind encourages litigants to focus the trial court's attention on an admissibility claim at the earliest opportunity and thus allows the court either to sustain the objection and avoid error in the first instance or to build a record that will facilitate an appellate court's review of the matter. In the absence of such a rule, litigants might deliberately invite error by withholding an objection to evidence from the trial court with the intention of urging an appellate court to reverse on that ground if the trial court's judgment resolving the entire case is unfavorable.[165]

The state interest in efficient litigation does not always justify withholding Supreme Court appellate jurisdiction.[166] Moreover, state procedural requirements can be manipulated to frustrate federal claims indirectly. Procedural issues of state law are invariably linked with federal questions in succession: A state court first decides that the party advancing a federal claim failed to comply with the applicable local rule for presenting the claim, then declines to reach the federal claim. That sequential arrangement alone means that the Supreme Court must calculate whether the state ground is sufficient to foreclose the Court's appellate jurisdiction of the underlying federal claim. Thus when a state court refuses to address a federal claim because of a litigant's procedural default, the Court must inquire into the *bona fides* of the state court's work.

The Court rarely finds state grounds actually to *be* inadequate. To do so is to confront state courts that have disposed of cases on grounds they regard as sufficient and to insist that the adjudication of a federal issue has been sacrificed without justification. The political and ideological implications of that kind of conflict counsel restraint. The Supreme Court employs a process model to determine whether to con-

162. See notes 122–27 and accompanying text.

163. Professor Meltzer provides an extensive catalog of the precedents. Daniel J. Meltzer, *State Court Forfeitures of Federal Rights*, 99 Harv. L. Rev. 1128 (1986).

164. Litigants who fail to comply with state procedural rules of this kind are often said to "waive" the claims in issue. That is a misnomer. A waiver is a knowing and deliberate act. State procedural rules typically cut off claims if they are not seasonably advanced, whether or not the parties concerned consciously decided to withhold them. If, then, litigants lose the opportunity to press claims because of procedural default, they *forfeit* those claims in service of the state's interests in efficient litigation.

165. Professor Resnik disputes the notion that litigants commonly "sandbag" the state courts in this way. She argues that it is unrealistic to think that litigants and their lawyers plot such "fantastically risk-prone" strategies, particularly in criminal cases. It is far more likely that if counsel fails to object to illegal evidence at the proper time, it is because of ignorance or neglect. Judith Resnik, *Tiers*, 57 So. Calif. L. Rev. 837, 896–98 (1984). Accord Meltzer, note 163, at 1196–99.

166. Justice Holmes' famous dictum makes (but plainly overstates) this point: "[T]he assertion of federal rights, when plainly and reasonably made, is not to be defeated under the name of local practice." *Davis v. Wechsler*, 263 U.S. 22, 24 (1923).

sider federal questions that state courts refuse to entertain because of procedural default.[167] The cases in point fall into four general categories: (1) cases in which state procedural rules violate federal law; (2) cases in which state rules are inconsistently applied; (3) cases in which state rules have too little rational basis to warrant foreclosing Supreme Court review of federal issues; and (4) cases in which state rules ordinarily are adequate to forestall Supreme Court review, but are inadequate when applied in extraordinary circumstances.[168]

Rules that violate federal law. A state ground of decision is inadequate if it depends on a state procedural rule that itself violates federal law, either in general or as the rule is applied in a particular instance. If a state rule is invalid as a federal matter, the Court has appellate jurisdiction to consider *that* federal issue, quite apart from the federal claim the state court failed to reach.[169] In *Brinkderhoff-Faris Trust & Savings Co. v. Hill*,[170] for example, the state court below deprived a taxpayer of property without due process by arbitrarily denying him an opportunity to attack a state tax on equal protection grounds. The Supreme Court reversed on the basis of the due process violation and remanded the case to state court for consideration of the equal protection claim.[171]

Modern illustrations tend to be cases in which state courts apply facially valid procedural rules in a fundamentally unfair way. In *Reece v. Georgia*,[172] an African American defendant claimed that blacks had been excluded from the grand jury that indicted him (for raping a white woman). The Georgia Supreme Court refused to consider that claim, because the defendant had failed to comply with a local rule requiring challenges to a grand jury array to be filed prior to indictment. The defendant had been indicted only three days after his arrest and before counsel had been appointed to represent him. In those circumstances, the Supreme Court held that the state's failure to give the defendant a "reasonable opportunity" to comply with the rule violated due process. Accordingly, his failure to comply supplied no adequate state ground for the state court's decision.

Due process cases are notoriously fact-sensitive. For every case like *Reece*, in which the individual prevailed, there are dozens of counter-examples in which litigants were unsuccessful. In *Michel v. Louisiana*,[173] decided with *Reece*, the Court rejected very similar due process arguments by African American defendants in Louisiana. And in *Herndon v. Georgia*,[174] the Court disclaimed jurisdiction to consider an obvious first amendment claim, because the defendant (an African American organizer

---

167. See Chapter I, notes 73–77 and accompanying text (discussing the process model).

168. Professor Glennon contends that many of these cases reflect the Warren Court's efforts to contend with state court racism during the civil rights movement of the 1960s. Glennon, note 155, at 885–902.

169. See Alfred Hill, *The Inadequate State Ground*, 65 Colum. L. Rev. 943, 944–45 (1965). This is true, at least, if the validity of the procedural rule under federal law is properly presented to the state courts and thus preserved for Supreme Court attention. See notes 60–65 and accompanying text.

170. 281 U.S. 673 (1930).

171. Id. at 682.

172. 350 U.S. 85 (1955).

173. 350 U.S. 91 (1955).

174. 295 U.S. 441 (1935).

for the Communist Party) had not advanced that claim until a motion for rehearing in state court. There were powerful reasons to decide *Michel* and *Herndon* the other way. But the Court plainly hesitated to confront the state courts in racially charged circumstances.[175]

Rules that are inconsistently applied. A state ground of decision can be inadequate if a state court enforces a rule inconsistently or springs a novel rule on litigants in the eleventh hour, when it is too late to comply.[176] In *NAACP v. Alabama ex rel. Patterson*,[177] the NAACP was held in contempt for refusing to produce its membership list for inspection by state authorities and appealed on the theory that the forced disclosure of its members' names would violate the first amendment. The Alabama Supreme Court refused to consider that federal claim, because the NAACP might have avoided contempt by resisting the original order to disclose the membership list in an action for a writ of prohibition. The state court had never before insisted on any such extraordinary procedure. Accordingly, the Supreme Court held that the NAACP's failure to follow that course did not furnish an adequate state ground for the state court's decision.[178]

One proposed extension on the *Patterson* theme is doubtful. In *Sullivan v. Little Hunting Park*,[179] Justice Douglas suggested that if a state court has authority to waive a rule, but does not always exercise that authority, it follows that the rule is inconsistently applied. In *Sullivan*, the Virginia Court of Appeals held that civil rights plaintiffs in a race discrimination case had committed procedural default under state law by failing to give opposing counsel a copy of the trial transcript. It was conceded that the state court had discretionary power to waive that rule to avoid a miscarriage of justice, but had declined to do so in *Sullivan*. In a separate opinion, Justice Harlan explained that if a state court's ability to make *ad hoc* exceptions to local procedural rules rendered its enforcement of those rules inadequate to support its judgments, state courts might respond by enforcing procedural rules relentlessly, without exceptions for cases in which justice called for dispensation. That, of course, would be perverse—and nothing that Justice Douglas would have wished to bring about.[180]

Rules that lack sufficient basis. A state ground of decision is inadequate if it depends on a peculiarly rigid rule that serves only trivial state interests. In *Staub v. City of Baxley*,[181] the state court refused to consider a first amendment attack on a city ordinance, because the plaintiff had challenged the statute in its entirety rather that specifying each section of the ordinance she meant to condemn. That, according to the Supreme Court,

---

175. Dissenting in *Herndon*, Justice Cardozo argued that the first amendment claim in that case had not become clear until the Georgia Supreme Court gave the statute a surprising construction in another case and that the defendant had then advanced his claim as soon as he reasonably could—in a motion for rehearing. 295 U.S. at 446–47 (dissenting opinion).

176. The selective enforcement of state law can violate the fourteenth amendment, as can the retroactive application of a forfeiture rule. Moreover, in cases under this heading, state courts may be charged with violating the underlying federal rights they purport to avoid—by erecting bogus state law grounds of decision for the deliberate purpose of frustrating federal law. See Hill, note 169, at 958–59; *Williams v. Georgia*, 349 U.S. 375, 399 (1955) (Clark, J., dissenting).

177. 357 U.S. 449 (1958).

178. Accord *NAACP v. Alabama ex rel. Flowers*, 377 U.S. 288 (1964); *Barr v. City of Columbia*, 378 U.S. 146 (1964).

179. 396 U.S. 229 (1969).

180. See Hill, note 169, at 985–86 n.174.

181. 355 U.S. 313 (1958).

was to demand "an arid ritual of meaningless form."[182] In *Shuttlesworth v. City of Birmingham*,[183] the Court took a similar view of a rule regarding the paper on which an appellate brief could be printed. And in *James v. Kentucky*,[184] the Court refused to credit a state procedural ground where the state courts had declined to consider a criminal defendant's federal claim because he had asked for a jury "admonition" when he should have asked for an "instruction." Here, too, there are close cases. Yet there are precedents enough to establish that some state procedural rules are insufficient to foreclose Supreme Court appellate review, even if those rules are not so baseless that they themselves violate the fourteenth amendment.[185]

Rules that are inadequate as applied. A state ground of decision can also be inadequate if it depends on a rule that is arbitrarily applied in a particular case, even if the rule is valid in general and its application, while arbitrary, stops short of constituting an independent constitutional violation. The most famous illustration is *Henry v. Mississippi*.[186] In that case, a defendant in a state criminal prosecution failed to comply with a state contemporaneous objection rule. Yet the defendant raised his federal objection to the admissibility of evidence later, in a motion for a directed verdict. According to Justice Brennan, that motion was the substantial equivalent of the motion the defendant should have filed at the time the evidence was offered. It came late, but it nonetheless served the state's legitimate interests in presenting the federal claim to the trial judge before the case went to the jury. Justice Brennan declined actually to conclude that the state's procedural ground was inadequate. Yet he did remand the case to permit the state supreme court to reconsider its decision not to address the federal claim because of the defendant's procedural default. The *Henry* decision has been criticized, primarily because it requires the Court to undertake *ad hoc* examinations of the way state courts implement their own procedural law. That, in turn, challenges state courts to shape local practice to suit the justices' predilections. The Court has not cited *Henry* favorably for many years. By most accounts, the analysis in that case is no longer viable. If a state court's application of a procedural rule establishes an independent constitutional violation, the resulting state ground of decision is inadequate.[187] Otherwise, the application of a rule, valid in itself, almost always produces a state ground of decision that is adequate to bar Supreme Court review.

There are, however, exceptions to this general proposition. In *Osborne v. Ohio*,[188] a state contemporaneous objection rule required the defendant to object to jury instructions at the time they were given. The defendant failed to comply with that rule. Yet he had raised his federal claim earlier in a motion to dismiss the charges before the trial began. In those circumstances, Justice White explained that no purpose was served by the state court's refusal to consider the federal claim because the defendant failed to re-

182. Id. at 320.
183. 376 U.S. 339 (1964).
184. 466 U.S. 341 (1984).
185. Justice Frankfurter wrote separately in *Staub* to argue that it *did* make sense to ask the plaintiff to attack each section of the ordinance in turn, in order to focus her federal claims in the interest of rigorous analysis.
186. 379 U.S. 443 (1965).
187. See notes 169–75 and accompanying text.
188. 495 U.S. 103 (1990).

peat it at the proper time. In *Lee v. Kemna*,[189] Justice Ginsburg relied on *Osborne* to find a state ground inadequate in similar circumstances.[190] The defendant in *Lee* claimed that he was denied due process when a trial judge refused to grant a continuance to allow him to locate alibi witnesses. Local procedural rules ostensibly required a timely written motion for a continuance, setting out the basis for the request and other details. In *Lee*, however, defense counsel was surprised by the sudden disappearance of his witnesses and thus had not prepared a written motion. The state supreme court declined to consider his federal claim because of that procedural default. Justice Ginsburg concluded that in the special circumstances of the *Lee* case, the state's procedural ground of decision was inadequate. The defendant had offered an oral motion, which served the state's legitimate interests.

The decisions in *Osborne* and *Lee* are virtually unique. In *Osborne*, Justice White's treatment of the adequacy question was summary at best. In *Lee*, Justice Ginsburg took pains to explain that state contemporaneous objection rules are usually "unassailable" and thus routinely establish adequate grounds of decision when applied in ordinary circumstances.[191] Dissenting in *Lee*, Justice Kennedy complained that the Court's decision revived *Henry*.[192] In response, Justice Ginsburg explicitly disclaimed that characterization. In *Henry*, she explained, the defendant was allowed to compensate for failing to offer a federal claim in a timely way by raising the claim later. In *Lee*, by contrast, the defendant met the substantive demands of local procedural law at the proper time, albeit without filing precisely the written motion that state law contemplated.[193] Setting *Henry* to one side, Justice Ginsburg relied, instead, on the precedent set in *Osborne* and on a laundry list of special circumstances in *Lee* that justified the Court's decision that the state's procedural ground was inadequate.[194] The implication is clear. In most instances, state grounds will not be found inadequate on the theory that state courts arbitrarily applied valid procedural rules (in the absence of an independent constitutional violation).

---

189. 534 U.S. 362 (2002).

190. The circumstances were dissimilar in one respect. In *Osborne*, the Court applied the adequate state ground doctrine in an ordinary case on direct review of a state court decision. In *Lee*, by contrast, the Court applied the doctrine in a case in which the petitioner had initially filed a habeas corpus petition in a federal district court and then sought Supreme Court direct review of the district court's decision denying him federal habeas relief. Ordinarily, one would expect the Court to be less generous to a habeas petitioner than to a litigant seeking direct review. See Chapter XII, text accompanying note 62. Yet the adequate state ground doctrine applies (by analogy) to habeas cases, and *Lee* is an illustration that its meaning does not change in the different context. See Chapter XII notes 209–11 and accompanying text. But see note 145 (suggesting that the Court may have adjusted the *Michigan v. Long* feature of the doctrine for application in habeas corpus cases).

191. 534 U.S. at 379.

192. Id. at 393–95 (dissenting opinion).

193. Id. at 386 & n.16 (majority opinion).

194. Justice Ginsburg explained that state's attorneys did not complain about the absence of a written motion until two years later when the case was on appeal, that the trial judge announced at the crucial point that he was unwilling to grant a continuance because he had no room on the calendar, that there were no state court precedents establishing that the rules requiring a written motion were to be rigidly applied, and, most importantly, that counsel did all he could do in the urgency of the circumstances to apprise the trial judge of the basis on which he sought a continuance. Id. at 380–85. It was almost certainly important, too, that the defendant in *Lee* was convicted on the basis of eye-witness testimony that the absent alibi witnesses might have rebutted. The Court was undoubtedly concerned that the defendant might be the innocent victim of misidentification.

2. Proper Disposition

When the Supreme Court concludes that a state ground of decision itself violates federal law, the Court typically reverses on that basis and remands the case to the state courts for consideration of the underlying federal claim. When the Court concludes that a state ground is inadequate, though not in itself invalid, the Court has no authority to reverse, unless and until it reaches the federal question the state court declined to consider. The Court hesitates to determine federal questions without a state court decision below. Accordingly, the Court occasionally contrives to channel cases back to state court in an informal way. The classic illustrations in point are *Henry v. Mississippi*[195] and *Williams v. Georgia.*[196] Both were sensitive individual liberty cases. Both involved African American defendants convicted in state court at a time when racial tensions ran high. The Court clearly meant to encourage the state courts to put state procedural niceties aside and determine the merits of the defendants' federal claims. In both instances, the Court was unsuccessful.[197]

Recall that in *Henry* Justice Brennan only suggested that the state's procedural ground of decision was inadequate, but nonetheless remanded the case to the state supreme court in hopes that court would address the defendant's federal claim, after all. Brennan dropped the heavy hint that the state court should overlook any supposed procedural default, unless the defendant had *deliberately* failed to file a contemporaneous objection advancing that federal claim in order to mislead the trial judge.[198] In *Williams*, the Court acknowledged the validity of a state rule requiring challenges to the jury venire to be filed before trial, but intimated that the state court had applied that rule inconsistently. There, too, the Court reversed and remanded in hopes that the state court would reach the merits of the prisoner's underlying claim. Academics debate whether *Henry* and *Williams* prove that the adequate state ground doctrine is more a body of *ad hoc* prudential judgments than it is legal doctrine at all.[199]

---

195. See notes 186–87 and accompanying text.

196. 349 U.S. 375 (1955).

197. Aaron Henry was ultimately vindicated in a habeas corpus proceeding in federal court. *Henry v. Williams*, 299 F. Supp. 36 (N.D. Miss. 1969). Aubry Williams was executed. See Del Dickson, *State Court Defiance and the Limits of Supreme Court Authority: Williams v. Georgia Revisited*, 103 Yale L.J. 1423 (1994).

198. Brennan thus suggested that the state's procedural ground of decision might be adequate only if the defendant had actually *waived* his federal constitutional claim. See note 164; Field, note 106, at 966–67. That idea has not survived. See Meltzer, note 163, at 1145. The Warren Court established a waiver standard for cases in which criminal defendants failed to comply with state procedural rules and then sought to raise federal claims via applications for the federal writ of habeas corpus. That rule, too, has been discarded in more recent decisions. See Chapter XII, notes 203–07 and accompanying text.

199. Professor Meltzer contends that the source of the adequacy doctrine is federal common law, which allows states to employ a variety of rules in different contexts but fixes a baseline (which itself varies with the circumstances) beneath which the states cannot go. Accordingly, the Court can vacate and remand a case if it finds a state law ground to be inadequate as a matter of federal common law, because state courts are obligated to apply that law just as would a federal court. Their failure to do so is reversible error. Meltzer, note 163, at 1132–33; see Chapter VI, note 100 and accompanying text. Professor Field argues that when the Court refuses to accept a state ground as adequate, it is not (necessarily) because that ground *is* inconsistent with federal common law, but rather because it *would* be if the Court were to create federal law for the occasion. According to Field, the Court's power to create that law enables the Court to decide, instead, to "bend existing state rules to make them consistent with federal interests." Field, note 106, at 969–70.

G. Standards of Review

In general, the standards the Supreme Court employs in reviewing state court judgments correspond to the three steps in the adjudicative function.[200] The Court extends great deference to state court determinations of historical facts and typically accepts findings of that kind if they are supported by "substantial evidence."[201] This is true as a generalization even with respect to findings touching constitutional claims.[202] In essence, the Court applies to state court findings the standard of review that Rule 52(a) of the Federal Rules of Civil Procedure prescribes for federal appellate review of factual findings by federal district courts. Under Rule 52(a), "[f]indings of fact, whether based on oral or documentary evidence, shall not be set aside unless clearly erroneous."[203] The Court equally defers to the state courts' rational inferences from historical facts.[204] By contrast, the Court exercises entirely fresh, *de novo* judgment regarding state court interpretations of federal law,[205] as well as state court applications of law to the facts of particular cases (determinations of so-called "mixed" questions of law and fact).[206]

The Court's authority to see that abstract principles of federal law are properly applied in actual cases was central to the great *Martin* case.[207] Hunter argued that if the Court had power to review the Virginia court's judgment at all, its power was limited to deciding whether the state court had correctly interpreted the treaties and did not extend to deciding whether the state court had correctly determined Martin's particular claim under the treaties, properly construed. Justice Story rejected that argument, explaining that the Court had appellate jurisdiction to review the state court's "decision" below. That decision must necessarily include both the state court's articulation of the abstract law of the matter and its application of that law to the instant facts.[208]

These generalizations hold in large measure, but they can be misleading. The Court routinely departs from them in sensitive contexts—sometimes to safeguard federal rights, sometimes to foster harmonious relations with state courts. In free speech cases, for example, the historical facts are invariably crucial, and an unsympathetic state court can skew proper constitutional analysis by misrepresenting the events on which first amendment principles are brought to bear. The Court has explained, accordingly, that it will reexamine state court findings of historical fact in speech cases as a safeguard

---

200. See Chapter I, text accompanying note 8.

201. *General Motors v. Washington*, 377 U.S. 436, 442 (1964). If the state courts fail to find the material facts, the Court typically hesitates to make the necessary findings itself on the basis of the record and thus remands for further fact-finding at the state level. E.g., *United Bldg. & Constr. Trades Council v. Mayor of Camden*, 465 U.S. 208 (1984).

202. Cf. Chapter V, note 49.

203. See *Hernandez v. New York*, 500 U.S. 352, 365 (1991); *Bose Corp. v. Consumers Union*, 466 U.S. 485, 499 (1984).

204. See *Hernandez*, 500 U.S. at 369 (deferring to a state court's inference that a prosecutor's explanation for striking Hispanic jurors was not pretextual).

205. Hill, note 169, at 945.

206. *Norris v. Alabama*, 294 U.S. 587, 590 (1935); *Fiske v. Kansas*, 274 U.S. 380, 385 (1927).

207. *Martin v. Hunter's Lessee*, 14 U.S. (1 Wheat.) 304 (1816); see notes 50–57 and accompanying text.

208. 14 U.S. at 358–59. Liebman and Ryan contend that *Martin* and other familiar precedents establish that all Article III courts exercising the federal judicial power must have authority to decide the "whole" case. Liebman & Ryan, note 56, at 696.

against that contingency.[209] In other cases, the Court hesitates to give even state court determinations of mixed questions the independent examination that conventional doctrine contemplates. In order to disclaim that kind of review, the Court sometimes characterizes issues that are quite plainly mixed as, instead, questions of historical fact, and on that basis invokes a highly deferential standard of review.[210]

H. Appellate Review of Federal Judgments

The Supreme Court has appellate jurisdiction to review judgments rendered by the inferior federal courts.[211] Pursuant to 28 U.S.C. §1254, the Court may review cases "in the courts of appeals," either at the instance of a party or by certification from the court of appeals itself.[212] The circuit courts, in turn, have appellate jurisdiction (pursuant to 28 U.S.C. §1291) to review "final decisions" by the district courts. In the vast majority of cases, accordingly, the Supreme Court's jurisdiction attaches to circuit court judgments that depend on final judgments at the district level. The Court cites cases involving the final judgment requirements in §1291 and §1257 interchangeably, as though the finality question is the same, irrespective of whether the tribunal below was a federal or state court.[213] Implementation of the finality rule under §1291 has generated a maze of exceptions.[214] The circuit courts have jurisdiction to consider interlocutory appeals in a range of circumstances described by 28 U.S.C. §1292.[215] There are proposals to jettison the general finality rule and the special rules for interlocutory appeals captured in §1292

209. *Bose*, 466 U.S. at 499; *Hurley v. Irish-American Gay, Lesbian and Bisexual Group of Boston*, 515 U.S. 557 (1995).

210. In habeas corpus cases, the Court candidly acknowledges that if the Court itself regards the state courts as the best decision-makers with respect to a question, it is inclined to resolve doubts about the nature of the question in favor of finding it to be one of historical fact—for the very purpose of routing it to the state courts. See Chapter XII, notes 276–78 and accompanying text.

211. The Supreme Court typically grants review only to examine a circuit court's determination of a *federal* issue. See *Brockett v. Spokane Arcades*, 472 U.S. 491, 499–500 (1990) (explaining that in the interests of economy the Court almost always accepts a circuit court's judgment regarding *state* law issues); but see *Leavitt v. Jane L.*, 518 U.S. 137 (1996) (accepting review in a case decided below on the basis of a state law issue and reversing on that same issue). See Chapter IV, notes 136–40 and accompanying text (discussing the academic debate over whether inferior federal courts are obliged to follow Supreme Court precedent).

212. The idea of certifying questions to the Court seems sensible enough in the abstract. A circuit court may genuinely need the Court's guidance on a point of federal law before disposing of a case in which that question figures. See Sup. Ct. R. 19 (prescribing the procedure for certification). In the modern era, however, the Court has virtually ceased accepting certified questions. See *Wisniewski v. United States*, 353 U.S. 901, 902 (1957) (declining to answer a question that had divided different panels of the same circuit court and instructing the circuit court itself to "reconcile its internal difficulties").

213. See notes 66–90 and accompanying text (discussing the finality rule under §1257 with respect to judgments in state court). In *Cohn*, however, Chief Justice Rehnquist argued that while efficiency may be the chief consideration with respect to the former, more sensitive federalism concerns are at stake with respect to the latter. See notes 66–68 and accompanying text.

214. See, e.g., *Firestone Tire & Rubber Co. v. Risjord*, 449 U.S. 368 (1981) (elaborating the "collateral order rule").

215. See Chapter X, notes 83, 490 (noting the availability of early appellate review in immunity cases); Chapter XI, notes 140–42 and accompanying text (discussing interlocutory appeals in abstention cases).

in favor of a policy allowing appeals in an appellate court's discretion.[216] The Supreme Court has authority pursuant to §1292(e) to promulgate different rules for interlocutory appeals, but has failed to exercise that authority. The Court also enjoys a supervisory power to superintend the procedures followed in the inferior federal courts.[217] Each of these features of the Court's appellate jurisdiction generates its own problems.[218]

I. Discretionary Review

With few exceptions, the Supreme Court has discretion both to decide what cases it will accept for appellate review and to prescribe the criteria it will use to make the choices it does.[219] The old Eighteenth Century writs of error under which litigants were entitled to appellate review as of right,[220] together with Twentieth Century rights of ap-

---

216. See, e.g., Robert J. Martineau, *Defining Finality and Appealability by Court Rule: Right Problem, Wrong Solution*, 54 U. Pitt. L. Rev. 717 (1993); Thomas D. Rowe, Jr., *Defining Finality and Appealability by Court Rule: A Comment on Martineau's Right Problem, Wrong Solution*, 54 U. Pitt. L. Rev. 795 (1993); John C. Nagel, *Replacing the Crazy Quilt of Interlocutory Appeals Jurisprudence with Discretionary Review*, 44 Duke L.J. 200 (1994).

217. *Mu'Min v. Virginia*, 500 U.S. 415, 422 (1991). See Sara Beale, *Reconsidering Supervisory Power in Criminal Cases: Constitutional and Statutory Limits on the Authority of the Federal Courts*, 84 Colum. L. Rev. 1433 (1984). Recall, too, Professor Pfander's argument that the Court enjoys a constitutionally rooted power to supervise lower federal courts via prerogative writs. Pfander, notes 9 & 14.

218. A party may seek review either "before or after" judgment, but the Court rarely finds it appropriate to act in advance of the circuit courts. See Sup. Ct. R. 11 (stating that the Court will grant *certiorari* prior to judgment at the circuit level only in cases of "imperative public importance"); *Clinton v. City of New York*, 524 U.S. 417, 455 (1998) (Scalia, J., concurring & dissenting) (finding it appropriate to consider the line-item veto case on an expedited basis). Pursuant to 28 U.S.C. §2253, habeas corpus petitioners who wish to appeal from unfavorable district court decisions must obtain a certificate of appealability from a single judge or circuit justice. In a series of decisions culminating in *House v. Mayo*, 324 U.S. 42 (1945), the Supreme Court held that a "case" was not "in" a circuit court of appeals unless and until a judge issued a certificate. Accordingly, the Court itself had no jurisdiction under §1254 to review the denial of a prisoner's request for a certificate—made to an individual judge. The Court overruled *House* (on this point) in *Hohn v. United States*, 524 U.S. 236 (1998). According to *Hohn*, the denial of a request for a certificate by an individual federal judge is itself a "case" within the meaning of §1254 and thus can be reviewed in the Supreme Court, provided the Court chooses to grant the prisoner's *certiorari* petition. Justice Kennedy explained that the rule in *Hohn* comports with the language of §1254 and, not coincidentally, permits the Court to fulfill its "normal function of reviewing possible misapplications of law" without resorting to extraordinary means. Id. at 251. In *House*, for example, the Court ultimately sustained its capacity to examine a certificate issue as a way of protecting its appellate jurisdiction by means of an order issued under the authority of the All-Writs Act. See Chapter II, note 58. For a discussion of the "certificate of appealability" requirement in habeas cases, see Chapter XII, notes 495–507 and accompanying text.

219. See, e.g., 28 U.S.C. §1253 (providing for appeals as of right in the relatively few cases decided by three-judge panels at the district level); 28 U.S.C. §2284 (providing for three-judge district court panels in legislative apportionment cases). Both §1257 (governing review of state court judgments) and §1254 (governing review of inferior federal court judgments) recognize that the Court "may" accept a case for appellate review. See generally Edward A. Hartnett, *Questioning Certiorari: Some Reflections Seventy-Five Years After the Judges' Bill*, 100 Colum. L. Rev. 1643 (2000) (providing an exhaustive treatment of the Court's discretionary control of its docket).

220. See Chapter II, text accompanying note 62.

peal,[221] are gone. They have been replaced by a modern statutory writ of *certiorari*, which borrows only one characteristic feature from its common law forerunner: its discretionary nature.[222] Litigants who suffer disappointing judgments on federal claims in either a state court or an inferior federal court may petition the Supreme Court for a writ of *certiorari* pursuant to §1257 or §1254, respectively. The Court receives thousands of petitions every year, but selects only about one hundred for full dress treatment.

Rule 10 of the Court's rules explains that a petition will be granted only for "compelling reasons" and "rarely" when the error the petitioner asks the Court to review is a mistaken "factual" finding or a "misapplication of a properly stated rule of law." Rule 10 offers an inexhaustive list of the kinds of cases that may warrant review: (1) cases in which inferior federal courts or state courts are divided over an "important matter" of federal law; (2) cases in which a federal court or a state court has decided an important question that "has not been, but should be" settled by the Supreme Court; and (3) cases in which a federal court or a state court has decided an important question "in a way that conflicts with" Supreme Court precedent.[223] The Court thus discourages petitions from litigants who complain only that the court below reached an erroneous judgment. The point is to screen the mass of cases in which lower courts may have made mistakes for those involving questions of larger moment for the legal system as a whole. The first illustrative category indicates that the Court means to settle disagreements between other courts in aid of uniformity. The second indicates that the Court means to decide hard cases in aid of accuracy. And the third signals that the Court means to superintend recalcitrant lower courts in aid of supremacy.

The Supreme Court is not a court of error. It does not operate on the private rights model, resolving isolated disputes and elaborating federal law only as a necessary by-product.[224] Instead, the Court proceeds on something approaching the public rights model.[225] The Court accepts cases for appellate review not to do justice in those particular disputes, but rather to use the cases it selects as vehicles for its law-declaration function.[226] By common account, the Court must proceed in this way if it is to have any practical chance to perform its referee function in a system that constantly generates questions, both profound and technical, all demanding authoritative answers. But the real story runs much deeper. The Supreme Court is not a "court" at all in the conven-

---

221. See Bennett Boskey & Eugene Gressman, *The Supreme Court Bids Farewell to Mandatory Appeals*, 121 F.R.D. 81 (1988).

222. At common law, courts issued the writ of *certiorari* to obtain the record of a case in an inferior court in order to assume responsibility for the matter. Since that writ was familiar, the drafters of the Evarts Act in 1891 borrowed it (or rather its name) when they concluded that at least some portion of the Supreme Court's appellate workload should no longer be mandatory. The statutory writ of *certiorari* prescribed by §1257 and §1254 must be distinguished from the common law writ itself in its modern form. The All-Writs Act (28 U.S.C. §1651) authorizes the Court to issue the common law writ, as well as other injunction-style orders. See note 218. Yet the Court reserves that authority for "the most critical and exigent circumstances" when "the legal rights at issue are indisputably clear." See *Brown v. Gilmore*, 533 U.S. 1301, 1303 (2001) (opinion of Rehnquist, C.J.) (quoted cases omitted).

223. This formulation does not track Rule 10's own internal organization, but it accurately reflects the rule's content in substance. Rule 10 also mentions cases in which a circuit court of appeals has "so far departed from the accepted and usual course of judicial proceedings, or sanctioned such a departure by a lower court, as to call for an exercise of" the Supreme Court's supervisory power. See note 217 and accompanying text.

224. See Chapter I, notes 61–72 and accompanying text.

225. See Chapter I, notes 78–91 and accompanying text.

226. But see Chapter IX, notes 11–34 and accompanying text (discussing advisory opinions).

tional sense. It is a peculiarly American invention that has evolved over two centuries to play an extremely important, hard-to-pin-down role in a marvelously complex political system that still purports to be (and we hope actually is) basically democratic.[227]

Not only does the Court select cases as vehicles for law-declaration. It also selects issues within cases in order to tailor its review to the matters that warrant attention. Rule 14 instructs petitioners to state the questions their cases present "concisely," so that the justices can identify plausible choices with a minimum of effort. If a case is selected, the Court commonly proceeds on the basis of the questions the petitioner articulates and limits itself to a consideration of those issues and any subsidiary questions "fairly included."[228] Often, however, the Court selects only one or more of the questions the petitioner identifies and denies review with respect to the others.[229] Occasionally, the Court introduces additional questions the petitioner did not advance,[230] or jettisons the petitioner's questions and substitutes a question or questions of its own.[231] The parties to a case the Court selects for appellate review thus may find themselves developing issues of federal law that the justices themselves have unilaterally injected into the case to make it serve some wider public purpose.

The Court has become increasingly bureaucratic in order to cope with the workload this screening function entails. The clerk's office guides litigants who wish to file *certio-*

---

227. For discussions, see Lisa Kloppenburg, How the Supreme Court Side Steps Hard Cases and Stunts the Development of the Law (2001); Samuel Estreicher & John Sexton, Redefining the Supreme Court's Role 128–36 (1986); Ashutosh Bhagwat, *Separate but Equal? The Supreme Court, The Lower Federal Courts, and the Nature of the Judicial Function*, 80 B.U. L. Rev. 967 (2000). Chief Justice Rehnquist has explained that in many instances the issues the Court must decide are not glamorous constitutional questions, but more rudimentary questions of federal statutory construction. The Court's answers to those questions are not accurate in an ultimate objective sense, but *are* authoritative and thus satisfying when only clarity is genuinely needed. William H. Rehnquist, *The Changing Role of the Supreme Court*, 14 Fla. St. U. L. Rev. 1, 11 (1986). If the justices initially select a case for review, but later conclude that it does not provide a good vehicle for clarifying the law, they can simply change their minds and dismiss the writ of *certiorari* as "improvidently granted." E.g., *Rogers v. United States*, 522 U.S. 252 (1998). See note 241 and accompanying text.

228. Sup. Ct. R. 14(1)(a).

229. The Court commonly grants review with respect to one or more of a petitioner's questions, determines those issues, and then remands for reconsideration of the petitioner's other questions in light of the Court's treatment of the issues actually decided. E.g., *Bragdon v. Abbott*, 524 U.S. 624, 654–55 (1998). Yet the Court is frequently less focused on arriving at an accurate outcome in the case at bar. In *Lindh v. Murphy*, 521 U.S. 320 (1997), the Court granted *certiorari* to decide whether a newly enacted statute, 28 U.S.C. §2254(d), applied to the pending case, but denied review with respect to the contingent question whether, if §2254(d) was applicable, the circuit court below had correctly applied it. In *Lindh*, then, the Court deliberately declined to consider whether the dispute at hand had been decided correctly and chose, instead, to pass only on an abstract question of law, antecedent to the dispute.

230. The classic illustration is the list of questions the Court asked the parties to brief and argue in *Brown v. Bd. of Ed.*, 345 U.S. 972 (1953). In *Garcia v. San Antonio Metro. Transit Auth.*, 468 U.S. 1213 (1984), the Court asked the parties to brief the question whether the previous decision in *Nat'l League of Cities v. Usery*, 426 U.S. 833 (1976), should be overruled. In *Wright v. West*, 502 U.S. 1021 (1991), the Court asked the parties to brief a question that had not arisen in the lower courts. See Chapter XII, text accompanying notes 364–65.

231. In *Hohn v. United States*, 524 U.S. 236 (1998), the Court bypassed the petitioner's issues and granted *certiorari* only on the different question whether the Court had jurisdiction to remand the case for further proceedings at the circuit level. When the Court concluded that it had jurisdiction, it remanded without going further. See note 218. For a useful (though dated) discussion, see Scott H. Bice, *The Limited Grant of Certiorari and the Justification of Judicial Review*, 1975 Wis. L. Rev. 343.

rari petitions and ensures that the petitions received are in proper order. Petitions are then channeled to a pool of law clerks, employed by individual justices. The clerks in the pool examine the petitions in turn, test them against the criteria in Rule 10, and write short memoranda recommending either that they be rejected or accepted. The justices themselves receive the memoranda in chambers, and they, together with their clerks, identify the cases they deem to be "certworthy." The Chief Justice prepares a "discuss list" of candidates, and the other justices add any additional cases that they wish the Court to review. Ultimately, the justices confer and make the final choices. Under the customary "Rule of Four," the vote of four justices is sufficient to grant a writ of *certiorari* and thus to place a case on the Court's docket for consideration on the merits.[232] When the Court grants *certiorari* in a case, it typically holds other cases presenting the same issue until it decides that case and then disposes of them summarily, typically by granting *certiorari*, vacating the judgment below, and remanding for reconsideration in light of the new decision. The "GVR" practice is meant to ensure even-handed treatment, lest a single case be selected from a stream of similar cases and resolved in one way, while others of like character are concluded in another way. [233]

The Court's refusal to accept a case for review leaves the lower court decision undisturbed and therefore usually makes that decision final. In that practical sense, a denial of *certiorari* has genuine significance. Yet it is not a judgment on the merits and approves neither the result below nor the analysis that produced that result. A *certiorari* denial has no value as precedent.[234] The justices may have all manner of reasons for declining review, or no particular reason at all. To avoid misunderstanding, they typically offer no public explanations.[235] Individual justices occasionally attach separate opinions, either concurring in the denial of *certiorari* or dissenting from that action. Those opinions can throw light on the Court's thinking, but they are not authoritative.[236] On occasion, the Court grants a writ of *certiorari* and summarily affirms or reverses the judgment below. Typically, a summary disposition is accompanied by a *per curiam*, which

---

232. See Joan M. Leiman, *The Rule of Four*, 57 Colum. L. Rev. 975 (1957); John P. Stevens, *The Life Span of a Judge-Made Rule*, 58 N.Y.U. L. Rev. 1, 10–13 (1983). For a more detailed account of the *certiorari* process, see H.W. Perry, Jr., Deciding to Decide (1991). Professor Straus has examined the Court's operations from the perspective of an administrative lawyer and formed the impression that in an attempt to keep its workload within manageable limits, the Court has made itself remote from much of the country's legal business. Peter L. Strauss, *One Hundred Fifty Cases Per Year: Some Implications of the Supreme Court's Limited Resources for Judicial Review of Agency Action*, 87 Colum. L. Rev. 1093 (1987). See also Kevin H. Smith, *Justice for All?: The Supreme Court's Denial of Pro Se Petitions for Certiorari*, 63 Albany L. Rev. 381 (1999) (offering empirical data on the way the Court exercises discretion in *forma pauperis* cases). The Court evidently does not employ the rule of four when it decides whether to entertain petitions for a writ of habeas corpus issuing "originally" from the Court itself. *In re Tarver*, 528 U.S. 1152 (2000) (denying a petition despite a notation that four justices would set it down for argument). See Chapter IV, note 36 and accompanying text; Chapter XII, note 545.

233. The proper management of "GVR" matters has occasionally been controversial within the Court. See, e.g., *Thomas v. Amer. Homes Products*, 519 U.S. 913 (1996).

234. The classic citation for this point is Justice Frankfurter's opinion respecting the denial of *certiorari* in *Maryland v. Baltimore Radio Show*, 338 U.S. 912, 917–18 (1950). Professor Linzer argues that the "orthodox" view of *certiorari* denials is "oversimplified" and that one can often find "hints" that "most" of the justices are not "strongly dissatisfied" with the decision below. Peter Linzer, *The Meaning of Certiorari Denials*, 79 Colum. L. Rev. 1227, 1229 (1979).

235. See *Singleton v. Commissioners*, 439 U.S. 940 (1978) (opinion of Blackmun, J.) (contending that reasons should not be given).

236. Professor Linzer relies in some measure on indications gleaned from separate opinions. Linzer, note 234.

explains the Court's rationale. Since the Court acts without benefit of briefs and argument, a *per curiam* generally is authoritative only with respect to the issues it explicitly addresses and resolves.[237] The Court employed the summary disposition device more commonly when it was obliged to consider cases on appeal and could not simply deny review to those it thought were not worthy of attention.

The parties invariably prepare extensive briefs. Very often, other individuals and organizations file independent *amicus curiae* briefs that draw the Court's attention to problems and arguments the parties may not fully explore. Not all *amici curiae* are ideologically motivated, but many repeat players certainly are. Their participation in cases before the Court underscores the significance of the Court's work for a wide range of social policies.[238] The rate at which *amicus* briefs are filed in the Supreme Court increased dramatically in the latter half of the Twentieth Century. In part, the increase can be ascribed to the Court's policy of accepting *amicus* briefs routinely. Under Rule 37, anyone may file a brief if the parties consent. If a party refuses, a would-be *amicus* can move the Court for leave to file, anyway. The Court, in turn, almost always grants permission. Since experienced lawyers know that, they almost always give consent and thus save everyone the bother of an additional motion.[239] *Amicus* briefs are decried in some quarters as an attempt by interest groups to lobby the Court. It is difficult to say how successful they are or even whether they have any influence at all on the justices' thinking. Yet empirical evidence suggests that *amicus* briefs are valuable if they offer arguments or information that the party briefs do not.[240]

The Court hears oral argument *en banc*, and soon thereafter the justices meet *in camera*. Occasionally, the justices conclude that the case is not appropriate for decision, after all, and thus dismiss the writ of *certiorari* as improvidently granted. Usually, the reason is that some procedural complication makes the case a poor vehicle for addressing the question the justices wanted to determine.[241] More often, the justices vote on the merits of the issue or issues presented. When the Chief Justice is in the majority, he assigns the Court's opinion to himself or to one of the associate justices in the majority. When the Chief Justice is in the minority, the senior associate justice in the majority makes the assignment. Individual justices may file separate concurring or dissenting opinions, expressing their personal views. If, for some reason, a case is heard by an even number of justices, and those justices divide evenly, the judgment below is typically "affirmed by an equally divided court" without explanatory opinion.[242] That kind of dispo-

---

237. Justice Marshall contended, however, that once the Court grants review in a case, it should take no definitive action before seeing the parties' briefs on the merits. *Montana v. Hall*, 481 U.S. 400, 410 (1987) (dissenting opinion).

238. See Gregg Ivers & Karen O'Connor, *Friends as Foes: The Amicus Curiae Participation and Effectiveness of the American Civil Liberties Union and Americans for Effective Law Enforcement in Criminal Cases, 1969–1982*, 9 Law & Policy 161 (1987).

239. Joseph D. Kearney & Thomas W. Merrill, *The Influence of Amicus Curiae Briefs on the Supreme Court*, 148 U. Penn. L. Rev. 743, 762 (2000).

240. Id. at 830 (summarizing the results of an exhaustive study of *amicus* briefs filed by the Solicitor General, the ACLU, and the AFL-CIO).

241. In *Adarand Constr. v. Pena*, 515 U.S. 200 (1995), the Court determined that a race-based set-aside program must be strictly scrutinized and remanded for the application of that demanding standard. Seven years later, the parties returned to the Court for review of the lower court's decision on the merits. The Court granted *certiorari* expecting to be able to decide whether the strict scrutiny standard had been properly applied. After briefing and argument, however, it became clear that the focus of the parties' dispute had changed so dramatically that the issue the Court had hoped to address was no longer presented. Accordingly, the Court dismissed the writ as improvidently granted. *Adarand Constr. v. Mineta*, 534 U.S. 103 (2001).

242. E.g., *Free v. Abbott Labs*, 529 U.S. 333 (2000).

sition is entitled to no precedential weight.[243] The justices are often sharply divided. A thin majority may be fragile, inviting advocates to probe for weaknesses in the future. In rare instances, dissenters disclaim propositions they find unacceptable.[244] If there is a majority in support of a single rationale, however, lower courts take that reasoning to be authoritative. When there is no majority support for a single analysis, lower courts take the holding to be based on the views of the justices who concur on the narrowest ground.[245] The Court typically announces decisions in public session. The justice who prepared the Court's opinion may summarize the result and the supporting analysis. The written opinions in cases are distributed at the same time and promptly come under the scrutiny of the hosts of observers who look to the Supreme Court's opinions as the final, authoritative statements of federal law.

243. See *Rutledge v. United States*, 517 U.S. 292, 304 (1996). Professor Baker has criticized the Court for failing in these cases to settle the questions of federal law the Court ostensibly granted review to decide. Thomas E. Baker, *Why We Call the Supreme Court "Supreme": A Case Study on the Importance of Settling the National Law*, 2 Green Bag 129 (2000).

244. See, e.g., Chapter X, note 190 and accompanying text (noting that four members of the Court consider the current majority's sovereign immunity decisions not to warrant respect as precedents).

245. *Marks v. United States*, 430 U.S. 188, 193 (1977).

Chapter VIII

Federal Questions in Federal District Court

Litigants who wish to advance federal claims in federal court usually must invoke the original jurisdiction of a United States district court. Article III contemplates that district courts may determine federal questions in a variety of contexts. Party-based categories of jurisdiction may offer opportunities. Cases in which states are involved sometimes turn on federal law,[1] as do controversies to which the United States is a party.[2] Categories of jurisdiction identified by subject matter usually implicate federal questions. Admiralty cases, for example, are frequently governed by federal statutes or federal common law.[3] The general class of cases "arising under" the "Constitution" or "Laws of the United States" is the most commodious source of federal question jurisdiction.[4]

A. Cases Arising Under Federal Law

The Supreme Court has always given the idea of a case arising under federal law a generous interpretation. In *Osborn v. Bank of United States*,[5] Chief Justice Marshall recognized that Article III specifies federal jurisdiction of *cases*, not *issues* within cases. Cases, in turn, often involve both questions of federal law and questions of state law, as well. If, then, a federal court is to adjudicate the "whole case," the court must be able to resolve both federal and state issues.[6]

In *Osborn*, the Bank of the United States sued officials of the state of Ohio in a federal circuit court, seeking an injunction requiring those officers to return money they had seized pursuant to an unconstitutional tax on the bank's assets. The statute creating the bank gave it authority to "sue and be sued" in "any Circuit Court of the United States." Chief Justice Marshall read that language to establish a circuit court's juris-

---

1. See notes 68–70 and accompanying text. Recall that inferior federal courts may have concurrent jurisdiction to determine the kinds of cases that Article III permits the Supreme Court to entertain as an original matter. See Chapter VII, note 3 and accompanying text.
2. See text accompanying note 98.
3. See notes 71–88 and accompanying text.
4. See notes 5–46 and accompanying text.
5. 22 U.S. (9 Wheat.) 738 (1824).
6. Id. at 819–23. See Chapter VII, notes 112–13 and accompanying text (discussing this idea in connection with the Supreme Court's appellate jurisdiction).

diction to entertain suits brought by or against the bank.[7] That construction of the statute, in turn, presented Marshall with the constitutional question whether cases involving the bank arose under federal law within the meaning of Article III.[8] The defendants argued that only the validity of the tax was a question of federal law, that other issues would surface in the case, and that Congress could not confer jurisdiction on a circuit court to consider those state law matters. Marshall responded that there was no *constitutional* barrier to the circuit court's adjudication of both federal and state issues. He gave two explanations.

First, it was enough that the bank's "right" would be "defeated by one construction [of federal law] and sustained by the opposite construction."[9] That initial explanation suggested that the circuit court's jurisdiction was comparatively narrow: A case had to turn on an actual question of federal law, and that federal question had to be apparent at the time the suit was initiated. Once the court assumed jurisdiction on the basis of such a federal issue, the court could consider any incidental state questions that emerged.[10] In *Osborn* itself, those contingencies were satisfied. The bank's claim against the Ohio defendants was a federal constitutional challenge to the tax, and that claim was clear at the outset of the litigation.[11]

Second, the suit by the bank arose under federal law for Article III purposes because a federal question formed an "ingredient" of the "original cause."[12] Congress had enacted the statute establishing the bank and giving it authority to file lawsuits. At the threshold of any suit, an opposing party might raise some question about the bank's ex-

---

7. It now appears that the explicit mention of suits in the federal circuit courts was crucial to Marshall's interpretation of the statute to confer jurisdiction on those courts. In *Amer. Nat'l Red Cross v. S.G.*, 505 U.S. 247 (1992), the Court read similar language in the congressional charter issued to the Red Cross to confer jurisdiction on the federal courts to entertain a state tort claim against the Red Cross. If the statutes in *Osborn* and *Red Cross* had only established that the bank and the Red Cross could "sue and be sued" in *some* court, without specifying a *federal* court, they would not have been understood to do jurisdictional work. In truth, those statutes did not read like jurisdictional statutes at all. They did not address the federal courts and empower them forthrightly, but instead addressed the bank and the Red Cross and thus appeared to affect the courts only indirectly—by authorizing the bank and the Red Cross to sue or to be sued *in* federal court. See note 131. Looking back, it seems perfectly clear that the statute in *Osborn* contemplated that the circuit courts would have jurisdiction to entertain suits by and against the bank, even if the language it used to accomplish that end left something to be desired. Moreover, Chief Justice Marshall plainly wanted to read the statute to create federal jurisdiction and was not in a mood to demand more clarity. It is questionable whether it was equally expedient to read the statute in *Red Cross* in the same way and thus to place ordinary state law claims in federal court merely because the Red Cross holds a charter containing the familiar "sue and be sued" boilerplate. See *Red Cross*, 505 U.S. at 267–69 (Scalia, J., dissenting); cf. Louise Weinberg, *The Power of Congress Over Courts in Nonfederal Cases*, 1995 B.Y.U. L. Rev. 731, 797–802 (describing *Red Cross* as "an intellectual muddle").

8. If Marshall had found no statutory jurisdiction for the bank's suit in *Osborn*, the constitutional question would not have arisen.

9. 22 U.S. at 822.

10. See notes 402–03 and accompanying text (explaining that this is the way supplemental jurisdiction works in modern federal district courts).

11. The bank's suit was actually in equity to enjoin a trespass and for the common law writ of replevin. That kind of action does not translate neatly into modern terms. It is possible that the federal issue would have emerged as the bank's response to the state's defense, in which case modern standards for invoking federal jurisdiction (by statute) would not have been satisfied. See notes 263–90 and accompanying text (describing the classic cases on the well-pleaded complaint rule).

12. 22 U.S. at 823.

istence as a corporate entity or its capacity to sue (in any court). Those objections, if raised, would turn on federal law—namely, the bank's charter. Marshall did not mean that a suit by the bank would arise under federal law *only* if an opposing party *actually* injected federal issues into a case in some way. He insisted that questions about the bank's credentials *could* be raised in "every possible case," and that was enough to make every action in which the bank was a party a case arising under federal law.[13]

Marshall's second explanation suggested that the circuit court's jurisdiction could be much more expansive. If the mere possibility that the bank's charter might be questioned would suffice, then the nature of the bank's legal claim in a lawsuit would make no difference. Marshall explained, for example, that a suit by the bank on an ordinary state contract claim would arise under federal law, even if neither party actually raised any federal issue for decision. In a companion case, *Bank of United States v. Planters' Bank*,[14] he held that just such a case arose under federal law for Article III purposes. Moreover, numerous other entities and organizations (apart from the bank) also depended on federal statutes for their existence and authority to conduct business. If any suit involving the bank arose under federal law, it appeared that a suit involving any federally chartered party would equally qualify. The Court later took that very position in the *Removal Cases*,[15] where private plaintiffs were allowed to sue federally chartered railroads in federal court, even though the plaintiffs' tort claims against the railroads turned entirely on state law.[16] Indeed, by Marshall's second account, the range of cases arising under federal law extended even further. If the *possibility* that a federal question would develop was sufficient, there was no self-evident reason why that question must go to the very existence of a federally incorporated institution or its capacity to sue. All manner of cases having nothing to do with federally incorporated entities would be cases arising under federal law for Article III purposes.[17]

---

13. Id. at 824.

14. 22 U.S. (9 Wheat.) 904 (1824).

15. *Pac. R.R. Removal Cases*, 115 U.S. 1 (1885).

16. Federal courts no longer have jurisdiction of actions merely because federally incorporated entities are involved, unless the United States owns more than half their stock. 28 U.S.C. §1349. In none of the three early cases, *Osborn*, *Planters' Bank*, or the *Removal Cases*, did the Court suggest that the federally chartered corporations involved were arms of the United States, so that federal judicial power could rest independently on the provision in Article III for controversies to which the United States itself is a party. See *Lebron v. Nat'l R.R. Passenger Corp.*, 513 U.S. 374, 398–99 (1995) (discussing *Planters' Bank*).

17. Dissenting in *Osborn*, Justice Johnson put two hypotheticals that demonstrated, to his satisfaction, that Marshall went too far. First, under federal revenue statutes, some contracts (themselves governed entirely by state law) had to be written on stamped paper (indicating that certain federal taxes had been paid). It was *possible*, according to Johnson, that a party to such a contract might raise some issue touching the required stamp and the taxes owed to the federal government. Second, the title to land in the territories could always be traced back to a patent issued by the government. It was *possible*, then, that a party to an ordinary real estate suit could raise some issue touching that original federal patent. By Marshall's account, then, ordinary contract and real property disputes were cases arising under federal law for Article III purposes. 22 U.S. at 874–76 (dissenting opinion). Marshall himself may have indicated some doubt about his interpretation of Article III when he rejected a third hypothetical. He agreed that a naturalized citizen, too, was a "mere creature of law," but he did not concede that, on that account, cases involving naturalized citizens arose under federal law simply because an opposing party might challenge their federally created credentials. According to Marshall, a naturalized citizen, unlike a federally chartered corporation, owed nothing further to Congress and possessed all the rights of native citizens. Id. at 827–28 (majority opinion). Marshall probably meant to say only that he could not envision any practical instance in which the

Marshall may have conceived that Article III must be interpreted expansively in order to accommodate both inferior courts' original jurisdiction and the Supreme Court's appellate jurisdiction.[18] Article III describes only one category of cases arising under federal law. Thus Marshall may have assumed that any appellate jurisdiction the Supreme Court draws from that category can be no greater than the original jurisdiction that the inferior federal courts obtain from it. If, then, Article III allows the Supreme Court *appellate* jurisdiction to adjudicate cases in which federal issues emerge only after litigation is under way, it must follow that Article III also allows federal trial courts *original* jurisdiction to entertain cases in which federal issues may (but may not) actually surface. That analysis may be true to the text of Article III, but it is not logically compelled. Even if it is assumed that the Supreme Court must have plenary jurisdiction to examine dispositive federal questions that come to light in cases after they are filed, it does not follow that federal trial courts equally require such an expansive purview.[19] Cases in which federal issues are only potentially implicated can proceed in state court and reach the Supreme Court later, if and when federal questions actually appear and become dispositive.[20]

The idea that cases can arise under federal law when federal issues are only potentially implicated is but a step away from the theory of "protective jurisdiction."[21] Academicians who promote that theory invariably rely on Marshall's analysis in *Osborn* to supply the fulcrum on which protective jurisdiction turns: Article III does not demand that a federal question must actually be presented for decision in a case, but only that it *might* be presented—*if* Congress were to use the legislative authority it has to create federal law for the occasion.[22] In a famous dissent in the *Lincoln Mills* case,[23] Justice Frankfurter urged the Court not to extend *Osborn* so far. Frankfurter insisted that the labor dispute in *Lincoln Mills* was controlled by state law. That meant (to Frankfurter) that there was no substantive federal law under which the case could arise for Article III purposes. Frankfurter considered the possibility that Congress could create federal

---

means by which a party had become a citizen could figure as an antecedent ingredient in a lawsuit. In that respect, he resisted Justice Johnson's charge that there were no limits at all on the cases that could arise under federal law for constitutional purposes. It has been argued that Marshall meant that the potential federal ingredient must be essential to the claimant's lawsuit (like the capacity to sue at all or to form the contract over which suit is initiated) and that any other kind of potential federal issue (like a federal defense or counterclaim offered by the defendant) would not suffice. See Note, *The Outer Limits of "Arising Under"*, 54 N.Y.U. L. Rev. 978, 987–88 (1982).

18. Marshall may also have embraced Hamilton's view that the federal government's judicial power must be coterminous with its legislative power. See Chapter II, note 48. That line of argument would have led Marshall to give the courts' power under Article III a capacious reading in order to keep pace with Congress' powers under Article I.

19. See Paul J. Mishkin, *The Federal "Question" in the District Courts*, 53 Colum. L. Rev. 157, 163 (1953).

20. See Chapter VII, notes 112–13 and accompanying text (discussing the same idea in connection with the *Murdock* case).

21. See Chapter VI, notes 139–43 and accompanying text (discussing protective jurisdiction in connection with removal under 28 U.S.C. §1442).

22. There is a connection between protective jurisdiction and the idea that cases in which federally chartered corporations are parties arise under federal law. The point of conferring jurisdiction on federal courts in cases involving federally chartered entities is to protect those entities from state court provincialism.

23. *Textile Workers Union v. Lincoln Mills*, 353 U.S. 448, 460–84 (1957); see notes 95–97 and accompanying text.

jurisdiction alone, without providing substantive federal law for the federal courts to apply. But he dismissed that idea, in part because it rested (illogically) on the "beguiling" syllogism that the "greater" power must include the "lesser."[24]

Of course, a federal statute by which Congress purports to establish federal court jurisdiction cannot itself supply the federal law under which a case can be said to arise. If it could, Congress would be able to bootstrap federal jurisdiction in every conceivable case simply by enacting a federal statute conferring jurisdiction and relying on that federal statute to provide the federal law required. The law under which a case arises is the legal standard the court may be asked to apply *in* the case.[25] Nor is it persuasive to argue that *every* jurisdictional statute necessarily authorizes the federal courts to fashion a federal common law of decision, which then can supply the law under which cases arise for Article III purposes.[26] There is also an argument that Article III itself prescribes the only valid forms of protective jurisdiction (e.g., diversity jurisdiction to safeguard out-of-state citizens from local prejudice) and forecloses others by negative implication.

The modern Court has indicated doubts about the "ingredient" test in general[27] and protective jurisdiction in particular.[28] Yet the Court has not revisited the question whether a purely speculative federal question will satisfy Article III. There was no need to do that in *Verlinden B.V. v. Central Bank of Nigeria*.[29] In that case, the Court upheld a provision of the Foreign Sovereign Immunities Act giving federal district courts jurisdiction over actions against foreign nations that, under the FSIA, cannot insist upon immunity. Chief Justice Burger explained that the FSIA both makes a federal court's jurisdiction contingent on a foreign nation's inability to claim immunity and establishes the standards for determining the immunity issue as a matter of federal law. The threshold question in every case, accordingly, is the (federal) question whether a nation is immune.[30] That federal question, in turn, makes every FSIA lawsuit a case arising under federal law for Article III purposes. Chief Justice Burger chided the lower court for relying on precedents regarding the statute that ordinarily confers jurisdiction on district courts in federal question cases: 28 U.S.C. §1331. The issue in *Verlinden* was not whether the quite different non-constitutional standards for invoking

24. *Lincoln Mills*, 353 U.S. at 473 (dissenting opinion); see Chapter I, notes 26–28 and accompanying text.

25. Justice Frankfurter also rejected Judge Wyzanski's suggestion that a statute giving federal courts jurisdiction to decide state law issues might be read to incorporate state law into federal law and, in that way, to generate a body of federal law under which cases might arise. *Lincoln Mills*, 353 U.S. at 472 (dissenting opinion); see *Textile Workers Union v. Amer. Thread Co.*, 113 F. Supp. 137, 140 (D. Mass. 1953).

26. See notes 99–101 and accompanying text.

27. In a related context, Justice Souter has noted potential constitutional difficulty with a statute allowing the Attorney General to invoke federal jurisdiction by unilaterally injecting the United States into a case as a party. *Gutierrez de Martinez v. Lamagno*, 515 U.S. 417, 443–44 (1995) (dissenting opinion).

28. See Chapter VI, notes 139–43 and accompanying text (discussing the *Mesa* case on removal jurisdiction).

29. 461 U.S. 480 (1983).

30. 28 U.S.C. §1330(a) (conferring jurisdiction on district courts to determine any claim against a foreign state "as to which the foreign state is not entitled to immunity" under the FSIA's standards).

31. See notes 263–90 and accompanying text.

jurisdiction under §1331 were met. Clearly, they were not.[31] The issue was, instead, whether Article III allowed Congress to establish a more capacious jurisdiction via the FSIA.[32]

It may prove necessary to explore the potential constitutional limits on "arising under" jurisdiction in certain bankruptcy cases.[33] Congress has considerable authority under the Commerce Clause to prescribe substantive federal law to govern the bulk of the transactions implicated in bankruptcies. Moreover, Congress has independent legislative power under the Bankruptcy Clause to "establish uniform Laws on the subject of Bankruptcies."[34] That legislative power entitles Congress to enact substantive federal bankruptcy rules governing the collection and distribution of a bankrupt's assets.[35] Concomitantly, Congress can confer jurisdiction on Article III courts to determine cases "arising under" those federal rules. In the main, however, the federal bankruptcy law that Congress has actually enacted (most recently in the Bankruptcy Act of 1984) does not establish federal grounds for recovery in bankruptcy cases, but rather provides federal machinery for reconciling competing state law claims against the estate.[36] If and when the issues to be decided rest entirely on state law, Congress' power to confer jurisdiction on Article III courts can be questioned.[37]

In many bankruptcy cases, the "ingredient" test in *Osborn* may answer. A trustee in bankruptcy is a federal officer whose credentials and functions are governed by federal law. The trustee, in turn, represents the bankruptcy estate, which is an independent federally created juridical entity entitled by federal law to sue or be sued.[38] At the outset of a bankruptcy proceeding involving the estate as a party, another party may raise some (federal) question regarding the status of the trustee or the bankruptcy estate. Even if no such issue is actually raised, there is a potential that it *might* be—which may be sufficient to allow Congress to place the matter in federal court.[39] Federal jurisdiction is more problematic in cases in which the claim at stake is said to be "related to" a bankruptcy.[40] In those cases, the estate itself may not be a party. Instead, competitors for some piece of the estate may be at war among themselves over matters entirely con-

---

32. 461 U.S. at 494–97.

33. See Susan Block-Lieb, *Permissive Bankruptcy Abstention*, 76 Wash. U. L.Q. 781, 831–34 (1998) (citing legislative history suggesting that the bankruptcy statutes were meant to extend federal jurisdiction as far as the Constitution allows).

34. U.S. Const. art. I, §8, cl.4.

35. See, e.g., *Young v. United States*, 122 S.Ct. 1036 (2002) (treating a time limitation affecting certain exceptions from potential discharge as a matter of federal law).

36. E.g., *Jaffke v. Dunham*, 352 U.S. 280 (1957). See Ralph Brubaker, *On the Nature of Federal Bankruptcy Jurisdiction: A General Statutory and Constitutional Theory*, 41 Wm. & Mary L. Rev. 743, 807 (2000).

37. Cf. *Celotex Corp. v. Edwards*, 514 U.S. 300, 307–08 (1995) (describing the federal courts' jurisdiction in bankruptcy as "of some breadth" but not "limitless").

38. 11 U.S.C. §323.

39. Professor Brubaker argues that since the bankruptcy estate is the real party in interest, federal jurisdiction must rest, if at all, on the possibility that the federal status of the estate may be challenged, not on the possibility that the federal *bona fides* of the trustee may be questioned. Brubaker, note 36, at 813–20. Brubaker explains that in reorganization cases the debtor-in-possession handles the functions that might otherwise be performed by a trustee. In those cases, by his account, the reorganization estate must be the federally created entity, the existence and status of which can be the basis for federal jurisdiction on the "ingredient" rationale. Id. at 822–31.

40. 28 U.S.C. §1334(b). See Darrell Dunham, *Bankruptcy Court Jurisdiction*, 67 U.M.K.C. L. Rev. 229 (1998) (surveying lower court attempts to determine whether issues are "related to" bankruptcy cases in the necessary sense).

trolled by state law. By some accounts, federal jurisdiction in cases of that kind can only be justified as "protective."[41] That rationale is, of course, suspect.[42] By other accounts, federal courts can exercise "ancillary" or "supplemental" jurisdiction to determine state law disputes "related to" a bankruptcy, but involving parties other than the bankruptcy estate.[43]

The scope of federal jurisdiction implicates sensitive political values. The more jurisdiction federal courts have, the more routinely they will compete for business with state courts and the more commonly they will come into conflict with the other branches of the central government. The less jurisdiction federal courts have, the less authority they will command to enforce federal law—often against assertions of power by the states and the other branches. The scope of jurisdiction also entails administrative considerations. Once federal courts are granted jurisdiction sufficient to perform their institutional role, more subtle adjustments may be warranted to manage the flow of cases. It is difficult to anticipate the many and varied problems that may arise at that stage, and a capacity to fine-tune jurisdictional arrangements can be essential. It would be cumbersome to make those adjustments as interpretations of the Constitution. Accordingly, the Court essentially paints Article III out of the picture. Congress makes the basic allocation of judicial power in the first instance.[44] Then, the Court can introduce refinements when it places an authoritative construction on the statutes that Congress enacts. In the end, there are few *constitutional* limits on the jurisdiction the federal courts *can* be given. But that only means that the jurisdiction the federal courts actually *have* is a non-constitutional question of statutory construction, imbued by the Court's sense of sound policy.

Dissenting in *Osborn*, Justice Johnson insisted that a case could arise under federal law for Article III purposes only if a federal question actually surfaced at some point. If

---

41. See Thomas Galligan, Jr., *Article III and the "Related to" Bankruptcy Jurisdiction: A Case Study in Protective Jurisdiction*, 11 U. Puget Sound L. Rev. 1 (1987).

42. See notes 21–24, 28 and accompanying text; Chapter VI, notes 139–43 and accompanying text.

43. The Court itself suggested this possibility in *Northern Pipeline Constr. Co. v. Marathon Pipe Line Co.*, 458 U.S. 50, 72 n.26 (1982). For an elaboration of the argument, see John T. Cross, *Congressional Power to Extend Federal Jurisdiction to Disputes Outside Article III: A Critical Analysis from the Perspective of Bankruptcy*, 87 Nw. U. L. Rev. 1188 (1993); notes 402–22 and accompanying text (discussing supplemental jurisdiction). Professor Cross acknowledges that some third-party disputes share no common factual basis with disputes that are within federal jurisdiction because they are at least potentially federal. He contends, however, that state law issues that are "logically related" should be equally cognizable. Cross, at 1247. The general supplemental jurisdiction statute, 28 U.S.C. §1367, grants federal courts jurisdiction to determine state law issues that are "so related" that they form "part of the same case or controversy." That formulation is conventionally thought to contemplate state issues that arise from a "common nucleus of operative fact." See *City of Chicago v. Internat'l College of Surgeons*, 522 U.S. 156, 165 (1997); notes 406–07 and accompanying text. Professor Brubaker notes another reason for leaving §1367 out of the explanation for federal bankruptcy jurisdiction. That statute confers jurisdiction on district courts, but does not (explicitly) extend that jurisdiction to the bankruptcy judges to whom district courts may refer bankruptcy business—including disputes between third parties over state law issues. Brubaker, note 36, at 926. See Chapter V, note 52 and accompanying text (noting that district courts must decline jurisdiction over state law claims that divide non-diverse third parties where one of those parties files a timely action in state court).

44. Professor Holt has explained that Article III left most features of the federal judiciary to Congress. Wythe Holt, *"Federal Courts as the Asylum to Federal Interests": Randolph's Report, the Benson Amendment, and the "Original Understanding" of the Federal Judiciary*, 36 Buffalo L. Rev. 341 (1987).

it appeared in the plaintiff's complaint, a federal court could consider the case as an original matter. If it did not, by Johnson's account, a federal trial court could not entertain the case initially. Yet if the plaintiff went to state court and the federal question emerged as the case progressed, a federal court could *then* exercise jurisdiction, either by removal or on appellate review of the state court's judgment.[45] Working from John Marshall's more generous interpretation of Article III, Congress and the Court have limited district court original jurisdiction to cases in which a federal claim appears in the plaintiff's complaint—but as a matter of non-constitutional policy.[46]

B. Federal Common Law

The federal question that triggers federal jurisdiction need not find its source in the Constitution or a statute. It can be a matter of federal common law created by the federal courts themselves. When federal common law governs a case, it supplies the law under which the case arises for jurisdictional purposes.[47] In any particular instance, the existence of controlling federal common law is itself a question of federal law: whether federal courts have the power and the duty to announce and enforce federal law of their own making in the class of cases to which the instant case belongs.[48]

Federal judge-made law is the exception, not the rule. State courts routinely create common law, just as courts of general jurisdiction always have within the Anglo-American system. Federal courts are not courts of general jurisdiction in that traditional sense.[49] They are restricted to the jurisdiction that Article III permits Congress to confer upon them, and, in turn, by the specific jurisdictional statutes that Congress, in its wisdom, decides to enact.[50] State courts can assume that they are entitled to fashion any legal standards needed to resolve the disputes that come before them, so long as they respect any relevant statutes or constitutional provisions.[51] Federal courts require greater justification when they take "molar" rather than "molecular" jumps.[52] The Supreme

45. *Osborn*, 22 U.S. at 888–89. See Chapter VI, notes 125–35 and accompanying text (discussing removal jurisdiction).

46. See notes 263–90 and accompanying text.

47. See *Illinois v. Milwaukee*, 406 U.S. 91, 99–100 (1972), *overruled on other gr'ds, Milwaukee v. Illinois*, 451 U.S. 304 (1981); accord *Nat'l Farmers Ins. Co. v. Crow Tribe*, 471 U.S. 845, 850 (1985). In the celebrated Supreme Court cases on federal common law, the jurisdictional statute in play was typically *not* §1331. Until the Supreme Court announced its decision, it was not clear that federal law controlled and might have supplied the basis for jurisdiction as an "arising under" matter.

48. *D'Oench, Duhme & Co. v. FDIC*, 315 U.S. 447 (1942).

49. See Chapter I, note 59 and accompanying text (discussing the "interstitial" character of federal law and federal courts according to the Hart and Wechsler paradigm).

50. See Chapter IV, notes 62–64 and accompanying text. Just as a particular grant of jurisdiction has its positive, power-creating side, it equally has its negative, power-denying side (in the obvious sense that the power it confers has limits).

51. As a matter of practice, state courts probably approach disputes from the other direction—looking first for a controlling statute and turning to their own law-making authority only when necessary. In the modern world, legislation often eclipses judge-crafted common law at both the federal and state levels.

52. *Southern Pac. R.R. v. Jensen*, 244 U.S. 205, 221 (1917) (Holmes, J., dissenting), quoted in Louise Weinberg, *Federal Common Law*, 83 Nw. U. L. Rev. 805, 806 (1989). Professor Weinberg argues that the federal courts' authority to create federal common law parallels Congress' power to

Court decided early on that there is no federal common law of crimes.[53] Federal criminal offenses are "solely creatures of statute."[54] And in *Erie R.R. Co. v. Tompkins*,[55] Justice Brandeis declared that there is no federal "general" common law in civil cases. Accordingly, federal courts are not entitled to create their own body of judge-made law to govern federal "diversity" suits involving citizens of different states.[56] In the wake of *Erie*, and pursuant to the Rules of Decision Act, federal courts typically apply state substantive law in diversity actions.[57] Nevertheless, federal courts *do* fashion federal rules of decision in cases falling within certain closely circumscribed "enclaves."[58]

Federal courts routinely exercise creative judgment when they interpret federal statutes. By most accounts, it is useless to attempt any clear distinction between interpretation and independent law declaration. That realistic point conceded, the lion's share of federal common law may arguably be explained away as so many instances of imaginative statutory interpretation, requiring no special explanation or justification as free-standing judge-made law.[59] Most authorities resist such a facile explanation, how-

---

enact legislation in the same context. She does recognize limits, however. She does not endorse federal common law crimes.

53. *United States v. Hudson & Goodwin*, 11 U.S. (7 Cranch) 32 (1812); *United States v. Coolidge*, 14 U.S. (1 Wheat.) 415 (1816). Justice Story evidently thought it was perfectly appropriate for federal courts to entertain common law prosecutions. The idea of common law crimes figured in Federalist arguments for an expansive national government generally. Nevertheless, the decision in *Hudson & Goodwin*, authored by Justice Johnson (the Court's Jeffersonian member), concluded the issue the other way. See Gary D. Rowe, *The Sound of Silence: United States v. Hudson & Goodwin, the Jeffersonian Ascendancy, and the Abolition of Federal Common Law Crimes*, 101 Yale L.J. 919 (1992); see generally Stewart Jay, *Origins of Federal Common Law: Part One*, 133 U. Pa. L. Rev. 1003 (1985); Stewart Jay, *Origins of Federal Common Law: Part Two*, 133 U. Pa. L. Rev. 1231 (1985).

54. *Dowling v. United States*, 473 U.S. 207, 213 (1985). Professor Kahan argues that Congress can give the courts "criminal lawmaking power" to fill in the details of "open-textured" statutes and that Congress has essentially done that in certain contexts—for example, in the RICO statute. 18 U.S.C. §1961, *et seq.* Dan M. Kahan, *Lenity and Federal Common Law Crimes*, 1994 Sup. Ct. Rev. 345. See Ben Rosenberg, *The Growth of Federal Criminal Common Law*, 29 Am. J. Crim. L. 193 (2002).

55. 304 U.S. 64, 78 (1938).

56. 28 U.S.C. §1332 (stating the scope of federal diversity jurisdiction today); see *Swift v. Tyson*, 41 U.S. (16 Pet.) 1 (1842) (articulating the understanding that *Erie* discarded—i.e., that "general" federal law controlled in diversity cases); John Hart Ely, *The Irrepressible Myth of Erie*, 87 Harv. L. Rev. 693 (1974) (providing a discussion).

57. See Chapter II, note 61 (explaining that the Rules of Decision Act derives from the Judiciary Act of 1789). Under the Rules of Decision Act, the "laws of the several states... shall be regarded as rules of decision," but only "where they apply" and where "the Constitution or treaties of the United States or Acts of Congress [do not] otherwise require or provide." 28 U.S.C. §1652. Accordingly, even in post-*Erie* cases in which diversity jurisdiction is invoked pursuant to 28 U.S.C. §1332, federal common law may control *if* that federal law applies and state law does not. E.g., *Boyle v. United Technologies Corp.*, 487 U.S. 500 (1988); see notes 102–03 and accompanying text.

58. *Texas Indus. v. Radcliff Materials*, 451 U.S. 630, 641 (1981). As Judge Friendly once explained, *Erie* and subsequent cases on federal common law produced "complementary concepts" that are "so beautifully simple, and so simply beautiful, that we must wonder why a century and a half were needed to discover them." While *Erie* put the federal courts out of the business of fashioning a large and unnecessary body of federal law for diversity cases, the new federal common law cases put the federal courts in the business of creating federal law where it is genuinely needed to promote federal interests. See Henry J. Friendly, *In Praise of Erie—and of the New Federal Common Law*, 39 N.Y.U. L. Rev. 383, 422 (1964).

59. Professor Westen and Professor Lehman advance this argument. See Peter Westen & Jeffrey S. Lehman, *Is There Life for Erie After the Death of Diversity?*, 78 Mich. L. Rev. 311, 332–33 (1980). Professor Field also thinks that a sufficient federal statutory basis of decision can typically be lo-

ever, particularly at a time when the Supreme Court's preferred approach to statutory construction is primarily textual.[60] If courts genuinely derive the rule they apply to a case from some statutory text, they do not create federal common law at all; the function of forging federal common law begins only where the function of interpretation ends.[61] Yet when the Court strays significantly from the language of a statute, it is hard to propose that the justices are still engaged in the "alchemy of construction."[62]

Justice Jackson contended that there are practical reasons why federal courts must be able to fashion common law. Congress, he said, cannot be expected to enact "all-complete statutory codes" that address every contingency that may arise.[63] Accordingly, federal courts must have authority to fill the gaps that statutes leave open in order to effectuate the policies that statutes are meant to promote.[64] Thus "wherever" federal courts must decide a federal question that "cannot be answered from federal statutes alone," they can "resort to all of the source materials of the common law" and select a legal principle they think appropriate.[65] Jackson's explanation is incomplete. The practical necessity of filling gaps in federal statutes may mute concerns that the courts are intruding upon Congress' legislative preserve. But the displacement of available state law demands independent explanation. It is not self-evident that when imperfect federal statutes need to be supplemented, federal courts must fashion rules of their own choosing. They may be able to locate corresponding state rules and feed them into the mix.[66]

---

cated. Martha A. Field, *Sources of Law: The Scope of Federal Common Law*, 99 Harv. L. Rev. 881, 887 (1986).

60. See Chapter I, notes 30–43 and accompanying text.

61. See Bradford R. Clark, *Federal Common Law: A Structural Reinterpretation*, 144 U. Pa. L. Rev. 1245, 1248 (1996).

62. *Lincoln Mills*, 353 U.S. at 462 (Frankfurter, J., dissenting).

63. *D'Oench*, 315 U.S. at 468–70 (concurring opinion).

64. Id. at 472. Accord *United States v. Little Lake Misere Land Co.*, 412 U.S. 580, 593 (1973).

65. *D'Oench*, 315 U.S. at 469. In these passages, Justice Jackson had in mind cases in which federal statutes reflect a clear federal policy, but fail to see to the details that must be addressed to promote that policy. In many instances, however, federal statutes leave gaps of a different order. They reach and control behavior in one context, but leave similar conduct in other contexts untouched. In cases of that kind, the Court must decide whether to fill in the latter gaps with federal common law (so that the same policy reaches similar behavior in similar contexts) or, instead, to draw the negative inference that the same policy does *not* apply across the board. The current Court's textualism may commonly suggest the latter course. In *Moragne v. States Marine Lines*, 398 U.S. 375 (1970), Congress enacted a statute permitting wrongful death actions after accidents on the high seas, but failed to enact a similar statute for accidents in waters within an individual state. The Court explained that the latter omission did not reflect deliberate policy but, instead, rested on historical anomalies. Accordingly, the Court held that as a matter of federal judge-fashioned maritime law, a longshoreman's widow could recover for his wrongful death, even though the accident had occurred in Florida waters. In *Dooley v. Korean Air Lines*, 524 U.S. 116 (1998), however, the Court held that survivors could not rely on "general" maritime law to recover for a decedent's pre-death pain and suffering. The statute in point in *Dooley* did not provide for that kind of relief, and the Court inferred that Congress meant to foreclose recovery under more general law by implication. Judge Mikva and Professor Pfander argue that federal courts should revive the *Moragne* approach in a different context: Rather than borrow state filing periods for federal rights of action, the courts should substitute the uniform four-year period that Congress has prescribed for federal rights of action established since 1990. Abner J. Mikva & James E. Pfander, *On the Meaning of Congressional Silence: Using Federal Common Law to Fill the Gap in Congress's Residual Statute of Limitations*, 107 Yale L.J. 393 (1997).

66. See notes 106–13 and accompanying text.

1. Classic illustrations

In two familiar instances, the Supreme Court has held that the existence of federal jurisdiction implies judicial authority to create the substantive law needed to resolve disputes: (1) controversies between states; and (2) admiralty cases.[67] At first glance, the rationale in these cases may appear to get the cart before the horse. One might have thought that it would be crucial first to establish that federal law of some ilk governs a dispute and then to conclude that a federal court can have jurisdiction to entertain a suit in which that federal law is applied. Recall, however, that Article III contemplates federal jurisdiction in lots of cases and controversies apart from cases "arising under" federal law. In suits relying on those other bases of jurisdiction, federal law need not provide the rules of decision. Diversity cases are the obvious illustration. So the existence of federal jurisdiction is not necessarily contingent on the character of the law that federal courts will implement.

Disputes between states. Recall that controversies between two or more states fall exclusively within the Supreme Court's original jurisdiction.[68] Boundary disputes and quarrels over water are the standard fare. When disputes of that kind arise, it would scarcely make sense for the Court to invoke the local law of one of the adverse parties. The very point of Supreme Court jurisdiction is to guarantee a neutral arbiter. And neutrality in disputes between states seems naturally to require, as well, the application of an independent body of governing law. Accordingly, the Supreme Court has long held that its jurisdiction in interstate cases implies an authority to craft federal rules of decision as needed.[69] Then again, the Court often refers to the law of the states concerned for guidance.[70]

Admiralty cases. Article III also contemplates federal jurisdiction in admiralty and maritime cases.[71] Acting on that constitutional authority, Congress has always granted federal courts jurisdiction to handle those matters. The current statute, 28 U.S.C. §1333, gives federal district courts an exclusive original jurisdiction to adjudicate admiralty cases, "saving to suitors in all cases all other remedies to which they are otherwise entitled."[72] Here again, the existence of jurisdiction implies the additional authority to articulate and enforce a uniform body of substantive law. The leading precedent is *Southern Pac. R.R. v. Jensen.*[73] At the outset, the Supreme Court almost certainly understood that there was a pre-Constitution (and thus non-federal) body of maritime law, largely captured in custom, old "sea codes," and contemporary treatises.[74] John Marshall

---

67. There is also a body of precedent holding that some aspects of the law of nations form a species of federal common law. For discussions, see Curtis A. Bradley & Jack L. Goldsmith, *Customary International Law as Federal Common Law: A Critique of the Modern Position*, 110 Harv. L. Rev. 815 (1997); Harold Koh, *Is International Law Really State Law?*, 111 Harv. L. Rev. 1824 (1998); Symposium, 42 Va. J. Intnat'l L. 365 (2002).

68. See Chapter IV, text accompanying note 5; Chapter VII, text accompanying note 22.

69. See *Kentucky v. Indiana*, 281 U.S. 163 (1930).

70. See Chapter VII, text accompanying notes 29–33.

71. See Chapter IV, text accompanying note 3.

72. This provision is the modern descendent of a similar provision in the Judiciary Act of 1789. See Chapter II, text accompanying notes 56–58.

73. 244 U.S. 205 (1917).

74. See William H. Theis, *United States Admiralty Law as an Enclave of Federal Common Law*, 23 Tulane Mar. L.J. 73, 76–79 (1998).

once explained that Article III simply recognized that law and authorized Congress to create federal courts with jurisdiction to administer it.[75] As the need arose, however, federal courts enlarged preexisting maritime law by adding their own judge-made principles and rules. By conventional account, those principles and rules constitute a species of federal common law.[76]

This does not mean that admiralty law is entirely a creature of judicial policy-making. Congress has enacted numerous statutes that override common law rules that the courts would otherwise enforce.[77] And in the wake of each succeeding statute, federal courts attempt to harmonize any further judicial law-making they think necessary with the policy that Congress has put in place.[78] Today, specialists debate whether it is accurate to characterize federal admiralty law as a body of judicial decisions, adjusted on occasion by statute, or, instead, a battery of federal statutes whose gaps are filled by judge-made common law.[79] The states, too, play a role. State legislatures often enact local measures regulating maritime affairs.[80] And the "saving to suitors" clause in §1333 allows suits in state court to vindicate claims anchored in either state or federal law.[81] Sometimes, federal judge-made maritime law trumps state law purporting to operate on the same subject matter. The Court explained in *Jensen* that state law is invalid if it "works material prejudice" to "general" maritime law or "interferes with the harmony and uniformity of that law."[82] Yet preemption is by no means automatic. Federal judge-made admiralty law does not displace state law in cases in which the states have a strong interest in enforcing local policy and there is no significant threat to uniformity.[83] Moreover, the Court integrates state regulations into the corpus of federal admiralty law wherever possible.[84] The practical result is that admiralty is actually a collage of principles and rules originating in a variety of places: federal judicial decisions, federal

---

75. *American Ins. Co. v. 356 Bales of Cotton (Canter)*, 26 U.S. 511, 545–46 (1828) (explaining that admiralty cases did not arise under federal law but were governed by maritime law "as old as navigation itself").

76. See Joel K. Goldstein, *Federal Common Law in Admiralty: An Introduction to the Beginning of an Exchange*, 43 St. Louis U. L.J. 1337, 1339 (1999).

77. E.g., *Dooley*, 524 U.S. at 123 (holding that the Death on the High Seas Act preempts judge-made admiralty law). Congress' power to enact maritime law is derived from two sources. The Commerce Clause grants Congress authority to regulate commerce in the form of navigation. *Gibbons v. Ogden*, 22 U.S. (9 Wheat.) 1 (1824). The admiralty provision in Article III independently (though implicitly) grants Congress power to make adjustments to the maritime law that existed prior to the Constitution and has been embellished since by the courts. See *Romero v. Intnat'l Term. Op. Co.*, 358 U.S. 354, 360–61 (1959); *Panama R.R. Co. v. Johnson*, 264 U.S. 375, 385–87 (1924). This second basis of legislative power may seem odd. But it has strong historical and practical support. At least in the modern world, it would be hard to accept the idea that Article III might implicitly empower federal courts to make up substantive federal non-constitutional common law that Congress is unable to displace.

78. *American Dredging Co. v. Miller*, 510 U.S. 443, 455 (1994).

79. See generally W. Eugene Davis, *The Role of Federal Courts in Admiralty: The Challenges Facing the Admiralty Judges of the Lower Federal Courts*, 75 Tulane L. Rev. 1355 (2001); Robert Force, *An Essay on Federal Common Law and Admiralty*, 43 St. Louis U. L.J. 1367 (1999).

80. See *American Dredging*, 510 U.S. at 452; *Yamaha Motor Corp. v. Calhoun*, 516 U.S. 199, 210 n.8 (1996).

81. See Ernest A. Young, *The Last Brooding Omnipresence: Erie Railroad Co. v. Tompkins and the Unconstitutionality of Preemptive Federal Maritime Law*, 43 St. Louis U. L.J. 1349, 1351–52 (1999).

82. *Jensen*, 244 U.S. at 216.

83. E.g., *Kossick v. United Fruit Co.*, 365 U.S. 731, 739 (1961).

84. See *Jerome B. Grubart v. Great Lakes Dredge & Dock Co.*, 513 U.S. 527, 545 (1995); e.g., *Moragne*, 398 U.S. at 405–06 (explaining that federal law controlled the availability of a wrongful death action but borrowing the content of that federal law from the law of most states).

statutes, and state law. Specialists debate, too, whether state law operates in some cases of its own force (that is, *as* state law) or, instead, only provides the absorbed content of federal admiralty law (so that it loses its character as state law and becomes itself federal). This ambiguity also attends other instances in which federal common law borrows from state sources.[85]

By some accounts, the premise of the *Jensen* decision (that admiralty jurisprudence is prototypically federal judge-made law) is no longer sound. Some commentators have urged the Court to abandon that notion, to rely in the main on federal statutes and state law (*qua* state law), and to approve judge-made federal common law only in circumstances calling for a uniform national rule that no federal statute currently provides.[86] Congress could presumably impose more systemic order in this field legislatively. But the great complexity of the task is daunting.[87] Meanwhile, the Supreme Court appears content to develop federal admiralty law incrementally.[88]

2. Other illustrations

Federal courts have authority to fashion federal common law in a sprinkling of other instances. Occasionally, Congress expressly delegates law-making authority to the courts. The best illustration is Rule 501 of the Federal Rules of Evidence, which specifies that certain evidentiary privileges are governed by "common law" principles "as interpreted by" the federal courts "in light of reason and experience."[89] In cases of express delegation, judicial law-making is non-controversial in most circles—provided that Congress could make the same law by statute.[90] Even when federal courts act on what

---

85. See notes 114–16 and accompanying text.

86. See, e.g., Bradford R. Clark, *Federal Common Law: A Structural Reinterpretation*, 144 U. Pa. L. Rev. 1245 (1996); Ernest A. Young, *Preemption at Sea*, 67 Geo. Wash. L. Rev. 273 (1998). Professor Theis contends that the case for uniformity holds only with respect to cases involving international maritime affairs. With respect to domestic admiralty cases, Theis argues that the states should have wide latitude to adopt and enforce local policies. Theis, note 74, at 121. Professor Force argues that an expansive admiralty jurisdiction in federal court primarily provides an escape route for litigants who want to avoid jury trial in state court. Force, note 79, at 1369. Professor Friedell contends that it is "too late" to suggest that it is unconstitutional for federal courts to make federal admiralty law. Steven F. Friedell, *The Diverse Nature of Admiralty Jurisdiction*, 43 St. Louis U. L.J. 1389, 1392 (1999).

87. The American Law Institute has acknowledged that reforms may be in order, but the ALI hesitates to propose a program for fear that it might inadvertently make things worse. See John Oakley, *Prospectus for the American Law Institute's Federal Judicial Code Revision Project*, 31 U.C. Davis L. Rev. 855, 884–87 (1998).

88. The Court was invited to revisit *Jensen* in the *American Dredging* case. Justice Stevens attached a concurring opinion suggesting that *Jensen* is now "untrustworthy." 510 U.S. at 458. Writing for the full Court, Justice Scalia explained that it would be inappropriate to reconsider such an important precedent without full briefing. Id. at 447 n.1. The Court has continued to elaborate admiralty as a matter of federal common law. E.g., *Norfolk Shipbuilding & Drydock v. Garris*, 532 U.S. 811 (2001); *McDermott v. AmClyde*, 511 U.S. 202 (1994); *East River S.S. Corp. v. Transamerica Delaval*, 476 U.S. 858 (1986).

89. The Federal Deposit Insurance Corporation Act also explicitly delegates law-making authority inasmuch as it provides that civil suits in which the FDIC is a party "shall be deemed to arise under the laws of the United States." *D'Oench*, 315 U.S. at 455 n.2.

90. Congress may also explicitly instruct federal courts to apply state law. For example, the Federal Tort Claims Act typically makes the United States liable for torts committed by its officers where the government, were it a private person, would be liable "in accordance with the law of the place where the act or omission occurred." 28 U.S.C. §1346(b). In a curious old case, *United States v.*

they regard as an *implicit* delegation of authority, they can be on solid ground. The federal common law the courts have developed in anti-trust cases is an example.[91] There are cases, however, in which judicial law-making evokes concern, because it threatens both to appropriate the legislative power of Congress (and thus to upset the separation of powers within the national government)[92] and to preempt state law (and thus to undermine the values associated with federalism).[93]

The Supreme Court precedents in point recognize three conditions that typically attend the creation of federal common law: (1) some kind of invitation from Congress or, at least, congressional acquiescence (typically a statutory grant of jurisdiction); (2) a significant interest on the part of the federal government (typically a regulatory, proprietary, or sovereign interest); and (3) a demonstrable need for a uniform rule across the country (as opposed to inconsistent rules supplied by different states).[94]

Congressional invitation or acquiescence. At the very least, Congress' acquiescence in judicial law-making is crucial, and something approaching an affirmative invitation is typically present. In two classic cases, *Textile Workers Union v. Lincoln Mills*[95] and *Clearfield Trust Co. v. United States*,[96] the Supreme Court relied, in part, on congressional grants of jurisdiction. In *Lincoln Mills*, a union sued an employer in a federal district court, invoking the court's jurisdiction under §301(a) of the Labor Management Relations Act to entertain suits to enforce labor agreements. Justice Douglas read §301(a) not only to confer jurisdiction on the district court, but also to express a "fed-

---

Standard Oil Co., 332 U.S. 301 (1947), the Court faced the inverse of the situation contemplated by §1346(b): a suit *by* the United States against a private company to recover damages for losing the services of a soldier who had been injured by a company truck. The Court held that federal law controlled that case, because the government's monetary assets were at stake. Yet the Court declined to fashion any federal common law for the occasion and, instead, invited Congress to enact a statute. That disposition defeated the government's claim for want of any basis for holding the company liable.

91. See, e.g., *Nat'l Soc'y of Prof. Engineers v. United States*, 435 U.S. 679, 688 (1978).

92. See Chapter I, notes 2–18 and accompanying text. Professor Redish contends that this is the principal concern raised by federal judicial law-making. He notes that the Rules of Decision Act does not mention federal common law, but (by his account) directs federal courts *always* to apply state law, unless a federal statute, a treaty, or the Constitution specifies otherwise. See note 57. Thus when federal courts presume to create federal common law, they not only usurp Congress' legislative authority, but actually violate an extant congressional enactment. See Martin H. Redish, *Federal Common Law, Political Legitimacy, and the Interpretive Process: An "Institutionalist" Perspective*, 83 Nw. U. L. Rev. 761, 786–801 (1989). Professor Weinberg understands federal common law cases to be instances in which the Constitution precludes the application of state law. Louise Weinberg, *The Curious Notion that the Rules of Decision Act Blocks Supreme Federal Common Law*, 83 Nw. U. L. Rev. 860, 865–66 (1989). Professor Meltzer adds that cases in which federal common law controls may be instances in which no state rules "apply" within the meaning of the Rules of Decision Act. Daniel J. Meltzer, *State Court Forfeitures of Federal Rights*, 99 Harv. L. Rev. 1128, 1168 n.194 (1986).

93. See Chapter I, notes 19–25 and accompanying text. Professor Field regards this as the chief (but easily surmountable) difficulty with federal common law. Field, note 59, at 924–26, 931.

94. Academicians offer their own variations on these themes. See Donald L. Doernberg, *Juridical Chameleons in the "New Erie" Canal*, 1990 Utah L. Rev. 759; Alfred Hill, *The Law-Making Power of the Federal Courts: Constitutional Preemption*, 67 Colum. L. Rev. 1024 (1967); Thomas W. Merrill, *The Common Law Powers of Federal Courts*, 52 U. Chi. L. Rev. 1 (1985); *Symposium*, 12 Pace L. Rev. 227 (1992).

95. 353 U.S. 448 (1957).

96. 318 U.S. 363 (1943).

eral policy that federal courts should enforce" labor agreements. In some instances, he said, the LMRA "expressly" specified substantive law for the federal courts to apply. But in other instances, the Act was silent, leaving problems in "the penumbra of express statutory mandates." In those instances, the courts themselves must create "federal law" consistent with the "policy of our national labor laws."[97] In *Clearfield*, the federal government sued a bank in a federal district court, invoking the court's jurisdiction under the precursor of 28 U.S.C. §1345 to entertain suits in which the United States was a party. The government contended that the bank was liable for the amount of a stolen government check. Justice Douglas said that the "rights and duties" of the United States regarding government checks were governed by "federal rather than local law." Since Congress had failed to enact substantive rules, it was "for the federal courts to fashion" their own rules "according to their own standards."[98]

The mere existence of jurisdiction is not ordinarily a sufficient basis for judicial law-making.[99] The cases on disputes between states and admiralty matters are exceptional.[100] The Court no longer takes the same view of judicial authority in ordinary §1332 diversity cases. The very point of *Erie* is that diversity jurisdiction does not empower the federal courts to create federal common law.[101] The Court has never proposed that §1331 implies power to make up federal law in garden variety federal question cases. Moreover, relying on a jurisdictional grant as the basis for federal common law creates an anomaly when cases controlled by that law are entertained in state court. State courts are ostensibly called upon to apply federal law and thus necessarily to contribute to its development. Yet *state* courts cannot rest their law-making authority on a grant of jurisdiction to the *federal* courts.

Federal interests. Federal judicial law-making is warranted only when significant federal interests are at stake. The government had regulatory interests in *Lincoln Mills* and proprietary interests in *Clearfield.* In *Boyle v. United Technologies Corp.*,[102] the government's sovereign interests were implicated. The father of a Marine Corps pilot who had died in a helicopter accident invoked a federal district court's diversity jurisdiction to determine a state tort claim against the manufacturer. The plaintiff contended that the manufacturer was liable for design defects in the helicopter, even though the design conformed to Marine Corps specifications. Justice Scalia said that if state tort law rendered the manufacturer liable for producing a helicopter that met Marine Corps standards, it was preempted by federal common law. He explained that the Federal Tort Claims Act would not have permitted the plaintiff to hold the government responsible for his son's death on the theory that the Marine Corps had misdesigned the helicopter. Imposing liability on the manufacturer was different, but not sufficiently different to warrant a contrary result. By Scalia's account, the same "uniquely federal" interests implicated in a suit against the government were also implicated in a suit against a private company for actions taken pursuant to a contract with the government.[103]

---

97. 353 U.S. at 455–57.
98. 318 U.S. at 366.
99. See *Radcliff Materials*, 451 U.S. at 640 (disclaiming the proposition that jurisdiction-granting statutes typically authorize federal courts to create federal common law).
100. See notes 68–88 and accompanying text.
101. See notes 55–56 and accompanying text; Alfred Hill, *The Erie Doctrine and the Constitution*, 53 Nw. U. L. Rev. 427 (1958).
102. 487 U.S. 500 (1988).
103. Id. at 505.

The need for a uniform rule. When federal interests obtain in a case, there is often value in a uniform body of national rules of decision, which can be supplied by federal courts in the form of federal common law. When uniformity is not important, federal courts may still find federal common law controlling, but may incorporate state law as the content of that federal common law. In that event, state law no longer operates as "an independent source of private rights."[104] But it does generate results, and those results can vary from state to state.[105] The question whether federal courts should borrow state law to fill in the content of federal common law calls for pragmatic judgment. Justice Douglas said in *Lincoln Mills* that in some circumstances the courts might resort to state law regarding labor contracts, provided state law was "compatible with the purpose of §301" and would "best effectuate" federal policy.[106] And in *Clearfield*, he recognized that federal courts might adopt state rules governing commercial paper. In that instance, however, he concluded that reliance on state law was "inappropriate" because it would subject the government's "rights and duties" to "exceptional uncertainty."[107]

Critics tend to accept the Court's judgment in *Lincoln Mills*, but to express more doubt regarding *Clearfield*.[108] The government plainly has an interest in consistent rules that will apply wherever it does business. Yet the states also have their own interests in vindicating the local commercial policies promoted by state law. If, in *Clearfield*, the Court had applied the law of the state concerned (Pennsylvania), private merchants in that state would have been able to rely on local commercial law, both in their transactions with other merchants and in their dealings with the government.[109] In more recent cases, the Court has acknowledged federal judicial authority to create federal law to govern commercial disputes, but has insisted that there must be stronger justification for actually imposing uniform national rules. In *Kamen v. Kemper Financial Svc.*,[110] the Court adopted a "presumption" in favor of incorporating state law into federal law, particularly in the commercial and corporate context.[111] And in *O'Melveny & Myers v.*

---

104. *Lincoln Mills*, 353 U.S. at 457.

105. The Court recognized this point in *Semtek v. Lockheed*, 531 U.S. 497 (2001). The issue in that case was the content of federal common law preclusion rules with respect to federal court judgments in diversity cases. Since the claims in those cases turn on state law, the Court found no need for a uniform national rule regarding preclusion. Accordingly, the Court borrowed the relevant state's preclusion law as the content of federal preclusion doctrine. Id. at 508. Cf. Chapter VI, notes 190–92 and accompanying text (discussing the *Elliot* case in which the Court also borrowed state preclusion law with respect to prior judgments by state administrative agencies). The Full Faith and Credit Statute, 28 U.S.C. §1738, deals only with the preclusive effects of *state court* judgments and thus was inapplicable in *Semtek*. See Chapter VI, notes 161–85 and accompanying text (discussing §1738 in cases to which it applies).

106. *Lincoln Mills*, 353 U.S. at 457.

107. *Clearfield*, 318 U.S. at 367.

108. At the time, it must be said, some observers doubted that the federal courts would be equal to the task set for them in *Lincoln Mills*. See, e.g., Alexander M. Bickel & Harry H. Wellington, *Legislative Purpose and the Judicial Process: The Lincoln Mills Case*, 71 Harv. L. Rev. 1, 22–23 (1957).

109. In light of *Clearfield*, federal common law controls the federal government's own "rights and duties" attending its commercial paper. It does not follow, however, that federal common law equally governs all cases involving government checks. In *Bank of America Nat'l Trust & Savings Ass'n v. Parnell*, 352 U.S. 29 (1956), a bank sued a private individual to recover the value of government securities said to be overdue. The Court applied federal common law to decide whether the bonds *were* overdue, but said that state law controlled the different question whether the defendant had accepted the bonds in good faith. The due dates of the bonds implicated the federal government's interests, but the defendant's good faith did not.

110. 500 U.S. 90, 98 (1991).

111. See *United States v. Kimball Foods*, 440 U.S. 715, 740 (1979) (choosing the "prudent course" of adopting "the readymade body of state law as the federal rule of decision").

FDIC,[112] the Court said that federal courts may properly fashion their own federal rules of decision only in those "few and restricted" instances in which the application of state law would conflict with an important federal policy.[113]

There is a difference between holding, on the one hand, that state law is controlling of its own force and holding, on the other, that state law is dispositive because it supplies the content of federal common law. If state law governs only because it is incorporated by federal law, both state and federal courts will in future enforce that law *as federal law*. Things can become conceptually murky when state courts enforce law that originally took shape as state law (over which state courts are authoritative), but that has become federal in nature (so that state court decisions are presumably subject to appellate review in the Supreme Court).[114] Safe to say, the Supreme Court is not about to accept appellate review in a case in which the state's highest court has determined a matter of state law and presume to review that judgment for error on the theory that the state law issue has been "federalized" by incorporation into federal common law. For this reason, the Court has said that when state law provides the rule of decision in a case, it is "only of theoretical interest whether the basis of that application" is the state's "own sovereign power" or "federal adoption" of a state's law.[115] The "incorporation" phenomenon can make matters complex in other ways, as well. Federal common law may not embrace the entirety of a state's legal rules in a given field, but only a few rules or a single rule; it may select only one feature of a rule and neglect its details; it may ignore other complicating aspects of state rules (e.g., state choice of law rules); and it may incorporate only the rules of law in some states, but not in others.[116]

Critics typically find *Boyle* the most troubling of the Court's modern precedents. In that case, Justice Scalia did not discard state law entirely in favor of a uniform body of federal judge-made rules. Instead, he held only that in a lawsuit generally controlled by state law, the defendant was entitled to a federal defense that state law otherwise denied. Bluntly stated, Justice Scalia injected federal common law into a state tort action only

---

112. 512 U.S. 79, 87 (1994). Professor Lund has criticized the *Kamen* and *O'Melveny* decisions for failing to appreciate the federal interests at stake. Paul Lund, *The Decline of Federal Common Law*, 76 B.U. L. Rev. 895 (1996).

113. Acting on this premise, the Court held in *Atherton v. FDIC*, 519 U.S. 213 (1997), that the standard of care to which managers at federally chartered banks are held is a matter of state law, albeit a federal statute establishes "gross negligence" as a federal floor (which controls in any state that would otherwise let bank managers get away with all manner of mayhem). If federal courts *lack* authority to create federal law, then any relevant state law controls of its own authority. E.g., *Wallis v. Pan Amer. Petroleum Corp.*, 384 U.S. 63 (1966) (holding that state law controlled in a dispute between private parties over a mineral lease issued by the federal government).

114. Cf. *Local 174 v. Lucas Flour Co.*, 369 U.S. 95, 102–03 (1962) (refusing to permit a state court to depart from the federal common law that controlled a case).

115. *O'Melveny*, 512 U.S. at 85. Moreover, since the Court's ability to ensure the supremacy, accuracy, and uniformity of federal law would not be implicated, in this instance the Court might conclude that a state court's disposition of a question of "federalized state law" constitutes an independent and adequate state ground of decision. See Chapter VII, notes 138–40 and accompanying text. In that vein, however, the Court would presumably assume jurisdiction to determine whether the state court's judgment has "fair support" and thus does not constitute an effort to frustrate the federal policies that caused the Court to introduce federal common law into the equation in the first place. See Chapter VII, notes 121–27 and accompanying text. In the *Semtek* case, Justice Scalia explained that a "federal reference to state law will not obtain... in situations in which state law is incompatible with federal interests." *Semtek*, 531 U.S. at 509; see note 105.

116. See Paul J. Mishkin, *The Variousness of "Federal Law": Competence and Discretion in the Choice of National and State Rules for Decision*, 105 U. Pa. L. Rev. 797, 804–08 (1957).

insofar as was essential to guarantee that a large manufacturing company could resist a products liability claim that would have been successful but for the intervention of federal law that the Court itself manufactured.[117] This from a member of the Court who usually insists that the courts must enforce the text of enacted statutes.[118] The body of judicial decisions and academic commentaries touching federal common law provides few occasions for ideological controversy. Yet *Boyle* may be evidence that in this context, too, the Court can excite criticism that its doctrinal innovations reflect unstated underlying values.[119]

C. Federal Rights of Action

Litigants who wish to invoke the federal courts' jurisdiction must have both a claim that is federal in character *and* authorization to vindicate that claim by means of a pri-

---

117. Dissenting in *Boyle*, Justice Brennan said that the justices had to assume for purposes of decision that if United Technologies had designed such a "death trap" for a commercial firm rather than for the Marine Corps, the pilot's father would have recovered on his state law claim. 487 U.S. at 515. Congress had previously failed to enact bills that would have insulated the company from liability. See Michael D. Green & Richard A. Matasar, *The Supreme Court and the Products Liability Crisis: Lessons From Boyle's Government Contractor Defense*, 63 So. Calif. L. Rev. 637, 669 (1990).

118. See Chapter I, notes 30–43 and accompanying text. Cf. Chapter VI, notes 34–35 and accompanying text (discussing Justice Scalia's position in the *Tafflin* case). Consider, for example, that the Court often invokes the canon of statutory construction which has it that when a statute explicitly establishes a policy for a list of items, it forecloses (by negative implication) the same policy for items not on the list. Even if it appears that the policy should be more generally applicable, it should be inferred that Congress has decided to limit its purview to the listed items. The statute in *Boyle* (the FTCA) insulated the government from liability but did not extend that policy to private companies contracting with the government. One might have expected Justice Scalia to infer, accordingly, that the FTCA denied a similar defense to a private contractor. Instead, he insisted that the same policy *should* apply to private defendants. And since Congress had not enacted a statute to that effect, he fashioned federal common law for the task. Most critics do not fault the Court simply for inconsistency—that is, for relying exclusively on rules of statutory construction in some instances while attending to policy considerations in others. The more telling criticism is that in cases in which rules of construction are deployed, the Court typically disclaims any capacity to consider policy implications, purporting to defer, instead, to the policy the Court ascribes to Congress, which enacted the statute as written. See, e.g., Chapter XII, text accompanying notes 178, 188, 533. Decisions like *Boyle* indicate, however, that the Court is not insensitive to policy at all, but rather exercises judgment in the context of statutory construction as in any other. The Court would do better to acknowledge that canons of construction do not (and should not) operate mechanically to grind out results for which the justices are in no way responsible.

119. Professor Weinberg, herself a strong proponent of federal common law, contends that the serious question today is not whether federal common law controls a case in general, but rather whether federal common law establishes affirmative federal claims for plaintiffs or, instead, gives corporations federal defenses that vanquish state tort law meant to protect consumers. Professor Weinberg faults Justice Scalia for promoting the government contractor defense while discounting the state policies served by products liability law. See Weinberg, note 92, at 848–49. Professor Lund, also a proponent of federal common law, juxtaposes Justice Scalia's opinion in *Boyle* with his quite different opinion for the Court in *O'Melveny*. See text accompanying notes 112–13. Lund regards *Boyle* as an instance in which the Court had every reason to allow state law to operate. See Lund, note 112, at 959–64. Professor Cass and Professor Gillette have traced out what they think are the incentives created by the government contractor defense established in *Boyle*. They contend that the implications are much more complex than the Court seems to appreciate. Ronald A. Cass & Clayton P. Gillette, *The Government Contractor Defense: Contractual Allocation of Public Risk*, 77 Va. L. Rev. 257 (1991).

vate lawsuit. In common parlance, an authorization to sue is called a "cause of action." That label can be confusing. The better designation is a "right of action"—a right to *litigate* a substantive claim. There is a difference between a federal claim and a federal right of action. The one is the plaintiff's argument that the defendant has violated some species of federal law (federal common law, a federal statute, or the Constitution). The other is a procedural vehicle for advancing that argument in court.[120] The dichotomy between a claim, on the one hand, and a means of access to court for the enforcement of that claim, on the other, challenges the familiar maxim that there can be no "right" without a "remedy." That adage only recognizes that we typically depend on courts to give meaning to legal claims by bringing judicial power to bear on violators—ordering them to cease unlawful behavior or to pay damages for the injuries they have caused.[121]

---

120. Courts and commentators alike typically employ the term "cause of action" to mean a private party's entitlement to sue for the enforcement of a federal legal standard (i.e., a federal statute, a rule of federal common law, or the Constitution)—that is, to mean a "right of action." Sometimes, however, courts and commentators use the same "cause of action" phrase to refer to the plaintiff's legal claim itself—the violation of law the plaintiff charges the defendant with committing. Sometimes, courts and commentators use the "cause of action" formulation to capture both ideas at once, and sometimes it is frankly hard to know *what* they mean. The difficulty is in part historical. The "cause of action" formulation dates from the early Nineteenth Century. It figured prominently in the Field Code, adopted in New York in 1848. In that context, a "cause of action" was a plaintiff's primary "right" to demand some behavior from the defendant, such that the defendant's breach of the duty to behave in that way constituted a "wrong." See Robert G. Bone, *Mapping the Boundaries of a Dispute: Conceptions of Ideal Lawsuit Structure From the Field Code to the Federal Rules*, 89 Colum. L. Rev. 1, 28 (1989). Under the Field Code, a plaintiff's ability to complain to a court that the defendant had committed a breach of duty was a different matter—a "remedial right." Id. at 12 n.21, 13–14, 28. When courts and commentators today refer to a "cause of action" as an entitlement to sue in some court to vindicate a substantive right, they are not using the "cause of action" rubric in the way it was employed in the Field Code. They are talking about something that the Field Code did not consider to be part of a "cause of action" at all. Then again, when courts and commentators use "cause of action" in more or less the way it was understood in the Field Code (i.e., to refer to a substantive claim), they invite misunderstanding—given the way in which others use the same language. In part, too, the difficulty is conceptual. In a common law system of the kind the states are understood to have, there are few occasions for separating plaintiffs' claims that they have been wronged from their authority to sue in court. Common law courts sit to enforce whatever claims a party may have; they recognize no independent question whether the party is authorized to ask them for help. Better said, in a common law scheme, lawsuits in court are the only game in town. There is no menu of enforcement mechanisms from which to choose. So a claim is meaningful only if it is enforceable by means of a private lawsuit. Anything that is not judicially enforceable is not a claim the law recognizes at all. In the common law context, then, the two ideas (a substantive claim and the authority to take that claim to court) genuinely (or at least typically) merge into one, and use of the single "cause of action" label creates no great uncertainty. By contrast, federal legal claims are *not* invariably enforceable by means of lawsuits filed in court. Federal courts do *not* sit routinely to enforce whatever claims parties might wish to present to them (even when those claims are federal in character), and a party's authorization to sue *does* present an independent question. Accordingly, it is essential to differentiate between claims, on the one hand, and rights of action, on the other. There is no easy escape from this terminological tangle. One can only parse opinions and academic discussions carefully in order to identify precisely what is being described: a legal claim (i.e., an assertion that the defendant has violated the law), a right of action (i.e., an authorization to ask a court to redress that violation in some way), or some combination of the two.

121. Herein more confusing nomenclature. When this common adage is used with reference to state law and access to state court, its essential message is typically accurate. Within a framework in which courts enjoy a general authority to adjudicate any and all claims that come through the door, a realist may sensibly conclude that there is no point in differentiating a claim, a right of action to enforce that claim in a lawsuit, the court's subject matter jurisdiction to entertain the lawsuit, and the relief the court will award if the plaintiff is successful on the merits. To the realist, all that matters is what a court can *do* on the plaintiff's behalf. When the adage is used with reference to federal

On examination, the relationship between abstract legal claims and judicial enforcement machinery is more complex where federal courts are concerned.

It is tempting to think that any claim that can be described as an individual "right" to some behavior by another party must necessarily entail a "right of action" to take a defendant to court, and that difficulties arise only when a plaintiff wishes to sue in order to hold a defendant accountable for violating a federal statute or constitutional provision that does not confer an individual "right" on the plaintiff.[122] Yet there are instances in which plaintiffs have federal rights, but no rights of action to enforce those rights in a lawsuit.[123] Congress has significant authority to prescribe the means by which federal law will be implemented. Congress may authorize private civil lawsuits as an effective, traditional means of forcing private citizens and companies or governmental officials to comply with federal law. But a private lawsuit is scarcely the only choice on the menu or, certainly, a necessary choice. In addition to private suits, or as an alternative, Congress may make violations of federal law a crime and invite the executive branch to prosecute violators in criminal proceedings. Or Congress may turn enforcement responsibility over to an administrative agency.[124] In any given instance, Congress is largely free to select whatever enforcement devices it pleases and is equally free to foreclose others—including lawsuits by individuals who wish to file their own actions in court.[125]

Constitutional law stands on a special footing. The Supreme Court itself has historically been willing to assume some responsibility for constitutional enforcement, in service of the Court's independent duty to see that the Constitution is respected as the supreme law. Nevertheless, the Court accords Congress general authority to make decisions regarding enforcement vehicles for constitutional, as well as non-constitutional, law.[126] As a practical matter, then, litigants who want to enforce federal law of any stripe in a lawsuit

---

law and access to federal court, its message (about the realistic relationship between claims and judicial enforcement of claims) can be obscured, and a different (misleading) message can emerge. In this context, the very distinctions the adage suggests can be ignored must, instead, be drawn with analytic rigor. The existence of a plaintiff's abstract claim that the defendant has violated federal law does not automatically entail either an authorization to advance that claim in a lawsuit or a federal court's jurisdiction to entertain such a suit. And the remedy a court may grant in the end is something else again. For clarity's sake, one might want to reserve the term "remedy" to describe the form of relief a court may award. But courts and commentators refuse to cooperate. They sometimes use that term to describe a right of action or *both* the right of action needed in a case *and* the form of relief a court may be persuaded to order.

122. See Chapter IX, notes 91–139, 319–80 and accompanying text (discussing the way ideas of this kind play out in the context of "standing" doctrine).

123. See notes 154–60, 223–30 and accompanying text. For critiques of the distinction between rights and rights of action, see John C. Jeffries, Jr., *Disaggregating Constitutional Torts*, 110 Yale L.J. 259 (2000); Daryl J. Levinson, *Rights Essentialism and Remedial Equilibration*, 99 Colum. L. Rev. 857 (1999); Donald H. Zeigler, *Rights, Rights of Action, and Remedies: An Integrated Approach*, 76 Wash. L. Rev. 67 (2001).

124. See Chapter V (discussing agencies and their relationship to Article III). If Congress does employ an agency for enforcement purposes in the first instance, the agency's performance is typically open to judicial review later—either by some means established by the statute itself, see Chapter V, text accompanying notes 18–19, or by the means provided by the Administrative Procedure Act. See notes 133, 137–39 and accompanying text.

125. The classic precedent is *Cary v. Curtis*, 44 U.S. (3 How.) 236 (1845). See Henry M. Hart, Jr., *The Power of Congress to Limit the Jurisdiction of Federal Courts: An Exercise in Dialectic*, 66 Harv. L. Rev. 1362, 1366–69 (1953).

126. Professor Dellinger contends that congressional authority regarding rights of action to enforce the Constitution (as opposed to federal statutes) can be derived from congressional authority

must demonstrate that Congress will allow the action and has not selected some alternative implementation scheme to the exclusion of litigation by private citizens.[127]

1. Rights of Action to Enforce Federal Statutes

Congress often authorizes private lawsuits for the enforcement of federal statutes. In the *Osborn* case, for example, the same "sue and be sued" language that John Marshall read to confer jurisdiction on the federal circuit court also performed two other functions.[128] It clarified that the bank, a newly constructed creature of statute, was competent to conduct its own litigation with other parties, and it authorized the bank and its adversaries to file lawsuits to settle their differences. In *Lincoln Mills*, Justice Douglas declined to read a similar "sue and be sued" provision in §301(b) of the LMRA to confer jurisdiction on federal district courts.[129] But he did read that provision both to establish unions as entities capable of litigating for themselves and to authorize them and their adversaries to litigate claims under labor contracts governed by federal common law. The bank in *Osborn* and the union in *Lincoln Mills* needed both kinds of help from Congress. The bank could be competent to engage in litigation only if Congress made that capacity one of the bank's statutory properties. The union was an unincorporated association that would not have had capacity to sue at common law. So the union, too, needed a statute in order to engage in litigation "as an entity."[130] In addition, the bank, the union, and their adversaries needed authorization from Congress to file lawsuits advancing federal legal claims. A right of action to enforce a federal legal standard is essential and often cannot be supplied by state law.[131]

There are some free-standing right-of-action statutes that serve generally as procedural vehicles by which litigants can enforce federal statutes by means of private law-

---

to prescribe the federal courts' jurisdiction. See Walter E. Dellinger, *Of Rights and Remedies: The Constitution as a Sword*, 85 Harv. L. Rev. 1532, 1546–47 (1972); Chapter IV, notes 62–71 and accompanying text.

127. See note 170 and accompanying text (discussing alternatives to §1983 actions); notes 223–30 and accompanying text (discussing alternatives to *Bivens* actions).

128. See note 7 and accompanying text.

129. Douglas had no need to rest on §301(b) for jurisdictional purposes, since §301(a) independently performed that function. See note 97 and accompanying text.

130. *Lincoln Mills*, 353 U.S. at 451.

131. See notes 291–331 and accompanying text. By contrast, state law does provide a party's right of action to enforce state law claims, in either federal or state court. Or, perhaps better said, state law typically builds a right of action into the state law claim itself. See note 120. When entities like the bank and the union sue on state law grounds, and equally when their adversaries sue them on state law grounds, the authority that Congress has granted for federal question litigation does not operate. In the *Planters' Bank* case, accordingly, the bank relied on its congressionally granted competency to sue, but not on its congressionally granted right of action. See note 14 and accompanying text. In *Amer. Nat'l Red Cross v. S.G.*, 505 U.S. 247 (1992), see note 7, private plaintiffs initially sued the Red Cross in state court, relying on state law both for their substantive tort claims and for their right to sue. They relied on the "sue and be sued" provision in the charter issued to the Red Cross only to establish the capacity of the Red Cross to be a defendant in a lawsuit. The Red Cross removed the state court action to federal court on the theory that the plaintiffs might have sued originally in the federal forum pursuant to the grant of jurisdiction that the "sue and be sued" provision also provided. Since the plaintiffs' claim rested exclusively on state law, they needed no federally created right of action. Then again, if they *did* need one, the same "sue and be sued" provision would presumably have provided it. See notes 294–99 and accompanying text (discussing these issues in connection with removal jurisdiction).

suits. The Ku Klux Klan Act, 42 U.S.C. §1983, is one,[132] the Administrative Procedure Act, 5 U.S.C. §702, is another,[133] and the Declaratory Judgment Act, 28 U.S.C. §2201, may be yet another.[134] Pursuant to §1983, a "party injured" can file "an action at law, suit in equity, or other proper proceeding for redress," naming as a defendant a "person" who, "under color of any statute, ordinance, regulation, custom, or usage of any State or Territory" subjects a "citizen" or "other person" to the "deprivation of any rights, privileges, or immunities secured by the Constitution and laws."[135] Modern decisions give that archaic language an authoritative interpretation. It neither establishes substantive rights nor confers jurisdiction on the federal courts. But it does supply a right of action to be employed by plaintiffs who wish to vindicate rights that have some independent source in the Constitution or other "laws" of the United States. Recall that §1983 actions can be filed either in federal court or in state court.[136]

Pursuant to §702, a "person" can seek judicial review of actions taken by certain federal administrative agencies, if the litigant either suffers "legal wrong" or is "adversely affected or aggrieved by agency action within the meaning of a relevant statute." If, then, Congress chooses to employ an agency to implement a federal statute in the first instance (perhaps to the exclusion of private suits), private litigants may sometimes enforce the statute at one step removed—by suing the *agency* to ensure that the agency does not violate the very statute it is charged to implement (or some provision of the Constitution). This right of action is not always open.[137] Yet when §702 *is* available, it performs (with respect to suits alleging that federal agencies have violated federal law) the same function that §1983 performs (with respect to suits alleging that state officials have violated certain federal rights). Section 702 neither creates substantive rights nor confers jurisdiction on the federal courts.[138] But it does provide a right of action for litigants whose interests fall "arguably within the zone of interests" protected by the statutes or constitutional provisions they contend federal agencies have violated.[139]

---

132. See Chapter II, notes 74–75 and accompanying text.

133. See Chapter II, note 78 and accompanying text.

134. See Chapter II, note 77 and accompanying text.

135. See notes 165–90 and accompanying text. The text of §1983 goes on to state that "in any action brought against a judicial officer for an act or omission taken in such officer's judicial capacity, injunctive relief shall not be granted unless a declaratory decree was violated or declaratory relief was unavailable." See Chapter X, note 434 and accompanying text.

136. See Chapter VI, note 51 and accompanying text. Plaintiffs in §1983 actions typically advance fourteenth amendment claims and invoke federal court jurisdiction under the general authority provided by 28 U.S.C. §1331. See text accompanying notes 234–35. By common account, the Reconstruction Congress enacted §1983 for the very purpose of enforcing the then-recent fourteenth amendment. See *Monroe v. Pape*, 365 U.S. 167, 171 (1961). An independent provision enacted at the same time originally supplied federal courts with the jurisdiction required to entertain §1983 actions, irrespective of the amount in controversy between the parties. See 28 U.S.C. §1343(3); Chapter II, note 74 and accompanying text. When Congress eliminated the amount-in-controversy requirement from §1331 in 1980, there was no longer any need for §1343(3). That statute remains in place, but it is now superfluous. The Court has not read §1983 to have significance for the "standing" of plaintiffs to appear in an Article III court. See Chapter IX, note 321.

137. Judicial review under §702 is contingent on a body of statutes and decisions that comprise a healthy portion of administrative law. For example, the APA applies only to certain departments and agencies, 5 U.S.C. §701, and judicial review is typically restricted to agency action that is "final" within the meaning of 5 U.S.C. §704.

138. *Califano v. Sanders*, 430 U.S. 99 (1977). Like §1983 suits in federal court, actions pursuant to §702 typically rely on §1331 for subject matter jurisdiction.

139. *Clarke v. Secur. Indus. Ass'n*, 479 U.S. 388, 399–400 (1987); see Chapter IX, notes 274–94 and accompanying text (discussing the zone test). By contrast to §1983, §702 does speak to the

Pursuant to §2201, a federal court "may" declare the "rights and other legal relations of any interested party seeking such declaration," if an "appropriate pleading" is filed in "a case of actual controversy" within the court's jurisdiction. That language, too, is opaque. According to the Supreme Court's decisions, §2201 neither creates substantive rights nor confers subject matter jurisdiction.[140] At a minimum, it enables federal courts to grant a declaratory judgment as a remedy—that is, as a form of judicial relief different from an award of damages or an injunction.[141] There is an argument that it does *only* that and does not *itself* create a right of action to sue in the first instance. Note in this vein that §2201 expressly licenses the federal courts and does not, in so many words, empower potential litigants. Moreover, §2201 *authorizes* the federal courts to issue declaratory judgments, but does not *require* them to do so. The discretionary character of declaratory relief may presuppose that litigants must establish a right of action on some independent basis. Since §2201 is addressed only to federal courts, it evidently supplies no right of action for suits in state court. In that way, too, §2201 differs from §1983 and thus arguably appears not to authorize suits in the first instance, but only to permit a certain form of relief in suits that are authorized by some independent source.[142]

There is also an argument that the Declaratory Judgment Act, like §1983 and §702, grants private plaintiffs permission to go to court, so long as they seek only declaratory relief.[143] Since declaratory judgments have no immediate coercive effect, they lend themselves to cases in which the parties have a genuine dispute regarding the law governing their relations, but will find it easy enough to reconcile their differences once a court announces where each party stands.[144] Declaratory judgments are also valuable

"standing" of the litigants it authorizes to sue. See Chapter IX, notes 107–20, 274–94 and accompanying text.

140. See Chapter IX, notes 16–24 and accompanying text (discussing the relationship between §2201 and Article III).

141. The next section following, 28 U.S.C. §2202, empowers federal courts to issue "[f]urther necessary or proper relief" against parties who defy an authoritative declaration of their rights and legal relations. Since §2202 authorizes injunctions to enforce declaratory judgments, it blurs the distinction between the two forms of relief. See Chapter IX, notes 416–20 and accompanying text (discussing declaratory actions in place of actions for injunctions); Chapter XI, notes 153–55, 204–21 and accompanying text (discussing decisions to abstain from exercising jurisdiction in declaratory judgment cases).

142. Professor Monaghan reads §2201 this way. Henry P. Monaghan, *Federal Statutory Review Under §1983 and the APA*, 91 Colum. L. Rev. 233, 238 (1991). On the district courts' discretion regarding declaratory relief, see *Wilton v. Seven Falls Co.*, 515 U.S. 277 (1995); *Public Svc. Comm'n v. Wycoff*, 344 U.S. 237, 241 (1952); Chapter XI, note 139 and accompanying text (discussing *Wilton)*.

143. In *Calderon v. Ashmus*, 523 U.S. 740 (1998), the lower court permitted a class of prison inmates to rely on §2201 to supply a right of action. The prisoners also cited §1983, but there was some doubt whether their claim (regarding the appropriate filing period for planned habeas corpus actions) rested on "rights" that §1983 might be used to vindicate. See notes 135–36, 174–87 and accompanying text. The Supreme Court decided *Ashmus* on constitutional grounds and did not address the capacity of the Declaratory Judgment Act to provide the prisoners with the right of action they needed. See Chapter IX, notes 22–24 and accompanying text. In *Golden State Transit Corp. v. City of Los Angeles*, 493 U.S. 103 (1989), the Court held that §1983 established a right of action for a suit seeking damages for a violation of the National Labor Relations Act. Justice Kennedy dissented from that holding (on the theory that the NLRA contained no "rights" that a §1983 action could enforce). But Kennedy suggested that the plaintiffs could sue for a declaratory judgment pursuant to §2201. Having set §1983 aside, Justice Kennedy may have meant that §2201 could supply an independent right of action, so long as the plaintiffs sought only declaratory relief. Id. at 119 (dissenting opinion). See notes 361–64 and accompanying text (revisiting the problem of finding a right of action in cases in which plaintiffs contend that federal statutes preempt state law).

144. See text accompanying note 354 (discussing *Franchise Tax Board* as an illustration).

when one party plans to behave in a way that will very likely prompt the other to take legal action. The classic illustrations are cases in which citizens wish to engage in behavior they believe to be constitutionally protected, but it appears that they will be prosecuted. In the absence of a declaratory judgment device, it would be necessary to take the planned action, suffer prosecution, and then advance a constitutional claim as a defense to the criminal charge. The Declaratory Judgment Act gives litigants the option of filing a pre-enforcement civil suit in which to litigate the constitutional claim affirmatively. A citizen should not be told that the only way to know a mushroom from a toadstool is to eat it.[145]

Declaratory judgments are not well adapted to redress past violations. In *Steel Co. v. Citizens for a Better Environment*,[146] the plaintiffs notified a company that it was in violation of a federal statute inasmuch as it had not filed periodic reports on its use of toxic materials. The company then supplied the reports, albeit out of time. At that point, the plaintiffs filed suit in federal court, seeking a declaratory judgment that the company had violated the statute in the past. In the Supreme Court, Justice Scalia explained that a declaratory judgment would do nothing to redress the injuries the plaintiffs insisted they had suffered because of the company's misbehavior. It would only restate a matter that was uncontested at the time of suit (i.e., that the defendant had previously violated the statute) and thus would be "worthless."[147]

Ordinarily, Congress enacts right-of-action statutes in connection with particular regulatory schemes. Congress initially establishes a legal standard that must be enforced by some means, and then, in further provisions of the same statute, Congress authorizes private enforcement lawsuits and confers jurisdiction on federal courts to entertain them.[148] Historically, the Court sometimes found private rights of action to be implied in federal statutes that did not create them in so many words.[149] Early on, in *J.I. Case v. Borak*,[150] the Court made "implied" rights of action the rule rather than the exception.

145. Edwin M. Borchard, Declaratory Judgments 967 (2d ed. 1941).

146. 523 U.S. 83 (1998).

147. Id. at 106. See Chapter IX, notes 244–47 and accompanying text (discussing the plaintiffs' "standing" in *Steel*).

148. The statute in *Testa v. Katt*, 330 U.S. 386 (1947), is an illustration. See Chapter VI, notes 41–44 and accompanying text. The Emergency Price Control Act involved in that case: (1) established maximum prices that manufacturers could charge for their products; (2) authorized buyers to sue sellers for overcharging; and (3) conferred jurisdiction on federal district courts "concurrently" with state courts to entertain suits to enforce federal price limits. In each instance, the Act performed functions essential to judicial enforcement. Initially, in (1), the Act created a federal legal standard. Next, in (2), the Act established buyers' right of action to file enforcement suits. Then, in (3), the Act conferred jurisdiction on the federal courts. In yet a fourth provision, the Act authorized courts to award triple damages and thus prescribed a "remedy." See note 121.

149. Professor Foy contends that courts have found rights of action implicit in legislative enactments since the formative period of English law and that the notion that courts might *not* enforce statutes in private litigation is an entirely modern idea. H. Miles Foy, III, *Some Reflections on Legislation, Adjudication, and Implied Private Actions in the State and Federal Courts*, 71 Cornell L. Rev. 501 (1986); see id. at 524, quoting Lord Coke: "[E]very Act of Parliament made against any injury, mischiefe, or grievance doth either expressly, or impliedly give a remedy to the party wronged, or grieved." But see note 120 (explaining that rights and rights of action go hand-in-hand in a common law system).

150. 377 U.S. 426 (1964) (finding a private right of action implied in the Securities and Exchange Act).

In the 1970s, in *Cort v. Ash*[151] and *Cannon v. University of Chicago*,[152] the Court discarded the *Borak* approach in favor of more *ad hoc* judgment. Today, however, the Court insists that Congress must be explicit. Writing for the Court in *Alexander v. Sandoval*,[153] Justice Scalia held that no private right of action exists to enforce a federal statute via private litigation unless Congress enacts text that itself displays that "intent."[154] Justice Scalia did not explicitly go further and demand a clear statement from Congress.[155] Yet it seems plain that he, at least, demands explicit statutory language, free of ambiguity. The dissenters in *Sandoval* clearly understood him to mean that the text is all that matters.[156]

The question in *Sandoval* was whether there was a private right of action to enforce a regulation adopted by the Department of Justice pursuant to Title VI of the Civil Rights Act of 1964. The Court had previously held that Title VI itself authorized private individuals to file suits for the enforcement of its substantive provisions barring intentional race discrimination in connection with programs funded by the federal government. However, the Court had not decided that any similar private right of action existed to enforce administrative regulations promulgated under the authority of Title VI. Justice Scalia allowed that the right of action previously recognized in suits to enforce the statute itself would equally serve in suits to enforce regulations "applying" the statute's prohibition on deliberate discrimination. But he refused to recognize a private right of action to enforce the particular regulation in *Sandoval*, which purported to go "beyond intentional discrimination" to bar grant recipients from adopting policies having a "disparate impact" on racial minorities.[157] Since Congress was immediately responsible only for the intention-based standard in the statute and not for the effect-based standard in the regulation, Justice Scalia refused to interpret the private right of action the Court had recognized for the enforcement of the former to extend similar authority to sue for the enforcement of the latter.[158]

---

151. 422 U.S. 66 (1975) (adopting a multi-factor "test" for determining whether implied private rights of action should be recognized).

152. 441 U.S. 677 (1979) (holding on the basis of *Cort* that Title IX of the Civil Rights Act of 1964 creates a private right of action).

153. 532 U.S. 275 (2001).

154. Justice Scalia referred both to "congressional intent" and to "statutory intent." Id. at 286–89. The former phrase may suggest some willingness to delve into what Congress meant to accomplish in enacting a statute, but the latter suggests that "intent" must be expressed in the text of the statute itself, without reference to any other source. See Chapter I, notes 35–37 and accompanying text.

155. Justice Scalia insisted that he relied on the Court's "standard test" for determining the existence of private rights of action. Accordingly, he declined to consider whether the Court should apply a clear statement rule to legislation in this context. 532 U.S. at 293. See Chapter I, notes 44–52 and accompanying text (discussing the clear statement doctrine). But see notes 176–81 and accompanying text (discussing the *Gonzaga* case).

156. See *Sandoval*, 532 U.S. at 311 (Stevens, J., dissenting) (joined by Souter, Ginsburg & Breyer, J.J.) (criticizing Justice Scalia for adopting the view that recognizing an "implied right of action" when "the text and structure of a statute do not absolutely compel such a conclusion" amounts to "judicial self-indulgence"). Scalia's personal disdain for legislative history is well known. See Chapter I, note 35.

157. 532 U.S. at 284–85. Justice Scalia assumed for purposes of the decision in *Sandoval* that the regulation in question was valid.

158. Many federal statutes that might be thought to contemplate private rights of action were enacted before the Court announced that it would no longer look behind the text. Congress pre-

There are numerous decisions on the books in which the Court has found private rights of action in the absence of explicit "statutory intent." Those decisions presumably remain intact. It is unlikely that the Court will revisit and overrule them simply because it now demands that Congress must state its intentions in the text of a statute.[159] It is well to note, too, that several justices regret the text-only analysis in *Sandoval* and would like to look beyond a statute's language for other evidence of congressional purpose.[160] Nevertheless, Justice Scalia's position in *Sandoval* is now authoritative. The Supreme Court has taken itself "out of the business"[161] of finding private rights of action that statutory text fails to specify.

If litigants wish to enforce federal legal standards in suits against federal agencies, §702 of the APA often can take them part of the way toward the statutory authority they need.[162] The Court has explained that §702 expresses a "presumption" in favor of judicial review in the cases to which it applies.[163] That makes sense, particularly where agency enforcement precludes first order private enforcement suits and limits private litigants to attacks on the way the agency performs. If even suits against the agency were barred, private litigants would be carved out of the picture entirely. Recall, however, that §702 authorizes private suits only on behalf of litigants whose interests arguably fall within the zone of interests protected by the statutes they seek to enforce.[164]

The Court's insistence that Congress must express its "intent" to establish private rights of action must be reconciled with the decisions interpreting §1983.[165] In *Maine v. Thiboutot*,[166] the Court held that §1983 sometimes can supply a right of action for the enforcement of federal statutes that have none of their own.[167] Justice Brennan acknowledged that §1983 more commonly serves litigants who wish to advance fourteenth amendment claims. Yet §1983 also creates a right of action on behalf of a party injured

---

sumably acted against the backdrop of the Court's more flexible position at the time. There is (or rather there was) an argument, accordingly, that when the Court turns to those older statutes it should not hold Congress to the *Sandoval* demand for specific text. See Robert H.A. Ashford, *Implied Causes of Action Under Federal Laws: Calling the Court Back to Borak*, 79 Nw. U. L. Rev. 227 (1984). But in *Sandoval*, Justice Scalia expressly disavowed that argument. *Sandoval*, 532 U.S. at 287–88 (insisting that "legal context matters only to the extent it clarifies text").

159. This is to say, the important decisions in *Borak* and *Cannon* continue to be viable. Justice Scalia noted in *Sandoval* that Congress had acknowledged the right of action recognized in *Cannon* in subsequent amendments to Title VI. Accordingly, "it is beyond dispute that private individuals may sue to enforce [that statute]." *Sandoval*, 532 U.S. at 280. Nevertheless, the Court's current rejection of implied actions can be registered in other ways. In *Barnes v. Gorman*, 122 S.Ct. 2097 (2002), for example, the Court held that private right of action for Title VI cases does not extend to suits for punitive damages.

160. *Sandoval*, 532 U.S. at 312 (Stevens, J., dissenting) (joined by Souter, Ginsburg & Breyer, J.J.) (arguing that an exclusive focus on text actually "blinds" the Court to "important evidence of congressional intent").

161. *Thompson v. Thompson*, 484 U.S. 174, 188 (1988) (Scalia, J., concurring).

162. See notes 137–39 and accompanying text.

163. *Clarke*, 479 U.S. at 398–99. See Chapter IX, note 279 and accompanying text.

164. See text accompanying note 139.

165. And (perhaps) the Declaratory Judgment Act. See notes 140–42 and accompanying text.

166. 448 U.S. 1 (1980).

167. This idea (that §1983 can provide a right of action to enforce a federal statute that itself establishes only the basis for a legal claim) underscores that rights of action and legal claims are not elements of a single phenomenon (and thus cannot be captured under a single "cause of action" label without risking confusion). See note 120.

by a violation of the "laws" of the United States.[168] The Court held in *Golden State Transit Corp. v. City of Los Angeles*[169] that if §1983 *can* provide litigants with a right of action to enforce a federal statute, the default position is that a §1983 suit *is* available. Congress can choose otherwise only by making itself clear, either by prohibiting §1983 actions expressly or by creating a "carefully tailored" alternative enforcement scheme with which §1983 actions would be inconsistent.[170] There is no doubt that the text of §1983 evinces a purpose to authorize private suits and thus satisfies *Sandoval*. Accordingly, to the extent the express right of action created by §1983 is available to private litigants who wish to enforce other federal statutes that fail to establish a right of action for themselves, the *Sandoval* decision has no practical effect.[171]

Then again, §1983 does not answer in the run of statutory cases. For one thing, plaintiffs in §1983 suits must claim that the defendant has acted under color of state law.[172] Thus §1983 is largely useful only when litigants sue state and local officials or private parties working with them.[173] For another, plaintiffs cannot rely on §1983 for a

---

168. See text accompanying note 136. Justice Brennan relied (uncharacteristically) on the textualism that is often reflected in opinions by more conservative members of the Court. See Chapter I, notes 30–43 and accompanying text. In dissent, Justice Powell insisted that Brennan had blinded himself to the "plain" meaning of §1983 in its "historical context." 448 U.S. at 12. Powell contended that the Reconstruction Congress used the general term "laws" when it actually meant to include only equal rights legislation. See Clive B. Jacques & Jack M. Beermann, *Section 1983's "And Laws" Clause Run Amok: Civil Rights Attorney's Fees in Cellualar Facilities Siting Disputes*, 81 B.U. L. Rev. 735, 786–91 (2001) (arguing that §1983 is unconstitutional to the extent it purports to authorize suits to enforce statutes that cannot rest themselves on Congress' power to enforce the fourteenth amendment); Chapter X, note 237 and accompanying text.

169. 493 U.S. 103 (1989).

170. Id. at 106–07. Litigants' entitlement to file §1983 actions is not defeated by the mere existence of alternative means of protecting their rights. Congress must do something more to make it clear that §1983 actions are unavailable. In *Middlesex County Sewerage Auth. v. Nat'l Sea Clammers Ass'n*, 453 U.S. 1 (1981), the Court found it sufficient that Congress had created a "comprehensive enforcement scheme" attended by its own procedural requirements—which litigants would bypass by "bringing suit directly under §1983." Id. at 20. The plaintiffs in *Sea Clammers* failed to satisfy notification standards required under the express right-of-action provisions in two federal environmental protection statutes. In *Smith v. Robinson*, 468 U.S. 992 (1984), the Court found a similar scheme sufficient to foreclose §1983 actions. In *Wright v. City of Roanoke*, 479 U.S. 418 (1987), the Court explained that the regulatory schemes in *Sea Clammers* and *Smith* left "no room" for §1983 actions. In the absence of comprehensive statutory schemes of that kind, the Court will "not lightly conclude that Congress intended to preclude reliance on §1983." Id. at 423–24. Cf. *Blessing v. Freestone*, 520 U.S. 329 (1997) (noting that *Sea Clammers* and *Smith* are the only cases in which the Court has found §1983 actions to be precluded in the absence of express language to that effect). Writing soon after *Thiboutot*, Professor Sunstein argued that §1983 actions should be available whenever they would not be inconsistent with another enforcement mechanism. Cass R. Sunstein, *Section 1983 and Private Enforcement of Federal Law*, 49 U. Chi. L. Rev. 394 (1982). At that time, however, the lower courts often found §1983 actions foreclosed. See George D. Brown, *Whither Thiboutot? Section 1983, Private Enforcement, and the Damages Dilemma*, 33 DePaul L. Rev. 31 (1983) (also describing unsuccessful proposals to overrule *Thiboutot* by statute).

171. Since the defendants in the *Sandoval* case acted under color of state law, Justice Stevens declared that §1983 would presumably supply the very right of action that the Court read Title VI not to provide. *Sandoval*, 532 U.S. at 300 (dissenting opinion) (joined by Souter, Ginsburg & Breyer, J.J.). But see Todd E. Pettys, *The Intended Relationship Between Administrative Regulations and Section 1983's Laws*, 67 Geo. Wash. L. Rev. 51 (1998) (contending that the term "laws" in §1983 does not include federal administrative regulations).

172. See text accompanying note 135.

173. See, e.g., *Edelman v. Jordan*, 415 U.S. 651 (1974) (ultimately holding that a §1983 suit was barred by state sovereign immunity); see Chapter X, notes 367–87 and accompanying text. The

right of action whenever they charge a state officer with "a violation of law."[174] Instead, they must allege that they have suffered a deprivation of "rights, privileges, or immunities" that are "secured" by federal law. Those "rights" must be "personal."[175] Moreover, in *Gonzaga University v. Doe*,[176] Chief Justice Rehnquist held that if Congress wants to create personal statutory rights enforceable via §1983, it must do it in "clear and unambiguous terms."[177] The Chief Justice acknowledged that in previous cases the Court had said that statutes creating certain "benefits" for individuals could be read to establish "rights" within the meaning of §1983.[178] He explained, however, that those decisions were not "models of clarity."[179] They evidently confused the lower courts.[180] To resolve any "resulting ambiguity," he announced that, henceforth, courts should determine the existence of statutory rights for §1983 purposes solely on the basis of the text of the relevant statute. The Chief Justice explained that in at least some instances a clear statement requirement is in order, demanding an extraordinary measure of textual specificity: If the creation of rights within the meaning of §1983 would alter "the usual constitutional balance" between the federal government and the states, Congress must make its intention to establish such rights "unmistakably clear."[181]

---

right of action established by §1983 does not work if the defendant is a state, but it does work when the defendant is a county or municipality (at least in some circumstances). See Chapter X, notes 237, 369, 388–94 and accompanying text.

174. *Golden State*, 493 U.S. at 106.

175. Id. at 112.

176. 122 S.Ct. 2268 (2002).

177. Id. at 2279.

178. In those cases, the Court had indicated that a statute created a right if it: (1) benefited individuals who might be §1983 plaintiffs; (2) imposed a "binding obligation" in mandatory (not precatory) terms; and (3) was not so "vague and amorphous" that its enforcement would "strain judicial competence." *Blessing*, 520 U.S. at 340–41, relying on *Golden State*, 493 U.S. at 106; *Wright*, 479 U.S. at 430; and *Wilder v. Virginia Hosp. Ass'n*, 496 U.S. 498, 509–11 (1990).

179. *Gonzaga*, 122 S.Ct. at 2272. In *Wright*, the Court allowed tenants in federally funded low income housing to file §1983 actions claiming that they had been denied the benefits of rent ceilings established by federal statutes and administrative regulations. Cf. *Dennis v. Higgins*, 498 U.S. 439 (1991) (holding that private businesses had a sufficient "right" under the Commerce Clause to conduct their affairs free of state regulation). In *Pennhurst State School & Hosp. v. Halderman*, 451 U.S. 1 (1981), however, the Court held that the Developmentally Disabled Assistance and Bill of Rights Act created no such rights. In *Suter v. Artist M.*, 503 U.S. 347 (1992), the Court held that the Adoption Assistance and Child Welfare Act rendered no rights, either. In the wake of *Suter*, Congress enacted further legislation in an apparent attempt to make §1983 actions available in that instance. See Brian D. Ledahl, *Congress Overruling the Courts: Legislative Changes to the Scope of §1983*, 29 Colum. J. Law & Soc. Prob. 411 (1996).

180. The Chief Justice noted, for example, that some circuit courts had drawn an analogy to the "zone of interests" idea in the law of standing—thus finding that plaintiffs advance "rights" enforceable pursuant to §1983 if they assert "interests" falling within the zone of interests protected by the statute the defendant allegedly violated. *Gonzaga*, 122 S.Ct. at 2275; see Chapter IX, notes 274–94 and accompanying text.

181. 122 S.Ct. at 2277, quoting *Atascadero State Hosp. v. Scanlon*, 473 U.S. 234, 242 (1985) (a sovereign immunity case). According to Chief Justice Rehnquist, Congress would alter the "usual" constitutional balance if it created personal rights in *Gonzaga*, where the plaintiff argued that federal law established a right to the confidentiality of academic records. A federal personal right of that kind would be in tension with the "tradition of deference to state and local school officials." Id. at n.5. The Chief Justice did not say flatly that the ordinary constitutional balance between federal and state power is altered in *every* instance in which Congress creates statutory rights enforceable by means of §1983. Justice Breyer and Justice Souter concurred in the result in *Gonzaga*. In their view, the existence of rights for §1983 purposes is a matter of "congressional intent," which need not depend exclusively on statutory text. Id. at 2279. Justice Stevens and Justice Ginsburg dissented.

Chief Justice Rehnquist explained that the most troubling cases in this context involve federal statutes that arguably create personal rights by fixing conditions on federal spending. In *Gonzaga* itself, the plaintiff sued the university for allegedly violating the Family Educational Rights and Privacy Act, which bars grant recipients from releasing personal information about students. According to the Chief Justice, conditions on federal grants are not typically enforced by private individuals who suffer some injury. They are, instead, enforced by federal granting agencies, which withdraw federal funding in case of a breach.[182] Especially in conditional spending cases, then, Congress must use "unambiguous" language if it means to create personal rights that, in turn, can be vindicated in §1983 actions that supplement the government's enforcement efforts.[183]

Chief Justice Rehnquist confirmed that there is a difference between asking, on the one hand, whether a statute creates a substantive right and asking, on the other, whether a statute creates a private right of action as an enforcement mechanism for a right. In §1983 cases like *Gonzaga*, only the former question is on the table. Nevertheless, he insisted that precedents regarding implied rights of action guide decisions like *Gonzaga*.[184] Reflecting back on the cases in which the Court once found rights of action implied, the Chief Justice Rehnquist insisted that the Court typically decided, as an antecedent matter, that the statutes involved created substantive rights. And when the Court looked for rights in that context, it demanded clear language in the text of the statute. In *Cannon*, for example, the Court explained that Title IX "explicitly" created personal rights and only then decided that Title IX also implied that those rights

182. 122 U.S. at 2272–73 (majority opinion). In an opinion for the Court in *Barnes v. Gorman*, 122 S.Ct. 2097 (2002), handed down three days before *Gonzaga*, Justice Scalia elaborated on the private right of action previously recognized for enforcing the personal rights established by Title VI of the Civil Rights Act. He explained that Title VI rests on Congress' power to put limits on federal spending. Those limits, in turn, may be analogized to the terms of a contract between the government and a grant recipient: the recipient agrees to adhere to conditions in exchange for the funds received. Justice Scalia did not propose in *Barnes* that grant conditions can *only* be enforced in the manner of contract law (by, for example, declaring a recipient in breach and cutting off funds). But he plainly regarded enforcement mechanisms of that sort as the baseline from which Congress may depart only by using explicit statutory language. In *Barnes* itself, Justice Scalia declined to allow a plaintiff (a "third party beneficiary" of the "contract" between the government and local officials) to sue for punitive as well as compensatory damages. See note 159 and accompanying text. Justice Scalia advanced a similar conceptual understanding of private suits to enforce grant conditions in a concurring opinion in the *Blessing* case. There, he suggested that private individuals never have rights within the meaning of §1983 if they argue only that a grant recipient has effectively breached its contract with the granting agency. *Blessing*, 520 U.S. at 349–50. Justice Scalia did not take that view in his opinion for the majority in *Barnes*.

183. Chief Justice Rehnquist did not propose that Congress cannot create rights within the meaning of §1983 in statutes enacted under the spending power. By contrast, he cited conditional spending measures that create rights with sufficient clarity—statutes that explicitly state, for example, that a "person" enjoys some entitlement. 122 S.Ct. at 2275 n.3. Nor did the Chief Justice limit the requirement that Congress must be specific to cases involving conditional spending statutes. He stated the holding in *Gonzaga* as an interpretation of §1983 generally, employed as a mechanism for enforcing statutory rights of any kind. Id. at 2279.

184. 122 S.Ct. at 2275–77. Of course, the Chief Justice did not mean that a statute can create a right only if it also creates a private right of action, as though a right is worthy of the name only if it can be vindicated in court in the traditional manner of the common law. That understanding would make the existence of §1983 unintelligible: If rights that are enforceable in §1983 actions could exist only if Congress created litigation rights to go with them, there would be no work left for §1983 to do (in cases involving statutory rights), far less any occasion for maintaining that §1983 actions are presumptively available, absent clear congressional indication to the contrary.

were enforceable in private lawsuits.[185] The Chief Justice held in *Gonzaga* that a court's "role in discerning whether personal rights exist" for purposes of §1983 should not "differ" from its "role in discerning whether personal rights exist in the implied right of action context."[186] In order to create rights for §1983 purposes, Congress must use "clear and unambiguous terms—no less and no more than what is required for Congress to create new rights enforceable under an implied private right of action."[187]

The Court has now renounced the idea of finding rights of action implied in federal statutes. That is the point of *Sandoval.* It is puzzling, then, that Chief Justice Rehnquist should reach back to *Cannon* and similar precedents. To be sure, he located language in those cases indicating that the Court read the statutes involved to establish personal rights explicitly. The reason for that, however, is fairly self-evident. If a statute clearly created personal rights, the Court found it easy, even natural, to read the statute also to imply that private lawsuits vindicating those rights were authorized.[188] That rationale was not at work in *Gonzaga*, where the existence of a right of action was not in question. The Chief Justice took no genuine analysis from *Cannon* and other implied right-of-action cases, but only lifted quotations from those cases that made his opinion appear more consistent with the past. It seems odd, or at least a little late, to instruct lower courts searching for rights within the meaning of §1983 to be guided by *Cannon's* approach to identifying rights, while instructing courts searching for rights of action apart from §1983 to set *Cannon* aside and follow *Sandoval.*[189]

In any event, the square holding in *Gonzaga* is perfectly clear, as is the analytic framework that *Gonzaga* erects in combination with *Sandoval.* In cases in which plaintiffs rely on the explicit right of action established by §1983, they can enforce only personal statutory rights created by clear and unambiguous terms in the text of the relevant statute. In §1983 cases, then, both rights and the procedural vehicle for vindicating those rights must be established by explicit statutory text. In cases in which plaintiffs do not rely on §1983, they must demonstrate that some other statute explicitly establishes a private right of action to vindicate their claims. In some of those cases, the claims to be enforced will sound in personal rights. When that is true (and those rights are themselves explicitly established), §1983 may also provide the requisite authority to sue.[190] In other cases, plaintiffs will advance claims under statutes that do

---

185. *Cannon v. University of Chicago*, 441 U.S. 677, 690 n.13 (1979); see note 152 and accompanying text.

186. 122 S.Ct. at 2276.

187. Id. at 2279.

188. If, by contrast, statutes did not furnish individuals with substantive rights explicitly, the case for relying on alternative enforcement mechanisms was obviously stronger. Dissenting in *Gonzaga*, Justice Stevens contended that the hard issue in the implied right-of-action cases was whether the Court should allow private individuals to sue in the absence of explicit text authorizing private suits, given Congress' traditional authority to decide how federal law should be implemented. According to Stevens, that separation-of-powers consideration is not implicated in §1983 cases, in which Congress plainly has created a private right of action. Id. at 2284 (dissenting opinion). In response, Chief Justice Rehnquist said that the loose "multi-factor" test the Court had used previously to determine whether statutes created rights for purposes of §1983 would not improve the courts' relations with Congress. Additionally, according to the Chief Justice, the identification of rights within the meaning of §1983 implicates the relations between the national government and the states. Id. at 2277 (majority opinion).

189. Recall, however, that *Sandoval* does not engage a clear statement requirement, while *Gonzaga* may. See notes 155, 181 and accompanying text.

190. See note 171 and accompanying text.

not create personal rights. In those cases, §1983 will not offer an alternative right of action.[191]

The explanations for *Sandoval* (if not *Gonzaga*) are plain enough. The Court puts decisions like *Borak* (and even *Cort* and *Cannon*) in the same category with the classic federal common law cases, *Lincoln Mills* and *Clearfield*.[192] When the Court approves private rights of action to enforce statutes in the absence of express authorization, the Court itself fashions a species of federal law. When, however, the Court demands explicit congressional "intent" in the text of a statute before making private suits available, the Court rests more comfortably on statutory construction. The considerations that attend judicial law-making in this context are the same considerations that attend judicial law-making elsewhere: (1) deference to Congress' primary responsibility to prescribe legislative policies and the way they will be implemented; and (2) deference to state court authority to adjudicate disputes that Congress does not assign to the federal judiciary.[193]

Deference to Congress. The Court now regards the authorization of private rights of action to enforce federal statutes as a legislative function. When Congress establishes enforcement schemes other than private lawsuits and fails affirmatively to provide for private suits as well, the Court draws the inference that the former occupy the field to the exclusion of the latter.[194] This approach has been questioned. When, following *Lincoln Mills* and *Clearfield*, federal courts create substantive federal law to provide rules of decision, they fashion legislative policies of their own choosing.[195] When, by contrast, federal courts approve private lawsuits to enforce statutes that Congress has enacted, they implement policies that Congress has articulated. The better question, then, may be whether private actions interfere with other enforcement mechanisms that Congress puts in place. There is a rich literature exploring the extent to which private rights of action may complement (or hinder) the enforcement efforts of federal agencies.[196]

If the Court relentlessly rejects private suits that augment rather than impede congressional policies, the implication may be that the Court does not mean to defer to Congress' policy prerogatives at all, but rather to resist the policy of permitting private litigants to enforce federal statutes. Decisions like *Sandoval*, which make it more difficult for Congress to authorize private parties to press lawsuits in *any* court, may be of a piece with decisions on "standing," which make it more difficult for Congress to autho-

---

191. The *Sandoval* case appears to state the law for all cases in which the question presented is whether a statute creates a private right of action, not just cases in which the question is whether a statute creates a right of action to enforce personal statutory rights. Congress often creates private rights of action to enforce species of federal law that cannot be characterized as personal rights. See Chapter IX, notes 91–120, 319–80 and accompanying text.

192. See notes 95–98 and accompanying text. See also *Bivens v. Six Unknown Named Agents*, 403 U.S. 388, 402 n. 4 (1971) (Harlan, J., concurring) (reading *Borak* this way).

193. See text accompanying note 94.

194. See notes 223–30 and accompanying text (discussing statutory schemes that displace private suits to enforce the Constitution). In an influential dissent in *Cannon*, Justice Powell condemned the approach in *Cort* as an "open invitation" to the federal courts to "legislate" private actions that Congress has not authorized. 441 U.S. at 731. Professor Weinberg dismisses the Court's concerns about judicial law-making as baseless. Weinberg, note 92, at 841.

195. See note 62 and accompanying text. But see text accompanying note 97 (noting the Court's insistence in *Lincoln Mills* that courts could develop federal common law for labor contracts as an extension of national policy initially prescribed by Congress).

196. See, e.g., Frank Easterbrook, *Foreward: The Court and the Economic System*, 98 Harv. L. Rev. 4 (1984); Richard B. Stewart & Cass R. Sunstein, *Public Programs and Private Rights*, 95 Harv. L. Rev. 1193 (1982).

rize private parties to proceed in an Article III court. In the standing context, some justices insist that the Court is obliged to prevent Congress from appointing "private attorneys general" to perform functions better left to the executive branch.[197]

Deference to state courts. The Court also hesitates to find implied authority for private suits, lest federal courts be charged with enlarging their own power unilaterally.[198] This explanation, too, has limited force. When federal courts construe their *jurisdiction* narrowly to ensure that they do not overstep the bounds that Congress has established, the usual consequence is that judicial business is channeled into state court. In this context, however, that is not the case. When federal courts decline to find rights of action implied in federal statutes, they typically close not only their own doors, but the doors of state courts, as well. If private litigants have no right of action to enforce a federal statute in federal court, they usually have no right of action to enforce the statute in state court, either.[199]

2. Rights of Action to Enforce the Constitution

In some instances, Congress explicitly empowers private litigants to initiate lawsuits advancing constitutional claims. The best example is §1983, which typically supplies a vehicle for suits to vindicate fourteenth amendment rights allegedly violated by defendants acting under color of state law.[200] Yet no statute so generally authorizes constitutional suits against defendants acting under color of *federal* law.[201] Accordingly, authority for private lawsuits to enforce the Constitution against federal officers must be found elsewhere. The Supreme Court routinely finds private rights of action implied in constitutional provisions. Nevertheless, modern decisions reflect the same doubts and concerns that figure in the cases on private suits to enforce federal statutes. Following the pattern set in the statutory cases, the Court has lost any enthusiasm it once had for "implied" constitutional actions and is now inclined to find private suits foreclosed by other enforcement mechanisms that Congress sets in place.

---

197. See Chapter IX, notes 121–39, 319–80.

198. According to Justice Powell, the idea that federal courts may volunteer their services "runs contrary" to the general principle that the courts should not expand their own jurisdiction beyond what Congress prescribes. *Cannon*, 441 U.S. at 746–47 (dissenting opinion), citing *American Fire & Cas. Co. v. Finn*, 341 U.S. 6, 17 (1951). Recall that Congress fixes the federal courts' jurisdiction within the limits established by Article III. Chapter IV, notes 62–71 and accompanying text.

199. State law may incorporate a federal statute and thus make a violation of that statute actionable as a matter of state law. Yet an authoritative decision that Congress has precluded private litigation to enforce the statute will control even in that event. See notes 305–06, 316 and accompanying text. In some instances, the federal courts' failure to find a current right of action implied only postpones federal court adjudication until after a federal administrative agency has acted, when §702 of the APA or some similar statute authorizes disappointed private litigants to challenge the agency's performance. See notes 133, 137–39 and accompanying text; Chapter V, text accompanying notes 18–19. In *Hilton v. South Carolina Pub. Ry. Comm'n*, 502 U.S. 197 (1991), state sovereign immunity barred a private action against the state in federal court, but the Court held that plaintiffs could nonetheless sue in state court. The state did not assert sovereign immunity against a suit in its own courts. The issue, then, was a matter of statutory construction: whether the relevant statute (the Federal Employers Liability Act) authorized private enforcement suits. The state courts below held that the FELA did not, but the Supreme Court overturned that construction. See Chapter VI, note 96 (discussing other aspects of *Hilton*).

200. See notes 132, 135–36 and accompanying text.

201. The Federal Tort Claims Act does not authorize suits against federal officers on constitutional grounds, though it does authorize suits against the government on parallel state tort claims arising from the same conduct. *Carlson v. Green*, 446 U.S. 14, 19–20 (1980).

Private suits for injunctive relief typically do not evoke controversy, despite Congress' failure to authorize actions of that kind explicitly.[202] If federal courts were to turn away litigants who seek only to bring an end to a current violation of the Constitution, or to prevent some future violation, they would decline to enforce the basic law in the most vivid way. Suits for monetary damages have always been more troubling.[203] In cases of that kind, Congress can waive the federal government's sovereign immunity.[204] Yet no statute actually *does* open the government routinely to constitutional suits for damages.[205] Accordingly, actions for compensatory relief typically attempt to saddle individual officers with personal liability. That prospect implicates additional considerations. The Supreme Court is reluctant to hold individual federal agents personally accountable for their behavior in the line of duty.[206]

The Court initially approached private actions for damages in *Bell v. Hood*.[207] The plaintiff in that case sued FBI agents in a federal district court, contending that they had violated his fourth amendment rights. The lower courts dismissed for lack of jurisdiction. Justice Black acknowledged that it was questionable whether the fourth amendment was enforceable in a private action for monetary relief. Yet he explained that whether or not such an action could be brought, the *question* whether it was available raised a substantial issue of federal law. Accordingly, the complaint could not fail for want of *jurisdiction*. Black reversed on that basis alone, leaving the right-of-action issue unresolved.[208]

The Court returned to that question a quarter century later in *Bivens v. Six Unknown Named Agents*.[209] The plaintiff in *Bivens* also sought damages from federal agents for a violation of his fourth amendment rights. The agents responded on two levels. First, they contended that the fourth amendment established no federal right of privacy, but only fortified a right of privacy created by state law. By their account, the plaintiff had to sue them in state court on a state tort theory. Then, if they resisted liability on the ground that they acted within their federal authority, the plaintiff would be entitled to counter that they exceeded that authority by violating the fourth amendment. Second, the agents argued that if the fourth amendment did establish a constitutional right of privacy, it was for Congress, not the courts, to decide whether that right should be enforceable in private lawsuits for damages. Justice Brennan rejected the notion that the fourth amendment could come into play only to defeat a defense to a state law tort claim and, turning to the question left open in *Bell*, said that a right of action to enforce the fourth amendment affirmatively *does* exist, even though neither

---

202. See Alfred Hill, *Constitutional Remedies*, 69 Colum. L. Rev. 1109 (1969).

203. Academicians debate whether actions for damages were generally available prior to the Court's modern decisions. Professor Collins thinks so; Professor Dellinger thinks not. See Michael G. Collins,"*Economic Rights," Implied Constitutional Actions, and the Scope of Section 1983*, 77 Gtn. L.J. 1493, 1517–25 (1989); Dellinger, note 126, at 1542.

204. See Chapter X, notes 41–51 and accompanying text.

205. The Federal Tort Claims Act waives the federal government's sovereign immunity for a wide range of suits, but not for constitutional actions. *FDIC v. Meyer*, 510 U.S. 471, 477–78 (1994).

206. See Chapter X, notes 452–57 and accompanying text (discussing the availability of official immunity). The Court is comparatively enthusiastic about lawsuits naming government officers as defendants but seeking forward-looking declaratory or injunctive relief. See Chapter X, notes 283–88, 308 and accompanying text. It is crucial to distinguish those suits from the actions under discussion here, which mean to hold government officers personally liable for damages. See Chapter X, notes 18–20 and accompanying text.

207. 327 U.S. 678 (1946).

208. Id. at 684.

209. 403 U.S. 388 (1971).

the fourth amendment itself nor any statute enacted by Congress expressly says as much.[210]

Justice Brennan's opinion in *Bivens* was perfectly clear in announcing the Court's result, less so in explaining the supporting rationale. Justice Harlan was more revealing in an important concurring opinion. Harlan, for his part, placed *Bivens* squarely within the body of decisions approving the creation of federal common law—stretching from *Lincoln Mills* and *Clearfield* through *Borak*.[211] Accepting that kind of judicial law-making responsibility, Harlan said the Court should ponder the same "range of policy considerations" that a legislature would examine if it were deciding whether to authorize suits by statute.[212] In that vein, Harlan explained that the plaintiff in *Bivens* could no longer benefit from an injunction. His rights had already been invaded; it was "damages or nothing."[213] Accordingly, Justice Harlan concluded that, on balance, a suit for damages should be allowed.[214]

Since *Bivens*, the Court has held that plaintiffs can file lawsuits seeking compensation for violations of other constitutional provisions. In *Davis v. Passman*[215] and *Carlson v. Green*,[216] Justice Brennan said that the Court presumes that private suits to enforce the Constitution are available to litigants who have no other "effective means" to protect their rights.[217] The justices who doubt the wisdom of "implied" constitutional actions

---

210. Id. at 395–97. Justice Brennan remanded the case to allow the lower courts to determine whether the agents were entitled to official immunity.

211. 403 U.S. at 403–04 (concurring opinion). See notes 95–98, 129–31, 150 and accompanying text.

212. 403 U.S. at 407. Justice Harlan explained that he could not distinguish suits for damages from suits for injunctions. Plaintiffs needed a right of action to sue at all, for either kind of remedy. In the past, he said, the Court had permitted plaintiffs to sue for injunctive relief without difficulty, resting solely on the federal courts' subject matter jurisdiction or, at any rate, *sans* any separate source for a right of action. That being true, Harlan concluded that plaintiffs seeking damages could equally proceed in the absence of an authorizing statute. Id. at 405.

213. Id. at 409–10. Unless the plaintiff in *Bivens* could demonstrate a credible threat that he might be mistreated in the same way in the future, he lacked "standing" to seek injunctive or declaratory relief. See Chapter IX, notes 240–41 and accompanying text (discussing the *Lyons* case).

214. In dissent, Justice Black insisted that the creation of a right of action was a legislative function, that by enacting §1983 Congress had established such a right of action for challenging the behavior of state officials, that Congress had plainly failed to enact an analog to §1983 for suits against federal officials, and that the Court should not take it upon itself to "legislate" such a right of action into existence by judicial decision. 403 U.S. at 427–28. Both Justice Black and Justice Blackmun argued that the recognition of private actions in *Bivens* would burden federal court dockets. Id. at 430 (Blackmun, J., dissenting). That particular argument was weak. It was conceded in *Bivens* that federal officers sued in state court on state tort theories would routinely remove the actions against them to federal court via 28 U.S.C. §1442. See Chapter VI, notes 136–43 and accompanying text. That being true, allowing private suits that might be filed originally in federal court would not (necessarily) contribute to federal docket congestion. 403 U.S. at 391 n.4 (majority opinion).

215. 442 U.S. 228 (1979) (involving fifth amendment due process).

216. 446 U.S. 14 (1980) (involving the eighth amendment).

217. *Davis*, 442 U.S. at 242. Professor Harrison argues that fourteenth amendment rights present a special case. The fourteenth amendment contains (in section five) a specific provision authorizing Congress to enforce its substantive provisions (collected in section one) by legislation. That, according to Harrison, suggests that section one cannot alone be the source of a right of action to sue (even for declaratory or injunctive relief) and that affirmative enforcement suits require independent statutory authority. Since §1983 often provides that statutory authority, the implications of Harrison's view are largely academic. But in instances in which §1983 or some other statute is not available, Harrison insists that individuals with fourteenth amendment claims are relegated to older, common law means of getting those claims into court—e.g., advancing them in reply to a defendant's defense to a state tort action. See text accompanying notes 209–10. In the absence of a federal

for compensation have typically prevented the extension of the rationale in *Bivens*, *Davis*, and *Green* to new contexts.[218] Three related questions bear consideration: (1) whether, in retrospect, *Bivens* must be regarded as an exercise in federal common law-making; (2) whether Congress can substitute other enforcement devices for private actions; and (3) whether, if so, alternative mechanisms must be the equal of private suits for compensatory relief.

The basis of the Bivens decision. Since the fourth amendment was the only positive law Justice Brennan discussed in *Bivens*, he may well have meant to rest his decision on that constitutional ground.[219] Yet Brennan expressly declined to decide whether a right of action for damages is "necessary" to enforce the fourth amendment. Congress had not attempted to negate private suits and thus had not presented the Court with the question whether a statute barring private actions would be valid.[220] Moreover, Brennan said that there were "no special factors" in *Bivens* "counselling hesitation" to recognize private suits.[221] That suggested that he (like Harlan) meant only to balance the competing considerations in aid of a reasoned non-constitutional holding. It appears, then, that *Bivens* is a species of federal common law.[222]

---

right-of-action statute, by Harrison's account, individuals who wish to challenge a state statute cannot sue for declaratory or injunctive relief, but must commit a violation and then defend against prosecution on fourteenth amendment grounds. John Harrison, *Jurisdiction, Congressional Power, and Constitutional Remedies*, 86 Gtn. L.J. 2513 (1998). But see Daniel J. Meltzer, *Congress, Courts, and Constitutional Remedies*, 86 Gtn. L.J. 2537, 2551 (1998) (criticizing Harrison's view as "radical").

218. E.g., *FDIC v. Meyer*, 510 U.S. 471 (1994) (declining to approve a *Bivens* action against a federal agency); *Correctional Serv. Corp. v. Malesko*, 534 U.S. 61 (2001) (also refusing to permit a *Bivens* action against a private corporation). Doubtful justices have not hesitated to speak their minds. In *Davis*, Justice Powell insisted that the Court should not regard private actions as a constitutional imperative, but should decide in each instance whether such suits should be allowed as a matter of "principled discretion." 442 U.S. at 251 (dissenting opinion). In *Malesko*, Justice Scalia and Justice Thomas dismissed *Bivens* as a "relic of the heady days" when the Court "assumed common-law powers to create causes of action." 534 U.S. at 75 (Scalia, J., concurring) (joined by Thomas, J.). In *Carlson*, then-Justice Rehnquist, for his part, urged the Court to overrule *Bivens* altogether. 446 U.S. at 31 (dissenting opinion).

219. Professor Bandes contends that *Bivens* at least *should* be understood as a constitutional decision. See Susan Bandes, *Reinventing Bivens: The Self-Executing Constitution*, 68 So. Calif. L. Rev. 289 (1995).

220. 403 U.S. at 397. See Chapter X, notes 310–39 and accompanying text (discussing Congress' capacity to foreclose officer suits that otherwise would elude state sovereign immunity under *Ex parte Young*).

221. 403 U.S. at 396.

222. Professor Monaghan reads *Bivens* this way. See Henry P. Monaghan, *Foreword: Constitutional Common Law*, 89 Harv. L. Rev. 1, 24–25 (1975). Professor Meltzer argues that *Bivens* cannot be understood entirely as a constitutional decision, but may be regarded as constitutionally "inspired." Meltzer, note 92, at 1128. If, however, *Bivens* is an instance of federal common law-making apart from constitutional interpretation, it must presumably rest on the justifications that have traditionally been given for the creation of federal common law. See text accompanying note 94. Professor Dellinger understands Justice Harlan to have based his position in *Bivens* on the proposition that federal courts can fashion common law under the implicit authority of the relevant jurisdictional statute: 28 U.S.C. §1331. Dellinger, note 126, at 1542–43. The difficulty with that explanation is that a grant of jurisdiction to federal courts cannot (even implicitly) supply law-making authority to *state* courts handling *Bivens* cases. See text accompanying note 101; Daniel J. Meltzer, *Deterring Constitutional Violations by Law Enforcement Officers: Plaintiffs and Defendants as Private Attorneys General*, 88 Colum. L. Rev. 247, 295 (1988). Professor Grey acknowledges that *Bivens* must be considered federal common law and thus can be overridden by statute. Yet since the efficacy of constitutional rights is implicated, she urges the Court to require a clear statement from Congress before

Alternative enforcement mechanisms. Justice Brennan explained in *Bivens* that Congress had not only failed to disclaim private enforcement suits, but had established no other "remedy" to which plaintiffs might be "remitted."[223] That suggested that Congress might yet shoulder responsibility for prescribing enforcement machinery. More recent decisions establish that Congress can create alternative enforcement mechanisms that displace private lawsuits.[224] In *Bush v. Lucas*,[225] the Court held that a federal employee who wished to sue his superior for an alleged violation of the first amendment had to be satisfied with the administrative procedures available to him under the federal civil service system. In *Schweiker v. Chilicky*,[226] the Court held that private plaintiffs with due process claims were obliged to use the administrative procedures provided by the Social Security Act. And in *Chappell v. Wallace*[227] and *United States v. Stanley*,[228] the Court held that soldiers could not sue for alleged constitutional violations arising from their military service and must, instead, seek relief through military channels.

The quality of alternatives. In *Bivens* itself, Justice Brennan explained that Congress had created no other enforcement mechanism that would be "equally effective."[229] That suggested (but did not squarely hold) that any alternative enforcement arrangements that Congress fashions to displace private suits must offer plaintiffs everything they might derive from the private actions that the Court itself authorized in *Bivens*. On this point, too, the *Bush*, *Chilicky*, *Chappell*, and *Stanley* decisions render a clear answer. None of the alternatives approved in those cases was the equivalent of a private lawsuit for damages. The Court nonetheless allowed them all to eclipse the plaintiffs' ability to file private lawsuits.[230]

---

reading legislation to displace *Bivens* actions. Betsy J. Grey, *Preemption of Bivens Claims: How Clearly Must Congress Speak?*, 70 Wash. U. L.Q. 1087 (1992).

223. 403 U.S. at 397.

224. Here again, it is clear that a legal claim (that a defendant has violated the fourth amendment) must be distinguished from a right of action (a private plaintiff's authorization to press that claim in court). When courts and commentators say that the question in a case is whether the plaintiff has a fourth amendment "cause of action," they *can* mean that the issue is whether the plaintiff has a plausible claim that the defendant has violated the fourth amendment. They can *also* mean that the question is whether Congress has displaced the right of action that the Court recognized in *Bivens*. See note 120 and accompanying text.

225. 462 U.S. 367 (1983).

226. 487 U.S. 412 (1988).

227. 462 U.S. 296 (1983).

228. 483 U.S. 669 (1987).

229. 403 U.S. at 397.

230. Moreover, the Court has suggested that the availability of *any* alternative enforcement mechanism will foreclose a *Bivens* action. *Malesko*, 534 U.S. at 72–74. For critiques of these decisions, see Joan Steinman, *Backing Off Bivens and the Ramifications of this Retreat for the Vindication of First Amendment Rights*, 83 Mich. L. Rev. 269 (1984); Barry Kellman, *Judicial Abdication of Military Tort Accountability: But Who Is to Guard the Guards Themselves?*, 1989 Duke L.J. 1597. Professor Nichol argues that conceiving of *Bivens* as a common law idea invites Congress to dilute the protections that private suits can supply by offering the victims of unconstitutional behavior alternative enforcement devices that make poor substitutes. Gene R. Nichol, *Bivens, Chilicky, and Constitutional Damages Claims*, 75 Va. L. Rev. 1117 (1989). By most accounts, a constitutional question would arise if Congress were to deny constitutional rights some indispensable minimum measure of enforcement. See Dellinger, note 126, at 1547–49. But see Chapter X (discussing sovereign immunity).

D. Statutory Jurisdiction

Litigants who have federal claims and a right of action to advance those claims in *some* court are not automatically entitled to do so in a *federal* court. To do that, they must independently establish that a federal district court has jurisdiction to entertain their lawsuits. The question whether a plaintiff has a right of action to press a federal claim in a private lawsuit is separate and apart from the question whether a district court has jurisdiction to receive it. If that were not true, the decisions regarding the existence of a right of action would be decisions on federal court jurisdiction. They are not. A right of action is only a plaintiff's authorization to enforce some species of federal law by means of a private lawsuit. Jurisdiction is judicial power to act in a case and thus to adjudicate a substantive legal claim, advanced by the plaintiff, that the defendant has violated federal law.[231] The Supreme Court underscores this point when it decides that a private litigant had no authority to sue and, for that reason, declines to address the different question whether, if the litigant had possessed a right of action, the district court below would have had jurisdiction.[232] And equally when the Court *assumes* that a litigant had authority to sue in order to dispose of a case on other grounds.[233]

Congress prescribes the district courts' jurisdiction by statute.[234] The principal jurisdictional statute for federal question cases is 28 U.S.C. §1331, which confers power on district courts to adjudicate "all civil actions arising under the Constitution, laws, or treaties of the United States." The text of §1331 tracks its parent provision in Article III.[235] Congress can extend jurisdiction to the Article III perimeter, and some members of the Reconstruction Congress that enacted §1331 probably meant to do just that.[236] But the Supreme Court has construed §1331 actually to grant judicial power on a much smaller scale.[237]

Subject matter jurisdiction is the threshold issue in every case.[238] Since a court's very authority to act depends on the existence of jurisdiction, it cannot properly address the merits of claims unless and until jurisdiction is confirmed.[239] Federal courts always have

---

231. See notes 258–62 and accompanying text (discussing *Bell v. Hood*); notes 120–21 and accompanying text. See also *Steel Co. v. Citizens for a Better Environment*, 523 U.S. 83, 88–93 (1998) (providing a good discussion); *Verizon v. Pub. Svc. Comm'n*, 122 S.Ct. 1753, 1758–59 (2002) (confirming *Steel's* explanation).

232. E.g., *Nat'l R.R. Passenger Corp. v. Nat'l Ass'n of R.R. Passengers*, 414 U.S. 453, 456 (1974).

233. E.g., *Owasso Indep. School Dist. v. Falvo*, 122 S.Ct. 934 (2002); *Northwest Airlines v. County of Kent*, 510 U.S. 355, 365 (1994). Cf. *Duke Power Co. v. Carolina Envt'l Study Grp.*, 438 U.S. 59, 71 (1978) (explaining that the non-jurisdictional question whether a plaintiff has a right of action need not be raised by the Court *sua sponte*). See notes 136, 138 (explaining that plaintiffs who rely on §1983 and §702 of the APA to supply them with a right of action independently look to §1331 to establish a federal court's jurisdiction).

234. See Chapter IV, notes 62–76 and accompanying text.

235. See text accompanying note 4.

236. Ray Forrester, *The Nature of a Federal Question*, 16 Tulane L. Rev. 362 (1942); see notes 5–46 and accompanying text (discussing the outer boundaries of Article III judicial power).

237. See Chapter I, text accompanying note 29 (noting that the Court has made the elaboration of §1331 its own preserve without any pretense of textualism).

238. But see Laura S. Fitzgerald, *Is Jurisdiction Jurisdictional?*, 95 Nw. U. L. Rev. 1207 (2001) (arguing that the Supreme Court itself does not always adhere to the "jurisdiction first" position).

239. Fed. R. Civ. P. 12(h)(3); *McNutt v. GMAC*, 298 U.S. 178, 182 (1936).

jurisdiction to determine, in the first instance, whether they have jurisdiction.[240] By convention, district courts presume that a suit does not fall within the jurisdiction conferred by §1331 and demand that the party asserting that it does bears the burden of "establishing the contrary."[241] The parties cannot create subject matter jurisdiction by consent or by oversight.[242] Accordingly, a party does not forfeit the ability to object to jurisdiction by failing to do so at the proper time—typically by means of a motion to dismiss the complaint.[243] Instead, objections to subject matter jurisdiction are in order at any time, even on appeal.[244] A federal court cannot fail to explore any doubts about its jurisdiction.[245] If doubts exist, the court must raise the jurisdictional issue *sua sponte*.[246] A federal court may not assume hypothetically that it has jurisdiction in order to dispose of a case on another ground.[247] If there are both non-constitutional and con-

---

240. *United States v. Ruiz*, 122 S.Ct. 2450, 2454 (2002).

241. *Kokkonen v. Guardian Life Ins. Co. v. Amer.*, 511 U.S. 375, 377 (1994).

242. *Sosna v. Iowa*, 419 U.S. 393, 398 (1975).

243. Fed. R. Civ. P. 12(b)(1). See notes 258–62 and accompanying text (discussing *Bell v. Hood*).

244. *Bender v. Williamsport Area School Dist.*, 475 U.S. 534, 541 (1986).

245. *Louisville & Nashville R.R. v. Mottley*, 211 U.S. 149, 152 (1908). If the Supreme Court notices that a lower federal court had no jurisdiction, the Court has appellate jurisdiction only to correct that error. *Gully v. Interstate Nat. Gas Co.*, 292 U.S. 16, 18–19 (1934).

246. *FW/PBS v. City of Dallas*, 493 U.S. 215, 231 (1990); *Duquesne Light Co. v. Barasch*, 488 U.S. 299, 306 (1989).

247. *Steel*, 523 U.S. at 88–89. In *Steel*, Justice Scalia explained that it was improper to assume that the plaintiffs had Article III standing to proceed in order to address the question whether they had a right of action to enforce the Emergency Planning and Community Right-to-Know Act. See notes 146–47 and accompanying text. The jurisdictional issue, then, was constitutional in character (the plaintiffs' ability to invoke Article III judicial power). See Chapter IX, notes 70–71 and accompanying text. Professor Idleman contends that *Steel's* rejection of "hypothetical jurisdiction" is limited, accordingly, to cases in which federal courts are tempted to leap-frog over potential constitutional questions about their power and does not (necessarily) prohibit courts from putting aside non-constitutional jurisdictional issues. Scott C. Idleman, *The Demise of Hypothetical Jurisdiction in the Federal Courts*, 52 Vand. L. Rev. 235, 297–99 (1999) (also pointing out that Justice Scalia's discussion of "hypothetical jurisdiction" may not have enjoyed support from a clear majority of the justices). Compare *Ashmus*, 523 U.S. at 745 (treating the question whether class plaintiffs presented an Article III "case or controversy" as antecedent to the question whether the suit was barred by state sovereign immunity), with *Vermont Agency v. United States ex rel. Stevens*, 529 U.S. 765, 778–80 (2000) (treating the question whether a federal statute authorized a private suit against a state as antecedent to the question whether the state could defeat the suit on the basis of sovereign immunity). Certainly, it is more troubling for courts to assume aside constitutional objections to jurisdiction than it is to assume aside non-constitutional objections. Professor Freer has pointed out that hypothesizing plaintiffs' Article III standing may lead to (unconstitutional) advisory opinions on other matters. Richard D. Freer, *Obervations on the Scope of the Supreme Court's Rejection of Hypothetical Jurisdiction*, 8 Fed. Lit. Guide Rptr. 247, 250 (1999); see Chapter IX, notes 11–34 and accompanying text. Professor Steinman notes that Justice Scalia also appeared to condemn the assumption of *statutory* jurisdiction. Joan Steinman, *After Steel Co.: Hypothetical Jurisdiction in the Federal Appellate Courts*, 58 Wash. & Lee L. Rev. 855, 859 (2001), quoting *Steel*, 523 U.S. at 101–02. Idleman, Freer, and Steinman identify circumstances in which hypothesizing at least statutory jurisdiction would make a good deal of sense. Steinman points out, however, that if the Court allows federal courts to lay aside non-constitutional jurisdictional concerns, it will still be difficult to distinguish categorically between questions that go to jurisdiction, on the one hand, and questions that do not, on the other—particularly at the appellate stage of proceedings. See, e.g., Chapter X, notes 67–70 and accompanying text (discussing the relationship between sovereign immunity and "jurisdiction").

stitutional questions about jurisdiction, a court should treat the non-constitutional questions first—and thus, perhaps, avoid the need to reach constitutional issues.[248]

In many of the classic cases in point, the Court formally construed jurisdictional statutes other than §1331. Occasionally, the statute at work was 28 U.S.C. §1338, which confers jurisdiction on district courts in civil actions "arising under" federal statutes relating to patents, trademarks, and similar matters. Since the Court has always applied the same "arising under" test to determine whether cases are within the jurisdiction prescribed by §1338 and §1331, precedents established in cases involving §1338 are typically also applicable to §1331.[249] In some of the most important cases, the plaintiff initially filed suit in state court, and it was the defendant who attempted to gain access to a federal district court by removing the suit pursuant 28 U.S.C. §1441. Removal is available only if the plaintiff might have sued in federal court in the first instance. Accordingly, the practical question in §1441 cases is whether, if the plaintiff had filed suit in federal court originally, the federal court would have had jurisdiction pursuant to §1331.[250]

Removal cases lend an air of artificiality to the Court's analysis of §1331. The Court finds itself asking whether plaintiffs have any genuine business in federal court when the plaintiffs themselves have never argued that they *should* be entitled to invoke federal jurisdiction. By hypothesis, they sued in state court. Moreover, since removal cases began in state court, it was typically state law that authorized the lawsuits the plaintiffs actually initiated. When the Court asks whether the plaintiffs might have started in a federal district court instead, the Court finds itself grappling with the proposition that *state* law might have supplied the right of action that litigants would have needed to enforce *federal* law in *federal* court. Rights of action created by state law are not easily reconciled with the language the Court uses to describe §1331 jurisdiction and with modern cases that largely give Congress the responsibility to decide whether federal law will be enforceable in private litigation.[251]

The foundational precedent on the meaning of §1331 was a removal case: *American Well Works Co. v. Layne & Bowler Co.*[252] American sued Layne in state court, alleging that Layne had injured American's manufacturing business by claiming that American was infringing Layne's patent and by threatening to sue American for infringement. Layne removed the suit to a federal district court on the theory that American might

---

248. Steel, 523 U.S. at 88–89; see Chapter I, text accompanying note 26. In *Ortiz v. Fibreboard Corp.*, 527 U.S. 815 (1999), for example, the Court explained that a question regarding class certification under Fed. R. Civ. P. 23 pertained to a district court's statutory jurisdiction and thus was "logically antecedent" to Article III concerns. Id. at 831, quoting *Amchem Products v. Windsor*, 521 U.S. 591, 612 (1997). Accordingly, the Court addressed the Rule 23 issue and resolved the case on that basis. Cf. *Ruhrgas AG v. Marathon Oil Co.*, 526 U.S. 574 (1999) (explaining that a court may properly address personal jurisdictional issues before non-constitutional subject matter jurisdictional concerns).

249. *Holmes Grp. v. Vornado Air Circulation Sys.*, 122 S.Ct. 1889, 1893 (2002); see notes 376–83 and accompanying text (discussing *Holmes*). Pursuant to 28 U.S.C. §1337, the district courts have jurisdiction of "any civil action or proceeding arising under any Act of Congress regulating commerce or protecting trade and commerce against restraints and monopolies." The Court has also used the same "arising under" test for determining whether cases fit under that jurisdictional heading. *Franchise Tax Bd. v. Constr. Laborers Vacation Trust*, 463 U.S. 1, 8 n.7 (1983).

250. See Chapter VI, note 133 and accompanying text.

251. See text accompanying notes 123–25, 223–30, 291–331.

252. 241 U.S. 257 (1916).

have placed it in federal court in the first instance pursuant to §1338. Justice Holmes held, however, that American's action could not have been filed originally in federal court, because it did not arise under federal law for purposes of §1338 or, by extension, §1331. According to Holmes, American's suit was essentially a tort action in the nature of trade libel, governed by state law. If Layne had done American any "wrong" at all, it was by doing injury to American's business, and whether Layne's behavior actually constituted such a "wrong" depended on state law.[253]

Justice Holmes might have said that a suit "arises under" the law that supplies a plaintiff's substantive claim against the defendant. Since, in *Well Works*, that law was state tort law, American could not have invoked federal jurisdiction in the first instance. In fact, Justice Holmes said that a suit "arises under the law that creates the *cause of action*."[254] That formulation has been the point of departure for interpreting §1331 ever since. And it has created no small amount of confusion. The problem is this: The Holmes formulation can be taken to mean that a civil action arises *not* under the law that creates the plaintiff's substantive *claim*, but rather under the law that creates the plaintiff's *right of action*—the law that authorizes the plaintiff to file a lawsuit to enforce a claim. In most instances, substantive claims and procedural vehicles for enforcing those claims have a common source. Where that is true, the distinction between the two makes no practical difference. Nevertheless, it is essential to keep that distinction clear in order to understand the cases in which legal arguments and the authority to make those arguments in court derive from different sources.

There are certainly Supreme Court opinions and academic commentaries that understand the Holmes formulation to mean that a civil action arises under the law that establishes a litigant's authority to go to court.[255] By that account, any case in which the Supreme Court has found §1331 jurisdiction to exist in the absence of a federally created right of action must be regarded as an exception to Holmes—justified, if at all, on some less neat and tidy basis. On the whole, however, the Court understands the Holmes formulation to mean that a civil action arises under the law that creates the plaintiff's substantive claim—the law that governs the parties' primary behavior, the law the plaintiff insists the defendant has violated, the law that makes the defendant's behavior a legal "wrong," the law that a federal court will be asked to use as the rule of

---

253. The procedural framework in *Well Works* was convoluted, even by federal courts standards. Recall that a district court's jurisdiction under §1338 is exclusive. See Chapter VI, note 22 and accompanying text. In *Well Works*, accordingly, Layne contended not merely that American *might* have sued in federal court, but that American had no other choice. The federal district court agreed with Layne that American's suit arose under federal patent law for purposes of §1338 jurisdiction. Yet that court dismissed Layne's removal petition anyway, because (at the time) the removal statute, §1441, allowed a case to reach federal court by means of removal only if the state court in which the case was originally filed had jurisdiction. According to the district court, the action might have been filed in federal court, and, indeed, could have been filed in no other court. But it could not reach the district court via removal. When Justice Holmes concluded that American's action could not have been brought in federal court at all and could only be handled in state court, he, too, decided that Layne's removal petition was without merit. Nevertheless, Holmes reversed the district court's order (dismissing Layne's petition on the basis of just the opposite conclusion regarding §1338 jurisdiction), so that the district court could remand the case back to state court where it belonged. Congress has since amended §1441, eliminating any requirement that the state court from which a case is removed must itself have jurisdiction.

254. 241 U.S. at 260 (emphasis added).

255. E.g., Donald L. Doernberg, Identity Crisis: Federal Courts in a Psychological Wilderness 153 (2000) (stating that Holmes' test "implicitly says that a federal issue is not sufficiently substantial to support jurisdiction unless the law that permits plaintiff to sue is federal law").

decision in a case in which it has jurisdiction.[256] The exceptions, then, are cases in which the plaintiff's legal argument is federal in nature, but nonetheless fails to establish §1331 jurisdiction for some other good and sufficient reason.[257]

The Court has fortified the Holmes test for §1331 jurisdiction with two supplemental rules: (1) the rule that jurisdiction can rest on a complaint that advances a substantial federal claim, even if it is unlikely that the plaintiff can prevail on the merits; and (2) the rule that the federal nature of the claim that triggers jurisdiction must appear on the face of the complaint.

1. The Substantial Claim Rule

The Court held in *Bell v. Hood*[258] that a plaintiff can invoke a federal district court's jurisdiction under §1331 by filing a complaint stating a substantial federal claim, even if

---

256. E.g., *Verizon*, 122 S.Ct. at 1759 (explaining that a district court had jurisdiction under §1331 because the plaintiffs' substantive "claim" turned on the proper interpretation of a federal statute or federal agency action).

257. See notes 300–31 (discussing *Merrell Dow*). Holmes himself had no occasion to distinguish between a substantive claim and a right of action to vindicate that claim. He had in mind state tort law, wherein those two ideas typically converge. See note 120. Moreover, Holmes could not anticipate modern decisions that isolate claims from the means by which they are implemented and so often foreclose private suits in favor of alternative enforcement mechanisms. See notes 120–230 and accompanying text. If Holmes had been thinking in modern terms, he would scarcely have proposed that a §1983 action to enforce the fourteenth amendment is within a district court's §1331 jurisdiction not because the fourteenth amendment is a federal constitutional provision, but because §1983 is a federal statute. Of course, Congress typically authorizes private lawsuits only for the purpose of enforcing federal law. So if it *were* true that §1983 actions arise under federal law because §1983 is federal, the results in ordinary cases would not change. Still, the distinction between claims and rights of action cannot be ignored. Consider the implications of a federal statute purporting to authorize private suits to enforce some species of *state* law. If it is circular to argue that a federal jurisdictional statute can itself supply the federal law under which a case arises for Article III purposes (and it is), then it is also circular to argue that a federal right-of-action statute can supply the federal law under which a civil action arises for purposes of §1331. See text accompanying note 25. A federal right-of-action statute authorizing private suits to enforce state law would reproduce in this different context the same constitutional questions that attend protective jurisdiction. See notes 21–24 and accompanying text. Consider, finally, another removal case. In *City of Chicago v. Intnat'l College of Surgeons*, 522 U.S. 156 (1997), Justice O'Connor recognized that a complaint advancing a fourteenth amendment claim arises under federal law for §1331 purposes, even though the procedural vehicle in which the claim is presented is a creature of state law. Id. at 529. In that case, ICS originally pressed a constitutional claim in an administrative review suit, authorized by state law and filed in state court. Nevertheless, the Court held that the defendants (state authorities) could remove the suit to federal court pursuant to §1441—because ICS might have invoked federal jurisdiction under §1331, if ICS had chosen to litigate in federal court in the first instance. The suit arose under federal law, because ICS's substantive fourteenth amendment claim was federal. There is language in Justice O'Connor's opinion suggesting that *Surgeons* was an *exception* to Holmes' general rule that the "cause of action" must be federal. Id. (conceding that the "cause of action" in *Surgeons* was created by state law but insisting that federal jurisdiction "might still" be established). The better (and far simpler) view is that, within the Holmes formulation, a "cause of action" means a substantive claim, not a procedural vehicle. See Chapter VI, notes 128–35 and accompanying text (discussing the connection between §1441 and §1331). Professor Oakley has identified even more ways in which commonly employed nomenclature creates confusion. Oakley proposes to clarify matters by specifying more rigorously what a "cause of action" entails. See John B. Oakley, *Federal Jurisdiction and the Problem of the Litigative Unit: When Does What "Arise Under" Federal Law?*, 76 Tex. L. Rev. 1829, 1858 (1998).

258. 327 U.S. 678 (1946); see notes 207–08 and accompanying text.

the claim is most unlikely to succeed. If the plaintiff's claim is "wholly insubstantial and frivolous," it will not suffice for jurisdiction. Otherwise, jurisdiction is established at the threshold and, once settled, empowers the court to decide other issues—including whether the plaintiff genuinely has a winning argument. Recall that the plaintiff in *Bell* contended that FBI agents had violated his fourth amendment rights and that he was entitled to damages. Justice Black found that complaint sufficient to establish jurisdiction, notwithstanding serious doubt (at the time) that the plaintiff actually had the affirmative constitutional claim he asserted and a right of action to enforce that claim in a suit for damages.[259] Black recognized that the plaintiff might have framed his complaint as an ordinary action in trespass, relying on the agents' violation of the Constitution to show that their behavior was tortious as a matter of state law. In that event, the complaint might not have established jurisdiction under §1331.[260] Black explained, however, that the plaintiff was master of his pleading and could decide, if he wished, to advance a forthright claim under the Constitution.[261] As long as that claim was not wholly frivolous, it could survive a motion to dismiss for want of jurisdiction.[262]

---

259. Recall that until the *Bivens* decision, there was a body of professional opinion to the effect that the fourth amendment established no constitutional right of privacy, but only served to defeat defenses to state tort actions. See text accompanying notes 209–10.

260. Defendants move under Rule 12(b)(1) to dismiss complaints for want of jurisdiction and under Rule 12(b)(6) to dismiss for want of a claim for which relief can be granted. This is ostensibly consistent with *Bell*, which channels arguments that claims cannot support jurisdiction because they are frivolous to disposition under Rule 12(b)(1) and routes arguments that plaintiffs have no right of action to disposition under Rule 12(b)(6). Nevertheless, things may not always fall into place so neatly. In the *Bell* situation itself, the Court later held (in *Bivens*) that private plaintiffs *do* have a right of action to enforce the fourth amendment in suits for damages. See notes 209–10 and accompanying text. In other contexts, the Court may ultimately decide that a right of action does *not* exist. If, in circumstances of that kind, a plaintiff should file a subsequent complaint insisting upon the very right of action the Court has just held not to exist, a district court might entertain a motion to dismiss under Rule 12(b)(1). With an authoritative determination against the plaintiff on the right-of-action question in place, a complaint that depends on such a right of action may be regarded as frivolous and thus subject to dismissal for want of jurisdiction.

261. 327 U.S. at 681, citing *The Fair v. Kohler Die & Specialty Co.*, 228 U.S. 22, 25 (1913). Dissenting in *Bell*, Chief Justice Stone expressed concern that the jurisdictional power of the federal courts should be contingent on the way plaintiffs draw their complaints. 327 U.S. at 685–86; see notes 388–401 and accompanying text (discussing federal preemption of state law); Chapter VI, text accompanying note 135 (also discussing preemption).

262. Accord *Steel*, 523 U.S. at 89; *Verizon*, 122 S.Ct. at 1758. The rule in *Bell* screens out only claims that are "completely devoid of merit." *Falvo*, 122 S.Ct. at 938. Even at that, however, *Bell* requires district courts to take a preliminary look at the merits to ensure that claims are not entirely frivolous. The Court made it clear in the *Steel* case that *Bell* nonetheless survives the Court's rejection of "hypothetical jurisdiction." *Steel*, 523 U.S. at 89. Chief Justice Rehnquist has argued that *Bell* does not map onto Fed. R. Civ. P. 12 at all well and thus should be reexamined. *Yazoo County Indus. Develop. Corp. v. Suthoff*, 454 U.S. 1157 (1982) (dissenting from the denial of *certiorari*). By his account, *Bell* contemplates triage in three tiers: first, a district court may dismiss frivolous complaints for want of jurisdiction; second, the court may dismiss non-frivolous complaints if they present no claim for which relief can be granted; and, third, the court must handle complaints that cannot be dismissed more thoroughly—by summary judgment or trial. According to the Chief Justice, Rule 12(b) contemplates only two tiers, both captured in Rule 12(b)(6): A district court simply screens all complaints for claims on which relief can be granted, dismissing those that do not measure up and giving more thorough treatment to those that do. The Chief Justice lays Rule 12(b)(1) aside. By his account, it is only because *Bell* made the substantiality of claims a jurisdictional matter that anyone has thought that Rule 12(b)(1) handles that kind of issue. But for *Bell*, Rule 12(b)(1) would not figure in §1331 cases, but would cover dismissals for lack of diversity or a sufficient amount in controversy. Apparently, Chief Justice Rehnquist would abandon the basic holding in *Bell* (that non-

2. The Well-Pleaded Complaint Rule

The substantial federal claim that triggers jurisdiction must appear on the face of a "well-pleaded" or "properly pleaded" complaint. The leading case in point is *Louisville & Nashville R.R. Co. v. Mottley*.[263] The Mottleys, husband and wife, had been involved in a rail accident. By way of settlement, the railroad gave them a contract under which they were entitled to travel by train free of charge. Congress later enacted a statute forbidding railroads to issue free passes. The railroad reneged on its contract with the Mottleys, citing the statute as justification. The Mottleys sued the railroad in federal court, seeking specific performance of the contract. They claimed that the new statute did not release the railroad from its duty to perform under the contract and that, if it did, it violated the fifth amendment. Justice Moody said that the Mottleys' claim against the railroad did not arise under federal law for purposes of §1331. Their affirmative claim was for breach of contract, based entirely on state law. They could plead the facts and the law regarding that claim without mentioning the federal issues they expected the railroad to raise by way of defense.[264] To the extent the Mottleys anticipated those federal issues in their complaint, they introduced matters that were not "well-pleaded" or "properly pleaded" in support of their affirmative claim.[265]

The well-pleaded complaint rule is usually an efficient device for identifying cases that satisfy the Holmes test for §1331 jurisdiction. Nevertheless, fair arguments abound regarding the classic cases. On first blush, the well-pleaded complaint rule appears to explain the result in *Well Works* itself. State tort law established both American's right to operate its enterprise free of interference from Layne and, as well, Layne's duty to forbear unfounded accusations and threats that injured American's business. Accordingly, American's claim could be articulated without reference to any federal matter. Anything American said in its complaint about the validity of Layne's patent anticipated a federal issue that would only emerge later, if at all, in Layne's answer to American's state law claim. It is quite possible to argue, however, that American's state trade libel claim necessarily entailed an allegation that Layne's statements were untrue. If so, American was required to allege that Layne's claim of patent infringement was false, which, of course, would have implicated a federal question.[266]

In *Shoshone Mining Co. v. Rutter*,[267] the Court held that an "adverse suit" filed by a miner in a federal district court in Idaho did not arise under federal law for purposes of §1331 jurisdiction. In the late Nineteenth Century, Congress enacted a statute under which federal land offices issued patents allowing miners to extract minerals from federal lands. Under that statute, a miner who wished to take minerals from a site filed an application for a patent with the closest land office. The land office published a notice

---

frivolous claims establish jurisdiction in the first instance) and would allow district courts to dismiss (on the merits) any claims they regard as insubstantial.

263. 211 U.S. 149 (1908).

264. See note 339 (elaborating this point).

265. The well-pleaded complaint rule underscores that the law that must be federal in a §1331 case is the law on which the plaintiff relies for a substantive claim, not the law that gives the plaintiff permission to use a lawsuit to press the claim. The purpose of a complaint is to allege the elements of a claim sufficiently to give the defendant notice, not to explain that Congress has authorized the suit. See note 257 and accompanying text.

266. See William Cohen, *The Broken Compass: The Requirement That a Case Arise "Directly" Under Federal Law*, 115 U. Pa. L. Rev. 890, 897 (1967).

267. 177 U.S. 505 (1900).

of the application and its intention to grant the miner a patent within a fixed period of time, if no competitor came forward. Another miner could challenge the applicant's entitlement to a patent by filing an "adverse claim" regarding the same site. Any miner who did so was obliged by the statute to commence an "adverse suit" in a "court of competent jurisdiction" to determine which of the two miners had the superior "right of possession." Under the federal statute, the court could make that determination on the basis of "local customs and rules of miners" or "the statute of limitations for mining claims of the state or territory" where the land was situated.[268]

Justice Brewer recognized that federal issues might be implicated in some adverse suits. But upon the whole, he thought federal law would have no role. The federal statute did not incorporate local customs or state statutes into federal substantive law. Instead, the statute contemplated that courts entertaining adverse suits would simply use local customs and state statutes to resolve the question of rightful possession on the basis of the facts. Typically, the only real issue would be which of the two miners had first marked the site in the customary manner. Certainly, it would be the rare case in which a court would be asked to decide any issue touching the federal statute that established the underlying scheme. Justice Brewer acknowledged that the federal statute "authorized" adverse suits, but he said that was not "in and of itself sufficient to vest jurisdiction" in a federal court. The law that had to be federal was not the law that allowed the adverse claimant to file suit, but the law that the court would apply *in* that suit: "A statute authorizing an action to establish a right is very different from one which creates a right to be established."[269]

It is debatable whether *Shoshone Mining* can be reconciled with the Holmes formulation and the well-pleaded complaint rule. On the one hand, that case does seem to fit. An adverse claimant's claim of possession depended (at least typically) on historical facts and local law. A well-pleaded complaint would (typically) have no occasion to recite any federal issue.[270] On the other hand, the federal statute not only authorized an adverse claimant to sue, but forced such a suit if the challenger had any hope of keeping the original applicant from securing a patent. It was that statute, moreover, that made local customs and state statutes applicable to adverse suits. The federal statute may not have incorporated local customs and state statutes into the fabric of federal law. But it did lend those customs and state statutes their authoritative force in the resolution of the rightful possession question, which, in turn, determined which of the two competing miners ultimately received a federal patent to take minerals from federal land. Arguably, then, an adverse claimant's claim did rely on federal law, and a well-pleaded complaint could say so.[271]

---

268. See *Blackburn v. Portland Gold Mining Co.*, 175 U.S. 571, 576–78 (1900) (quoting the federal statute in full).

269. *Shoshone Mining*, 177 U.S. at 510–13.

270. Professor Shapiro adds that it made sense in *Shoshone Mining* to bar federal jurisdiction of most adverse suits in order to ensure that miners could obtain the decisions they needed from nearby state courts and were not forced to travel significant distances through the wilderness to appear before a federal court. David L. Shapiro, *Jurisdiction and Discretion*, 60 N.Y.U. L. Rev. 543, 569–70 (1985).

271. Professor Doernberg finds *Shoshone Mining* inconsistent with *Well Works*. Donald L. Doernberg, *There's No Reason For It; It's Just Our Policy: Why the Well-Pleaded Complaint Rule Sabotages the Purposes of Federal Question Jurisdiction*, 38 Hastings L.J. 597, 627 n.139 (1987). But in taking that position Doernberg appears to assume that the Holmes formulation, articulated in *Well Works*, contemplates that a civil action arises under the law that creates the plaintiff's authority to sue. See note 255 and accompanying text. It is hard to fault *Shoshone Mining* for rejecting the argument that adverse suits arose under federal law merely because a federal statute authorized miners to

In *Moore v. Chesapeake & Ohio Ry.*,[272] the Court held that a worker's suit against a railroad did not arise under federal law for purposes of §1331. The plaintiff in that case alleged that he had been injured on the job and was due compensation under the state workers compensation law.[273] He contended that he could neither be found guilty of contributory negligence nor held to have assumed the risk, because the accident was the result of the railroad's violation of federal law. According to the plaintiff, the railroad had failed to maintain the equipment on which he was working according to standards established by the Federal Safety Appliance Act. Under state law, the railroad could not set up contributory negligence or assumption of risk to avoid liability in any case in which the railroad had violated federal laws enacted to protect employee safety. Chief Justice Hughes said that the plaintiff's claim was based entirely on state workers compensation law.[274]

It is also debatable whether *Moore* corresponds to the Holmes formulation and the well-pleaded complaint rule. On the one hand, *Moore* does appear to fit, more neatly perhaps than *Shoshone Mining*. The plaintiff did not claim that he was entitled to recover solely because the railroad had violated federal law. He rested his affirmative claim on the state workers compensation statute. He could articulate that claim without mentioning federal law. The only federal question that could arise in the case would come in later—if the railroad attempted to avoid liability by asserting contributory negligence or assumption of risk. Even then, nothing federal would be implicated until the plaintiff responded that those defenses were unavailable, because the railroad had violated federal law. And even *then*, federal law would be involved only because state law incorporated its standards for the limited purpose of restricting the railroad's defenses. On the other hand, it was quite clear in *Moore* that the federal questions the plaintiff anticipated were likely to emerge and, when they did, the court adjudicating the case would have to consult the federal Act in order to resolve them.[275]

---

take their claims to court, irrespective of the nature of their arguments for rightful possession. See Oakley, note 257, at 1841–42 n.63. In *Puerto Rico v. Russell*, 288 U.S. 476 (1933), Puerto Rico sued an association of companies in the Insular Court in San Juan, seeking to collect taxes levied on the companies' land. The companies attempted to remove the action to the United States District Court for Puerto Rico on the theory that the suit arose under federal law. The validity of the tax in question had been contested for years, and Congress had ultimately enacted a statute authorizing Puerto Rico to collect the monies that were due by means of a lawsuit (rather than by simply seizing property). Justice Stone explained that "even though [Puerto Rico] derived its authority to maintain the suit" from an "Act of Congress," the suit "did not arise under the laws of the United States within the meaning of the jurisdictional statutes." Puerto Rico's suit was to recover taxes levied by the Puerto Rican legislature, not to "enforce a right created by a law of the United States." The complaint raised no issue with respect to the federal authorizing statute: "Federal jurisdiction may be invoked to vindicate a right or privilege claimed under a federal statute. It may *not* be invoked where the right asserted is non-federal, merely because the plaintiff's right to sue is derived from federal law.... *The federal nature of the right to be established is decisive—not the source of the authority to establish it.*" Id. at 483 (emphasis added).

272. 291 U.S. 205 (1934).

273. The plaintiff also claimed the railroad was liable under the Federal Employers Liability Act, but the Court's treatment of that claim did not raise jurisdictional questions.

274. The consequence of the holding in *Moore* was that the plaintiff's claim under state law could remain in federal court only as a diversity matter under 28 U.S.C. §1332. That meant that venue was proper in Indiana rather than Kentucky.

275. See text accompanying note 312 (discussing the Court's explanation of *Moore* in the *Merrell Dow* case); Chapter VI, notes 3–38 and accompanying text (discussing state court jurisdiction to determine federal issues).

In *Smith v. Kansas City Title & Trust Co.*,[276] the Court held that a suit by a stockholder to enjoin company managers from purchasing federal bonds *was* a civil action arising under federal law for §1331 purposes. The corporation's charter barred unlawful investments. The plaintiff claimed that the bonds in question were unlawful, because they were issued by federal land banks pursuant to statutes that Congress had no constitutional power to enact. Justice Day said that the legal claim in the plaintiff's complaint was his constitutional attack on the federal statutes creating the land banks. Since the plaintiff's "right to relief" turned on a construction of federal statutes and the Constitution, the suit arose under federal law.[277] Justice Holmes dissented. He insisted that the shareholder's only claim was that management was about to violate the corporation's charter. According to Holmes, any duties the charter imposed on management were matters of state law. Holmes acknowledged that state law incorporated federal law inasmuch as state law barred management from purchasing securities issued under an unconstitutional federal statute. But even then, according to Holmes, the plaintiff's claim still rested formally on state law: Federal law had "relevance and effect" only because state law "took it up." By Holmes' account, "[t]he mere adoption" of federal law by state law, where federal law had "no force *proprio vigore*," could not make the shareholder's lawsuit arise under federal law.[278]

The decision in *Smith* may be the most unruly of the classic precedents. On the one hand, *Smith* seems consistent with the well-pleaded complaint rule. To plead the claim that management was about to violate the corporate charter (and thus state law), the shareholder had to allege that management was poised to make an unlawful investment. And to plead that there was something unlawful about the federal bonds, the shareholder had to describe the federal constitutional flaw he saw in them.[279] Thus the complaint did justifiably mention a federal issue. On the other hand, the shareholder advanced no claim that management's mere purchase of the bonds violated federal law. By contrast, he alleged only that the purchase violated state law, which prohibited management from investing in securities whose issuance was independently unlawful (under either state or federal law). Holmes himself thought that *Smith* could not be squared with his previous opinion for the Court in *Well Works*. Holmes did not mention the well-pleaded complaint rule. Instead, he insisted that, under *Well Works*, all that mattered was the source of the plaintiff's claim. And in *Smith* the shareholder's claim was formally based on state law. As Holmes explained, the shareholder would have had no occasion to contend that the bonds violated federal law if state law had not conditioned management's authority to buy them on their validity.

The *Smith* case is sometimes depicted as an exception to the Holmes formulation, because the Court approved §1331 jurisdiction even though state law created the shareholder's "cause of action"—namely, the shareholder's authority to sue. To be sure, *Smith* is the only Supreme Court precedent that comes to mind in which a plaintiff who looked to state law for the authority to sue was able to invoke §1331 jurisdiction originally, instead of beginning in state court and reaching federal court by removal. But it is confusing to suggest that *Smith* conflicts with the Holmes formulation because state law

---

276. 255 U.S. 180 (1921).

277. See text accompanying notes 313, 325–31 (discussing the Court's explanation of *Smith* in *Merrell Dow*).

278. 255 U.S. at 214–15.

279. Professor Doernberg explains that the shareholder's complaint would have been dismissed for "insufficiency" if it had not pleaded the "illegality of the bonds." Doernberg, note 271, at 629 n.147.

provided the shareholder with a right of action. Here again, it makes far more sense to understand the Holmes formulation to mean that federal jurisdiction turns on the source of the substantive *claim* that the litigant seeks to advance *by means of* a lawsuit.[280] Holmes himself objected to the decision in *Smith* not on the ground that state law authorized the shareholder to take his claim to court, but rather on the ground that the claim he advanced in court was that management was about to violate state law.[281] The difference between the Court and Holmes was not that the Court rejected Justice Holmes' view that §1331 jurisdiction demanded that the plaintiff's substantive legal claim must be federal. It was that the Court concluded that the shareholder's substantive claim *was* federal because his formal state law claim incorporated a federal element. Holmes argued that so long as the formal shell of the claim was a matter of state law, the incorporation of a federal element did not make the claim federal for §1331 jurisdictional purposes.[282]

Together, the Holmes formulation and the well-pleaded complaint rule screen cases fairly well. The Holmes test demands that the plaintiff's substantive claim must be federal. Whether or not a claim *is* federal can sometimes be debated; *Smith* is an illustration. But in the run of cases the federal character of a claim is perfectly clear. The well-pleaded complaint rule ensures that district courts can determine whether such a federal claim exists simply by reading the complaint, without pausing to hear arguments about issues that might emerge at a later stage.[283] The well-pleaded complaint rule's rigidity has been

---

280. See notes 256–57 and accompanying text.

281. *Smith*, 255 U.S. at 214 (dissenting opinion). See notes 313, 325–31 and accompanying text. Professor Shapiro finds *Smith* hard to square with other classic precedents, but *not* because the plaintiff's right of action was created by state law. For example, Shapiro finds *Smith* inconsistent with *Shoshone Mining*: "In *Smith*, the presence of a federal ingredient made relevant by state law was sufficient to confer jurisdiction, but in *Shoshone*, a federally created claim that turned on issues of state law was not." Shapiro, note 270, at 570.

282. The shareholder in *Smith* almost certainly lacked "standing" to sue federal authorities directly to challenge the validity of the land banks and their bonds. Paradoxically, the Supreme Court found §1331 jurisdiction lacking in *Shoshone Mining* and *Moore* (which were traditional bi-polar disputes in which individuals pressed personal legal claims), but sustained §1331 jurisdiction in *Smith* (where the suit was plainly a device for testing the constitutionality of a statute that affected the entire country). See Chapter IX, notes 167–200 and accompanying text (discussing the insufficiency of most "generalized grievances" to establish "standing").

283. Thus a "civil action" arising under federal law for purposes of §1331 cannot depend on the *possibility* that a federal issue *might* emerge. See notes 12–46 and accompanying text (discussing the broader scope accorded to "cases" arising under federal law for purposes of Article III). In *Gully v. First Nat'l Bank*, 299 U.S. 109 (1936), state authorities sued a nationally chartered bank in state court to collect taxes. The bank attempted to remove the suit to federal court on the theory that the state had power to impose the taxes only because a federal statute allowed national banks to be taxed at the state level and the complaint might have been drawn to state a federal issue for purposes of §1331 jurisdiction. Justice Cardozo responded that the state tax officials' claim was wholly one of state law. It was true that the state relied on federal law for its authority to impose the tax in the first instance. But that matter of federal law was not actually implicated in the suit and thus could not establish §1331 jurisdiction. Id. at 116. Cases involving real estate actions make the same point. Recall that Justice Johnson worried in *Osborn* that Marshall's "ingredient" test would make every lawsuit involving western lands a case arising under federal law for Article III purposes—because one of the parties might conceivably contest the original patent issued by the federal government. See note 17. The Court has always been sensitive to that argument in its interpretation of §1331. On the whole, the Court has held that plaintiffs who trace their title to a grant by the federal government cannot, for that reason alone, invoke §1331 jurisdiction when they sue others for possession or title. The old real property cases typically took the form of ejectment actions, in which plaintiffs were not required to plead the original source of their claims. See Chapter VII, note 45 (explaining the ele-

questioned. Justice Cardozo once warned (in *dictum*) that it can be hazardous to "define broadly and in the abstract" what constitutes an action arising under federal law: "What is needed is something of that common-sense accommodation of judgment to kaleidoscopic situations which characterizes the law in its treatment of problems of causation."[284] Nevertheless, a categorical rule is generally thought to be justified on pragmatic grounds. The threshold question of jurisdiction should be easy to settle *without* the exercise of judgment—so that suits in which federal courts have no power to act can be dispatched in favor of matters that the courts have authority to address.[285]

The well-pleaded complaint rule is plainly underinclusive inasmuch as it bars jurisdiction in cases in which non-frivolous federal issues will predominate. The only issues

---

ments of ejectment in connection with the *Fairfax* litigation). That may explain *Shoshone Mining*, at least in part. Moreover, once land is conveyed into private hands, federal law has done its work. Thereafter, the rights and duties attending the land are governed by state law. The Court took a different view in the special circumstances presented in *Oneida Indian Nation v. County of Oneida*, 414 U.S. 661 (1974). In that case, Indian tribes successfully invoked federal jurisdiction on the ground that their claims to the land in question did not rest merely on an original transfer from the federal government, but on the government's continuing protection of the tribes' interests in possession. In *Louisville & Nashville R.R. Co. v. Rice*, 247 U.S. 201 (1918), the Court held that common carriers can invoke federal jurisdiction under §1337 to resolve disputes over ordinary freight charges, because the Interstate Commerce Act obligates them to collect the fees authorized by that Act. The *Rice* decision is hard to square with *Gully* and the real property cases. See note 249 (noting that the Court generally reads §1331 and §1337 in the same way). Yet the Court has reaffirmed its old decision, albeit in a case in which the circuit court below had presumed to say that *Rice* was no longer sound. *Thurston Motor Lines v. Jordan K. Rand*, 460 U.S. 533 (1983).

284. *Gully*, 299 U.S. at 117. Professor Cohen argues that it would be better for district courts to make *ad hoc* discretionary judgments about whether cases warrant federal adjudication. Cohen, note 266. Professor Shapiro thinks discretion of that kind at the threshold of litigation in the district courts would be unmanageable. Shapiro argues, however, that the Supreme Court may sensibly create exceptions to the Holmes formulation and the well-pleaded complaint rule when those formulae either include a body of cases that should not be in federal court or exclude a body of cases that should be. Shapiro, note 270, at 588–89. If the Court's classic precedents in point cannot easily be reconciled, Shapiro thinks it is because the Court has exercised discretionary judgment at that level.

285. The American Law Institute endorses the well-pleaded complaint rule chiefly for this pragmatic reason. ALI, Study of the Division of Jurisdiction Between State and Federal Courts 170 (1969). Professor Chadbourn and Professor Levin once proposed that the rule should be relaxed enough to allow jurisdiction if the plaintiff anticipates a federal defense and the defendant readily concedes that the defense will be raised. James H. Chadbourn & A. Leo Levin, *Original Jurisdiction of Federal Questions*, 90 U. Pa. L. Rev. 639, 674 (1942). Professor Trautman also contended that a "general allegation" of a federal issue should be sufficient to establish jurisdiction until pre-trial procedure progresses to the point at which the actual existence of such a question can be ascertained. Herman L. Trautman, *Federal Right Jurisdiction and the Declaratory Remedy*, 7 Vand. L. Rev. 445, 460 (1954). Professor Mishkin concedes that jurisdiction must turn on the content of the complaint, for the necessary and sufficient reason that the district court has only the complaint to go on. Mishkin argues, however, that jurisdiction need not depend on what is "properly" pleaded to state the plaintiff's claim. Complaints in diversity actions independently allege diverse citizenship for jurisdictional purposes alone. Similar special jurisdictional pleading might be allowed in federal question cases. Mishkin, note 19, at 164. Professor Mishkin contends, moreover, that the well-pleaded complaint rule is not so neat and tidy as it may seem inasmuch as it depends on an unstated and contestable understanding of what counts as "proper" pleading. Id. at 176. None of the Court's cases identifies the body of pleading rules to which district courts are to refer, and in some instances the need to plead something of a federal nature can be debated. Recall in this connection that notice pleading is ordinarily sufficient in federal lawsuits. To the extent the well-pleaded complaint rule contemplates that plaintiffs will spell out the elements of their claims, it is in some tension with Fed. R. Civ. P. 8. See Chapter IX, notes 142–43 and accompanying text (discussing the pleading standards that must be met to establish "standing").

dividing the parties in *Mottley* were federal in nature: whether the new statute abrogated the contract and, if it did, whether it was constitutional.[286] After the Supreme Court held that the Mottleys could not sue originally in federal court, they filed suit in state court. The railroad could not remove the action to federal court pursuant to §1441, because (as the Supreme Court had just explained) the Mottleys could not have begun there originally. The federal issues promptly surfaced in the litigation in state court and proved to be decisive. The Supreme Court thus had appellate jurisdiction to examine the state courts' disposition of those questions.[287] Equally in *Moore*, Chief Justice Hughes conceded that if the case went to state court and the state court decision ultimately turned on federal issues, the Supreme Court would have appellate jurisdiction.[288]

The well-pleaded complaint rule does not foreclose jurisdiction in the kinds of cases that are most important for federal courts to handle: cases in which plaintiffs advance forthright claims under the Constitution or federal statutes. Even when the federal character of claims is less obvious, plaintiffs can often establish §1331 jurisdiction. A claim is federal for jurisdictional purposes even if, as was true in *Smith*, it is formally a matter of state law—so long as it incorporates a federal element. A claim is "substantial" for jurisdictional purposes if it is non-frivolous in the *Bell v. Hood* sense.[290] In many instances, moreover, Congress grants litigants with federal claims a right of action to file suits that will invoke §1331 jurisdiction in the district courts. In ordinary §1983 actions, for example, plaintiffs have Congress' permission to use a private lawsuit to enforce federal law (that is, they have a right of action), and they can properly plead the elements of a claim that is both federal in character and "substantial" in merit (for example, a violation of the fourteenth amendment).[289]

E. Rights of Action Revisited

When Congress does *not* authorize private litigants to go to court, the situation is altered. Recall that there is a difference between a federal district court's jurisdiction to entertain a lawsuit, on the one hand, and a litigant's right of action to file the lawsuit in the first instance, on the other.[291] A litigant who attempts to initiate suit to enforce federal law in federal district court without a right of action typically suffers dismissal on that (non-jurisdictional) basis.[292] Nevertheless, the existence (or not) of a private right of action has implications for the separate question of district court jurisdiction. Congress' failure to include private lawsuits on the list of approved devices for enforcing a federal statute implies a preference for enforcement by alternative means (for example,

---

286. See notes 263–65 and accompanying text.
287. *Louisville & N.R.R. v. Mottley*, 219 U.S. 467 (1911).
288. *Moore*, 291 U.S. at 214; see notes 272–75; Chapter VII, notes 132–37 and accompanying text (discussing the Supreme Court's appellate jurisdiction in cases in which state law incorporates federal law).
290. See notes 258–62 and accompanying text.
289. See note 136 and accompanying text.
291. See notes 231–33 and accompanying text.
292. See notes 120–27 and accompanying text.

suits in federal court by a federal administrative agency or private suits in state court).[293] Accordingly, the Supreme Court has held that in some instances district courts have no §1331 jurisdiction to adjudicate suits brought by private litigants seeking to enforce federal statutes, unless Congress has created a private right of action for the occasion.

The relationship between these two ideas (a district court's §1331 jurisdiction and a private litigant's right of action) comes to light in removal cases.[294] A litigant begins a lawsuit in *state* court, advancing a non-frivolous federal substantive claim. Then, the defendant attempts to remove the suit to federal district court. Recall that a district court has removal jurisdiction under §1441 only if the plaintiff might have invoked the federal court's original jurisdiction in the first instance.[295] If there is a federal right of action that would have authorized the plaintiff to sue originally in federal court, there is no difficulty. If, however, there is no such federal right of action, the question arises whether district court jurisdiction might have been achieved in its absence. There are instances in which jurisdiction can be established under §1441 without benefit of a federal right of action. In *Lapides v. Bd. of Regents*,[296] a private plaintiff filed a §1983 action in state court, contending that the state of Georgia had violated both the fourteenth amendment and various provisions of state law.[297] The state removed the case to federal court pursuant to §1441. In the Supreme Court, Justice Breyer explained that the state was not a "person" subject to suit under §1983. Accordingly, the plaintiff's fourteenth amendment claim was subject to dismissal for lack of a federally created right of action.[298] Nevertheless, Justice Breyer explained that the removed case was still within the district court's jurisdiction until that court disposed of the plaintiff's state law claims.[299]

The *Lapides* case confirms the distinction between a federal right of action, on the one hand, and federal court subject matter jurisdiction, on the other. But in cases like *Lapides*, the point is largely formal. As a practical matter, the removal cases in which the right-of-action/jurisdiction distinction is important are cases in which plaintiffs file lawsuits in state court, advancing claims that are formally grounded in *state* law but are federal for jurisdictional purposes because they incorporate a federal element. By hypothesis in that kind of case, the plaintiff characterizes his or her claim as a matter of state law and chooses to press that claim in state court. The question, then, is whether the defendant can override the plaintiff's choice of forum and transfer the case to federal court even if, had the plaintiff tried to go to federal court in the first instance, there would have been no federally created right of action authorizing the suit. In *Merrell*

---

293. In a case involving a constitutional as opposed to a statutory claim, a federal right of action is typically in place, either explicitly (via §1983) or implicitly (via a *Bivens* analysis). See notes 200, 209–10 and accompanying text. Congress may enact statutes that limit private suits to enforce constitutional rights. See notes 223–30 and accompanying text. Yet the Court hesitates to permit Congress to foreclose federal court adjudication of constitutional claims. See Chapter IV, notes 112–17 and accompanying text.

294. See notes 250–51; Chapter VI, notes 128–35 and accompanying text.

295. See Chapter VI, note 129 and accompanying text.

296. 122 S.Ct. 1640 (2002).

297. The defendant was actually a state board of regents, which was treated as the state itself. See Chapter X, note 58 and accompanying text.

298. See text accompanying note 135; Chapter X, note 369 and accompanying text.

299. *Lapides*, 122 S.Ct. at 1643. See also Chapter X, notes 82, 181–87 and accompanying text (discussing the sovereign immunity issue the Court ultimately resolved in *Lapides*). Of course, the district court would not have actually determined the plaintiff's state law claims after dismissing his federal claim for want of a right of action. See notes 417–18 and accompanying text (discussing a district court's discretion to dismiss state law claims).

Dow Pharmaceuticals v. Thompson,[300] the Court held that a defendant (usually) cannot invoke a federal district court's jurisdiction in those circumstances.

The Thompsons' child was born with deformities, allegedly because the mother had taken the drug Bendectin during pregnancy. They sued the manufacturer, Merrell Dow, in state court, advancing negligence and products liability claims in six separate counts. In their fourth count, the Thompsons alleged that the company had failed to put a proper warning label on the bottle and thus had "misbranded" the drug in violation of the federal Food, Drug, and Cosmetic Act. That count advanced the claim that, under state law, the company's violation of the FDCA established a rebuttable presumption of negligence. Merrell Dow removed the lawsuit to federal district court under §1441. The district court accepted jurisdiction, citing the *Smith* case as the apparently controlling precedent.[301] The court of appeals reversed. In the Supreme Court, Justice Stevens affirmed the circuit court's judgment that the district court lacked jurisdiction, but on the strength of a different analysis.[302]

The removal posture of the case was crucial. The Thompsons did not argue that the FDCA itself or any other federal statute gave them a right of action to enforce the FDCA in private litigation. Nor did they attempt to invoke §1331 as the jurisdictional basis for an action in federal court. They advanced state tort claims against the company in state court and alleged a violation of the FDCA in their fourth count only in service of a state law claim of negligence. Nevertheless, given the way removal jurisdiction operates, Justice Stevens addressed the artificial question whether the Thompsons might have established original jurisdiction in federal court in the first instance.[303] He assumed for purposes of decision that Congress had enacted no statute authorizing private plaintiffs to file lawsuits seeking to enforce the FDCA.[304] That assumption made it necessary to determine whether the absence of a federally created right of action had some bearing on the district court's jurisdiction. Justice Stevens explained that Congress' failure to create such a litigation right *did* make a jurisdictional difference.

Justice Stevens recognized that *state* law authorized the Thompsons to litigate their claim in *state* court. State tort law incorporated the labeling standards established by the FDCA. Accordingly, insofar as the state courts were concerned, the Thompsons had a state tort claim against Merrell Dow because they alleged that the company had violated the FDCA. In addition, insofar as the state courts were concerned, the Thompsons were entitled to advance that claim in a lawsuit—in the same way that any other state tort claim could be vindicated in private litigation.[305] Justice Stevens had no difficulty with that. He did not propose that Congress had forbidden private suits to enforce

300. 478 U.S. 804 (1986).

301. *Smith v. Kansas City Title & Trust Co.*, 255 U.S. 180 (1921); see notes 276–82 and accompanying text (discussing *Smith*). Having accepted jurisdiction, the district court granted Merrell Dow's motion to dismiss on *forum non conveniens* grounds.

302. The court of appeals held that to the extent the fourth count advanced a federal claim, it was not "necessary" to the Thompsons' lawsuit, because the jury could find the company negligent without also finding a violation of the FDCA. Justice Stevens rejected that analysis. 478 U.S. at 817 n.15. As long as there is one substantial federal question in a case, a district court has jurisdiction under §1331, even though most of the other issues are matters of state law. See text accompanying note 258; see also notes 402–22 and accompanying text (discussing supplemental jurisdiction).

303. See text accompanying note 250.

304. The circuit court had so held, and both parties agreed on this point.

305. See note 120 (explaining that any claims that state law recognizes in the abstract are typically enforceable in private lawsuits).

the FDCA in *state* court.[306] The question in *Merrell Dow* was whether the Thompsons might have established jurisdiction in a federal district court under §1331, relying on the FDCA to supply the content of their substantive claim (thus making it federal), without any congressional authorization to vindicate that claim by means of a private lawsuit in federal court.

Justice Stevens acknowledged that in order to answer that question he would have to square the Court's precedents regarding §1331 jurisdiction with its precedents regarding federal rights of action. The classic cases on §1331 jurisdiction were decided before the Court developed the modern doctrine regarding private rights of action. In those older decisions, the Court probably assumed that if federal courts were found to have jurisdiction it would follow that someone would be able to exploit that jurisdiction by filing an appropriate lawsuit. In any event, the Court did not pause to consider whether some federal statute authorized the plaintiffs concerned to invoke federal court jurisdiction when it existed. The *Smith* case provides an illustration.[307] In that case, Justice Day focused exclusively on whether the shareholder's claim was sufficiently federal to trigger §1331 jurisdiction. Concluding that it was, he decided that federal claim on the merits. Today, private litigants who press federal claims in federal court must demonstrate both the federal court's jurisdiction and their own authority to sue. That is the point of the decisions leading down to *Sandoval*.[308] In *Merrell Dow*, then, it was necessary to revisit the old jurisdictional cases, particularly *Smith*, in light of more recent decisions on federal rights of action.[309]

Initially, Justice Stevens said that "the congressional determination that there should be no federal remedy for the violation of this federal statute [the FDCA]" was "tantamount to a congressional conclusion that the presence of a claimed violation of the statute as an element of a state cause of action [was] insufficiently 'substantial' to confer federal-question jurisdiction."[310] He then dropped a footnote to explain what he meant by a "substantial" federal claim in this context. In that footnote, he reconciled numerous precedents on §1331 jurisdiction, including *Smith*, around a common theme: Federal claims invoke federal court jurisdiction under §1331 when the "federal interests" at stake warrant adjudication in a federal district court.[311] According to Justice Stevens, the federal interests were modest in *Shoshone Mining* and *Moore*, where finding §1331 jurisdiction would have drawn numerous mining and workers compensation claims into the federal district courts, there to be adjudicated primarily on the basis of state law.[312] The federal interest in *Smith* was compelling by comparison. By approving §1331 jurisdiction in that case, the Court allowed a federal district court to entertain a constitutional attack on the validity of a federal statute. Otherwise, the state courts in Missouri

---

306. *Merrell Dow*, 478 U.S. at 816 (recognizing that the Thompsons' claim might be addressed in state court and that the Supreme Court might review the resulting judgment).

307. See notes 276–82 and accompanying text.

308. *Alexander v. Sandoval*, 532 U.S. 275 (2001); see notes 153–58 and accompanying text.

309. Professor Luneburg applauds *Merrell Dow* for recognizing that the situation called for the exercise of judicial discretion to assign meaning to §1331 that could not be ascribed to congressional intent at the time of enactment. William V. Luneburg, *Nonoriginalist Interpretation—A Comment on Federal Question Jurisdiction and Merrell Dow Pharmaceuticals, Inc. v. Thompson*, 48 U. Pitt. L. Rev. 757 (1987).

310. 478 U.S. at 814.

311. Id. at 814–15 n.12.

312. See notes 267–75 and accompanying text.

would have shouldered that responsibility.[313] Finally, Justice Stevens stated his conclusion: "[A] complaint alleging a violation of a federal statute as an element of a state cause of action, when Congress has determined that there should be no private, federal cause of action for the violation, does not state a claim" triggering §1331 jurisdiction.[314]

In dissent, Justice Brennan insisted that *Smith* was controlling.[315] The Thompsons' fourth count advanced a state law negligence claim that incorporated the federal labeling requirements established by the FDCA. Since that claim was not frivolous, according to Brennan, it would have sufficed for §1331 jurisdiction if the Thompsons had filed their suit in federal court. Justice Brennan acknowledged Stevens' desire to reconcile the Court's recent decisions on federally created rights of action. He, too, assumed for purposes of discussion that Congress had not authorized private litigants to file lawsuits to enforce the FDCA. Yet Justice Brennan saw no basis in that for construing the jurisdictional statute, §1331, to foreclose the Thompsons' (hypothetical) suit. He pointed out that the enforcement actions that Congress *had* authorized (civil suits by the Food and Drug Administration and criminal prosecutions) would be filed in federal district court. To Brennan, then, it was "rather strange" that Justice Stevens should take Congress to have disclaimed enough federal interest in the interpretation of the FDCA to warrant federal jurisdiction of a private lawsuit.[316]

In all candor, Justice Stevens' opinion for the Court was frightfully, not to say willfully, ambiguous.[317] Accordingly, the precise holding in *Merrell Dow* can be debated—and has been (exhaustively) in academic circles. According to some observers, *Merrell Dow* held that determinations of §1331 jurisdiction require more *ad hoc* consideration than previously believed. This, notwithstanding the conventional understanding that plaintiffs can invoke §1331 jurisdiction simply by properly pleading a claim that is both federal in character and "substantial" in the *Bell v. Hood* sense.[318] In *Merrell Dow*, Justice Stevens suggested that admittedly non-frivolous federal claims are sufficient only if they are "substantial" in a different sense: They must evoke federal interests that are better protected by original district court jurisdiction than they would be by original adjudica-

---

313. See Chapter VI, notes 3–38 and accompanying text (discussing concurrent jurisdiction of federal question cases in state court).

314. 478 U.S. at 817.

315. Id. at 820 (dissenting opinion). Justice Brennan insisted that *Smith's* "continuing vitality" was "beyond challenge" and reminded Justice Stevens that the Court had "reaffirmed" the holding in that case very recently—in Brennan's own opinion for a unanimous Court in *Franchise Tax Bd. v. Constr. Laborers Vacation Trust*, 463 U.S. 1 (1983); see notes 352–67 and accompanying text.

316. Justice Brennan conceded that Congress' failure to create a private right of action to enforce the FDCA in any court might be understood as an implicit prohibition on private suits in both federal and state court. But he did not understand Justice Stevens to rest on that ground. In Brennan's view, then, Congress was content both that FDCA claims would be litigated in federal court (at someone's behest) and that private suits might be initiated in state court. Putting those two ideas together, he insisted that Congress' failure to create a right of action for a private suit filed originally in federal court should not be taken as an indication that Congress disapproved of federal court jurisdiction in a removal setting. *Merrell Dow*, 478 U.S. at 831–32 (dissenting opinion).

317. For openers, the terminology was confusing. Justice Stevens used the label "federal remedy" to mean a federally created private right of action—that is, congressional authorization of private suits to enforce the FDCA. He used the label "state cause of action" to mean *both* a state tort claim (the plaintiffs' right under state law to demand that the company take reasonable care in the preparation and distribution of its products) *and* state law authority to take such a state tort claim to court. See notes 120–21 (discussing the confusion this terminology can generate).

318. See note 258 and accompanying text.

tion in state court, subject to appellate review in the Supreme Court. If that is true in the run of cases, then the well-pleaded complaint rule may be undermined. Recall that the great value of that rule is that it operates mechanically, so that district courts need not devote substantial resources to determining their power to entertain a lawsuit.[319] It seems clear (enough), however, that district courts are not always obliged to consider the federal interests to be served by §1331 jurisdiction. Instead, they must do so only in cases involving claims like the claim in *Merrell Dow* itself (claims that are formally matters of state law but are federal because they take their content from a federal statute), pressed without benefit of a federally created right of action.[320] In the run of cases, *Bell v. Hood* remains controlling and any non-frivolous federal claim is sufficient to establish a federal court's jurisdiction.[321]

Other observers understand *Merrell Dow* to mean that a federally created right of action is always necessary to §1331 jurisdiction and, by extension, to removal jurisdiction pursuant to §1441.[322] This, notwithstanding the conventional understanding that jurisdiction and a right of action are not the same thing.[323] Justice Stevens made it clear that the point of the exercise in *Merrell Dow* was to explain the relationship between those two ideas. And he stated flatly that a decision by Congress not to authorize private suits to enforce a federal statute is "tantamount" to a determination that the "federal interests" to be served by original jurisdiction in the district courts are insufficient. If that is true in the run of cases, then what really counts is not whether courts regard the federal interests in district court jurisdiction to be important enough. Instead, it is whether Congress has already concluded that those interests are *not* sufficient and has expressed that conclusion (implicitly) by failing to authorize private litigants to sue. This, too, misreads *Merrell Dow*. Once again, Justice Stevens appeared to contemplate a case-by-case examination of the nature of the federal interests at stake only in cases involving

---

319. Justice Brennan objected that Justice Stevens' analysis would abandon the relative certainty and efficiency of the well-pleaded complaint rule in favor of an "infinitely malleable" (and thus unmanageable) test for jurisdiction. 478 U.S. at 821 n.1 (dissenting opinion).

320. Since *Merrell Dow*, the Court has insisted that the well-pleaded complaint rule must be scrupulously enforced. In *Oklahoma Tax Comm'n v. Graham*, 489 U.S. 838 (1989), the Court summarily reversed a circuit decision for failure to do so. The *Graham* case arose in a removal posture, but the Court did not mention *Merrell Dow*, the source of the plaintiff's right of action, or the relative importance of the federal interests involved.

321. See note 262 and accompanying text. In *City of Chicago v. Intnat'l College of Surgeons*, 522 U.S. 156 (1997), Justice O'Connor noted that ICS did not resist federal jurisdiction on the theory that its federal claim was "so insubstantial as not to establish federal jurisdiction." Id. at 168. See note 257. On that point, she cited *Merrell Dow*, not *Bell v. Hood*. It is hard to think, however, that Justice O'Connor meant to suggest that the *Bell* test for substantiality was not controlling. She also cited *Duke Power Co. v. Carolina Envt'l Study Grp.*, 438 U.S. 59 (1978), on the same point. That case *did* rely on *Bell*. Id. at 70–71. Moreover, the federal claim in *Surgeons* was constitutional. See notes 406–10 and accompanying text.

322. See Comment, *Understanding Merrell Dow: Federal Question Jurisdiction for State-Federal Hybrid Cases*, 77 Wash. U. L.Q. 219 (1999) (collecting lower court cases that apparently take this view).

323. See notes 231–33 and accompanying text. If §1441 conditioned a defendant's ability to remove on the plaintiff's hypothetical ability to satisfy all the prerequisites for suing in federal court in the first instance, §1441 might plausibly be construed to require a defendant to demonstrate both that a district court would have had subject matter jurisdiction and that the plaintiff would have had a right of action. As it is, §1441 does not lend itself to that interpretation. By its terms, §1441 authorizes removal in "any civil action" in which a federal district court would have had "original jurisdiction." The *Lapides* case confirms that the absence of a federal right of action does not deprive a federal court of subject matter jurisdiction of a removed case. See notes 296–99 and accompanying text.

claims that are formally matters of state law but incorporate a federal statutory component, advanced without benefit of a federally created right of action.[324]

The *Merrell Dow* case is best understood as a bridge between the Court's modern right-of-action cases, on the one hand, and older jurisdictional precedents, on the other—in particular the *Smith* case. All observers recognize that Justice Stevens made peace with *Smith*. That has to be significant. By acknowledging *Smith* as a viable precedent, Justice Stevens confirmed two propositions for which that precedent stands. One of those propositions is, again, that §1331 jurisdiction does not always depend on the existence of a federally created right of action. Justice Day cited no federal statute authorizing the suit in *Smith*, and still he sustained the district court's jurisdiction.[325] The other proposition in *Smith* is the idea for which that case is best known: A substantive legal claim can be federal for §1331 purposes even if it is formally an alleged violation of state law—as long as it rests, in turn, on an incorporated federal element. Recall that in *Smith* itself, the shareholder successfully invoked §1331 jurisdiction by alleging a violation of state corporate law that would be established only if the bonds were issued under an invalid federal statute.[326] If the shareholder in *Smith* was able to establish §1331 jurisdiction, one would have thought that the Thompsons in *Merrell Dow* might equally have done so. They would have had no federally created right of action, but the shareholder in *Smith* had none, either. The Thompsons' claim would have been federal only inasmuch as their state negligence theory incorporated an allegation that Merrell Dow had violated the FDCA. But the shareholder in *Smith* also advanced a claim that was formally a matter of state law, but contained a federal element. The trick to understanding the decision in *Merrell Dow* is to identify the distinction Justice Stevens drew between that case and *Smith*.

Justice Stevens distinguished the two cases on the ground that especially important federal interests were served by district court jurisdiction in *Smith*. Recall that the incorporated federal component of the claim in that case was constitutional in character. The success of the shareholder's overarching state claim turned not on whether management was about to violate a federal statute, but rather on whether Congress had power to enact the statute in the first place. That question was best addressed originally in a federal district court. The alternative was unsatisfactory by comparison: a suit in state court. In *Merrell Dow*, by contrast, the success of the Thompsons' state negligence claim turned only on whether the company had violated a federal statute. That claim lacked the same purchase on original district court jurisdiction. Accordingly, Justice Stevens explained that the Thompsons' claim should be adjudicated in state court. Thereafter, the Supreme Court could address any dispositive federal issues on direct review.[327]

---

324. Confusing verbiage notwithstanding, Justice Stevens should not be understood to have meant that, after all, a civil action arises under the law that establishes a litigant's authority to sue. To decide *Merrell Dow* on that theory, he would have had to adopt a troubling understanding of the Holmes formulation in *Well Works*. See notes 255–57 and accompanying text. Certainly, if he had meant that, he would simply have said as much and stopped. Doernberg, note 255, at 157.

325. Of course, Justice Day did not stop to consider the need for any such authority to sue in *Smith*. If a case like *Smith* were to arise today, the Court presumably *would* take up the non-jurisdictional question of the plaintiff's right of action—i.e., authority from some source, express or implied, to use a private lawsuit to attack the constitutionality of the federal statute authorizing the bonds.

326. See text accompanying notes 276–78.

327. Justice Stevens recognized that the Supreme Court has appellate jurisdiction to review state court judgments on FDCA issues. He relied on the Court's appellate jurisdiction to ensure accuracy and uniformity in the interpretation of the FDCA, despite the inability of federal district courts to entertain private suits in the first instance. 478 U.S. at 816 & n.4; see Chapter VII, notes 132–37 and

In the end, Justice Stevens limited the decision in *Merrell Dow* to the circumstances of that case, as distinguished from the circumstances in *Smith.* He addressed only cases in which Congress fails to create a private right of action to enforce a federal *statute.* Within that (small) category of cases, he addressed only cases involving claims that are formally based on state law, but which are nonetheless federal for §1331 purposes because they incorporate an alleged violation of a federal statute. And in that (even smaller) category of cases, he said that §1331 jurisdiction (and thus §1441 jurisdiction) usually does not exist. That is so because a decision by Congress not to authorize private suits to enforce a federal statute usually counts as a decision that a state law claim that incorporates an alleged violation of that statute implicates no federal interests especially warranting original district court jurisdiction. Justice Stevens acknowledged, however, that *some* formally state law claims incorporating a federal element *can* trigger §1331 jurisdiction, even when Congress creates no attendant private right of action. That (evidently) is because Congress' failure to authorize private suits does not *always* imply that no federal interests command original district court adjudication. The claim in *Smith* (incorporating an allegation that a federal statute violated the Constitution) is an illustration.[328]

It is possible that *Merrell Dow* draws a sharp line between claims that incorporate federal statutory issues, on the one hand, and claims that incorporate federal constitutional issues, on the other. That understanding would make some sense. It would not only reconcile *Merrell Dow* with *Smith,* but would also spare district courts the burden of determining on an *ad hoc* basis whether federal interests especially warrant original district court jurisdiction. Instead, district courts would have to decide only whether an incorporated federal element is statutory or constitutional.[329] Statutory elements would never justify jurisdiction. Nevertheless, the better understanding is that some claims that incorporate federal statutory elements do warrant §1331 jusrisdiction. Accordingly, *Merrell Dow* contemplates case-by-case judgments regarding the federal interests that would be promoted by district court jurisdiction when litigants attempt to invoke federal jurisdiction without benefit of congressional authorization in order to advance claims grounded in state law incorporating federal statutory law as its content.[330] That

---

accompanying text (discussing the Court's appellate jurisdiction to review a state court judgment in the kind of case that the Thompsons initiated in state court). For an elaboration, see Patti Alleva, *Prerogative Lost: The Trouble with Statutory Federal Question Doctrine After Merrell Dow*, 52 Ohio St. L.J. 1477, 1484, 1502 (1991).

328. But see Note, *Mr. Smith goes to Federal Court: Federal Question Jurisdiction over State Law Claims Post-Merrell Dow*, 115 Harv. L. Rev. 2272, 2290 (2002) (contending that the Court should also take into account competing state interests in keeping formally state claims in state court).

329. The Court sustained removal jurisdiction in the *Surgeons* case, where the plaintiff in state court advanced a fourteenth amendment claim. See notes 257, 406–10 and accompanying text. In constitutional cases, of course, the Court typically finds rights of action either expressly set forth in statutes like §1983 (which would have been available in *Surgeons*) or implied in the constitutional provisions involved. See notes 200–10 and accompanying text. Then again, in *Lapides*, Justice Breyer confirmed a district court's supplemental jurisdiction of state law claims that depended, in the first instance, on §1331 jurisdiction of a fourteenth amendment claim for which §1983 provided no federal right of action. See note 299 and accompanying text. In cases in which the Court has considered whether suits begun in state court can be removed on the theory that they advance federal common law claims, the Court has not cleanly isolated the right-of-action issue from the question whether federal common law does genuinely control. See notes 398–401 and accompanying text.

330. The editors of the Hart and Wechsler casebook once suggested that, immediately prior to *Merrell Dow*, the prerequisites for §1331 jurisdiction could be captured in three propositions: (A) "A case 'arises under' federal law for purposes of the general federal question statute if it is brought to

understanding makes more sense. It asks district courts to work harder to determine their jurisdiction, but only in an extremely narrow class of cases. In truth, the cases in question are primarily removal cases like *Merrell Dow* itself, in which a plaintiff's hypothetical ability to establish §1331 jurisdiction is important only because removal jurisdiction under §1441 is tethered to original jurisdiction under §1331. As a practical matter, *Merrell Dow* (sometimes) prevents a defendant named in a state court lawsuit from trumping the plaintiff's choice of the state forum for the adjudication of a claim that the plaintiff is content to characterize as a matter of state law.[331]

F. Declaratory Judgment Actions

1. In General

Litigants who seek declaratory relief pursuant to the Declaratory Judgment Act would seem to satisfy the well-pleaded complaint rule simply by drawing a complaint to request an authoritative decision on a federal issue.[332] It is not that simple. Instead, declaratory plaintiffs proceeding under 28 U.S.C. §2201 can invoke §1331 jurisdiction only if the federal issue on which they want the court to rule would equally secure federal jurisdiction in a suit for a more traditional (coercive) form of relief, such as compensatory damages or an injunction. There are two schools of thought about how this works.

By one account, a declaratory plaintiff can establish federal jurisdiction only if he or she might have invoked §1331 by filing a well-pleaded complaint seeking coercive relief. By this (conservative) account, the Declaratory Judgment Act does nothing to enhance a plaintiff's ability to establish federal jurisdiction. It only allows a plaintiff to seek (and authorizes federal courts to grant) declaratory relief—either alone or in company with traditional remedies. The point of reading §2201 and §1331 this way is clear: If a plaintiff can establish jurisdiction by requesting a declaration regarding an issue that would not appear in a complaint for a different form of relief, the plaintiff can circumnavigate

enforce a right of action created by federal law"; (B) "A case also 'arises under' federal law for the same purposes if it is brought to enforce a right of action created by state law, if under orderly rules of pleading and proof the plaintiff, as part of his case in chief, must establish the correctness and applicability of federal law in order to prevail"; and (C) "No case other than those described in Propositions A and B 'arises under' federal law within the meaning of the general federal question statute." The Federal Courts and the Federal System 995 (Bator, Meltzer, Mishkin & Shapiro eds. 1988). In that summary, the editors used "right of action" to mean substantive claim. After all, a lawsuit is brought to "enforce" a legal claim, not a procedural vehicle for advancing a claim. Accordingly, they meant Proposition A to describe most cases and Proposition B to describe *Smith*. After *Merrell Dow*, the editors suggested that a fourth proposition might be necessary to complete the picture: (D) "The rules stated in propositions A and B shall not apply to [categories of] cases where the court concludes that considerations of judicial administration and the degree of federal concern justify a refusal to exercise federal jurisdiction." Id. at 1021 (asking rhetorically whether the words in brackets should be included).

331. See Arthur R. Miller, *Artful Pleading: A Doctrine in Search of Definition*, 76 Tex. L. Rev. 1781, 1786–91 (1998) (discussing lower court decisions). Still, there plainly are unsettled questions attending *Merrell Dow*. Cf. Oakley, note 87, at 878–79 (listing *Merrell Dow* on the agenda for ALI attention)

332. See notes 140–42 and accompanying text (discussing the Declaratory Judgment Act).

the well-pleaded complaint rule, provided he or she requests only declaratory relief. While this account is true to the well-pleaded complaint rule, it does not necessarily serve the policies on which that rule rests. In the cases in which the well-pleaded complaint rule was fashioned, the point was to ensure that courts could easily determine their jurisdiction by looking only at the face of a complaint. In declaratory judgment cases, that purpose is served: A declaratory plaintiff obviously must plead the federal issue or issues on which clarity is sought.[333]

By another account, a declaratory plaintiff can establish federal jurisdiction if *either* the plaintiff or the *declaratory defendant* might have established jurisdiction in a coercive action. By this second (more generous) account, a declaratory plaintiff need not advance a federal claim of his own, but can establish jurisdiction on the basis of a federal claim that the declaratory defendant might raise—if the declaratory defendant were to sue the declaratory plaintiff for damages or an injunction. The rationale for this second account is also clear: The Declaratory Judgment Act authorizes litigants to obtain clarity regarding their rights and legal relations, so that they can proceed with their lives without undertaking (or risking) coercive lawsuits. If parties differ over a federal issue, it should make no difference which of them initiates the legal proceeding in which that issue can be resolved.[334] In the early years, it was commonly argued that the most refreshing feature of the Declaratory Judgment Act was that it would permit a plaintiff to advance a federal issue that, under common law pleading standards geared to other forms of relief, would not have been introduced until the defendant answered and, perhaps, not before the plaintiff replied.[335]

The competition between these two accounts has roots in *Skelly Oil v. Phillips Petroleum.*[336] Skelly contracted to sell natural gas to Phillips, so that Phillips, in turn, could supply it to a distributor, the Michigan-Wisconsin Pipeline Company. The contract contained a provision allowing Skelly to back out if Michigan-Wisconsin failed to obtain a "certificate of public convenience and necessity" (authorizing Michigan-Wisconsin to operate its pipeline) from the Federal Power Commission by a date certain. The FPC issued a provisional certificate. Skelly found that insufficient and notified Phillips that the deal was off. Phillips then sued Skelly in federal district court, invoking juris-

333. See notes 263–65 and accompanying text. This, of course, is an incomplete response. If it is routinely possible to invoke §1331 jurisdiction by properly pleading a request for a clarifying judgment on a federal question, plaintiffs who cannot establish jurisdiction in an action for coercive relief have an incentive to file a declaratory suit in hopes of winning a declaratory judgment that will probably bring the defendant around. Recall that a declaratory judgment can be enforced, if necessary, by a follow-on injunction. 28 U.S.C. §2202; see note 141. At the very least, a party who arms himself with a declaratory judgment is likely to obtain a favorable settlement.

334. See *Developments in the Law: Declaratory Judgments*, 62 Harv. L. Rev. 787, 802–03 (1949) (taking this view); accord Oakley, note 87, at 877 (nonetheless listing the question on the ALI's agenda).

335. E.g., Trautman, note 285, at 463. Put more bluntly, the argument is that it would be a good idea, not a bad one, to let a plaintiff who otherwise would have to go to state court (because of the well-pleaded complaint rule as it operates in suits for non-declaratory relief) instead to litigate in federal court when he or she is confident that clarity regarding a federal issue will substantially resolve a dispute with the defendant. By all accounts, the well-pleaded complaint rule routinely channels cases out of federal court even though it is perfectly obvious that the issues dividing the parties are federal. See notes 286–88 and accompanying text. That result is justified only if it is a necessary cost of ensuring that district courts can determine their jurisdiction on the basis of the original complaint alone. Since complaints for declaratory relief do specify the federal question to be decided, the mechanical quality of the well-pleaded complaint rule is preserved.

336. 339 U.S. 667 (1950).

diction under §1331 and seeking a declaratory judgment that the provisional certificate was valid and that Skelly was not entitled to renege. That question was federal, according to Phillips, because the contract incorporated federal standards for a timely FPC certificate.

In the Supreme Court, Justice Frankfurter said that, even so, Phillips could not establish §1331 jurisdiction. Insofar as Phillips was concerned, the action was for breach of contract, governed by state law. The federal issue (if any there was)[337] would be introduced only when (and if) Skelly filed an answer insisting that it was entitled to exploit the escape clause (on the theory that the certificate did not meet federal standards). Phillips had no affirmative federal claim of its own, but only wished to defeat Skelly's anticipated federal defense. Justice Frankfurter acknowledged that by requesting a declaratory judgment that Skelly's potential defense was invalid, Phillips had pled a federal issue. But Frankfurter insisted that Phillips could not establish §1331 jurisdiction in a suit for declaratory relief, unless Phillips could equally establish jurisdiction in a suit for damages or an injunction. The Declaratory Judgment Act, he said, was "procedural only" and could do nothing to assist Phillips in establishing jurisdiction that Phillips would have been unable to achieve in a suit for a traditional remedy.[338]

Justice Frankfurter's opinion in *Skelly* embraced the first account of the Declaratory Judgment Act's effect on §1331 jurisdiction—namely, the view that §2201 has no effect at all. Frankfurter explained that the declaratory plaintiff (Phillips) could not establish federal jurisdiction to seek a declaratory judgment against the declaratory defendant (Skelly), because Phillips could not have invoked federal jurisdiction to sue Skelly for some other form of relief. If, for example, Phillips had sued Skelly for damages, the well-pleaded complaint rule would have prevented Phillips from injecting a federal issue into its complaint by anticipating Skelly's federal defense. Frankfurter insisted that the Declaratory Judgment Act could not help a plaintiff like Phillips gain access to federal court when, but for the Act, that plaintiff would have been relegated to state court.[339]

It is possible nonetheless to find support in *Skelly* for the second account of the way jurisdiction works in declaratory actions. If the point is only that the Declaratory Judgment Act does not expand the federal courts' jurisdiction pursuant to §1331, it should make no difference which of the two parties (the declaratory plaintiff or the declaratory defendant) would have been able to establish jurisdiction in an action for coercive relief. So long as one of them could have satisfied the well-pleaded complaint rule in a traditional lawsuit against the other, the case should count as one that a federal court might

---

337. Writing separately in *Skelly*, Chief Justice Vinson said he doubted that there was any federal question in the case at all. He was not convinced that the parties could manufacture federal jurisdiction under §1331 by building a federal issue into a term in a private contract. 339 U.S. at 679.

338. Id. at 671 (majority opinion), quoting *Aetna Life Ins. v. Haworth*, 300 U.S. 227, 240 (1937). When, in *Haworth*, Chief Justice Hughes said that the Declaratory Judgment Act is "procedural only," he meant that the Act makes no attempt to authorize advisory opinions in violation of Article III. See Chapter IX, text accompanying note 21.

339. *Skelly*, 339 U.S. at 672: "Whatever federal claim Phillips may be able to urge would in any event be injected into the case only in anticipation of a defense to be asserted by petitioner [Skelly]." The traditional way of making this point is to ask whether the Mottleys might have established §1331 jurisdiction in their suit against the railroad if they had sought a declaratory judgment that the federal statute in that case did *not* give the railroad a valid basis for refusing to perform under the contract. See notes 263–65 and accompanying text (discussing the *Mottley* case). Given what Frankfurter said in *Skelly*, it seems most unlikely that he would have allowed that.

have considered apart from the Declaratory Judgment Act. One might sensibly say that the Act does not expand the federal courts' traditional jurisdiction merely because it permits a declaratory plaintiff to anticipate a declaratory defendant's federal defense—in a case in which the declaratory defendant might have turned that defense into an affirmative claim in an action against the declaratory plaintiff for coercive relief.[340]

Justice Frankfurter did not pause to ask whether Skelly might have established federal jurisdiction in a coercive lawsuit against Phillips. If he had, he presumably would have considered an action for rescission and restitution—filed by Skelly to rid itself of a contract that (in Skelly's view) was null and void and to recoup any expenses Skelly had incurred. In a complaint for that kind of relief, Skelly would presumably have alleged that the escape clause allowed Skelly to renege, because the FPC certificate had not been obtained on time as a matter of federal law. That allegation would arguably have satisfied the well-pleaded complaint rule. If Justice Frankfurter had run the argument out in this way and *still* held that Phillips could not establish federal jurisdiction for a declaratory action against Skelly, it would follow that he meant what he said in the opinion he actually wrote: Phillips was unsuccessful because Phillips itself could not have invoked federal jurisdiction in a coercive action against Skelly.

Then again, if Frankfurter had considered the possibility of a suit by Skelly, he might have said that Skelly could *not* establish federal jurisdiction in an action for rescission. After all, Skelly's formal claim would have been that the contract was invalid (a question of state law), and Skelly would have pled a federal issue only as an element of that overarching state law theory. Arguably at least, federal law might not have genuinely supplied the source of Skelly's substantive claim for coercive relief. Following Holmes, Frankfurter might have said that so long as the formal shell of Skelly's claim was a matter of state law, the incorporation of a federal condition was inconsequential.[341] Thus a hypothetical action for rescission filed by Skelly would have arisen under state law and would not have been cognizable in federal court. If Justice Frankfurter had run the argument out in this different way and *then* held that Phillips could not establish federal jurisdiction for a declaratory action against Skelly, it would (or might) follow that he *really* meant something that he did *not* say expressly: Jurisdiction did not exist in *Skelly* because the Declaratory Judgment Act could not expand the federal courts' jurisdiction in a much more fundamental way—namely, by drawing into federal court a dispute that *no one* would have been able to place there in a suit for a traditional remedy.

This last understanding of *Skelly* posits that litigants may have federal defenses that cannot be turned into affirmative federal claims that independently establish §1331 jurisdiction: If Phillips had sued Skelly for breach of contract, Skelly would have had a federal theory to put forward as a basis for defeating liability. Yet if Skelly had sued Phillips for rescission, Skelly would not have been able to advance that same federal theory as an affirmative claim and, on that basis, to invoke federal jurisdiction. The idea is scarcely illogical. And it may help to sort out the confusing way that *Skelly* has been described in subsequent cases. Upon the whole, the modern Court is inclined to embrace the first account of the relationship between §2201 and §1331. But the Court has not

340. See generally Martin H. Redish, Federal Jurisdiction: Tensions in the Allocation of Judicial Power 108–14 (2d ed. 1990). Professor Redish does not make this particular point (explicitly), but he does provide a good (critical) discussion of *Skelly* and subsequent decisions.

341. See text accompanying note 278 (discussing Justice Holmes' argument that there was no federal jurisdiction in the *Smith* case where state law incorporated a federal legal standard).

squarely rejected the second account and, in fact, may preserve that approach in its boilerplate doctrinal statements.[342]

In *Franchise Tax Bd. v. Constr. Laborers Vacation Trust*,[343] Justice Brennan said that *Skelly* has "come to stand for the proposition that 'if, but for the availability of the declaratory judgment procedure, the federal claim would arise only as a defense to a state created action, jurisdiction is lacking.'"[344] In *Textron Lycoming Reciprocating Engine Div. v. UAW*,[345] Justice Scalia said that, according to *Skelly*, "a declaratory action asserting a federal defense to a nonfederal claim [is] not a 'civil action'" within the meaning of §1331.[346] And in *Public Svc. Comm'n v. Wycoff*,[347] Justice Jackson said that "where the complaint in an action for declaratory judgment seeks in essence to assert a defense to an impending or threatened state court action, *it is the character of the threatened action*, and *not of the defense*, which will determine whether there is federal-question jurisdiction in the District Court."[348]

Those statements are potentially misleading. They create the erroneous impression that declaratory plaintiffs cannot establish §1331 jurisdiction even under the first (conservative) account of jurisdiction in declaratory actions—that is, when declaratory plaintiffs advance affirmative federal claims that might also be properly pled to establish federal jurisdiction in a suit for damages or an injunction. Frankfurter said nothing like that in *Skelly*. His point was that Phillips had no federal claim at all, but only a state law contract claim. Frankfurter did not suggest that litigants who *do* have federal claims of their own are unable to file declaratory judgment actions in federal court because, if they were sued by someone else on a state law theory, they would introduce those federal claims as defenses. One of the key objectives of the Declaratory Judgment Act is to permit litigants who have federal claims to sue for clarity regarding those claims before

342. See text accompanying notes 344–48; notes 368–75 and accompanying text (discussing the *Textron* case). Professor Trautman decried *Skelly* as "unnecessary and unfortunate in an area of the law" that was "already unnecessarily complex." Trautman, note 285, at 468. The American Law Institute has proposed that *Skelly* be overruled by statute. ALI Study, note 285, at 171. Professor Doernberg and Professor Mushlin contend that the legislative history indicates a purpose to allow jurisdiction in some of the very instances in which *Skelly* finds it wanting. Donald L. Doernberg & Michael B. Mushlin, *The Trojan Horse: How the Declaratory Judgment Act Created a Cause of Action and Expanded Federal Jurisdiction While the Supreme Court Wasn't Looking*, 36 U.C.L.A. L. Rev. 529, 547–73 (1989).

343. 463 U.S. 1 (1983).

344. Id. at 16, quoting Federal Practice and Procedure §2767, at 744–45 (Wright, Miller & Kane eds. 1983).

345. 523 U.S. 653 (1998).

346. Id. at 658–59.

347. 344 U.S. 237 (1952).

348. Id. at 248 (emphasis added). In *Franchise Tax Board*, the Court forthrightly delineated district court jurisdiction under §1441 and §1331. See notes 352–67 and accompanying text. In *Textron*, the Court formally addressed district court jurisdiction under §301(a) of the LMRA. See notes 368–75 and accompanying text. In *Wycoff*, the Court purported to decide only that the plaintiff could not obtain declaratory relief. In that case, a private film company sued state regulatory authorities in federal court, seeking a declaratory judgment that its business constituted interstate commerce and was therefore exempt from state regulation. There was no hard evidence that state regulators planned any action against the company. Accordingly, Justice Jackson concluded that the company's federal action was either premature for purposes of obtaining discretionary declaratory relief or unripe in the constitutional sense. See notes 141–42 and accompanying text (noting that declaratory relief is discretionary); Chapter IX, notes 416–20 and accompanying text (discussing ripeness). Jackson's comment about jurisdiction may fairly be regarded as *dicta*—offered to explain why declaratory relief was unavailable unless and until the company was actually at risk from state regulatory agents.

they are named as defendants in suits filed by others (advancing either federal or state claims) and, in that posture, must turn their federal claims into defenses. Legions of cases demonstrate that litigants can secure §1331 jurisdiction for anticipatory declaratory actions.[349]

The formulations in *Franchise Tax Board*, *Textron*, and *Wycoff* make sense, however, if they are understood as (inartful) attempts to say something else. The Court may mean that declaratory plaintiffs cannot establish federal jurisdiction if they depend on potential federal arguments that would be advanced by declaratory *defendants*. That reading reflects the first account of jurisdiction in declaratory judgment cases—namely, the understanding that declaratory plaintiffs must advance their own federal claims and cannot depend in any way on what declaratory defendants may say or do. It fits the opinion that Justice Frankfurter actually wrote in *Skelly*. Then again, the Court may mean that declaratory plaintiffs cannot rely on a declaratory defendant's federal argument if it could arise *only* as a defense—and thus could not be turned into an affirmative claim that would establish federal jurisdiction in a coercive lawsuit *brought by the declaratory defendant*. If this is what the Court means, then it may follow that the second (comparatively generous) account of the way the Declaratory Judgment Act works is sustained: Declaratory plaintiffs cannot establish §1331 jurisdiction in *every* case in which the declaratory defendant will raise a federal defense. But they can invoke §1331 jurisdiction if they anticipate the kind of federal defense that, turned into an affirmative claim on behalf of the declaratory defendant, would establish jurisdiction in an action for coercive relief.

2. Modern Precedents

Some lower court cases hold that declaratory plaintiffs can anticipate federal claims that declaratory defendants might advance in coercive suits. In those cases, companies

349. See note 145 and accompanying text. E.g., *Shaw v. Delta Airlines*, 463 U.S. 85 (1983); see notes 362–63 and accompanying text; *Steffel v. Thompson*, 415 U.S. 452 (1974); see Chapter IX, notes 418–20 and accompanying text. Then again, litigants need a right of action to do so. In *Steffel*, §1983 answered on that account. The right-of-action issue in *Shaw* was problematic. See note 364. If litigants with federal claims do not sue first, but wait until an adversary sues them in state court for a violation of state law, they usually will not be able to remove the actions brought against them to federal court. See Chapter VI, notes 131–32 and accompanying text. But it is a mistake to conclude that litigants who would not be able to remove state law suits against them on the basis of their own federal defenses cannot turn their potential federal defenses into affirmative federal claims in prior, anticipatory declaratory judgment actions. That is precisely what litigants who have their own federal claims usually *can* do. It is, again, the very point of the Declaratory Judgment Act—a point that Justice Frankfurter appreciated and respected in *Skelly*. Justice Jackson did not suggest in *Wycoff* that the plaintiff company in that case was attempting to get round the removal statute. He did say that "federal courts will not seize litigation from state courts merely because one, normally a defendant, goes to federal court to begin his federal-law defense before the state court begins the case under state law." *Wycoff*, 344 U.S. at 248. But at that point he was explaining that the company would have an opportunity to mount its constitutional attack on state regulation if and when state authorities actually filed an enforcement action in state court and that the Supreme Court itself might review the state courts' disposition. It is possible that Jackson was groping toward ideas that the Supreme Court has more recently elaborated as abstention doctrines, under which federal courts decline to exercise jurisdiction when state court proceedings against the plaintiff are pending or about to begin. Anticipatory declaratory judgment actions figure significantly in the cases on abstention. See Chapter XI, notes 153–55, 207–15 and accompanying text.

invoke federal jurisdiction pursuant to §1338 to seek declaratory judgments that they are not liable on federal claims that declaratory defendants are in a position to press against them. The Seventh Circuit decision in *Edelmann v. Triple-A Specialty*[350] is the leading illustration. Edelmann let it be known in the trade that Triple-A was infringing Edelmann's patent on a hydrometer. Triple-A sued Edelmann in federal court, seeking a declaration that Triple-A was *not* infringing Edelmann's patent. Edelmann objected to the district court's jurisdiction on the ground that the patent statutes created no substantive or litigation rights in alleged infringers and that Triple-A only wished to defeat Edelmann's potential federal claim of patent infringement.[351] The court conceded that, prior to the Declaratory Judgment Act, only patentees were able to invoke federal jurisdiction to sue alleged patent infringers and thus to vindicate their own federal patent claims. The court held, however, that §2201 allows alleged infringers to sue patentees. It is that proposition in *Edelmann* that continues to engender debate.

In *Franchise Tax Board*, construction companies in California established CLVT to hold funds for their employees' annual vacations. CLVT qualified as an "employee benefit plan" within the meaning of the federal Employee Retirement Income Security Act and thus was subject to extensive federal regulation. The Tax Board was the California agency with responsibility for collecting state taxes. If the Tax Board could not collect from taxpayers directly, it was authorized under state law to collect indirectly—by requiring a trust fund like CLVT to pay over funds held for the benefit of delinquents. On finding that CLVT was holding funds on behalf of three delinquent individuals, the Board directed CLVT to transmit to the Board an amount equal to those employees' outstanding tax bills. CLVT asked the United States Department of Labor whether it could comply. The Labor Department advised CLVT that ERISA preempted the tax laws of California and barred CLVT from surrendering trust monies to the Tax Board. On the basis of that opinion, CLVT declined to forward the funds. The Tax Board sued CLVT in state court, advancing two claims. First, the Board claimed that CLVT was obliged under state law to transmit the requested funds. Second, the Board sought a declaratory judgment that ERISA did not preempt the Board's state law authority to collect the taxes and that CLVT had a legal duty under state law to comply. CLVT removed the case to a federal district court. In the Supreme Court, the question was whether the district court would have had jurisdiction under §1331, if the Board had originally filed suit in federal court.[352] Writing for a unanimous Court, Justice Brennan said that neither of the Board's claims would have established §1331 jurisdiction.

Brennan disposed of the first claim summarily. That was solely a state tax collection claim that stood entirely on state law and could be articulated in the Board's complaint without mention of any federal issue. Accordingly, it would not have satisfied either the Holmes test for §1331 jurisdiction or the well-pleaded complaint rule.[353] Brennan found it harder to dispose of the second claim. He recognized that the case presented a classic occasion for a declaratory judgment action. The only genuine issue on which the parties disagreed was whether ERISA preempted the Board's efforts to reach funds that CLVT held in trust. Once that federal issue was resolved, they would easily settle their accounts accordingly.[354] Nevertheless, Brennan found *Skelly* controlling. The Board's re-

350. 88 F.2d 852 (7th Cir.), *cert. denied*, 300 U.S. 680 (1937).

351. For a description of the federal rights created by the patent and copyright laws and their implications for federal court jurisdiction, see Judge Friendly's opinion in *T.B. Harms v. Eliscu*, 339 F.2d 823 (2d Cir. 1964).

352. See text accompanying notes 250–51.

353. See notes 252–57, 263–65 and accompanying text.

354. See text accompanying note 144.

quest for a declaratory judgment on the federal preemption question would not have established §1331 jurisdiction. The Board advanced no affirmative claim that federal law *did* preempt state law, but rather hoped to show that federal law did *not* preempt state law—so that the *defendant's* federal preemption argument would be defeated. If the Board had not sought a declaratory judgment, but some other form of relief, there would have been no occasion to mention CLVT's federal preemption defense in the complaint.[355]

Justice Brennan recognized that *Skelly* had interpreted the federal Declaratory Judgment Act, while the Tax Board had sued under the California state declaratory judgment statute. As a formal matter, then, state pleading rules governed the issues on which the Board could seek a judgment—pleading rules that might not contain an analog of *Skelly*. Yet Brennan nonetheless relied on *Skelly* for what he regarded as a pragmatic reason. If he conceded that the Board might have invoked §1331 jurisdiction for a suit authorized by a state declaratory judgment statute to which *Skelly* did not apply, he would invite the Board (and future plaintiffs, as well) to elude *Skelly* routinely, simply by relying on state declaratory judgment statutes with more liberal pleading standards rather than on §2201. In this, Justice Brennan was apparently haunted by the threat that troubled Justice Stevens in *Merrell Dow*—namely, the specter of plaintiffs litigating federal issues in federal court on the basis of an authority provided by state law.[356] Justice Brennan dealt with the issue differently. He held, in essence, that the state declaratory judgment statute could not help the Board establish §1331 jurisdiction where *Skelly*'s interpretation of the federal Declaratory Judgment Act, were it applicable, would not allow it.

Justice Brennan acknowledged that "[f]ederal courts have regularly taken original jurisdiction over declaratory judgment suits in which, if the declaratory judgment defendant brought a coercive action to enforce its rights, that suit would necessarily present a federal question."[357] He cited *Edelmann* by name as an illustration.[358] If he saw any tension between *Edelmann* and *Skelly*, he said nothing about it. Nor did he suggest that patent cases are governed by a special rule.[359] Instead, he treated *Edelmann* as yet another precedent ostensibly bearing on §1331 jurisdiction. Accordingly, he considered whether the Tax Board would have been able invoke §1331 jurisdiction in the first instance on the theory that CLVT might have done so in a suit for coercive relief against the Board.[360]

It appeared that CLVT might well have established jurisdiction to sue the Board for an injunction—by advancing an affirmative federal claim that ERISA preempted the Board's state law authority. Justice Brennan referred to prior cases in point.[361] He might

355. This was clear enough from Justice Brennan's treatment of the Board's first claim under state law for the taxes the Board insisted were due. That was the only claim for coercive relief that the Board might have advanced.

356. See text accompanying note 300.

357. *Franchise Tax Board*, 463 U.S. at 19; see notes 334–35 and accompanying text.

358. 463 U.S. at 19 n.19.

359. But see text accompanying note 372 (discussing Justice Scalia's reference to this part of *Franchise Tax Board* in his opinion for the Court in *Textron*).

360. Justice Brennan quoted Justice Jackson's *dictum* in *Wycoff* and explained that *Edelmann* is consistent with it. 463 U.S. at 16 n.14, 19 n.19; see text accompanying note 348. That was true enough, but the point only underscored the tension between *Edelmann* and Frankfurter's opinion in *Skelly*. See text accompanying note 369.

361. Specifically, he cited *Lake Carriers' Ass'n v. MacMullan*, 406 U.S. 498 (1972), and two circuit court cases indicating that parties who are subject to federal regulation can establish §1331 jurisdiction to sue state officials for injunctions against state regulations that conflict with their fed-

also have relied on another case, decided on the very day that he delivered his opinion in *Franchise Tax Board.* In *Shaw v. Delta Airlines*,[362] Justice Blackmun held that Delta could invoke federal jurisdiction in a suit for injunctive and declaratory relief against New York authorities who threatened to force the airline to comply with state statutes preempted by ERISA.[363] In addition, Justice Brennan recognized that special provisions in ERISA would have covered a suit by CLVT. One section, §502(a)(3), authorized any "participant, beneficiary, or fiduciary" subject to ERISA to file "a civil action" seeking an injunction against any defendant who violated ERISA's substantive provisions. Another section, §502(e)(1), conferred jurisdiction on federal district courts to entertain suits filed under the authority provided in §502(a)(3).[364]

Justice Brennan concluded, however, that CLVT's apparent ability to establish federal jurisdiction to sue the Board for an injunction could not translate into an ability on the part of the Board to establish federal jurisdiction to sue CLVT for a declaratory judgment. Brennan quoted Justice Cardozo's warning that jurisdictional issues require judgment.[365] In this instance, he said there were two reasons why, in good judgment, he could not say that the Board might have sued in federal court in the first instance. First,

---

eral obligations and that, since they can sue for injunctive relief, they can equally sue for declaratory relief. 463 U.S. at 20 n.20.

362. 463 U.S. 85 (1983).

363. Unlike *Shaw*, *Franchise Tax Board* involved an attempt to evade state taxes. Justice Brennan declined to say whether the Tax Injunction Act would have precluded a suit by CLVT. 463 U.S. at 20 n.21. See Chapter XI, note 35 and accompanying text (taking fleeting note of the Tax Injunction Act).

364. Since *Shaw*, too, was an ERISA case, Justice Blackmun might have relied on these same provisions both for the airline's right of action and for the district court's jurisdiction. Cf. *Devlin v. Scardelletti*, 122 S.Ct. 2005 (2002) (involving a suit by the trustees of a retirement plan governed by ERISA against a class composed of individual members of the plan). He did not. Instead, he relied on *Mottley*, *Smith*, and other cases indicating that litigants can establish federal jurisdiction under §1331 if they advance affirmative federal claims in their complaints. See notes 263–65, 276–82 and accompanying text. Blackmun did not explain where the litigants in those cases found their rights of action. Nor did he explain where, apart from §502(a)(3), the airline in *Shaw* might have found authority to sue. Given the Court's modern decisions requiring litigants to show wherein Congress has given them permission to enforce federal statutes via private litigation, that was a significant omission. Blackmun's failure to address the right-of-action question is even more problematic today, in light of *Merrell Dow*. See text accompanying note 310 (discussing the connection drawn in *Merrell Dow* between the existence of a federal right of action and §1331 jurisdiction). Justice Blackmun referred obliquely to *Ex parte Young*, 209 U.S. 123 (1908), which again begged the right-of-action question. See Chapter X, notes 310–13 and accompanying text. In *Shaw* itself, the airline sought both injunctive and declaratory relief. If the Declaratory Judgment Act is an independent right-of-action statute, then §2201 could answer in that case with respect to the latter remedy. See notes 143–45 and accompanying text. The Court has said that §1983 is "presumptively available" to plaintiffs contending that federal statutes preempt state regulations. E.g., *Livadas v. Bradshaw*, 512 U.S. 107, 133 (1994). Yet the right of action provided by §1983 is limited to claims of the character of personal legal rights. See notes 174–87 and accompanying text (discussing the *Gonzaga* case). It has been suggested that Justice Blackmun meant to recognize a right of action implied in the Supremacy Clause, serving litigants who wish to advance affirmative federal preemption claims. The Federal Courts and the Federal System 947–48 (Fallon, Meltzer & Shapiro eds. 1996). Professor Monaghan insists that *Shaw* "seems wrong" if it purports to hold that "any federal immunity holder" can have "automatic access to federal courts for declaratory and injunctive relief." Monaghan, note 142, at 241–42. Professor Sloss argues, by contrast, that *Shaw* is correct and bolsters the argument that the Supremacy Clause implicitly authorizes preemption suits in a wide variety of circumstances. David Sloss, *Ex parte Young and Federal Remedies for Human Rights Treaty Violations*, 75 Wash. L. Rev. 1107, 1176 (2000).

365. See text accompanying note 284.

state authorities would not be "significantly prejudiced" if they were unable to invoke the jurisdiction of the federal courts in order to collect state taxes. They could easily take that peculiarly local business to state court. Second, the special provisions in ERISA plainly addressed only suits *by* institutions like CLVT and did not provide for suits *against* them. Brennan said he could not fairly read those sections of ERISA to empower a litigant like the Tax Board indirectly via the analysis in *Edelmann*.

Both Justice Brennan's reasons for distinguishing *Edelmann* have appeal, though both equally have weaknesses. By common account, the result he reached in the end was sensible. The case was, after all, a tax collection proceeding by state authorities who had never wanted to be in federal court in the first place. In general, matters of that kind are best left to the state courts.[366] If litigants like CLVT wish to air their federal preemption claims in federal court, they typically can do so by filing their own lawsuits before state officials initiate litigation in state court. Once again, the removal posture of a case infused it with intellectual difficulty that would not have been presented in an ordinary §1331 case filed originally in a federal district court.[367]

In the *Textron* case, the UAW sued Textron in federal court, seeking a declaratory judgment that a collective bargaining agreement was invalid. The union invoked the district court's jurisdiction under §301(a) of the Labor Management Relations Act.[368] Justice Scalia explained that §301(a) reaches only actions to enforce labor agreements, not actions challenging the validity of agreements in the absence of breach. Accordingly, the union's claim depended entirely on state contract law, and the district court should have dismissed the action for want of jurisdiction. The UAW countered that its pursuit of a declaratory judgment altered the case. The union argued that it made no difference that its own claim rested on state law. The district court's jurisdiction to entertain its declaratory action could rest on the federal claim that Textron would have against the union in a coercive action for breach of the collective bargaining agreement. Justice Scalia rejected that argument, as well.[369] He insisted that neither the UAW nor the Solic-

366. Even if Justice Brennan did not formally rely on the Tax Injunction Act, he reached a result that seems in keeping with the general policy of that Act. See note 363 (noting Brennan's failure to decide whether the Tax Injunction Act bars declaratory suits to avoid state taxes).

367. See text accompanying notes 250–51.

368. See text accompanying note 97. In addition to §301(a), the UAW also cited §1331 (on the theory that the suit arose under federal common law). Justice Scalia declined to address that possibility because it was not within the question on which *certiorari* had been granted. See Chapter VII, text accompanying note 228. He nonetheless discussed the case law pertaining to §1331.

369. Justice Scalia said that the UAW's argument made assumptions that the Court could not indulge. The first was that "facts which were the *converse* of *Skelly Oil*—i.e., a declaratory-judgment complaint raising a *nonfederal* defense to an anticipated *federal* claim—*would* confer §1331 jurisdiction." 523 U.S. at 659 (emphasis in original). The union did contend that it could invoke federal jurisdiction on the basis of a federal coercive action that Textron might file. But it is hard to see why that argument depended on an assumption that the facts in *Textron* differed in a meaningful way from the facts in *Skelly*, far less that the fact patterns in the two cases were polar opposites. The relevant facts were actually similar. In both instances, a declaratory plaintiff hoped to establish federal jurisdiction by anticipating a federal argument that the declaratory defendant might advance. The UAW contended (as any prudent litigant would) that its position was consistent with *Skelly*. But the union placed primary reliance on the Supreme Court's suggestion in *Franchise Tax Board* that cases like *Edelmann* are sound and that (*Skelly* notwithstanding) declaratory plaintiffs *can* invoke federal jurisdiction on the basis of federal claims that lie only in the mouth of the defendant. Justice Scalia correctly observed that the union's position arguably conflicted with the well-pleaded complaint rule. But that only underscored that the union hoped to succeed where Phillips had failed. Professor Collins has pointed out that Scalia's comparison of *Skelly* and *Textron* overlooked the telling distinction between the two cases. Phillips was in a position to identify an extant federal defense that Skelly

itor General (who appeared as *amicus* in *Textron*) could point to a decision by the Supreme Court or "any other federal court" upholding federal jurisdiction "on the basis of the anticipated claim against which the declaratory-judgment plaintiff presents a nonfederal defense."[370]

Justice Scalia did not purport actually to decide that §1331 jurisdiction cannot be established on the basis of an anticipated claim by the declaratory defendant. He said only that it is "not clear" that jurisdiction can be established in that way and that it "can be argued" that declaratory plaintiffs who anticipate federal claims by the defendant are no more entitled to invoke federal jurisdiction than are plaintiffs in ordinary actions who allege only state law claims and anticipate federal defenses or counterclaims from the defendant—namely, plaintiffs who are routinely foreclosed under the well-pleaded complaint rule.[371] Justice Scalia acknowledged that *Franchise Tax Board* had observed "with seeming approval" that jurisdiction had been established on the basis of a defendant's federal claim in cases like *Edelmann*. He explained, "*however*," that the "cases brought forward to support" that understanding were suits by alleged patent infringers to declare a patent invalid, "*which of course themselves raise a federal question*."[372] He thus intimated that *Edelmann* may be viable, but only in patent infringement cases or, at most, in cases in which declaratory plaintiffs advance no affirmative claims of their own, but exclusively seek judicial declarations that they are not liable on federal claims for coercive relief that declaratory defendants might advance.[373] In cases of that kind, plaintiffs make no request for declarations regarding any state law claims they may have; by hypothesis, they possess no such claims. The only issues in view are necessarily federal. Declaratory suits by alleged patent infringers are good illustrations. Alleged infringers have no federal rights of their own to assert and frequently have no state law claims, either.[374] When they sue a patent holder, they invariably present only quintes-

---

would almost certainly raise. The UAW was *not* in a position to allege an existing federal claim on the part of Textron. The UAW had not violated the collective bargaining agreement, so Textron had no current complaint at all, federal or otherwise.

370. 523 U.S. at 660. Writing separately in *Textron*, Justice Breyer suggested a middle ground. By his account, a declaratory plaintiff can establish jurisdiction on the basis of the declaratory defendant's federal claim, but only when the declaratory defendant's coercive action advancing that federal claim against the declaratory plaintiff is imminent—in the sense that it already counts as an "actual" case or controversy. Id. at 665 (concurring opinion). Justice Breyer noted that the Declaratory Judgment Act specifically authorizes federal courts to declare "the rights and other legal relations of any interested party." See text accompanying note 140. So a federal court having jurisdiction of a declaratory defendant's federal claim can equally issue an authoritative declaration regarding a declaratory plaintiff's state law defense to that claim. By Breyer's account, it makes no difference that the declaratory plaintiff's state claim does not itself establish jurisdiction; that state claim still can be adjudicated in a declaratory judgment action once jurisdiction has been established via the declaratory defendant's federal claim. Justice Breyer drew support for this view from *Franchise Tax Board's* reference to *Edelmann*. His approach is appealing inasmuch as it would allow a party like the union in *Textron* to file suit in federal court without committing a breach that invites the employer to sue for coercive relief. See note 145 and accompanying text (explaining that declaratory judgment actions are supposed to allow litigants to force litigation without putting themselves at risk of suit for violating the very legal standards on which they need clarity).

371. 523 U.S. at 659.

372. Id. at 660 n.4 (emphasis added).

373. See note 351 and accompanying text.

374. Professor Doernberg and Professor Mushlin think of *Edelmann* as the declaratory judgment analog of *Well Works*. See notes 252–53 and accompanying text. Doernberg & Mushlin, note 342, at 574–77. Recall that in *Well Works*, Justice Holmes held that an alleged patent infringer could not invoke federal jurisdiction for a suit against a patentee, because the alleged infringer's claim

sentially federal issues: whether the holder's patent is valid and, if so, whether the alleged infringer has infringed that patent.[375]

In *Holmes Grp. v. Vornado Air Circulation Sys.*,[376] Holmes sued Vornado in federal district court, advancing a variety of state tort theories and, in addition, a request for a declaratory judgment that Holmes was not infringing Vornado's "trade dress" regarding the design of a fan grill.[377] Holmes invoked the district court's jurisdiction on the basis of §1331, §1332 (the diversity jurisdiction statute), and §1367 (the supplemental jurisdiction statute).[378] Since the trade dress issue was based on the Lanham Act, Holmes might also have relied on §1338, which confers permissive jurisdiction on district courts in cases arising under federal trademark statutes. Yet Holmes did not cite §1338. Vornado responded to Holmes' complaint by offering a (compulsory) counterclaim that Holmes was violating Vornado's patent. If Vornado had sued Holmes in the first instance, that patent infringement claim would have been within the district court's exclusive jurisdiction under §1338. Inasmuch as Vornado advanced the patent infringement claim as a counterclaim, however, its jurisdictional significance was problematic. The district court entertained Holmes' suit, sided with Holmes on the merits of the trade dress claim, and issued a declaratory judgment that Holmes was not infringing Vornado's trade dress rights.[379]

Vornado sought appellate review in the Court of Appeals for the Federal Circuit.[380] The governing statute, 28 U.S.C. §1295(1), makes that court's appellate jurisdiction turn on whether the district court's original jurisdiction rested, in whole or in part, on §1338. A further proviso states, however, that cases involving trademarks "and no other claims" under §1338 are subject to appellate review in the regional circuit courts of appeals. Both sides agreed that Holmes' complaint in the district court included no claim under the patent laws. Holmes itself insisted that even its trade dress claim did not im-

---

sounded in trade libel under state law. If there was a federal question in dispute in *Well Works*, it would only be introduced by the defendant patentee. In *Well Works*, however, the infringer alleged facts that made out a claim under state law. Alleged infringers may not be able to do that in all cases. A company may be accused of patent infringement (and thus have every reason to sue for a declaration of non-infringement), but not yet be able to allege that the patent holder has committed acts that injure the alleged infringer in a way that makes a state tort action available or feasible.

375. Moreover, there are equitable considerations in patent cases. Companies accused of patent infringement immediately begin to accrue liability for damages. If they cannot sue their accusers to settle matters early, they may run up massive liability waiting for patentees to sue *them* for infringement. See Lisa A. Dolak, *Declaratory Judgment Jurisdiction in Patent Cases: Restoring the Balance Between the Patentee and the Accused Infringer*, 38 B.C. L. Rev. 903 (1997). Alleged patent infringers thus genuinely need the ability to take the initiative. The legislative history behind the Declaratory Judgment Act suggests that at least some proponents had alleged patent infringers in mind as potential beneficiaries of the declaratory judgment device. Doernberg & Mushlin, note 342, at 564.

376. 122 S.Ct. 1889 (2002).

377. A "trade dress" infringement claim rests on the theory that the "design or packaging" of a product may be sufficiently distinct that it identifies the product with its manufacturer. When that occurs, use of the design by another company can create confusion regarding the "origin, sponsorship, or approval" of the product. See *Traffix Devices v. Marketing Displays*, 532 U.S. 23, 28 (2001).

378. See text accompanying notes 402–03.

379. The district court also enjoined Vornado from continuing to charge Holmes with violating its trade dress. That court stayed consideration of Vornado's patent infringement counterclaim until its treatment of Holmes' claims could be considered on appeal. If the declaratory judgment and the injunction favoring Holmes withstood review, the district court indicated that it would dismiss Vornado's counterclaim. The district court did not specify the jurisdictional basis on which it acted in awarding Holmes either declaratory or injunctive relief.

380. See Chapter II, note 79 and accompanying text.

plicate §1338, because Holmes had pressed that claim under alternative heads of jurisdiction (§1331, §1332, and §1367). In any case, according to Holmes, even if the district court might have exercised §1338 jurisdiction over the trade dress claim, that hypothetical point made no difference with respect to the Federal Circuit's jurisdiction on appeal. Under the proviso in §1295(1), the Federal Circuit had no appellate jurisdiction if the district court's original jurisdiction under §1338 depended on the presence of a trademark, as opposed to a patent law, claim. Vornado, for its part, contended that its own patent infringement counterclaim triggered the district court's jurisdiction under §1338 for purposes of the Federal Circuit's appellate jurisdiction under §1295(1).[381] The Federal Circuit embraced Vornado's argument. In the Supreme Court, Justice Scalia reversed. He explained that §1338, like §1331, is subject to the well-pleaded complaint rule. Accordingly, the district court's jurisdiction depended exclusively on the claims that Holmes alleged in its original complaint and could not rest on any defense or counterclaim that Vornado offered in response.[382] Since Holmes had advanced no claim arising under the patent laws, Justice Scalia vacated the Federal Circuit's judgment and remanded with instructions to transfer the case to the Court of Appeals for the Tenth Circuit.

In the end, the *Holmes* decision said nothing regarding *Edelmann's* continuing viability, either as an interpretation of §1338 or, more importantly, as an indication of the proper interpretation of §1331. Justice Scalia squarely decided only that the Federal Circuit had no jurisdiction to review the district court's judgment. To reach that decision, he held that, in a case in which a declaratory plaintiff fails to seek a declaration that the plaintiff is not infringing the defendant's patent, a district court has no jurisdiction under §1338 even though the defendant files a compulsory patent infringement counterclaim. That holding did not (necessarily) establish that a declaratory plaintiff cannot

381. Both Vornado and Holmes were jockeying for strategic advantage. In earlier litigation between Vornado and another company, the Court of Appeals for the Tenth Circuit had found Vornado's trade dress claim regarding the fan grill without merit. Holmes chose to sue Vornado in the United States District Court for the District of Kansas in hopes that the Tenth Circuit's previous decision in that other case would be given preclusive effect—both in the district court and on appeal in the Tenth Circuit itself. Holmes deliberately avoided relying on §1338 as the basis for the district court's jurisdiction in order to ensure that any appeal in the case would go to the Tenth Circuit rather than to the Federal Circuit, where Holmes was less sure of a favorable outcome. Vornado obviously hoped to frustrate Holmes' strategy by pressing its own patent infringement counterclaim in the district court and then arguing before the Federal Circuit that the counterclaim was sufficient to justify the Federal Circuit's appellate jurisdiction. Initially, Holmes' strategy was successful. The district court did hold that the previous Tenth Circuit decision was entitled to preclusive effect against Vornado. Vornado, too, was at first successful. The Federal Circuit took jurisdiction and reversed. Ultimately, however, Holmes prevailed when the Supreme Court reversed the Federal Circuit.

382. Vornado argued that Congress' purpose in establishing the Federal Circuit would be better served by permitting a patent infringement counterclaim in the district court to be a sufficient basis for Federal Circuit appellate jurisdiction. In that way, the Federal Circuit would be able to establish and maintain greater national uniformity regarding patent law matters. There are good and familiar reasons for demanding that original jurisdiction in a district court must turn on the issues that appear at the outset of a case and thus can be pleaded in the complaint. Those reasons have no force with respect to appellate jurisdiction, which can easily depend on issues that emerge after a case is under way. See notes 18–20 and accompanying text. Justice Scalia acknowledged that it might be sensible to channel most or all patent issues to a single national appellate court. As a matter of fact, however, there are numerous circumstances in which regional circuit courts, and even state courts, routinely handle patent law issues. In any event, he insisted, the Supreme Court's function is not to determine what result would effectuate congressional policy, but rather to determine "what the words of the statute must fairly be understood to mean." 122 S.Ct. at 1895.

invoke §1338 jurisdiction if the plaintiff *does* insert in an original complaint a request for a declaratory judgment that the plaintiff is not infringing the defendant's patent. That, of course, is what happened in *Edelmann*. Nor did the *Holmes* decision specify whether the *Edelmann* model may operate outside the context of §1338. As a matter of fact, the district court in *Holmes* may have had all the jurisdiction it needed by virtue of §1332 and §1367 and required nothing more from §1338 or §1331 to justify its power to consider the federal issues in the case.[383]

In light of the extant case law, the viability of *Edelmann's* analysis remains debatable. Certainly, plaintiffs can obtain §1331 jurisdiction if they want clarity regarding their own affirmative federal claims—claims that they themselves might place in well-pleaded complaints seeking a traditional coercive form of relief. No one has ever suggested otherwise.[384] In light of *Skelly*, however, plaintiffs cannot invoke §1331 jurisdiction by requesting a declaratory judgment that a potential federal argument available to the defendant is invalid, where that argument would arise exclusively as a defense rather than as a legal claim for some form of relief.[385] It is not clear whether plaintiffs can invoke §1331 jurisdiction by requesting a declaratory judgment that a potential federal argument available to a defendant is invalid where that federal argument might be translated into a federal claim for coercive relief. Academic observers commonly contend that plaintiffs should be able to establish §1331 jurisdiction if they seek a declaration regarding the validity of a federal claim for coercive relief available to the defendant.[386] At the very least, jurisdiction should be available if declaratory plaintiffs request only a declaration regarding the merits of such a potential federal claim by the defendant and do not also request a declaration regarding the validity of their own state law claims. This last possibility tracks Justice Scalia's aside in *Textron*.[387]

G. Preemption

Arguments that federal law preempts state law are commonly adjudicated in state court. Plaintiffs are masters of the theories they wish to litigate and choose to advance state law claims in the first instance. Defendants then argue federal preemption in defense, but cannot remove on that basis. In some instances, however, federal law occupies the entire field in which disputes arise, displacing any state law that would otherwise operate. When that is true, plaintiffs are not free to characterize their claims as state law matters. By hypothesis, there *is* no state law, but only superseding federal

---

383. If diversity jurisdiction pursuant to §1332 was good, the district court had power on that basis to consider Holmes' request for a declaratory judgment that it was not infringing Vornado's trade dress. There was no need also to rely on §1331 and thus to implicate Holmes' capacity to trigger §1331 jurisdiction by seeking a declaration that a potential trade dress infringement claim belonging to Vornado was invalid.

384. See text accompanying note 349.

385. See text accompanying note 339.

386. For example, Professor Monaghan admits the possibility that the Declaratory Judgment Act "permits party realignment and alteration in the timing of an otherwise proper federal court suit." Monaghan, note 142, at 240. Yet he warns that the existence of a right of action as a vehicle for suit remains an independent problem. See note 349.

387. See text accompanying note 373.

law.[388] Plaintiffs' claims are therefore necessarily federal in nature. It follows *ceteris paribus* that they might have filed suit in federal court in the first instance, invoking jurisdiction under §1331. Accordingly, defendants are entitled to remove.[389]

The Supreme Court hesitates to find "complete" preemption and invariably demands a clear statement of congressional "intent" to displace state law entirely.[390] In *Avco v. Aero Lodge*,[391] an employer sued a union in state court for an injunction against a labor strike. The union removed the suit to federal court on the theory that §301 of the Labor Management Relations Act preempted state law regarding labor contracts and occupied the field with federal common law. Accordingly, the employer had no state law contract action against the union, but only a federal common law claim—which would have justified federal jurisdiction if the employer had sued in federal court in the first instance. Justice Douglas agreed. Given *Lincoln Mills*, an action to enforce a general labor contract was governed by federal substantive law, wherever the plaintiff chose to file it.[392] In *Caterpillar v. Williams*,[393] however, Justice Brennan explained that *Avco* meant only that §301 federalized claims under a collective bargaining agreement. State law remained available to individual employees suing to enforce personal employment contracts. Those employees could characterize their claims as state law matters and thus avoid removal.

The cases on ERISA follow a similar pattern. In *Metropolitan Life Ins. Co. v. Taylor*,[394] Justice O'Connor explained that ERISA displaced state law with respect to the kinds of claims about which Congress was primarily concerned: suits *by* "participants, beneficiaries, and fiduciaries."[395] Accordingly, an employee no longer had any state claims to ad-

---

388. In the instances in which the Court has found federal preemption to have this effect, the content of the federal law that displaces state law is largely federal common law fashioned by the federal courts. Recall that when federal common law governs at all, it governs irrespective of whether a case is handled in federal or state court. See note 114 and accompanying text.

389. See Chapter VI, text accompanying note 135; Comment, *Federal Preemption, Removal Jurisdiction, and the Well-Pleaded Complaint Rule*, 51 U. Chi. L. Rev. 634, 664–65 (1984). By contrast, if defendants merely have ordinary issue or claim preclusion defenses to state claims filed in state court, they cannot remove—even if those defenses are anchored in federal law. *Rivet v. Regions Bank*, 522 U.S. 470 (1998). In *Rivet*, the Court disclaimed a notorious footnote in *Federated Dep't Stores v. Moitie*, 452 U.S. 394, 397 n.2 (1981), which had suggested that a defendant could remove on the strength of an argument that a plaintiff's state claim was precluded by a federal judgment in a prior action. Justice Ginsburg explained in *Rivet* that while a claim preclusion defense to a state claim may be federal in character, it can no more be the basis for removal than can other federal defenses. It is only when the defendant shows that the *plaintiff's* claim is necessarily federal (because it is completely preempted by federal law) that removal is available. For a discussion of the problems the footnote in *Moitie* had created, see Miller, note 331, at 1800–18.

390. E.g., *Pilot Life Ins. Co. v. Dedeaux*, 481 U.S. 41, 55–57 (1987). In this instance, the Court has consulted legislative history much more than usual. See, e.g., id. at 46, 55; but see Chapter I, notes 35–37 and accompanying text (discussing the Court's typical preference for resting judgment on the text of a statute rather than on background materials).

391. 390 U.S. 557 (1968).

392. See *Textile Workers Union v. Lincoln Mills*, 353 U.S. 448 (1957); notes 95–98. Douglas recognized that the Norris-LaGuardia Act would bar the federal court to which the action was removed from issuing the injunction that the employer had hoped to win from the state courts. But he explained that the "nature of the relief" that the federal court might award after it adjudicated a suit could not affect the court's jurisdiction to adjudicate in the first instance. Jurisdiction, he said, depended entirely on the federal nature of the employer's claim, coupled with the defendant's choice to remove. 390 U.S. at 560.

393. 482 U.S. 386 (1987).

394. 481 U.S. 58 (1987).

395. See text accompanying note 364.

vance regarding the way her demand for benefits had been handled by Metropolitan (an employee benefit plan within the meaning of the Act). Those claims had been federalized. Since the employee might have filed suit in federal court in the first instance, Metropolitan was entitled to remove. In *Franchise Tax Board*,[396] however, Justice Brennan held that ERISA did not displace state law with respect to claims about which Congress was *not* primarily concerned: suits by other parties (like the Tax Board) *against* "participants, beneficiaries, and fiduciaries" (like CLVT). Accordingly, the Tax Board's claims had not been federalized, and CLVT could not remove.[397]

Justice Brennan fortified his conclusion in *Franchise Tax Board* with a separate argument. In *Avco*, the LMRA not only displaced state substantive law, but also provided the plaintiff in that case with a federal right of action to vindicate its federalized claim in the courts.[398] In *Franchise Tax Board*, by contrast, ERISA did not provide litigants like the Board with a federal right of action. Brennan took that as further evidence that Congress had not meant ERISA to federalize the claims the Board wished to advance. Later, in *Caterpillar*,[399] Justice Brennan explained that Congress can manifest a purpose to preempt formerly state law claims without ensuring that plaintiffs can obtain the same "remedy" in federal court that they might have obtained from the state courts.[400] In *Franchise Tax Board*, then, Brennan regarded Congress' failure to provide the Board with a *right of action* as probative evidence that Congress did not mean to federalize the Board's claims. But in *Caterpillar*, he said that Congress' failure to ensure that a plaintiff might obtain a particular form of *relief* lacked the same significance in determining the congressional design.[401]

---

396. *Franchise Tax Bd. v. Constr. Laborers Vacation Trust*, 463 U.S. 1 (1983); see notes 352–67 and accompanying text.

397. In *Rush Prudential HMO v. Moran*, 122 S.Ct. 2151 (2002), an individual sued an HMO in state court under a state statute providing for independent medical review of the denial of health benefits. The HMO removed the action on the theory that ERISA preempted the state statute. The federal district court concluded that ERISA did not completely preempt the statute and thus remanded the case to state court. After additional complicated litigation, the case reached the Supreme Court, where Justice O'Connor held that the state statute was not preempted. Nevertheless, Justice O'Connor declined simply to sustain the district court's original disposition. Since a claim under the state law "would seem to be akin to a suit to compel compliance" with a health care plan pursuant to a provision of ERISA, she hesitated to approve the district court's judgment that, for want of complete preemption, removal was unavailable. Id. at 2157 n.2. For (pre-*Rush*) discussions, see Mary P. Twitchell, *Characterizing Federal Claims: Preemption, Removal, and the Arising-Under Jurisdiction of the Federal Courts*, 54 Geo. Wash. L. Rev. 812, 840–70 (1986); Note, *Understanding Preemption Removal Under ERISA §502*, 72 N.Y.U. L. Rev. 578 (1997).

398. Recall the Court's holding in *Lincoln Mills* that §301(b) creates a federal right of action for suits the federal courts have jurisdiction to entertain pursuant to §301(a) and in which they apply federal common law. See text accompanying note 131.

399. See note 393 and accompanying text.

400. *Caterpillar*, 482 U.S. at 391 n.4.

401. See note 121 (discussing the difference between rights of action and remedies). In light of *Merrell Dow*, this may make a certain amount of sense. The absence of a federally created right of action may rob a federal court of jurisdiction, even though the substantive claim at bar is federal. See notes 300–31 and accompanying text. Yet one would not have expected to hear this from Justice Brennan, given his dissent in *Merrell Dow*. See notes 315–16 and accompanying text. Professor Hirshman has written a searching history and analysis of the interplay between the right-of-action cases and federal jurisdiction—up to and including *Franchise Tax Board*. Linda R. Hirshman, *Whose Law Is It, Anyway? A Reconsideration of Federal Question Jurisdiction Over Cases of Mixed State and Federal Law*, 60 Ind. L.J. 17 (1984).

H. Supplemental Jurisdiction

A federal district court's jurisdiction to adjudicate a "civil action" under §1331 depends on the existence of a substantial federal claim. The scope of that jurisdiction, once established, extends further. Pursuant to 28 U.S.C. §1367(a), the court has "supplemental" jurisdiction[402] over "all other claims that are so related" to the federal claim "that they form part of the same case or controversy under Article III."[403] In *Raygor v. Regents*,[404] the Court declined to read §1367 to confer jurisdiction over state law claims against states that refuse to waive sovereign immunity. If the statute were to extend supplemental jurisdiction in that way, it would invite constitutional objections.[405] Beyond the special sovereign immunity context, however, the Court has read §1367 liberally. In *City of Chicago v. Intnat'l College of Surgeons*,[406] Justice O'Conner said that a "case" within the meaning of Article III (and, by extension, supplemental jurisdiction under §1367) generally extends to state claims that "derive from a common nucleus of operative fact."[407]

In *Surgeons*, the Commission on Chicago Historical and Architectural Landmarks designated a building owned by ICS as an historical landmark. ICS sought judicial review of the Commission's action in state court. In that suit, ICS argued both that the Commission should have allowed ICS an exemption on the basis of economic hardship and that the landmarks ordinance on which the Commission relied violated the fourteenth amendment. The Commission removed the case to federal court on the theory

---

402. This comparatively new statute substitutes the term "supplemental" jurisdiction for more traditional terminology. The shift was deliberate. Previous nomenclature could be confusing. Typically, courts referred to the exercise of jurisdiction over additional claims as "pendent" jurisdiction and to the exercise of jurisdiction over additional parties as "ancillary" jurisdiction. Occasionally, however, courts used the label "pendent" jurisdiction to identify either additional claims or additional parties introduced by the plaintiff and "ancillary" jurisdiction to identify additional claims or parties introduced by the defendant. Under §1367, one label covers all variations on the same theme: power to consider matters that are related to cases over which a federal court has jurisdiction but would not otherwise fall within the court's authority to address. This said, it must also be said that §1367 does not occupy the field, but only codifies "much of the common-law doctrine of ancillary jurisdiction" that courts otherwise enjoy. *Peacock v. Thomas*, 516 U.S. 349, 354 n.5 (1996). Given the sweep of supplemental jurisdiction under §1367, it is hard to anticipate what occasion federal district courts might have to rest on a residual basis of power to *decide* issues. More often, they may rely on extra-§1367 authority to *forgo* decisions on state claims in their discretion. See note 417 and accompanying text.

403. This general rule, established by §1367(a), is subject to exceptions, identified by §1367(b), for claims advanced in certain diversity actions.

404. 534 U.S. 533 (2002).

405. See Chapter X, notes 244–51 and accompanying text.

406. 522 U.S. 156 (1997); see note 257.

407. 522 U.S. at 165, quoting *United Mine Workers v. Gibbs*, 383 U.S. 715, 725 (1966). Professor Matasar argues that this definition neglects the more expansive definitions of a case envisioned by the civil rules on joinder of claims and parties. Richard A. Matasar, *Rediscovering "One Constitutional Case": Procedural Rules and the Rejection of the Gibbs Test for Supplemental Jurisdiction*, 71 Calif. L. Rev. 1399 (1983). For an exhaustive discussion, see Susan Bandes, *The Idea of a Case*, 42 Stan. L. Rev. 227 (1990). In this context, the *Osborn* "ingredient" test for identifying Article III cases will not answer. See text accompanying note 12. By hypothesis, federal courts can identify both the federal question that triggers jurisdiction and the state claims over which they are asked to exercise supplemental jurisdiction.

that ICS might have filed its action there pursuant to §1331.[408] Justice O'Connor agreed that the fourteenth amendment claim would have triggered §1331 jurisdiction and that removal was therefore proper.[409] Moreover, she explained that §1367(a) extended the federal court's jurisdiction to ICS's state claim that the Commission had reached an erroneous decision. Justice O'Connor recognized that the state claim was a peculiarly local matter. To determine it, a federal court would have to review the Commission's record, giving deference to the Commission's expertise and judgment. Yet since §1367(a) explicitly refers to "all" other claims within a constitutional "case," Justice O'-Connor refused to make any exceptions.[410]

Chief Justice Marshall recognized in *Osborn* that some measure of supplemental jurisdiction is a practical necessity if federal courts are to adjudicate the "whole case."[411] In other instances, the Court has identified three additional reasons for extending a federal court's reach beyond the claims that originally trigger jurisdiction. In *Hurn v. Oursler*,[412] the Court recognized that supplemental jurisdiction is necessary in some cases to avoid a multiplicity of suits regarding the same subject matter. If a plaintiff has

---

408. See text accompanying notes 250–51.

409. Justice O'Connor was persuaded that §1367 applies to §1441 cases. *Surgeons*, 522 U.S. at 165–66. See id. at 176 n.1 (Ginsburg, J., dissenting) (expressing agreement on the point). See Joan Steinman, *Supplemental Jurisdiction in §1441 Removed Cases: An Unsurveyed Frontier of Congress' Handiwork*, 35 Ariz. L. Rev. 305 (1993). But see Oakley, note 87, at 1028–29 (reporting that the ALI recommends restricting §1367 to original jurisdiction cases).

410. Justice O'Connor acknowledged *Chicago R.I. & P.R. Co. v. Stude*, 346 U.S. 574 (1954), in which the Court held that a case requiring a district court to consider state issues previously determined by a state administrative agency would not qualify as an original diversity action, but, instead, would contemplate impermissible appellate jurisdiction. See Chapter VI, notes 196–225 and accompanying text. Yet she explained that under §1367, it was enough that ICS's federal claim would have established a "civil action" for purposes of §1331. Professor Woolhandler and Professor Collins read *Surgeons* to avoid either endorsing or overruling *Stude*. When the Court accepts a case in which *Stude* figures more directly, they urge the Court to jettison that case. Their survey of historical materials persuades them that it is not at all out of character or troubling for federal courts to determine state law issues that call for some measure of deference to state agencies. Ann Woolhandler & Michael G. Collins, *Judicial Federalism and the Administrative States*, 87 Calif. L. Rev. 613 (1999). Justice O'Connor was plainly sensitive in *Surgeons* to the history behind the enactment of §1367 in 1991. In *Finley v. United States*, 490 U.S. 545 (1989), a widow sued the United States in federal court, claiming that the FAA was responsible for the death of her husband and children in an airline accident. That claim was within the federal court's exclusive jurisdiction under the Federal Tort Claims Act. The plaintiff also included a state tort claim that a private company had negligently positioned the power lines with which the plane collided. Justice Scalia said that the federal court had no supplemental jurisdiction over the latter claim. He acknowledged that Article III would allow Congress to extend supplemental jurisdiction to claims against additional parties. Yet he declined to reach that result without more explicit guidance from Congress. The following year, Congress provided that very guidance in the form of §1367. In *Surgeons*, accordingly, the justices acquiesced in a clear statement responding to *Finley*. For discussions of *Finley* and §1367, see Denis F. McLaughlin, *The Federal Supplemental Jurisdiction Statute—A Constitutional and Statutory Analysis*, 24 Ariz. St. L.J. 849 (1992); Richard D. Freer, *Compounding Confusion and Hampering Diversity: Life After Finley and the Supplemental Jurisdiction Statute*, 40 Emory L.J. 445 (1991); *Essays, Compounding or Creating Confusion About Supplemental Jurisdiction? A Reply to Professor Freer*, 40 Emory L.J. 943 (1991) (Rowe, Burbank & Mengler).

411. *Osborn*, 22 U.S. at 822; see text accompanying note 6.

412. 289 U.S. 238 (1933). In *Hurn*, the Court linked supplemental jurisdiction to the law of preclusion—by permitting federal courts to determine state claims that were part of the plaintiff's "cause of action" and thus would ordinarily be foreclosed in future litigation between the two parties. This is one instance in which the Supreme Court has acknowledged the confusion that surrounds the "cause of action" formulation. The *Hurn* approach to supplemental jurisdiction has been discarded in favor of the approach codified in §1367(a).

both federal and state claims to advance, and the federal claim must be filed in federal court because it is within the federal court's exclusive jurisdiction, the federal court must have supplemental jurisdiction to determine the state claim as well. Otherwise, the plaintiff will be forced to press the state law claim in a separate lawsuit in state court. In *United Mine Workers v. Gibbs*,[413] the Court recognized that similar, though less severe, difficulties arise when federal jurisdiction of a federal claim is not exclusive. In that event, supplemental jurisdiction in federal court is not essential to avoid more than one suit; the plaintiff is free to take both federal and state claims to state court. Yet if that is the result, the plaintiff will be denied the very promise that §1331 holds out—namely, the ability to advance federal claims in federal court. Finally, in *Siler v. Louisville & Nashville R.R. Co.*,[414] the Court explained that supplemental jurisdiction provides federal courts with the opportunity to avoid federal constitutional issues by resolving disputes on state law grounds.

A federal question can invoke §1331 jurisdiction only if it is substantial. Recall, however, that in *Bell v. Hood*[415] the Court indicated that any non-frivolous claim will suffice. The Court recognizes that plaintiffs may be tempted to inject questionable federal claims into their complaints in hopes of obtaining federal jurisdiction over related state law issues.[416] In the main, however, the check on that kind of strategic behavior is not a demanding test for determining whether a federal court has power to consider state issues. It is, instead, the district court's discretion to forgo the *exercise* of that power. Pursuant to §1367(c), district courts may decline to exercise supplemental jurisdiction over a state claim if: (1) the claim "raises a novel or complex issue of State law;" (2) the claim "substantially predominates" over the federal claim that triggered jurisdiction in the first place; (3) the federal claim that triggered jurisdiction is dismissed, leaving only state claims in the case; or (4) in "exceptional circumstances," there are "other compelling reasons for declining jurisdiction." Even this list of open-ended standards is not exhaustive. In *Surgeons*, Justice O'Connor read §1367(c) to reflect the considerations that the Court itself had previously identified: "[A] federal court should consider and weigh in each case, and at every stage of the litigation, the values of judicial economy, convenience, fairness, and comity."[417] The framework, then, is straightforward. A non-frivolous federal claim carries with it supplemental jurisdiction of related state issues, unless and until a district court determines, on one or more of these grounds, to dismiss state claims in its discretion.[418]

District court authority to dismiss supplemental state claims can produce inconvenient results. In the first instance, §1367 invites a plaintiff to aggregate federal and related state claims in a single lawsuit in federal court. Concomitantly, state preclusion law typically encourages the plaintiff to press all related claims in a single lawsuit on pain of forfeiting claims that are omitted.[419] A plaintiff who advances both federal and

---

413. 383 U.S. 715 (1966).

414. 213 U.S. 175 (1909). But see Chapter X, notes 361–66 and accompanying text (discussing the way the *Pennhurst* decision regarding state sovereign immunity can affect this feature of supplemental jurisdiction in some instances).

415. 327 U.S. 678 (1946); see notes 258–62 and accompanying text.

416. See *Hagans v. Lavine*, 415 U.S. 528, 552 (1974) (Powell, J., dissenting) (insisting that federal claims must have more than a "glimmer of merit" to justify exercising supplemental jurisdiction over state law claims).

417. 522 U.S. at 173, quoting *Carnegie-Mellon v. Cohill*, 484 U.S. 343, 350 (1988).

418. See *Lapides*, 122 S.Ct. at 1643 (confirming a district court's jurisdiction after all federal claims are dispatched but before related state law claims are similarly dismissed).

419. See Chapter VI, note 164 and accompanying text (discussing claim preclusion).

state claims in federal court appears, then, to be proceeding in precisely the way that the federal statute and state preclusion law suggest. Thereafter, however, the federal district court may decide to dismiss some or all state claims in its discretion. And in the interim, the time for filing those state claims in state court may have run out. To avoid that problem, §1367 tolls the relevant state statute of limitations while state claims are pending in federal court.[420] In the *Raygor* case, the Court construed the tolling provision not to apply to state law claims that are dismissed in federal court on the basis of a state's sovereign immunity.[421] Once again, the Court cited the constitutional concerns that would be presented if the statute were read to preserve state law claims subject to sovereign immunity.[422]

---

420. Professor Oakley has explained that the tolling provision not only avoids unfairness, but also protects the integrity of the federal courts' discretion into the bargain. In the absence of this provision in §1367, district courts might feel pressed to retain state law claims after the state filing deadline has passed, even if they would otherwise use their discretion to dismiss them in favor of state court adjudication. Oakley, note 87, at 945. Cf. *Cohill*, 484 U.S. at 352–53 (1988) (recognizing these problems).

421. See note 404 and accompanying text.

422. See Chapter X, notes 244–51 and accompanying text. Specifically, §1367(d) states that state filing periods are tolled with respect to state law claims that are "dismissed" under §1367(a). Specialists debate whether the tolling provision applies only to claims dismissed in the exercise of the district court discretion established by §1367(c), or to claims dismissed for other reasons, as well. In *Raygor*, the Supreme Court dealt exclusively with state claims dismissed on the basis of state sovereign immunity. 534 U.S. at 546. See Chapter VI, note 104 (noting constitutional doubts about federal statutes prescribing procedures for state courts to follow when they determine state law claims).

Chapter IX

Justiciability

Litigants who seek adjudication in federal court must satisfy a series of doctrines that, taken together, establish the conditions under which a matter is "justiciable" in an Article III tribunal. These justiciability doctrines bear their own names. Yet they illustrate not different ideas, but different circumstances in which the Supreme Court recognizes and elaborates the same operative themes. In the main, the justiciability doctrines reflect and foster structural values: the separation of powers and federalism. They differentiate the judiciary's role from the legislative and executive responsibilities of Congress and the President and screen some matters out of federal court and into the hands of local authorities and state courts. Justiciability doctrines also serve functional objectives. They ensure that federal courts adjudicate legal questions in light of facts and arguments marshaled by genuine adversaries who have an incentive to explore all relevant considerations. Sound judicial process, in turn, produces workable decisions not only for the litigants at bar, but also for others whose interests may be affected and for the public at large.

State courts need not employ the justiciability doctrines that govern access to the federal courts.[1] Accordingly, when a federal court declines to entertain a suit for want of justiciability, a state court may be open to receive it.[2] State courts often have their own justiciability doctrines that bar access there as well. In that event, issues are denied adjudication in any court at all.[3] This is not an occasion when state courts are obliged to entertain federal claims. If a question is non-justiciable in federal court, it is by hypothesis a matter that can be resolved without adjudication of any kind. State courts thus have a valid excuse for withholding the state forum.[4]

The Supreme Court has developed standing doctrine primarily as a check on the behavior of the inferior Article III courts. The Court itself performs unique referee functions that call for greater flexibility.[5] Nevertheless, standing doctrine formally governs the exercise of federal judicial power at all levels, and what the Court specifies regarding the lower courts' purview equally applies to the Court's own preserve. The Court sometimes defuses the resulting tension when it can open its own doors to litigants without,

1. *Intnat'l Primate Protection League v. Administrators of Tulane Ed. Fund*, 500 U.S. 72, 78 n.4 (1991); *Pernell v. City of San Jose*, 485 U.S. 1, 8 (1988).

2. See Christopher S. Elmendorf, *State Courts, Citizen Suits, and the Enforcement of Federal Environmental Law by Non-Article III Plaintifffs*, 110 Yale L.J. 1003 (2001) (arguing that environmentalists who lack "standing" to enforce federal regulatory statutes in federal court may find state courts more hospitable).

3. But see Helen Hershkoff, *State Courts and the 'Passive Virtues': Rethinking the Judicial Function*, 114 Harv. L. Rev. 1833 (2001) (urging state courts not to adopt federal justiciability law wholesale but rather to develop independent state law doctrines tailored to local conditions).

4. See Chapter VI, notes 97–106 and accompanying text.

5. See Chapter VII, text accompanying notes 224–27.

at the same time, opening the doors of the district courts. In *ASARCO v. Kadish*,[6] for example, the Court acknowledged that the plaintiff in the state courts below would not have had standing to begin in an Article III court. Yet the plaintiff had won in state court. With the case in that posture, the Court explained that the *defendant* had a sufficient interest in upsetting the state court judgment to invoke the Court's appellate jurisdiction. In cases like *ASARCO*, accordingly, the justiciability doctrines that channel litigation to state court in the first instance do not foreclose federal adjudication later in the Supreme Court.[7]

Roughly speaking, the justiciability doctrines govern *what* matters are susceptible to determination in federal court, *who* can invoke federal judicial power, and *when* federal court action is timely.[8] Some of the most basic doctrines go to *what* matters are justiciable in the sense that they disclaim duties the federal courts cannot perform: Federal courts cannot issue "advisory" opinions, render judgments that are not "final" within the judicial branch, or resolve "political" questions. The doctrine of "standing" originally identified *who* may sue in an Article III court and continues to address that question today. The "ripeness" and "mootness" doctrines govern *when* issues can be considered. It is dangerous, however, to take generalizations of this kind very far. For example, in the context of standing the Court has made it perfectly clear that *who* is entitled to be in an Article III tribunal is *not* the whole of the matter at all or anything like it.[9] All the justiciability doctrines serve the same master: the Supreme Court's sense of the federal judiciary's role in relation to the other branches of the central government and the states. The Court commonly cites decisions rendered under the various justiciability doctrines interchangeably and thus underscores the cross-currents running between them.

In recent years, standing has become the central focus. Other justiciability doctrines spin off from standing and the ideas that standing entails. Standing doctrine, in turn, is the product of a profound struggle between competing conceptions of the federal courts, conceptions that are roughly captured in the private rights model of adjudication and its rival, the public rights model.[10] That struggle has obvious political and ideological significance. And it is not yet at an end. Standing doctrine is therefore unruly, even incoherent, and by some accounts manipulable. The key to understanding is an appreciation of the jurisprudential backdrop and the monumental difficulties the Supreme Court faces in creating intellectual order out of so much conflicting material.

---

6. 490 U.S. 605 (1989).

7. The outcome might have been different if the plaintiff had *lost* in state court and then sought Supreme Court review. See *Doremus v. Bd. of Ed.*, 342 U.S. 429 (1952) (declining to find standing in that kind of case). For arguments that state courts should be required to observe federal justiciability standards, see William A. Fletcher, *The "Case or Controversy" Requirement in State Court Adjudication of Federal Questions*, 78 Calif. L. Rev. 263 (1990); Jonathan D. Varat, *Variable Justiciability and the Duke Power Case*, 58 Tex. L. Rev. 273 (1980).

8. See Henry P. Monaghan, *Constitutional Adjudication: The Who and When*, 82 Yale L.J. 1363 (1973).

9. See text accompanying notes 121–22.

10. See Chapter I, notes 61–72, 78–91 and accompanying text.

A. Basic Doctrines

1. Advisory Opinions

Federal courts cannot offer opinions that are merely advisory in the sense that they have no decisive consequences. The classic illustration came early. In 1793, President Washington asked his Secretary of State (Jefferson) to seek advice from the Supreme Court regarding the interpretation of treaties with European nations. When Jefferson wrote to the justices, however, they declined to act as consultants. In a famous letter addressed to Washington himself, the justices said there were "strong arguments" against the "propriety" of "deciding" questions "extrajudicially"—namely, the "lines of separation drawn by the Constitution between the three departments of the government."[11]

By conventional account, judicial advice on legal questions outside the context of an actual lawsuit does not constitute *judicial* action at all, but is, instead, a species of executive or legislative behavior beyond the judicial purview. Justice Frankfurter explained, accordingly, that Article III bars advisory opinions insofar as it limits the exercise of judicial power to "cases" or "controversies" and thus restricts federal courts to the resolution of actual disputes pursuant to the private rights model.[12] When a federal court is asked merely to express its opinion on a matter in the abstract, it has no genuine case or controversy to determine and thus has no justification for taking action *as a court.*[13]

The ban on advisory opinions also reflects pragmatic methodological considerations.[14] By resisting involvement in the formulation of legal positions in the first instance, federal courts make themselves available to consider problems afresh at a later time, when it is essential to do so in order to resolve an actual case. Courts deliver better answers when issues are presented by self-interested advocates in the context of a discrete fact pattern. When they determine questions in the abstract, they are more

---

11. See Correspondence of the Justices, August 8, 1793, reprt'd in The Federal Courts and the Federal System 93 (Fallon, Meltzer & Shapiro eds. 1996). The justices called attention to the specific provision in Article II authorizing the President to "require the Opinion, in writing, of the principal Officer in each of the Executive Departments, upon any Subject relating to the Duties of their respective Offices." U.S. Const. art. II, §2, cl.1. That provision implied that Washington was limited to seeking advice from within the executive branch. The justices may actually have resisted any general role as advisors to the President in order to husband their resources and establish their independence within the new national scheme. Chief Justice Jay had previously prepared (but may not have sent) a letter to Washington challenging the constitutionality of forcing the justices to "ride circuit." Russell Wheeler, *Extrajudicial Activities of the Early Supreme Court*, 1973 Sup. Ct. Rev. 123, 148. See Chapter II, note 54 and accompanying text.

12. See Felix Frankfurter, *A Note on Advisory Opinions*, 37 Harv. L. Rev. 1002 (1924).

13. In this instance, an interpretation placed on the Constitution's text serves the structural values associated with the separation principle. See Chapter I, text accompanying note 17. Professor Pushaw contends that the private rights model befits Article III "controversies" defined by the identity of the parties. But he argues that the founding generation regarded "cases" implicating federal questions as occasions for elaborating the law, apart from any immediate need to do so in order to resolve disputes. Robert J. Pushaw, Jr., *Article III's Case/Controversy Distinction and the Dual Functions of Federal Courts*, 69 Notre Dame L. Rev. 447 (1994). See Chapter II, note 27 (noting alternative understandings).

14. See *United States v Freuhauf*, 365 U.S. 146, 157 (1961); Chapter I, notes 61–72 and accompanying text (discussing traditional adjudication under the private rights model).

likely to make mistakes or to announce sweeping principles that must be abandoned later when it appears that a more variegated approach is required.[15]

Concerns about advisory opinions figured in the formulation of the Declaratory Judgment Act.[16] In *Willing v. Chicago Aud. Ass'n*,[17] Justice Brandeis warned that "the power conferred upon the federal judiciary" did not extend to awarding a "declaratory judgment" that merely clarified a legal issue. That warning raised concern that the Court would find a general statute empowering the federal courts to issue declaratory judgments to be an invalid attempt to authorize advisory opinions. Soon thereafter, however, the Court accepted appellate jurisdiction in *Nashville, C. & St. L. Ry. v. Wallace*,[18] in which the plaintiff had sued in state court for a declaratory judgment (authorized by state law) that a state tax violated the Constitution. In *Wallace*, Justice Stone explained that since the plaintiff might have sought injunctive relief, his decision to seek only a declaration of his rights did not deprive the matter of its character as an Article III "case."[19]

Encouraged by *Wallace*, Congress enacted the Declaratory Judgment Act, 28 U.S.C. §2201, which enables federal courts to issue declaratory judgments "in a case of actual controversy." The Supreme Court upheld the new Act in *Aetna Life Ins. Co. v. Haworth*.[20] Chief Justice Hughes was satisfied that Congress had made no attempt to authorize advisory opinions, because §2201 limits declaratory judgments to "cases" on which the federal courts are entitled to rule. In a famous line, Hughes said that the "operation" of the Declaratory Judgment Act is "procedural only" in that it provides "remedies" and defines "procedure" for suits that, by hypothesis, satisfy the constitutional requirements for federal adjudication.[21] Accordingly, litigants can use the Declaratory Judgment Act to obtain authoritative declarations that will resolve a current case or controversy.

Litigants cannot use §2201 to obtain clarity regarding particular *issues* that will be presented in a future case or controversy. In *Calderon v. Ashmus*,[22] California prison inmates alleged that they planned to file individual habeas corpus petitions attacking their criminal convictions (and death sentences) in federal court. Pursuant to 28 U.S.C. §2263 (then recently enacted), California could insist that those petitions had to be filed within 180 days after the completion of direct review in state court—*if* California provided lawyers to help prisoners under sentence of death in state postconviction proceedings.[23] Otherwise, the prisoners had a year in which to file their petitions. State officials declared that California had done what was necessary to trigger the 180-day filing period. The prisoners in *Ashmus* contended that California did not qualify and, accordingly, that they had twice that long to prepare their petitions. They alleged that they were in the very dilemma that the Declaratory Judgment Act was meant to address.

---

15. See notes 401–03 and accompanying text (discussing this rationale in connection with the ripeness doctrine).
16. See Chapter II, note 77 and accompanying text.
17. 277 U.S. 274 (1928).
18. 288 U.S. 249 (1933).
19. Id. at 264.
20. 300 U.S. 227 (1937).
21. Id. at 240. But see Chapter XI, note 214 (discussing Chief Justice Rehnquist's suggestion that declaratory judgments may not be entitled to preclusive effect). For a discussion of the functions of modern declaratory actions, see Chapter VIII, notes 140–47 and accompanying text.
22. 523 U.S. 740 (1998).
23. See Chapter XII, notes 67, 133 and accompanying text.

They needed clarity regarding their rights in order to plan their future behavior. Without an authoritative declaration that California did *not* qualify, the prisoners would be forced to act within 180 days rather than run the risk that their position would ultimately be rejected. In the Supreme Court, Chief Justice Rehnquist said that the prisoners' class action was not justiciable. Individual prisoners would have (individual) Article III cases when they filed their own habeas corpus petitions and, at that time, would be entitled to a judgment regarding the correct filing period. But the prisoners' anticipatory suit did not itself constitute a case or controversy, because it could not entirely resolve the "underlying" disputes between the prisoners and their keepers (i.e., the validity of the prisoners' detention).[24]

A justiciable case or controversy demands actual parties with demonstrable opposing positions. Certainly, collusive suits will not do.[25] But the requirement of genuine adversaries runs deeper. The modern Court frequently cites *Muskrat v. United States*[26] for this fundamental point.[27] In that case, Cherokee Indians complained that Congress had unconstitutionally restricted their ability to sell certain land. Congress responded by enacting a special statute authorizing the Cherokees to file suit in federal court to obtain a judicial determination of the validity of what Congress had done. When the Cherokees initiated an action, the Court ruled that it did not qualify as a justiciable case or controversy: The suit did not constitute a genuine effort to enforce the Cherokees' constitutional rights, but was instead an artificial device for obtaining a judicial opinion on an abstract question of constitutional law. The federal government was not really an adverse party, and other private citizens who had a stake in the matter were not involved. In other instances, however, the Court has allowed Congress to establish mechanisms for obtaining clarity. In *South Carolina v. Katzenbach*,[28] for example, the Court approved Section Five of the Voting Rights Act of 1965, which authorizes states to seek special declaratory judgments regarding the effect of changes in local voting rules on the ability of racial minorities to participate in elections.[29]

The prohibition on advisory opinions is well settled. It nonetheless bears critical examination. In related contexts, proponents of the private rights model insist that federal judicial power tracks the authority that "Colonial courts and the courts of Westminster" exercised "when the Constitution was framed."[30] The evidence suggests, however, that

24. *Ashmus*, 523 U.S. at 746. The result, of course, was that prisoners in California were forced to file individual habeas corpus petitions within 180 days, irrespective of whether California was legally entitled to demand that they proceed so quickly. No one would be so foolish as to deliberately file later in order to be in a position to litigate the issue and obtain an authoritative judgment.

25. See, e.g., *United States v. Johnson*, 319 U.S. 302 (1943) (refusing to consider an action filed by a plaintiff who had been recruited by the defendant to file a lawsuit that the defendant could control).

26. 219 U.S. 346 (1911).

27. E.g., *Moore v. Charlotte-Mecklenburg Bd. of Ed.*, 402 U.S. 47, 48 (1971); see *Steel Co. v. Citizens for a Better Environment*, 523 U.S. 83, 101 (1998) (citing *Muskrat* in support of a holding that federal courts cannot assume "hypothetically" that an Article III case or controversy exists in order to dispose of a matter on other grounds); Chapter VIII, note 247.

28. 383 U.S. 301 (1966).

29. But see *Texas v. United States*, 523 U.S. 296 (1998) (holding that an attempt by Texas to obtain a declaratory judgment that a new state statute would not dilute minority voting power was not yet ripe for adjudication); see notes 394–420 and accompanying text (discussing the ripeness doctrine).

30. *Coleman v. Miller*, 307 U.S. 433, 460 (1939) (Frankfurter, J.); see note 89 and accompanying text.

courts in England did not find advisory opinions to be "extrajudicial" at all.[31] The constitutional justifications for the prohibition on federal advisory opinions are also open to question. Originalists find little evidence in point. James Madison's statement that federal courts would determine only "cases of a Judiciary Nature" begged the question.[32] The Supreme Court pays lip service to the ban on advisory opinions. Yet there are countless ways in which federal courts routinely express themselves beyond the narrow requirements of particular cases.[33] In its own work, the Court itself routinely addresses abstract legal questions when it manipulates the issues presented in appellate cases in order to isolate the matters on which it wishes to rule.[34]

2. Finality

Just as federal courts are barred from issuing advisory opinions on abstract questions, they are equally barred from determining actual disputes if their orders are not final, but rather are subject to review in the executive or legislative branches. The working idea is much the same in both instances. If judicial opinions are not binding on the other branches, either because they are merely advisory (and thus can be ignored) or because they are not final (and thus can be overturned), they are not independently *judicial* in character. Instead, they are in service of the executive and legislative authorities whose decisions will actually control.[35] When courts render determinations that are not final, they invade the preserves of the other branches by doing preliminary executive or legislative work *for* officials who bear ultimate decision-making responsibility. Those executive or legislative officers, in turn, invade the preserve of the judiciary by presuming to reexamine court decisions rather than accepting them as authoritative pronouncements of law.[36]

The classic illustration is *Hayburn's Case*.[37] In 1792, Congress enacted the Invalid Pensions Act, which established pensions for veterans disabled in the Revolutionary War. To be eligible, applicants had to show that they had served honorably and that they had suffered wounds in the fighting. At the time, Congress had no experience with administrative agencies and turned to the federal circuit courts to receive applications, apply the criteria, and forward recommendations to the Secretary of War. The Secretary

---

31. See Stewart Jay, Most Humble Servants: The Advisory Role of Early Judges (1997); Chapter II, notes 1–4 and accompanying text; but see Robert J. Pushaw, Jr., *Why the Supreme Court Never Gets Any 'Dear John' Letters: Advisory Opinions in Historical Perspective*, 87 Gtn. L.J. 473 (1998) (suggesting that advisory opinions were thought to be more troubling in this country).

32. See Chapter II, text accompanying note 25. Recall that Madison himself championed the council of revision idea. According to conventional wisdom, the delegates rejected that proposal on the theory that the justices should not participate in the legislative function. See Chapter II, text accompanying notes 10, 22–24.

33. See Ronald J. Krotoszynski, Jr., *Constitutional Flares: On Judges, Legislatures, and Dialogue*, 83 Minn. L. Rev. 1 (1998) (providing numerous illustrations).

34. See Chapter VII, text accompanying notes 224–31. Professor Lee notes that the Court expresses concern about the "advisory" aspects of opinions in circumstances in which the Court does not mean that judicial action would violate Article III. The ban on advisory opinions, then, may actually entail generalized prudential considerations regarding the exercise of federal judicial power. See Evan Tsen Lee, *Deconstitutionalizing Justiciability: The Example of Mootness*, 105 Harv. L. Rev. 603, 644–49 (1992).

35. See *Chicago & Southern Air Lines v. Waterman*, 333 U.S. 103, 113–14 (1948) (making the connection expressly).

36. See Chapter I, notes 2–18 and accompanying text (discussing the separation principle).

37. 2 U.S. (2 Dall.) 408 (1792).

could either accept or reject the courts' recommendations. If he decided that a circuit court had made a mistake, he reported his decision to Congress. Thus the Secretary and Congress retained authority to make final decisions awarding or denying benefits.

When a circuit court in Pennsylvania declined to entertain a claim under the Act, Attorney General Randolph asked the Supreme Court to issue a writ of mandamus requiring that court to cooperate. Initially, the Court balked at Randolph's request, advanced without reference to any particular applicant and without any explicit authorizing statute. Randolph withdrew as Attorney General and reappeared as private counsel to William Hayburn, the applicant whose claim the circuit court had refused to consider.[38] At that point, the Court took the matter under advisement. Congress promptly amended the Act to eliminate the circuit courts' role. The Supreme Court, accordingly, never rendered an authoritative judgment on whether the Act imposed unconstitutional duties on the federal judiciary. Three circuit courts *did* address the issue. Since Supreme Court justices staffed those courts, their discussions were plainly significant.[39] All three declined to make preliminary determinations that the Secretary of War and Congress were free to reject.[40]

---

38. Professor Bloch suggests various reasons why the Court may have thought that Randolph needed to involve an individual claimant. The Court may have been concerned that if the Attorney General acted on behalf of the federal government alone in seeking a writ of mandamus running to a federal court, there would be no Article III case or controversy because the United States would appear on both sides of the litigation—in its executive and judicial forms, respectively. The Court may also have been worried that the United States lacked standing to complain that the circuit court had refused to process benefits claims. The government could not lose money if the statute was not enforced, but would have to pay benefits if the writ issued and the circuit court was forced to approve at least some claims. See notes 223–47 and accompanying text (discussing the modern concept of redressability). The Court may also have doubted that mandamus was the proper remedy. See Susan Low Bloch, *The Early Role of the Attorney General in Our Constitutional Scheme: In the Beginning There Was Pragmatism*, 1989 Duke L.J. 561, 599–600. Marcus and Teir contend (primarily on the basis of Justice Iredell's notes) that the Court would have allowed Randolph to act without involving Hayburn if Randolph had first obtained Washington's express approval. Maeva Marcus & Robert Teir, *Hayburn's Case: A Misinterpretation of Precedent*, 1988 Wis. L. Rev. 527. The concerns that Professor Bloch identifies would not trouble the Court today. See, e.g., *United States v. Nixon*, 418 U.S. 683, 696–97 (1974) (rejecting President Nixon's argument that the Watergate special prosecutor's subpoena of the famous "Nixon tapes" presented a non-justiciable intrabranch dispute); *Tutun v. United States*, 270 U.S. 568, 577 (1926) (holding that an individual's uncontested application for naturalization constituted a "case" on which a federal court could act—because the federal government was at least a "possible adverse party"). See generally Michael Herz, *United States v. United States: When Can the Federal Government Sue Itself?*, 32 Wm. & Mary L. Rev. 893 (1991). The Attorney General now routinely litigates federal questions in federal court, though typically in circumstances in which some statute appears to authorize suit. See Chapter X, note 1 and accompanying text.

39. See Chapter II, note 54 and accompanying text (explaining that the early circuit courts had no judges of their own and depended on Supreme Court justices "riding circuit"). None of the circuit courts issued an opinion. All expressed their views in letters to President Washington. It may be that the justices hoped to impress on Washington personally their objections to circuit-riding. If the Act had been approved, they would have had to travel to sit in circuit courts all the more often in order to handle the increased caseload. See note 11. All six of the justices agreed that the duties imposed on the circuit courts were not judicial in nature and that the Act was, to that extent, invalid. See Bloch, note 38, at 591–92.

40. In one of the cases, the justices said that Congress could appoint them as individuals to make the necessary determinations as special commissioners (not as Article III judges). That maneuver was plainly meant to defuse the immediate constitutional question. Yet it raised another: the question whether Article III judges can be assigned extra-Article III duties to be performed in an executive capacity. See Chapter IV, notes 110–11 and accompanying text.

The authority to be gleaned from *Hayburn's Case* can be questioned. The precise issues that troubled the justices are unclear. Nevertheless, it is settled today that Congress cannot assign federal courts the duty to enter judgments that are subject to executive or legislative revision.[41] By a parity of reasoning, Congress cannot force courts to reopen judgments that they consider to be closed. The Supreme Court said as much in *Plaut v. Spendthrift Farm*.[42] Previously, the Court had held that suits under the Securities and Exchange Act must be filed within a year after the discovery of a claim.[43] On the basis of that decision, lower courts dismissed a number of actions that had been filed too late. Ostensibly to avoid injustice, Congress enacted a statute authorizing the courts to reopen those cases. Writing for the Court in *Plaut*, Justice Scalia held the statute invalid inasmuch as it attempted to upset Article III court judgments that were already final.[44]

3. Political Questions

Federal courts cannot entertain questions that are "political" and thus properly to be answered by the politically accountable (executive and legislative) branches of the government. This idea, too, sounds in the separation of powers and the private rights model for judicial action. The precedents in point began with *Marbury v. Madison*,[45] where Chief Justice Marshall recognized that federal courts have no authority to "inquire" how the President decides matters the Constitution assigns to his "discretion."[46] By some accounts, Marshall meant that when the President (or Congress) has constitutionally anchored discretion, there are no judicially enforceable standards to be met. The branch of the government that enjoys discretion simply makes (and is entitled to make) whatever decision it chooses, without fear that the courts may find it erroneous. Formally, a decision of that kind cannot *be* erroneous and therefore is not susceptible to judicial review.

The ban on advisory opinions bars federal courts from deciding *legal* issues abstracted from *disputes*.[47] Complementing that idea, the ban on political questions bars federal courts from resolving *disputes* implicating issues that are not *legal*—because they are not susceptible to authoritative judicial orders that the other branches are bound to respect. The Constitution rarely leaves matters to the unbridled discretion of the President or Congress, but typically circumscribes their power with legal restraints that the courts can enforce. In *Marbury*, for example, Chief Justice Marshall said that Marbury's entitlement to his commission was not a political issue in the constitutional sense. Neither Jefferson nor Madison had any general Article II power to decide in his

---

41. *Waterman*, 333 U.S. at 113–14. In *Seminole Tribe v. Florida*, 517 U.S. 44 (1996), Justice Stevens argued that an obscure provision of the Indian Gaming Act violates this principle. Under that Act, a federal court is expected to name a mediator to help a state negotiate with an Indian tribe planning a gambling casino. If the parties decline to embrace a mediator's proposal, they have recourse not to the court, but to the Secretary of the Interior. See Chapter X, notes 141–49 and accompanying text (discussing other aspects of *Seminole Tribe*).

42. 514 U.S. 211 (1995).

43. *Lampf, Pleva v. Gilbertson*, 501 U.S. 350 (1991).

44. Justice Scalia explained that Congress can affect the results in pending cases in a variety of other ways—by, for example, adjusting the applicable substantive law or by waiving defenses. See Chapter IV, notes 90–92 and accompanying text.

45. 5 U.S. (1 Cranch) 137 (1803). See Chapter I, notes 65–70 and accompanying text.

46. *Marbury*, 5 U.S. at 170.

47. See text accompanying notes 12–13.

discretion whether to deliver the commission. Marbury claimed a legal right to delivery, and Marshall acknowledged that there was some federal *law* on which Marbury could rely—law that the Court would have been able to enforce if it had possessed the necessary jurisdiction.[48]

The Supreme Court is of two minds about political questions. On the one hand, the Court sometimes takes *Marbury* itself as the guide and suggests that to find a question political is simply to render a judicial decision that the Constitution assigns the question to one of the political branches. This approach deprives the political question doctrine of any genuine function as an explanation for *failing* to exercise judicial power. While the Court declines to grapple with the question on its own terms, the Court nonetheless renders an authoritative decision on the meaning of the Constitution—namely, that the decision reached by another branch of the government is (necessarily) correct.[49] On the other hand, the Court also sometimes suggests that the identification of a question as political is *not* itself an interpretation of the Constitution, but is, instead, a matter of pragmatic judgment. According to this second approach, the political question doctrine is a prudential device for avoiding sensitive questions, particularly in volatile circumstances in which workable judicial solutions are difficult to deliver.[50]

Both approaches figure in the classic political question cases, often reinforcing each other but nonetheless creating a measure of intellectual tension. In *Luther v. Borden*,[51] Chief Justice Taney said that the Constitution gave Congress the authority to decide

---

48. See Chapter I, text accompanying note 68.

49. This first approach has wide support in the academic literature. See, e.g., Herbert Wechsler, Principles, Politics and Fundamental Law 11–14 (1961). Professor Henkin argues that most of the Court's political question cases are actually instances in which the Court has made this kind of threshold constitutional determination and that others can be explained as occasions on which the Court has hesitated to award equitable relief. Louis Henkin, *Is There a Political Question Doctrine?*, 85 Yale L.J. 597 (1976). Professor Scharpf proposes a third theme—namely, that some questions would present intractable logistical and other functional difficulties. See Fritz W. Scharpf, *Judicial Review and the Political Question: A Functional Analysis*, 75 Yale L.J. 517 (1966).

50. This approach is typically associated with Professor Bickel, who argued that the courts must calibrate the exercise of judicial power so that they do not compromise their legitimacy by assuming responsibilities they are not equipped to meet or issuing orders they cannot enforce. To Bickel, a pragmatic political question doctrine should work together with other discretionary doctrines (not themselves prescribed by the Constitution, though fully consistent with it) to ensure proper judicial restraint in a variety of delicate circumstances. See Alexander Bickel, The Least Dangerous Branch 125–26 (1962); Alexander Bickel, *Foreword: The Passive Virtues*, 75 Harv. L. Rev. 40 (1962). See generally David L. Shapiro, *Jurisdiction and Discretion*, 60 N.Y.U. L. Rev. 543 (1985). The discretionary features of the political question doctrine have received a good deal of academic attention, most of it critical. Professor Redish contends that any element of the doctrine that cannot be set down to judicial interpretation of the Constitution should be discarded. Martin H. Redish, *Judicial Review and the Political Question*, 79 Nw. U. L. Rev. 1031 (1984). Accord Erwin Chemerinsky, *Cases Under the Guarantee Clause Should be Justiciable*, 65 U. Colo. L. Rev. 849 (1994); Louise Weinberg, *Political Questions and the Guarantee Clause*, 65 U. Colo. L. Rev. 887 (1994); Michael Tigar, *Judicial Power, the "Political Question Doctrine," and Foreign Relations*, 17 U.C.L.A. L. Rev. 1135 (1970). Professor Nagel suggests (or perhaps laments) that academics' impatience with the political question doctrine reflects a growing consensus that adjudication has merged with policy-making and that it therefore makes no sense to continue the pretense that courts can reserve their authority for "principled" duties. Robert F. Nagel, *Political Law, Legalistic Politics: A Recent History of the Political Question Doctrine*, 56 U. Chi. L. Rev. 643, 658 (1989). Professor Mulhern contends that the stubborn persistence of the political question doctrine should prompt academicians to acknowledge that courts share responsibility for interpreting the Constitution with the other branches of the government. J. Peter Mulhern, *In Defense of the Political Question Doctrine*, 137 U. Pa. L. Rev. 97 (1988).

51. 48 U.S. (7 How.) 1 (1849).

whether to accept the credentials of individuals who claimed to be the elected representatives and senators from Rhode Island. It followed that Congress equally had the authority to decide whether those officers represented the lawful government of that state. Taney acknowledged that the Guarantee Clause obliged "the United States" to "guarantee to every State" a "Republican Form of Government."[52] But he said that a claim under that clause raised a political issue to the extent it asked the courts to review Congress' decision to receive the representatives and senators who were already seated. In some respects, Taney appeared to rest the decision in *Luther* on an interpretation of the Constitution. Yet he also noted the difficulties that would follow if rival political camps could draw the federal courts into local struggles for power.[53]

The Warren Court attempted to reconcile the two approaches within a single formula. In *Baker v. Carr*,[54] Justice Brennan explained that the political question doctrine contemplates a "case-by-case inquiry." Courts determine whether a question is political in light of six factors, no one of which is decisive: (1) a "textually demonstrable constitutional commitment of the issue to a coordinate political department;" (2) a "lack of judicially discoverable and manageable standards for resolving it;" (3) the "impossibility of deciding without an initial policy determination of a kind clearly for nonjudicial discretion;" (4) the "impossibility of a court's undertaking independent resolution without expressing lack of the respect due coordinate branches of government;" (5) "an unusual need for unquestioning adherence to a political decision already made;" and (6) "the potentiality of embarrassment from multifarious pronouncements by various departments on one question."[55] The first factor reflects the *Marbury* approach to political questions. The other five, together with Brennan's introductory reference to "case-by-case" inquiries, reflect the pragmatic approach.

Invoking the six-part formulation in *Baker* itself, Justice Brennan concluded that an equal protection attack on the apportionment of the Tennessee state legislature did *not* raise a political question. He distinguished *Luther* on two grounds. First, while the Con-

---

52. U.S. Const. art. IV, §4.

53. The *Luther* case arose in connection with the unsettled affairs in Rhode Island in the wake of Dorr's Rebellion. Academicians debate the precise issues presented in the case, as well as the decisive elements of Taney's opinion for the Court. See William Wiecek, The Guarantee Clause of the United States Constitution (1972); Arthur Bonfield, *The Guarantee Clause of Article IV, Section 4: A Study in Constitutional Desuetude*, 46 Minn. L. Rev. 513 (1962). Both approaches to the political question doctrine also figured in famous cases in the middle third of this century: *Colegrove v. Green*, 328 U.S. 549 (1946) (holding that a Guarantee Clause claim regarding the apportionment of congressional districts in Illinois was non-justiciable); *Coleman v. Miller*, 307 U.S. 433 (1939) (holding that a claim regarding a state's ratification of a proposed constitutional amendment was also political). Foreign affairs cases provide an obvious occasion for finding issues to be political. See, e.g., *Banco Nat'l de Cuba v. Sabbatino*, 376 U.S. 398 (1964) (declining to recognize an exception to the "act of state doctrine" because of the possibility of interfering with the executive's conduct of foreign affairs). But it would be misleading to suggest that *any* issue touching foreign relations is for that reason alone non-justiciable. Compare *Goldwater v. Carter*, 444 U.S. 996 (1979) (Rehnquist, J., concurring) (arguing that a challenge to the President's decision to terminate a treaty presented a political question), with *Japan Whaling Ass'n v. Amer. Cetacean Society*, 478 U.S. 221 (1986) (holding that an attack on the failure of the Secretary of Commerce to certify that the Japanese whaling fleet jeopardized international agreements *was* justiciable). Cf. *Gilligan v. Morgan*, 413 U.S. 1 (1973) (holding that an attack on the way the national guard is trained raises a political question for Congress). See generally Thomas Franck, Political Questions/Judicial Answers: Does the Rule of Law Apply to Foreign Affairs (1992); Louis Henkin, Foreign Affairs and the Constitution (1972).

54. 369 U.S. 186 (1962).

55. Id. at 217.

stitution assigned Congress the authority to decide whether representatives and senators actually represented valid state governments, the Constitution did not assign to Congress (or the President) the authority to decide whether state legislatures were validly apportioned. Second, the Equal Protection Clause implicated in *Baker* offered "judicially manageable" standards that the Guarantee Clause did not. Brennan's reasoning has been questioned.[56] But it freed the Court to find apportionment cases justiciable and thus to be in a position three years later to announce the famous "one-person, one-vote" standard in *Reynolds v. Sims*.[57] Justice Brennan and the other justices in the *Baker* majority plainly saw a compelling need to prescribe constitutional standards for apportionment cases, because incumbents would rarely be willing to change even plainly unrepresentative systems in fear that reforms would favor their opponents. The *Baker* decision thus illustrates the Court's willingness to decide thorny questions that the justices might prefer to leave to politics when it appears that political bodies are paralyzed and cannot effectively respond.[58]

The Court also applied the six-part formula in *Powell v. McCormack*.[59] In that instance, Adam Clayton Powell asked the federal courts to review the House of Representatives' refusal to seat him as his district's representative. The House had found Powell "unqualified" because he had been accused of stealing public funds and other unseemly behavior. Chief Justice Warren recognized that the Constitution made the House "the Judge of the Elections, Returns and Qualifications of its own Members."[60] But he insisted that the Constitution also specified what those "Qualifications" were: candidates need only be twenty-five years of age, citizens of the United States, and residents of their districts.[61] The Constitution assigned the House the authority to apply those three standards, not to introduce additional qualifications that members must meet. If the House had found Powell unqualified for failing one of the three prescribed tests, an objection from Powell might have raised a political question. But the attempt to hold Powell to *different* standards presented a justiciable issue that federal courts could consider.

The Court continues to invoke the *Baker* formulation in political question cases, but plainly gives decisive weight to the first of the six elements. In *Nixon v. United States*,[62] Chief Justice Rehnquist explained that "in the first instance" courts must "interpret the text" of the pertinent constitutional provision and "determine whether and to what extent the issue is textually committed" to another branch. Courts must also consider whether the question is subject to "judicially manageable standards." But that inquiry is "not completely separate." The absence of manageable standards "may strengthen the conclusion that there is a textually demonstrable commitment to a coordinate branch."[63] The *Marbury* approach thus appears to be on the ascendant, the prudential

56. Justice Frankfurter argued in dissent that the plaintiffs were advancing "a Guarantee Clause claim masquerading under a different label." Id. at 297 (dissenting opinion).

57. 377 U.S. 533 (1964).

58. See Louis Pollak, *Judicial Power and "the Politics of the People"*, 72 Yale L.J. 81, 88 (1962). Justice Frankfurter argued that if state legislatures were unrepresentative, it was for an "informed, civically militant electorate" to force incumbents to make reforms, despite their personal interests. *Baker*, 369 U.S. at 270 (dissenting opinion).

59. 395 U.S. 486 (1969).

60. U.S. Const. art. I, §5, cl.1

61. U.S. Const. art. I, §2, cl.2.

62. 506 U.S. 224 (1993).

63. Id. at 228–29.

approach on the decline.[64] This is in keeping with the Court's emphasis on textualism, albeit the text in this instance is the Constitution itself.[65]

In *Nixon*, a former federal district judge sought judicial review of his impeachment conviction in the Senate. He complained that the Senate had delegated responsibility for collecting evidence against him to a committee and had convicted him on the basis of the committee's report in violation of the constitutional requirement that the Senate "shall have the sole Power to try all Impeachments."[66] Chief Justice Rehnquist found the validity of the Senate's procedure to present a political question. He rested primarily on an interpretation of the relevant text, concluding that by giving the Senate the "sole" power to try impeachment cases the Constitution committed the question "whether an individual should be acquitted or convicted" to the Senate exclusively, without possibility of judicial review.[67] Rehnquist said that the other elements of the *Baker* formulation fortified that conclusion: The term "try" lacks "sufficient precision to afford any judicially manageable standard of review" for examining the Senate's work;[68] judicial review of impeachment convictions would produce unsettlement; and, if a claim were found to be meritorious, it would be difficult to fashion appropriate relief.[69]

---

64. Justice Souter explicitly adopted the prudential approach in *Nixon*, but in a lone concurring opinion that no other justice joined. Id. at 252.

65. See Chapter I, notes 30–43 and accompanying text. This emphasis on constitutional text does not (necessarily) signal enthusiasm for deciding politically sensitive issues. The Court found the question in *Nixon* to be non-justiciable. Moreover, the Court often relies on other justiciability doctrines to avoid questions it wishes to sidestep, at least for the moment. See notes 77, 185 and accompanying text (standing); note 427 and accompanying text (mootness). Nevertheless, some academics argue that the Court is less inclined than it once was to avoid politically charged cases. By some accounts, the Court has developed greater confidence that its judgment is superior to that of other institutions. See, e.g., Rachel E. Barkow, *More Supreme Than Court? The Fall of the Political Question Doctrine and the Rise of Judicial Supremacy*, 102 Colum. L. Rev. 237 (2002).

66. U.S. Const. art. I, §3, cl.6.

67. 506 U.S. at 231. The Chief Justice fortified his interpretation of constitutional text both with references to the (thin) history behind the text and with inferences from structure—namely, the general scheme the Constitution contemplates for channeling impeachment decisions to the House (for charges) and then to the Senate (for trials), with no explicit provision for judicial involvement. Id. at 236. See Chapter III, text accompanying notes 37–40. Professor Brown has questioned the assumption that judicial review of the procedure by which the Senate acts would necessarily be the equivalent of judicial review of a Senate "decision on the merits." Rebecca L. Brown, *When Political Questions Affect Individual Rights: The Other Nixon v. United States*, 1993 Sup. Ct. Rev. 125, 130–31.

68. 506 U.S. at 230. Rehnquist concluded that since the Constitution prescribes other, comparatively specific requirements for Senate trials (e.g., a two-thirds majority vote for conviction), the "Framers" apparently did not "intend" that the courts should construe the ambiguous term "try" to demand that particular procedures be followed. Id. Concurring in the judgment in *Nixon*, Justice White said it was "not without irony" that the Court should disclaim an ability to identify standards for "procedural justice." Id. at 248. Professor Weinberg suggests that the Chief Justice "cannot have been wearing a very straight face" when he advanced that argument. For "if courts do not know whether or not a case has been tried, nobody knows." Weinberg, note 50, at 915.

69. With respect to these points, the Chief Justice set aside the particular case at bar (involving the impeachment of a district judge) and anticipated, instead, the more troubling case of a presidential impeachment. If the President were not removed from office by a Senate conviction alone, but could seek judicial review of the Senate's action, the country might be thrown into dangerous uncertainty while time-consuming judicial proceedings progressed. And if the courts should find the President's claims of mistreatment meritorious, the indelicacy of a judicial order for his reinstatement would be self-evident. These questions are less troubling in the context of judicial impeachments, where other measures may be available. See Chapter III, notes 44–49 and accompanying text.

B. Standing: Background

Article III courts can entertain only suits advanced by parties who have "standing."[70] Some features of standing doctrine are derived from Article III and the separation principle. They are irreducible constitutional prerequisites to the exercise of federal judicial power and must be satisfied in every instance. Plaintiffs have standing in this constitutional sense if they demonstrate: (1) "injury in fact" that is (2) "fairly traceable to" and thus "caused [by]" the defendant's allegedly unlawful behavior, and (3) "likely [to] be redressed by a favorable decision" and an award of the "requested relief."[71] Other aspects of standing are "prudential" in nature. They rest on non-constitutional policy considerations and may be relaxed in some circumstances. Familiar illustrations include: (1) the rule that litigants ordinarily cannot establish standing on the basis of injuries that are "widely shared" with other people;[72] (2) the rule that litigants ordinarily will be heard to advance only their own legal rights and not the rights of third parties;[73] and (3) the rule that litigants suing federal administrative agencies pursuant to the Administrative Procedure Act must suffer injuries to interests that fall "arguably" within the "zone of interests" protected by the federal law they wish to enforce.[74]

The distinction between constitutional and non-constitutional standing doctrine can be misleading. Obviously, the constitutional aspects of standing are not self-evident in the text of the Constitution or its structure. The Court has constructed those standing requirements as a matter of judgment—precisely in the way the Court has generated prudential standing rules. The Court uses the distinction between constitutional and non-constitutional standing to identify the power it is willing to share with Congress. When the Court declares that an aspect of standing doctrine is a constitutional requirement, it claims for itself the authority to elaborate that doctrinal feature as constitutional law, not subject to congressional override or adjustment. When the Court characterizes an aspect of standing doctrine as prudential, it opens the doctrine in that respect to statutory alteration. By this means, the Court allows Congress some voice in identifying the litigants who may pass through the federal court house doors, and, at the same time, reserves the capacity to close those doors if Congress becomes (in the Court's view) overly generous.[75]

Standing jurisprudence is notoriously hard to manage. By some accounts, the Court's decisions on standing make sense only if they are understood as disguised judgments on the merits, the justices' assurances to the contrary notwithstanding. Put crudely, the Court may grant standing to litigants whose substantive claims it approves and may refuse standing to litigants whose claims it disdains.[76] By other accounts, the Court often deploys standing doctrine to *avoid* the substance of claims when the justices cannot agree

---

70. The term "standing" is derived from the Latin phrase "*locus standii*" (a place to stand), used in England to describe one's capacity to "stand" before Parliament to address a bill.

71. See notes 141–247 and accompanying text.

72. See notes 172–74 and accompanying text.

73. See notes 250–73 and accompanying text.

74. See notes 274–94 and accompanying text.

75. See Gene R. Nichol, Jr., *Justice Scalia, Standing, and Public Law Litigation*, 42 Duke L.J. 1141, 1160 (1993) (making this point).

76. See Mark V. Tushnet, *The New Law of Standing: A Plea for Abandonment*, 62 Cornell L. Rev. 663 (1977); Richard J. Pierce, Jr., *Is Standing Law or Politics?*, 77 N. Car. L. Rev. 1741 (1999).

on a proper disposition on the merits.[77] It would be a mistake to dismiss standing doctrine so easily. The cases under this heading are often ideologically charged and socially sensitive. Doubtless the Court's views on the merits of claims influence both its analysis and its results. Yet the same can be said with respect to many other features of federal courts law. There is a good deal to be learned by taking the Court's decisions for what they purport to be and trying to understand standing doctrine by its own terms.

Standing is formally an issue in every instance in which Article III courts exercise judicial power, irrespective of the subject matter or the identity of the parties. In many instances, standing is readily apparent. Private citizens who invoke diversity jurisdiction for suits against other private citizens on state law claims easily meet applicable standing requirements. They sue over injuries to genuine interests (which take the form of personal legal rights created and made actionable by state law); the defendants they name appear to be the responsible wrongdoers; and if their claims prove to be meritorious, they can be awarded compensation to make them whole. Private citizens who invoke federal question jurisdiction often find standing more difficult to achieve. The federal statutes or constitutional provisions they wish to enforce may (or may not) establish personal legal rights of the kind the courts entertain with comfort. Congress may (or may not) provide them with a right of action to enforce those statutes or constitutional provisions in private lawsuits in federal court, seeking the relief they desire.[78]

The conceptual underpinnings of standing doctrine have developed as a reflection of, and as a reaction to, the evolution of the modern administrative state. The Supreme Court has permitted Congress to fashion extensive federal regulatory law and to establish federal agencies to administer it. Yet the Court has also struggled to locate and defend a proper place for the federal judiciary in the resulting structure.[79] The Court's judgment regarding the federal courts' proper role has shifted over time. Typically, the problems that arise follow a pattern: Congress first enacts a federal statute that prohibits certain behavior but fails to create any concomitant, correlative rights in anyone to be free of that behavior. Next, Congress establishes federal administrative machinery to enforce the new regulatory law, subject to some form of judicial review at the behest of a designated class of private citizens. Then, private plaintiffs contend that they are within the class of litigants entitled to sue either the agency itself (to ensure that the

---

77. In *Raines v. Byrd*, 521 U.S. 811 (1997), for example, the Court held that members of Congress lacked standing to attack the Line Item Veto Act, which gave the President authority to disapprove only selected provisions in legislative spending bills. By denying standing to the plaintiffs in *Raines*, the Court only postponed an examination of the Act's validity. At some point, the President would cancel a particular spending measure, and the "putative beneficiaries" of that provision would then suffer a "cognizable injury" that would allow them to sue for judicial relief. Id. at 834 (Souter, J. concurring). The Court did not suggest in *Raines* that the validity of the Act presented a non-justiciable political question. See notes 45–69 and accompanying text. It did not. Nevertheless, by deploying standing doctrine to deflect the plaintiffs' claims, the Court avoided for the moment a politically sensitive controversy. See note 65. In the next Term, when plaintiffs who could show economic injury from the President's actual use of the new statute filed suit, the Court found the law invalid (by a sharply divided vote). *Clinton v. City of New York*, 524 U.S. 417 (1998). For a speculative essay on why the justices may have wished to postpone treatment of the new law (and why they chose standing doctrine as a means to that end), see Neal Devins & Michael A. Fitts, *The Triumph of Timing: Raines v. Byrd and the Modern Supreme Court's Attempt to Control Constitutional Confrontations*, 86 Gtn. L.J. 351 (1997). See also Note, *Standing in the Way of Separation of Powers: The Consequences of Raines v. Byrd*, 112 Harv. L. Rev. 1741 (1999); note 220 (discussing the *Warth v. Seldin* case).

78. See Chapter VIII, notes 120–230 and accompanying text.

79. See Chapter V (discussing the federal courts' competition from administrative agencies).

agency performs its functions consistent with the statute it is charged to implement) or other private parties (to ensure that they comply with federal mandates that the agency does not properly enforce). Not every controversial standing decision follows this pattern. But the standing doctrine the Supreme Court applies in all cases is intelligible only if its origins in cases of this kind are understood and kept in mind.

The idea that litigants need standing to challenge governmental power shares a common history with the idea that the sovereign is immune from suit.[80] In early England, the king was the *source* of law and by hypothesis could not *violate* it. The courts were the king's alter ego. What they did, they did in his name. It followed that the king was not subject to suit. He could not (acting through his own judges) find himself guilty of violating his own law, such that his victim was entitled to judicial relief. The same was true for the king's agents, who enjoyed his immunity from suit so long as they acted on his authority. In time, however, English courts adopted a fictitious means of eluding royal immunity. They split the king's men into two persons, the one sovereign (and still insulated from suit as was the king himself), the other private (and subject to suit in the same way that other Englishmen were held to account). The courts declared that agents were acting in their private capacity whenever they violated the rights of others. It thus became possible, after all, for plaintiffs to force the king's agents (and through them the king himself) to conform to the developing common law of England.

In this country, suits challenging official conduct took essentially the same form: lawsuits by private citizens (claiming a breach of private common law rights) against government officials (treated as private citizens who had violated the private rights of others).[81] In federal question suits against governmental authorities, just as in ordinary cases involving private plaintiffs and defendants, the courts' primary function was to resolve disputes over plaintiffs' assertions of private rights.[82] The private rights model of adjudication predominated in the federal courts until the Progressive Era, when it came under pressure from suits reflecting the public rights model.[83]

---

80. Professor Vining provides the account summarized in the text. Joseph Vining, Legal Identity 20–27 (1978). Professor Jaffe offered a similar account. Louis L. Jaffe, *Suits Against Governments and Officers: Sovereign Immunity*, 77 Harv. L. Rev. 1 (1963). See Chapter X, notes 8–16 and accompanying text (discussing the federal government's sovereign immunity).

81. E.g., *Perkins v. Lukens Steel Co.*, 310 U.S. 113 (1940) (determining the Secretary of Labor's amenability to suit on the basis of common law rules applicable to private agents and principals).

82. See Chapter I, notes 61–72 and accompanying text.

83. See Chapter I, notes 78–91 and accompanying text. Professor Sunstein develops this history and its significance. See Cass R. Sunstein, *Standing and the Privatization of Public Law*, 88 Colum. L. Rev. 1432 (1988). See also Lee A. Albert, *Standing to Challenge Administrative Action: An Inadequate Surrogate for Claim for Relief*, 83 Yale L.J. 425 (1974); Richard B. Stewart, *The Reformation of American Administrative Law*, 88 Harv. L. Rev. 1669, 1679–80, 1717–18 (1975). The notion that only litigants asserting personal rights could seek judicial relief was not monolithic, either in England or in America. Recall that colonial courts did not limit themselves to supplicants of that description. See Chapter II, notes 1–3 and accompanying text. Moreover, both English and American courts issued common law writs on behalf of citizens who advanced no rights of their own, but wished only to force government officials to conform their behavior to law. See Raoul Berger, *Standing to Sue in Public Actions: Is it a Constitutional Requirement?*, 78 Yale. L.J. 816 (1969); Louis L. Jaffe, *Standing to Secure Judicial Review: Public Actions*, 74 Harv. L. Rev. 1265 (1961). But see Bradley S. Clanton, *Standing and the English Prerogative Writs: The Original Understanding*, 63 Brooklyn L. Rev. 1001 (1997) (arguing that Berger and Jaffe exaggerated the extent to which litigants could use prerogative writs to invoke judicial power in England in the Eighteenth Century); James Leonard & Joanne C. Brant, *The Half-Open Door: Article III, the Injury-in-Fact Rule, and the Framers' Plan for Federal Courts of Limited Jurisdiction*, 54 Rutgers L. Rev. 1, 86 (2001) (insisting that there is sufficient his-

New kinds of federal regulatory statutes and corresponding administrative agencies generated new forms of litigation. Both the subjects of regulation (chiefly industrial corporations) and its beneficiaries (primarily competitors, workers, and consumers) sought access to the courts to vindicate their interests. Corporations typically *resisted* regulation, contending either that government officials had exceeded any lawful authority the new statutes gave them or, if they had not, that the statutes they enforced were unconstitutional. By contrast, competitors, workers, and consumers typically *exploited* regulation, contending that government officials had lawful authority, but failed to use it properly. Corporations went to court to advance their own private rights. Competitors, workers, and consumers went to court to obtain benefits that would flow from forcing regulated industries and government agents to comply with federal statutes. If rights were at stake in suits by the beneficiaries of regulation, they were not personal, *private* rights, but *public* rights: the rights of Americans at large to demand that companies and governmental officials conduct themselves according to law.[84]

Academics gave the plaintiffs in the new public rights cases a name. Professor Hohfeld had previously developed a symmetrical conceptual framework in which one party's right was set opposite an opposing party's correlative duty to respect that right. Professor Jaffe argued that the plaintiffs in cases that fit the traditional, private rights model were "Hohfeldian" in the sense that they sought to litigate some question regarding their own legal rights. The plaintiffs in the new public rights cases were "non-Hohfeldian." They had enough interest in litigation to give them an incentive to sue, but they did not advance legal rights to demand that defendants perform duties owed to them personally.[85]

---

torical evidence to warrant the conclusion that the "framers" of the Constitution meant to restrict federal courts to suits by parties advancing "grievances about violations of their rights").

84. The nomenclature here is conventional, but problematic. The law of standing typically draws a crucial distinction between litigants who have personal *rights* that they wish to enforce in federal litigation and litigants who have only personal *interests*, but wish to vindicate someone else's rights or to enforce a federal legal standard that begets no personal rights in anyone. Nevertheless, courts and commentators refer interchangeably to litigation to enforce "public rights" and litigation in the "public interest." See Chapter I, note 83; see also Chapter V, notes 96–119, 122 (discussing the "public rights" label in connection with adjudication by administrative agencies and legislative courts).

85. Louis L. Jaffe, *The Citizen as Litigant in Public Actions: The Non-Hohfeldian or Ideological Plaintiff*, 116 U. Pa. L. Rev. 1033 (1968); see Wesley N. Hohfeld, *Some Fundamental Legal Conceptions as Applied in Judicial Reasoning*, 23 Yale L.J. 16 (1913). Professor Jaffe explained that it would only confuse analysis to say that plaintiffs who are given authority to sue must, for that reason alone, be understood to have a "legally protected interest" or, in Jaffe's lexicon, a "right," to the treatment they demand. Jaffe, at 1033–34. Jaffe recognized only two kinds of litigants: Hohfeldian plaintiffs who assert legal rights for standing purposes, on the one hand, and non-Hohfeldian plaintiffs who assert no such rights, on the other. He drew no (clear and working) distinction *within* the non-Hohfeldian category between plaintiffs who assert some personal interest that distinguishes them from the crowd and plaintiffs who are entirely fungible with all others in "large, indeterminate groups" and who sue entirely for ideological reasons. Professor Fallon also appears to treat non-Hohfeldian litigants as an indivisible class. As he describes them, they claim no "injuries" that are "easily definable in terms of personal, financial loss or other harms actionable at common law," nor a breach of "a legal duty running personally to them." Instead, they "aspire to secure the enforcement of legal principles that touch others as directly as themselves and that are valued for moral or political reasons independent of economic interests." Richard H. Fallon, Jr., *Of Justiciability, Remedies, and Public Law Litigation: Notes on the Jurisprudence of Lyons*, 59 N.Y.U. L. Rev. 1, 4 (1984). Yet standing analysis demands finer distinctions. See notes 274–94 and accompanying text (discussing the way the zone test allows some litigants who assert no rights to sue but nonetheless excludes purely ideological plaintiffs); notes 172–74 and accompanying text (discussing the way in which the

The Supreme Court initially reacted negatively to non-Hohfeldian plaintiffs. Conservative and progressive justices alike maintained that litigants had standing to appear in federal court only to enforce their own legal rights in the traditional way.[86] Early signals of the Court's commitment to the private rights model came in Justice Brandeis' reservations about declaratory judgment actions in *Willing*[87] and in the Court's refusal to entertain a taxpayer suit challenging a federal statute in *Frothingham v. Mellon*.[88] In the ensuing years, Justice Frankfurter became the chief architect of standing doctrine. In his famous (not to say notorious) words, prerequisites for litigant standing served to reserve adjudication in Article III courts for "matters that were the traditional concern of the courts at Westminster" at the time the Constitution was adopted.[89] Frankfurter recognized that private legal rights flowed not only from the common law, but also from statutes and the Constitution, and that standing doctrine must acknowledge that litigants asserting statutory and constitutional rights could have access to the federal courts. He insisted, however, that plaintiffs must advance *rights* of some character. By his account, litigants ordinarily could not sue in federal court to advance just *any* interests they might have in seeing defendants comply with federal law, but only to press "*legal* interest[s]": *private legal rights* anchored in the common law, a statute, or the Constitution.[90]

Beginning in the 1930s, Congress countered the Court's standing doctrine with a different kind of legislation.[91] In §402(b) of the Communications Act of 1934, for example, Congress authorized anyone "aggrieved" by the actions of the Federal Communications Commission to seek review in the courts. That provision (and others like it in statutes touching other agencies) did not purport to create a *substantive* right that, in turn, could be the basis for litigant standing (to enforce that right) in a federal lawsuit.

Court has distinguished between litigants whose injuries are "widely shared" from litigants whose injuries are "abstract and indefinite").

86. The Court had used the term "standing" on numerous occasions, but had never before elaborated a doctrine of that name as a significant barrier to litigants' access to the federal courts. See Louis L. Jaffee, *Standing to Secure Judicial Review: Private Actions*, 75 Harv. L. Rev. 255, 256 (1961); Steven L. Winter, *The Metaphor of Standing and the Problem of Self-Governance*, 40 Stan. L. Rev. 1371, 1376 & n.26 (1988). Frankfurter and Landis did not mention standing in their treatise on the federal courts. Felix Frankfurter & James Landis, The Business of the Supreme Court: A Study in the Federal Judicial System (1928).

87. *Willing v. Chicago Aud. Ass'n*, 277 U.S. 274 (1928); see note 17 and accompanying text.

88. 262 U.S. 447 (1923); see text accompanying note 153. Professor Sunstein has explained that conservative justices were content to allow only corporations resisting regulation to sue and that Justice Brandeis cooperated because he thought suits by beneficiaries threatened the development of an enlightened administrative state that would displace the common law system. Sunstein, note 83, at 1437–38. Professor Winter has described Brandeis' influence in *Frothingham* and related cases. Winter, note 86, at 1376–79. Neither *Willing* nor *Frothingham* mentioned standing explicitly, but both those early cases demonstrated the Court's concerns about novel forms of litigation that departed from the traditional model.

89. *Coleman v. Miller*, 307 U.S. at 460 (Frankfurter, J.).

90. Id. at 465. Here again, conventional jargon can be confusing. When Justice Frankfurter referred to legally protected "interests," he meant legal *rights*. He did not mean personal *interests* that would be served if the courts forced defendants to obey the law. See note 85 (discussing Professor Jaffe's explanation); Administrative Law: Cases and Materials 305–06 (Cass, Diver & Beermann eds. 1994). For a different account of the nature and origins of standing doctrine, see Maxwell L. Stearns, *Standing Back from the Forest: Justiciability and Social Choice*, 83 Calif. L. Rev. 1309 (1995) (offering a public choice perspective); Maxwell L. Stearns, *Standing and Social Choice: Historical Evidence*, 144 U. Pa. L. Rev. 309 (1995) (offering a revisionist explanation of the Court's decisions).

91. See Sunstein, note 83, at 1438–43.

Instead, it created a *litigation* right. It simply authorized a class of people (persons "aggrieved" by agency action) to take their complaints to court. Judge Frank captured the idea in yet another metaphor still in use today. He noted that Congress commonly authorized the Attorney General to litigate on behalf of the public.[92] According to Frank, Congress could equally appoint non-Hohfeldian "aggrieved" persons as "private attorneys general" and empower them to sue in federal court to ensure, on behalf of the public, that federal law was enforced.[93]

The Supreme Court essentially adopted that view of the matter in *FCC v. Sanders Bros. Radio Station*.[94] The FCC awarded a license to the Telegraph Herald in Dubuque, authorizing that company to establish a new radio station in an area in which Sanders already operated a station. Sanders sought judicial review of the FCC's decision on the theory that Sanders was "aggrieved" inasmuch as the new station would compete with Sanders' existing business. Sanders had no private *right* to be operate without competition, derived from the common law, the Communications Act, or the Constitution.[95] Justice Roberts nevertheless sustained Sanders' standing on the basis of §402(b). That provision, he explained, reflected a decision by Congress that litigants like Sanders, who were "injured" by the FCC's actions, had a sufficient "interest" to bring any errors of law the FCC might commit to the attention of the courts. Roberts confirmed in *Sanders* that Congress had "power" to "confer such standing" on private litigants.[96] In *Scripps-Howard Radio v. FCC*,[97] Justice Frankfurter himself conceded that, pursuant to §402(b), litigants who had no personal rights of their own nonetheless had standing "as representatives of the public interest."[98]

The Communications Act cases, *Sanders* and *Scripps-Howard*, put the standing issue graphically. The primary substantive legal standard the Act required the FCC to follow in deciding whether to issue licenses was whether the "public convenience, interest, or necessity" would be served.[99] The plaintiff in *Sanders* contended on the merits that the Commission had not developed sufficient evidence to warrant the conclusion that granting a license to the Telegraph Herald met that standard. The plaintiff in *Scripps-Howard* claimed that the FCC had awarded a license to a competitor in violation of its own rules (and due process). The Commission held no hearing in which the plaintiff might have shown that it was not in the "public interest" to introduce a new station into

---

92. See note 38.

93. *Assoc. Indus. v. Ickes*, 134 F.2d 694, 704 (2d Cir.), *vacated on other gr'ds*, 320 U.S. 707 (1943). Professor Johnson has suggested that the "private attorney general" metaphor leaves the erroneous impression that the private litigants it describes can simply supplant the Attorney General of the United States, enforcing whatever federal laws they think need enforcing. In fact, private litigants can achieve standing in federal court only if they assert some personal and concrete injury. Stephen M. Johnson, *Private Plaintiffs, Public Rights: Article II and Environmental Citizen Suits*, 49 Kan. L. Rev. 383, 418 (2001). See note 85 and accompanying text (discussing similar imprecision regarding Hohfeldian/non-Hohfeldian terminology); notes 144–200 and accompanying text (discussing current doctrine); notes 308–18 and accompanying text (discussing the "agency" and "assignment" theories).

94. 309 U.S. 470 (1940).

95. Id. at 475. See *Tennessee Elec. Power Co. v. TVA*, 306 U.S. 118, 137–38 (1939).

96. 309 U.S. at 477.

97. 316 U.S. 4 (1942).

98. Id. at 14. The question in *Scripps-Howard* was whether a radio station that claimed only a competitive interest (but no legal rights) could obtain a stay of an FCC order granting a license to another station, pending the court's review of whether the FCC had followed applicable legal standards. Justice Frankfurter held that the reviewing court could grant such a stay.

99. 47 U.S.C. §307(a).

the area. Professor Jaffe explained that *Sanders* and *Scripps-Howard* recognized standing in non-Hohfeldian plaintiffs. In those cases, the Court explicitly denied that the plaintiffs had a "substantive right to be free of competition," but nonetheless allowed them to sue. Jaffe insisted that it would be circular to say that, since the plaintiffs in *Sanders* and *Scripps-Howard* had standing they must necessarily have had a primary "right" under the Communications Act to be treated in the way they demanded. If the kind of legal right that had always sufficed for standing was merely a right to "have the law enforced," then, to Jaffe, the requirement of a "right" for standing was "meaningless." In *Sanders* and *Scripps-Howard*, the plaintiffs obtained standing without asserting any primary rights at all, but rather on the basis of a *litigation* right (a right to go to federal court) conferred by Congress in the absence of primary rights. They were simply authorized to ask the federal courts to enforce the law.[100]

In some minds, suits by private attorneys general who claimed no invasion of their own primary rights came perilously close to requests for advisory opinions.[101] Moreover, the public interest that private litigants proposed to vindicate was not monolithic. Non-Hohfeldian plaintiffs might press only their own narrow perspectives and fail adequately to represent the interests of others with different points of view.[102] Nevertheless, the Court struck a tacit bargain with Congress and the public rights suits that Congress wished to authorize. Justice Frankfurter summarized the resulting arrangement in a classic concurring opinion in *Joint Anti-Fascist Refugee Comm. v. McGrath.*[103] Congress would be permitted to decide, on a case-by-case basis, whether the country would be well served by allowing non-Hohfeldian private litigants access to the federal courts under specified statutes. Yet in the absence of a special standing provision like §402(b) authorizing suits with respect to a particular agency's performance, private litigation would be restricted to Hohfeldian plaintiffs advancing their own legal rights.[104] Frankfurter explicitly tied the baseline rights-based test for standing to the separation of powers.[105] By his account, however, the separation principle, in turn, served democratic ends: By restricting standing to litigants advancing personal legal rights, standing doctrine kept unelected federal judges from frustrating policies forged democratically by Congress. If, then, Congress itself wished to further its policy objectives in some field by authorizing private citizens to file lawsuits in the absence of personal legal rights, it would make no sense to frustrate that politically accountable judgment in the name of democracy.[106]

100. Jaffe, note 85, at 1035–36.

101. See, e.g., Albert, note 83, at 481; see notes 6–22 and accompanying text (discussing the ban on advisory opinions).

102. See note 252 and accompanying text (discussing this point in connection with third-party claims).

103. 341 U.S. 123, 152 (1951) (concurring opinion).

104. See *Perkins*, 310 U.S. at 125.

105. See Chapter I, notes 2–18 and accompanying text.

106. See Pierce, note 76, at 1767–68. Frankfurter himself was an adherent of the Legal Process School whose views about the law of federal courts often tracked the Hart and Wechsler paradigm. In the case of standing, he hoped to allocate dispute-resolution authority to courts (with a comparative advantage in that field) and policy-making authority to Congress (the institution better suited to that task). See Chapter I, notes 53–60 and accompanying text. Professor Hart himself expressed views about standing similar to Frankfurter's. E.g., Henry M. Hart, Jr., *The Power of Congress to Limit the Jurisdiction of the Federal Courts: An Exercise in Dialectic*, 66 Harv. L. Rev. 1362, 1377 (1953). Professor Pushaw has traced Frankfurter's work in detail. See Robert J. Pushaw, Jr., *Justiciability and Separation of Powers: A Neo-Federalist Approach*, 81 Cornell L. Rev. 393, 458–63 (1996).

In 1946, Congress enacted the Administrative Procedure Act and, concomitantly, the general provision on judicial review now codified in 5 U.S.C. §702. That provision authorized a "person" to seek judicial review if he or she either suffered a "legal wrong" because of agency action or was "adversely affected or aggrieved by agency action within the meaning of a relevant statute."[107] By some accounts, §702 merely codified the existing state of affairs. The reference to a "legal wrong" reflected the traditional rights-based test for standing: One suffered a legal *wrong* when a legal *right* was violated. The reference to persons "adversely affected or aggrieved" within the meaning of a relevant statute referred to litigants whom Congress had independently authorized to challenge actions by certain agencies. A "relevant" statute was a provision like §402(b) of the Communications Act—a statute authorizing private litigants who claimed no rights of their own to sue on behalf of the public to ensure that a particular agency complied with the law.[108] In *Ass'n of Data Processing Svc. Orgs. v. Camp*,[109] however, the Court read §702 in an entirely different way.[110]

In *Data Processing*, the Comptroller of the Currency ruled that banks could provide data processing services to their customers. Independent data processing companies challenged that ruling on the ground that it violated the Bank Services Corporation Act, which limited banks to "bank services." The plaintiff companies did not claim that the Act gave them any legal right to be free of competition. Like the competing radio station in *Sanders*, they claimed only that they suffered economic harm from the Comptroller's ruling, because it allowed banks to enter their market. Justice Douglas acknowledged that, in the main, the Court had held that only plaintiffs who claimed an invasion of a "legal right" had standing to sue in federal court. The *Sanders* case was an exception that could be explained on the basis of §402(b), which was inapplicable to the case at hand.[111] Douglas nonetheless held, in effect, that the conception of standing the Court had embraced in *Sanders* was not limited to that case, but was transferable to all standing cases.

By Douglas' account, the plaintiffs in *Data Processing* had standing to attack the Comptroller's ruling because: (1) they suffered "injury in fact" resulting from that ruling, and (2) their interests were "arguably" within the "zone of interests... protected or regulated by the statute or constitutional guarantee" that, in their view, the ruling violated.[112] The plaintiffs had to demonstrate factual "injury" as a constitutional prerequisite for standing. Without that, they had no actual dispute with the Comptroller, no case or controversy within the meaning of Article III. The plaintiffs needed an interest that was "arguably" within the "zone of interests" protected by the Bank Services Corporation Act in order to satisfy the additional non-constitutional requirement for standing

107. See Chapter II, note 78 and accompanying text.

108. See, e.g., Louis L. Jaffe, Judicial Control of Administrative Action 528–30 (1965); Richard B. Stewart, *Standing for Solidarity*, 88 Yale L.J. 1559, 1569 (1979). An influential Justice Department memorandum declared that §702 was only a "general restatement of the principles of judicial review embodied in many statutes and judicial decisions." U.S. Dep't of Justice, Attorney General's Manual on the Administrative Procedure Act 93 (1947). Professor Duffy explains that the DOJ's strategy was to limit the extent to which the new APA provision would be read to change extant judge-made standing law. John F. Duffy, *Administrative Common Law in Judicial Review*, 77 Tex. L. Rev. 113, 130–34 (1998).

109. 397 U.S. 150, 153 (1970).

110. For a discussion of §702's function as a right-of-action statute, see Chapter VIII, notes 133, 137–39 and accompanying text.

111. 397 U.S. at 153 n.1.

112. Id. at 152–53.

that Congress had created in §702—namely, the requirement that they must be "adversely affected" or "aggrieved" within the meaning of that Act.[113] It was clear enough that the Act limited banks to "banking" primarily to safeguard accounts.[114] Justice Douglas was satisfied, however, that the competitive interests of the data processing companies were also "arguably" included.[115]

In effect, Douglas read §702 of the Administrative Procedure Act to do for all litigants seeking to challenge the actions of all agencies (covered by the APA) what Justice Roberts had read §402(b) of the Communications Act to do for litigants seeking to challenge actions of one agency (the FCC). This is to say, Douglas held that Congress had decided against appraising the advisability of private suits with respect to each agency in turn (an approach that would have produced a series of agency-specific provisions like §402(b)). Instead, Congress had deputized private attorneys general *en masse* to litigate with all manner of agencies.[116] But Douglas did more than that. He repudiated the rights-based test for standing that had formed the previous baseline and replaced it with a new harm-based test. Douglas did not deny that litigants whose interests had the legal status of rights could establish standing. The "legal wrong" language in §702 reaffirmed that litigants had standing to sue if they claimed that an agency had violated their "legal rights." But he insisted that litigants were not generally *required* to advance legal rights. They were, instead, generally able to achieve standing on the basis of an "injury" to an "interest," whether or not the law made that interest a legal right. According to Justice Douglas, standing demanded only a sufficient "personal stake in the outcome" of a lawsuit to create an incentive to supply effective advocacy.[117] A harm-based test served that purpose. Frankfurter's "legal interest" test (that is, the rights-based test) went not to the plaintiffs' standing to appear in an Article III court, but to "the merits" of their legal claims.[118]

The harm-based test the Court adopted in *Data Processing* was not merely an interpretation of §702, limited to attacks on federal agency action. It was a comprehensive reconceptualization of standing, applicable in every context in which the standing question might arise. That reconceptualization accommodated the very public rights litigation that the Court had previously discouraged. The harm-based test made it possible for litigants to gain access to federal court on the basis of observable, value-neutral *facts*, without any necessary reference to *law*.[119] That, in turn, allowed non-Hohfeldian private attorneys general to use federal litigation as a means of prompting federal agencies to enforce statutes on civil rights, consumer affairs, the environment, and other matters

---

113. Professor Davis had previously contended that the reference to anyone "adversely affected" dispensed with any non-constitutional standing requirement and authorized anyone with factual injury to sue. 3 Kenneth C. Davis, Administrative Law Treatise 232 (1958).

114. The legislative history suggests that some members of Congress were concerned that if banks extended their operations to other activities, they might put their reserves at risk and compromise the safety of savings and checking accounts.

115. Having settled the standing question, Justice Douglas turned to (and rejected) the argument that Congress had absolutely precluded judicial review of the Comptroller's ruling. 397 U.S. at 157; see Chapter IV, notes 112–21and accompanying text.

116. See Administrative Law, note 90, at 310.

117. *Data Processing*, 397 U.S. at 151–52, citing *Flast v. Cohen*, 392 U.S. 83, 101 (1968). See notes 155–66 and accompanying text.

118. 397 U.S. at 153–54. See notes 381–93 and accompanying text (discussing the link between standing and the merits of litigants' claims).

119. Professor Nichol explains that "injury in fact" is to be "distinguished, one supposes, from injury protected by law." Gene R. Nichol, Jr., *Rethinking Standing*, 72 Calif. L. Rev. 68, 74 (1984).

of general public interest. For many observers, the occasion called for celebration. Private litigants could force agencies to do the job that Congress had given them. In a famous opinion delivered just after *Data Processing*, Judge Skelly Wright declared that the federal courts now had a "duty" to ensure that "important legislative purposes, heralded in the halls of Congress, [were] not lost or misdirected in the vast hallways of the federal bureaucracy."[120]

In the years since, the Supreme Court has brought harm-based standing doctrine along an uneven path. At the time *Data Processing* was decided, the Court insisted that standing had nothing to do with the separation of powers. Instead, according to the Court, the constitutional requirements for standing existed only to ensure effective advocacy.[121] Today, by contrast, the Court considers the separation of powers to be the "single basic idea" on which "the law of Article III standing is built."[122] Standing requirements not only sharpen legal issues for adjudication, but confine judicial law-making to the resolution of actual disputes and divert broader issues of public law and policy to the political arena. By common account, this shift in rationale can be traced to Justice Scalia. In a widely noted lecture delivered in 1983 (before he joined the Court), Scalia criticized the harm-based conception of standing for the very reason that it encourages public rights litigation.[123] He acknowledged that if effective advocacy were the issue, he would not *reject*, but would *prefer*, ideologically committed organizational advocates, which promise to build a more convincing case than would a single, isolated individual.[124] He contended, however, that the harm-based test neglects the separation principle, which, in his view, restricts the federal judiciary to its proper institutional role. By Scalia's account, the Court should abandon the harm-based test entirely and resurrect the rights-based test that *Data Processing* discarded.[125]

Specifically, Justice Scalia contended that the judicial branch should be confined to "protecting individuals and minorities against impositions of the majority" rather than

---

120. *Calvert Cliffs Coordinating Comm. v. U.S. Atomic Energy Comm'n*, 449 F.2d 1109, 1111 (D.C. Cir. 1971).

121. See *Data Processing*, 397 U.S. at 151–52; *Flast*, 392 U.S. at 100.

122. *Allen v. Wright*, 468 U.S. 737, 752 (1984). Accord *Spencer v. Kemna*, 523 U.S. 1, 10 (1998); *Lewis v. Casey*, 518 U.S. 343, 353 n.3 (1996). Justice O'Connor began her important opinion for the Court in *Allen* with a quotation from Judge Robert Bork: "All of the doctrines that cluster about Article III—not only standing but mootness, ripeness, political question, and the like—relate in part, and in different though overlapping ways, to an idea, which is more than an intuition but less than a rigorous and explicit theory, about the constitutional and prudential limits to the powers of an unelected, unrepresentative judiciary in our kind of government." *Vander Jagt v. O'Neil*, 699 F.2d 1166, 1178–79 (D.C. Cir. 1983) (concurring opinion).

123. Antonin Scalia, *The Doctrine of Standing As An Essential Element of the Separation of Powers*, 17 Suffolk U. L. Rev. 881 (1983).

124. Id. at 891.

125. Professor Bandes agrees that ideological plaintiffs make more effective advocates and argues, for that reason, that Justice Scalia's alternative ideas about standing are perverse. According to Bandes, Scalia's approach requires organizations like the Sierra Club and the American Civil Liberties Union to locate an individual who meets the requirements for standing and recruit that person as a surrogate. In the end, then, the entire affair becomes pretense—a suit that has the appearance of a traditional common law action, but is actually contrived to satisfy standing prerequisites. Susan Bandes, *The Idea of a Case*, 42 Stan. L. Rev. 227, 299 (1990). Professor Tushnet contends that organizational litigants often have strategic reasons for involving individuals. Mark V. Tushnet, *The Sociology of Article III: A Response to Professor Brilmayer*, 93 Harv. L. Rev. 1698, 1713 (1980). Professor Brilmayer argues that, if that is so, then Tushnet and others should not object to standing doctrine that requires organizations to find willing individuals to serve as plaintiffs. Lea Brilmayer, *A Reply*, 93 Harv. L. Rev. 1727 (1980).

"prescribing how the other two branches should function in order to serve the interest *of the majority itself*."[126] In his view, litigants who wish to challenge the way they themselves are regulated by law should always have standing, but litigants who wish to challenge the way in which government regulates other people, organizations, and companies should not. Justice Scalia's approach was reminiscent of Justice Frankfurter's account in the *McGrath* case.[127] Unlike Frankfurter, however, Justice Scalia maintained that the separation principle is not simply a device for preventing judges from undermining democratically adopted policies. In Scalia's view, private litigants lacking personal legal rights should be denied access to the federal courts even if Congress, in the exercise of politically accountable judgment, enacts legislation authorizing suits advancing the general public interest. Thus Justice Scalia's approach would contemplate a return not to the standing doctrine that prevailed just prior to *Data Processing* in 1961, but rather to the doctrine that prevailed prior to the *Sanders* case in 1940, when the Supreme Court generally denied standing to the beneficiaries of social welfare legislation.[128]

Justice Scalia expanded on his views in an important dissent from the Court's judgment in *Friends of the Earth v. Laidlaw*.[129] By his account, there are two (related) reasons why Congress should not be able to authorize "private" attorneys general to enforce federal statutes. First, the separation principle is a matter of constitutional law that the Court must enforce despite the wishes of another branch, however politically accountable that branch may be. Second, Congress is not the only department affected. Private enforcement suits interfere with the President's performance of his Article II duty and responsibility to execute federal law.[130] According to Justice Scalia, the executive branch is empowered to decide when and how federal statutes are to be enforced, and Congress has no authority to turn that power over to private individuals and groups with their own self-interested or ideological agenda.[131] In environmental cases like *Laidlaw*, Justice Scalia insisted that private groups not subject to "public control" can manipulate the enforcement function to achieve objectives that the executive branch might not pursue.[132] That, in his view, is constitutionally unacceptable. If the executive is not meeting his enforcement responsibilities, the remedy is at the polls, not in the courts.[133]

---

126. Scalia, note 123, at 894 (emphasis in original).

127. See notes 103–06 and accompanying text.

128. See Pierce, note 76, at 1773. See notes 86–90 and accompanying text.

129. 528 U.S. 167, 198 (2000) (dissenting opinion).

130. U.S. Const. art. II, §3 (providing that the President "shall take Care that the Laws be faithfully executed').

131. *Laidlaw*, 528 U.S. at 209. The Court has said in other contexts that a "governmental unit whose domain is...narrowed" cannot consent to a breach of the separation of powers principle as elaborated by the Court. *New York v. United States*, 505 U.S. 144, 182 (1992).

132. *Laidlaw*, 528 U.S. at 209. See also *FEC v. Akins*, 524 U.S. 11, 36 (1998) (Scalia, J., dissenting) (also invoking Article II in support of an argument that private litigants lacked standing to sue over an alleged violation of a federal statute); note 178 and accompanying text (discussing *Akins*).

133. See *Lujan v. Defenders of Wildlife*, 504 U.S. 555, 577 (1992) (Scalia, J.); notes 190–94 and accompanying text. In *Lujan* (apparently) and *Laidlaw* (explicitly), Justice Scalia ultimately rested on Article III alone. 504 U.S. at 578; 528 U.S. at 209. The parties in *Laidlaw* did not brief the question whether Article II was implicated. See 528 U.S. at 197 (Kennedy, J., concurring) (noting that the Article II issues were "[d]ifficult and fundamental" and thus were "best reserved for a later case"). Cf. *Vermont Agency v. United States ex rel. Stevens*, 529 U.S. 765, 778 n.8 (2000) (noting but failing to consider whether *qui tam* lawsuits violate Article II); see notes 305–18 and accompanying text (discussing *Stevens*). It remains to be seen whether a standing analysis based independently on Article II will depart significantly from the Article III analysis that Justice Scalia has now sketched

The extent to which Justice Scalia's views have influenced the Court's standing decisions is debatable. Certainly, the Court has not discarded the harm-based test. Nor has the Court adopted Scalia's concerns that public rights lawsuits threaten the executive's preserve.[134] Yet the emphasis on the separation-of-powers rationale often leads the justices to worry aloud about whether litigants are asking the judiciary to resolve public policy issues better left to the legislative and executive branches. In many (though by no means all) cases, the Court arguably resolves its doubts about policy-oriented litigation by insisting on ever more tangible personal injuries as a constitutional prerequisite for standing. By some accounts, the evolving harm-based test for standing may actually reintroduce the rights-based test it was supposed to supersede.[135] As the Court searches for a context in which to determine what qualifies as a sufficient factual injury, it falls back into reflexive reliance on the kinds of personal interests that warranted judicial attention at common law. In consequence, the rights-based test for standing may be alive and well, after all, hiding behind the formal requirement of personal injuries to interests apart from legal rights. Moreover, the resulting ersatz rights-based standing doctrine may be more virulent than the original article. Since it purports not to rely on law at all, it discourages any open examination of the collective public interests that modern regulatory statutes hope to promote.[136]

This turn of events has elicited mixed reactions in the academic community. Observers who were enthusiastic about *Data Processing* are obviously displeased.[137] Yet oth-

---

out. Professor Sunstein dismisses any Article II argument. In his view, the President's authority to administer statutes is actually a *duty*, and Congress should be able to authorize private litigants to sue to enforce that duty in the courts. Cass R. Sunstein, *Article II Revisionism*, 92 Mich. L. Rev. 131, 134 (1993). But see Harold J. Krent & Ethan G. Shenkman, *Of Citizen Suits and Citizen Sunstein*, 91 Mich. L. Rev. 1793 (1993) (arguing that Congress cannot appoint private attorneys general who eclipse the executive department entirely). According to reports, the executive branch cannot effectively enforce federal environmental protection and civil rights laws without supplemental private lawsuits. See Johnson, note 93, at 385 (reporting that private citizens file the lion's share of suits under the Clean Water Act); Myriam E. Gilles, *Reinventing Structural Reform Litigation: Deputizing Private Citizens in the Enforcement of Civil Rights*, 100 Colum. L. Rev. 1384, 1404–12 (2000) (reporting that the Department of Justice has filed relatively few suits to enjoin patterns of police violence). See also William Casto, The Supreme Court in the Early Republic 137–39 (1995) (reporting that it was commonly understood early on that private citizens could press federal criminal prosecutions if the Attorney General declined to do so).

134. Writing for the Court in *Laidlaw*, Justice Ginsburg described Justice Scalia's concerns about executive prerogatives as "overdrawn." 528 U.S. at 188 n.4. Ginsburg explained that the statute the private plaintiffs were attempting to enforce (the Clean Water Act) explicitly authorized the government to intervene in any private suit of which it disapproved and, in that posture, to bring its views to the court's attention. In the particular case at hand, moreover, the Department of Justice had filed an *amicus* brief supporting the plaintiffs' standing to sue. Id. Justice Scalia responded that an authority to intervene was insufficient. Even if the government could "foreclose" a private action by "itself bringing" the very suit that private litigants wished to advance, the result would be litigation according to "private direction." That, according to Justice Scalia, would be "constitutionally bizarre." Id. at 210 (dissenting opinion). Scalia acknowledged that the DOJ was on the plaintiffs' side in the instant case. But he insisted that "acquiescence and approval by a single Administration" did not "deserve passing mention." Id. Justice Stevens has rejected any argument that Article II brings something to the standing table that Article III does not. See *Stevens*, 529 U.S. at 789 (Stevens, J., dissenting) (joined by Souter, J.); *Steel Co. v. Citizens for a Better Environment*, 523 U.S. 88, 127–28 (1998) (Stevens, J., concurring in the judgment).

135. See note 380.

136. See notes 374–80 and accompanying text (elaborating on these points).

137. E.g., John D. Echeverria & Jon T. Zeidler, Barely Standing: The Erosion of Citizen "Standing" to Sue to Enforce Federal Environmental Law (1999) (reporting the views of the Environmental Policy Project at Georgetown University Law Center).

ers cautiously applaud the Court's inclination to look beyond factual harm to underlying legal arrangements. They hope that if the Court looks once again at the way in which the law recognizes factual harms, it will be more willing than it was a half-century ago to grant standing to litigants who wish to vindicate the kinds of interests that federal regulatory statutes aim to advance. If the Court were to do that, its renewed attention to the legal station of factual injuries might paradoxically produce more (not fewer) public rights lawsuits—the very result that Justice Scalia finds disquieting.[138] The justices occasionally send signals indicating a willingness to be more flexible.[139] Those signals are tentative, however, evoking more speculation in the academic literature than authoritative decisions in the United States Reports.

C. Standing: Constitutional Prerequisites

To satisfy Article III requirements for standing, plaintiffs must assert (and ultimately must prove) that they have suffered, are suffering, or will imminently suffer: (1) factual injury, (2) caused by the defendant, and (3) likely to be redressed by an award of the requested relief.[140] These standing prerequisites are not "mere" matters of "pleading." They form "an indispensible part of the plaintiff's case."[141] Accordingly, plaintiffs must demonstrate each element of standing doctrine (in the manner prescribed for the successive stages of a lawsuit), just as they must demonstrate the elements of their claims on the merits. Modern "notice pleading" conventions do not apply.[142] Initially, plaintiffs must generally allege facts which, if true, would establish these three (related) elements. At the summary judgment stage, they can no longer rely on general averments alone, but must set forth the relevant facts more specifically and supply supporting affidavits or other evidence. By the time a case comes to judgment, plaintiffs must actually prove the existence of injury, causation, and redressability.[143]

1. Injury in Fact

The "injury" requirement appears to demand only that litigants truthfully assert some non-trivial factual harm. When Justice Douglas initially coined the "injury in

138. See text accompanying note 380.
139. See notes 346–73 and accompanying text.
140. *Allen*, 468 U.S. at 751; *Lujan*, 504 U.S. at 560–61.
141. *Lujan*, 504 U.S. at 561.
142. Id.
143. Id. (describing this progression). In some instances, then, plaintiffs' success in convincing the Supreme Court that they have standing may turn on the stage at which the court below arrived at its judgment. If the district court dismissed the complaint under Rule 12, the plaintiffs must only persuade the Court that their general allegations were sufficient. If the district court granted the defendant's motion for summary judgment under Rule 56, the plaintiffs must persuade the Court that they offered more specific factual assertions and adequate supporting evidence. And if the district court conducted a trial before rendering judgment, the plaintiffs must convince the Court that they carried their burden of proving, by a preponderance of the evidence, all (contested) elements of standing. See *Laidlaw*, 528 U.S. at 198 (Scalia, J., dissenting) (underscoring that plaintiffs' burden increases as a case proceeds toward judgment and is at its zenith when the district court has held a trial and reached a judgment on the merits). See note 219 and accompanying text.

fact" formulation in *Data Processing*, that is probably exactly what he meant.[144] The current Court continues to insist that the injury required for standing is *de facto* harm and that (at the constitutional level) standing "in no way depends on the merits" of a litigant's claim that "particular conduct is illegal."[145] Yet not every factual harm will do. The Court draws distinctions within the category of factual injuries, labeling some injuries "judicially cognizable"[146] while finding others to be inadequate. Judicially cognizable injuries are "concrete" and "particularized" in the sense that they affect plaintiffs in a "personal and individual way."[147]

Leading cases elaborating the "injury" requirement may be organized in four categories: (1) cases in which litigants allege hard, quantifiable, economic losses; (2) cases in which taxpayers allege pecuniary harm when the federal government spends money from the public treasury; (3) cases in which litigants assert "generalized grievances;" and (4) cases in which litigants characterize their injuries in a way that necessarily implicates the content of the legal claims they wish to advance, despite the harm-based test for standing the Court purports to employ.

Economic harm cases. Litigants who allege economic injuries at the hands of defendants rarely have difficulty establishing standing. If, for example, a commercial company asserts that it has lost profits as a result of another private firm's violation of federal law, there is typically no doubt that a lawsuit seeking compensation from the offending firm is a "case" or "controversy" within the meaning of Article III.[148] Similarly, if a company alleges that it has suffered economic harm because a governmental agency has unlawfully saddled it with some regulatory burden, the company usually has standing to sue the agency for appropriate relief.[149] Standing is sometimes more controversial in cases in which a company complains not about its own treatment, but rather about the way a governmental agency is regulating other firms. Cases of that kind, of course, are the very cases that trouble Justice Scalia.[150] Nevertheless, there, too, the plaintiff company's allegation of economic effects usually satisfies the constitutional "injury" requirement.[151] Finally, if a company sells or otherwise assigns its business losses to another firm, the successor firm can assert those losses as the basis for its own standing to sue either an offending private firm or a governmental agency for appropriate redress.[152]

Taxpayer cases. In the main, litigants cannot establish standing to litigate in an Article III court on the theory that they pay taxes and therefore are injured when the federal government spends *their* money. The classic precedent is *Frothingham v. Mellon*.[153] In

144. See note 112 and accompanying text. But see notes 374–77 and accompanying text (discussing the arguable links between what is perceived as factual harm and the surrounding legal environment).

145. *Warth v. Seldin*, 422 U.S. 490, 500 (1975).

146. *Allen*, 468 U.S. at 752.

147. *Lujan*, 504 U.S. at 560 n.1; accord *Raines*, 521 U.S. at 819.

148. E.g., *Brunswick Corp. v. Pueblo Bowl-O-Mat*, 429 U.S. 477 (1977); but see id. at 489 (explaining that Congress may make additional demands that exceed the constitutionally required "injury casually linked to" the defendant's unlawful conduct).

149. E.g., *Stark v. Wickard*, 321 U.S. 288, 309–10 (1944).

150. See text accompanying notes 126–127.

151. E.g., *Nat'l Credit Union Admin. v. First Nat'l Bank*, 522 U.S. 479, 488 n.4 (1998); see notes 277–78 and accompanying text.

152. *Poller v. CBS*, 368 U.S. 464, 465 (1962) (providing an illustration but offering no discussion of the standing question).

153. 262 U.S. 447 (1923).

that case, a taxpayer challenged a statute under which the federal government funded medical services. She contended that the statute violated the Commerce Clause and due process. Justice Sutherland recognized that the plaintiff had an economic interest in money held by the treasury. But that interest was "minute and indeterminate." If an expenditure of federal funds had any effect on it at all, that effect was "remote, fluctuating and uncertain."[154] Accordingly, Sutherland refused to allow the plaintiff to proceed. He did not say that Mrs. Frothingham lacked "standing." But he made it clear that her case was not a matter of which an Article III court could take cognizance.

In one instance, however, litigants *can* obtain a foothold in federal court on the basis of their status as federal taxpayers. In *Flast v. Cohen*,[155] Chief Justice Warren held that taxpayers have standing to attack a federal spending measure, ostensibly on the basis of their remote pecuniary interest in the state of the national fisc, if (and only if) they contend that the government is using public funds to finance religion in violation of the Establishment Clause. Warren distinguished *Frothingham* in *Flast*. He explained that the plaintiffs in *Flast* had standing because they showed *both* a nexus between their status (as taxpayers who contributed to the government's coffers) and the kind of legislative enactment they wished to challenge (a spending measure that disbursed public money) *and* a nexus between their status (as taxpayers) and the constitutional provision they contended the statute violated (the Establishment Clause—the chief purpose of which is to prohibit taxation for religious ends). By demonstrating the first nexus, the plaintiffs in *Flast* satisfied the constitutional "injury" requirement for standing; by demonstrating the second, they met an additional, non-constitutional standing requirement that the Court created for the occasion. The plaintiff in *Frothingham*, too, met the constitutional "injury" test, but failed the second, prudential standard.[156]

The decision in *Flast* illustrates the Warren Court's effort to break the hold that the rights-based test for standing then had on access to the federal courts.[157] That case roughly coincided with *Data Processing* and thus reflected the Court's nascent idea that standing should turn on the existence of factual injury, even the modest factual injury that any federal taxpayer might suffer from an expenditure of federal funds. Moreover, Chief Justice Warren plainly had a substantive agenda. He meant to allow litigants to advance claims that government was financing sectarian activities in violation of the Establishment Clause where, previously, no one had been able to do so for lack of standing. To that end, he articulated a formula for taxpayer standing that neatly fit the Establishment Clause claims he wished to make justiciable. Insofar as the constitutional

154. *Frothingham*, 262 U.S. at 487.

155. 392 U.S. 83 (1968).

156. Professor Davis explained that despite some ambiguity in the *Flast* opinion, the Court regarded the injury in that case to be the admittedly "trifling" economic harm that taxpayers suffer when the government spends public money. See Kenneth C. Davis, *Standing: Taxpayers and Others*, 35 U. Chi. L. Rev. 601, 609–12 (1968). See also *Doremus v. Bd. of Ed.*, 342 U.S. 429, 434–35 (1952) (explaining that state taxpayers can establish standing when they press "good-faith pocketbook" actions); cf. *Zelman v. Simmons-Harris*, 122 S.Ct. 2460 (2002) (entertaining a suit by state taxpayers without discussion of any standing difficulties). See notes 290–92 and accompanying text (explaining that the second nexus that Chief Justice Warren described in *Flast* was actually the zone test that the Court would soon announce in *Data Processing*). Mrs. Frothingham could not connect her status as a taxpayer (i.e., her economic interest in the treasury) to the Commerce Clause and due process claims she wished to advance, because those constitutional provisions are not especially conceived as limits on federal spending.

157. See notes 103–06 and accompanying text (describing the state of standing doctrine at the time).

element of that formula went, however, Warren was satisfied with a kind of injury that has not been sufficient in any other context since.

Concurring in *Flast*, Justice Stewart took a position more in keeping with the rights-based test for standing that (in 1968) was formally still in play. He argued that taxpayers had a constitutional *right* under the Establishment Clause to resist taxes supporting religion and that they therefore had standing, on the strength of that *right*, to challenge federal payments to parochial schools.[158] Stewart's view has won a measure of support in the academic community.[159] In the *Valley Forge* case,[160] however, the Court denied that the Establishment Clause confers on all taxpayers a "shared individuated" constitutional right to be free of taxation for religious purposes.[161] Accordingly, *Flast* cannot be justified in hindsight as a decision that simply permitted litigants to proceed in an Article III court on the basis of injuries to interests that the Constitution transforms into legal rights. Instead, *Flast* must rest on the theory that federal taxpayers suffer sufficient factual harm to establish standing (in the constitutional sense) when they challenge a governmental spending measure.[162]

Dissenting in *Flast*, Justice Harlan dismissed the idea that a disbursement of funds from the federal treasury could visit any genuine factual injury on individual taxpayers. In his view, the plaintiffs' suit should be understood as a "public action" in which the plaintiffs hoped to serve as "private attorneys general" representing the "public interest."[163] Suits of that kind, in his view, put serious strains on the judicial function. Accordingly, Harlan argued that the Court should not approve them unilaterally, but should await authorizing legislation. If Congress enacted a statute giving non-Hohfeldian plaintiffs standing to advance Establishment Clause attacks on federal spending measures, he was content that the separation-of-powers considerations would be defused.[164] Chief Justice Warren did not respond to Harlan's argument explicitly, but he necessarily rejected it inasmuch as he concluded that the taxpayer-plaintiffs in *Flast* satisfied all the prerequisites for standing, without benefit of congressional action.

The *Flast* case thus counts as one modern instance in which the Court held that private litigants satisfied the constitutional prerequisites for standing on the basis of injuries that all federal taxpayers might assert regarding the expenditure of funds from the national treasury. That said, it must also be said that the Court has refused to extend *Flast* beyond its facts. The taxpayer-plaintiffs in *Valley Forge* claimed that a federal agency had given a private sectarian college a parcel of public property in violation of the Establishment Clause. Chief Justice Rehnquist restricted *Flast* to taxpayer attacks on federal statutes (rather than actions by federal agencies), and to attacks on statutes enacted pursuant to the spending power (rather than dispositions of federal property

---

158. 392 U.S. at 114 (concurring opinion); see text accompanying notes 116–18.

159. See note 378.

160. *Valley Forge Christian College v. Americans United for Separation of Church and State*, 454 U.S. 464 (1982).

161. Id. at 482.

162. To be sure, taxpayers must also establish a nexus between their status as taxpayers and the statute or constitutional provision they wish to enforce. Yet that second, judicially imposed, non-constitutional standing requirement does nothing to ensure that the particular taxpayer-plaintiffs at bar assert factual injuries that are concrete and personal to them.

163. 392 U.S. at 120 (dissenting opinion); see note 346 and accompanying text. But see notes 130–31 and accompanying text (calling into question Congress' capacity to "waive" separation principle considerations).

164. 392 U.S. at 130–33.

under the Property Clause).[165] He thus left *Flast* in place to control only the specific class of cases for which the analysis in that decision was tailored.[166]

Generalized grievance cases. Apart from taxpayer cases subject to *Flast*, litigants usually lack standing if they assert only "generalized grievances."[167] The "generalized grievance" formulation is notoriously ambiguous. On the one hand, the Court insists that factual injuries will suffice for Article III standing only if they are both "concrete" and "particularized."[168] That formulation suggests that "generalized grievances" can never suffice for Article III standing. A few precedents appear to say as much.[169] On the other hand, the Court has explained that *some* "generalized grievances" *can* satisfy the constitutional "injury" requirement and that "the rule barring generalized grievances" is a *non-constitutional* standing barrier that the Court has erected as a matter of policy.[170] The reason for denying a judicial forum for the consideration of "generalized grievances" is plain enough. Common concerns about public policy may be "more appropriately addressed in the representative branches."[171] The important question is the *source* of the rule that "generalized grievances" are typically not justiciable. If that rule is a matter of non-constitutional judicial policy, Congress can override it by legislation. If it is a matter of constitutional law, Congress cannot.

In *FEC v. Akins*,[172] Justice Breyer explained that the precedents referring to "generalized grievances" typically concern two kinds of injuries: (1) injuries that are "widely shared" with large numbers of other people; and (2) injuries that are by nature "abstract and indefinite."[173] The distinction between the two is of constitutional moment. Injuries that are "generalized" only because they are "widely shared" typically fail to establish standing on non-constitutional, prudential grounds. By contrast, injuries that are "generalized" because they are "abstract and indefinite" fail to establish standing on constitutional, Article III grounds.[174]

By this account, plaintiffs pressing "widely shared" injuries may be successful in establishing standing, but only if they have help from Congress. The *Akins* case provides

165. U.S. Const. art. IV, § 3, cl.2.

166. Then-Professor Fletcher once suggested that it would "dignify" *Valley Forge* to treat it as "anything more than an intellectually disingenuous way to undercut *Flast*." See William A. Fletcher, *The Structure of Standing*, 98 Yale L.J. 221, 268 (1988).

167. *United States v. Richardson*, 418 U.S. 166, 176–77 (1974), quoting *Ex parte Levitt*, 302 U.S. 633, 634 (1937).

168. *Lujan*, 504 U.S. at 560 n.1.

169. In *United States v. Hays*, 515 U.S. 737 (1995), for example, Justice O'Connor initially recalled that the "irreducible constitutional minimum of standing" contains the three familiar elements: injury, causation, and redressability. Then, she explained that "[i]n light of *these* principles," the Court has "refused to recognize a generalized grievance against allegedly illegal governmental conduct as sufficient for standing to invoke the federal judicial power." Id. at 743 (emphasis added).

170. *Allen*, 468 U.S. at 751 (opinion of O'Connor, J.).

171. Id.

172. 524 U.S. 11 (1998).

173. Id. at 24. Justice Breyer acknowledged that the Court has sometimes "styled" the ban on "generalized grievances" as a non-constitutional prudential standing rule and that it has sometimes treated it as a limit on the factual injuries that meet constitutional standards for standing. Id. at 23.

174. Justice Breyer recognized that Article III "limits Congress' grant of judicial power to 'cases' or 'controversies'" and explained that, among other things, "[t]hat means that [plaintiffs] must show...'injury in fact'." Id. at 20, citing *Lujan*, 504 U.S. at 560–61, and *Bennett v. Spear*, 520 U.S. 154, 167 (1997). Then he explained that an "abstract" harm deprives a case of the "concrete specificity that...prevents a plaintiff from obtaining what would, in effect, amount to an advisory opinion." Id. at 24.

an illustration. The Federal Election Campaign Act required "political committees" to file reports identifying their principal benefactors and expenditures. That Act also authorized "[a]ny person" who believed that a violation of the Act had occurred to file a complaint with the Federal Election Commission. The plaintiffs filed a complaint, contending that the American Israel Public Affairs Committee was a "political committee" and had failed to file the required reports. The Commission determined that AIPAC was not a "political committee" within the meaning of the Act and thus had not acted unlawfully. The plaintiffs then sued the Commission pursuant to yet another provision of the Act authorizing "[a]ny party aggrieved by" a Commission order to seek judicial review in a district court. They alleged that they were "aggrieved" by the Commission's decision because, as voters, they needed the information that would be contained in the reports in order to evaluate candidates that AIPAC supported and to track and publicize AIPAC's political influence. Justice Breyer acknowledged that the plaintiffs' interest in AIPAC's contributor list was "widely shared" by voters at large. Yet he held that an injury to that interest was nonetheless sufficient to establish Article III standing.[175]

Justice Breyer explained that the Court itself typically does not entertain suits by plaintiffs claiming only "widely shared" injuries, which may find a "political" forum "readily available."[176] He suggested that, for the same reason, the Court might hesitate to construe a federal statute to confer standing on would-be plaintiffs asserting only injuries they have in common with many others. He insisted, however, that "widely shared" injuries are not "automatically disqualif[ied]" as the basis for standing in an Article III court. Congress can make them justiciable. In *Akins*, the Federal Election Campaign Act *did* confer standing on any voters seeking disclosure of the information the Act required "political committees" to release. Moreover, the plaintiffs' "informational injury" was "directly related to voting, the most basic of political rights." Accordingly, Justice Breyer concluded that the plaintiffs' injury was "concrete and specific" (that is, *not* "abstract and indefinite"). And Congress did not lack "constitutional power to authorize its vindication in the federal courts" merely because it was "widely shared."[177]

---

175. *Akins*, 524 U.S. at 25. Professor Nichol argues that the Court would do better to adopt a presumption that generalized grievances will not suffice and then allow some interests of that kind to establish standing when the Court itself (rather than Congress) concludes that there is a "special need for intervention" by the courts. Gene R. Nichol, Jr., *Injury and the Disintegration of Article III*, 74 Calif. L. Rev. 1915, 1944 (1986).

176. 524 U.S. at 24.

177. Id. at 24–25. This crucial passage hedged a bit. Justice Breyer did not say flatly that the plaintiffs' "informational injury" alone was sufficient. He added that, in the case at hand, the plaintiffs' interest in the information they sought was linked "directly" to their interest in voting. Read narrowly, then, *Akins* may stand only for the proposition that plaintiffs' "widely shared" injury to an interest in obtaining information is sufficient for Article III standing when an allegation of "informational injury" is supplemented by an allegation that denial of the information in question will undercut intelligent political activity. Professor Sunstein reads *Akins* as a much more expansive decision and argues that Breyer's reference to the interest in voting was no more than an "exclamation point." Cass R. Sunstein, *Informational Regulation and Information Standing, Akins and Beyond*, 147 U. Pa. L. Rev. 613, 655 (1999). Yet Sunstein concedes this potential basis for limiting the precedential value of *Akins* considerably. Id. at 645. Professor Gilles thinks Sunstein's ambitions for *Akins* overlook the specific "factual allegations" on which the Court relied. Myriam E. Gilles, *Representational Standing: U.S. ex rel. Stevens and the Future of Public Law Litigation*, 89 Calif. L. Rev. 315, 331 n.97 (2001). In light of *Akins*, the decision in *Raines v. Byrd*, 521 U.S. 811 (1997), may be understood as a case in which Congress could *not* confer standing on litigants, because their injuries were not only widely shared, but were also abstract. See note 77. Members of Congress complained that the Line Item Veto Act authorized the President to cancel spending measures and thus to dilute the

Dissenting in *Akins*, Justice Scalia insisted that Justice Breyer was "wrong" to think that "generalized grievances" had previously excited constitutional concern only when they were "abstract." According to Scalia, "widely shared" injuries, too, had been insufficient for Article III standing in the past.[178] Scalia argued that Breyer ignored the requirement that plaintiffs' injuries must be "particularized." Scalia himself took "particularized" and "generalized" injuries to be mutually exclusive, the one being constitutionally sufficient for standing, the other being constitutionally insufficient. Nevertheless, in his opinion for the Court, Justice Breyer drew the constitutional line in a different place—*within* the category of injuries that the Court has (loosely) labeled as "generalized."[179] Scalia's position, shared by Justices O'Connor and Thomas, may well influence the Court's treatment of close cases in the future. Yet Justice Breyer's explanation of current doctrine is now controlling: The rule barring generalized grievances is not always a constitutional obstacle to standing. With respect to injuries that are "generalized" only because they are "widely shared," the rule is prudential and may be overridden or adjusted by Congress.[180]

By contrast, injuries that are "generalized" because they are "abstract and indefinite" are constitutionally inadequate to support standing, irrespective of any legislation that Congress enacts. In *Akins*, Justice Breyer gave as one example "the injury to the interest in seeing that the law is obeyed."[181] Several precedents illustrate this proposition. In *Schlesinger v. Reservists Committee to Stop the War*,[182] the Court refused to allow citizen-plaintiffs standing to challenge members of Congress who held military commissions in alleged violation of the Incompatibility Clause.[183] And in *United States v. Richardson*,[184] the Court similarly denied taxpayer-plaintiffs standing to attack Congress' failure to

---

effect of their votes for those bills. Chief Justice Rehnquist explained that the plaintiffs could not allege that they would be denied an opportunity to vote on any particular bill. Nor could they claim that their votes would be discounted and that a bill they supported would fail only because their participation in the legislative process was entirely nullified. They were affected by the Act in precisely the same way that other members of the House and Senate were affected. Congress had explicitly granted members authority to attack the Act in federal court. Accordingly, the Chief Justice acknowledged that standing could not be denied on prudential grounds. 521 U.S. at 820 n.3. Yet since the plaintiffs' injuries were both "widely dispersed" and "wholly abstract," there was nothing that Congress could do to get them into federal court. Id. at 829.

178. 524 U.S. at 35 (dissenting opinion). Justice Scalia cited his own discussion of generalized grievances in *Lujan*, in which, he insisted, it was clear enough that "widely shared" injuries were constitutionally inadequate. See notes 190–94 and accompanying text.

179. If, Scalia contended, "concrete generalized grievances (like concrete particularized grievances) are OK, and abstract generalized grievances (like abstract particularized grievances) are bad—one must wonder why we ever *developed* the superfluous distinction between generalized and particularized grievances at all." 524 U.S. at 34 (emphasis in original). Given Justice Breyer's prevailing position in *Akins*, there is a way in which Justice Scalia is right: It probably is confusing to continue using "generalized grievances" as an overarching category, when the constitutionally significant injury classes are subunits of that category: "widely shared" and "abstract and indefinite" injuries. Consider, however, that standing is usually barred for both kinds of generalized grievances. The point in *Akins* is only that some of them are insufficient for constitutional reasons and some for non-constitutional reasons.

180. This does not (necessarily) conclude Congress' role with respect to standing, nor even with respect to what counts as *de facto* injury for constitutional standing purposes. See notes 346–80 and accompanying text.

181. 524 U.S. at 24.

182. 418 U.S. 208 (1974).

183. U.S. Const. art. I, §6, cl.2.

184. 418 U.S. 166 (1974).

publish the CIA's budget in alleged violation of the Statement of Account Clause.[185] The injuries implicated in *Reservists* and *Richardson* existed in a factual sense. But those factual injuries would not suffice, because they were *both* "widely shared" *and* "abstract" within the meaning of *Akins*.[186]

Other leading precedents may be understood in the same way. In *Sierra Club v. Morton*,[187] for example, the club charged that the United States Forest Service's approval of a ski resort in the Mineral King Valley violated federal environmental protection statutes and regulations. The club alleged that it would be harmed if the project proceeded, because it had an interest in conserving the nation's natural resources. Justice Stewart responded that the club's concerns for the environment were inadequate for Article III standing. He suggested, however, that some of the club's members might be able to assert sufficient injury as individuals, provided they sincerely alleged that they used the particular area to be developed and personally stood to suffer the loss of its pristine beauty if the resort was constructed.

There was no statute in *Sierra Club* purporting to authorize organizations especially concerned about the environment to sue on their own account.[188] If such a statute had been in place, perhaps the Court would have allowed it to eliminate any concern that the club's asserted injury was "widely shared." Yet Stewart's decision that the club lacked a sufficient injury arguably rested on the ground that the club's commitment to the en-

---

185. U.S. Const. art. I, §9, cl.7. Chief Justice Burger conceded in *Richardson* that if the taxpayers in that case had no standing, it might well be that no one did. That was not disturbing, he said, because it only signified that the question itself might be political. 418 U.S. at 179. See notes 45–69 and accompanying text. Burger thus suggested that standing doctrine and the political question doctrine can reinforce each other as independent, but related, explanations for routing delicate issues to the political branches. Professor Bandes argues, by contrast, that the Chief Justice merely shored up "one dubious assumption" about the federal courts' role "with another." Bandes, note 125, at 268.

186. Justice Scalia contended that *Richardson* should have produced a different result in *Akins*. By his account, *Richardson* squarely stated that voter interests in obtaining information in the government's hands did not establish a justiciable controversy. 524 U.S. at 35. Justice Breyer responded that *Richardson* was actually decided on the narrow ground that the plaintiff in that case lacked standing for want of a nexus between his status as a taxpayer and his substantive claim (that the Statement of Account Clause mandated release of the CIA's budget). Id. at 22; see notes 155–56 and accompanying text (discussing such a nexus as an element of the *Flast* analysis for taxpayer standing). If, by contrast, "the plaintiff had asserted his standing to sue as a voter rather than a taxpayer," Breyer said the Court would have been faced in *Richardson* with the question whether "'*general directives* [of the Constitution]...[are] subject to enforcement by individual citizens.'" Id., quoting *Richardson*, 418 U.S. at 178 (emphasis in *Richardson*). The answer to that question, according to Breyer, would have "rested in significant part upon the Court's view of the Accounts Clause." Id. This last suggestion warrants attention. Justice Breyer may have contemplated that the Court would (or may yet) apply to the Accounts Clause the kind of analysis the Court applied to the Establishment Clause in *Flast*. Professor Sunstein has argued that, instead, Breyer's reference to the Accounts Clause "suggests unambiguously" that standing turns on whether the legal standard that litigants wish to enforce establishes their "right to bring suit." Sunstein, note 177, at 642. Sunstein apparently has in mind either the kind of argument that Justice Stewart advanced (unsuccessfully) in *Flast*, see text and accompanying note 158, or the argument that Sunstein himself and others have championed—namely, that Congress can establish sufficient "perceived harm" to satisfy the constitutional test for standing simply by enacting a statute authorizing litigants to sue in federal court. See notes 376, 379 and accompanying text.

187. 405 U.S. 727 (1972).

188. The club proceeded under §702 of the Administrative Procedure Act. See notes 107–18 and accompanying text.

vironment generally was "abstract and indefinite" by comparison to the interests of individual club members. It may be, then, that *Sierra Club* is consistent with *Akins*. Certainly, the problem in *Sierra Club* was not that environmental harm could not constitute *de facto* injury for Article III standing purposes. The Court explicitly disclaimed that understanding. Instead, the problem was that the club was not "among" those suffering that kind of injury from the Mineral King Valley project.[189]

Two other important cases may also be brought into line, albeit with some effort. In *Lujan v. Defenders of Wildlife*,[190] environmentalists sued to enforce a provision of the Endangered Species Act requiring the Secretary of the Interior to consult with other agencies regarding the effect of construction projects on rare flora and fauna. The plaintiffs alleged that they had previously visited sites where exotic animals (crocodiles in Egypt, elephants and leopards in Sri Lanka) were at risk from development and intended to return in hopes of actually seeing those creatures in their natural habitats. Justice Scalia acknowledged that the "desire" to "observe an animal species, even for purely aesthetic purposes" was "undeniably" an interest, an injury to which could establish standing in a proper case.[191] He concluded, however, that the plaintiffs in *Lujan* had failed to allege personal injuries of that kind. Their previous visits to Egypt and Sri Lanka "prove[d] nothing," and their professed "intent" to return was speculative in the absence of "concrete plans."[192] In *Lujan*, there *was* a "citizen-suit" statute purporting to confer standing on "any person" who wished to contend that a governmental agency

---

189. 405 U.S. at 735. An organization can establish standing on the basis of injuries it suffers *as* an organization. In *Havens Realty Corp. v. Coleman*, 455 U.S. 363 (1982), the Court found it sufficient that a group advocating open housing alleged that it had been forced to expend additional resources to assist its clients because of the defendant's practice of steering racial minorities into segregated areas. An organization can also litigate on behalf of its members if: (1) the members themselves have standing to sue; (2) the interests the suit seeks to protect are "germane" to the organization's purposes; and (3) the litigation does not require that individual members participate in order to develop either the merits of the claim or the form of appropriate relief. *Hunt v. Washington State Apple Adv. Comm'n*, 432 U.S. 333, 343 (1977). See *UAW v. Brock*, 477 U.S. 274, 290 (1986) (rejecting the argument that members should be required to advance common claims in class actions). Units of government may have standing to advance both their own sovereign or quasi-sovereign interests and the interests of citizens. See *Alfred L. Snapp & Son v. Puerto Rico*, 458 U.S. 592 (1982). For a discussion of *parens patriae* litigation, see Ann Woolhandler & Michael G. Collins, *State Standing*, 81 Va. L. Rev. 387 (1995).

190. 504 U.S. 555 (1992).

191. Id. at 562. Justice Scalia said in *Lujan* that the constitutional "injury in fact" test requires an "invasion of a legally-protected interest." Id. at 555. That phrase suggested the rights-based test for standing that Scalia himself has promoted. See text accompanying note 128; note 85 (discussing Professor Jaffe's analysis). Professor Sunstein has argued that Scalia deliberately used the "legally-protected interest" formulation in *Lujan* as an "unambiguous sign" that the rights-based test is back. Sunstein, note 177, at 641 & n.41. But it is hard to think that Justice Scalia was attempting to discard the harm-based test on the full Court's behalf, without acknowledgment. In the next following passages, he went immediately on to the conventional question whether the plaintiffs suffered factual harm. Writing for the Court in *Steel Co. v. Citizens for a Better Environment*, 523 U.S. 83 (1998), Justice Scalia stated the constitutional requirement as "concrete injury in fact." Id. at 105.

192. Id. at 562–64. In a concurring opinion, Justice Kennedy suggested that the plaintiffs might yet be able to allege sufficient injury if they purchased airline tickets or even if they merely announced a "date certain" on which they would return to the sites they had previously visited. Id. at 579. The plaintiffs in *Lujan* advanced other, more creative interests peculiar to environmental litigation. But Justice Scalia dismissed those contentions summarily. Professor Carlson has suggested various ways in which environmental concerns are unique. Ann E. Carlson, *Standing for the Environment*, 45 U.C.L.A. L. Rev. 937 (1998).

acted in violation of the Endangered Species Act.[193] Still, if the constitutional deficit was not that the plaintiffs advanced "widely shared" injuries, but that they asserted only "abstract and indefinite" harm, the result in *Lujan* can be squared with *Akins*. In this vein, Justice Scalia explained that the plaintiffs in *Lujan*, like the club in *Sierra Club*, had not shown themselves to be "among the injured."[194]

In *Allen v. Wright*,[195] a class of African American children challenged IRS standards for determining whether private schools were entitled to tax exempt status. The plaintiffs alleged that the standards did not screen out schools that refused to admit black students and thus effectively allowed segregationist academies to receive favorable tax treatment in violation of federal statutes. Justice O'Connor understood the plaintiffs to allege two kinds of injury. First, they contended that they suffered harm "by the mere fact" that the government was giving financial aid to "discriminatory private schools." Second, they argued that the tax exemptions the IRS had granted to segregationist schools made those private schools more attractive to white students and thus "impaired" the plaintiffs' ability to attend desegregated public schools.

Justice O'Connor rejected the plaintiffs' first contention. To the extent the children advanced an interest in seeing the IRS comply with federal law, their injury was no more "judicially cognizable" than the injuries in *Reservists* and *Richardson*. Citizens, she explained, "have no standing to complain simply that their government is violating the law."[196] The children in *Allen* came no closer to the mark to the extent they alleged "stigmatic injury" or "denigration" from government complicity in racial discrimination. Injuries of that kind were not cognizable, because the children themselves "were not personally subject to the challenged discrimination." Justice O'Connor found the *Allen* plaintiffs' second contention sufficient to establish injury for standing purposes. Their interest in attending desegregated public schools was "concrete" and "personal" by comparison to their interest in government compliance with federal anti-discrimination law.[197]

The difference between the injuries Justice O'Connor found inadequate in *Allen* and the injury she found sufficient was arguably the difference between "abstract and indefinite" injuries and more "concrete" harm.[198] Moreover, O'Connor did not squarely deny that the plaintiffs could establish constitutional standing on the basis of "widely shared" injuries. She resisted the notion that any African American citizen who is offended by race discrimination can, on that basis alone, allege the injury necessary to challenge the

---

193. 16 U.S.C. §1540(g).

194. 504 U.S. at 563, quoting *Sierra Club*, 405 U.S. at 734–35. Once the Court specifies what is required in cases like *Sierra Club* and *Lujan*, plaintiffs may be able to compensate and comply. On remand in *Sierra Club* itself, individual members of the club alleged that they used the valley for recreational purposes and thus suffered the kind of personal injury that the Supreme Court had found wanting in the club itself. The district court agreed. *Sierra Club v. Morton*, 348 F. Supp. 219 (N.D. Calif. 1972). In *Friends of the Earth v. Laidlaw*, 528 U.S. 167 (2000), individual members of other environmental groups alleged that they lived near, or frequented the area around, a hazardous waste incinerator. On that basis, they achieved standing to challenge the operating company's compliance with the Clean Water Act.

195. 468 U.S. 737 (1984).

196. Id. at 756.

197. Id. at 754–56.

198. At least, her decision may lend itself to this understanding in order to hammer it into line behind the more recent decision in *Akins*.

discrimination in federal court.[199] And she insisted that only African Americans who suffer "personal" injuries can make the required showing.[200] Yet her interpretation of the "injury" requirement did not seriously diminish the number of litigants in *Allen.* O'-Connor recognized that the plaintiffs represented millions of children who could allege the very kind of injury she found to be sufficient for constitutional standing purposes.

Recharacterized injury cases. In other instances, the Court has adjusted the harm-based conception of standing in another way—by consulting the legal claims that litigants wish to pursue in order to characterize the injuries they allege for standing purposes. In *Regents of the University of California v. Bakke*,[201] an unsuccessful white applicant for admission to medical school challenged the school's affirmative action program under which seats in the entering class were set aside for minority candidates. On first blush, it appeared that the plaintiff could show no personal injury. His ideological objection to race-based admissions policies would not suffice, and he could not demonstrate that the personal disappointment he had suffered in being denied admission was related to the affirmative action program about which he complained. Justice Powell nevertheless sustained standing in *Bakke* by recharacterizing the plaintiff's injury: Because of his race, he had not been considered for one of the sixteen places reserved for minority candidates. He had suffered personal harm not by being denied admission, but by being denied the opportunity to compete for all the seats in the class on a racially neutral basis.[202]

In *Northeastern Florida Chapter of Ass'n Gen. Contractors v. Jacksonville*,[203] white contractors attacked a local program reserving a percentage of the city's construction contracts for minority businesses. The plaintiffs in *Jacksonville* could not demonstrate that they had actually lost contracts because of the set-aside program for minorities and thus appeared to lack the injury required for standing. Writing for the Court, however, Justice Thomas characterized their injury as the denial of an opportunity to compete for city jobs on a racially neutral basis. Citing *Bakke*, Justice Thomas explained that since the plaintiffs claimed that the city had established a scheme for distributing contracts that made it harder for them to succeed, they did not have to show that they would have obtained contracts if the scheme had not existed. The required injury could be found in the "denial of equal treatment" under a racially discriminatory program.[204]

---

199. Justice O'Connor insisted that if "stigmatic injury" were enough, it would follow that an African American in Hawaii could challenge an IRS tax exemption granted to a private school in Maine. 468 U.S. at 771 n.3.

200. O'Connor explained, for example, that if the children in *Allen* had alleged that they had been denied admission to private schools on racial grounds, the case would have been different. In that event, they would have suffered judicially cognizable injury and thus would have had standing to challenge their exclusion in a suit against the offending school. E.g., *Runyan v. McCrary*, 427 U.S. 160 (1976).

201. 438 U.S. 265 (1978).

202. Id. at 281 n.14.

203. 508 U.S. 656 (1993).

204. Id. at 666. Professor Ely argues that the Court's decisions approving standing in racial gerrymandering cases can be explained in a similar way. See, e.g., *Shaw v. Reno*, 509 U.S. 630 (1993); *Miller v. Johnson*, 515 U.S. 900 (1995). In those cases, white voters challenged apportionment plans that placed them in congressional districts that had deliberately been drawn to ensure that African American voters would hold a majority. The Court sustained standing in each instance. In *Miller*, Justice Kennedy said that the plaintiffs had sufficient injury, because they suffered the stigma of being treated according to racial stereotypes and because their moral worth as citizens had been challenged. Id. at 911–12, 915. Injuries of that kind would appear to be generalized grievances, abstract in nature. See text accompanying note 174; text accompanying notes 196–200 (discussing the *Allen* case). Cf. *Sinkfield v. Kelley*, 531 U.S. 28 (2000) (holding that residents of abutting districts

Both *Bakke* and *Jacksonville* can be explained as cases in which the plaintiffs established standing by forthrightly asserting interests having the status of legal rights and thus had no need to contend that they were entitled to proceed on the basis of factual injury alone.[205] In both instances, the plaintiffs contended that the actions of the defendants violated their constitutional right to equal protection of the laws. Yet neither Justice Powell in *Bakke* nor Justice Thomas in *Jacksonville* explained his analysis in that way. Instead, both located the plaintiffs' injuries within the harm-based framework in *Data Processing*. That was problematic. In both cases, it was possible to characterize the plaintiffs' injuries as a denial of an opportunity to compete only by reference to the content of their legal theories—namely, their constitutional claims to be treated as equals. By some accounts, *Bakke* and *Jacksonville* implicitly conceded that the injury requirement is not, after all, entirely separate from the legal theories that litigants wish to advance.[206] In point of fact, the reasoning in those cases threatens to dissolve entirely the distinction between standing, on the one hand, and the merits of claims, on the other.

In *Texas v. Lesage*,[207] an unsuccessful applicant for admission to the University of Texas sued the school for damages, claiming that he had been rejected on racial grounds. The school responded with uncontested evidence that the plaintiff would not have been admitted even if the admissions policy had been "completely colorblind." The

---

lack standing because they are not personally denied equal treatment), relying on *Hays*, 515 U.S. at 746. Professor Ely contends that the Court should simply have recharacterized the plaintiffs' injuries. By his account, when white voters are placed in districts in which African American voters are in the majority, it is for the very purpose of ensuring that African Americans will be able to elect African American representatives if they wish, while white "filler people" will be unable to elect white representatives. As distasteful as racial bloc voting may be, Ely argues that white voters have a legitimate interest in "a meaningful shot at helping to elect a representative" of their own race. Accordingly, filler people are personally harmed for standing purposes when they are deprived of that opportunity. John Hart Ely, *Standing to Challenge Pro-Minority Gerrymanders*, 111 Harv. L. Rev. 576, 594 (1997). For a critique of Ely's analysis, see Samuel Issacharoff & Pamela S. Karlan, *Standing and Misunderstanding in Voting Rights Law*, 111 Harv. L. Rev. 2276 (1998). Professor Dow argues the since state legislatures are overwhelmingly white, white voters who object to apportionment schemes that prevent them from helping to elect white representatives should be relegated to political remedies. David R. Dow, *The Equal Protection Clause and the Legislative Redistricting Cases—Some Notes Concerning the Standing of White Plaintiffs*, 81 Minn. L. Rev. 1123 (1997). See Note, *Expressive Harms and Standing*, 112 Harv. L. Rev. 1313 (1999) (arguing that the Court's decisions are inconsistent with respect to injuries resulting from governmentally expressed messages).

205. See text accompanying notes 116–18 (explaining that allegations of the invasion of legal rights count as allegations of factual harm).

206. The Court has cited *Jacksonville* for the proposition that parties who are denied a "benefit" in a "bargaining process" may be injured for standing purposes. *Clinton v. City of New York*, 524 U.S. 417, 433 n.22 (1998); see note 77. Dissenting in *Clinton*, Justice Scalia insisted that a "mere detriment to one's 'bargaining position'" is insufficient and that only a "demonstrated" loss of the bargain itself will do. According to Scalia, *Jacksonville* depends entirely on the right to equal protection and stands only for the proposition that the "denial of equal treatment" qualifies as "injury." 524 U.S. at 457 (dissenting opinion). Professor Sunstein contends that the injuries in some or most of the Court's other standing cases might also have been recharacterized in a way that would have rendered them more likely to suffice for standing purposes. Cass R. Sunstein, *Standing Inquiries*, 1993 Sup. Ct. Rev. 37, 50–51. Sunstein acknowledges that if the Court had recharacterized injuries in the manner he suggests, it would necessarily have had to refer to the legal claims that the plaintiffs concerned wished to advance—namely, claims to certain opportunities said to be conferred by the statutes and constitutional provisions in issue. Professor Spann regards *Bakke* and *Jacksonville* as illustrations of a "racially suspicious" tendency to deny standing to racial minorities who attack patterns of mistreatment, but to grant standing to groups of whites who wish to challenge affirmative action programs. Girardeau A. Spann, *Color-Coded Standing*, 80 Cornell L. Rev. 1422, 1423 (1995).

207. 528 U.S. 18 (1999) (*per curiam*).

district court granted summary judgment on that basis. The circuit court reversed on the theory that the plaintiff could establish a constitutional violation by showing that he had been rejected at a time when the school was operating a racially discriminatory admissions scheme. In the circuit court's view, the plaintiff had standing to advance that claim under *Bakke* inasmuch as he was deprived of the opportunity to compete for admission on a racially neutral basis. The Supreme Court reversed the circuit decision *per curiam*. Since the the applicant would have been rejected in any event, it was clear that the school could not be liable on the merits. It followed, according to the Court, that there was no "cognizable injury." That assessment collapsed the merits of the fourteenth amendment claim into standing.[208]

2. Causation

Litigants seeking access to federal court must show a "causal connection" between their injuries and the defendant's allegedly unlawful behavior.[209] This second constitutional prerequisite for standing is sensible enough, even logically implied. Yet it can be unpredictable.

In some instances, the Court is surprisingly easy to please. In *United States v. SCRAP*,[210] members of an organization called Students Challenging Regulatory Agency Procedures (SCRAP) contended that the Interstate Commerce Commission had taken action that frustrated their enjoyment of the parks in Washington, D.C. Since the students alleged that they visited the parks that would be affected, the Court held that they had asserted adequate personal injuries for standing purposes. Coming to causation, the Court accepted the students' allegation that the ICC's conduct compromised their recreational activities. By the students' account, the ICC failed to prepare an environmental impact statement before deciding to maintain a surcharge on railroad freight rates, the surcharge would keep freight rates high, the cost of shipping refuse away would escalate, less refuse would be removed, recyclable bottles and cans would accumulate in public areas, and, accordingly, the plaintiffs' enjoyment of those facilities would be diminished. In *Duke Power Co. v. Carolina Envt'l Study Grp.*,[211] the Court accepted an equally tenuous causal chain. The plaintiffs in that case argued that the Price-Anderson Act, which limited power company liability in the case of nuclear accident, violated due process. They alleged injury to their use and enjoyment of a lake near their homes: The Act encouraged the power company to construct a nuclear facility on the lake, the plant would emit particles and heat, the lake water would be affected, and, in the end, the plaintiffs' enjoyment of the lake would be compromised.

In other instances, the Court has found causal connections insufficiently clear and definite. Typically, the Court faults causal chains that are contingent on the behavior of intermediate actors. In *Simon v. Eastern Kentucky Welfare Rights Org.*,[212] low income people challenged an IRS decision no longer to require hospitals to provide free care to indigents in order to secure tax exempt status. The plaintiffs easily alleged judicially cognizable injury: the loss of medical care. But the Court was not convinced that their

208. Id. at 21.
209. *Lujan*, 504 U.S. at 560.
210. 412 U.S. 669 (1973).
211. 438 U.S. 59, 74 (1978).
212. 426 U.S. 26 (1976).

injury was caused by the IRS action. The plaintiffs insisted that the IRS ruling would eliminate the hospitals' incentive to treat them and that the hospitals would respond by cutting costs they no longer were required to bear. Justice Powell responded that it was "speculative" whether the hospitals would react to the new IRS ruling in the way the plaintiffs predicted.

In *Warth v. Seldin*,[213] numerous individuals and organizations, alleging a variety of injuries, attacked a city zoning ordinance on the ground that it effectively precluded the construction of low income housing for racial minorities. Justice Powell concluded that all the plaintiffs lacked standing, some of them for want of a causal connection between the ordinance and their injuries. Three individuals, for example, alleged that they wished to relocate to the town, but could not do so because they could afford to live only in a low income project: The ordinance made it difficult for companies to build low income projects, it was for that reason that no suitable projects had been built, and, accordingly, the ordinance was the cause of their difficulties. Powell faulted that causal chain, because it depended on contractors who were willing to build low income housing but were frustrated by the ordinance. The plaintiffs had not demonstrated that there *were* any such contractors waiting in the wings. Accordingly, they had not shown that the ordinance caused their injuries.[214]

The African American children in *Allen v. Wright*[215] also failed to establish causation. By their account, the IRS was employing standards that allowed private segregationist schools to obtain tax exemptions, those schools thus received subsidies that allowed them to operate as havens for white flight from public schools, the resulting exodus from public schools handicapped desegregation efforts, and, in the end, the plaintiffs lost the chance to receive a desegregated public education. According to Justice O'Connor, "the line of causation" between the award of tax exemptions to private schools and the injuries of which the plaintiffs complained was "attenuated." The unpredictable intermediate actors in *Allen* were private schools and the parents of white children. The plaintiffs had not demonstrated that enough private schools were receiving improper tax exemptions to make any "appreciable difference" to the attempts by public schools in the plaintiffs' communities to desegregate. Nor had the plaintiffs established that improper tax exemptions actually affected either the admissions policies of the private schools concerned or the decisions of white parents to enroll their children in those schools. Accordingly, it was not clear (enough) that, if the IRS had actually granted tax exemptions to segregationist private academies in violation of federal law, that unlawful action made any difference to the public schools the plaintiffs attended.[216]

---

213. 422 U.S. 490 (1975).

214. The plaintiffs identified two unsuccessful proposals for housing developments in recent years, but failed to show that those buildings, had they been constructed, would have supplied the plaintiffs with apartments they could afford. Even if the ordinance had frustrated those two projects, and even if some low income people had suffered injury in the process, the three particular plaintiffs in *Warth* could not demonstrate that they themselves would have been among the injured. See text accompanying notes 189, 194. Professor Sager argues that it should have been unnecessary for the plaintiffs to show that the ordinance actually deprived them of the "ultimate benefit" of affordable housing and that it should have sufficed that the ordinance forestalled an "intermediate" state of affairs in which the plaintiffs' chances of securing housing would be improved. Lawrence G. Sager, *Insular Majorities Unabated: Warth v. Seldin and City of Eastlake v. Forest City Enterprises, Inc.*, 91 Harv. L. Rev. 1373, 1385–86 (1978). See notes 201–06 and accompanying text (describing the way in which injuries can sometimes be recharacterized as lost opportunities).

215. 468 U.S. 737 (1984); see notes 195–200 and accompanying text.

216. 468 U.S. at 757–59.

The Court's decisions on causation have been questioned. At the very least, those decisions apply pleading standards that are unusually exacting, even for standing cases.[217] Arguably, the Court examines fact-specific complaints inconsistently. In *SCRAP* and *Duke Power*, the Court accepted the plaintiffs' allegations that the companies concerned would respond to economic incentives in a predictable self-interested way. Yet in *Simon*, *Warth*, and *Allen*, the Court found allegations of that kind to be speculative.[218] The procedural posture of a case may offer a partial explanation in some instances, but not in all.[219]

The apparent inconsistency in the cases may reflect the Court's level of enthusiasm for adjudicating the claims that plaintiffs seek to advance. The Court may be generous to plaintiffs attempting to construct causal chains when it wants to reach the merits and needs to approve the plaintiffs' standing in order to do so. But the Court may be more demanding when it wishes to avoid the merits and thus needs a door-closing device that forecloses adjudication. In *Duke Power*, for example, the Court plainly wanted to reach the merits of the plaintiffs' challenge to the Price-Anderson Act in order to reverse the lower court's decision declaring that statute unconstitutional. In other instances, perhaps including *Warth*, *Simon*, and *Allen*, the Court may have been less anxious to grapple with the merits of the plaintiffs' substantive claims.[220]

---

217. See notes 142–43 and accompanying text. Dissenting in *Allen*, Justice Stevens complained that Justice O'Connor was applying intricate pleading rules "that would have gladdened the heart of Baron Parke." Id. at 785 n.2, quoting Abram Chayes, *The Role of the Judge in Public Law Litigation*, 89 Harv. L. Rev. 1281, 1305 (1976). In a separate dissent in *Allen*, Justice Brennan unsuccessfully urged the Court to remand the case so that the plaintiffs could amend their complaint in light of the Court's pleading requirements. 468 U.S. at 775 n.6. Cf. *Havens*, 455 U.S. at 377–78 (following that course).

218. On this point, Justice Stevens said that the causation analysis in *Allen* required only a "restatement of elementary economics" of the kind the Court acknowledges in other contexts. 468 U.S. at 788 (dissenting opinion), citing *Regan v. Taxation With Representation*, 461 U.S. 540 (1983). Professor Nichol describes the allegation in *Allen* as "simple: tax exempt status makes private schools economically more attractive." Gene R. Nichol, Jr., *Abusing Standing: A Comment on Allen v. Wright*, 133 U. Pa. L. Rev. 635, 639 n. 26 (1985).

219. In *SCRAP*, for example, the sufficiency of the plaintiffs' allegations regarding standing was determined in the context of the ICC's motion to dismiss under Rule 12(b). In that posture, the Court assumed both that the plaintiffs' allegations were true and that general allegations embraced more specific assertions. That may explain the Court's generous examination of the complaint in *SCRAP*. See notes 142–43 and accompanying text. But it does not defuse the tension between *SCRAP* and other cases in this line. The *Simon* case was handled in a Rule 56 posture. But both *Warth* and *Allen* were Rule 12 cases, albeit the motion in *Warth* was considered in light of "extensive supportive materials." 422 U.S. at 497. In retrospect, *SCRAP* probably should be dismissed as a sport.

220. Professor Sager contends that *Warth* rests on the premise that federal courts ordinarily should leave zoning matters to state courts. Sager, note 214, at 1391. Consider, however, that *Warth* was decided in 1975. It was not until *Washington v. Davis*, 426 U.S. 229 (1976), that the Court announced its novel formula for handling equal protection challenges to rules and practices that are race-neutral on their face, but impose burdens disproportionately on racial minorities. Then, a year after *Davis*, the Court concluded in *Village of Arlington Heights v. Metro. Hous. Develop. Corp.*, 429 U.S. 252 (1977), that plaintiffs attacking exclusionary zoning practices like those in *Warth* had established a sufficient causal chain and thus had standing to obtain an adjudication of their claim on the merits. The plaintiffs in *Arlington Heights* did connect themselves to a particular low income housing project they insisted was stalled by the ordinance in that case, and the Court distinguished *Warth* on that basis. Nevertheless, it seems inescapable that the Court wanted to avoid the substantive claim in *Warth* until the justices had settled on an analysis to fit it and that, once they announced such an analysis in *Davis*, they were more willing to revisit the issues in *Warth* in a new case (*Arlington Heights*) which then could serve as a vehicle for elaborating the *Davis* approach. Pro-

By other accounts, the Court's cases regarding causation support the thesis that decisions on standing are often actually decisions on the merits.[221] That is invariably true when, to satisfy the threshold requirement for standing, plaintiffs allege not only factual injury but also an invasion of a positive legal right. In cases of that kind, causation necessarily merges with the merits—namely, whether the defendant has, indeed, violated the plaintiffs' legal rights. Even in cases in which plaintiffs allege only an injury to an interest for standing purposes, causation approaches the merits. The same allegations plaintiffs offer to establish a causal connection between their injury and the defendant's action are often equally crucial to their legal claim that the defendant's action is unlawful. In *Allen*, for example, Justice O'Connor said that the plaintiffs had not alleged an adequate causal chain in part because it was unclear that the IRS permitted enough ineligible private schools to receive tax exemptions to compromise efforts to desegregate the public schools the plaintiffs attended. Yet that incorporated the very legal claim the plaintiffs advanced—namely, the claim that the IRS was allowing private segregationist academies to obtain tax exemptions to which they were not lawfully entitled.[222]

3. Redressability

The Supreme Court originally equated the causation requirement with the prospect of effective judicial relief. Chief Justice Burger explained that the only question was whether the injury asserted for standing purposes "fairly" could be "traced" to the defendant, so that if a court found a plaintiff's claim to be meritorious, the court could coerce the defendant to do something that redressed the plaintiff's injury.[223] Today, however, the Court treats "redressability" as a third constitutional prerequisite for standing. Justice O'Connor explained in *Allen* that "[t]o the extent there is a difference" between causation and redressability, it is that causation links the defendant's allegedly unlawful behavior to the plaintiff's injury, while redressability links the plaintiff's injury to the relief the plaintiff asks a court to award if it finds a claim to be meritorious.[224] That distinction granted, the Court nonetheless typically collapses its search for causal connections into its evaluation of the likelihood of effective judicial relief.

In *Allen*, Justice O'Connor purported to rest her result on the ground that the plaintiffs had failed to demonstrate causation. They had not established that their judicially cognizable injury was "fairly traceable to the assertedly unlawful conduct of the IRS." O'Connor explained, however, that the causal linkage broke down, because it was unclear "whether withdrawal of a tax exemption from any particular school would lead the school to change its policies." That, of course, went not to the causation question

---

fessor Nichol contends that the justices' views regarding the claims plaintiffs seek to advance "will likely affect the standing determination as long as judges with strong feelings about substantive claims decide jurisdictional issues." Nichol, note 218, at 650. Professor Logan argues that causation is too fluid to be considered a constitutional mandate and would better be treated as a prudential consideration. David A. Logan, *Standing to Sue: A Proposed Separation of Powers Analysis*, 1984 Wis. L. Rev. 37, 82.

221. See note 76 and accompanying text.

222. See text accompanying note 195. Professor Nichol has noted the overlap between causation and the merits of the claim in *Allen*. Nichol, note 218, at 640 n. 27.

223. *Duke Power*, 438 U.S. at 74. See also *Warth*, 422 U.S. at 505 (explaining that plaintiffs must allege that their injuries are the "consequence" of the defendant's actions "or" that the relief they seek will "remove the harm").

224. 468 U.S. at 753 n.19.

(whether existing IRS rules allowed private schools to obtain tax exemptions they did not deserve, effectively subsidized white flight from public schools, and thus caused the plaintiffs to lose their chance for desegregated public education), but rather to the redressability question (whether, if the plaintiffs were successful on the merits, a court could remedy the plaintiffs' injury by forcing the IRS to use more effective standards that would deny tax exemptions to undeserving private schools, create an incentive for those schools to admit black students in order to obtain lawful exemptions, eliminate private schools as a haven for white flight, and thus make it easier for public schools to desegregate).[225]

Occasionally, the Court treats redressability in isolation from causation. At the same time, the crucial element of the analysis is similar—namely, whether a chain of events that plaintffs construct depends on the behavior of some independent actor. Plaintiffs will be unsuccessful if there are gaps in the linkage they assert between the relief they seek from the courts and the injuries of which they complain. In the *Lujan* case,[226] for example, Justice Scalia said that redressability would present a problem for the plaintiffs even if they formed definite plans to visit sites where construction projects threatened endangered species and thus established sufficient personal injury. If they succeeded on the merits of their claim, the only relief they could win was an order requiring the Secretary to consult with the federal agencies involved in those projects. Since those agencies were not themselves defendants, however, the court could not order *them* to consult with the Secretary. Moreover, even if all the government's arms agreed to consider the effects of the projects on endangered animals, the plaintiffs had not shown that officials in Egypt and Sri Lanka would pay any heed. They might disturb the animals' habitats, whether or not their American sponsors approved.

Justice Scalia's conclusion regarding redressability in *Lujan* received only plurality support. In apparently similar cases, the Court has demonstrated more flexibility. In *Bennett v. Spear*,[227] for example, ranchers contended that the Fish and Wildlife Service failed to comply with the Endangered Species Act in developing a plan to keep the water levels in two reservoirs relatively high to protect an endangered species of sucker fish. According to the ranchers, the plan allowed too little water to escape for their commercial and recreational use. It appeared, however, that the Service had formal authority only to advise another agency, the Bureau of Reclamation, which had responsibility for physically adjusting the water in the lakes. And the plaintiffs had neglected to name the Bureau as a defendant. Nevertheless, in his opinion for the Court in *Bennett*, Justice Scalia himself found redressability no bar, because the named agency, the Fish and Wildlife Service, had the capacity to coerce the unnamed agency, the Bureau, into line.[228]

---

225. Id. at 753, 758. This same pattern is often repeated. In *Linda R.S. v. Richard D.*, 410 U.S. 614 (1973), the mother of an illegitimate child claimed that the child's father was not making support payments because officials pressed prosecutions only against the delinquent fathers of legitimate children. Justice Marshall said that the plaintiff had failed to allege a "sufficient nexus between her injury and the government action" she wished to challenge, in part because the only relief a court could award was an order requiring the defendants to prosecute cases involving illegitimate children. That might result in a prosecution of the father of the plaintiff's child, perhaps even in his incarceration. But it would not ensure that she would receive the support payments she was due.

226. *Lujan v. Defenders of Wildlife*, 504 U.S. 555 (1992); see notes 190–94 and accompanying text.

227. 520 U.S. 154 (1997).

228. Id. at 169–71. See notes 325–29 and accompanying text (discussing other aspects of *Bennett*).

Justice Scalia warned in *Bennett* that plaintiffs' standing would be questionable if their injuries could be redressed only by the "*independent*" action of some "third party not before the court."[229] But in *Utah v. Evans*,[230] the full Court was again more flexible. In that case, the state of Utah sued federal officers responsible for the census on the theory that their sampling techniques violated federal statutes and the Constitution.[231] Specifically, Utah claimed that the use of "hot deck imputation" methodology produced census results that would have the effect of eliminating one of Utah's representatives in the House of Representatives and giving that place to a new representative from North Carolina. In its prayer for relief, Utah sought a declaration that the census report the defendant officers had filed was unlawful and an injunction requiring them to recalculate their results and file a corrected report. North Carolina intervened to contest Utah's standing.

It was conceded that the injury that Utah meant to avoid was the loss of its representative. According to North Carolina, neither a declaration that the federal officers had miscounted the population nor even an injunction requiring them to count again and revise their figures could redress that injury. North Carolina argued that a federal statute required the defendants to file their report by a date certain and they had done so. Thereafter, pursuant to the statute, the President had sent a statement to Congress, specifying the allocation of representatives that the census report indicated each state should have. Next, also according to the statute, the Clerk of the House had sent certificates to the governors of Utah and North Carolina (as well as the governors of other states) indicating the number of seats each state would have in the next Congress. At that point, according to the text of the statute, each state was entitled to the number of places specified in its certificate. By North Carolina's account, then, the governing statute made the existing allocation of seats inviolate until the next census. Even if the statute permitted an adjustment, an actual reallocation of seats in the House could be achieved only if the President and Congress took some corrective action. Of course, Utah had not named (and could not name) either the President or Congress as party defendants.[232]

Writing for the Court, Justice Breyer rejected North Carolina's arguments in turn. He acknowledged that the statute's literal terms suggested that a certificate showing a state's allocation could not be changed after a specified time. But he declined to read that statute "so absolutely."[233] The statute did not "expressly say" that a certificate could not be altered even if errors were found in the census report on which it was based. Accordingly, the statute lent itself to a more "flexible" construction, allowing a certificate to be altered if serious clerical or mathematical errors were detected. And if a certificate could be changed in the case of errors in calculations, Justice Breyer concluded that it also could be changed in the case of legal error identified by a court, "leading to a court-required revision" of the underlying census report.[234] Turning to the argument that the President and Congress were not named defendants, Justice Breyer said the Court would assume that they would acknowledge a judicial determination that the census was invalid and act accordingly.[235]

---

229. 520 U.S. at 169 (emphasis in original), quoting *Lujan*, 504 U.S. at 560–61.

230. 122 S.Ct. 2191 (2002).

231. See Chapter IV, notes 73–74 and accompanying text (discussing other features in *Evans*).

232. See Chapter X, notes 431, 438 and accompanying text (discussing immunity).

233. 122 S.Ct. at 2198.

234. Id.

235. On this point, Justice Breyer had the benefit of a previous opinion by Justice O'Connor in *Franklin v. Massachusetts*, 505 U.S. 788, 803 (1992).

Only Justice Scalia dissented from Justice Breyer's treatment of the redressability question. He embraced North Carolina's reading of the statute and thus agreed that the allocation of seats in the next House of Representatives was fixed and unalterable in the absence of overriding legislation. On the more general question of the linkage between the relief Utah hoped to obtain from the courts and the state's ultimate goal, Justice Scalia argued that in *Evans*, finally, the Court surely had a case in which the "unfettered choices" made by "independent" actors could forestall the result that a plaintiff hoped to achieve. In particular, Justice Scalia insisted that the Court displayed "gross disrespect" for the President by assuming that if the courts held that the defendant officers had computed the population by unlawful means and ordered them to correct their report, the President would "obediently" follow the new advice from his "subordinates" and alter his statement to Congress.[236] Justice Scalia's isolation in *Evans* may indicate that most members of the Court are not enthusiastic about a strict redressability analysis. Then again, it seems clear that the other justices wanted to recognize Utah's standing in order to reach the merits and settle the legal issues regarding computation methodology for purposes of the next census. On the merits, Justice Breyer held that "hot deck imputation" violates neither federal statutes nor the Constitution.

Redressability analysis, flexible as it is in cases like *Evans*, can be relaxed in another way in cases in which litigants advance "procedural rights." Justice Scalia acknowledged in *Lujan* that litigants who contend only that they are entitled to certain procedures need not satisfy "all the normal standards for redressability and immediacy." [237] For example, a private citizen who lives near a site that a federal agency has approved for a new dam may well have standing to sue the agency in federal court for failing to prepare an environmental impact statement (typically required by the National Environmental Protection Act). That neighbor can allege concrete factual injury to the enjoyment of his contiguous real estate. If, however, his legal claim is limited to an alleged violation of the "procedural right" to the preparation of an impact statement, his prayer for relief will be restricted to an order requiring the agency to prepare the statement. The plaintiff will not be in a position to seek, and certainly cannot win, an order affecting the dam project itself, once an impact statement has been secured. If the dam will be built anyway, it would seem that the relief the plaintiff seeks and obtains (an impact statement) will not redress his injury (the diminution in the value of his property). But that is the point. The neighbor will not be held to the usual redressability requirement. He will have standing to press his procedural right to an impact statement if he requests an order requiring the agency to cure its unlawful failure to prepare a statement in the first place.[238]

At all events, the redressability requirement makes access to the federal courts contingent on the kind of relief that litigants desire. Simply put, litigants must establish standing with respect to each judicial remedy they pursue. If they name a remedy that is not reasonably likely to redress their factual injuries, they will lack standing to pursue that form of relief, even though they may have standing to seek other remedies. When plaintiffs have suffered harm in the past and seek backward-looking relief in the nature of damages, redressability is rarely problematic. A monetary award forthrightly com-

---

236. 122 S.Ct. at 2224 (dissenting opinion). Justice Scalia did not pause to name any particular chief executive who might be offended by the suggestion that he would comply with the judgment of a federal court.

237. *Lujan*, 504 U.S. at 572 n.7.

238. Id. The *SCRAP* case is a concrete illustration. See note 210 and accompanying text.

pensates for losses already sustained. When, by contrast, plaintiffs seek forward-looking declaratory or injunctive relief, redressability can present a constitutional bar.[239]

Litigants who assert only injury in the past cannot seek declaratory or injunctive relief, which speaks to the future and thus cannot redress the injury alleged. The leading illustration is *City of Los Angeles v. Lyons.*[240] The plaintiff in that case complained that the Los Angeles police used life-threatening "choke holds" to subdue suspects, that sixteen people had lost their lives in that way, and that he himself had been strangled into unconsciousness. Contending that the choke holds were unconstitutional, he sued the police both for compensatory damages and for an injunction barring use of the holds. In the Supreme Court, Justice White acknowledged that the plaintiff had standing to sue for damages, but held that he did not have standing to sue for injunctive relief. An injunction could only protect the plaintiff from being subjected to a choke hold on some other occasion. But he could not plausibly allege either that he would be arrested again or that, if he were, the police would restrain him in the same way. Justice White therefore concluded that the plaintiff lacked constitutional standing to seek the particular form of relief he requested.[241]

Litigants who anticipate future injury *can* seek declaratory and injunctive relief. Yet they may also sometimes seek a monetary award for the purpose of deterring defendants from committing further injurious acts. In *Friends of the Earth v. Laidlaw*,[242] private plaintiffs alleged that they frequented the area near a waste disposal plant and stood to be injured if the defendant company resumed its polluting ways at the plant. They sought not only an injunction barring further violations of federal anti-dumping laws, but also the assessment of monetary civil penalties for the violations to date. Justice Ginsburg acknowledged that the fines would be paid to the federal government, so there was no argument that the money would somehow compensate the plaintiffs for injuries in the past. Yet she explained that the fines nonetheless would redress the plaintiffs' prospective injuries inasmuch as they would discourage additional pollution at the site. Monetary awards are primarily tailored to compensate for losses already incurred and affect the future only indirectly. Yet they can also deter future misconduct.[243] When it appears that deterrence is reasonably likely to occur, the redressability requirement is satisfied.

---

239. See Chapter X, notes 446–94 and accompanying text (explaining that defendant officers may be immune from suit for compensatory relief). To the extent this feature of standing doctrine prefers actions for damages to suits for injunctions, it is in some tension with the Court's historical willingness to entertain private suits against government officers for injunctive relief and its comparative hesitancy over suits for compensatory damages. See Chapter VIII, note 212. Injunctions are appealing inasmuch as they force officials to comply with the law. On the other hand, in the context of standing, the Court insists that litigants' desire to see the law enforced is insufficient. See text accompanying notes 181, 196.

240. 461 U.S. 95 (1983).

241. The *Lyons* analysis is not airtight. In *Kolender v. Lawson*, 461 U.S. 352 (1983), the plaintiff alleged that he had been arrested under a vague statute on fifteen occasions within a period of two years. That record established a "credible threat" that he would be arrested again and thus established his standing to seek injunctive relief. Id. at 355 n.3. See note 420 and accompanying text (discussing the need for a similar "credible threat" to sue for declaratory relief). Justice White also said in *Lyons* that, apart from Article III standing difficulties, the plaintiff could not meet the non-constitutional standards for obtaining injunctive relief. Professor Fallon argues that to the extent the Court was primarily concerned with the nature of the relief the plaintiff sought, it would have done better to decide the case on that non-constitutional basis. See Fallon, note 85, at 8.

242. 528 U.S. 167 (2000).

243. See generally Daniel J. Meltzer, *Deterring Constitutional Violations by Law Enforcement Officials: Plaintiffs and Defendants as Private Attorneys General*, 88 Colum. L. Rev. 247 (1988).

Redressability nonetheless poses a serious barrier to standing in many cases. In *Steel Co. v. Citizens for a Better Environment*,[244] for example, the plaintiffs collected and distributed information about the use of hazardous materials. They notified a company that it had failed to file reports regarding its use of toxic chemicals, as required by the Emergency Planning and Community Right-to-Know Act. The company filed the overdue reports, and the Environmental Protection Agency declined to take punitive action. The plaintiffs then sued the company, alleging that their "right to know" about the use of toxic substances and their "interests" in protecting the environment were "adversely affected" by the company's failure to supply information in a timely way. The plaintiffs alleged that the effects of the company's default lingered after the company submitted tardy reports, because the plaintiffs needed a steady flow of current data to fuel their public education campaign. Justice Scalia assumed for purposes of decision that the plaintiffs had alleged cognizable injury in fact for standing purposes.[245] He concluded, however, that they lacked standing because their injuries were not redressable.

Justice Scalia took each of the plaintiffs' requests for relief in turn. He agreed that they might win a declaratory judgment that the defendant had filed the required reports after they were due. But since that violation of the Act was uncontested, such a declaration would be "worthless."[246] He acknowledged that the plaintiffs had requested an order authorizing them to inspect the company's records and premises to ensure that the company complied with the Act. Citing *Lyons*, however, he said an injunctive order of that kind would not be available, because the district court would not assume that the company's misconduct in the past demonstrated a sufficient likelihood of misbehavior in the future. Finally, Justice Scalia dismissed out of hand the argument that the plaintiffs might recoup the money they had spent in pressing the lawsuit. Even if they obtained a reimbursement order, it would not redress the injuries that were said to have justified the suit originally. Certainly, he said, the prospect of being reimbursed for the costs of litigation could not independently establish injury for standing purposes. If that were true, plaintiffs would be able to manufacture injury in fact routinely,

---

244. 523 U.S. 83 (1998).

245. Id. at 105. Justice Scalia said that the Court had never decided whether "being deprived of the information" that the Act required companies to report was a "concrete" injury for standing purposes. He noted, however, that some of the plaintiffs in *Steel* resided in the community in which the company operated and that they did not merely allege that they had the kind of interest in the information that anyone might claim, but insisted that they had a "particular plan" for using it. Id. at 1017–18. See text accompanying notes 86–90 (discussing the Court's early misgivings about recognizing standing in the beneficiaries of regulatory programs); notes 167–200 and accompanying text (discussing generalized grievances). In the *Akins* case, the Court held that plaintiffs suffered concrete factual injury when they were deprived of information they insisted a political committee was obligated by law to divulge. See note 177 and accompanying text. Justice Breyer recognized that the plaintiffs in that case might never get the information they wanted, even if they were correct that the statute required it to be made available. The agency involved, the Federal Election Commission, had authority to waive that requirement in its discretion. Nevertheless, Justice Breyer dismissed any concerns regarding either causation or redressability on the ground that the plaintiffs were entitled to an authoritative judicial statement of the law as the basis for the agency's exercise of discretion. *Akins*, 524 U.S. at 25. Professor Sunstein has suggested that Justice Breyer essentially acted upon Justice Scalia's own assurances in *Lujan* that litigants claiming violations of procedural rights will be spared a rigorous redressability requirement. See text accompanying notes 237–38. Sunstein, note 177, at 650.

246. See notes 16–21 and accompanying text (discussing the argument that declaratory judgments are advisory opinions).

merely by investing funds in the very lawsuits they needed injury to launch in the first instance.[247]

D. Standing: Non-Constitutional Prerequisites

Some features of standing doctrine are not constitutional imperatives, but rest on a different, non-constitutional footing. Two implications attend the prudential nature of these ideas. First, the Court explicitly claims more discretion when it describes and applies non-constitutional rules of "self-restraint" than it claims when it elaborates standing rules it ascribes to the separation principle and Article III.[248] Second, Congress can establish or eliminate prudential standing rules by statute.[249]

1. Third-Party Claims

Once litigants satisfy the constitutional prerequisites for standing and gain a foothold in federal court, they usually can advance only the legal claims they themselves have against the defendant. The progenitor precedent for this basic idea is *Yazoo & Mississippi Valley R.R. v. Jackson Vinegar Co.*[250] In that case, the railroad attacked the constitutionality of a state statute not only as it had been applied in the case at bar, but also as it might be applied in other readily foreseeable contexts. The Supreme Court limited its consideration of the railroad's claim to the circumstances in which the state courts had enforced the statute below. The principle derived from *Yazoo* is that litigants must be content to press the claims they have at present and cannot ask the federal courts to anticipate claims that might arise from a different pattern of facts.[251]

---

247. *Steel*, 523 U.S. at 107; see *Diamond v. Charles*, 476 U.S. 54, 70–71 (1986) (holding that an intervenor's interest in avoiding attorney fees was insufficient to maintain standing to appeal from an unfavorable judgment). The plaintiffs in *Steel* also offered to show redressability on the ground that they might obtain an order requiring the company to pay fines for failing to file the reports on time. Justice Scalia rejected that argument on the ground that the money would be paid into the federal treasury and thus could not compensate the plaintiffs for the injuries they had suffered. He did not discuss the possibility that fines might deter future harms. In *Steel*, however, it was conceded that the company's unlawful behavior had ceased and thus needed no deterrence. In *Laidlaw*, Justice Ginsburg distinguished *Steel* on that basis. 528 U.S. at 187–88. Dissenting in *Laidlaw*, Justice Scalia argued that "deterrence" is "speculative as a matter of law" and therefore never satisfies the redressability requirement. Id. at 205.

248. *Craig v. Boren*, 429 U.S. 190, 193 (1976).

249. See text accompanying note 75. E.g., *United Food & Commercial Workers Union v. Brown Grp.*, 517 U.S. 544 (1996) (holding that Congress could legislatively eliminate a prudential feature of the Court's doctrine regarding "organizational standing").

250. 226 U.S. 217 (1912).

251. The railroad in *Yazoo* argued that a Mississippi statute violated due process inasmuch as it imposed a $25 fine on the railroad if it failed to settle any claim for lost or damaged freight within a fixed period. In the particular case at bar, the railroad had been fined for missing the deadline with respect to a legitimate claim. The Court sustained the statute on that basis. The railroad contended that the statute would also authorize a fine in the case of an extravagant claim that the railroad could not be expected to settle. The Court refused to consider that argument until a case involving an unreasonable claim actually arose. Id. at 219–20.

Extrapolating from *Yazoo*, the Court typically insists that litigants are equally barred from advancing legal claims that belong to a third party—someone who does not formally appear on either side of the dispute at hand. Even though the actual parties to a suit have by hypothesis initiated an Article III "case" on which federal judicial power can be exercised, it still is intuitively sensible that, within that case, they should not be claiming that someone else's rights have been violated. If individuals whose rights are actually at stake are not complaining, the Court hesitates to anticipate the claims they *might* one day advance on their own behalf. Parties who assert the rights of others may generate unfavorable results that will frustrate those whose rights are actually affected, if and when they file their own lawsuits.[252]

It may be misleading to regard the rule against third party claims as an aspect of standing doctrine. By hypothesis, litigants who are in federal court in the first instance have met the constitutional prerequisites for standing. The question, then, is not whether they have any business in an Article III court, but whether the business they concededly have can include advancing claims on behalf of others. Nevertheless, the prohibition on third-party claims is commonly regarded as a feature of prudential standing doctrine.[253]

The general prohibition on third-party claims applies both to plaintiffs and to defendants. Of course, defendants have constitutional standing inasmuch as they suffer injury simply from being named in a lawsuit (and will suffer still more injury if they are found liable). The arguments they can advance by way of defense, however, implicate other prudential considerations. In the leading case, *Barrows v. Jackson*,[254] the plaintiff sued a white property holder for selling land to an African American buyer in violation of a racially restrictive covenant. The Court wrestled with the question whether the defendant should be permitted to answer that the covenant violated the equal protection rights of the buyer (concluding in the end that the defendant *could* advance that argument).

In some circumstances, the rationales for the general rule against third-party claims do not hold, and the Supreme Court, accordingly, allows exceptions: (1) cases in which litigants are specially positioned to advocate *jus tertii* on behalf of other people; and (2) cases in which litigants attack statutes for overbreadth in violation of the first amendment.

Jus tertii cases. Litigants can advance legal claims that belong to others if two factors counsel an exception from the general rule against third-party arguments. First, the absent parties must face obstacles to proceeding on their own behalf. In that event, it cannot be assumed that the absent parties have failed to file suit because they consider the rights at stake unimportant. The obstacle need not prevent the absent parties from litigating altogether. In some instances, the Court has found it sufficient that they would engage significant personal costs if they were to file their own suits. In the leading case, *Singleton v. Wulff*,[255] the Court allowed physicians to advance the rights of their patients

---

252. Professor Brilmayer defends constitutional and non-constitutional standing rules to the extent they discourage representative litigation that may compromise the interests and rights of those who are said to be represented. Lea Brilmayer, *The Jurisprudence of Article III: Perspectives on the "Case or Controversy" Requirement*, 93 Harv. L. Rev. 297 (1979). But see notes 308–18 and accompanying text (discussing Congress' ability to make private litigants its agents or assignees for standing purposes).

253. See Henry P. Monaghan, *Third Party Standing*, 84 Colum. L. Rev. 277, 278 n.6 (1984).

254. 346 U.S. 249 (1953).

255. 428 U.S. 106 (1976).

to obtain abortions. Justice Blackmun explained that female patients might have sued on their own behalf, but, in order to do so, would have risked exposing their private decisions regarding procreation.[256] In *Craig v. Boren*,[257] Justice Brennan permitted a liquor store proprietor to press the rights of her teenage male customers.

Second (and in addition), litigants who wish to advance the claims of others must bear some relationship to the absent persons. If, for example, the parties to a case at bar hold a position of trust with respect to the other persons, or have some contractual relationship to them, it may follow that the parties in court can supply effective advocacy. Their own interest in vindicating the rights of others is more concrete, their willingness and capacity to press those rights vigorously more certain. On this point, too, the Court is often generous to litigants seeking, in effect, to represent absent friends and associates. The bartender's intimate and supportive relationship with her regulars in *Craig* was one thing, the physician's fleeting ministrations to his patients in *Wulff* quite another.[258]

It may be that the exceptions have virtually swallowed the general rule against *jus tertii* standing. The Court makes *ad hoc* judgments on whether claims should be heard and very often concludes that they should.[259] That flexibility, in turn, may reflect the Court's

---

256. Justice Blackmun also said that any individual's claim might be rendered moot before a decision could be rendered. That legal impediment was only "technical," however, inasmuch as the Court had previously held that women could typically avoid dismissal on mootness grounds. Id. at 117. See note 436 and accompanying text (discussing the mootness doctrine in abortion cases).

257. 429 U.S. 190 (1976). In *Powers v. Ohio*, 499 U.S. 400 (1991), the Court held that a white criminal defendant can advance the equal protection claims of blacks who are excluded from the jury. The Court reasoned that individual veniremen have little incentive to shoulder the burdens of litigation to press their own claims. See also *Campbell v. Louisiana*, 523 U.S. 392 (1998) (relying on *Powers* in a case involving racially discriminatory exclusions of blacks from grand juries). In *Miller v. Albright*, 523 U.S. 420 (1998), the daughter of an American serviceman advanced her alleged father's equal protection claim against a federal statute requiring men (but not women) to take special measures to ensure that their illegitimate children born overseas become American citizens. The full Court passed on the merits of the claim and purported not to address the plaintiff's standing. Justice Breyer wrote a concurring opinion explaining that the father faced obstacles to suit on his own behalf. In a separate opinion, Justice O'Connor contended, however, that *Powers* established that the absent party must face genuinely "daunting" hurdles, not present in *Miller*. Id. at 449. Justice Scalia offered the blazing insight that the doctrine on this point "is in need of what may charitably be called clarification." Id. at 454–55 n.1.

258. In fact, the Court described the plaintiff in *Craig* as a "licensed vendor of 3.2% beer." See also *United States Dep't of Labor v. Triplett*, 494 U.S. 715 (1990) (permitting an attorney to advance the claims of his clients); *Maryland v. Joseph H. Munson Co.*, 467 U.S. 947 (1984) (allowing a professional fund raiser to press claims belonging to his sources). Cf. Ara B. Gershengorn, *Private Party Standing to Raise Tenth Amendment Commandeering Challenges*, 100 Colum. L. Rev. 1065 (2000) (arguing that private citizens may be good champions for state complaints that federal legislation invalidly commandeers state officers). In *Bush v. Gore*, 531 U.S. 98 (2000) (*per curiam*), the Court considered claims that George W. Bush advanced on behalf of voters without pausing to consider whether Bush should be allowed to proceed as their representative. In that instance, evidence gathered later indicated that a majority of those voters, if asked, would have chosen somebody else.

259. The *Craig* case may illustrate. In that case, Justice Brennan set aside the usual rule against third-party claims not because the parties whose rights were at stake faced special obstacles or because the plaintiff bore them a special relationship, but because the lower court had already passed on the merits. The defendant had raised no objection, and there was no reason to think that the issues would be presented more fully if the Court waited until teenage boys sued on their own behalf. A teenage boy had appeared as a plaintiff in *Craig* in the lower courts. But he had reached the age of 21 before the case arrived in the Supreme Court, and his personal claim was moot. See text accompanying note 434 (explaining that many short-lived disputes become moot). In some instances, the Court is much more suspicious of third-party claims. See, e.g., *Whitmore v. Arkansas*, 495 U.S. 149 (1990) (refusing to allow one death row inmate to press a constitutional claim on behalf of another

recognition that the classic rationales for the baseline rule against third-party claims underestimate the burdens of modern litigation. Ordinary citizens may fail to press their own claims chiefly because they find lawsuits daunting. It may be appropriate, then, to allow litigants who have constitutional standing (and thus have a sufficient stake in the outcome to ensure effective advocacy) to litigate issues, even though they do not themselves share the legal claims they seek to advance.[260]

Overbreadth cases. In ordinary *jus tertii* cases, the litigants at bar seek to advance claims that belong to other people who are identified or at least identifiable. In a related class of free speech cases, litigants press claims that belong to other people who are neither identified nor identifiable, but whose existence is hypothetical. In keeping with the *Yazoo* principle, litigants who challenge a federal or state statute usually can argue only that the statute is invalid as applied in the circumstances of their own case.[261] The Supreme Court recognizes an exception, however, in some instances in which litigants claim that statutes violate freedom of speech protected by the first amendment. No exception is necessary so long as litigants argue only that a statute violates their own first amendment rights, as the statute has been *applied* in the particular case at hand. An exception is necessary, however, if litigants argue that a statute is overbroad *on its face* and *would* violate the rights of *others* if it were applied in different circumstances.[262]

---

who declined to proceed for himself). For a realistic appraisal of the consequences of cases like *Whitmore*, see Ann Althouse, *Standing, In Fluffy Slippers*, 77 Va. L. Rev. 1177 (1991).

260. Professor Sedler argues that most of the decisions in question can (and should) be understood as determinations that the litigants at bar were not asserting third-party claims at all, but their own personal rights. Sedler contends that the litigants in those cases themselves had rights to engage in activities with others and that those personal rights were put at risk when their colleagues and associates suffered some invalid burden. Professor Sedler explains *Craig*, for example, as a case in which a state statute that denied equal protection to the liquor store proprietor's male customers equally interfered with the proprietor's "liberty" and "property." Robert A. Sedler, *The Assertion of Constitutional Jus Tertii: A Substantive Approach*, 70 Calif. L. Rev. 1308, 1333 (1982). Professor Monaghan offers a similar general theory, which generates a similar revisionist explanation for *Craig*. Monaghan, note 253, at 300. In some instances, however, Sedler and Monaghan disagree. For example, Professor Sedler contends that the physicians in *Wulff* could assert their own constitutional right to receive fees for performing abortions in common with dispensing other medical services. Professor Monaghan, by contrast, argues that a litigant has a personal right to advance only if the statute or other action under attack constitutes a "more direct and meaningful interference" with an "interactive transaction" involving the litigant and the absent person. Monaghan, note 253, at 307. Monaghan finds that missing from *Wulff*. For a sophisticated exchange regarding third-party standing, see Mathew D. Adler, *Rights Against Rules: The Moral Structure of American Constitutional Law*, 97 Mich. L. Rev. 1 (1998); Richard H. Fallon, Jr., *As-Applied and Factual Challenges and Third-Party Standing*, 113 Harv. L. Rev. 1321 (2000); Mathew D. Adler, *Rights, Rules, and the Structure of Constitutional Adjudication: A Response to Professor Fallon*, 113 Harv. L. Rev. 1371 (2000).

261. In *United States v. Salerno*, 481 U.S. 739 (1987), the Court said that a plaintiff attacking a statute on its face "must establish that no set of circumstances exists under which the Act would be valid." Id. at 745. Professor Dorf contends that, if that passage is taken literally, facial attacks should be virtually non-existent. Litigants who show that a statute cannot constitutionally be applied in the circumstances of their cases succeed on that basis and have no occasion to argue as well that the statute cannot be applied in other circumstances. Litigants who fail to demonstrate that the statute is invalid as applied lose on both counts. By showing that the statute can operate constitutionally in at least one instance, they disable themselves (under *Salerno*) from attacking the statute on its face, i.e., as it might apply in other circumstances. Michael C. Dorf, *Facial Challenges to State and Federal Statutes*, 46 Stan. L. Rev. 235, 239 (1994).

262. Determining whether a statute affects speech in the necessary way can be tricky. In *Los Angeles Police Dep't v. United Reporting Pub.*, 528 U.S. 32 (1999), a commercial publishing firm challenged the facial validity of a state statute making the names of arrested persons available only to the press and certain not-for-profit organizations. The Court disallowed that argument on the basis of

The Court allows an exception from the *Yazoo* principle for first amendment overbreadth cases, because the very existence of an overbroad statute can have a "chilling effect" on free speech.[263] If the statute *appears* to penalize expression that is actually protected, it may discourage would-be speakers who will censor themselves rather than risk prosecution. In *Coates v. City of Cincinnati*, for example,[264] the Court held that a city ordinance that made it an offense for three or more people to assemble in public in a manner "annoying to persons passing by" was plainly overbroad. Justice Stewart said there was no need to investigate the "details of the conduct found to be annoying" in the particular case at hand, because it was "the ordinance on its face" that set "the standard of conduct" and warned "against transgression."[265]

Statutes are often both overbroad (because they purport to reach protected expression) and vague (because they fail to specify the behavior they reach and thus may condemn protected speech). Yet a statute can be overbroad, even though it is perfectly clear. Overbreadth is a first amendment doctrine concerned with the chilling effect a statute may have on expression; vagueness is a due process doctrine concerned with fair notice of what a statute means.[266] Courts can save statutes that are overbroad or vague as written by giving them an authoritative narrowing construction.[267] If a statute as written is flawed only for overbreadth, a court can give it a saving construction after an individual has been charged and still, perhaps, apply the statute (in its new form) to the litigant at bar. By hypothesis in an overbreadth case, the individual's attack on the statute's facial validity is in service of the rights of other speakers not before the court. Once the court eliminates the chilling effect on those speakers by construing the statute narrowly, the individual litigant no longer has a first amendment objection to the court's application of the statute in the circumstances of his case.[268] If a statute as written is vague, a court cannot repair the damage to an individual after he or she has been charged with a violation. The gravamen of the evil in a vagueness case is lack of fair notice, which cannot be

---

the general rule that litigants are permitted only to contend that a statute cannot validly be applied to them. The exception for an overbreadth facial attack was unavailable because the statute did not discourage public expression, but only limited access to information.

263. Professor Dorf argues that statutes should be subject to challenge for overbreadth not only if they affect free speech, but also if they affect other constitutional rights to engage in "primary conduct." He recognizes, however, that few constitutional rights are of that order. Dorf, note 261, at 264–65. See *Planned Parenthood v. Casey*, 505 U.S. 833 (1992) (entertaining a facial attack on an abortion regulation affecting the substantive right to procure an abortion without undue burdens); *Kolender v. Lawson*, 461 U.S 352 (1983) (allowing a litigant to whom a statute could plainly apply to attack the statute on its face for vagueness—on behalf of other potential defendants). Professor Fallon thinks overbreadth analysis has been limited to speech cases in the main because of the special values associated with expression. Richard H. Fallon, Jr., *Making Sense of Overbreadth*, 100 Yale L.J. 853 (1991). Cf. *Janklow v. Planned Parenthood*, 517 U.S. 1174 (1996) (Scalia, J., dissenting from the denial of *certiorari*) (urging the Court to reconsider whether abortion regulations are subject to facial challenge).

264. 402 U.S. 611 (1971).

265. Id. at 616. See also *Gooding v. Wilson*, 405 U.S. 518 (1972) (invalidating a statute that made it an offense to use "opprobrious words"). Professor Fallon has explained that some overbroad statutes may threaten a greater chilling effect on speech than others. Fallon, note 263.

266. See Note, *The First Amendment Overbreadth Doctrine*, 83 Harv. L. Rev. 844, 852–58 (1970).

267. See *Osborne v. Ohio*, 495 U.S. 103 (1990).

268. Id. at 115. In one famous case, *Shuttlesworth v. City of Birmingham*, 394 U.S. 147 (1969), the Court refused to allow the Alabama Supreme Court to cure overbreadth on appeal and, on that basis, to affirm the convictions of civil rights demonstrators. But *Shuttlesworth* was almost certainly a creature of its civil rights context.

remedied by construing a statute narrowly after a citizen has had to guess at its meaning as written.[269]

An overbroad statute that cannot be saved by construction is constitutionally invalid in any circumstances—including cases in which a more narrowly drawn statute might be invoked to punish an individual's expressive behavior.[270] Accordingly, litigants whose own conduct might be penalized under a valid statute nonetheless escape punishment by establishing that the actual statute brought to bear on them is overbroad with respect to other, hypothetical speakers. The Court's enthusiasm for overbreadth is not so strong now as it once was. In *Broadrick v. Oklahoma*,[271] the Court held that in cases in which "conduct" as well as expression is involved, statutes can be attacked on their face only if they are "substantially" overbroad.[272] But the Court does continue to apply the analysis.[273]

2. The Zone Test

Litigants who satisfy the constitutional prerequisites for standing sometimes must satisfy a second non-constitutional rule. They must show that the injuries they have suffered, or are about to suffer, implicate interests that are "arguably within the zone of interests" protected or regulated by the statute or constitutional provision they seek to enforce. The Court initially announced this zone test in *Data Processing* as a non-constitutional requirement for standing that Congress had fashioned for litigants proceeding under the authority of §702 of the Administrative Procedure Act.[274] The zone test unquestionably counts as a prudential barrier to standing; Justice Douglas might have read §702 to dispense with any standing requirement beyond the constitutional prerequisites.[275] In retrospect, however, it seems plain that Douglas meant the zone test as a litigant-friendly alternative to a competing interpretation of §702 that

269. *Shuttlesworth*, 394 U.S. at 155. It is not always necessary to invalidate an overbroad statute in its entirety. Sometimes, courts can sever offending features and leave the rest in place. State courts are authoritative with respect to state statutes. See Chapter VII, notes 104–06 and accompanying text. Accordingly, the federal courts' ability to save overbroad statutes in that way is more limited with respect to state statutes than it is with respect to federal statutes. But see *Brockett v. Spokane Arcades*, 472 U.S. 491 (1985) (holding that the overbroad features of a state statute could be stripped out on the authority of a severability clause).

270. Professor Monaghan argues that the overbreadth cases should be understood not as instances in which the Court allows an exception to the usual prohibition on third-party claims, but rather as instances in which the Court recognizes "first party" claims on behalf of litigants advancing overbreadth arguments. According to Monaghan, a litigant "always" has a "right to be judged in accordance with a constitutionally valid rule of law." Henry P. Monaghan, *Overbreadth*, 1981 Sup. Ct. Rev. 1, 3. By his account, a statute that makes it an offense to whistle is facially invalid and thus cannot be constitutionally invoked even against a defendant who disrupts a courtroom proceeding by whistling. Henry P. Monaghan, *Harmless Error and the Valid Rule Requirement*, 1989 Sup. Ct. Rev. 195, 196.

271. 413 U.S. 601 (1973).

272. Cf. *Joseph H. Munson*, 467 U.S. at 978 (Rehnquist, J., dissenting) (expressing general doubts about permitting facial attacks on statutes).

273. Everybody's favorite illustration is *City of Los Angeles v. Jews for Jesus*, 482 U.S. 569 (1987) (invalidating a blanket prohibition on all "First Amendment activities" at the Los Angeles airport).

274. See text accompanying note 107.

275. That is what Justice Brennan would have done. In an opinion concurring in the result in *Data Processing*, Brennan insisted that Douglas should have approved the plaintiffs' standing on the basis of their economic injuries alone, without reference to the zone test as an additional non-constitutional requirement, and then should have gone immediately to the preclusion question. Bren-

would have been considerably less generous.[276] In 1970, the zone test was far more important for the cases it allowed into the federal courts than it was for the cases it excluded. For the most part, that remains true today.

The leading illustrations are cases like *Nat'l Credit Union Admin. v. First National Bank*,[277] in which commercial firms assert economic interests in the way federal agencies regulate their competitors. Under §109 of the National Credit Union Act, credit unions can serve only customers who are connected by a common occupational bond or who reside in a defined geographic area. The NCUA interpreted §109 to allow credit unions to serve multiple unrelated groups of customers, so long as the customers in each group shared a common bond. That interpretation permitted credit unions to expand their customer base and thus to compete with banks for depositors—causing banks economic injury in fact. In *First National Bank*, Justice Thomas held that banks had standing to challenge the NCUA's interpretation, because their competitive interests were arguably within the zone of interests protected by §109.

Justice Thomas conceded that neither the text of §109 nor its legislative history indicated that Congress had enacted §109 with the specific "intent" or "purpose" to protect banks from competition. He acknowledged that the legislative history showed, instead, that Congress meant to ensure that credit unions would have a "cooperative nature" and would provide discrete groups of customers with a safe place to put their money and a ready pool of funds from which to borrow. Thomas insisted, however, that litigants can satisfy the zone test even though there is no "evidence" that Congress intended that they should benefit from the statute they wish to enforce. Litigants have an interest that is "arguably" within the zone if there is a "link" between that interest and the interests that a statute was actually enacted to serve. Thomas found such a connection in *First National Bank.* The immediate objective of §109 was to limit the customers (and thus the markets) that credit unions could reach. That was also the banks' immediate objective. Therein a link. It made no difference that Congress' *reason* for limiting credit union markets (the creation of a cooperative atmosphere) was not the banks' reason (the profit motive).[278] Other decisions in recent years reflect a similarly generous understanding of the zone test.[279]

---

nan agreed that no statute precluded review of the Comptroller's ruling. *Data Processing*, 397 U.S. at 159.

276. See notes 107–10 and accompanying text.

277. 522 U.S. 479 (1998).

278. Id. at 492–94. In dissent, Justice O'Connor charged Justice Thomas with eviscerating the zone test entirely, thus allowing any litigant who satisfies the constitutional prerequisites for standing to challenge agency action under §702. According to O'Connor, the zone test requires "*some* indication in the statute, beyond the mere fact that its enforcement has the effect of incidentally benefiting the plaintiff, from which one can draw an inference that the plaintiff's injury arguably falls within the zone of interests sought to be protected by that statute." Id. at 517 (emphasis in original). In response, Justice Thomas said that he (and thus the majority) differed with Justice O'Connor not over the content of the zone test, but only over its application in the case at bar. He insisted that there *was* at least *some* indication in §109 that the banks were arguably within the zone, because both Congress and the banks wished to limit the business that credit unions could undertake. The banks were "more than merely incidental beneficiaries of §109's effects on competition." Id. at 494 n.7 (majority opinion).

279. In *FEC v. Akins*, 524 U.S. 11 (1998), Justice Breyer said that voters who wanted information about a political committee satisfied the zone test, because nothing in the relevant statute suggested that Congress meant to "exclude" their interests from the zone of interests protected by that statute. Id. at 20; see notes 172–80 and accompanying text. In *Clarke v. Secur. Indus. Ass'n*, 479 U.S. 388 (1987), Justice White explained that §702 expresses a "presumption" in favor of judicial review in

Of course, §702 authorizes only *some* private litigants to enforce federal legal standards in court—and not only in court, but in federal court. This is to say, §702 both creates a right of action for, and confers standing on, only litigants whose interests are within the zone.[280] In any given case, then, courts cannot determine whether the zone test is met by examining §702 alone, but must press on to decide whether the particular private litigants at the door have interests that fall arguably within the zone of interests protected by the statutes they wish to enforce.[281] Since it is enough that litigants' interests are even *arguably* within the zone, however, it is not essential that they be expressly identified as the targets or beneficiaries of the statutes they claim the agency has violated.[282] The zone test is a "guide for deciding whether... a particular plaintiff should be heard to complain of a particular agency decision." Litigants will fail the zone test only if their interests are "so marginally related to or inconsistent with the purposes implicit in the statute that it cannot be assumed that Congress intended to permit the suit."[283]

The zone test bears a family resemblance to the rule against third-party claims. Roughly speaking, litigants whose own interests are *not* within the zone are foreclosed, because they are attempting to litigate on behalf of other people whose interests *are* within the zone.[284] Yet the two ideas are not identical. The zone test concerns the factual *injuries* sufficient to establish standing for access to federal court in the first instance. The ban on third-party claims concerns the *violations of law* that litigants assert once they are inside the door.[285] Recall that the crucial (though controversial) point of *Data*

---

the cases to which it applies and that the zone test is not "especially demanding." Id. at 399. In *Clarke*, White held that securities dealers who competed with banks had interests that were within the zone of interests protected by the McFadden Act's limits on branch banking. Accordingly, they could challenge a ruling by the Comptroller of the Currency allowing banks to establish offices outside their home states. In *Lujan v. Nat'l Wildlife Fed.*, 497 U.S. 871 (1990), Justice Scalia held that environmentalists' interests were within the zone of interests protected by the Federal Land Policy and Management Act's specifications for opening public land to development. The plaintiffs' difficulty in that case was not the zone test, but their failure to allege sufficient personal use of particular areas to capitalize on the Court's willingness to consider their interests to be arguably protected by the FLPMA. Litigants do fall short on occasion. In *Air Courier Conf. v. Amer. Postal Workers Union*, 498 U.S. 517 (1991), the Court held that the interests of postal workers in retaining jobs did not fall within the zone of interests protected by the Postal Reorganization Act's provisions on maintaining the Postal Service's monopoly. Cf. *Bennett v. Spear*, 520 U.S. 154 (1997); notes 325–29 and accompanying text.

280. See Chapter VIII, notes 137–39 and accompanying text.

281. In this sense, §702 is like §1983. Both are free-standing right-of-action provisions that require an examination of the underlying statutes or constitutional provisions litigants seek to enforce in order to determine whether the particular litigants at bar are eligible to proceed. In §702 cases, would-be litigants must advance interests that arguably fall within the zone of interests protected by the statutes or constitutional provisions they claim the defendant has violated. In §1983 cases, would-be litigants must allege a violation of (someone's) "rights" under color of state law. See Chapter VIII, notes 135–36 and accompanying text.

282. Justice White once explained that it is easier for litigants to show that their interests fall within the zone of interests protected by a statute for purposes of §702 than it is for litigants to show, under "conditions that make the APA inapplicable," that they nonetheless have a right of action implied from the statute involved. *Clarke*, 479 U.S. at 400 n.16. That, however, was before the Court brought an end to implied actions entirely. See Chapter VIII, notes 153–61 and accompanying text. *A fortiori*, litigants can pass the zone test in the absence of any specific statutory text making it clear that they are entitled to sue.

283. *Clarke*, 479 U.S. at 399.

284. See Laurence H. Tribe, American Constitutional Law 434 (3d ed. 2000).

285. *Duke Power v. Carolina Envt'l Study Grp.*, 438 U.S. 59, 80–81 (1978).

Processing was to distinguish the threshold matter of standing, on the one hand, from the further question of the legal claims to be adjudicated, on the other. The constitutional prerequisites for standing comport with that rationale inasmuch as they rest standing on the nature of personal injuries rather than on the content of legal claims. The zone test compromises the point inasmuch as it requires an examination of the statute or constitutional provision litigants wish to enforce in order to determine whether their interests are arguably within the zone of interests protected. Nevertheless, the zone test does *not* obliterate the distinction entirely by collapsing the *interests* litigants must allege for standing into the *violations of law* that litigants assert the defendant committed when causing injury to those interests.[286] The zone test illustrates that it is necessary to draw distinctions between groups of non-Hohfeldian plaintiffs. Plaintiffs need not assert legal rights to pass the zone test; they need only have interests that are arguably within the zone. So they are plainly non-Hohfeldian. Yet they do have interests that distinguish them from the public at large—typically economic interests that were not actionable at common law. Certainly, they do not (necessarily) proceed solely for ideological purposes.[287]

The zone test primarily controls cases arising under the APA, in which litigants rely on §702 for authority to challenge actions taken by federal agencies.[288] Nevertheless, the Court has occasionally utilized the zone test outside the context of §702 and has indicated that it is a feature of general prudential standing doctrine.[289] The Court invoked essentially the same idea as early as *Flast v. Cohen*.[290] Recall that Chief Justice Warren held that the taxpayers in that case had standing to challenge a federal spending measure because they could demonstrate both a nexus between their status as taxpayers and the expenditures they attacked and a nexus between their status and the constitutional provision they contended was violated—the Establishment Clause being a limitation on spending. The first nexus stated the constitutional prerequisite for standing: injury caused by the enactment under attack.[291] The second was the zone test traveling under

286. See text accompanying notes 112–18. Justice Powell explained in *Warth* that the "source" of a plaintiff's claim to relief can have "critical importance" with respect to prudential standing rules. 422 U.S. at 500. Then again, the causation requirement does sometimes approach the merits. See notes 221–22 and accompanying text.

287. But see note 85 (discussing different assessments).

288. *Clarke*, 479 U.S. at 400 & n.16.

289. E.g., *Bennett*, 520 U.S. at 162–63 (listing the zone test along with the ban on third-party claims and thus as a "prudential standing requirement of general application"). See also *Allen*, 468 U.S. at 751; *Devlin v. Scardelletti*, 122 S.Ct. 2005, 2009 (2002); *Valley Forge*, 454 U.S. at 474–75. In two other cases, the Court consulted the zone test, but easily found it to be satisfied. In *Boston Stock Exchange v. State Tax Comm'n*, 429 U.S. 318 (1977), taxpayers sued state authorities in state court, contending that a state tax violated the Commerce Clause. Justice White explained in a footnote that the plaintiffs had "standing under the two-part test" in *Data Processing*. Id. at 320–21 n.3. Since the taxpayers were asserting "their right under the Commerce Clause to engage in interstate commerce free of discriminatory taxes...they [were] arguably within the zone of interests" protected by the prohibition against discriminatory taxation established by the Commerce Clause. In *Dennis v. Higgins*, 498 U.S. 439 (1991), Justice White cited the footnote in *Boston Stock Exchange* in aid of a holding that private businesses have a "right" to be free of discriminatory taxes that is enforceable in a §1983 action. Id. at 449. See Chapter VIII, notes 175–83 and accompanying text. The assertion of a *legal right* is sufficient for standing wholly apart from the zone test. See text accompanying notes 116–18.

290. 392 U.S. 83 (1968); see notes 155–62 and accompanying text.

291. See notes 112–13 and accompanying text.

another name: injury to interests that were within the zone of interests protected by the statute or constitutional provision said to be violated.[292] In other cases, the Court has disclaimed the zone test apart from §702. In *Duke Power*,[293] Chief Justice Burger acknowledged that the plaintiffs' interest in the lake was not connected to their due process claim. But he confined the second nexus requirement in *Flast* (that is, the zone test) to taxpayer suits and thus held that the plaintiffs in *Duke Power* had standing without satisfying that test.[294]

E. Standing: Congressional Power

It is common to say that Congress has power to "confer" standing on private litigants. That formulation can be misleading. For one thing, it suggests that a federal statute regarding standing can work in only one direction, always enlarging (but never restricting) litigants' capacity to proceed in an Article III court. That is not so. Standing statutes typically work in both directions. A statute that grants standing to a class of litigants both authorizes the members of that class to sue in federal court and also disqualifies (by negative implication) other would-be litigants who fall outside the class. Congress *can* enact standing legislation that operates exclusively to the advantage of potential litigants. But to do that, Congress must enact a statute clearly authorizing *anyone* to litigate in an Article III court. That kind of statute contains no non-constitutional criteria for litigants to meet and, indeed, eliminates all non-constitutional standing criteria that the Court would otherwise enforce.[295]

---

292. See Fallon, note 85, at 20; Nichol, note 119, at 96. In *Invest. Co. Inst. v. Camp*, 401 U.S. 617 (1971), decided just after *Data Processing*, investment companies attacked a ruling by the Comptroller of the Currency allowing banks to offer investment accounts. In a *per curiam*, the Court went directly to whether the ruling violated the Glass-Steagall Act's protections of competitors and, holding that it did, explained that there could be "no real question" that the plaintiffs' interests fell within the zone for standing purposes. Id. at 621. That disposition has been criticized for dodging the zone test. See Note, *A Defense of the Zone of Interests Standing Test*, 1983 Duke L.J. 447, 453. Yet if a litigant advances an interest that a statute elevates to the character of a legal right, it *does* follow that the litigant has standing—provided the litigant demonstrates causation and seeks a remedy that satisfies the redressability requirement. See text accompanying notes 209–47 and accompanying text.

293. 438 U.S. 59 (1978); see note 211 and accompanying text.

294. The plaintiffs also alleged that they would suffer injuries to their lives and property if a nuclear accident occurred. The Chief Justice agreed that those injuries *were* connected to their due process claim. 438 U.S. at 78 n.23. Yet since he did not rely on injuries of that kind in satisfaction of the constitutional requirements for standing in *Duke Power*, he could not recruit them to service with respect to the zone test, either. Id. at 78–79.

295. Professor Anthony has explained that when Congress establishes non-constitutional standing criteria in a given context, those criteria occupy the field to the exclusion of any other non-constitutional standards. It follows that litigants who satisfy the requirements specified have standing so long as they meet the constitutional prerequisites. There is (or should be) no occasion for asking them also to satisfy other non-constitutional standing requirements that Congress has not brought into play. Robert A. Anthony, *Zone-Free Standing for Private Attorneys General*, 7 Geo. Mason L. Rev. 237 (1999). Anthony faults Justice Breyer in *Akins*, 524 U.S. at 20, and Justice Scalia in *Bennett*, 520 U.S. at 163, for ambiguous statements suggesting that the zone test is generally applicable, even when Congress establishes different prudential standing criteria. Professor Anthony is clearly correct. Any language in *Akins* and *Bennett* indicating otherwise was either ill-advised or offered for

For another thing, the proposition that Congress can "confer" standing suggests that Congress has complete authority to decide who gets to appear in federal court. That is not so, either. Even when Congress enacts a statute abolishing all non-constitutional standing barriers, litigants still must satisfy the constitutional prerequisites for standing established in the Court's decisions. In the end, then, even a federal statute purporting to authorize *anyone* to litigate in an Article III court actually permits only some litigants to do so: litigants meeting judicially determined constitutional standards.[296] Recall in this vein that the function served by the distinction between constitutional and non-constitutional standing rules is the delineation of the role the Court allows Congress to play in the identification of litigants who can invoke federal judicial power.[297]

1. Hohfeldian Plaintiffs

It is well-settled, of course, that Congress can transform concrete factual interests into personal legal rights and that the holders of those rights (Hohfeldian plaintiffs) have standing to enforce them in federal court.[298] That much has been true since *Marbury v. Madison*.[299] To take a modern example, §804 of the Fair Housing Act makes it unlawful "[t]o refuse to sell or rent" a dwelling to "any person because of race, color, religion, sex, or national origin" or to "represent to any person because of race, color, religion, sex, or national origin, that any dwelling is not available" for sale or rent when, in fact, the dwelling *is* available for occupancy.[300] The Court has read that statute not only to specify the way in which real estate brokers and landlords are to behave, but also to establish personal legal rights in buyers and tenants. In *Havens Realty Corp. v. Coleman*,[301] two "testers," one African American and one white, contended that a broker had violated §804 by falsely telling the black tester that apartments were *not* available, while truthfully telling the white tester that they *were*. Justice Brennan interpreted §804 to confer on "all 'persons' a *legal right* to truthful information about available housing." Accordingly, the African American tester had standing, because she claimed that the broker had violated her statutory right to the truth. The white tester, who had been told the truth, could not allege a similar violation and thus lacked standing on this basis.[302]

---

emphasis. Anthony himself suggests plausible ways to read those opinions not to propose that the zone test (or any other non-constitutional standing doctrine) survives Congress' explicit prescription of the prudential standing rules for litigants seeking to enforce a particular statute. Anthony, at 251–54.

296. See text accompanying note 71.

297. See text accompanying note 75.

298. See text accompanying notes 90, 116–18 (discussing the sufficiency of legal rights for standing purposes).

299. 5 U.S. (1 Cranch) 137, 163 (1803); Chapter I, text accompanying note 67; but see note 181 and accompanying text (explaining that "abstract and indefinite" interests are constitutionally inadequate and thus cannot support standing even if Congress labels them legal "rights").

300. 42 U.S.C. §3604.

301. 455 U.S. 363 (1982).

302. Id. at 373 (emphasis added). See notes 361–62 and accompanying text (explaining that the white tester might still establish standing on the basis of an injury to an interest). Litigants who advance legal rights must also show causation and redressability. The former merges with the merits, but the latter may be problematic. See notes 240–47 and accompanying text.

2. Representative Plaintiffs

Congress can authorize private litigants to proceed in federal court in a representative capacity. The precedents suggest three possibilities: (1) litigants who stand to win a bounty if they prevail in a federal lawsuit; (2) litigants who proceed in federal court as the designated agents of the United States; and (3) litigants who proceed as assignees of interests that the United States itself enjoys.

Bounty hunters. The Court has implied that Congress might manufacture a sufficient personal interest in the outcome of cases by offering a cash reward to litigants who are successful. In the *Lujan* case, Justice Scalia did not state affirmatively that a bounty scheme would satisfy constitutional standing requirements. But he implied as much by explaining that the plaintiffs in *Lujan* could claim no promise of a prize and thus could not establish standing on that basis.[303] Some academics have expressed the view that a bounty scheme would satisfy Article III.[304] On reflection, however, the idea is almost certainly unsound. The promise of a prize may give a litigant a personal economic "stake in the outcome" of a federal lawsuit. Yet in *Vermont Agency v. United States ex rel. Stevens*,[305] Justice Scalia himself recognized that anyone who places a bet on the result in a pending case can claim a similar prospect of gain. Recall, moreover, that an injury is constitutionally sufficient to establish standing only if it is *caused* by the defendant's allegedly unlawful behavior.[306] A bounty is related only to the outcome of a lawsuit, not to the primary behavior on the defendant's part that forms the basis of the plaintiff's claim in the first instance. Injury to an interest that is only a "by-product" of litigation cannot count as "judicially cognizable" factual injury for Article III standing purposes.[307]

Government agents. The Court has also acknowledged that Congress can designate a private litigant to prosecute a federal lawsuit as the government's agent. In *Stevens*, Justice Scalia explained that agents need no personal injuries of their own, but can act on the government's behalf.[308] The government suffers injury to its "sovereignty" when its laws are violated and injury to its propriety interests when its treasury is looted.[309] In *Stevens* itself, the agency theory was unavailable.[310] The plaintiff in that case proceeded under the False Claims Act, which creates a *qui tam* arrangement by which private citi-

---

303. *Lujan*, 504 U.S. at 573; see notes 190–94 and accompanying text. Justice Scalia mentioned bounties again in *Steel*, 523 U.S. at 106; see notes 244–47 and accompanying text. In a separate opinion in *Steel*, Justice Stevens implied that he, too, would find the promise of a cash reward sufficient to establish injury in fact.

304. E.g., Cass R. Sunstein, *What's Standing After Lujan? Of Citizen Suits, "Injuries," and Article III*, 91 Mich. L. Rev. 163, 232–33 (1992); Gene R. Nichol, Jr., *Justice Scalia, Standing, and Public Law Litigation*, 42 Duke L.J. 1141, 1165 (1993).

305. 529 U.S. 765 (2000).

306. Id. at 772. See notes 209–22 and accompanying text.

307. *Stevens*, 529 U.S. at 773. See note 247 and accompanying text (discussing similar problems under the heading of redressability).

308. *Stevens*, 529 U.S. at 772.

309. Id. at 771. For discussions of the federal government's standing to sue, see Edward Hartnett, *The Standing of the United States: How Criminal Prosecutions Show That Standing Doctrine is Looking for Answers in All the Wrong Places*, 97 Mich. L. Rev. 2239 (1999); Larry W. Yackle, *A Worthy Champion for Fourteenth Amendment Rights: The United States in Parens Patriae*, 92 Nw. U. L. Rev. 111 (1997).

310. In simple form, the agency model is familiar. The government frequently retains private lawyers to handle litigation. See Gilles, note 133, at 1424–32 (offering illustrations).

zens (called "relators") are authorized to file federal lawsuits to recover funds of which the federal government has been defrauded.[311] Under the Act, the government is entitled to intervene and assume primary responsibility for lawsuits brought by private relators. If the government does not intervene, relators are entitled to proceed alone and, if successful, to pocket a percentage of the award. As Justice Scalia conceived the scheme, relators do not act merely as representatives of the government, but also as parties in their own right. Accordingly, the plaintiff in *Stevens* could not claim to be the government's agent laboring in the expectation of receiving a fee for services rendered. Despite the result in *Stevens*, the agency theory can operate in other cases in which private litigants act exclusively for the government. If Congress employs the agency vehicle in other contexts, it may be able to accomplish, in effect, what the Court's standing doctrine has kept it from doing by more conventional means. Then again, the agency device is presumably available only in cases in which private litigants wish to sue other private parties or (perhaps) the states[312] and not when they wish to sue their own principal: the federal government or one of its arms.[313] Moreover, some justices may insist upon a large measure of "public control" in order to safeguard the executive's responsibility for enforcing federal law.[314]

Government assignees. Congress can also assign its interests in litigation to private citizens. This third theory *was* available in *Stevens*. Justice Scalia recognized that private companies have long been permitted to assign interests to others and that the assignee companies have been entitled to rely on the assigned interests to establish standing in suits against others.[315] He saw no reason that the federal government cannot do the same thing. The False Claims Act is not written in assignment terms. Yet Justice Scalia concluded that the Act can nonetheless be "regarded" as an assignment arrangement. Perhaps importantly, Scalia explained that assignments to *qui tam* relators are not complete, but "partial."[316] By that, he may have meant to underscore that the False Claims Act does not contemplate that the government relinquishes to assignees all capacity to direct litigation in federal court. The retention of some "public control" may, once again, be crucial to defuse potential constitutional objections.[317] Like agents of the fed-

311. For previous discussions of standing in *qui tam* actions, compare Evan Caminker, *The Constitutionality of Qui Tam Actions*, 99 Yale L.J. 341 (1989) (arguing that suits envisioned by the False Claims Act could be sustained), with James T. Blanch, *The Constitutionality of the False Claims Act's Qui Tam Provision*, 16 Harv. J. L. & Pub. Policy 701 (1993) (arguing the contrary).

312. See Chapter X (discussing the possibility that state sovereign immunity may defeat some suits against unconsenting states).

313. Professor Gilles sees great promise in the agency model. She predicts, however, that the Court will import ordinary agency law principles into its analysis. Accordingly, a valid agency arrangement must preserve the government's ability as principal to control the litigation that its agents pursue. Gilles, note 177, at 348–64.

314. See note 132 and accompanying text. In this vein, Professor Gilles anticipates that valid agency statutes must at least preserve the level of executive control that the Court found in the independent counsel provisions of the Ethics in Government Act. *Morrison v. Olsen*, 487 U.S. 654 (1988). Gilles, note 177.

315. See note 152 and accompanying text.

316. *Stevens*, 529 U.S. at 774 n.4.

317. Professor Gilles offers this explanation for Justice Scalia's insistence that the assignment approved in *Stevens* was "partial." Gilles, note 177, at 345–48. In addition, Gilles anticipates another important limitation on the assignment model. The common law typically permits the assignment only of property interests and not interests more personal to the would-be assignor. For example, assignments of claims for business losses are valid, but assignments of claims for personal injury are not. Reasoning by analogy, Professor Gilles predicts that the Court will allow the federal government effectively to "confer" standing on private litigants by assignment only with respect to govern-

eral government, assignees of the government's interests probably are unable to sue the government itself. That limitation, in turn, restricts the value of assignments as a means of empowering private litigants to advance federal claims in federal court.[318]

3. Non-Hohfeldian Plaintiffs

Congress can authorize non-Hohfeldian private citizens to seek federal judicial enforcement of federal law, even though that law does not furnish them with personal legal rights.[319] This is the authority that has attracted primary attention. It contemplates that Congress need not create primary rights in anyone, but can limit itself to creating *litigation* rights in plaintiffs who assert interests alone. Recall that all litigants in federal court need a procedural vehicle: a right of action to vindicate their claims by means of private lawsuits.[320] There is a difference, however, between a statute establishing a right of action to litigate in *some* court, on the one hand, and a statute establishing a right of action to litigate in an *Article III court*, on the other. Only the latter implicates standing.[321] Congress commonly establishes federal rights of action to proceed in federal court in connection with particular statutory schemes and, in so doing, defines the class of authorized private litigants in the way Congress sees fit.[322] In some instances, too, Congress enacts general standing statutes authorizing litigants to appear in federal court to advance a wide range of claims. That, of course, is the model at work in §702 of the APA, which authorizes suits against most federal agencies by anyone who is "adversely affected or aggrieved." The Court, in turn, has read that to mean anyone whose interests fall arguably within the zone of interests protected by the statute he or she wishes to enforce.[323]

---

ment interests of a propriety nature (like the monetary claim in *Stevens*). By contrast, Gilles thinks the Court will not permit the government to assign its sovereign interest in law enforcement. To tolerate that would be to invite Congress to use the assignment model to circumnavigate the usual constitutional rule that Congress cannot authorize litigants to sue in federal court solely to seek compliance with federal law.

318. See Gilles, note 177, at 363.

319. *Data Processing*, 397 U.S. at 154. Accord *Bennett*, 520 U.S. at 165.

320. See Chapter VIII, notes 120–230 and accompanying text (discussing rights of action generally).

321. For example, adjacent provisions of the Fair Housing Act (§810 and §812) independently state that the rights established by §804 "may be enforced by civil actions in appropriate United States district courts." Those additional provisions confer standing (within limits) inasmuch as they specify the federal forum. Other statutes simply authorize litigants to file lawsuits without more and thus do nothing toward establishing standing to sue in federal court. The most familiar illustration is 42 U.S.C. §1983. See *O'Shea v. Littleton*, 414 U.S. 488, 493–94 n.2 (1974) (confirming that §1983 does not address standing). This is why, in §1983 cases like *Wulff* and *Craig*, see notes 255–57 and accompanying text, the Court invoked its own prudential standing rules without reference to anything Congress might have said with respect to standing. As a matter of statutory construction, the Court did not understand §1983 to deal with standing at all. Academicians who urge the Court to make the existence of a right of action central in standing cases sometimes argue that §1983 should be understood to have implications for standing, after all. E.g., David P. Currie, *Misunderstanding Standing*, 1981 Sup. Ct. Rev. 41, 45; Sunstein, note 206, at 46.

322. See, e.g., 7 U.S.C. §2305(c) (authorizing a person "injured in his business or property" to sue to enforce fair trade statutes); 15 U.S.C. §298(b) (authorizing "competitors, customers, or subsequent purchasers" to sue to enforce gold and silver standards).

323. See notes 112, 274–87 and accompanying text. Congress often borrows the specific language in §702 for use in standing statutes governing suits to enforce particular statutes. Recall, for example, that the statute in the *Akins* case, the Federal Election Campaign Act, authorizes any

Occasionally, Congress is more expansive still, empowering non-Hohfeldian litigants to proceed in an Article III court without specifying that they must be connected in any way to the statutes they insist have been violated. This is the way Congress not only disclaims congressionally created non-constitutional standing rules like the zone test, but also sweeps aside any prudential standing requirements that the courts would ordinarily invoke.[324] In *Bennett v. Spear*,[325] Justice Scalia explained that the Court applies a clear statement rule to ensure that any particular standing statute genuinely means to be so generous.[326] If, however, Congress uses language that is sufficiently exacting, Congress can eliminate all non-constitutional barriers and thus confer standing on "everyman" (who satisfies the constitutional prerequisites).[327]

The *Bennett* case is the leading illustration. Recall that the ranchers contended that the Fish and Wildlife Service failed to comply with the Endangered Species Act in framing a plan for protecting sucker fish in reservoirs under the government's control. The ranchers contended that the plan deprived them of the water needed to keep their stock alive and their sailboats afloat. The circuit court below ruled that the ranchers' interests were not within the zone of interests protected by ESA. After all, the ranchers hoped to reduce the water available for the fish and thus to defeat the Act's purpose to preserve an endangered species. Justice Scalia rejected that judgment with respect to some of the ranchers' claims on the ground that their economic interests *were* "arguably" within the zone of interests protected by the specific provisions of ESA they contended the Service had violated. With respect to other claims, Justice Scalia said that it made no difference whether the ranchers satisfied the zone test, because Congress had superseded that test. The special "citizen-suit" provision in ESA[328] eliminated all non-constitutional barriers that would otherwise have applied. The ranchers' economic injury satisfied the "injury in fact" constitutional requirement for standing. Accordingly, they were free to contest what they viewed as a violation of the Act, even though they were antagonistic to its primary objectives.[329]

Congress cannot dispense with judicially cognizable injury in fact, causation, and redressability. In the *Lujan* case,[330] Justice Scalia explained that those requirements are "irreducible" constitutional conditions that Congress is not free to discard.[331] Congress may conclude that anyone willing to undertake the burdens of suit will serve well

---

"party aggrieved" by a Commission order to seek judicial review. See note 175 and accompanying text. When Justice Breyer interpreted that language, he sensibly did so in light of the precedents construing §702. *Akins*, 524 U.S. at 19. In dissent, Justice Scalia read the "party aggrieved" formulation more narrowly. Id. at 32. In *Dep't of Commerce v. United States House of Representatives*, 525 U.S. 316 (1999), Justice O'Connor said that Congress had "eliminated any prudential concerns" about standing by "providing that '[a]ny person *aggrieved*'" could sue. Id. at 328 (emphasis added). There were no dissents from that understanding. Yet it seems odd that the Court did not give the term "aggrieved" at least the modest content it has in §702 and elsewhere.

324. See text accompanying note 295.

325. 520 U.S. 154 (1997); see notes 227–28 and accompanying text.

326. See Chapter I, notes 44–52 and accompanying text.

327. *Bennett*, 520 U.S. at 166; accord *Raines v. Byrd*, 521 U.S. 811, 820 n.3 (1997).

328. See text accompanying note 193.

329. 520 U.S. at 163–68. Professor Soifer is astonished that the ranchers did not challenge the EPA's determination that the fish were genuinely endangered. After all, the birth rate of suckers can be computed by the minute.

330. *Defenders of Wildlife v. Lujan*, 504 U.S. 555 (1992); see notes 190–94 and accompanying text.

331. *Lujan*, 504 U.S. at 560.

enough. But the Court maintains that the constitutional aspects of standing doctrine do not merely ensure effective advocacy. They elaborate the separation of powers.[332] In *Lujan*, accordingly, Justice Scalia read the "citizen-suit" provision in the Endangered Species Act to leave the constitutional prerequisites intact.[333]

The lower court in *Lujan* held that the plaintiffs had standing because they suffered "procedural" injury that would not have existed apart from ESA.[334] Initially, that court read the Act not only to establish the Secretary's legal duty to consult with the agencies handling construction projects, but also to give private individuals a "correlative procedural right" to that consultation. Next, the circuit court read the "citizen-suit" provision to give all "persons" a further "procedural right" to vindicate that "right to consultation" by means of a lawsuit in federal court.[335] In the Supreme Court, Justice Scalia acknowledged that Congress can create "procedural" rights that Article III courts can enforce. Yet he explicitly rejected the idea that Congress can manufacture the constitutionally required "injury in fact" by creating in "*all* persons" a "self-contained, noninstrumental 'right' to have the Executive observe the procedures required by law."[336] He insisted, by contrast, that the Court had never allowed Congress to confer standing on private litigants merely by giving them "procedural" rights "unconnected" to anyone's "own concrete harm."[337]

Justice Scalia's analysis of the "procedural right" argument in *Lujan* was scarcely surprising. Even under the rights-based test for standing, the personal legal rights that were sufficient to win access to federal court were linked to some underlying factual harm to a preexisting interest.[338] The Court did not conceive that litigants had (or could have) legal rights with no basis in genuine interests that could be injured in fact. When the Court abandoned the rights-based formula for standing and substituted the harm-based test, it meant only to say that, in future, litigants need no longer contend that they had personal legal rights to enforce. It would suffice to allege only factual harm to interests, without regard to whether Congress granted anyone a legal right against that harm. Certainly, however, litigants still needed judicially cognizable *de facto* injuries to satisfy the constitutional prerequisites for standing.[339]

---

332. See note 122 and accompanying text.

333. See text accompanying note 194.

334. *Defenders of Wildlife v. Lujan*, 911 F.2d 117, 121 (8th Cir. 1990).

335. This can be confusing. The circuit court construed the Act to create two legal rights and characterized both of them as procedural. First, the provision requiring the Secretary to consult with other agencies gave everyone a right in that consultation. That right was procedural in character inasmuch as it implicated only the process by which development projects were discussed rather than the actual construction those discussions produced. Second, the separate "citizen-suit" provision gave everyone an additional right to enforce the first procedural right in federal court. That second right was also procedural in nature; it was a right of action providing private litigants with a procedural vehicle for filing a lawsuit advancing a claim that the first right had been violated. That right of action, in turn, had standing implications since it specified that the lawsuits it authorized could be filed in federal court.

336. *Lujan*, 504 U.S. at 573 (emphasis in original).

337. Id. at 571–73 & n.8. Recall Justice Scalia's illustration of this point. See notes 237–38 and accompanying text. A person who lives near the site of a proposed dam may well have standing to challenge a federal agency's failure to procure an environmental impact statement. Federal statutes create both the agency's legal duty to prepare such a statement and a private procedural right to enforce that duty in federal court. But it is a neighbor's personal, concrete interest in avoiding a dam next door that establishes his or her constitutional standing. Someone who lives a great distance away has no similar injury to assert and thus cannot constitutionally take advantage of the statutory rights that Congress creates. 504 U.S. at 572 n.7.

338. See note 90 and accompanying text.

339. See notes 117–19 and accompanying text.

It is hard to think that Congress might validly authorize litigants to proceed in an Article III court on the basis of legal rights (either substantive or procedural) that have no analog in preexisting interests that can be injured in fact in the familiar "judicially cognizable" sense. If Congress could do that, it could affix the "legal right" label to anything (including everyone's "abstract and indefinite" interest in seeing that federal law is followed) and then "confer" standing (on anyone and everyone) to vindicate that right in federal court. Congressional power of that magnitude cannot be reconciled with the great body of the Court's harm-based standing jurisprudence. Small wonder that in the next few paragraphs of his opinion in *Lujan*, Justice Scalia rehearsed the precedents holding that litigants cannot achieve constitutional standing on the basis of "generalized grievances" devoid of "concrete injury."[340]

This is not to say, however, that *Lujan* and other precedents bar private non-Hohfeldian plaintiffs from enforcing environmental protection laws and other statutes promising general benefits to the public at large. Litigation of that kind is typically within bounds, albeit litigants sometimes fail to measure up. Individuals usually can allege genuine personal factual injuries from foul air and water.[341] In this vein, moreover, *FEC v. Akins*[342] indicates that private litigants will have standing to enforce the wide range of federal statutes that hope to achieve regulatory ends by demanding the disclosure of information to the public.[343] So-called "citizen-suit" provisions like the one in the Endangered Species Act are now common.[344] They sweep aside all non-constitutional standing barriers and, as a practical matter, permit ideologically committed private litigants to advance their notions of the public interest. Nevertheless, those statutes invariably state that the private litigants they empower will proceed on their own behalf and not simply on behalf of the public. And, of course, they must satisfy the constitutional prerequisites for standing, including the requirement that they suffer concrete personal injury in fact.[345]

---

340. *Lujan*, 504 U.S. at 576.

341. See note 194 and accompanying text.

342. 524 U.S. 11 (1998); see notes 172–77 and accompanying text.

343. Even in dissent in *Akins*, Justice Scalia arguably acknowledged that Congress may give "all persons" standing to enforce the provisions of the Freedom of Information Act. 5 U.S.C. §552. See 524 U.S. at 30–31. See generally Sunstein, note 177 (providing a survey of federal "informational" statutes containing generous standing provisions).

344. E.g., 42 U.S.C. §7604 (the Clean Air Act provision); 33 U.S.C. §1365 (the Clean Water Act provision). See *Dep't of Energy v. Ohio*, 503 U.S. 607, 613 n.5 (1992) (citing the Clean Water Act provision with apparent approval).

345. See Robin K. Craig, *Will Separation of Powers Challenges 'Take Care' of Environmental Citizen Suits? Article II, Injury-in-Fact, Private 'Enforcers,' and Lessons from Qui Tam Litigation*, 72 U. Colo. L. Rev. 93 (2001). Professor Sunstein reads *Lujan* and other cases to allow standing to litigate alleged violations of various federal statutes protecting animal welfare. Cass R. Sunstein, *Standing for Animals (with Notes on Animal Rights)*, 47 U.C.L.A. L. Rev. 1333 (2000). Naturalists or tourists who have tickets in their pockets are not the only candidates. Other litigants may suffer economic losses from a violation of a statute regulating the treatment of animals. Sunstein concedes that under current law animals themselves have no standing to vindicate their own interests through litigation in Article III courts. Yet in his view that is only because the relevant federal statutes expressly limit standing to "persons." According to Sunstein, there is no obvious constitutional objection to animal-plaintiffs in Article III courts. Accordingly, Congress could open the federal court house doors to beasts themselves (represented by human guardians *ad litem*) simply by elimininating the current "persons only" signs. Id. at 1359–67. This last point is, of course, controversial outside Animal Farm.

4. Undeveloped Possibilities

Signals from the Court. Some justices have suggested that Congress should be able to go further than *Lujan* and other leading precedents contemplate. Recall Justice Harlan's dissent in *Flast,* in which Harlan said that, for his part, Congress should be able to confer standing even on litigants who allege no factual injury.[346] If the underlying issue is the separation of powers, Harlan argued that Congress should be able to consent to an exercise of judicial power when it sees no threat to its own sphere. Justice White may have agreed. In a brief concurring opinion in *Trafficante v. Metro. Life Ins. Co.,*[347] he said that he would have had "great difficulty" concluding that the plaintiffs presented a "case or controversy," if §810 of the Fair Housing Act had not granted them authority to "sue in court."[348]

If, *contra* Harlan and White, Congress' capacity to confer standing is limited to litigants who are factually injured, it would seem to follow that Congress has no capacity at all to extend standing beyond what the Court's constitutional standing rules permit. That appears to be the lesson to be taken from the *Lujan* case.[349] A legislative body has power to change the *legal* landscape by enacting new *laws,* but no (commonly understood) power to change the *physical* landscape by altering *facts.* Facts are empirically derivable truth (as best we can determine it). Facts are prior to law; they are not of it. Nevertheless, there is a body of opinion to the effect that Congress *can* make adjustments in the factual circumstances on which standing depends within the harm-based framework.

Even in *Lujan,* Justice Scalia endorsed Justice Powell's statement in *Warth* that the "injury" required by Article III "may exist solely by virtue of statute,"[350] as well as Justice Marshall's *dictum* in *Linda R.S. v. Richard D.*[351] that "Congress may enact statutes creating legal rights, the invasion of which creates standing, even though no injury would exist without the statute."[352] Justice Scalia explained that in the cases on which Powell and Marshall relied, Congress had elevated "to the status of *legally cognizable* injuries *concrete, de facto* injuries that were *previously inadequate in law.*"[353] Yet he distinguished between federal statutes that broaden "the categories of injury that may be alleged in support of standing," on the one hand, and statutes that abandon "the requirement that the party seeking review must himself have suffered an injury," on the other.[354]

Writing separately in *Lujan,* Justice Kennedy arguably opened the door a bit wider. He agreed that there must be an "outer limit" on congressional power "to confer rights of action" and that Article III requires litigants to show that they suffer injury in a "concrete and personal way." He suggested, however, that "[a]s government policies and programs become more complex," the Court should be "sensitive to the articulation of new rights of action that do not have clear analogues in our common-law tradition."[355] Ac-

---

346. See *Flast v. Cohen,* 392 U.S. 83, 131 (1968) (dissenting opinion); see notes 163–64 and accompanying text.

347. 409 U.S. 205 (1972).

348. Id. at 212; see note 369 and accompanying text.

349. *Lujan v. Defenders of Wildlife,* 504 U.S. 555 (1992); see notes 190–94 and accompanying text.

350. 422 U.S. at 500; see notes 213–14 and accompanying text.

351. 410 U.S. 614 (1973); see note 225.

352. 410 U.S. at 617 n.3.

353. 504 U.S. at 578 (emphasis added).

354. Id., quoting *Sierra Club,* 405 U.S. at 738.

355. *Lujan,* 504 U.S. at 580 (Kennedy, J., concurring) (joined by Souter, J.).

cording to Kennedy, Congress can "*define injuries* and *articulate chains of causation* that will give rise to a case or controversy *where none existed before*." Yet Congress must "at the very least identify the injury it seeks to vindicate and relate the injury to the class of persons entitled to bring suit," rather than authorizing "anyone" to proceed.[356]

Justice Breyer's opinion for the Court in *Akins* also contains hints in this direction.[357] Breyer stated that the plaintiffs in that case alleged "genuine 'injury in fact'" flowing from their deprivation of information that could be of use to them. That factual injury presumably existed apart from the Federal Election Campaign Act. Yet in the same breath, Breyer explained that the plaintiffs contended that the Act required AIPAC to divulge the information they needed.[358] That arguably implied a link between the plaintiffs' allegation of factual injury from the denial of information, on the one hand, and Congress' decision to make it unlawful to withhold that very information from them, on the other. *After* he referred to the plaintiffs' contention that the Act guaranteed them the data they wanted, Justice Breyer explained that there was no reason to doubt their claim that the information would help them evaluate candidates that AIPAC supported and that their injury "consequently" appeared to be "concrete and particular," thus sufficient to establish Article III standing.[359]

These passages in the *Lujan* and *Akins* opinions are enigmatic. Some of the difficulty lies in the *Linda R.S. dictum*, which mixes *legal rights* with *injuries*. Since *Data Processing*, the Court has distinguished between those two ideas. There are at least three ways to resolve the ambiguity.

Initially, *Linda R.S.* may confirm that Congress can enact statutes that turn interests into rights and that litigants who claim a violation of those rights satisfy the threshold constitutional requirement for standing. Having legal rights to advance, they have no need to seek standing on an exclusively fact-based ground.[360] Justice Brennan read the *Linda R.S. dictum* this way in *Havens*.[361] If that understanding is correct, *Linda R.S.* makes the unremarkable point that a violation of a legal right (resting on law as well as facts) *a fortiori* does the same *work* that injury in fact alone performs in some standing cases. In *Havens*, Justice Brennan drew a sharp distinction between the black tester (who had been given false information and thus had standing on the basis of a violation of her legal rights under §804) and the white tester (who had received accurate information and thus could not claim that his legal right to truthful information had been violated). Justice Brennan said that the white tester might obtain standing on the basis of an *injury* to his *interest* in living in an integrated community. But that was a different allegation that would have to be developed on remand.[362]

Alternatively, *Linda R.S.* may only acknowledge that Congress can enact statutes specifying non-constitutional standing rules that displace any prudential rules that the Court would otherwise apply. As Justice Scalia noted in *Lujan*, the two cases that Justice Marshall cited in *Linda R.S.* involved statutes of that kind. In *Hardin v. Kentucky Utili-*

356. Id. (emphasis added).

357. *FEC v. Akins*, 524 U.S. 11 (1998); see notes 172–77 and accompanying text.

358. *Akins*, 524 U.S. at 21.

359. Id.

360. See notes 104, 116–18, 298–301 and accompanying text.

361. *Havens Realty Corp. v. Coleman*, 455 U.S. 363, 373–74 (1982); see notes 301–02 and accompanying text. Professor Fallon also understands *Linda R.S.* this way. To test congressional power with respect to standing, Fallon posits the creation of what he calls, interchangeably, statutory "rights" or "legal interests." Fallon, note 85, at 19, 49.

362. 455 U.S. at 374–77.

ties Co.,[363] a private utility company contended that the Tennessee Valley Authority had unlawfully sold electricity outside a prescribed area. Justice Black held that the company's economic interest in avoiding competition met the requirements for standing, because the statute the company charged the TVA with violating reflected "a legislative purpose to protect a competitive interest."[364] In *Data Processing*, Justice Douglas said that "no explicit statutory provision" had been "necessary to confer standing" in *Hardin*, because the plaintiff company was "within the class of persons that the statutory provision was designed to protect." Douglas thus read *Hardin* to mean that the utility company needed no "specific" standing statute authorizing aggrieved citizens to sue the TVA in particular. The company was entitled to rely on the general standing provision in §702 of the APA, which authorized the company to sue the TVA, provided the company's interests were arguably within the zone of interests protected by the statute limiting the TVA's service area.[365]

In the other case, *Trafficante*,[366] tenants of an apartment building contended that the landlord discouraged African American applicants from renting rooms in violation of §804 of the Fair Housing Act.[367] They did not argue that the landlord had violated their legal rights under §804, but they insisted that they nonetheless had standing because they suffered factual injury: They were deprived of the benefits of living in a racially integrated building. Justice Douglas read one of the attendant standing provisions in the Act (§810) to eliminate any non-constitutional standing limits that otherwise would apply.[368] That left only the question whether the plaintiffs' interest in integrated housing supplied factual injury for constitutional standing purposes. Douglas held that it did. Justice White then added his concurring opinion, in which he suggested that §810 was sufficient in itself to satisfy Article III, even if the plaintiffs' alleged injury would not otherwise have sufficed.[369]

In *Lujan* itself, Justice Scalia suggested a third meaning for *Linda R.S.*, *Hardin*, and *Trafficante*. Recall what he said: Congress can identify "concrete, de facto injuries" that "previously" were "inadequate in law" and can elevate those injuries to "legally cognizable" status.[370] This third account is difficult to follow. The injuries in those cases were

---

363. 390 U.S. 1 (1968).

364. Id. at 6.

365. *Data Processing*, 397 U.S. at 155; see notes 274–87 and accompanying text (discussing the zone test). Alternatively, Justice Black may have conceived that the statute in *Hardin* gave the competing utility company a *legal right* to be free of competition from the TVA outside the area in which the statute authorized the TVA to seek customers. If that is what he meant, *Hardin* did nothing new, but only applied the Court's then-familiar rights-based conception of standing. See text accompanying notes 103–06 (explaining standing doctrine just prior to *Data Processing*).

366. See notes 347–48 and accompanying text.

367. See text accompanying note 300.

368. See note 321.

369. See text accompanying note 348. White's tone suggested not that he would cheerfully have gone further than Douglas, but rather that he joined Douglas only grudgingly. Nevertheless, White said that §810 was crucial to his conclusion that Article III standing existed. He therefore necessarily contemplated a role for Congress that Douglas did not broach. Douglas noted legislative history suggesting that some members of Congress were concerned about the kind of interest the plaintiffs alleged. But that part of his opinion went not to whether the plaintiffs had injuries at all, but to whether the standing provision (§810) was actually so sweeping as its language suggested. Douglas did not propose that §810 made the plaintiffs' allegations sufficient for Article III standing. He said that §810 eliminated any non-constitutional limits and that no constitutional question was presented because the plaintiffs had alleged *factual* injury "with particularity." 409 U.S. at 211 (majority opinion).

370. See text accompanying note 353.

not previously "inadequate in law" to qualify as factual injuries for constitutional standing purposes. Both the interest in avoiding competition and the interest in living in integrated housing existed prior to the creation of the TVA and the enactment of the Fair Housing Act. Those interests were personal to the plaintiffs in *Hardin* and *Trafficante* and thus were "cognizable" without reference to any law that Congress created.[371] The plaintiffs in those cases needed a statute not to establish factual injuries to genuine interests, but rather to escape the Court's rights-based test for standing under which *injuries* to *interests*, however concrete, would not suffice.[372]

Then again, Justice Scalia himself may think that it was a mistake to regard factual injuries alone to be sufficient for standing. In his view (at least as he expressed himself in 1983), it *should* have been necessary for the plaintiffs in *Hardin* and *Trafficante* to advance legal rights, not just concrete factual injuries.[373] Recall, too, that Justice Scalia's principal holding in *Lujan* was that Congress cannot manufacture an Article III case or controversy by establishing legal rights with no connection to any factual injury to pre-existing interests. It is hard to think, then, that Justice Scalia meant to credit the idea that Congress may grant standing to litigants who otherwise would fail the harm-based test. By contrast, he almost certainly meant to suggest (again) that the Court should recover the rights-based test for standing that he himself believes to be a better means of keeping judicial power within proper borders.

The suggestive passages in the *Lujan* and *Akins* opinions indicate that at least some justices may be coming to doubt the premise of the harm-based test for standing—that is, the idea that the constitutional prerequisites for standing can rest entirely on matters of fact, divorced from law. Conceivably, this renewed attention to the statutes that Congress enacts will lead the Court to accept Justice Scalia's invitation to restrict standing to Hohfeldian plaintiffs. It is also possible, however, that the Court may permit federal statutes to delineate interests that can be injured where, absent statute, those interests would have been less visible. If that is the course the Court follows, its new attention to Congress may make it more (not less) receptive to non-Hohfeldian plaintiffs seeking to enforce federal regulatory legislation.

Academic theories. Some academics have never been fully satisfied with the harm-based test for standing. In their view, the Court in *Data Processing* properly rejected the rights-based test, because it limited standing to interests having only one kind of legal station: the character of personal legal rights. Yet it was unnecessary (and unwise) to hold that standing should be determined on the basis of interests without reference to any other kind of legal recognition that interests may enjoy. Instead, according to some academics, the Court should acknowledge that Congress can identify and illuminate genuine human interests that previously were not fully appreciated, and even that Congress can develop satisfying accounts of the way in which unlawful conduct injures interests of that kind.[374]

On reflection, there is undeniable insight in the notion that what counts as a factual injury brought about by a violation of law is, after all, typically related to the law that is said to have been violated. Put the other way, law normally does not accord the status of

371. Recall that the Court recognized as early as *Sanders* that competitors suffer factual injury. See notes 94–96 and accompanying text.

372. See text accompanying note 90.

373. See notes 123–28 and accompanying text.

374. E.g., Donald L. Doernberg, *"We the People": John Locke, Collective Constitutional Rights, and Standing to Challenge Government Action*, 73 Calif. L. Rev. 52 (1985); Winter, note 86.

legal rights to human interests that have no basis in fact. The common law did not give a citizen an abstract legal claim to demand that his neighbor exercise reasonable care, but only a legal claim against actual (factual) injury caused by negligence. Nor did traditional statutes lay down rules for citizens to follow without regard to any purpose to avoid or discourage identifiable (factual) injuries. If some injuries seem to have an obvious basis in fact without reference to any law (a punch in the nose, for example), it may be only because the law establishing the legal right to be free of physical assaults is so deeply entrenched in American culture that its existence is universally accepted without conscious consideration.[375]

In a strong form, this insight about the relationship between factual injuries and legal rights can lead to an extravagant (and unattractive) argument: Factual injuries do not exist *as judicially cognizable injuries*, unless and until the law gives them legal status.[376] In a weaker form, the same insight can lead to an argument that is more widely appealing: Factual injuries precede law. But once those injuries receive legal status (of some kind), human perceptions of them are typically altered, sometimes in extremely important ways. Accordingly, injuries cannot be fully appreciated without some attention to the recognition that law gives them. By this more modest account, the point is not that law is the exclusive source of value, but rather that law reflects and projects value in a subtle, sometimes unconscious manner.

Modern federal regulatory statutes often recognize factual harm (and seek to prevent it) in ways that were unknown to the common law and the traditional statutes that the old rights-based test for standing had in view. Today, Congress does not attempt always (or even often) to protect identifiable individuals from injury, but rather fashions general regulatory schemes to achieve systemic improvements for society as a whole: racial integration, safe factories, and, to be sure, clean air and water. Violations of regulatory statutes produce harms. But those harms are not discrete injuries to some individuals as distinguished from others, but more diffuse deprivations of the generalized social benefits that Congress means to achieve. If the Court were to pay more respect to the regulatory programs that Congress enacts to address the general public interest, the Court might be more willing to grant standing to litigants alleging harm to those same interests. After all, the point of adopting the harm-based test for standing in the first place was to allow private litigants to use the federal judiciary to enforce federal legal stan-

375. For elaboration, see Albert, note 83; Fletcher, note 166; Sunstein, note 206.

376. Professor Sunstein has argued, for example, that if a woman had complained of sexual harassment before Congress enacted a statute establishing a legal right against that form of abuse, her injury would have seemed "purely ideological." Sunstein, note 177, at 640. Similarly, Professor Albert has argued that it would have been "inconceivable" to recognize environmental damage or anticompetitive injuries before Congress enacted legislation protecting interests of that kind by law. Albert, note 83, at 491. Surely these arguments grossly overstate the extent to which law drives human values. Consider that members of Congress must themselves perceive that genuine (factual) harms exist and need attention, else they would not propose responsive legislation. More fundamentally, all manner of suffering associated with poverty, racism, and other social ills occurs every day without eliciting efforts for amelioration through law. Professor Sunstein has acknowledged as much in the course of elaborating his approach to standing more fully. His argument is not that human beings cannot suffer harm in the absence of some legal recognition of that harm, but rather that the *legal system* does not acknowledge purely factual harm that enjoys no legal station of any kind. Recall in this vein that standing to sue in an Article III court is not established by factual injury of *any* kind, but only by "judicially cognizable" injury. See text accompanying notes 146–47. Sunstein contends that when the Court determines whether an injury is "judiciably cognizable" for standing purposes, it necessarily relies (consciously or unconsciously) on understandings influenced by the legal culture.

dards that beget no personal rights but nonetheless certainly *do* recognize *interests* that can be *injured* and thus generate genuine disputes.[377]

Many academics have proposed that standing doctrine should accommodate the links between what society perceives as interests that can be injured and the status that law gives to those interests. By some accounts, the question whether litigants have standing to enforce federal regulatory statutes should collapse entirely into the question whether Congress has authorized private suits in federal court.[378] Bluntly stated, the idea is this: Standing to advance a federal statutory claim (in both the constitutional and non-constitutional senses) should be entirely a matter for Congress to rule. Congressional authorization to institute litigation in federal court should be both a sufficient and a necessary prerequisite for standing. Factual injury alone, devoid of any legal recognition, should be neither necessary nor sufficient.[379] That approach would depart dramatically from the conceptual framework the Court now employs inasmuch as it

377. See notes 119–20 and accompanying text.

378. See, e.g., Albert, note 83; Erwin Chemerinsky, *A Unified Approach to Justiciability*, 22 Conn. L. Rev. 677 (1990); Currie, note 321; Fletcher, note 166; Sunstein, note 304. In cases in which litigants seek to enforce the Constitution, Fletcher and Sunstein would let the particular provision in question be the source of both the right to be enforced and the authority for litigation. For example, Fletcher endorses the position that Justice Stewart took regarding the Establishment Clause claim in *Flast*—namely, that taxpayers have standing to enforce the Establishment Clause because that clause itself gives taxpayers a judicially enforceable right to be free of taxation for religious purposes. See notes 158–59 and accompanying text.

379. See Sunstein, note 177, at 639. Professor Sunstein may be the most aggressive proponent of this approach. He does not fault Justice Scalia for contending that standing should turn on the status that law gives to human interests. Sunstein himself thinks that is inevitable. In his view, the "legal system does not 'see' an injury unless some law has made it qualify as such." Id. at 640. Sunstein denies the possibility of determining whether litigants have been injured for standing purposes without consulting what "people within the legal culture" consider to be "actual cognizable" harms. Id. at 641. Sunstein *does* fault Justice Scalia for using the harm-based test for standing to demand personal and particularized injuries reflecting common law thinking about interests that warrant judicial attention. According to Sunstein, Congress is entitled to decide that more general interests are sufficient. If Congress does that, the Court should acquiesce. Congressional action defuses any separation-of-powers questions, Scalia's concerns for executive authority notwithstanding. Sunstein concedes that his theory would empower Congress to extend standing well beyond current doctrinal limits. He argues, however, that the Court can now say that a purely ideological desire to see some aspect of federal law respected is not a sufficiently concrete interest only because the law has not given that desire legal recognition. If, however, Congress were to enact a statute creating a right to a state of affairs in which that feature of federal law is followed, Sunstein thinks the Court should acknowledge the statute as an identification of the desire for enforcement as an interest sufficient for Article III standing. Professor Sunstein does not distinguish cleanly and consistently between statutes that create primary legal rights, on the one hand, and statutes that create rights of action, on the other. The hypotheticals he offers to illustrate his approach indicate that he would have the Court find standing if Congress creates rights of either character. See id. at 671 (proposing that Congress might create standing by enacting a statute giving "everyone" a "property interest" in clear skies over the Grand Canyon); id. at 641 n.144 (suggesting that Congress might also create standing by enacting a statute authorizing "anyone" to sue over allegedly unlawful race discrimination occurring "anywhere" in the country). Sunstein recognizes that his position is inconsistent with *Lujan*. And he concedes that *Lujan* has not been overruled. Id. at 643 n.154. Yet Sunstein cites certain language in that opinion, see text accompanying notes 350–53, as well as Justice Kennedy's concurring opinion, see notes 355–56 and accompanying text, as evidence that the Court is moving in his direction. Sunstein thinks Justice Breyer's opinion for the Court in *Akins* constitutes a "reformulation" of standing doctrine that largely places matters in Congress' hands. Id. at 641; see also id. at 617 (arguing that *Akins* "appears to vindicate" Kennedy's separate opinion in *Lujan*). Professor Johnson and Professor Gilles think Professor Sunstein reads too much into *Akins*. See Johnson, note 93; Gilles, note 177.

would discard the search for factual injury and concentrate, instead, on the instructions that Congress supplies regarding the judicial enforcement of its enactments.

By other accounts, the question whether litigants have standing should simply pay more attention to the interests that federal statutes identify: In the absence of a federal statute authorizing federal litigation, the Court may conclude that litigants lack sufficient factual interest in the enforcement of a regulatory scheme. Yet when Congress enacts a statute explicitly authorizing private suits, the Court should acknowledge Congress' identification of what may be diffuse (but nonetheless real) interests and thus conclude that litigants have standing. By these accounts, judicially cognizable *de facto* injury remains a constitutional prerequisite for standing. A federal statute purporting to "confer" standing is neither necessary nor sufficient in itself to create an Article III case or controversy. But such a statute can and should influence the Court's decision on whether litigants advancing congressionally identified interests satisfy the Court's constitutional standards for access to the Article III judiciary.[380]

F. Standing and the Merits

Hohfeldian plaintiffs who seek standing on the basis of their own personal legal rights make arguments at the standing stage that are essentially a preview of the presentations they will make regarding their claims on the merits. Non-Hohfeldian plaintiffs who seek standing on the basis of factual injuries do not (necessarily). There is always some overlap. The causation and redressability features of harm-based standing doctrine contemplate some attention to the violations of law that non-Hohfeldian litigants contend are responsible for their injuries.[381] Prudential standing doctrines invariably implicate the merits of legal claims more forthrightly.[382] Yet the very point of the harm-based framework is to separate standing from the merits in order to enable non-Hohfeldian plaintiffs to litigate legal issues on behalf of the public.[383]

The working premise is that litigants who achieve standing on the basis of injuries are in a position to succeed on the merits if they can establish that the defendant has violated, is violating, or will imminently violate the law. That violation of law need not constitute a breach of any legal duty the defendant owes to the plaintiffs personally; it need not be conceived as a violation of their personal legal rights. It can be, and often is, simply a violation of some federal statute or constitutional provision specifying the way in which the defendant must behave. Once again, the *Bennett* case[384] provides an example. The ranchers in that case satisfied the requirements for harm-based standing and were therefore entitled to press a variety of legal claims against the defendant agency. One of those claims was that in implementing various provisions of the Endangered Species Act, the Fish and Wildlife Service had acted "arbitrarily and capriciously"

380. For example, Professor Nichol argues that the Court's approach to factual injuries is unjustifiably wedded to common law thinking and that the Court would do better to open its mind to the collective public rights that federal law entails. Nichol, note 304, at 1156–60. Professor Winter, too, finds the Court's framework to be overly individualistic. See Winter, note 86.

381. See notes 221–22, 246–47 and accompanying text.

382. See text accompanying notes 281–87 (discussing the zone test).

383. See notes 116–18 and accompanying text.

384. *Bennett v. Spear*, 520 U.S. 154 (1997); see notes 325–29 and accompanying text.

or "otherwise not in accordance with law."[385] A claim of that kind could not usefully be understood as a claim that the agency had violated the ranchers' personal legal rights. It was simply a claim that the agency had violated the law (in a way that harmed the ranchers who on the basis of that harm had standing to sue to enforce the law).

This proposition, solid as it is, nonetheless can be obscured in some cases. Recall that in *Data Processing*, Justice Douglas said that the plaintiff companies had standing under §702 inasmuch as they suffered injury to interests that were arguably within the zone of interests protected by the Bank Services Corporation Act.[386] In a final paragraph, he said that whether anything in that Act gave the plaintiffs a "legal interest" that "protect[ed] them against violations," and whether the actions of the Comptroller "did in fact violate" the Act, were questions that went to "the merits" and thus remained to be resolved in the lower courts.[387] That final paragraph implied that Douglas' analysis of standing did not vanquish Frankfurter's "legal interest" requirement after all, but merely shifted attention to that requirement to a later stage of the proceedings when litigants would still be expected to demonstrate that their own legal rights were violated.[388] Having obtained standing on the basis of *interests* with which the statute was arguably *concerned*, they could succeed on the merits only by demonstrating personal legal *rights* that the statute actually *established*.[389]

It would not be illogical to treat the relationship between harm-based standing and the merits in that way. Standing might be understood as a rule of pleading that screens out litigants who have so little interest that they do not warrant judicial attention at all and reserves judicial resources for litigants who attempt to establish a violation of their own legal rights. Yet if that were all that the harm-based test for standing meant, it would not be so important as, in fact, it is. By contrast to the suggestion in *Data Processing*, litigants who achieve standing on the basis of judicially cognizable injuries to interests are not (constitutionally) limited to pressing legal claims that their personal rights have been violated. Instead, they are entitled to advance claims that a defendant has simply violated the law, whether or not that law begets personal rights in them or in anyone else.[390]

Of course, non-Hohfeldian litigants invariably attempt to convince federal courts to interpret federal law to their advantage. In so doing, they commonly contend that the

385. 5 U.S.C. §706.

386. See text accompanying notes 112–15.

387. *Data Processing*, 397 U.S. at 158. Justice Douglas himself placed quotation marks around the phrase "legal interest." Justice Brennan left essentially the same impression. He said that once the plaintiffs established standing on the basis of "injury in fact," the inquiry would proceed to "the merits—to whether the specific legal interest claimed" by the plaintiffs was "protected by the statute" and "whether the protested agency action invaded that interest." *Barlow v. Collins*, 397 U.S. 159, 175 (1970) (dissenting opinion). Cf. *Invest. Co. Inst.*, 401 U.S. at 620 (reading *Data Processing* to mean that the question whether Congress has actually "prohibited" competition of which plaintiffs complain is a "question for the merits").

388. See text accompanying notes 90, 103–06, 112–20 (discussing the "legal interest" test and Douglas' rejection of it in *Data Processing*).

389. See The Federal Courts and the Federal System 176 (Fallon, Meltzer & Shapiro eds. 1996).

390. Professor Stewart argues that the "considerations that a litigant may advance on the merits should normally be no broader or narrower than those that the litigant may assert to secure standing." Otherwise, litigants with special concerns of their own may misrepresent the interests of others. Conflicts of interest, in turn, can produce poor decisions. See Stewart, note 108, at 1573 n.62. See also note 252 and accompanying text (discussing similar arguments regarding third-party claims). The conventional answer is that Congress addresses concerns of that kind when it decides to authorize private attorneys general and establishes the criteria they must meet to qualify as the public's champions. See note 116 and accompanying text (discussing the congressional judgment ascribed to the statutory zone test).

purpose of a statute or constitutional provision is to protect the kinds of interests they themselves have. There is a genuine sense, then, in which litigants within the harm-based conception of standing *do* often press their own interests at the merits stage. In *Bennett*, for example, the ranchers contended that the Fish and Wildlife Service had violated the Endangered Species Act by failing to take account of the economic injuries the ranchers would suffer.[391] And in the *Steel* case, the plaintiffs argued that the company had violated their "right to know" the information the company had concealed.[392] Nevertheless, there is no formal requirement that litigants must contrive to couch a legal claim that the defendant has violated the *law* as a claim that the defendant has violated their individual *legal rights*.[393]

G. Ripeness

Federal courts can entertain claims only if they are "ripe" for adjudication. Claims are ripe when they are presented for decision in the context of an extant case or controversy within the meaning of Article III.[394] As a formal matter, accordingly, the ripeness doctrine adds nothing to the constitutional prerequisites for standing, but only focuses attention on whether the harm that litigants allege is sufficiently "imminent" to create the injury that standing requires.[395]

In the leading case, *United Public Workers v. Mitchell*,[396] federal employees challenged a provision of the Hatch Act barring them from taking an "active part" in political cam-

---

391. *Bennett*, 520 U.S. at 160; see notes 325–29 and accompanying text.

392. *Steel Co. v. Citizens for a Better Environment*, 523 U.S. 83 (1998); see notes 244–47 and accompanying text.

393. In *Sierra Club v. Morton*, 405 U.S. 727 (1972), the Court said that the radio station cases, *Sanders* and *Scripps-Howard*, establish that litigants who achieve standing on the basis of some cognizable injury are then in a position simply to contend that an agency "has failed to comply with its statutory mandate." 405 U.S. at 737; see notes 187–89 and accompanying text (discussing the *Sierra Club* case); notes 94–98 and accompanying text (discussing *Sanders* and *Scripps-Howard*). In *First National Bank*, the Court upset an agency interpretation of a federal regulatory statute at the behest of competitor banks who barely passed the zone test, far less asserted any legal rights with respect to the agency's action. See notes 277–79 and accompanying text. In *TVA v. Hill*, 437 U.S. 153 (1978), biologists and other individuals who used the Little Tennessee Valley area where the Tellico Dam was being built sued the TVA for violating the Endangered Species Act by destroying the snail darter's habitat. The plaintiffs had the benefit of the "citizen-suit" provision in the ESA, but they asserted no personal legal rights. The Court forthrightly addressed the question whether constructing the dam violated the Act and held that the plaintiffs were entitled to a permanent injunction against further work on the project. Of course, Congress may establish special statutory limits on the private actions that litigants can bring. In *Bennett*, for example, Justice Scalia examined the intricacies of ESA and the APA to determine which provisions permitted the ranchers to advance their various claims. And in some instances litigants may have difficulty identifying particular remedies that will redress their injuries in the constitutional sense. See notes 223–47 and accompanying text.

394. *Babbitt v. Farm Workers*, 442 U.S. 289, 297 (1979).

395. See text accompanying note 141 (noting that "imminent" injury is necessary for standing). Professor Nichol contends that the ripeness doctrine should be (and often is) more flexible than rules governing standing and that it is unwise to regard ripeness as an Article III requirement. See Gene R. Nichol, Jr., *Ripeness and the Constitution*, 54 U. Chi. L. Rev. 153 (1987). Professor Pushaw points out that ripeness *is* distinguishable from other constitutional requirements in that federal adjudication may be available once the factual and legal issues have matured. Pushaw, note 106, at 493.

396. 330 U.S. 75 (1947).

paigns. The Civil Service Commission had already charged one of the plaintiffs with engaging in prohibited activity and had prepared an order for his dismissal. Justice Reed found that plaintiff's first amendment claim ripe for consideration. Reed explained, however, that the claims advanced by the other plaintiffs were premature. Those plaintiffs alleged in a general way that they wished to engage in the kinds of activities the Act condemned and that they feared that they, too, would be discharged. But they did not detail the precise activities they had in mind. Without more specificity, Justice Reed said it was speculative whether they would actually do anything that the Commission would regard as a violation of the Act so as to prompt any disciplinary action against them. Alternatively, Reed might have rested the decision in *Mitchell* on conventional standing doctrine: The plaintiffs failed satisfactorily to allege that the Commission was causing them any current or imminent injury by frustrating actual plans for political activities.[397]

1. Relevant Considerations

In practice, the Court has identified four considerations regarding ripeness that do not always track the constitutional features of standing: (1) whether the legal claims that litigants advance especially warrant early judicial attention; (2) whether the issues and factual circumstances will be sharper at a later time; (3) whether the postponement of adjudication will avoid interference with the work of other non-judicial authorities; and (4) whether the postponement of adjudication will visit hardships on the parties.

Claims that warrant early attention. In some instances, litigants advance claims that can be determined on legal grounds alone, without attention to factual circumstances. In cases of that kind, there is little to be gained from delay. First amendment overbreadth claims fit this description.[398] Since the litigants at bar attack overbroad statutes on their face, without regard to the circumstances in which the statutes have been applied, it is feasible to adjudicate the merits in a comparatively abstract way. In *Adler v. Bd. of Ed.*,[399] for example, the Court allowed public school teachers to challenge the infamous Feinberg Law in New York, under which teachers were to be dismissed if they belonged to organizations advocating the overthrow of the government. Only Justice Frankfurter argued that the plaintiffs' overbreadth claim in *Adler* was not ripe, but that was because Frankfurter alone thought the validity of the Feinberg Law depended on the way it was applied.[400]

Postponement in aid of a better record. Courts prefer to examine legal issues on the basis of a fully developed factual record, which both demonstrates the need for adjudication and supplies the wherewithal for sound decisions.[401] If, then, litigants present is-

397. Dissenting in the *Duke Power* case, Justice Stevens insisted that the prospect of a nuclear accident was so remote that the plaintiffs' due process attack on the Price-Anderson Act could not be ripe for adjudication. *Duke Power v. Carolina Envt'l Study Group*, 438 U.S. 59, 102–03 (1978); see note 211 and accompanying text. In response, Chief Justice Burger explained that his conclusion that the plaintiffs had standing equally meant that their claim was ripe. Id. at 81 (majority opinion).

398. See notes 261–73 and accompanying text.

399. 342 U.S. 485 (1952).

400. Id. at 504 (dissenting opinion). See Scharpf, note 49, at 532. The plaintiffs in *Mitchell* also attacked the Hatch Act on its face. It seems clear, however, that the Court regarded that claim as frivolous and thought that only a particularly egregious application of the Act could violate the first amendment. See *United States Civil Service Comm'n v. Nat'l Ass'n of Letter Carriers*, 413 U.S. 548 (1973) (rejecting an overbreadth attack on one provision of the Act).

401. See notes 14–15 and accompanying text; Chapter I, notes 61–72 and accompanying text.

sues in a contingent posture, there may be a good deal to gain by delaying judicial action until the circumstances become more concrete. In some instances, unexpected events may defuse the parties' dispute and make it unnecessary to adjudicate at all.[402] In other instances, events will make the factual basis for decision more definite. In *Mitchell*, for example, it was not clear that the plaintiffs would follow through with any plans to become involved in political activities or, if they did, that the Commission would decide to invoke the Act against them. If, by contrast, the plaintiffs were ultimately charged with a violation, there would be a definite description of their conduct to work with in determining whether their first amendment claims were meritorious.[403]

Postponement to avoid interference with other authorities. Courts attempt to avoid premature consideration of legal claims that might frustrate the performance of other bodies. In *Abbott Laboratories v. Gardner*,[404] Justice Harlan explained that declining adjudication on ripeness grounds keeps courts from becoming entangled in "abstract disagreements" with administrative agencies and concomitantly protects agencies from "judicial interference" before they have "formalized" their own decisions and brought them to bear on individuals.[405] Harlan identified two factors that govern judgment: the "fitness of the issues for judicial decision" and the "hardship to the parties" if adjudication is deferred. In *Abbott Labs* itself, the plaintiffs were drug companies who challenged a regulation requiring them to identify the drugs they sold by their generic names. Justice Harlan concluded that the question whether the regulation was valid was ripe for adjudication, because it was a purely legal issue that was "fit" for immediate consideration and because postponing review would work a hardship on the companies. If they chose to comply with the regulation in the short term, they would have to revise all their advertising literature; if they chose to defy it, they would risk prosecution.[406]

---

402. E.g., *Texas v. United States*, 523 U.S. 296, 302 (1998) (finding a matter not to be ripe because it was "too speculative whether the problem" the plaintiff presented would "ever need solving"). See notes 421–41 and accompanying text (discussing mootness).

403. See *Babbitt*, 442 U.S. at 300 (explaining that delay for purposes of developing a better record is appropriate even when there is no serious doubt that a rule will be enforced). Cases in which litigants wish to challenge criminal statutes also offer illustrations. Until individuals make a definite record of the behavior in which they want to engage, and until prosecuting officers make it clear that planned behavior is subject to prosecution, courts may hesitate to find claims to be ripe. E.g., *Poe v. Ullman*, 367 U.S. 497 (1961). Nevertheless, the Supreme Court has allowed litigants to seek anticipatory relief from the enforcement of criminal statutes, so long as the prospect of prosecution is not entirely speculative. In *Pierce v. Society of Sisters*, 268 U.S. 510 (1925), the Court found it sufficient that local authorities had declared that they would prosecute parents who failed to send their children to public school in defiance of a state statute. By most accounts, the decisions in point are inconsistent, and the results may best be explained on other grounds. The Court plainly did not want to address the merits of the prohibition on contraceptives in *Poe*. In *Epperson v. Arkansas*, 393 U.S. 97 (1968), by contrast, the Court was eager to invalidate the notorious "Monkey Law" and thus found the question ripe even though no one stood to be prosecuted. Of course, when prosecution is likely, litigants suffer hardship if they are unable to gain access to federal court and must endure criminal charges and trials in order to advance their claims in state court. See Chapter VIII, notes 143–45 and accompanying text (discussing the availability of declaratory judgment actions in these circumstances).

404. 387 U.S. 136 (1967).

405. Id. at 148. Judicial review of actions taken by federal administrative agencies is governed by federal statutes and judicial decisions meant to discourage premature judicial consideration of intermediate agency behavior. The ripeness doctrine complements that body of law.

406. Id. at 149, 153. In practice, the ripeness doctrine tends to allow the subjects of regulation (like the drug companies in *Abbott Labs*) to attack agency rulings before they go into effect, but to force the beneficiaries of regulation to await an appellate form of judicial review later. The subjects of regulation typically must alter their behavior in response to a ruling as long as it is in place. Ben-

Early adjudication to avoid hardship. Courts generally take into account the costs to the litigants if judicial action is deferred—not just in cases in which federal agencies are involved. When this consideration predominates, it is hard to think that ripeness doctrine is entirely a creature of Article III. The convenience of the parties is irrelevant to the character of their dispute as a constitutional case or controversy. In *Duke Power*,[407] Chief Justice Burger placed concerns for the parties under the heading of the "*prudential considerations* embodied in the ripeness doctrine." In that vein, he said that prudence argued for immediate attention to the plaintiffs' claim. Delay would undermine the Price-Anderson Act's purpose to reassure the nuclear power industry and would foreclose any relief to which the plaintiffs might be entitled if the Act was unconstitutional. The only point of deferring judgment to a later time would be to await a nuclear disaster, after which it would become clear whether Congress had set aside sufficient funds to cover potential losses. That scenario was a bit drastic.[408]

2. Ripeness and Remedies

The ripeness doctrine overlaps not only with the constitutional aspects of standing, but also with the equitable and discretionary considerations attending the availability of injunctive and declaratory relief. In *O'Shea v. Littleton*[409] and *Rizzo v. Goode*,[410] residents of Cairo, Illinois and Philadelphia filed class actions against local authorities alleging that the police in those cities systematically enforced the law in a racially discriminatory manner. The plaintiffs alleged that African Americans were singled out for arrest, subjected to excessive bonds, and otherwise mistreated because of their race. In both instances, the Supreme Court found the issues not to be ripe, because the supporting allegations were vague and speculative.

In *O'Shea*, Justice White explained that the constitutional question whether the plaintiffs' claims were ripe for adjudication "shade[d] into" the non-constitutional question whether they could be awarded injunctive relief. The plaintiffs had not established that they were personally threatened with "substantial and immediate irreparable injury" in circumstances in which equitable relief was necessary because there were no "adequate remedies at law." Their allegations were speculative, and if they themselves ultimately suffered the kind of race discrimination they anticipated, they would be able to press their constitutional claims in the course of the state legal proceedings against them. Moreover, any injunction the district court issued would apply to uncertain future events in an attempt to preempt unlawful race discrimination of unknown propor-

---

eficiaries typically suffer no significant harm until an agency acts upon them personally in some manner. In *Ohio Forestry Ass'n v. Sierra Club*, 523 U.S. 98 (1998), for example, the Court held that the Sierra Club's challenge to a Forest Service logging plan was not ripe for adjudication. The plan was a precondition to logging that would injure club members, but it did not, in itself, actually authorize timber to be harvested. Before anyone could begin cutting trees, the Service would have to take additional procedural steps in proceedings in which the club could participate. And then any final decision to permit cutting would be subject to the ordinary appellate review process.

407. *Duke Power Co. v. Carolina Envt'l Study Grp.*, 438 U.S. 59 (1978); see note 211 and accompanying text.

408. *Duke Power*, 438 U.S. at 81–82 (emphasis added).

409. 414 U.S. 488 (1974).

410. 423 U.S. 362 (1976).

tions. An injunction of that kind, White said, would draw the federal district court into an "ongoing federal audit of state criminal proceedings."[411]

The decisions in *O'Shea* and *Rizzo* illustrate the Supreme Court's growing concerns in the 1970s about federal public rights litigation.[412] In cases involving segregation in public schools, racially discriminatory voting schemes, and poor conditions in state mental hospitals and prisons, federal district courts had issued elaborate injunctive decrees forcing state officials to reform the way they managed state functions and institutions. Equitable relief of that kind put pressure on federalism.[413] The Court responded by recruiting the ripeness doctrine, coupled with limits on equitable relief, to discourage litigation that, in the Court's view, had veered too far from the traditional private rights model of adjudication. Having linked Article III justiciability doctrines to the availability of equitable relief in class action cases like *O'Shea* and *Rizzo*, the Court carried that theme over to more traditional lawsuits. In the choke hold case, *Lyons*,[414] Justice White also found it premature to consider a single plaintiff's suit for an injunction, because the plaintiff's allegations about the future were speculative.[415]

Cases in which litigants seek declaratory relief sometimes follow a similar pattern. A declaratory judgment is not an equitable remedy. Accordingly, the classic conditions for injunctions are inapplicable.[416] Nevertheless, federal courts have discretion regarding declaratory relief, and, in practice, they exercise that discretion with ripeness in mind.[417] In *Steffel v. Thompson*,[418] the plaintiff alleged that local police officers had warned him that if he continued to distribute leaflets protesting the Vietnam War, he would be arrested and prosecuted for criminal trespass. The plaintiff left the scene, but soon thereafter filed an action in federal court, seeking a declaratory judgment that he was entitled to pass out the leaflets and that a prosecution for trespass would violate the first amendment.[419] He alleged that he wished to resume distributing handbills at the same location, but feared that, if he did so, he would be arrested. The prosecutor named as defendant stipulated that the plaintiff's concern was warranted. The anticipatory nature of the suit raised questions about both ripeness and discretion to award declaratory relief.

Justice Brennan concluded that the plaintiff in *Steffel* could proceed. With respect to ripeness, Brennan explained that the risk of future prosecution created current harm: The plaintiff wanted to continue distributing leaflets, but he could not do so without bearing serious costs. His plans were concrete, the threat of prosecution real. Accordingly, his claim was ripe for judicial determination. With respect to declaratory relief, Brennan explained that one of the central purposes of the Declaratory Judgment Act

---

411. 414 U.S. at 500.

412. See Chapter I, note 90 and accompanying text.

413. See Chapter I, notes 19–25 and accompanying text.

414. See notes 240–41 and accompanying text.

415. Professor Fallon contends that the Court reacted in *Lyons* to the remedial difficulties that had been presented in the large class action cases, *O'Shea* and *Rizzo*. In *Lyons*, however, an injunction would not have disrupted local police functions on anything like the same scale. See Fallon, note 85, at 44.

416. *Zwickler v. Koota*, 389 U.S. 241, 254 (1967).

417. See Chapter VIII, notes 141–42 and accompanying text.

418. 415 U.S. 452 (1974).

419. See Chapter XI, notes 207–12 and accompanying text (discussing the abstention issues in *Steffel*).

was to furnish litigants with a mechanism for enforcing their federal rights without subjecting themselves to the costs and embarrassments of a criminal prosecution. A declaration that would provide clarity to both sides was, then, appropriate.[420]

H. Mootness

Federal courts cannot consider claims after the disputes in which they arose have been resolved by other means and are now "moot." The mootness doctrine mirrors the ripeness doctrine. Ripeness is concerned that federal adjudication not come too soon, while mootness is concerned that it not come too late. Like ripeness, mootness is formally a feature of the Article III requirement that federal judicial power can operate only upon a case or controversy.[421] Mootness is routinely linked to standing: The Supreme Court holds a case to be moot when, at some point during the litigation, something occurs to eliminate the injury on which a litigant relies for standing. Mootness is equally linked to the ban on advisory opinions: When a dispute has disappeared, nothing a federal court says or does will have any practical effect on the parties' positions.[422]

In *DeFunis v. Odegaard*,[423] the Court initially granted review to consider a constitutional attack on a race-conscious admissions program at the University of Washington Law School. By the time the case was ready for decision, the plaintiff had been admitted to the school and was in his last year of study. School authorities assured the Court that they had no intention of preventing the plaintiff's graduation, irrespective of the outcome of the lawsuit. At that point, the Court issued a *per curiam* finding the matter moot. The injury the plaintiff had alleged no longer sustained his standing to sue for the relief he had sought two years earlier: an injunction requiring that he be admitted to the entering class.[424]

---

420. Even so, since the Vietnam War had wound down while the litigation in *Steffel* proceeded, Justice Brennan remanded for a current determination whether the petitioner retained an active interest in distributing the handbills. In *Ellis v. Dyson*, 421 U.S. 426 (1975), the Court explained that declaratory actions of the kind *Steffel* approved depend on the existence of a "credible threat" that the plaintiff will be prosecuted. Id. at 434–35.

421. *Spencer v. Kemna*, 523 U.S. 1, 7 (1998).

422. It is not essential that the same injury that originally established standing must remain in place throughout the litigation, but only that some injury must always be present to preserve the plaintiff's personal stake in the outcome. In criminal cases, for example, federal courts can entertain attacks on convictions after the convicts concerned have served their sentences. Criminal convictions typically carry collateral legal consequences: convicts are not permitted to join certain professions, engage in certain businesses, or obtain certain licenses. Those disabilities constitute continuing harms. They are so common that the Court presumes they exist and that, because of them, cases involving criminal convictions are not typically moot. See *Sibron v. New York*, 392 U.S. 40, 55 (1968). But see *Spencer*, 523 U.S. at 10–12 (disparaging *Sibron* and declining to adopt a similar presumption that revocations of parole have collateral consequences). Cf. *Dove v. United States*, 423 U.S. 325 (1976) (holding that a convict's death moots an appeal).

423. 416 U.S. 312 (1974).

424. Mootness, like redressability, attends to the nature of the relief a plaintiff seeks. A case is moot, accordingly, if the relief sought is either unavailable or ineffective to remedy the plaintiff's complaint. Professor Fallon has suggested that the *Lyons* choke hold case might well have been handled as a matter of mootness. See Fallon, note 85, at 24–28. It is questionable whether a shift in labels would have made any difference.

The Court once embraced the general proposition that mootness is only "standing set in a time frame."[425] More recently, the Court has explained that statement as pithy, but "not comprehensive."[426] Like the ripeness doctrine, the mootness doctrine is fluid in operation. It is hard, then, to accept the notion that mootness is truly a constitutional doctrine—particularly in a case like *DeFunis*, in which the parties had labored to present an important federal question in a concrete posture for decision. By common account, the Court often employs mootness as a means of avoiding issues it is not yet ready to decide.[427] In other instances, moreover, the Court recognizes special exceptions that rescue issues from mootness on pragmatic grounds: (1) cases in which the defendant voluntarily ceases the behavior under attack but is free to resume it in the future; (2) cases in which plaintiffs advance claims that exist only for a short time but by their nature are likely to recur; and (3) cases in which plaintiffs represent a class of litigants with similar claims.

Voluntary cessation. In some instances, cases become moot because the party said to be acting unlawfully voluntarily ceases the offending behavior. Unilateral action of that kind can eliminate the dispute between the parties and, concomitantly, the justification for federal adjudication. This occurs, of course, when the party advancing the claim seeks declaratory or injunctive relief looking to the future—the kind of relief that is unnecessary if the opposing party has already decided to do what an injunction would require. The Supreme Court is suspicious, however, that litigants may use the mootness doctrine strategically, changing their behavior just long enough to win dismissal on mootness grounds. Accordingly, the Court typically does not allow voluntary cessation to render a case moot if the party whose behavior is challenged acts only in response to litigation.[428] In general, the Court demands solid assurances that litigants will not resume the conduct that gave rise to the dispute.[429]

The Court is also sensitive to the practical implications of declaring a matter no longer justiciable after a lower court has reached a judgment on the merits. In *City of Erie v. Pap's*,[430] the Court refused to hold that a challenge to an ordinance banning nude dancing was moot. The nightclub that had filed the suit had gone out of business and sold its property. In part, Justice O'Connor explained that the club was still incorporated and might yet resume operation. The telling point, though, was the decision below. The club had obtained a judgment in state court invalidating the ordinance on

---

425. *Arizonans for Official English v. Arizona*, 520 U.S. 43, 68 n.22 (1997), quoting Monaghan, note 8, at 1384.

426. *Friends of the Earth v. Laidlaw*, 528 U.S. 167, 190 (2000).

427. Chief Justice Rehnquist has said that, for his part, mootness is a prudential device for orchestrating the exercise of judicial power and not a constitutional prohibition. *Honig v. Doe*, 484 U.S. 305, 331 (1988) (concurring opinion). Professor Lee develops that thesis and, in particular, attacks the received wisdom that to decide an issue that is moot by conventional standards would be to render an advisory opinion. Lee, note 34; see notes 11–34 (discussing advisory opinions).

428. E.g., *United States v. W.T. Grant Co.*, 345 U.S. 629, 632 (1953).

429. In *City of Mesquite v. Aladdin's Castle*, 455 U.S. 283 (1982), the Court declined to hold that an attack on a city ordinance governing "amusement establishments" was moot. The ordinance had been repealed after a lower court held it invalid. But local authorities made it clear that they would reenact the ordinance if it was approved by the Supreme Court. In the *Laidlaw* case, see notes 242–43 and accompanying text, the Court declined to hold that environmentalists' attack on the operation of an incinerator was moot. The facility had been closed, and, for that reason, the lower court had denied an injunction against further pollution. Nevertheless, the Court regarded the prospect of future violations at the site to be sufficiently in dispute to keep the matter in court.

430. 529 U.S. 277 (2000).

first amendment grounds, and the city had sought Supreme Court review. The club then closed its business before it responded to the city's petition for *certiorari*. The club did not mention the changed circumstances until after the Court granted review. It appeared, accordingly, that the club meant to deprive the Court of the opportunity to reexamine the state court's decision in the club's favor.[431] The Court distinguished *Pap's* in *City News & Novelty v. City of Waukesha*.[432] In that case, another "adult enterprise" challenged a city ordinance, *lost* in state court, went out of business, and still tried to press its constitutional claims in the Supreme Court. Justice Ginsburg explained that the dispute could be adjudged moot without leaving the city under the "weight of an adverse judgment."[433] With the matter in that posture, Justice Ginsburg *did* declare the case moot, albeit she listed additional reasons for concluding that it did not properly present the issue on which the Court had expected to rule.

Short-term disputes. Many short-lived disputes become moot before a final judgment can be rendered and thus are denied federal adjudication. In one class of short-term disputes, however, the Supreme Court recognizes an exception to the mootness doctrine: disputes that promise to recur periodically, only to be mooted in each instance. When an interest has ceased to exist, but is "capable of repetition yet evading review," a federal court can adjudicate, mootness notwithstanding.[434] It is not enough that others may suffer the same kind of injury in the future. The "capable of repetition" exception to mootness is available only if the plaintiff in the lawsuit at hand is likely to be in the same position again.[435] The best illustration is an attack on an abortion regulation. On the theory that "[p]regnancy often comes more than once to the same woman," the Court allows a single plaintiff to press a lawsuit of that kind, even after her pregnancy is terminated.[436]

Class actions. Class action lawsuits can also avoid mootness. In form, either the named plaintiff or the class must have a justiciable claim at every stage of the proceedings, from the filing of the complaint through final judgment. In practice, litigants can rely on fictional "relation back" devices to fill in gaps when they appear. If a named plaintiff's claim survives until the class is certified, the class becomes the plaintiff and the entire lawsuit can proceed, even if the named plaintiff's claim later becomes moot. In cases of that kind, the named plaintiff carries the case until it is handed off to the full class.[437] In some circumstances, the lawsuit can proceed even if the named plaintiff's claim becomes moot *before* the trial court certifies the class. If the named plaintiff's claim is so "inherently transitory" that it disappears before the court can rule on a motion to certify the class, the court's later order certifying the class relates back to the time the request for certification was filed. The actual gap between the time the named plaintiff's claim becomes moot and the time the class is certified is filled in by means of the "relation back" doctrine.[438] Finally, if the trial court *declines* to certify the class as re-

431. Id. at 305 (Scalia, J., concurring in the judgment) (nonetheless contending that the case was moot).

432. 531 U.S. 278 (2001).

433. Id. at 284.

434. *Southern Pac. Terminal Co. v. ICC*, 219 U.S. 498, 515 (1911).

435. *Weinstein v. Bradford*, 423 U.S. 147, 149 (1975).

436. *Roe v. Wade*, 410 U.S. 113, 125 (1973). See Comment, *A Search for Principles of Mootness in the Federal Courts: Part One—The Continuing Impact Doctrines*, 54 Tex. L. Rev. 1289 (1976).

437. *Franks v. Bowman Trans. Co.*, 424 U.S. 747 (1976). The only remaining issue is whether the named plaintiff whose personal claim is moot continues to be a proper representative of the class. See *Kremens v. Bartley*, 431 U.S. 119 (1977).

438. *Gerstein v. Pugh*, 420 U.S. 103 (1975).

quested and the named plaintiff's claim becomes moot, the matter *still* can proceed in order to give the appellate courts an opportunity to review the trial court's determination of the certification question.[439] The named plaintiff retains a sufficient interest in the motion for class certification to sustain the matter as an Article III case. If the trial court's determination is reversed on appeal and certification is ultimately granted, that certification order, too, relates back and saves the lawsuit from mootness.[440]

The Court's decisions regarding mootness, particularly the decisions involving class actions, are plainly more generous to litigants than are the Court's parallel decisions on standing. By some accounts, greater flexibility is warranted in this context, because the civil rules governing class actions are sharper tools for managing class litigation than is Article III.[441]

439. *United States Parole Comm'n v. Geraghty*, 445 U.S. 388 (1980).

440. Id. at 404; but see id. at 405–07 (warning that the named plaintiff's representative status may be questioned independently).

441. Professor Greenstein provides a discussion. See Richard K. Greenstein, *Bridging the Mootness Gap in Federal Court Class Actions*, 35 Stan. L. Rev. 897 (1983).

Chapter X

Suits against Government and Government Officers

Lawsuits by or against government or government officers constitute a sizeable share of federal question litigation in federal court. Suits by government are typically conducted by executive officers or agencies, acting under statutory authority either to protect government's sovereign and proprietary interests[1] or to seek judicial enforcement of the Constitution, statutes, regulations, or administrative rulings.[2] Actions of that kind occasionally raise important questions.[3] And recent developments promise to bring those difficulties to the fore.[4] On the whole, however, suits by *private* litigants *against* government or government officers form the corpus on which federal courts doctrine operates. The Supreme Court keeps the law governing litigation with the federal government and federal officers on a parallel track with the law governing litigation with the states and state officers—subject to statutes that Congress adds to the mix.[5] In both instances, the starting place is sovereign immunity.[6] Private litigants who satisfy the justiciability doctrines, and who demonstrate both a right of action to vindicate their federal claims in court and a federal district court's jurisdiction to entertain those claims, still may be thwarted if the party they name as defendant is immune from suit.[7]

---

1. The Attorney General typically has authority to litigate on behalf of the federal government. 28 U.S.C. §516. Other officers and entities have authority to do so within their own fields. See *FDIC v. Meyer*, 510 U.S. 471, 475 (1994) (discussing the "sue and be sued" authority that Congress sometimes confers on federal agencies); Chapter VIII, note 7 and accompanying text (discussing the same boilerplate authority given to some federally chartered corporations). Barring special statutory exception, the district courts have jurisdiction to entertain all suits "commenced by the United States, or by any agency or officer thereof expressly authorized to sue by Act of Congress." 28 U.S.C. §1345.

2. See Chapter V, text accompanying notes 18–19 (discussing enforcement actions by federal administrative agencies).

3. See Edward Hartnett, *The Standing of the United States: How Criminal Prosecutions Show That Standing Doctrine is Looking for Answers in All the Wrong Places*, 97 Mich. L. Rev. 2239 (1999); Henry P. Monaghan, *The Protective Power of the Presidency*, 93 Colum. L. Rev. 1 (1993).

4. See notes 257–75 and accompanying text.

5. See notes 52–66, 276–77, 424–30 and accompanying text.

6. See Chapter IX, notes 80–83 and accompanying text (discussing the link between sovereign immunity and "standing" doctrine).

7. See notes 67–70 and accompanying text (discussing the way in which sovereign immunity may be treated as "jurisdictional").

A. Suits Against the Federal Government

1. In General

The Constitution does not explicitly establish the federal government's sovereign immunity. By contrast, Article III includes controversies "to which the United States shall be a Party" within the federal judicial power.[8] Nevertheless, the Supreme Court has always recognized that the central government cannot be sued without its consent.[9] The government's sovereign immunity defeats suits brought either by private citizens or by public entities,[10] in either federal or state court,[11] advancing either federal or state claims,[12] and seeking either compensatory or injunctive (or declaratory) relief.[13] Apart from the historical account,[14] the Court explains the government's immunity on pragmatic grounds: Private suits for damages would divert public resources into the pockets of individual plaintiffs and away from the uses that government has chosen by democratic means.[15] Private suits for injunctive orders requiring the government to alter its behavior would stop the government "in its tracks," frustrating the administration of the public's business.[16]

2. Officer Suits

Despite the federal government's sovereign immunity, private litigants often can challenge actions taken on the government's behalf by suing federal officers rather than the government itself.[17] The cases in point fall into two categories: (1) cases in which private litigants mean to impose personal liability on government officers as individuals; and (2) cases in which private litigants sue government officers only as a legal fiction in order to obtain relief against the government by indirection.

---

8. See Chapter IV, text accompanying note 4.

9. *United States v. Testan*, 424 U.S. 392, 399 (1976); see *Cohens v. Virginia*, 19 U.S. (6 Wheat.) 264, 411–12 (1812) (*dictum*). The Court has acknowledged that Native American tribes enjoy a similar immunity, defeasible by federal legislation. See *Kiowa Tribe v. Manufacturing Tech.*, 523 U.S. 751 (1998).

10. Cf. *West v. Gibson*, 527 U.S. 212, 222 (1999) (acknowledging the argument that absent consent the government would be immune from liability for damages assessed by the EEOC).

11. See *Alden v. Maine*, 527 U.S. 706, 749 (1999) (confirming that the federal government enjoys immunity both in federal and in state court).

12. See *Dep't of the Army v. Blue Fox*, 525 U.S. 255 (1999) (involving a private contract suit in federal court asserting an equitable lien against funds held by the Army); *United States v. Stanley*, 483 U.S. 669 (1987) (involving a private tort suit in federal court seeking compensatory damages).

13. See *United States v. Sherwood*, 312 U.S. 584 (1941); *Naganab v. Hitchcock*, 202 U.S. 473 (1906).

14. See Chapter IX, notes 80–83 and accompanying text.

15. *Dugan v. Rank*, 372 U.S. 609, 621 (1963). See Harold J. Krent, *Reconceptualizing Sovereign Immunity*, 45 Vand. L. Rev. 1529 (1992) (elaborating these rationales); Roger C. Cramton, *Nonstatutory Review of Federal Administrative Action: The Need for Statutory Reform of Sovereign Immunity, Subject Matter Jurisdiction, and Parties Defendant*, 68 Mich. L. Rev. 387, 396–97 (1970) (offering a critical account). Sovereign immunity is widely condemned in the academic literature. See, e.g., Erwin Chemerinsky, *Against Soverign Immunity*, 53 Stan. L. Rev. 1201 (2001) (contending that sovereign immunity undermines political accountability and conflicts with numerous conventional constitutional themes).

16. *Larson v. Domestic & Foreign Commerce Corp.*, 337 U.S. 682, 704 (1949).

17. See Chapter IX, text accompanying notes 81–83.

Suits to impose personal liability. The federal government's immunity is not implicated when private litigants sue federal officers in a genuine attempt to impose personal liability on the officers themselves. Typically, plaintiffs claim that federal officers have violated the plaintiffs' rights under state tort law or the Constitution. So-called *Bivens* actions provide the best modern illustration.[18] Liability depends on the circumstances. Behavior that would ordinarily count as an assault or a violation of the fourth amendment may have been perfectly lawful if, at the time, government officers were subduing a violent suspect. In some circumstances, officers can defeat personal liability on the basis of their own official immunity.[19] But they cannot assert the federal government's sovereign immunity. The federal government is not liable as the defendants' employer on the theory of *respondeat superior*. If plaintiffs are ultimately successful, they obtain compensatory damages to be paid out of the pockets of the officers concerned.[20]

Suits to affect the government. The federal government's sovereign immunity is sometimes (but not always) implicated when private litigants sue federal officers in an attempt to reach the government indirectly.[21] John Marshall suggested in the *Osborn* case that plaintiffs can always elude the government's sovereign immunity, so long as they do not name the government itself as a formal defendant party of record—irrespective of what plaintiffs actually hope to gain from litigation.[22] That view no longer holds.[23] The Court now looks beyond the formal pleadings to determine whether a suit is actually against the federal government. Nevertheless, officer suits do provide private litigants with a practical means by which to challenge the validity of governmental behavior.

Actions for common law writs are prototypical officer suits, neatly avoiding the government's sovereign immunity. Recall that Chief Justice Marshall said in *Marbury v. Madison* that, in a case of proper jurisdiction, a federal court might have issued the writ of mandamus to require the Secretary of State to deliver Marbury's commission.[24] Actions for injunctive relief against federal officers can also evade the government's immunity, provided plaintiffs advance constitutional claims.[25] When defendant officers comply with writs and injunctions, they do not act as individuals, but rather on behalf of the

---

18. See *Little v. Barreme*, 6 U.S. (2 Cranch) 170 (1804) (holding a naval officer personally liable for trespass committed under color of official authority); Chapter VIII, notes 200–30 and accompanying text (discussing private *Bivens* suits against federal officers to vindicate federal constitutional rights).

19. See notes 424–94 and accompanying text.

20. The federal government can indemnify federal officers. But see Cornelia T.I. Pillard, *Taking Fiction Seriously: The Strange Results of Public Officials' Individual Liability Under Bivens*, 88 Gtn. L.J. 65 (1999) (reporting that few plaintiffs are actually compensated).

21. On the use of fictional officer suits to avoid sovereign immunity, see Kenneth C. Davis, *Suing the Government by Falsely Pretending to Sue an Officer*, 29 U. Chi. L. Rev. 435 (1962); Louis L. Jaffe, *Suits Against Governments and Officers: Sovereign Immunity*, 77 Harv. L. Rev. 1 (1963).

22. *Osborn v. Bank of United States*, 22 U.S. (9 Wheat.) 738, 856–57 (1824) (actually referring to a state's sovereign immunity); see text accompanying note 114; Chapter VIII, notes 5–20 and accompanying text (discussing other aspects of *Osborn*).

23. See *In re Ayers*, 123 U.S. 443, 487 (1887) (also a state sovereign immunity decision); notes 280–85 and accompanying text.

24. 5 U.S. (1 Cranch) 137, 173 (1803); see Chapter I, text accompanying note 68. Mandamus remains the most useful of the common law writs. Today, pursuant to 28 U.S.C. §1361, federal district courts have original jurisdiction to entertain "any action in the nature of mandamus to compel an officer or employee of the United States or any agency thereof to perform a duty owed to the plaintiff." See Clark Byse & Joseph V. Fiocca, *Section 1361 of the Mandamus and Venue Act of 1962 and "Nonstatutory" Judicial Review of Federal Administrative Action*, 81 Harv. L. Rev. 308 (1967).

25. E.g., *Shields v. Utah Idaho Central R.R.*, 305 U.S. 177, 183–84 (1938).

government. Nevertheless, they cannot set up the government's sovereign immunity.[26] In the leading case, *United States v. Lee*,[27] the Court held that a private citizen could sue federal officers in an ejectment action in order to regain possession of real estate. At the time, the plaintiff in *Lee* was unable to seek compensatory damages in the Court of Claims.[28] If sovereign immunity had barred his suit to eject government agents from the land, he would have been deprived of his property without just compensation.[29]

In the middle of the Twentieth Century, the Court found officer suits ineffective to avoid sovereign immunity when plaintiffs advanced non-constitutional tort or contract claims.[30] In *Larson v. Domestic & Foreign Commerce Corp.*,[31] for example, a private company contracted to buy coal from the War Assets Administration. Thereafter, the agency canceled the contract. The company sued Larson, the chief administrator, for an injunction ordering him to deliver the coal.[32] Chief Justice Vinson allowed Larson to assert the government's immunity and, on that basis, to defeat the company's suit. Vinson assumed that Larson had violated the contract and that if he had been an agent for a private seller, the plaintiff would have been entitled to an injunction. As it was, however, Vinson said that Larson had acted within his statutory authority to superintend sales of government coal. That made Larson's action "inescapably the action of the

26. See, e.g., *Heckler v. Ringer*, 466 U.S. 602 (1984) (allowing a suit against the Secretary of Health and Human Services); *Minnesota v. Hitchcock*, 185 U.S. 373 (1902) (permitting a suit against the Secretary of the Interior); cf. *Schneider v. Smith*, 390 U.S. 17 (1968) (permitting a suit for a declaratory judgment against the Commandant of the Coast Guard). See also Chapter XII, notes 38–43 and accompanying text (discussing petitions for the writ of habeas corpus running to federal officers). The writs of mandamus and habeas corpus are authorized by independent statute. Other common law writs may be issued pursuant to the All-Writs Act, 28 U.S.C. §1651. See Chapter II, note 58. None of the statutes regarding writs purports to waive the government's sovereign immunity. Each presupposes that petitions for writs addressed to individual federal officers do not implicate that immunity. See *Seminole Tribe v. Florida*, 517 U.S. 44, 177–78 (1996) (Souter, J., dissenting) (actually referring to state sovereign immunity).

27. 106 U.S. 196 (1882).

28. See note 45 and accompanying text (discussing the Tucker Act of 1887).

29. In *Lee*, Robert E. Lee's son initially filed the ejectment action in state court, claiming that federal agents had seized the Lee family estate pursuant to an unlawful tax foreclosure. The agents removed the suit to federal court, then moved to dismiss on sovereign immunity grounds. Recall that federal agents can remove, provided they assert federal defenses. 28 U.S.C. §1442; see Chapter VI, notes 136–43 and accompanying text. Justice Miller acknowledged that, in truth, Lee meant to challenge the government's actions. The idea that Lee was suing only the officers as individuals was a legal fiction. If he obtained a judicial order requiring the agents to return the land, he would receive everything that he might have gained if he had been able to sue the government as a corporate entity. Yet Justice Miller found that fiction acceptable for the very reason that it *did* avoid the government's sovereign immunity. He explained that if the government was dissatisfied with the way its interests were treated in a suit against its agents, the government was free to initiate litigation on its own behalf. Recall that in a suit like *Lee* in the form of ejectment, the formal determination of title to real estate was submerged in a contest over a (fictional) lease. See Chapter VII, note 45. The government was not bound by a judgment imposing personal liability on its officers. See *Carr v. United States*, 98 U.S. 433 (1878). But see *Montana v. United States*, 440 U.S. 147 (1979) (holding that under modern preclusion doctrine the government *is* bound if it takes an active role in litigation).

30. See generally *Developments in the Law: Remedies Against the United States and its Officers*, 70 Harv. L. Rev. 827, 831–32, 854–61 (1957).

31. 337 U.S. 682, 693 (1949).

32. The company invoked the district court's jurisdiction on the theory that it had already obtained title to the coal pursuant to the contract and thus had a federal claim to delivery (resting on the federal contract).

United States" and the company's effort to enjoin Larson "an effort to enjoin the United States."[33] Chief Justice Vinson distinguished *Lee* on the theory that the plaintiff in that case alleged a violation of the Constitution and had no other way to vindicate his claim.[34] In the *Larson* case, by contrast, there was no allegation that the government's agent had "taken" the company's property unconstitutionally, and the company might have sought compensation in the Court of Claims.[35]

The analysis in *Larson* threatened to vanquish officer suits entirely, except in cases in which federal agents acted beyond their statutory authority or violated federal constitutional rights. By Vinson's account, federal officers could routinely assert the government's sovereign immunity when they were sued regarding actions taken in their official capacity.[36] In subsequent cases, the Court took *Larson* just that far. In *Malone v. Bowdoin*,[37] the Court said that ejectment actions against federal agents could not be maintained in the absence of a constitutional claim. And in *Hawaii v. Gordon*,[38] the Court said that suits that "nominally" sought injunctive relief against government officers would be treated as suits against the sovereign itself if, in fact, they would "operate" against the government.[39] Academics criticized *Larson* and its progeny and, in time, Congress responded by enacting statutes that superseded those decisions by waiving the

---

33. *Larson*, 337 U.S. at 703.

34. See text accompanying notes 28–29.

35. *Larson*, 337 U.S. at 703 n.27. Dissenting in *Larson*, Justice Frankfurter insisted that *Lee* and other cases stood for the general proposition that sovereign immunity would not defeat a suit naming a federal officer and alleging a common law tort. Id. at 722. Justice Douglas concurred on the theory that the Court's decision was limited to cases involving government property. Id. at 705. For a discussion of the officer suit device in *Lee* and *Larson*, see Jonathan R. Siegel, *Suing the President: Nonstatutory Review Revisited*, 97 Colum. L. Rev. 1612, 1622–44 (1997).

36. Professor Byse has explained that, in this, Vinson's analysis in *Larson* proved too much. If federal agents could set up the government's immunity to defeat any suit challenging their official behavior, then the "officer suit" device would no longer allow private litigants to challenge governmental action indirectly. Any suit attacking the conduct of government agents *qua* agents (other than constitutional actions) would constitute an action against the government itself. If courts are to review officer behavior, it must be possible for government agents to have official "authority" to make "erroneous as well as correct determinations." Clark Byse, *Proposed Reforms in Federal "Nonstatutory" Judicial Review: Sovereign Immunity, Indispensable Parties, Mandamus*, 75 Harv. L. Rev. 1479, 1491 (1962). Professor Alexander and Professor Lee contend that it is impossible to distinguish systematically between conduct that exceeds an officer's authority and conduct that constitutes a mere mistake in the exercise of authority. Larry Alexander & Evan Tsen Lee, *Is There Such a Thing as Extraconstitutionality?: The Puzzling Case of Dalton v. Spencer*, 27 Ariz. St. L.J. 845 (1995). Cf. notes 289–300 (discussing analogous problems in cases involving state sovereign immunity and fourteenth amendment claims). In a notorious footnote in *Larson*, Chief Justice Vinson only added to the confusion. He said that a suit "may fail, as one against the sovereign, even if it is claimed that the officer being sued has acted unconstitutionally or beyond his statutory powers, if the relief requested cannot be granted by merely ordering the cessation of the conduct complained of but will require affirmative action by the sovereign or the disposition of unquestionably sovereign property." 337 U.S. at 691 n.11. On the one hand, the footnote confirmed that officer suits would remain available in some instances. On the other, it suggested that suits could be maintained only for negative (as opposed to affirmative) injunctive relief—even when litigants pressed constitutional claims. It is true that negative injunctions that require officers to cease unlawful behavior have a much longer history than do affirmative injunctions that command them to take prescribed action in the future. Yet the Court has allowed officer suits for both kinds of injunctions in cases involving the states, sovereign immunity notwithstanding. See notes 299–300 and accompanying text.

37. 369 U.S. 643, 646–47 (1962).

38. 373 U.S. 57, 58 (1963).

39. Id. at 58.

government's immunity in most instances. Conventional wisdom has it that *Larson* and its progeny would control today (unless overruled), but for statutes consenting to the kinds of suits involved in those cases.[40]

3. Waivers of Immunity

Congress can waive the federal government's sovereign immunity, thus permitting suits that would otherwise be barred. The Supreme Court insists, however, that waiver statutes must be "strictly construed...in favor of the sovereign."[41] This is to say, the Court invokes the doctrine of clear statement: a waiver must be "unequivocally expressed" in the text of a statute.[42] On the whole, the Court has read the statutes in point to be sufficiently clear.[43] In direct response to *Larson*, *Malone*, and *Gordon*, Congress inserted a general waiver of immunity for suits challenging agency action into §702 of the Administrative Procedure Act: "An action in a court of the United States seeking relief other than money damages and stating a claim that an agency or officer or employee thereof acted or failed to act in an official capacity or under color of legal authority shall not be dismissed nor relief therein denied on the ground that it is against the United States." The APA now states explicitly that the United States "may be named as a defendant" in such an action and that a "judgment or decree may be entered against the federal government itself."[44]

Other illustrations abound. The Tucker Act, first enacted in 1887, waives the government's immunity respecting certain claims for monetary relief: constitutional "takings" claims, claims under federal statutes, and most federal contract claims.[45] The Tucker Act expressly excludes tort actions. But the Federal Tort Claims Act, first enacted in 1946, waives the government's immunity for a wide range of suits in which private plaintiffs

40. Professor Pfander argues, however, that those cases neglected the first amendment right to "petition" the government for redress of grievances. By Pfander's account, that right extends to petitions directed to the courts and thus establishes a constitutional basis for suits against the government that sovereign immunity cannot deny. James E. Pfander, *Sovereign Immunity and the Right to Petition: Toward a First Amendment Right to Pursue Judicial Claims Against the Government*, 91 Nw. U. L. Rev. 899 (1997). Criticisms of *Larson* are legion. See, e.g., Byse, note 36; Cramton, note 15; Davis, note 21; Jaffe, note 21; Seigel, note 35.

41. *Blue Fox*, 525 U.S. at 261.

42. *Lane v. Pena*, 518 U.S. 187, 192 (1996); *Library of Congress v. Shaw*, 478 U.S. 310, 318 (1986).

43. E.g., *Henderson v. United States*, 517 U.S. 654 (1996); *United States v. Mitchell*, 463 U.S. 206 (1983). In *FDIC v. Meyer*, 510 U.S. 471 (1994), the Court construed the conventional "sue and be sued" formulation in the statute creating the FDIC as a sufficient waiver. See Chapter VIII, notes 7, 128–31 and accompanying text (noting other functions ascribed to the "sue and be sued" phrase).

44. This language, added to §702 in 1976, follows immediately the language authorizing private suits and conferring standing on "aggrieved" parties who pass the zone test. See Chapter VIII, notes 137–39 and accompanying text; Chapter IX, text accompanying note 107. For background, see Cramton, note 15. If *Larson* were to arise today, §702 would produce a different result. Another statute, codified at 28 U.S.C. §1346(f), waives the government's immunity for purposes of suits to quiet title to real estate. That statute would now produce a different result in *Malone*.

45. 28 U.S.C. §1346(a)(2). The Court of Federal Claims (a legislative court) has jurisdiction over most Tucker Act suits for monetary relief, subject to appellate review in the Court of Appeals for the Federal Circuit (an Article III court). E.g., *Franconia Assoc. v. United States*, 122 S.Ct. 1993 (2002); see Chapter II, text accompanying note 79. Plaintiffs who seek injunctive or declaratory relief on constitutional grounds can sue federal officers in a district court. *Eastern Enterprises v. Apfel*, 524 U.S. 498 (1998).

claim tortious injury at the hands of federal employees.[46] The FTCA covers negligence claims and some intentional torts.[47] It excludes claims that federal employees failed properly to perform a "discretionary function,"[48] most claims by military personnel,[49] and constitutional claims that can be the basis for *Bivens* suits.[50] The Suits in Admiralty Act waives the government's immunity regarding a range of maritime claims.[51]

B. Suits against a State

1. In General

The Constitution is no more explicit about the states' sovereign immunity than it is about that of the federal government. Here, too, Article III appears to contemplate suits in which the states are parties, with no specification that the states can only be plaintiffs or defendants by their own consent.[52] Nevertheless, the Supreme Court has held that the Constitution recognizes state sovereign immunity that generally tracks the immunity that the central government enjoys. The states, too, typically can defeat lawsuits brought in federal court, in state court, or in a federal administrative agency,[53] advancing either federal or state claims,[54] seeking either compensatory or injunctive (or de-

---

46. 28 U.S.C. §1346(b), §§2671-80. Recall that the FTCA incorporates state law to provide rules of decision. See Chapter VIII, note 90.

47. See Jack Boger, Mark Gitenstein & Paul Verkuil, *The Federal Tort Claims Act Intentional Torts Amendment: An Interpretative Analysis*, 54 N. Car. L. Rev. 497 (1976).

48. See *Berkovitz v. United States*, 486 U.S. 531 (1988) (reviewing the precedents in point); Note, *The Federal Tort Claims Act: A Proposal for Institutional Reform*, 100 Colum. L. Rev. 1538 (2000) (arguing that this exception is often used to defeat negligence claims).

49. See *Feres v. United States*, 340 U.S. 135 (1950); *United States v. Stanley*, 483 U.S. 669 (1987); cf. *United States v. Johnson*, 481 U.S. 681 (1987) (expressing dissatisfaction with the "*Feres* doctrine" but declining to discard it). See also Chapter VIII, notes 102–03, 117–19 and accompanying text (discussing the *Boyle* case).

50. *Meyer*, 510 U.S. at 477–78; see Chapter VIII, notes 209–18 and accompanying text. The district courts have exclusive jurisdiction of FTCA cases. A private plaintiff may allege a state tort arising out of circumstances that might also give rise to a constitutional violation. In that way, a case can be squeezed under the FTCA. But, of course, the government's liability then turns exclusively on state tort law, apart from the Constitution.

51. 46 U.S.C. §741 *et seq.* See *Henderson*, 517 U.S. at 656.

52. See Chapter IV, text accompanying note 4.

53. See, e.g., *Seminole Tribe v. Florida*, 517 U.S. 44 (1996) (involving a suit in federal court); *Alden v. Maine*, 527 U.S. 706 (1999) (involving a suit in state court); *Fed. Maritime Comm'n v. South Carolina State Ports Authority*, 122 S.Ct. 1864 (2002) (involving a complaint before a federal agency).

54. See, e.g., *Hans v. Louisiana*, 134 U.S. 1 (1890) (involving a constitutional claim); *Seminole Tribe*, 517 U.S. at 712 (involving a federal non-constitutional claim); *Lapides v. Bd. of Regents*, 122 S.Ct. 1640 (2002) (involving state law claims); *Pennhurst State School & Hosp. v. Halderman*, 465 U.S. 89 (1984) (same). In the *Lapides* and *Pennhurst* cases, the Court recognized state sovereign immunity with respect to state claims in *federal* court. See notes 181–87, 350–60 and accompanying text. In *Alden v. Maine*, the Court held that a state can assert a federal constitutional exemption from suit in state court. In *Alden*, however, the plaintiffs advanced federal statutory claims in a lawsuit authorized by Congress. See notes 175–80 and accompanying text (discussing the attendant complexities). Of course, some states allow themselves the luxury of a local, domestic sovereign immunity based on state law. See Chapter VI, notes 50–52, 72–73 and accompanying text.

claratory) relief.[55] Importantly, however, suits against state officers successfully evade state sovereign immunity in the very kinds of cases in which suits against federal officers do not always avoid the federal government's immunity.[56]

In the typical case, a state cannot be named as a formal party defendant without its consent.[57] An agency, department, or board exercising statewide authority counts as a state for these purposes.[58] Yet a political subdivision (a city, county, or local agency) or a typical multi-state entity does not. Local governmental bodies and entities are not sovereign themselves, but have only the status and authority granted to them by their (sovereign) states.[59] Most multi-state organizations are not extensions of the states involved, but exist only by agreement between those states and Congress. They are not themselves constituent elements of the constitutional scheme. No state's autonomy is threatened when they are sued.[60]

There is one important exception to state sovereign immunity that does not obtain with respect to the central government's similar privilege. State immunity operates only as a defense against lawsuits brought by *private* litigants—not by another state or by the federal government.[61] The Constitution contemplates that two states must be able to

55. See, e.g., *Alden*, 527 U.S. at 712 (involving a suit for monetary relief); *Alabama v. Pugh*, 438 U.S. 781 (1978) (involving a suit for injunctive relief).

56. See notes 30–40 and accompanying text (explaining that suits advancing non-constitutional claims against federal officers might be barred absent consent).

57. *Pugh*, 438 U.S. at 782.

58. *Ford Motor Co. v. Dep't of Treasury*, 323 U.S. 459 (1945). Questions occasionally arise over whether particular bodies count as the state for these purposes. See, e.g., *Lapides*, 122 S.Ct. at 1645 (assuming that the governing board of a state university can assert the state's immunity); cf. *Raygor v. Regents*, 534 U.S. 533 (2002) (recognizing a potential sovereign immunity issue in a case in which the defendant was a state university). For discussions, see John R. Pagan, *Eleventh Amendment Analysis*, 39 Ark. L. Rev. 447 (1986); Note, *Clothing State Governmental Entities with Sovereign Immunity: Disarray in the Eleventh Amendment Arm-of-State Doctrine*, 92 Colum. L. Rev. 1243 (1992).

59. *Lincoln County v. Luning*, 133 U.S. 529, 530 (1890); see *Mt. Healthy Bd. of Ed. v. Doyle*, 429 U.S. 274, 280 (1977) (declining to treat a local school board as an arm of the state for sovereign immunity purposes). Given the modern development of home rule, cities and counties now enjoy many of the attributes traditionally associated with sovereignty. Some critics argue, accordingly, that *Luning* is outdated. For a defense of *Luning's* result (but not its analysis), see Melvyn R. Durchslag, *Should Political Subdivisions be Accorded Eleventh Amendment Immunity?*, 43 DePaul L. Rev. 577 (1994). Professor Durchslag acknowledges that cities and counties qualify as the state for purposes of the fourteenth amendment. But, in his view, it does not follow that they must equally be regarded as the state for purposes of state immunity. If cities and counties were exempt from the fourteenth amendment, states could frustrate the individual rights that amendment protects simply by delegating authority to political subdivisions. Other constitutional references to a state cannot plausibly include cities and counties. Diversity jurisdiction surely does not exist simply because a citizen of Boston sues a citizen of Cambridge (even if Ronald Reagan *did* think he was in a foreign country whenever he visited Harvard). According to Durchslag, the analogy to the term "state" in the tenth amendment provides more food for thought. See *Nat'l League of Cities v. Usery*, 426 U.S. 833, 855 n.20 (1976) (holding that cities and counties *do* count as the state for purposes of the tenth amendment—whatever those purposes may be); notes 96–97 and accompanying text (noting the parallels between the tenth and eleventh amendments).

60. *Hess v. Port Auth.*, 513 U.S. 30 (1994). The Court said in *Hess* that state sovereign immunity may be implicated if a multi-state entity is deliberately "structured" to be entitled to the immunity that the member states themselves enjoy. The key issue (evidently) is whether the member states are responsible for the multi-state organization's debts. Id. at 44–45. But see id. at 61–62 (O'Connor, J., dissenting) (arguing that a state's liability for a multi-state entity's debts should be sufficient but not necessary to bring sovereign immunity into play).

61. See note 10 and accompanying text.

settle their accounts in a neutral tribunal—typically supplied by the Supreme Court itself in the exercise of original jurisdiction.[62] More importantly, the Constitution also contemplates that the United States must be able to resolve its disputes with an autonomous state. In the leading case, *United States v. Texas*,[63] the Court explained that suits by the federal government are exempted from state immunity, because: (1) the states must be subject to suits lest the federal government be required to subject them to military force;[64] and (2) the states implicitly surrendered their immunity by joining the Union.[65] Suits at the instance of sister states are rare and inconsequential. Suits by the federal government (and its arms) are much more common and, by some accounts, promise a practical device for breaching state sovereign immunity and forcing states to conform their behavior to law.[66]

2. Waivers of Immunity

States can waive their federal constitutional immunity from suit. Unlike the federal government, the states often fail to do so by express legislation. Yet the Supreme Court sometimes finds state waivers nonetheless. The Court occasionally refers to state sovereign immunity as though it goes to a court's subject matter "jurisdiction."[67] That is loose talk.[68] Immunity is not "jurisdictional" in the ordinary "subject matter" sense that its existence constitutes a defect in judicial power to entertain a lawsuit. If that were true, a state would be unable to consent to be sued in circumstances in which immunity is available.[69] A state's privilege to resist suit is better understood as a defense that a state is free to assert or not as it pleases. Nevertheless, state sovereign immunity "sufficiently *partakes of the nature of* a jurisdictional bar" that immunity is sometimes treated *in the way* that a jurisdictional deficit would be handled.[70] Four means of establishing a state's consent to be sued warrant attention: (1) waiver by positive enactment; (2) waiver by knowing action; (3) waiver by voluntary litigation behavior; and (4) waiver by default.

---

62. *Kansas v. Colorado*, 206 U.S. 46 (1907). See Chapter VII, notes 6–8 and accompanying text (discussing the Court's original jurisdiction to resolve disputes between two states).

63. 143 U.S. 621 (1892). In *Texas*, the federal government invoked the Supreme Court's original jurisdiction. See Chapter VII, notes 26–28 and accompanying text.

64. Recall what Hamilton had to say about this. See Chapter II, text accompanying note 49. But see *Principality of Monaco v. Mississippi*, 292 U.S. 313 (1934) (holding that a state can set up sovereign immunity to defeat a suit brought by a foreign nation in federal court).

65. See *Blatchford v. Indian Village of Noatak*, 501 U.S. 775, 782 (1991).

66. See notes 257–75 and accompanying text.

67. E.g., *Seminole Tribe*, 517 U.S. at 76 (concluding that a suit was barred by state immunity and therefore ordering it dismissed "for lack of jurisdiction"). The eleventh amendment suggests a "jurisdictional" limitation inasmuch as it prescribes the way in which "the Judicial Power of the United States" is to be construed. See *Alden*, 527 U.S. at 754 (suggesting that suits against unconsenting states are "not within the judicial power of the United States and [cannot] be heard in federal courts"). But see notes 117–22 and accompanying text (explaining that state sovereign immunity does not depend on the text of the eleventh amendment).

68. See Antonin Scalia, *Sovereign Immunity and Nonstatutory Review of Federal Administrative Action: Some Conclusions from the Public Lands Cases*, 68 Mich. L. Rev. 867, 920 (1970).

69. *Wisconsin Dep't of Corrections v. Schacht*, 524 U.S. 381, 389–91 (1998) (making this point while purporting to reserve the question whether state immunity is "a matter of subject-matter jurisdiction"). See Chapter VIII, note 242 and accompanying text (explaining that the parties cannot establish subject matter jurisdiction by consent).

70. *Edelman v. Jordan*, 415 U.S. 651, 678 (1974) (emphasis added).

Waiver by positive enactment. A state certainly can waive sovereign immunity by enacting a statute that consents to all suits or to suits in specified classes of cases.[71] A statute of that kind can attach limitations that affect the state's exposure—for example, a filing deadline.[72] Similarly, a state can enact a statute authorizing a state officer to waive the state's immunity *ad hoc*.[73] When plaintiffs rely on express waiver, however, the Supreme Court applies a clear statement rule.[74] The legislature must articulate its consent in "the most express language or by such overwhelming implication from the text" that there can be "no room for any other reasonable construction."[75] A statute that purports only to waive the immunity that *state* law establishes for purposes of suits in state court does not waive the immunity the state derives from the federal Constitution.[76]

Waiver by knowing action. A state can waive its federal immunity by taking part in a federal regulatory program or by accepting federal funds when Congress has specified that those actions will open the state to suits from which it would otherwise be immune.[77] Here again, a clear statement rule applies. In this instance, it is Congress that must use exacting language in establishing the regulatory scheme or conditional funding program in order to alert the state to the consequences of its conduct. If Congress is sufficiently clear, the state's voluntary behavior will constitute a waiver of sovereign immunity.[78] Congress cannot, however, simply tell a state that if it engages in an activity, otherwise lawful, it will be amenable to suits that it would ordinarily be able to resist. In cases of that kind, it makes no difference how clearly Congress articulates its policy. The state itself must explicitly declare its willingness to be sued.[79]

Waiver by voluntary litigation behavior. A state can waive its federal immunity by voluntarily invoking a court's jurisdiction in circumstances in which the state might avoid involvement. Of course, state sovereign immunity is implicated only when a state occupies a defensive position in litigation. Yet there are numerous circumstances in which states are not simply named (involuntarily) as defendants in the first instance, but take some independent action of their own to engage a court's attention. For exam-

---

71. *Port Auth. v. Feeney*, 495 U.S. 299 (1990).

72. *Beers v. Arkansas*, 61 U.S. (20 How.) 527 (1858). See notes 244–51 and accompanying text (discussing the *Raygor* case); see also Chapter VIII, notes 404–05, 421–22 and accompanying text.

73. See Daniel J. Meltzer, *Overcoming Immunity: The Case of Federal Regulation of Intellectual Property*, 53 Stan. L. Rev. 1331, 1387 nn.191–92 (2001) (collecting cases in which lower courts have examined state statutes for this kind of authorization).

74. See notes 141–42 and accompanying text (discussing a similar clear statement doctrine applicable to waiver by the federal government).

75. *Feeney*, 495 U.S. at 305–06.

76. *Ry. Co. v. Whitton's Adm'r*, 80 U.S. (13 Wall.) 270 (1871). Accord *Florida Dep't of Health & Rehab. Servs. v. Florida Nursing Home Ass'n*, 450 U.S. 147, 149–50 (1981) (finding it insufficient that a state statute authorized a state agency to "sue or be sued"); *Kennecott Copper Corp. v. State Tax Comm'n*, 327 U.S. 573, 577–79 (1946) (holding that consent to suit in "any court of competent jurisdiction" would not do).

77. See *College Savings Bank v. Florida PrePaid Postsecondary Ed. Bd.*, 527 U.S. 666, 686–87 (1999) (confirming this form of waiver).

78. Cf. *South Dakota v. Dole*, 483 U.S. 203, 207 (1987) (explaining that unambiguous language is essential to establishing a condition on federal spending). But see Lauren Ouziel, *Waiving States' Sovereign Immunity from Suit in Their Own Courts: Purchased Waiver and the Clear Statement Rule*, 99 Colum. L. Rev. 1584 (1999) (arguing that a clear statement should not be required in spending power cases); note 253 (noting that some academics anticipate future adjustments in this doctrine).

79. *College Savings*, 527 U.S. at 676. See notes 74–75 and accompanying text.

ple, a state may intervene as a defendant in an ongoing suit,[80] advance a claim against the estate in a pending bankruptcy proceeding,[81] or remove a suit from state court to federal court.[82] Voluntary actions of that kind count as a waiver of any immunity the state would otherwise have. There is no doctrine of clear statement in this context. Even if a state has not explicitly authorized a state's attorney to waive the state's immunity, still the attorney's voluntary actions in litigation bind the state. The rationale is not simply that a state can be held to its own choices, but also that any other rule would risk inconsistency and injustice. If a state were able both to invoke a court's jurisdiction and to insist on immunity, the state might manipulate litigation to its own advantage.[83]

Waiver by default. In the main, states are not held to waive their immunity when state's attorneys simply fail to object at the proper time, perhaps because of ignorance or neglect. In this context, at least, the Court insists that "constructive consent" is insufficient to justify the "surrender of constitutional rights."[84] There are cases, accordingly, in which states have successfully asserted sovereign immunity only at the appellate level.[85] Nevertheless, the Court itself feels no obligation to raise sovereign immunity *sua sponte*.[86] And there are cases in which the Court has refused to consider tardy immunity arguments.[87]

3. The Eleventh Amendment

State sovereign immunity is sometimes called "eleventh amendment immunity."[88] That label is a "misnomer."[89] State sovereign immunity (in the constitutional sense)

---

80. *Clark v. Barnard*, 108 U.S. 436 (1883).

81. *Gardner v. New Jersey*, 329 U.S. 565 (1947).

82. *Lapides*, 122 S.Ct. at 1644.

83. The decision in the removal case, *Lapides*, was prefigured by Justice Kennedy's concurring opinion in *Schacht*. 524 U.S. at 393. Justice Kennedy explained, for example, that a state might initially submit to a court's jurisdiction, but then claim sovereign immunity later to frustrate an unfavorable judgment. Cf. *Puerto Rico Aqueduct & Sewer Auth. v. Metcalf*, 506 U.S. 139, 147 (1993) (holding that a district court's denial of a state's motion to dismiss on sovereign immunity grounds is immediately appealable); see Chapter VII, note 215 and accompanying text (noting that this is an exception to the final judgment rule).

84. *Edelman*, 415 U.S. at 673. Compare Chaper XII, notes 205–07 and accompanying text (discussing decisions in which the Court routinely visits a forfeiture on individuals who fail to raise constitutional claims seasonably).

85. *Edelman*, 415 U.S. at 678 (apparently confirming that late assertions of sovereign immunity are typically acceptable).

86. See *Patsy v. Bd. of Regents*, 457 U.S. 496, 515–16 n.19 (1982).

87. E.g., *Blessing v. Freestone*, 520 U.S. 329, 340 n.3 (1997) (declining to consider an immunity claim that state's attorneys had neither preserved below nor presented in the petition for *certiorari*). If a state failed to advance an immunity defense in the lower courts because of ignorance or neglect (rather than as a matter of deliberate strategy) and still is foreclosed from raising the defense in the Supreme Court, the state has not actually *waived* immunity, but has *forfeited* that defense. See Chapter VII, note 64.

88. E.g., *Seminole Tribe*, 517 U.S. at 58.

89. *Alden*, 527 U.S. at 713. Writing for the Court in *Alden*, Justice Kennedy also described the "eleventh amendment immunity" formulation as a "convenient shorthand." Id. That characterization is questionable. By Justice Kennedy's own account, the eleventh amendment suggests a fairly narrow form of state sovereign immunity (if it can be said to suggest sovereign immunity at all). Accordingly, it is confusing to mention the eleventh amendment as any part of a label for a much more muscular immunity, derived from independent constitutional sources.

does not rest on the eleventh amendment or on any other particular provision, but is derived from "the structure of the original Constitution itself."[90] The eleventh amendment does not mention sovereign immunity expressly, but rather purports to prescribe the way in which the federal judicial power (established by Article III) is to be understood: "The Judicial Power of the United States *shall not be construed* to extend to any suit in law or equity, commenced or prosecuted *against* one of the United States *by Citizens of another State*, or *by Citizens or Subjects of any Foreign State*."[91] That text actually undercuts, by negative implication, the sweeping state sovereign immunity the Court has recognized. Notice, for example, that the eleventh amendment refers only to suits brought in federal court by citizens of other states or foreign nations.[92] Moreover, it says nothing explicitly about suits advancing federal claims (rather than the non-federal claims typically associated with "diversity" actions).[93] By the Court's account, however, a state is constitutionally immune from suits brought in federal or *state* court (or in federal agencies), *by its own citizens*, pressing *federal* claims.[94] The Court recognizes these and other textual difficulties. Nevertheless, the Court interprets the eleventh amendment to fortify the much more capacious immunity to which the states are entitled under the Constitution as a whole.[95]

Recall that the Court reads the tenth amendment to confirm certain constitutional restrictions on federal *legislative* power notwithstanding the text of that amendment, which scarcely is up to the job.[96] There, too, the real source of constitutional limitations is an inference from the general structure of the governmental scheme the Court understands the Constitution to contemplate. It may not be surprising, then, that the Court should equally read the eleventh amendment to signify constitutional limitations on federal *judicial* power that the text of the eleventh amendment alone does support. In some of the most important modern decisions on state immunity from lawsuits, the Court relies on both the eleventh amendment and the tenth—always as evidence of larger constitutional themes that transcend those particular provisions.[97] There is, however, a large body of precedent that singles out the eleventh amendment, some of it quite recent. That body of precedent continues to influence modern decisions about sovereign immunity even though the Court has now integrated the eleventh amendment (along with the tenth) into a larger doctrinal picture.

The story goes this way. Sovereign immunity was an established feature of English law at the time the Constitution was written and ratified.[98] The Constitutional Conven-

---

90. Id. at 728.

91. U.S. Const. amend. XI (emphasis added).

92. See notes 125–27 and accompanying text (discussing academic theories that rely upon these points).

93. See Chapter VIII, notes 55–57 and accompanying text.

94. See notes 138–210 and accompanying text.

95. See notes 117–22 and accompanying text.

96. See Chapter VI, notes 82–92 and accompanying text (discussing the tenth amendment in connection with Congress' authority to compel state courts to adjudicate federal claims).

97. See notes 211–23 and accompanying text. For discussions of the intersection between the tenth and eleventh amendments, see George D. Brown, *State Sovereignty Under the Burger Court—How the Eleventh Amendment Survived the Death of the Tenth: Some Broader Implications of Atascadero State Hospital v. Scanlon*, 74 Gtn. L.J. 363 (1985); Calvin R. Massey, *State Sovereignty and the Tenth and Eleventh Amendments*, 56 U. Chi. L. Rev. 61 (1989).

98. Judge Gibbons contends that sovereign immunity existed at the time, but was relatively unimportant. He notes that the original charter in the Massachusetts Bay Colony expressly disavowed the idea as early as 1620. John J. Gibbons, *The Eleventh Amendment and State Sovereign Immunity: A Reinterpretation*, 83 Colum. L. Rev. 1889, 1896 (1983).

tion nonetheless placed suits involving the states as parties on the Article III menu, ostensibly indicating that the states would not have immunity from suit in the Supreme Court or in any inferior federal courts that Congress might create. Some Anti-Federalists took exception.[99] In response, both Madison and Hamilton gave assurances that Article III would not empower federal courts to entertain suits against the states without their consent.[100] Some ratifying conventions were dissatisfied and proposed amendments that would have made state immunity explicit.[101] Madison declined to include a provision of that kind in the group of amendments he drafted for consideration in the first congressional session.[102]

Two years later, in *Chisholm v. Georgia*,[103] the Supreme Court held that it could consider a contract action by a citizen of South Carolina against the state of Georgia. Chisholm represented the estate of a merchant who had sold military hardware to Georgia in 1777, but had never received payment. He filed suit in the Supreme Court itself, invoking the Court's original jurisdiction under the Judiciary Act of 1789 to adjudicate "all controversies of a civil nature" involving a state as a party.[104] The justices issued *seriatim* opinions. Justice Blair and Justice Cushing said that the Court's power rested on the provision in Article III extending the federal judicial power to controversies "between a State and Citizens of another State," together with the further provision that the Supreme Court had original jurisdiction in cases "in which a State shall be a Party."[105] Chief Justice Jay and Justice Wilson acknowledged Georgia's claim of immunity, but rejected it out of hand. By their account, Article III discarded the "feudal" doctrine of sovereign immunity. Justice Iredell dissented, primarily on the theory that the Judiciary Act did not confer *statutory* jurisdiction to entertain the case.[106]

The *Chisholm* case plainly precipitated the eleventh amendment. Yet historians differ over the best understanding of what happened immediately following that decision and in later years.[107] The Supreme Court has embraced this version of the events: *Chisholm* pro-

---

99. See Chapter II, text accompanying note 34.

100. Madison expressed this view to the Virginia convention. Hamilton said essentially the same thing in Federalist 81, addressed to the New York convention. See Chapter II, text accompanying note 50. Judge Gibbons argues that a close reading of both Madison and Hamilton reveals more ambiguity than is conventionally recognized. He contends, for example, that Hamilton may actually have meant to say only that private citizens would have no *right of action* to sue an unconsenting state in federal court, not that a state would be *immune* from suit. Gibbons, note 98, at 1911.

101. The New York convention offered such an amendment.

102. Chapter II, text accompanying note 36.

103. 2 U.S. (2 Dall.) 419 (1793).

104. 1 Stat. 73, 80; see Chapter II, text accompanying note 56. Everyone concerned recognized that the occasion was momentous. Attorney General Randolph appeared as counsel to Chisholm in order to make the case for federal judicial power; the state of Georgia refused to appear at all in order to underscore its contrary position.

105. See Chapter IV, text accompanying note 4. Recall that the Supreme Court's original jurisdiction is self-executing and thus requires no confirming statutory basis. See Chapter VII, note 11 and accompanying text.

106. Given the self-executing nature of the Supreme Court's original jurisdiction, and the similarity between the language of the Judiciary Act provision and the language of Article III, it is difficult to find Iredell's analysis persuasive. Professor Orth argues that Iredell clutched at a statutory ground for denying jurisdiction in hopes of avoiding a confrontation over the larger question of constitutional power. John V. Orth, *The Truth About Justice Iredell's Dissent in Chisholm v. Georgia*, 73 N. Car. L. Rev. 255, 267–68 (1994).

107. See note 128 and accompanying text.

duced a "shock of surprise."[108] Scarcely anyone was prepared for the Court's holding that Article III obliterated the states' immunity with respect to suits in federal court.[109] Several members of Congress immediately proposed constitutional amendments to overturn the Court's decision. The idea was not to establish a new constitutional immunity for the states nor to codify the immunity they had previously enjoyed. Instead, it was simply to disavow the particular decision in *Chisholm*.[110] That limited objective accounts for the eleventh amendment's otherwise curious language. By its express terms, it declares that the federal judicial power shall not be "construed" to reach a suit against a state by citizens of "another" state or citizens of a foreign nation—that is, the kind suit involved in *Chisholm*.[111]

The Court avoided a serious analysis of the eleventh amendment for many years. John Marshall made very little of it. In *Cohens v. Virginia*,[112] he said that the eleventh amendment was concerned only with original jurisdiction in an Article III court. Accordingly, it did not apply to a case reaching the Supreme Court on appellate review of a state court judgment—even though, at that point, the state was no longer the moving party, but was defending the decision below.[113] In the *Osborn* case, Marshall offered the short-lived thesis that, even in original jurisdiction cases, the eleventh amendment was implicated only if a state was formally named as the defendant.[114] Historians debate the implications of other cases.[115] The Nineteenth Century decision that mattered most was *Hans v. Louisiana*.[116]

In *Hans*, the state of Louisiana sold bonds promising a high rate of interest. Later, the state adopted an amendment to the state constitution that effectively reduced the return on those bonds. One of the bondholders, himself a citizen of Louisiana, sued the state in a federal circuit court, claiming that the change in state law amounted to an un-

---

108. *Principality of Monaco*, 292 U.S. at 325.

109. I Charles Warren, The Supreme Court in United States History 91–96 (1935).

110. *Alden*, 527 U.S. at 719–27.

111. See text accompanying note 103. Professor Pfander contends that the "shall not be construed" phraseology reflects an attempt to adopt an "explanatory" or "declaratory" provision, which would explain that, contra *Chisholm*, states could be sued in federal court only with respect to debts they incurred after the new Constitution was adopted and not for debts held over from the pre-Constitution period. James E. Pfander, *History and State Suability: An "Explanatory" Account of the Eleventh Amendment*, 83 Cornell L. Rev. 1269, 1276–79 (1998). See Clyde Jacobs, The Eleventh Amendment and Sovereign Immunity 68–69 (1972) (suggesting a variety of explanations for the "shall not be construed" formulation). See also note 67.

112. 19 U.S. (6 Wheat.) 264, 411–12 (1821).

113. The petitioner in *Cohens* was a citizen of Virginia, the state in which he had been convicted and thus the state that opposed him in the Supreme Court. Since the eleventh amendment refers expressly only to suits by citizens of "another" state, it was possible to hold, on that basis alone, that the eleventh amendment was inapplicable. Marshall did not rely on that narrow ground. Moreover, he reaffirmed *Cohens* in *Worcester v. Georgia*, 31 U.S. (6 Pet.) 515 (1832), in which the defendant was a citizen of Vermont. The *Cohens* rule survives today, despite its apparent conflict with the large body of immunity law barring federal courts from entertaining actions against states as an original matter. See *McKesson Corp. v. Div. of Alcoholic Beverages & Tobacco*, 496 U.S. 18, 26–28 (1990) (confirming *Cohens*); *South Central Bell Tel. Co. v. Alabama*, 526 U.S. 160, 165–66 (1999) (squarely declining an invitation to "overrule" *McKesson*); Chapter VI, note 76. Professor Jackson has examined the analytical difficulties that *Cohens* presents. Vicki C. Jackson, *The Supreme Court, the Eleventh Amendment, and State Sovereign Immunity*, 98 Yale L.J. 1, 39 (1988).

114. See note 22 and accompanying text.

115. See Gibbons, note 98, at 1959–78.

116. 134 U.S. 1 (1890).

constitutional impairment of contract.[117] The plaintiff contended that the eleventh amendment was limited to "diversity" actions against a state by citizens of "another" state.[118] Accordingly, it did not bar his suit against his own state. Chief Justice Bradley refused to take the eleventh amendment's language literally. Bradley said it would have made no sense for Congress to promulgate an amendment that barred only suits by citizens of other states, but left a state vulnerable to suits by its own citizens. The idea must have been to correct the *Chisholm* decision in a more fundamental way—by reaffirming state immunity from suit as a general matter. According to Bradley, Article III had never been meant to deny the states' immunity, and the eleventh amendment merely confirmed that understanding.

The Supreme Court's interpretation of the eleventh amendment in *Hans* has always excited criticism. On occasion, some justices have proposed that the Court should overrule that case.[119] The full Court, however, has not only endorsed *Hans*, but has built upon it.[120] Concomitantly, the Court has rejected numerous alternative interpretations, most of which depend on the eleventh amendment's actual language. The Court has attempted to defuse the significance of arguments about the eleventh amendment's text by recasting that text in a modest supporting role with respect to state sovereign immunity. At this point, it might be just as well to lay aside altogether both the eleventh amendment and rejected constructions of it, lest old debates that have now been settled hang on to confuse prevailing doctrine and future developments. At the very least, one would think that no one should any longer use the "eleventh amendment immunity" misnomer. Nevertheless, the eleventh amendment cannot be neglected entirely. For one thing, the Court itself continues to cite (and even to rely on) the eleventh amendment in cases implicating state immunity from suits in federal court.[121] For another, many precedents were established before state immunity slipped the eleventh amendment mooring. Those precedents must now be repackaged as elaborations of sovereign immunity as a structural inference. Yet they apparently remain viable.[122]

Alternative accounts of the eleventh amendment also rule us from the grave. Those accounts provide an analytic framework for appraising and criticizing the Court's authoritative interpretation of the Constitution. Moreover, the justices who now sit on the Supreme Court are sharply divided in this field. Justices who dissent from the Court's current course typically rely on the very arguments that the majority engages and rejects. It is well to bear those arguments in mind, even if they do not command the full Court's respect.

---

117. U.S. Const. art. I, §10, cl.1. The decision in *Hans* was prefigured by other bond cases. See *Louisiana v. Jumel*, 107 U.S. 711 (1883) (holding that out-of-state bondholders could not avoid state sovereign immunity by naming state officers as defendants); *Virginia Coupon Cases*, 114 U.S. 269, 337–38 (1885) (Bradley, J., dissenting) (insisting that state sovereign immunity barred federal question suits as well as contract actions). For a discussion of those (and related) decisions with particular attention to the availability of suits in *state* court, see Ann Woolhandler, *The Common Law Origins of Constitutionally Compelled Remedies*, 107 Yale L.J. 77 (1997).

118. See text accompanying note 91.

119. See, e.g., *Welch v. Texas Dep't of Highways*, 483 U.S. 468, 496 (1987) (Brennan, J., dissenting) (joined by Marshall, Blackmun & Stevens, J.J.); *Atascadero State Hosp. v. Scanlon*, 473 U.S. 234, 301–02 (1985) (Brennan, J., dissenting) (joined by Marshall, Blackmun & Stevens, J.J.).

120. See text accompanying notes 141–42.

121. E.g., *Lapides*, 122 S.Ct. at 1646; *Verizon v. Public Svc. Comm'n*, 122 S.Ct. 1753, 1760 (2002). See notes 187, 332–39 and accompanying text.

122. See notes 161–69 and accompanying text (describing Justice Kennedy's discussion of the precedents in *Alden*).

4. Alternative Interpretations

Numerous academics have urged the Court to discard *Hans* and begin afresh.[123] Others have been more cautious. If the Court were to overrule *Hans*, it would assume judicial authority to alter the balance of federal and state power. It would also upset arrangements built up around the *Hans* baseline for nearly a century. By many accounts, then, it would be more prudent to read the Constitution to recognize state immunity in many circumstances, but also to empower Congress to override that immunity by statute. That course would not only shift responsibility to the political branch. It would permit Congress to decide on a case-by-case basis whether the success of a regulatory program depends on making the states themselves subject to unconsented lawsuits.[124] Most of the alternative interpretations offered in the law reviews would have the practical effect of leaving Congress free to control state immunity legislatively. Those alternative interpretations fall into four groups: (1) diversity theories; (2) conspiracy theories; (3) common law theories; and (4) forum-allocation theories.

Diversity theories. Many academicians contend that the text of the eleventh amendment *should* be taken literally. By this account, the eleventh amendment does not address sovereign immunity at all, but merely amends Article III by deleting from the federal judicial power two kinds of diversity actions: (1) suits by citizens of one state against another state; and (2) suits by citizens of a foreign nation against a state.[125] In its strong form, the diversity interpretation insists that the eleventh amendment is exclusively concerned with lawsuits that would otherwise be within the federal judicial power because of the identity of the parties. Accordingly, the eleventh amendment does not apply to suits against a state resting on Article III's provisions for cases identified by

---

123. E.g., Vicki C. Jackson, *One Hundred Years of Folly: The Eleventh Amendment and the 1988 Term*, 64 So. Calif. L. Rev. 51, 103 (1990). For an entertaining (though dated) treatment of the tortured decisional law that *Hans* begets, see William Burnham, *Beam Me Up, There's No Intelligent Life Here: A Dialogue on the Eleventh Amendment with Lawyers from Mars*, 75 Neb. L. Rev. 551 (1996). For a sympathetic discussion of *Hans* and sovereign immunity generally, see Alfred Hill, *In Defense of Our Law of Sovereign Immunity*, 42 B.C. L. Rev. 485 (2001).

124. E.g., John Nowak, *The Scope of Congressional Power to Create Causes of Action Against State Government and the History of the Eleventh and Fourteenth Amendments*, 75 Colum. L. Rev. 1413 (1975). See also Brown, note 97, at 394. Professor Althouse has urged the Court to evaluate *Hans* in light of the modern federal interests at stake (rather than contested historical accounts). Ann Althouse, *When to Believe a Legal Fiction: Federal Interests and the Eleventh Amendment*, 40 Hastings L.J. 1123 (1989). See also Carol F. Lee, *Sovereign Immunity and the Eleventh Amendment: The Uses of History*, 18 Urban Lawyer 519, 549 (1986) (arguing that the justices' appraisal of historical materials was guided by their own "substantive values"). Professor Shreve once suggested that the Court should shift its focus away from the eleventh amendment to Article III and the constitutional structure generally, thus to work out the appropriate balance between the federal judiciary and the states in a more comprehensive policy-driven manner. Gene R. Shreve, *Letting Go of the Eleventh Amendment*, 64 Ind. L.J. 601 (1989). That is what the Court has done, though the Court has not reached the results that Professor Shreve had in mind.

125. See William A. Fletcher, *A Historical Interpretation of the Eleventh Amendment: A Narrow Construction of an Affirmative Grant of Jurisdiction Rather than a Prohibition Against Jurisdiction*, 35 Stan. L. Rev. 1033 (1983). For a critique, see William P. Marshall, *The Diversity Theory of the Eleventh Amendment: A Critical Evaluation*, 102 Harv. L. Rev. 1372 (1989). For Fletcher's response, see William A. Fletcher, *The Diversity Explanation of the Eleventh Amendment: A Reply to Critics*, 56 U. Chi. L. Rev. 1261 (1989). See generally *Exchange on the Eleventh Amendment*, 57 U. Chi. L. Rev. 117 (1990) (Massey, Marshall & Fletcher).

subject matter—most importantly, the provision for cases arising under federal law.[126] In its weak form, the diversity theory has it that the eleventh amendment bars all suits in the two categories it mentions, irrespective of the Article III basis they would otherwise have. Accordingly, the eleventh amendment *does* apply to federal question suits against a state, if they are filed by citizens of other states or foreign nations.[127]

Conspiracy theories. Other academics reach the same practical result as the academicians who promote the diversity theory: The eleventh amendment bars federal suits against the states only in the two instances it expressly mentions and *not* in federal question cases. But conspiracy theory proponents offer a different explanation for that result. Key public figures manipulated both the original adoption of the eleventh amendment and its interpretation in *Hans* for near-term tactical purposes. By this account, *Chisholm* was not the surprise the Court pretends it was. Instead, Madison, Hamilton, Jefferson, and Jay intended that the federal courts would entertain suits against the states. If they misrepresented that reality to the ratifying conventions, they did so as a political strategy. In particular, those key figures had in mind suits by Tories and British nationals seeking to collect on Revolutionary War debts. The treaties that ended the war committed the United States to honoring claims of that kind. When proposals to overrule *Chisholm* surfaced, Madison and the others contrived to limit the eleventh amendment to diversity actions in order to preserve the federal courts' authority to entertain federal claims based on the treaties.[128] Thereafter, they avoided a confrontation regarding the eleventh amendment's application to federal question cases by channeling treaty cases to an international commission.[129]

Similar political machinations explain what happened a hundred years later in connection with a different set of public finance cases culminating in *Hans*.[130] The bonds

---

126. E.g., Akhil R. Amar, *Of Sovereignty and Federalism*, 96 Yale L.J. 1425, 1473 (1987); Gibbons, note 98, at 2004. Apart from federal question cases, there are other categories of jurisdiction in Article III that do not depend on party status. For an analysis of the eleventh amendment's application to admiralty cases, see David J. Bederman, *Admiralty and the Eleventh Amendment*, 72 Notre Dame L. Rev. 935 (1997).

127. E.g., Lawrence C. Marshall, *Fighting the Words of the Eleventh Amendment*, 102 Harv. L. Rev. 1342, 1368 (1989). Professor Sherry has pointed out that, at the time *Hans* was decided, the Court did not distinguish clearly between diversity actions and federal question suits. Under *Swift v. Tyson*, 41 U.S. 1 (1842), federal "general" common law controlled the former. According to Sherry, the Court may have failed fully to appreciate the significance of extending the eleventh amendment to federal question claims. For that reason, Sherry thinks it should be relatively easy to overrule *Hans* on the ground that subsequent developments have undermined its intellectual footing. Suzanna Sherry, *The Eleventh Amendment and Stare Decisis: Overruling Hans v. Louisiana*, 57 U. Chi. L. Rev. 1260 (1990).

128. Judge Gibbons argues that *Chisholm* was far less important than other cases pending at the time, which advanced *federal* treaty claims against state defendants. Gibbons, note 98, at 1916–26. Professor Nelson contends, alternatively, that when Madison and Hamilton said that states would not be "amenable" to suit without consent, they actually were thinking of the settled notion that the states could not be "commanded to appear" in court. Accordingly, they had in mind something akin to personal (not subject matter) jurisdiction. Caleb Nelson, *Sovereign Immunity as a Doctrine of Personal Jurisdiction*, 115 Harv. L. Rev. 1559, 1575–76 (2002).

129. Gibbons, note 98 at 1939–40. Professor Pfander argues that *Chisholm* was a shock, but not for the reason the Supreme Court gives. In his view, members of Congress were surprised not that the Court took jurisdiction of any case in which a state was named as an unconsenting defendant, but that the Court entertained a case in which the plaintiff meant to hold a state to account for an obligation that preexisted the Constitution. See Pfander, note 111, at 1278.

130. Professor Orth develops this account. John V. Orth, The Judicial Power of the United States: The Eleventh Amendment in American History (1987). For a critique, see Michael G. Collins, *The Conspiracy Theory of the Eleventh Amendment*, 88 Colum. L. Rev. 212 (1988).

that Louisiana and other states issued were actually used by Reconstruction governments in the former Confederacy to run up heavy debts. When opponents of those governments regained power, they took any steps they could to avoid paying unfair interest. The change in state law in *Hans* was only one of several devices to that end—all of them vulnerable to attack as violations of the Contract Clause. In order to be successful in repudiating bonds, the new southern leaders needed cooperation from the courts. State courts collaborated, but federal courts posed a genuine threat. It was essential, then, that the Supreme Court should read the eleventh amendment as a blanket prohibition on suits against a state, even if the plaintiffs were citizens of the defendant state and even if they claimed that the repudiation of their bonds violated federal law. That is the interpretation that *Hans* supplied.[131]

Common law theories. Still other academicians contend that the eleventh amendment does not constitutionalize state sovereign immunity, but only establishes that the Constitution itself is neutral on the question. If the states enjoyed immunity in their own courts prior to the Constitution, it can only have been because immunity existed at that time as a species of common law, carried over from England.[132] In *Chisholm*, the Supreme Court misread Article III to eliminate that immunity. Then, when the eleventh amendment corrected *Chisholm*, it restored the *status quo ante*—namely, the states' immunity as a matter of non-constitutional law. Of course, Congress can change non-constitutional law by statute. By this account, the Court may honor the states' immunity from suit in the absence of statute, but the Court should sustain legislation that Congress enacts to abrogate that immunity in the exercise of a legislative power delegated to Congress by Article I.[133]

Forum-allocation theories. Finally, some academics contend that the eleventh amendment allows the states to choose the courts in which they will answer federal claims.[134] In its strong form, the forum-allocation theory has it that the states are constitutionally obligated to open themselves to suit in one place or the other. If they are unwilling to waive their eleventh amendment immunity from suit in federal court, they

---

131. Historians who paint this picture of events contend that the Compromise of 1877 figured mightily in the mix. After the election of 1876, the electoral college was deadlocked between Hayes (the Republican candidate) and Tilden (the Democrat). The House of Representatives appointed a commission to determine which of the two should receive twenty contested electoral votes. The commission included five members of the Supreme Court, among them Justice Bradley, who prepared the commission report giving those votes to Hayes. When some Democrats in Congress attempted to override the commission's decision, key southern Democrats declined to cooperate. Professor Orth contends that they were pacified by tacit commitments from Republicans in Congress to bring an end to Reconstruction and from the Court to foreclose debt collection cases in the federal courts. When Justice Bradley wrote the Court's opinion in *Hans*, so the argument goes, he effectively delivered on that political promise. Orth, note 130, at 79.

132. Professor Field has advanced this argument. Martha A. Field, *The Eleventh Amendment and Other Sovereign Immunity Doctrines*, 126 U. Pa. L. Rev. 515 (1978); Martha A. Field, *The Eleventh Amendment and Other Sovereign Immunity Doctrines: Congressional Imposition of Suit Upon the States*, 126 U. Pa. L. Rev. 1203 (1978). See Chapter IX, notes 80–81 and accompanying text.

133. Professor Tribe argues that since the eleventh amendment prescribes the way in which the federal judicial power is to be "construed," it addresses only the courts and not Congress. Laurence H. Tribe, *Intergovernmental Immunities in Litigation, Taxation, and Regulation: Separation of Powers Issues in Controversies About Federalism*, 89 Harv. L. Rev. 682, 694 (1976). But see note 111. Professor Jackson argues that the Supreme Court itself should overrule *Hans* and adopt a diversity theory of the eleventh amendment. If the Court were to do that, she contends that state sovereign immunity might continue to function—but as a non-constitutional feature of the federal law of remedies. Jackson, note 113, at 72.

134. Professor Vazquez has elaborated this approach. Carlos M. Vazquez, *What Is Eleventh Amendment Immunity?*, 106 Yale L.J. 1683 (1997).

cannot resist suit in state court on the basis of sovereign immunity.[135] In its weak form, the forum-allocation theory has it that Congress can override state assertions of immunity. Whether or not Congress can or does abrogate the states' eleventh amendment immunity from suits in federal court, Congress can always force the states to answer federal claims in their own courts.[136] This last interpretation draws support from precedents suggesting that state courts are constitutionally obliged to entertain federal claims, particularly constitutional "takings" and due process claims.[137]

5. Current Doctrine

The Court explained its current understanding of the constitutional status of state sovereign immunity in three leading cases: *Seminole Tribe v. Florida*,[138] *Alden v. Maine*,[139] and *Fed. Maritime Comm'n v. South Carolina State Ports Authority*.[140] Those cases essentially presented a question of legislative power—namely, whether the Constitution permits Congress to subject unwilling states to lawsuits brought by private litigants. To resolve that question, it was necessary more fully to justify and specify the state sovereign immunity the Court had previously associated with the eleventh amendment. That task, in turn, entailed the integration of ideas fashioned in the eleventh amendment cases into a larger conceptual framework, drawing as well on the tenth amendment and on inferences from the constitutional structure.

According to the Court, the existence and scope of the states' constitutional immunity is not entirely and always a preliminary matter, which then has necessary implications for what Congress can do by legislation. The point is not simply that the Constitution authorizes states to assert sovereign immunity as a defense to any and all private suits in any forum, and Congress can do nothing about it. Would that it were that simple. Instead, the Constitution recognizes state sovereign immunity as a means by which states can resist the exercise of federal power in either its judicial or its legislative forms. The key to the states' constitutional immunity is not the nature of the claims that private litigants advance, the forum in which they file suit, or the form of relief they seek. Instead, state sovereign immunity is engaged when the federal government attempts to subject the states to the indignity of uninvited private suits. If private litigants sue a state in federal court, the state can assert sovereign immunity to resist the exercise of federal *judicial* power. If private litigants sue a state in state court in reliance on a federal statute authorizing the suit, the state can assert sovereign immunity to resist that exercise of federal *legislative* power. And if private litigants file claims against a state before a federal administrative agency, the state again can assert sovereign immunity to resist the exercise of federal *legislative* power to commission a federal entity to perform adjudicative functions that track the exercise of federal judicial power.

Each of the three principal cases warrants careful attention. None of the three offers a free-standing account of state sovereign immunity groomed to particular circum-

135. Professor Monaghan offers this view. Henry P. Monaghan, *The Sovereign Immunity "Exception"*, 110 Harv. L. Rev. 102, 125 (1996).

136. See Vazquez, note 134, at 1690–93.

137. See Chapter VI, notes 64–69 and accompanying text (discussing the *Reich* and *McKesson* cases).

138. 517 U.S. 44 (1996).

139. 527 U.S. 706 (1999).

140. 534 U.S. 533 (2002).

stances: *Seminole Tribe* covering suits in federal court, *Alden* covering suits in state court, and *Ports Authority* addressing suits before federal agencies. Instead, all three cases elaborate a single constitutional doctrine and only illustrate its application in different settings. Nevertheless, these decisions build on each other. Accordingly, the Court's analysis is best digested if they are taken *seriatim*.

Suits in federal court. In *Seminole Tribe*, the federal Indian Gaming Act entitled an Indian tribe to operate a gambling facility under a compact with the state in which the facility was located. The state was obliged to negotiate with the tribe in order to arrive at an arrangement agreeable to both. If the state failed to negotiate, the Act authorized the tribe to file an action in federal district court naming the state as the defendant. Relying on that provision, the Seminole Tribe sued the state of Florida and its governor, seeking an order requiring the state to negotiate an agreement for gambling activities the tribe wished to conduct in that state. Florida set up sovereign immunity to defeat the suit. In the Supreme Court, Chief Justice Rehnquist sustained the state's position in an opinion for himself and four others.[141]

The Chief Justice first reaffirmed the holding in *Hans* that the states' constitutional immunity from suit in an Article III court is not restricted to the kinds of cases identified by the text of the eleventh amendment. He readily engaged the attacks that academics had launched against *Hans*. He dismissed the diversity, conspiracy, and common law theories in turn. Diversity theories, he said, depend on "blind deference" to the eleventh amendment's text. Conspiracy theories conflict with the Court's own "shock" thesis. Common law theories miss the point of the error in *Chisholm*. It is not that *Chisholm* misunderstood Article III to deny state immunity and that the eleventh amendment established that Article III was meant to be neutral. Instead, according to Chief Justice Rehnquist, the original Constitution recognized state sovereign immunity as a constitutional mandate, and the eleventh amendment confirmed *that*. By this account, the Constitution as a whole guarantees the states an ability to resist most unconsented lawsuits, anything in Article III or the eleventh amendment to the contrary notwithstanding. Justice Souter filed a lengthy dissent in *Seminole Tribe*, in which he rehearsed various alternative interpretations of the eleventh amendment.[142] Chief Justice Rehnquist responded that Souter's analysis was "cobbled together from law review articles" and Souter's "own version of historical events." Rehnquist preferred to rest on the Court's case law—namely, the precedent set by *Hans*.[143]

Having established the constitutional foundation of state immunity, the Chief Justice turned to the tribe's argument that the Indian Gaming Act nonetheless entitled the tribe to sue the state in federal court. Initially, he examined the Act closely and determined that it was a genuine attempt by Congress to authorize the tribe's suit.[144] That construction of the Act led him to the further question whether Congress had power to abrogate Florida's immunity from such a suit. He acknowledged that, in *Pennsylvania v. Union Gas Co.*,[145] a plurality of the justices had said that Congress could override state immunity as an exercise of its power to regulate commerce.[146] Yet he squarely overruled *Union*

141. 517 U.S. at 76 (joined by O'Connor, Scalia, Kennedy & Thomas, J.J.).

142. Id. at 100 (dissenting opinion) (joined by Ginsburg & Breyer, J.J.). Justice Stevens filed a separate dissent.

143. Id. at 68 (majority opinion).

144. See note 233 and accompanying text (explaining that abrogation requires a clear statement from Congress).

145. 491 U.S. 1 (1989).

146. Concurring in *Union Gas*, Justice Stevens explained that, in his view, the eleventh amendment constitutionalizes sovereign immunity in the two kinds of cases it mentions explicitly and

Gas on that point.[147] The Chief Justice also recognized that many of the alternative accounts of the eleventh amendment offered by academics suggest theoretical bases for upholding a general abrogation power in Congress. Having rejected those theories in favor of *Hans v. Louisiana*, however, he found nothing in them to justify congressional legislation that can trump the states' constitutional privilege.[148] Justice Souter and the other dissenters disagreed.[149]

Suits in state court. In *Alden v. Maine*, the federal Fair Labor Standards Act required the states to pay their employees an accelerated rate for overtime work. A group of probation officers in Maine alleged that they had not received that rate. Maine had in fact failed to comply with the FLSA. After negotiating with the employees, the state agreed to change its ways in the future.[150] Nevertheless, the state refused to reimburse the probation officers for overtime payments they had been denied in the past. The officers sued Maine in state court, seeking monetary compensation. The state asserted sovereign immunity. In the Supreme Court, Justice Kennedy recognized that the FLSA explicitly purported to confer on state workers a private right of action to sue the state itself. The Court had recognized as much on other occasions.[151] Yet he insisted that no state had previously asserted state sovereign immunity as a defense to such a suit. In this case, however, Maine advanced a federal sovereign immunity argument. And no statute in Maine waived that immunity expressly. Accordingly, the question presented was whether Congress, in the exercise of one of its Article I powers, can subject an unconsenting state to a suit brought by private plaintiffs in the state's own courts. Justice Kennedy concluded that Congress cannot. The Chief Justice and the other three justices who had joined the majority opinion in *Seminole Tribe* equally joined Justice Kennedy's opinion in *Alden*.

Justice Kennedy explained that state sovereign immunity is anchored in the Constitution and is not, accordingly, "defeasible by federal statute."[152] He thus followed Chief Justice Rehnquest in *Seminole Tribe*: A state's constitutionally rooted sovereign immunity must necessarily win any fight with a mere statute.[153] In *Seminole Tribe*, however, the state of Florida resisted suit in a *federal* court. There was, then, a federal *judicial* affront to state sovereignty, apart from the federal *legislative* affront created by Congress' attempt to abrogate the state's immunity. In *Alden*, by contrast, the state of Maine objected to a suit brought by private litigants in its own courts. The only self-evident federal action about which the state could complain was entirely legisla-

---

that, as to those cases, Congress has no power to abrogate the states' immunity. According to Stevens, however, the kind of immunity recognized in *Hans* for other kinds of cases (i.e., federal question suits by citizens against their own states) is entirely a matter of non-constitutional law that Congress can override when it exercises any of its enumerated powers. Id. at 23–24.

147. 517 U.S. at 66. In fact, Congress purported to enact the Indian Gaming Act pursuant to its power to regulate commerce "with the Indian Tribes" rather than its power to regulate commerce "among the several States." U.S. Const. art. I, §8, cl.3. The Chief Justice attached no significance to that point. For background on the sovereignty of Indian tribes, see Judith Resnik, *Dependent Sovereigns: Indian Tribes, States, and the Federal Courts*, 56 U. Chi. L. Rev. 671 (1989).

148. 517 U.S. at 68–73.

149. See notes 142–43 and accompanying text.

150. *Alden*, 527 U.S. at 759.

151. The Court had previously construed the FLSA to establish a private right of action and, in fact, had held that state employees could sue state employers in state court to enforce their statutory rights. *Hilton v. South Carolina Pub. Ry. Comm'n*, 502 U.S. 197 (1991); see note 161.

152. 527 U.S. at 733.

153. But see notes 230–33 and accompanying text (explaining that Congress can abrogate state immunity by means of legislation authorized by section five of the fourteenth amendment).

tive: Congress' decision to pursue its policy objectives by subjecting the state to lawsuits. Justice Kennedy recognized this key difference between *Seminole Tribe* and *Alden*, and he addressed it forthrightly. By his account, the Constitution safeguards states against overreaching by either the judicial or the legislative branches of the national government. One illustration of that constitutional design is that the Constitution usually denies Congress power to subject the states to suits by private litigants in *any* court.[154]

Justice Kennedy restated the Court's resolve not to be bound by the literal text of the Constitution and again insisted that the eleventh amendment actually supports a more sweeping brand of immunity. Yet he soon abandoned the eleventh amendment itself and turned to alternative sources for state immunity—sources that, he explained, establish the states' federal constitutional privilege to resist suits in their own courts. He did not explicitly address forum-allocation accounts of immunity in the academic literature. But he plainly rejected those theories.[155] In the main, he relied on the Constitution's overarching structure and on the special constitutional position of the states implied by various provisions, including the tenth amendment.[156] Justice Kennedy explained that the Constitution recognizes the states as sovereign entities that retain the dignity (if not the "full authority") of sovereignty.[157] By inference, then, the states enjoy the immunity to which the sovereign was entitled in England. That structural inference is supported, in turn, by the founding generation's original understanding of the Constitution, by congressional practices after the Constitution was adopted, and by the Court's own precedents.

Regarding original understanding, Justice Kennedy cited evidence suggesting that participants in Philadelphia and at the state ratifying conventions did not anticipate that the Constitution would strip the states of immunity when they were sued in federal court. He conceded that there is no evidence suggesting that anyone proposed that the Constitution would authorize states to assert immunity from suit in their own courts. He explained, however, that "silence" in this instance is "instructive." By his account, state immunity from lawsuits in state court was "so well established" that "no one conceived it would be altered by the new Constitution."[158] Indeed, according to Justice Kennedy, the commitment to immunity was so strong that the Constitution "never would have been ratified" without it.[159] Coming to common practices in the wake of the Constitution, Justice Kennedy insisted that there was no pattern of federal legislation contemplating that the states might be named as defendants in state court. Some modern statutes, like the FLSA itself, may fit that description. But they are too recent to lend meaning to an interpretation of the original Constitution.[160]

---

154. 527 U.S. at 730 (stating that the constitutional "design" protects the states not only from "federal jurisdiction" in Article III courts but also from excesses of congressional power under Article I). Justice Kennedy conceded that Congress has power to subject the states to lawsuits where there is "'compelling evidence' that the states were required to surrender [that] power to Congress pursuant to the constitutional design." Id. at 731, quoting *Blatchford*, 501 U.S. at 781. He found that kind of implicit consent in cases involving suits by the federal government. See note 65 and accompanying text. But he refused to find the same kind of implicit consent in cases in which private litigants sue states on the basis of an authority granted by Congress.

155. See notes 134–37 and accompanying text.

156. See notes 96–97 and accompanying text.

157. 527 U.S. at 715.

158. Id. at 741.

159. Id. at 727, quoting *Atascadero*, 473 U.S. at 239 n.2.

160. Id. at 745.

Turning to the Court's precedents, Justice Kennedy acknowledged that some cases had suggested that states have a federal constitutional immunity only against suits brought in federal court. He dismissed some statements in those cases as *dicta*, but he gave other decisions more attention.[161] He explained, for example, that in the tax reimbursement case, *Reich v. Collins*,[162] the plaintiff's entitlement to sue for a refund in state court arose from the constitutional right at stake. Recall that in *Reich* the state had exacted taxes from the plaintiff on the promise that there would be an opportunity to contest the validity of those taxes in later proceedings. In those circumstances, the state had a due process duty to make good on its prior commitment.[163] Justice Kennedy explained that in *Howlett v. Rose*[164] the only question was whether a local school board (not entitled to the state's federal constitutional immunity) could assert "state-law" immunity to defeat a federal claim advanced by means of a §1983 action in state court.[165] And he said that in the old *Crain* case[166] the Court assumed that the state was immune from suit in both federal and state court. That, in his telling, is why (in *Ex parte Young* decided the same day) the Court allowed private plaintiffs to sue state officers (rather than the state itself) in a suit for forward-looking injunctive relief.[167] On first blush, the precedent set in *Nevada v. Hall*[168] appeared to be more difficult to get around. In that case, the Court held that the state of Nevada had no federal immunity in a (state law)

161. Kennedy explained, for example, that in *Hilton v. South Carolina Pub. Ry. Comm'n*, 502 U.S. 197 (1991), the state had apparently consented to be sued, albeit perhaps in the erroneous belief that it had no choice. See Chapter VI, note 96 (discussing *Hilton*).

162. 513 U.S. 106 (1994); see Chapter VI, notes 65–69 and accompanying text.

163. The state did not rely on sovereign immunity in *Reich*. Professor Vazquez has suggested that, if *Reich* was correctly decided, then lots of cases should fall into place behind that precedent. In his view, for example, the plaintiffs in *Alden* itself had a property interest in the wages to which they were entitled under federal law. Accordingly, the state of Maine should have been under a due process obligation to provide them with a forum. Carlos Manuel Vazquez, *Sovereign Immunity, Due Process, and the Alden Trilogy*, 109 Yale L.J. 1927 (2000). Cf. Chapter VI, note 70 and accompanying text (discussing due process as a basis for state courts' obligation to enforce federal law). Professor Meltzer has argued that a uniform conception of state immunity is hard to square with the Court's tax cases. Compare *Reich* (holding that state courts must be open to at least some suits claiming reimbursement for invalid taxes), with *Great Northern Life Ins. Co. v. Read*, 322 U.S. 47 (1944) (holding that a state was immune from a suit in federal court advancing the same kind of claim). Daniel J. Meltzer, *State Sovereign Immunity: Five Authors in Search of a Theory*, 75 Notre Dame L. Rev. 1011, 1033–34 n.97 (2000). It *is* hard to reconcile *Reich* and *Read* with the notion that state immunity is indifferent to forum. But as a practical matter there is no real doubt about what has happened. Justice Kennedy's protests to the contrary notwithstanding, prior to *Alden* the Court typically assumed that state immunity existed only in federal court and that suits that were barred there could usually go forward in state court. Professor Seamon reads *Alden* to suggest that the states are free to defeat constitutional "just compensation" claims on the basis of sovereign immunity, but he thinks that due process should override immunity in that context. Richard H. Seamon, *The Asymmetry of State Sovereign Immunity*, 76 Wash. L. Rev. 1067, 1112 (2001).

164. 496 U.S. 356 (1990).

165. See Chapter VI, notes 50–56 and accompanying text. Recall, however, that the classic decisions distinguishing political subdivisions from the states were said to be interpretations of the eleventh amendment. See note 59 and accompanying text. Now that the Court has adopted a different basis for state immunity, something more may be required to explain why cities and counties cannot invoke it. See Richard H. Seamon, *The Sovereign Immunity of States in Their Own Courts*, 37 Brandeis L.J. 319, 389–90 (1999) (arguing that units of local government should be entitled to invoke the immunity recognized in *Alden*).

166. 209 U.S. 211 (1908).

167. *Ex parte Young*, 209 U.S. 123 (1908); see notes 283–88 and accompanying text. For a discussion of this and other accounts of *Crain*, see Chapter VI, notes 72–79 and accompanying text.

168. 440 U.S. 410 (1979).

tort lawsuit brought by a private citizen of California in a California state court. Nevada plainly would have been immune from the plaintiff's suit if it had been brought in federal court. Yet the Court explained that the suit in another state's courts was different—different enough to deny Nevada a federal privilege to defeat a suit filed there. In *Alden*, Justice Kennedy distinguished *Hall* on the ground that in *Hall* the Court held only that a state has no immunity from suit in another state's courts—not that a state can be sued in its own courts.[169]

Justice Kennedy collapsed his elaboration of the structural basis for state immunity into a discussion of the limits on congressional power.[170] Specifically, he made these points: If Congress could abrogate the states' immunity, it could "thrust" them into the "disfavored status" of debtors. That status, in turn, would deny states the "dignity and respect" to which they are entitled as "members of the federation."[171] It would be more "offensive" for Congress to subject the states to suit in their own courts than to force them to respond to suits in federal court. To press state courts into service would be to turn states' own institutions against them, thus to "commandeer" state "political machinery" in the pursuit of Congress' policy objectives.[172] Since the federal government retains immunity from suit in either federal or state court, it is only consistent to allow the states a "reciprocal privilege."[173] By forcing states to respond to suits for monetary relief, Congress would expose state treasure to the claims of private citizens. That, in turn, might interfere with the states' capacity to allocate scarce resources through the political process. By requiring states to prefer the claimants that Congress authorizes to sue, Congress would substitute its priorities for those the states might choose and thus corrupt ordinary channels of political accountability. By effectively giving state courts the authority to make budgetary judgments; Congress would "blur" the "distinct responsibilities" of state judicial and legislative institutions. Since Congress usually cannot abrogate state immunity from suit in federal court, it cannot recruit federal courts to service in furthering congressional objectives regarding the way the states should behave. It would be anomalous for Congress to have power to press state courts into that very service. Finally, suits against states without their consent are arguably not "judi-

---

169. 527 U.S. at 739–40. Justice Stevens wrote the majority opinion in *Hall*. In dissent, then-Justice Rehnquist contended that Nevada should be accorded immunity from suit in a sister state's courts. Both Justice Stevens and Justice Rehnquist plainly assumed that Nevada would have been entitled to immunity from the plaintiff's state law suit if it had been filed in a Nevada state court. But neither stated explicitly that Nevada's immunity in that instance would have rested on the Constitution rather than on whatever immunity Nevada law allowed. It is most unlikely that Justice Stevens would have taken that view. Justice Rehnquist, however, was another story. Much of what he said regarding the federal constitutional immunity he thought Nevada should enjoy in the courts of California might equally have been said to support a similar federal immunity in Nevada's own courts. Indeed, Rehnquist's dissent in *Hall* was in many ways a prelude to Justice Kennedy's opinion for the Court in *Alden*.

170. For this reason, it is difficult to say whether Justice Kennedy meant that Congress' attempt to abrogate state immunity in *Alden* outstripped the "internal restraints" on the commerce power, or that the statute in *Alden* (otherwise valid as an exercise of the commerce power) violated an "external" restraint located elsewhere in the Constitution—namely, in inferences from the structure of the Constitution as a whole. Chapter IV, notes 131–32 and accompanying text. If a choice had to be made, the smart money would be on the latter understanding. Certainly, Justice Kennedy did not suggest that the FLSA invalidly regulates activities not substantially connected to interstate commerce. But a choice probably doesn't have to be made. The fact of the matter is that Justice Kennedy did not appear to draw the familiar distinction between internal and external restraints.

171. 527 U.S. at 749.

172. Id.

173. Id. at 750.

cial" matters within the meaning of Article III. It would be novel to allow Congress power nonetheless to force matters of that kind into state court.[174]

Justice Kennedy offered these structural considerations to explain both that the states enjoy a constitutionally grounded sovereign immunity and that Congress has no general power to abrogate that immunity by authorizing private suits in state court.[175] Yet his heavy emphasis on the perils of congressional overreaching was telling. By common account, he meant only to recognize a constitutional limitation on congressional legislative power. The holding in *Alden* is that a state enjoys a federal constitutional immunity against a private suit advancing a federal claim against the state in state court—where Congress presumes to empower the private plaintiff to bring the suit despite the state's objections. Justice Kennedy did not mean to say that a state enjoys a free-standing federal constitutional immunity that it can use to defeat private suits that arrive in state court *sans* congressional imprimatur. The *Alden* decision does not stand for that startling proposition. The federal structure is not at risk if neither federal judicial nor federal legislative power is exercised.[176]

This said, it must also be said that some features of Justice Kennedy's analysis in *Alden* invite the interpretation that the states have a federal constitutional immunity to defeat suits in state court, even when federal legislative power is not at work. The rationales that Justice Kennedy offered for the states' constitutional immunity suggest a monolithic privilege to defy private lawsuits on any theory in any forum, an immunity that could conceivably operate independently of an attempt by Congress to subject the states to suit.[177] Then again, Congress ordinarily is in some wise responsible for private litigants' asserted ability to advance federal statutory or constitutional claims in private lawsuits. Plaintiffs must have a private right of action, which is typically supplied by a federal statute.[178] As a practical matter, then, the only cases in which a federal constitutional immunity might operate routinely in the absence of some enabling action by Congress would be suits by private litigants against the states in their own courts, alleging violations of *state* law. Of course, cases like that are subject to whatever state-law immunity the states provide for themselves.[179] The only function that an additional federal immunity might serve would be to parry an attempt by Congress to force the states

---

174. See notes 67–70 and accompanying text (discussing the "jurisdictional" properties of immunity). For a point-by-point critique of Justice Kennedy's arguments regarding political accountability, see William P. Marshall & Jason S. Cowart, *State Immunity, Political Accountability, and Alden v. Maine*, 75 Notre Dame L. Rev. 1069 (2000).

175. Professor Pfander has said that the Court "achieved its result by transforming its rule of state sovereign immunity into an implicit restriction on the power of Congress." James E. Pfander, *Once More Unto the Breach: Eleventh Amendment Scholarship and the Court*, 75 Notre Dame L. Rev. 817, 821 (2001). That seems accurate. Yet it might equally be said that the Court leveraged a limit on Congress back into an immunity for the states.

176. See text accompanying note 154.

177. For example, Justice Kennedy explained that the Constitution was meant to perpetuate an immunity that states had always had. That pre-Constitution immunity obviously was not limited to federal claims authorized by Congress. He also said that the federal government has immunity from all manner of suits (wherever filed) and that the states' immunity is similar. Obviously, the immunity that the national government enjoys does not insulate the government only from suits that its own legislature authorizes. Consider, too, that to the extent state immunity exists to protect state treasuries, it arguably should make no difference whether plaintiffs seek damages in suits that Congress permits them to press against the states themselves.

178. See Chapter VIII, notes 128–57 and accompanying text.

179. See note 54.

to tolerate suits against their will. That, of course, would reintroduce an exercise of federal legislative power of the kind that *Alden* plainly addresses.[180]

The decision in *Lapides v. Bd. of Regents*[181] throws no significant light on the reach of *Alden's* analysis. A private plaintiff filed a §1983 action in state court, naming as defendants a state board of regents and individual state officers, and seeking monetary relief on the basis of both federal and state claims (over which the district court had supplemental jurisdiction pursuant to 28 U.S.C. §1367). The defendants removed the case to a federal district court pursuant to 28 U.S.C. §1441.[182] The board then moved for dismissal on the ground that the plaintiff's suit against the board itself (a statewide entity) was barred by sovereign immunity.[183] In the Supreme Court, Justice Breyer recognized that the board had a federal constitutional immunity to assert (grounded, he said, on the eleventh amendment). Yet in the circumstances of *Lapides*, he held that the board's voluntary invocation of the federal court's jurisdiction surrendered that immunity.[184]

The board conceded that a state statute waived the state's state-law immunity from suit on the state law claims in *state* court. But the board insisted that the statute did not waive the state's federal constitutional immunity from suit on those claims in *federal* court. At first glance, then, it may appear that the *Lapides* case was litigated and decided on the premise that the board removed the suit in order to obtain the benefits of a federal constitutional sovereign immunity in federal court that it could not assert in state court. The board explained, however, that it joined the individual officer defendants in removing the case to federal court only to improve the chances that those defendants would escape liability on the basis of official immunity.[185] Accordingly, the board did not (necessarily) assume that the federal constitutional immunity recognized in *Alden* was unavailable in state court for want of any attempt by Congress to force the state to submit to suit in its own courts. For his part, Justice Breyer certainly assumed that the board enjoyed federal constitutional immunity from suit on state claims—without any suggestion that the basis of that immunity was coercion by Congress.[186] But he took that view only because the case had been removed to federal court, where he insisted the eleventh amendment was controlling. In the end, *Lapides* may be notable primarily for

---

180. Then again, if a state has no federal constitutional immunity to defeat a state law claim advanced in state court without congressional authorization, Justice Kennedy must contemplate a four-space matrix with one obvious quadrant unchecked: As a matter of federal constitutional law, the states can resist suits brought in federal court on federal grounds, suits brought in federal court on state grounds, and suits brought in state court on federal grounds. But states must stand and deliver if they are sued in state court on state grounds, except to the extent they provide themselves with immunity as a matter of state law. This last exception seems out of step with the monolithic conception of federal constitutional immunity that Justice Kennedy appeared to envision in *Alden*. If it is, though, the lesson may be (again) that Justice Kennedy's analysis of constitutional structure in *Alden* was far from rigorous.

181. 122 S.Ct. 1640 (2002).

182. See Chapter VIII, notes 296–99 and accompanying text (discussing *Lapides* in connection with federal question jurisdiction); Chapter VI, notes 128–32 and accompanying text (discussing removal jurisdiction).

183. See note 58 (explaining that state universities count as the state for immunity purposes).

184. See note 82 and accompanying text.

185. See notes 446–94 and accompanying text.

186. Justice Breyer did not treat §1983 or §1367 as an attempt by Congress to abrogate state sovereign immunity. See text accompanying notes 237, 247–49. Instead, he explained that the board was not a "person" within the meaning of §1983. Accordingly, the federal district court was obliged to dismiss the plaintiff's federal claims for want of a right of action. 122 S.Ct. at 1643. See note 369 and accompanying text; Chapter VIII, text accompanying note 135.

its reliance on the "specific text" of the eleventh amendment, notwithstanding that *Alden* treated that amendment as a distraction from the real sources of the states' federal constitutional immunity from unwanted private suits.[187]

Dissenting in *Alden*, Justice Souter contended that Justice Kennedy's analysis rendered the text of the Constitution irrelevant to the immunity question, except to the extent Kennedy relied on the tenth amendment to "confirm" the existence of state immunity.[188] Souter acknowledged Kennedy's resistance to the idea that state immunity was only a matter of common law before the Constitution was adopted. He charged, then, that Kennedy must conceive that state immunity existed as a species of natural law, which then was carried over into the Constitution. Souter denied that any natural law conception of state sovereign immunity was widely accepted in Philadelphia or at the ratifying conventions. By his account, there was no consensus about sovereign immunity of any stripe, certainly no consensus that immunity was "fundamental in the sense of being unalterable."[189] Justice Souter also disputed Justice Kennedy's reading of other historical events and the precedents. In his view, the *Alden* decision only perpetuated and exacerbated the flawed analysis in *Seminole Tribe*, from which Souter and the three justices who signed his dissent had also dissented. Subsequently, all four dissenters (Justices Souter, Stevens, Ginsburg, and Breyer) declared that *Seminole Tribe* and *Alden* are so fundamentally mistaken that they are not entitled to respect as authoritative Supreme Court precedents.[190]

Academic commentaries on *Seminole Tribe* and *Alden* are typically critical.[191] At the very least, the justices who formed the majority in those cases departed from their usual

---

187. Justice Breyer acknowledged precedents holding that the federal government does *not* waive its immunity by invocating a court's jurisdiction. Those precedents seemed probative in light of *Alden's* insistence that the states' immunity springs from the same structural sources. Justice Breyer answered, however, that the eleventh amendment made the difference. 122 S.Ct. at 1646. The *Lapides* decision was unanimous. No one wrote separately to explain any connection to *Alden* or to disclaim Justice Breyer's (needling) invocation of the eleventh amendment's text. Presumably, the five justices who discounted the eleventh amendment's significance in *Seminole Tribe* and *Alden* failed to proof read the final draft of Breyer's opinion.

188. 527 U.S. at 760–62 (Souter, J., dissenting) (joined by Stevens, Ginsburg & Breyer, J.J.).

189. Id. at 764.

190. *Kimel v. Florida Bd. of Regents*, 528 U.S. 62, 97–98 (2000) (dissenting opinion).

191. See, e.g., Vicki C. Jackson, *Principle and Compromise in Constitutional Adjudication: The Eleventh Amendment and State Sovereign Immunity*, 75 Notre Dame L. Rev. 953, 970 (2000) (contending that *Seminole Tribe* and *Alden* should be overruled before they do any more damage); Laura S. Fitzgerald, *Beyond Marbury: Jurisdictional Self-Dealing in Seminole Tribe*, 52 Vand. L. Rev. 407 (1999) (suggesting that *Seminole Tribe* provides additional evidence that the Court itself means to control access to the federal forum). Professor Nowak charges the justices in the majority with reviving the attitudes usually ascribed to the Court just after the Civil War. John E. Nowak, *The Gang of Five & the Second Coming of the Anti-Reconstruction Supreme Court*, 75 Notre Dame L. Rev. 1091 (2000). Professor Sherry reports a joke going around Washington on the day *Alden* was decided: The Y2K bug arrived early, and five of the justices thought it was 1900. Suzanna Sherry, *States Are People Too*, 75 Notre Dame L. Rev. 1121 (2000). But see Ann Althouse, *On Dignity and Deference: The Supreme Court's New Federalism*, 68 U. Cin. L. Rev. 245, 258 n.58 (2000) (arguing that "*Alden* preserves a good balance"); Daniel A. Farber, *Pledging a New Allegiance: An Essay on Sovereignty and the New Federalism*, 75 Notre Dame L. Rev. 1133 (2000) (arguing that the immunity cases join other recent decisions that collectively paint a coherent picture of the form of government the Court's majority conceives the country to have); Hill, note 123 (contending that the sovereign immunity cases do not seriously threaten the enforcement of federal law); cf. Jay Tidmarsh, *A Dialogic Defense of Alden*, 75 Notre Dame L. Rev. 1161 (2000) (arguing that the *result* in *Alden* may be explained as a prudential judgment about the best way to promote the structure of the Constitution in the near term).

insistence on adhering to the text of the Constitution.[192] By some accounts, it was pure cynicism for the majority to cite the eleventh and tenth amendments as though to draw textual support from them, but nonetheless to refuse to be limited by their explicit language. The "originalist" methodology in *Alden* is especially unappealing, because it prefers the thinking behind the text to the text itself.[193] Even at that, Justice Kennedy's historical evidence was thin. He cited materials suggesting that important figures conceived that the Constitution would not *abolish* state immunity. But he offered no evidence that they thought the Constitution would affirmatively *incorporate* immunity as itself a feature of federal constitutional law.[194] His reliance on the "sounds of silence" is widely regarded as so much bootstrapping.[195] By other accounts, Kennedy's appeal to federal structure was also unconvincing. Everyone concedes that the states enjoy some form of autonomy. But it is arguably a stretch from that proposition to a federal constitutional sovereign immunity from suits authorized by Congress in state court.[196]

Suits in federal agencies. The *Ports Authority* case presented state sovereignty issues in yet another configuration. A private company filed a claim before the Federal Maritime Commission, charging that the South Carolina State Ports Authority had violated the Shipping Act of 1994 by refusing to allow the company to berth its cruise ship in the Port of Charleston.[197] The Ports Authority was a state entity able to assert the state's sovereign immunity, provided there was any immunity to assert. The Ports Authority answered both by denying any violation of the Shipping Act and by insisting that the complaint should be dismissed on sovereign immunity grounds. According to the Ports Authority, "the Constitution" barred "Congress from passing a statute" authorizing a private company to file a complaint with the Commission and thus to "sue" the state.[198] An administrative law judge sustained the Ports Authority's argument in light of *Seminole Tribe*, but the Commission set the ALJ's recommendation aside. The Ports Authority sought review in the Court of Appeals for the Fourth Circuit. That court reversed the Commission's decision and remanded the case with instructions to dismiss the complaint, just as the ALJ had initially recommended. In the Supreme Court, Justice Thomas affirmed that decision, thus upholding the Ports Authority's sovereign immunity position. The four justices who, with Thomas, formed the majorities in *Seminole*

192. See Donald L. Doernberg, Identity Crisis: Federal Courts in a Psychological Wilderness 125 (2000) (arguing that *Alden* is "quite remarkable" in this respect); Michael C. Dorf, *No Federalists Here: Anti-Federalism and Nationalism on the Rehnquist Court*, 31 Rutgers L.J. 741, 745 (2000) (pointing out that the justices who "ignore" the text of the eleventh amendment are also the justices who frequently argue that the Court should not discover individual rights that have no textual basis).

193. See Ernest A. Young, *Alden v Maine and the Jurisprudence of Structure*, 41 Wm. & Mary L. Rev. 1601 (2000).

194. See Daan Braveman, *Enforcement of Federal Rights Against States: Alden and Federalism Non-Sense*, 49 Am. U. L. Rev. 611, 641 (2000).

195. See, e.g., John R. Prince, *Caught in a Trap: The Romantic Reading of the Eleventh Amendment*, 48 Buffalo L. Rev. 411, 478 (2000). Professor Pfander has argued that Justice Kennedy based "a jurisprudence of original intention" on his own "intuitive reconstruction of the framers' likely attitude toward an issue that did not arise during the debates over ratification." Pfander, note 175, at 832.

196. In this vein, Professor Weinberg has argued that *Alden* undermines the foundation of the Hart and Wechsler paradigm, which assumes that state courts are typically available to do any judicial business that needs doing. See Chapter I, notes 53–60 and accompanying text. Louise Weinberg, *Of Sovereignty and Union: The Legends of Alden*, 76 Notre Dame L. Rev. 1113, 1141 (2001).

197. The Ports Authority somehow got the idea that the people of Charleston could live just as long and could be just as happy without another sea-going gambling casino. Go figure.

198. 122 S.Ct. at 1869 (quoting from the record below).

Tribe and *Alden* joined his opinion. The dissenters in *Seminole Tribe* and *Alden* dissented again in *Ports Authority*.[199]

The Maritime Commission is not, of course, either a federal court or a state court. It is an independent federal administrative agency or, for constitutional purposes, the equivalent of a federal legislative court.[200] Justice Thomas readily acknowledged, accordingly, that *Seminole Tribe* and *Alden* were arguably distinguishable. He assumed *arguendo* that the Commission does not exercise "the judicial power of the United States" within the meaning of Article III.[201] Formally, then, the state had no complaint that it was subject to invalid federal judicial power—not, at least, in the way that Florida was in *Seminole Tribe*. Yet Justice Thomas insisted that the Commission performs adjudicative functions that amount to the same thing. Moreover, Congress enacted the Shipping Act and authorized the Commission to entertain the company's claim against the state. According to Justice Thomas, that statutory scheme constituted an invalid exercise of federal legislative power and thus a sufficient federal affront to the state's dignity to bring state sovereign immunity into play. He then found it easy enough to hold that the state's immunity, previously elaborated in *Seminole Tribe* and *Alden* for suits brought in federal and state court, extended as well to a suit before the Commission. Realistically speaking, he said, it would be "quite strange" to hold that Congress cannot subject a state to suit in federal court, but that Congress can force a state to answer charges before "court-like administrative tribunals."[202]

The government lawyers defending the Commission's action offered three primary arguments for distinguishing the proceeding before the Commission from the judicial proceeding in *Seminole Tribe*. First, they argued that the Commission's decisions were not self-executing. To enforce a judgment, the Commission was required to file suit in a federal district court, seeking a judicial order forcing a recalcitrant party to obey.[203] Second, they contended that the Commission was not authorized to order the state to make monetary payments as reparations for a violation of the Shipping Act. Accordingly, the state's treasury was not at risk.[204] Third, government lawyers argued that the Commission needed the ability to entertain complaints against states in order to establish and maintain a uniform national policy regarding maritime commerce. Justice Thomas rejected those arguments in turn. He insisted that the means by which the Commission's orders were enforced made no "meaningful" difference. Even if only a federal court could actually force the state to comply with a Commission decision, the state was obliged to participate in the agency proceedings in order to protect its interests. If the state refused to raise and litigate its arguments before the agency, it would forfeit those arguments later, if and when the agency reached a decision unfavorable to the state and went to court for an enforcement order.[205] Coming to the argument that the state treasury was not at risk, Justice Thomas insisted that sovereign immunity does not depend on the consequences that may follow an adjudicative proceeding, but rather

199. See note 190 and accompanying text.

200. See Chapter V.

201. 122 S.Ct. at 1871. See Chapter V, note 1 and accompanying text.

202. Id. at 1875.

203. See Chapter V, notes 18–19 and accompanying text.

204. See notes 173–74 and accompanying text (noting Justice Kennedy's discussion of state budgetary concerns in *Alden*); notes 340–49 and accompanying text (discussing officer suits for compensatory relief).

205. 122 S.Ct. at 1876. Justice Thomas intimated that the case might be different if the state were entitled to bypass the agency and nonetheless receive "full *de novo*" review of an agency order in an Article III court. Id. at n.15. See Chapter V, note 17 and accompanying text.

protects a state from suit in the first instance, whatever form the relief awarded may take. Finally, Justice Thomas conceded that sovereign immunity often disrupts uniform national policy and even that sovereign immunity frustrates efficient and convenient agency enforcement of federal law. Yet, by his account, that is inconsequential inasmuch as the Court's duty is to interpret the Constitution's "design" as it was devised by "the Framers."[206]

Justice Thomas hastened to make it clear that the state's immunity operated only to defeat a private plaintiff's complaint before the Commission and did not prevent the agency itself or the Attorney General from prosecuting a state for an alleged violation of the Act. In that respect, he sounded a familiar theme: If the federal government itself is the moving party in an enforcement action, the state cannot set up sovereign immunity as a defense.[207] The constitutional defect in the scheme in *Ports Authority* was that the government did not assume political responsibility for enforcing federal law, but, instead, purported to authorize private litigants to summon a state into an adjudicative proceeding to answer a private claim. The "preeminent purpose" of sovereign immunity is to spare a state that indignity.[208]

Justice Breyer filed an important dissent in *Ports Authority*, joined by the other three justices who also dissented in *Seminole Tribe* and *Alden*. In this instance, however, he did not repeat the arguments that he and others had offered before. Instead, Justice Breyer challenged the analogy that Justice Thomas drew between federal agencies and federal courts. According to Breyer, agencies are better understood as arms of the federal executive branch. They may proceed via adjudicative proceedings that "resemble" the work of courts. Yet their only genuine function is to determine whether the government should go to a federal court to seek a coercive order running to some party, including a state.[209] Justice Thomas rejected that conception as unrealistic. As the Fourth Circuit put it, a proceeding before an agency ALJ "walks, talks, and squawks very much like a lawsuit."[210] Accordingly, the analogy between agency proceedings and judicial proceedings is close enough to engage a state's constitutional sovereign immunity defense.

6. Congressional Power

Current sovereign immunity law blends the Court's previous interpretations of Article III and the eleventh amendment into a larger conceptual doctrine. That larger doctrine, in turn, is itself part of an even larger body of jurisprudence regarding the ability of Congress to legislate with respect to the states. It would be a mistake to neglect that jurisprudence and the sharp disagreements it has generated among the justices. Indeed, the Court's decisions on sovereign immunity may best be understood as the most recent reports from one of many theaters in which the justices are constantly battling each other for the one-vote advantage that, as a practical matter, determines whether a federal statute is valid. The opinion that Justice Kennedy wrote for the Court in *Alden*

206. 122 S.Ct. at 1877–79.

207. See notes 63–65, 257–75 and accompanying text.

208. 122 S.Ct. at 1874.

209. See Chapter V, notes 15–16 and accompanying text.

210. 122 S.Ct. at 1869, quoting *South Carolina State Ports Authority v. Fed. Maritime Comm'n*, 243 F.3d 165, 174 (4th Cir. 2001).

opens a window on the justices' quarrels regarding the relationship between Congress' ability to override state sovereign immunity from suits, on the one hand, and other authorities that Congress occasionally asserts, on the other.

The issue in *Alden*, again, was Congress' power to abrogate state immunity. Yet as Justice Kennedy grappled with that question, he rehearsed familiar arguments about Congress' authority to subject the states to federal regulatory programs in the first instance.[211] He acknowledged that the Fair Labor Standards Act applied to the state of Maine's employment practices and, accordingly, that Maine was obliged to pay its employees the wages specified in that Act. The state itself conceded as much.[212] Yet Justice Kennedy nonetheless leaned on themes that have ignited an intense debate within the Court regarding the authority of Congress to address the states. He intimated, for example, that Congress' attempt to subject the state to suit amounted to commandeering state institutions in violation of the principle recognized in *Printz v. United States*.[213] More fundamentally, he described an attempt by Congress to abrogate state immunity as an effort to "regulate" the states by making private litigants Congress' "proxy" with the authority "to levy" on "state treasuries" in order to advance policies that Congress selects.[214] That comment and others sprinkled through Justice Kennedy's opinion elicited a charge from Justice Souter, in dissent, that the Court means to frustrate valid congressional regulatory statutes by indirection—that is, by arming recalcitrant states with immunity against enforcement suits.[215]

The leading case on congressional regulation of the states, *Garcia v. San Antonio Metro. Trans. Auth.*,[216] itself involved the FLSA. In that case, Justice Blackmun held that Congress typically can force states to follow directives applied to private industry.[217] There were strong dissents in *Garcia*, even vows to overrule that case when the opportunity arises.[218] It is scarcely surprising, then, that the justices who lost in *Garcia* should regroup in *Alden* to protect the states from suits to enforce the very federal statute that those justices think should not apply to the states at all.[219] Nor is it surprising that justices who are content with the regulatory beachhead in *Garcia* should oppose what they reasonably may regard as a retreat in *Alden*. Given the monumental stakes in this great debate over congressional power, it is not surprising either that the dissenters in *Alden*, for their part, should refuse to credit the Court's decision in that case.[220]

---

211. See *Atascadero*, 473 U.S. at 303 (Blackmun, J., dissenting) (stating that the two lines of decisions "spring from the same soil").

212. 527 U.S. at 759.

213. 521 U.S. 898 (1997). See *Alden*, 527 U.S. at 748–53; text accompanying note 172. See also Chapter VI, notes 86–90 and accompanying text (discussing *Printz*). Nevertheless, Justice Kennedy explicitly disclaimed any suggestion that *Alden* undermines *Testa v. Katt*, 330 U.S. 386 (1947); see Chapter VI, note 85 and accompanying text. The state of Florida also raised the "anti-commandeering" argument in *Seminole Tribe*, but the Chief Justice failed to reach the issue. Professor Monaghan has suggested that the sovereign immunity analysis in *Seminole Tribe* was so weak that even the tenth amendment would have provided a "more secure foundation" for the Court's result. Monaghan, note 135, at 119.

214. 527 U.S. at 750.

215. Id. at 809 (Souter, J., dissenting).

216. 469 U.S. 528 (1985).

217. Writing for the Court in *New York v. United States*, 505 U.S. 144 (1992), Justice O'Connor distinguished the Court's approval of congressional regulation of states in *Garcia* from the Court's disapproval of congressional "commandeering" of state agencies to carry out federal programs. Id. at 160.

218. E.g., *Garcia*, 469 U.S. at 580 (Rehnquist, J., dissenting).

219. See Meltzer, note 163, at 1027–37.

220. See note 190 and accompanying text.

The *Garcia* and *Alden* decisions do not conflict as a matter of logic. It is possible to hold (as the Court plainly *has* held) that a state can be at once obligated to comply with a federal statute and immune from a lawsuit brought by private citizens to enforce it. Yet there is some tension between the two propositions, and that tension renders both *Garcia* and *Alden* (and the legal analysis they represent) "unstable."[221] The realistic explanation for the maintenance of both precedents is that neither bloc of sitting justices has the votes to have its way across the board. There is no majority to revisit *Garcia*, but there *is* a majority to frustrate the implementation of federal statutes that *Garcia* makes possible by allowing states to resist (some) enforcement lawsuits via sovereign immunity.[222] The resulting *impasse* (if *impasse* it is) provides a graphic illustration of the ideological debates that so often drive the law governing federal courts.[223]

Justice Kennedy insisted in *Alden* that state sovereign immunity poses no serious threat to the enforcement of federal law. He noted that states almost always comply with federal law voluntarily and, in some instances, are willing to consent to be sued and thus forgo their immunity. Beyond those possibilities, he noted that private litigants can sometimes achieve their goals by suing cities and counties, which do not share the immunity the Constitution accords to member states.[224] He confirmed that private litigants can employ officer suits to obtain injunctive relief that effectively forces states to comply with federal law in the future.[225] And he noted that plaintiffs can obtain monetary relief if they sue state officers personally and seek compensation from the officers' own pockets.[226] Finally, Justice Kennedy recognized that if Congress concludes that it is essential to subject states to suit, there usually is a way to do it apart from exercising Article I regulatory power.

---

221. Meltzer, note 163, at 1015.

222. See Dorf, note 192, at 746.

223. See Ann Althouse, *The Alden Trilogy: Still Searching for a Way to Enforce Federalism*, 31 Rutgers L.J. 631, 685 (2000) (noting that "a one-vote shift in the balance of power" could "consign" academic criticisms of the Court's work to "the dustbin of legal scholarship"). Professor Fried has suggested that *Garcia* is the "bad case of the tail wagging the dog." Charles Fried, *Supreme Court Folly*, N.Y. Times (July 6, 1999). Yet many other observers think that *Garcia* was rightly decided and that *Seminole Tribe* and *Alden* should be reexamined. E.g., Vicki C. Jackson, *Seductions of Coherence, State Sovereign Immunity, and the Denationalization of Federal Law*, 31 Rutgers L.J. 691, 712 (2000) (criticizing *Alden* for allowing states to refuse to meet their financial obligations); Ana Maria Merico-Stephens, *Of Maine's Sovereignty, Alden's Federalism, and the Myth of Absolute Principles: The Newest Oldest Question of Constitutional Law*, 33 U.C. Davis L. Rev. 325, 388 (2000) (contending that *Alden* makes a "political choice" better left to Congress). The decisive vote appears to rest with Justice Kennedy. It may be that he has developed his own unique vision of the federal structure and has attempted in this series of decisions to give effect to that vision. Then again, Justice Kennedy may be as confused as the rest of us. Cf. Meltzer, note 163, at 1042–45 (arguing that Kennedy's opinions cannot be reconciled).

224. See note 59 and accompanying text. This last avenue is not a means by which the states themselves can be brought to heel. Yet in many circumstances, private plaintiffs may be able to construct lawsuits against local authorities that will do the work of suits against the states themselves.

225. See notes 56, 283–88, 308 and accompanying text.

226. See notes 278, 348–49, 372–76 and accompanying text. But see notes 424–94 and accompanying text (discussing official immunity). Professor Meltzer has explained, however, that it would be "jarring" if individual state officers should be held personally liable for damage awards in the millions, even if the states were generally to indemnify them. Daniel J. Meltzer, note 163, at 1019. Others contend that it would be grossly inefficient to force private plaintiffs to seek compensatory relief in the form of suits against individual officers in order to trigger state indemnification and curious in the extreme to read the Constitution to prefer awkward arrangements of that kind to ordinary suits against the states themselves. See, e.g., Carlos Mauel Vazquez, *Eleventh Amendment Schizophrenia*, 75 Notre Dame L. Rev. 859, 876–87 (2000).

If there really are so many ways to hold recalcitrant states to account, the Court's seemingly significant immunity decisions may turn out to have no real theoretical bite. Certainly, state sovereign immunity is a serious nuisance. Yet it may be largely a symbolic matter, celebrating the dignity due the states and little else.[227] The practical point may be only that the Court's constitutional decisions make it necessary for Congress to achieve its ends by means of more carefully conceived and worded legislation. That, in turn, makes it easier for the opponents of regulation to forestall effective legislative action. In any event, it appears that Congress' inability to abrogate state sovereign immunity under any of its Article I powers is not always fatal. There are other ways by which Congress usually can ensure that states pay damages if they fail to comply with federal law. Justice Kennedy listed them in *Alden*. Congress can: (1) abrogate state immunity insofar as section five of the fourteenth amendment allows; (2) induce the states to consent to suit by offering them incentives to do so; and (3) authorize enforcement suits by the federal government itself.

Abrogation under section five. The decisions in *Seminole Tribe*, *Alden*, and *Ports Authority* establish that Congress cannot abolish state sovereign immunity under any of its Article I powers.[228] Congress can, however, abrogate the states' federal constitutional immunity when it acts pursuant to section five of the fourteenth amendment.[229] Writing for the Court in *Fitzpatrick v. Bitzer*,[230] then-Justice Rehnquist explained that Congress' power under section five was added to the Constitution *after* the eleventh amendment was in place and thus can be read to make a prospective change regarding state sovereignty.[231] More fundamentally, the fourteenth amendment's substantive provisions (the Equal Protection and Due Process Clauses) are expressly "directed at the States" and thus invite enforcement legislation that targets the states themselves.[232] To ensure that Congress genuinely "intends" to abrogate state immunity, the Court employs another clear statement rule. Congress must make "its intention unmistakably clear."[233] The justices often disagree over whether a statute is specific enough to satisfy the clear statement rule. Occasionally, the Court is willing to consult legislative history.[234] In the main, however, the Court insists upon exacting language in the text of an enacted statute.[235] In *Quern v. Jordan*,[236] the Court held that §1983 is not sufficiently clear and thus does not abrogate state immunity in the manner approved in *Fitzpatrick*.[237]

---

227. See Frank B. Cross, *Realism About Federalism*, 74 N.Y.U. L. Rev. 1305, 1323–24 (1999).

228. *Florida Prepaid Postsecondary Ed. Bd. v. College Savings Bank*, 527 U.S. 627, 636 (1999).

229. See *Alden*, 527 U.S. at 756; *Seminole Tribe*, 517 U.S. at 59.

230. 427 U.S. 445 (1976).

231. For a discussion of the significance of this timing point, see Vicki C. Jackson, *Holistic Interpretation: Fitzpatrick v. Bitzer and Our Bifurcated Constitution*, 53 Stan. L. Rev. 1259 (2001).

232. *Fitzpatrick*, 427 U.S. at 453.

233. *Atascadero*, 473 U.S. at 242 (declining to find the Rehabilitation Act of 1973 to be sufficiently clear). Justice Kennedy explained in *Hilton v. South Carolina Pub. Ry. Comm'n*, 502 U.S. 197 (1991), that the requirement of a clear statement to effect an abrogation of state sovereign immunity is itself a feature of that immunity and thus has the status of constitutional law. Id. at 205–06.

234. E.g., *Hutto v. Finney*, 437 U.S. 678 (1978).

235. E.g., *Dellmuth v. Muth*, 491 U.S. 223 (1989). Writing for the Court in *Dellmuth*, Justice Kennedy disclaimed legislative history entirely. He said that Congress need not mention state immunity by name, but he plainly indicated that, if Congress genuinely wishes to be successful, it must list the states themselves as potential defendants. Id. at 230.

236. 440 U.S. 332 (1979).

237. By conventional account, §1983 is anchored in section five. Justice Brennan recalled in *Quern* that the preamble to the original statute in 1871 stated that the Act was meant "to enforce the Provisions of the Fourteenth Amendment." Id. at 332 n.3 (concurring opinion). Thus §1983 presumably *could* abrogate state immunity (in some way) if it were clear enough on the point. See

The exception for statutes pursuant to section five has been criticized.[238] Yet it may achieve a defensible compromise. Congress is deprived of the extensive capacity to subject the states to lawsuits that its generous Article I powers would otherwise entail. But Congress enjoys abrogation power in cases in which state immunity may be most problematic—namely, cases in which states refuse to comply with federal civil rights laws. In *Fitzpatrick*, for example, the Court held that Congress could subject the states to suit when private litigants allege a violation of the Civil Rights Act of 1964.

Prior to the recent immunity decisions, it was typically unnecessary to ascertain the precise constitutional power on which federal statutes could be said to rest. If any power sufficed, a statute could be sustained.[239] Today, that is only partially true. It still makes no difference what power Congress exercises if the point is only to regulate the states. So long as a regulatory statute is valid under either Article I or section five, the statute can establish the states' primary legal obligations. If, however, Congress wishes to authorize private litigants to file enforcement lawsuits, then only Congress' power under section five will do. This means, of course, that the scope of section five power is crucial. The Court has recently turned to that question in a series of cases.[240] In those cases, it is typically conceded that statutes are valid under Article I insofar as they impose legal duties on the states. The serious question has been whether the same statutes can also rest on section five, so that their provisions authorizing private enforcement suits for damages are equally valid. The Court has concluded that most of the statutes it has examined cannot be justified under section five.[241] Accordingly, they cannot deprive the states of sovereign immunity. If they are to be enforced, they must be enforced by some alternative means.[242] Academic commentaries typically suggest that the Court's developing section five doctrine is driven by its sovereign immunity decisions. The Court insists that the availability of abrogation under section five allows the states to be called to account for at least some violations of federal law and thus mitigates the effects of sovereign immunity. Yet the Court has kept the scope of section five power fairly narrow, lest it open a breach in the states' sovereign immunity defenses.[243]

Chapter II, notes 75–76 and accompanying text; Chapter VIII, notes 132, 135–36 and accompanying text. But see Clive B. Jacques & Jack M. Beermann, *Section 1983's "And Laws" Clause Run Amok: Civil Rights Attorney's Fees in Cellular Facilities Siting Disputes*, 81 B.U. L. Rev. 735, 786–91 (1999) (contending that section five cannot support §1983 insofar as it purports to authorize private suits to enforce federal statutes that cannot themselves rest on section five).

238. Academics debate whether the Court's distinction between section five and Article I is convincing and (if not), whether it is *Seminole Tribe* or *Fitzpatrick* that should go. See Daniel J. Meltzer, *The Seminole Decison and State Sovereign Immunity*, 1996 Sup. Ct. Rev. 1, 20–24 (critiquing the distinction); Hill, note 123 (contending that *Fitzpatrick* is unjustified).

239. *Woods v. Cloyd W. Miller Co.*, 333 U.S. 138, 144 (1948).

240. The Court began with *City of Boerne v. Flores*, 521 U.S. 507 (1997), the case in which the Court found the Religious Freedom Restoration Act unconstitutional.

241. See, e.g., *Bd. of Trustees of the University of Alabama v. Garrett*, 531 U.S. 356 (2001); *Kimel v. Florida Bd. of Regents*, 528 U.S. 62 (2000). Numerous statutes have yet to be examined. For illustrations, see *Seminole Tribe*, 517 U.S. at 77 n.1 (Stevens, J., dissenting); Martha A. Field, *The Seminole Case, Federalism, and the Indian Commerce Clause*, 29 Ariz. St. L.J. 3, 15–16 (1997); H. Stephen Harris & Michael P. Kenny, *Eleventh Amendment Jurisprudence After Atascadero: The Coming Clash With Antitrust, Copyright, and Other Causes of Action Over which the Federal Courts Have Exclusive Jurisdiction*, 37 Emory L.J. 645 (1988).

242. See *Garrett*, 531 U.S. at 376 (Kennedy, J., concurring) (acknowledging this consequence).

243. See Evan H. Caminker, *"Appropriate" Means-Ends Constraints on Section 5 Powers*, 53 Stan. L. Rev. 1127 (2001); Ruth Colker, *The Section Five Quagmire*, 47 U.C.L.A. L. Rev. 653 (2000); Robert Post & Reva Siegel, *Equal Protection by Law: Federal Antidiscrimination Legislation After Mor-*

Concomitantly, the Court has relied on the doctrine of clear statement to protect the states without formally finding an unconstitutional attempt to abolish their immunity. In *Raygor v. Regents*,[244] employees of the University of Minnesota sued the university in a federal district court, claiming age discrimination in violation of the federal Age Discrimination in Employment Act. They also advanced state law claims over which the court had supplemental jurisdiction pursuant to 28 U.S.C. §1367.[245] The district court granted the university's motion to dismiss both the federal and the state claims on the basis of sovereign immunity. The plaintiffs then filed suit in state court, pressing only the state law claims. At that point, the university moved to dismiss because the applicable state statute of limitations had run. The plaintiffs contended that §1367 effectively extended the filing period in state court by tolling it for the time the parties were in federal court. In the Supreme Court, Justice O'Connor construed §1367 not to confer jurisdiction on federal district courts to hear state law claims against unconsenting states. Concomitantly, she construed the tolling provision not to suspend a state statute of limitations with respect to state law claims dismissed in federal court on the basis of state sovereign immunity.[246]

Justice O'Connor explained that if §1367 were read to confer jurisdiction on district courts to entertain state law claims against unconsenting states, it could be sustained only on the theory that Congress can validly abrogate a state's federal constitutional immunity from claims of that sort advanced in federal court. Accordingly, the clear statement requirement applicable to abrogation must be satisfied.[247] If §1367 were read to toll the filing period for state claims in state court, it could be sustained only on the theory that Congress can validly adjust a condition a state establishes regarding its willingness to suffer suit in its own courts. Justice O'Connor conceded uncertainty about whether a federal statute having that effect would also have to be justified as a valid abrogation of state immunity. Yet she insisted that it would raise "serious" constitutional doubts."[248] Accordingly, exacting statutory language was again required. Justice O'Connor found §1367 insufficiently explicit either to confer jurisdiction on federal courts to adjudicate state claims against states or to toll the filing deadline for state claims rerouted to state court after dismissal in federal court.[249]

If the Court were to reach the question, it is most unlikely that the Court would approve §1367 as an abrogation of state sovereign immunity from suits on state claims in federal court. That immunity is well established, and there is no apparent way that a

---

rison and Kimel, 110 Yale L.J. 441 (2001); Tracey A. Thomas, *Congress' Section 5 Power and Remedial Rights*, 34 U.C. Davis L. Rev. 673 (2001).

244. 534 U.S. 533 (2002).

245. See Chapter VIII, notes 402–22 and accompanying text.

246. See Chapter VIII, notes 404–05, 421–22 and accompanying text.

247. 534 U.S. at 541.

248. Id. at 543. In this, Justice O'Connor understood that the state had waived sovereign immunity for state law claims in state court, but had conditioned that waiver on a plaintiff's compliance with the accompanying statute of limitations. If federal law tolled that statute of limitations, it would expose the state to liability for a longer period than the state itself had agreed to put itself at risk.

249. In dissent, Justice Stevens argued that federal statutes that toll state filing periods are common and perfectly sensible devices for avoiding unfairness. By his account, they affect state sovereignty only modestly. They do not presume to determine "*whether*" unconsenting states will be subject to suit at all, but only "*when*" states that have already consented remain vulnerable. 534 U.S. at 552 (dissenting opinion) (emphasis in original). Writing for the Court, Justice O'Connor rejected that argument on the ground that the states are entitled to name the terms on which they consent to suits that they could resist entirely. Id. at 543 (majority opinion).

statute authorizing supplemental jurisdiction generally can override it, even by means of the most specific language.[250] The possibility that the Court might have sustained the tolling provision applied to state claims against unconsenting states in state court is problematic. With respect to that question, it may be crucial in *Raygor* that the Court avoided a forthright constitutional decision and, instead, rested on the doctrine of clear statement.[251]

Inducements to consent. Congress can induce the states to waive sovereign immunity by offering them incentives to do so. For example, Congress can condition states' participation in federal regulatory programs or the receipt of federal funding on their willingness to consent to be sued for damages should some dispute arise.[252] Conditional spending is a routinely employed means of achieving regulatory goals and probably offers the most promising vehicle in this context. Recall, however, that Congress must make it clear to the states that the acceptance of federal money comes with this string attached.[253] In *Alden*, moreover, Justice Kennedy specified that Congress may only

250. Justice O'Connor focused exclusively on whether the text of §1367 is sufficiently clear to count as an attempt to abrogate the kind of immunity recognized in *Pennhurst*. She did not mention that, in any case, abrogation authority is now limited to section five of the fourteenth amendment. See notes 228–31. She referred to section five only when she responded to the plaintiffs' argument that the tolling provision in §1367 could be justified as a means of preventing due process violations arising from unfair state litigation tactics. She recognized, for example, that a state might insist that plaintiffs raise all their claims in federal court, postpone an objection on sovereign immunity grounds until it is too late for plaintiffs to sue in state court, and then insist that a suit in state court is untimely. Justice O'Connor rejected that argument because, again, the tolling provision does not clearly specify that it protects state claims dismissed in federal court on sovereign immunity grounds. *Raygor*, 534 U.S. 546.

251. The *Raygor* case (like *Alden*) raised only a question of congressional power with respect to state immunity. The Court had no occasion to specify what, if any, federal constitutional immunity the states may enjoy regarding state law claims in state court in cases in which no federal statute is implicated. See notes 177–80 and accompanying text. Concurring in *Raygor*, Justice Ginsburg noted that Justice O'Connor did not "invoke" *Alden*. 534 U.S. at 548 n.1. It appears, then, that Justice Ginsburg thought that the analysis in *Raygor* did not depend on any assumptions about state sovereign immunity anchored in the Constitution. Ginsburg agreed, however, that a clear statement requirement was appropriate in order to avoid "difficult constitutional questions." Id. Apart from federal constitutional state sovereign immunity, it is hard to know what those questions might be. Perhaps Justice Ginsburg meant to flag the concerns that some academics have raised about federal legislation purporting to establish procedural rules to be followed by state courts adjudicating state law claims. See Chapter VI, note 104. Those concerns, however, generally rest in some wise on state immunity. Moreover, if federally prescribed rules for the conduct of state court litigation on state issues raise constitutional problems at all, it would seem that they must do so in all their applications—not just in cases in which the states themselves or state officers may assert state sovereign immunity. So the potential constitutional questions about the tolling provision in §1367 would presumably remain (and perhaps do remain) even after Justice O'Connor's construction of that provision.

252. See notes 77–79 and accompanying text; Kit Kinports, *Implied Waiver After Seminole Tribe*, 82 Minn. L. Rev. 793 (1998).

253. See note 78 and accompanying text. Some academics question whether the Court will continue for long its willingness to allow Congress essentially to buy out state sovereignty by making the surrender of immunity a condition for receiving federal funds. It seems odd that the Court should think that straightforward abrogation threatens core constitutional values if Congress can accomplish the same regulatory goals by another means. See, e.g., Rebecca E. Zietlow, *Federalism's Paradox: The Spending Power and Waiver of Sovereign Immunity*, 37 Wake Forest L. Rev. 141 (2002); cf. Lynn A. Baker, *Conditional Federal Spending After Lopez*, 95 Colum. L. Rev. 1911 (1995). Yet if the only real point of the immunity cases is that uninvited private suits deny states the dignity to which they are entitled, the Court may well be content when Congress allows the states the choice (however formal) of refusing to be bribed. Zietlow, at 203–06. Recall that in *Ports Authority*, Justice

"seek" the states' "voluntary consent."[254] The Court held in *College Savings Bank v. Florida Prepaid Postsecondary Ed. Bd.*[255] that if Congress fails to give states anything in return for their consent to be sued, but only purports to prevent them from conducting otherwise lawful operations *unless* they consent, then the states themselves must explicitly waive their immunity.

Justice Scalia acknowledged in *College Savings* that it would be possible to recognize "constructive consent," provided Congress uses exacting language so that states understand (or can be held to understand) that they will be treated as though they have consented to be sued. Nevertheless, he declined. In part, the explanation is pragmatic. The Court does not want to invite Congress to rewrite statutes that previously purported simply to abrogate state sovereign immunity so that they, instead, unilaterally impose "constructive consent" on the states. That would be too easy and thus would frustrate the state immunity recognized in *Seminole Tribe* and *Alden*. According to the Court, unless a state obtains some *quid pro quo* that renders its agreement to be sued genuinely voluntary, state sovereign immunity needs the protection that the express waiver requirement provides.[256]

Suits by the federal government. Congress can exploit the longstanding rule that state sovereign immunity does not operate in suits brought by the federal government.[257] If Congress thinks that states themselves should be subject to suit, Congress can commission the Attorney General or some other appropriate officer or agency to initiate legal action.[258] In *Alden*, Justice Kennedy distinguished between suits by the federal government itself and suits by private citizens acting with congressional authorization. Government prosecutors and regulators exercise discretion and sue when, in their judgment, the public interest will be promoted. Private citizens sue whenever it serves their own purposes, without any necessary concern for the public. According to Justice Kennedy, the Constitution allows Congress to provide for suits by federal officials who exercise politically accountable judgment before haling states into court. But it does not allow Congress to turn enforcement authority over to private citizens, who are not similarly answerable to the electorate.[259]

Thomas declared that the "preeminent purpose" of state immunity is to protect the states from the indignity of private suits. See text accompanying note 208. See generally Christina Bohannan, *Beyond Abrogation of Sovereign Immunity: State Waivers, Private Contracts, and Federal Incentives*, 77 N.Y.U. L. Rev. 273 (2002) (contending that inducements to consent remain viable and potentially may significantly blunt the impact of the Court's aggressive stance regarding state immunity).

254. 527 U.S. at 755.

255. 527 U.S. 666 (1999).

256. On this point, Justice Scalia explicitly overruled *Parden v. Terminal Ry.*, 377 U.S. 184 (1964). See *College Savings*, 527 U.S. at 680–83. A bill introduced by Senator Leahy proposes to condition the states' ability to hold intellectual property on their express consent to be sued for patent violations. S. 1835, 106th Cong., 1st Sess. (1999). See Meltzer, note 73, at 1380–89 (mulling this possibility); Mitchell N. Berman, R. Anthony Reese & Ernest A. Young, *State Accountability for Violations of Intellectual Property Rights: How to "Fix" Florida Prepaid (And How Not To)*, 79 Tex. L. Rev. 1037, 1146–47 (2001) (questioning its likely success). Cf. Paul J. Heald & Michael L. Wells, *Remedies for the Misappropriation of Intellectual Property by State and Municipal Governments Before and After Seminole Tribe: The Eleventh Amendment and Other Immunity Doctrines*, 55 Wash. & Lee L. Rev. 849 (1998) (offering a rigorous treatment of these problems prior to *College Savings*).

257. See notes 63–66 and accompanying text.

258. See note 1 and accompanying text.

259. In *Alden* itself, Kennedy noted that Congress had enacted a statute authorizing the Secretary of Labor to sue the states for alleged violations of the FLSA. If the Secretary had initiated suit under that statute, there evidently would have been no sovereign immunity impediment. Yet the Secretary did not file suit. Kennedy took that to mean that the responsible federal officers had decided that it was not in the public interest to take legal action against the state of Maine to recover

This preference for government enforcement actions over private lawsuits sounds a familiar theme. Recall that some members of the Court have contended that private litigants should be denied standing to sue, lest they displace the executive's authority and responsibility to see that federal law is respected. In that context, too, some justices have expressed concern that private litigants are not politically accountable.[260] There is, of course, an important difference. In the standing context, the private litigants who have attracted attention are non-Hohfeldians seeking forward-looking injunctive relief that changes the way government officers (or corporations) behave in the future. Here, by contrast, private litigants wish to press their own personal legal rights under federal statutes and typically seek backward-looking compensation for their economic losses. Nevertheless, when Hohfeldian private plaintiffs presume to sue the states, the Court insists that they must be turned away at least in part *because* they act only for themselves.[261] In the standing context, the personal Hohfeldian perspective is an asset; in this context, that same perspective is a liability. The Court's position on immunity seems doubly curious. If the point of the exercise is to interpret the Constitution to keep the federal government out of the states' hair, it seems odd that the Court should end up encouraging the government to bring its considerable resources to bear on the states forthrightly.[262]

Justice Kennedy said in *Alden* that the central government can sue the states "on behalf of" private individuals.[263] He did not say that the government can obtain monetary damages that can be distributed to the individuals affected. But that further proposition is a fair inference.[264] So-called *parens patriae* suits for the benefit of constituents present difficulties that Justice Kennedy did not address.[265] Yet they have been employed in the

---

the probation officers' back wages. That, he insisted, had analytical significance. *Alden*, 527 U.S. at 759.

260. See Chapter IX, notes 130–34, 314 and accompanying text.

261. Professor Woolhandler has explained, however, that suits for monetary relief were historically available against states only to protect traditional property interests, not the "new property" interests of workers in public jobs. Ann Woolhandler, *Old Property, New Property, and Sovereign Immunity*, 75 Notre Dame L. Rev. 919 (2000).

262. See William A. Fletcher, *The Eleventh Amendment: Unfinished Business*, 75 Notre Dame L. Rev. 843, 847 (2000).

263. *Alden*, 527 U.S. at 759.

264. There is no Supreme Court precedent squarely on point. Yet the statute that Justice Kennedy himself cited in *Alden*, 29 U.S.C. §216(c), expressly authorizes the Secretary of Labor to sue for monetary relief and to turn funds recovered over to deserving employees. See *EEOC v. Waffle House*, 534 U.S. 279 (2002) (apparently approving a suit by the EEOC against a private employer for backpay and compensation to be distributed to individual employees). Writing for the Court in *Pennhurst State School & Hosp. v. Halderman*, 465 U.S. 89 (1994), Justice Powell said that the federal government's participation as a plaintiff in a suit against a state does not permit the court to "order the State to pay damages to other [private] plaintiffs." Id. at 103 n.12. A suit in which the government seeks direct payments to private citizens is one thing. A suit in which the government itself recovers money and then transmits it to private individuals is another. The Court has drawn this distinction in cases in which one state sues another for monetary damages. So long as the plaintiff state has its own sovereign or quasi-sovereign interest in the litigation, the defendant state cannot set up sovereign immunity as a defense. That is true even when the plaintiff state intends all along to distribute the proceeds to individual citizens. *Kansas v. Colorado*, 533 U.S. 1, 8 (2001).

265. See, e.g., Larry W. Yackle, *A Worthy Champion for Fourteenth Amendment Rights: The United States in Parens Patriae*, 92 Nw. U. L. Rev. 111, 161–72 (1997) (discussing among other things the preclusive effects of government suits).

past and may well do greater service in the post-*Alden* world.[266] It seems likely that any arrangements that Congress establishes in this connection must meet two requirements. A scheme can be valid if it contemplates suits against states in which: (1) the federal government itself has genuine interests to vindicate; and (2) the executive branch both decides whether to bring suit in the first instance and also controls the litigation thereafter.

The rationales for the federal government's exemption from state immunity operate only when the government *qua* government is the "real party in interest."[267] Certainly, only the government itself is in a position to exert military force to have its way with the states. Private litigants may send in lawyers, but they cannot send in the Marines. Equally, the states can sensibly be said to have consented to be sued only when the government advances its own interests. It is hard to think that the implicit waiver theory works if the central government merely lends its name to suits that are really private.[268] The *kind* of government interest that will suffice is problematic. The government has sovereign and quasi-sovereign interests in the promotion of federal law for the benefit of the public.[269] So all suits that press federal legal claims against states can be said to be in aid of the government's interest in law enforcement. In consequence, the government may be able to launch whatever enforcement actions it likes, obtaining compensation for private citizens into the bargain. Yet precedents in the standing context indicate that *parens patriae* suits must press public interests that transcend the concerns of private individuals.[270] Moreover, the limitations on Congress' power to confer standing on private litigants may also signify. Recall in this vein Congress' capacity to make private citizens its agents or to assign to them its own litigation interests.[271] Given the invitation in

266. Cf. Ann Woolhandler & Michael G. Collins, *State Standing*, 81 Va. L. Rev. 387 (1995) (exhaustively treating the standing of states to sue in *parens patriae*).

267. Evan H. Caminker, *State Immunity Waivers for Suits by the United States*, 98 Mich. L. Rev. 92, 95 (1999).

268. Cf. *Kansas v. Colorado*, 533 U.S. at 7–8 (recalling precedents holding that a state cannot defeat another state's immunity simply by becoming a nominal plaintiff in a suit actually pursued by private parties). Professor Caminker argues that an individual state would have had ample incentives to authorize the federal government to sue *other* states for projecting their power beyond their borders. To accomplish that end, each state would have concomitantly consented to be sued itself. Caminker, note 267, at 110.

269. See *Alfred L. Snapp & Son v. Puerto Rico*, 458 U.S. 592 (1982) (listing these interests as the basis for the standing of individual states to litigate in federal court on behalf of constituents); *Massachusetts v. Mellon*, 262 U.S. 447, 485–86 (1923) (indicating that the federal government can also sue in *parens patriae*).

270. See, e.g., *General Tel. Co. v. EEOC*, 446 U.S. 318 (1980) (stating that the EEOC has standing to sue in the public interest); *Pasadena City Bd. of Ed. v. Spangler*, 427 U.S. 424, 430–31 (1976) (explaining that the federal government can maintain a suit after the claims of individual plaintiffs become moot); cf. *Snapp*, 458 U.S. at 607 (explaining that a state need not sue on behalf of the general public so long as its concerns go beyond those of some "identifiable group of individual residents"). In *United States v. San Jacinto Tin Co.*, 125 U.S. 273 (1888), the Court said that the government could not institute suit to rescind an allegedly invalid land patent if the suit was entirely for the benefit of an individual and the United States had neither an independent pecuniary interest nor any relevant obligation to the general public. In that case, the Court ultimately found it sufficient that the government was protecting the integrity of federal patents—even though it was clear that the suit *was* for the benefit of a single person, who stood to get the land himself if the government was successful and, indeed, had signed a bond indemnifying the government in order to persuade the Attorney General to act. Id. at 286–87.

271. See Chapter IX, notes 308–18 and accompanying text.

Alden, it seems likely that the federal government can serve as a champion for private citizens and, in that role, can obtain compensation for them that they cannot obtain for themselves. Still, it is risky to assume that the federal government can maneuver around the state immunity recognized in *Alden* by routinely making itself a collection agency for private creditors.[272]

Independent separation-of-powers considerations suggest that Congress cannot go it alone. The legislative branch may authorize government suits in the first instance. That requires a politically accountable judgment that the public interest will be served in at least some cases. But in *Alden*, Justice Kennedy said that a political filter is needed *ad hoc*—with respect to "each suit prosecuted against a State."[273] It may be that Kennedy contemplates that officers in the executive branch must make case-by-case judgments about whether the public interest warrants the extraordinary step of naming a state as a defendant.[274] Here again, it is hard to think that themes that have previously surfaced in cases on standing are not equally triggered in connection with state sovereign immunity. In the standing context, some justices have worried that Congress loosely deputizes private litigants to perform a function that, in their minds, the Constitution assigns to the executive branch. In this context, too, some justices may be similarly concerned if Congress authorizes suits on the federal government's behalf that do not preserve a sufficient measure of control for federal prosecutors or agencies.[275]

C. Officer Suits

Private litigants can often employ officer suits to avoid the states' immunity.[276] Recall that suits against federal officers do not implicate the federal government's sovereign

272. The federal government also has its own proprietary interests. When those interests correlate with the interests of private citizens, the government should be able to sue a state on its own behalf and, concomitantly, on behalf of private citizens similarly affected. Then again, suits of that kind are less promising vehicles for law enforcement than suits implicating the government's sovereign or quasi-sovereign interests. See Chapter IX, note 317.

273. 527 U.S. at 756.

274. By some accounts, the political judgments that government agents make would typically render enforcement actions by the federal government poor substitutes for self-interested private suits. The budgets for agency litigation are notoriously under-funded. Even if federal authorities were given the necessary resources, they would often see too little public interest in suing simply to obtain compensation for a limited number of individuals. Harms to individuals entitled to compensation may actually be inversely proportional to the public interest. Cf. Meltzer, note 163, at 1022. But see Caminker, note 267, at 122 (arguing that federal prosecutors may be underwhelmed by the "dignity" owed to states and may be perfectly willing to pursuit lawsuits that have merit).

275. Professor Caminker has argued that the existing *qui tam* scheme in the False Claims Act should be sustained under this heading. Caminker, note 267. See *Vermont Agency v. United States ex rel. Stevens*, 529 U.S. 765, 787 (2000) (avoiding the question by construing that Act not to authorize suits against states). Professor Siegel has suggested more novel possibilities. Johathan R. Siegel, *Congress's Power to Authorize Suits Against States*, 68 Geo. Wash. L. Rev. 44, 70–72 (1999). Siegel concedes, however, that if Congress can readily circumnavigate state immunity, it is hard to take seriously the Court's insistence that immunity is (or was) so fundamental to the constitutional design. Certainly, it is hard to think that ratification actually "turned on the slight difference between what the Supreme Court's decisions apparently forbid and what, in practice, they allow Congress to accomplish." Id. at 48. See also Jonathan R. Siegel, *The Hidden Source of Congress's Power to Abrogate State Sovereign Immunity*, 73 Tex. L. Rev. 539 (1995) (offering pre-*Alden* arguments).

276. See text accompanying note 17 (discussing suits against federal officers).

immunity if litigants genuinely mean to impose personal liability on the officers themselves.[277] The same is true of suits against state officers seeking compensatory damages out of the officers' own pockets.[278] Officer suits can also affect the states themselves, albeit indirectly.

1. Suits for Prospective Relief

At the time that *Hans v. Louisiana* was decided, the Supreme Court threatened to do, with respect to suits against state officers, what it would later do, in *Larson* and its progeny, with respect to suits against federal officers.[279] In another state bond case, *In re Ayers*,[280] the plaintiffs attempted to obtain full value for their bonds by surrendering them to the state of Virginia as tax payments. The Virginia legislature enacted a statute authorizing state officers to proceed against the bondholders for cash. Some of the bondholders sued the state attorney general in federal court, seeking an injunction against those proceedings on the theory that they amounted to an unconstitutional impairment of the bond contracts.[281] Justice Matthews held that the suit against the attorney general was barred by the state's federal constitutional sovereign immunity. That suit, according to the Court, was in actuality an action to enforce the plaintiffs' contract with the state. The attorney general might be held personally liable for any torts he committed and thus might be forced to compensate his victims out of his own pocket. But he could not be held to account for breach of a contractual obligation that the state had undertaken and thus be made to deliver on the state's commitments.[282]

Ten years later, however, the Court adopted a different view in *Ex parte Young*,[283] one of the most important decisions the Court has ever rendered regarding the federal courts. Shareholders sued the Minnesota attorney general in federal court, seeking an injunction against enforcement of railroad freight rates fixed by state law. They insisted that the rates were confiscatory and thus violated the fourteenth amendment.[284] In *Young*, by contrast to *Ayers*, the Court held that the state's federal constitutional immunity did not bar the plaintiffs' suit. Justice Peckham acknowledged that the state itself was immune. But the attorney general could not set up the state's immunity to defeat the action against him. Justice Peckham distinguished *Ayers* on the theory that the plaintiffs in that case had attempted to enforce a contract with the state and thus to reach the state treasury. By most accounts, however, that

277. See notes 18–20 and accompanying text.

278. But see notes 452–57 and accompanying text (discussing official immunity).

279. See notes 31–35 and accompanying text (discussing *Larson*).

280. 123 U.S. 443 (1887).

281. The federal court issued an injunction, and when the attorney general failed to comply with it, the court held him in contempt and placed him in custody. The attorney general then petitioned the Supreme Court for a writ of habeas corpus, and the Court considered the matter in that posture.

282. See Woolhandler, note 117 (providing an exhaustive discussion of the bond cases in the period).

283. 209 U.S. 123 (1908).

284. In *Young*, too, the state attorney general put the sovereign immunity issue before the Supreme Court in a petition for a writ of habeas corpus that would free him from detention for contempt of a district court injunction. See note 281 (describing the similar procedural path that the suit in *Ayers* took to the Court).

distinction did not ring true. In *Young*, too, the plaintiffs sued a state officer only as a means of affecting the state itself.[285]

It is easy to misunderstand *Ex parte Young*. Justice Peckham invoked the familiar fiction that an officer suit is not a suit against the state itself, even when the idea is to reach the state indirectly through its agents.[286] That, in itself, is confusing enough. Peckham confused matters still more. He said that if the attorney general's conduct violated due process, he could claim no state authority for his behavior and must have acted as a private citizen. That will not do. It calls to mind Chief Justice Vinson's troubling analysis in *Larson*.[287] The Constitution addresses only governmental action. If, in order to elude state sovereign immunity in *Young*, Justice Peckham had to deny that the attorney general acted for the state, then the entire case should have collapsed for want of any "state action" bringing the fourteenth amendment into play. Whatever Peckham may have said in *Young*, that case cannot mean that state sovereign immunity does not bar suits against state officers for violations of the fourteenth amendment because those officers do not act for the state. If officers don't act for the state, they can't violate the fourteenth amendment at all. Properly framed, *Ex parte Young* stands for a different proposition: When state officers are charged with violating federal law, they cannot set up the state's federal constitutional sovereign immunity to defeat suits for prospective relief.[288]

The Court made this clear in *Home Telephone & Telegraph v. Los Angeles*.[289] In that case, Chief Justice White explained that state and local officers *do* act for the state when they perform their official duties, even if it turns out that their behavior violates state law. The telephone company sued city officials in federal court, seeking an injunction against rates the company insisted were in violation of due process.[290] The officials responded that if the company was right that the rates violated due process, then they had no authority to enforce those rates and thus did not act for the state when they did so. The state constitution also barred confiscatory rates. The officers conceded that if the state constitution allowed the rates about which the company complained, the company could charge them with acting for the state. But to do that, the company would first have to sue them in state court and obtain an authoritative determination that their enforcement of the rates conformed to state law. Only then would the company be in a position to argue that the defendant officials acted for the state; only then would the company be able to advance a fourteenth amendment claim. Chief Justice White held, however, that the officers acted for the state in the fourteenth amendment "state action"

---

285. Dissenting in *Young*, Justice Harlan insisted that the plaintiffs had sued the attorney general only because he *was* the attorney general and thus meant, by enjoining his behavior on the state's behalf, to affect the state itself. 209 U.S. at 174.

286. Some observers contend that the officer suits recognized in *Young* do not really depend on a fiction, but rather have a solid historical foundation in the law of sovereign immunity. See Chapter IX, notes 80–83 and accompanying text. It may be that no fiction is required to maintain that plaintiffs can obtain compensation out of officers' own pockets. In cases of that kind, the state is neither sued nor held liable. Yet a fiction *is* required to maintain that plaintiffs are not suing the state itself when they name state officers for the very purpose of obtaining injunctive orders that those officers will follow as they perform their official duties for the state. See Eric H. Zagrans, *Under Color of What Law: A Reconstructed Model of Section 1983 Liability*, 71 Va. L. Rev. 499, 563 n.338 (1985).

287. *Larson v. Domestic & Foreign Commerce Corp.*, 337 U.S. 682 (1949); see notes 31–36 and accompanying text.

288. See notes 301–02, 308 and accompanying text.

289. 227 U.S. 278 (1913).

290. State sovereign immunity was not implicated, because the defendants were city officials. See note 59 and accompanying text. Those officers were, however, "state" officials for purposes of the fourteenth amendment.

sense, because they exercised "state power." The state "clothed" them with official authority, and that was sufficient for fourteenth amendment purposes.[291]

Chief Justice White acknowledged that a previous case, *Barney v. City of New York*,[292] had suggested that "state action" for fourteenth amendment purposes must necessarily be anchored in state positive law—e.g., a state statute or constitutional provision. But White rejected that notion out of hand. Later, in a concurring opinion in *Snowden v. Hughes*,[293] Justice Frankfurter suggested that *Barney* should be revived. Otherwise, the actions of a "policeman on the beat would be state action for purposes of suit in a federal court."[294] It may have seemed to Frankfurter that a police officer who violates state positive law cannot be said to act for the state in the fourteenth amendment sense. But that is precisely what *Home Telephone* held, and it is precisely what the Court has held ever since.[295] To do otherwise would be to rob the fourteenth amendment of capacity to check state executive officers who abuse their authority. Justice Souter has explained that if "compliance with state law authority were a defense" to an officer suit under *Ex parte Young*, "there would be precious few *Young* suits."[296]

Frankfurter's approach would have routed cases out of federal court and into state court. Consider the scenario he envisioned: Plaintiffs who complain that state officers are violating the fourteenth amendment would first sue in state court and, in that forum, would try to establish that the officers' conduct conforms to state law. If successful, the plaintiffs would then be able to contend that the state law that authorizes that behavior must itself violate the fourteenth amendment. It is scarcely sensible to think that plaintiffs would file lawsuits in state court to argue that state officers are *complying* with state law. If it were necessary for plaintiffs to go to state court at all, they would naturally contend that defendant officers are *violating* state law. Moreover, lest plaintiffs fall victim to preclusion, they would also advance their fourteenth amendment claims in state court. If the state courts were to hold for the plaintiffs on state law grounds, the fourteenth amendment issues would not be reached. If the state courts were to determine fourteenth amendment claims, their judgments would be reviewable in the Supreme Court, but would probably be entitled to preclusive effect in an inferior federal court.[297] In the end, plaintiffs would be channeled out of federal court and into state court for the adjudication of fourteenth amendment claims that do not challenge formal state enactments.

That is precisely what Justice Frankfurter thought should happen.[298] But the full Court plainly rejected his point of view. Instead, *Ex parte Young* and *Home Telephone* neatly reconcile state sovereign immunity with the fourteenth amendment in a way that permits officer suits for injunctive relief. According to *Young*, state officers performing official state functions cannot use the state's immunity to fend off suits challenging their behavior on the state's behalf. According to *Home Telephone*, state officers nonetheless act for the state for purposes of the fourteenth amendment, even if their behavior violates state law. Private citizens may therefore seek injunctive or declaratory relief from

291. 227 U.S. at 288–89.

292. 193 U.S. 430 (1904).

293. 321 U.S. 1 (1944).

294. Id. at 16.

295. See notes 372–76 and accompanying text (discussing the related idea of officer behavior "under color" of state law for purposes of §1983).

296. *Idaho v. Coeur d'Alene Tribe*, 521 U.S. 261, 310 (1997) (dissenting opinion).

297. See Chapter VI, notes 161–85 and accompanying text (discussing issue preclusion in cases of this kind).

298. See notes 293–95 and accompanying text.

current or future violations of federal law at the hands of state officials without pausing to consider, much less to litigate, whether state officers are also violating or threatening to violate state law.[299] But for *Young* and *Home Telephone*, the large body of modern civil rights and civil liberties litigation would not exist.[300]

Modern pleading practice contemplates that officer suits will routinely be employed to produce changes in the way a state behaves, operating through its agents. When plaintiffs sue a state official seeking injunctive or declaratory orders that will, in fact, cause the officer to take action for the state, they can name the defendant officer in a "personal" or "individual" capacity. That would be in keeping with the fiction that the officer can be held to account as an ordinary citizen. Nevertheless, plaintiffs can (and more commonly do) name a state officer in an "official" capacity. That formulation reflects the reality of what is afoot: The action is not against the officer personally, but against the "office" the officer holds.[301] Relevant procedural rules encourage plaintiffs to name state officers in an official capacity in order to clarify their actual objectives. Officers sued in their official capacity can be described by their titles (rather than their personal names), and if they leave office while a lawsuit is pending, their successors in office are substituted as defendants by operation of law.[302]

In a curious opinion announcing the Court's judgment in *Idaho v. Coeur d'Alene Tribe*,[303] Justice Kennedy suggested that *Ex parte Young* is not the routinely available device for eluding state immunity that it is generally supposed to be. The tribe sued Idaho officials in federal court, seeking a declaration that the tribe had rightful title to a parcel of real estate and an injunction barring the defendant officers from exercising any regulatory authority with respect to the land. Justice Kennedy marshaled a five-member majority to support his holding that the suit was barred by state sovereign immunity, *Ex parte Young* notwithstanding.[304] In the main, he explained that the suit was effectively an action to quiet title to the property and that it implicated "special sovereignty interests" in land, water, and regulatory authority that ordinary officer suits do not.[305]

---

299. For example, *Ex parte Young* explains why state prisoners need not be concerned about state sovereign immunity when they petition the federal courts for a writ of habeas corpus running to the wardens of state penitentiaries (but effectively challenging their convictions in state court). See *Seminole Tribe*, 517 U.S. at 178 (Souter, J., dissenting).

300. The Court did not have civil rights and civil liberties cases in mind in 1908. By all accounts, *Ex parte Young* was of a piece with *Lochner v. New York*, 198 U.S. 45 (1905). The Court needed a means of circumventing state immunity in order to enforce economic due process claims in the federal forum. See Michael G. Collins, *Economic Rights, Implied Constitutional Actions and the Scope of Section 1983*, 77 Gtn. L.J. 1493, 1494–95 (1989); Herbert Hovenkamp, *Judicial Restraint and Constitutional Federalism: The Supreme Court's Lopez and Seminole Tribe Decisions*, 96 Colum. L. Rev. 2213, 2246 (1996).

301. *Brandon v. Holt*, 469 U.S. 464, 470–71 (1985); *Hutto v. Finney*, 437 U.S. 678, 693 (1978); see *Will v. Michigan Dep't of State Police*, 491 U.S. 58, 71 (1989); but see notes 347–48 and accompanying text (discussing suits for compensatory relief).

302. Fed. R. Civ. P. 25(d). See *Hafer v. Melo*, 502 U.S. 21, 25 (1991); *Brandon*, 469 U.S. at 470–71.

303. 521 U.S. 261 (1997).

304. Justices Stevens, Ginsburg, and Breyer joined Justice Souter's dissent both from the Court's holding and from its analysis. Id. at 297 (dissenting opinion).

305. Id. at 281 (plurality opinion). Writing for the Court in *California v. Deep Sea Research*, 523 U.S. 491 (1998), Justice O'Connor explained that state sovereign immunity does not affect suits in which federal courts exercise *in rem* jurisdiction over personal property not in the state's possession. In a concurring opinion, Justice Kennedy suggested that federal constitutional state sovereign immunity might be inapplicable to *any* suit involving *in rem* jurisdiction of personal items (like the sunken cargo in *Deep Sea Research*). Id. at 510.

Apart from that holding, Justice Kennedy offered a novel explanation of *Ex parte Young*. Joined in this only by Chief Justice Rehnquist, Kennedy said that plaintiffs' ability to advance officer suits under *Young* depends on a "careful balancing and accommodation of state interests" on a "case-by-case" basis. Courts, he said, must consider the availability of a lawsuit in state court, the nature of the federal claims to be considered, and any "special factors counselling hesitation."[306] The dissenters in *Coeur d'Alene* dismissed Justice Kennedy's attempt to "redefine" the *Young* doctrine.[307] Justice O'Connor also disclaimed Kennedy's discussion of *Young* in a sharply worded concurring opinion, joined by Justice Scalia and Justice Thomas. By Justice O'Connor's (controlling) account, *Young* continues to supply a means of avoiding state sovereign immunity when plaintiffs sue state officials alleging an "*ongoing* violation of federal law" and seeking "*prospective* rather than *retrospective*" relief.[308] Accordingly, federal courts are not to determine the availability of an officer suit on the basis of an *ad hoc* examination of factors.[309]

An officer suit pursuant to *Ex parte Young* performs only one function: It evades the state's sovereign immunity. Plaintiffs must independently satisfy the other requirements for obtaining federal adjudication of their claims on the merits. For example, plaintiffs must have a right of action—that is, an authorization to take their claims to court. In many instances, plaintiffs can rely on §1983 for that purpose.[310] If §1983 had been un-

306. *Coeur d'Alene*, 521 U.S. at 280, quoting *Bivens*, 403 U.S. at 396; see Chapter VIII, text accompanying note 221. While Justice Kennedy said that the "nature" of a plaintiff's claim should be a factor for consideration, he did not suggest that officer suits should be allowed in federal court only to advance constitutional (rather than federal statutory) claims. Even if a claim is statutory, it remains part of the supreme law, and its enforcement against state officers comports with the supremacy point of *Young*. Nevertheless, Professor Jackson argues that Kennedy's opinion in *Coeur d'Alene* and Chief Justice Rehnquist's opinion for the Court in *Seminole Tribe* illustrate a resurgence of the "federalist" perspective on the role of federal courts. Vicki C. Jackson, *Coeur d'Alene, Federal Courts and the Supremacy of Federal Law: The Competing Paradigms of Chief Justices Marshall and Rehnquist*, 15 Const. Comm. 301 (1998); see Chapter I, note 20 and accompanying text. In *Corey v. White*, 457 U.S. 85 (1982), the Court held that a state's federal constitutional sovereign immunity barred a federal interpleader action that, in form, alleged no violation of federal law of any kind, but merely asked the federal court to decide which of two competing states was entitled to administer Howard Hughes' estate. Since *Corey* was a dispute between two states, the rule of decision was a matter of federal common law. Yet in the peculiar procedural posture of the case, neither side alleged that the other was actually *violating* that law.

307. *Coeur d'Alene*, 521 U.S. at 298 (Souter, J., dissenting).

308. Id. at 294 (O'Connor, J., concurring) (emphasis in original). See *Verizon v. Pub. Svc. Comm'n*, 122 S.Ct. 1753, 1760 (2002) (embracing Justice O'Connor's account of *Ex parte Young* on behalf of the full Court); but see id. at 1761 (Kennedy, J., concurring) (reiterating his position *Coeur d'Alene*).

309. After the tribe itself was barred from suing the state of Idaho, the United States advanced similar claims in an independent lawsuit, advancing both its own sovereign and quasi-sovereign interests and the interests of the tribe, as well. That lawsuit was successful. *Idaho v. United States*, 533 U.S. 262, 271 n.4 (2001) (explaining that Idaho could not set up state sovereign immunity to defeat a suit brought by the United States). See notes 63–66 and accompanying text (explaining that suits by the United States are exempt from state sovereign immunity). If it was Justice Kennedy's suggestion that courts must make *ad hoc* judgments about the availability of *Ex parte Young* that troubled the other justices, it may be that they would warm to a systematic attempt to define entire categories of cases in some rule-oriented way and to carve those categories out of *Young* at wholesale. For a discussion, see Eric B. Wolff, *Coeur d'Alene and Existential Categories for Sovereign Immunity Cases*, 86 Calif. L. Rev. 879 (1998).

310. See Chapter VIII, notes 132, 135–36, 166–83 and accompanying text. In *McKune v. Lile*, 122 S.Ct. 2017 (2002), for example, the Court entertained a §1983 action filed by a prison inmate against state officers alleged to be threatening to punish him for asserting the privilege against self-

derstood in 1908 in the way it is understood today, the suit in *Ex parte Young* would have been filed as a §1983 action. At that time, however, §1983 served only plaintiffs pressing personal liberty claims, not the "property" claims the shareholders in *Young* meant to vindicate.[311] In the event, the Court did not rely on §1983 (or any other statute) to supply a right of action in *Young*. The explanation is probably that the Court attached no great significance to the "right of action" issue with which the justices are so vitally concerned today or, rather, that they operated on the common law assumption that a right and an ability to complain to a court about a violation of that right were one and the same.[312] It is important to understand, however, that the existence of a right of action and the effect of state sovereign immunity are now analytically distinct ideas. The Court in *Young* decided both questions in favor of the plaintiffs, but provided an explanation only for the latter.[313]

Recall, too, that a district court's subject matter jurisdiction is yet another matter, distinguishable both from the sovereign immunity defense and from a plaintiff's right of action. The Court itself can be maddeningly confusing about these different (albeit related) ideas.[314] Chief Justice Rehnquist's opinion in *Seminole Tribe*[315] provides an illustration. In one part of his analysis in *Seminole Tribe*, the Chief Justice suggested that he meant to make some adjustment in the meaning of *Ex parte Young* as a device for eluding state sovereign immunity. He then mingled the availability of an officer suit under *Young* with "jurisdiction." Finally, he actually held that an officer suit was barred for want of a right of action.

Chief Justice Rehnquist initially read the Indian Gaming Act to prescribe a suit against a state in its own name as the mechanism for forcing the state to negotiate with an Indian tribe over the tribe's plans to operate a casino.[316] He found a suit of that kind to be barred by state sovereign immunity. Thereafter, he turned to the tribe's alternative theory that it could sue the governor as a state officer, relying on *Ex parte Young* to defuse the state's immunity. He rejected that argument as well and, in so doing, invited the understanding that he meant to revise the status of *Young* as a constitutional matter.[317] He explained that by specifying a suit against the state as the

---

incrimination (established by the fifth amendment and protected against state authority by the fourteenth).

311. E.g., *Holt v. Indiana Mfg. Co.*, 176 U.S. 68, 72 (1900) (limiting §1983 to "civil rights" claims); see *Lynch v. Household Finance Corp.*, 405 U.S. 538 (1972) (surveying early attempts to distinguish "liberty" claims and "property" claims for purposes of §1983).

312. See Chapter VIII, note 120. Some observers contend that the Court operated on the assumption that a right of action was implied in the fourteenth amendment. E.g., Daniel J. Meltzer, *The Seminole Decision and State Sovereign Immunity*, 1996 Sup. Ct. Rev. 1, 38; Monaghan, note 213, at 130–31. See Chapter VIII, note 215 and accompanying text (noting that the Court has found a right of action implied in the Due Process Clause of the fifth amendment). Others argue that *Young* proceeded from the premise that the Supremacy Clause creates a right of action to sue state officers for injunctive relief whenever they violate the Constitution. See Chapter VIII, note 364 and accompanying text.

313. Whatever the Court may have been thinking in *Young*, Professor Harrison urges the current Court to hold that the fourteenth amendment only nullifies state action inconsistent with its substantive provisions and that a right of action to advance a claim in court must have an independent source—e.g., a statute like §1983. John Harrison, *Jurisdiction, Congressional Power, and Constitutional Remedies*, 86 Gtn. L.J. 2513 (1998). See Chapter VIII, note 217.

314. See Chapter VIII, notes 291–331 (discussing the linkage in some cases between the existence of a right of action and the interpretation of adjacent jurisdictional statutes).

315. *Seminole Tribe v. Florida*, 517 U.S. 44 (1996); see notes 141–49 and accompanying text.

316. See text accompanying note 144.

317. See Vicki C. Jackson, *Seminole Tribe, the Eleventh Amendment, and the Potential Evisceration of Ex parte Young*, 72 N.Y.U. L. Rev. 495, 530, 542 (1997).

means by which the Act was to be enforced, Congress had indicated that it had no wish to authorize an officer suit, as well. The Act prescribed a "detailed remedial scheme" complete with a variety of limitations on the suit it authorized against the state. If the Court allowed the tribe to repackage its action as an officer suit against the governor, the Court would not only defeat Congress' purpose to authorize only a suit against the state, but also would override the limitations that Congress had fixed for a suit of that kind by itself permitting the tribe to employ an officer suit that would be free of those restrictions.[318]

When he expressed his conclusion on this point, the Chief Justice explained that since *Ex parte Young* was "inapplicable," the tribe's action in *Seminole Tribe* was barred by state sovereign immunity and thus "must be dismissed for lack of *jurisdiction*."[319] That was misleading. There was no genuine question regarding the district court's subject matter jurisdiction to entertain the tribe's lawsuit. If the state of Florida had consented to the tribe's suit, the district court would have proceeded with the case in the ordinary course. The Act itself conferred jurisdiction for purposes of a suit against a state. Likewise, there was no question that the district court had jurisdiction to entertain an officer suit against the governor. The special jurisdictional provision in the Act would not have answered, but the general federal question jurisdictional statute, 28 U.S.C. §1331, certainly would have.[320] The Chief Justice must have used the term "jurisdiction" loosely—as the Court is wont to do in sovereign immunity cases.[321] He should have said that since Congress had implicitly foreclosed an officer suit, the tribe's suit against the state was the only legal action to be considered. And since the suit against the state was barred by sovereign immunity, it was subject to dismissal. That dismissal was not for want of subject matter jurisdiction in the ordinary sense. Yet sovereign immunity "partakes of the nature of a jurisdictional bar" and thus often has the effect of a jurisdictional defect.[322]

The Chief Justice also should have explained that if he permitted the tribe to shift to a suit against the governor (in order to avoid the state's sovereign immunity via *Ex parte Young*), it would do the tribe no good. The tribe still would face the problem of finding an authority to sue the governor in some other source. Since no other source existed, a suit by the tribe against the governor would be subject to dismissal on that basis alone. In fact, Chief Justice Rehnquist came ever so close to explaining his result in precisely that way. He drew an analogy to *Schweiker v. Chilicky*,[323] one of the cases in which the Court had previously held that a federal statutory scheme implicitly displaced *Bivens* actions that the Court otherwise would have allowed. He recognized that the issue in *Seminole Tribe* was not the same: In *Chilicky*, the question was whether the Court should fashion a private right of action as a matter of judge-crafted common law in a context in which Congress had established a more restricted enforcement scheme by

318. *Seminole Tribe*, 517 U.S. at 75–76.The Chief Justice noted, for example, that under the Act a state that refused to accept a mediator's recommendation was not subject to any coercive sanction. Instead, the Secretary of the Interior was authorized to establish the conditions under which the tribe's casino would operate. In an officer suit, by contrast, the governor might be held in contempt.

319. Id. at 76 (emphasis added).

320. See Chapter IV, notes 72–76 and accompanying text (explaining that an extant basis of federal court jurisdiction cannot be repealed by implication); accord *Verizon*, 122 S.Ct. at 1759 (holding that §1331 was not foreclosed by a statute that arguably conferred a more limited jurisdiction).

321. See notes 67–70 and accompanying text.

322. *Edelman v. Jordan*, 415 U.S. 651, 678 (1974) (opinion for the Court by Rehnquist, J.); see notes 341–45 and accompanying text.

323. 487 U.S. 412 (1988).

statute.[324] In *Seminole Tribe*, the question was whether the Court should invoke the *Ex parte Young* fiction to elude state sovereign immunity in a context in which Congress had authorized a more limited suit against a state in its own right. Nevertheless, he insisted that the same general principle applied in both instances.

Chief Justice Rehnquist hastened to make it clear that the case would have been different if Congress had authorized an officer suit against the governor, apart from or in addition to a suit against the state.[325] In that event, an officer suit would not have frustrated Congress' express enforcement program, but rather would have been part and parcel of it.[326] In the end, then, the problem the tribe could not surmount was neither the governor's ability to assert the state's immunity to defeat an officer suit (the governor had no such capacity) nor some defect in the district court's jurisdiction to entertain an officer suit (there was no such defect), but rather the absence of congressional authorization to enforce the Act via private litigation against a state officer.[327] Reflecting on that understanding, one might wonder why the Chief Justice did not consider whether §1983 could supply the necessary procedural vehicle.[328] One answer is that the tribe did not advance that argument. A better answer is that the Indian Gaming Act created no "rights" redressable via §1983.[329] The best answer is that §1983 lawsuits, like *Bivens* actions, can be displaced by alternative enforcement schemes that occupy the field.[330] Having held that Congress had foreclosed an officer suit against the governor, Chief Justice Rehnquist presumably would have held in the same breath that Congress had eclipsed a §1983 action by necessary implication.[331]

This general understanding of *Seminole Tribe* is confirmed by *Verizon v. Pub. Svc. Comm'n*.[332] The Telecommunications Act of 1996 obligated companies providing telephone service to form agreements regarding their related activities, subject to approval by a state public utility authority. The Verizon company entered an agreement with the WorldCom firm. The companies quarreled about whether that agreement obligated Verizon to compensate WorldCom for certain uses of WorldCom's facilities. Verizon complained to the Maryland Public Service Commission, contending that under the Act and a recent FCC order the commission was obliged to hold that the agreement did not require the disputed payments. The state commission held that state contract law re-

---

324. See Chapter VIII, notes 224–26 and accompanying text.

325. *Seminole Tribe*, 517 U.S. at 75 n.17.

326. See Wayne L. Baker, *Seminole Speaks to Sovereign Immunity and Ex Parte Young*, 71 St. John's L. Rev. 739 (1997) (explaining that even after *Seminole Tribe* Congress might resolve matters simply by amending the Act to authorize officer suits).

327. Note that Chief Justice Rehnquist did not anticipate the revisionist appraisal of *Young* itself that he and Justice Kennedy later advanced (for themselves alone) in *Coeur d'Alene*. See notes 303–09 and accompanying text.

328. Recall that §1983 can authorize a suit to enforce at least some federal statutes. See Chapter VIII, notes 166–71 and accompanying text.

329. See Chapter VIII, notes 175–83 and accompanying text.

330. E.g., *Middlesex County Sewerage Auth. v. Nat'l Sea Clammers Ass'n*, 453 U.S. 1 (1981). See Chapter VIII, notes 169–70 and accompanying text. According to Professor Currie, "*Seminole Tribe* was just another application of the *Sea Clammers* principle." David P. Currie, *Ex Parte Young After Seminole Tribe*, 72 N.Y.U. L. Rev. 547, 549 (1997). Accord Monaghan, note 135, at 128–29.

331. But see Meltzer, note 238, at 39–40 (contending that in the absence of clear statutory language to the contrary the Court should have held that §1983 provided a right of action to enforce the Act in a suit against a state officer).

332. 122 S.Ct. 1864 (2002).

quired Verizon to pay. Verizon then filed suit in a federal district court, seeking declaratory and injunctive relief on the theory that the commission's action was preempted by federal law. Verizon named the individual members of the state commission as defendants and invoked federal jurisdiction under §1331. The defendants responded on three fronts. First, they argued that a special jurisdictional provision in the Telecommunications Act denied the district court jurisdiction to entertain Verizon's preemption claim and thus foreclosed jurisdiction under §1331 by negative implication. Second, they argued that the Act gave Verizon no private right of action to challenge the commission's order and, accordingly, that the district court had no jurisdiction to adjudicate such a suit. Third, they argued that the Act established a particularized remedial scheme that displaced an officer suit against individual commissioners. Accordingly, *Ex parte Young* did not defuse a sovereign immunity defense.

In the Supreme Court, Justice Scalia squarely rejected the defendants' first and third arguments. He held that the Telecommunications Act did not explicitly purport to withdraw the district court's ordinary jurisdiction to adjudicate preemption claims under §1331.[333] In that vein, he confirmed that federal jurisdiction cannot be repealed by implication.[334] He also held that the Act did not foreclose an officer suit against individual commissioners. He explained that the Telecommunications Act established no "detailed and exclusive remedial scheme like the one in *Seminole Tribe*" that implicitly precluded an action relying on *Ex parte Young*.[335] Specifically, he said that the Telecommunications Act, by contrast to the Indian Gaming Act, displayed no "intent to foreclose *jurisdiction* under *Ex parte Young*."[336] In referring to "jurisdiction," however, he only followed the Court's (unfortunate) tendency to describe sovereign immunity in jurisdictional terms.[337] Justice Scalia was circumspect with respect to the argument that Verizon had no right of action to attack the commission's order and that the district court therefore had no jurisdiction. He explained that he had no occasion to express an opinion on the "premise" of that argument (that is, the defendants' contention that Verizon had no right of action). Even if the defendants were right about that, it would make no jurisdictional difference. In the Court's cases, "the absence of a valid (as opposed to arguable) cause of action does not implicate subject matter jurisdiction."[338] Since the lower court had rested its judgment against Verizon on jurisdictional grounds, Justice Scalia reversed and remanded for further proceedings. That left the potentially dispositive right-of-action question to the circuit court in the first instance.[339]

---

333. See *Shaw v. Delta Airlines*, 463 U.S. 85 (1983); Chapter VIII, note 362 and accompanying text.

334. See note 320 and accompanying text.

335. *Verizon*, 122 S.Ct. at 1761.

336. Id. (emphasis added).

337. See notes 67–70 and accompanying text.

338. 122 S.Ct. at 1758, citing *Steel Co. v. Citizens for a Better Environment*, 523 U.S. 83, 89 (1998). In *Steel*, of course, the Court relied on *Bell v. Hood*. See Chapter VIII, note 262 and accompanying text.

339. Justice Scalia probably understood that Verizon *did* have a right of action to challenge the commission's order. Apart from the Telecommunications Act, there is a body of precedent supporting private suits by litigants who claim that they are subject to state regulation that conflicts with federal law and thus advance preemption arguments under the Supremacy Clause. See Chapter VIII, notes 361–64 and accompanying text (discussing the right-of-action issues in those cases). Justice Scalia explained, in any case, that neither Verizon's assertion of a right of action nor its substantive claim was "wholly insubstantial and frivolous." Accordingly, the district court had jurisdiction to entertain those arguments. See Chapter VIII, notes 258–62 and accompanying text (discussing *Bell v. Hood*).

2. Suits for Retrospective Relief

Plaintiffs can use officer suits to elude the state's sovereign immunity only if they seek injunctive or declaratory orders that terminate or forestall a current or impending violation of federal law. Plaintiffs who sue state officers seeking relief with respect to a violation of their federal rights in the past are understood to sue the state itself—and state immunity establishes a bar. If, for example, plaintiffs seek compensatory damages to be paid from the state treasury, the state is the "real, substantial party in interest," even if individual state officers are the "nominal defendants."[340] In the leading modern case, *Edelman v. Jordan*,[341] private plaintiffs claimed that they had been denied federal monetary aid under a Social Security program administered by state officials. They filed a §1983 action in federal court, naming state officers as defendants and contending that those officers had denied them the payments to which they were entitled—in violation of federal regulations and the fourteenth amendment. The plaintiffs sought a declaration that the defendants had acted unlawfully and an injunction requiring them to give the plaintiffs the money that had been wrongfully withheld. Then-Justice Rehnquist held that the action was barred by state sovereign immunity.

Justice Rehnquist explained that the plaintiffs' suit was not an attempt to hold the state officers individually liable for unpaid benefits and thus to seek compensation from those officers personally. Instead, the plaintiffs clearly meant to reach the state treasury. They hoped to hold the state itself accountable for a "monetary loss" resulting from a "past breach of a legal duty" by the state's agents. In that critical respect, the plaintiffs' action was more like *Ayers* than *Ex parte Young*.[342] Justice Rehnquist acknowledged that *Young* would permit plaintiffs to obtain forward-looking injunctive orders that might entail the expenditure of state funds in the future. But *Young* did not justify an injunction that would constitute, in effect, an award of compensatory damages against the state for failing to meet legal obligations in the past.

The distinction in *Edelman* between prospective and retrospective relief is hard to defend. State officers will inevitably spend state funds in order to comply with any injunctive order, even one that addresses only the future.[343] Justice Rehnquist explained in *Edelman* that prospective orders are comparatively manageable inasmuch as the state has an opportunity to budget for any increased disbursements that must be made. Orders that require a state to make unplanned expenditures to compensate for past misdeeds are, by their nature, more likely to disrupt the state's current efforts to manage its own affairs.[344] Yet courts can always establish a future payment schedule for compen-

---

340. *Ford Motor Co.*, 323 U.S. at 464. Recall, however, that plaintiffs face no similar sovereign immunity barrier if they sue state officers for compensation to be paid from the officers' own pockets. See notes 18–20 and accompanying text (explaining this point with respect to suits against federal officers).

341. 415 U.S. 651 (1974).

342. *In re Ayers*, 123 U.S. 443 (1887); see text accompanying notes 280–82.

343. See Pamela S. Karlan, *The Irony of Immunity: The Eleventh Amendment, Irreparable Injury, and Section 1983*, 53 Stan. L. Rev. 1311, 1314 (2001) (explaining that the costs of complying with injunctions often far exceed the amounts that might be awarded as compensatory damages).

344. 415 U.S. at 666 n.11. The circuit court below in *Edelman* treated the plaintiffs' prayer for relief as a request for "equitable restitution." Justice Rehnquist rejected that characterization of the case. Id. at 668. It is not coincidental that Rehnquist offered a similar analysis of the effects on state budgets in his opinion for the Court in *Nat'l League of Cities v. Usery*, 426 U.S. 833 (1976). See notes 96–97, 211–23 (noting the parallels between the Court's decisions on congressional power and its decisions regarding state sovereign immunity). There is, however, a long tradition distinguishing

satory damages, so that states can equally budget for making backward-looking payments. As a practical matter, *Edelman* puts a state that concededly violated federal law in the past in a better position than a state that is attempting to comply with federal law in the future.[345]

The distinction in *Edelman* is also hard to administer.[346] Yet it survives intact. Plaintiffs who sue state officials seeking compensation for violations of federal law in the past must look to the officers' themselves, not to the treasury of the state the officers serve.

(for immunity purposes) between actions sounding in contract and actions sounding in tort. See Jaffe, note 21, at 29.

345. The Court has explained that *Edelman* was not exclusively concerned with the effect on the state's budget, but saw that effect as evidence that the state was the real party in interest. *Corey*, 457 U.S. at 90–91. Cf. *Arizonans for Official English v. Arizona*, 520 U.S. 43, 69 n.24 (1997) (indicating that *Edelman* bars even a nominal award of damages if it is to be paid from the state treasury). Professor Jeffries has argued that the law should prefer forward-looking injunctions (however costly) to backward-looking compensatory awards for a different reason. By his account, reparatory awards to the victims of past wrongs soak up scarce state funds that would be better spent on implementing changes that will forestall similar wrongs in the future. The expenditure of public funds to prevent future harms, in turn, works a redistribution of wealth to younger generations that stand to benefit from desirable innovations in the content and implementation of federal law. John C. Jeffries, Jr., *The Right-Remedy Gap in Constitutional Law*, 109 Yale L.J. 87 (1999). Professor Hills has offered a public choice account of the Court's distinction between injunctions and monetary awards. By his account, limiting relief to injunctions enhances the ability of local elected officials to superintend the appointed bureaucrats who administer state agencies. Bureaucrats who support the aims that plaintiffs seek to further may not seriously resist damage awards, which are typically paid from the state's general treasury. So elected officials need the protection that state immunity offers against inappropriate financial liability. Bureaucrats are more likely to resist injunctions, because their agencies typically bear the costs of implementation. In the case of injunctions, then, local elected officials need less insurance against illegitimate liability. Moreover, according to Hills, elected officials are in a position to superintend bureaucrats as they spend state funds in the course of implementing forward-looking injunctions. See Roderick M. Hills, Jr., *The Eleventh Amendment as a Curb on Bureaucratic Power*, 53 Stan. L. Rev. 1225 (2001). Professor Pfander has pointed out that Congress evidently hopes to defuse any untoward incentives among agency officials by insisting that agencies reimburse the general treasury for disbursements made to cover damage awards. Pfander, note 175, at 836 n.77 (describing the Judgment Fund, 31 U.S.C. §1304).

346. In *Quern v. Jordan*, 440 U.S. 332 (1979), the Court held that the district court could order the state officers in *Edelman* to spend state funds in order to notify the members of the plaintiff class that they could still seek payments via state administrative procedures. But in *Green v. Mansour*, 474 U.S. 64 (1985), the Court held that state sovereign immunity barred a suit for a declaratory judgment that state officials had violated federal law regarding AFDC benefits and an order requiring state officials to notify individuals of their entitlement to benefits. In *Green*, the state officers had already conformed to federal law and there was no prospective injunction to which a notification order could be attached. In *Milliken v. Bradley*, 433 U.S. 267 (1977), the Court found no sovereign immunity bar to an injunction requiring state officers to expend state funds to pay for remedial programs for students whose education suffered because they had been assigned to racially segregated schools. In *Hutto v. Finney*, 437 U.S. 678 (1978), the Court approved an award of attorneys fees "ancillary" to a prospective injunction regarding prison conditions. The fees compensated counsel for work in the past, but the Court treated them as tantamount to court costs. In *Papasan v. Allain*, 478 U.S. 265 (1986), the Court held that state sovereign immunity prevented children from obtaining funding for their schools on the theory that state officials had unlawfully administered public lands held in trust for the schools. The Court rejected the argument that the state officers were engaged in an ongoing breach of the trust, but, instead, read the complaint to seek redress for a violation of federal law in the past. For an argument that the Court has not consistently applied its own doctrine, see Carlos Manuel Vazquez, *Night and Day: Coeur d'Alene, Breard, and the Unraveling of the Prospective/Retrospective Distinction in Eleventh Amendment Doctrine*, 87 Gtn. L.J. 7 (1998) (suggesting that the Court should distinguish instead between compensatory damages and other forms of relief).

Pleading practice bears this out. If a plaintiff names a state officer in an official capacity, seeking backward-looking compensatory relief, the plaintiff will be understood to be seeking money from the state's treasury and thus to be suing the state. In that event, the plaintiff faces a sovereign immunity bar, unless Congress has abrogated the state's immunity or the state has consented to the suit.[347] Plaintiffs who hope to impose liability on individual officers must name those officers in an individual or personal capacity in order to signal that they do not hope to reach the state treasury. That will eliminate sovereign immunity from the picture.[348] If a plaintiff sues an officer in the officer's individual capacity for compensation from the officer's personal assets and the officer leaves office before the matter is settled, the plaintiff must pursue the named defendant into private life. If a plaintiff names an officer in an individual capacity and the officer dies before execution on a judgment, the plaintiff must pursue the decedent's personal estate.[349]

3. Suits to Enforce State Law

When plaintiffs file officer suits in federal court, advancing both federal claims and supplemental state claims for injunctive or declaratory relief, only the federal claims can have the benefit of *Ex parte Young*. In *Pennhurst State School & Hosp. v. Halderman*,[350] residents at a state hospital for the mentally ill sued state and county officials, contending that those officers were operating the institution in violation of a federal statute, relevant state statutes, and the fourteenth amendment. The district court sustained all three claims and issued an injunction requiring the defendant officers to make sweeping changes in the way the institution would be managed in the future. The circuit court affirmed, but only on the basis of the federal statutory claim. The Supreme Court overturned that judgment on the ground that the federal statute did not establish substantive federal rights in the plaintiffs.[351] On remand, the circuit court turned next to the plaintiffs' state claims in order to avoid the fourteenth amendment issue, if possible.[352] When the circuit reaffirmed its judgment on the basis of state law, the Supreme Court reversed yet again.

Justice Powell explained that officer suits in federal court pursuant to *Ex parte Young* can be justified in order to "vindicate federal rights and hold state officials responsible

347. *Kentucky v. Graham*, 473 U.S. 159, 166 (1985) (explaining that a suit naming an officer of a governmental entity in an official capacity is "treated as a suit against the entity" in "all respects other than name"); *Will*, 491 U.S. at 71 (confirming the point).

348. *Hafer*, 502 U.S. at 30.

349. *Graham*, 473 U.S. at 166 n. 11. But see notes 424–94 and accompanying text (discussing official immunity). A state may voluntarily indemnify state officers who are held personally liable. Insurance typically has no affect on state sovereign immunity. *Jackson v. Georgia Dep't of Transp.*, 16 F.3d 1573 (11th Cir. 1994). Cf. *Regents of the University of California v. Doe*, 519 U.S. 425, 431 (1997) (explaining that a state does not surrender its immunity by purchasing insurance and thus making a private insurance company liable to pay judgments). Professor Jeffries finds *Edelman* analytically unsound, but thinks no great harm is done. Plaintiffs can impose personal liability on individual officers, and when that happens the state is likely to be "bound by conscience" to indemnify them. John C. Jeffries, Jr., *In Praise of the Eleventh Amendment and Section 1983*, 84 Va. L. Rev. 47, 61 (1998). But see Mark R. Brown, *The Failure of Fault Under §1983: Municipal Liability for State Law Enforcement*, 84 Cornell L. Rev. 1503 (1999) (arguing that most victims of public wrongdoing go without relief).

350. 465 U.S. 89 (1984).

351. See Chapter VIII, text accompanying note 175.

352. See Chapter VIII, note 414 and accompanying text (discussing the *Siler* case).

to 'the supreme authority of the United States.'"[353] When, by contrast, plaintiffs seek to enforce state law, there is no such justification for denying a state's sovereign immunity from suit in federal court.[354] Justice Powell plainly assumed in *Pennhurst* that the state's federal constitutional immunity would not defeat a suit on the plaintiffs' state law claims in state court.[355] If states can resist state claims in state court as well as in federal court, plaintiffs have no tribunal at all in which to litigate—absent a state's willingness to consent to be sued despite its immunity.[356]

The result in *Pennhurst* might have been predicted. The plaintiffs' suit was a public rights class action inviting the district court to issue a structural injunction requiring far-reaching changes in the operation of a state institution.[357] The district court's injunctive order was comprehensive and contemplated the appointment of a special master to monitor its implementation over time. In the 1980s, that was precisely the kind of lawsuit the Court meant to discourage.[358] Nevertheless, the means by which the Court brought the district court to heel was surprising. Justice Powell might have focused on the scope of the relief below and set about curbing the district court's aggressive use of federal equitable remedies.[359] Instead, he located a federal constitutional bar to the lawsuit in the first instance. Historians debate whether *Pennhurst* had intellectual precursors. Prior to that case, state sovereign immunity had been concerned with plaintiffs' choice of defendants and their requests for relief, not with the nature of their substantive claims.[360]

---

353. *Pennhurst*, 465 U.S. at 105, quoting *Ex parte Young*, 209 U.S. at 160.

354. Justice Powell spent most of his opinion responding to a vigorous dissent by Justice Stevens. The two debated a welter of old decisions, particularly *Larson*, in hopes of fortifying their opposing positions. See notes 31–35 and accompanying text. Powell contended that *Larson* demonstrates that officer suits are not typically available to advance non-constitutional claims, unless agents act entirely *ultra vires* "without any authority whatever." Id. at 102 n.11, quoting *Larson*, 337 U.S. at 694. Stevens, for his part, insisted that *Larson* actually stands for the proposition that officers act *ultra vires* whenever they commit acts that are either unauthorized or forbidden by statute. Professor Shapiro faults Justice Powell for carrying the (erroneous) *Larson* decision a step further into even more error. By Shapiro's account, the only basis Justice Powell had for concluding that the defendants in *Pennhurst* had acted within their statutory authority was the lower court's decision that they could rely on qualified immunity to avoid personal liability for damages. See notes 446–94 and accompanying text. Justice Powell thus contrived to translate a form of personal immunity meant to safeguard individual officers' assets into a blanket governmental immunity from suit for injunctive relief. David L. Shapiro, *Wrong Turns: The Eleventh Amendment and the Pennhurst Case*, 98 Harv. L. Rev. 61, 75–76 (1984).

355. The Court's more recent decision in *Alden v. Maine* arguably draws that assumption into question. See notes 177–80 and accompanying text.

356. Apart from the federal constitutional immunity implicated in *Alden*, the states have always been able to assert their own local, state-law immunity from suit in state court. That possibility certainly existed at the time *Pennhurst* was decided and, *ceteris paribus*, might have defeated the state claims in that case once the plaintiffs moved to state court.

357. See Chapter I, notes 78–91 and accompanying text.

358. Professor Rudenstine and Professor Dwyer regard *Pennhurst* as primarily a response to what the Court considered to be overly aggressive "institutional" litigation. David Rudenstine, *Pennhurst and the Scope of Federal Judicial Power to Reform Social Institutions*, 6 Cardozo L. Rev. 71 (1984); John P. Dwyer, *Pendent Jurisdiction and the Eleventh Amendment*, 75 Calif. L. Rev. 129 (1987).

359. See Chapter IX, notes 409–15 and accompanying text (describing the Court's use of the ripeness doctrine to limit the availability of injunctive relief in class action civil rights cases).

360. Most academic treatments of *Pennhurst* are critical. E.g., Louise Weinberg, *The New Judicial Federalism: Where Are We Now?*, 19 Ga. L. Rev. 1075, 1078–79 (1985); George D. Brown, *Beyond Pennhurst—Protective Jurisdiction, the Eleventh Amendment, and the Power of Congress to Enlarge Federal Jurisdiction in Response to the Burger Court*, 71 Va. L. Rev. 343 (1985); Erwin

The decision in *Pennhurst* has implications for supplemental jurisdiction over state law claims.[361] By hypothesis, state officers can assert the state's immunity from suit on a state claim in a federal district court.[362] Accordingly, the court will have no opportunity to dispose of a dispute on state grounds rather than face a federal issue. That is the ordinary path prescribed by *Siler v. Louisville & Nashville R.R. Co.*[363] But it is not open in cases controlled by *Pennhurst*.[364] More fundamentally, *Pennhurst* forecloses supplemental jurisdiction altogether when a plaintiff sues state officers, thus frustrating (in this kind of case) the rationales that underlie 28 U.S.C. §1367. A plaintiff who wishes to advance both federal and state claims against state authorities faces unattractive options. Federal adjudication of the state claim is unavailable. A state court may be open to consider that claim, provided the defendant state officers do not set up sovereign immunity there, as well. Accordingly, the plaintiff can choose either to file a single action in state court (joining both federal and state claims), or to file two actions (one in federal court to advance the federal claim and another in state court to press the state claim). In the first scenario, the plaintiff must surrender the very thing that §1367 appears to offer: an ability to litigate a federal claim in federal court without sacrificing a related state claim. In the second, the plaintiff can preserve the federal forum for the federal claim, but only at the cost of inefficiency. If the plaintiff chooses to sue in both courts at once, further questions arise. The state court may be willing to stay its hand while the federal court proceeds.[365] If, however, the state court plunges ahead and completes its work first, the

---

Chemerinsky, *State Sovereignty and Federal Court Power: The Eleventh Amendment After Pennhurst v. Halderman*, 12 Hastings Const. L.Q. 643 (1985); Robert H. Smith, *Pennhurst v. Halderman: The Eleventh Amendment, Erie, and Pendent State Law Claims*, 34 Buffalo L. Rev. 227 (1985). Professor Jackson notes, however, that to the extent *Pennhurst* invokes immunity because a federal claim is *not* at stake, that case has the virtue of drawing attention back to what Jackson regards as the proper purview of state sovereign immunity—namely, suits that are in federal court on some basis other than the existence of federal question jurisdiction. Jackson, note 113, at 52. Professor Amar agrees, but finds the point only to underscore what Amar regards as the Court's erroneous decision in *Hans* that sovereign immunity covers federal question cases. Amar, note 126, at 1476–77. Professor Althouse applauds *Pennhurst* for inviting state courts to police their own precincts. Ann Althouse, *How to Build a Separate Sphere: Federal Courts and State Power*, 100 Harv. L. Rev. 1485 (1987).

361. See Chapter VIII, note 414 and accompanying text.

362. Of course, *Pennhurst* does not affect *every* supplemental jurisdiction case, but only those in which plaintiffs sue state officers. Moreover, Justice Powell suggested in a footnote that the sovereign immunity bar recognized in *Pennhurst* affects only officer suits for injunctive relief, not suits for compensatory damages to be paid by individuals. 465 U.S. at 111 n.21. Accordingly, plaintiffs who sue state officers for damages on federal grounds can still attach supplemental claims (for damages) on state law theories. Justice Powell did not mention suits for declaratory relief, but it is hard to think that sovereign immunity does not treat declaratory judgments like injunctions in this context. Professor Shapiro suggests that if declaratory relief can be granted, but no follow-on injunctions can issue, it is still likely that declaratory judgments themselves can have preclusive effect between the parties. Shapiro, note 354, at 82.

363. 213 U.S. 175 (1909); see Chapter VIII, note 414 and accompanying text.

364. See Robert A. Schapiro, *Polyphonic Federalism: State Constitutions in the Federal Courts*, 87 Calif. L. Rev. 1409, 1423 (1999).

365. The federal district court would have no obvious reason to stay its treatment of the federal claim while the state court considers the state claim. The *Pullman* abstention doctrine contemplates postponements of that kind only when a litigant invokes a federal court's supplemental jurisdiction over related state law issues. See Chapter XI, notes 80–84 and accompanying text. For a discussion of the complications created by the combination of *Pennhurst* and *Pullman*, see Keith Werhan, *Pullman Abstention After Pennhurst: A Comment on Judicial Federalism*, 27 Wm. & Mary L. Rev. 449 (1986).

resulting state judgment will be reviewable only in the Supreme Court. It will almost certainly be entitled to some form of preclusive effect in the federal district court in which the plaintiff's federal claim is pending.[366]

D. The Ku Klux Klan Act

Officer suits naming state agents as defendants typically rely on 42 U.S.C. §1983 for the right of action required.[367] The Supreme Court recognizes as much and has construed §1983 to conform to the immunity environment in which officers suits typically operate. Recall that §1983 does not abrogate a state's federal constitutional sovereign immunity from unconsented suits.[368] Consistently, the Court has held that a state is not a "person" within the meaning of §1983 and thus cannot be named as a defendant in a §1983 action.[369]

The Court has also conformed §1983 to *Home Telephone*.[370] In that case, the Court clarified an element of a substantive fourteenth amendment claim (the requirement that the action of which the plaintiff complains must be ascribable to the state). In this context, the task has been to explain an element of the right of action that §1983 supplies for advancing substantive claims (often fourteenth amendment claims). By its terms, §1983 authorizes lawsuits only against defendants who act under "color" of a state "statute, ordinance, regulation, custom or usage."[371] In *Monroe v. Pape*,[372] the Court held that the "color of law" requirement in §1983 tracks the "state action" requirement in the fourteenth amendment. Officers act under color of state law when they exercise the offi-

---

366. See Chapter VI, notes 161–95 and accompanying text (discussing preclusion); Shapiro, note 354, at 80–81. Presumably, litigants cannot be faulted for failing to advance state claims in federal court in the teeth of a sovereign immunity bar. Yet they might well be expected to press federal claims in state court. So state preclusion law might well foreclose a federal claim that was not, but might have been, advanced in state court along with related state claims. Moreover, state law may give preclusive effect to findings of fact made by the state court for purposes of determining the state claim but equally pertinent to the federal claim.

367. See Chapter II, text accompanying notes 74–76; Chapter VIII, notes 132, 200 and accompanying text.

368. See note 237 and accompanying text.

369. *Will*, 491 U.S. at 71. See also *Ngiraingas v. Sanchez*, 495 U.S. 182 (1990) (holding that an American territory is not a person for §1983 purposes). Nor is a state a "person" for purposes of being a plaintiff in a §1983 action. *South Carolina v. Katzenbach*, 383 U.S. 301, 323–24 (1966); cf. *Breard v. Greene*, 523 U.S. 371, 378 (1998) (explaining that the same goes for a foreign nation). The Court said in *Will* that an officer sued in an official capacity for compensatory relief counts as the state and thus is not a person for §1983 purposes. That comports with the understanding that suits of that kind are genuinely against the state itself. See note 347 and accompanying text. The Court made it clear, however, that an officer sued in an official capacity for injunctive relief *is* a person. Accordingly, §1983 can supply the right of action required for modern suits of the kind the Court approved in *Ex parte Young*. *Will*, 491 U.S. at 71 n.10; see notes 301–02 and accompanying text. Nevertheless, in light of *Will*, plaintiffs cannot sue a *state* in a §1983 action (in either state or federal court), even if the state consents. 491 U.S. at 85 (Brennan, J., dissenting) (lamenting this implication); *Arizonans for Official English*, 520 U.S. at 69 (confirming it).

370. See notes 289–300 and accompanying text.

371. See Chapter VIII, text accompanying note 135.

372. 365 U.S. 167 (1961).

cial authority in which they are "clothed," even if they actually violate state law.[373] The plaintiffs in *Monroe* filed a §1983 action against Chicago police officers, contending that the officers had violated the plaintiffs' fourteenth amendment rights by breaking into their home and conducting an unreasonable search. The officers responded that they had not acted under color of state law for purposes of §1983, because Illinois law did not authorize them to commit the acts of which the plaintiffs complained. In the Supreme Court, Justice Douglas explained that the defendant officers *had* acted under "color" of state law and thus could be sued in a §1983 action, irrespective of whether they had violated state law.[374] In that §1983 action, the officers could be held liable for violating the plaintiffs' fourteenth amendment rights—again without regard to whether the officers had violated state law, as well.[375] According to Justice Douglas, §1983 provides plaintiffs with a right of action for vindicating federal rights that is "supplementary" to any action they might file in state court, pressing parallel state claims arising from the same episode.[376]

In dissent, Justice Frankfurter insisted that the "color of law" requirement in §1983 should be understood to incorporate (in essence) the view that he previously took (without success) regarding "state action" for fourteenth amendment purposes.[377] In most instances, according to Frankfurter, state officers act under color of state authority only if some species of positive state law authorizes their behavior. If plaintiffs wish to charge state officers with misusing their official positions to commit unauthorized acts, the proper course is to file suit in state court in order to allow those courts to enforce state tort law. By Frankfurter's account, an "unlawful intrusion by a policeman in

373. Justice Douglas relied on *United States v. Classic*, 313 U.S. 299 (1941); *Screws v. United States*, 325 U.S. 91 (1945); and *Williams v. United States*, 341 U.S. 97 (1951). In those cases, the Court construed other statutes from the Reconstruction era, which contain the same "color of law" language found in §1983. In the main, defendants act under color of law (and thus are subject to suit via §1983) if their behavior can be ascribed to the state (and thus counts as state action for purposes of the fourteenth amendment). That is what makes §1983 the common right-of-action vehicle for fourteenth amendment claims. Most defendants in §1983 suits are employees of state or local government. Conceptually, however, the "color of law" category is larger than the "state action" category. Otherwise, the Court would be unable to reach the fourteenth amendment "state action" question in a §1983 action. Every case would be resolved on the basis of the analytically prior, nonconstitutional question whether the defendant acted under color of law. As it is, the Court assumes (*sub silentio*) that a defendant's behavior was under color of law for §1983 purposes and then focuses on whether that action was ascribable to the state for purposes of the fourteenth amendment. Some cases are easy, others more controversial. In *Lugar v. Edmondson*, 457 U.S. 922 (1982), Justice White mustered only a bare majority for a holding that the conduct of private parties is state action when they participate jointly with state officials in the seizure of disputed property. See Chapter XI, notes 257–58 and accompanying text (discussing the *Lugar* dissenters' disinclination to rely on that case in *Pennzoil v. Texaco*).

374. The Court has since held that §1983 actions can be filed in both federal and state court. See Chapter VI, text accompanying note 54. In *Monroe*, however, the point was that the plaintiffs were entitled to choose the federal forum if they wished, relying on §1983 for a right of action and on a separate statute, §1343(3), for the district court's jurisdiction. Today, §1983 actions invariably rest on §1331 for subject matter jurisdiction in federal court. See Chapter VIII, note 136.

375. Recall that §1983 supplies no substantive rights itself, but serves only as a procedural vehicle for pressing other rights (typically fourteenth amendment rights) in court.

376. 365 U.S. at 183. Douglas relied on legislative history indicating that Congress enacted §1983 *because* the Ku Klux Klan, often acting in concert with local authorities, was abusing private citizens in the teeth of state statutes condemning Klan violence.

377. See notes 293–98 and accompanying text.

Chicago" should entail no "different consequences" than an "unlawful intrusion by a hoodlum." Justice Frankfurter acknowledged that §1983 authorizes suits against officers acting under color of "custom or usage" and that, in that way, appears not to require that they have explicit authority in a formal state statute. Yet he contended that any qualifying "custom or usage" must be so settled and systematic as to have the "cast of law."[378]

With respect to "state action" (for purposes of the fourteenth amendment), Justice Frankfurter insisted that no instance of officer behavior should count, unless and until a state court delivers an authoritative judgment that it conforms to state law.[379] That arrangement would drive fourteenth amendment suits against abusive state executive officers into state court. Plaintiffs would retain only the ability to attack state statutes or constitutional provisions as themselves inconsistent with federal law. With respect to action under "color of law" (for purposes of §1983), Frankfurter was less severe. On that account, he said it should be enough if plaintiffs can point to some state statute or clear systematic practice authorizing the officers' behavior. As a practical matter, however, Frankfurter's view of the "color of law" requirement would also channel plaintiffs into state court in cases in which they allege that executive officers have abused their official authority. That, in turn, would produce the same consequences that would have attended his interpretation of "state action."[380]

Justice Frankfurter plainly hoped to interpret §1983 in a way that would divert litigation into state court. But in 1961, when *Monroe* was decided, the Supreme Court just as plainly meant to open the federal courts for the adjudication of federal claims, particularly civil rights and civil liberties claims under the fourteenth amendment. By holding that §1983 supplied the required right of action, the Court built upon the foundation laid in *Ex parte Young* and *Home Telephone* to erect a general framework for litigation of that kind. Prior to *Monroe*, §1983 had largely been used only in officer suits seeking injunctive relief from ongoing violations of federal law. In *Monroe*, the Court recruited

---

378. 365 U.S. at 236 (dissenting opinion). Frankfurter thus insisted that the plaintiffs' suit in *Monroe* could not go forward on the basis of their general allegation that the defendant officers had violated the fourteenth amendment—ignoring unquestioned evidence that state law, too, condemned the same conduct. Frankfurter acknowledged, however, that the plaintiffs alleged that the officers acted in some respects on the basis of settled and systematic practices. He conceded that the §1983 action might be allowed to proceed, limited to those particular allegations. Frankfurter's unsuccessful proposal for interpreting §1983 thus tracked the interpretation the Court has given the civil rights removal statute, 28 U.S.C. §1443. See Chapter VI, notes 144–60 and accompanying text.

379. 365 U.S. at 211.

380. Concurring in *Monroe*, Justice Harlan said he would have found the debate between Douglas and Frankfurter "close" if the Court had not previously adopted Justice Douglas' interpretation of the "color of law" formulation. See note 373. Yet on the merits of Frankfurter's position, Harlan said he could not be persuaded that the Reconstruction Congress that wrote §1983 would have wished to force plaintiffs into state court in the absence of a formal enactment or settled practice authorizing officer behavior. The point of enacting §1983 was not that state law formally permitted state officers to mistreat the citizenry, but that citizens were being mistreated despite the requirements of state law. 365 U.S. at 487. Professor Zagrans contends that Frankfurter had the better of the historical argument. Zagrans, note 286. Professor Winter sides with Douglas. Steven L. Winter, *The Meaning of "Under Color of" Law*, 91 Mich. L. Rev. 323 (1992). Dissenting in *Crawford-El v. Britton*, 523 U.S. 574 (1998), Justice Scalia expressed sympathy for Frankfurter's position on the "color of law" question. Id. at 611. Justice Thomas joined Scalia's attack on *Monroe's* analysis. But see David Achtenberg, *A Milder Measure of Villainy: The Unknown History of 42 U.S.C. §1983 and the Meaning of Under Color of Law*, 1999 Utah L. Rev. 1 (offering additional legislative history supporting *Monroe*).

§1983 to service as a vehicle for officer suits seeking compensatory relief for violations in the past.[381] Today, the availability of a §1983 action in federal court is typically the *sine qua non* of a successful challenge to the actions of state officers.[382]

The text of §1983 merely establishes a right of action and does not address ancillary questions that can arise. The Supreme Court fashions rules and procedures for §1983 actions as a matter of federal common law, typically by borrowing from the law of tort and analogous state law rules.[383] Pursuant to 42 U.S.C. §1988, the losing party can be taxed for the winner's reasonable attorney fees. Liability for attorney fees under §1988 follows liability on the merits. Accordingly, if state officers are held personally liable for damages, they must equally pay the plaintiffs' attorney fees. The state that employs them cannot be liable to pay damages, both because the state cannot be a defendant in a §1983 action and because a state enjoys sovereign immunity. Accordingly, a state cannot be liable for attorney fees in a suit for damages.[384] If, on the other hand, attorney fees are awarded in officer suits for injunctive or declaratory relief, state officers can be ordered to pay fees from state sources, state sovereign immunity notwithstanding.[385] Suc-

---

381. On the significance of *Monroe* in this respect, see Michael Wells, *Constitutional Torts, Common Law Torts, and Due Process of Law*, 72 Chicago-Kent L. Rev. 617, 620 (1997); Christina B. Whitman, *Emphasizing the Constitutional in Constitutional Torts*, 72 Chicago-Kent L. Rev. 661, 664–66 (1997). Professor Weinberg points out that the Court decided *Monroe* in the midst of its decisions applying the Bill of Rights to the states. She argues that *Monroe* supplied a means of enforcing those rights (most of them rights against abusive police behavior) in cases in which plaintiffs had already been harmed and wanted compensation for their injuries. Louise Weinberg, *The Monroe Mystery Solved: Beyond the "Unhappy History" Theory of Civil Rights Litigation*, 1991 B.Y.U. L. Rev. 737, 757.

382. For exhaustive treatments of §1983, see Sheldon H. Nahmod, Civil Rights and Civil Liberties Litigation: The Law of Section 1983 (4th ed. 1997); *Developments in the Law: Section 1983 and Federalism*, 90 Harv. L. Rev. 1133 (1977). For an ideological assessment of §1983 and its potential, see Jack M. Beermann, *A Critical Approach to Section 1983 With Special Attention to the Sources of Law*, 42 Stan. L. Rev. 51 (1989).

383. The Court occasionally relies upon 42 U.S.C. §1988, which instructs federal courts to apply state law in §1983 actions when federal law is "deficient." E.g., *Wilson v. Garcia*, 471 U.S. 261 (1985) (adopting a state statute of limitations); *Robertson v. Wegmann*, 436 U.S. 584, 594–95 (1978) (adopting a state rule of survivorship). But see *Felder v. Casey*, 487 U.S. 131 (1988) (rejecting a state notice requirement because it would routinely frustrate the enforcement of federal rights). For discussions of §1988, see Seth F. Kreimer, *The Source of Law in Civil Rights Actions: Some Old Light on Section 1988*, 133 U. Pa. L. Rev. 601 (1985); Theodore Eisenberg, *State Law in Federal Civil Rights Cases: The Proper Scope of Section 1988*, 128 U. Pa. L. Rev. 499 (1980). Here again, the Court departs from the textualism that characterizes its construction of other statutes. See Harold S. Lewis, Jr. & Theodore Y. Blumoff, *Reshaping Section 1983's Asymmetry*, 140 U. Pa. L. Rev. 755, 760 (1992) (describing §1983 as "almost entirely a judicial construct"); Chapter I, notes 30–43 and accompanying text (discussing the Court's usual emphasis on the text of statutes). Professor Beermann argues that the Court eschews a more textual approach to §1983, because it would not serve the Court's "conservative agenda." Jack M. Beermann, *Common Law Elements of the Section 1983 Action*, 72 Chicago-Kent L. Rev. 695, 699 (1997). Professor Wells contends that §1983 will not bear the meaning required of a workable right-of-action statute. He argues that the Court should set §1983 aside, find a right of action implied in the Due Process Clause, and proceed to elaborate that right of action as a matter of constitutional tort law. Michael Wells, *The Past and the Future of Constitutional Torts: From Statutory Interpretation to Common Law Rules*, 19 Conn. L. Rev. 53 (1986). See note 312 (discussing the possibility of a right of action implied in the fourteenth amendment); Chapter VIII, notes 209–14 and accompanying text (discussing implied actions generally).

384. *Graham*, 473 U.S. at 167–68.

385. See note 346 (noting the *Hutto* case).

cessful plaintiffs typically recover fees under §1988.[386] Successful defendants can do so only if the actions against them are frivolous or vexatious.[387]

1. Suits Against Cities and Counties

While a state cannot be a "person" within the meaning of §1983, a city or county can be. The Supreme Court held as much in *Monell v. Dep't of Social Svc.*[388] Recall that cities and counties have no federal constitutional sovereign immunity from suit.[389] The construction that *Monell* placed on §1983 is inconsequential in cases in which plaintiffs seek injunctive or declaratory relief. Plaintiffs are able to name cities and counties as corporate entities. But that formality adds nothing of substance. Plaintiffs can pursue the same kinds of prospective relief in officer suits against individual local officials. The *Monell* decision is significant, by contrast, if plaintiffs sue for retrospective relief. Given *Monell*, plaintiffs can use §1983 suits to seek compensation directly from local government coffers. Justice Brennan explained in *Monell*, however, that cities and counties cannot be held liable to pay compensation for the misdeeds of their agents on the principle of *respondeat superior*.[390] They are accountable in money damages only for actions traceable to a "law, statute, ordinance, regulation, custom, or usage" that can "fairly be said to represent official policy."[391] As a practical matter, then, *Monell* does with respect to the liability of cities and counties what Justice Frankfurter tried (but failed) to do with respect to the liability of individual state officers: To obtain compensation, plaintiffs must tie a violation of their federal rights to a general policy or custom ascribable

386. *Maher v. Gagne*, 448 U.S. 122 (1980).

387. *Hughes v. Rowe*, 449 U.S. 5 (1980).

388. 436 U.S. 658 (1978). The Court took the other view in *Monroe*, but *Monell* squarely overruled *Monroe* on this point, relying on a reassessment of the relevant legislative history. Id. at 690. Cf. *Mt. Healthy Bd. of Ed. v. Doyle*, 429 U.S. 274, 277–79 (1977) (noting but failing to decide the question whether a local school board can be subject to suit under §1983).

389. See note 59 and accompanying text.

390. Justice Stevens dissented on this point. Professor Kramer and Professor Sykes contend that Stevens had the better of the argument. Larry Kramer & Alan O. Sykes, *Municipal Liability Under §1983: A Legal and Economic Analysis*, 1987 Sup. Ct. Rev. 249, 261–62. Cf. *Bd. of County Comm'rs v. Brown*, 520 U.S. 397, 430 (1997) (Breyer, J., dissenting) (urging the Court to reconsider *Monell's* rejection of *respondeat superior* liability).

391. 436 U.S. at 691, 694, quoting the text of §1983. The rule is not that a city or county can be liable only if a policy or custom itself violates a plaintiff's federal rights. The rule is that a city or county can be liable only if there is a "direct causal link" between a policy or custom and the action of the employee that, in turn, violates the plaintiff's rights, *City of Canton v. Harris*, 489 U.S. 378, 385 (1989), so that the policy or custom is the "moving force" behind the violation that occurs. *Brown*, 520 U.S. at 404. In *Harris*, accordingly, the Court said that the city would be liable for failing to train police officers if it were shown to maintain a policy of "deliberate indifference" to the federal rights of persons with whom poorly trained officers would come into contact. The Court remanded the case in order that the plaintiff could attempt to demonstrate such a policy. In the wake of that resounding victory, there was no noticeable upturn in the number of successful §1983 actions grounded on a "failure to train" theory. Even if a city or county authorizes unconstitutional activity, there can be no corporate liability unless some officer actually commits a violation. *City of Los Angeles v. Heller*, 475 U.S. 796 (1986). For a discussion of the advantages and disadvantages of *respondeat superior* in §1983 cases, see Lewis & Blumoff, note 383; Note, *Government Tort Liability*, 111 Harv. L. Rev. 2009 (1998).

to the corporate body.[392] Legislative enactments will suffice. Customs that are so widespread as to have the force of law will also answer, even though they have not been formally approved. Isolated decisions by the governing bodies concerned will do, albeit those decisions are not framed as general rules.[393] The Court has had difficulty with cases in which individual city or county officers have authority to make general policy and plaintiffs claim they have done so when making particular decisions.[394]

2. Constitutional Torts

The right of action established by §1983 bears an uneasy relationship to the law of tort. In the groundwork case, *Monroe v. Pape*,[395] Justice Douglas declared that §1983 "should be read against the background of tort liability that makes a man responsible for the natural consequences of his actions."[396] Plaintiffs who employ §1983 must necessarily seek to vindicate some right secured by federal law. The content of a claim advanced in a §1983 lawsuit is neither more nor less than the content of the federal right

392. See notes 293–98 and accompanying text. If the point is to deter violations of federal rights, there is a case to be made for visiting liability on officers personally. See Peter H. Schuck, Suing Government: Citizen Remedies for Official Wrongs 68 (1983). If, however, the point is compensation for victims, most commentators argue that it is important to reach the public treasury. E.g., Brown, note 349; Ronald A. Cass, *Damage Suits Against Public Officers*, 129 U. Pa. L. Rev. 1110 (1981); Jon O. Newman, *Suing the Lawbreakers: Proposals to Strengthen the Section 1983 Damage Remedy for Law Enforcers' Misconduct*, 87 Yale L.J. 447 (1978); Peter Schuck, *Municipal Liability Under Section 1983: Some Lessons from Tort Law and Organization Theory*, 77 Gtn. L.J. 1753 (1989). According to one (dated) study, police misconduct suits rarely produce compensation awards. *Project: Suing the Police in Federal Court*, 88 Yale L.J. 781 (1979). For updated discussions, see Pillard, note 20; Symposium, *Section 1983 Municipal Liability in Civil Rights Litigation*, 48 DePaul L. Rev. 619 (1999).

393. E.g., *Owen v. City of Independence*, 445 U.S. 622 (1980) (holding a city liable for the city council's violation of due process in summarily dismissing an employee); *Newport v. Fact Concerts*, 453 U.S. 247 (1981) (holding a city responsible for the city council's violation of the first amendment in summarily canceling a concert).

394. Compare *Pembaur v. City of Cincinnati*, 475 U.S. 469 (1986) (holding a county liable for an authoritative decision by a prosecutor), with *City of St. Louis v. Praprotnik*, 485 U.S. 112 (1988) (declining to hold a city liable for the actions of two senior supervisors in dismissing a subordinate). In both *Pembaur* and *Praprotnik*, the Court took account of local law in making the determination whether the relevant officer enjoyed policy-making authority. In *McMillian v. Monroe County*, 520 U.S. 781 (1997), the Court held that, as a matter of state law, a sheriff acting in a law enforcement capacity was a state, not a county, officer. Accordingly, the plaintiffs' claim for compensatory relief could succeed only if it was repackaged as a suit to obtain damages from the sheriff personally. For a discussion of *Pembaur*, *Praprotnik*, and related cases, see Jack M. Beermann, *Municipal Responsibility for Constitutional Torts*, 48 DePaul L. Rev. 627, 652–65 (1999).

395. See notes 372–76 and accompanying text. For discussions of these problems, see Susan Bandes, *Monell, Parratt, Daniels & Davidson: Distinguishing a Custom or Policy from a Random, Unauthorized Act*, 72 Iowa L. Rev. 101 (1986); Michael J. Gerhardt, *The Monell Legacy: Balancing Federalism Concerns and Municipal Accountability Under Section 1983*, 62 So. Calif. L. Rev. 539 (1989).

396. 365 U.S. at 187. Douglas offered this statement by way of distinguishing civil actions for damages under §1983 from criminal prosecutions under 18 U.S.C. §242, in which it is necessary for the prosecution to prove that a defendant acted "wilfully" and thus with a "specific intent to deprive a person of a federal right." *Monroe*, 365 U.S. at 187, quoting *Screws*, 325 U.S. at 103. Douglas did not mean that tort law determines the state of mind required for civil liability under §1983. He meant that §1983 does not require proof that a defendant was aware of the plaintiff's federal rights and subjectively intended to violate those rights.

the plaintiff hopes to establish. Suits under §1983 actions merely supply occasions for interpreting and applying federal constitutional and statutory rights on their own (federal) bottom.[397] Most Supreme Court decisions reflect this understanding. The Court elaborates the meaning of federal claims without suggesting that it makes any difference that plaintiffs present those claims in a §1983 action rather than by some other means.[398]

In *Parratt v. Taylor*,[399] for example, a state prison inmate ordered a hobby kit from a mail order house. The kit was lost or stolen after its arrival at the institution. The prisoner filed a §1983 action in federal court, contending that the defendants (the manager of the prison's hobby center and the warden) had deprived him of his property without due process of law. The prisoner did not explicitly allege that the defendants acted deliberately; his complaint could be read to complain only that they had been negligent. Then-Justice Rehnquist first decided what he regarded as a question of statutory interpretation: whether negligence would "support a claim for relief under §1983." He found nothing in §1983 to condition liability on "a particular state of mind" and thus relied on Justice Douglas' statement in *Monroe* that the ordinary "natural consequences" rule in tort law should apply.[400] That was a mistake. Later, in *Daniels v. Williams*,[401] Justice Rehnquist repudiated *Parratt* on this point. He explained that if a defendant's liability turns on a "state of mind," it is only because that mental state is an element of the claim that the plaintiff advances in a §1983 action. Treating the "state of mind" issue in that way, Justice Rehnquist decided in *Daniels* that negligence cannot constitute a "deprivation" of property within the meaning of the Due Process Clause.[402]

Nevertheless, in cases in which plaintiffs seek compensatory damages (either from officers themselves or from a city or county), the Court often insists that §1983 "creates a species of tort liability."[403] By referring to tort law, the Court may only mean to recognize that a defendant's behavior often constitutes both a violation of the plaintiff's federal rights for purposes of §1983 and a common law wrong, compensable under state law.[404] Alternatively, the Court may mean to acknowledge that it consults tort principles

---

397. Many provisions of the Constitution have roots in the common law, and the Supreme Court routinely consults common law materials in coming to an authoritative decision regarding their meaning. That, however, is only familiar interpretive methodology. It does not deny that the law being interpreted has an independent federal existence.

398. See *Baker v. McCollan*, 443 U.S. 137 (1979) (explaining that it is insufficient for plaintiffs in §1983 actions to allege the elements of common law torts and that it is essential that they allege violations of federal rights). Professor Whitman applauds this approach and discourages the notion that the common law of tort can provide a "useful model for constitutional decision-making." Whitman, note 381, at 661.

399. 451 U.S. 527 (1981).

400. See text accompanying note 396.

401. 474 U.S. 327, 330 (1986).

402. See *Brown*, 520 U.S. at 405 (confirming that §1983 itself contains no "state-of-mind" requirement and that plaintiffs must establish only the "state of mind required to prove the underlying violation"); *Farmer v. Brennan*, 511 U.S. 825, 834 (1994) (explaining that the "deliberate indifference" state of mind necessary to a meritorious eighth amendment claim is a function of the eighth amendment itself). Professor Gildin points out that the defendant's state of mind may figure in the availability of qualified immunity. Gary S. Gildin, *The Standard of Culpability in Section 1983 and Bivens Actions: The Prima Facie Case, Qualified Immunity and the Constitution*, 11 Hofstra L. Rev. 557, 560 (1983); see notes 446–94 and accompanying text.

403. *Memphis Community School Dist. v. Stachura*, 477 U.S. 299, 305 (1986).

404. See notes 374–76 and accompanying text.

when it chooses federal rules to govern various aspects of §1983 litigation and liability, apart from the nature of the claims that plaintiffs' advance.[405] There are decisions, however, in which it is hard to isolate the Court's references to tort law from its articulation of the elements of plaintiffs' federal claims.[406] Those decisions have baffled the lower courts and spawned yet another body of academic literature.

The overlap between §1983 suits advancing federal claims and state tort actions has important implications for the allocation of business between federal and state courts. Critics charge that by linking §1983 lawsuits to the common law of tort, the Court trivializes the federal rights that §1983 exists to enforce and lays the groundwork for relegating the enforcement of those rights to state court.[407] The Court makes it appear that

---

405. See *Carey v. Piphus*, 435 U.S. 247, 258 (1978) (explaining that "tort rules of damages" may typically be applied to §1983 actions). Professor Jeffries has explored the difficulties of computing damages to compensate plaintiffs in §1983 actions. E.g., John C. Jeffries, Jr., *Compensation for Constitutional Torts: Reflections on the Significance of Fault*, 88 Mich. L. Rev. 82 (1989); John C. Jeffries, Jr., *Damages for Constitutional Violations: The Relation of Risk to Injury in Constitutional Torts*, 75 Va. L. Rev. 1461 (1989). For a critique of Jeffries, see Sheldon H. Nahmod, *Constitutional Damages and Corrective Justice: A Different View*, 76 Va. L. Rev. 997 (1990).

406. In *Heck v. Humphrey*, 512 U.S. 477 (1994), a prison inmate filed a §1983 action in federal court, contending that state law enforcement officers had conducted an unreasonable criminal investigation, destroyed evidence, and contrived to introduce inadmissible evidence at his trial—leading to his unconstitutional conviction. He sought compensatory damages, but no injunctive relief. Justice Scalia said that the prisoner was effectively challenging the validity of his conviction, even if he was not seeking immediate release from custody. Accordingly, he was attempting to employ §1983 as a substitute for the more conventional vehicle for attacking criminal convictions—a petition for a writ of habeas corpus. The question, then, was whether the prisoner could proceed under §1983 (on the theory that he was entitled to compensation for an invalid conviction) *before* he established that the conviction was invalid by the ordinary means (a habeas corpus action). One might have expected Justice Scalia to resolve that question as a matter of statutory construction, reconciling §1983 with the statutes governing habeas corpus actions. Instead, he repeated the boilerplate that §1983 "creates a species of tort liability" and insisted that he could decide whether there was a "bar" to the plaintiff's §1983 action only by looking "first to the common law of torts." Turning to tort law, Scalia said that the "closest analogy" to the plaintiff's constitutional claim was an action for malicious prosecution. That kind of tort action contemplated that a plaintiff must first undermine the validity of a conviction by some other means and only thereafter seek compensatory damages. Importing that feature of the common law malicious prosecution tort into the plaintiff's instant §1983 action, Scalia concluded that the §1983 action was premature. The prisoner must first dislodge his conviction via habeas corpus proceedings or some comparable form of action. In dissent, Justice Souter (and three other justices) did not "object to referring to the common law" for guidance, but rather complained that Justice Scalia had allowed common law principles to override the first order of business: the proper construction of §1983. Souter then went on to offer a different assessment of the way analogous common law actions should bear on the question at hand. Professor Beermann reads *Heck* to suggest that §1983 plaintiffs must plead and prove the elements of common law torts, after all. Beermann, note 383, at 711–14. See Chapter XII, notes 561–73 and accompanying text (discussing *Heck's* relationship to habeas corpus).

407. Professor Eisenberg and Professor Schwab contend that the Court's decisions uniformly hope to limit access to the federal courts. Theodore Eisenberg & Stewart J. Schwab, *The Reality of Constitutional Tort Litigation*, 72 Cornell L. Rev. 641, 646–47 (1987). Professor Nahmod argues that by using the "rhetoric" of tort to describe §1983 actions, the Court hopes to "marginalize" §1983 litigation. Sheldon H. Nahmod, *Section 1983 Discourse: The Move From Constitution to Tort*, 77 Gtn. L.J. 1719, 1719–20 (1989). Justice Blackmun once said that the Court is "inclined to cut back on §1983 in any way" it can, short of "ignoring the language of the statute" and existing precedent. Harry A. Blackmun, *Section 1983 and Federal Protection of Individual Rights—Will the Statute Remain Alive or Fade Away?*, 60 N.Y.U. L. Rev. 1, 23 (1985). For exhaustive treatments of the cases in point, see Constitutional Torts (Nahmod, Wells & Eaton eds. 1995); Christina B. Whitman, *Government Responsibility for Constitutional Torts*, 85 Mich. L. Rev. 225 (1986); Christina B. Whitman, *Constitutional Torts*, 79 Mich. L. Rev. 5 (1980).

§1983 lawsuits threaten to shift traditional state tort claims to federal court, as plaintiffs repackage their theories for recovery as federal claims in order to litigate them under the authority provided by §1983.[408] Then, the Court justifies new limits on federal rights as a necessary response to that threat. The best illustrations are cases in which plaintiffs assert the most amorphous kind of constitutional claim: arbitrary action in violation of due process. Claims of that sort often absorb forms of wrongful treatment conventionally redressed in tort. Ostensibly to discourage plaintiffs from using §1983 to advance due process claims in federal court, the Supreme Court interprets due process itself in a way that channels litigants into state court.[409]

In *Parratt*, Justice Rehnquist understood the prisoner to advance a procedural due process claim: His property had been taken without a hearing. Rehnquist agreed that due process mandated some kind of procedure before the state "finally" deprived the prisoner of his hobby kit. But in the circumstances in *Parratt*, it was useless to propose that a hearing should have been held before the hobby kit disappeared. Since the loss or theft of the kit was "tortious," it was a "random and unauthorized" act, not the sort of thing that the state might have anticipated. Accordingly, the Due Process Clause must be satisfied by process after the fact. That process, in turn, need not be supplied by the defendants themselves at the penitentiary. It could be offered later in state court, when the prisoner sued the defendants in tort.[410] Justice Rehnquist concluded, accordingly, that

408. E.g., Marshall S. Shapo, *Constitutional Tort: Monroe v. Pape and the Frontiers Beyond*, 60 Nw. U. L. Rev. 277, 323–24 (1965). The promise of attorney fees in §1983 actions creates an additional incentive to characterize claims as federal in nature. See notes 384–87 and accompanying text. Since §1983 actions can be filed in state court, however, plaintiffs who package their claims as alleged violations of federal rights primarily to obtain attorney fees may choose to remain in the state forum. Even then, however, the elaboration of the substantive content of federal rights can be skewed if litigants merely contrive to extend those rights to cover tortious behavior in order to be in a position to win attorney fees. For a discussion, see Stewart J. Schwab & Theodore Eisenberg, *Explaining Constitutional Tort Litigation: The Influence of the Attorney Fees Statute and the Government as Defendant*, 73 Cornell L. Rev. 719, 780 (1988) (reporting inconclusive results from an empirical study).

409. E.g., *Collins v. City of Harker Heights*, 503 U.S. 115, 127 (1992) (acknowledging the Court's reluctance to elaborate the scope of substantive due process "because guideposts for responsible decisionmaking in this uncharted area are scarce and open-ended"); *Paul v. Davis*, 424 U.S. 693, 701 (1976) (expressing concern that §1983 could become a "font of tort law"); *Crawford-El*, 523 U.S. at 611 (Scalia, J., dissenting) (insisting that the Court's interpretation of §1983 in *Monroe* engages the Court in "a losing struggle to prevent the Constitution from degenerating into a general tort law"). Professor Wells acknowledges that the Court cannot very well hold that a state officer's every tortious act is a violation of the victim's constitutional rights. Tort law is subject to adjustment in the ordinary majoritarian manner. If it were constitutionalized to any significant degree, the courts (and particularly the federal courts) would displace state legislatures in the formulation of social policy on a wide scale. Wells argues that the Court should nonetheless welcome the insight that substantive due process governs cases on the boundary of constitutional law and common law tort and should rationalize its cases under a general substantive due process heading. The Court should "pay attention" to tort law, but the Court should not regard tort law as a "source" of constitutional law and certainly should not adopt a rule simply *because* it has a basis in common law. Instead, by Wells' account, the Court should elaborate *constitutional* tort law in a way that vindicates constitutional rights. Michael Wells, *Constitutional Remedies, Section 1983 and the Common Law*, 68 Miss. L.J. 157 (1998). Professor Whitman argues that "torts is a distraction" and that, to the extent the Court allows itself to worry about moving matters that might be handled as state tort actions into federal court, the Court permits the law of torts to "drive thinking about constitutional substance." Whitman, note 381, at 661.

410. In the particular case at bar, Justice Rehnquist noted that Nebraska had established a special mechanism for adjudicating prisoner claims of the kind the plaintiff wished to advance in federal court. Professor Kupfer detects tension between *Parratt's* ready acceptance of state process and

the prisoner had not "alleged a violation" of due process, because he had not challenged the adequacy of the process the state offered in the form of state judicial proceedings.[411]

The decision in *Parratt* rested on an interpretation of procedural due process. Justice Rehnquist posited a deprivation of property; the only question was when and how the state was obliged to provide the process that was due. Yet by holding that the state could satisfy due process by offering the plaintiff an opportunity to sue in state court, Rehnquist effectively barred the prisoner (and others like him) from using §1983 to press complaints in federal court. Any procedural due process claim was incomplete, unless and until the plaintiff gave the state courts an opportunity to examine the matter.[412] Justice Rehnquist did not hide the forum-allocation implications of the *Parratt* case. He explained that any other interpretation would have allowed plaintiffs to turn ordinary tortious injuries into constitutional claims to be litigated in federal court in §1983 actions.[413]

Monroe's emphasis on the value of litigation in federal court. Susan G. Kupfer, *Restructuring the Monroe Doctrine: Current Litigation Under Section 1983*, 9 Hastings Const. L.Q. 463 (1982). See also Leon Friedman, *Parratt v. Taylor: Opening and Closing the Door on Section 1983*, 9 Hastings Const. L.Q. 545 (1982).

411. The assumed negligence of the defendants' behavior in *Parratt* was not critical to the characterization of that behavior as "random and unauthorized." In *Hudson v. Palmer*, 468 U.S. 517 (1984), the Court applied the same characterization to intentional (tortious) conduct. By insisting that the prisoner's procedural due process claim must acknowledge not only any process that the prison officials offered (or failed to offer), but also the process provided by state courts, Justice Rehnquist presupposed that all the arms of the state could help satisfy the claim. That put pressure on the *Ex parte Young* "officer suit" fiction on which he implicitly rested to avoid state sovereign immunity. See notes 283–88 and accompanying text. Perhaps he can be forgiven for leaving that particular stone unturned.

412. Even when a state erroneously deprives an individual of liberty or property, it does not necessarily follow that the state has violated the individual's right to procedural due process. *Martinez v. California*, 444 U.S. 277, 284 n.9 (1980).

413. 451 U.S. at 544. It is well to consider what Justice Rehnquist did *not* hold in *Parratt*. He did *not* deny that the defendant officers had acted under color of state law. Given *Monroe*, those officers clearly *had* acted under color of law for purposes of §1983 and, given *Home Telephone*, they had equally acted for the state for purposes of the fourteenth amendment. See notes 372–75 and accompanying text. Nevertheless, Professor Alexander argues that Rehnquist actually departed from *Monroe* and *Home Telephone* and, in essence, held that state officers do not act for the state when they violate state law. Larry Alexander, *Constitutional Torts, the Supreme Court, and the Law of Noncontradiction: An Essay on Zinermon v. Burch*, 87 Nw. U. L. Rev. 576, 582 (1993). Justice Rehnquist did *not* hold that the prisoner in *Parratt* was required to exhaust state opportunities for adjudicating his claim before seeking federal adjudication. Litigants ordinarily need not exhaust state procedures before filing §1983 actions. *Patsy v. Bd. of Regents*, 457 U.S. 496 (1982); see Chapter XI, notes 47–51 and accompanying text; but see Chapter XI, note 36 (noting that prison inmates are now obliged to exhaust administrative remedies). The point in *Parratt* was not, in any case, that the state courts of Nebraska should be given the first opportunity to resolve the prisoner's claim that he had not received the process he was due. It was that the plaintiff had not been denied that process, because he had never given the state an opportunity to provide it to him: He had not filed suit in state court after suffering the loss of his property. Finally, Justice Rehnquist did *not* hold that the federal district court should have abstained from considering the prisoner's due process claim until the state courts resolved the question whether he had a meritorious state tort claim. See Chapter XI, notes 64–69 and accompanying text. Rehnquist did not propose that consideration of the prisoner's procedural due process claim should be postponed. He addressed it squarely and decided it against the plaintiff—on the theory that the prisoner had not been *denied* process that he had never sought. Professor Fallon concedes that Justice Rehnquist did not rest on abstention, but argues that the *Parratt* decision would have made more sense if he had. Richard H. Fallon, Jr., *Some Confusions About Due Process, Judicial Review, and Constitutional Remedies*, 93 Colum. L. Rev. 309, 345 (1993).

In *Zinermon v. Burch*,[414] the Court underscored that *Parratt* was a procedural due process decision. The plaintiff was found wandering the streets in a disoriented condition. He was taken to a state mental health facility, where he signed forms requesting "voluntary" admission. Under state law, the facility was entitled to accept voluntary patients only if they gave informed consent. There was no established procedure for determining whether a patient was capable of giving consent. Later, the plaintiff sued the staff members who admitted him in a §1983 action in federal court. Justice Blackmun took the plaintiff's claim to be that he had been denied procedural due process inasmuch as the defendants had committed him without engaging any procedure for determining his ability to make an intelligent decision. Distinguishing *Parratt*, Blackmun held that claim to be complete and adjudicable in federal court.[415]

Justice Blackmun explained that when a plaintiff's claim is that state officers acted in a "random and unauthorized" manner, pre-deprivation process is unnecessary and post-deprivation process by means of a state tort lawsuit will suffice. That was *Parratt*. In *Zinermon*, however, the hospital staff members did not act in a "random and unauthorized" way. They followed instructions. The difficulty arose because those instructions were incomplete. The state might well have anticipated the need for some process to determine a patient's capacity to give consent before the patient was deprived of liberty. But the state had established no such process. The plaintiff therefore could allege a complete procedural due process claim in a §1983 action without going to state court—namely, a claim that he had been denied the pre-deprivation process to which he was entitled.[416]

Plaintiffs whose procedural due process claims fall on the *Parratt* (rather than the *Zinermon*) side of the line must give the state courts an opportunity to supply the process that is due. The means for testing the adequacy of that state process is problematic. A federal district court will typically be barred from entertaining a §1983 action in which a plaintiff complains about procedural irregularities in state court.[417] The Supreme Court has appellate jurisdiction to examine any state court failure to provide due process. But, of course, that avenue is more theoretical than real. If the Court accepts a case for review, the standards the Court should apply are unclear. The prece-

---

414. 494 U.S. 113 (1990).

415. Professor Alexander faults Justice Blackmun for drawing the substance/process line in *Zinermon* and insists that, in doing so, Blackmun surrendered the opportunity that case presented to revisit (and overrule) *Parratt*. Alexander, note 413, at 587–88.

416. In dissent, Justice O'Connor accepted Justice Blackmun's premise that both *Zinermon* and *Parratt* were procedural due process cases. But she insisted that Blackmun's analysis is unworkable, because it requires courts to decide at the threshold of every case whether a need for process might have been anticipated. O'Connor argued, instead, for a blanket rule that post-deprivation process is always sufficient when plaintiffs do not attack the adequacy of existing procedural arrangements, but complain that procedures were not put in place where the need for them might have been forecast.

417. See Chapter VI, notes 161–225 and accompanying text (discussing the *Rooker* doctrine and preclusion rules applicable pursuant to the Full Faith and Credit Statute). Professor Blum has suggested that if a plaintiff initially files a §1983 action pressing a procedural due process claim, the federal court can hold that action in abeyance pending the plaintiff's pursuit of relief in state court. Later, if the plaintiff is dissatisfied with the process in state court and returns to federal court, the court can reinstate the action and review the adequacy of what the state courts did. Karen M. Blum, *Applying the Parratt/Hudson Doctrine: Defining the Scope of the Logan Established State Procedure Exception and Determining the Adequacy of State Postdeprivation Remedies*, 13 Hastings Const. L.Q. 695, 726–28 (1986). See Chapter XI, notes 96–102 and accompanying text (describing a similar procedure in state-question abstention cases).

dents in point suggest that state process may be constitutionally adequate even if state procedures are truncated and even if state immunity doctrine bars suit altogether.[418] If a state can provide the process that is due by summarily dismissing an action on the basis of sovereign immunity, then *Parratt's* interpretation of procedural due process is devastating to claims of that nature.[419]

The analysis of procedural due process claims in *Parratt* and *Zinermon* does not suffice in cases in which litigants advance substantive due process claims. In that instance, the constitutional violation is complete at the time of the defendant's initial conduct. No amount of procedure can make up for it. The Supreme Court elaborated on the substance/process distinction in *County of Sacramento v. Lewis*.[420] Police officers in a squad car chased two teenage boys on a motorcycle at speeds in excess of a hundred miles per hour. When the motorcycle tipped over on a curve, the police were going too fast to stop and skidded over one of the boys, killing him on the spot. The decedent's parents filed a §1983 action against the officers involved, claiming that their actions violated due process. In the Supreme Court, Justice Souter acknowledged that the parents did not contend that state procedures were inadequate in any way, but rather that the officers had abused their executive power. That claim was complete and adjudicable, wholly apart from the availability of state process.[421]

---

418. See, e.g., *Daniels*, 474 U.S. 332, 342 (Stevens, J., concurring); see also *Albright v. Oliver*, 510 U.S. 266, 285–86 (1994) (Kennedy, J., concurring) (suggesting that a minimum of state process will suffice). Cf. *Lujan v. G & G Fire Sprinklers*, 532 U.S. 189, 197 (2001) (holding that due process would be satisfied if a state made "ordinary judicial processes available" to a private party seeking to enforce a contract with the state).

419. See Chapter VI, notes 57–79 and accompanying text. Then, too, if this is *Parratt's* end-product, there may be a conflict with the decisions requiring the states to provide compensation in due process "takings" cases. It is hard to think that the Court can hold that the states must give the well-heeled classes a judicial remedy for unlawful deprivations of real estate, but then can find it constitutionally satisfying for a state to refuse hospital patients any redress at all for deprivations of physical liberty. The Court relied on *Parratt* by analogy in *Williamson County Regional Planning Comm'n v. Hamilton Bank*, 473 U.S. 172, 194–96 (1985), when it held that a "takings" claim is not mature until local condemnation proceedings are complete and the state has arguably failed to provide just compensation. Then again, the Court has an unnerving habit of describing *Williamson* as a matter of "ripeness." E.g., *Palazzolo v. Rhode Island*, 533 U.S. 606, 618 (2001).

420. 523 U.S. 833 (1998).

421. Some commentators argue that *Parratt*, too, was actually a substantive due process case. The prisoner in that instance did not want more process, but simply complained that he had been victimized arbitrarily. See, e.g., Fallon, note 413, at 343–44; Michael Wells & Thomas A. Eaton, *Substantive Due Process and the Scope of Constitutional Torts*, 18 Ga. L. Rev. 201, 215–23 (1984); Henry P. Monaghan, *State Law Wrongs, State Law Remedies, and the Fourteenth Amendment*, 86 Colum. L. Rev. 979, 984–86 (1986). The Court deliberately treated the claim as a matter of procedural due process. Otherwise, the Court's wholly procedural analysis would be unintelligible. In a concurring opinion in *Albright*, Justice Kennedy nonetheless said that *Parratt* would be rendered a "dead letter" if plaintiffs could demonstrate that a state tort action was not sufficient to respond to their substantive due process claims. 510 U.S. at 285. But see *Lewis*, 523 U.S. at 856 (Kennedy, J., concurring) (acknowledging that "certain actions" are barred by substantive due process "no matter what procedures attend them"). Writing for the Court in *Florida Prepaid v. College Savings Bank*, 527 U.S. 627 (1999), Chief Justice Rehnquist said that a state's infringement of a patent, standing alone, does not violate the Constitution, but a state's failure to provide some avenue by which injured patent holders can vindicate their claims may violate due process. Id. at 643. Professor Wells has explained that if the Chief Justice meant to deal only with the possibility of an offense to *procedural* due process, his account may be sustainable. Wells points out, however, that an instance of patent infringement may count as a violation of *substantive* due process. Michael Wells, *"Available State Remedies" and the Fourteenth Amendment: Comments on Florida Prepaid v. College Savings Bank*, 33 Loy. L.A. L. Rev. 1665 (2000).

The Court is especially suspicious that substantive due process claims are only state tort claims dressed in federal clothing. In an apparent effort to delineate more clearly between state and federal theories, the Court declines to recognize substantive due process claims at all, if plaintiffs' contentions can fairly be recharacterized as claims under independent provisions of the Bill of Rights, incorporated by the fourteenth amendment.[422] In cases in which no provision of the Bill of Rights fits, the Court grapples with substantive due process theories on their own bottom. Yet the Court insists that only the most arbitrary and oppressive treatment can actually establish a violation. In *Lewis*, for example, Justice Souter explained that the plaintiffs could win only by showing that the officers' behavior "shock[ed] the conscience."[423]

E. Official Immunity

In addition to sovereign immunity (which protects government itself), defendants in officer suits may be able to defeat lawsuits challenging their behavior on the basis of official immunity (which protects government agents). Official immunity doctrine is largely the same for both federal and state officers, as well as for officers serving cities and counties.[424] The official immunity issue typically arises when plaintiffs sue federal officers, relying on a right of action implied in a constitutional provision,[425] and when

422. E.g., *Albright*, 510 U.S. at 271–73; *Graham v. Connor*, 490 U.S. 386 (1989); see *Whitley v. Albers*, 475 U.S. 312 (1986) (finding a substantive due process claim essentially subsumed by an eighth amendment claim). Cases like *Albright* and *Connor* are a twist on the old "incorporation" cases, in which many of the justices hesitated to permit litigants to rely on provisions of the Bill of Rights and preferred that they proceed on the basis of due process alone. See *Adamson v. California*, 322 U.S. 46, 124 (1947) (Frankfurter, J., concurring). Now, the Court insists that litigants must press Bill of Rights claims rather than substantive due process claims.

423. 523 U.S. at 846–47, relying explicitly on *Rochin v. California*, 342 U.S. 165 (1952). Professor Urbonya has reviewed the pre-*Lewis* lower court decisions puzzling out the elements of "excessive force" claims. See Kathryn R. Urbonya, *Establishing a Deprivation of a Constitutional Right to Personal Security Under Section 1983: The Use of Unjustified Force by State Officials in Violation of the Fourth, Fifth, and Fourteenth Amendments*, 51 Albany L. Rev. 171 (1987).

424. *Butz v. Economou*, 438 U.S. 478, 503–04 (1978). Professor Vazquez has suggested that a change in the status of official immunity may be in store. Recall that the states themselves enjoy a federal constitutional immunity from many private suits for damages. See notes 52–61 and accompanying text. In *Alden v. Maine*, however, Justice Kennedy explained that plaintiffs might still obtain compensation by suing state officials personally. 527 U.S. at 757; see note 226 and accompanying text. Professor Vazquez suggests that if plaintiffs barred from suing the states begin suing state officers individually, and if the states routinely indemnify those officers, the result will be a general pattern of damage awards for which the states are responsible—the very thing the sovereign immunity cases condemn. Of course, the states would have a formal choice in the matter; they might refuse to indemnify their officers. Yet in the absence of indemnity, a lot of people would not accept public employment. See notes 452–55 and accompanying text. Professor Vazquez puts a case in which Congress abolishes official immunity by statute. If Congress were to do that, states would be under enormous pressure to indemnify all state officers. Absent even the protection that official immunity provides, nobody in his or her right mind would take a public job. Vazquez predicts that if Congress were to dilute official immunity significantly, the Court might respond by holding that official (as well as sovereign) immunity is constitutionally grounded. That would be necessary to keep Congress from circumnavigating *Alden* by essentially coercing states into indemnifying state officers held personally liable in suits that *Alden* allows the states themselves to resist. Vazquez, note 226, at 902.

425. See Chapter VIII, notes 209–17 and accompanying text.

plaintiffs sue state and local officers, relying on §1983 to supply the required right of action.[426] Implied actions and §1983 actions are not generally subject to official immunity because of anything Congress has done.[427] The Supreme Court fashions official immunity doctrine as a species of judge-made federal law. To do so, the Court draws on two sources: (1) the immunities that governmental officers enjoyed in 1871, when §1983 was enacted; and (2) the Court's own judgment regarding the nature and scope of the immunities that should be recognized today in light of relevant policy considerations. Here again, the Court relies on tort law to elaborate federal rules for liability in lawsuits advancing constitutional claims.[428]

When officers assert that they are immune, the Supreme Court ascertains whether some similar form of immunity existed in 1871. If no such immunity was recognized at that time, the Court declines to recognize it today, even if there is a plausible reason for doing so.[429] If an immunity did exist in 1871, the Court determines the governmental function that immunity protected and the extent to which potential liability might affect officers' performance of that function today. Official immunity comes in two flavors: (1) absolute immunity; and (2) qualified immunity.[430]

---

426. See notes 132, 135–36, 200 and accompanying text. Only government officers are entitled to official immunity. In *Wyatt v. Cole*, 504 U.S. 158 (1992), the plaintiff filed a §1983 action against private citizens, contending that they had acted in concert with state officers (and thus under color of state law) but were not entitled to invoke official immunity. The Supreme Court agreed on the immunity point. Since the defendants were not state officers, they had no *official* immunity of any kind. The Court followed *Wyatt* in *Richardson v. McKnight*, 521 U.S. 399 (1997), where the defendants were prison guards employed by a private management firm. Justice Scalia and three other justices dissented in *Richardson* on the ground that the guards performed a function that was historically "public."

427. The one exception is the newly enacted prohibition on injunctive suits against judicial officers acting under color of state law. See note 434 and accompanying text. The Court generally assumes that §1983 presupposes the immunities that existed at the time it was adopted. Writing before the 1996 amendment, Professor Matasar insisted that since §1983 said nothing about immunities of any kind, the Court should infer that none was available. Richard A. Matasar, *Personal Immunities Under Section 1983: The Limits of the Court's Historical Analysis*, 40 Ark. L. Rev. 741, 771 (1987). Professor Wells contends that the Court should read §1983 not to embrace the 1871 baseline, but to delegate to the Court itself an authority to fashion immunity rules that serve the purposes of §1983 and the constitutional rights that §1983 is typically employed to enforce. Wells, note 409.

428. See notes 403–06 and accompanying text. The Court explained in *Tower v. Glover*, 467 U.S. 914 (1984), that it has no "license" to establish immunities in §1983 actions on the basis of its own views of "sound public policy" and that it will determine in every instance whether "§1983's history or purposes" contemplate an immunity. Id. at 920–24. But, in fact, the Court's actual analysis is driven by history and policy and draws nothing of significance from the statute itself.

429. In *Tower*, the Court held that public defenders have no official immunity from suit—because public defenders did not exist in 1871. 467 U.S. at 921.

430. Professor Jeffries has offered a critique of these methodological devices and the arcane inquiries they entail. He contends that the Court would do better to discard (in this context) the distinction between a violation of federal rights, on the one hand, and liability for damages, on the other. In its place, Jeffries would have the Court make explicit judgments about whether particular federal rights warrant enforcement via monetary remedies. John C. Jeffries, Jr., *Disaggregating Constitutional Torts*, 110 Yale L.J. 259 (2000). Jeffries contends that prohibiting monetary relief for the violation of some rights may promote the development of those rights. If courts are assured that they can spare executive officers any liability to pay damages, they may be more willing to find officer behavior wrongful in the first instance. Moreover, the award of injunctive orders instead of compensatory damages shifts scarce resources to the comparatively more important task of ensuring respect for rights in the future. Jeffries, note 345, at 90.

1. Absolute Immunity

Officers performing legislative functions had absolute immunity in 1871. Legislative affairs were thought to be so sensitive that it was intolerable that legislators should be exposed to suit in any way. The Court takes the same view of the matter today. If legislators abuse their authority, disgruntled constituents can call them to account at the polls. Accordingly, officers are absolutely immune from suit with respect to legislative functions, irrespective of whether plaintiffs seek compensatory damages or prospective injunctive or declaratory relief.[431] Officers performing judicial functions are largely treated in the same way. They, too, were absolutely immune from suit for compensatory damages in 1871—ostensibly to ensure that they did not temper their judgments to forestall litigation and liability. Officers performing judicial functions are equally immune from suit for monetary relief today.[432] Judges were not historically immune from suits for prospective relief.[433] But an amendment to §1983 enacted in 1996 prohibits suits for injunctions against a "judicial" officer for "an act or omission taken in a judicial capacity," unless the officer first violates a declaratory judgment or declaratory relief is "unavailable."[434] By extension of the analysis regarding judges, the Supreme Court has held that officers performing prosecutorial functions, as well as jurors and witnesses, are also absolutely immune from liability for compensatory damages.[435]

It is not enough that officers hold formal titles suggesting that they are entitled to absolute immunity. The behavior of which plaintiffs complain must genuinely fall within the governmental function to which absolute immunity attaches. The Court is inclined to be generous to legislators and judges. In *Tenney v. Brandhove*,[436] for example, the Court said that legislators acted in their legislative capacity in the conduct of a committee investigation of "un-American activities."[437] In *Stump v. Sparkman*,[438] the Court held

---

431. *Eastland v. United States Servicemen's Fund*, 421 U.S. 491 (1975) (relying on the Speech and Debate Clause protecting members of Congress); *Supreme Court of Virginia v. Consumers' Union*, 446 U.S. 719, 732–33 (1980) (holding that judges performing legislative functions are entitled to legislative immunity); *Bogan v. Scott-Harris*, 523 U.S. 44 (1998) (holding that members of local legislative bodies also enjoy absolute immunity from liability for damages). See generally Robert Reinstein & Harvey Silverglate, *Legislative Privilege and the Separation of Powers*, 86 Harv. L. Rev. 1113 (1973).

432. *Pierson v. Ray*, 386 U.S. 547 (1967) (involving ordinary judges); *Butz v. Economou*, 438 U.S. 478 (1978) (involving administrative law judges operating within federal agencies).

433. *Pulliam v. Allen*, 466 U.S. 522 (1984).

434. The 1996 amendment purports to overrule *Pulliam*, which had previously held that state judges are not immune from suits for prospective relief. An accompanying amendment to 42 U.S.C. §1988 makes state judges immune from liability for attorney fees. For background, see Don Kates, *Immunity of State Judges Under the Federal Civil Rights Acts: Pierson v. Ray Reconsidered*, 65 Nw. U. L. Rev. 615 (1970).

435. *Imbler v. Pachtman*, 424 U.S. 409 (1976) (prosecutors); *Briscoe v. LaHue*, 460 U.S. 325 (1983) (jurors and witnesses). When public prosecutors prefer charges and conduct judicial proceedings, their functions are indistinguishable for these purposes from the functions of judges. See Note, *Delimiting the Scope of Prosecutorial Immunity from Section 1983 Damage Suits*, 52 N.Y.U. L. Rev. 173 (1977). The witnesses in *Briscoe* were police officers. That made it easier for the plaintiff to contend that they acted under color of state law for purposes of §1983.

436. 341 U.S. 367 (1951).

437. Id. at 369.

438. 435 U.S. 349 (1978). The President is absolutely immune from suit regarding activities within the scope of his duties, *Nixon v. Fitzgerald*, 457 U.S. 731 (1982), but not regarding private conduct occurring before he took office. *Clinton v. Jones*, 520 U.S. 681 (1997).

that a judge acted in his judicial capacity when he summarily ordered a young woman to be sterilized without her knowledge.[439] According to *Stump*, judges surrender their absolute immunity only if they take action "in the clear absence of all jurisdiction."[440] The Court is less generous to prosecutors who extend their activities outside conventional bounds. In *Mitchell v. Forsyth*[441] and *Burns v. Reed*,[442] the Court held that prosecutors surrender their absolute immunity when they assume responsibility for directing police investigations.[443]

Absolute immunity is an affirmative defense. Plaintiffs are not obliged to anticipate that defense in an original complaint.[444] In most instances, however, defendants can and do insist upon immunity early in the process in order to avoid the burdens of discovery and trial. Typically, the availability of absolute immunity can be determined from the face of the complaint, and when that is so the matter can be resolved on the defendant's motion to dismiss for failure to state a claim for which relief can be granted.[445]

2. Qualified Immunity

Officers performing executive functions had qualified official immunity in 1871—not a blanket shield against suits of any kind for any form of relief, but a contingent immunity from suits for compensatory damages.[446] Executive officers enjoy that same kind of immunity today. Until recently, the Court held that qualified immunity had both ob-

---

439. See Irene Rosenberg, *Stump v. Sparkman: The Doctrine of Judicial Impunity*, 64 Va. L. Rev. 833 (1978). See also *Mireles v. Waco*, 502 U.S. 9 (1991) (holding that a judge acted in his judicial capacity when he ordered a public defender to be seized "with excessive force"). But see *Forrester v. White*, 484 U.S. 219 (1988) (holding that a judge did not act in a judicial capacity when he fired a probation officer). Occasionally, officers who are not denominated "judges" nonetheless perform judicial functions of a sort and thus claim absolute immunity—usually without success. E.g., *Antoine v. Byers & Anderson*, 508 U.S. 429 (1993) (holding that a court reporter did not act in a judicial capacity when preparing a trial transcript); *Cleavinger v. Saxner*, 474 U.S. 193 (1985) (holding that prison authorities did not act in a judicial capacity for these purposes when they presided at disciplinary proceedings).

440. *Stump*, 435 U.S. at 349, relying on *Bradley v. Fisher*, 80 U.S. 335, 351 (1871).

441. 472 U.S. 511 (1985).

442. 500 U.S. 478 (1991).

443. See also *Buckley v. Fitzsimmons*, 509 U.S. 259 (1993) (denying prosecutors absolute immunity with respect to statements made at a press conference); *Kalina v. Fletcher*, 522 U.S. 118 (1997) (holding that a prosecutor acted as a complaining witness when she signed an affidavit supporting an arrest warrant and thus was not entitled to absolute immunity).

444. *Gomez v. Toledo*, 446 U.S. 635, 639–41 (1980); *Connor*, 490 U.S. at 399 n.12. The Supreme Court has rejected attempts by lower courts to impose special pleading standards on plaintiffs in *Bivens* and §1983 actions. *Leatherman v. Tarrant County Narcotics Unit*, 507 U.S. 163 (1993). While those "heightened" standards went to the specificity of plaintiffs' allegations regarding the merits of their claims, they were also meant to force plaintiffs to anticipate and defuse potential immunity defenses. Cf. *Crawford-El*, 523 U.S. at 594–96 (declining to require plaintiffs to prove by "clear and convincing evidence" that defendants had the state of mind required for liability).

445. Fed. R. Civ. P. 12(b)(6). Professor Chen has explained that absolute immunity defenses tend to be relatively categorical and thus lend themselves to resolution on the pleadings. Alan K. Chen, *The Ultimate Standard: Qualified Immunity in the Age of Constitutional Balancing Tests*, 81 Iowa L. Rev. 261, 262 (1994).

446. Recall that officer suits for injunctive or declaratory relief were and remain devices for holding government to account for ongoing violations of federal law. See notes 283–88, 307–09 and accompanying text.

jective and subjective elements: Officers could avoid liability if they neither knew nor should have known that they were violating federal law and thus acted in good faith and without malice.[447] In *Harlow v. Fitzgerald*,[448] however, Justice Powell explained that qualified immunity now depends entirely on "the objective reasonableness of an official's conduct."[449] Officers "performing discretionary functions" generally "are shielded from liability from civil damages insofar as their conduct does not violate clearly established statutory or constitutional rights of which a reasonable person would have known."[450] Qualified immunity is restricted to "discretionary" functions because it is only with respect to that kind of behavior that executive officers need protection if they are to do their jobs properly.[451]

The task of specifying the qualified immunity doctrine for executive officers requires striking a balance between the desire to compensate plaintiffs whose rights have been violated, on the one hand, and the desire to respect a range of "special federal policy concerns," on the other.[452] Those policy concerns are pragmatic. Officers performing executive functions occupy the spectrum from cabinet ministers to police officers on the beat.[453] According to the Court, they should not be faced with the "specter of damages liability for judgment calls made in a legally uncertain environment."[454] The threat of trials and liability in other than extraordinary circumstances might discourage competent people from accepting public employment or, having done so, from aggressively discharging their duties.[455] Particularly in cases involving law enforcement officers, public safety suffers if officers are over-deterred and thus fail to pursue and apprehend suspects.[456] Moreover, when executive officers are forced to defend themselves at trial, "society as a whole" must bear the "expenses of litigation" and the "diversion of official energy from pressing public issues."[457]

Two aspects of qualified immunity doctrine warrant special attention: (1) the standard to which executive officers are held if they are to be immune; and (2) the procedural arrangements for addressing qualified immunity defenses.

---

447. E.g., *Wood v. Strickland*, 420 U.S. 308 (1975). See William Theis,"*Good Faith" as a Defense to Suits for Police Deprivations of Individual Rights*, 59 Minn. L. Rev. 991 (1975) (criticizing the subjective elements of the analysis in cases like *Wood*).

448. 457 U.S. 800 (1982).

449. Id. at 818.

450. Id. Professor Nahmod contends that *Harlow* marked a general retreat from the promise that *Bivens* suits and §1983 actions would effectively enforce federal rights. Sheldon H. Nahmod, *Constitutional Wrongs Without Remedies: Executive Official Immunity*, 62 Wash. U. L.Q. 221 (1984). For a discussion of qualified immunity, see Kit Kinports, *Qualified Immunity in Section 1983 Cases: The Unanswered Questions*, 23 Ga. L. Rev. 597 (1989). For an early description of the lower courts' reception of *Harlow*, see Comment, *Harlow v. Fitzgerald: The Lower Courts Implement the New Standard for Qualified Immunity Under Section 1983*, 132 U. Pa. L. Rev. 901 (1984).

451. Officers have no immunity from suit when they misperform "ministerial" duties imposed upon them by statute. See *Davis v. Scherer*, 468 U.S. 198, 196–97 n.14 (1984). In cases of that kind, the courts can evaluate officers' conduct without presuming to second-guess genuine judgment of any kind. Cf. note 48 and accompanying text (noting that the Federal Tort Claims Act similarly singles out discretionary functions for special treatment).

452. *Reynoldsville Casket Co. v. Hyde*, 514 U.S. 749, 758 (1995).

453. E.g., *Butz v. Economou*, 438 U.S. 478 (1978) (involving the agribusiness shill who served as Secretary of Agriculture in the Nixon Administration); *Malley v. Briggs*, 475 U.S. 335 (1986) (involving local police officers).

454. *Ryder v. United States*, 515 U.S. 177, 185 (1995).

455. *Harlow*, 457 U.S. at 814.

456. *Anderson v. Creighton*, 483 U.S. 635, 638 (1987).

457. *Harlow*, 457 U.S. at 814.

The standard. Executive officers are immune unless they violated federal legal rules that were "clearly established" at the time they acted.[458] The purpose of fixing clearly established law as the standard is to ensure that officers had "fair warning" that their behavior was unlawful.[459] The key to the analysis is the level of generality at which a legal rule must have been clearly established.[460] A rule can be stated abstractly, thus providing guidance for officers to follow in a variety of circumstances. For example, the fourth amendment bars "unreasonable" searches. That "reasonableness" standard has been clearly established since 1791.[461] If fourth amendment law, stated in those general terms, were sufficient to provide fair warning in every case, no police officer who conducted an "unreasonable" search would be entitled to immunity. In each instance, however, a good deal of *ad hoc* judgment is required to determine whether a particular search is "reasonable." Accordingly, the general "reasonableness" rule (clearly established as it may be in the abstract) fails to provide much guidance to officers in the field. A legal rule can also be stated at a lower level of generality. A rule of that kind generates more predictable results in actual cases and thus can deliver sufficient warning to defeat qualified immunity. In *Anderson v. Creighton*,[462] Justice Scalia explained that the legal rule that an officer is charged with violating must have been clearly established at a more "particularized" level: the "reasonableness" of the kind of search conducted in the case at bar.[463]

The Court determines whether the law that executive officers violated was clearly established primarily by examining the judicial precedents that were then in existence. If those precedents articulated the law at a level that provided the officers with fair warning that their conduct was unlawful, the officers are not immune from suits by their victims. If those precedents were insufficiently clear, the officers can be said to have acted in an objectively reasonable way even if what they did constituted a violation of a plaintiff's rights. Nobody thinks that executive officers actually read (or can be expected to read) judicial opinions in order to make themselves familiar with even clearly established rules of law. The Court only pretends that officers can obtain guidance in that way.[464] If actual knowledge were relevant, officers would have the perverse incentive to remain willfully ignorant. The fundamental point is that the "fair warning/clearly estab-

458. Id. at 818; see text accompanying note 450.

459. *United States v. Lanier*, 520 U.S. 259, 270 (1997). In the *Lanier* case, the Supreme Court construed 18 U.S.C. §242, which makes it a criminal offense to "deprive a person of rights protected by the Constitution or laws of the United States." The circuit court had reversed a conviction under that statute, in part on the theory that the defendant could be criminally responsible for depriving his victim of a federal right only if that right was even more clearly established than it would have had to be to defeat qualified immunity in a civil action. In the Supreme Court, Justice Souter rejected that construction of §242. He explained that defendants can be held either criminally liable under §242 or civilly liable under qualified immunity doctrine on the basis of the same showing of a violation of "clearly established" law.

460. The "generality" question is common in the law of federal courts. See, e.g., Chapter IV, notes 88–91 (discussing the unruly formal distinction between a legal standard and the sum of the results in a series of adjudications); Chapter XII, notes 343–55, 393–408 and accompanying text (discussing "new rules" of law within the meaning of the *Teague* doctrine and "clearly established" law within the meaning of §2254(d)).

461. Or at least since 1949, when the Court initially held that "arbitrary intrusions by the police" violate the fourteenth amendment. *Wolf v. Colorado*, 338 U.S. 25 (1949).

462. 483 U.S. 635 (1987).

463. Id. at 639.

464. See Lewis & Blumoff, note 383, at 783 (noting that the objective test for immunity is anchored in a "fiction"—the "fragile belief" that a "cop on the beat appreciates the current state of constitutional law").

lished law" formulation is neither more nor less than a means by which the Court finds a middle ground between two untenable extremes: holding executive officers accountable for every violation they commit or holding them accountable for none.

Justice Scalia explained in *Anderson* that there need be no previous "on all fours" decision squarely holding that the "very action" taken by an executive officer was unlawful. In *Hope v. Pelzer*,[465] prison guards handcuffed an inmate to a "hitching post" as punishment for "disruptive conduct." The Court of Appeals for the Eleventh Circuit held that the officers were immune, because there was no "materially similar" precedent clearly establishing that their conduct violated the eighth amendment.[466] In the Supreme Court, Justice Stevens disclaimed the circuit's "rigid gloss" on the standard for judging qualified immunity cases. The "salient question" is not whether some similar precedent specified that particular conduct was unlawful. Instead, the question is simply whether analogous precedents gave officers fair warning.[467]

Relevant precedents must be arranged in a hierarchy. Analogous Supreme Court decisions provide the best guidance regarding clearly established law. Among federal precedents, circuit decisions come next, and district court decisions come last. In *Hope*, Justice Stevens said that some of the Supreme Court's own precedents "arguably" provided the guards with the fair warning they were due. But certainly the Eleventh Circuit's own precedents were adequate.[468] Justice Stevens acknowledged that some district court precedents suggested that using the hitching post was not necessarily unconstitutional. Yet he dismissed those cases because they were distinguishable, unreported, and, in any event, "no match" for circuit-level decisions.[469]

---

465. 122 S.Ct. 2508 (2002).

466. Id. at 2515.

467. Id. at 2516; see also id. at 2515, quoting *Anderson*, 483 U.S. at 640 (stating that the precedent must have made it "apparent" that the officers' conduct was unlawful).

468. In *Lanier*, the circuit court below held that a federal criminal statute, 18 U.S.C. §242, did not give fair warning of the behavior it condemned unless the Supreme Court itself had issued a precedent or precedents clarifying a federal right and thus informing potential defendants of what would constitute a violation of that right. Justice Souter rejected that argument. He explained that lower court decisions can clarify the law both for purposes of determining whether defendants are immune from liability for damages and for purposes of determining whether defendants are criminally liable under §242. 520 U.S. at 269; see note 459.

469. Id. at 2519. It is hard to credit Justice Stevens' point that the district court decisions were unpublished. Again, no one conceives that immunity turns on the genuine likelihood that officers will be familiar with current constitutional jurisprudence. The district court decisions were rendered by courts in Alabama, where the dispute in *Hope* arose. And they involved complaints that prisoners had been handcuffed to restraining bars. If the guards in *Hope* were aware of any judicial decisions at all (which is questionable), they were more likely to be aware of those district court decisions than the decisions that the Eleventh Circuit or the Supreme Court itself had published in books stacked on library shelves. Justice Stevens also noted that the Justice Department had advised Alabama authorities that use of the hitching post violated the eighth amendment. Id. at 2518. In addition, he noted that the Alabama Department of Corrections had adopted a regulation for employing the hitching post and that the guards in *Hope* had failed to follow that regulation. Id. at 2517. Justice Thomas, for his part, argued that there was no evidence showing that the officers in *Hope* had ever been advised of the Justice Department's recommendation. Id. at 2526 (dissenting opinion). There again, it is hard to think that actual knowledge had anything to do with the analysis. It is probably a good guess that the guards *did* know about the DOJ report. Then again, the state regulation (had the guards seen it) plainly would have suggested to them that the hitching post was still a valid means of punishing prisoners for serious infractions. Justice Thomas argued that the record failed to demonstrate that the particular punishment dealt to the plaintiff amounted to a violation of the regulation. Id. at 2526.

The Court's insistence that clearly established law must be defined at a fairly low level of generality can produce confusing analysis. The availability of immunity often turns on a fact-sensitive examination of the circumstances of an individual case. That, in turn, overlaps with the merits of some federal claims.[470] Consider, again, cases in which plaintiffs allege that government officers violated their rights under the fourth amendment by subjecting them to unreasonable searches. In cases of that kind, executive officers commit a violation in the first instance by acting "unreasonably" in the circumstances presented. Nevertheless, officers are entitled to immunity if they could "reasonably" have understood that their behavior was lawful—because, at the time, the precedents did not clearly establish otherwise.[471] Writing for the Court in *Saucier v. Katz*,[472] Justice Kennedy recognized the difficulty of proposing that officers can escape liability for damages by showing that they "'reasonably' acted unreasonably."[473] Nevertheless, he insisted that the merits of a fourth amendment claim must be distinguished (and must be examined separately) from the question whether qualified immunity is available. There are two reasons for this. One is that the distinction between the merits of a claim and the availability of qualified immunity operates well (enough) in most instances, and it would be needlessly complex to create an exception for cases involving fourth amendment claims. The other is that trial judges should ordinarily determine the availability of qualified immunity before trial. If the immunity issue were collapsed into the merits in every fourth amendment case, trial judges would end up sending all cases to trial (and probably to the jury).[474]

Procedure. The question whether a plaintiff's federal rights have been violated is analytically prior to the question whether a defendant officer is immune from suit. Accordingly, Chief Justice Rehnquist explained in *Siegert v. Gilley*[475] that a court entertaining a civil action for damages against an executive officer must determine at the outset whether the plaintiff has alleged a violation of federal law.[476] This does not mean that courts routinely undertake a thoroughgoing adjudication of claims on the merits before they turn to the availability of immunity. Instead, they initially decide only whether a plaintiff's allegations, taken in the light most favorable to the plaintiff, would make out a meritorious claim.[477] The idea is to screen for cases that warrant trial. If the plaintiff's allegations would not establish a valid claim, the court must dismiss the complaint without going further. If, however, the allegations would establish a violation of a federal right, then the court turns to the immunity question—that is, the question whether that right was clearly established at the time the defendant acted.[478]

---

470. See Kathryn R. Urbonya, *Problematic Standards of Reasonableness: Qualified Immunity in Section 1983 Actions for a Police Officer's Use of Excessive Force*, 62 Temple L.Q. 61 (1989).

471. See text accompanying note 450 (quoting *Harlow*).

472. 533 U.S. 194 (2001).

473. Id. at 203, quoting *Anderson*, 483 U.S. at 643.

474. Professor Rudovsky has elaborated the effect of the Court's analysis on actual litigation. David Rudovsky, *The Qualified Immunity Doctrine in the Supreme Court: Judicial Activism and the Restriction of Constitutional Rights*, 138 U. Pa. L. Rev. 23 (1989). Professor Nourse contends that the "clear law" orientation in these and other cases suggests simplicity, but actually masks a welter of subtle jurisprudential questions touching the essential variability of law. Victoria F. Nourse, *Making Constitutional Doctrine in a Realist Age*, 145 U. Pa. L. Rev. 1401 (1997). See Chapter XII, notes 438–65 and accompanying text (discussing the "clearly established law" formulation in habeas corpus cases).

475. 500 U.S. 226 (1991).

476. Accord *McCollan*, 443 U.S. at 140; *Wilson v. Layne*, 526 U.S. 603, 609 (1999).

477. *Siegert*, 500 U.S. at 232–33.

478. *Saucier*, 533 U.S. at 200 (2001).

The Court usually insists that federal courts should avoid constitutional questions whenever possible.[479] Justice Souter explained in the *Lewis* case, however, that qualified immunity cases warrant a departure from that policy in order to ensure that federal courts clarify the standards of conduct that government officers are obliged to meet.[480] If courts were to bypass the threshold question whether a plaintiff has alleged a violation of a federal right, and were to go immediately to the availability of an immunity defense, they would routinely leave the law in a state of uncertainty. Many cases, perhaps most, would be resolved on the ground that the plaintiff's right was not established clearly enough at the time of the episode. Precedents of that kind provide no clarity regarding the true content of federal rights and thus leave both citizens and public officials in doubt. The better course, accordingly, is "to determine the right before determining whether it was previously established with clarity."[481]

Recall that plaintiffs who have suffered injury at the hands of executive officers often lack standing to seek injunctive or declaratory relief.[482] If lawsuits fail for want of standing, courts have no occasion to address the merits of plaintiffs' claims. If that were true as well in cases in which plaintiffs seek retrospective relief in the form of damages, plaintiffs would have no avenue by which to obtain a merits adjudication. It is important, then, that when plaintiffs seek monetary relief, courts do not "skip ahead" to defendant officers' immunity, but, instead, address the merits as an antecedent matter.[483] By this means, courts are able to contribute to the corpus of federal law, even though defendant officers may ultimately escape liability.[484] The system is not perfect. In *Ashcroft v. Mattis*,[485] police officers shot and killed a teenage boy. The boy's father sued both for damages and for a declaratory judgment that the state statutes authorizing the police to use deadly force were unconstitutional. The defendant officers successfully asserted immunity from liability for damages. The Supreme Court then issued a *per curiam* explaining that the father could no longer maintain an Article III case or controversy. The boy was dead and thus beyond any threat of further deadly force, the father was due no compensatory damages, and a declaratory judgment would be hypothetical.[486]

---

479. Chapter I, note 26 and accompanying text.

480. *County of Sacramento v. Lewis*, 523 U.S. 833 (1998); see notes 420–23 and accompanying text.

481. 523 U.S. at 841–42 n.5. Concurring in the judgment in *Lewis*, Justice Stevens proposed that when plaintiffs advance claims that are "both difficult and unresolved," it would be better for courts to address the immunity issue first and thus (perhaps) avoid "unnecessary" constitutional adjudication. Speaking for the full Court, Justice Souter explicitly rejected that idea.

482. See Chapter IX, notes 239–41 and accompanying text.

483. *Saucier*, 433 U.S. at 201.

484. There is no doubt that litigants seeking compensatory damages have standing to sue in an Article III court, even if it turns out (after litigation) that they cannot actually win that relief. There would be a redressability issue only if the relief prisoners seek would not redress their injuries, even if they were to obtain it. See Chapter IX, text accompanying note 224. Nor is there any doubt that a federal court can pass on the merits of a claim as an analytically anterior matter before turning to the further question whether compensatory relief can be granted. Federal judgments on the merits are not advisory merely because a particular form of relief is not forthcoming.

485. 431 U.S. 171 (1977).

486. Professor Wells argues that society at large suffers if courts are unable to enforce the Constitution *either* in cases in which plaintiffs seek prospective relief *or* in cases in which they seek compensatory damages. By his account, qualified immunity doctrine places too much emphasis on concerns that officers may be over-deterred and too little on concerns that they may violate federal law. Wells thinks that it would be preferable to hold government officials to a higher standard and to in-

Like absolute immunity, qualified immunity is an affirmative defense that must be raised by the defendant at the proper time.[487] Unlike absolute immunity, qualified immunity typically demands attention to the circumstances of the defendant's behavior and thus rarely can be settled on a motion to dismiss. The Court held in *Hunter v. Bryant*,[488] however, that qualified immunity can often be determined on a motion for summary judgment—and ordinarily should be handled in that way to spare a defendant officer any further unnecessary burdens. When an officer moves for summary judgment, the plaintiff must proffer evidence to demonstrate the existence of triable issues.[489] Inasmuch as the officer's immunity turns on whether particular conduct violated clearly established law, immunity issues may be resolved on the basis of the evidence the plaintiff proffers and briefs exploring the precedents in existence at the time.[490]

Qualified immunity is structured to ensure that plaintiffs are compensated when executive officers abuse their authority by taking actions they should know are unlawful. The Court held in *Owen v. City of Independence*[491] that those purposes would not be served by according immunity to a city or county. The policies that justify sparing individual officers from liability do not obtain with respect to units of government.[492] Accordingly, cities and counties cannot assert qualified immunity from suits for damages, even if the officers whose behavior is in question can assert immunity to avoid personal liability.[493]

---

duce public employers to purchase insurance to indemnify officers who get out of line. Current law unjustifiably visits costs on the innocent victims of government's uninsured agents. Wells, note 409.

487. *Gomez*, 446 U.S. at 639–41; *Connor*, 490 U.S. at 399.

488. 502 U.S. 224 (1991).

489. See *Celotex Corp. v. Catrett*, 477 U.S. 317 (1986). Here again, the Supreme Court has refused to approve special pleading requirements meant to force plaintiffs to anticipate immunity defenses in the first instance. See note 444. Professor Chen contends that qualified immunity (as opposed to absolute immunity) is comparatively fact-sensitive and *cannot* typically be handled on motion for summary judgment. See Chen, note 445; Alan R. Chen, *The Burdens of Qualified Immunity: Summary Judgment and the Role of Facts in Constitutional Tort Law*, 47 Am. U. L. Rev. 1 (1997). In his view, the Court's decisions elaborating the content of the qualified immunity defense are in conflict with its apparent desire to minimize the costs of constitutional litigation by resolving cases at the summary judgment stage.

490. If a district court's decision on summary judgment rests entirely on a matter of law, it is immediately subject to appeal. *Mitchell v. Forsyth*, 472 U.S. 511 (1985). See Chapter VII, note 215 (discussing this rule in connection with the final judgment requirement). If it rests on a determination of fact, it is not. *Johnson v. Jones*, 515 U.S. 304 (1995). If an officer is unsuccessful on interlocutory appeal from a district court's denial of a motion to dismiss, the officer may file a motion for summary judgment and, if necessary, take an interlocutory appeal from the district court's judgment on that. *Behrens v. Pelletier*, 516 U.S. 299 (1996). But see *Johnson v. Fankell*, 520 U.S. 911 (1997) (holding that the states are free to adopt different rules for interlocutory appeals on immunity issues for purposes of §1983 actions in state court). The Court held in *Elder v. Holloway*, 510 U.S. 510 (1994), that an appellate court should take account of any extant precedents, even if neither party presented those precedents to the court below.

491. 445 U.S. 622 (1980).

492. See text accompanying notes 452–56.

493. The Court did not address absolute immunity in *Owen*, but by a parity of reasoning it would seem that cities and counties should be denied either form of immunity. This is not to suggest that it is easy to saddle local government with liability for the sins of its executive agents. Because units of local government do not share qualified immunity with their employees, plaintiffs sometimes seek compensation from cities and counties on the theory that they failed properly to train their officers. Suits of that kind are possible, but only barely. See note 390. In *FDIC v. Meyer*, 510 U.S. 471 (1994), the Court expressed concern that if plaintiffs cannot hold federal officers personally liable, they will compensate by suing the federal agencies that employ them. To nip that pos-

In the end, qualified immunity doctrine is tailored to the values and policies obviously at stake when a private litigant sues an executive officer, seeking to establish a violation of federal law and to hold the officer personally liable. In order to achieve clarity regarding federal rights for the future, the court initially determines whether the plaintiff has alleged a violation of federal law. If so, the court turns to the further question whether the defendant can be held personally accountable. At that stage, the public's interest in effective and aggressive law enforcement is paramount. Executive officers are not steeped in current constitutional law and, in any event, they have neither the resources nor the time to resolve thorny legal questions before taking action in the field. Accordingly, the court will hold an officer liable only if the precedents that existed at the time he acted gave him fair warning that his conduct violated the plaintiff's federal rights.[494]

---

sibility in the bud, Justice Thomas held that agencies are not subject to *Bivens* suits. Id. at 485. See Chapter VIII, note 218 and accompanying text (discussing *Bivens*).

494. See text accompanying notes 459, 467–71.

Chapter XI

Abstention

When the prerequisites for federal adjudication of federal claims are satisfied, federal district courts still may decline to *exercise* their power. Inferior federal courts have no discretion to turn business away *ad hoc*. That is a luxury reserved for the Supreme Court.[1] Yet the district courts do *abstain* in a variety of circumstances prescribed by a body of quasi-constitutional principles, statutes, and judge-made doctrines.

Recall that state courts typically have concurrent jurisdiction to determine federal question cases.[2] It is quite possible that the same parties can be involved in litigation in both state and federal court at the same time, perhaps quarreling over the same issues in both places. In principle, that prospect presents no difficulty, but follows as the natural implication of a bifurcated system.[3] State courts are constitutionally barred from interfering with proceedings in federal court.[4] Federal courts are not constitutionally barred from interfering with proceedings in state court. Yet federal courts generally have no cause either to enjoin parallel state proceedings or to stay their own hand. Instead, lawsuits can proceed in state and federal court on separate tracks.[5] Trial court errors can be corrected on direct review. Thereafter, the law of preclusion will determine whether there is anything left for the other set of courts to decide.[6] Nevertheless, there are competing considerations: the special value that may attach to federal adjudication of federal claims, the costs attending a multiplicity of suits, and the conflicts that simultaneous lawsuits often entail. Accordingly, both Congress and the Supreme Court have devised ways to channel business into state court in the first instance and to prevent federal courts from taking simultaneous parallel action. The task of allocating judicial responsibility is problematic. The statutes and rules in this context are both complex in themselves and riddled with exceptions.

A. Statutory Limitations

1. The Anti-Injunction Act

The Anti-Injunction Act, 28 U.S.C. §2283, bars a "court of the United States" from granting an injunction "to stay proceedings in a State court" except: (1) "as expressly au-

1. See Chapter VII, notes 219–45 and accompanying text.
2. See Chapter VI, notes 3–38 and accompanying text.
3. See *Kline v. Burke Constr. Co.*, 260 U.S. 226 (1922).
4. See Chapter VI, notes 121–24 and accompanying text.
5. *Kline*, 260 U.S. at 230.
6. See Chapter VI, notes 161–225 and accompanying text (discussing the preclusive effects of state judgments in subsequent federal proceedings and *Rooker/Feldman*).

thorized by Act of Congress;" (2) "where necessary in aid of its jurisdiction;" or (3) "to protect or effectuate its judgments." In *Atlantic Coast Line R.R. v. Brotherhood of Locomotive Engineers*,[7] Justice Black explained that §2283 is a "clear-cut prohibition qualified only by specifically defined exceptions." Moreover, inasmuch as §2283 "rests on the fundamental constitutional independence of the States and their courts," Justice Black insisted that the three exceptions "should not be enlarged by loose statutory construction." In *Atlantic Coast Line*, accordingly, he held that a union could not obtain a federal injunction that would keep an employer from maintaining an action in state court, even though the employer was seeking state court relief that would violate federal labor law. Black explained that although the injunction was addressed to one of the parties and not directly to the state court, it was nonetheless an injunction "to stay proceedings in State court" and thus was barred by §2283.[8]

Despite Justice Black's rhetoric in *Atlantic Coast Line*, the Anti-Injunction Act has never functioned as a sweeping restraint on federal court authority to issue injunctions that interfere with state functions. The Act protects only state *judicial* proceedings and has no application to the hosts of cases involving state administrative action.[9] It protects judicial proceedings only if they are already pending when a federal court is asked to take action.[10] It has no effect in cases in which the federal government or a federal agency seeks an injunction.[11] Nor does it limit the ability of strangers to a pending state court action to obtain a federal injunction that affects the state court proceeding.[12]

When it was first enacted in 1793, the Anti-Injunction Act had nothing to do with circumscribing the authority of the inferior federal courts.[13] Later, when the Court

---

7. 398 U.S. 281 (1970).

8. Id. at 287, 295. Justice Black noted that if the state court reached an erroneous judgment, the union could attack it in the state appellate courts and, if necessary, in the Supreme Court on *certiorari*. Id. at 296; see Chapter VII, notes 58–59, 219–22 and accompanying text.

9. E.g., *Lynch v. Household Fin. Corp.*, 405 U.S. 538, 553 (1972) (finding §2283 inapplicable to a prejudgment garnishment conducted by a deputy sheriff without judicial involvement). Nor does §2283 affect cases in which federal courts are asked to enjoin proceedings in foreign courts. But see Comment, *Comity Be Damned: The Use of Antisuit Injunctions Against the Courts of a Foreign Nation*, 147 U. Pa. L. Rev. 409 (1998) (contending that §2283 would make a fitting model for those cases).

10. *Dombrowski v. Pfister*, 380 U.S. 479, 485 n.2 (1965); see note 149.

11. *Leiter Minerals v. United States*, 352 U.S. 220, 225–26 (1957); *NLRB v. Nash-Finch Co.*, 404 U.S. 138, 144–46 (1971).

12. *Hale v. Bimco Trading*, 306 U.S. 375 (1939). The point of §2283 is not that a federal court can never bar anyone from pursuing an action in state court, but that when two parties are already engaged in state court litigation, a federal court cannot lend one of them a hand by issuing an injunction that forces the other to desist. The mere existence of a state court lawsuit involving some parties does not prevent someone else from seeking federal injunctive relief, even if that relief will run to one of the parties to the current state proceeding and even if it bears on the issues the state court is considering. See *County of Imperial v. Munoz*, 449 U.S. 54 (1980) (explaining that federal courts can act only on behalf of genuine "strangers").

13. Professor Mayton has developed irresistible evidence that the language in the 1793 Act that later was to become the Anti-Injunction Act actually addressed only Supreme Court justices "riding circuit." See Chapter II, note 54 and accompanying text. By Mayton's account, the legislation enacted in 1793 *did* contain some restrictions on federal courts generally. See Chapter II, text accompanying notes 67–69. Yet in this particular instance Congress meant to *extend* the authority of individual justices. The All-Writs Act authorized the Supreme Court and inferior courts to issue common law writs, but failed to authorize individual circuit justices to do so. See Chapter II, note 58. Congress thus inserted a provision in the 1793 Act giving circuit justices power to issue writs, but added as a proviso that they could not use their new authority to enjoin state proceedings.

came to regard it as a general limitation on federal court power, the Court read it to allow for exceptions in a range of circumstances in which the Court thought injunctions were warranted.[14] In *Toucey v. United States*,[15] however, the Court changed its position. In that case, Justice Frankfurter read the Act to establish an unqualified prohibition on injunctions. Accordingly, he concluded that a federal district court could not prevent a party who had lost a case in federal court from filing a subsequent suit in state court in an attempt to relitigate the matter. Congress soon amended the Act not only to overrule *Toucey*, but also to incorporate some of the exceptions the Court had previously recognized. The exceptions now codified in §2283 have not been narrowly construed in the way that Justice Black declared they should be. By some accounts, they have largely swallowed any general (statutory) rule barring federal injunctions against state court proceedings.

Expressly authorized injunctions. In *Mitchum v. Foster*,[16] the Court held that 42 U.S.C. §1983 qualifies as an "Act of Congress" that "expressly" authorizes federal courts to issue injunctions that would otherwise be barred. Accordingly, when private plaintiffs file §1983 actions in federal court, seeking injunctions against state judicial proceedings, §2283 poses no barrier. In a single stroke, *Mitchum* eliminated the Anti-Injunction Act as a factor in the most sensitive instances (cases in which federal injunctions against state proceedings may be needed to keep state officers from using state courts to violate federal rights), but in which state interests in state court litigation are high (because state authorities naturally wish to use their own courts to enforce state law). In *Atlantic Coast Line*, Justice Black insisted that the very point of §2283 is that state courts are willing to respect federal rights and that if they make a mistake, they can be corrected on direct review. In *Mitchum*, Justice Stewart explained that the point of §1983 is that "state officers" may be "antipathetic" to federal rights and that their "failings" may extend to state courts.[17]

Nothing in §1983 "expressly" approves injunctions against state judicial proceedings. Justice Stewart explained, however, that §1983 is an integral element of the body of leg-

---

Then, in the middle of the Nineteenth Century, the Supreme Court picked the latter language out of context and treated it as a restriction on federal courts at large. *Peck v. Jenness*, 48 U.S. (7 How.) 612 (1849). That misconstruction was codified in 1874. William T. Mayton, *Ersatz Federalism Under the Anti-Injunction Statute*, 78 Colum. L. Rev. 330 (1978). If Mayton is right about the history behind the Anti-Injunction Act (and he almost certainly is), the Court's handling of the Act parallels its handling of the eleventh amendment. Both the statute and the constitutional amendment may have been misinterpreted early on. But the modern Court has its own reasons for leaving those mistakes in place. It is not merely that the Court hesitates to overrule old precedents. The Court thinks it is good policy that federal courts should not routinely enjoin state court proceedings and that the states should be immune from many private lawsuits. Then again, the Court allows exceptions in each instance in hopes of striking an appropriate balance. See Chapter X (discussing the Court's sovereign immunity decisions).

14. For a discussion of illustrative cases, see Edgar N. Durfee & Robert L. Sloss, *Federal Injunction Against Proceedings in State Courts: The Life History of a Statute*, 30 Mich. L. Rev. 1145 (1932); Telford Taylor & Everett I. Willis, *The Power of Federal Courts to Enjoin Proceedings in State Courts*, 42 Yale L.J. 1169 (1933).

15. 314 U.S. 118 (1941).

16. 407 U.S. 225 (1972).

17. *Atlantic Coast Line*, 398 U.S. at 296; *Mitchum*, 407 U.S. at 242. The two cases illustrate the internal debate over parity that is constantly waged within the Court. See Chapter I, notes 79–91 and accompanying text. Professor Fallon regards *Atlantic Coast Line* as a decision reflecting the federalist perspective on federal-state relations and *Mitchum* as an illustration of the nationalist perspective. Richard H. Fallon, Jr., *The Ideologies of Federal Courts Law*, 74 Va. L. Rev. 1141, 1165 n.92, 1166 n.93 (1988); see Chapter I, note 20 and accompanying text.

islation enacted by the Reconstruction Congress for the very purpose of "altering the relationship between the States and the Nation with respect to the protection of federally created rights." He said that §1983 authorizes actions for federal equitable relief against state authorities and thus can be "given its intended scope" only if federal courts are able to stay state court proceedings.[18] At the same time, Stewart disclaimed any purpose to "question or qualify" the conventional "principles of equity, comity, and federalism" that restrain federal courts when they are asked to interfere with litigation in state court. That disclaimer left the practical consequences of *Mitchum* in some doubt. Federal district courts entertaining §1983 actions are not barred by §2283 from issuing injunctions that short-circuit pending state court proceedings. Yet they are restricted by judicially fashioned limitations that typically have much the same effect.[19]

Injunctions in aid of jurisdiction. By common account, this second exception is meant to reconcile the Anti-Injunction Act with the All-Writs Act, 28 U.S.C. §1651, which explicitly authorizes federal courts to issue writs "in aid of their respective jurisdictions."[20] A federal court must have jurisdiction on some independent basis. Then, pursuant to the additional authority provided by §1651, and under this exception to §2283, the court can issue orders that stay state proceedings "in aid of" that previously established jurisdiction.[21] This exception accommodates two kinds of cases in which the Supreme Court found injunctions warranted prior to *Toucey*: (1) cases in which lawsuits have been removed to federal court;[22] and (2) cases in which federal jurisdiction is *in rem* and thus depends on the federal court's possession or control of some physical object.[23] In the former cases, the state court from which a suit has been removed has lost jurisdiction by operation of law and thus poaches on the federal court's preserve if it threatens to continue.[24] In the latter cases, the federal court's ability to deal with a "res" would be impaired if a state court were to assert jurisdiction over the same object.[25]

---

18. 407 U.S. at 242; see Chapter II, notes 74–76. Judge Wood once said that, according to *Mitchum*, "expressly authorized" actually means "implicitly authorized." Diane P. Wood, *Fine-Tuning Judicial Federalism: A Proposal for Reform of the Anti-Injunction Act*, 1990 B.Y.U. L. Rev. 289, 297, relying on David P. Currie, *The Federal Courts and the American Law Institute, Part II*, 36 U. Chi. L. Rev. 268, 322 (1969). Professor Nichol argues that *Mitchum* rests on "an essentially accurate vision" of the legislative "intent" behind §1983. Gene R. Nichol, Jr., *Federalism, State Courts, and Section 1983*, 73 Va. L. Rev. 959, 1000 (1987). Professor Redish faults *Mitchum* for looking beyond the text of §1983. Martin H. Redish, *The Anti-Injunction Statute Reconsidered*, 44 U. Chi. L. Rev. 717, 735 (1977). In *Vendo Co. v. Lektro-Vend Corp.*, 433 U.S. 623 (1977), the Court held that §16 of the Clayton Act is not a statute expressly authorizing federal injunctions against state judicial proceedings. There was no majority opinion. For an appraisal of various justices' views, see Redish, at 739–43.

19. 407 U.S. at 243; see notes 130–281 and accompanying text (discussing the judicially crafted doctrine the Court has developed to substitute for §2283 in §1983 actions).

20. See note 13.

21. In *Amalgamated Clothing Workers v. Richman Bros.*, 348 U.S. 511 (1955), the Court found this exception unavailable, because the federal court had no independent basis of jurisdiction "in aid of" which an injunctive order could operate.

22. E.g., *French v. Hay*, 89 U.S. (22 Wall.) 250 (1874).

23. E.g., *Kline v. Burke Constr. Co.*, 260 U.S. 226 (1922).

24. Professor Redish argues that federal injunctions may be warranted in removal cases on the independent ground that they are "expressly" authorized by the removal statute, 28 U.S.C. §1441. He agrees that *in rem* cases fit under this heading, but insists that the "in aid of jurisdiction" exception should be broad enough to include many other cases in which state proceedings present a "substantial" threat to efficient federal adjudication. Redish, note 18, at 744, 753–60.

25. This second exception may also permit federal injunctions when state proceedings interfere with complex federal lawsuits, particularly suits in the class action form. Steven M. Larimore, *Ex-*

Injunctions to protect or effectuate judgments. The final exception in §2283 covers cases in which a federal court initially reaches a judgment, but the losing party continues to press a parallel action in state court, hoping for a favorable judgment there. The party who prevailed in federal court may be content simply to insist upon preclusion in state court and to appeal from any unfavorable state court decision on the preclusion issue. Yet under this exception, a federal court can issue a preemptive federal injunction.[26]

By some accounts, Congress should amend the Act yet again, this time either establishing a single general standard to apply in every instance or specifying more carefully when federal injunctions are warranted and when they are barred.[27] By other accounts, the courts should make decisions on an *ad hoc* basis in light of relevant considerations.[28] Already, in light of *Mitchum*, §2283 is largely limited to disputes between private litigants, many of which turn on state law and reach federal court on the basis of diversity jurisdiction. Those are scarcely cases in which federal injunctions would be appropriate, even apart from a special statute in point.[29] Meanwhile, various abstention doctrines fashioned by the Supreme Court largely prescribe the circumstances in which federal injunctive relief can be available in more politically volatile federal question cases.

2. Other Statutes

Other statutes bear on the federal courts' ability to issue injunctive relief regarding federal issues: (1) three-judge court statutes; (2) the Johnson Act; and (3) the Tax Injunction Act.

Three-judge court statutes. Congress sometimes specifies that only three-judge panels at the district court level have authority to issue injunctive relief, subject to direct appellate review in the Supreme Court.[30] Three-judge courts are notoriously unpopular within the judicial branch—for four related reasons: (1) they challenge the integrity

---

ploring the Interface Between Rule 23 Class Actions and the Anti-Injunction Act, 18 Ga. L. Rev. 259 (1984).

26. In *Chick Kam Choo v. Exxon Corp.*, 486 U.S. 140 (1988), the Supreme Court called this the "relitigation" exception. Id. at 147. It permits a prevailing party in federal court to obtain a federal injunction against any further proceedings in state court seeking a different outcome on issues the federal court has already adjudicated. Professor Martinez argues that *Chick Kam Choo* also permits a federal court to enjoin state proceedings regarding issues that might have been, but were not, adjudicated in the prior federal proceeding. George A. Martinez, *The Anti-Injunction Act: Fending Off the New Attack on the Relitigation Exception*, 72 Neb. L. Rev. 643 (1993). In *Parsons Steel v. First Alabama Bank*, 474 U.S. 518 (1986), the Court explained that the federal court must act before the state proceeding itself comes to a close. At that point the Full Faith and Credit Statute, 28 U.S.C. §1738, instructs the federal court to give the state judgment the preclusive effect it would have in the courts of the state concerned. See Chapter VI, note 161 and accompanying text. Judge Wood has suggested that *Parsons* may create a perverse incentive. If the party that prevailed in federal court raises preclusion as a defense in state court and *loses* on that point, there is no recourse to the federal court that previously decided the issue. Accordingly, to be safe, a litigant may bypass any presentation of the preclusion issue in state court and go immediately to federal court for a federal injunction that stops the state proceeding in its tracks. Wood, note 18, at 305–06.

27. E.g., Currie, note 18, at 329 (proposing a single general standard); ALI, Study of the Division of Jurisdiction Between State and Federal Courts 51–52 (1969) (proposing a longer list of exceptions).

28. Judge Wood identifies the options, including repeal of §2283. She proposes rewriting what are now statutory exceptions as a set of (more flexible) principles. Wood, note 18, at 318–20.

29. Mayton, note 13, at 355.

30. See 28 U.S.C. §1253; Chapter VII, note 219.

and capacity of individual district judges; (2) they draw heavily on judicial resources; (3) they bypass the corrective function of the circuit courts of appeals; and (4) they burden the Supreme Court. When Congress provides for three-judge courts, it is usually to signal displeasure with what the courts are doing at the moment.[31] For example, only three-judge courts can issue injunctions in suits attacking the constitutionality of legislative apportionment schemes[32] and injunctions requiring the release of convicts to reduce overcrowding in state penitentiaries.[33]

The Johnson Act. Pursuant to 28 U.S.C. §1342, the district courts are generally barred from issuing injunctions that "enjoin, suspend, or restrain" a state regulatory body's orders regarding utility rates. The Johnson Act insulates rate orders from federal interference on four conditions: (1) federal jurisdiction is based solely on diversity of citizenship or on the presence of a federal constitutional question; (2) the relevant state order does not interfere with interstate commerce; (3) the agency issued the order only after notice and a hearing; and (4) the utility company that is subject to the order has a "plain, speedy and efficient remedy" in state court. Each of the four conditions can generate litigation.[34]

The Tax Injunction Act. Pursuant to 28 U.S.C. §1341, the district courts are barred from issuing injunctions that "enjoin, suspend or restrain" the enforcement of state taxes. The Tax Injunction Act specifies only one precondition: The taxpayer must have a "plain, speedy and efficient remedy" in state court. This Act, too, can generate litigation.[35]

B. Exhaustion of Non-Judicial Remedies

Some statutes require litigants to "exhaust" state non-judicial remedies before filing lawsuits in federal court.[36] Exhaustion requirements are by nature rules of timing alone.

---

31. Immediately following *Ex parte Young*, 209 U.S. 123 (1908); see Chapter X, notes 283–88 and accompanying text, Congress enacted statutes specifying that only three-judge courts could enjoin state statutes. The concern then was that the federal courts would frustrate economic regulation. See Chapter X, note 300. Those statutes were repealed in 1976.

32. 28 U.S.C. §2284(a). For a discussion, see Napoleon B. Williams, Jr., *The New Three-Judge Courts of Reapportionment and Continuing Problems of Three-Judge-Court Procedure*, 65 Gtn. L.J. 971 (1977); Michael E. Solimine, *The Three-Judge District Court in Voting Rights Litigation*, 30 U. Mich. J. L. Ref. 79 (1996).

33. 18 U.S.C. §3626(a)(3)(B). This provision was added in 1996. For a discussion of the larger bill and the political backdrop, see Mark V. Tushnet & Larry W. Yackle, *Symbolic Statutes and Real Laws: The Pathologies of the Antiterrorism and Effective Death Penalty Act and the Prison Litigation Reform Act*, 47 Duke L.J. 1 (1997).

34. For a discussion of the Johnson Act, see Federal Practice and Procedure: Jurisdiction, §4236 (Wright, Miller & Cooper eds. 1988).

35. Recall, for example, the argument in *Franchise Tax Board v. Constr. Laborers Vacation Trust*, 463 U.S. 1 (1983), that the Tax Injunction Act bars a fiduciary subject to ERISA from suing state tax authorities in federal court, seeking an injunction against a third-party assessment. See Chapter VIII, note 363. For a discussion of the Tax Injunction Act, see Federal Practice and Procedure, note 34, at §4237.

36. E.g., Title VII of the Civil Rights Act of 1964, 42 U.S.C. §2000e-5(c) (requiring plaintiffs to exhaust state administrative procedures for resolving employment discrimination claims before filing federal court actions under the Act); Civil Rights of Institutionalized Persons Act, 42 U.S.C. §1997e (requiring state prison inmates to exhaust certain state administrative procedures for resolving claims about their treatment before filing §1983 actions). In this context, it is conventional to refer generally to state administrative arrangements for addressing complaints as "remedies." See Chapter VIII, note 121.

They hold out the promise of federal adjudication at some point, but they postpone that adjudication until litigants have first taken their quarrels to state authorities. Exhaustion rules both respect state arrangements for resolving disputes and reap the benefits of those procedures. If state non-judicial authorities give litigants the relief they want, there will be no need for federal court adjudication at all. If state non-judicial authorities do not satisfy litigants entirely, they still may develop the record in a way that makes later federal adjudication more efficient. Decisions by state non-judicial authorities are not ordinarily entitled to preclusive effect in federal court. If they were, the exhaustion requirement would cease to be merely a rule of timing. A scheme that compromises the capacity of the federal courts to adjudicate a dispute at some point cannot properly be called an exhaustion rule.[37]

The Supreme Court enforces exhaustion doctrines of its own creation in two instances: (1) when there are further opportunities for litigants to affect the state legislative policy they wish to attack in federal court; and (2) when there are state administrative procedures for resolving their difficulties without the need for litigation.[38]

Legislative remedies. A federal lawsuit is premature if it challenges state legislative action that is incomplete. Ordinarily, litigants attack enacted statutes, and there is no basis for suggesting that they are obliged to pursue political strategies for persuading the legislature to change what it has already done. In some circumstances, however, states

---

37. See note 166 (discussing this point in the context of the federal-question abstention doctrine). In *Kremer v. Chem. Constr. Corp.*, 456 U.S. 461 (1982), and *University of Tennessee v. Elliott*, 478 U.S. 788 (1986), the Court recognized that Title VII both requires litigants to exhaust state administrative remedies before filing federal employment discrimination actions and guarantees litigants who ultimately file federal lawsuits the opportunity for *de novo* adjudication in federal court. The litigant in *Kremer* engaged preclusion only because he went beyond state administrative procedures and sued for relief in state court—thus bringing the Full Faith and Credit Statute into play. The litigant in *Elliott* engaged preclusion only with respect to his voluntary presentation of *constitutional* claims to the state agency in that case. See Chapter VI, notes 186–92 and accompanying text. The Court typically requires litigants to exhaust *federal* administrative remedies and nevertheless gives preclusive effect to agency findings of fact. See *McKart v. United States*, 395 U.S. 167 (1961); but see *McCarthy v. Madigan*, 503 U.S. 140, 146 (1992) (describing exceptions); *Astoria Fed. Savings & Loan Ass'n v. Solimino*, 501 U.S. 104 (1991) (explaining that Congress can deny preclusion by statute). To that extent, the Court departs from the conventional understanding that an exhaustion rule is exclusively a rule of timing.

38. Of course, there is no ordinary doctrine requiring litigants to exhaust state *judicial* opportunities to press federal claims. When litigants proceed in state court and attempt to revisit the same issues later in federal court, the Full Faith and Credit Statute typically instructs federal courts to give the previous state judgment the preclusive effect it would have under state law. See Chapter VI, note 161 and accompanying text. But see Chapter XII, note 4 and accompanying text (noting that federal habeas corpus is an exception). The general rule that litigants must exhaust *federal* administrative remedies is meant to ensure that all the adjudicative institutions established by Congress (including both courts and agencies) function efficiently together. Chapter IX, notes 404–06 and accompanying text (discussing the related doctrine of ripeness). Yet the Court allows exceptions when non-judicial remedies do not promise fair and effective machinery or when they threaten undue delays. E.g., *McCarthy v. Madigan*, 503 U.S. 140 (1992) (declining to require a federal prison inmate to exhaust administrative remedies before filing a *Bivens* action against penal authorities). See Chapter VIII, notes 209–30 and accompanying text (discussing *Bivens*). Professor Power has reviewed the Court's cases and concluded that they form no coherent doctrine. Robert C. Power, *Help Is Sometimes Close at Hand: The Exhaustion Problem and the Ripeness Solution*, 1987 U. Ill. L. Rev. 547. In *Darby v. Cisneros*, 509 U.S. 137 (1993), the Court held that in cases controlled by the Administrative Procedure Act, litigants need exhaust only the remedies that Congress prescribes by statute and need not pursue additional administrative procedures that the Court itself might otherwise have required.

allocate legislative power in an unconventional way. In the leading case, *Prentis v. Atlantic Coast Line Co.*,[39] the state of Virginia authorized an administrative agency to make an initial legislative judgment regarding the maximum rates that railroads could charge, but then gave the Virginia Supreme Court authority to set the agency's rate order aside and substitute an order of its own making. Justice Holmes explained that an arrangement of that kind did not merely subject the agency's action to judicial review in state court. Instead, it conferred independent *legislative* power on the state supreme court. Accordingly, Holmes held that the railroad must complain to that court that the agency had fixed the rate too low and, in that way, allow all the state's legislative institutions to operate as planned. Thereafter, if the railroad was dissatisfied with the state court's legislative decision, the railroad would be free to attack that legislative action in a federal lawsuit.[40]

The *Prentis* doctrine is conventionally regarded as a rule of exhaustion. Yet it may be more accurate to regard it as a rule of finality. The idea is that, in some circumstances, local legislative action does not take its final authoritative form until private litigants press for an ultimate resolution. The means for doing that may have the look and feel of a lawsuit in state court. But in theory the state court performs a legislative function.[41] Unless the arrangement is unduly burdensome, private litigants may fairly be asked to play their role in the state legislative process before seeking genuine judicial relief in court.[42] The *Prentis* doctrine is analogous to the Court's decisions regarding claims that state authorities have taken property without giving just compensation. In order to be in a position to complain that the compensation the state has awarded is insufficient, litigants must advance their claims before all the state entities with authority to make adjustments in their favor.[43]

---

39. 211 U.S. 210 (1908).

40. Holmes made it clear that the railroad's lawsuit in that instance would be filed in the appropriate federal trial court for the exercise of original jurisdiction. Since the state supreme court's action was legislative in nature, the railroad could not seek appellate review of its order directly in the Supreme Court of the United States. The Supreme Court reviews judgments by state courts (acting in a judicial capacity), not state legislatures (or state courts acting in a legislative capacity). See Chapter VII, note 59 and accompanying text (discussing the scope of the Court's appellate jurisdiction of state court judgments).

41. In *Prentis*, Justice Holmes was confident that the state supreme court acted in a legislative capacity. In *Bacon v. Rutland R.R.*, 232 U.S. 134 (1914), by contrast, he concluded that the Vermont Supreme Court had only the conventional authority to review a utility rate order in a judicial capacity. Accordingly, the *Prentis* doctrine did not apply, and the railroad in *Bacon* was entitled to sue in federal court. If the railroad had sought judicial review in the Vermont Supreme Court, it would almost certainly have been unable to sue thereafter in a federal trial court. See Chapter VI, notes 161–225 (discussing the preclusive effects of state court judgments and the *Rooker/Feldman* doctrine). These cases place a premium on characterizing the nature of the state court's function as either judicial or legislative. See Chapter VI, notes 189–92, 206–08 and accompanying text (discussing the same problem with respect to §1738 and *Rooker/Feldman*). In *Oklahoma Packing Co. v. Oklahoma Gas & Elec. Co.*, 309 U.S. 4 (1940), the Court indicated that it may rely in part on a state court's own characterization of its function.

42. See *Pac. Tel. & Tel. Co. v. Kuykendall*, 265 U.S. 196 (1924) (permitting a federal court to act before a state court had completed a final leg of the state legislative process—because state law allowed no stay of the rates under attack while the company's arguments were heard in state court).

43. E.g., *Williamson County Regional Planning Comm'n v. Hamilton Bank*, 473 U.S. 172 (1985) (requiring a plaintiff to complete all available administrative procedures for obtaining a zoning adjustment). Professor Ryckman has explained that land use cases are peculiarly local and that zoning boards and planning commissions invariably offer developers the best chance of getting what they want. William E. Ryckman, Jr., *Land Use Litigation, Federal Jurisdiction, and the Abstention Doctrines*, 69 Calif. L. Rev. 377 (1981) (nonetheless detailing the way in which land use cases are af-

Administrative remedies. A federal lawsuit can also be premature if there is some workable administrative means for addressing the matter that has not yet been engaged. In *Fair Assessment in Real Estate Ass'n v. McNary*,[44] taxpayers contended that state officials had administered state taxes in violation of the fourteenth amendment. In hopes of eluding the Tax Injunction Act, the plaintiffs framed their suit in federal court as a §1983 action seeking compensatory damages for invalid assessments and penalties.[45] Then-Justice Rehnquist set §1341 aside and rested judgment on a construction of §1983. He found the prospect of disrupting tax collections intolerable and held, accordingly, that §1983 would not allow taxpayers to bypass the state administrative remedies available to them.[46]

In *Patsy v. Bd. of Regents*,[47] the Court held that litigants need not exhaust state administrative remedies before filing §1983 actions attacking other kinds of state action. Justice Marshall emphasized the historic purpose of §1983 as a means of seeking prompt judicial redress for violations of federal rights.[48] On the surface, *Patsy* operates in this context much in the way that *Mitchum v. Foster* operates in the context of the Anti-Injunction Act—exempting the most politically sensitive cases from a rule that would otherwise burden would-be federal plaintiffs.[49] In practice, *Patsy* may be more potent than *Mitchum*. The Court has made up for *Mitchum* by fashioning its own doctrinal rules limiting §1983 injunctive actions against state proceedings.[50] But the Court has not filled the gap that *Patsy* created in the exhaustion doctrine. Accordingly, plaintiffs who wish to file §1983 actions can typically bypass state administrative remedies, if they wish.[51]

---

fected by the various abstention doctrines). There is also a surface analogy to the *Parratt* and *Zinermon* cases, in which the Court finds some procedural due process claims incomplete if plaintiffs have not taken advantage of state tort lawsuits that might provide the process that is due. See Chapter X, note 419 (noting that the Court relied on *Parratt* in *Williamson*). There, however, the Court finds the process that state courts offer (in a judicial capacity) to be sufficient to satisfy constitutional standards. The *Parratt* and *Zinermon* cases are not, then, cases about postponing federal court adjudication of claims until state court means of redressing those claims have been exhausted. See Chapter X, note 413.

44. 454 U.S. 100 (1981).

45. See text accompanying note 35.

46. 454 U.S. at 113–15. In an important concurring opinion, Justice Brennan agreed that, if the exhaustion of state administrative remedies was required before taxpayers could file suit in state court, the same should be true if they wished, instead, to file suit in federal court. Id. at 117. Professor Bravemen argues that *McNary's* loose rationale cannot easily be limited to taxation cases and thus poses a threat to §1983 actions in other kinds of cases. Daan Bravemen, *Fair Assessment and Federal Jurisdiction in Civil Rights Cases*, 45 U. Pitt. L. Rev. 351, 366–70 (1984). Bravemen notes, however, that the Court was divided over the proper analysis to be applied in *McNary* and that the decision in that case may not bear heavy precedential weight. The Court relied on *McNary* in *Nat'l Private Truck Council v. Oklahoma Tax Comm'n*, 515 U.S. 582 (1995) (holding that taxpayers cannot avoid the Tax Injunction Act by filing §1983 actions in *state* court seeking injunctions against the collection of state taxes). In *Quackenbush v. Allstate Ins. Co.*, 517 U.S. 706 (1996), the Court characterized the *McNary* and *Nat'l Private Truck* cases as interpretations of §1983.

47. 457 U.S. 496 (1982).

48. Justice Marshall also noted that Congress has enacted a special statute requiring state prison inmates to exhaust state administrative remedies. See note 36. Accordingly, it appears by negative inference that in the run of §1983 actions, exhaustion is not required. 457 U.S. at 507–12.

49. See notes 16–17 and accompanying text.

50. See notes 144–49 and accompanying text.

51. Recall that litigants have an incentive to bypass state administrative agencies to avoid the preclusive effects of their determinations. See Chapter VI, notes 193–95 (discussing the *Elliott* decision).

C. Abstention and Discretionary Remedies

The Supreme Court has fashioned a series of abstention doctrines limiting the exercise of federal jurisdiction that might interfere with state interests and proceedings. Some separately described doctrines are actually only precedents with inexact implications for other cases.[52] Others have developed well beyond their intellectual roots.[53] Certainly, all the doctrines under this general heading are related to each other inasmuch as they draw upon common themes. Justice Powell once declared that the abstention doctrines are not "rigid pigeonholes into which federal courts must try to fit cases," but rather "reflect a complex of considerations" for softening federal-state relations.[54] Nevertheless, it would be a mistake to collapse all the abstention doctrines, each with its own peculiar features, into a single multi-faceted idea.[55] Justice Scalia has acknowledged that the "policy considerations" supporting the doctrines are sufficiently "distinct" to justify "independent analysis."[56]

The abstention doctrines are rooted in the preconditions for particular kinds of relief, particularly injunctions. Yet the law governing remedies does not fully account for the body of decisions under this heading. Abstention is another device for allocating authority and responsibility between federal and state courts. Into the bargain, abstention moderates the friction that inevitably develops between two sets of courts functioning together in a single judicial system.[57] Federal courts abstain not only on the ground that the maxims of equity foreclose injunctive relief. They also abstain on the basis of comity—the respect federal courts owe to the states and their courts within the overarching constitutional scheme.[58] Accordingly, abstention is not limited to cases in

52. See notes 104–43 and accompanying text (describing the *Burford*, *Thibodaux*, and *Colorado River* cases).

53. See notes 144–295 and accompanying text (describing the *Younger* doctrine).

54. *Pennzoil v. Texaco*, 481 U.S. 1, 11 n.9 (1987).

55. Professor Althouse thinks it is unlikely that Powell intended his "offhanded comment" to have "doctrine-shattering" implications. Ann Althouse, *The Misguided Search for State Interest in Abstention Cases: Observations on the Occasion of Pennzoil v. Texaco*, 63 N.Y.U. L. Rev. 1051, 1072–73 (1988).

56. *NOPSI v. Council of New Orleans*, 491 U.S. 350, 359–60 (1989); see notes 110–15 and accompanying text.

57. In *Grupo Mexicano de DeSarrollo v. Alliance Bond Fund,* 527 U.S. 308 (1999), the Court explained that the federal courts' authority to issue equitable relief turns on the traditional principles that had developed in England at the time the Constitution was adopted. Professor Fiss questions the Court's reliance on traditional preconditions for equitable relief to resolve federalism issues. By his account, it would be the purest accident if rules fashioned to govern the relations between Chancery and Common Pleas in medieval England should somehow manage to strike just the right balance between federal and state judicial authority in this country today. Owen Fiss, *Dombrowski*, 86 Yale L.J. 1103, 1107 (1977). In truth, according to Fiss, the Court does not simply apply equitable principles in abstention cases, but rather uses the language of equity to explain policy choices regarding the exercise of federal judicial power.

58. The term "comity" is borrowed from the law of nations. The Supreme Court explained "comity" in that context in *Hilton v. Guyot*, 159 U.S. 113, 163–64 (1895): "'Comity,' in the legal sense, is neither a matter of absolute obligation, on the one hand, nor of mere courtesy and good will, upon the other." It is "the recognition which one nation allows within its territory to the legislative, executive or judicial acts of another nation, having due regard both to international duty and convenience." Courts and commentators also use the comity idea in working out the relations between individual states. In that context, comity usually connotes something akin to reciprocity. See Larry Kramer, *Rethinking Choice of Law*, 90 Colum. L. Rev. 277 (1990); Louise Weinberg, *Against*

which litigants seek equitable relief. In some instances, abstention is appropriate when litigants pursue declaratory judgments and, occasionally, monetary damages—the form of relief historically understood to be quintessentially legal rather than equitable in character.[59]

The relief that litigants seek from the federal courts nonetheless has decisive implications for the form that abstention may take. In cases in which courts have discretion regarding the relief sought, they may abstain either by postponing federal adjudication or by surrendering jurisdiction entirely in favor of litigation in state court. In cases in which courts have no such discretion, they can abstain only by staying their hand in the near term and not by relinquishing adjudicative power altogether. Federal courts have discretion regarding equitable relief (like injunctions) and certain other modern remedies (for example, declaratory judgments).[60] They have no similar discretion regarding monetary relief. Accordingly, they may abstain with respect to claims for compensatory damages only by postponement. To dismiss claims for damages outright would be a breach of the federal courts' duty with respect to claims of that kind. To postpone the exercise of jurisdiction is not, however, an "abnegation of judicial duty," but rather constitutes a "wise and productive discharge of it."[61]

In the leading case, *Quackenbush v. Allstate Ins. Co.*,[62] a state insurance commissioner was appointed trustee of a failed insurance company. Acting in that capacity, the commissioner sued the Allstate company in state court, seeking compensatory damages on state law contract and tort theories. Allstate removed the case to federal district court. The commissioner asked the federal court to abstain on the theory that federal court adjudication of the dispute would disrupt the state's effort to resolve the many difficulties associated with the failed company's liquidation. The federal district court accepted that argument and remanded the case to state court. In the Supreme Court, Justice O'-Connor explained that, in those circumstances, a remand on the basis of abstention was unwarranted. It would mean not merely delaying the federal court's exercise of jurisdiction, but effectively dismissing the suit and remitting the matter to state court without recourse. Since the commissioner sought compensatory damages rather than a form of relief over which the district court had discretion, abstention in the form of renouncing jurisdiction could not be sustained.[63]

Comity, 80 Gtn. L.J. 53 (1991). In the context of federal-state judicial relations, comity refers to the "proper respect" the federal courts accord to state functions and, in particular, state judicial functions. *Younger v. Harris*, 401 U.S. 37, 44 (1971); cf. *Calderon v. Thompson*, 523 U.S. 538, 552 (1998) (noting that comity is owed both to state courts and to state executive officers). Critics complain that the content of comity is "undefined" and that decisions anchored in comity are at best unpredictable and at worst unprincipled. See, e.g., Shirley M. Hufstedler, *Comity and the Constitution: The Changing Role of the Federal Judiciary*, 47 N.Y.U. L. Rev. 841, 867 (1972). Professor Wells argues, however, that it is the very "shapelessness" of comity that makes the idea so valuable to the Supreme Court. Michael Wells, *The Role of Comity in the Law of Federal Courts*, 60 N. Car. L. Rev. 59, 86 (1981).

59. See Chapter V, note 148 and accompanying text (noting the historical difference between claims tried before a jury in the "law" courts and claims tried without a jury in courts of "equity").

60. See Chapter VIII, notes 134, 140–45 and accompanying text.

61. *Louisiana Power & Light Co. v. Thibodaux*, 360 U.S. 25, 29 (1959).

62. 517 U.S. 706 (1996).

63. The *Quackenbush* case involved the kind of "administrative" abstention associated with *Burford v. Sun Oil Co.*, 319 U.S. 315 (1943); see notes 104–18 and accompanying text. But Justice O'-Connor tailored her analysis to cover other forms of abstention, as well. See Comment, *Burford Abstention in Actions for Damages*, 99 Colum. L. Rev. 1871 (1999) (contending that *Burford* abstention is never appropriate when litigants seek monetary relief). Justice O'Connor acknowledged that fed-

D. State-Question Abstention

Federal courts often have authority to determine state issues that are related to the federal questions that trigger jurisdiction pursuant to §1331. Yet they may abstain from exercising their jurisdiction in order to give state courts an opportunity to pass on questions of state law. In *Railroad Comm'n of Texas v. Pullman Co.*,[64] the Texas Railroad Commission issued an order requiring all trains operated in Texas to be under the supervision of Pullman conductors rather than porters. At the time, Pullman conductors were invariably white; porters were invariably black. The railroad sued for an injunction in federal court, contending that the Commission's order both violated federal law (the Commerce Clause and the fourteenth amendment) and exceeded the Commission's authority under state law. The district court issued the injunction, but the Supreme Court held that the court should have abstained.

Justice Frankfurter initially relied on traditional equitable considerations. He said that the railroad had no "right" to injunctive relief, despite the merits of its claims, and that, instead, the request for an injunction was addressed to the "sound discretion" of the court.[65] In England, injunctions were typically awarded only by Chancery, and then only if there was no "adequate remedy" in the "law" courts and injunctive relief was essential to spare litigants "irreparable" harm, both "great and immediate."[66] Frankfurter recognized that the district court below had jurisdictional power to entertain the lawsuit and to award appropriate relief. He insisted, however, that the historical preconditions for equitable relief could do service in the cause of federalism: Federal district courts should withhold equitable relief for the purpose of avoiding needless friction with the states and state courts.[67]

Next, Justice Frankfurter insisted that if the railroad's state claim was meritorious, the case should be resolved on that basis alone. In that event, the federal constitutional issues would not arise.[68] With respect to state issues, he explained that federal courts always run the risk that they may misconceive state law. Erroneous federal decisions regarding state law may dispose of particular cases. But in future cases, state courts can provide the really authoritative judgment. Frankfurter explained that federal court "forecasts" about state law can easily be displaced by later state court decisions and are therefore wasteful and potentially offensive to the states. Moreover, in the near term, erroneous federal rulings on state issues may interfere with "sensitive" state policies. If, then, the parties have "an easy and ample means" of obtaining an authoritative judgment from the state courts, federal courts should postpone their own work to allow the parties to seek that judgment.[69]

Over his career, Justice Frankfurter attempted to divert litigation into state court in a number of ways. It is important to understand the analytic differences between his tac-

---

eral courts often dismiss federal actions for *forum non conveniens*. She insisted, however, that those cases are governed by other considerations that do not attend abstention in any of its forms. *Quackenbush*, 517 U.S. at 722–23.

64. 312 U.S. 496 (1941).

65. Id. at 500, quoting *Beal v. Missouri Pac. R.R.*, 312 U.S. 45, 50 (1941).

66. For a synopsis of the classic materials, see Donald H. Zeigler, *Rights Require Remedies: A New Approach to the Enforcement of Rights in the Federal Courts*, 38 Hastings L.J. 665, 667–71 (1987).

67. 312 U.S. at 500–01.

68. Recall the Court's policy of avoiding constitutional questions whenever possible. See Chapter I, note 26.

69. 312 U.S. at 499–501.

tics. There is a certain similarity between the abstention doctrine Frankfurter established in *Pullman* and the arguments he pressed (unsuccessfully) in *Snowden v. Hughes*[70] and *Monroe v. Pape*.[71] In *Snowden* and *Monroe*, Frankfurter argued (in the main) that plaintiffs with federal claims should be sent to state court in pursuit of authoritative decisions on whether state officers have taken action consistent with state law. By Frankfurter's (erroneous) account, state court decisions regarding state law have a crucial bearing on the plaintiffs' federal claims (the applicability of the fourteenth amendment and the availability of §1983). In *Pullman*, by contrast, Frankfurter held that plaintiffs should be sent to state court in pursuit of authoritative state court decisions on independent (though related) state claims that, if successful, would obviate the need to determine their federal claims.[72]

State-question abstention has followed an uneven course since *Pullman*. In some ways, abstention under this heading has gained ground. Despite Justice Frankfurter's heavy reliance on equitable discretion, the Court has invoked *Pullman* abstention in actions "at law" for damages.[73] Moreover, the Court has held that §1983 actions are not exempt from state-question abstention.[74] By contrast, §1983 suits frequently provide the occasion for abstention when there are federal constitutional claims to be deferred.[75] In other respects, state-question abstention has lost ground, primarily because of the costs it visits upon the parties.[76] Academicians debate the merits of the Court's work. By some accounts, state-question abstention is inconsistent with the separation of powers inasmuch as it defies Congress' primary authority to establish the federal courts' jurisdiction.[77] By other accounts, state-question abstention (properly orchestrated) is one of many defensible devices by which the courts determine when to exercise the jurisdiction that Congress confers.[78] By many accounts, state-question abstention is objectionable

70. 321 U.S. 1 (1944).

71. 365 U.S. 167 (1961). See Chapter X, notes 293–98, 377–80 and accompanying text.

72. See also Chapter X, note 413 (explaining the difference between *Pullman* abstention and the Court's analysis of procedural due process in *Parratt*). Professor McManamon has traced Justice Frankfurter's many efforts to achieve similar practical ends. Mary Brigid McManamon, *Felix Frankfurter: The Architect of "Our Federalism"*, 27 Ga. L. Rev. 697 (1993). Professor Purcell argues that Frankfurter had two objectives: to preserve the quality of federal adjudication and to minimize federal court interference with the states and their courts. Edward A. Purcell, Jr., *Reconsidering the Franfurtarian Paradigm: Reflections on Histories of Lower Federal Courts*, 24 Law & Soc. Inquiry 679, 698–706 (1999).

73. E.g., *Clay v. Sun Ins. Office*, 363 U.S. 207 (1960); *Fornaris v. Ridge Tool Co.*, 400 U.S. 41 (1970). In both *Clay* and *Fornaris*, the effect of abstention was the postponement rather than the surrender of federal adjudicative authority. See notes 62–63 and accompanying text.

74. *Harrison v. NAACP*, 360 U.S. 167 (1959).

75. The Court did not mention §1983 in *Pullman* itself, which preceded *Monroe v. Pape* by twenty years. See Chapter X, notes 372–76 and accompanying text (discussing *Monroe*). Today, an action like the one in *Pullman* would be authorized by §1983, albeit an attempt to obtain injunctive relief regarding a violation of state law would implicate state sovereign immunity as interpreted in *Pennhurst State School & Hosp. v. Halderman*, 465 U.S. 89 (1984); see Chapter X, notes 350–66 and accompanying text.

76. See notes 96–102 and accompanying text.

77. Professor Redish once pressed this view. Martin H. Redish, *Abstention, Separation of Powers, and the Limits of the Judicial Function*, 94 Yale L.J. 71 (1984). Professor Wells thinks the argument pays insufficient attention to the Court's responsibility for elaborating the statutes that Congress enacts—particularly §1983. Michael Wells, *Why Professor Redish is Wrong About Abstention*, 19 Ga. L. Rev. 1097 (1985). Cf. note 143 (noting that Redish has adopted a different perspective more recently).

78. Professor Shapiro promotes this position. David L. Shapiro, *Jurisdiction and Discretion*, 60 N.Y.U. L. Rev. 543 (1985). He argues that Congress cannot hope to "answer in gross" the many

inasmuch as it postpones (and can frustrate) litigants' access to the federal courts for the adjudication of federal constitutional claims.[79]

1. Prerequisites

Justice Frankfurter summed up the abstention doctrine associated with *Pullman* this way: When (1) a plaintiff in federal court asserts both federal constitutional and state law claims for equitable relief; (2) the resolution of the state claim might dispose of the matter without recourse to the constitutional claim; (3) the state question is unsettled, so that there is a serious chance that the federal court will fail to predict the way in which the state courts will ultimately decide it; and (4) the state courts offer an effective means of obtaining an authoritative judgment on the state issue—then the federal court should postpone a federal decision on either claim pending state court adjudication of the state claim.

Alternative federal and state claims. State-question abstention presupposes that plaintiffs advance both federal and state claims. Federal courts have no occasion to abstain on the theory that plaintiffs *might* have added supplemental state claims to their complaints. To rest abstention on claims that plaintiffs choose not to present would be to neglect plaintiffs' traditional ability to select their own theories.[80] Moreover, it would require federal courts to entertain arguments from defendants who wish to explore the corpus of state law in search of claims that plaintiffs have overlooked or deliberately eschewed.[81] At the same time, state-question abstention undermines supplemental jurisdiction. The principal point of 28 U.S.C. §1367 is to ensure that litigants with federal claims are able to obtain an adjudication of those claims in federal court without aban-

---

questions that arise regarding the prudent exercise of federal judicial power and that the courts are "functionally better adapted to engage in the necessary fine tuning." Id. at 574. Professor Friedman contends that the Supreme Court employs abstention as a means of deciding whether cases warrant federal court treatment at the *trial* level or can be handled sufficiently well on appellate review from state court judgments. Barry Friedman, *A Revisionist Theory of Abstention*, 88 Mich. L. Rev. 530, 533, 577–80 (1989). Professor Redish has responded to Shapiro and Wells. See Martin H. Redish, The Federal Courts in the Political Order 51–67 (1991).

79. See Martha A. Field, *Abstention in Constitutional Cases: The Scope of the Pullman Abstention Doctrine Today*, 122 U. Pa. L. Rev. 1071, 1095–96 (1974). Charles A. Wright, *The Abstention Doctrine Reconsidered*, 37 Tex. L. Rev. 815, 817–18 (1959).

80. See Chapter VIII, note 261 and accompanying text.

81. Some lower court decisions indulge defendants in this way. E.g., *Intnat'l Brotherhood of Electrical Workers v. Public Svc. Comm'n*, 614 F.2d 206, 213 n.2 (9th Cir. 1980) (indicating that a plaintiff's failure to advance a state claim is not decisive). Yet there is no Supreme Court precedent for it. Chief Justice Burger once argued (unsuccessfully) that federal courts should abstain in cases in which plaintiffs raise federal constitutional claims but fail to add state constitutional claims of a similar order. *Wisconsin v. Constantineau*, 400 U.S. 433, 439 (1971) (dissenting opinion). Justice Blackmun concurred in *Pennzoil v. Texaco*, 481 U.S. 1 (1987), on the theory that abstention was justified for the reasons given in *Pullman*—even though the plaintiff (Texaco) had advanced no formal state law claim and the defendant (Pennzoil) had abandoned the argument that *Pullman* abstention was warranted. The parties had nonetheless briefed a variety of state law questions, and Blackmun thought it was appropriate to allow the state courts to examine those questions in hopes that Texaco's federal constitutional claim could be avoided. Id. at 27; see note 266. Professor Althouse argues that *Pennzoil* was not an appropriate case for *Pullman* abstention, because the state law issues were not susceptible to resolution in a way that would obviate the federal constitutional question. See note 263 (explaining that the only possibility was that the state courts might elaborate an obscure provision of the state constitution). Althouse, note 55, at 1072.

doning related state claims.[82] Yet when federal courts abstain in favor of state adjudication of state claims, that purpose is sacrificed to comity and federalism. Abstention discourages plaintiffs from invoking a federal district court's supplemental jurisdiction over related state law claims.[83] If plaintiffs follow that course, they risk the postponement of their federal claims while they are obliged to litigate their state claims in state court.[84]

Avoidance of constitutional claims. State-question abstention chiefly hopes to make it unnecessary to grapple with federal constitutional claims.[85] The Court acted on this same principle in *Siler v. Louisville & Nashville R.R. Co.*[86] In *Siler*, however, the Court held only that a federal court should address potentially dispositive state issues before taking up federal constitutional questions. The *Pullman* decision goes a step further—channeling state questions into state court. The Court has said that abstention is warranted only if a plausible determination of a state law question will obviate federal constitutional issues.[87] But the Court has also found abstention appropriate if the state courts' treatment of state issues may improve the record on which federal constitutional issues will be adjudicated.[88]

Unsettled state law. State-question abstention is justified only when a state law claim is so unsettled that there is a serious risk that a federal district court will reach an erro-

---

82. See Chapter VIII, text accompanying notes 412–13.

83. In some instances, federal courts may avoid abstention by dismissing supplemental state claims in their discretion. See Chapter VIII, notes 417–18 and accompanying text. Professor Schapiro has explained, however, that district courts should not assume that whenever *Pullman* abstention is appropriate, they are necessarily entitled to avoid it by eliminating related state claims. Robert Schapiro, *Polyphonic Federalism: State Constitutions in the Federal Courts*, 87 Calif. L. Rev. 1409, 1422 (1999).

84. In some instances, too, plaintiffs who attempt to invoke federal supplemental jurisdiction over related state claims risk dismissal of those claims on state sovereign immunity grounds. Recall that the *Pennhurst* decision allows state officers to set up state sovereign immunity to defeat private suits advancing state law theories, even when only injunctive relief is sought. See Chapter X, notes 350–60 and accompanying text. The *Pennhurst* case, in turn, creates some tension with abstention under *Pullman*. If a plaintiff files suit in federal court advancing both a federal claim and a state claim, the court may be obliged to dismiss the state claim on sovereign immunity grounds and thus may not be in a position to abstain in favor of state court consideration of that claim. See Keith Werhan, *Pullman Abstention After Pennhurst: A Comment on Judicial Federalism*, 27 Wm. & Mary L. Rev. 449, 487 (1986). See also notes 96–102 and accompanying text (discussing the procedural scenarios). Professor Schapiro contends that *Pullman*, *Siler*, and *Pennhurst* "pull in many contradictory directions." Schapiro, note 83, at 1424. Recall, too, the possibility that states may be able to set up federal constitutional state sovereign immunity to defeat state claims in state court as well as in federal court. See Chapter X, notes 150–80 and accompanying text (discussing *Alden v. Maine*). If that is the case, plaintiffs with state law claims may have nowhere to turn.

85. Professor Bezanson contends that if abstention is warranted to avoid constitutional issues, it is equally justified to avoid non-constitutional federal questions. Randall P. Bezanson, *Abstention: The Supreme Court and Allocation of Judicial Power*, 27 Vand. L. Rev. 1107, 1112 (1974). The Court has not taken that view. See *Propper v. Clark*, 337 U.S. 472, 490 (1949).

86. 213 U.S. 175 (1909); see Chapter VIII, text accompanying note 414.

87. *Baggett v. Bullitt*, 377 U.S. 360, 375–77 (1964). Accordingly, *Pullman* abstention demands that federal district courts attend to the relationship between state law issues and federal constitutional questions arranged in tandem. That, of course, is the kind of relationship that the Supreme Court sometimes addresses when it implements the adequate state ground doctrine. See Chapter VII, notes 122–27 and accompanying text.

88. E.g., *Lake Carriers' Ass'n v. MacMullan*, 406 U.S. 498, 510–12 (1972); *Zwickler v. Koota*, 389 U.S. 241, 248–49 (1967). Professor Bezanson draws an analogy to the ripeness doctrine, which also postpones federal adjudication in part to achieve a better basis for judgment on constitutional claims. Bezanson, note 85, at 1118–19; see Chapter IX, notes 394–420.

neous judgment. The "relevant inquiry" is not whether there is a "bare, though unlikely, possibility" that the state courts "*might*" decide a state issue in a way that avoids a constitutional claim. The state law issue must be genuinely "uncertain" and "obviously susceptible" to a construction of that kind.[89] Abstention is not to be used as a thinly veiled invitation to the state courts to "rewrite" state statutes in order to forestall federal constitutional issues.[90]

State court machinery. State-question abstention depends on a reasonably efficient means for obtaining an authoritative state court judgment on the plaintiff's state claim. Plaintiffs who are diverted to state court usually must initiate entirely new lawsuits, typically in the form of actions for declaratory relief. Litigation of that kind can consume years before reaching final judgment.[91] Most states facilitate abstention by inviting federal courts to "certify" unsettled questions of state law to the state's highest court for expedited treatment. The Supreme Court encourages the district and circuit courts to exploit mechanisms of that kind[92] and itself occasionally takes advantage of them.[93] Yet certification does not always answer.[94] The functional difficulty of obtaining authorita-

---

89. *Hawaii Housing Auth. v. Midkiff*, 467 U.S. 229, 237 (1984) (emphasis in original).

90. *City of Houston v. Hill*, 482 U.S. 451, 470–71 (1987). It is insufficient that the state courts have never construed a statute and a federal court would have to do so on a clean slate. The statute must be unclear, and there must be a plausible construction of it that would avoid the federal constitutional issue, or at least place that question in a different posture. See *Brockett v. Spokane Arcades*, 472 U.S. 491 (1985). Cases involving ambiguous state constitutional provisions are problematic. Even though the text of such a provision may track the language of a parallel provision of the United States Constitution, the state courts may not (and perhaps should not) give it the same interpretation. And since state constitutional law is typically underdeveloped, there may be few state precedents on which to base a genuine prediction. In *Reetz v. Bozanich*, 397 U.S. 82 (1970), the Court found abstention warranted, because the state constitutional claim rested on peculiar provisions of the Alaska constitution that had never been addressed by the courts of that state. In *Examining Bd. of Engineers v. Flores de Otero*, 426 U.S. 572 (1976), the Court found abstention unjustified, because the state constitutional claim rested on a state analog of the federal Equal Protection Clause. The Court explained in *Otero* that if abstention were warranted in every case in which a plaintiff advanced a claim based on a "broad and sweeping" state constitutional provision, state-question abstention would no longer be an exception to the exercise of federal jurisdiction, but would become the rule. Id. at 598. The Court said in *Harris County Comm'rs Court v. Moore*, 420 U.S. 77 (1975), that abstention is appropriate if a state claim rests on a state statute that is part of an integrated scheme of local statutes, regulations, and constitutional provisions that "as a whole calls for clarifying interpretation by the state courts." Id. at 84 n.8.

91. For discussions of the burdens and delays that state-question abstention entails, see Donald S. Chisum, *The Tensions of Judicial Federalism*, 33 Stan. L. Rev. 1161, 1179 (1981); Philip B. Kurland, *Toward a Co-operative Judicial Federalism: The Federal Court Abstention Doctrine*, 24 F.R.D. 481, 489 (1959).

92. E.g., *Bellotti v. Baird*, 428 U.S. 132, 151 (1976). Certification can "simplif[y]" abstention, *Planned Parenthood Ass'n v. Ashcroft*, 462 U.S. 476, 493 n.21 (1983), but does not alone *justify* abstention. *Hill*, 482 U.S. at 470–71. In *Arizonans for Official English v. Arizona*, 520 U.S. 43 (1997), the Court suggested that the availability of certification should cut in favor of abstention in case involving "novel" or "unsettled" questions of state law. Id. at 76.

93. E.g., *Fiore v. White*, 528 U.S. 23 (1999) (directing a question to a state supreme court).

94. Some certification schemes authorize state supreme courts to answer only questions from other appellate courts—not federal district courts. When state supreme courts can (and are willing to) respond, they necessarily do so without a trial and the usual development of the issues. For discussions of these and other functional shortcomings, see Paul A. LeBel, *Legal Positivism and Federalism: The Certification Experience*, 19 Ga. L. Rev. 999 (1985); Bruce M. Selya, *Certified Madness: Ask a Silly Question...*, 29 Suffolk U. L. Rev. 677 (1995); M. Bryan Schneider, *But Answer Came There None: The Michigan Supreme Court and the Certified Question of State Law*, 41 Wayne L. Rev. 273 (1995). The Chief Justice has warned that certification can be burdensome and time-consuming. *Lehman Bros. v. Schein*, 416 U.S. 386, 394–95 (1974) (concurring opinion). The American Law In-

tive state court judgments within a reasonable time has always been and remains the principal flaw in the framework that Justice Frankfurter envisioned.[95]

2. Procedure

The point of state-question abstention pursuant to *Pullman* is not (necessarily) to relinquish responsibility for a case entirely, but to defer adjudication in order to avoid wrestling with the plaintiff's federal constitutional claim.[96] The federal court retains formal jurisdiction of the matter, but stays further federal proceedings while the plaintiff takes the state question to state court.[97] When the state courts entertain the state claim, they are entitled to know that the plaintiff also has a related federal constitutional claim. The federal environment in which a state claim is situated can affect its proper resolution. Accordingly, the plaintiff must apprise the state courts of both the state claim and the federal claim.[98] Having gone that far, the plaintiff may decide to abandon the federal forum altogether and commit both claims for resolution in state court. In that instance, the plaintiff will typically be bound by the state courts' ultimate decision on both claims, subject to Supreme Court appellate review if the federal claim is dispositive.[99] The federal district court in which the plaintiff originally filed suit will have no jurisdiction to review the state court judgment for error and will, instead, give that judgment the preclusive effect it would have in another state court.[100]

In *England v. Louisiana State Bd. of Med. Examiners*,[101] the Court held that a plaintiff who does *not* wish to commit both state and federal claims to the state courts need not do so. Justice Brennan explained that the plaintiff can alert the state courts to both issues, but reserve the right to return to the federal district court once the state courts have given the state law claim an authoritative adjudication. In that instance, the federal court's formal retention of jurisdiction permits that court to resume responsibility for the case. Thereafter, the litigation can continue through the federal judicial system in

---

stitute has developed a model act in hopes of perfecting the mechanism. That model, too, has flaws. See Ira P. Robbins, *The Uniform Certification of Questions of Law Act: A Proposal for Reform*, 18 J. Legis. 127 (1992). For an endorsement of state certification schemes, see Bradford R. Clark, *Ascertaining the Laws of the Several States: Positivism and Judicial Federalism After Erie*, 145 U. Pa. L. Rev. 1459, 1544–64 (1997).

95. See David P. Currie, *The Federal Courts and the American Law Institute: Part II*, 36 U. Chi. L. Rev. 268, 317 (1969).

96. *Growe v. Emison*, 507 U.S. 25, 32 n.1 (1993). See note 85 and accompanying text.

97. The Supreme Court of Texas once refused to entertain a declaratory judgment action regarding an unsettled question of state law while the plaintiff's original lawsuit was formally pending in federal court. To satisfy that court, the Supreme Court said in the *Moore* case that a district court in Texas could formally dismiss an action in order to ensure that the plaintiff could gain access to the Texas state courts following the federal court's abstention. *Moore*, 420 U.S. at 88–89. The Court explained that the dismissal would be without prejudice to the plaintiff's return to federal court later, after the Texas courts had resolved the state law issue that triggered abstention. Other state courts are more cooperative, and formal dismissal is unnecessary.

98. *Gov't & Civic Employees Org. Comm. v. Windsor*, 353 U.S. 364 (1957).

99. See Chapter VII, notes 58–90. If a party fully commits all issues to the state courts, the federal district court's formal retention of jurisdiction is inconsequential, and the final judgment rendered in state court is subject to Supreme Court review in the ordinary manner. *NAACP v. Button*, 371 U.S. 415, 427 (1963).

100. See Chapter VI, notes 161–225 (discussing the preclusive effects of state court judgments and the *Rooker/Feldman* doctrine).

101. 375 U.S. 411 (1964).

the ordinary course. By all accounts, the procedure described in *England* is awkward for both litigants and courts. Its only redeeming feature is that it protects the plaintiff's opportunity to advance federal claims in federal court, provided the plaintiff has the resources and stamina to make use of it.[102]

E. Special State Interests

Federal courts may abstain from exercising jurisdiction in three additional contexts, primarily (though not exclusively) identified by the special state interests at stake. District courts either postpone or relinquish jurisdiction if federal court action would: (1) disrupt coordinated arrangements under which state administrative agencies and courts regulate matters of peculiar complexity and local importance; (2) risk an erroneous judgment on a difficult issue of state law touching a state's sovereign interests; or (3) duplicate litigation already pending in state court in special circumstances warranting deference. By most accounts, the Supreme Court decisions under these headings articulate no reliable formulaic principles or rules. They are authoritative precedents not to be ignored. But, in truth, they represent no predictable abstention *doctrines* at all. When they are honored, it is often in the breach.[103]

1. State Administrative Interests

In *Burford v. Sun Oil Co.*,[104] the Court grappled with a scheme under which Texas regulated the East Texas Oil Field.[105] The Texas Railroad Commission had broad discretionary authority to maintain the proper balance between economically beneficial drilling in the near term, on the one hand, and safeguards for the future of the field, on the other. State trial courts in Austin had authority to work with the Commission to ensure that the oil field was supervised in an effective, geologically sound manner. The Commission issued an order permitting Burford to drill new wells. The Sun Oil Company filed suit in federal court, contending that the order violated both state law and the fourteenth amendment. The case did not satisfy the criteria for state-question abstention. The company sought equitable relief with respect to federal and state claims, but there was no reason to regard the relevant state law as unsettled or to think that the state courts might resolve the state claim in a way that would make it unnecessary to reach

102. The American Law Institute has recommended that the *England* procedure should be discarded. According to the ALI, state-question abstention usually should be available only when the value of sending litigants to state court is so great that federal district courts are justified in surrendering jurisdiction entirely, leaving it to the Supreme Court to correct state court errors on direct review. Yet the ALI would eliminate state-question abstention in race discrimination cases like *Pullman*. ALI, Study of the Division of Jurisdiction Between State and Federal Courts 49–50, 282–86 (1969).

103. See notes 104–06, 119–20, 132–36 and accompanying text.

104. 319 U.S. 315 (1943).

105. The wells that a private operator drilled in that area drew oil not only from beneath the operator's own land, but from the extensive reservoir of oil beneath all the land in the field. Moreover, even a single well reduced the underground pressure throughout the field and thus made it more difficult and expensive to extract oil from other sites. Texas depended on the oil field to generate economic activity and tax revenues.

the federal constitutional issue.[106] Nevertheless, the Supreme Court held that abstention was warranted.

Justice Black offered no doctrinal explanation, but rested, instead, on an extensive review of the facts. He emphasized the special nature of the administrative scheme in Texas and the expertise required for regulating such a vital and economically important local resource. Moreover, he said that the state courts authorized to review the Commission's decisions were "working partners" with the Commission, performing a function that was neither wholly legislative in the sense of the *Prentis* case,[107] nor wholly judicial, either. If the federal court were to involve itself in that scheme, it might disrupt the state's attempt to achieve uniform decisions on largely technical questions. Given those special circumstances, Black said that a "sound respect for the independence of state action" required a federal "equity court" to dismiss the oil company's federal lawsuit.[108]

The Supreme Court has relied on *Burford* to justify abstention in only one other case, decided nearly a half century ago.[109] Yet the Court has occasionally recalled *Burford* with apparent approval, albeit stating the message in the case only vaguely. In *NOPSI v. Council of New Orleans*,[110] the Court gave this account: So long as "timely and adequate state-court review is available," a federal court "sitting in equity must decline to interfere with" state administrative agencies when there are "difficult questions of state law bearing on policy problems of substantial public import whose importance transcends the result in the case then at bar" or when the "exercise of federal review" of state questions would be "disruptive of state efforts to establish a coherent policy with respect to a matter of substantial public concern."[111] Then again, the Court made it clear in *NOPSI* that *Burford* does *not* require federal district courts to dismiss routine cases in which plaintiffs mount federal attacks on orders issued by state regulatory agencies.[112]

In *NOPSI*, an electrical power company (NOPSI) agreed to contribute to the costs of constructing two nuclear plants. The price of electricity went down, the costs of building the plants went up, and construction was suspended. The Federal Energy Regulatory

106. Id. at 339–42 (Frankfurter, J., dissenting).

107. See notes 39–43 and accompanying text (discussing *Prentis*).

108. 319 U.S. at 334 (majority opinion). Professor Young has parsed Justice Black's "rambling" opinion for these and other points. Gordon G. Young, *Federal Court Abstention and State Administrative Law From Burford to Ankenbrandt: Fifty Years of Judicial Federalism Under Burford v. Sun Oil Co. and Kindred Doctrines*, 42 DePaul L. Rev. 859, 877–78 (1993).

109. In *Alabama Pub. Svc. Comm'n v. Southern Ry.*, 341 U.S. 341 (1951), state regulators denied the railroad's request to drop two intrastate routes. There was a procedure for seeking review of that order in state court. Like the oil company in *Burford*, the railroad filed suit in federal court, attacking the order on both state and fourteenth amendment grounds. Chief Justice Vinson said that intrastate railroad traffic was generally a matter of state concern and that since state law concentrated supervisory authority in a particular state court, the railroad must pursue relief from that court. Id. at 348. In *McNeese v. Bd. of Ed.*, 373 U.S. 668 (1963), the Court declined to invoke *Burford* in a school desegregation context. In that case, the Court said that *Burford* is limited to circumstances in which a federal issue is "entangled in a skein of state law" that "must be untangled before the federal case can proceed." Id. at 674.

110. 491 U.S. 350 (1989).

111. Id. at 361. Justice Scalia borrowed some of this language from *Colorado River Water Conservation Dist. v. United States*, 424 U.S. 800, 814 (1976), where the Court had previously used it to describe the abstention usually associated with the *Thibodaux* decision. See text accompanying notes 119–20.

112. See also *Quackenbush v. Allstate Ins. Co.*, 517 U.S. 706 (1996) (refusing to approve *Burford* abstention in a case presenting "nothing more than a run-of-the-mill contract dispute"); notes 62–63 and accompanying text.

Commission (FERC) determined the losses that should be allocated to NOPSI. NOPSI then asked the local regulatory agency (the Council) to fix intrastate power rates at a level that would allow NOPSI to recoup the losses that FERC identified. The Council set the case for a hearing. NOPSI immediately filed suit in federal court, seeking a declaratory judgment that the Council was obliged to approve the requested rates and an injunction ordering the Council to do so. The district court dismissed that suit, relying on *Burford* abstention and the Johnson Act as alternative grounds.[113] The Council then initiated an investigation of NOPSI's involvement in the power plant deal. During the investigation, NOPSI filed a second federal lawsuit. The district court also dismissed that suit, invoking both *Burford* and the ripeness doctrine.[114] The Council ultimately issued an order establishing lower rates than NOPSI had requested. NOPSI then filed both a petition for review of the Council's order in state court and a third lawsuit in federal court. The district court dismissed the federal action, but the Supreme Court reversed.

NOPSI advanced no significant claims under state law. Nor did NOPSI contest the way in which the Council had weighed "state-law" factors in reaching its decision. Instead, in both its state and federal court actions, NOPSI primarily contended that the Council's rate order was preempted by federal law (because it conflicted with FERC's determination of NOPSI's share of the expenses associated with the new plants). Justice Scalia explained that there was nothing especially complex about the regulatory scheme in the case. Nor did the review proceeding in state court exhibit the special features the Court had found significant in *Burford*. NOPSI's federal preemption claim went to the validity of the rate order on its face and could be determined without going beyond the order's "four corners." Accordingly, the district court's adjudication of that claim would not disrupt the state agency's efforts to enforce local regulatory law in an accurate, uniform, and efficient manner.[115]

In the wake of *NOPSI*, the only safe (though admittedly narrow) formulation for *Burford* abstention must be gleaned from the facts of *Burford* itself: Abstention is warranted if the exercise of federal jurisdiction will seriously interfere with coordinated state regulatory schemes in which administrative agencies and state courts function as partners to bring technical expertise to bear on peculiarly complex and important local matters—involving at least some questions of state regulatory law.[116] If this is what *Bur-*

---

113. See note 34 and accompanying text (discussing the Johnson Act).

114. See Chapter IX, notes 394–420 and accompanying text (discussing ripeness).

115. 491 U.S. at 361–63. The pendency of the parallel state court action did not, in itself, warrant abstention pursuant to *Burford* or any other abstention doctrine. See notes 271–78 and accompanying text.

116. Professor Young has explored the lower court decisions elaborating *Burford*. Some adopt this narrow formulation, but others give *Burford* a much broader purview. Young, note 108, at 900–02. See also Julie A. Davies, *Pullman and Burford Abstention: Clarifying the Roles of State and Federal Courts in Constitutional Cases*, 20 U.C. Davis L. Rev. 1 (1986) (also reporting wide variations in lower court decisions). In *Ankenbrandt v. Richards*, 504 U.S. 689 (1992), the Court reaffirmed that federal district courts have no diversity jurisdiction to issue divorce, alimony, and child custody decrees. The Court noted that the district courts may also abstain in other kinds of domestic relations cases on the basis of *Burford*. Id. at 705–06. That suggested (but did not decide) that *Burford* abstention may yet extend beyond the factual setting in *Burford* itself. There is nothing to suggest, however, that *Burford* could sensibly be extended to the lengths that some lower courts have taken that case. For discussions of the jurisdictional rule in *Ankenbrandt*, see Naomi R. Cahn, *Family Law, Federalism, and the Federal Courts*, 79 Iowa L. Rev. 1073 (1994); Michael A. Stein, *The Domestic Relations Exception to Federal Jurisdiction: Rethinking an Unsettled Federal Courts Doctrine*, 36 B.C. L. Rev. 669 (1995). The Court has also held that federal courts generally do not handle probate matters. See *Markham v. Allen*, 326 U.S. 490 (1946). See Peter Nicolas, *Fighting the Probate Mafia: A Dissection of the Probate Exception to Federal Court Jurisdiction*, 74 So. Calif. L. Rev. 1479, 1528–36

ford means, however, it may have been overtaken by more recent developments. It is possible that the suit in *Burford* might have been filed pursuant to §1983. Today, plaintiffs in §1983 actions need not exhaust state administrative remedies.[117]

The abstention doctrine associated with *Burford* (if doctrine it is) differs from state-question abstention under *Pullman* in two important respects: (1) the point of *Burford* abstention is to avoid disrupting state affairs, not needless consideration of federal constitutional questions; and (2) the consequence of *Burford* abstention may be relinquishment of federal responsibility for both state and federal claims rather than postponement of federal adjudication—provided the court has discretion regarding the relief at stake.[118]

2. State Sovereign Interests

In *Louisiana Power & Light Co. v. City of Thibodaux*,[119] the city initiated an action in state court to condemn property owned by the company. The company removed the

(2001) (exploring the extent to which *Burford* or the other abstention doctrines explain and justify the "probate exception"). Professor Wells argues that *Burford* is addressed to business regulation cases, which no longer present serious federal constitutional questions and are thus best left to state law, enforced by state courts. Wells, note 58, at 77.

117. See notes 47–51 and accompanying text (discussing the *Patsy* case); Chapter VIII, notes 135–36 (describing the prerequisites for a §1983 action); but see Chapter VI, notes 186–95 and accompanying text (noting that litigants who choose to pursue relief in state administrative agencies may find that they cannot revisit factual issues in later litigation in federal court). Some academics find *Burford* unobjectionable, even desirable. E.g., Bezanson, note 85, at 1124; Calvin R. Massey, *Abstention and the Constitutional Limits of the Judicial Power of the United States*, 1991 B.Y.U. L. Rev. 811, 849. Others are critical. Professor Young argues that *Burford* is an artifact of the formative period of American administrative law and illustrates the Court's early efforts to accommodate both state and federal agencies. Young, note 108, at 886–94. Professor Woolhandler and Professor Collins contend that *Burford* reflects exaggerated concerns that federal courts will be drawn into shaping state administrative law and, at that, will appear to be exercising a form of appellate review of state administrative orders. They argue that federal courts have historically handled similar kinds of matters and that the routine invocation of abstention in cases involving state administrative action is not only unnecessary, but in tension with the jurisdiction that Congress has conferred via §1331 and §1332. While diversity may not be popular in academic circles, it can be defended as a means of protecting out-of-state litigants from bias in local courts. And as long as diversity jurisdiction exists, Woolhandler and Collins argue that *Burford* abstention can be justified only when federal plaintiffs advance rudimentary claims that state agencies have acted arbitrarily in isolated instances. Ann Woolhandler & Michael G. Collins, *Judicial Federalism and the Administrative States*, 87 Calif. L. Rev. 613 (1999). Woolhandler and Collins contend that federal courts can mitigate any genuine interference with state administrative mechanisms by giving agency determinations the kind of (relaxed) review they enjoy as a matter of state law. See Chapter VIII, note 410 (discussing the *Surgeons* and *Stude* cases).

118. Justice Black explicitly approved the district court's dismissal of the action in *Burford*. But see notes 60–63 and accompanying text (explaining that the Court has since limited *Burford* abstention to postponements in cases in which federal plaintiffs seek non-discretionary relief). Justice Frankfurter dissented in *Burford* and concurred on other grounds in *Southern Ry*. See note 109. In both instances, Frankfurter argued that abstention can be justified only to avoid needless constitutional adjudication and that, in any event, should only postpone the exercise of federal jurisdiction. Frankfurter insisted that abstention is not warranted merely because a federal district court may reach a decision on a state law question that differs from the decision that a state court would render. He denied that his analysis in *Pullman* implies that conclusion. By his account, the very point of federal diversity jurisdiction is that a comparatively neutral federal court is a better judge of state law than the courts of either interested state. *Burford*, 319 U.S. at 344–45 (dissenting opinion).

119. 360 U.S. 25 (1959).

suit to federal court on the basis of diversity. The only dispute was over the city's authority to condemn land at all. The relevant state statute appeared to give the city the necessary power, but an opinion by the state attorney general denied it. There was no state court precedent regarding the statute's meaning. The Supreme Court upheld the district court's decision to abstain while the company pursued a declaratory judgment action in state court, seeking a definitive construction of the statute. Justice Frankfurter explained that the "special nature of eminent domain," together with the sensitivity of determining the relations between a state and one of its subdivisions, justified abstention. The case called for a determination of a question of state law that was "intimately involved with sovereign prerogative." Only the state courts could make that determination authoritatively. The attorney general's opinion clouded the issue, presenting a genuine risk that the federal court might reach an erroneous result. That, in turn, would produce needless friction with the state courts.[120]

The decision in *Thibodaux* shared some features with *Pullman*: It would have been hard to "forecast" the way the state courts would construe the statute, and the district court did not dismiss the federal suit, but held it on the docket pending resolution of the state suit.[121] Yet the chief rationales for abstention in *Pullman* were missing. The company did not seek an injunction, so the court could not rest its decision to abstain on equitable considerations. And there was no reason to think that the state courts might interpret the state statute in a way that would make it unnecessary to decide a federal constitutional question. Since the case was in federal court only on the basis of diversity, the federal court could be expected to decide state law questions, with or without significant guidance from state precedents.[122] The only special factors were the state's sovereign interests in eminent domain and the authority delegated to a political subdivision. Justice Brennan dissented in *Thibodaux*. Then, in an opinion for the Court in *Allegheny County v. Frank Mashuda Co.*,[123] decided on the same day, Brennan disclaimed abstention in another eminent domain case that was distinguishable from *Thibodaux* only on the most tenuous grounds.[124]

---

120. Id. at 28.

121. Since *Thibodaux* was a diversity case in which the only immediately contested question was the proper construction of the state statute, it was not entirely clear why Justice Frankfurter found it important that the district court had merely stayed the federal action rather than dismissing it outright. Once the state courts settled the question whether the city had state law authority to condemn the property, there would be nothing left to decide. Frankfurter may have thought it essential for the federal court to keep the case formally on the federal docket to ensure that the state proceedings were handled efficiently. He may also have anticipated that, if the condemnation ultimately went forward, the company might contest the adequacy of the compensation—a federal matter.

122. See *Meredith v. Winter Haven*, 320 U.S. 228, 234 (1943) (stating the general rule that abstention is inappropriate in a diversity case merely because the state law issues to be decided are difficult). See note 118 (discussing Justice Frankfurter's previous criticism of abstention in diversity cases). In *Thibodaux*, Frankfurter distinguished *Meredith* on the ground that, in that case, the lower court had dismissed a federal lawsuit entirely rather than retaining jurisdiction pending litigation in state court. *Thibodaux*, 360 U.S. at 27 n.2.

123. 360 U.S. 185 (1959).

124. In *Mashuda*, Brennan essentially reiterated the arguments he had just made in dissent in *Thibodaux*. Frankfurter, for his part, joined Justice Clark's dissent in *Mashuda*—which cited essentially the same grounds that Frankfurter had just given (for the Court) to justify abstention in *Thibodaux*. Justice Stewart and Justice Whittaker saw the two cases differently. In *Thibodaux*, the key issue was the proper interpretation of a state statute; in *Mashuda*, the chief question was whether property had been taken for a public use. Professor Friedman suggests that the two cases were distinguishable inasmuch as the question in *Mashuda* was essentially one of "fact," making that diversity action the kind of matter that Congress might sensibly have wished to channel to a compara-

The Supreme Court has never relied on *Thibodaux* to justify abstention in any other case.[125] Yet the Court has cited *Thibodaux* with apparent approval, much in the way it has cited *Burford*.[126] In *Colorado River Water Conservation Dist. v. United States*,[127] Justice Brennan said that *Thibodaux* calls for abstention when a case presents "difficult questions of state law bearing on policy problems of substantial public import whose importance transcends the result in the case then at bar."[128] That formulation is far too broad to be accurate. Not only does it reach beyond cases implicating special questions of sovereignty, but (taken literally) it covers a host of ordinary diversity actions in which federal courts may wish to wash their hands of intricate state law questions.[129] In the *NOPSI* case, Justice Scalia borrowed Brennan's description of *Thibodaux* to form part of his account of *Burford*.[130] It may be, then, that the Court now regards *Thibodaux* and *Burford* as illustrations of the same general idea.[131]

3. Parallel Litigation in State Court

In *Colorado River*,[132] the Court revisited the classic problem: parallel lawsuits involving the same parties and issues, proceeding simultaneously in federal and state court. Colorado maintained a special system of "water courts" to resolve disputes over water rights in each of seven districts. The federal government asserted water rights in areas located in some of those districts. The government had participated in state court suits in some districts, but was not involved in any of several such actions pending in District No. 7. To advance its claims to water in that district, the government filed suit in federal

---

tively neutral federal court. Friedman, note 78, at 582–83. Recalling the *Thibodaux* and *Mashuda* cases in *Quackenbush*, Justice O'Connor explained the different results in those cases on a familiar ground: In *Thibodaux*, the district court had only stayed federal proceedings, but in *Mashuda* the district court had dismissed the federal action entirely. *Quackenbush*, 517 U.S. at 720–21; see notes 60–63 and accompanying text.

125. There are, however, largely unexplained decisions that call *Thibodaux* to mind. E.g., *Kaiser Steel Corp. v. W.S. Ranch Co.*, 391 U.S. 593 (1968) (ordering the lower court to stay a federal diversity action pending a state declaratory judgment suit regarding water rights under state law); *Lehman Bros. v. Schein*, 416 U.S. 386 (1974) (ordering the circuit court handling a diversity suit to use a state certification scheme to obtain an answer to a question of state law).

126. See text accompanying notes 109–12.

127. 424 U.S. 800 (1976).

128. Id. at 814.

129. Professor Hickman argues that if abstention is justified at all in diversity cases, it must be narrowly restricted. Kelly D. Hickman, *Federal Court Abstention in Diversity of Citizenship Cases*, 62 So. Calif. L. Rev. 1237 (1989).

130. See note 111 and accompanying text.

131. But see James C. Rehnquist, *Taking Comity Seriously: How to Neutralize the Abstention Doctrine*, 46 Stan. L. Rev. 1049, 1083 (1994) (noting once again that *Burford* calls for the dismissal of federal suits while *Thibodaux* calls only for postponement). Professor Young argues that while the Court's literal descriptions suggest that *Thibodaux* abstention is a "variety" of *Burford* abstention, it would make more sense to regard *Burford* as a subset of *Thibodaux*. After all, *Burford* is typically linked to federal deference to state administrative agency proceedings, but *Thibodaux* is not. Young, note 108, at 874–75. Professor Woolhandler and Professor Collins critique *Burford* abstention for the reason that it appears to single out state administrative cases for special treatment. They note that the Court may have been moved by a similar impulse in *Thibodaux*, but they regard *Burford* as especially troubling in that respect. Woolhandler & Collins, note 117. In truth, the justices (or their law clerks) are probably passing along cut-and-paste boilerplate in heartless disregard for academics attempting to understand their results and rationales.

132. See note 127 and accompanying text.

court, naming competing private water users as defendants and seeking a declaratory judgment. The defendants invoked the McCarran Amendment to join the government as a party to one of the actions already under way in state court and moved for dismissal of the government's federal suit in deference to the parallel state proceedings.[133] The district court agreed to dismiss the federal suit, and the Supreme Court affirmed.

Justice Brennan acknowledged that the pendency of an action in state court is "no bar to proceedings concerning the same matter" in federal court.[134] By contrast, federal courts ordinarily have an "unflagging" duty to exercise the jurisdiction that Congress gives them. Abstention is the "exception, not the rule."[135] Brennan summarized the cases in which the Court had found abstention appropriate in the past (including *Burford* and *Thibodaux*) and conceded that none of those cases called for abstention in the case at bar. Nevertheless, in the "particular" circumstances presented in *Colorado River*, Justice Brennan concluded that abstention was warranted in the interests of "[w]ise judicial administration, giving regard to conservation of judicial resources and comprehensive disposition of litigation."[136]

Justice Brennan offered no doctrinal formulation to account for abstention in *Colorado River*. Instead, he explained that several factors (no one of which was "necessarily determinative") counseled against the exercise of federal jurisdiction: The McCarran Amendment established a "clear federal policy" of avoiding "piecemeal adjudication of water rights." The state court action had been filed first, and the government's action in federal court had not progressed beyond the initial pleading stage. The federal action would be tried in Denver, some distance from District No. 7, where most of the private defendants resided. And the government had previously been willing to participate in state court actions in other districts.[137] The Court was divided in *Colorado River*. In dissent, Justice Stewart dismissed as insubstantial all the factors that Justice Brennan mentioned.[138]

The Court has relied on *Colorado River* in more recent instances.[139] Yet in so doing, the Court has consistently reiterated that *Colorado River*, like its cousins (*Burford* and

---

133. The McCarran Amendment, 43 U.S.C. §666, allows plaintiffs to make the United States a defendant in "any" suit "for the adjudication of rights to the use of water," provided that the government owns the relevant water. The Amendment waives the immunity the government would otherwise enjoy. See Chapter X, notes 41–51 and accompanying text.

134. 424 U.S. at 817, quoting *McClellan v. Garland*, 217 U.S. 268, 282 (1910); see note 5 and accompanying text.

135. 424 U.S. at 813.

136. Id. at 817, quoting *Kerotest Mfg. Co. v. C-O-Two Fire Equip. Co.*, 342 U.S. 180, 183 (1952). In *Kerotest*, the Court considered the question whether one federal court should stay its hand in deference to parallel litigation in another federal court.

137. 424 U.S. at 818–20.

138. Justice Stewart distinguished the cases indicating that a court may prudently stay its own proceedings when another court has control of a "res" and an attempt to adjudicate rights in the same "res" may produce conflict. Id. at 822–24; see notes 23–25 and accompanying text. Stewart insisted that neither the federal court nor the state court in *Colorado River* needed physical control of the water in Colorado streams in order to adjudicate disputes over rights to that water.

139. In *Arizona v. San Carlos Apache Tribe*, 463 U.S. 545 (1983), the Court followed *Colorado River* in a factually similar water rights case in which the tribe (rather than the federal government) was the plaintiff in federal court. In *Iowa Mut. Ins. Co. v. LaPlante*, 480 U.S. 9 (1987), the Court approved abstention in a diversity case in deference to pending proceedings in an Indian tribal court. And in *Growe v. Emison*, 507 U.S. 25 (1993), the Court relied on *Colorado River* in directing a three-judge district court to stay its hand in a legislative apportionment case. The Court referred to *Colorado River* in the *NOPSI* case, but primarily only for *Colorado River's* summary of *Burford*. See note 111 and accompanying text. In *Wilton v. Seven Falls Co.*, 515 U.S. 277 (1995), the Court upheld a district court's decision to dismiss a federal diversity action filed by an insurance company seeking a declaratory judgment that it was not obliged to indemnify an oil company for its losses in litigation.

Thibodaux), illustrates an exception to the general rule that federal courts are duty-bound to exercise the jurisdiction that Congress confers upon them. The difficulty, once again, is that the Court's attempt to generalize its thinking produces a formulation that is far too elastic to be taken seriously—for example, the general notion that district courts may abstain in the name of "wise judicial administration." District court decisions to abstain are reviewable,[140] and the Court weights the appellate process *against* abstention. A district court order refusing to abstain is not sufficiently final to be immediately appealable.[141] An order staying or dismissing an action *is* final and can be reviewed.[142] Nevertheless, most academic commentary on *Colorado River* is critical.[143]

Soon after the insurance company filed that suit, the oil company sued the insurance company in state court, seeking to recover under the policy in the ordinary course. In the Supreme Court, Justice O'Connor acknowledged that there were no exceptional circumstances of the kind that *Colorado River* required. The lawsuit in state court would take up the same (state law) issues, but that in itself was insufficient to warrant abstention—particularly in a case in which the state court lawsuit was filed *after* the suit in federal court. O'Connor sustained abstention, however, because federal declaratory relief is discretionary and she could not say that the district court had abused its discretion by taking the parallel litigation in state court into account in deciding whether a declaratory remedy was warranted. See Chapter VIII, notes 140–42 and accompanying text (noting that the Declaratory Judgment Act only *enables* federal courts to award declaratory relief); note 60 and accompanying text (explaining that federal courts may abstain with respect to suits for declaratory relief by dismissing them entirely—because declaratory relief is discretionary). The analysis in *Wilton* is problematic, given that the abstention doctrines generally rest on the threshold notion that litigants have no absolute right to the relief they seek in federal court. See notes 65–66 and accompanying text (noting Justice Frankfurter's discussion of the nature of equitable relief in *Pullman*); notes 153–55 and accompanying text (noting Justice Black's discussion of the nature of declaratory relief in *Samuels*). One might have thought, accordingly, that the abstention doctrines capture and specify the content of the federal courts' discretion in the cases to which they apply, leaving federal courts with no reservoir of discretion to divest themselves of cases that the abstention doctrines do not foreclose. As it turns out, it just is not that simple. The abstention doctrines do add a measure of clarity, but they do not occupy the field. In *Wilton*, it must be said, the insurance company did not seek federal declaratory relief for any of the classic reasons. See Chapter VIII, notes 144–45 and accompanying text. Moreover, the company advanced no federal claims, but invoked federal jurisdiction only to obtain federal adjudication of state claims on which the state courts were authoritative. If, then, there was ever a case for approving a district court's decision to abstain in the absence of exceptional circumstances, *Wilton* was that case.

140. E.g., *Moses H. Cone Mem. Hosp. v. Mercury Constr. Corp.*, 460 U.S. 1 (1983) (holding that a district court had abused its discretion by declining a contract action).

141. *Gulfstream Aerospace Corp. v. Mayacamas Corp.*, 485 U.S. 271 (1988).

142. *Moses H. Cone*, 460 U.S. at 8–13. See Chapter VII, note 215 and accompanying text (discussing the finality rule).

143. Professor Mullenix argues that abstention can be warranted by comity and federalism, but cannot be justified "for reasons of sound judicial administration." Accordingly, she thinks *Colorado River* should be discarded. Linda S. Mullenix, *A Branch Too Far: Pruning the Abstention Doctrine*, 75 Gtn. L.J. 99, 156 (1986). Professor Redish once argued that *Colorado River* could not be squared with Congress' power to establish the federal courts' jurisdiction. Redish, note 77, at 96–98. More recently, he has acknowledged that the Court was not persuaded. As a matter of policy, Redish thinks that either the Court or Congress should make *Colorado River* abstention the rule rather than the exception. Martin H. Redish, *Interstemic Redundancy and Federal Court Power: Proposing a Zero Tolerance Solution to the Duplicative Litigation Problem*, 75 Notre Dame L.Rev. 1347, 1370 (2000). Professor Sonenshein agrees that *Colorado River* was unjustified at its inception, but contends that it can be revised to provide more guidance to the lower courts. David A. Sonenshein, *Abstention: The Crooked Course of Colorado River*, 59 Tulane L. Rev. 651 (1985). Professor Friedman finds *Colorado River* "anomalous," apart from other abstention decisions depending on comity and federalism. Friedman, note 78, at 592. Professor Bartels considers *Colorado River* to rest primarily on a construction of the McCarren Amendment and thus doubts that the case bears significance in other contexts—for example, the context of civil rights. Robert Bartels, *Avoiding a Comity of Errors: A*

F. Federal-Question Abstention

In a final class of cases, federal courts entertaining §1983 actions may abstain for the express purpose of permitting state courts to adjudicate federal claims in pending (or soon to be initiated) litigation in state court. On first blush, this last form of abstention is not surprising. The Anti-Injunction Act, §2283, ordinarily bars federal courts from issuing injunctions that interfere with pending state proceedings.[144] Recall, however, that §2283 is inapplicable to §1983 actions. According to the *Mitchum* decision, federal courts must have authority to enjoin pending state proceedings in §1983 cases in order to protect individual rights secured by federal law.[145] In this last class of cases, federal courts abstain nonetheless in obedience to doctrine that the Supreme Court has elaborated, apart from any statute.

In the leading case, *Younger v. Harris*,[146] John Harris was arrested for distributing leaflets advancing the Progressive Labor Party's agenda. He was charged under the California "syndicalism" statute, which made it a crime to advocate political change by violent means. Harris contended that the syndicalism law was invalid on its face for overbreadth.[147] The state courts rejected that argument and set the case for trial. Harris then filed a §1983 suit in federal court, seeking an injunction against the state prosecution on the theory that it would violate his first amendment rights.[148] The district court issued the injunction, but the Supreme Court held that the district court should have abstained.[149]

Model for Adjudicating Federal Civil Rights Suits that "Interfere" with State Civil Proceedings, 29 Stan. L. Rev. 27, 58 (1976). But see Rehnquist, note 131 (arguing that *Colorado River* is the one form of abstention that *can* be justified—provided it is reduced to a simple rule that the federal courts should routinely defer to state court lawsuits that are already under way and offer litigants an adequate opportunity to litigate their federal claims).

144. See text accompanying note 7.

145. See notes 16–17 and accompanying text.

146. 401 U.S. 37 (1971).

147. See Chapter IX, notes 261–73 and accompanying text.

148. At the time *Younger* was before the Court, *Mitchum* had not yet been decided. See notes 16–17 and accompanying text. Since Harris was a defendant in a pending state criminal prosecution, Justice Black might have invoked the Anti-Injunction Act to condemn the district court's injunction or, in the alternative, might have taken the view the Court would ultimately take in *Mitchum*—namely, that §2283 was inapplicable to a lawsuit filed under the authority of §1983. Instead, Black rested the decision in *Younger* entirely on non-statutory grounds and explicitly declined to say whether §2283 was otherwise controlling "in and of itself." Black relied on §2283 only as evidence that Congress had always manifested a "desire to permit state courts to try state cases free from interference by federal courts." 401 U.S. at 43.

149. The lower courts in *Younger* relied on the Supreme Court's then-recent precedent in *Dombrowski v. Pfister*, 380 U.S. 479 (1965). In that case, the Court had approved an injunction against a prosecution under a virtually identical syndicalism statute in a Louisiana case. Writing for the Court, Justice Brennan said in *Dombrowski* that a defense to a charge under an overbroad statute would not be adequate. Prospective defendants suffered "irreparable harm" because of the "chilling effect" on their freedom of speech, which arose from the *threat* of prosecution. It would not do to hold that anyone who refused to be chilled could raise a free speech defense at trial. The point was to address and relieve the chilling effect on the less intrepid. The only mechanism for dealing effectively with an overbroad statute, according to Brennan, was an affirmative civil suit for injunctive or declaratory relief in which the statute could be struck from the books entirely, not merely rendered ineffective as applied to an individual case. Id. at 488–89. By all accounts, *Younger* departed from *Dombrowski*. The violent shift between the two cases may be the most vivid illustration of the way the Court's approach to federal courts questions changed with the change in its membership. Between 1965 and 1971, the Warren Court's "liberal" majority was replaced by a more "conservative" cohort of Nixon appointees. See Chapter I, note 90 and accompanying text. The Court was divided

Justice Black started where Justice Frankfurter had begun in *Pullman*, using traditional restraints on equitable relief to condition federal court orders affecting state court proceedings.[150] Black recalled that under a "basic doctrine of equity jurisprudence," courts should not "restrain a criminal prosecution" when the defendant has an "adequate remedy at law" and will suffer no "irreparable" injury if the injunction is denied.[151] He explained that Harris had an adequate remedy at law inasmuch as he was free to press his first amendment claim as a defense to the charge against him in state court. If the statute under which he was charged was overbroad as written, the state courts might well save it by giving it a narrow construction. Apart from equity, Justice Black relied on comity as an "even more vital" consideration. In turn, Black merged comity ("a proper respect for state functions") with "Our Federalism." Federal courts must strike a balance, neither according "blind deference" to the states nor interfering "unduly" with state activities. Ordinarily, he explained, federal injunctions against pending state criminal prosecutions tip that balance and should be denied.[152]

---

in *Dombrowski*, as it was later in *Younger*. In *Dombrowski*, Brennan wrote for a five-member Court (himself, Warren, Douglas, Goldberg, and White). Harlan and Clark dissented; Black and Stewart did not participate. During the interim between the two cases, Fortas and Marshall replaced Goldberg and Clark, and Burger and Blackmun replaced Warren and Fortas. Then, in *Younger*, Black wrote for only a plurality (himself, Burger, and Blackmun). Harlan and Stewart concurred to make a majority of five. Brennan also concurred (with Marshall and White), but only with respect to Black's discussion of injunctions (not declaratory judgments). See note 155; text accompanying note 209. Douglas dissented.

150. See notes 65–66 and accompanying text.

151. *Douglas v. City of Jeannette*, 319 U.S. 157, 162–65 (1943); see *Stefanelli v. Minard*, 342 U.S. 117 (1951) (holding that federal courts should not enjoin the use of illegally seized evidence in a state trial). Professor Soifer and Professor Macgill have shown that injunctions were historically much more readily available than Justice Black suggested. Aviam Soifer & H. C. Macgill, *The Younger Doctrine: Reconstructing Reconstruction*, 55 Tex. L. Rev. 1141, 1148–55 (1977). Professor Laycock takes a similar view. Douglas Laycock, *Federal Interference with State Prosecutions: The Cases that Dombrowski Forgot*, 46 U. Chi. L. Rev. 636 (1979).

152. 401 U.S. at 44–49. Justice Black had it that the phrase "Our Federalism" enjoys an old and venerable lineage in American jurisprudence. As a matter of fact, Justice Frankfurter introduced that phrase when he joined the Court in 1939. Michael G. Collins, *Whose Federalism?*, 9 Const. Comm. 75 (1992); see also notes 70–72 and accompanying text. Since Justice Black relied on comity and federalism in *Younger*, as well as on equitable considerations, it is open to argue that the federal-question abstention doctrine he elaborated in that case reaches §1983 suits for damages. The Supreme Court has never squarely decided the question. But see *Deakins v. Monaghan*, 484 U.S. 193, 205 (1988) (White, J., concurring) (giving a positive answer). In *McNary*, the Court cited *Younger* in partial support of its holding that §1983 does not authorize a federal suit for damages arising from wrongful state taxation. See notes 44–46 and accompanying text. The core of the idea in *Younger* is that federal courts should not interfere with pending state prosecutions. Interference is perfectly obvious if federal courts presume to enjoin state proceedings, less so if federal courts merely exercise jurisdiction over legal actions involving the same parties and issues. Recall that another abstention case, *Colorado River*, purports to describe the circumstances in which federal courts should abstain in favor of parallel state proceedings in order to avoid a duplication of effort. See notes 132–36 and accompanying text. Parallel federal §1983 suits for damages and state criminal prosecutions would not appear to meet the *Colorado River* standards (such as they are). Cf. *Heck v. Humphrey*, 512 U.S. 477 (1994) (interpreting §1983 not to be available to most prison inmates seeking compensatory damages for unconstitutional criminal convictions); see Chapter XII, notes 561–73 and accompanying text (discussing *Heck* and related decisions). If *Younger* were ever to be applied in a case involving a suit for damages, the federal court would presumably be limited to postponing the exercise of jurisdiction. See notes 60–61 and accompanying text.

Justice Black took the same view of declaratory relief. Writing for the Court in a companion case, *Samuels v. Mackell*,[153] he acknowledged that declaratory judgments are not governed by the same equitable rules and traditions attending injunctions. But he insisted that declaratory relief is discretionary and that comity and federalism can inform that discretion.[154] By Black's account, federal declaratory judgments interfere with state criminal proceedings in virtually the same way as injunctions. He assumed that any declaratory judgment that a district court rendered would be entitled to preclusive effect in state court. If the state courts declined to respect it, the district court would have authority to issue an injunction after all, as a means of enforcing the declaratory judgment. Accordingly, federal courts should ordinarily refuse to issue declaratory judgments regarding the validity of pending state criminal prosecutions.[155]

The abstention doctrine associated with *Younger* and *Samuels* differs fundamentally from the abstention doctrine associated with *Pullman*.[156] Federal courts do not *stay* federal §1983 actions, forcing litigants to file *new* lawsuits in state court in order to give the state courts an opportunity to determine potentially dispositive issues of *state* law.[157] Under the *Younger* doctrine, federal courts *relinquish* federal jurisdiction entirely, forcing litigants to be satisfied with already *pending* actions in state court, in which state courts will determine *federal* claims.[158] When district courts conclude that *Younger* and *Samuels* bar federal injunctive or declaratory relief, they dismiss the §1983 actions before them in favor of pending state proceedings.[159] In *Huffman v. Pursue*,[160] the Court

---

153. 401 U.S. 66 (1971).

154. See Chapter VIII, notes 141–42 and accompanying text; Chapter IX, notes 416–20 and accompanying text.

155. Justice Brennan concurred on this point in *Samuels*, but only because the indictment in that case had been filed before the federal suit was initiated. In a separate opinion in yet another companion case, *Perez v. Ledesma*, 401 U.S. 82 (1971), Brennan distinguished cases in which §1983 plaintiffs seek declaratory relief in federal court *before* charges are filed in state court. See notes 207–09 and accompanying text (discussing Brennan's subsequent opinion for the Court in *Steffel v. Thompson*).

156. This last abstention doctrine is also distinguishable from *Burford*, *Thibodaux*, and *Colorado River*. In *Thibodaux*, the Court approved a stay of federal litigation in favor of a state court determination of a doubtful question of state law. In *Burford* and *Colorado River*, the Court ordered abstention dismissals knowing that the state courts would decide federal issues. But in neither of those cases was that the point of abstention.

157. See notes 96–97 and accompanying text.

158. See notes 60–61 and accompanying text (explaining that the surrender of jurisdiction can be justified in case involving suits for discretionary relief). The Supreme Court also supervises the implementation of *Younger* and *Samuels* differently from the way it superintends the application of *Pullman*. None of the abstention doctrines purports to deny the federal courts' subject matter jurisdiction, but only to orchestrate the exercise of jurisdiction the federal courts are understood to enjoy. Accordingly, if defendants in federal actions fail to request abstention, federal courts are not required to address the question *sua sponte*. In *Ohio Bureau of Employment Svc. v. Hodory*, 431 U.S. 471 (1977), the Court said that if state authorities do not invoke *Younger* abstention, and thus "voluntarily" agree to litigate in federal court, the federal court may proceed. The "principles of comity do not demand that the federal court force the case back into the State's own system." Id. at 480. The Court explained, however, that it would not quickly approve such a waiver of *Pullman* abstention. In cases otherwise controlled by *Younger*, the consequence of accepting a waiver is that a federal court (rather than a state court) will pass on a federal claim for injunctive or declaratory relief. In cases subject to *Pullman*, by contrast, the consequence of accepting a waiver is that the federal court will forgo the chance to avoid a federal constitutional question. But see *Pennzoil*, 481 U.S. at 11 n.9 (declining to rest on *Pullman* because the interested party had abandoned its argument for abstention on that basis); note 266.

159. E.g., *Hicks v. Miranda*, 422 U.S. 332, 352 (1975).

160. 420 U.S. 592 (1975).

held that state court cases are "pending" within the meaning of *Younger* and *Samuels* not only while they are before state trials courts, but also over the course of direct review within the state court system. Accordingly, litigants whose federal §1983 actions are dismissed must advance their federal theories both at the trial court level in state court and (if they suffer defeat at that level) in the state appellate courts.[161]

Litigants whose federal theories are finally rejected in state court may seek appellate review in the Supreme Court.[162] Litigants who suffer criminal conviction and are sentenced to imprisonment may be able to petition a federal court for a writ of habeas corpus.[163] In that indirect way, they may put federal claims about their treatment before an inferior federal court at a later time.[164] Apart from habeas corpus, however, there is no mechanism by which §1983 plaintiffs whose actions are dismissed under *Younger* and *Samuels* can return to federal district court.[165] Inferior federal courts have no appellate jurisdiction to review state court decisions for error, and, in the main, they are obliged to give state court judgments preclusive effect.[166]

---

161. In *Huffman*, state authorities filed a state court action against the proprietor of a motion picture theater, charging that the theater was exhibiting obscene films. As soon as the trial court issued an order barring further showings, the proprietor filed a federal §1983 action attacking the state obscenity statute on first amendment grounds. Then-Justice Rehnquist said that the state court proceeding was still pending inasmuch as the proprietor had a right to appeal the trial court's order to higher state courts. It did not matter that, by seeking appellate review, the theater proprietor would no longer be responding to state charges brought by state officials in state court, but would become the moving party asking the state appellate courts to determine a federal issue.

162. See Chapter VII, notes 219–22 and accompanying text.

163. See Chapter XII, notes 44–74 and accompanying text.

164. Inasmuch as John Harris was at risk of a criminal conviction in state court and a potential sentence to confinement, the Court's decision in *Younger* did not (necessarily) mean that Harris would never have an opportunity to press his first amendment claim in a federal district court. If he landed in jail after conviction, he would be able to seek a federal writ of habeas corpus. In that rough sense, *Younger* itself *postponed* federal district court adjudication (for some individuals). See Harry T. Edwards, *The Changing Notion of "Our Federalism"*, 33 Wayne L. Rev. 1015, 1030–31 (1987). In *Huffman*, by contrast, the Court extended the *Younger* abstention doctrine to a *civil* proceeding in state court, which allowed for no punishment by imprisonment and, accordingly, no possibility of subsequent district court adjudication in habeas corpus. Cases like *Huffman* plainly establish that the consequence of federal-question abstention is not typically a deferral of federal district court adjudication, but a surrender of jurisdiction to state courts whose judgments will almost always be final. See Larry W. Yackle, *Explaining Habeas Corpus*, 60 N.Y.U. L. Rev. 991, 1045–46 (1985). Justice Rehnquist acknowledged as much in *Huffman* and discounted objections with the explanation that litigants are not always entitled to a federal trial-level tribunal for the determination of federal claims. *Huffman*, 420 U.S. at 605–06. For further discussion of *Younger's* application to civil proceedings, see notes 237–78 and accompanying text.

165. The federal-question abstention doctrine in *Younger* recognizes no analog to *England*. See notes 101–02 and accompanying text.

166. See Chapter VI, notes 161–225 and accompanying text. Justice Rehnquist described the result in *Huffman* in an unfortunate way: The theater proprietor "must *exhaust* his state appellate remedies *before* seeking relief" in a federal district court "unless he can bring himself within one of the exceptions specified in *Younger*." *Huffman*, 420 U.S. at 608 (emphasis added). Clearly, Rehnquist did not mean to announce a genuine exhaustion doctrine—a rule of timing that merely postponed federal adjudication until the state courts had an opportunity to pass on federal claims. See notes 36–37 and accompanying text. If, in *Huffman*, the state's highest court rejected the proprietor's first amendment claim, that judgment would probably be entitled to preclusive effect pursuant to the Full Faith and Credit Statute. The proprietor might seek *certiorari* review in the Supreme Court, but he would not ordinarily be able to relitigate his federal claim in a federal district court. See *Ellis v. Dyson*, 421 U.S. 426, 437 (1975) (Powell, J., dissenting) (explaining the usual scenario). Justice Rehnquist indicated as much when he noted, in an aside, that he would have reached the same result if the time for filing an appeal in state court had expired. In that event, the proprietor would

The general rule that plaintiffs in federal §1983 actions cannot obtain injunctions or declaratory judgments against pending state criminal prosecutions is consistent with the statutes governing removal. Recall that under 28 U.S.C. §1441, defendants in state court cannot ordinarily remove the actions against them to federal court on the basis of a federal defense.[167] In both instances, the default position is that state court litigation, once under way, will be allowed to take its course without federal interference. Many observers propose that §1441 should be amended to permit removal on the basis of a federal defense in *civil* litigation. But no one seriously contends that defendants in state *criminal* actions should be able to remove whenever they advance federal defenses.[168] Accordingly, if federal-question abstention were limited to the rule announced in *Younger*, this final category of abstention cases would be largely non-controversial. As it is, however, federal-question abstention is intensively controversial—not for what it was in *Younger* itself, but for what it has become in the years since.[169]

By some accounts, federal-question abstention conflicts with *Mitchum's* explanation of §1983.[170] If the point of §1983 is to empower federal courts to enforce federal rights that state courts may fail to respect, it is hard to justify curtailing federal judicial authority on the theory that state courts are, after all, perfectly reliable. Moreover, §1983 states a national policy ascribable to Congress. Once the Supreme Court has given that statute an authoritative interpretation (as it did in *Mitchum*), the Court cannot easily fashion a limiting doctrine that denies federal courts the very remedial authority that Congress, by hypothesis, has decided they should have. To the extent federal-question abstention approaches the kind of blanket prohibition on injunctions in §1983 cases that §2283 would have imposed (absent *Mitchum*), this judicially created doctrine arguably undermines Congress' authority to prescribe the means by which federal rights will be enforced.[171]

(ordinarily) have no recourse to *any* court. 420 U.S. at 611 n.22. But see Chapter VI, notes 181–82 and accompanying text (discussing exceptions to preclusion when state court procedures offer no opportunity for full and fair adjudication); Chapter VII, notes 160–94 and accompanying text (discussing the Supreme Court's authority to reach federal issues when state procedural grounds are inadequate to sustain a judgment disposing of a federal claim).

167. See Chapter VI, notes 128–32 and accompanying text; but see Chapter VI, notes 136–60 and accompanying text (discussing the limited circumstances in which defendants in state court *can* remove on the basis of a federal defense).

168. See Chapter VI, notes 156–57. Federal-question abstention recognizes exceptions for cases in which the process in state court is flawed. See notes 178–203 and accompanying text. Recall that the Court has not employed the process model to determine the availability of removal pursuant to §1443. See Chapter VI, notes 154–55 and accompanying text. Accordingly, litigants can avoid federal-question abstention in circumstances in which they would not be able to remove the actions against them to federal court. Then again, since federal courts rarely conclude that state procedural machinery is inadequate, the distinction makes little practical difference.

169. See notes 195, 236, 239, 293 and accompanying text.

170. *Mitchum v. Foster*, 407 U.S. 225 (1972); see notes 16–17 and accompanying text.

171. Professor Redish recognizes that at least some of the justices may think that *Mitchum* was wrongly decided and thus regard *Younger* and *Samuels* as consistent with congressional will, as expressed in the Anti-Injunction Act. In his opinion for the Court in *Younger*, Justice Black relied on §2283 as evidence of Congress' general desire to free state court proceedings from federal interference. See note 148. If, however, the Court continues to accept *Mitchum's* account of §1983, Redish contends that *Younger* constitutes "judicial usurpation of legislative authority." Redish, note 77, at 88. See also Donald L. Doernberg,"*You Can Lead a Horse to Water…": The Supreme Court's Refusal to Allow the Exercise of Original Jurisdiction Conferred by Congress*, 40 Case Western Res. L. Rev. 999, 1017 (1990) (describing *Younger* as the "clearest" of several examples of the Court's "abdication" of jurisdiction that Congress has prescribed); Nichol, note 18, at 992 (contending that "*Younger* largely takes away what *Mitchum* grants"). Professor Althouse suggests that the 1971 decision in *Younger*

By other accounts, federal-question abstention is yet another illustration of the modern Court's commitment to the private rights model of adjudication.[172] Both *Younger* and *Samuels* contemplate that would-be federal §1983 plaintiffs can just as easily vindicate their federal claims in state court. In some instances, that may be true. But it certainly is not true in all. Federal courts entertaining civil §1983 actions for injunctive or declaratory relief are in a position to protect federal rights in a variety of ways. They can issue temporary orders that protect citizens from prosecution while federal claims are under consideration. If they conclude that federal claims are meritorious, they can grant permanent prospective relief that will safeguard citizens in the future. And they can issue orders on behalf of classes of plaintiffs, so that anyone whose federal rights are at stake can benefit. By contrast, state criminal courts have authority only to determine whether a state statute can validly be applied to a particular defendant.[173] Of course, litigants who want and need prospective relief for an entire class may be able to obtain it via civil actions in *state* court.[174] But if it is once recognized that litigants must launch separate civil actions to achieve what they cannot accomplish by defending against isolated criminal charges, it would seem that they should be entitled to do so in federal court, if they wish.[175]

By still other accounts, federal-question abstention illustrates the current Court's general tendency to deny access to federal courts in a wide variety of circumstances in which individuals seek protection from the excesses of state officials. The Court insists upon parity between federal and state courts and, on that basis, justifies routing federal

---

was essential to the *Mitchum* decision in 1972. By her account, the Court was willing to release its grip on a statutory basis for curbing the district courts only after it had established an independent, judge-crafted basis for doing much the same thing. The Court may have preferred to rely on its own doctrine rather than a statute simply to achieve greater flexibility. Ann Althouse, *The Humble and the Treasonous: Judge-Made Jurisdiction Law*, 40 Case Western Res. L. Rev. 1035, 1043 (1990). Professor Beermann doubts that the separation principle can answer the sensitive ideological questions that abstention entails. Jack M. Beermann,"*Bad" Judicial Activism and Liberal Federal-Courts Doctrine: A Comment on Professor Doernberg and Professor Redish*, 40 Case Western Res. L. Rev. 1053 (1990). Professor Wells argues that it is unrealistic to draw any distinction between the creative statutory construction the Court undertakes in cases like *Mitchum* and the elaboration of doctrine the Court undertakes in cases like *Younger*. Wells, note 77; see also Michael Wells, *The Role of Comity in the Law of Federal Courts*, 60 N. Car. L. Rev. 59 (1981).

172. See Chapter I, notes 61–72 and accompanying text.

173. Under classic precedents, a remedy at law is "adequate" only if it is as "complete, practical and efficient as that which equity could afford." *Terrace v. Thompson*, 263 U.S. 197, 214 (1923). Professor Laycock argues that since state criminal prosecutions often cannot meet that standard, private litigants should be allowed to seek injunctive and declaratory relief in federal §1983 actions in many more cases than the Court's abstention doctrine allows. Douglas Laycock, *Federal Interference with State Prosecutions: The Need for Prospective Relief*, 1977 Sup. Ct. Rev. 193. Professor Zeigler contends that private litigants need access to the federal courts via §1983 class actions in order to achieve systemic reforms of state criminal process—the kinds of reforms that state courts are unlikely to undertake in the context of individual prosecutions. Donald H. Zeigler, *Federal Court Reform of State Criminal Justice Systems: A Reassessment of the Younger Doctrine from a Modern Perspective*, 19 U.C. Davis L. Rev. 31 (1985). The New York State Bar Association has published guidelines that federal district courts might follow in order to ensure that they abstain in class action cases only when the policies on which *Younger* rests will actually be promoted. For a discussion, see Georgene M. Vairo, *Making Younger Civil: The Consequences of Federal Court Deference to State Court Proceedings*, 58 Fordham L. Rev. 173 (1989).

174. See Chapter VI, note 54 and accompanying text.

175. See *NOPSI*, 491 U.S. at 359, quoting *Willcox v. Consolidated Gas Co.*, 212 U.S. 19, 40 (1909): "The right of a party plaintiff to choose a Federal court where there is a choice cannot be properly denied."

question business to the latter as a routine matter.[176] If this is what *Younger* and *Samuels* mean, this last form of abstention reflects an agenda with sensitive political implications: a general "devolution of power" to the states.[177]

1. The Process Model

There are exceptions to federal-question abstention. In *Younger*, Justice Black said that federal courts need not abstain in three kinds of cases: (1) cases in which the proceedings in state court constitute "bad faith and harassment;" (2) cases in which the state statute involved is not only arguably invalid on its face, but "flagrantly and patently violative of express constitutional prohibitions in every clause, sentence and paragraph, and in whatever manner and against whomever an effort might be made to apply it;" and (3) cases involving "other unusual situations calling for federal intervention."[178] The Court has assimilated those exceptions into the process model: Federal courts need not abstain if the process available in state court fails to offer an adequate opportunity for the adjudication of federal claims.[179]

Bad faith and harassment. This exception plainly goes to the integrity of the adjudicative process in state court. It encompasses prosecutions pressed without any genuine expectation that a valid conviction can be secured, but only to punish individuals by subjecting them to burdensome and expensive legal proceedings.[180] The leading precedent in the Supreme Court is *Dombrowski v. Pfister*,[181] decided before (and distinguished in) *Younger*. In *Dombrowski*, local prosecutors in Louisiana repeatedly charged civil rights workers with violating a facially overbroad statute, but routinely dismissed the charges on the eve of trial—just before the state courts would have had an opportunity to consider the defendants' first amendment claims.[182] The idea at work in this first exception, accordingly, is that federal courts can issue injunctions or declaratory judg-

---

176. See Chapter I, notes 92–104 and accompanying text. On this point, Professor Wells argues that the Court does not genuinely think that federal and state courts are fungible at all. By contrast, the Court recognizes that federal courts are more likely to find individual claims meritorious, while state courts are more likely to side with state officials. Capitalizing on the *absence* of parity, the Court uses abstention to achieve substantive results—by deliberately diverting cases into state court, where state interests are more likely to prevail. Wells himself deplores the results the Court appears to have in mind, but he contends that the use of forum-allocation rules is a legitimate means of achieving substantive ends without making overt changes in formal constitutional doctrine. Michael Wells, *Is Disparity a Problem?*, 22 Ga. L. Rev. 283, 326–27 (1988).

177. Soifer & Macgill, note 151, at 1141. See Louise Weinberg, *The New Judicial Federalism*, 29 Stan. L. Rev. 1191, 1203 (1977) (depicting *Younger* as an aspect of a "jurisdictional counterrevolution" in which an increasingly conservative Court has denied access to federal courts for the enforcement of federal rights); Zeigler, note 66, at 689 (arguing that *Younger* frustrates federal court vindication of federal rights and should be "abandoned").

178. 401 U.S. at 53–54.

179. See Chapter I, notes 73–77 and accompanying text.

180. See *Kugler v. Helfant*, 421 U.S. 117, 126 n.6 (1975).

181. 380 U.S. 479 (1965).

182. Justice Brennan discussed this aspect of the record in *Dombrowski*, but he plainly relied on the related, but analytically distinct, ground that the plaintiffs advanced a first amendment overbreadth claim. See note 149. When Justice Black seized upon Brennan's reference to "bad faith and harassment," he did it as a deliberate device for limiting *Dombrowski* to that kind of case. See Fiss, note 56, at 1120. For a survey and analysis of lower court decisions, see C. Keith Wingate, *The Bad Faith-Harassment Exception to the Younger Doctrine: Exploring the Empty Universe*, 5 Rev. Litigation 123 (1986).

ments regarding pending state proceedings when the procedural machinery at the state level is inadequate to protect federal rights.[183]

Flagrantly invalid state statutes. This second exception is obviously extremely narrow. The Court has never found a statute to fit it. If a statute were so obviously unconstitutional, the state courts would presumably recognize as much and refuse to enforce it—making federal injunctive relief unnecessary, even if it is available.[184] Moreover, if state prosecuting authorities or state courts were to enforce such a statute, their actions would very likely be in bad faith, collapsing this second exception into the first.[185] The point, again, is that abstention is unwarranted when pending state court proceedings offer no opportunity for full and fair adjudication.[186]

Other unusual circumstances. This final exception bears the marks of a catch-all category to cover circumstances that are difficult to anticipate. In fact, the Supreme Court has relied on it only once. In *Gibson v. Berryhill*,[187] the Court approved an injunction against a pending state license-revocation proceeding.[188] The licensing board was presumptively biased, because its members had a financial incentive to revoke the licenses of their competitors. The point of *Berryhill*, then, was once again that the process available at the state level was fundamentally flawed.[189] In this instance, the Court invokes the process model in its traditional formulation: Other unusual circumstances are limited to conditions that "render the state court incapable of fairly and fully adjudicating the federal issues before it."[190]

The Court elaborated the process orientation of the three *Younger* exceptions in *Moore v. Sims*.[191] State authorities assumed temporary custody of minor children thought to be the victims of parental abuse and initiated proceedings in state court, seeking judicial approval for placing the children with their grandparents. The parents employed a variety of state law devices for regaining custody of the children. The litigation in state court became confused, and the parents soon filed a §1983 action in federal court, advancing federal constitutional arguments against the state statutory scheme under which the state authorities purported to act. The parents primarily contended that the state scheme violated procedural due process inasmuch as it authorized state officials to detain children for a considerable period of time without a hearing.[192] The

183. Professor Fiss makes this connection. See Fiss, note 57, at 1114–15.

184. Michael G. Collins, *The Right to Avoid Trial: Justifying Federal Court Intervention into Ongoing State Court Proceedings*, 66 N. Car. L. Rev. 49, 67 (1987).

185. Ralph V. Whitten, *Federal Declaratory and Injunctive Interference With State Court Proceedings: The Supreme Court and the Limits of Judicial Discretion*, 53 N. Car. L. Rev. 591, 618–19 (1975).

186. Justice Stevens has argued that if this exception to abstention is concerned with the adequacy of state process, it should allow a federal district court to act when §1983 plaintiffs challenge the validity of the very state procedural machinery they will have to engage if the district court abstains. *Trainor v. Hernandez*, 431 U.S. 434, 469–70 (1977) (dissenting opinion); *Juidice v. Vail*, 430 U.S. 327, 339–41 (1977) (concurring opinion). The full Court has rejected Stevens' view. See, e.g., *Moore v. Sims*, 442 U.S. 415, 426–27 n.10 (1979).

187. 411 U.S. 564 (1973).

188. See *Kugler*, 421 U.S. at 125 n.4 (recalling *Berryhill* as a case in which the Court relied on the "extraordinary circumstances" exception).

189. Since the board itself was biased, it could not be relied upon to consider the validity of its own composition. The licensee had a right to appeal an adverse decision to the state courts, but he could not retain his license while that appeal was pending. Collins, note 184, at 70.

190. *Kugler*, 421 U.S. at 124–25.

191. 442 U.S. 415 (1979).

192. They also contended that the state failed to provide for guardians *ad litem* to represent children, authorized the severance of parental rights on the basis of a preponderance of the evidence (rather than "clear and convincing" proof), and permitted state officials to collect and disseminate

district court issued a preliminary injunction barring state officers from proceeding any further in state court while the district court considered the parents' constitutional challenge. After trial, the district court found the state statutory scheme invalid on its face and issued a permanent injunction against its use. The Supreme Court reversed on the theory that the district court should have abstained.

Then-Justice Rehnquist acknowledged that *Moore* differed from *Younger*. When the parents filed their §1983 suit, they were not defendants in any state court proceeding in which they might have advanced their claims against the state scheme as a defense. The only state proceeding pending at all was the action to deprive the parents of custody. That action turned on the "best interests" of particular children, quite apart from the constitutional validity of the general statutory framework. Justice Rehnquist explained, however, that abstention was appropriate if the parents had the "opportunity" to "present" their other claims in that proceeding. It was unclear whether Texas procedure would allow the parents to do that. But Justice Rehnquist insisted that doubts should be resolved in favor of abstention. He rejected the district court's suggestion that abstention was unwarranted because the parents' claims were "broad and novel." According to Justice Rehnquist, the "breadth" of the parents' challenge to the state statutory system "militated in *favor* of abstention, not *against* it." If federal courts presumed to entertain claims of that kind, state courts would be denied the opportunity to give state statutes a "narrowing" construction that would "obviate" federal issues.[193]

Taken literally, *Moore* contemplates that abstention is warranted in any instance in which federal §1983 plaintiffs are involved in a state court proceeding into which they might inject the federal issues they wish to litigate in federal court.[194] The question is not whether the state proceeding necessarily implicates those federal issues, so that the state courts will pass on them in due course. Instead, the question is whether the state proceeding can be made to accommodate federal theories that otherwise would not be addressed. That, in turn, approaches the proposition that litigants are not, after all, entitled to choose a federal forum if they wish, but must put their federal claims before state courts when those courts offer an adequate procedural opportunity to do so.[195] Recall, however, that the parents in *Moore* did not merely choose to file a §1983 action in federal court at a time when they happened to be involved in related proceedings in state court. They sought and obtained an injunction against those state proceedings (and any other proceedings like them).[196]

---

data regarding *suspected* child abuse without an adequate judicial determination of *actual* mistreatment.

193. 442 U.S. at 425 (emphasis in original). See text accompanying notes 150–52 (discussing Justice Black's reliance on the same point in *Younger*).

194. In dissent, Justice Stevens contended that the pending child custody proceeding bore no more relation to the claims in the parents' federal §1983 action than a pending traffic violation charge would have. *Moore*, 442 U.S. at 435–36.

195. Professor Marcus criticizes the Court's decisions on this ground and proposes a more complicated (but still workable) alternative. She would have federal district courts determine not whether there is some discernible bar to state court consideration of federal claims, but whether federal claims will "probably" be adjudicated in the state proceedings to which federal courts defer. Maria L. Marcus, *Wanted: A Federal Standard for Evaluating the Adequate State Forum*, 50 Md. L. Rev. 131 (1991).

196. Justice Rehnquist was also troubled by the scope of the district court's order in *Moore*. He wondered aloud whether the plaintiffs had standing to press all the claims the district court explored. 442 U.S. at 428–29. See Chapter IX.

The appearance of the process model at this juncture further delineates the practical effect of the Court's decision in *Mitchum* (exempting §1983 actions from the Anti-Injunction Act).[197] If §2283 were applicable, federal courts entertaining §1983 actions would be barred from issuing injunctions that interfere with pending state court proceedings, subject to the other exceptions that §2283 itself recognizes.[198] As it is, §2283 is inapplicable, and the Court's own federal-question abstention doctrine fills the void. Under that doctrine, federal courts entertaining §1983 suits are also ordinarily barred from issuing injunctions or declaratory judgments that interfere with pending state criminal proceedings.[199] But the exceptions are different. Federal-question abstention acknowledges not the exceptions listed in §2283, but the different exceptions listed in *Younger*. Those exceptions, in turn, boil down to cases in which state court process fails to provide an opportunity for adequate adjudication of federal claims.

Federal-question abstention assumes parity, proceeds on the private rights model, and recognizes exceptions in familiar circumstances: when the processes in state court break down.[200] This form of abstention thus restrains federal judicial power while state court proceedings are *pending* in much the way that the Full Faith and Credit Statute restrains federal judicial power when state court proceedings are *complete*. Recall that under 28 U.S.C. §1738, federal courts give state court judgments the preclusive effect they would have in state court. Ordinarily, federal claims that were, or might have been, advanced in state court are foreclosed thereafter. There is an exception, however, for circumstances in which litigants are denied an opportunity for "full and fair" adjudication in the initial state proceeding.[201] Here again, then, the Court achieves a certain symmetry. Positing that state court litigation is satisfying in the main, the Court generally insists that litigants must present their federal claims to those courts and accept the judgments the state courts render.[202] Yet recognizing that inadequate state procedures undermine the reliability of state decisions, the Court allows for exceptions (in both instances) on procedural grounds.[203]

---

197. See notes 16–19 and accompanying text.

198. See notes 20–26 and accompanying text.

199. But see notes 207–12 and accompanying text (discussing the inapplicability of federal-question abstention when no state proceeding is pending); cf. notes 237–78 and accompanying text (discussing the extension of federal-question abstention to civil proceedings in state court).

200. See Chapter I, notes 61–77, 92–104 and accompanying text.

201. See Chapter VI, notes 181–82 and accompanying text. But see Chapter VI, notes 154–57 (noting that the process model does not control the availability of civil rights removal under §1443).

202. Subject to the theoretical possibility of direct review in the Supreme Court and, in some instances, a petition for federal habeas corpus.

203. In this abstention context, however, the Court has not suggested that state processes are adequate if they comport with due process in the fourteenth amendment sense. See Chapter VI, notes 183–84 and accompanying text (discussing the *Kremer* decision regarding "full and fair adjudication" in the preclusion context). Professor Bator endorsed the Court's process-oriented sense of the circumstances that warrant federal intervention. Paul M. Bator, *The State Courts and Federal Constitutional Litigation*, 22 Wm. & Mary L. Rev. 605, 626–27 (1981). Professor Collins is also sympathetic. Collins, note 184. Professor Rosenfeld prefers an analogy to the Tax Injunction Act's condition that the state courts must offer a "plain, speedy, and effective" means of addressing federal claims. S. Stephan Rosenfeld, *The Place of State Courts in the Era of Younger v. Harris*, 59 B.U. L. Rev. 597 (1979); see note 35 and accompanying text. For a review of lower court decisions, see Brian Stagner, *Avoiding Abstention: The Younger Exceptions*, 29 Texas Tech. L. Rev. 137 (1998). The Judiciary Act of 1789 included a provision barring federal courts of equity from entertaining suits for injunctions when there was a "plain, adequate, and complete" remedy at law. That section contemplated, however, that such a remedy at law would be found on the "law side" of a *federal* court—not

2. Anticipatory Actions

In *Younger* and *Samuels*, the Supreme Court elaborated federal-question abstention for cases in which federal courts are asked to issue injunctions or declaratory judgments that interfere with state criminal proceedings that are already under way.[204] In cases of that kind, district courts always decline to intervene, unless the proceedings pending in state court fail to provide an opportunity for full and fair adjudication of federal claims. If no state proceedings are pending, district courts fall back on the general prerequisites for equitable and declaratory relief. Plaintiffs seeking injunctions must demonstrate irreparable harm for which there is no adequate remedy at law. Plaintiffs seeking declaratory judgments must show a sufficient need for clarity to warrant discretionary relief.[205]

There are differences between §1983 plaintiffs who ask federal courts to interfere with pending state prosecutions and §1983 plaintiffs who ask federal courts to protect them from prosecution in the future. Plaintiffs who are already under indictment have an ostensibly adequate means of vindicating their federal claims in state court: They can raise those claims as defenses to the pending state prosecution. Federal injunctive or declaratory relief will disrupt ongoing state processes. By contrast, plaintiffs who have not been indicted have no immediate means of advancing their federal claims in state court. To obtain an adjudication of those claims, they must launch new litigation in one set of courts or the other. Together, §1983 and §1331 ostensibly entitle them to choose the federal courts, if they wish. Federal courts do not disturb state processes simply by exercising their jurisdiction when no state court has taken, or has been asked to take, any action with respect to the matter.[206]

There are also differences between §1983 plaintiffs who ask federal courts to interfere with state prosecutions regarding *past* behavior and §1983 plaintiffs who seek federal protection from prosecution for *future* behavior. Plaintiffs who are charged or threatened with prosecution on the basis of past behavior have already placed themselves at risk. Plaintiffs who have not taken the same risks may be shrinking violets by comparison, but they may also be more appealing candidates for federal litigation: They wish to conform their behavior to the law and seek assurance that the behavior in which they want to engage *is* lawful. Accordingly, they ask federal courts to determine *ex ante* whether they are entitled to carry out their plans and, if they are, either to enjoin state officials from prosecuting them or to declare that prosecution would violate their federal rights.

---

in a state criminal proceeding. See *Guaranty Trust Co. v. York*, 326 U.S. 99 (1945). It was repealed in 1948 when Congress abandoned the old dichotomy between law and equity.

204. Justice Black explicitly declined to decide whether the same abstention doctrine applies in cases in which federal courts are asked to issue injunctions or declaratory judgments regarding prospective prosecutions. *Younger*, 401 U.S. at 41; *Samuels*, 401 U.S. at 73–74.

205. See text accompanying notes 65–66 (describing the traditional limits on equitable relief); Chapter VIII, text accompanying notes 141–42 (discussing the discretionary character of declaratory relief). It may be helpful to think of the federal-question abstention doctrine in *Younger* and *Samuels* as a distillation of the traditional criteria for equitable and declaratory relief for purposes of cases in which certain state proceedings are pending. Yet the Supreme Court sometimes insists upon flexibility beyond what the abstention doctrines entail. See note 139 (discussing the *Wilton* case). Moreover, *Younger* and *Samuels* surface in other contexts where their particular doctrinal features do not operate. When, for example, the Court invokes *Younger* because district court action would disrupt state executive functions, there is no occasion for asking whether proceedings in state court are adequate to address plaintiffs' federal claims. See notes 288–95 and accompanying text.

206. See Chapter VIII, text accompanying notes 234–38.

The Supreme Court has grappled with these distinctions in a series of cases. In *Steffel v. Thompson*,[207] the Court held that the *Younger/Samuels* formulation is inapplicable to cases that have the strongest purchase on federal court action: cases in which §1983 plaintiffs seek federal declaratory relief from the threat of prosecution for planned conduct in the future.[208] Justice Brennan insisted that the state interests that explain abstention when state proceedings are pending do not hold when a state prosecution is yet to be initiated. Moreover, he said that the Declaratory Judgment Act is meant to provide a "milder alternative" to injunctions in anticipatory suits.[209]

The holding in *Steffel* is solid and reliable. Yet Brennan's two explanations are problematic. The first understates the disruptive effects of federal declaratory judgments that preempt prospective state prosecutions. The second overstates the distinction between declaratory judgments and injunctions. By emphasizing the virtues of declaratory actions, Justice Brennan left the impression that the result might have been different if Steffel had sought an injunction. That is unlikely. The point of the Declaratory Judgment Act is to make it *unnecessary* for district courts to issue injunctions in anticipatory actions, not to foreclose injunctive relief when it is warranted. Apart from *Steffel*, the Court has recognized that both declaratory judgments and injunctions can disrupt state proceedings.[210] And in numerous other cases, including *Ex parte Young*,[211] the Court has held that injunctions, too, can be granted when plaintiffs need protection from future state prosecutions.[212]

---

207. 415 U.S. 452 (1974).

208. Recall that the plaintiff in *Steffel* had not been formally charged when he filed suit in federal court, but it was clear that he would be arrested and prosecuted if he tried to distribute his leaflets again. See Chapter IX, notes 418–20 and accompanying text. In his earlier opinion for the Court in *Dombrowski*, Justice Brennan had it that it is *most* important that federal courts entertain actions challenging the facial validity of state statutes. See note 149. In *Steffel*, however, he explained that even when federal §1983 plaintiffs claim that a valid statute will be unconstitutionally applied to them, a federal court can act—so long as no prosecution is yet under way.

209. 415 U.S. at 467, quoting his own concurring opinion in *Perez*, 401 U.S. at 111. See note 155.

210. See text accompanying notes 153–55 (discussing Justice Black's explanation in *Samuels*).

211. 209 U.S. 123 (1908); see Chapter X, notes 283–85 and accompanying text.

212. The shareholder plaintiffs in *Young* sought a federal injunction that would shield their railroad and its employees from future prosecution for charging higher rates than state law permitted. Justice Peckham said that a federal court would not "of course" interfere with a pending state prosecution, but could enjoin a future prosecution in exceptional circumstances warranting equitable relief. 209 U.S. at 162. Peckham explained that the railroad faced irreparable injury for which there was no adequate remedy at law. The only way to test the validity of the rates fixed by state law was to violate that law on one occasion and then challenge its constitutionality as a defense to a criminal charge. Since the penalties for even one violation were stiff, Peckham doubted that the railroad could find employees willing to put themselves at risk. If a cooperative employee could be found, the railroad would still have to engage lengthy state proceedings in an attempt to establish its constitutional claim. In the interim, it would have to comply with rate limits it insisted were confiscatory. And if the railroad ultimately established that those regulations were invalid, it might not be able to recover its lost revenues. Id. at 163–65. Recalling *Young* in *Idaho v. Coeur d'Alene Tribe*, 521 U.S. 261 (1997), Justice Kennedy said that there was no available state court forum in that case at all. Id. at 2035; see Chapter X, notes 303–04 and accompanying text. That was an overstatement—as Justice Souter explained in dissent in *Coeur d'Alene*. 521 U.S. at 315–16. The holding in *Young* was that it would have been exceptionally burdensome for the railroad to press its federal claims as a defense to a state criminal action. Accordingly, there was no adequate remedy at law, and a federal court could issue an injunction that would preempt prosecution. Professor Laycock contends that in the wake of *Young*, and despite cases like *Douglas*, see note 151, federal courts often issued injunctions to protect litigants from *future* prosecution. Laycock, note 173, at 197.

In the end, accordingly, neither anticipatory §1983 suits for declaratory judgments nor anticipatory §1983 suits for injunctions are governed by *Younger/Samuels*. Both are controlled, instead, by more general discretionary and equitable considerations.[213] Typically, plaintiffs request both forms of relief. When district courts are satisfied that relief of some kind is in order, they turn to the further question whether declaratory relief alone will suffice (at least in the near term). The decisive factor is the extent to which a declaratory judgment will spare §1983 plaintiffs the risks and burdens associated with prospective prosecution. Local authorities will often respect a federal declaration that prosecution would be unlawful. If prosecuting officers initiate state proceedings in the teeth of a federal declaration, the state courts will give the federal judgment preclusive effect.[214] If the state courts, too, refuse to respect a declaratory judgment, then, as a last resort, the federal district court can issue an injunction directing local prosecutors to desist.[215]

In some circumstances, immediate injunctive relief may be warranted.[216] In *Wooley v. Maynard*,[217] the plaintiff had been prosecuted on three occasions for obscuring the state's charming pastoral motto ("Live Free or Die") on the license plate of his car. He filed a §1983 action in federal court, in which he contended that the state statute forcing him to display the motto violated his first amendment rights. Chief Justice Burger said that in those circumstances the district court could properly issue an injunction against future prosecutions. There was no indication in *Wooley* that a declaratory judgment

---

213. This is the understanding to be gleaned both from the precedents as a whole and from most explicit statements from the Court. E.g., *Ankenbrandt*, 504 U.S. at 705 (stating that the Court has "never applied the notions of comity so critical to *Younger's* 'Our Federalism' when no state proceeding [is] pending"). There is, however, a body of opinion within the Court that *Younger* and *Samuels* should control anticipatory suits, as well. That minority sentiment occasionally appears in opinions for the full Court, written by individual members who continue to press their position. E.g., *Morales v. TWA*, 504 U.S. 374, 381 n.1 (1992) (indicating that *Younger* imposes "heightened requirements for an injunction to restrain an already-pending or an about-to-be-pending state criminal action") (opinion for the Court by Scalia, J.).

214. Concurring in *Steffel*, then-Justice Rehnquist suggested the novel theory that a federal declaratory judgment issued in a §1983 suit might not be entitled to preclusive effect in subsequent proceedings in state court. *Steffel*, 415 U.S. at 479. By his account, a federal declaratory judgment is "simply a statement" that local authorities may "choose" either to accept or to ignore. Such a declaration of rights may well persuade local officials to drop their plans to prosecute, or it may persuade the state courts to dismiss any charges that are brought. But, according to Rehnquist, if a declaratory judgment has greater effect (as a "giant step toward... an injunction"), it ceases to be distinguishable from an injunction at all. Id. at 481–82. But see id. at 477 (White, J., concurring) (indicating that declaratory judgments should have the usual preclusive effect). Professor Shapiro contends that federal declaratory judgments are entitled to preclusive effect and would otherwise be unintelligible. David L. Shapiro, *State Courts and Federal Declaratory Judgments*, 74 Nw. U. L. Rev. 759, 764–65 (1979). See also Chapter IX, notes 16–21 and accompanying text (discussing the historical debate over whether declaratory judgments constitute unconstitutional advisory opinions). In the typical case, a federal declaratory judgment will not cover all the issues in a subsequent state prosecution. Yet it will often capture the crucial issue: the validity of an individual's federal defense to a charge laid on the basis of an anticipated set of facts.

215. Recall that federal district courts are authorized to issue injunctions to enforce previously issued declaratory judgments. See Chapter VIII, note 141.

216. E.g., *Bellotti v. Baird*, 443 U.S. 622, 651 (1979) (approving anticipatory injunctive relief without discussion); see *Zablocki v. Redhail*, 434 U.S. 374, 380 n.5 (1978) (explaining that *Younger* did not bar a district court from enjoining a prospective civil proceeding threatened by local authorities).

217. 430 U.S. 705 (1977).

alone would deter local authorities from initiating further actions against the plaintiff. He was at risk whenever he left his driveway.[218]

This does not mean that injunctions or declaratory judgments are routinely available. The prerequisites for both are demanding.[219] Recall, moreover, that those prerequisites converge on the requirements for standing and ripeness.[220] Plaintiffs must time their applications to the federal courts with care. If they proceed too soon (before state charges are imminent), they may find that their injuries are insufficiently concrete, their claims premature. If they proceed too late (when state charges are about to be laid), they may find that they have lost the race to court, that state authorities have managed to initiate state proceedings, and that federal-question abstention as articulated in *Younger/Samuels* is controlling.[221]

Plaintiffs who file anticipatory suits in federal court can sometimes obtain temporary orders that maintain the *status quo* while their requests for injunctive or declaratory relief are under consideration. In *Doran v. Salem Inn*,[222] the proprietors of two fashionable night spots filed a §1983 action in federal court, contending that a city ordinance banning "topless" dancing violated their first amendment rights. They sought both injunctive and declaratory protection from prosecution under the ordinance. The district court issued a preliminary injunction barring local authorities from charging the taverns until the court could determine the merits of their claims and decide whether to issue declaratory or (permanent) injunctive relief. Thereafter, the tavern operators resumed the nude performances that would otherwise have put them at risk of prosecution. The Supreme Court sustained the district court's preliminary injunction.

Then-Justice Rehnquist explained that since the tavern operators sought federal relief when no state prosecution was pending, their cases were not governed by *Younger/Samuels*.[223] He acknowledged that the conventional equitable standards for the issuance of a preliminary injunction are strict: Applicants must show that they will suf-

---

218. Id. at 712. Chief Justice Burger explained that the plaintiff's three prior convictions in state court did not preclude federal court action, because the plaintiff sought no relief with respect to those convictions and requested only injunctive relief regarding future exposure. Id. at 711. That will not wash. The point of preclusion is that issues that were, or might have been, determined previously ordinarily cannot be revisited in subsequent litigation. Plainly, at least some issues of fact had been determined in the three prior prosecutions and, arguably, some key issues of law—namely, federal constitutional law. See David P. Currie, *Res Judicata: The Neglected Defense*, 45 U. Chi. L. Rev. 317, 334–46 (1978); see Chapter VI, notes 161–64 and accompanying text. Recall, however, that *Wooley* was decided three years before *Allen v. McCurry*, 449 U.S. 90 (1980), in which the Court squarely held that §1983 actions are subject to the Full Faith and Credit Statute. See Chapter VI, notes 167–74 and accompanying text. Dissenting in *Wooley*, Justices White, Blackmun, and Rehnquist said nothing about preclusion, but insisted that local authorities should have been given a chance to comply with a declaratory judgment.

219. E.g., *Boyle v. Landry*, 401 U.S. 77 (1971) (holding that African Americans who had not been personally mistreated by the Chicago police could not allege irreparable injury for purposes of a suit contesting a pattern of racially charged police misconduct in the city).

220. See Chapter IX, notes 409–15 and accompanying text.

221. See notes 227–30 and accompanying text (explaining that litigants who file federal §1983 actions just before state authorities file state charges may still be channeled into the after-filed proceedings in state court).

222. 422 U.S. 922 (1975).

223. Writing in 1975, Justice Rehnquist limited his account of this point to the plaintiffs' request for a declaratory judgment and explicitly noted that the Court had not yet decided whether *Younger/Samuels* applied to suits for an injunction against future prosecution. 422 U.S. at 930; see note 204 and accompanying text. Since then, the Court has made it clear that the *Younger/Samuels*

fer irreparable harm while their claims are under review and that they are "likely to prevail on the merits."[224] In the circumstances of *Salem Inn*, however, he could not say that the district court had abused its discretion in finding those standards satisfied.[225] Without a federal order protecting them from prosecution in the near term, the tavern proprietors would have been forced to choose between violating the ordinance (and inviting prosecution), on the one hand, or complying with it (and losing business), on the other. By choosing the former course, they would have surrendered their attempt to obtain a federal adjudication of their claims; by choosing the latter, they would have jeopardized their livelihood.[226]

Plaintiffs cannot always escape *Younger/Samuels* abstention by filing §1983 actions in federal court before state authorities formally initiate prosecutions in state court. In *Hicks v. Miranda*,[227] Justice White said it would "trivialize" the "principles" of *Younger/Samuels* to let the applicability of the federal-question abstention doctrine turn on the outcome of a race to the court house.[228] In *Hicks*, local authorities charged two employees of a movie theater with the criminal offense of purveying obscene material.[229] The theater owners then filed a §1983 action in federal court, seeking a declaration that the state obscenity statute was unconstitutional and an injunction against its enforcement. Shortly thereafter, local officials added the owners as defendants in the criminal prosecution previously filed against their employees. At that time, the federal district court entertaining the owners' §1983 action had received motions to dismiss and for summary judgment. But it had conducted no hearings and issued no orders. Justice White held that since the owners had been named in a state criminal prosecution "before any proceedings of substance on the merits" in their federal action, the case was controlled by *Younger/Samuels*.[230]

At first glance, *Hicks* appears to be in tension with *Salem Inn*.[231] In *Salem Inn*, remember, the Court allowed federal §1983 plaintiffs to obtain a preliminary injunction insulating them from prosecution in state court while their federal lawsuit was under consideration. It may seem, then, that if the plaintiffs in *Hicks* had obtained a near-term protective order of that kind, the local authorities would not have been able to short circuit their federal action by quickly filing state charges. In *Salem Inn*, however, the preliminary injunction protected the bar operators only from prosecution on the basis of *future* behavior.[232] In *Hicks*, the theater owners would have needed protection

---

doctrine controls only in cases in which state proceedings are under way (or soon will be). See notes 207–15 and accompanying text.

224. 422 U.S. at 931.

225. The Supreme Court's appellate review of a district court's decision to grant preliminary relief is limited to deciding whether the district court's judgment constitutes an "abuse of discretion." Id. at 931–32.

226. See note 212 (discussing the similar considerations in *Ex parte Young*). Of course, whatever commercial value the nude dancing may have had, the taverns contended that their ability to express themselves would suffer. Justice Rehnquist warmed more easily to the argument that profits were at stake.

227. 422 U.S. 332 (1975).

228. Id. at 350.

229. State authorities also initiated a civil proceeding in which the owners were summoned to show why the film in question ("Deep Throat") was not obscene.

230. 422 U.S. at 349.

231. See notes 222–26 and accompanying text.

232. Justice Rehnquist explained in *Salem Inn* that a third tavern operator was not entitled to a preliminary injunction, because that operator had already defied state authorities and violated the ordinance. Rehnquist thus made it clear that a federal district court cannot protect a litigant from future prosecution on the basis of past behavior. Professor Laycock contends that, even if the third

from prosecution for past behavior. The state officials in *Hicks* filed criminal charges against the theater owners after they were already in federal court. But the basis of those charges was the prior exhibition of the movie. Nothing in *Salem Inn* suggests that citizens can violate state statutes and then thwart state prosecution by promptly filing federal §1983 lawsuits and obtaining preliminary injunctions against prosecution in state court.[233]

The decision in *Hicks* plainly *is* in tension with *Steffel* and *Wooley*.[234] Those cases appear to make the formal initiation of state proceedings crucial to deciding whether federal court action is controlled by *Younger/Samuels* or by the traditional standards for injunctive and declaratory relief: If state court proceedings are pending, *Younger/Samuels* controls; if not, traditional standards govern. According to *Hicks*, however, the crucial question is not whether a federal §1983 action is filed before the plaintiffs in that action are prosecuted in state court. Local prosecutors can *lose* the race to the court house and *still* rely on *Younger/Samuels* to defeat a federal §1983 action filed previously by individuals who were more fleet afoot. In light of *Hicks*, the dates on which federal and state proceedings are initiated are not conclusive. The decisive question is whether proceedings in the federal lawsuit have moved beyond the "embryonic" stage.[235]

It does seem formalistic to make the applicability of *Younger/Samuels* turn entirely on whether a federal §1983 action is filed before or after an indictment is returned in state court. Yet it makes important conceptual sense. By some accounts, *Hicks* allows federal-question abstention to undermine the statutory scheme by which Congress makes federal courts available to adjudicate federal claims. Plaintiffs who file federal lawsuits when no state court proceedings are pending do so on the authority they are given by §1983, invoking the jurisdiction that federal courts are given by §1331. Yet *Hicks* permits state officials to retrieve federal questions that have been properly pre-

---

operator was properly denied a preliminary injunction that would block prosecution for a past violation, that operator should have been entitled to a preliminary order protecting him from prosecution for future violations. With respect to future violations, the third operator was in the same position as the two operators who *did* obtain preliminary injunctions. Laycock, note 173, at 206–07.

233. If plaintiffs' federal claims turn out to be without merit, the preliminary injunctions that have shielded them from prosecution will be withdrawn, and they may face charges for offenses committed under its aegis. It seems unfair that anyone should suffer for behavior that was effectively sanctioned by federal order at the time it occurred. Yet it is conceptually difficult to contend that a federal court can immunize conduct that later, on more thorough consideration, is determined to be criminal. See *Edgar v. MITE Corp*., 457 U.S. 624, 647 (1982) (Stevens, J., concurring) (indicating that federal courts cannot insulate private behavior to that extent).

234. The *Hicks* case is equally in tension with *Ex parte Young*. See notes 211–12 and accompanying text. Justice Peckham explained in *Young* that a federal court that "first" assumes jurisdiction to consider plaintiffs' federal claims retains authority, "to the exclusion of all other courts," until its duty is "fully performed." When a state official who is a defendant in a federal lawsuit subsequently initiates a state criminal prosecution regarding the "same right" that is in issue in federal court, the federal court "may enjoin" the state criminal action. *Young*, 209 U.S. at 161–62.

235. *Salem Inn*, 422 U.S. at 929. This different criterion is comparatively amorphous and thus more difficult for the lower courts to apply. The Supreme Court has offered little guidance regarding when proceedings in federal court have progressed far enough that an after-filed state court action can no longer trigger *Younger/Samuels*. The Court has declined to decide whether federal proceedings on an application for a temporary restraining order will suffice. But the Court has held that the issuance of a preliminary injunction *does* count as a proceeding "of substance on the merits." *Midkiff*, 467 U.S. at 238. A temporary restraining order can be considered *ex parte*; a preliminary injunction can be considered only after the defendant has an opportunity to respond, typically in a hearing.

sented to the federal courts, drag those questions into state court, and hold them there until the state courts render decisions that are effectively final.[236]

3. Civil Proceedings in State Court

Federal-question abstention is not limited to cases in which §1983 plaintiffs seek injunctive or declaratory relief from *criminal* prosecutions pending in state court. Federal courts also abstain when §1983 plaintiffs seek relief from some *civil* proceedings in which particularly important state interests are implicated. In *Huffman v. Pursue*,[237] then-Justice Rehnquist recognized that abstention in favor of civil actions cannot rest on the special equitable rule that Justice Black emphasized in *Younger*—namely, the rule that courts of equity ordinarily do not enjoin criminal prosecutions.[238] Rehnquist explained, however, that other considerations fortifying *Younger* (comity and federalism) are sometimes implicated "as much" with respect to civil actions as they are with respect to criminal actions. Federal court orders preempting civil proceedings: (1) prevent the state from "effectuating its substantive policies;" (2) frustrate the state's attempt to provide a "forum competent to vindicate any constitutional objections interposed against those policies;" (3) duplicate proceedings already under way in state court; and (4) cast doubt on the state courts' ability to enforce federal law.[239]

Those four consequences would appear to attend federal injunctive or declaratory relief with respect to *any* pending state proceedings. Yet Justice Rehnquist added two further points about *Huffman* that bear significant limiting potential. The state proceeding in that case was an action to abate a movie theater as a public nuisance. According to Justice Rehnquist, it was important that: (1) state officials were the moving parties in that proceeding; and (2) while state law regarded the proceeding as civil in nature, it was "more akin to a criminal prosecution than are most civil cases."[240] The same two conditions also obtained in *Moore v. Sims*,[241] where the Court invoked federal-question abstention in favor of child custody proceedings initiated by the responsible state authorities.[242]

The two limiting factors did *not* appear in two other cases: *Juidice v. Vail*[243] and *Pennzoil v. Texaco*.[244] In *Juidice*, a New York statute allowed private creditors who had won judgments against private debtors to obtain subpoenas requiring debtors to appear and divulge their assets. If debtors failed to comply, the state courts could hold them in contempt and jail or fine them in order to force them to cooperate. A class of debtors filed a federal §1983 action, contending that the state scheme violated the fourteenth amendment. They named state judges who had issued contempt orders as defendants and sought an injunction ordering the judges to cease.[245] The district court distinguished

236. Professor Fiss describes a state prosecutor's capacity under *Hicks* as a "reverse removal power." Fiss, note 57, at 1136.

237. 420 U.S. 592 (1975); see notes 160–61 and accompanying text.

238. See text accompanying note 151.

239. 420 U.S. at 604.

240. Id.

241. 442 U.S. 415 (1979); see notes 191–96 and accompanying text.

242. See also *Trainor v. Hernandez*, 431 U.S. 434 (1977) (holding that abstention was required in deference to a state civil action to recover state funds that had allegedly been obtained unlawfully).

243. 430 U.S. 327 (1977).

244. 481 U.S. 1 (1987).

245. Two of the plaintiffs sought damages for past violations of their federal rights, but those claims were dismissed on the basis of the judges' immunity. Today, state judges might have immu-

Huffman, held the statute authorizing contempt orders unconstitutional, and enjoined the judges from relying on it in the future. The Supreme Court held that the district court should have abstained.

Then-Justice Rehnquist acknowledged that the moving parties in state court were private creditors (rather than state officers) and that the state proceedings were ordinary loan-default matters (not civil enforcement actions akin to criminal prosecutions). He also acknowledged that the state's interest in enforcing its "contempt process" was less important than its interest in enforcing its criminal laws and, perhaps, less important than its interest in maintaining "quasi-criminal" proceedings like the nuisance action in *Huffman*. Nevertheless, the state's interest in its contempt process was "of sufficiently great import" to warrant abstention. The contempt power "lies at the core" of the state's administration of its courts.[246] The debtor-plaintiffs in the federal §1983 action had been given an opportunity to present their federal objections both to the state trial courts that held them in contempt and to the state appellate courts. That was sufficient to dispose of any of the recognized exceptions to *Younger/Samuels*.[247]

In *Huffman*, *Moore*, and *Juidice*, the Court declined to hold that federal-question abstention obliges federal courts to defer to *all* civil proceedings pending in state court.[248] Obviously, *Younger/Samuels* cannot extend to ordinary state lawsuits involving only private parties. Recall that the Court's judicially created abstention doctrine governs only when plaintiffs seek declaratory judgments or injunctions in federal §1983 actions.[249] Plaintiffs must, then, name defendants who act "under color" of state law.[250] The defendants in §1983 actions are almost always state officers, and plaintiffs almost always want relief from state proceedings in which those state officers are the moving parties. Plaintiffs ordinarily have no basis for filing a federal §1983 action against state officials, seeking a federal order protecting them from pending state lawsuits brought by other private litigants (strangers to the §1983 action). Without some basis for proceeding under §1983 in federal court, plaintiffs will be denied the relief they seek against privately initiated proceedings in state court—not because federal courts invoke *Younger/Samuels*, but because (in the absence of a §1983 action) the Anti-Injunction Act establishes an independent statutory bar.[251] If the Court's interpretation of §1983 in *Mitchum* has any practical significance at all, federal-question abstention under *Younger/Samuels* cannot be coextensive with §2283.[252] Yet the further the Court extends abstention into the domain of privately initiated state proceedings, the less likely it is that federal courts will have §1983 actions before them in which they might issue injunctions or declaratory judgments against those proceedings. At some point, *Younger/Samuels* loses meaning, because §1983 no longer provides a mechanism for avoiding §2283. And at that point, the statute takes over.[253]

---

nity in a case like *Juidice*, even if plaintiffs request only injunctive relief—unless the judges concerned first refuse to comply with a declaratory judgment. See Chapter X, note 434 and accompanying text.

246. 430 U.S. at 335.

247. Id. at 337. See text accompanying note 203.

248. *Huffman*, 420 U.S. at 594; *Moore*, 442 U.S. at 423 n.8; *Juidice*, 430 U.S. at 236 n.13.

249. See text accompanying note 19.

250. See Chapter VIII, text accompanying note 135; Chapter X, notes 373–74 and accompanying text.

251. But see notes 20–26 and accompanying (discussing two other exceptions to §2283).

252. See notes 16–19, 170–71 and accompanying text.

253. See text accompanying note 29 (explaining that there is little reason think that federal courts should routinely enjoin state court litigation between private parties).

The contempt case, *Juidice*, was singular in this respect inasmuch as the plaintiffs in federal court sued state officials (the judges) for using heavy-handed tactics to help private loan companies collect their bad debts. If a federal injunction had been available in that case, it would have run to state judicial officers. That was a rare instance, then, in which a federal §1983 action against state officials might have produced injunctive or declaratory relief affecting litigation in state court involving only private named parties. Moreover, it was a case in which a federal order would have interfered with state officials' performance of an important state function—namely, the exercise of the contempt power. So *Juidice* was *both* a case in which §1983 was available to circumnavigate §2283 *and* a case in which an important state interest justified abstention in the absence of §2283.[254]

The *Pennzoil* case was also extraordinary, but in a different way. In that case, a private plaintiff was able to file a federal §1983 action against another private party. Pennzoil initially sued Texaco in state court in Texas, contending that Texaco had interfered with Pennzoil's contract with another oil company. The understandably incensed jury gave Pennzoil an award of damages that seemed, in all justice, to fit Texaco's offense rather well: $10 billion, give or take a billion. Under Texas law, Pennzoil was entitled to the assistance of local constables to collect. Texaco could avoid immediate execution of the judgment pending review in the state appellate courts, if Texaco would only be so good as to post a bond in the amount of the judgment. Texaco found a bond of that magnitude a bit steep to be covered out of petty cash. So Texaco filed something else: a §1983 action against Pennzoil in a federal district court in New York.[255] In that federal lawsuit, Texaco claimed that the Texas state judgment violated various provisions of the Constitution and two federal statutes and that the sizeable bond that Texas required for an appeal in state court violated the fourteenth amendment. The district court enjoined Pennzoil from attempting to enforce the Texas judgment. In the Supreme Court, Justice Powell explained that the district court should have abstained in light of "the principles of federalism enunciated in" *Younger*.[256]

The first order of business was to decide whether Texaco could properly rely on §1983 to advance its claims in federal court. If not, the Anti-Injunction Act presumably foreclosed the district court's order. To proceed under §1983, Texaco had to establish that Pennzoil acted under color of state law. In separate opinions concurring in the judgment, four justices said that Pennzoil *would* act under color of law as soon as it invoked the Texas scheme for enforcing the state judgment and thus began working in concert with the state constabulary.[257] Writing for the Court, Justice Powell side-stepped the "color of law" issue and went directly to whether the circumstances warranted abstention.[258] He conceded that the equitable basis of *Younger* would not answer. But he insisted that comity mandated abstention nonetheless. His explanation was circular: Comity "mandates" abstention when

---

254. See Althouse, note 55, at 1080.

255. Texaco contended that venue was proper in New York because its offices were there and it was there that it would file for bankruptcy if its §1983 action proved unsuccessful. The (geographically challenged) district court contrived to find venue appropriate on the theory that Texaco's federal claims "arose" in lower Manhattan. 28 U.S.C. §1391(b). Pennzoil did not object to venue and thus forfeited any argument in that respect. See 481 U.S. at 23–24 (Marshall, J., concurring in the judgment).

256. 430 U.S. at 10.

257. E.g., id. at 30 n.1 (Stevens, J., concurring in the judgment). See Chapter X, note 373 (discussing *Lugar v. Edmondson*).

258. Justice Powell dissented in *Lugar*, joined by then-Justice Rehnquist and Justice O'Connor (who joined Powell's opinion in *Pennzoil*).

"certain" civil proceedings are pending in state court and the state's interests are "so important that exercise of federal judicial power would disregard the comity between the States and the National Government."[259]

Justice Powell rested primarily on *Juidice*. By his account, the state interest the Court had found sufficient to warrant abstention there (the interest in effectuating state court judgments via the contempt power) was equally implicated in *Pennzoil*. The district court's order barring Pennzoil from executing the state judgment interfered with the state's interest in "enforcing the orders and judgments" of its courts in cases pending before those courts.[260] Powell's reliance on *Juidice* has been questioned. By some accounts, *Juidice* attached importance not to the enforcement of state judgments by means of the contempt power, but rather to the contempt power itself—used by state courts in all manner of circumstances.[261] Recall, too, that the injunction in *Juidice* ran to the state judges who exercised the contempt power and thus plainly interfered with the state's interest in the preservation of that power. By contrast, the district court's injunction in *Pennzoil* ran to a private company (Pennzoil) and affected the state's sovereign interests only indirectly.[262]

Justice Powell also said that abstention was required in order to avoid an unwarranted federal court determination of Texaco's federal constitutional claims. If Texaco pressed its claims in state court, those courts might construe the statute requiring such a significant bond in a way that would save it from constitutional attack.[263] Powell acknowledged that the avoidance of federal constitutional issues is typically the point of *Pullman* abstention.[264] But he explained (fairly enough) that *Younger* abstention, too, allows state courts an opportunity to find alternative state law grounds for resolving disputes, thus defusing federal questions.[265] By now, however, Powell was plainly dissembling. He was convinced that Texaco's lawsuit did not belong in federal court, and he was merely offering additional observations to fortify the conclusion that abstention was appropriate.[266] Other members of the Court groped for still other approaches to the case, arguing among themselves over whether *Rooker/Feldman* should control.[267]

---

259. 481 U.S. at 11.

260. Id. at 13–14.

261. Professor Althouse takes this view. Althouse, note 55, at 1080–81.

262. In fact, Texas filed an *amicus* brief in the district court, denying any interest at all in the matter. According to Professor Althouse, Justice Powell's opinion in *Pennzoil* "made a rather dramatic new extension of *Younger*, applying it to a case with no state official as defendant, where the state's interest was so insignificant that the state itself disclaimed it." Id. at 1082.

263. Justice Powell noted that the Texas courts might read the statute with the "open courts" provision of the state constitution and conclude that it did not authorize a bond that no litigant could afford. Id. at 11–12.

264. See notes 85–88 and accompanying text.

265. 481 U.S. at 11–12; see notes 150–52, 193 and accompanying text.

266. 481 U.S. at 11 n.9. Writing separately, Justice Blackmun relied on *Pullman* forthrightly. That was a neat trick inasmuch as Texaco had advanced no supplemental state law claims. See notes 80–82 and accompanying text. It appears that Blackmun reached for *Pullman* in order to avoid joining Justice Powell in what Blackmun regarded as a dangerous extension of *Younger*. 481 U.S. at 27–29 (Blackmun, J., concurring). Justice Powell declined to rest formally on *Pullman*, because Pennzoil had not argued the point. That was also a neat trick inasmuch as the Court had previously said that it would not permit the parties to control the application of *Pullman* abstention. See note 158.

267. See Chapter VI, notes 196–225 and accompanying text. Justice Marshall thought so. 481 U.S. at 24–25 (concurring opinion). Justice Scalia thought not—because the federal court had not been asked actually to second-guess a previous state court decision on the merits of Texaco's federal claims. Id. at 18 (concurring opinion). Justice Brennan and Justice Stevens preferred to reach the

In the end, the result in *Pennzoil* was scarcely surprising. Yet its precedential significance is problematic. By some accounts, *Pennzoil* was unique—the product of a silly judgment in state court, audacious forum-shopping, and the complexities that invariably attend litigation over great sums of money.[268] Justice Powell himself disclaimed any doctrinal innovation. He insisted that *Pennzoil* involved the same state interest previously found to be important in *Juidice* and dropped a footnote setting aside the question whether *Younger* governs cases in which the states have no special interest in private litigation pending in state court.[269] At all events, *Pennzoil* offers a good case study of the intersections among §1983, §2283, the abstention doctrines, and related ideas (like *Rooker/Feldman*).[270]

The Supreme Court declined in *NOPSI* to advance federal-question abstention further into new territory.[271] Recall that NOPSI filed simultaneous suits in state and federal court, advancing the same federal preemption claim in both places. The district court relied primarily on *Burford* to dismiss the federal suit, but the circuit court invoked *Younger* as well. In the Supreme Court, Justice Scalia rejected the idea that federal courts have discretion to dismiss lawsuits simply because the parties are also litigating the same issues in state court. Recalling Justice Brennan's declaration in *Colorado River*, he said that federal courts have an "unflagging" obligation to decide cases within their jurisdiction, and he depicted *Younger* as only one of a "class of cases" in which federal courts withhold otherwise authorized equitable relief to avoid "undue interference with state proceedings."[272] Justice Scalia explained that the state court review proceeding in *NOPSI* was not of the "type" to which *Younger* was applicable. He acknowledged that the Court had applied *Younger* to civil actions in *Huffman*, *Juidice*, and *Pennzoil*. But he insisted that the Court had never suggested that *Younger* also applies to state court review of executive or legislative action. To press *Younger* that far, he said, would make a "mockery" of the understanding that abstention is the exception, not the rule.[273]

---

merits rather than rest on any door-closing device. They would have rejected Texaco's challenge to the bond scheme.

268. Justice Marshall offered something of this view, putting *Pennzoil* down as yet another illustration of Holmes' warning that "hard cases make bad law." Id. at 26 (concurring opinion), quoting *Northern Secur. Co. v. United States*, 193 U.S. 197, 400 (1904) (Holmes, J., dissenting).

269. 481 U.S. at 14 n.12. Professor Althouse regards *Pennzoil* as convincing evidence that the Court has lost sight of the thinking that generated *Younger* in the first place—namely, the assumption that state courts are typically ready, willing, and able to adjudicate federal claims effectively. As the Court has extended *Younger* to civil actions, the Court has used as a limiting "principle" the requirement that abstention is warranted only when states have especially important interests in the state court litigation in question. Yet it is when important state interests are at stake, according to Althouse, that state courts may *not* offer the kind of disinterested adjudication that *Younger* presupposes. On the one hand, *Pennzoil* appears to be a surprising and troubling further extension of *Younger* into a context in which an especially important state interest is difficult to find. Yet on the other, *Pennzoil* may represent the strongest case for abstention—for the very reason that in the *absence* of an important state interest in the enforcement of a private judgment, the state courts are ostensibly neutral and thus constitute "trustworthy" tribunals for the adjudication of federal questions. Althouse, note 55, at 1087–88.

270. The Court has not elaborated on *Pennzoil* since that case was decided. Reviewing lower court decisions three years later, Professor Baker reported inclusive results. Thomas E. Baker,"*Our Federalism" in Pennzoil Co. v. Texaco, Inc. or How the Younger Doctrine Keeps Getting Older Not Better*, 9 Rev. Litigation 303 (1990).

271. *NOPSI v. Council of New Orleans*, 491 U.S. 350 (1989); see notes 110–15 and accompanying text).

272. 491 U.S. at 359.

273. Id. at 368.

It would be a mistake to read *NOPSI* as a belated attempt to put the *Younger* genie back in the equity bottle.[274] Justice Scalia himself recognized that Justice Black rested in *Younger* "primarily" on comity and federalism.[275] Moreover, *NOPSI* offered no occasion for a thoroughgoing examination of *Younger* and its progeny. NOPSI did not seek injunctive or declaratory relief against a pending suit filed in state court by state officials seeking to enforce a regulatory agency determination anchored in state law. By contrast, NOPSI itself sued state authorities in state court hoping to resist the agency's order.[276] Accordingly, the *NOPSI* case was not about whether a federal district court should entertain a §1983 action seeking a federal court injunction or declaration terminating a pending state court proceeding in which the §1983 plaintiff was a defendant. It was about whether a federal court should allow a litigant to press a federal claim in both federal and state court at the same time. Parallel lawsuits can create friction. That was true in *NOPSI*, where state authorities were parties to NOPSI's suit in state court and important state regulatory interests were implicated.[277] Justice Scalia recognized that if the federal district court reached a judgment first, its disposition might well affect (or even preempt) the parallel state court action. Yet neither *Younger* nor any other precedent suggests that federal courts must (or can) decline jurisdiction on those grounds alone.[278]

4. State Administrative Proceedings

Federal-question abstention is applicable to cases in which federal §1983 plaintiffs seek injunctive or declaratory relief from proceedings pending before state administrative agencies, provided those proceedings are *judicial* in nature.[279] In *Middlesex County Ethics Comm. v. Garden State Bar Ass'n*,[280] an attorney filed a federal §1983 action, seeking an injunction against the enforcement of a bar association rule forbidding lawyers to make public statements "prejudicial to the administration of justice." At the time, the

274. Professor Brown has suggested that Justice Scalia's rhetoric about the obligation to exercise jurisdiction "reads like a reprint of Professor Redish's article." George D. Brown, *When Federalism and Separation of Powers Collide—Rethinking Younger Abstention*, 59 Geo. Wash. L. Rev. 114, 150 (1990). See note 77 and accompanying text. At the same time, Scalia also cited Professor Shapiro's article—which takes a decidedly different set of positions. See note 78.

275. *NOPSI*, 491 U.S. at 364; see note 152 and accompanying text.

276. Justice Scalia noted that NOPSI filed the state court action only because the district court had dismissed its prior federal actions and might well dismiss its third. 491 U.S. at 357. By the time the case reached the Supreme Court, NOPSI's suit in state court had been consolidated with an independent suit (by the Council) for a state declaratory judgment validating the rate order and with a third suit (against the Council) by a consumer group hoping to prevent the Council from acceding to NOPSI's demands. Since NOPSI sought no federal relief respecting those lawsuits, their existence did not trigger *Younger* abstention. Justice Scalia noted them in a footnote. 491 U.S. at 358 n.3.

277. See text accompanying note 239.

278. Whatever may be the scope of the abstention doctrine associated with *Colorado River*, it plainly falls well short of a general rule that federal courts must defer to parallel litigation in state court in any and all circumstances. See note 135 and accompanying text. Most academics doubt the wisdom of extending *Younger* abstention to ordinary civil cases in state court. For a rare endorsement, see Howard B. Stravitz, *Younger Abstention Reaches a Civil Maturity: Pennzoil Co. v. Texaco, Inc.*, 57 Fordham L. Rev. 997 (1989).

279. See Chapter VI, text accompanying notes 186–89 (discussing the adjudicative functions that state agencies perform); cf. Chapter V, text accompanying note 1 (noting that federal agencies commonly adjudicate claims).

280. 457 U.S. 423 (1982).

lawyer was charged with violating that rule, and his case was pending before a state ethics committee impaneled under the auspices of the state supreme court. In those circumstances, Chief Justice Burger sustained the district court's decision to abstain. Burger explained that the ethics committee proceeding satisfied the three conditions for triggering *Younger*: (1) it was judicial in nature; (2) it implicated an important state interest; and (3) it provided the §1983 plaintiff with an "adequate opportunity" to litigate his first amendment claim. Burger acknowledged that the committee itself might not supply the necessary adjudication. But he explained that, if the committee rejected the attorney's constitutional defense, he would be entitled to seek appellate review in the state courts, which *would* consider his claim.[281]

Federal-question abstention is *not* applicable if federal §1983 plaintiffs seek relief from state administrative proceedings that are *legislative* in nature. The characterization a state places on a proceeding carries some weight.[282] Yet federal courts make their own independent appraisals. The question can be close in some instances, the difference between judicial and legislative action being elusive. On the whole, state agency proceedings are judicial in the relevant sense if they manifest the usual features of adjudication (the determination of historical facts, the identification of the proper legal standard, and the application of that standard to the facts). Agency proceedings are legislative when they undertake the formulation of substantive policy for the future.[283]

In a final effort to invoke *Younger* in *NOPSI*, the Council contended that the district court was obliged to abstain in favor of the Council's own administrative proceeding and that, in turn, the district court was equally obliged to abstain in favor of the state courts' review of the Council's order.[284] For the first point, the Council relied on *Middlesex*; for the second, the Council cited *Huffman*, albeit by analogy.[285] Justice Scalia rejected both parts of the Council's argument. Initially, he explained that the Council's proceeding was not "judicial in nature," but was essentially legislative. Accordingly, *Middlesex* did not control. That point raised another. Recalling the *Prentis* case, Justice Scalia conceded that the district court could not enjoin a state legislative process,

281. Id. at 433–36 & n.15. The decision in *Middlesex* was arguably narrow. The ethics committee was not an ordinary state administrative agency, but was formally an instrumentality of the state courts. Even Justice Brennan concurred in the Court's judgment—though he reaffirmed his view that *Younger* is "in general inapplicable to civil proceedings." Id. at 438. In *Ohio Civil Rights Comm'n v. Dayton Christian Schools*, 477 U.S. 619 (1986), however, the Court invoked *Younger* to foreclose federal interference with a state civil rights agency's investigation of a religious school. The Commission's orders were reviewable in state court, and it was in state court that the school would receive an opportunity to litigate its first amendment claims. But there was no other relationship between the state agency and the state courts. Then-Justice Rehnquist dismissed any apparent tension with the rule that §1983 plaintiffs need not exhaust state administrative remedies. See notes 47–51 and accompanying text (discussing *Patsy*). The religious school was not required to initiate a proceeding before the Commission as a means of seeking affirmative relief prior to filing a federal §1983 action. The Commission had itself instituted an investigation of the school for alleged violations of the school's employees' rights.

282. In the *Dayton* case, the Court distinguished one precedent on the ground that state law indicated that the agency in that case did not act in a judicial capacity. *Dayton Christian Schools*, 477 U.S. at 627 n.2.

283. See Chapter I, notes 7, 61–62 and accompanying text.

284. See notes 271–73 and accompanying text.

285. See notes 160–61 and accompanying text (explaining that in the *Huffman* case the Court held that a state *judicial* proceeding is "pending" for purposes of *Younger* throughout the process of appellate review in higher state courts).

either—while it was under way.[286] In *NOPSI*, however, the Council's legislative action had come to an end before NOPSI filed its two lawsuits (attacking the Council's legislative product) in federal and state court. Unlike the state court in *Prentis* (which exercised legislative authority), the state court in *NOPSI* was charged with the ordinary judicial responsibility to determine whether NOPSI's attack on the Council's order was meritorious. Accordingly, the Council's analogy to *Huffman* was of no moment. Once the Council completed its legislative activity (by producing the order), NOPSI was free to attack that order in state court, in federal court, or in both courts at once.[287]

5. State Executive Activities

Federal-question abstention is also applicable in some cases in which federal §1983 plaintiffs seek injunctive or declaratory relief with respect to certain kinds of executive activity. Recall that in *O'Shea v. Littleton*[288] and *Rizzo v. Goode*,[289] the Supreme Court held that federal district courts could not issue orders barring the police in Chicago and Philadelphia from continuing a pattern of abusive behavior, typically targeting racial minorities. In the main, the Court held in both cases that the plaintiffs' federal claims were not ripe for adjudication in an Article III court.[290] That ground was sufficient in itself (formally speaking) to dispose of the two cases. Yet in both instances the Court went on to rely in the alternative on equitable considerations, comity, and federalism. And in so doing, the Court explicitly invoked *Younger* and cases in the *Younger* line.

In *O'Shea*, Justice White said that *Younger* reaffirmed that federal courts should not ordinarily restrain state criminal prosecutions. That idea led to another: The need for a "proper balance" between "federal and state *courts*" counsels restraint regarding injunctions against "state officers engaged in the *administration* of the State's criminal laws."[291] In *Rizzo*, then-Justice Rehnquist also acknowledged that the "principles of federalism" elaborated in *Younger* and its progeny are "entitled to the greatest weight" in cases in which federal courts are asked to enjoin state criminal prosecutions. Yet he, too, insisted that the same "principles" have "applicability where injunctive relief is sought, *not* against the *judicial* branch of... state government, but against those in charge of an *executive* branch of... state or local government."[292]

---

286. *Prentis v. Atlantic Coast Line Co.*, 211 U.S. 210 (1908); see notes 39–43 and accompanying text.

287. Since Justice Scalia held that the Council's own action was not judicial in nature and thus did not bring *Younger* abstention into play, he had no occasion to decide whether the Council's analogy to *Huffman* was sound. He only assumed the validity of that analogy for purposes of analysis. 491 U.S. at 369. Concurring in the judgment, Justice Blackmun was "not entirely persuaded" that the question was actually "open." Id. at 374–75 (concurring opinion). Recall that in *Dayton Christian Schools*, Justice Rehnquist said that the school would have an opportunity to press its federal claim in state court, on judicial review of the agency's action in that case. See note 281. Justice Scalia acknowledged in *NOPSI* that, in that way, *Dayton Christian Schools* "suggested" that (by analogy to *Huffman*) a state administrative proceeding that is sufficiently judicial to invoke *Younger* remains pending while the agency's order is reviewed in state court. 491 U.S. at 369 n.4 (majority opinion).

288. 414 U.S. 488 (1974).

289. 423 U.S. 362 (1976).

290. See Chapter IX, notes 409–14 and accompanying text.

291. *O'Shea*, 414 U.S. at 499 (emphasis added).

292. *Rizzo*, 423 U.S. at 380 (emphasis added).

These passages do not simply cite *Younger* and related abstention cases as illustrations of the way in which equitable restraint, comity, and federalism temper federal court action with respect to the states. They purport actually to extend at least the "principles" associated with *Younger* to entirely different precincts: federal court actions challenging state executive activities. It is hard to think that the idea in *Younger* can range so far afield and still retain any trace of its original character. By some accounts, *O'Shea* and *Rizzo* abandon any pretense that the Supreme Court is elaborating coherent doctrine governing abstention and essentially concede that *Younger* is a short-hand for a general refusal to entertain civil rights actions for the vindication of fourteenth amendment rights against state power.[293] All the same, *O'Shea* and *Rizzo* were decided in the middle 1970s, when the Court was taking aggressive steps to bring the expansive Warren Court period to a close.[294] More recent decisions touching *Younger* suggest that the Court may now be less intent on withholding federal judicial power in cases in which §1983 and §1331 authorize its use.[295]

---

293. E.g., H. Jefferson Powell, *The Compleat Jeffersonian: Justice Rehnquist and Federalism*, 91 Yale L.J. 1317, 1343–44 (1982); Soifer & Macgill, note 151, at 1215; Weinberg, note 177, at 1215–22.

294. See Chapter I, text accompanying note 90.

295. See notes 271–73 and accompanying text.

Chapter XII

Habeas Corpus

The writ of habeas corpus is the traditional Anglo-American vehicle for inquiring into the validity of personal detention. The writ takes its name, "you have the body," from the basic purpose it serves.[1] Historically, the writ has been an unusually efficient and expeditious device for ensuring that prisoners do not suffer deprivations of liberty without prompt judicial attention. In addition, the writ has been an instrument of governmental administration, both holding government to answer in independent courts and reconciling conflicts of jurisdiction between different courts competing for hegemony. The writ often figures in federal court battles with the executive and legislative branches of the national government and equally in confrontations between federal courts and the states and state courts. Habeas corpus cases thus invariably implicate the separation principle and federalism.[2]

A. Function and History of the Writ

Prisoners in state custody typically seek federal habeas corpus relief *after* state courts have had an opportunity to determine their claims.[3] As a formal matter, applications for the federal writ are not subject to state preclusion rules under the Full Faith and Credit Statute.[4] On first blush, then, federal habeas appears to offer (on a deferred basis) what federal-question abstention and so many other doctrines usually deny at earlier stages—namely, a federal forum for the adjudication of federal claims. The writ occasionally functions in precisely that way. Nevertheless, modern habeas corpus is so tightly restricted that litigants who are unable to gain access to federal court before or during state proceedings are also typically foreclosed thereafter. Various statutes and judge-made doctrines establish door-closing rules in the interests of federalism and comity.[5]

---

1. II Pollock & Maitland, History of English Law 593 n.4 (1898).

2. Recall that some of the most famous cases in federal courts law originated as petitions for the writ of habeas corpus. In *Ex parte McCardle*, the Supreme Court maneuvered for position with respect to Congress. See Chapter IV, notes 12–25 and accompanying text. And in *Ex parte Young*, the Court grappled with the relationship between the federal judiciary and the states. See Chapter X, notes 283–88 and accompanying text.

3. See notes 89–131 and accompanying text (discussing the exhaustion doctrine).

4. *Kremer v. Chem. Constr. Corp.*, 456 U.S. 461, 485 n.27 (1982); see Chapter VI, note 170 and accompanying text.

5. See notes 194–264 and accompanying text (discussing procedural default doctrine).

The origins of habeas corpus can be traced to the early central courts in England.[6] Initially, those courts issued the writ to obtain the presence of individuals so that matters in which they were involved could be considered.[7] Later, the common law courts (King's Bench and Common Pleas) used the writ to draw litigation away from local manorial courts and to bring cases under the King's central authority.[8] Later still, those courts also relied on the writ in their competition with Chancery, which administered the King's equity.[9] Ultimately, they used the writ to challenge the King's own prerogatives.[10] In the Seventeenth Century, John Selden and Lord Coke fashioned habeas corpus into a procedural device for enforcing the thirty-ninth chapter of Magna Charta, which, by their (creative) account, barred the King from summarily sending Englishmen to the Tower of London. According to Selden and Coke, imprisonment at the King's command alone violated the "law of the land," which Coke abbreviated as "due process."[11] The English Habeas Corpus Act of 1679 established procedures for using the writ routinely to prevent the Crown from holding prisoners in jail for lengthy periods awaiting trial. Thereafter, Parliament occasionally denied the writ *ad hoc* to petitioners the King imprisoned for "high treason." On the whole, however, habeas corpus continued to develop as the Great Writ of Liberty.[12]

American colonists laid claim to the writ of habeas corpus as one of the rights they were due as Englishmen. But historians have no clear picture of the writ's actual use in the colonial period.[13] It was not until after the Constitution was adopted that most states enacted American versions of the English Act of 1679. By some accounts, the paucity of earlier statutes actually demonstrates that habeas was well entrenched: The colonists may have thought the writ was so fundamental that it needed no codification in legislation or state constitutions.[14]

1. The Suspension Clause

The delegates to the Philadelphia Convention referred to the writ of habeas corpus in the text of the new Constitution, but only in the oblique Suspension Clause: "The Privilege of the Writ of Habeas Corpus shall not be suspended unless when in Cases of Re-

6. See 9 William S. Holdsworth, History of English Law 108–09 (4th ed. 1926); Daniel J. Meador, Habeas Corpus and Magna Carta 7–9 (1966).

7. Robert J. Sharpe, The Law of Habeas Corpus 2 n.1 (1976).

8. See Robert Walker, The Constitutional and Legal Development of Habeas Corpus as the Writ of Liberty 25 (1960) (linking the writ to the "centralization of judicial power in the hands of the royal courts").

9. Holdsworth, note 6, at 109–10.

10. In the typical scenario, Chancery issued an injunction forbidding would-be litigants to sue in the law courts and, if they failed to comply, ordered them imprisoned for contempt. Then, the law courts protected their own turf by issuing the writ of habeas corpus to discharge the prisoners and allow them to sue, after all.

11. Meador, note 6, at 14–20; Walker, note 8, at 24; William F. Duker, *The English Origins of the Writ of Habeas Corpus: A Peculiar Path to Fame*, 53 N.Y.U. L. Rev. 983, 1031–32 (1978).

12. Rollin C. Hurd, A Treatise on the Right of Personal Liberty and on the Writ of Habeas Corpus 122–27 (1858).

13. See Dallin H. Oaks, *Habeas Corpus in the States—1776–1865*, 32 U. Chi. L. Rev. 243 (1965); Neil McFeeley, *The Historical Development of Habeas Corpus*, 30 Sw. L.J. 585 (1976).

14. This was Professor Chafee's view. Zechariah Chafee, Jr., *The Most Important Human Right in the Constitution*, 32 B.U. L. Rev. 143, 146 (1952).

bellion or Invasion the public Safety may require it."[15] That language does not explicitly confer jurisdiction on federal courts to issue the writ. Instead, it presupposes that the writ already exists and addresses only the circumstances in which access to it can be suspended—presumably by Congress.[16] The records of the Convention, such as they are, provide little interpretive help. The delegates debated only whether to allow suspension in cases of emergency.[17]

By some accounts, the Suspension Clause amounts to very little. At most, it contemplates that *state* courts may have power to issue the writ of habeas corpus and limits Congress' authority to interfere with that jurisdiction. Parliament had routinely suspended the writ in particular cases in order to keep "treasonous" dissenters in prison. Colonial assemblies adopted "suspension" statutes that temporarily denied the writ to certain classes of people or in certain geographic areas. Accordingly, the Convention may have meant only to prevent the new American Congress from taking similar *ad hoc* action.[18] By other accounts, the Suspension Clause means a great deal. Three positions have substantial support in Supreme Court opinions and the attendant academic literature. According to one view, the Suspension Clause constitutes a self-executing source of *federal* judicial power, authorizing federal courts to issue the writ of habeas corpus in appropriate cases: The Suspension Clause may not obligate Congress to create inferior federal courts. But if Congress chooses to establish inferior courts, Congress cannot deny those courts power to entertain habeas corpus applications.[19] According to a second view, the Suspension Clause may not itself establish federal judicial power to entertain petitions for habeas corpus relief. Nevertheless, it recognizes that the common law writ was generally available in 1787 and limits Congress' capacity to deny federal courts the authority to issue the writ in similar cases in the future.[20] According to a third view,

---

15. U.S. Const. art. I, §9, cl.2.

16. Note that the Suspension Clause is located in §9 of Article I (where certain limitations on congressional power are collected), not in Article II (where the executive's powers are listed). In 1861, President Lincoln purported to suspend the writ in order to permit union troops to administer martial law in civilian areas. Chief Justice Taney wrote an order in *Ex parte Merryman*, 17 F. Cas. 144 (1861), stating that only Congress had that power. Military leaders ignored Taney's opinion at the time. Congress later defused the issue by enacting legislation ratifying Lincoln's action. Martin S. Sheffer, *Presidential Power to Suspend Habeas Corpus: The Taney-Bates Dialogue and Ex parte Merryman*, 11 Okla. City U. L. Rev. 1 (1986). See Chapter V, text accompanying notes 82–95 (noting the argument that the Suspension Clause limits the executive's ability to deliver the trial of suspected "terrorists" entirely into the hands of military tribunals established by presidential decree).

17. Professor Freedman argues that the delegates in Philadelphia and at the ratifying conventions did not debate whether federal courts would have power to issue the writ, because there was widespread agreement that those courts *would* have that jurisdiction as a matter of course. Eric M. Freedman, *The Suspension Clause in the Ratification Debates*, 44 Buffalo L. Rev. 451 (1996).

18. Justice Scalia suggested this possibility in his dissent in *INS v. St. Cyr*, 533 U.S. 289, 337–38 (2001); see Chapter IV, notes 32–41 and accompanying text. The Chief Justice and Justice Thomas joined Scalia's opinion in its entirety. Justice O'Connor joined other sections, but did not endorse Justice Scalia's discussion of the Suspension Clause. For academic commentaries giving the Suspension Clause roughly this narrow scope, see William F. Duker, A Constitutional History of Habeas Corpus 126–56 (1980); Akhil R. Amar, *Of Sovereignty and Federalism*, 96 Yale L.J. 1425, 1509 (1987); Rex A. Collings, Jr., *Habeas Corpus for Convicts—Constitutional Right or Legislative Grace?*, 40 Calif. L. Rev. 335, 345 (1952). Professor Meltzer has pointed out that this interpretation of the Suspension Clause necessarily denies that *Tarble's Case* was a constitutional decision. Daniel J. Meltzer, *Congress, Courts, and Constitutional Remedies*, 86 Gtn. L.J. 2537, 2566–67 (1998). See Chapter VI, note 107 and accompanying text.

19. E.g., Francis Paschal, *The Constitution and Habeas Corpus*, 1970 Duke L.J. 605.

20. Justice Stevens suggested this understanding in his opinion for the Court in *St. Cyr*. See 520 U.S. at 301.

the Suspension Clause has no bearing unless and until Congress confers some form of habeas jurisdiction on federal courts. Thereafter, it limits Congress' ability to change its mind and withdraw that jurisdiction. By this last account, the Suspension Clause may speak only to temporary "suspensions" of the writ, leaving Congress free to eliminate federal habeas jurisdiction permanently.[21]

If it is posited that the Suspension Clause ensures some constitutional footing for federal court authority, further debates typically slide into quarrels about the scope of the federal courts' purview in habeas corpus cases. Two questions are paramount: (1) whether the Suspension Clause is exclusively concerned with prisoners held in executive detention without trial or, instead, also addresses prisoners serving sentences after conviction; and (2) whether the Suspension Clause is exclusively concerned with prisoners held by federal authorities or, instead, also addresses prisoners in state custody. Originalists typically insist that the Suspension Clause guarantees the writ of habeas corpus only in the form it took in England in 1787. Beginning from that premise, different originalists give different answers to these two key questions, depending on their reading of the relevant historical materials.[22] Other observers deny that the Suspension Clause codifies the writ as it existed in 1787 and contend, by contrast, that it constitutionalizes a dynamic procedural device that was changing even then and has never ceased to evolve over time.[23] Other commentators, too, disagree among themselves, but typically argue that the Suspension Clause can and should be understood to ensure federal court authority to entertain petitions from convicts in the custody of state, as well as federal, authorities.[24]

---

21. Justice Scalia also discussed this rough understanding of the Suspension Clause in his *St. Cyr* dissent. See id. at 337–41. Justice Stevens explicitly disclaimed it. Id. at 304 n.24 (majority opinion). In response, Justice Scalia insisted that if it is true (as Justice Scalia believes it is) that Congress can decline to establish federal habeas jurisdiction in the first place, it necessarily follows that Congress can permanently withdraw that which it initially extends (provided Congress does so explicitly). The evil to which the Suspension Clause is directed, Justice Scalia suggested, is congressional tampering with habeas jurisdiction on a selective, temporary basis. A capacity to manipulate habeas jurisdiction only in certain circumstances can lend itself to abuse in ways that a capacity to make more sweeping and permanent changes cannot.

22. Justice Brennan once said that the writ *did* extend to convicts in 1787. *Fay v. Noia*, 372 U.S. 391, 403 (1963), citing the English precedent in *Bushell's Case*, 124 Eng. Rep. 1006 (1670). See also *McNally v. Hill*, 293 U.S. 131, 135 (1934) (explaining that the Suspension Clause "implicitly recognize[s]" the "use of the writ" by sentenced prisoners). According to Chief Justice Burger, however, courts in 1787 had no authority to issue the writ on behalf of petitioners held in jail under court order. In Burger's view, then, the Suspension Clause allows Congress to deny the writ to convicts, even if they claim to have been tried and sentenced in violation of federal law. *Swain v. Pressley*, 430 U.S. 372, 386 (1977) (Burger, C.J., concurring). It is scarcely surprising that there is no abundance of early precedent regarding the availability of the writ for convicts. It was not until the 1830s that incarceration became a common means of punishing criminal offenders. Prior to that time, a criminal conviction and sentence typically terminated pre-trial detention and subjected offenders to some form of torture as punishment. Marc M. Arkin, *The Ghost at the Banquet: Slavery, Federalism, and Habeas Corpus for State Prisoners*, 70 Tulane L. Rev. 1, 10–11 & n.40 (1995). The Court held in *Ex parte Dorr*, 44 U.S. (3 How.) 103 (1845), that the federal courts' habeas corpus jurisdiction did not (at that time) reach prisoners in state custody. But the Court did not mention the Suspension Clause in *Dorr*.

23. In a famous brief, Professor Freund once contended that "[w]e shall have to look to history for the essentials of the Great Writ, but not to one point in that history." Brief for Respondent, *United States v. Hayman*, 342 U.S. 205 (1952). For an illustration of a non-originalist interpretation of the Suspension Clause focusing on immigration cases, see Gerald L. Neuman, *Habeas Corpus, Executive Detention, and the Removal of Aliens*, 98 Colum. L. Rev. 961, 970 (1998).

24. Professor Steiker argues that the fourteenth amendment "constitutionalized" federal court responsibility to determine federal claims in criminal cases and thus imposed an obligation on Con-

The Supreme Court has never given the Suspension Clause an authoritative interpretation. Chief Justice Marshall intimated in *Ex parte Bollman*[25] that federal court authority to issue the writ depends entirely on the jurisdictional statutes that Congress enacts: "[T]he power to award the writ by any of the courts of the United States must be given by *written law*."[26] That suggested that the Suspension Clause has no independent significance and that Congress may give federal courts jurisdiction in habeas corpus cases or not, as Congress pleases—within the ordinary parameters established by Article III. Then again, Marshall's purpose in *Bollman* was to disclaim any common law authority to issue the writ. He mentioned the Suspension Clause only in passing. Accordingly, he did not specify that only a *statute* could supply the "written law" required (rather than the Suspension Clause itself). Moreover, Marshall *did* say this in *Bollman*: "[Congress] must have felt, with peculiar force, the *obligation* of providing efficient means by which this great *constitutional* privilege should receive life and activity; for if the means be not in existence, the privilege itself would be lost."[27]

Since Congress has generally provided for federal jurisdiction in habeas corpus cases, the Court has had few occasions to consider whether a restriction on that jurisdiction might be unconstitutional. The Judiciary Act of 1789 granted federal courts authority to entertain habeas corpus petitions from prisoners in federal custody.[28] Other statutes expanded that jurisdiction incrementally.[29] Then, during Reconstruction, the 1867 Act opened federal courts to petitions from state prisoners claiming to be deprived of their liberty in violation of federal law.[30] The derivative modern statute, 28 U.S.C. §2241, describes federal habeas corpus jurisdiction in the negative: "Writs of habeas corpus may be granted by the Supreme Court, any justice thereof, the district courts and any circuit judge within

---

gress to extend habeas jurisdiction to applications from state convicts. Jordan Steiker, *Incorporating the Suspension Clause: Is There a Constitutional Right to Federal Habeas Corpus for State Prisoners?*, 92 Mich. L. Rev. 862 (1994).

25. 8 U.S. (4 Cranch) 75 (1807); see Chapter IV, note 36.

26. Id. at 94 (emphasis added).

27. Id. at 95 (emphasis added). The issue in *Bollman* was whether the Supreme Court had authority to entertain an "original" habeas corpus petition. In the *St. Cyr* case, Justices Stevens and Scalia fought a footnote battle over what Marshall said, or meant to say, in *Bollman*. Compare 533 U.S. at 304 n.24 (opinion of Stevens, J.) (placing emphasis on Marshall's reference to Congress' "obligation" regarding this "constitutional privilege"), with id. at 340 (Scalia, J., dissenting) (reading Marshall's statement that federal jurisdiction "must be given by written law" to contemplate a federal statute). For a close examination of Marshall's opinion in *Bollman* (as well as a novel understanding of the Suspension Clause), see Eric M. Freedman, Habeas Corpus: Rethinking the Great Writ of Liberty 20–25 (2001).

28. See Chapter II, note 57 and accompanying text.

29. In 1833 and 1842, respectively, Congress gave federal courts power to issue the writ on behalf of federal officials and foreign nationals held in state custody. See Armistead M. Dobie, *Habeas Corpus in the Federal Courts*, 13 Va. L. Rev. 433, 442 (1927).

30. It has been argued that the 1867 Act was actually meant to make the writ available to emancipated slaves and indentured servants held in a state of peonage after the Civil War. Lewis Mayers, *The Habeas Corpus Act of 1867: The Supreme Court as Legal Historian*, 33 U. Chi. L. Rev. 31 (1965). That understanding depends on thin evidence regarding the drafters' personal intentions. Those drafters promoted the bill to their colleagues as a means of extending the writ to state prisoners generally. See Larry W. Yackle, *Form and Function in the Administration of Justice: The Bill of Rights and Federal Habeas Corpus*, 23 U. Mich. J. L. Ref. 685, 695–98 (1990). Professor Forsythe contends that the "plain language" of the 1867 Act makes it clear that convicts would not be eligible petitioners. He fortifies that interpretation with other remnants of legislative history which, in his view, demonstrate that the proponents' floor speeches do not tell the full story. Clarke D. Forsythe, *The Historical Origins of Broad Federal Habeas Review Reconsidered*, 70 Notre Dame L. Rev. 1079, 1105–17 (1995).

their respective jurisdictions." But the writ "shall not extend to a prisoner" unless "[h]e is in custody in violation of the Constitution or laws or treaties of the United States."[31]

The Court occasionally relies on the Suspension Clause for leverage in reaching an appropriate construction of §2241 and related statutes. In partial justification for reading statutory language to leave federal court authority intact, the Court explains that an alternative construction would raise Suspension Clause questions. The Court did that in *INS v. St. Cyr*,[32] and there are other illustrations.[33] The *St. Cyr* case did not implicate the really sensitive constitutional questions. The petitioner there was a convict, but he did not challenge the validity of his conviction. He challenged his treatment by federal executive officers, not a state prison warden.[34] Other cases *do* involve convicts attempting to attack criminal convictions. Sometimes, those convicts complain that they are held in state, not federal, custody.[35] The Court is clearly at pains to avoid grappling with the Suspension Clause and determining what, if anything, that clause adds to Article III. In *Felker v. Turpin*,[36] for example, Chief Justice Rehnquist only assumed for purposes of analysis that the Suspension Clause "refers to the writ as it exists today, rather than as it existed in 1789."[37]

2. Challenges to Executive Detention

Habeas corpus is not limited to applicants who contend they are detained unlawfully in connection with criminal charges. Deprivations of liberty are rare apart from the criminal process, but not unknown. Illustrations include selective service cases in which petitioners face involuntary conscription into the military services and immigration cases in which petitioners face physical detention and removal from the country. Congress occasionally enacts legislation curbing judicial review of induction decisions. Yet

---

31. 28 U.S.C. §2241(a), (c)(3). Read literally, §2241 confers jurisdiction on both the Supreme Court and its individual justices, on the district courts as corporate bodies, but then only on circuit judges individually. In practice, those distinctions make no difference. Circuit judges almost never entertain petitions addressed to them personally, and circuit courts routinely handle habeas cases on appeal from district courts. See also 28 U.S.C. §2241(b) (authorizing individual Supreme Court justices and circuit judges to transfer habeas petitions to a district court). For more background, see Larry W. Yackle, Postconviction Remedies 80–84 (1981).

32. 533 U.S. 289 (2001); see Chapter IV, notes 43–45 and accompanying text.

33. E.g., *Hayman*, 342 U.S. at 223. See Chapter I, text accompanying note 26 (noting the avoidance principle generally).

34. Justice Stevens was careful to point out that, in these respects, the petitioners in *St. Cyr* advanced comparatively non-controversial claims to habeas jurisdiction. 533 U.S. at 300–01.

35. E.g., *United States v. MacCollom*, 426 U.S. 317, 322–23 (1976) (mentioning but avoiding a Suspension Clause argument in a case involving a federal convict); *Jones v. Cunningham*, 371 U.S. 236, 238 (1963) (declaring in a case involving a state convict that the habeas corpus statutes implement the "constitutional command that the writ of habeas corpus be made available"); see *Schlup v. Delo*, 513 U.S. 298, 343 (1995) (Scalia, J., dissenting) (referring to Congress' authority to curtail federal habeas corpus for state prisoners "within the very broad limits set by the Suspension Clause").

36. 518 U.S. 651 (1996).

37. Id. at 664. The Court's primary focus in *Felker* was on the Article III implications of a statute that (arguably) deprived the Court itself of jurisdiction to supervise actions taken at the circuit level. See Chapter IV, notes 31–36 and accompanying text. Professor Fallon and Professor Cole contend that the Suspension Clause cannot be considered in isolation from Article III and due process. Richard H. Fallon, Jr., *Applying the Suspension Clause to Immigration Cases*, 98 Colum. L. Rev. 1068 (1998); David Cole, *Jurisdiction and Liberty: Habeas Corpus and Due Process as Limits on Congress's Control of Federal Jurisdiction*, 86 Gtn. L.J. 2481 (1998).

in a celebrated World War II case, *Estep v. United States*,[38] some of the justices explained that the usual means by which federal claims were adjudicated could be curtailed *because* disappointed inductees could still file applications for habeas corpus relief.[39]

Immigrants threatened with removal were traditionally entitled to challenge their treatment in federal habeas corpus proceedings. The Court held as much in one of the early Chinese exclusion cases, *United States v. Jung Ah Lung*.[40] In the immigration context, the Court has sometimes permitted Congress to immunize executive actions from judicial examination. In the leading case, *Nishimura Ekiu v. United States*,[41] Justice Gray relied expressly on the theory that immigration cases implicate "public rights" that need not be subject to adjudication in the courts.[42] Nevertheless, the Court does not lightly construe federal statutes to deny federal courts jurisdiction to entertain habeas petitions from petitioners challenging actions by immigration authorities. In the *St. Cyr* case, the Court held that Congress had not disturbed district court jurisdiction to determine questions of federal statutory law raised by petitioners invoking federal jurisdiction pursuant to §2241.[43]

3. Challenges to Criminal Convictions

The most controversial habeas corpus cases involve prison inmates who have been convicted of criminal offenses and sentenced to incarceration or death. According to conventional theory, a habeas corpus proceeding is not part of the criminal prosecution undertaken by government prosecutors. A prisoner who files a petition initiates an original civil lawsuit, naming the custodian (usually the prison warden) as the respondent and hoping to show that the custodian has no lawful basis for depriving the prisoner of liberty. The federal court entertaining the petition is not (typically) concerned with

---

38. 327 U.S. 114 (1946).

39. Id. at 146 (Burton, J., dissenting).

40. 124 U.S. 621 (1888).

41. 142 U.S. 651 (1892).

42. See Chapter V, notes 97–100 and accompanying text (discussing *Murray's Lessee*); Chapter V, notes 121–28 and accompanying text (linking "public rights" to federal regulatory schemes). But see Jonathan L. Hafetz, *The Untold Story of Noncriminal Habeas Corpus and the 1996 Immigration Acts*, 107 Yale L.J. 2509 (1998) (contending that habeas corpus was available in deportation cases at common law and that it would be unconstitutional for Congress to restrict federal courts to constitutional claims). Professor Fallon contends that immigration cases illustrate the difficulties of assimilating the public rights tradition into a coherent modern framework. In his view, the argument that immigration cases simply *are* public rights cases and therefore can be determined without judicial involvement at all proves too much. To reconcile immigration cases with developed understandings in adjacent fields, the public rights idea should be reconceptualized as a recognition that Congress can specify the form that Article III court participation should take. In many instances, according to Fallon, after-the-fact judicial attention, via habeas corpus or some other procedural vehicle, is both necessary and sufficient to satisfy the Suspension Clause, Article III, and due process. See Fallon, note 37; Chapter V, notes 132, 141–43 and accompanying text (noting that the existence of Article III court review is a factor affecting the validity of non-Article III adjudication).

43. *INS v. St. Cyr*, 533 U.S. 289 (2001); see notes 32–34; Chapter IV, notes 32–48, 75–76 and accompanying text. Professor Neuman and Professor Cole have developed elaborate arguments that the Suspension Clause bars Congress from absolutely foreclosing habeas jurisdiction in immigration cases. Neuman, note 23; Cole, note 37. See Chapter IV, notes 112–21 (discussing the preclusion of judicial review generally). Professor Meltzer has doubts about the argument that aliens have a constitutional right of access to a federal court. But he thinks aliens probably do have a right of access to some court, perhaps a state court. Meltzer, note 18, at 2566–74.

whether the prisoner is guilty or innocent.[44] Nor does the federal court presume (formally) to second-guess the court that conducted the criminal trial and imposed the sentence.[45] Instead, the federal court focuses exclusively on the validity of the prisoner's current detention. As a practical matter, however, the custodian invariably offers the conviction and sentence as the explanation for the prisoner's custody. And when the federal court evaluates that explanation, the court typically also examines federal issues that the sentencing court determined previously. In a real sense, then, federal habeas corpus is a device by which prisoners can ask federal courts to revisit prior judgments regarding federal claims. Current statutes confirm this role for the writ. Most criminal prosecutions occur in state court. Under 28 U.S.C. §2254, federal courts "shall" entertain applications for habeas relief filed by prisoners complaining that they are in "custody" pursuant to the judgment of a state court.[46]

Congress occasionally adjusts this conceptual picture and, in so doing, recognizes what petitioners genuinely mean to accomplish. For example, Congress has largely eliminated the ability of *federal* convicts to attack their convictions and sentences under §2241 and substituted a motion procedure to perform the same function. Pursuant to 28 U.S.C. §2255, a prisoner who claims "the right to be released" from confinement under a federal sentence imposed in violation of federal law may "move the court which imposed" the sentence "to vacate, set aside or correct" it. A prisoner who is authorized to file a §2255 motion can petition for habeas corpus relief under §2241 only if a §2255 motion is "inadequate or ineffective to test the legality of his detention."[47] The Supreme Court sustained §2255 in *United States v. Hayman*.[48] Chief Justice Vinson assumed (but did not decide) that the Suspension Clause would bar Congress from abrogating the writ of habeas corpus, even in cases in which prisoners are serving sentences for crimi-

44. *Noia*, 372 U.S. at 422–24. Since federal habeas courts have jurisdiction only to consider federal claims, it would be strange if they were expected to attend to fact-sensitive questions of criminal liability under state law. Nevertheless, there is a body of opinion to the effect that federal habeas corpus requires some morally persuasive justification. The idea that federal courts can detect mistaken convictions may answer. Henry Friendly, *Is Innocence Irrelevant? Collateral Attack on Criminal Judgments*, 38 U. Chi. L. Rev. 142 (1970). Thinking along these lines typically produces procedural rules for the conduct of habeas litigation that privilege legal claims linked in some way to actual innocence. See, e.g., notes 231–42, 279, 291, 516, 550 and accompanying text. See note 71 (noting a proposal by Professor Hoffmann and Professor Stuntz to use a "colorable" showing of innocence in a different way).

45. *Coleman v. Thompson*, 501 U.S. 722, 730 (1991).

46. Recall that district courts have no appellate jurisdiction to review state court judgments for error in the ordinary course. See Chapter VI, notes 196–225 and accompanying text (discussing the *Rooker/Feldman* doctrine). Nevertheless, habeas has an undeniable appellate flavor, and some academics contend that it is best understood as an appellate mechanism. E.g., Barry Friedman, *A Tale of Two Habeas*, 73 Minn. L. Rev. 247 (1988); Barry Friedman, *Pas De Deux: The Supreme Court and the Habeas Courts*, 66 So. Calif. L. Rev. 2467 (1993); James S. Liebman, *Apocalypse Next Time?: The Anachronistic Attack on Habeas Corpus/Direct Review Parity*, 92 Colum. L. Rev. 1997 (1992).

47. Cases in which a §2255 motion is inadequate in this sense are virtually non-existent. In *Triestman v. United States*, 124 F.3d 361 (2d Cir. 1997), the court held that §2255 was inadequate (and that a habeas corpus petition under §2241 was therefore available), because §2255 would not permit a prisoner to file a second application advancing a novel non-constitutional federal claim. In *Triestman*, however, the prisoner's claim could not have been included in his previous §2255 motion and serious constitutional questions would have been presented if he were denied any opportunity to advance that claim at all. Obviously, a §2255 motion is not inadequate in the run of cases in which prisoners are unsuccessful in one §2255 motion and cannot file another under the rules governing successive applications. *Jiminian v. Nash*, 245 F.3d 144, 147–48 (2d Cir. 2001); see notes 508–52 and accompanying text (discussing successive §2254 habeas petitions and §2255 motions).

48. 342 U.S. 205 (1952).

nal offenses. But he read §2255 to authorize an equally "independent" inquiry into the "validity" of federal custody. Since federal prisoners lost nothing in the switch from §2241 to §2255, there was no constitutional difficulty. Today, §2255 provides federal prisoners with a means of access to federal court that is "exactly commensurate" with the writ of habeas corpus that was previously available to them.[49] The only practical difference is that, previously, habeas corpus petitions under §2241 were filed in a district court near the place of confinement, while §2255 motions are filed in the sentencing court.[50]

It is debatable whether federal prisoners should be entitled to attack criminal judgments after appellate review is complete—by means of §2255 motions or any other vehicle. It is more debatable whether state prisoners should be entitled to advance §2254 petitions for habeas corpus relief from state criminal convictions and sentences. Federal habeas corpus proceedings in the wake of state criminal prosecutions appear to be inefficient, even redundant. Elsewhere, statutes and judge-crafted doctrines channel federal question litigation either to state court or to federal court, and proponents of federal adjudication are pressed to explain why a federal forum should be available. In this context, litigants who have once *been* to state court claim an entitlement to litigate *again* in federal court.

The explanation is historical and functional. Federal habeas corpus for state prisoners is largely the product of the Supreme Court's efforts in the middle decades of the Twentieth Century to improve the quality of state criminal justice. In the famous "incorporation" decisions, the Court read the fourteenth amendment to make the procedural safeguards prescribed in the Bill of Rights applicable to criminal cases tried in state court.[51] Simultaneously, the Court expanded the scope of federal habeas corpus so that federal courts could enforce those rights. The Court recognized that it could not police fifty state courts by exercising appellate jurisdiction alone and so turned to the lower federal courts as surrogates. On examination, then, the availability of federal

49. *Hill v. United States*, 368 U.S. 424, 427 (1962). See also *Heflin v. United States*, 358 U.S. 415, 418 n.7 (1959) (stating that a §2255 proceeding is equally "an independent civil suit"). The characterizations of §2255 in *Hayman*, *Hill*, and *Heflin* are hard to reconcile with *United States v. Morgan*, 346 U.S. 502 (1954), where the Court said that a §2255 motion is of the "same general character" as a petition for a writ of coram nobis—which is traditionally understood to be a further step in a criminal case and *not* an independent civil proceeding. Id. at 505 n.4. The point, however, is that §2255 affords federal prisoners the same postconviction access to a federal judicial forum that was previously achieved by means of habeas corpus.

50. But see notes 141–42, 547–52 and accompanying text (noting that AEDPA sometimes treats §2255 motions and habeas corpus petitions differently). By all accounts, Congress created §2255 motions primarily as a docket control measure. Previously, district courts located near major federal penitentiaries were swamped with §2241 habeas corpus petitions. Moreover, those courts faced practical difficulties. The relevant files and records were in the sentencing court, and if a hearing was necessary the witnesses were typically near that court, as well. By rerouting prisoners to the sentencing court, Congress hoped to achieve greater efficiency in the adjudication of the same kinds of claims. See John J. Parker, *Limiting the Abuse of Habeas Corpus*, 8 F.R.D. 171 (1948). Prisoners convicted in the local courts of the District of Columbia are similarly barred from seeking federal habeas relief from district courts and must, instead, file postconviction motions in the courts in which they were sentenced. The Supreme Court sustained that scheme in *Swain v. Pressley*, 430 U.S. 372 (1977), relying heavily on an analogy to §2255. The statute controlling District of Columbia cases tracks the language of §2255 verbatim—and thus includes the (formally important) proviso that habeas corpus remains available if the motion remedy proves to be "inadequate or ineffective to test the legality" of a prisoner's detention. But see note 47.

51. See Kenneth Pye, *The Warren Court and Criminal Procedure*, 67 Mich. L. Rev. 249 (1968); Henry Friendly, *The Bill of Rights as a Code of Criminal Procedure*, 53 Calif. L. Rev. 929 (1965).

habeas after state courts have completed their work is not anomalous. Habeas provides prisoners deprived of their liberty an opportunity to press any federal claims they may have in federal court at a time when federal adjudication can no longer interfere with ongoing proceedings in state court.[52]

By most accounts, the idea that federal habeas should be a sequel to state criminal proceedings began with Justice Holmes' great dissent in Leo Frank's case.[53] It took hold in Holmes' opinion for the Court in *Moore v. Dempsey*,[54] emerged fully developed in *Brown v. Allen*,[55] and then flowered in a trilogy of decisions in the Warren Court period—*Fay v. Noia*,[56] *Townsend v. Sain*,[57] and *Sanders v. United States*.[58] As the Court explained in *Brown*, a previous state court judgment on a federal claim was entitled only to the "weight that federal practice [gave] to the conclusion of a court of last resort of another jurisdiction."[59] By the middle 1960s, habeas corpus proceedings under the authority of §2241 and §2254 had become the procedural analog of the Warren Court's innovations in criminal procedure, providing the federal machinery for bringing new constitutional values to bear in concrete cases.[60] To some, federal habeas corpus for state prisoners is the embodiment of all that was *right* about the Warren Court and the vision that Court offered of a meaningful system of American liberty, underwritten by independent Article III courts willing and able to check the coercive power of government. To others, by contrast, federal habeas is the paradigm of all that was *wrong* with the Warren Court—namely, that Court's distrust of the states and state courts and its celebration of individual liberty at the expense of order and stability. In habeas corpus cases, accordingly, the familiar debates over federalism and parity surface yet again.[61]

---

52. See generally William J. Brennan, Jr., *Federal Habeas Corpus and State Prisoners: An Exercise in Federalism*, 7 Utah L. Rev. 423 (1961); Robert M. Cover & T. Alexander Aleinikoff, *Dialectical Federalism: Habeas Corpus and the Court*, 86 Yale L.J. 1035 (1977); Daniel J. Meador, *The Impact of Federal Habeas Corpus on State Trial Procedures*, 52 Va. L. Rev. 286 (1966); Larry W. Yackle, *The Habeas Hagioscope*, 66 So. Calif. L. Rev. 2331, 2337–2349 (1993).

53. *Frank v. Mangum*, 237 U.S. 309, 346 (1915): Habeas corpus "comes in from the outside, not in subordination to the proceedings, and although every form may have been preserved opens the inquiry whether they have been more than an empty shell."

54. 261 U.S. 86 (1923).

55. 344 U.S. 443, 506 (1953) (concurring opinion).

56. 372 U.S. 391 (1963).

57. 372 U.S. 293 (1963).

58. 373 U.S. 1 (1963).

59. 344 U.S. at 458. The *Brown* case is conventionally taken to rest on the proposition that federal court adjudication in habeas corpus begins on a clean slate, *de novo*. That is the way Justice Jackson characterized the Court's analysis in his separate opinion concurring in the judgment. Id. at 546. But see notes 315–494 and accompanying text (discussing the *Teague* doctrine and the effect that §2254(d) gives to previous state court decisions on the merits).

60. For reviews of these developments, see Paul M. Bator, *Finality in Criminal Law and Federal Habeas Corpus for State Prisoners*, 76 Harv. L. Rev. 441 (1963); Freedman, note 27; Henry M. Hart, Jr., *Foreword: The Time Chart of the Justices*, 73 Harv. L. Rev. 84 (1959); Gary Peller, *In Defense of Federal Habeas Corpus Relitigation*, 16 Harv. C.R.-C.L. L. Rev. 579 (1982); Keith G. Meyer & Larry W. Yackle, *Collateral Challenges to Criminal Convictions*, 21 Kan. L. Rev. 259 (1973); *Developments in the Law: Federal Habeas Corpus*, 83 Harv. L. Rev. 1038 (1970). Professor Woolhandler argues that most accounts of older cases fail to appreciate that the development of habeas corpus as a vehicle for enforcing federal rights was linked to the contemporaneous development of other devices for holding government agents responsible. Ann Woolhandler, *DeModeling Habeas*, 45 Stan. L. Rev. 575 (1993).

61. See generally Chapter I, notes 19–25, 92–104 and accompanying text (reviewing the arguments touching federalism and parity). For an illustrative appraisal of federal habeas corpus when Edwin Meese was Attorney General, see U.S. Dep't of Justice, Report to the Attorney General: Fed-

Just as the Warren Court developed constitutional safeguards and habeas corpus in a creative way to advance that Court's civil liberties agenda, the justices who arrived in the 1970s exercised equally active imaginations in an effort to reestablish comparative discipline. Soon after the Court's membership changed, its decisions touching criminal procedure and habeas corpus also shifted—notwithstanding that "the statutory language authorizing" federal habeas "remained unchanged."[62] The Rehnquist Court has sometimes squarely overruled Warren Court precedents and sometimes forged its own novel doctrines to circumscribe the writ. In this rough sense, the Court's decisions regarding federal habeas corpus parallel its decisions regarding the Ku Klux Klan Act (§1983), civil rights removal, immunity, and federal-question abstention. In each instance, the Court has fashioned extremely complex doctrines in a perpetual effort to strike the balance the justices think proper between federal judicial power and state prerogatives. Special procedural rules for handling §2254 petitions and §2255 motions sometimes facilitate the processing of cases in the district courts.[63] Nevertheless, petitions and motions challenging criminal convictions form a significant part of the federal courts' responsibilities.

The controversy over habeas corpus is also fueled by the contemporaneous national debate over capital punishment. In some minds, habeas corpus serves only to postpone lawful executions. Habeas litigation in capital cases is especially complicated and time-consuming, both because prisoners' claims are often thorny and because the habeas process in capital cases has itself become increasingly convoluted (largely through the introduction of intricate doctrines ostensibly meant to keep inferior federal courts from unduly interfering with executions). Death penalty proponents are suspicious that their adversaries defend habeas corpus primarily to frustrate capital punishment by the back door. Many Supreme Court decisions illustrate the Court's attempts to accommodate the special demands that capital litigation places on the judicial system.[64]

Given the political implications, Congress, too, has responded. After debating a host of habeas corpus bills over a thirty-year period, Congress enacted the Antiterrorism and Effective Death Penalty Act of 1996.[65] Some provisions in the 1996 Act apply to all habeas corpus cases. They appear in a series of cut-and-paste amendments to preexist-

---

eral Habeas Corpus Review of State Judgments (1988). For a critique of that report, see Yackle, note 30. Professor Bator was the Warren Court's principal critic. See Bator, note 60. He contended that habeas corpus should generally be governed by the process model. Prisoners convicted in state court should not be entitled to claim that the state courts reached an erroneous outcome regarding a federal issue, but only that the process the state courts employed to arrive at a judgment was inadequate to ensure sound decision-making. For a critique of Bator's argument, see Larry W. Yackle, *Explaining Habeas Corpus*, 60 N.Y.U. L. Rev. 991, 1014–19 (1985).

62. *Wainwright v. Sykes*, 433 U.S. 72, 81 (1977).

63. Rules Governing Section 2254 Cases in the United States District Courts (typically called the §2254 Rules); Rules Governing Section 2255 Proceedings in the United States District Courts (typically called the §2255 Rules).

64. For an exhaustive treatment, see James S. Liebman & Randy Hertz, Federal Habeas Corpus Practice and Procedure (4th ed. 2001).

65. See Chapter IV, notes 33–36 and accompanying text. See also Yackle, note 52 (discussing prior bills); Larry W. Yackle, *The Reagan Administration's Habeas Corpus Proposals*, 68 Iowa L. Rev. 609 (1983) (examining the Reagan Administration's initiative); Larry W. Yackle, *A Primer on the New Habeas Corpus Statute*, 44 Buffalo L. Rev. 381 (1996) (offering a grossly oversimplified summary of the 1996 Act); Marshall J. Hartman & Jeanette Nyden, *Habeas Corpus and the New Federalism After the Antiterrorism and Effective Death Penalty Act of 1996*, 30 John Marshall L. Rev. 337 (1997) (also providing a summary).

ing sections of Chapter 153 of the Judicial Code, 28 U.S.C. §2241, *et seq.*[66] Other provisions of the Act address only death penalty cases. Those provisions are collected in Chapter 154 of the Judicial Code, 28 U.S.C. §2261, *et seq.*[67] By some accounts, AEDPA creates a dilemma. If the Court construes a provision essentially to codify a restriction on habeas that the Court itself had previously adopted, the justices may be charged with treating the Act as meaningless. Yet if the Court strains to read every provision to change preexisting arrangements, it may often thwart the Act's genuine purpose to endorse and reinforce the Court's efforts to curb the writ and, into the bargain, manufacture needless inefficiency, confusion, and injustice.[68] At all events, AEDPA has altered the Supreme Court's approach to many important habeas corpus questions. The Court is now less inclined to regard habeas cases as an occasion for fashioning policy of its own choosing and more inclined to see its task as interpreting AEDPA's precise text. Reliance on the text of AEDPA's provisions is problematic. By all accounts, those provisions provide a very good example of very bad legislative drafting.[69] The Court some-

---

66. The Supreme Court held in *Lindh v. Murphy*, 521 U.S. 320 (1997), that one provision in Chapter 153, 28 U.S.C. §2254(d), does not apply to cases already "pending" on the date of enactment (April 24, 1996). See notes 368–494 and accompanying text (discussing §2254(d)). The primary rationale in *Lindh* was that language in Chapter 154 plainly made that chapter applicable to cases already under way and thus, by negative implication, indicated that the amendments to Chapter 153 would operate only on petitions filed in the future. Nevertheless, the Court held in *Slack v. McDaniel*, 529 U.S. 473 (2000), that a different provision in Chapter 153, 28 U.S.C. §2253, is applicable to cases that were pending when AEDPA became law.

67. The provisions in Chapter 154 are applicable only to habeas corpus petitions filed in states that establish a system for providing indigent death row prisoners with competent and properly compensated counsel in *state* postconviction proceedings. That optional framework was suggested by a committee of the Judicial Conference of the United States, appointed by Chief Justice Rehnquist and chaired by Justice Powell. The 1996 Act also incorporates some of the Powell Committee's other proposals, but by no means all. See *Symposium*, 19 Capital U. L. Rev. 599 (1990) (reviewing the Powell Committee's recommendations); Ronald J. Tabak & J. Mark Lane, *Judicial Activism and Legislative "Reform" of Federal Habeas Corpus: A Critical Analysis of Recent Developments and Current Proposals*, 55 Albany L. Rev. 1, 56–84 (1991) (offering a similar review). The Powell Committee's program was hotly debated within the Judicial Conference. Senior circuit judges insisted that it would limit the federal courts too much and would render the habeas process even more complex into the bargain. See Donald P. Lay, *The Writ of Habeas Corpus: A Complex Procedure for a Simple Process*, 77 Minn. L. Rev. 1015, 1048–63 (1993). For discussions of Chapter 154 and preliminary reports on state attempts to obtain the benefits of its provisions, see Comment, *The Option Not Taken: A Progressive Report on Chapter 154 of the Anti-Terrorism and Effective Death Penalty Act*, 9 Cornell J. L. & Pub. Policy 607 (2000); Comment, *Opting for Death: State Responses to the AEDPA's Opt-In Provisions and the Need for a Right to Post-Conviction Counsel*, 1 U. Pa. J. Const. L. 661 (1999). For a rare holding that a state's system for supplying counsel in state postconviction proceedings met federal standards and thus invoked Chapter 154, see *Spears v. Stewart*, 283 F.3d 992 (9th Cir. 2002) (considering the Arizona system). For a proposal to make greater demands on the states in exchange for expedited federal habeas proceedings in death penalty cases, see Andrew Hammel, *Diabolical Federalism: A Functional Critique and Proposed Reconstruction of Death Penalty Federal Habeas*, 39 Am. Crim. L. Rev. 1 (2002).

68. See Mark V. Tushnet & Larry W. Yackle, *Symbolic Statutes and Real Laws: The Pathologies of the Antiterrorism and Effective Death Penalty Act and the Prison Litigation Reform Act*, 47 Duke L.J. 1 (1997) (contending that many of the key provisions in the 1996 Act ratify changes that the Supreme Court had already instituted on its own). For a (tedious) section-by-section discussion of the 1996 Act and early returns from the lower courts, see Larry W. Yackle, *Developments in Habeas Corpus*, The Champion, Part I, Sept./Oct. 1997, at 14; Part II, Nov. 1997, at 16; Part III, Dec. 1997, at 16.

69. In the *Lindh* case, Justice Souter labored through numerous AEDPA provisions in a valiant effort to identify a single theme that would reconcile them all. When he finished, he confessed that he could not account for the text of one last paragraph. Despairing, he left that "loose end" dan-

times disclaims any attention to policy at all. More often, the Court ascribes policy implications to Congress' inartful language.[70]

Numerous academics criticize both the conceptual framework within which habeas corpus is understood and the statutes and doctrines that framework produces.[71] Some are moved by the success rate for habeas corpus actions in federal court, which is quite low (about 4%). That figure arguably reflects prisoners' inability to marshal their claims and thread their way through the maze of procedural obstacles that lie in their path on the way to an adjudication on the merits. It is important to understand that most convicts serving prison terms have no lawyers to assist them.[72] The data may also suggest that state courts usually catch federal errors and, consequently, that subsequent federal litigation may not be worth the candle.[73] In death penalty cases, however, both state and federal courts find error at an extremely high rate (over 50%).[74]

B. Prerequisites

1. The Custody Doctrine

Litigants who wish to invoke a federal district court's jurisdiction pursuant to §2241 and §2254 must allege that they are in "custody" in violation of federal law.[75] Custody is

---

gling, explaining that "in a world of silk purses and pigs' ears, the Act is not a silk purse of the art of statutory drafting." *Lindh*, 521 U.S. at 336.

70. See Chapter I, notes 30–43 and accompanying text (describing the Court's "textualism"). For illustrations, see, e.g., notes 173–90, 524–33 (and accompanying text).

71. See Brian M. Hoffstadt, *How Congress Might Redesign a Leaner, Cleaner Writ of Habeas Corpus*, 49 Duke L.J. 947 (2000) (surveying the literature). Professor Hoffmann and Professor Stuntz argue that federal habeas should be understood as a stage in the criminal process and that the scope of the federal courts' purview should turn on the purposes of criminal prosecutions—ascertaining guilt, while respecting procedural rights. Hoffmann and Stuntz would have federal courts exercise an entirely independent and rigorous examination of any claims advanced by prisoners who make a colorable showing of innocence. But they would have federal courts defer to any "reasonable" state court decisions on claims by prisoners who fail to draw their guilt into question. Joseph L. Hoffmann & William J. Stuntz, *Habeas After the Revolution*, 1993 Sup. Ct. Rev. 65, 69. Professor Steiker proposes that prisoners under sentence of death ordinarily should be permitted to appeal their state convictions and sentences directly to federal circuit courts of appeal. Prisoners should file habeas corpus petitions at the district court level only when existing state court records provide an insufficient factual basis for determining the merits of federal claims. See Jordan Steiker, *Restructuring Post-Conviction Review of Federal Constitutional Claims Raised by State Prisoners: Confronting the New Face of Excessive Proceduralism*, 1998 U. Chi. Legal F. 315. For a critique of the Hoffmann/Stuntz and Steiker models, see Larry W. Yackle, *The Figure in the Carpet*, 78 Tex. L. Rev. 1731 (2000).

72. See Richard Faust, Tina J. Rubenstein & Larry W. Yackle, *The Great Writ in Action: Empirical Light on the Federal Habeas Corpus Debate*, 18 N.Y.U. Rev. L. & Soc. Change 637, 660 (1991) (reporting data from New York City showing that "professional representation is the single best predictor of success in federal habeas corpus").

73. See Daniel J. Meltzer, *Habeas Corpus Jurisdiction: The Limits of Models*, 66 So. Calif. L. Rev. 2507, 2523–24 (1993) (contending that the low success rate is a factor to be considered).

74. During the period from 1973 to 1995, state courts found serious error in 47% of the cases in which death sentences were imposed at the trial court level. Thereafter, federal courts found serious error in 40% of the *remaining* cases, i.e., the cases in which state courts had previously affirmed convictions and capital sentences. James S. Liebman, Jeffrey Fagan & Valerie West, A Broken System: Error Rates in Capital Cases, 1973–1995 (June 20, 2000).

75. See text accompanying note 31.

a jurisdictional prerequisite, bearing a correlative relationship to the function of habeas corpus: to secure the release of a person suffering wrongful detention.[76] Applicants for the writ must be held in some form of custody from which they wish to be discharged. As a practical matter, however, the custody requirement operates as a gate-keeping device, screening cases according to the nature of the individual interests at stake. All litigants in federal court must have some kind of concrete injury to establish standing.[77] The custody requirement further subdivides the field of litigants by identifying those who can have access to federal court after state court proceedings are complete, without facing state preclusion rules.[78]

Federal courts exercising habeas corpus jurisdiction have no authority to overturn convictions or to set aside sentences, but can only order custodians to release prisoners for want of a lawful basis for their detention.[79] Ordinarily, however, courts stay release orders to give prosecutors an opportunity to cure the deficiencies that the habeas corpus proceeding has uncovered—typically by conducting a new trial that does not repeat the federal errors that were committed previously. In some instances, moreover, prisoners win orders releasing them from some sentences, but still remain in prison serving other valid terms.[80]

The custody doctrine does not demand actual incarceration, but can be satisfied by constructive restraints on liberty. In selective service and immigration cases, for example, petitioners often suffer milder limits on their freedom and the threat of actual incarceration in the future.[81] In cases touching criminal prosecutions, it is enough if petitioners are subject to bail or parole conditions.[82] The flexibility of the custody idea is a function of the Supreme Court's desire (during the 1960s) to open federal habeas corpus to a wide range of petitioners—particularly convicts seeking, in effect, to attack their convictions and sentences collaterally. It takes time to get to federal court with a

---

76. *Maleng v. Cook*, 490 U.S. 488, 490–91 (1989).

77. See Chapter IX, notes 140–208 and accompanying text.

78. See note 4 and accompanying text. Custody is also a jurisdictional prerequisite for motions by federal convicts pursuant to §2255. In the case of litigants convicted in federal court, however, the absence of custody is not fatal. The Court held in *Morgan* that federal convicts who have completed their sentences can file petitions for the writ of coram nobis in the sentencing court. *Morgan*, 346 U.S. at 512–13; see note 49. By means of that old writ, authorized by the All-Writs Act (28 U.S.C. §1651), federal convicts can advance the same claims that they would otherwise press in a §2255 motion. The All-Writs Act does not itself confer jurisdiction to entertain an application for a writ of coram nobis. A federal court's jurisdiction to do so rests on its original jurisdiction in the criminal prosecution about which the applicant complains. Convicts challenging state convictions thus cannot seek coram nobis relief, but can only pursue a writ of habeas corpus. When a federal court entertains a habeas corpus application from a convict attacking a state court judgment, the court has no prior criminal jurisdiction to rely upon. Accordingly, the state prisoner must invoke §2241 as an independent basis of jurisdiction. That jurisdiction is contingent on custody.

79. *Noia*, 372 U.S. at 431.

80. For a general discussion of the relief available in federal habeas proceedings, see Yackle, note 31, at 527–45. Prisoners who are successful in attacking federal convictions or sentences pursuant to §2255 *can* obtain orders that "vacate, set aside, or correct" their sentences. The same is true of prisoners who are successful in coram nobis proceedings. See note 78.

81. See text accompanying notes 38–43.

82. *Hensley v. Municipal Court*, 411 U.S. 345 (1973) (bail); *Jones v. Cunningham*, 371 U.S. 236 (1963) (parole); see *Justices of Boston Municipal Court v. Lydon*, 466 U.S. 294 (1984) (finding that a prisoner released on personal recognizance after a preliminary bench trial was in custody for purposes of federal habeas corpus). Cf. Wayne A. Logan, *Federal Habeas in the Information Age*, 85 Minn. L. Rev. 147 (2000) (arguing that convicts forced to register as "sex offenders" are in custody for habeas purposes).

petition for habeas corpus relief. If the custody doctrine required physical detention, many would-be applicants would be turned away, having been released from that kind of restraint during the interim.

A federal habeas court determines whether a prisoner is in custody at the time a petition is filed. Once jurisdiction attaches, it continues notwithstanding that the prisoner may be fully relieved of all restraints before a final judgment is entered.[83] The only question is whether the matter will at some point be rendered moot because the applicant no longer has enough interest to keep an Article III case or controversy alive. Typically, habeas actions do not become moot. The Court presumes that a petitioner suffers legal consequences from a criminal conviction after the attendant sentence has been served.[84] In this same vein, the Court accommodates habeas applications from prisoners who are sentenced to serve multiple terms of confinement. A petitioner may attack one of two concurrent sentences, despite the understanding that the other (unchallenged) sentence will keep the petitioner in jail, whatever happens. Equally, a prisoner can challenge one of two consecutive sentences, even though the petitioner is not yet serving the sentence under attack. The Court aggregates consecutive sentences for purposes of ascertaining custody.[85]

A prisoner who has been fully discharged after completing an isolated sentence is no longer in custody under that sentence and thus cannot initiate a straightforward habeas challenge to the conviction that gave rise to it.[86] If, however, the prisoner is subsequently sentenced to a new term that is enhanced on the basis of the conviction underlying the previously completed sentence, the prisoner may be able to reach the older conviction indirectly—by attacking detention under the *new* sentence on the ground that it rests on an invalid prior judgment.[87] Then again, a prisoner who is in custody under such an enhanced sentence is not yet entitled to a decision on the merits. Typically, federal adjudication of claims touching older convictions will be procedurally foreclosed.[88]

2. The Exhaustion Doctrine

Pursuant to 28 U.S.C. §2254(b), prisoners attacking custody in the hands of state officials ordinarily must exhaust state judicial opportunities to litigate federal claims before presenting those claims to a federal court in a petition for a writ of habeas corpus. The exhaustion of state procedures is not a formal jurisdictional prerequisite. The statute enacted by Congress codifies the Supreme Court's holding in *Ex parte Royall*.[89] In that case, a criminal defendant filed a petition in federal court while he was awaiting trial in state court. Justice Harlan recognized that the district court had jurisdiction to entertain the petition. But in light of the comity owed to the state and its courts, Harlan said that the district court should have declined to exercise its jurisdiction while the state criminal prosecution was under way.[90]

---

83. *Carafas v. LaVallee*, 391 U.S. 234 (1968).
84. See Chapter IX, note 422.
85. *Peyton v. Rowe*, 391 U.S. 54 (1968); *Garlotte v. Fordice*, 515 U.S. 39 (1995).
86. *Maleng*, 490 U.S. at 492–93.
87. *Lackawanna County Dist. Attorney v. Coss*, 532 U.S. 394, 401–02 (2001).
88. See notes 243–57 and accompanying text.
89. 117 U.S. 241 (1886).
90. See *Bowen v. Johnston*, 306 U.S. 19, 27 (1939) (explaining that the exhaustion doctrine "is not one defining power but one which relates to the appropriate exercise of power"); Chapter XI, note 58 and accompanying text (explaining the idea of comity).

Under other Supreme Court precedents, as well as §2254(b), prisoners must seek relief in state court, unless the state court opportunities that appear to be "available" are actually "ineffective" to protect federal rights. There are certainly cases in which it is so clear that the state courts are unwilling to consider prisoners' claims that there is no point in requiring prisoners to make the attempt.[91] Those cases do not establish that the exhaustion doctrine can be *avoided*, but rather illustrate the way the exhaustion doctrine can be *satisfied*. The point is not that prisoners are excused when state court litigation is unlikely to be successful, but that prisoners are obliged to pursue only state court opportunities that are genuinely open to *be* exhausted at the time a federal petition is filed.

The exhaustion doctrine has two objectives: (1) to avoid federal interference with state processes; and (2) to preserve the state courts' role in the making and enforcement of federal law.[92] To accomplish those ends, federal courts decline to entertain premature petitions for federal relief. Prisoners must first identify their claims to the state courts, so that those courts have a fair chance to address them. Prisoners need not cite "book and verse on the federal constitution," but they are obligated to identify the "substance" of their federal claims for consideration in state court.[93] Certainly, prisoners cannot present the state courts with one claim and then advance a "clearly distinct" claim in federal court.[94] It is not enough merely to identify a legal claim in the abstract. Prisoners must also present the state courts with allegations of the facts on which claims may be said to rest.[95]

When a petition fails to satisfy the exhaustion requirement, a federal court does not disclaim jurisdictional power to act, but only postpones the exercise of jurisdiction. Ordinarily, the proper disposition of a premature petition is dismissal "without prejudice" to a renewed application for the writ, filed when no state court avenues for litigation remain open.[96] Alternatively, by some accounts, district courts may stay any action on a premature petition, hold the petition in abeyance, and then proceed with it after the prisoner has satisfied the exhaustion requirement. A stay may be preferable to a dismissal without prejudice in cases in which the filing deadline for seeking federal habeas relief is likely to arrive before the prisoner can exhaust state opportunities for enforcing his claims and return to federal court.[97] Here again, the point of habeas corpus is to provide a federal forum, but at a time when state proceedings are finished and federal adjudication is no longer disruptive.[98]

---

91. See note 116.

92. For a discussion of the exhaustion doctrine's development, see Larry W. Yackle, *The Exhaustion Doctrine in Federal Habeas Corpus: An Argument for a Return to First Principles*, 44 Ohio St. L.J. 393 (1983).

93. *Picard v. Connor*, 404 U.S. 270, 276–78 (1971).

94. Id. See also *Anderson v. Harless*, 459 U.S. 4 (1982); *Duncan v. Henry*, 513 U.S. 364 (1995).

95. See *Vasquez v. Hillery*, 474 U.S. 254, 257–60 (1986) (concluding that a prisoner's offer of additional evidence did not "fundamentally alter the legal claim" presented to the state courts and thus did not reflect a failure to exhaust state court avenues for litigating that claim).

96. *Slayton v. Smith*, 404 U.S. 53 (1971).

97. *Duncan v. Walker*, 533 U.S. 167, 182–83 (2001) (Stevens, J., concurring in part); see note 191 and accompanying text. See generally notes 132–93 and accompanying text (discussing filing deadlines). One might have expected that the ordinary disposition would be a stay of federal proceedings rather than dismissal. That, after all, is the practice in abstention cases in which federal courts postpone the exercise of jurisdiction. See Chapter XI, text accompanying note 97 (describing state-question abstention). Dismissals without prejudice have the virtue of leaving federal dockets uncluttered. Yet in light of the potential filing deadline difficulties, it would seem that, in many cases, stays do a better job of effectuating the exhaustion doctrine's rationales.

98. Litigants who press claims in state court in the first instance and come away with an unfavorable judgment usually cannot try again in federal court. The Full Faith and Credit Statute in-

The exhaustion doctrine typically prevents prisoners who are charged with criminal offenses from escaping into federal court to advance federal claims and, instead, forces them to offer those claims as defenses at trial and on appeal in state court. The exhaustion requirement thus complements the law of removal and the federal-question abstention doctrine.[99] Generally speaking, then, federal courts usually decline to interfere with ongoing state prosecutions for any of several overlapping reasons: because there is no general statute authorizing removal on the basis of a federal defense, because federal injunctive or declaratory relief is inappropriate while pending state proceedings provide an opportunity for litigating federal claims, *and* because a petition for a writ of habeas corpus is premature when ostensibly effective state court avenues for litigation have yet to be exhausted. When federal courts *do* act, it is again for reasons that justify various forms of federal intervention. Removal is almost never available.[100] But federal courts can issue injunctive, declaratory, or habeas relief on those (rare) occasions when the state court proceedings under way do not provide an adequate opportunity for enforcing federal rights.[101] If prisoners have claims that cannot be vindicated

structs federal courts to give prior state judgments the preclusive effect that state law would accord them. See Chapter VI, notes 161–64 and accompanying text. Federal habeas corpus is an exception. See note 4 and accompanying text. Otherwise, the requirement that prisoners exhaust state judicial remedies *before* filing federal petitions would be unintelligible. See Chapter XI, text accompanying notes 36–37 (explaining the nature of an exhaustion doctrine).

99. See Chapter VI, notes 144–60 and accompanying text (discussing civil rights removal); Chapter XI, notes 146–55 and accompanying text (discussing abstention with respect to state criminal prosecutions). For a discussion, see Michael G. Collins, *The Right to Avoid Trial: Justifying Federal Court Intervention into Ongoing State Court Proceedings*, 66 N. Car. L. Rev. 49 (1987).

100. The Court has given the civil rights removal statute, 28 U.S.C. §1443(1), an extremely narrow interpretation. The idea is that transferring state criminal prosecutions to federal court would be far too disruptive and that, when necessary, federal courts can protect defendants from inadequate state process by issuing injunctive or habeas relief. See Chapter VI, 144–60 and accompanying text. Cf. Yackle, note 61, at 1019 (contending that prisoners' access to federal district courts *after* conviction by means of habeas corpus is best explained as a sensible trade-off for their inability to remove their prosecutions to federal court in the first instance on the basis of federal defenses).

101. A special statute, 28 U.S.C. §2251, empowers federal courts to stay state proceedings while a federal habeas "proceeding" is "pending." That statute is typically used only to stay the execution of prisoners under sentence of death. For a discussion, see *Barefoot v. Estelle*, 463 U.S. 880 (1983). In *Lonchar v. Thomas*, 517 U.S. 314 (1996), the Court held that a prisoner was entitled to a stay of execution even though he had deliberately postponed filing a petition until the day he was scheduled to die. The petition in *Lonchar*, however tardy, was the prisoner's first attempt to obtain federal habeas relief. The Court is much less generous in cases in which prisoners seek stays while second or successive petitions are under consideration. See, e.g., *Bowersox v. Williams*, 517 U.S. 345, 346 (1996) (holding that a stay is appropriate in a successive petition posture only when there are "substantial grounds for relief"); accord *Bagley v. Byrd*, 533 U.S. 973, 975 (2002) (Rehnquist, C.J., dissenting from the denial of the respondent's application to vacate a stay). It will surprise no one that petitions for stays in capital cases often divide the justices along ideological lines. See, e.g., *Moore v. Texas*, 122 S.Ct. 2350, 2354 (2000) (Scalia, J., dissenting from an order granting a stay) (insisting that stays of execution invite "meritless last minute applications to disrupt the orderly administration of the death penalty"). Under 28 U.S.C. §2262, petitioners under sentence of death are entitled to a stay while an initial federal petition is under consideration, but only if they file for federal relief within the applicable filing period and make a "substantial showing of the denial of a Federal right." If a prisoner misses the filing deadline, fails to make the necessary showing, or is denied relief at the district court level, §2262 bars any federal court from staying the execution further, unless a court of appeals gives the prisoner permission to lodge a second or successive petition. See notes 132–65 and accompanying text (discussing filing deadlines); notes 508–52 and accompanying text (discussing second and successive federal petitions). Since §2262 appears in the optional Chapter 154, it controls only cases arising from states that invoke that chapter. See note 67. Indigent prisoners who wish to attack capital sentences in federal court are entitled to appointed counsel at government ex-

by raising them as defenses in state court, federal habeas is available even before trial.[102] Then again, prisoners must first exhaust any pre-trial avenues for relief that state courts may offer.[103]

In many instances, prisoners must also engage any state postconviction procedures available after their convictions are affirmed on direct review. Postconviction petitions and motions take various forms. Typically, they are filed in the trial court in which the conviction was obtained, seeking correction of fundamental errors that were not cured at trial or on direct review—including errors of constitutional moment. The need to engage state postconviction processes typically turns on the nature of the claims in question. Prisoners who advance claims that can be determined on the basis of the record made at trial can usually satisfy the exhaustion doctrine by presenting those claims to the appellate courts on direct review of a criminal conviction. Prisoners who press claims that can be determined only if the record is expanded typically must file postconviction petitions or motions that can prompt an evidentiary hearing.[104] If infe-

---

pense. 21 U.S.C. §848(q). That right to counsel would be frustrated if prisoners were forced to file *pro se* habeas petitions in order to initiate federal habeas "proceedings," thus to engage a federal court's jurisdiction to issue a stay. The Court held in *McFarland v. Scott*, 512 U.S. 849 (1994), that a prisoner's application for an order appointing counsel counts as a habeas "proceeding" within the meaning of §2251. Accordingly, a federal court has jurisdiction to stay the prisoner's execution while counsel prepares a federal petition on the prisoner's behalf.

102. E.g., *Braden v. 30th Judicial Circuit Court*, 410 U.S. 484 (1973) (entertaining a pre-trial federal habeas corpus petition filed by a prisoner contending that state authorities had denied him a speedy trial by failing to schedule a trial at all); *Arizona v. Washington*, 434 U.S. 497 (1978) (entertaining a pre-trial habeas petition filed by a prisoner who claimed that a state trial would itself constitute double jeopardy).

103. *Braden*, 410 U.S. at 491. For example, state law may permit a criminal defendant to raise a federal objection to a criminal prosecution before trial begins and, if he is unsuccessful with that claim in the trial court, to obtain immediate appellate review in the state's highest court. If a prisoner uses that means of litigating a claim through the state hierarchy, the exhaustion doctrine is satisfied and does not prevent the exercise of federal habeas corpus jurisdiction before the trial in state court. There is, however, another obstacle. The federal-question abstention doctrine may nonetheless obligate a federal court to dismiss a habeas petition filed while a state criminal prosecution is pending. See Chapter XI, notes 146–55 and accompanying text (discussing *Younger v. Harris*). There is an argument that the exhaustion doctrine alone strikes the balance between federal and state interests in this context and that, once that doctrine is satisfied, it is not only unnecessary but inappropriate for a federal court to abstain from exercising jurisdiction over a habeas petition. But see *In re Justices*, 218 F.3d 11 (1st Cir. 2000) (rejecting that argument). The counterarguments are straightforward. States might hesitate to allow pre-trial appeals on federal issues if, in consequence, they surrendered the protection that abstention ordinarily gives to pending state criminal proceedings. Id. at 19. Moreover, if a federal habeas court abstains notwithstanding satisfaction of the exhaustion doctrine, the prisoner may prevail at trial or on direct review on the basis of some other claim, thus obviating any need for a federal habeas court to examine the claim the prisoner litigated prior to trial. In rare instances, prisoners may have no opportunity for full and fair adjudication of their claims at trial in state court, making abstention unavailable. See Chapter XI, notes 178–203 and accompanying text. That is the case *a fortiori* with respect to claims based on federal rights that are violated by trial itself. See note 102 and accompanying text.

104. The nomenclature here can be confusing. State "postconviction" petitions or motions are actually (typically) vehicles for attacking criminal convictions or sentences after the highest state court has affirmed the trial court's work on appeal. They occur, then, not simply after conviction, but after the ordinary appellate process following conviction. They exist, in the main, to ensure one last opportunity for state courts to catch serious errors, particularly federal constitutional errors, that were not detected and corrected at trial or on direct review. See note 315 (explaining why state postconviction proceedings are said to constitute "collateral review"). See generally Yackle, note 31, at 264–86. For discussions of the postconviction procedures that states typically offer (and their shortcomings), see Larry W. Yackle, *The Misadventures of State Postconviction Remedies*, 16 N.Y.U.

rior state courts react negatively, prisoners must press on to the highest state court in which an appeal is available.

There is often considerable uncertainty regarding the state opportunities for litigation that will be regarded as "available" within the meaning of §2254(b). On the one hand, prisoners need not invoke exotic mechanisms that are "available" only in form. If, indeed, prisoners attempt to satisfy the exhaustion doctrine in that way, they will be unsuccessful. In *Pitchess v. Davis*,[105] the Court found it insufficient that a prisoner had raised a federal claim in a pre-trial petition for a writ of prohibition in the California Supreme Court. California had not identified petitions of that kind as an accepted means of challenging criminal convictions. And it could not be said that the prisoner had given the state supreme court a fair chance to consider his claim simply because he had filed such a petition and that court had dismissed it on procedural grounds. In *Castille v. Peoples*,[106] the Court found it insufficient that a prisoner had raised a claim for the first time in a petition for allocatur in the state's highest court. There, too, the prisoner presented his claim in a procedural context in which it was unlikely that the state court would entertain the merits.

On the other hand, prisoners sometimes must exhaust state court litigation opportunities that the states concerned actually discourage prisoners from using (procedural avenues, accordingly, that almost always end in dismissal on procedural grounds). In many states, prisoners have no right of appeal to the highest state court, but can only apply for discretionary review. That state court (typically the state supreme court) thus functions in much the way that the Supreme Court itself operates—accepting for review only cases that have larger significance.[107] Nevertheless, the Court held in *O'Sullivan v. Boerckel*[108] that prisoners ordinarily must seek discretionary review in the highest state court in order to satisfy the exhaustion doctrine and keep their claims alive for federal habeas.[109]

State supreme courts may not welcome a federal rule that requires prisoners to press ordinary federal claims in petitions for discretionary review in the teeth of state procedural rules that invite only especially important or novel issues.[110] The *Boerckel* decision

---

Rev. L. & Soc. Change 359 (1988); James C. Harrington & Anne More Burnham, *Texas's New Habeas Corpus Procedure for Death-Row Inmates: Kafkaesque—And Probably Unconstitutional*, 27 St. Mary's L.J. 69 (1995). By some accounts, federal habeas corpus would be less important than it is if state postconviction procedures were more effective in identifying and redressing violations of federal rights in criminal cases. The 1996 Act ostensibly hopes to foster improvements by encouraging the states to provide indigent death row inmates with lawyers in state postconviction proceedings. In exchange, the Act offers states a variety of procedural advantages in the federal habeas corpus proceedings that come later—for example, a shorter filing period. See text accompanying notes 65–67, 133.

105. 421 U.S. 482 (1975).

106. 489 U.S. 346 (1989).

107. See Chapter VII, notes 219–45 (describing the Supreme Court's discretionary control of its docket).

108. 526 U.S. 838 (1999).

109. Compare Chapter VII, notes 60–65 and accompanying text (discussing a similar understanding of the preservation rule).

110. Justice O'Connor acknowledged as much in her opinion for the Court in *Boerckel*. 526 U.S. at 847. The Illinois rule in *Boerckel* expressly encouraged prisoners to select from their list of claims only those contentions that warranted discretionary review. Specifically, the rule explained that the Illinois Supreme Court would consider "the general importance" of a question, the existence of a "conflict" on the question among the intermediate appellate courts, the "need" for the exercise of the state supreme court's supervisory authority, and the "final or interlocutory" character of the issue. Ill. Sup. Ct. R. 315.

arguably undermines cordial relations with state courts and, into the bargain, complicates litigation both in state court and in federal court thereafter.[111] Yet states' only recourse is to eliminate discretionary review from their "normal" appellate scheme, thus making that avenue "unavailable."[112] States that do that may be able to spare themselves (and prisoners) the bother of petitions for discretionary review that state supreme courts do not wish to receive.[113] Some state supreme courts have responded by specifying that they regard petitions for discretionary review as unnecessary. Justice Souter suggested in *Boerckel* that explicit statements to that effect should be effective. But he had to write separately to make that point.[114]

Prisoners need not engage in redundant litigation. It is typically sufficient if they exhaust one of several alternative procedures in state court.[115] Once the highest state court has had an opportunity to pass on a claim and has failed to render a favorable judgment, the exhaustion doctrine is satisfied and federal habeas corpus need be postponed no longer.[116] Of course, a prisoner cannot force a state court actually to address a claim. It is enough if the highest state court has a fair opportunity to reach the merits, even if the court declines to do so on procedural grounds or overlooks or disregards the claim without explanation.[117] Pursuant to §2264(a), a federal court entertaining a habeas corpus petition from a prisoner on death row can ordinarily consider only claims that were previously "raised" and "decided on the merits" in state court. That provision must presuppose that the state courts addressed and resolved properly presented claims. Otherwise, it would foreclose federal adjudication of claims the state courts chose to ignore, even though those claims were presented for decision.[118]

The exhaustion doctrine has only to do with *state* opportunities for litigation. Prisoners need not petition the Supreme Court of the United States for discretionary review before they proceed to federal habeas corpus at the federal district court level. If a pris-

---

111. See Note, *Requiring Unwanted Habeas Corpus Petitions to State Supreme Courts for Exhaustion Purposes: Too Exhausting*, 79 Minn. L. Rev. 1197 (1995).

112. *Boerckel*, 526 U.S. at 847.

113. Cf. *Michigan v. Long*, 463 U.S. 1032 (1983) (allowing state courts to specify that their judgments rest exclusively on state law and thus to avoid Supreme Court appellate review); see Chapter VII, notes 142–48 and accompanying text.

114. 526 U.S. at 849–50 (concurring opinion). See *Mattis v. Vaughn*, 128 F.Supp.2d 249, 256–61 (E.D. Pa. 2001) (reporting that Pennsylvania has followed Justice Souter's suggestion).

115. *Wade v. Mayo*, 334 U.S. 672, 678 (1948).

116. But see note 103 (discussing the effect of the federal-question abstention doctrine). Prisoners rarely can satisfy the exhaustion doctrine by showing that the state courts have rejected the same claim in another prisoner's case and are unlikely to change their minds. The likelihood that a claim will be successful is not the criterion. The Supreme Court itself occasionally credits the argument that resort to the state courts would be "futile." But the circumstances are limited. In *Lynce v. Mathis*, 519 U.S. 433 (1997), the Court agreed that a prisoner should not be required to take his claim to state court because it was clear that the state courts would not be receptive. But in that case the respondent failed to raise the exhaustion issue either in the circuit court below or, more importantly, in the Supreme Court. Id. at 436 n.4. On some occasions, the Court has recognized that state avenues are unavailable because of a prisoner's procedural default. E.g., *Engle v. Isaac*, 456 U.S. 107, 125–26 n.28 (1982). See text accompanying note 194 (explaining that when prisoners satisfy the exhaustion requirement by committing default in state court they are likely to suffer dismissal outright). For a general discussion of how exhausting the exhaustion doctrine can be, see Yackle, note 31, at 251–93.

117. *Smith v. Digmon*, 434 U.S. 332 (1978).

118. The Powell Committee, which provided the model for §2264(a), recommended that federal courts should be limited to claims that were "actually presented and litigated" (not "decided") in state court. See note 67.

oner does file a *certiorari* petition in the Supreme Court and review is denied (as is usually the case), the Supreme Court's disposition has no effect on later habeas proceedings in a district court.[119] If, however, the Supreme Court accepts a case for review and determines the merits of the prisoner's claim, that decision *does* foreclose a later habeas application to a district court.[120]

Prisoners sometimes file habeas corpus petitions containing multiple claims, some of which are ready for federal adjudication and some of which are not. The Supreme Court held in *Rose v. Lundy*[121] that district courts should dismiss "mixed" petitions in their entirety. The point is to encourage prisoners to exhaust state opportunities for litigating all their claims and then to aggregate those claims in a single federal petition. In effect, *Lundy* puts prisoners to a choice. On the one hand, they can accept dismissal of an entire "mixed" petition, pursue available state court litigation opportunities for the claims that are premature, and then return to federal court when they have satisfied the exhaustion doctrine with respect to all claims.[122] That option necessarily defers federal adjudication of the claims that are currently ready for consideration. On the other hand, prisoners can abandon any claims that are not yet cognizable and proceed with claims the state courts have had the opportunity to consider.[123]

Pursuant to §2254(b)(2), a federal district court "may" ignore a prisoner's failure to exhaust, provided the court denies relief "on the merits." If federal courts were to do that routinely, they would deny state courts any opportunity to consider the claims in question and would therefore sacrifice the policies that explain the exhaustion doctrine in the first place. It is sensible to make that sacrifice only when claims are so frivolous that there is no chance that the state courts would sustain them. In cases of that kind, it would be wasteful to dismiss for failure to exhaust and thus to condemn both prisoners and state courts to futile litigation. Accordingly, a federal court should leapfrog over the exhaustion requirement and deny relief on the merits only when it is "convinced" that a claim has "no merit" and that it would be useless to send the prisoner to state court.[124] The capacity to deny claims on the merits is especially valuable in cases otherwise controlled by *Lundy*. If the claims that a prisoner has not yet presented to the state courts are so worthless that they can be dispatched pursuant to §2254(b)(2), a federal court

---

119. *Brown v. Allen*, 344 U.S. at 488–97 (Frankfurter, J., concurring); see Chapter VII, note 234 and accompanying text. Cf. Sup. Ct. R. 20.4(b) (explaining that the denial of an "original" habeas petition is not an adjudication on the merits and thus does not preclude a later petition addressed to a lower court).

120. 28 U.S.C. §2244(c); see Yackle, note 31, at 566–77.

121. 455 U.S. 509 (1982).

122. If a prisoner's initial petition is dismissed without prejudice under the *Lundy* decision, a second petition (filed after the prisoner has satisfied the exhaustion requirement with respect to all claims) is not subject to dismissal under the rules governing second or successive applications for federal relief. *Slack*, 529 U.S. at 486–89; see note 515.

123. In some circuits, district courts explain these options to *pro se* petitioners and record the choices made for future reference. E.g., *Solis v. Garcia*, 219 F.3d 922, 925 n.3 (9th Cir. 2000). Writing for the Court in *Lundy*, Justice O'Connor said that a prisoner who strips premature claims out of his petition runs the "risk" that those claims will be foreclosed, if and when they are renewed in a subsequent habeas application. 455 U.S. at 520–21. The lower courts took that to be a gentle way of saying that any claims dropped from a current petition are barred later. The Supreme Court has said nothing to the contrary since *Lundy*. See *Slack*, 529 U.S. at 487 (repeating the warning in *Lundy* without elaboration); notes 508–52 and accompanying text (discussing the standards for second and successive petitions).

124. *Hoxsie v. Kerby*, 108 F.3d 1239, 1243 (10th Cir. 1997).

can proceed with other potentially meritorious claims that are ready for federal attention.[125]

State authorities may forgo the exhaustion requirement and submit a claim for federal adjudication before the state courts have had an opportunity to consider it.[126] Yet they cannot forfeit the state's interests through inattention. States' attorneys have a duty to advise district courts about whether, in their view, prisoners have exhausted available state procedures.[127] In the run of cases, accordingly, the exhaustion issue should not be overlooked unintentionally. Yet if states' attorneys fail to raise an exhaustion doctrine objection, the state's prerogatives are nonetheless preserved. Under §2254(b)(3), states' attorneys can forgo exhaustion only if they do so "expressly." A state will not otherwise be "deemed to have waived the exhaustion requirement or be estopped from reliance" on it.[128]

In the main, both §2254(b) and judicial decisions celebrate the exhaustion requirement as an essential ingredient of habeas corpus jurisprudence. Nevertheless, another statute, 28 U.S.C. §2264, arguably dispenses with exhaustion once a petitioner under sentence of death files a federal petition. Under §2264(a), a district court entertaining an application from a death row prisoner must determine at the threshold whether federal adjudication is foreclosed because a claim was not presented in state court.[129] If the court determines that a claim is not precluded because of default, the next section, §2264(b), instructs the district court to consider the claim in light of three specified paragraphs of §2254. Importantly (or so it would seem), the paragraph that codifies the exhaustion doctrine, §2254(b), is not among them. One available inference is that §2264 jettisons the exhaustion requirement in the interests of speeding capital cases through the federal courts.[130] If that is what §2264 means, however, the implication is

---

125. If a district court denies a claim pursuant to §2254(b)(2), it presumably must do so without relying on the relief-limiting provisions in 28 U.S.C. §2254(d), which are applicable only in cases in which a state court previously adjudicated a claim on the merits. See notes 376–92 and accompanying text.

126. See *Granberry v. Greer*, 481 U.S. 129, 134–35 (1987) (explaining that district courts nonetheless may insist on exhaustion when there are reasons for thinking that the interests of state courts in adjudicating claims are paramount).

127. Id.

128. Notwithstanding §2254(b)(3), it is questionable whether states' attorneys are free to withhold any argument about a prisoner's satisfaction of the exhaustion requirement until a federal court has invested resources in an adjudication of the merits or, worse yet, until the court has determined that a claim is meritorious and is poised to award relief. See *Harding v. North Carolina*, 683 F.2d 850 (4th Cir. 1982) (refusing to allow states' attorneys to waive exhaustion on the condition that the federal court would rule against the prisoner on the merits). Of course, if a claim is so frivolous that it can be denied on the merits pursuant to §2254(b)(2), it makes no difference whether the state waives exhaustion. The point here is that states' attorneys should not be able to manipulate the exhaustion doctrine with respect to a potentially meritorious claim—allowing a claim of that order to proceed in federal court in hopes that it will be rejected, but then insisting on exhaustion in the eleventh hour if it appears that the prisoner is likely to win. Cf. Chapter X, notes 80–83 and accompanying text (explaining that states sometimes surrender sovereign immunity by engaging in manipulative litigation tactics); Chapter XI, notes 227–30 (discussing prosecutors' capacity to invoke federal-question abstention only if they act before a federal court has conducted "proceedings of substance on the merits").

129. See notes 194–264 and accompanying text.

130. Since §2264 appears in the optional Chapter 154, it is applicable only to capital cases and then only to cases arising from states that have invoked that chapter. See note 67. For a discussion of §2264's implications for procedural default in state court, see notes 258–64 and accompanying text.

startling: District courts in capital cases controlled by §2264 are neither obliged nor *permitted* to enforce the exhaustion requirement, even if the respondent asks that the state courts be given the chance to consider a prisoner's claim.[131]

3. Filing Deadlines

In general. Prisoners seeking federal habeas relief from state custody must initiate federal proceedings within fixed filing periods. Pursuant to 28 U.S.C. §2244(d)(1), prisoners must be in federal court within one year after the latest of four dates: (A) the date on which the state court "judgment" under attack becomes "final" by the "conclusion of direct review or the expiration of the time for seeking such review;" (B) the date on which an unlawful state "impediment" to filing is removed; (C) the date on which the "constitutional right" asserted is "initially recognized by the Supreme Court," provided that right has been "newly recognized by the Supreme Court and made retroactively applicable to cases on collateral review;" or (D) the date on which the "factual predicate" of a claim is discoverable "through the exercise of due diligence." Prisoners challenging federal convictions or sentences via §2255 motions must also file within one year after any of four roughly corresponding dates, described in paragraphs (1)–(4), albeit some inconsistencies between §2244(d)(1) and §2255 may invite different computations.[132] Pursuant to §2263, state prisoners under sentence of death must meet a 180-day filing deadline, running from "final State court affirmance of the conviction and sentence on direct review or the expiration of the time for seeking such review."[133] All these provisions were enacted as part of AEDPA.[134] They are plainly geared to preexisting features of habeas corpus law bearing on the time that prisoners need to prepare and lodge federal petitions. By all accounts, they bristle with interpretive difficulties.[135]

---

131. Startling though it may be, this is precisely what the Powell Committee recommended. See Powell Committee Report, note 67, at 51–53.

132. See notes 141–42 and accompanying text.

133. Pursuant to a further provision in §2263, death-sentenced prisoners can apply for a thirty-day extension. Section 2263 also appears in the optional Chapter 154 and thus is applicable only in cases from qualifying states. See note 67. Other provisions in Chapter 154 attempt to expedite death penalty cases in another way. Under §2266, federal courts must handle petitions filed by death-sentenced prisoners on fixed timetables. The initial provision of Chapter 154, 28 U.S.C. §2261(a), limits the application of that chapter to "cases arising under section 2254 brought by prisoners in State custody." Nevertheless, §2266(a) also extends the timetables to §2255 motions from federal prisoners under sentence of death. Legislatively imposed timetables for Article III court proceedings can be problematic. See William F. Ryan, *Rush to Judgment: A Constitutional Analysis of Time Limits on Judicial Decisions*, 77 B.U. L. Rev. 761 (1997). In this instance, however, federal courts have a fair measure of flexibility. Pursuant to paragraphs (b)(4)(B) and (c)(4)(B) of §2266, a state is authorized to "enforce" the timetables by petitioning for a writ of mandamus. An appellate court can mandate only that the court before which an issue is pending must decide that question, not that the court must reach a particular outcome. *Will v. United States*, 389 U.S. 90, 98 n.6 (1967). The contemplation of §2266, then, is that the timetables established for federal court action on capital habeas petitions only encourage courts to act as quickly as they can to discharge their Article III duties. This also appears to be the contemplation of paragraphs (b)(5) and (c)(5) of §2266, which call on the Administrative Office of United States Courts to file periodic reports on compliance with the timetables.

134. See text accompanying note 65.

135. See Tushnet & Yackle, note 68, at 26–30 (offering a brief discussion); Yackle, note 68 (running on at some length). See also Michael Mello, *Suspending Justice: The Unconstitutionality of the Proposed Six-Month Time Limit on the Filing of Habeas Corpus Petitions by State Death Row Inmates*,

Paragraph (A) of §2244(d)(1) specifies that state prisoners have one year in which to get an application for the writ before a federal court, running from the date the state court judgment becomes "final" at the conclusion of "direct review" or the expiration of the time for "seeking" direct review. That date is not the date on which the highest state court affirms a criminal conviction on appeal from the trial court in which it was obtained. It is the date on which the Supreme Court disposes of a petition seeking *certiorari* review of a state appellate court's decision affirming a conviction or, in a case in which a prisoner does not seek Supreme Court review, the date on which the time for filing a *certiorari* petition expires.[136] Few prisoners file *certiorari* petitions after their convictions are affirmed at the state appellate court level.[137] Effectively, then, most prisoners must reach federal court within a year and three months after the highest state court affirms their convictions and sentences on direct review.[138] Certainly a prisoner stops the clock when he formally files a petition.[139] Other actions may also suffice—for

---

18 N.Y.U. Rev. L. & Soc. Change 451 (1991) (arguing that the filing deadlines are invalid); Peter Sessions, *Swift Justice?: Imposing a Statute of Limitations on the Federal Habeas Corpus Petitions of State Prisoners*, 70 So. Calif. L. Rev. 1513 (1997) (contending that the deadlines are unfair). Because the filing deadlines are not jurisdictional limits, they may be understood to establish affirmative defenses, which must be asserted by the respondent or forfeited. See notes 126–28 and accompanying text (discussing the respondent's obligations with respect to the exhaustion doctrine). But see *Herbst v. Cook*, 260 F.3d 1039, 1042–43 (9th Cir. 2001) (holding that a district court may raise the filing deadline issue *sua sponte* provided the prisoner has an opportunity to respond).

136. *Williams v. Artuz*, 237 F.3d 147, 151 (2d Cir. 2001). Cf. *Griffith v. Kentucky*, 479 U.S. 314, 321 n.6 (1987) (recognizing that proceedings in the Court itself count as part of the direct review process). See also notes 315–21 and accompanying text. In describing the procedural history of the case in *Carey v. Saffold*, 122 S.Ct. 2134 (2002), Justice Breyer said that the prisoner's "conviction" became final on a date certain in 1992. Id. at 2137. Justice Breyer did not pause to explain how he arrived at that conclusion. In fact, the prisoner in *Saffold* ceased his efforts in state court after an intermediate appellate court affirmed his conviction. He did not petition the California Supreme Court for review and thus was never in a position to file a petition for *certiorari* in the United States Supreme Court. See Chapter VII, notes 60–65 and accompanying text (explaining that litigants typically must present claims to the highest state court before asking the Supreme Court for review).

137. Recall that prisoners are not required to seek appellate review in the Supreme Court in order to exhaust state remedies. See notes 119–20 and accompanying text.

138. See Sup. Ct. R. 13 (allowing ninety days to file a petition for *certiorari*); but see notes 166–93 and accompanying text (discussing the tolling provision in paragraph (2) of §2244(d)).

139. The circuits are divided over whether the one-year period is computed according to Fed. R. Civ. P. 6(a). Compare *Hernandez v. Caldwell*, 225 F.3d 435 (4th Cir. 2000) (relying on Rule 6), with *Crutcher v. Cockrell*, 301 F.3d 656 (5th Cir. 2002) (finding Rule 6 inapplicable). See §2254 Rule 11 (authorizing the application of ordinary civil rules in habeas cases); §2255 Rule 12 (similarly authorizing the application of the civil rules in §2255 cases). Ordinarily, a prisoner who meets the deadline by filing a petition may amend that petition later under Fed. R. Civ. P. 15, in which case the amendment "relates back" to the date the original petition was filed. Valid amendments under Rule 15 are not barred even if they occur after the statutory filing time has run. *Pruitt v. United States*, 274 F.3d 1315 (11th Cir. 2001) (*per curiam*). The idea in Rule 15 is to permit litigants to correct technical flaws or to clarify or elaborate claims. If, then, a prisoner offers an amendment that is "far removed from his original claims," the amendment will not "relate back" to the time of original filing and may be cut off if the filing deadline has arrived. *Pruitt*, 274 F.3d at 1319. Pursuant to §2266(b)(3)(B), a prisoner challenging a death sentence can amend a petition after the respondent files an answer only if the prisoner satisfies the standards for filing a second or successive petition. See §2244(b); notes 508–52 and accompanying text. Since §2266 appears in the optional Chapter 154, it applies only in states that trigger the provisions in that chapter by establishing a qualifying scheme for providing indigents under sentence of death with counsel in state postconviction proceedings. See note 67. Cf. *Calderon v. Ashmus*, 523 U.S. 740, 750 (1998) (Breyer, J., concurring) (noting this feature of Chapter 154).

example, a motion for the appointment of counsel to prepare a formal habeas petition.[140]

Paragraph (1) of §2255 similarly gives prisoners attacking federal judgments one year in which to file, running from the date on which a "judgment of conviction becomes final." Notice, however, that paragraph (1) does not mention the time required for seeking appellate review. In §2255 cases, then, a prisoner may have time to appeal to the appropriate circuit court, but not to petition the Supreme Court for *certiorari* review thereafter.[141] Yet that construction would confuse and frustrate the regular process of appellate review. It would be more sensible to read paragraph (1)'s reference to a "final" judgment of conviction to allow both for appellate review in a circuit court of appeals and for *certiorari* proceedings in the Supreme Court. Accordingly, most prisoners contemplating §2255 motions should have a year and ninety days following the affirmance of their convictions and sentences at the circuit level.[142]

The same result, more or less, should be reached in most death penalty cases governed by §2263, albeit the basic time period allowed is only half so long. Paragraph (a) of §2263 starts the filing period on the date that a *state* court affirms a prisoner's conviction and sentence on direct review or the date on which the time for seeking "such" review expires. There is no mention of proceedings in the Supreme Court thereafter. Yet paragraph (b) tolls the filing period from the date a prisoner files a petition for *certiorari* in the Supreme Court until the date on which the Court disposes of that petition. The result is roughly the same, though the mechanism for arriving at that result is different.[143]

Paragraph (B) of §2244(d)(1) and paragraph (2) of §2255 draw on Supreme Court decisions that forgive prisoners' failure to comply with procedural rules if the "cause" of their default lies with negligent or abusive government officials.[144] If government officers prevent a prisoner from filing a habeas petition or a §2255 motion by placing an unlawful "impediment" in his way, the one-year filing period begins to run only after that impediment is removed. If, for example, a prosecutor withheld exculpatory evidence from the prisoner at trial and the prisoner does not become aware of that evidence until his only avenue of attack is to file a §2254 petition or a §2255 motion, the clock starts on the date the evidence becomes known, thus ensuring that the prisoner

---

140. See note 101. The circuit courts have divided over whether an extant motion for the appointment of counsel made a habeas case "pending" at the time AEDPA was adopted (thus rendering most provisions in the new Act inapplicable). See note 66. Compare *Sandoval v. Calderon*, 231 F.3d 1140, 1145 (9th Cir. 2000) (holding that a motion for appointment of counsel was sufficient), with *Williams v. Cain*, 125 F.3d 269, 274 (5th Cir. 1997) (holding that only a formal petition would do). Cf. *Fierro v. Cockrell*, 294 F.3d 674, 680 (5th Cir. 2002) (holding that an application to a circuit court for permission to file a second or successive petition at the district level does not initiate a habeas proceeding in a way that stops the clock). See also note 146 (discussing the mailbox rule).

141. E.g., *Gendron v. United States*, 154 F.3d 672 (7th Cir. 1998) (*per curiam*) (so holding).

142. See *Kaufmann v. United States*, 282 F.3d 1336, 1338 (11th Cir. 2002) (taking this view but recognizing a division on the question among the circuits).

143. The result is only roughly the same, because the tolling provision in paragraph (b) of §2263 stops the clock only when a petition for *certiorari* is filed. Under paragraph (A) of §2244(d)(1), and (probably) under paragraph (1) of §2255, the filing period does not begin until *certiorari* proceedings in the Supreme Court are finished or the time for filing a *certiorari* petition has run out. See notes 166–93 and accompanying text (discussing the operation of the tolling provision in paragraph (2) of §2244(d) for §2254 habeas cases not controlled by §2263).

144. See notes 214–28 and accompanying text.

has time to prepare and file a petition or motion.[145] Paragraph (B) of §2244(d)(1) and paragraph (2) of §2255 control very few cases. In part, that is because government officers rarely keep prisoners from filing timely federal petitions and motions and, if they do, it is hard for prisoners to prove it. Moreover, the condition that the "impediment" must itself violate federal law is an important limitation.[146]

Paragraph (C) of §2244(d)(1) and paragraph (3) of §2255 draw on the Court's decisions regarding procedural default and on its decisions governing claims that can be sustained only if changes in the law are given retrospective effect. Concomitantly, those provisions reset the clock for (some) prisoners seeking to file second or successive federal petitions or motions.[147] Some decisions on default recognize that a prisoner has "cause" for failing to advance a claim depending on a new legal right if, at the crucial juncture, the Court has not yet announced the existence of the right.[148] At the same time, the decisions on changes in the law generally bar the retroactive enforcement of new rules except in narrow circumstances.[149] The existence of a new right thus comes to nothing, unless that right fits one of the exceptions to the ban on "new rule" claims and thus is retroactively available in collateral proceedings like federal habeas corpus.[150] In

---

145. The existence of an "impediment" within the meaning of these provisions is fact-sensitive and thus may require a federal evidentiary hearing to resolve conflicting accounts of the events. See note 216 (noting that federal fact-finding proceedings are sometimes needed to determine the existence of "cause" for procedural default in state court).

146. The Supreme Court has recognized that prison inmates must rely on guards and prison administrators to handle their mail and thus does not hold prisoners accountable for the time that prison authorities take to convey petitions to the courts. *Houston v. Lack*, 487 U.S. 266 (1988) (holding that prisoners' papers are deemed to be filed when they are placed in the prison mailbox). The "mailbox rule" applies when federal courts compute the filing periods for lodging habeas petitions. E.g., *Huizar v. Carey*, 273 F.3d 1220 (9th Cir. 2001). But courts do not rely on paragraph (B) of §2244(d)(1) or on paragraph (2) of §2255 as a source of authority, presumably because a prison official who takes undue time to funnel a prisoner's petition to court does not necessarily act in violation of federal law. But see *Ex parte Hull*, 312 U.S. 546 (1941) (holding that some forms of interference are unconstitutional).

147. See notes 508–52 and accompanying text (discussing §2244(b) and the provisions in §2255 governing multiple motions). Prisoners who have been unsuccessful with one application for federal collateral relief and want to try again typically must rely on paragraphs (C) or (D) of §2244(d)(1) or on paragraphs (3) or (4) of §2255, which promise an extension on the single year allowed by the basic provisions in paragraph (A) of §2244(d)(1) and paragraph (1) of §2255. It is no accident, then, that the standards established by those provisions correspond to the standards for filing second or successive petitions or motions. See *Libby v. Magnusson*, 177 F.3d 43, 47–49 (1st Cir. 1999) (offering a good discussion). What *is* surprising is that the fit between the filing deadline provisions and the provisions on second or successive applications is not tighter than it is.

148. See notes 218–21 and accompanying text (discussing *Reed v. Ross*).

149. See notes 315–42 and accompanying text (discussing the *Teague* doctrine and the two exceptions to *Teague's* general ban on the retroactive enforcement of "new rules"). The precise reference in paragraph (C) is to a new "right" that is made retroactively applicable to "cases on collateral review." In theory, of course, habeas corpus cases like *Teague* do not contemplate that federal courts "review" state court judgments. When the Court is careful, it recognizes as much. E.g., *INS v. St. Cyr*, 533 U.S. at 311–12 (distinguishing habeas adjudication from "judicial review"). Yet both the Court and Congress often refer to habeas as "collateral review" in order to distinguish proceedings with respect to the writ from "direct review"—i.e., an initial appeal from a trial court. E.g., *Teague v. Lane*, 489 U.S. 288, 305–16 (1989); see note 315. By all accounts, the "collateral review" phrase in paragraph (C) refers primarily to habeas corpus proceedings.

150. In all candor, paragraph (C) may have few practical applications. The Court holds out the possibility that some prisoners may avoid dismissal for default on the theory that they could not anticipate a novel theory and that prisoners who escape dismissal on that ground may be able to establish that their novel theories are available retroactively. But the standards prisoners must satisfy in

attempting to account for these conditions, paragraphs (C) and (3) raise numerous interpretation questions.

At the outset, paragraph (C) of §2244(d)(1) starts the clock ticking when a "constitutional" claim is initially recognized and made available in habeas corpus. Paragraph (3) of §2255 similarly starts the filing period for §2255 motions running on the date that a "right" is initially recognized, provided the right is retroactively available. Yet paragraph (3) does not describe the right as "constitutional." The appearance of the "constitutional" modifier in paragraph (C) of §2244(d)(1) and its omission from paragraph (3) of §2255 invites the inference that the filing period for habeas petitions by state prisoners demands a new right with some constitutional footing, but the filing period for §2255 motions does not. Both prisoners seeking federal habeas relief from state judgments and prisoners challenging federal convictions and sentences can advance non-constitutional federal claims.[151] There is no self-evident reason for making filing deadlines turn on whether prisoners press one kind of claim rather than the other. This same interpretive problem is reproduced with respect to numerous other AEDPA provisions, some of which use the "constitutional" modifier and some of which do not—without apparent explanation for the inconsistency.[152] The best resolution of the problem, here and elsewhere, is to put it down to poor draftsmanship. Paragraph (C) and other provisions use the label "constitutional" not to preclude cognizable non-constitutional claims, but simply (and loosely) to *identify* cognizable claims, which typically *are* constitutional but need not be.[153]

Paragraph (C) of §2244(d)(1) and paragraph (3) of §2255 start the filing period from the date on which the "right" the prisoner asserts is "initially recognized by the Supreme Court—if that right is both "newly recognized by the Supreme Court" and "made retroactively applicable to cases on collateral review."[154] Read literally, that for-

---

both respects are demanding. Not many prisoners actually stand to benefit from the extra time that paragraph (C) allows.

151. See note 297 and accompanying text.

152. See §2244(b)(2)(A) (referring to a "new rule of constitutional law" in a provision affecting prisoners' ability to file more than one federal petition); §2253(c)(2) (referring to "constitutional" rights in a provision governing appellate review); §2254(e)(2)(A)(i) (also referring to a "new rule of constitutional law" in a provision affecting prisoners' ability to obtain a federal evidentiary hearing); §2255 (using the same phrase in a provision affecting federal prisoners' ability to file a second or successive motion attacking a federal conviction or sentence); but see §2262(b)(3) (stating that stays of execution expire if prisoners under sentence of death fail to "make a substantial showing of the denial of a Federal right"); §2264(a)(3) (contemplating that death-sentenced prisoners may advance claims asserting a "new Federal right"). See notes 286–87, 499–505, 519 and accompanying text.

153. But see *United States v. Lopez*, 248 F.3d 427, 430 (5th Cir. 2001) (reading §2255 to allow for new statutory rights but suggesting that §2244(d)(1)(C) does not). In some contexts, it would be especially hard to read references to constitutional claims and issues to exclude non-constitutional matters by negative implication. See notes 499–505 and accompanying text (discussing the problem with respect to §2253 on certificates of appealability).

154. This language appears redundant inasmuch as it refers to the recognition of a new right twice in succession. The point of adding the condition that the right in question must be "newly recognized" is to clarify that paragraph (C) extends the time that a prisoner would otherwise have to file under the general filing period prescribed in paragraph (A). The idea is not to start the filing period on the date of some familiar Supreme Court decision that announced a new right at the time (e.g., *Gideon v. Wainwright* in 1963). It is to give a prisoner extra time if the Court announces a new right after the usual starting date for the one-year filing period—i.e., the conclusion of direct review or the date on which the time for filing a *certiorari* petition expires. See notes 136–38 and accompanying text. Prisoners usually contend that their claims do *not* depend on "new" rules of law—for the obvious reason that claims that *do* depend on something new are almost always foreclosed. See notes 315–67 and accompanying text. Nevertheless, in this context prisoners find themselves ar-

mulation suggests that a decision by the Court itself may be necessary to identify a right as "new," to settle the "retroactivity" question, or both. Then, if the Supreme Court makes those necessary judgments itself, the filing period begins to run not from the date of the decision that comes last, but from the date of the decision initially recognizing the right—whenever it arrives. The wisdom of requiring action by the Court for this (or any) particular purpose is questionable.[155] Nevertheless, the Court held in *Tyler v. Cain*[156] that similar language in §2244(b)(2)(A) requires a Supreme Court holding on retroactivity for purposes of determining whether successive petitions can be filed.

The *Tyler* decision is problematic on its own ground. Requiring a Supreme Court holding on retroactivity in the context of successive petitions creates complications that a different interpretation would have avoided.[157] Requiring a Supreme Court holding on retroactivity in filing deadline cases would not raise the same problems. In this instance, it would make sense to require a Supreme Court holding on retroactivity to start the filing period running. In the successive petition context, requiring a Supreme Court holding on retroactivity has the pernicious effect of preventing prisoners from going to federal court even though the substance of the standards in §2244(b)(2) are met: A new rule has been announced and it *should* be retroactively available. In the filing deadline context, requiring a Supreme Court holding on retroactivity to start the filing period running would have the salutary effect of allowing prisoners to forgo filing petitions until it is clear that the substantive standards in paragraphs (C) and (3) are satisfied: A new right has been recognized, and it has been held to be enforceable in §2254 or §2255 proceedings.

A filing period works well only if it begins on an easily identified date certain. If the Court uses a single case both to announce a new right and to hold that right retroactively available in collateral proceedings, there is no great difficulty. The filing period begins running on the date of that decision. In this vein, the Court has said that its practice is to make both decisions in a single case.[158] The Court may, however, use one case as a vehicle for recognizing a new right and wait for another to hold that the new right is retroactively applicable to habeas corpus cases. That, in fact, is the most likely scenario, albeit the announcement of a new rule in any circumstances is an extremely

---

guing that they are asserting "new" rights in order to extend the filing period. See *United States v. Hopkins*, 268 F.3d 222 (4th Cir. 2001) (rejecting a prisoner's argument that he relied on a newly recognized right and thus finding his §2255 motion untimely). Here again, however, the complexities of §2244(d) are hardly worth the candle. Prisoners who convince the federal courts that their claims are "new" can obtain more time in which to file only if the novel theories on which they rely are retroactively available, which, again, is almost never the case.

155. After all, the Court has responsibilities across the breadth of American public law and, by all accounts, needs a great deal of flexibility in order deploy its scarce capacity when and where it is needed most. See Chapter VII, notes 219–45.

156. 533 U.S. 656 (2002); see notes 524–33 and accompanying text.

157. See notes 527–33 and accompanying text.

158. *Teague*, 489 U.S. at 300; see notes 319–23 and accompanying text. Justice O'Connor explained in *Teague* that if the Court uses a case as a vehicle for announcing a new rule of law, the Court must be willing to apply that rule to the case at bar. Otherwise, the announcement of the rule would be an advisory opinion. But see Chapter IX, notes 33–34 and accompanying text) (discussing the Court's practice of clarifying the law beyond the requirements of particular cases). She insisted that all similarly situated habeas petitioners are entitled to be treated in the same way. It follows that if the Court applies a new rule to one habeas applicant, it must apply the rule to others (assuming aside any procedural complexities).

rare event.[159] The Court has explained that it typically considers novel theories only in cases that reach the Court on direct review rather than in habeas proceedings.[160] If the Court recognizes a new rule in a direct review posture, it has no occasion to address the question whether that rule will also be enforceable in habeas corpus.[161] If, then, paragraph (C) of §2244(d)(1) and paragraph (3) of §2255 start the filing period running on the date the Court merely recognizes a new right, without yet deciding whether it is enforceable in habeas proceedings, prisoners will be induced to file federal lawsuits as soon as (they think) the Court has recognized a new right that the Court will ultimately make retroactively available to them.[162] Far better to read those provisions to start the filing period only when the Court makes the retroactivity decision. Then prisoners will be prodded into action only when their petitions stand a genuine chance of success and thus warrant access to a federal court: when the Court has both recognized a new right and held that it is enforceable in collateral proceedings.[163]

Unfortunately, the texts of these provisions in AEDPA make it harder to require a Supreme Court holding on retroactivity in this context (where it makes sense) than it is in the context of second or successive petitions or motions (where it is problematic). There is a difference between the filing deadline provisions in paragraph (C) of §2244(d)(1) and paragraph (3) of §2255, on the one hand, and the successive petition provisions in paragraph (A) of §2244(b)(2) and §2255, on the other. The successive petition provisions explicitly refer to a new rule "*made* retroactive to cases on collateral review *by the Supreme Court*." The filing deadline provisions refer to rights that have been

---

159. See *O'Dell v. Netherland*, 519 U.S. 1050 (1996) (granting *certiorari* in a habeas corpus case to determine whether a rule announced in a previous decision on direct review would be given retroactive effect in collateral proceedings).

160. See *Teague*, 489 U.S. at 310; notes 315–21 and accompanying text.

161. To do so, the Court would have to render an advisory opinion—if, that is, Justice O'Connor's discussion of the Article III issue in *Teague* is taken seriously.

162. The Court obviously has other business to do and may take some considerable time to decide whether a new right is retroactively applicable to habeas cases. In some instances, the Court may never itself pass on the question, bowing instead to a consensus among the circuit courts, one way or the other. See Chapter VII, note 223 and accompanying text (explaining that the Court often fails to grant review unless there is a division of authority below).

163. See *In re Vial*, 115 F.3d 1192, 1197 n.9 (4th Cir. 1997) (stating that the clock starts only after the Supreme Court has made a determination on retroactivity). Justice Breyer said in *Tyler* that, in light of the construction placed on paragraph (A) of §2244(b)(2) in that case, this construction of paragraph (C) of §2244(d)(1) is necessary to give prisoners a chance to file second or successive petitions advancing novel claims. See 533 U.S. at 677 (Breyer, J., dissenting); notes 534–36 and accompanying text. If the filing period were to begin on the date the Court recognizes a new right without specifying its retroactive application, a prisoner who can assert that right only in a second or successive petition would face a ticking clock, but would have no way to stop it. He would be forced to await a subsequent Supreme Court decision on retroactivity (rendered in some other prisoner's case) and only then would be entitled to file a petition on his own behalf. If the filing period were to expire in the interim, the prisoner would be foreclosed. But see notes 192–93 and accompanying text (discussing equitable tolling). That result might be unconstitutional. Cf. *Logan v. Zimmerman Brush*, 455 U.S. 422, 433 (1982) (holding that it violates due process to deprive an individual of a property interest on the basis of a rule of timing the individual cannot satisfy). The Fifth Circuit acknowledged all this in the *Lopez* case, but nonetheless insisted that the filing period must begin running at the time the Supreme Court recognizes the substance of a new right. According to that court, the possibility that the Supreme Court might never decide the retroactivity question actually fortifies the view that the filing period cannot await a Supreme Court decision. If it did, the filing deadline would never arrive "and any petitioner's out-of-time motion would be timely." *Lopez*, 248 F.3d at 433.

"initially recognized *by the Supreme Court*" and "newly recognized *by the Supreme Court*," but then simply "*made*" retroactively applicable to cases on collateral review. That formulation attaches the modifying phrase "by the Supreme Court" to the recognition of a new right, thus (if *Tyler* is probative) requiring a Supreme Court holding on that issue. Yet since the same modifying phrase is not (necessarily) attached to the different matter of retroactivity, it is open to argue that a Supreme Court holding on retroactivity is not required to start a new filing period running.[164]

Paragraph (D) of §2244(d)(1) and paragraph (4) of §2255 rely on Supreme Court decisions on procedural default and on other provisions in AEDPA that forgive prisoners who do their best to uncover factual support for their claims but are unsuccessful. In those related fields, the telltale requirement is "diligence" on the prisoner's part. The same is true here: The filing period begins to run on the date a prisoner discovers the "factual predicate" of his claim, provided he could not have discovered the facts earlier by the exercise of "due diligence."[165]

Tolling. Pursuant to §2244(d)(2), the one-year filing period for state prisoners seeking federal habeas relief is tolled while a "properly filed" application for "State postconviction or other collateral relief with respect to the pertinent judgment or claim is pending." Pursuant to §2263(b)(2), the 180-day filing period for death penalty cases is tolled "from the date on which the first petition for post-conviction review or other collateral relief is filed until the final State court disposition of such petition."[166] Those tolling provisions are essential to accommodate the exhaustion doctrine. But for tolling, the combination of filing deadlines and exhaustion would be unintelligible: Filing deadlines necessarily encourage prisoners to seek federal habeas relief early, while the exhaustion requirement demands that they postpone federal petitions until state court opportunities to litigate their federal claims have been tried. There is no similar tolling provision in §2255. The reason, presumably, is that prisoners challenging federal convictions or sentences typically have no exhaustion requirement to meet.[167]

The tension between filing deadlines and exhaustion is modest in cases in which prisoners satisfy the exhaustion doctrine with respect to all their claims by presenting those claims to the state's highest court on direct review of their convictions. In cases of that kind, prisoners typically have an initial ninety days (the period for seeking *certiorari* in the Supreme Court) and then a full year in which to file a habeas petition in the

164. See *Lopez*, 248 F.3d at 433 (so holding). Cf. §2254(e)(2)(A)(i) (using a "made retroactive... by the Supreme Court" formulation similar to the one in paragraph (A) of §2244(b)(2) in a provision governing the availability of federal evidentiary hearings); see text accompanying note 279.

165. See notes 280–83 and accompanying text (discussing §2254(e)(2) and the *Michael Williams* case). Here again, a federal hearing may be necessary to determine whether a prisoner exercised the diligence required. E.g., *Aron v. United States*, 291 F.3d 708 (10th Cir. 2002).

166. Section 2263 governs only cases arising from states that have done what is necessary to have the benefits of the provisions in Chapter 154. See note 67.

167. A prisoner may claim that a federal sentence was enhanced on the basis of an invalid prior conviction in state court. See *Daniels v. United States*, 532 U.S. 374 (2000); note 246 and accompanying text. If, in that kind of case, state avenues for attacking the prior state conviction remain open, a prisoner may wish to challenge the old conviction in state court and may argue that the tolling provision in §2244(d)(2) should apply by extension. Alternatively, the prisoner may be entitled to equitable tolling. See notes 192–93 and accompanying text. At least, such a prisoner should be able to file a §2255 motion advancing the "enhancement" claim against his federal sentence within the ordinary filing period, then ask the court to postpone consideration of that claim while he goes to state court to attack the prior conviction. See notes 97, 257 and accompanying text.

district court.[168] However, in cases in which prisoners have claims that still can be considered in state postconviction proceedings, the possible scenarios become complex. Recall that the "mixed petition" doctrine established in *Rose v. Lundy* demands that all the claims a prisoner wishes to advance must sink or swim together.[169] On the surface, it would appear that a prisoner is in a quandary if he has some claims that are ready for federal habeas corpus and other claims that are not. If the prisoner withholds the former claims in the near term while taking other claims to state postconviction proceedings, the filing period may run out before state proceedings are completed.

The tolling provision in §2244(d)(2) defuses the problem. The disjunctive "or" between "judgment" and "claim" makes it plain that the filing period is tolled not only with respect to claims that a prisoner is pressing in state postconviction proceedings, but also with respect to all other claims addressed to the same "judgment."[170] That includes claims that the prisoner is not currently presenting to the state courts—namely, claims that are ready for federal habeas consideration but are held up while the prisoner satisfies the exhaustion doctrine with respect to other claims. Then, when state postconviction proceedings are completed, the prisoner can aggregate all claims in a single federal habeas petition in the manner prescribed by *Lundy*. Thus with the benefit of the tolling provision prisoners can delay claims that are ready for federal consideration until other claims catch up, even though more than a year and ninety days passes in the interim.[171] The analogous provision for capital cases in §2263(b)(2) states that the filing period is tolled from the date on which a prisoner's "first petition" is filed until "final" state court disposition of that petition. That provision appears to operate in the same way, stopping the clock while state court proceedings are under way without regard to the claims asserted.[172]

The tolling provision in §2244(d)(2) suspends the filing deadline as soon as an application for state postconviction relief is "properly filed" in state court. Writing for the Court in *Artuz v. Bennett*,[173] Justice Scalia explained that an application is "filed" when it is accepted by the appropriate state court officer (typically the court clerk).[174] It is "properly" filed if, at that time, it satisfies state rules governing filing—namely, rules prescribing the form of the instrument, the filing fee, time limits, the proper office at the court house, and any special requirements affecting postconviction petitions.[175] If

168. Recall, however, that most prisoners must prepare their own petitions without professional help.

169. See notes 121–23 and accompanying text.

170. *Sweger v. Chesney*, 294 F.3d 506, 515–18 (3d Cir. 2002).

171. If the tolling provision's only purpose is to accommodate the exhaustion doctrine, a petition for state postconviction relief may be sufficient only if it advances one or more federal claims that may be cognizable in federal court. *Austin v. Mitchell*, 200 F.3d 391, 394 (6th Cir. 1999). Yet the statute itself does not qualify the tolling function of a state petition according to the claims advanced. *Carter v. Litscher*, 275 F.3d 663, 665 (7th Cir. 2001). And there is a policy basis for finding a state postconviction petition sufficient even if it contains only state law claims for relief. It makes sense to postpone federal habeas adjudication of any federal claims a prisoner may have until the state courts have had a chance to address other claims that, if accepted, may make it unnecessary for the prisoner to petition for federal relief at all. *Carter*, at 665; *Ford v. Moore*, 296 F.3d 1035 (11th Cir. 2002) (*per curiam*).

172. See Chapter XI, note 85 and accompanying text (discussing a similar rationale for the state-question abstention doctrine).

173. 531 U.S. 4 (2000).

174. Id. at 8.

175. Id. Justice Scalia explained, for example, that some states require prisoners to obtain leave of court before filing applications for postconviction relief. He drew an analogy to the requirement that prisoners seeking appellate review of federal habeas corpus judgments must obtain a "certificate

formal rules of that kind are met, it makes no difference whether the claims contained in an application are meritorious or subject to dismissal on procedural grounds.[176] In *Bennett* itself, the state complained that the prisoner's claims were procedurally barred because he had, or might have, pressed them earlier on direct review of his criminal conviction. Justice Scalia found that beside the point. An individual "claim" may well be subject to dismissal because of procedural default. But claims are not "filed"; they are "*presented* or *raised*."[177] When, then, §2244(d)(2) refers to "applications" that are "properly filed," it must mean only entire applications, without regard to the prospects that the individual claims contained within it will be successful. The state argued in *Bennett* that unscrupulous prisoners might frustrate the federal deadlines by filing applications advancing bogus claims for state postconviction relief. Justice Scalia responded that a federal district court should be able to determine whether an application tolls the filing deadline for a federal habeas petition without investigating the possibility that the claims contained in it will ultimately be dismissed. In any event, he said, "policy concerns" must be left to Congress. The Court's role is to give the text its "only permissible interpretation."[178]

Once an application for state postconviction relief is "properly filed," it tolls the federal filing period while that application is "pending." In *Carey v. Saffold*,[179] Justice Breyer explained that an application ordinarily is "pending" while it is actually before a state court, during any period after one state court has acted and a higher state court takes up the application on appellate review, and until the highest state court reaches a final judgment.[180] Justice Breyer initially explained that his copy of Webster's defines the term "pending" to mean, among other things, "until the... completion of." Applying that definition to the term in §2244(d)(2), Breyer concluded that an application is "pending" until the state courts have finally disposed of it. Justice Breyer quickly added, however, that the state's competing interpretation would create a conflict with the exhaustion doctrine. By the state's account, §2244(d)(2) tolls the filing deadline only while an application for state postconviction relief is actually before a state court and not during any intervals between one state court and the next. Justice Breyer responded that, if that were the law, a prisoner might be unable to negotiate all the appellate levels of state court postconviction process before his federal filing period expires. By construing §2244(d)(2) to toll the federal filing period for all the time required to process a state petition, Justice Breyer ensured that prisoners can satisfy both the filing deadline and the exhaustion doctrine. Importantly, he explained that a prisoner must meet any state filing deadlines for appealing from one state court to another and that it is for state courts to decide whether a prisoner has done so.

Under the peculiar statutory arrangement in California, where the *Saffold* case arose, a prisoner did not file one application for state postconviction relief, which, in turn,

---

of appealability." See notes 495–98 and accompanying text. A state rule demanding that kind of permission at the time of filing also counts as a rule that must be satisfied if an application is to be regarded as "properly filed" within the meaning of §2244(d)(2).

176. *Bennett*, 531 U.S. at 9.

177. Id. at 10 (emphasis in original).

178. Id.

179. 122 S.Ct. 2134 (2002).

180. Recall that the Court has taken this same view regarding the question whether a state court suit is "pending" for purposes of the federal-question abstention doctrine. See Chapter XI, note 161 and accompanying text.

was processed through multiple levels of state court review. Instead, a prisoner filed multiple independent applications, one in each state court in succession. Justice Breyer explained that, in the main, that oddity of California practice made no functional difference. He recognized, however, that because each state court entertained a separate petition, a prisoner was not obliged to meet fixed filing deadlines, but was required only to file a new petition in each successive court within a "reasonable" time. That feature of the California system made it likely that a federal court would have greater difficulty determining whether a prisoner had acted seasonably as a matter of state law, thus to decide whether the federal filing period was tolled. According to Justice Breyer, though, it was for the state of California to decide how to process applications for state postconviction relief. If California found its current arrangements inconvenient in light of the effect on the federal tolling provision, California was free to change state law.[181]

Dissenting in *Saffold*, Justice Kennedy insisted that Justice Breyer paid too little attention to California's special system. Since California contemplated not one but multiple applications for state relief, Justice Kennedy argued that §2244(d)(2) could properly be construed to toll the federal filing period only while each separate application was pending before a court and not during any dead time between independent applications in different courts.[182] Justice Kennedy insisted that the real statutory construction question was not the meaning to be assigned to the term "pending," but rather the meaning to be assigned to the term "application." In California, each separate application initiated a new and different proceeding during which that particular application could be said to be pending. Justice Kennedy also contended that in California and most other states, prisoners are formally entitled to file independent "original" applications for habeas corpus relief at any time. Accordingly, under Justice Breyer's interpretation of §2244(d)(2), it will be impossible for a federal court ever to conclude that the federal filing period is no longer tolled—because prisoners always can claim that they have yet to complete all the available means of obtaining state postconviction relief. To that, Justice Breyer responded that federal courts can and will hold prisoners to the ordinary filing deadlines recognized by state law and will not be hoodwinked into believing that state postconviction proceedings are always timely. Again, according to Justice Breyer, if

181. In *Saffold* itself, the California Supreme Court dismissed the prisoner's application for state postconviction relief "on the merits and for lack of diligence." The Court of Appeals for the Ninth Circuit understood that to mean that the state court had ruled on the merits of the prisoner's claim and had not relied on the procedural ground that the prisoner had failed to file his state papers in time. Justice Breyer insisted, however, that the state court's handling of the timing issue was ambiguous. Accordingly, he remanded the case to the circuit court with instructions to reconsider whether the state court had actually concluded that the prisoner had filed within a "reasonable" time as required by state law. He made it clear that the circuit court could not assume that the state court had found the prisoner's application timing solely because the state court also stated that the claim was dismissed "on the merits." But he left it to the circuit court to consider other arguments regarding the meaning to be attached to the state court's action. In passing, Justice Breyer mentioned that the circuit court might certify the question to the California Supreme Court. 122 S.Ct. at 2141; see Chapter XI, notes 92–93 and accompanying text. But he did not order the circuit court to obtain clarity in that way. Recall that the Supreme Court itself typically treats a state court decision relying alternatively on federal and state grounds to rest, well enough, on the state ground alone. See Chapter VII, notes 117–21 and accompanying text. Then, too, the Court assumes that a state court rests on a federal ground (rather than on a state procedural bar rule) when the state court's opinion appears to do so and does not explicitly indicate otherwise. Chapter VII, notes 141–55 and accompanying text. The Court has applied the latter approach to habeas cases. See Chapter VII, note 145.

182. *Saffold*, 122 S.Ct. at 2142 (dissenting opinion) (joined by Rehnquist, C.J. and Scalia & Thomas, J.J.).

the special arrangements in California invite unscrupulous prisoners to manipulate the process, California can change its own law.[183]

The filing period for federal habeas corpus petitions is not tolled during the time a petition is under consideration in *federal* court. Justice O'Connor explained in *Duncan v. Walker*[184] that §2244(d)(2) postpones the deadline only while an application for "State post-conviction or other collateral review" is pending. Within that formulation, the term "State" modifies both "post-conviction" and "other collateral review." Accordingly, "other collateral review" cannot include *federal* habeas corpus. By Justice O'Connor's account, any other construction would deprive the modifier "State" of meaning. The phrase "other collateral review" need not refer to federal habeas corpus. It may be included only to acknowledge the "diverse terminology" used by the states to describe their schemes for examining claims after trial and direct review are completed. Extrapolating from *Duncan*, it appears that the filing period is not tolled while a prisoner seeks, or is entitled to seek, *certiorari* review in the Supreme Court following the denial of relief in state postconviction proceedings.[185] The tolling provision for death penalty cases, §2263(b)(2), also appears to start the clock again when a "State court" finally disposes of a prisoner's petition for postconviction relief in state court.[186]

The *Duncan* interpretation of the tolling provision in §2244(d)(2) *does* create serious conflicts with the exhaustion doctrine. A prisoner may file a federal habeas petition in the belief that all the claims contained in it are ready for federal adjudication. The federal district court may take substantial time to decide whether that is so. If the district court later concludes that state procedures have not been exhausted regarding even a single claim, the court will ordinarily dismiss the entire petition. By that time, the prisoner may be unable to satisfy the exhaustion requirement with respect to that claim and return to federal court before the federal filing period expires.[187] In *Duncan*, however,

---

183. Id. at 2141 (majority opinion).

184. 533 U.S. 167 (2001).

185. Recall that paragraph (A) of §2244(d)(1) explicitly starts the filing period after the time for seeking direct review expires. See text accompanying note 136. An application for state postconviction relief would not appear to be "properly filed" and "pending" during a period in which a prisoner is entitled to seek direct review but does not actually do so. *Smaldone v. Senkowski*, 273 F.3d 133, 136–38 (2d Cir. 2001). If, however, a prisoner *does* file a timely petition for *certiorari* at this stage, there may be a sound argument that §2244(d)(2) tolls the filing period until the Supreme Court disposes of that petition. But see *Crawley v. Catoe*, 257 F.3d 395, 398–401 (4th Cir. 2001) (allowing no tolling while a petition for *certiorari* was actually pending). Consider, in this vein, that the Supreme Court might grant a petition for *certiorari* and thus put some issue in a prisoner's case on the docket for examination. That usually doesn't happen. See note 316 and accompanying text. But in the unlikely event the Court were to break from usual practice, it would be odd if the filing period for advancing a habeas corpus petition at the district court level were to continue running, so that the prisoner would be forced to press ahead in a district court while the Supreme Court proceedings are under way. Then again, if the filing period is tolled while a petition for *certiorari* is pending in this context, prisoners might be encouraged to file petitions that are almost certainly destined to be denied. But see Chapter VII, notes 219–27 and accompanying text (explaining that the Court rarely grants review in any kind of case in any posture). Cf. *Fierro*, 294 F.3d at 681 n.12 (declining to decide whether the filing period is equitably tolled while a circuit panel decides whether to give a prisoner permission to file a second or successive petition in a district court).

186. See text accompanying note 143.

187. See notes 121–25 and accompanying text (discussing *Rose v. Lundy*). The scenario is bleak enough if it is assumed that the only difficulty is that district courts take time to decide exhaustion doctrine questions. Consider, though, that district courts may also reach erroneous decisions on exhaustion issues. Thus a prisoner who has complied with the exhaustion doctrine may suffer an erroneous dismissal and then find that the filing deadline has come and gone while he was engaged in

Justice O'Connor insisted that requiring prisoners to bear the risk that one of their claims is premature will encourage them to use care in exhausting state procedures before filing a petition in the first instance. Any potential unfairness is a policy matter for Congress. The Court's "sole task" is to construe the text of §2244(d)(2) according to its "language and purpose."[188]

Justice O'Connor's explicit reference to "purpose" suggests that she was not entirely indifferent to the implications of the *Duncan* decision. She may have been persuaded that §2244(d)(2), as she understands it, actually strikes a proper balance between the policy of expediting federal habeas corpus proceedings, on the one hand, and the policy of requiring prisoners to exhaust state avenues for relief, on the other. Then again, Justice O'Connor failed to acknowledge one inescapable consequence: A prisoner who understands that the filing period is running while his federal petition is pending may file a simultaneous application for state postconviction relief—not because he genuinely thinks that further state court litigation is necessary to satisfy the exhaustion doctrine, but because only an application for state relief will toll the filing period. The *Duncan* decision thus encourages prisoners to file the very redundant applications for state postconviction relief that the respondent in *Bennett* worried that the decision in that case would make possible.[189] Dissenting in *Duncan*, Justice Breyer contended that the real flaw in O'Connor's construction of the tolling provision is that it threatens to mistreat unwitting petitioners who will *not* comprehend that the clock is still running after they file in federal court. Breyer insisted that §2244(d)(2) is actually ambiguous and thus should be read to toll the federal filing period while federal petitions are pending.[190]

The federal courts may take steps to mitigate unfairness ascribable to the filing deadlines for federal habeas petitions. First, district courts need not dismiss habeas petitions for failure to satisfy the exhaustion doctrine. Instead, they can hold premature petitions on the federal docket while prisoners return to state court for further litigation. In that way, federal courts can spare deserving prisoners the risk that their claims will be time-barred.[191] Second, district courts can relax the filing deadlines according to the equities of particular cases. The filing periods in §2244(d)(1) are not hard jurisdictional limits on the exercise of federal judicial power. Instead, they are subject to "equitable tolling" beyond the limits of the statutory tolling provision in §2244(d)(2).[192] If courts were ex-

---

further litigation in state court that should not have been required in the first place. See *Jorss v. Gomez*, 266 F.3d 956, 958 (9th Cir. 2001) (using equitable tolling to avoid unfairness in a case of that kind).

188. *Duncan*, 533 U.S. at 181.

189. See text accompanying notes 177–78.

190. 533 U.S. at 185 (dissenting opinion) (joined by Ginsburg, J.). See also Stephen Breyer, *Our Democratic Constitution*, 77 N.Y.U. L. Rev. 245, 267–68 (2002) (continuing the argument that the decision in *Duncan* closes the doors to the federal courts in a "random" way that should not be thought to be Congress' purpose).

191. Justice Stevens has endorsed this possibility for avoiding unfairness. *Duncan*, 533 U.S. at 182–83 (concurring opinion); see notes 184–90 and accompanying text. Writing for the Court in *Duncan*, Justice O'Connor noted the point but declined to address it. 533 U.S. at 181 (majority opinion). See *Nowaczyk v. Warden*, 299 F.3d 69 (1st Cir. 2002) (providing a good discussion); *Delaney v. Matesanz*, 264 F.3d 7, 14–15 n.5 (1st Cir. 2001) ("commending" a stay rather than a dismissal when there is a "realistic danger" that the filing period will expire while a prisoner goes back to state court); *Zarvela v. Artuz*, 254 F.3d 374 (2d Cir. 2001) (instructing district courts to issue stays conditional on prisoners' expeditious pursuit of state relief and prompt return to federal court thereafter).

192. Justice Stevens has also endorsed equitable tolling. *Duncan*, 533 U.S. at 183. The circuit courts uniformly recognize that equitable tolling is available.

cessively free with equitable tolling, the formal statutory limits would be meaningless. Accordingly, equitable tolling is itself sharply limited in habeas corpus cases.[193]

C. Procedural Default in State Court

1. In General

Petitioners satisfy the exhaustion doctrine if, at the time they file federal habeas corpus petitions, there is no available and effective state court opportunity to litigate their federal claims. It often happens that no state court opportunities are *currently* open, but only because petitioners failed to advance their claims in previous proceedings in the manner prescribed by state law, and, for that reason, the state courts are no longer willing to entertain them. For example, defense attorneys frequently fail to comply with contemporaneous objection rules during trial. The defendants concerned then forfeit any other state court opportunities to litigate the claims that counsel neglects. State courts are generally entitled to penalize defaulters in that way, and their ultimate judgments rest, accordingly, on adequate state procedural grounds—even if meritorious federal claims are ignored because of counsel's blunders. Adequate state grounds of decision prevent the Supreme Court from considering underlying federal claims on direct review.[194] They also (usually) bar federal district courts from considering those claims in §2254 habeas corpus proceedings. Commonly, then, petitioners satisfy the exhaustion doctrine (and thus avoid a postponement of their claims), but only for a reason that bars federal adjudication entirely. They escape the exhaustion doctrine's frying pan only to fall irretrievably into the procedure default doctrine's fire.

In the main, the idea is not that federal courts have their own ideas about the way prisoners should litigate federal claims in state court and that, if prisoners fail to proceed in that manner, they lose the opportunity they would otherwise have to seek federal habeas corpus relief. Instead, federal default doctrine reinforces *state* procedural rules and, to that end, gives effect to forfeitures that the state courts impose for default as a matter of state law. Thus state law establishes the conditions that bring federal default doctrine into play. If the state courts do not initially find a prisoner in default and refuse to consider a claim for that reason, but, instead, determine the claim on the merits, a federal district court will equally proceed to the merits.[195] If states' attorneys wish to contend that a claim is barred because of default, they must advance that contention

193. See *Drew v. Moore*, 297 F.3d 1278, 1284 (11th Cir. 2002) (explaining that prisoners must show that they exercised "diligence" but that compliance with filing deadlines was beyond their control); *Smith v. McGinnis*, 208 F.3d 13, 17 (2d Cir. 2000) (explaining that equitable tolling is reserved for "rare and exceptional circumstances"). It may be necessary to convene a federal evidentiary hearing to determine whether equitable tolling is warranted. E.g., *Neverson v. Bissonnette*, 261 F.3d 120, 126–27 (1st Cir. 2001).

194. See Chapter VII, notes 160–99 and accompanying text (describing state contemporaneous objection rules and the reasoning the Supreme Court employs to determine whether forfeitures imposed for violating rules of that kind are adequate to foreclose appellate review).

195. *County Court of Ulster County v. Allen*, 442 U.S. 140, 148 (1979) (making it clear that a federal habeas court will decline to consider a claim only if the state courts have refused or would refuse to do so); *Rezin v. Wolff*, 439 U.S. 1103 (1979) (White, J., dissenting) (explaining that the Supreme Court's default doctrine does not "impose its own contemporaneous objection rule independent of state rules").

in federal court. Since federal jurisdiction is not at stake, a federal district court has no obligation to raise the matter *sua sponte.*[196] In the main, then, federal default doctrine operates very much in the way that the Full Faith and Credit Statute would, if that statute were applicable to federal habeas proceedings.[197]

In one instance, however, the Court has fashioned an independent federal default rule that may supersede state procedural arrangements. Recall that the Court held in *O'Sullivan v. Boerckel*[198] that prisoners must advance all their federal claims in a petition for discretionary review addressed to a state supreme court, even if a state rule instructs them to limit their arguments to particular kinds of claims.[199] If prisoners fail to include a claim in that kind of petition, they commit "procedural default" even though they have violated no state procedural rule.[200] The prisoner in *Boerckel* itself complied with state procedural law. He raised all his federal claims in an intermediate state appellate court. But he omitted some of those claims from his petition for discretionary review in the Illinois Supreme Court, because those claims did not meet the criteria the local rule prescribed for discretionary review. If he had later presented those same claims in an application for state postconviction relief, he would have been turned away—not on the procedural ground that he should have included them in his petition for discretionary review in the state supreme court, but on the substantive ground that the intermediate state appellate court had rejected them on the merits. In *Boerckel,* accordingly, the Court established a free-standing federal rule regarding the way litigants must behave in state court proceedings.

There is no general statute governing the effect that federal courts entertaining habeas corpus petitions should give to procedural default in state court.[201] The Supreme Court has fashioned its own body of doctrinal rules for the occasion. By all accounts, those rules have shifted with the ebb and flow of the Court's enthusiasm for habeas corpus over time. In the 1960s, the Court was suspicious of state procedural schemes that denied federal claims any judicial forum at all and thus threatened to frustrate implementation of "incorporated" constitutional safeguards. The Warren Court largely (though sometimes grudgingly) granted that state courts could visit forfeitures on criminal defendants for procedural default in state proceedings. And that Court largely (though sometimes grudgingly) respected the adequate state ground doctrine as a limit on its own appellate jurisdiction to review state court judgments directly.[202] But the Warren Court insisted that state procedural grounds of decision would not commonly foreclose adjudication of federal claims by federal district courts in habeas corpus proceedings.

In theory, of course, federal courts entertaining habeas petitions do not *review* state court *judgments* at all, but rather act on prisoners' allegedly unlawful custody. In *Fay v.*

---

196. The Court held in *Trest v. Cain,* 522 U.S. 87 (1997), that federal courts are not *required* to take up the default issue *sua sponte,* but found it unnecessary to decide whether they *can.*

197. But see note 4 and accompanying text.

198. 526 U.S. 838 (1999).

199. See notes 108–14 and accompanying text.

200. 526 U.S. at 846–48.

201. But see notes 129–31, 258–64 and accompanying text (discussing §2264 governing death penalty cases arising in states that trigger Chapter 154); notes 279–91 and accompanying text (discussing §2254(e)(2) governing default with respect to fact-finding in state court); notes 508–52 and accompanying text (discussing §2244(b)(2) governing second or successive federal petitions).

202. Recall the Warren Court's occasional decisions finding state procedural grounds inadequate in cases in which it appeared that litigants' race figured in the dispositions in state court, as well as the *Henry* and *Williams* cases in which the Court encouraged state courts to relax local forfeiture rules. See Chapter VII, notes 195–99 and accompanying text.

Noia,[203] Justice Brennan gave the theoretical conception of the writ practical significance. He explained that district courts could act on habeas petitions without upsetting the state convictions that wardens offered to justify prisoners' detention. Even if those judgments were formally valid (in the sense that they rested on adequate state grounds), district courts could look behind them and examine federal claims that the state courts refused to consider. Brennan recognized that would-be habeas petitioners had an obligation to exhaust state court opportunities to litigate their federal claims and acknowledged that some device was necessary to discourage prisoners from ignoring the state courts, accepting forfeiture under state law, and then presenting their claims for the first time in federal court. Accordingly, he said that federal district courts should decline to entertain claims that prisoners intentionally withheld from the state courts "for strategic, tactical, or any other reasons that [could] fairly be described as the deliberate bypassing of state procedures." Yet the "deliberate bypass" standard contemplated that petitioners could be shut out of federal court only if they themselves decided to forgo state court opportunities to advance federal claims. That standard thus permitted prisoners to seek federal relief on the basis of claims that state courts found to be barred because of procedural default ascribable to defense counsel's ignorance or neglect.[204]

When the Supreme Court began to curtail habeas corpus in the 1970s, the deliberate bypass rule for default cases was one of the first features of the Warren Court's structure to go. In *Wainwright v. Sykes*,[205] then-Justice Rehnquist said that *Noia* failed to give sufficient respect to the state interests served by contemporaneous objection rules, invited petitioners and their lawyers to "sandbag" the state courts, and generally treated state criminal trials as a "tryout on the road" to federal habeas corpus rather than as the "main event" for the adjudication of all issues pertaining to criminal cases.[206] He therefore discarded the deliberate bypass rule and substituted a doctrinal formulation that

---

203. 372 U.S. 391 (1963).

204. Justice Brennan described the paradigm case as one in which a prisoner "after consultation with competent counsel or otherwise, understandingly and knowingly forewent the privilege of seeking to vindicate his federal claims in the state courts." A deliberate bypass could be found, he said, only on the basis of a "considered choice of the petitioner." A "choice made by counsel not participated in by the petitioner" would "not automatically bar relief." Id. at 439. Taken literally, then, Brennan had it that default could not foreclose federal habeas even if counsel deliberately withheld claims for tactical purposes, unless prisoners themselves were consulted and approved. He probably meant that aspect of the deliberate bypass rule as a hedge against the tendency to presume that counsel's actions have a tactical basis and to impute that purpose to their clients.

205. 433 U.S. 72 (1977).

206. See Chapter VII, note 165 and accompanying text (describing the "sandbagging" argument). The deliberate bypass rule itself addressed the very problem that concerned the Court in *Sykes* inasmuch as that rule cut off federal habeas if prisoners intentionally withheld claims from the state courts. Yet since the deliberate bypass rule demanded that petitioners themselves must have participated in a decision to forgo state court litigation, it drastically limited the occasions on which federal courts could actually find federal habeas foreclosed. By most accounts, it was unrealistic to think that counsel could consult with their clients in the heat of a trial, and, if they did, it was difficult to prove it. See *Sykes*, 433 U.S. at 93 (Burger, C.J., concurring); *Henderson v. Kibbe*, 431 U.S. 145, 512 (1977) (Burger, C.J., concurring). Accordingly, while the deliberate bypass rule prevailed, tactical decisions to bypass the state courts may have escaped without detection. Then again, by some accounts, it is unlikely that defense lawyers actually engage in sandbagging. Professor Givelber has explored the institutional reasons why lawyers representing capital clients at successive stages of state proceedings often fail to raise claims in a way that preserves them for litigation later in federal court. Daniel Givelber, *Litigating State Capital Cases While Preserving Questions*, 29 St. Mary's L.J. 1009 (1998).

revived (but added to) the adequate state ground doctrine.[207] Generally speaking, *Sykes* and subsequent decisions established a new baseline. While the *Noia* approach to default cases prevailed, procedural default in state court did *not* foreclose federal habeas corpus, except in cases in which there was good reason for *penalizing* a failure to comply with state procedural rules. Under *Sykes* and its progeny, procedural default in state court *does* foreclose federal habeas corpus, except in cases in which there is good reason for *excusing* a failure to comply with state procedural rules.

2. Current Doctrine

Modern procedural default doctrine can be complicated. At the outset, a federal district court must make the same assessments that the Supreme Court makes when it determines whether a state judgment rests on an adequate state ground. The initial questions are matters of state law: There must *be* a state procedural rule requiring a prisoner to raise a federal claim in a particular way or at a particular time. The prisoner must have failed to comply with that rule. And, for that reason, the state courts must be unwilling to consider the claim.[208] Next, the district court must determine whether the state courts' procedural disposition of the claim would constitute an adequate and independent state ground of decision that would defeat jurisdiction in the Supreme Court, if the case were before the Court on direct review.[209] In this respect, current law departs from the Warren Court, which found the adequate state ground doctrine inapplicable in habeas corpus. The adequate state ground doctrine does not limit district court jurisdiction in habeas cases in the way it restricts the Supreme Court's appellate jurisdiction. Nevertheless, that doctrine applies in habeas cases in the interests of "federalism and comity."[210] If the state courts' procedural ground for refusing to consider a federal claim would not be adequate to foreclose Supreme Court review, a district court will overlook

---

207. Justice Rehnquist did not act abruptly in *Sykes*, but built upon other decisions handed down since *Noia*. For contemporaneous commentary, see Yale Rosenberg, *Jettisoning Fay v. Noia: Procedural Defaults by Reasonably Incompetent Counsel*, 62 Minn. L. Rev. 341 (1978); Ralph Spritzer, *Criminal Waiver, Procedural Default and the Burger Court*, 126 U. Pa. L. Rev. 473 (1978); Peter W. Tague, *Federal Habeas Corpus and Ineffective Representation of Counsel: The Supreme Court Has Work to Do*, 31 Stan. L. Rev. 1 (1978).

208. See text accompanying note 195. Cf. John H. Blume & Pamela A. Wilkins, *Death by Default: State Procedural Default Doctrine in Capital Cases*, 50 S. Car. L. Rev. 1 (1998) (explaining how difficult it is for prisoners to thread their way through the state courts without committing default under some state rule).

209. The procedural ground must be both adequate and independent. In *Stewart v. Smith*, 122 S.Ct. 2578 (2002) (*per curiam*), a state court in Arizona dismissed a prisoner's application for post-conviction relief on the basis of a state rule restricting postconviction proceedings to claims of "sufficient constitutional magnitude." The Court used the Arizona certification system to ask the state supreme court whether the administration of that rule required state courts to consider the merits of prisoners' federal claims. See Chapter XI, notes 92–94 and accompanying text. The Arizona court replied that the rule called on state courts only to classify federal claims (as either of sufficient magnitude or not), but not to evaluate the merits of any particular claim. That response persuaded the Supreme Court that the rule and its operation in Arizona were entirely matters of state law, independent of any federal considerations. Accordingly, the Court remanded for attention to further questions— e.g., the adequacy of the state's independent ground of decision and the prisoner's ability to overcome the state's reliance on state grounds, both independent and adequate.

210. *Lambrix v. Singletary*, 520 U.S. 518, 523 (1997).

the prisoner's default and proceed to the merits.[211] If the state courts' procedural justification for declining to consider a claim would cut off Supreme Court review, the district court typically will refuse to entertain the claim.

There are, however, two exceptions. A district court can consider a claim on the merits despite an adequate state procedural ground for rejecting it—if: (1) the prisoner shows both "cause" for having failed to raise the claim properly in state court and "actual prejudice" resulting from the default;[212] or (2) the prisoner demonstrates that the federal error that went uncorrected in state court "probably resulted in the conviction of one who is actually innocent."[213]

Cause. Statutes and court rules commonly allow exceptions for "cause shown" and contemplate that courts will exercise *ad hoc* judgment about whether litigants offer a sufficient excuse for failing to meet procedural requirements. In this context, however, cause has a more definite meaning. Certainly, petitioners cannot demonstrate cause by showing that they or their attorneys inadvertently overlooked federal claims that should have been raised in state court. The very point of *Sykes* is that petitioners now routinely forfeit the opportunity to litigate claims in both state and federal court, even though neither they nor counsel knowingly meant to do so. Justice O'Connor explained in *Murray v. Carrier*[214] that petitioners can establish cause only by showing that "some objective factor *external to the defense* impeded counsel's efforts to comply with the state's procedural rule." For example, cause can be shown: (1) if, at the time counsel might have advanced a claim in state court, the factual or legal basis for the claim was not "reasonably available;"[215] (2) if state authorities interfered with counsel's ability to com-

---

211. E.g., *Lee v. Kemna*, 534 U.S. 362 (2002); see Chapter VII, notes 189–94 and accompanying text. Notice that the revival of the adequate state ground doctrine for use in habeas cases can improve some prisoners' chances of obtaining a foothold in federal court. If a prisoner can persuade a district court that the procedural ground on which a state court purported to rest would *not* be adequate to bar Supreme Court direct review, the prisoner can avoid dismissal for default in a habeas corpus proceeding without establishing "cause" and "prejudice" or probable innocence. See notes 212–42 and accompanying text. Robson and Mello contend that *Sykes* actually (and perhaps surprisingly) resurrected *Henry v. Mississippi*. Ruthann Robson & Michael Mello, *Ariadne's Provisions: A "Clue of Thread" to the Intricacies of Procedural Default, Adequate and Independent State Grounds, and Florida's Death Penalty*, 76 Calif. L. Rev. 87, 118 (1988). But see Chapter VII, notes 186–94 and accompanying text (discussing *Henry*). Professor Natali has pointed out that state procedural rules and state practices with respect to them can change over time, sometimes for the better. For these purposes, however, the question is whether a state procedural ground of decision was adequate at the time a state court relied on it to foreclose a prisoner's claim. Louis M. Natali, Jr., *New Bars in Pennsylvania Capital Post-Conviction Law and Their Implications for Federal Habeas Corpus Review*, 73 Temple L. Rev. 69 (2000).

212. *Sykes*, 433 U.S. at 85. The "cause" and "prejudice" ideas initially appeared in *Davis v. United States*, 411 U.S. 233 (1973), a case involving a §2255 motion attacking a federal conviction and thus implicating Fed R. Crim. P. 12. In that case, then-Justice Rehnquist drew upon Rule 12 for the cause standard and on precedents for the prejudice test, but reworked the latter into an additional hurdle for prisoners to clear. The precedents interpreting Rule 12 had it that federal prisoners who could not show cause for failing to comply with procedural rules could avoid a forfeiture by showing prejudice. In *Davis*, by contrast, Justice Rehnquist insisted that §2255 movants must show *both* cause *and* prejudice. See Louis Michael Seidman, *Factual Guilt and the Burger Court: An Examination of Continuity and Change in Criminal Procedure*, 80 Colum. L. Rev. 436, 463 (1980). Next, in *Francis v. Henderson*, 425 U.S. 536 (1976), Justice Stewart imported the cause-and-prejudice doctrine into habeas corpus actions involving state prisoners. For a critique, see Alfred Hill, *The Forfeiture of Constitutional Rights in Criminal Cases*, 78 Colum. L. Rev. 1050, 1056 (1978).

213. *Murray v. Carrier*, 477 U.S. 478, 496 (1986).

214. Id. at 488 (emphasis added).

215. Id.

ply with a rule, making compliance "impracticable;"[216] or (3) if counsel's failure to follow a procedural rule was so fundamentally incompetent and prejudicial as to constitute ineffective assistance of counsel in violation of the fourteenth amendment (which incorporates the sixth amendment).[217] Each of these illustrations of cause, in turn, begets its own further intricacies.

The proposition that prisoners cannot be expected to anticipate changes in the law is not so obvious as it may seem. To be sure, the Court held in *Reed v. Ross*[218] that a prisoner established cause by showing that the claim he wished to advance in federal habeas corpus (an attack on a burden-shifting jury instruction) was novel and that his attorney could not reasonably have anticipated it in time to raise it at trial in state court (fifteen years earlier). The *Reed* decision has never been overruled, but its value as precedent is questionable. Justice O'Connor has explained that while defense attorneys need not be "visionaries," they must use the "tools" they have to identify and appreciate creative claims and have no cause for withholding any claim simply because the existing precedents suggest that it is unlikely to succeed.[219] Moreover, doctrines developed since *Reed* typically bar habeas petitioners from pressing claims based on new rules of federal law, even if they *did* press those same claims at the proper time when their cases were in state court.[220] There are circumstances, however, in which novel claims remain cognizable, and *Reed* may support an argument for cause in cases of that kind. Then again, the jury instruction claim in *Reed* itself would be unlikely to qualify.[221]

The idea that prisoners should not be held responsible for their lawyers' mistakes is also problematic. The fact is that prisoners typically *are* saddled with the consequences of bad representation in state court. Counsel error constitutes cause only if it rises (or, better said, sinks) to the level of an independent constitutional violation. The point is not that lawyers can perform so poorly that they cease to be defendants' agents, but that the state bears overarching responsibility for ensuring that the defense function meets minimal constitutional standards. Accordingly, ineffective assistance in the constitutional sense qualifies as a factor "external to the defense" itself. Of course, habeas peti-

---

216. Id. In *Amadeo v. Zant*, 486 U.S. 214 (1988), the Court found cause for counsel's failure to raise a jury discrimination claim at trial, because prosecutors had concealed crucial evidence supporting that claim and thus interfered with counsel's ability to identify and advance the claim in compliance with state procedural rules. In *Strickler v. Greene*, 527 U.S. 263 (1999), the Court found cause for counsel's failure to request information from the prosecution, because the state had led counsel to believe that there was nothing to disclose. The existence of cause often depends on factual circumstances that were not explored in state court (when the reasons for a prisoner's default may not have been pertinent) and thus must be developed by a federal district court entertaining a habeas petition. See *Jenkins v. Anderson*, 447 U.S. 231, 234–35 n.1 (1980).

217. Justice O'Connor conceded this for the Court in *Carrier*, 477 U.S. at 488, and again in *Coleman v. Thompson*, 501 U.S. 722, 755 (1991).

218. 468 U.S. 1 (1984).

219. *Engle v. Isaac*, 456 U.S. 107, 131 (1982). Accord *Smith v. Murray*, 477 U.S. 527, 535 (1986).

220. See notes 315–67 and accompanying text (discussing the *Teague* doctrine); notes 368–94 and accompanying text (discussing 28 U.S.C. §2254(d)). See also Marc M. Arkin, *The Prisoner's Dilemma: Life in the Lower Federal Courts after Teague v. Lane*, 69 N. Car. L. Rev. 371, 407–19 (1991) (describing *Teague's* effect on *Reed* in the lower courts); Yackle, *Primer*, note 65, at 419 n.124 (suggesting that conservative justices' dissatisfaction with *Reed* may have produced *Teague*). Cf. Tung Yin, *A Better Mousetrap: Procedural Default as a Retroactivity Alternative to Teague v. Lane and the Antiterrorism and Effective Death Penalty Act of 1996*, 25 Am. Crim. L. Rev. 203 (1998) (arguing that *Reed* should be overruled so that procedural default doctrine can displace the *Teague* doctrine and §2254(d) as the means by which novel claims are foreclosed in federal habeas proceedings).

221. See notes 335–42 and accompanying text (discussing the exceptions recognized in *Teague*).

tioners who prove that their right to effective assistance was violated in state court can seek federal habeas relief on that independent basis, whether or not they can also advance federal claims that ineffective counsel failed to raise. So the only prisoners who can rely on counsel error to overcome procedural default with respect to other claims are prisoners who probably have no need to do so—namely, prisoners who can seek federal habeas relief on the independent basis that their constitutional right to effective representation was violated in state court.[222]

The constitutional standards for effective assistance are notoriously generous to the lawyers concerned. The Court held in *Strickland v. Washington*[223] that counsel's performance need only be minimally competent and that, even when it is not, there is no constitutional violation unless the defendant is actually prejudiced. Moreover, the constitutional right to effective assistance attaches only at the trial and appellate stages of the process in state court and not to the postconviction stage. Invoking a "greater power" argument, Justice O'Connor has explained that since prisoners have no constitutional right to demand counsel in state postconviction proceedings, they equally have no right to demand that the lawyers they are given as a matter of grace perform effectively. Accordingly, the most egregious negligence of counsel in representing a prisoner seeking state postconviction relief cannot violate the Constitution and thus cannot establish cause for procedural default.[224]

The Court has held, in addition, that prisoners who argue ineffective assistance as the basis for cause must satisfy the exhaustion doctrine with respect to that contention.[225] Understand the scenario: A prisoner seeks federal habeas corpus relief on the basis of some claim (a *Miranda* claim, for example) that his lawyer failed to raise in state court. The prisoner tries to overcome counsel's default by showing that the lawyer's performance was constitutionally ineffective and therefore constitutes cause. In order to advance that argument for cause in federal court, the prisoner must first present the state courts with the substantive claim that counsel's conduct failed to meet constitutional standards. In some cases, there may be an avenue for litigating that claim in state court. In many instances, however, it will be too late. A claim that counsel performed ineffectively will itself be procedurally barred because it, too, was never raised in state court. Where that is true, the prisoner satisfies the exhaustion doctrine.[226] But then he faces yet a second procedural default problem. He must establish cause for failing to raise the ineffective assistance claim in state court, thus to put himself in a posi-

222. There are additional complications making it all the more difficult for prisoners to satisfy the *Strickland* standards. In many jurisdictions, a claim that counsel rendered ineffective assistance at trial is not cognizable on direct review, but must wait for state postconviction proceedings. The primary rationale is that ineffective assistance claims typically depend on evidence not contained in the record on appeal. Moreover, the lawyer who represented a convict at trial often handles the appeal as well, and it would be awkward (and unethical) for that attorney to take responsibility for making the case against his own performance. If the prisoner is given a lawyer at all in state postconviction proceedings later, he gets (or should get) a different attorney who is able to set about making the case (for ineffective assistance either at trial or on appeal) objectively. In some jurisdictions, however, a claim of ineffective assistance at trial must be raised on direct review. If it is not, it is procedurally barred in later postconviction proceedings. Where that is the practice, a prisoner who is represented on appeal by the same lawyer who conducted his trial faces a dilemma (as does the attorney). See Anne M. Voigts, *Narrowing the Eye of the Needle: Procedural Default, Habeas Reform, and Claims of Ineffective Assistance of Counsel*, 99 Colum. L. Rev. 1103 (1999).

223. 466 U.S. 668 (1984).

224. *Coleman*, 501 U.S. at 753–54.

225. Id. at 756.

226. See text accompanying note 194.

tion to argue that the same violation of his right to effective assistance establishes cause, in turn, for failing to raise the separate *Miranda* claim that he wanted to raise in federal court in the first place.[227]

Prejudice. Prisoners who hope to avoid dismissal on the basis of procedural default typically must establish both cause and actual prejudice. Justice O'Connor said in *United States v. Frady*[228] that in cases in which prisoners claim that jury instructions given in state court violated due process, prejudice is established only if the instructions "so infected the entire trial that the resulting *conviction*" was unfair.[229] That formulation of prejudice insists that a prisoner must show not only that federal error affected the fairness of the proceedings in state court, but that it affected the outcome—the accuracy of the determination of guilt. Justice O'Connor did not explain precisely how great the effect on the outcome must be, nor whether an effect on outcome is necessary with respect to other kinds of claims.[230]

---

227. *Edwards v. Carpenter*, 529 U.S. 446 (2000). Writing for the Court in *Carpenter*, Justice Scalia explained that a prisoner in these circumstances might yet get his original claim before a federal district court by showing cause (as well as prejudice) on both levels. He noted, however, that prisoners hoping to establish cause for failing to raise ineffective assistance claims in state postconviction proceedings must do so on some basis other than another episode of counsel ineffectiveness at that stage. Recall that counsel mistakes at the postconviction stage cannot constitute cause. See text accompanying note 224. Justice Breyer filed an opinion concurring only in the judgment in *Carpenter*. He conceded that Justice Scalia's opinion for the Court made a certain amount of sense, given the procedural default doctrine that had gone before. But that proved to Breyer that the only people who can appreciate it are people who "like difficult puzzles." Id. at 458.

228. 456 U.S. 152 (1982).

229. Id. at 169 (emphasis added). Justice O'Connor explained in *Frady* that the cause-and-prejudice formulation elaborated in *Sykes* and other cases involving state prisoners also applies to cases (like *Frady*) involving federal prisoners pursuing §2255 relief. That was unremarkable, given *Davis v. United States*. See note 212. Yet since the Court explains and defends the *Sykes* doctrine primarily on the basis of the comity federal courts owe to the states, it is not self-evident that collateral attacks on federal convictions should be reflexively handled in the same way.

230. Justice O'Connor was at pains in *Frady* to limit her discussion of prejudice to the circumstances in that case and to disclaim any more general elaboration of the prejudice idea for other cases and claims. 456 U.S. at 168. Professor Jeffries and Professor Stuntz suggest that the formulation O'Connor used to describe prejudice in *Frady* approximates the formulation the Court uses to describe the prejudice element of ineffective assistance of counsel claims, where prisoners must show a "reasonable probability that, but for counsel's unprofessional errors, the result of the proceeding would have been different." In that context, a "reasonable probability" is a "probability sufficient to undermine confidence in the outcome." *Strickland*, 466 U.S. at 694. Jeffries and Stuntz think that is about right—an effect greater than what would create a "reasonable doubt" yet less than what would make an acquittal "more likely than not." John C. Jeffries, Jr. & William J. Stuntz, *Ineffective Assistance and Procedural Default in Federal Habeas Corpus*, 57 U. Chi. L. Rev. 679, 684–85 (1990). Jeffries and Stuntz propose that the Court should abandon its focus on compliance with state procedural rules and attend to the nature of the claims prisoners advance in federal court—and should suspend rigid procedural bar rules when federal courts have the chance to correct an erroneous conviction or sentence of death. Professor Dooley proposes that the Court should jettison default rules altogether, allow federal courts to consider especially compelling claims, and simply foreclose other claims on the theory that they are by nature insufficient to warrant consideration in federal court. Laura Gaston Dooley, *Equal Protection and the Procedural Default Bar Doctrine in Federal Habeas Corpus*, 59 Fordham L. Rev. 737, 769–70 (1991). Professor Marcus offers a nuanced appraisal of both cause and prejudice and proposes that the two ideas should operate more closely together. For example, Marcus contends that defense counsel's neglect (short of a sixth amendment violation) should constitute cause, if the prisoner makes a showing of significant prejudice—namely, "factual innocence or a defect in the truth-seeking process." Maria L. Marcus, *Federal Habeas Corpus After State Court Default: A Definition of Cause and Prejudice*, 53 Fordham L. Rev. 663, 733 (1985). See note 212 (noting that older interpretations of Rule 12 allowed prejudice to make cause unnecessary).

Innocence. The Court is confident that the cause-and-prejudice formulation will typically capture cases in which a genuine miscarriage of justice would ensue if default were not excused. Nevertheless, "in an extraordinary case, where a constitutional violation has probably resulted in the conviction of one who is actually innocent," a federal court can address the merits of a claim "even in the absence of a showing of cause."[231] A safety valve for cases in which prisoners show "probable innocence" is hard to reconcile with the traditional understanding of habeas corpus or, for that matter, with federal jurisdiction generally. Virtually everyone agrees that it was for state courts (and juries) to determine whether defendants actually committed the criminal acts with which they were charged and that federal courts should limit their purview to the constitutionality of the legal procedures by which state courts set about reaching those judgments.[232] Nevertheless, there is some appeal in the idea that genuine concerns about prisoners' guilt should justify reaching legal claims that would otherwise be dismissed on procedural grounds.[233]

Even as the Court brooks some attention to actual innocence in habeas, however, the Court plainly hesitates to invite petitioners to advance innocence arguments routinely. In an apparent effort to keep this last escape route within narrow bounds, the Court has stated the controlling test in some of the most Byzantine language in all the law of federal courts. Writing for the Court in *Schlup v. Delo*,[234] Justice Stevens said that a prisoner who hopes to satisfy the "probable innocence" standard must "support his allegations of constitutional error with new reliable evidence—whether it be exculpatory scientific evidence, trustworthy eyewitness accounts, or critical physical evidence—that was not presented at trial." On the basis of that evidence, the prisoner must show that "it is *more likely than not* that *no reasonable juror* would have convicted him in light of the new evidence."[235]

Dissenting in *Schlup*, Chief Justice Rehnquist said that Stevens' formulation mixed a "quintessential charge to a finder of fact" (the "more likely than not" standard) with "an equally quintessential conclusion of law" (the "no reasonable juror would have convicted" standard).[236] That was a fair point. Yet the Chief Justice himself proposed an alternative formulation even less intelligible—the formulation that Justice Kennedy had previously articulated in *Sawyer v. Whitley*[237] for use in cases in which prisoners contend that they have been erroneously sentenced to death. In that context, a prisoner must show "by clear and convincing evidence that but for constitutional error, no reasonable juror would [have found] the petitioner eligible for the death penalty."[238] Justice Stevens, for his part, explained that prisoners like *Schlup* (whose claims go to the validity of a conviction) must make a showing that is stronger than what is needed to establish prej-

231. *Carrier*, 477 U.S. at 496. Writing for the Court in *Carrier*, Justice O'Connor did not mention the usual requirement that petitioners must also show prejudice. Prisoners who show probable innocence demonstrate prejudice *a fortiori*. See notes 236–40 (discussing Justice Stevens' explanation of the relationship between prejudice and probable innocence in *Schlup*).

232. In the *Isaac* case, Justice O'Connor summarily rejected the argument that the *Sykes* approach to default should be relaxed when prisoners advance claims going to factual innocence. *Isaac*, 456 U.S. at 129 (explaining that the habeas corpus statutes do not distinguish among federal claims).

233. See notes 295–96 and accompanying text (discussing the *Herrera* case).

234. 513 U.S. 298 (1995).

235. Id. at 327 (emphasis added).

236. Id. at 339 (dissenting opinion).

237. 505 U.S. 333 (1992).

238. Id. at 348.

udice, but not so strong as what is required of prisoners in cases like *Sawyer* (whose claims go only to their eligibility to receive a death sentence). Both *Schlup* and *Sawyer* involved second or successive federal petitions from a single prisoner and thus formally elaborated the doctrine applicable to cases of that kind. Yet at the time those decisions were rendered, the Supreme Court used the same rules both to determine the effect of default in prior state court proceedings and to determine the effect of default in prior federal proceedings.[239] Baroque as the Court's standards may be, they are beacons of simplicity and clarity by comparison to the statutes that now govern second or successive petitions.[240]

Procedural default doctrine is actually more complicated still. In *Bousley v. United States*,[241] the Court elaborated the "innocence" safety valve for cases in which prisoners attack pleas of guilty. The prisoner in *Bousley* (actually a federal convict proceeding under §2255) initially pled guilty to a charge of using a firearm in connection with a drug offense—on the mistaken understanding that mere possession of a gun constituted "use." Thereafter, the Supreme Court held that "use" demanded more active employment of a weapon. The prisoner then contended that his failure to insist on that interpretation of the statute should be excused, because he was actually innocent. The record did not demonstrate that he had brandished a weapon or otherwise "used" one in a way contemplated by the statute. In the Supreme Court, Chief Justice Rehnquist acknowledged that the prisoner was entitled make a showing of "actual innocence" if he could. But the Chief Justice explained that the government would be entitled to rebut the prisoner's argument regarding his innocence with any additional (admissible) evidence of his guilt, even if that evidence had not been presented at the earlier proceeding in which the guilty plea was taken. Moreover, the Chief Justice anticipated that in some cases the government may have withheld additional charges in connection with a plea agreement. Where that is so, the government is entitled to introduce evidence of a prisoner's guilt on those other charges. And in order to succeed, the prisoner must establish his probable innocence of those offenses, as well.[242]

3. Sentence Enhancement Cases

In general, when a state conviction ceases to be open to attack in its own right, it is regarded as "conclusively valid." If it is used later to enhance a different sentence imposed for another offense, the new sentence usually cannot be challenged in federal habeas corpus on the ground that it depends on an unlawful prior conviction.[243] In the

239. See note 546.

240. See, e.g., text accompanying note 516.

241. 523 U.S. 614 (1998).

242. Id. at 624. By some accounts, a prisoner's successful habeas challenge to a conviction that rests on a negotiated plea of guilty constitutes a breach of the plea agreement. If that understanding is valid, the prosecution should no longer be bound by the agreement and thus should be entitled to indict the prisoner on charges the prosecution previously agreed to drop. But see Note, *The Danger of Winning: Contract Law Ramifications of Successful Bailey Challenges for Plea-Convicted Defendants*, 72 N.Y.U. L. Rev. 841 (1997) (contending otherwise).

243. If the prior conviction *was* constitutionally flawed, it is hard to deny that the new sentence, too, is unlawful *ceteris paribus* to the extent it was influenced (in a non-harmless way) by the old conviction. In *Johnson v. Mississippi*, 486 U.S. 578 (1988), the Court said that "allowing" a death sentence to stand "although it was based on a reversed [prior] conviction" violates the eighth amendment. Id. at 585. Yet subject to narrow exceptions, the true merits of such a claim typically do not signify for want of any federal court with authority to *reach* the merits in these procedural

typical case, the prisoner has served the sentence that was imposed for the prior conviction and is therefore no longer in the custody of that sentence. Accordingly, a federal court has no jurisdiction to entertain a habeas corpus petition attacking the conviction on which that sentence was based. Moreover, the prisoner is often barred from challenging the old conviction because he failed to comply with ordinary state and federal procedural requirements. The state filing period has run, and state procedural default rules typically frustrate a tardy petition for relief in state court.[244] The federal filing period, too, has expired, and federal procedural default rules equally render federal habeas corpus unavailable.

A prisoner *is* in custody, however, under the sentence he is now serving. Accordingly, a federal district court has jurisdiction to entertain a claim that the current sentence was enhanced on the basis of an invalid prior conviction that itself is no longer subject to attack. Moreover, the prisoner may be able to satisfy state and federal procedural requirements with respect to an independent "enhancement" claim against his current sentence. Nevertheless, Justice O'Connor held in *Lackawanna County Dist. Attorney v. Coss*[245] that enhancement claims are almost always procedurally foreclosed *en masse*.[246] She explained that a general rule barring enhancement claims both protects state interests in the finality of criminal convictions and also spares federal courts the burden of investigating stale proceedings to determine whether some federal error may have occurred.[247]

On the one hand, the general rule announced in *Coss* seems harsh. It prevents a challenge to an enhanced sentence even in the rare case in which a prisoner can clear all the usual procedural hurdles in the way of a challenge to a prior conviction and is prevented from attacking that conviction only for want of custody. On the other hand, it would be surprising if a prisoner advancing an enhancement claim were effectively able to circumnavigate both the custody requirement with respect to the prior conviction and the procedural requirements attending a habeas challenge to that conviction. The petitioner in *Coss* argued that he himself had done everything he could to attack his prior conviction in a timely way. Yet the thrust of his argument was that his efforts in that direction did not matter. Since he was formally challenging only his current sen-

---

circumstances. The prior conviction is conclusively presumed to be valid in the sense that there is no longer any way to attack it. Accordingly, it is *treated* as though it is valid, whether or not it would be adjudged to be sound if there were some way to obtain a judicial decision on the question.

244. In the *Johnson* case, the state court below explained its refusal to reconsider a death sentence in part on the ground that the prisoner had failed to raise an enhancement claim on appeal from his death sentence. In the Supreme Court, Justice Stevens concluded that the state court had not consistently required prisoners to raise "enhancement" claims on direct review and therefore declined to credit that procedural ruling as an adequate and independent state ground of decision. *Johnson*, 486 U.S. at 587–89. See notes 209–11 and accompanying text.

245. 532 U.S. 394 (2001).

246. Justice O'Connor noted that, in *Daniels v. United States*, 532 U.S. 374 (2001), the Court had adopted this general rule for cases involving prisoners challenging federal sentences pursuant to 28 U.S.C. §2255. See notes 47–50 and accompanying text. The decision in *Daniels*, in turn, had borrowed the rule from yet another case in another context. In *Custis v. United States*, 511 U.S. 484 (1994), the Court held that defendants in federal sentencing proceedings usually cannot argue that prior criminal convictions are invalid and thus cannot lawfully influence a new federal sentence. In *Coss*, Justice O'Connor extended the same general rule to habeas corpus cases involving prisoners challenging state sentences. *Coss*, 532 U.S. at 403–04.

247. Writing for the Court in *Daniels*, Justice O'Connor explained that states typically rely on criminal convictions, the sentences for which have been served, to decide whether citizens should be granted various privileges (like professional licenses or permits to own firearms). *Daniels*, 532 U.S. at 379–80. See Chapter IX, note 422 and accompanying text. She also insisted that federal courts would have difficulty locating, recovering, and deciphering the records of old criminal prosecutions.

tence, he suggested that he should be entitled to proceed if he satisfied the usual procedural requirements for obtaining federal habeas relief with respect to the enhancement claim alone—irrespective of whether, or how well, he had used the opportunities he once had to attack the previous conviction at the time it was entered. The Court found that position unattractive.

There is one exception to the general rule foreclosing enhancement claims, and there may be two. The one that plainly exists is for cases in which prisoners claim that a current sentence was influenced by a previous conviction obtained in violation of the basic right to counsel recognized in *Gideon v. Wainwright*.[248] A claim under *Gideon* enjoys a "special status" because the complete denial of counsel reveals a "unique constitutional defect" in state proceedings, undercutting the state court's "jurisdiction."[249] Genuine state interests in preserving that kind of conviction are minimal, if they exist at all. Moreover, the records of prior state prosecutions readily disclose whether counsel was present. So a federal district court can determine whether *Gideon* was followed without recovering and searching an entire case file. A prisoner who claims that a current sentence is invalid because it was enhanced on the basis of a *Gideon*-flawed prior conviction must satisfy the procedural prerequisites for habeas relief with respect to the enhancement claim. He must exhaust state remedies regarding that claim, avoid or overcome procedural default regarding that claim, and file a petition in advance of the applicable filing deadline. But he need not satisfy the same requirements with respect to the underlying *Gideon* claim against the previous conviction itself.[250]

The exception that *may* exist is for cases in which prisoners had no opportunity to challenge prior convictions and thus cannot be blamed for failing to do so. Justice O'-Connor gave two examples: a case in which state authorities prevented a prisoner from advancing his federal claim against an old conviction and a case in which a prisoner discovers evidence showing his innocence only after the doors to the courts have closed. She related those possibilities, in turn, to the circumstances in which relevant statutes relax general procedural bar rules on the ground that prisoners were unable to act at the time usually prescribed.[251] In cases of that kind, a challenge to a current (enhanced) sentence may be the "first and only" opportunity to press a claim against the previous conviction. Accordingly, the general rule that enhancement claims are not cognizable may give way. Justice O'Connor neither adopted this second exception in principle nor explored its potential content.[252] It seems likely, however, that the Court will embrace it in a proper case.[253]

---

248. 372 U.S. 335 (1963).

249. *Coss*, 532 U.S. at 404.

250. See *United States v. Tucker*, 404 U.S. 443 (1972); *Burgett v. Texas*, 389 U.S. 109 (1967).

251. *Coss*, 532 U.S. at 405, citing §2244(d)(1)(B) (starting the filing period for §2254 petitions only after state authorities cease actions that prevent prisoners from initiating legal action); §2244(b)(2)(B) (permitting prisoners to file second or successive §2254 habeas petitions if they discover claims going to actual innocence after an initial petition has been denied). See notes 132, 516 and accompanying text. The leeway these provisions allow defaulting prisoners overlaps with, but is even tighter than, the latitude they are permitted under the ordinary doctrine the Court itself has established for procedural default cases. See notes 214–27 and accompanying text (discussing the circumstances that constitute "cause" for default in state court).

252. Perhaps to avoid getting into it, Justice O'Connor concluded that the prisoner in *Coss* was not in a position to make this kind of argument. On reviewing the record below, she concluded that his new sentence had not actually been affected by prior convictions at all. 532 U.S. at 406.

253. For his part, Justice Scalia said that it might be preferable to deal with the "odd case" in which a prisoner has yet to have even one opportunity to press a claim by holding that the courts of the state in which the allegedly invalid conviction was obtained have a due process obligation to set

Justice O'Connor limited the general rule excluding enhancement claims to cases in which there is no longer any means by which a prisoner can challenge a prior conviction itself. There may be cases, however, in which some state avenue for litigation is still open. When that is true, the prisoner plainly must pursue that state court opportunity to attack the prior judgment. If he is successful, he certainly will wish to claim that the new sentence must be adjusted accordingly.[254] That enhancement claim, too, must be pressed first in state court. Then, if the state courts reject the enhancement claim, the prisoner may seek federal habeas corpus relief. When a case is in that posture, the general rule against enhancement claims may be inapplicable. The underlying rationales do not obtain: By hypothesis, the state has no legitimate interest in the finality of the prior conviction, and the federal court need not expend any effort to determine whether that conviction was invalid.[255] Of course, if a prisoner does not begin to attack a prior conviction until it has already been used to enhance a new sentence, the filing deadline for a habeas challenge to the enhanced sentence may arrive before the prisoner can obtain a decision invalidating the old conviction.[256] To avoid filing period complications, a district court might entertain an enhancement claim notwithstanding the general rule against them, hold the claim on the docket while the prisoner attacks the prior convic-

---

aside procedural niceties and entertain the prisoner's challenge to that conviction—if the old conviction is to justify enhancing another sentence. *Daniels*, 532 U.S. at 386–87 (concurring opinion). In the *Johnson* case, the prisoner's death sentence in Mississippi depended in part on a previous conviction in New York. After the death sentence was approved on direct review in Mississippi, the courts in New York invalidated the prior conviction there. The prisoner petitioned the Mississippi Supreme Court to reconsider the death sentence at that point, but the Mississippi court refused on various grounds. The United States Supreme Court then held that "the Federal Constitution require[d] a reexamination" of the prisoner's death sentence and remanded the case to the Mississippi Supreme Court. *Johnson*, 486 U.S. at 584.

254. If the prisoner is unsuccessful in state court, the game is up. Justice O'Connor stated squarely that the general rule excluding enhancement claims comes into play as soon as an attack on the prior conviction is foreclosed—"either because [the prisoner] failed to pursue otherwise available remedies *or because he failed to prove a constitutional violation.*" *Daniels*, 532 U.S. at 383 (emphasis added); accord *Coss*, 532 U.S. at 403.

255. Justice O'Connor broached this scenario in *Daniels*, but only obliquely. The prisoner in that case attacked a federal sentence on the theory that it had been unlawfully extended on the basis of prior state convictions. Justice O'Connor explained that the federal sentencing court would have been unable to examine those convictions at the time that court imposed the federal sentence. See note 246. If, however, the prisoner were able to upset the previous convictions at some later date, Justice O'Connor recognized that he might ask that his federal sentence be revisited. She declined to express an opinion on "the appropriate disposition of such an application." *Daniels*, 532 U.S. at 382. Recall, however, that the Court held in *Johnson v. Mississippi* that a state court cannot ignore a post-sentencing judgment upsetting a prior conviction on which a death sentence is based. See note 243. In *Johnson*, though, the Court declined to credit the state court's procedural basis for refusing to reconsider the prisoner's capital sentence. See note 244. Most circuits allow prisoners an opportunity to challenge a federal sentence when a state conviction on which the federal sentence was based is invalidated in state court. See *United States v. Doe*, 239 F.3d 473, 475 (2d Cir. 2001) (collecting illustrations). In some instances, §2255 motions have served as the vehicle. E.g., *United States v. Walker*, 198 F.3d 811 (11th Cir. 1999).

256. Arguably, the filing period for an enhancement claim should not begin running until the prisoner obtains an order invalidating the prior conviction that allegedly influenced his current term. Recall that §2244(d)(1)(D) starts the clock on the date a prisoner "could have discovered" the "factual predicate" for his claim "through the exercise of due diligence." See text accompanying note 165. Yet a state court judgment does not obviously count as a "factual" matter. See *Brackett v. United States*, 270 F.3d 60, 68–70 (1st Cir. 2001) (measuring the filing deadline for enhancement claims from the date the prisoner first became aware of the historical facts supporting his claim against the prior conviction). Cf. note 170 and accompanying text (explaining that the federal filing period is tolled only during the pendency of a state postconviction petition challenging the same judgment).

tion in state court, and then take up the enhancement claim if and when the prisoner returns with a state court judgment upsetting the previous conviction.[257]

4. Capital Cases

Procedural default in some death penalty cases is governed by statute: 28 U.S.C. §2264.[258] Initially, §2264(a) restricts a federal district court to claims that were previously "raised" and "decided on the merits" in state court, unless "the failure to raise" a claim "properly" was: (1) the "result of State action in violation of the Constitution or laws of the United States;" (2) the "result of the Supreme Court's recognition of a new Federal right that is made retroactively applicable;" or (3) "based on a factual predicate that could not have been discovered through the exercise of due diligence in time to present the claim for State or Federal post-conviction review." Then, pursuant to §2264(b), "[f]ollowing review subject to subsections (a), (d), and (e) of section 2254, the district court shall rule on the claims properly before it."[259]

This provision does not codify the Court's default doctrine in so many words. But it does largely incorporate the Court's illustrations of cause. Paragraph (1) excuses default that can be ascribed to the state. It covers both cases in which state authorities interfered with counsel's ability to comply with state procedural rules and cases in which defense counsel's performance fell below constitutional standards. Paragraph (2) covers cases in which counsel could not reasonably anticipate the emergence of a new claim. Paragraph (3) covers cases in which counsel could not discover facts to support a more conventional claim.[260] Section 2264 does not contain anything like the ordinary requirement that prisoners show not only cause, but prejudice.[261] Nor does it explicitly capture the Court's "probable innocence" safety valve.[262]

Recall that the Court's own default doctrine usually only reinforces *state* default rules.[263] Section 2264 is not (expressly) contingent on state law in the same way and thus

---

257. See note 97 and accompanying text.

258. Since §2264(a) forms part of the optional Chapter 154, it applies only in death penalty cases arising from states that have invoked that chapter. See note 67.

259. See notes 129–31 and accompanying text (discussing the implications of §2264(b) for the exhaustion doctrine).

260. See text accompanying notes 215–17. At least, this seems to be the meaning to be drawn from a formulation that, read literally, makes no sense at all. Explicitly, §2264(a)(3) states that a federal habeas court shall not consider a claim "unless the failure to raise the claim properly is... based on a factual predicate that could not have been discovered... in time to present the claim for State or Federal post-conviction review." Presumably, the idea is that the claim itself (not a prisoner's "failure to raise" the claim) is "based on a factual predicate that could not have been discovered" earlier.

261. See notes 228–30 and accompanying text.

262. The Court excuses default in "probable innocence" cases in an abundance of caution to ensure that no miscarriage of justice occurs. See text accompanying note 231. That suggests a constitutional footing. Professor Berger contends that, at the very least, death-sentenced prisoners have a constitutional right to seek relief (in some court) on the basis of new evidence undermining guilt and that ordinary procedural bar rules should not operate in cases of that kind. Vivian Berger, *Herrera v. Collins: The Gateway of Innocence for Death-Sentenced Prisoners Leads Nowhere*, 35 Wm. & Mary L. Rev. 943, 949–50 (1994). In order to avoid the delicate constitutional questions that would be presented if §2264 were read to foreclose prisoners who may actually be innocent, it may be sensible to read it to presuppose the "probable innocence" feature of the Court's doctrine.

263. See note 195 and accompanying text.

might be read to establish an entirely independent federal law of default that cuts off federal adjudication of federal claims whether or not the state courts refused, or would refuse, to consider them. A construction of that kind would be extraordinary, however. It would vanquish an elaborate body of settled doctrine without explanation (and only by negative implication). And it would contemplate that federal courts must construct yet another body of *federal* default law to be applied to *state* criminal proceedings in order to determine whether federal habeas adjudication should be available. It is more plausible to read §2264 to presuppose the familiar environment in which the federal law of default is triggered by a threshold determination that a claim was, or would be, foreclosed in state court as a matter of state law. In this vein, §2264(a) refers (ambiguously) to claims that were not raised "properly" in state court. That suggests a state law definition of what counts as "proper."[264]

D. Evidentiary Hearings

Prisoners seeking federal habeas corpus relief typically advance fact-sensitive federal claims. Several statutes, together with the §2254 and §2255 Rules,[265] prescribe the means by which district courts can develop the factual record.[266] The Court held in *Townsend v. Sain*[267] that, as a general matter, a federal court is under an obligation to conduct an evidentiary hearing if a petition alleges facts that, if true, would establish a meritorious claim and if the respondent, in turn, disputes those allegations.[268] Nevertheless, pursuant to 28 U.S.C. §2254(e), federal courts often decline to hold hearings because: (1) the relevant facts were previously determined in state court; or (2) the prisoner committed procedural default with respect to fact-finding in state court and, for that reason, is not entitled to a hearing in federal court.

1. State Court Findings of Fact

Pursuant to §2254(e)(1), federal courts must typically presume that "a determination of a factual issue by a State court" is correct.[269] Once the presumption in favor of

264. See note 175 and accompanying text (explaining that a "properly filed" petition for state postconviction relief for purposes of §2244(d)(2) is one that complies with state rules governing filing).

265. See note 63 and accompanying text.

266. For a discussion of pleading, discovery, and other preliminary matters, see Yackle, note 31, at 429–78.

267. 372 U.S. 293 (1963).

268. Id. at 317. By some accounts, §2254 Rule 8 gives federal courts discretion to forgo hearings that would not be "meaningful." E.g., *McDonald v. Johnson*, 139 F.3d 1056, 1060 (5th Cir. 1998); but see *Nieblas v. Smith*, 204 F.3d 29, 32 (2d Cir. 1999) (insisting that a district court retains power to hold a hearing if the *Townsend* standards are satisfied); see *Murphy v. Johnson*, 205 F.3d 809, 815–17 (5th Cir. 2000) (providing a discussion). Rule 8 implicitly allows federal courts to employ other means of complementing the state court file. *Cardwell v. Greene*, 152 F.3d 331, 338–39 (4th Cir. 1998). See, e.g., §2254 Rule 6 (authorizing discovery); §2254 Rule 7 (authorizing an "expansion of the record").

269. Similarly, federal courts must accord the same presumption to unarticulated findings that are logically implied by a state court's decision on the merits of a claim. *Marshall v. Lonberger*, 495 U.S. 422, 433 (1983) (construing a previous iteration of the statute).

a state factual finding is engaged, it can be rebutted only by "clear and convincing evidence" that the state court reached an erroneous determination. State court findings of fact are typically examined generously. Recall, for example, that in direct review cases the Supreme Court overturns factual findings only if they are "clearly erroneous."[270] In this instance, however, state findings receive more than the usual measure of respect. In effect, §2254(e)(1) recognizes a kind of issue preclusion with respect to state findings of fact, as distinct from conclusions of law and determinations of "mixed" questions of law and fact.

It is hard to think that federal courts must presume the accuracy of any state court findings—no questions asked.[271] In the preclusion context, the Court has said that federal courts need not respect state judgments unless litigants had a full and fair opportunity to litigate their claims.[272] Similarly in this context, federal courts may be entitled to hold the process by which state courts reach factual findings to some minimal procedural standards of fairness and regularity.[273] Consider, too, that §2254(e)(1) must be reconciled with §2254(d)(2), which has it that a federal court may award relief on the merits if a previous state court adjudication "resulted in a decision" that was "based on an unreasonable determination of the facts in light of the evidence presented in the State court proceeding."[274] Under §2254(d)(2), a federal court can scarcely be indifferent to the process by which a state court reached a factual finding or the evidentiary support that finding enjoyed. In order to determine whether findings of fact were reasonable in light of the evidence presented in state court, a federal court must have something in the way of a state record of that evidence.

Ordinarily, courts with jurisdiction to determine claims have authority to decide all the material issues. In this instance, Congress has allocated responsibility for particular issues within an individual case: In the main, questions of fact are given to state courts, while questions of law and "mixed" questions remain with federal courts.[275] Recall, however, that in most instances federal adjudication substitutes for state adjudication and does not follow state court litigation *seriatim*. In the special context of habeas corpus, federal litigation comes later. By the time a prisoner negotiates the state system and seeks habeas corpus relief from a federal court, the state courts have typically already heard what the witnesses have to say about the facts underlying federal claims and have

---

270. See Chapter VII, notes 203–04 and accompanying text.

271. Under previous law, the presumption in favor of state findings was contingent on a written statement of the state court's conclusions, sound process in state court, and fair support in the evidentiary record. Taken literally, §2254(e)(1) preserves the presumption, but eliminates the contingencies. Compare *Valdez v. Cochrell*, 274 F.3d 941, 947–54 (5th Cir. 2002) (reading the statute precisely that way), with *Miller v. Champion*, 161 F.3d 1249, 1254 (10th Cir. 1998) (holding that the presumption in favor of state findings is implicitly conditioned on a full and fair hearing in state court). The facts a state court found to exist may have been affected by the legal standard the state court brought to bear. If that legal standard was erroneous, it is questionable whether findings intimately linked with it should be presumed to be accurate. See *Mask v. McGinnis*, 233 F.3d 132, 140 (2d Cir. 2000) (declining to invoke the presumption in circumstances of that kind).

272. See Chapter VI, notes 181–85 and accompanying text.

273. See *Valdez*, 274 F.3d at 959–68 (Dennis, J., dissenting). In a statement issued on the day he signed AEDPA into law, the President said this: "If [§2254(e)] were read to deny litigants a meaningful opportunity prove the facts necessary to vindicate Federal rights, it would raise serious constitutional questions. I do not read it that way." Statement of the President, Office of the Press Secretary (April 24, 1996). See generally Larry W. Yackle, *Federal Evidentiary Hearings Under the New Habeas Corpus Statute*, 6 B.U. Pub. Int. L.J. 135, 140–41 (1996).

274. See notes 418–27 and accompanying text.

275. See Chapter I, notes 63–64 and accompanying text.

chosen to believe one version of the story over another. In this context, moreover, it is not just that one set of courts has already found the facts and it appears wasteful and potentially antagonistic to propose that another set of courts should start over on a clean slate. Federal habeas typically comes some time after state court proceedings are complete. The passage of time since the critical events occurred may frustrate another round of fact-finding. Witnesses may be unavailable, memories may be faded, and physical evidence may be lost. Federal courts might restrict themselves to an appraisal of the state court record. Yet the judge who saw the witnesses first-hand was probably in the best position to sort truth from falsehood. Accordingly, it may make some sense to accord state findings of fact a presumption of accuracy (so long as those findings were reached by means of a full and fair process).

The presumption in favor of state findings of fact places heavy weight on the familiar fact/law distinction. It is one thing to accept state findings of historical facts and quite another to accept state court applications of law to those historical facts. Findings of fact rest in the main on credibility choices; applications of law are the crux of judicial judgment on the merits of claims. The Supreme Court is acutely aware that the characterization of an issue as factual or mixed determines the court that will have primary adjudicatory responsibility. When issues are plainly mixed, the Court acknowledges as much and finds the presumption in favor of factual findings inapplicable.[276] Nevertheless, the Court is frank to say that it sometimes approaches cases from the opposite direction, first deciding as a matter of policy whether it would be best if state or federal courts decided a question and then characterizing the question as either factual or mixed in order to channel it to the courts the justices prefer.[277] Certainly, the Court often characterizes issues as factual when, in all candor, they require more than a relatively objective determination of what happened in the course of some historical episode.[278]

2. Procedural Default Revisited

Pursuant to §2254(e)(2), federal courts may sometimes deny prisoners federal evidentiary hearings on the basis of default with respect to fact-finding in state court: "If the applicant has failed to develop the factual basis of a claim in State court proceedings," a federal court "shall not hold an evidentiary hearing on the claim," unless "the applicant shows" that: (A) the claim relies on (i) "a new rule of constitutional law, made retroactive to cases on collateral review by the Supreme Court, that was previously unavailable" or (ii) "a factual predicate that could not have been previously discovered through the exercise of due diligence;" "and" (B) "the facts underlying the claim would

276. See *Sumner v. Mata*, 455 U.S. 591, 597 (1982) (acknowledging that the presumption applies only to questions of historical fact and not to mixed issues). See, e.g., *Thompson v. Keohane*, 516 U.S. 99 (1995) (holding that the "custody" of a suspect at the time of an interrogation is a mixed question to which the presumption does not apply); *Miller v. Fenton*, 474 U.S. 104 (1985) (holding that the "voluntariness" of a confession is a mixed question); *Cuyler v. Sullivan*, 446 U.S. 335 (1980) (holding that the "effectiveness" of defense counsel is also a mixed question).

277. *Miller*, 474 U.S. at 114.

278. E.g., *Wainwright v. Witt*, 469 U.S. 412 (1985) (concluding that the "bias" of a juror is a matter of historical fact to which the presumption attaches); *Maggio v. Fulford*, 462 U.S. 111 (1983) (holding that a defendant's "competency" to stand trial is equally factual). See Chapter VII, notes 200–06 and accompanying text.

be sufficient to establish by clear and convincing evidence that but for constitutional error, no reasonable factfinder would have found the applicant guilty of the underlying offense."[279]

By its terms, §2254(e)(2) limits federal hearings only if "the applicant"..."failed" to develop the facts in state court. Accordingly, the Court held in *Michael Williams v. Taylor*[280] that a federal habeas court must determine, as an initial matter, whether a prisoner seeking a federal evidentiary hearing was himself responsible for inadequate factfinding in state court. If the federal court finds that the prisoner was not at fault, the court may hold a hearing without requiring the prisoner to satisfy the standards prescribed in paragraphs (A) and (B). This result makes sense, both as a construction of the statute's text and as a matter of policy. It would be hard to justify a "no fault" rule foreclosing federal evidentiary hearings without regard to *why* the facts were not developed in state court.[281]

Writing for the Court in *Michael Williams*, Justice Kennedy explained that it is not enough that the prisoner requested an evidentiary hearing in state court. He nonetheless "failed" to develop the facts within the meaning of §2254(e)(2) if he did not undertake a "diligent search for evidence" supporting his claims and present the state courts with allegations of pertinent facts on the basis of that evidence. In *Michael Williams* itself, Justice Kennedy concluded that the prisoner had not exercised the necessary diligence in developing the factual basis for a claim that the prosecution had withheld material evidence. The prisoner's lawyer requested psychological reports regarding all prosecution witnesses. But by Justice Kennedy's account, he might have "done more" to obtain a particular report on an especially important witness. That report would have showed that the witness had initially disclaimed any knowledge of the alleged homicide. Thus it would have fortified the claim that the prosecution withheld evidence that would have helped the defense mount an effective cross-examination. Justice Kennedy found the prisoner's diligence sufficient with respect to other claims—that a would-be juror gave misleading answers to questions on *voir dire* and that the prosecutor, who knew the truth, was silent when he might have set the record straight. Justice Kennedy explained that defense counsel had no reason to know what was going on. Accordingly,

279. Prior to the 1996 Act, the Court held in *Keeney v. Tamayo-Reyes*, 504 U.S. 1 (1992), that the doctrine the Court had previously created in *Sykes* for cases in which prisoners failed to raise claims in state court equally applied to cases in which prisoners raised claims, but neglected fully to develop the supporting facts. This provision supersedes *Tamayo-Reyes*. Unlike *Tamayo-Reyes* (but like the provision in §2264) §2254(e)(2) fails to state explicitly that its application depends on a threshold determination that the state courts have imposed, or would impose, a forfeiture sanction as a matter of state law. See *Burris v. Parke*, 116 F.3d 256, 258 (7th Cir. 1997) (reading §2254(e)(2) to operate independently of state law). See notes 263–64 and accompanying text.

280. 529 U.S. 420 (2000).

281. The President made this point in his signing statement when he said that "[§2254(e)] applies to situations in which 'the applicant has failed to develop the factual basis' of his or her claim. Therefore, [§2254(e)] is not triggered when some factor that is not fairly attributable to the applicant prevented evidence from being developed in State court." Signing Statement, note 273. Section 2254(e)(2) governs only federal evidentiary hearings on prisoners' claims for relief—not hearings on other matters. When, for example, the parties dispute the facts regarding the existence of "cause" for procedural default in state court, a federal court can hold a hearing to determine what happened without first deciding whether the applicant might have developed the facts in state court. See note 216 and accompanying text. The text itself may be dispositive; §2254(e)(2) explicitly refers to hearings on a "claim." Moreover, it would be hard to suggest that prisoners should have diligently attempted to develop facts that would become meaningful only later for purposes of sorting out federal procedural default doctrine. *Cristin v. Brennan*, 281 F.3d 404, 415–19 (3d Cir. 2002).

he could not be faulted for failing to visit the hall of records and learning the truth for himself. The juror had previously been married to a prosecution witness, and the prosecutor himself had represented the juror in the divorce proceeding.

The respondent in *Michael Williams* argued that by construing the opening paragraph of §2254(e)(2) to allow a hearing if a prisoner diligently attempted to develop the facts, Justice Kennedy deprived paragraph (A)(ii) of meaning. That paragraph states that a federal hearing is prohibited if the factual predicate of a claim "could not have been previously discovered through the exercise of due diligence."[282] Justice Kennedy responded that, by its terms, paragraph (A)(ii) addresses cases in which the facts "*could* not have been discovered." That means, he explained, that the evidence in question "did not exist" to *be* discovered, irrespective of the diligence the prisoner might have exercised.[283] Evidently, Justice Kennedy had in mind entirely new materials (like scientific test results or recanting witness statements) that came into being only after state court proceedings were completed.

In cases in which §2254(e)(2) controls, prisoners can obtain a federal hearing only if they satisfy the standards in paragraphs (A) and (B). Those standards resemble the standards in §2244(d)(1), governing filing deadlines,[284] and §2244(b)(2), governing second or successive federal petitions.[285] Here again, some familiar problems appear. Notice, for example, that paragraph (A)(i) refers to new rules of "constitutional" law, thus raising again the question whether non-constitutional rules are excluded by negative implication.[286] It is hard to think that a prisoner who failed to develop the facts with respect to a non-constitutional claim in state court is out of luck in federal court no matter how "new" a claim may be, no matter how difficult it would have been to discover its "factual predicate" earlier, and no matter how closely the claim is linked to innocence.[287]

---

282. See text accompanying note 279.

283. 529 U.S. at 435–36 (emphasis added).

284. See text accompanying note 132.

285. See text accompanying note 516. Paragraphs (A) and (B) establish standards for determining whether prisoners may obtain a hearing despite their failure to exercise diligence in state court. The model at work, accordingly, is akin to the model for procedural default cases in which prisoners failed to comply with state procedural rules and, for that reason, typically cannot advance claims at all in federal court unless they pass the tests prescribed in the Court's decisions on "cause" and "prejudice" or "probable innocence." See notes 214–42 and accompanying text. There is an available argument that the standards in paragraphs (A) and (B) of this provision on federal hearings should apply as well in cases in which prisoners failed to raise claims in state court, thus displacing the Court's doctrinal rules in that context: Prisoners who neglected to raise claims at all arguably also failed to develop the underlying facts, which should bring paragraphs (A) and (B) into play. Yet the Court's favorite canon of statutory construction cuts in the opposite direction: The text of §2254(e)(2) is limited to cases in which prisoners seek federal evidentiary hearings. By negative implication, then, the policy in §2254(e)(2) does not apply to procedural default cases not involving hearings. But see notes 433–35 and accompanying text (explaining that §2254(d) almost certainly extends its influence beyond cases in which it formally controls).

286. See notes 151–53 and accompanying text.

287. Recall that paragraph (a)(2) of §2264, applicable in some death penalty cases, contemplates that a prisoner may advance a claim based on a "new Federal right." Nothing in that paragraph indicates that the right must be constitutional in character. Then, paragraph (b) of §2264 instructs federal courts to conduct their proceedings "subject to subsections (a), (d), and (e)" of §2254. That suggests that a non-constitutional claim cognizable under paragraph (a)(2) may be entitled to a federal hearing under §2254(e) and, accordingly, that the reference to "constitutional" claims in paragraph (A)(i) of §2254(e)(2) does not preclude such a hearing.

Paragraph (A)(i) also refers to rules "made retroactive to cases on collateral review by the Supreme Court." That formulation, too, is problematic.[288] A federal evidentiary hearing is always difficult inasmuch as the court must recreate events after a considerable passage of time. If a hearing is postponed until the Supreme Court itself holds that a new rule of law is retroactively available, that difficulty will be aggravated. Notice, too, that this provision on hearings must be reconciled with the related filing deadline provision. If paragraph (C) of §2244(d)(1) starts the filing period running as soon as the Court recognizes a new right, even though the Court has not yet determined that the right is retroactive, and if paragraph (A)(i) of §2254(e)(2) bars a federal hearing in the absence of a Court holding on retroactivity, prisoners will face a ticking clock with no capacity to do what the filing deadline demands—namely, file federal petitions ready, willing, and able to adduce supporting evidence in a timely manner.[289]

The standards for obtaining federal hearings in paragraphs (A) and (B) of §2254(e)(2) are stated in language that is virtually identical to the language in paragraphs (A) and (B) of §2244(b)(2), which establishes the standards for second or successive federal petitions. Yet the standards are organized differently in the two sections. In paragraph (A) of §2254(e)(2), there is a disjunctive "or" between subparagraphs (i) and (ii), indicating that a prisoner can satisfy paragraph (A) either by advancing a claim that relies on a new and retroactive rule or by showing that he could not have discovered the facts supporting a more conventional claim at the time he was in state court. Then, there is a conjunctive "and" between paragraphs (A) and (B), indicating that a prisoner who satisfies paragraph (A) must also meet the standard in paragraph (B). Paragraph (B), in turn, insists that the facts underlying the prisoner's claim must go to innocence in an extremely convincing way. In §2244(b)(2), by contrast, there is a disjunctive "or" between paragraphs (A) and (B), indicating that a prisoner can file a second or successive petition if he satisfies the standards in either paragraph. Paragraph (A) thus permits a prisoner to file another petition advancing a claim based on a new and retroactive rule, whether or not the rule is related to innocence. One would have thought that the standards for obtaining federal evidentiary hearings would be less rigid than the standards for filing multiple federal petitions. Prisoners seeking hearings have not necessarily been in federal court before; prisoners advancing second or successive petitions obviously have been to the well on at least one previous occasion. In this respect, however, the standards for obtaining federal hearings are more demanding.[290]

Both paragraph (B) of §2254(e)(2) and subparagraph (B)(ii) of §2244(b)(2) state that the new facts that a prisoner offers must undermine the judgment that the prisoner

288. See notes 154–64, 524–35 and accompanying text. Both paragraph (A) of §2254(e)(2) and paragraph (A) of §2244(b)(2) refer to new rules that have not only been made retroactively applicable to habeas cases, but also were "previously unavailable." By contrast, neither the corresponding filing deadline provision, paragraph (C) of §2244(d)(1), nor §2264(a)(2) includes that condition. In the context of §2254(e) on the availability of federal hearings, the phrase "previously unavailable" may mean unavailable at the time a prisoner was in state court for fact-finding proceedings. In the context of §2244(b)(2), it may mean unavailable at the time a prisoner filed a previous federal petition.

289. See notes 529–35 and accompanying text (discussing a similar scenario in successive petition cases).

290. See notes 518–20 and accompanying text (elaborating further on the differences between §2254(e)(2) and §2244(b)(2)).

is "guilty of the underlying offense." That formulation is problematic for any claim that goes not to the validity of a conviction, but rather to the legality of a sentence imposed after conviction. Many prisoners whose claims exclusively challenge death sentences may be unable either to obtain evidentiary hearings or to file second or successive federal petitions.[291]

E. Cognizable Claims

Federal district courts entertaining §2254 habeas corpus petitions are authorized to determine whether the custody of which prisoners complain is "in violation of the Constitution or laws or treaties of the United States."[292] When, accordingly, prisoners successfully clear the procedural hurdles set before them, they are typically in a position to contend that the criminal convictions and sentences that custodians offer to justify their detention are insufficient. In the run of cases, prisoners argue that their convictions or sentences are invalid because they were obtained in violation of prisoners' federal rights before, during, or after trial. Claims under international treaties are possible, but rare.[293] Most prisoners advance claims under the Constitution; some assert violations of some feature of federal non-constitutional law.

1. Constitutional Claims

Prisoners almost always advance constitutional claims anchored in the procedural safeguards prescribed by the Bill of Rights, applicable to state cases via the fourteenth amendment. For example, habeas petitioners may allege that they were convicted on the basis of involuntary confessions, that their trials were corrupted by racial discrimination, or that their defense attorneys rendered ineffective assistance.[294] Recall that federal district courts do not typically concern themselves with prisoners' guilt or innocence. In *Herrera v. Collins*,[295] a prisoner advanced the claim that he was innocent of the offense of which he had been convicted and that it would therefore violate the fourteenth amendment to put him to death. In the Supreme Court, Chief Justice Rehnquist took pains to separate federal habeas corpus from any routine assessment of prisoners' guilt. Habeas corpus addresses the procedures that federal law puts in place to avoid convicting the innocent, not the ultimate decision whether, after a trial consistent with those procedures, the jury reached an accurate verdict. The Chief Justice assumed for

291. See *LaFevers v. Gibson*, 238 F.3d 1263, 1267 (10th Cir. 2001) (surveying lower court decisions); notes 521–22 and accompanying text.

292. See text accompanying note 31.

293. E.g., *Breard v. Greene*, 523 U.S. 371 (1998) (*per curiam*) (implicitly acknowledging that a claim anchored in a treaty was cognizable but holding that it was barred in light of procedural default in state court).

294. For a survey of illustrative claims, see Ira P. Robbins, Habeas Corpus Checklists, Ch. 6 (2000). The federal courts' jurisdiction to consider prisoners' federal claims for habeas relief does not include supplemental jurisdiction to take up related state law claims. See *Pulley v. Harris*, 465 U.S. 37, 41 (1984) (confirming that state law claims are not cognizable in federal habeas proceedings).

295. 506 U.S. 390 (1993).

purposes of analysis that "in a capital case, a truly persuasive demonstration of 'actual innocence' made after trial would render the execution of a defendant unconstitutional, and warrant federal habeas relief if there were no state avenue open to process such a claim."[296] But he failed to elaborate that idea.

2. Non-Constitutional Claims

Prisoners who press non-constitutional federal claims for habeas corpus relief can encounter difficulty. Non-constitutional claims are cognizable only if they reveal "fundamental defects" that "inherently" result in "a complete miscarriage of justice."[297] Moreover, one extremely important non-constitutional claim is by nature unenforceable in habeas corpus, except in extraordinary circumstances. In *Stone v. Powell*,[298] the Supreme Court held that prisoners cannot ordinarily attack their detention on the ground that they were convicted on the basis of evidence obtained in violation of the fourth amendment. Justice Powell explained in *Stone* that the fourth amendment exclusionary rule is not a personal right, but is rather a judicially fashioned evidentiary standard meant to enforce the fourth amendment by deterring police misconduct. It is applicable only to proceedings in which that deterrent purpose is served sufficiently to make it worthwhile to forgo the conviction of defendants who are demonstrably guilty. If unlawfully seized evidence is excluded at trial, or if a violation of the exclusionary rule forms the basis for reversal on direct review, the Court is satisfied that the officers whose conduct is faulted will get the point and mend their ways. If, by contrast, federal courts grant habeas corpus relief on the basis of the exclusionary rule, the Court is not convinced that the rule's deterrent purpose is achieved. Habeas corpus adjudication often comes too late to carry any genuine deterrent impact.

Justice Powell explicitly disclaimed any intention of touching federal court jurisdiction, even when prisoners seek habeas relief on the basis of exclusionary rule claims.[299]

---

296. The opening the Chief Justice allowed for demonstrations of actual innocence is extremely narrow. Even so, it has excited interest in academic and political circles. It may seem sensible to lawyers that federal courts should attend only to federal legal issues and should leave assessments of guilt to juries. Yet the point of procedural safeguards is chiefly (though not entirely) to avoid erroneous convictions. It is small wonder, then, that some limited attention to the accuracy of criminal judgments should be admitted in federal habeas. Recall that courts administering procedural default doctrine have occasion to address prisoners' arguments that they are probably innocent. See notes 231–42 and accompanying text. There, however, a showing of probable innocence serves only as a "gateway" to the consideration of conventional legal claims and does not itself count as a claim on which habeas relief may be awarded. *Schlup*, 513 U.S. at 315. If it offends the Constitution to execute an innocent person, it must equally offend the Constitution to imprison such a person. Accordingly, the suggestion in *Herrera* that showings of innocence may be cognizable cannot be limited to death penalty cases. Professor Steiker has developed an argument that federal habeas courts can entertain "bare-innocence" claims. Jordan Steiker, *Innocence and Federal Habeas*, 41 U.C.L.A. L. Rev. 303 (1993). By contrast, Professor Berger concludes (reluctantly) that federal courts should not ordinarily second-guess trial court determinations of guilt. Berger, note 262.

297. *Reed v. Farley*, 512 U.S. 339, 354 (1994) (involving a claim that state authorities had violated an interstate compact). Of course, state prisoners rarely have non-constitutional claims at all. Federal prisoners proceeding under §2255 are much more likely to complain that their convictions or sentences rest on violations of federal statutes or court rules. There, too, only "fundamental defects" will suffice. *Hill v. United States*, 368 U.S. 424 (1962) (involving an alleged violation of Fed. R. Crim. P. 32); *United States v. Timmreck*, 441 U.S. 780 (1979) (involving an alleged violation of Fed. R. Crim. P. 11).

298. 428 U.S. 465 (1976).

299. Id. at 494 n.37.

The point of *Stone* is not the nature and scope of habeas corpus, but rather the nature and purpose of the exclusionary rule. Nevertheless, when Justice Powell described the exceptional circumstances in which federal courts can entertain exclusionary rule claims, he relied on a familiar device for allocating judicial authority: the process model.[300] Federal district courts can consider exclusionary rule claims if prisoners were denied an "opportunity" for "full and fair adjudication" in state court.[301] By making an "opportunity" for state court adjudication critical, Justice Powell declared that federal courts should rebuff not only claims previously treated and rejected in state court, but also claims that were not, but might have been, determined there. He thus interpreted the exclusionary rule to introduce both issue and claim preclusion into habeas corpus cases involving exclusionary rule claims: If state courts consider a prisoner's claim and find it wanting, the prisoner is typically barred from attempting to relitigate that claim in federal court. If state courts offer a prisoner a means of litigating an exclusionary rule claim and the prisoner does not seize that opportunity, federal habeas corpus is also foreclosed.[302]

3. Harmless Error

If a federal court determines that a claim is meritorious, the court turns to the analytically subsequent question whether the error it has identified was harmless.[303] If the court concludes that the error was harmless, it withholds habeas relief on that basis.[304]

---

300. See Chapter I, notes 73–77 and accompanying text.

301. *Stone*, 428 U.S. at 481–82.

302. The consequences of *Stone* were immediate and dramatic. Federal enforcement of the exclusionary rule in habeas corpus proceedings ground to a halt. See Philip Halpern, *Federal Habeas Corpus and the Mapp Exclusionary Rule After Stone v. Powell*, 82 Colum. L. Rev. 1 (1982). Thereafter, some members of the Court contended that other claims should be handled in the same way. E.g., *Duckworth v. Eagan*, 492 U.S. 195, 205 (1989) (O'Connor, J., concurring) (joined by Scalia, J.) (offering *Miranda* claims as candidates). Yet the full Court explained in a series of decisions that *Stone* is limited to the fourth amendment exclusionary rule. E.g., *Withrow v. Williams*, 507 U.S. 680 (1993) (holding that *Miranda* claims are cognizable in the ordinary course). See *Kimmelman v. Morrison*, 477 U.S. 365 (1986) (holding that prisoners can contend that their sixth amendment rights were violated when defense counsel failed to raise an exclusionary rule objection to unlawfully seized evidence). In 1982, the Reagan Administration proposed an amendment to §2254, which would have barred federal district courts from awarding habeas relief on the basis of any claim that had previously been "fully and fairly" adjudicated in state court. The Reagan Administration's Proposed Reforms in Habeas Corpus Procedures (1982); see note 65. That initiative would have made *issue* preclusion the rule for all manner of claims advanced in federal habeas proceedings. Attorney General Smith conceded at the time that the point of the scheme was "simple abolition" of the writ for state prisoners. William F. Smith, *A Proposal for Habeas Corpus Reform*, in Criminal Justice Reform: A Blueprint (McGuigan & Rader eds. 1983). The Reagan Administration's plan was unsuccessful in Congress. See Yackle, note 52, at 2357–64.

303. The Court explained in *Lockhart v. Fretwell*, 506 U.S. 364 (1993), that a court properly takes up the harmless error question only if it first determines that error did actually occur. Id. at 369 n.2. Professor Kamin has pointed out that this sequencing of the issues preserves federal courts' capacity to speak clearly about the content of federal rights in the first instance. If courts were to begin by deciding whether error, if it existed, was harmless anyway, they would compromise their basic law-declaration function. Sam Kamin, *Harmless Error and the Rights/Remedies Split*, 88 Va. L. Rev. 1 (2002). See notes 315–67 and accompanying text (discussing the *Teague* doctrine); Chapter X, notes 446–94 and accompanying text (discussing qualified immunity).

304. See *Milton v. Wainwright*, 407 U.S. 371 (1972).

Some "structural defects" so undermine the integrity of the process that they can never be harmless.[305] In most instances, however, federal courts identify errors at trial that can be overlooked if they had no significant impact on the proceedings. When the Supreme Court considers cases on direct review of state court judgments, it employs a demanding test: The state must demonstrate that error was harmless "beyond a reasonable doubt."[306] In *Brecht v. Abrahamson*,[307] Chief Justice Rehnquist explained that a "less onerous" standard is applicable to cases reaching federal court via petitions for federal habeas corpus relief. In habeas cases, trial errors were harmless if they had no "substantial and injurious effect or influence" on the outcome of a prisoner's trial.[308] Under that standard, error was harmless in the absence of "actual prejudice."[309] In habeas, too, the burden of showing error to be harmless lies with the state. In *O'Neal v. McAninch*,[310] Justice Breyer said that when the evidence is in "equipoise," and a district court is in "grave doubt," the court should treat an error as if it had the necessary substantial effect on the verdict.[311]

Chief Justice Rehnquist acknowledged in *Brecht* that the habeas corpus statutes prescribe no standard for harmless error. Accordingly, he fashioned an appropriate test as a matter of judicial policy. As the Chief Justice explained it, the benefits of applying the "beyond a reasonable doubt" standard to habeas cases would be modest: State courts generally enforce constitutional rights and require no strong measures to "deter" them from committing constitutional error at trial.[312] The costs of employing that more demanding standard would be significant by comparison—namely, the demonstrable interference with state judgments, the bother and expense of curative state proceedings, and the possibility that guilty prisoners may escape punishment if the evidence supporting their guilt has become stale and they are acquitted after retrial.[313] Those costs attend any case in which a federal court awards relief. Chief Justice Rehnquist's explanation for *Brecht* is thus another illustration of the current Court's tendency to curb federal habeas corpus for state prisoners.[314]

---

305. See *Arizona v. Fulminante*, 499 U.S. 279, 290 (1991) (citing a violation of the right to counsel as an illustration).

306. *Chapman v. California*, 386 U.S. 18, 24 (1967). Since the Supreme Court itself uses the "beyond a reasonable doubt" standard on direct review, the state courts below are equally obliged to use that standard when they review trial errors directly. The *Chapman* approach to harmless error in cases on direct review has constitutional overtones. But see Daniel J. Meltzer, *Harmless Error and Constitutional Remedies*, 61 U. Chi. L. Rev. 1, 26 (1994) (arguing that *Chapman* states a proposition of federal common law—applicable both in the Court itself and in state court); see Chapter VIII, notes 47–119 and accompanying text (discussing federal common law).

307. 507 U.S. 619 (1993).

308. Id. at 637, quoting *Kotteakos v. United States*, 328 U.S. 750, 776 (1946).

309. Id. In *Brecht*, the state courts had properly applied the *Chapman* standard, and it may have been for that reason that the Supreme Court thought it sufficient if a federal habeas court applied a less demanding test. In a case in which the state courts did not bring *Chapman* to bear, it may be appropriate for a federal habeas court itself to use that standard rather than the standard in *Brecht*. See *Orndorff v. Lockhart*, 998 F.2d 1426, 1430 (8th Cir. 1993). See note 409 (discussing the effect of §2254(d) on harmless error analysis).

310. 513 U.S. 432 (1995).

311. Id. at 444–45.

312. *Brecht*, 507 U.S. at 636.

313. Id. at 637.

314. For critiques of *Brecht*, see James S. Liebman & Randy Hertz, *Brecht v. Abrahamson: Harmful Error in Habeas Corpus Law*, 84 J. Crim. L. & Criminology 1109 (1994); Yackle, note 52, at 2408–15.

F. The Ban on New Rules

1. In General

Prisoners seeking federal habeas relief also encounter difficulty if they advance claims that depend on novel theories of law. The Supreme Court draws a sharp line between cases the Court itself considers on "direct review" from a state court judgment affirming a conviction, on the one hand, and cases that arrive in federal court by means of "collateral review," on the other. Collateral review cases include those in which the Court examines state court judgments denying relief in state postconviction proceedings and cases in which prisoners reach federal court by petitioning for the writ of habeas corpus.[315] When litigants press new theories on direct review, the Court entertains their arguments routinely and formulates the rule of law it thinks appropriate, however much the resulting rule may depart from the past. When, by contrast, litigants advance new theories in a collateral review posture, virtually the opposite default position obtains: Claims that depend on the creation of new rules of law are *not* usually cognizable.

The Supreme Court rarely grants *certiorari* review when the state court judgment below was a denial of state postconviction relief.[316] As a practical matter, then, the ban on "new rule" claims affects federal habeas corpus, which supplies the typical means by which prisoners find their way to federal court after the state's highest court has affirmed their convictions and sentences on direct review and any direct review *certiorari* proceedings in the Supreme Court are complete. It is scarcely coincidental that the effect of the ban on "new rule" claims in collateral review cases should primarily be felt in federal habeas. In the leading case, *Teague v. Lane*,[317] Justice O'Connor explained that the ban orchestrates federal-state relations and ensures in yet another way that lower federal courts accord proper comity to state courts. The "new rule" ban achieves that end by adjusting the availability of a particular federal remedy: the writ of habeas corpus.[318] Justice O'Connor did not rest the *Teague* ban on "new rule" claims on the Con-

---

315. This can be confusing. If the Court reviews a state court judgment rendered in state postconviction proceedings, that review is "direct" in the sense that the Court examines the validity of a decision rendered by the highest state court below. The point, though, is that the Court does not straightforwardly examine for error that court's earlier judgment affirming the conviction and sentence on "direct review" from the trial court. Courts and lawyers conventionally refer to "direct review" as "appellate review" or (redundantly) as "direct appeal" in order to distinguish the initial review of a trial court judgment by appellate courts from "collateral review," which typically occurs via independent "postconviction" petitions or motions filed at the trial court level and thus is "collateral" to the original trial and appellate proceedings. See note 104. Strictly speaking, federal habeas corpus is not a form of "review" at all. See notes 44–46 and accompanying text. Yet habeas is often called "collateral review"—again, in order to clarify that habeas is not part of the "direct review" process, which proceeds vertically from the original conviction at the state trial court level, through the state appellate courts, to the Supreme Court. See note 149.

316. See *Kyles v. Whitley*, 498 U.S. 931, 932 (1990) (Stevens, J., concurring) (explaining that state postconviction procedures often inject complexity into cases and thus make *certiorari* grants undesirable). Moreover, the deadline for filing a federal habeas petition is probably not tolled during the time required to petition the Court for *certiorari* review of a state court judgment on a state postconviction petition. See note 185 and accompanying text. Accordingly, prisoners are discouraged from seeking Supreme Court review of state court decisions rendered at the postconviction stage of state proceedings.

317. 489 U.S. 288 (1989).

318. Id. at 308. See note 90 (discussing comity as the rationale for the exhaustion doctrine). Professor Fallon and Professor Meltzer contend that *Teague* should be understood as an attempt to

stitution or any statute enacted by Congress. Instead, the *Teague* doctrine is a creature of the Court's own policy-making.

Whenever the Court announces a new rule, the Court maintains that fairness demands the application of that new rule not only to the litigant in the case at bar, but also to all other litigants similarly situated. This is true if the Court creates a new rule in a case on direct review; it is also true if the Court announces a new rule in a case on collateral review.[319] *Ceteris paribus*, similarly situated litigants are in the same position as the party in the instant case, which provided the Court with a vehicle for creating the rule. It would be unfair, then, to treat them differently merely because the Court plucked someone else's case out of the stream of cases presenting the same issue. The Court recognizes that by applying a new rule to a case in which the state courts may have rejected a claim in reliance on prior precedents, the Court necessarily gives the new rule "retroactive" effect. And the Court is acutely aware that retroactive changes in the law are disruptive. Nevertheless, in cases on direct review, the Court finds it essential to entertain novel theories in order to function as the system's ultimate referee. The Court must shoulder the responsibility to address any innovative claims a party may have in order to articulate the supreme law in an accurate and uniform manner. If the Court announces a new rule, the unsettlement caused by extending that rule to similarly situated litigants must be endured. The Court thus applies the new rule to the instant case, to future cases, and to any cases pending at trial or on direct review—including cases in which the state courts have already rejected the same claim in light of prior precedents, but in which their judgments are still subject to direct review in the Supreme Court. It would violate "basic norms of constitutional adjudication" to refuse to apply a newly declared rule of federal law to a criminal case in which the judgment is not yet final when the rule is announced.[320]

By contrast, the Court insists that in cases that arrive in federal court on collateral review, the same justification for considering novel theories does not hold. By hypothesis, habeas corpus petitioners hope to affect state judgments that *are* final in the sense that they are no longer subject to appellate review for error. Federal adjudication of claims in habeas proceedings need not be, and typically is not, an occasion for the authoritative specification of federal law, now and for the foreseeable future. The purpose served by federal habeas is different, pedestrian by comparison. In *Teague*, Justice O'Connor explained that, theory to one side, the practical function of the federal writ is "deterrence"—namely, to give state courts an incentive "to conduct their proceedings in a

---

adjust the remedies available in circumstances in which the law is in flux. Richard H. Fallon, Jr. & Daniel J. Meltzer, *New Law, Non-Retroactivity, and Constitutional Remedies*, 104 Harv. L. Rev. 1731, 1766, 1813–20 (1991). Recall that Congress generally has considerable authority to determine what remedies are available to enforce federal law. Chapter VIII, notes 124–27, 194–97, 223–30 and accompanying text. See notes 409–27 and accompanying text (discussing the way in which §2254(d) governs the availability of federal habeas relief).

319. *Teague*, 489 U.S. at 300.

320. *Griffith v. Kentucky*, 479 U.S. 314, 322 (1987). The Court takes the same view of changes in the law affecting ordinary civil litigation. See *Harper v. Virginia Dep't of Taxation*, 509 U.S. 86 (1993). Then again, litigants in cases still subject to direct review may be unable to take advantage of a new rule if they failed to comply with state procedures for raising an appropriate claim in state court proceedings. See Chapter VII, notes 164–68 and accompanying text. If a new rule were announced and applied in a federal habeas case, thus becoming available to other prisoners whose convictions are final, most would-be beneficiaries would presumably be foreclosed on procedural grounds. But see notes 218–21.

manner consistent with established constitutional standards."[321] State courts, in turn, can only be expected to recognize rules of federal law that are well settled. If federal district courts give retroactive effect to a new rule that is announced after a conviction is already final, they achieve little deterrent effect.[322] Accordingly, the disruptions that would be caused by announcing new rules and extending their benefits to all similarly situated prisoners are not justified. To avoid those disruptions, federal habeas courts usually do not entertain claims that depend on novel theories and thus avoid placing themselves in a position to announce new rules and extend their benefits to prisoners whose convictions and sentences are already final.[323]

The limitation that *Teague* imposes on federal habeas corpus is not jurisdictional. The custodian must object that a prisoner's claim is barred because it necessarily depends on a new rule.[324] When the custodian raises a sufficient objection, the district

---

321. 489 U.S. at 306, quoting *Desist v. United States*, 394 U.S. 244, 262–63 (1969) (Harlan, J., dissenting). Justice O'Connor generally relied for her analysis on Justice Harlan's opinions objecting to the Warren Court's enthusiasm for habeas corpus. See also *Mackey v. United States*, 401 U.S. 667, 692–93 (1971) (concurring opinion). Recall that in traditional theory habeas corpus does not focus on previous court judgments at all, but attaches to the prisoner's current detention. See notes 44–46 and accompanying text. Obviously, there is a certain rhetorical tension between Justice O'-Connor's opinion in *Teague*, which had it that the point of federal habeas is to "deter" state courts from ignoring federal constitutional standards, and Chief Justice Rehnquist's insistence in *Brecht* that state courts need nothing to "deter" them from violating federal rights. See note 312 and accompanying text. But that tension is entirely verbal and bears no programmatic implications. Justice O'Connor did not bring heavier weaponry to bear on state courts in order to achieve deterrence, but (once again) curtailed the authority of federal courts entertaining habeas petitions from state prisoners. Professor Hoffmann explains that the deterrence theory of habeas corpus embraced in *Teague* has conceptual implications. Joseph L. Hoffmann, *The Supreme Court's New Vision of Federal Habeas Corpus for State Prisoners*, 1989 Sup. Ct. Rev. 165. Professor Lee has compared and contrasted the deterrence theory of the writ with the approaches suggested in prior decisions and in the academic literature. Evan Tsen Lee, *Theories of Federal Habeas Corpus*, 72 Wash. U. L.Q. 151 (1994).

322. In this instance, then, the Court conceives that the point of habeas jurisdiction itself is to deter misconduct by state officials. Accordingly, the Court has adjusted habeas corpus to correspond to that purpose. In *Stone v. Powell*, by contrast, the Court limited habeas in response to the deterrent purpose of the exclusionary rule. See notes 298–302.

323. The Warren Court, too, sometimes denied retroactive effect to novel principles of constitutional law. In the 1960s, when that Court frequently gave constitutional safeguards an innovative interpretation, there was a very practical reason for giving at least some of those new ideas prospective effect only. If the establishment of a new rule of law inevitably meant that cases decided under previous understandings had to be revisited, the Court would have hesitated to be so creative in the first place. If, however, the Court could avoid upsetting old convictions, it could move the law along at lower cost. When, accordingly, the Warren Court reached a decision that made a "clear break" with precedent, the Court sometimes declared that the new rule would not apply retroactively. *Desist*, 394 U.S. at 248. If a "clear break" decision was not essential to protect the innocent, and if its application would upset reliance interests, the Court denied its benefits to prisoners whose claims rested on prior events or judgments. See, e.g., *Linkletter v. Walker*, 381 U.S. 618, 636–37 (1965) (holding that the fourth amendment exclusionary rule announced in *Mapp v. Ohio* would not be applied retroactively); *Pickelsimer v. Wainwright*, 375 U.S. 2 (1963) (applying the right to counsel announced in *Gideon v. Wainright* retrospectively). The Warren Court drew no distinction between cases on direct and collateral review, but announced the rules of law it thought proper in both contexts. Then, the Court turned to the retrospective reach of a decision as a separate question. In every case, the Warren Court wrestled with that question by, first, deciding whether a rule was truly new (and thus presented a retroactivity question at all) and, second, weighing the values served by retrospective application against the effect on state interests.

324. *Collins v. Youngblood*, 497 U.S. 37, 40–41 (1990). See *Goeke v. Branch*, 514 U.S. 115 (1995) (concluding that the state had sufficiently preserved a *Teague* issue below); *Schiro v. Farley*, 510 U.S.

court addresses the "new rule" question before going further.[325] Initially, the court must ascertain the date on which the prisoner's conviction became final. That is not the date on which the state's highest court affirmed the conviction. It is the date on which the Supreme Court denied *certiorari* or, if no petition for *certiorari* was filed, the date on which the time for filing a petition expired.[326] Next, the court sorts through the case law that existed on that date and identifies the "old" rule controlling at the time. That is the rule the court applies to the prisoner's current claim. Accordingly, the general ban on "new" rules is best understood as a choice-of-law doctrine. The analysis required by *Teague* selects the legal rule that governs a claim advanced in an application for the writ of habeas corpus. Specifically, a federal court entertaining a habeas corpus petition applies the rule of law that prevailed when the prisoner's conviction became final on direct review, not (necessarily) the rule that prevails when the prisoner appears in federal court later.[327]

Of course, the Supreme Court might hand down a decision concededly announcing a new rule after the date on which the state's highest court affirms a prisoner's conviction but before the time for seeking *certiorari* has run out or the Supreme Court concludes the appellate process by acting on a petition for *certiorari* review. In that event, the prisoner is entitled to the benefit of the new rule in federal habeas, even though the state courts have had no opportunity to consider it on direct review. The Court might also render a decision announcing a new rule after a prisoner's conviction and sentence are final, but before the highest state court considers a claim based on the new rule in state postconviction proceedings. In that event, the state court does have an opportunity to apply the new rule. Nevertheless, the state court may be able to ignore the new rule without fear that its judgment will be effectively upset either by the Supreme Court or by inferior federal courts in habeas corpus proceedings.[328] These complications conceded, the Court has a reason for choosing the date on which a state conviction be-

---

222 (1994) (indicating that a belated *Teague* argument might be heard as a means of defending a lower court judgment on alternative grounds).

325. *Caspari v. Bohlen*, 510 U.S. 383, 389 (1994) (summarizing the analysis in *Teague* cases); *Horn v. Banks*, 122 S.Ct. 2147, 2150–51 (2002) (*per curiam*) (confirming *Caspari* on this point). While any *Teague* issues in a case should be treated before a federal court reaches the merits of a claim, any procedural bar issues ordinarily should be treated before *Teague*. *Lambrix v. Singletary*, 520 U.S. 518, 524–25 (1997).

326. *O'Dell v. Netherland*, 521 U.S. 151, 157 (1997).

327. See *Wright v. West*, 505 U.S. 277, 310–13 (1992) (Souter, J., concurring). If the court identifies the applicable rule, applies it to the circumstances of a particular case, and reaches the conclusion that the claim is meritorious, it still is not clear that the court must order the prisoner released unless the error is cured. If the error was harmless in the sense that it had no substantial effect on the outcome in state court, the prisoner is not entitled to relief. See notes 303–14 and accompanying text. Moreover, relief may be denied on a different basis pursuant to §2254(d). See notes 409–27 and accompanying text.

328. See notes 476–79 and accompanying text. If the state court fails to give the prisoner the benefit of a new rule established since the prisoner's conviction became final, the Supreme Court will not reverse. In operation, the *Teague* doctrine does not simply forgive state courts for failing to enforce rules of which they are unaware. Instead, *Teague* makes a new rule unavailable to prisoners in collateral proceedings, whether the state court is aware of the new rule or not. If the state court applies a new rule and sustains the prisoner's claim, the Supreme Court's reaction will turn on an assessment of the state court's reasons. If the state court enforces the new rule in the erroneous belief that it is required by federal law to do so, the Court will presumably reverse. If, however, the state court understands that the new rule is not cognizable as a matter of federal law, but enforces it anyway, the Court may conclude that the state court's decision rests on an independent state ground. See Chapter VII, notes 116–59 and accompanying text.

comes final as the cut-off. The conceptual rationale in *Teague* demands a clear delineation between cases in which "new rule" claims are routinely articulated and applied in the interests of fairness, on the one hand, and cases in which "new rule" claims are not ordinarily cognizable, on the other. Any case that is still formally subject to direct review in the Supreme Court must fall in the former category. By contrast, any case in which the prisoner's claim can be considered only in a collateral posture must fall in the latter category.[329]

Caveat. The *Teague* doctrine significantly restricts the capacity of federal courts to adjudicate claims that prisoners are in custody in violation of federal law. In all candor, however, the reason is *not* that *Teague* bars federal habeas courts from giving retroactive effect to authentic changes in the content of legal standards. The real story is buried in the meaning *Teague* attaches to "new rules." By defining "new" rules (that federal habeas courts usually cannot enforce) in an extraordinarily expansive way, the Court necessarily defines "old" rules (that habeas courts *can* apply) in an extremely narrow manner. In consequence, federal courts are prevented from adjudicating claims that do not depend on legal principles that are genuinely "new" in any ordinary sense. That being so, *Teague* has implications both for the conceptual understanding of federal habeas corpus associated with *Brown v. Allen* in 1953[330] and for the limitations on habeas relief established by AEDPA in 1996.[331] The Court insists that *Teague* demands an analysis that is "distinct" from the inquiries mandated by 28 U.S.C. §2254(d).[332] Yet there is a relationship between *Teague* and that statute.[333] If the two are to live together peaceably, the definitions of "new" and "old" rules for *Teague* purposes must be adjusted: "old" rules within the meaning of *Teague* must be redefined as "clearly established" law within the meaning of §2254(d).[334]

2. Exceptions

There are two exceptions to the usual prohibition on "new rule" claims in habeas corpus proceedings: (1) new rules that place "certain kinds of primary, private individual conduct beyond the power of the criminal law-making authority to proscribe;" and (2) rules "without which the likelihood of an accurate conviction is seriously diminished."[335] The first exception is narrow, meant primarily to cover cases in which federal *substantive* law develops to insulate citizens from criminal punishment at all.[336] The sec-

329. Professor Hoffmann argues, by contrast, that the "theoretical underpinnings" of *Teague* "virtually compel" making the crucial point the date on which the highest state court acts on a prisoner's claim. Joseph L. Hoffmann, *Retroactivity and the Great Writ: How Congress Should Respond to Teague v. Lane*, 1990 B.Y.U. L. Rev. 183, 216 n.135. Cf. notes 472–79 and accompanying text (discussing the analog issue regarding §2254(d)).

330. 344 U.S. 443 (1953); see note 55 and accompanying text.

331. See note 65 and accompanying text.

332. *Banks*, 122 S.Ct. at 2151.

333. See notes 401–02 and accompanying text.

334. See notes 446–61 and accompanying text.

335. *Teague*, 489 U.S. at 311, 313. Justice O'Connor borrowed these two exceptions from Justice Harlan, but in a modified form. Harlan would have extended the second exception to any rule requiring "procedures" that are "implicit in the concept of ordered liberty." *Mackey*, 401 U.S. at 693 (concurring opinion), quoting *Palko v. Connecticut*, 302 U.S. 319, 325 (1937). Justice O'Connor rejected that possibility as too generous and substituted the requirement that rules covered by the second exception must go to the accuracy of the guilt-determination function.

336. One of Justice Harlan's examples was the rule announced in *Griswold v. Connecticut*, 381 U.S. 479 (1965), where the Court held that Connecticut violated substantive due process by making

ond exception is also narrow, here again importing an explicit attention to guilt or innocence into habeas corpus doctrine. To fit within the second exception, a rule must meet two requirements. It must "seriously diminish the likelihood of obtaining an accurate conviction," and it must "alter our understanding of the bedrock procedural elements essential to the fairness of a proceeding."[337] Justice O'Connor said in *Teague* that it is "unlikely" that there are many new rules so essential to accurate decision-making, but yet to emerge.[338] In the current climate, that is understatement worthy of the British aristocracy. The Court has identified no new rules that fit the second exception, and it may ultimately prove to be a null set.[339]

It would be hard to justify the *Teague* ban on "new rule" claims if these exceptions at least were not recognized. Accordingly, the exceptions may have some basis in due process.[340] The truth of the matter is, however, that the exceptions are defined so nar-

---

it a crime for married people to use contraceptives. *Mackey*, 401 U.S. at 692 n.7 (concurring opinion). In an opinion for the Court in *Penry v. Lynaugh*, 492 U.S. 302 (1989), Justice O'Connor held that the first exception captured a claim that a prisoner with the mental capacity of a child could not be executed. O'Connor acknowledged that the claim in *Penry* did not fit precisely. But she candidly expanded the first exception to reach new rules that bar certain punishments for a "class of defendants" identified by "status or offense." Id. at 330. On the merits, the Court rejected the prisoner's claim. But see *Atkins v. Virginia*, 122 S.Ct. 2242 (2002) (ultimately holding that the eighth amendment bars the execution of "mentally retarded" convicts).

337. *Sawyer v. Smith*, 497 U.S. 227, 242 (1990), quoted in *Tyler v. Cain*, 533 U.S. 656, 665 (2001).

338. *Teague*, 489 U.S. at 313.

339. But see notes 525–33 and accompanying text (noting the possibility that the *Cage* decision fits the second *Teague* exception).

340. In *Fiore v. White*, 531 U.S. 225 (2001), the prisoner was convicted of violating a Pennsylvania statute making it a crime to conduct a waste disposal business without a permit. In fact, the prisoner had a permit to operate his facility, but he was convicted nonetheless. An intermediate state appellate court affirmed the conviction on the theory that if the defendant was shown to have conducted his business well beyond the authority granted by a permit, he could be held to have operated without a permit at all. The state supreme court declined to entertain the prisoner's argument that the statute should be read literally. Thereafter, the state supreme court reviewed a co-defendant's conviction arising from the same episode and, in that case, ruled after all that the statute condemned only operators who failed to obtain a permit of any kind. The prisoner then filed an application for state postconviction relief, hoping to have the benefit of the new decision. His petition was denied, both because his claim had been rejected previously on direct review and because his appeal was no longer pending when the state supreme court delivered its decision in the co-defendant's case. The prisoner then sought federal habeas corpus relief, claiming that the state courts denied him due process by sustaining his conviction while reversing the conviction of his co-defendant. The Supreme Court ultimately granted *certiorari* to determine the merits of that due process claim. The Court postponed consideration of the question until the state supreme court answered a certified question: whether the construction placed on the state statute in the co-defendant's case was correct at the time the two men were convicted. See Chapter XI, notes 92–94 and accompanying text (discussing certification). In response, the state supreme court explained that its decision in the co-defendant's case did not announce a "new rule of law," but merely clarified the statute's meaning. At that point, Justice Breyer explained for the Court that the due process question the Court had originally meant to decide was no longer presented. Since the prisoner had a permit, he could not be convicted of violating the statute as authoritatively construed. Id. at 228–29, relying on *In re Winship*, 397 U.S. 358 (1970) (holding that due process requires the prosecution to prove all elements of an offense). Accordingly, Breyer remanded the case to the circuit court for the award of federal habeas corpus relief. Cf. *Bousley v. United States*, 523 U.S. 614 (1998) (treating a case involving clarification of a federal criminal statute in the same way but withholding §2255 relief until the lower court assessed the government's argument that the prisoner was foreclosed for procedural default); see notes 241–42 and accompanying text. The result in *Fiore* made it unnecessary to decide whether due process would equally have been violated if the state supreme court had regarded its

rowly that they have no significant field of operation. Moreover, their microscopic content makes various provisions in AEDPA equally marginal—provisions that depend on the existence of new "rules" or new "rights" having retroactive application in collateral proceedings.[341] If those provisions incorporate by reference *Teague's* account of what counts as "new" and contemplate that a new rule or right is retroactively enforceable in habeas only if it fits one of the two exceptions, they, too, have virtually no serious consequences for any body of cases (and certainly offer nothing to justify the adjacent interpretive difficulties they entail).[342]

3. The Definition of New Rules

The Supreme Court has defined "new rules" for *Teague* purposes in two kinds of cases: (1) cases in which prisoners advance claims that depend on some recent precedent that arguably changed the law from what it was at the time their convictions became final; and (2) cases in which prisoners press claims that do not rely on any particular recent precedent, but nonetheless rest on a legal theory that the district court arguably can accept only by itself announcing and applying a change in the law.

Recent precedents. Cases in which prisoners rely on recent precedents readily lend themselves to a retroactivity analysis. In the paradigm case, a prisoner files a habeas corpus petition citing a recent Supreme Court decision that has just resolved a division among the lower courts on a legal issue. It is fair to ask whether that decision changed the law from what it was previously. If it did *not*, but, instead, merely explained that some lower courts were mistaken about the legal rule in question, the prisoner does not need the recent decision in order to prevail. The district court can rely on earlier precedents that the Court has reaffirmed. If, by contrast, the Court's recent decision *did* change the law, the situation is altered. Pursuant to *Teague*, the district court usually cannot entertain a claim based on that decision.

If the *Teague* doctrine barred prisoners from invoking recent decisions that obviously establish new propositions of law, its practical effect would be modest and its intellectual foundations largely non-controversial. According to the Court, however, decisions do not have to be especially creative in order to establish new rules. In *Teague*, Justice O'Connor said that "a case announces a new rule when it breaks new ground or imposes a new obligation" on the government.[343] In other cases, the Court has explained that "clear breaks" from precedent are not necessary: "[G]radual developments in the law over which reasonable jurists may disagree" can also produce entirely new rules.[344]

Innovative claims. Cases in which prisoners cite no particular recent precedent do not immediately appear to present a retroactivity problem at all. But on examination, the same policy is at stake: Just as *Teague* bars a federal district court from entertaining

---

new construction of the state statute as "new" law, but refused to apply that new law to a case in which the conviction was final before the new decision was rendered.

341. See notes 147–64, 288–89, 523–35 and accompanying text.

342. But see notes 446–61 and accompanying text (explaining that §2254(d) alters *Teague's* definitions of new and old rules).

343. *Teague*, 489 U.S. at 301. Justice O'Connor explained in *Teague* itself that since the Court had previously held that racial groups need not be proportionately represented on juries, a rule requiring juries to reflect the racial make-up of the community would be new.

344. *Sawyer v. Smith*, 497 U.S. 227, 234 (1990). See note 323 (explaining that the Warren Court considered only "clear breaks" from the past to be "new" for retroactivity purposes).

a claim that depends on a recent Supreme Court decision announcing a new rule, *Teague* equally bars a district court from itself fashioning a new rule and then applying that rule to resolve a prisoner's pending habeas corpus claim. To assess the originality of the rule of law on which a prisoner relies, a district court must do essentially the same thing that it would do to determine the novelty of a recent Supreme Court decision. The task is to look back at the precedents that were in place at the time the prisoner's conviction became final and to determine whether those precedents stood even then for the legal rule that the prisoner wishes to enforce. If so, the district court can apply that rule without doing anything new. If not, the district court must itself announce and apply a new rule of law in order to sustain the prisoner's claim. That, of course, is what *Teague* usually prohibits.

Here, too, the Supreme Court's conception of new rules is expansive. Habeas corpus petitioners do not have to ask a federal district court to be very imaginative at all in order to be charged with seeking the creation of a new rule of law. Unless previous precedents "dictated"[345] or "compelled"[346] the conclusion that a prisoner's claim was valid when his conviction became final, a district court would have to create a new rule of law in order to find the prisoner's claim meritorious today. Moreover, the district court's "application" of a settled rule of law to the facts of an analogous case may also "involve a new rule."[347] That is so, because even a familiar rule can be "extended" if it is applied in a "novel setting."[348] A district court thus establishes a new rule whenever it reaches a decision different from an "outcome" that was "susceptible to debate among reasonable minds" at the time a prisoner's conviction became final.[349]

4. Comparison with Qualified Immunity

The *Teague* doctrine shares intellectual features with qualified immunity doctrine.[350] If all the Court's statements are taken literally, *Teague* arguably insulates state court judgments on federal claims as much or more than qualified immunity protects executive of-

345. *Teague*, 489 U.S. at 301.

346. *Saffle v. Parks*, 494 U.S. 484, 488 (1990).

347. *Sawyer*, 497 U.S. at 234.

348. *Stringer v. Black*, 503 U.S. 222, 228 (1992).

349. *Butler v. McKellar*, 494 U.S. 407, 415–17 (1990). Justice Harlan, for his part, recognized that a decision regarding the novelty of a rule would often be close. In his view, the "content" of constitutional principles rarely changes "dramatically from year to year." What may appear on first glance to be the announcement of a "new rule," may, instead, be "simply" the application of a "well-established constitutional principle" to a "closely analogous" case. *Desist*, 394 U.S. at 263 (dissenting opinion). Harlan insisted that a rule is not new for retroactivity purposes unless, before the prisoner's conviction and sentence became final, the Supreme Court of the United States would have *rejected* the legal standard on which a prisoner relies. Under the current Court's formulations, a rule *is* new unless it can be said that, at that time, the Supreme Court would have *accepted* the prisoner's argument—and the state courts unaccountably failed to comprehend as much. The Court may rely on Harlan for the general framework in *Teague* (i.e., the general prohibition on "new rule" claims in habeas corpus). Yet the Court plainly draws no support from Harlan regarding the crucial question whether a rule is genuinely new. Professor Heald contends that the *Teague* doctrine would be more sensible if the Court were to revive Justice Harlan's understanding of what qualifies as new law. Paul J. Heald, *Retroactivity, Capital Sentencing, and the Jurisdictional Contours of Habeas Corpus*, 42 Ala. L. Rev. 1273, 1321 (1991). Professor Hoffmann, too, advocates a definition of new rules that conforms more closely to Harlan's views. Hoffmann, note 329.

350. See Chapter X, notes 446–94 and accompanying text.

ficers from personal liability for monetary damages. It is hard to think that is what the Court really means. Qualified immunity doctrine fixes a generous standard for executive officers, because those state agents (particularly the police) must take immediate action in the field when there is no opportunity to sort through complex legal issues. The *Teague* doctrine cannot sensibly regard state judges in the same way. Judges have the time, the resources, and the professional credentials (not to mention the duty) to make reasoned judgments. Moreover, the stakes are different: State judges are not personally exposed to liability, and it is hard to think that qualified men and women will be discouraged from accepting positions on state courts simply because prisoners are granted new trials when federal courts find their federal claims to be meritorious.[351] Federal courts expect comparatively little of cops on the beat and comparatively more of state judges with lawyers and libraries at their disposal.[352] Nevertheless, it is well to compare *Teague* with qualified immunity in at least two respects: (1) the standards the Court has announced in the two contexts; and (2) the procedures the Court has prescribed for enforcing those standards.

Standards. In qualified immunity cases, the standard to which executive officers are held is formed by the legal rule that was "clearly established" at the time they acted. The point is to give officers a certain amount of leeway. They are forgiven for some deviations. But they are not immune if they violated rights that were so well established that they reasonably should have known that their conduct was unlawful. Recall that the Court determines whether rights were clearly established in the necessary sense by examining the analogous precedents then in place. If those precedents gave officers fair warning, qualified immunity is unavailable.

In *Teague* cases, the standard to which state courts are held is stated differently, yet with some similarities. According to the decisions to date, federal habeas courts do not ask whether the legal rule on which a prisoner's claim depends was "clearly established" at the time his conviction became final.[353] Nor do federal courts ask whether contemporaneous precedents gave state courts fair warning that some trial procedure violated federal law. Yet federal habeas courts *do* ask whether it was "objectively unreasonabl[e]" to reject a prisoner's claim.[354] A federal habeas court cannot sustain a prisoner's claim whenever the federal court is confident that the claim was meritorious in light of the precedents that were available to guide the state courts. If it would not have been "un-

351. Dissenting in *Snead v. Stringer*, 454 U.S. 988 (1981), then-Justice Rehnquist actually proposed that "fewer and fewer capable lawyers [could] be found to serve on state benches when they [might] find their considered decisions overturned by the ruling of a single federal district judge." Id. at 993. That was a stretch.

352. See *West*, 505 U.S. at 303–05 (O'Connor, J., concurring in the judgment). The Supreme Court does not cite qualified immunity and *Teague* cases interchangeably as though the two doctrines are essentially the same. Of course, the claims advanced in §1983 actions for damages and habeas corpus petitions are often different. The former commonly involve fourth amendment or substantive due process claims against the police; the latter can implicate all manner of procedural safeguards attending criminal cases. Yet there is a not insignificant overlap, too. See notes 553–73 and accompanying notes (discussing the Court's efforts to deal with cases in which prisoners have claims that can be cognizable both in §1983 actions and in habeas). For a discussion of the similarities and differences between immunity doctrine and *Teague*, see Kit Kinports, *Habeas Corpus, Qualified Immunity, and Crystal Balls: Predicting the Course of Constitutional Law*, 33 Ariz. L. Rev. 115 (1991). See notes 428–88 and accompanying text (comparing qualified immunity and *Teague* with the analysis mandated by §2254(d)).

353. But see notes 446–61 and accompanying text (revisiting this issue in connection with §2254(d)).

354. *O'Dell*, 521 U.S. at 156.

reasonable" to reject the claim, the district court would have to create a new rule of law in order to find the claim meritorious. And that, of course, *Teague* usually forbids.

In qualified immunity cases and in *Teague* cases, as well, the key question is the level of generality at which rules of law are understood and stated. In both contexts, the Court articulates legal rules at a low level of generality. But the reason the Court gives for doing that in immunity cases is different from the reason it gives in *Teague* cases. In qualified immunity cases, the Court specifies rules more particularly in order to ensure that executive officers have fair warning of the kind of behavior that violates federal law. The Court does not suggest that officers are entitled to be warned about future changes in the rules. The objective is not to protect executive officers from liability for failing to anticipate the creation of new rules. Instead, the Court proceeds from the premise that officers violated legal rules that existed at that time (whether or not those rules have since been adjusted). The point of immunity is that there are sound policy reasons for absolving executive officers of personal liability despite their failure to comply with extant federal law.

In *Teague* cases, by contrast, the Court identifies rules at a low level of generality in order to establish a baseline from which to measure changes in the law. If a legal rule is stated abstractly, it need not be changed in order to be applied to a variety of fact patterns. In each instance, the rule remains constant even as significant judgment is required to determine its bearing on the case at hand. If, by contrast, a legal rule is articulated in more specific terms, it cannot accommodate the same range of applications without periodic adjustment in its content. The Court articulates "old" rules at a low level of generality in order to ensure that federal habeas courts will not be able to find prisoners' claims meritorious without relying on or establishing entirely "new" rules. The Court thus prevents federal district courts from entertaining claims that state courts rejected (or, at least, might reasonably have rejected). The Court does not (necessarily) suggest that any state court judgment that was or might have been "objectively reasonable" was, for that reason, *correct* at the time. Under the *Teague* doctrine, it is unnecessary to determine what the correct disposition of a claim was or would have been. The availability of a "reasonable" judgment against the prisoner at the time his conviction became final is sufficient without more to make it necessary for a federal court to rely on a new rule in order to render a judgment in his favor.[355]

Procedures. Courts handling qualified immunity and *Teague* cases proceed through the issues in a different sequence. In an immunity case, the court first decides whether the plaintiff has alleged a violation of a federal right and *then* turns to the different question whether that right was clearly established at the time the defendant officer acted. The court is therefore able to determine forthrightly the current scope of the federal right in issue.[356] In a *Teague* case, by contrast, a federal habeas court has no occasion to elaborate the content of a legal rule at present, but, at most, only articulates and applies the law as it was when the prisoner's conviction became final. Once the custodian raises an objection that a claim rests on a new rule, the district court deals with that question prior to, and perhaps instead of, making any determination about whether the prisoner has a meritorious claim in light of current legal standards. By the

355. But see text accompanying note 367 (noting Justice O'Connor's account in *West*); notes 364–67 and accompanying text.

356. See Chapter X, notes 475–84 and accompanying text.

Court's own account, *Teague* largely eliminates habeas corpus as a mechanism for the development of federal law.[357]

5. Practical Implications

The *Teague* doctrine bears implications for the fundamental proposition in *Brown v. Allen* that federal courts entertaining habeas petitions do not bow to previous state court decisions on the merits of federal claims, but rather exercise their own independent "*de novo*" judgment.[358] A federal court's determination of whether a rule is new for *Teague* purposes does not depend on anything the state courts said or did in the instant case. Instead, the federal court examines the precedents at the time the prisoner's conviction became final and decides whether those precedents compelled a judgment that the prisoner's claim was meritorious even then. By all accounts, however, the *Teague* doctrine constitutes yet another attempt by the Court to orchestrate the relationship between state and federal governmental authority. In many instances, the claims that state prisoners advance in federal habeas corpus petitions *were* previously examined and rejected in state court. Accordingly, federal adjudication of those claims puts federal courts in the posture of second-guessing state courts, in fact if not in theory.[359] The Supreme Court acknowledges that, as a result, prior state court judgments can effectively be set at naught and thus describes *Teague* as a check on federal judicial power to affect state court judgments: Federal habeas courts "will not disturb" a state conviction or sentence unless the state court acted "objectively unreasonably."[360] The very point of *Teague* is to "validate reasonable, good-faith interpretations of existing precedents made by the state courts."[361]

The *Teague* doctrine has come under intense criticism in academic circles. By some accounts, *Teague* is a transparent machination for circumnavigating *Brown*. Taken for all they are worth, the Court's various descriptions of new rules threaten to capture *all* claims advanced in federal habeas petitions—both claims seeking incremental developments in the content of legal standards and claims seeking the application of settled standards to different factual circumstances. Claims calling for any kind of serious judgment on questions of law, and equally claims calling for the resolution of mixed questions of law and fact, appear to demand the creation of entirely new rules of law that, given *Teague*, are typically unenforceable in habeas proceedings.[362] According to intem-

357. The retroactivity question is "properly treated as a threshold question" because, once a new rule is applied to the petitioner at bar, it must equally be applied to all other petitioners similarly situated. *Teague*, 489 U.S. at 300; see note 319 and accompanying text. That means, accordingly that "habeas corpus cannot be used as a vehicle to create new constitutional rules of criminal procedure unless those rules would be applied retroactively to all defendants on collateral review through one of the two exceptions [the Court has] articulated." Id. at 316. With respect to the sequencing of issues, *Teague* is out of step both with qualified immunity and with the harmless error doctrine. See note 303 and accompanying text.

358. See *Brown v. Allen*, 344 U.S. 443 (1953); see notes 55–60 and accompanying text.

359. See note 46 and accompanying text.

360. *O'Dell*, 521 U.S. at 156.

361. *Butler*, 494 U.S. at 414.

362. For criticisms of *Teague* in this vein, see Barry Friedman, *Habeas and Hubris*, 45 Vand. L. Rev. 797 (1992); James S. Liebman, *More Than "Slightly Retro": The Rehnquist Court's Rout of Habeas Corpus Jurisdiction in Teague v. Lane*, 18 N.Y.U. Rev. L. & Soc. Change 537 (1991); Kathleen Patchel, *The New Habeas*, 42 Hastings L. J. 939 (1991). On the wider jurisprudential implications of the Court's insistence that rules of law change so easily and rapidly, see Markus Dirk Dubber, *Prudence and Substance: How the Supreme Court's New Habeas Retroactivity Doctrine Mirrors and Affects*

perate critics, *Teague's* understanding of new rules is pure pretense. The content of legal rules obviously evolves over time. But it rarely lurches from an extremely well settled proposition that can produce only one reasonable result to an entirely different "new rule." Certainly, law does not shift so dramatically with anything like the frequency that *Teague* contemplates. The entire *Teague* doctrine would be utterly bizarre if it were not so obviously contrived to deprive the federal courts of the ability to vindicate federal claims in habeas corpus proceedings.[363]

The justices explored *Teague's* implications for *Brown* in *Wright v. West*,[364] an otherwise obscure case from Virginia. In that case, the Court asked the parties to brief not only the issues they had presented to the lower courts, but also a general question that the justices articulated on their own: Should a federal court entertaining a habeas petition from a prisoner in custody pursuant to the judgment of a state court "give deference to the state court's application of law to the specific facts of the petitioner's case" or "review the state court's determination *de novo*?" That question posed a choice between two possibilities, neither of which was consistent with conventional understanding. District courts had never (formally) purported to "give deference" to state court determinations of mixed questions. Nor had they (formally) purported to "review" state court decisions. Nevertheless, the question captured the gist of the controversy surrounding *Teague*.

After wrestling with its own question, the Court disposed of *West* without reaching and resolving it. In an opinion announcing the Court's judgment on the prisoner's individual claims, Justice Thomas made it clear that he is prepared to hold that district courts should "defer" to state court determinations of all factual, legal, and mixed issues and to rely on *Teague* and its progeny for support. In his view, it is enough if federal courts retain authority to decide "independently" whether state courts reached "reasonable" judgments.[365] Other justices explained *Teague* differently. Justice Kennedy denied that *Teague* is on a "collision course" with federal court authority to decide mixed questions independently. By his account, *Teague* spares the states from a regime in which their judgments are effectively upset by "changing a rule [of law] once thought correct but now understood to be deficient on its own terms." Justice Kennedy added that some rules are by their nature general, meant to guide judgment in a variety of fact patterns. When rules of that kind are applied, they rarely produce a result "so novel" that a "new rule" emerges.[366] Justice O'Connor also insisted that *Teague* is genuinely concerned with changes in the law. In her view, *Teague* does not demand that federal habeas courts allow "a state court's *incorrect* legal determination" to stand "because it was reasonable." By contrast, the *Teague* doctrine preserves the federal courts' duty and responsibility to determine whether a state court judgment was "correct" in light of the law as it was at the time a prisoner's conviction became final.[367]

Substantive Constitutional Law, 30 Am. Crim. L. Rev. 1 (1992); Fallon & Meltzer, note 318; Linda Meyer, *"Nothing We Say Matters": Teague and New Rules*, 61 U. Chi. L. Rev. 423 (1994).

363. Yackle, note 52, at 2386–93. More charitable observers recognize that *Teague's* distinction between old rules and new is hard to manage in a system of law in which judges are "trained to find old traces for new trails." Patrick E. Higginbotham, *Reflections on Reform of §2254 Habeas Petitions*, 18 Hofstra L. Rev. 1005, 1024 (1990).

364. 505 U.S. 277 (1992).

365. Id. at 287–88. The Chief Justice and Justice Scalia joined Justice Thomas on this point.

366. 505 U.S. at 306–08 (Kennedy, J., concurring in the judgment). See also *Gray v. Netherland*, 518 U.S. 152, 183 (1996) (Ginsburg, J., dissenting) (joined by Stevens, Souter & Breyer, J.J.) (insisting that "*Teague* is not the straightjacket the Commonwealth misunderstands it to be").

367. 505 U.S. at 305 (O'Connor, J., concurring in the judgment) (emphasis added).

G. Effect of Prior State Court Decisions

The disagreement among the justices in *Wright v. West*[368] set the stage for Congress to act. Justice O'Connor virtually invited Congress into the fray when she explained that Justice Thomas' position was untenable in part because Congress had not enacted legislation contemplating that federal courts entertaining habeas petitions should "defer" to "reasonable" state court judgments.[369] The result was a key provision in AEDPA, 28 U.S.C. §2254(d), which states that "an application for a writ of habeas corpus on behalf of a person in custody pursuant to the judgment of a State court shall not be granted with respect to any claim that was adjudicated on the merits in State proceedings" unless the "adjudication" of the claim: (1) "resulted in a decision that was contrary to, or involved an unreasonable application of, clearly established Federal law, as determined by the Supreme Court of the United States;" or (2) "resulted in a decision that was based on an unreasonable determination of the facts in light of the evidence presented in the State court proceeding."

By some accounts, this statute is constitutionally questionable to the extent it restricts the federal courts' ability to adjudicate federal claims properly within their jurisdiction.[370] If it required federal courts essentially to rubberstamp state court decisions on the merits of claims, its constitutionality presumably would be debatable.[371] Most observers agree, however, that §2254(d) is constitutionally sound so long as it is understood only to adjust the relief that federal courts can award a prevailing litigant.[372] Congress generally enjoys power to prescribe the means by which even constitutional rights are enforced.[373] As a practical matter, §2254(d) is commonly said to require federal habeas courts to give some measure of "deference" to previous state court decisions on the merits of prisoners' federal claims.[374] That characterization may be fair enough as a gross generalization.[375] Yet the precise content of the deference owed to state court judg-

---

368. See notes 364–67 and accompanying text.

369. *West*, 505 U.S. at 305–06 (concurring opinion).

370. The prisoner in *Terry Williams v. Taylor*, 529 U.S. 362 (2000), asked the Court to decide whether §2254(d) is unconstitutional because it invades the independence of Article III courts, suspends the writ, or both. See notes 15–37 and accompanying text. The Court denied review on all constitutional questions.

371. See note 35 (noting that the Supreme Court occasionally suggests that the Suspension Clause guarantees federal habeas jurisdiction to entertain petitions from state convicts); Chapter IV, notes 77–92 and accompanying text (discussing Article III limits on congressional authority to affect judicial outcomes). See also notes 406–08 and accompanying text (discussing constitutional arguments regarding the statute's focus on Supreme Court precedents to the exclusion of decisions by other courts).

372. Liebman and Ryan are satisfied that §2254(d) does not intrude upon the authority of Article III courts to adjudicate, at least so long as the statute is understood to restrict federal court authority no more than the *Teague* doctrine did previously. James S. Liebman & William F. Ryan, *"Some Effectual Power": The Quantity and Quality of Decisionmaking Required of Article III Courts*, 98 Colum. L. Rev. 696 (1998). See also Kent S. Scheidegger, *Habeas Corpus, Relitigation, and the Legislative Power*, 98 Colum. L. Rev. 888 (1998) (contending that §2254(d) is constitutional inasmuch as it affects only the availability of habeas relief).

373. See note 318; Chapter VIII, notes 223–30 and accompanying text.

374. E.g., *Bell v. Cone*, 122 S.Ct. 1843 (2002).

375. The term "deference" does not appear in the statute, but it does appear in the (perfunctory) conference report on AEDPA. H.R. Rep. No. 104–518, 1996 U.S. Code & Admin. News 944. Cf. *Burford v. United States*, 532 U.S. 59 (2001) (interpreting 18 U.S.C. §3742(e)—a statute that *does* explicitly instruct federal appellate courts to give "due deference" to district court applications of federal sentencing guidelines). It seems plain that §2254(d) does not contemplate that federal courts

ments requires a rigorous interpretive exercise. The statute's effect can best be examined under four headings: (1) a previous state court adjudication on the merits as a condition precedent to §2254(d)'s application to a case; (2) the restriction of the federal courts' purview to claims based on federal law that the Supreme Court had "clearly established" at the time the state court rendered its decision; (3) the limitations on federal authority to grant habeas relief; and (4) a comparison with the ban on new rules and qualified immunity.

1. Adjudication on the Merits

Section 2254(d) does not confer on inferior federal courts an appellate jurisdiction to review state court judgments for error.[376] By contrast, this statute preserves the traditional architecture of habeas corpus as an original civil action in which federal jurisdiction is based on custody alleged to be in violation of federal law. Nevertheless, it does explicitly direct federal courts to examine previous state court proceedings regarding federal claims and, in that respect, departs from the traditional model.[377] By its terms, §2254(d) establishes limitations on a federal court's ability to award habeas relief. Those limitations become applicable if a state court previously "adjudicated" a claim "on the merits" and that adjudication "resulted" in a "decision." Plainly, the state court's decision-making process (its "adjudication") must have focused on the "merits" of the claim.[378] It would hardly make sense to refer to an adjudication on the merits at all, if a state court decision on some other basis would suffice. Accordingly, it seems clear that the state court's ultimate "decision" with respect to a claim must also have been on the merits.

In *Semtek v. Lockheed*,[379] Justice Scalia explained that an adjudication has traditionally been said to be "on the merits" if a court "actually 'pass[es] on the substance of a [particular] claim.'"[380] The practical significance of a traditional "merits" adjudication is that it produces, in turn, a "*judgment* 'on the merits,'" which begets preclusive effects.[381] The "on the merits" formulation sometimes carries a different meaning. In *Semtek* itself,

---

will defer to state court decisions in the way (or for the reasons) they defer to decisions by federal administrative agencies pursuant to *Chevron v. Natural Resources Defense Council*, 467 U.S. 837 (1984); see Chapter I, note 41. *Terry Williams*, 529 U.S. at 387 n.3 (plurality opinion by Stevens, J.) (disclaiming any analogy to *Chevron*).

376. Consider, for comparative purposes, 28 U.S.C. §1257, which confers appellate jurisdiction on the Supreme Court to "review" state court judgments for error. See Chapter VII, text accompanying note 59. There is no serious argument that §2254(d) confers on federal district courts an appellate jurisdiction to superintend state courts as though state courts were inferior tribunals situated beneath district courts in a radical new hierarchical structure. Federal habeas corpus has always had an appellate quality, coming as it typically does after state courts have passed on prisoners' claims. See note 46. Yet the state courts' station within the federal judicial system is well established, and it would take more than the elliptical language in §2254(d) to change it. See Chapter VI (explaining the many ways in which the co-equal status of state courts and lower federal courts plays out).

377. Compare notes 358–61 and accompanying text (discussing the *Teague* doctrine).

378. An *adjudication* is not itself a *decision*. A decision is the *result* of an adjudication. An adjudication, accordingly, is something more than a disposition that concludes judicial consideration of a claim. It is a decision-making process for *reaching* a dispositive judgment.

379. 531 U.S. 497 (2001).

380. Id. at 501–02, quoting Restatement (Second) of Judgments §19, Comment (a).

381. Id. at 502 (emphasis added). See Chapter VI, notes 161–95 and accompanying text (discussing preclusion).

Justice Scalia concluded that Fed. R. Civ. P. 41(b) employs the phrase only to mean "the opposite of a 'dismissal without prejudice'" to refiling a claim in the same court.[382] It is hard to think that §2254(d) can use the "on the merits" formulation in that unorthodox way. The exhaustion doctrine demands that prisoners pursue relief in state court as long as some avenue remains open.[383] Any state court decision dismissing a claim without prejudice leaves the prisoner with an obligation to refile the claim in state court in the appropriate manner. Accordingly, a state court adjudication and decision on the merits cannot very well mean *anything but* a dismissal without prejudice. If that were so, it would cover any action a state court took with respect to a claim that allowed a prisoner to press on to federal court. That, in turn, would eliminate a prior state court adjudication and decision on the merits as a meaningful condition for the application of §2254(d). A condition that is always satisfied is no condition at all. Of course, a state court adjudication on the merits for purposes of §2254(d) cannot formally preclude a federal court's consideration of a claim.[384] Yet it seems clear that §2254(d) incorporates the essence of the traditional "on the merits" idea. Accordingly, §2254(d)'s limitations on federal habeas relief are implicated only if a state court previously investigated whether a claim had sufficient factual and legal support to establish a violation of federal law and decided that the claim did not.[385]

This understanding comports with the apparent rationale behind §2254(d): Federal courts usually should withhold relief if a state court has already considered a claim with care and has reached a reasoned decision that a prisoner is not imprisoned in violation of federal law. In any particular instance, then, §2254(d) contemplates that a federal court will determine whether the state court has actually done that. If a state court examined the substantive *bona fides* of a federal claim and found the claim wanting, a federal habeas court should grant relief only if the state court's decision fails one of the tests established by paragraphs (1) and (2). If, however, a state court disposed of a claim on some other basis (for example, a procedural ground), the rationale for restricting federal habeas corpus relief does not obtain and paragraphs (1) and (2) do not apply.[386]

---

382. Accordingly, when a federal district court exercising diversity jurisdiction dismisses a state law claim on the merits, Rule 41(b) does not prescribe the preclusive effects of the court's judgment in future litigation in another court. 531 U.S. at 505–06. In *Semtek*, a federal district court initially dismissed Semtek's state claims against Lockheed "on the merits" in light of the California statute of limitations. Semtek then sued Lockheed in a Maryland state court, advancing the same claims. A Maryland state appellate court read Rule 41(b) to mean that, as a matter of federal law, the federal court's previous order of dismissal was entitled to preclusive effect. In the Supreme Court, Justice Scalia held that the preclusive effects of a federal court's judgment on a state claim in a diversity action are governed by the law that would be applied by the courts of the state in which the federal court sits.

383. See notes 89–131 and accompanying text.

384. Federal habeas remains an exception to 28 U.S.C. §1738. See note 4 and accompanying text.

385. See *Schoenberger v. Russell*, 290 F.3d 831, 837 (6th Cir. 2002) (Keith, J., concurring) (explaining that most circuits take this position).

386. *Fisher v. Texas*, 169 F.3d 295, 300 (5th Cir. 1999). Of course, federal habeas consideration of the claim may be foreclosed under the default doctrine. See notes 194–264 and accompanying text. By hypothesis, however, when a federal court turns to §2254(d), it has already decided that the claim in question is not procedurally barred. The policy reflected in §2254(d) works best in cases in which state courts are alerted to the existence of federal claims but decline on procedural grounds to address the merits. In some instances, however, prisoners do not raise federal claims at all in state court and nonetheless satisfy the (demanding) standards for pressing those claims in federal court. See notes 208–42 and accompanying text. In cases of that kind, state courts have not actually decided to rest on procedural grounds. Cf. note 116 (explaining that the exhaustion doctrine is some-

It is often difficult to determine whether a state court adjudicated and rejected the substance of a claim. When state court opinions are vague or ambiguous, federal habeas courts may employ the techniques they use to make the determination whether a state court relied on an adequate and independent state ground of decision. For purposes of that question, a federal court assumes that a state court judgment rests on federal grounds if it "fairly appears" to do so.[387] In this context, it would make sense to assume that a state court adjudicated and decided the merits of a claim if its opinion fairly appears to rely on federal principles. In some instances, then, one part of the analysis a federal court engages to determine the (antecedent) question whether a claim is procedurally foreclosed may double as an analysis for determining whether §2254(d)'s relief-limiting provisions are applicable.[388] Of course, that technique is of no help if the state court disposed of a claim without appearing to rely primarily on the federal merits. The obvious illustration is a case in which a state court rejected a claim without explanation.[389]

A state court adjudication and decision on the merits may invoke the relief-limiting provisions in §2254(d) even if the state court's opinion failed to refer to the Supreme Court decisions bearing on a prisoner's federal claim. In *Early v. Packer*,[390] the Court explained that a state court decision on the merits was not "contrary to" the law the Court had "clearly established" at the time merely because the state court cited none of the Court's relevant precedents. As long as the state court's "reasoning" and "result" did not "contradict" those precedents, it made no difference whether the state court was even aware of them. If that was so, it follows that the state court decision in *Packer* counted as a decision on the merits (thus invoking §2254(d) in the first place) even though it was rendered without reference to the Court's contemporaneous holdings. Still, it seems clear that the state court had to offer some account of its "reasoning" in order to make it possible to decide whether its analysis *did* contradict controlling Supreme Court cases or, certainly, whether it applied the federal law established by those cases unrea-

---

times satisfied on the theory that state courts *would* find claims procedurally barred if they were asked). Nevertheless, it seems clear that §2254(d) is not triggered for want of a state court adjudication and decision on the merits.

387. See Chapter VII, note 144 and accompanying text.

388. Notice that the combination of the adequate state ground doctrine and §2254(d) gives respondents an option. On the one hand, a respondent may argue that a previous state court decision rested on state procedural grounds in hopes that the federal court will agree, find that state ground adequate, reject the prisoner's arguments regarding cause, prejudice, or innocence, and decline to consider the merits of the claim. On the other, a respondent may contend that a state court adjudicated a claim on the merits in hopes that the federal court will agree, conclude that §2254(d) is triggered, reject the prisoner's arguments under paragraphs (1) and (2), and decline to issue federal habeas relief.

389. Other techniques may be available when a state court gives no indication of its rationale. Recall that in the adequate-state-ground context an unexplained disposition in the highest state court is not decisive. A federal habeas court will look "through" a decision of that kind to decisions lower down in the state court hierarchy and determine, on that basis, whether a prisoner's claim was rejected on the basis of federal law. See Chapter VII, note 149. The same methodology may answer here. See *Johnson v. Nelson*, 142 F.Supp.2d 1215, 1221–22 (S.D. Calif. 2001) (finding no reasoned decision on the merits by a state supreme court and then looking beyond that decision to a dispositive decision by an intermediate level court). The Fifth Circuit has identified three factors that bear on whether a state decision rested on the substantive merits of a claim: "(1) what the state courts have done in similar cases; (2) whether the history of the case suggests that the state court was aware of any ground for not adjudicating the case on the merits; and (3) whether the state courts' opinions suggest reliance upon procedural grounds rather than a determination of the merits." *Green v. Johnson*, 116 F.3d 1115, 1121 (5th Cir. 1997).

390. 2002 WL 31444316 (U.S. Sup. Ct. 2002) (*per curiam*).

sonably. The framework that §2254(d) puts in place cannot function effectively if state courts do not supply opinions identifying the federal legal rules they brought to bear and explaining their application of those rules to particular cases.[391]

If there is no qualifying state court adjudication and decision on the merits, §2254(d) is inapplicable and a federal court's ability to grant federal habeas relief is not conditioned on the standards in paragraphs (1) and (2).[392] If there *is* a state court adjudication and decision on the merits, §2254(d) comes into play and specifies the federal court's further duties.

2. Clearly Established Law

Section 2254(d) contemplates that a federal habeas court will not examine a prisoner's claim in light of federal legal standards as they are at the time the federal court acts. Instead, the federal court will consider only federal law that the Supreme Court itself had "clearly established" when the state court rejected the claim.[393] The Court elaborated the "clearly established" law idea in *Terry Williams v. Taylor*.[394] Justice Stevens' opinion, joined in its entirety by three other justices, analyzed the case at hand and announced the Court's conclusion in the prisoner's favor.[395] Justice O'Connor's opinion,

---

391. In *Packer*, the state court relied on state court decisions holding trial judges to more demanding standards than did the Court's precedents elaborating pertinent federal constitutional law. That (evidently) demonstrated that the state court did not slight the prisoner's federal due process claim (that the trial judge in his case had presssured the jury into returning a verdict). The lower federal court in *Packer* understood the state court to have ignored the federal claim and rested its decision on state law grounds alone. *Packer v. Hill*, 291 F.3d 569, 579 n.11 (9th Cir. 2002). If that characterization was accurate, however, the state court's decision was not "on the merits" in the necessary sense that it rejected the substance of the claim as a matter of federal law. A state court determination that a prisoner's rights under *state* law were not violated can no more trigger §2254(d) than can a state court disposition resting on a prisoner's failure to comply with state procedural rules. The rationale behind §2254(d)'s limitations on federal habeas relief is that a state court decision on the *federal* merits of a claim is due some measure of deference. Some circuits hold that a state court opinion explaining the court's reliance on federal law is an essential prerequisite to the invocation of §2254(d). E.g., *Appel v. Horn*, 250 F.3d 203, 210-12 (3d Cir. 2001); *Dibenedetto v. Hall*, 272 F.3d 1, 6-7 (1st Cir. 2001). Others regard a state court decision rejecting the substance of a claim to be sufficient, however perfunctory the state court's explanation of its result may be. E.g., *Barnabei v. Angelone*, 214 F.3d 463, 469 (4th Cir. 2000); *Sellan v. Kuhlman*, 261 F.3d 303, 312 (2d Cir. 2001). Compare Adam N. Steinman, *Reconceptualizing Federal Habeas Corpus for State Prisoners*, 2001 Wis. L. Rev. 1493, 1528-30 (arguing that the point of §2254(d) is that federal habeas courts should "defer" to proper state court *reasoning* but not to state court *results* alone), with Scott Dodson, *Habeas Review of Perfunctory State Court Decisions on the Merits*, 29 Am. J. Crim. L. 223 (2002) (contending that decisions on the merits engage §2254(d) irrespective of whether they are accompanied by an articulated rationale).

392. Courts typically explain that they revert to what they did in habeas cases prior to the enactment of §2254(d). E.g., *Dibenedetto*, 272 F.3d at 7. But see notes 433–35 and accompanying text (discussing the likelihood that §2254(d) informs the threshold *Teague* analysis). Some circuits do not set §2254(d) aside entirely. Instead, when a state court either fails to render a decision on the merits or fails to supply an opinion explaining a merits analysis, they have it that a federal habeas court must conduct an independent examination of the entire record, determine the reasoning the state court might have offered for denying a claim on the merits, and then decide whether that reasoning would have been either "contrary to" clearly established law or "unreasonable." E.g., *Delgado v. Lewis*, 181 F.3d 1087, 1091 (9th Cir. 1999).

393. See note 404 and accompanying text.

394. 529 U.S. 362 (2000).

395. Id. at 367 (opinion of Stevens, J.) (joined by Souter, Ginsburg & Breyer, J.J.).

joined in critical respects by four different justices, supplied a general interpretation of §2254(d).[396] Justice O'Connor and Justice Kennedy joined the portions of Justice Stevens' opinion that they regarded as consistent with Justice O'Connor's explanation of the statutory framework.[397] Those sections of Stevens' opinion are thus authoritative, along with almost all of Justice O'Connor's discussion of the meaning of §2254(d) in general.[398]

The prisoner in *Terry Williams* was convicted in a Virginia state court and sentenced to death. In a petition for state postconviction relief, he contended that his lawyer had rendered ineffective assistance at the sentencing phase of the trial. The attorney failed to present evidence in mitigation that might have persuaded the jury to spare the prisoner's life. The state trial-level judge applied the *Strickland* standard and concluded that the claim was meritorious.[399] The Virginia Supreme Court reversed. That court agreed that counsel's performance "fell below an objective standard of reasonableness" and thus failed to satisfy the primary *Strickland* test. Nevertheless, the state supreme court held that the prisoner had not suffered sufficient prejudice to warrant the conclusion that his right to effective representation had been denied. The *Strickland* decision defined prejudice as a "reasonable probability that, but for counsel's unprofessional errors, the result of the proceeding would have been different." According to the Virginia Supreme Court, however, a more recent decision, *Lockhart v. Fretwell*,[400] modified that definition. The prisoner filed a petition for a writ of habeas corpus in federal court. In the Supreme Court, Justice Stevens explained that despite §2254(d), the prisoner was entitled to federal habeas relief.

Justice Stevens explained that the "threshold" question "under AEDPA" is whether a prisoner "seeks to apply a rule of law that was clearly established at the time his state-court conviction became final."[401] That statement was revealing in a number of respects. Notice in particular that Justice Stevens merged the "clearly established" law formulation in §2254(d) with key features of the *Teague* doctrine.[402] He was also incomplete. Justice O'Connor joined Stevens' account of the "threshold" question, but she added that the issue is actually whether the prisoner relies on a rule of federal law that was "clearly established... *by the Supreme Court of the United States*."[403] Justice O'Connor explained, in turn, that "clearly established" law for purposes of §2254(d) "refers to" the Supreme Court's own "holdings" at the time of the "relevant state-court decision."[404] If a

---

396. Id. at 399 (opinion of O'Connor, J.) (joined by Kennedy, J.). The Chief Justice, Justice Scalia, and Justice Thomas joined the part of Justice O'Connor's opinion explicating the statute generally. But they did not endorse her discussion of the justices' internal debate in *Wright v West*, 502 U.S. 277 (1992); see notes 364–67 and accompanying text. And they dissented from the Court's disposition of the case. 529 U.S. at 416 (Rehnquist, C.J., concurring in part & dissenting in part) (joined by Scalia & Thomas, J.J.). Justice Scalia disclaimed a footnote in Justice O'Connor's opinion referring to the legislative history behind §2254(d).

397. 529 U.S. 413 (opinion of O'Connor, J.) (joined by Kennedy, J.).

398. All but the footnote that Justice Scalia refused to credit. Id. at 408 n.* (relying on floor speeches by Senators Hatch and Specter to support the conclusion that an "unreasonable application" means an unreasonable application of the law to the facts of a particular case).

399. *Strickland v. Washington*, 466 U.S. 668 (1984); see note 223 and accompanying text.

400. 506 U.S. 364 (1993).

401. 529 U.S. at 390 (joined by O'Connor & Kennedy, J.J.). Accord *Cone*, 122 S.Ct. at 1850 ("first" addressing the question whether a state court identified and applied the rule of law that the Court's holding in *Strickland* had clearly established at the time the state court acted).

402. See notes 446–61 and accompanying text.

403. See text accompanying note 369.

404. 529 U.S. at 412. Justice O'Connor was arguably ambiguous. It is possible that she meant only to acknowledge that "clearly established" law for §2254(d) purposes must be ascribed to the

federal habeas court decides that a state court decision rejecting a prisoner's claim was correct in light of the Court's holdings in place at the time, that decision is dispositive. The claim must be dismissed.[405]

The idea that inferior federal courts may only compare state court decisions with Supreme Court holdings is problematic. Article III judges at every level operate as independent jurists, not as agents of the Supreme Court. They are duty-bound to make their best judgments about what federal law demands, and those judgments stand until they are overturned on appellate review. There is an argument, then, that Congress intrudes upon Article III independence if it presumes to prescribe the sources that federal judges can consult—even if Congress specifies Supreme Court precedents *en masse*.[406] There is, however, a less troublesome explanation of §2254(d)'s focus on Supreme Court holdings. The idea may be only to remind inferior federal courts that state courts are their co-equals in a single system, that state courts do not answer to federal district and circuit courts, and that both state and inferior federal courts *do* answer only to the Supreme Court.[407] By this account, §2254(d) is consistent with conventional thinking about the federal hierarchy. A state court's judgment was not necessarily mistaken merely because it conflicted with precedents in the lower federal courts. Instead, a state court decision was erroneous if it failed to comport with federal *law* as it was then clearly established. That federal law was captured in any existing Supreme Court decisions, as well as in the decisions of other courts (state and federal) that presumably thought they were following the Supreme Court's lead. A previous state court decision was wrong, then, if it was inconsistent with precedents (from whatever court) that accurately portrayed the law that was clearly established at the time—that is, the law that the Supreme Court itself had specified. Section 2254(d) thus allows federal habeas courts to compare state court decisions with precedents outside the Supreme Court—so long as those precedents are treated as evidence of what the Supreme Court itself had declared the law to be.[408]

Court itself and thus to its contemporaneous holdings. That, however, is obvious and scarcely worth pointing out at all. The serious question is the content of "clearly established" law in this context. When Justice O'Connor said that the statutory phrase "clearly established Federal law, as determined by the Supreme Court"..."refers to the holdings, as opposed to the dicta, of this Court's decisions," she almost certainly meant to say that those holdings and "clearly established" law are one and the same thing. That is a matter of genuine importance. See notes 446–61 and accompanying text.

405. E.g., *Weeks v. Angelone*, 528 U.S. 225, 237 (2000); *Ramdass v. Angelone*, 530 U.S. 156, 178 (2000).

406. Judge Ripple has argued that §2254(d) is unconstitutional to the extent it tells a federal habeas court that a state court decision must be found sufficient to foreclose habeas relief in any instance in which there was no telling Supreme Court precedent at the time and thus no clearly established law "as determined by the Supreme Court" that the state court neglected (or could have neglected). *Lindh v. Murphy*, 96 F.3d 856, 886–88 (7th Cir. 1996) (dissenting opinion). But see *O'Brien v. DuBois*, 145 F.3d 16, 21 (1st Cir. 1998) (insisting that a prisoner "need not point a habeas court to a factually identical" Supreme Court precedent). Professor Jackson suggests that Article III guarantees inferior federal court decisions respect as precedents for *stare decisis* purposes and that if §2254(d) bars *any* consideration of lower court precedents at all, it may be inconsistent with that constitutional principle. Vicki C. Jackson, *Introduction: Congressional Control of Jurisdiction and the Future of the Federal Courts—Opposition, Agreement, and Hierarchy*, 86 Gtn. L.J. 2445, 2470 (1998).

407. See *Lockhart*, 506 U.S. at 376 (1993) (Thomas, J., concurring) (explaining that state courts have no obligation to follow inferior federal court precedents).

408. See *O'Brien*, 145 F.3d at 21 (expressing this view). But see *Miller v. Straub*, 299 F.3d 570, 578–79 (6th Cir. 2002) (holding that §2254(d) prohibits reliance on lower court decisions).

3. Limitations on Relief

If a federal court decides that a previous state court decision on the merits of a claim was erroneous in light of the Supreme Court holdings at the time, the court still may be prevented from awarding habeas relief pursuant to the remaining provisions of §2254(d). Specifically, §2254(d) bars federal relief unless the state court decision in question fails one of the three tests stated in paragraphs (1) and (2). Paragraph (1) contains two clauses, each establishing an independent test: the "contrary to" clause and the "unreasonable application" clause. Paragraph (2) contains a further "unreasonable determination" clause and thus a third test.[409]

The "contrary to" clause. A state court decision may fail the test established by the "contrary to" clause in two ways: by applying a rule that is "substantially different" from the rule reflected in contemporaneous Supreme Court precedents, or by arriving at a result that is different from the result the Court itself reached in a prior case in which the facts were "materially indistinguishable."[410] Read this way, the "contrary to" clause is unlikely to control many cases. State courts usually can articulate abstract rules accurately and can reach correct results when there is a probative Supreme Court precedent in place.[411] Yet state courts sometimes misstate or misunderstand even familiar Supreme

---

409. These limitations on relief are separate and apart from the restriction established by the harmless error doctrine. See notes 303-14 and accompanying text. Moreover, they limit habeas relief for different reasons. The harmless error doctrine bars federal relief if the error in state court had no substantial effect on the outcome of the trial—however far off the mark a state court was in rejecting the prisoner's claim. The restrictions on relief in paragraphs (1) and (2) of §2254(d) bar federal habeas relief because a state court decision was neither "contrary to" Supreme Court holdings nor unreasonably off the mark. The order in which a federal court should address these issues is problematic. It would seem that the harmless error question should come first, immediately following a federal court's determination that error occurred in state court proceedings. The relief-limiting provisions in §2254(d) should come into play later. They presuppose that the error in state court was *not* harmless, but they may nonetheless may bar an award of the writ on different grounds. In *Early v. Packer*, however, the Court said that the lower court would have acted properly if it had first determined (accurately) that a state court decision failed the "contrary to" test in paragraph (1) of the statute and then had turned to the harmless error issue. See notes 390-91 and accompanying text. If a state court itself relied on the harmless error doctrine to deny relief with respect to a claim, a federal habeas court must apply the relief-limiting provisions in §2254(d) to that previous state court decision on the federal question whether the error was harmless. E.g., *Saiz v. Burnett*, 296 F.3d 1008, 1011-12 (10th Cir. 2002). That scenario is also problematic. In many instances, the state court will have applied not the *Brecht* test prescribed for harmless error analysis in federal habeas corpus, but rather the *Chapman* test prescribed for direct review in state court. If, then, a federal habeas court asks whether a state court decision applying *Chapman* was contrary to, or involved an unreasonable application of, the Supreme Court's holding in *Chapman*, the habeas court may be charged with breaching its obligation to employ the *Brecht* standard (as opposed to *Chapman*).

410. *Terry Williams*, 529 U.S. at 406 (opinion of O'Connor, J.).

411. The Court explained in *Woodford v. Visciotti*, 2002 WL 31444314 (U.S. Sup. Ct. 2002), that the "contrary to" test is to be applied in light of the "presumption that state courts know and follow the law." Recall, moreover, that the Court said in *Early v. Packer* that a state court can pass the "contrary to" test without actually citing and relying upon controlling Supreme Court precedents. See notes 390-91 and accompanying text (discussing *Packer*). In the *Cone* case, Chief Justice Rehnquist held that the Tennessee Court of Appeals had correctly identified *Strickland* as the governing holding and that, "[c]onsequently," there was "no merit" to the prisoner's argument that the state court's decision was "contrary to" clearly established law within the meaning of §2254(d)(1). 122 S.Ct. at 1852. That suggested that a state court can satisfy the "contrary to" test merely by stating the Supreme Court's pertinent holdings correctly. In *Terry Williams*, however, Justice O'Connor made it clear that a state decision can be "contrary to" a Supreme Court holding if the state decision arrives

Court holdings. In *Terry Williams* itself, the Virginia Supreme Court misapprehended the *Strickland* decision. Justice Stevens explained that the *Lockhart* case did not modify *Strickland* at all and, accordingly, that the state supreme court's decision in reliance on *Lockhart* was "contrary to" *Strickland*. For that reason, §2254(d) did not foreclose the award of habeas relief.[412]

The "unreasonable application" clause. A state court decision may also fail the test established by the "unreasonable application" clause in two ways: by "correctly [identifying] the governing legal rule" but "unreasonably" [applying] that rule "to the facts" of a particular case,[413] or by either "unreasonably" extending a legal rule to a "context" in which it "should not apply" or failing to extend a rule to a context in which it "should apply."[414] Read this way, the "unreasonable application" clause is likely to affect numerous cases. Justice O'Connor said that a federal habeas court is not barred from awarding habeas relief simply because "reasonable *jurists*" could think that a previous state court decision was correct. The "unreasonable application" clause is not concerned with unreasonable *judges*, but with "objectively unreasonable" state court *decisions*.[415] She explained, however, that a federal court is barred from granting habeas relief on the sole ground that a prior state court determination of a mixed question was wrong at the time it was rendered in light of contemporaneous Supreme Court holdings. Instead, a federal court can award habeas relief only if the state court determination was "also" unreasonable.[416] In *Terry Williams*, the Virginia Supreme Court not only employed a mistaken understanding of *Strickland*, but also applied *Strickland* unreasonably. Accordingly, the state court's decision failed the tests established by both the "contrary to" and the "unreasonable application" clauses.[417]

The "unreasonable determination" clause. A state court decision fails the test established by the "unreasonable determination" clause in §2254(d)(2) if the decision is "based on an unreasonable determination of the facts in light of the evidence presented in the State court proceeding." The idea at work here is plain enough: If the state court misapprehended the underlying facts, the court may have reached an unreliable decision regarding a claim, even if its handling of the legal issues was otherwise flawless. The reference in §2254(d)(2) to an "unreasonable" determination of the facts tracks the reference in §2254(d)(1) to an "unreasonable" application of law. It appears, then, that §2254(d)(2) permits habeas relief only if a state court's decision was anchored in a determination of the facts that was not only wrong, but was "also" unreasonable.[418]

---

at a result that cannot be reconciled with the result the Supreme Court itself reached in the controlling case. *Terry Williams*, 529 U.S. at 406. Accordingly, a state court is not home free if it merely states Supreme Court doctrine accurately. Justice O'Connor's explanation of the "contrary to" test also indicates that the distinction between that test and the "unreasonable application" test is not always bright and clear. See notes 413–17 and accompanying text.

412. *Terry Wiliams*, 529 U.S. at 391–97; see text accompanying note 400.

413. Id. at 407–08 (opinion of O'Connor, J.).

414. Id. at 407.

415. Id. at 409–10 (rejecting the lower court's reliance on a "reasonable jurist" standard). See Evan Tsen Lee, *Section 2254(d) of the New Habeas Statute: An (Opinionated) User's Manual*, 51 Vand. L. Rev. 103 (1998) (anticipating that the Court would take this position).

416. *Terry Williams*, 529 U.S. at 411 (opinion of O'Connor, J.).

417. In *Cone*, the prior state court decision rejecting a *Strickland* claim failed neither test. In that case, the state court correctly identified *Strickland* as the controlling legal standard. See note 411. And the Chief Justice could not say that the state court's application of *Strickland* was "objectively unreasonable." 122 S.Ct. at 1854.

418. See note 416 and accompanying text. Accord *Weaver v. Bowersox*, 241 F.3d 1024, 1030 (8th Cir. 2001). It is often difficult to say whether an issue before a state court was a question of fact alone or a mixed question of law and fact. See notes 276–78 and accompanying text. It may con-

Section 2254(d)(2) must be reconciled with §2254(e)(1), which instructs federal courts regarding the effect they must give to state court findings of fact.[419] That task demands nice distinctions.[420] Between them, §2254(d)(2) and §2254(e)(1) contemplate that a federal habeas court can at once presume the accuracy of facts found in state court and conclude that the decision a state court ultimately reached on the merits of a federal claim was based on an unreasonable determination of the facts. That proposition sounds odd, but it is not illogical. Recall that a prisoner can rebut the presumption in favor of state findings by producing "clear and convincing" evidence that the state court was wrong. Of course, if a prisoner defeats the presumption established by §2254(e)(1), a federal habeas court would almost certainly *have* to say that the state court's findings were to that extent unreasonable within the meaning of §2254(d)(2).[421] In this instance, the order in which a federal court should proceed seems clear. It would make no sense to start with §2254(d)(2). If the court were to do that, it would be attempting to decide whether a state court decision was based on an unreasonable determination of the facts *before* ascertaining *what* facts the state court found that can be accepted as accurate. The question of relief under §2254(d)(2) seems plainly to be subsequent to the preliminary questions addressed by §2254(e)(1).

Section 2254(d)(2) must also be squared with §2254(e)(2), which instructs federal courts regarding the availability of federal evidentiary hearings.[422] Herein more interpretive issues. By hypothesis, §2254(e)(2) allows a federal hearing in at least some cases and thus contemplates that, in those instances, federal courts will take new evidence beyond the evidence that was presented in state court. Yet §2254(d)(2) generally prohibits federal relief unless the state court based its decision on an unreasonable determination of the facts in light of the evidence the state court itself considered. Here, too, the order in which a federal court must proceed seems clear. It would make no sense to begin with the question of relief under §2254(d)(2). If the court were to do that, it would limit its attention to the evidence that was presented in state court and decide whether federal relief is barred on that basis alone. That, in turn, would rob §2254(e)(2) of any meaning. If the court were to decide that habeas relief is foreclosed because the state court reasonably found the material facts in reliance on the evidence the state court saw, it would be

---

comitantly be difficult to say whether the potential flaw in the state court's work should be judged under §2254(d)(2) or under the "unreasonable application" clause in §2254(d)(1). See *Torres v. Prunty*, 223 F.3d 1103, 1107 (9th Cir. 2000) (making this point). If a federal court concludes that a previous state court decision was based on an unreasonable determination of the facts within the meaning of §2254(d)(2), it does not follow on that ground alone that the federal court must grant relief. All that follows logically is that federal relief is not prohibited. The prisoner still must convince the federal court that his claim was meritorious and non-harmless in light of the Supreme Court precedents that were in place at the time. *Francis S. v. Stone*, 221 F.3d 100, 115 (2d Cir. 2000). Yet the court will almost certainly have addressed that question as an antecedent matter. See notes 409, 491.

419. See notes 269–78 and accompanying text.

420. See *Green v. White*, 232 F.3d 671, 672 n.3 (9th Cir. 2000) (opinion of Lay, C.J.) (noting that these two provisions are both addressed to the significance of state factual findings). The two provisions derive from different prior legislative bills and were brought together in the bill that became the 1996 Act without any public discussion or explanation of how they would function together. See Yackle, *Primer*, note 65, at 427 (tracing the idea of an "unreasonable" determination of the facts to a Justice Department memorandum explaining the Reagan Administration's program).

421. Cf. *Torres*, 223 F.3d at 1110 n.6 (explaining that by holding that a state court finding was unreasonable the court had necessarily concluded that the prisoner had shown by clear and convincing evidence that the finding was erroneous).

422. See notes 279–91 and accompanying text.

futile to turn thereafter to the question whether the federal court can and should take additional evidence in a hearing of its own. Section 2254(e)(2) is intelligible only if it governs the way a federal court is to construct the record on which it will decide the ultimate question whether a prisoner is entitled to federal habeas relief. In combination with §2254(e)(2), §2254(d)(2) makes sense only if it limits a federal court to an examination of evidence before the state courts in cases in which no federal hearing is held and thus no new evidence emerges in federal court.[423] Here again, the question of relief under §2254(d) is not the first, but the last, question on which a federal court must rule.

Together, §2254(e)(1), §2254(e)(2), §2254(d)(2) render a complicated yet coherent analytical program for a federal court to follow. Initially, pursuant to §2254(e)(1), the court presumes that the findings of fact in state court were correct. The prisoner can rebut that presumption with respect to any particular finding only by producing clear and convincing evidence that the state court was mistaken.[424] The prisoner may also request a federal hearing to determine facts that were not developed in state court. In that event, the court must turn to §2254(e)(2). If it was the prisoner's fault that the facts were not developed, the court can grant a hearing only if the prisoner satisfies the standards set out in §2254(e)(2)(A) and (B).[425] If the prisoner was not at fault, or if he manages to meet those standards, the federal court can hold a hearing—and *will* if the facts alleged would establish a meritorious claim.[426] After a hearing, the court itself may make findings of fact that supplement the findings reached by the state court. At that point, the federal court has captured the evidence and facts, true or presumed to be true, that form the predicate for determining whether habeas relief is barred by §2254(d)(2). If the federal court granted no federal hearing and thus took no additional evidence, the court must decide whether the state court's findings were unreasonable in light of the evidence the state court considered. If, however, the federal court held its own hearing and added new evidence to the record, the court must decide whether the state court's findings were unreasonable in light of that evidence, as well.[427]

This construction accounts for the allowance that §2254(e)(2) makes for federal hearings in some cases. It also makes sense as a matter of policy. It is defensible to say, on the one hand, that federal habeas relief should be barred when federal and state courts have a reasonable disagreement about the facts in light of a common body of evidence. When a state court arrives at a finding of fact (a finding it would reach again

---

423. But see *Jeffries v. Wood*, 114 F.3d 1484, 1506 (9th Cir. 1997) (Kozinski, J., dissenting) (contending that if federal habeas courts look beyond the record that was before the state courts they may encourage prisoners to "circumvent" §2254(d) by "planting factual errors in state court dispositions").

424. See notes 269–70 and accompanying text. Nothing in §2254(e)(1) or in any other statutory provision specifies the procedural arrangements for giving the prisoner an opportunity to present rebutting evidence. A prisoner may, of course, argue that the very evidence the state court considered demonstrates that its factual finding was wrong. Yet a prisoner may also wish to introduce new evidence to make the required clear and convincing showing. That may necessitate a federal hearing. Section 2254(e)(2) often bars a federal hearing into the facts supporting a prisoner's claim for habeas relief. It is far from clear, however, that §2254(e)(2) governs the availability of the kind of hearing contemplated by §2254(e)(1). See notes 281, 285. Of course, if §2254(e)(2) is applicable at this stage, a prisoner may nonetheless escape its general prohibition on federal hearings if he exercised the necessary diligence in state court. See notes 280–83 and accompanying text.

425. See notes 284–90 and accompanying text.

426. See *Matheney v. Anderson*, 253 F.3d 1025, 1039 (7th Cir. 2001), citing *Townsend v. Sain*, 372 U.S. at 312–13; text accompanying note 267.

427. *Sanna v. DiPaolo*, 265 F.3d 1, 10 (1st Cir. 2001).

even though a federal court disagrees), it is defensible to maintain that the state court's view should control, so long as it is reasonable. It is not defensible, however, to propose that federal relief should equally be barred when a federal court arrives at a different factual determination on the basis of a different body of evidence. By hypothesis in a case of that kind, the state court made a finding in reliance on an incomplete evidentiary record. With the advantage of additional information, the state court might not reach that same conclusion again. Accordingly, in a case in which §2254(e)(2) permits a federal court to take more evidence, the federal court may award habeas relief without simply substituting its own judgment for that of the state court. For all that appears, the state court itself would reach the same factual finding, given the benefit of evidence that previously escaped its attention.

4. Comparison with the Ban on New Rules and Qualified Immunity

The arrangements established by §2254(d) must be reconciled with the larger body of habeas law, some of it prescribed by other statutes, most of it created by the Supreme Court—initially in *Brown v. Allen* and more recently in the *Teague* line of cases. It is also well to keep in mind that the Court has employed similar doctrinal formulations to describe the qualified immunity that executive officers can assert to defeat suits for damages. The overlap between §2254(d) and *Teague* is obvious enough. Justice O'Connor acknowledged in *Terry Williams* that §2254(d) speaks to the Court's internal debate in *West* and establishes the effect that federal habeas courts must give to previous state court determinations regarding mixed questions of law and fact.[428] She declined to say, however, whether §2254(d) enacts Justice Thomas' position in *West* regarding the federal courts' proper role.[429] The statute neither displaces nor codifies the *Teague* doctrine wholesale. It is accurate to say only that §2254(d) absorbs the central ideas in *Teague* into a statutory framework for handling habeas petitions seeking, in effect, to upset prior state court decisions on the merits of prisoners' claims. Three features of §2254(d) especially invite comparisons with *Teague* and qualified immunity: (1) the significance of the requirement in §2254(d) that there must be a prior state court adjudication and decision on the merits; (2) the standards to which federal courts hold a previous state court decision; and (3) the procedural steps by which federal courts bring those standards to bear.

Adjudication on the merits. Recall that the *Teague* doctrine is not (necessarily) concerned with cases in which state courts addressed and rejected prisoners' claims on the merits. To conduct a *Teague* analysis, a federal court need not examine a prior state court judgment at all. Instead, the federal court surveys the precedents that were in place when the prisoner's conviction became final and determines whether those precedents compelled a judgment for the prisoner.[430] Qualified immunity doctrine governs the circum-

428. *Terry Williams*, 529 U.S. at 411–12; see notes 364–67 and accompanying text.

429. 529 U.S. at 411 (explaining that the relationship between §2254(d) and Justice Thomas' argument is "beside the point"). See also Note, *Rewriting the Great Writ: Standards of Review for Habeas Corpus Under the New 28 U.S.C. §2254*, 110 Harv. L. Rev. 1868, 1882 (1997) (reading §2254(d) to establish a "reasonableness" standard for mixed questions but failing to mention Justice Thomas).

430. See notes 358–61 and accompanying text.

stances in which executive officers can escape liability for damages in civil lawsuits filed originally in federal court. In those cases, there is rarely any prior state court judgment regarding the defendant officers' behavior, thus no occasion for a federal court to address previous state court proceedings.[431] By contrast, §2254(d) applies to a claim advanced in a habeas petition only if a state court previously disallowed the claim on the merits.[432]

If §2254(d) is inapplicable to a claim, the consequences are problematic. In that event, a federal habeas court arguably should address the claim as it would have prior to the enactment of AEDPA, subject to the *Teague* doctrine as that doctrine then stood.[433] Alternatively, §2254(d) may occupy the field, controlling cases to which it applies and uprooting (by negative implication) any doctrinal arrangements (like *Teague*) that the Court had previously adopted to accomplish similar ends. Accordingly, in a case in which §2254(d) is inapplicable, a federal habeas court should proceed as it would have prior to *Teague* itself and thus should determine the merits of the claim on the basis of current law.[434] Neither of those positions has to be adopted. The better solution for cases in which §2254(d) does not formally apply extrapolates from the statute by analogy. Section 2254(d) seems plainly to adopt the policy that prisoners' claims are to be judged against federal law as it was clearly established by the Supreme Court at some earlier time. That statutory definition of the controlling law in cases to which §2254(d) applies may sensibly be employed in all cases, including cases in which §2254(d) does not formally control. If, then, there is no state court merits adjudication and decision in the mix, a federal habeas court still should restrict itself to evaluating a claim on the basis of the rules of federal law reflected in the Supreme Court's holdings at the time a prisoner's conviction became final.[435]

It does not follow that the relief-limiting provisions in §2254(d) should also spill over to cases in which §2254(d) does not apply. If that were the law, the requirement of prior state court merits adjudication to bring the statute formally into play would have no meaning. All the same implications would obtain irrespective of whether a state court adjudicated and decided a claim on the merits. Moreover, it would be difficult to apply the relief-limiting provisions in the absence of a prior state court decision. A fed-

431. If a claim against a state officer *was* previously adjudicated in state court, the state court's judgment is typically entitled to preclusive effect in any subsequent suit for damages in federal court. See Chapter VI, notes 161–95 and accompanying text.

432. See notes 376–89 and accompanying text.

433. The Court made it clear in *Banks* that *Teague* remains in place in cases in which §2254(d) is applicable. That does not mean (necessarily) that *Teague* is unaffected by §2254(d). Nor does it mean that all the features of the *Teague* doctrine (for example, the definitions of "new" and "old" rules) survive intact.

434. Or, perhaps, according to the Court's previous doctrinal arrangements for handling habeas claims resting on "clear breaks" from precedent. See note 323. This alternative has its attractions as a matter of policy. If the purpose of §2254(d) is to encourage state courts to adjudicate the merits of federal claims, it would make sense to subject their judgments based on other grounds to more aggressive federal consideration. Certainly, it would make sense to set *Teague* aside. Realistically speaking, the *Teague* doctrine has always been a contrivance for forcing federal habeas courts to "defer" to previous state court judgments on the merits. See notes 358–63 and accompanying text. Justice Thomas essentially said as much in *West*. See text accompanying note 365. Now that Congress has adopted a statutory mechanism that serves the same purpose, the Court might sensibly hold that its own *Teague* doctrine has been superseded. Indeed, there is a case for discarding *Teague* in all cases, including cases in which §2254(d) is applicable. That approach would relieve the headaches created by the combination of *Teague* and §2254(d) in a single stroke. See, e.g., 446–88 and accompanying text. As matters stand, however, *Teague* continues to operate in cases in which §2254(d) also applies.

435. But see notes 472–79 and accompanying text (discussing the different cut-off dates for purposes of *Teague* and §2254(d)).

eral habeas court does not need a state decision in view in order to identify contemporaneous Supreme Court holdings and apply them to a current claim. But by most accounts, a federal court *does* need a state court decision (and, indeed, an explanatory opinion) in order to determine whether that decision fails the "contrary to" test, the "unreasonable application" test, or the "unreasonable determination" test.[436] It would make sense, then, in cases in which there is no prior state adjudication and decision on the merits, for a federal habeas court to borrow the "clearly established" law standard from §2254(d), but to set aside the relief-limiting provisions that the statute would bring into play if it were applicable.

This solution serves the purpose that can fairly be ascribed to §2254(d). In the main, the idea is to encourage state courts to examine and determine the merits of prisoners' federal claims in light of extant Supreme Court holdings. If a state court does that, it is assured that its decision will not be effectively upset simply because a federal habeas court thinks the decision is erroneous. Instead, a state decision on the merits prevails unless it fails one of the tests in paragraphs (1) and (2). If, however, a state court declines to deliver a merits decision, there is no self-evident reason why a federal court should withhold relief if the federal court is persuaded that the claim was valid at the time.[437]

Standards. When §2254(d) is applicable, it limits federal habeas corpus relief to claims depending on federal legal rules that were "clearly established" by the Supreme Court when the state court acted. That standard resembles the standard in *Teague* cases, where federal habeas courts usually apply only "old" rules.[438] The language the Court uses to describe the standard in qualified immunity cases is even closer: Executive officers are immune unless they acted unreasonably by violating legal rules that were "clearly established."[439] These parallels noted, the cross-currents running between §2254(d), *Teague*, and qualified immunity are actually more nuanced.

As a general matter, the Court insists that the inquiries required by *Teague* and §2254(d) are "distinct" from each other. In *Horn v. Banks*,[440] the prisoner was convicted and sentenced to death in a Pennsylvania state court. After his conviction and sentence became final on direct review, the Supreme Court held in *Mills v. Maryland*[441] that a state cannot require a jury to reach unanimous agreement regarding the existence of a mitigating factor before the jury can take that factor into account in deciding whether to impose capital punishment. The prisoner filed an application for postconviction relief in state court, contending that the jury in his case had been instructed in a way that *Mills* prohibited. The Pennsylvania Supreme Court held that the jury instruction was consistent with *Mills*. In habeas corpus proceedings in federal court, the Court of Appeals for the Third Circuit declined to consider whether *Mills* established a "new rule" within the meaning of *Teague* or, if *Mills* did create a new rule, whether that rule fit one of the two exceptions to the ban on "new rule" claims. Since the state supreme court

---

436. See notes 391–92 and accompanying text.

437. This assumes, of course, that there are no independent procedural reasons for refusing to get into the merits in the first place.

438. See *Neelley v. Nagle*, 138 F.3d 917, 922–23 (11th Cir. 1998) (explaining that *Teague* and §2254(d) call for a "similar analysis" of whether a rule of law was clearly established at the crucial time); see notes 446–61 and accompanying text.

439. See Chapter X, note 450 and accompanying text.

440. 122 S.Ct. 2147 (2002) (*per curiam*).

441. 486 U.S. 367 (1988).

had applied *Mills*, the federal circuit court thought that the *Teague* "retroactivity" issue was not "implicated."[442] In passing, the circuit court also questioned whether *Teague* has "continued force independent of AEDPA."[443] Focusing exclusively on §2254(d), the circuit court concluded that the state court had "unreasonably applied" *Mills* and therefore that federal habeas corpus relief was available. The Supreme Court summarily reversed. In a *per curiam*, the Court denied that it had ever suggested that §2254(d) relieves federal courts of the duty to address *Teague* arguments or that habeas relief may issue "automatically" whenever the statute establishes no bar.[444] In short, a federal court entertaining a habeas corpus petition cannot bypass the *Teague* choice-of-law issue and dispose of a claim solely on the basis of §2254(d).[445]

To say that §2254(d) does not displace the *Teague* doctrine is not, of course, to say that §2254(d) has no bearing on *Teague* at all. The *Teague* doctrine and the statute cannot simply ignore each other; they must learn to live together. Justice O'Connor explained in *Terry Williams* that a rule that rests entirely on Supreme Court precedents and qualifies as "old" for purposes of *Teague* also counts as "clearly established" law for purposes of §2254(d).[446] That follows *a fortiori*. It would be hard to deny that a rule of law was clearly established if it was ascribable to the Supreme Court and dictated a result favorable to the prisoner.[447] It does not follow (and Justice O'Connor did not say) that any rule that counts as clearly established law within the meaning of the statute necessarily counts as an old rule as old rules have been defined in the *Teague* cases. On examination, that definition of old rules is no longer tenable. If it were preserved intact, it would render the relief-limiting provisions in §2254(d) unintelligible. In the parlance of *Teague*, the definition of old rules itself embodies a "reasonableness" test. A rule is old only if it admitted a single reasonable result: a judgment sustaining the prisoner's claim. If old rules (defined that way) were congruent with clearly established federal law, there would be no room in which the "unreasonable application" clause[448] could sensibly operate. The *Teague* doctrine alone would prevent federal courts from considering attacks on reasonable state court decisions, thus eliminating the possibility that the statute might bar habeas relief on the ground that a state court decided a cognizable claim unreasonably.

Recall the syntax. Pursuant to the "unreasonable application" clause, a federal court is barred from granting relief if a previous state court decision involved an "unreasonable application of...clearly established" law. If that were read to mean that a federal court can award relief only if a state court unreasonably applied an old rule as defined in the *Teague* cases, the federal court would have to undertake *two* "reasonableness" inquiries *seriatim*. Initially, the federal court would have to ascertain the only reasonable result that contemporaneous precedents would permit and determine whether the state court's decision comported with that result, so that the state court acted "reasonably." Then, the federal court would have to decide whether the state court's decision consti-

442. *Banks v. Horn*, 271 F.3d 527, 543 (3d Cir. 2001).

443. Id. at 541 n.13, quoted in *Banks*, 122 S.Ct. at 2151.

444. 122 S.Ct. at 2151.

445. Since the Court acted in *Banks* on the basis of the *certiorari* papers alone, the justices did not see fully developed briefs from the parties or *amici*. There were no dissents. Summary actions stand only for the propositions they specifically articulate and do not offer more general guidance as precedents. See Chapter VII, note 237 and accompanying text.

446. 529 U.S. at 412.

447. Bear in mind, however, that the cut-off dates are different for old rules within the meaning of *Teague* and clearly established law within the meaning of §2254(d). See notes 315, 328–29, 404, 472–79 and accompanying text.

448. Or the "unreasonable determination" clause. See notes 418–27 and accompanying text.

tuted an unreasonable application of the law reflected in that very result—from which, by hypothesis, it would have been unreasonable to depart in the first place. To avoid that silly result, the Court must recognize that clearly established law is not coextensive with old rules as defined in the *Teague* cases, that clearly established law covers comparatively more ground, and that the Court's prior holdings capture that wider territory.[449]

The explanation for this riddle is plain enough. Both the *Teague* doctrine and §2254(d) protect "reasonable" state court decisions. But they do it in different ways. The *Teague* doctrine does it by packing peculiar meaning into the conception of old rules. The Court articulates legal rules at a case-specific level of generality and, even then, treats any reasonable judgment on a claim as sufficient. A reasonable decision then becomes the baseline, a departure from which constitutes a new rule. In a case in which a state court rejected a prisoner's claim, a federal habeas court's duty is to ascertain the only reasonable result that a court could reach at the time the prisoner's conviction became final and then determine whether the state court correctly arrived at that result. Section 2254(d) fosters deference to reasonable state court decisions by limiting the federal courts' authority to grant habeas relief.[450] If a federal habeas court determines that a state court reached the wrong result in light of clearly established law, the "unreasonable application" clause still bars federal relief unless the state court decision was also unreasonable. Under the statute, then, a federal court's duty is to ascertain the correct result regarding a prisoner's claim at the time and then determine whether a state court came reasonably close to that. If so, habeas relief is unavailable. The intellectual footwork is different, but the practical result is much the same.[451]

The *Teague* doctrine and §2254(d) cannot simply function in sequence, each performing the same function, each protecting reasonable state court decisions on federal claims, each doing it in its own way. The answer to the riddle, then, is to amend *Teague's* definition of old rules to comport with the definition of clearly established law for purposes of the statute: the Supreme Court holdings in place at the relevant time.[452] If rules of law embedded in the Court's holdings fix the baseline for the *Teague* "retroac-

---

449. Justice O'Connor may have intimated this understanding in *Terry Williams* when she said that the "clearly established" federal law phrase bears "only a slight" relationship to *Teague*. 529 U.S. at 412. By some accounts, she meant only to say that old rules as defined in the *Teague* cases do not have to be ascribed to the Supreme Court itself. That, however, would have been misleading inasmuch as it typically takes solid Supreme Court precedent to forge an old rule. See, e.g., *Clemons v. Delo*, 124 F.3d 944, 955 n.11 (8th Cir. 1997) (stating that only the Supreme Court itself can establish a rule that "dictates" one result), quoted in *Tyler v. Cain*, 533 U.S. 656, 676 (2001) (Breyer, J., dissenting). It is inconceivable that Justice O'Connor did not appreciate the obvious relationship between *Teague* and §2254(d) or the necessity of reconciling the definition of old rules with the statute's limitations on habeas relief.

450. 529 U.S. at 412 (opinion of O'Connor, J.). Judge Easterbrook has explained that §2254(d) "preserves rather than undermines federal courts' independent interpretive power" inasmuch as federal courts "are free to express an independent opinion on all legal issues in [a] case." This statute "does no more than regulate relief." *Lindh*, 96 F.3d at 868–70.

451. For related discussions, see Alan K. Chen, *Shadow Law: Reasonable Unreasonableness, Habeas Theory, and the Nature of Legal Rules*, 2 Buffalo Crim. L. Rev. 535 (1999); Larry W. Yackle, *The Figure in the Carpet*, 78 Tex. L. Rev. 1731, 1745–56 (2000); Note, *The Path to Habeas Corpus Narrows: Interpreting 28 U.S.C. §2254(d)(1)*, 96 Mich. L. Rev. 434 (1997).

452. The choice of appropriate cut-off dates for old rules and clearly established law is another, related but distinguishable, matter. Different cut-off dates cannot be preserved without producing difficulty. See notes 472–79 and accompanying text. But different cut-off dates *can* be preserved without producing the same intellectual confusion generated by the combination of the definition of old rules in the *Teague* cases and §2254(d)'s reliance on clearly established law as the operative standard.

tivity" analysis, that analysis can be undertaken as an initial matter, and still there will be room for §2254(d)'s relief-limiting provisions to operate thereafter. A federal habeas court will identify the rule of law it is entitled to apply to a claim (the rule that Supreme Court precedents established), decide whether a prior state court decision comported with that rule of law, and then, if the state court decision was erroneous, decide whether paragraphs (1) and (2) of §2254(d) nonetheless bar habeas relief.[453]

In *Terry Williams*, both Justice Stevens and Justice O'Connor recognized that *Teague* and §2254(d) fit together in this way. Recall that Justice Stevens said that the "threshold" question "under AEDPA" is whether a prisoner's claim depends on a "rule of law" that was "clearly established" at the time his conviction became final.[454] That statement plainly referred to *Teague*. The Court has always regarded the *Teague* choice-of-law question to be first in line for determination once a claim is found to satisfy procedural requirements.[455] Notice, too, that Stevens identified the time at which the applicable rule prevailed as the date on which the prisoner's conviction became final. That, of course, is the cut-off date that distinguishes between cases on direct and collateral review and thus determines, within *Teague's* framework, whether "new rule" claims are cognizable.[456] In the next breath, moreover, Justice Stevens explained that *Strickland* "dictated" the analysis that the Virginia Supreme Court was obliged to employ, thus indicating that *Strickland* stated an old rule within the meaning of *Teague*.[457] Justice Stevens also had §2254(d) in mind. He explained that he was articulating the initial question "under AEDPA," and he substituted the "clearly established law" standard in §2254(d) for the definition of old rules in the *Teague* cases. The *Strickland* case, he said, both "dictated" the controlling rule for *Teague* purposes and supplied the pertinent "clearly established" law within the meaning of §2254(d).[458]

Justice O'Connor joined this part of Justice Stevens' opinion and thus endorsed both his analytic framework and his account of *Strickland*. She added only two clarifications: (1) the Court's own holdings form the content of "clearly established" law within the meaning of §2254(d); and (2) the cut-off date under the statute is the date of "the relevant state-court decision."[459] Between them, accordingly, Justice Stevens and Justice O'-Connor harmonized *Teague* with §2254(d) not by separating the two, but by collapsing the core of *Teague's* choice-of-law analysis into the statute's search for clearly established law. This is not to suggest that the statute eclipses *Teague*. Remember *Banks*.[460] It is to suggest, however, that one feature of *Teague* (the Court's prior definition of old rules) will move over to make room for the statute. The resulting package is untidy, scarcely the sort of thing anyone would construct writing on a clean slate. But in general part the framework is coherent. A federal court first addresses the choice-of-law question

---

453. This same redefinition of old and new rules can be applied, in turn, to other provisions of AEDPA that depend on new rules or new rights having retroactive effect in collateral proceedings. See notes 154–64, 288–89, 524–35 and accompanying text.

454. 529 U.S. at 390; see text accompanying note 401.

455. See note 325 (explaining that procedural questions are antecedent to *Teague*).

456. See notes 315, 329 and accompanying text.

457. 529 U.S. at 391. See text accompanying note 345.

458. See text accompanying note 369.

459. 529 U.S. at 412 (opinion of O'Connor, J.); see notes 403–04, 472–79 and accompanying text.

460. See notes 440–45 and accompanying text.

that remains the province of *Teague*. Now, however, the rule that controls in a habeas case is not an old rule as previously defined, but the rule that the Court's holdings established. Subsequently, the court determines whether a state court decision that is erroneous in light of those holdings is nonetheless sufficient to bar an award of the federal habeas remedy under §2254(d)'s relief-limiting provisions.[461]

The measure of "reasonableness" that state courts are allowed is yet another matter. In the *Teague* cases, the Court is wont to say that a state court could reasonably reject a claim if its validity was "susceptible to debate among reasonable minds."[462] In *Terry Williams*, however, Justice O'Connor expressly disclaimed the "reasonable judge" standard for use in cases governed by the "unreasonable application" clause in §2254(d)(1).[463] Few observers think there is much to be made of the difference between the loose rhetoric in *Teague* cases and Justice O'Connor's more circumspect opinion in *Terry Williams*.[464] Under the *Teague* doctrine, too, the Court is plainly concerned that state courts render objectively reasonable decisions.[465]

There are two other loose ends touching the intersections between *Teague* and §2254(d): (1) the fate of the exceptions to *Teague's* general ban on "new rule" claims; and (2) the effects of the different cut-off dates employed by *Teague* and the statute.

Recall that the Court has not enforced *Teague's* general ban on "new rule" claims relentlessly, but has allowed certain exceptions.[466] As a matter of experience, those exceptions may come to very little. But they do exist. Section 2254(d) mentions neither the *Teague* exceptions nor any others. It is open to argue, then, that in this respect the statute is less forgiving than *Teague* and that federal habeas courts are barred from awarding relief to any prisoners advancing any claims, unless a prior state court decision fails one of the tests in the relief-limiting provisions.[467] That interpretation will not wash. When the Court explained in *Banks* that *Teague* survives §2254(d), the Court explicitly mentioned the *Teague* exceptions.[468] If §2254(d) were read not to allow those exceptions, they would be meaningless.[469] Moreover, other provisions in AEDPA refer to "new" rules of law that are "retroactively applicable" to cases reaching the federal courts in habeas corpus proceedings.[470] Those provisions typically relax procedural

---

461. See notes 489–91 and accompanying text.

462. *Butler*, 494 U.S. at 417; see note 349 and accompanying text.

463. See note 415 and accompanying text.

464. Notice, in this vein, that certificates of appealability can be issued only if "reasonable jurists" could debate whether a claim warrants appellate review. See text accompanying note 498. There, too, the Court is only being sloppy. It is judgment that must be "reasonable," not judges.

465. Since *Terry Williams*, some circuit courts have offered their own specifications of the meaning of an "unreasonable application" of federal law within the meaning of §2254(d). E.g., *Francis S.*, 221 F.3d at 111 (explaining that "some increment of incorrectness beyond error is required"); *Van Tran v. Lindsey*, 212 F.3d 1143, 1153 (stating that the state decision must reflect "clear error"). Professor Pettys has identified a variety of other venues in which courts make roughly analogous judgments. But he finds no analogy genuinely satisfying. Todd E. Pettys, *Federal Habeas Corpus Relief and the New Tolerance for "Reasonably Erroneous" Applications of Federal Law*, 63 Ohio St. L.J. 731 (2002).

466. See notes 335–39 and accompanying text.

467. See Liebman & Ryan, note 372, at 867–68.

468. *Banks*, 122 S.Ct. at 2150 n.5.

469. Of course, the exceptions are so narrow as to be practically meaningless, anyway, even if they are constitutionally grounded. See notes 340–42 and accompanying text.

470. See notes 154–64, 288–89, 524–35.

hurdles that otherwise would prevent prisoners pressing "new rule" claims from seeking habeas relief. They do so, presumably, on the theory that some new rules are retroactively applicable because they fit one of the *Teague* exceptions. Their purposes would be frustrated if §2254(d) were read to deny similar exceptions by negative implication.[471]

The *Teague* doctrine generally bars a federal habeas court from entertaining a claim based on a rule of law that emerged after a prisoner's conviction and sentence became final on direct review.[472] By contrast, §2254(d) specifies that a federal habeas court is to ask whether a state court's decision on the merits of a claim conformed to clearly established law at the time the state court acted.[473] That is often the date on which the highest state court affirmed a prisoner's conviction and sentence on direct review. But it may also be the date on which the highest state court rejected the claim in state postconviction proceedings. Both *Terry Williams* and *Banks* are illustrations.[474] When a state court adjudicates the merits at the postconviction stage, the §2254(d) cut-off date comes after the cut-off date for *Teague* purposes. The different cut-off dates can have practical significance in some cases.[475]

In *Banks*, for example, the Pennsylvania Supreme Court rejected the prisoner's *Mills* claim on the merits in the course of state postconviction proceedings occurring some years after *Mills* was decided.[476] The Third Circuit held that in those circumstances the *Teague* "retroactivity" question was no longer relevant. The Supreme Court rejected that idea out of hand. Yet the Court did not suggest that the circuit court was wrong in thinking that, at the time the state supreme court acted, the *Mills* decision constituted clearly established law for purposes of §2254(d). It follows that a prisoner can be denied an opportunity to press a claim in federal habeas corpus on the basis of the *Teague* choice-of-law doctrine even in a case in which the state's highest court reached an erroneous decision on the claim in light of clearly established federal law that the state court knew to exist at the time.[477] It doesn't matter if a state court openly defied a Supreme Court decision "on all fours"—if a claim based on that decision is not cognizable in habeas corpus in the first place.[478] This, notwithstanding that the rationale for barring "new rule" claims is to ensure that federal

---

471. Cf. *Tyler*, 533 U.S. at 665 (discussing the *Teague* exceptions in a case involving the provisions of AEDPA governing successive petitions); see notes 524–33 and accompanying text (discussing *Tyler*).

472. See text accompanying notes 323–27.

473. See text accompanying note 404.

474. See text accompanying notes 399, 441–42.

475. See Liebman & Ryan, note 372, at 867–68; Lee, note 415, at 118–22.

476. *Banks*, 271 F.3d at 541. See notes 440–45 and accompanying text.

477. In *Banks* itself, neither the Third Circuit nor the Supreme Court actually decided whether the prisoner's *Mills* claim was foreclosed by *Teague*. The Third Circuit held only that *Mills* constituted clearly established law at the time the Pennsylvania Supreme Court considered the prisoner's claim—not, necessarily, before the cut-off date for *Teague* purposes. The *Teague* cut-off date was earlier: the date on which the prisoner's conviction and sentence became final on direct review.

478. This arrangement may encourage states to adopt state law versions of the *Teague* doctrine, so that state courts, too, decline to consider novel claims in state postconviction proceedings and thus avoid putting themselves in the position of the Pennsylvania Supreme Court in *Banks*. Yet it seems ironic that the *Teague* doctrine, fashioned by the Supreme Court to orchestrate relations between federal and state courts, should end up as the policy of individual states for purposes of their own domestic affairs.

habeas corpus serves its purpose to deter state courts from neglecting settled principles of federal law.[479]

The relationship between the standards in §2254(d) and qualified immunity cases is probably remote, despite the appearance of the "clearly established law" formulation in both contexts.[480] Just as the policy considerations that drive qualified immunity doctrine do not travel well to habeas corpus cases governed by *Teague*, they do not travel well to cases implicating §2254(d), either.[481] In *Terry Williams*, Justice Stevens explicitly rejected any analogy to qualified immunity, albeit in a part of his opinion that did not enjoy majority support.[482] Justice O'Connor said nothing about immunity in her controlling opinion interpreting §2254(d). Two matters touching qualified immunity nonetheless warrant attention for comparative purposes: (1) the significance of lower court precedent; and (2) the acceptability of back-to-back "reasonableness" determinations.

Pursuant to §2254(d), only the Supreme Court can clearly establish federal law for state courts to follow. In qualified immunity cases, lower court precedents can supply executive officers with the guidance required.[483] This apparent difference between §2254(d) and qualified immunity suggests, on the surface, that §2254(d) gives state courts more leeway than qualified immunity allows executive officers. Here again, however, the verbal formulations used to describe legal doctrine may not reflect reality. There is room, in any event, for federal habeas courts implementing §2254(d) to look beyond Supreme Court precedents.[484]

In habeas cases implicating both §2254(d) and *Teague*, clearly established federal law cannot be the equivalent of old rules as previously defined. If that were the law, the relief-limiting provisions in the statute would have no operational impact. Federal habeas courts would have to undertake two "reasonableness" determinations in sequence, which, in turn, would produce an intellectual muddle.[485] The initial "reasonableness" determination made for purposes of the *Teague* choice-of-law question would always be dispositive.[486] Recall, however, that in *Saucier v. Katz*[487] the Court held that some fourth amendment cases contemplate a similarly troubling succession of "reasonableness" questions in the context of qualified immunity.[488] In *Saucier*, however, the Court was moved by the undesirability of making a special exception for fourth amendment cases and the desirability of assigning the immunity question to judges rather than juries. Neither of those considerations obtains in habeas corpus cases governed by §2254(d). In §2254(d) cases, two "reasonableness" determinations in tandem would not be the exception, but the rule—making habeas corpus logically troublesome in most instances, not just in a few. More importantly, in

479. Somehow, these dots don't seem to connect. But, again, this possibility is created not by any necessary difference between old rules and clearly established law, but rather by the different cut-off dates employed by the *Teague* doctrine and §2254(d).

480. See Chapter X, note 450 and accompanying text.

481. See notes 350–52 and accompanying text. Both Judge Easterbrook and Judge Selya suggest that courts handling habeas cases pursuant to §2254(d) should rely on habeas corpus precedents applying the *Teague* doctrine rather than on §1983 precedents applying qualified immunity doctrine. *Lindh*, 96 F.3d at 869–70; *O'Brien*, 145 F.3d at 24–25.

482. 529 U.S. at 380 n.12.

483. See Chapter X, notes 468–69 and accompanying text.

484. See notes 406–08 and accompanying text.

485. See text accompanying note 449.

486. See text accompanying notes 448–49.

487. 533 U.S. 194 (2001).

488. See Chapter X, text accompanying notes 473–74.

habeas cases the confusion of two "reasonableness" determinations can be neither justified nor defused by assigning one determination to the court and the other to a jury.

5. Procedures

The steps of a habeas court's analysis under §2254(d) mesh fairly well with the *Teague* doctrine. The respondent is free to object to the consideration of a claim on the ground that it depends on a new rule. The Supreme Court confirmed in *Banks* that when an objection is raised, a habeas court must deal with it before going further. At the same time, that *Teague* choice-of-law question converges on the question under §2254(d) whether a previous state court decision comported with clearly established federal law—that is, contemporaneous Supreme Court holdings.[489] If the federal court decides that the state court decision was correct in light of those holdings, the court must dismiss the claim.[490] If the federal court concludes that the state court decision was erroneous in view of the Supreme Court's holdings then in place, the court must turn to the provisions in paragraphs (1) and (2) of §2254(d). The tests contained in the "contrary to" clause, the "unreasonable application" clause, and the "unreasonable determination" clause then determine whether federal habeas relief is foreclosed.[491]

The steps in a qualified immunity analysis are different. There, a federal court entertaining an original suit for damages against an executive officer first determines whether the plaintiff has alleged facts that, if true, would establish a violation of a federal right. At the threshold, then, the court does not actually determine whether the plaintiff's allegations *are* true. In a habeas corpus case, by contrast, §2254(d) contemplates that a federal court *will* ascertain the facts (within the limits of §2254(e))[492] and thus will actually adjudicate the merits of a claim (albeit only by comparing the state court's decision with the law that was clearly established at the time).[493] In a qualified immunity case, the court appraises the sufficiency of the plaintiff's allegations on the basis of current law and turns to the question whether the defendant officer violated clearly established law only later, for purposes of determining the officer's entitlement to immunity.[494] In a

---

489. See notes 450–61 and accompanying text; but see notes 472–79 and accompanying text (discussing the different cut-off dates).

490. In many instances, there will be no occasion for a federal evidentiary hearing. Under §2254(e)(1), federal courts ordinarily presume that state court findings are correct. And under §2254(e)(2), federal courts deny evidentiary hearings to prisoners who failed to develop facts when they had an opportunity to do so in state court. If, however, §2254(e) permits federal fact-finding proceedings, federal courts ascertain the facts as part of the adjudication of claims on the merits. See notes 265–91 and accompanying text.

491. A federal habeas court presumably should decide initially whether a state court decision was erroneous in light of the Court's contemporaneous holdings and then turn, if necessary, to the question whether an incorrect decision nevertheless was close enough to forestall federal habeas relief. E.g., *Andrade v. Attorney General*, 270 F.3d 743, 753 (9th Cir. 2001), *cert. grt'd*, 122 S.Ct. 1434 (2002). But see *Penry v. Johnson*, 532 U.S. 782, 794–95 (2000) (arguably disposing of a claim on the basis of §2254(d)'s relief-limiting provisions alone); *Bell v. Jarvis*, 236 F.3d 149, 158–63 (4th Cir. 2000) (declining any "independent" decision on whether a state court decision was correct at the time and confining consideration to whether the state decision was "contrary to" clearly established law or "unreasonable").

492. See notes 265–91 and accompanying text.

493. See notes 395–405 and accompanying text.

494. See Chapter X, notes 475–84 and accompanying text.

habeas case, the court typically has no occasion to address current law, but rather focuses exclusively on the law as it was clearly established previously.

H. Appellate Review

Under 28 U.S.C. §2253, prisoners who are unsuccessful with §2254 habeas petitions or §2255 motions at the district court level may appeal to a circuit court of appeals and, from there, to the Supreme Court by means of *certiorari*. Pursuant to paragraph (b) of §2253, however, they are entitled to do so only if a "circuit justice or judge" issues a "certificate of appealability." Typically, prisoners request a certificate from the district judge.[495] If that judge refuses, prisoners may approach a circuit judge or a justice of the Supreme Court.[496] The standard for obtaining a certificate is familiar. According to paragraph (c)(2) of §2253, a prisoner must make "a substantial showing of the denial of a constitutional right." In *Slack v. McDaniel*,[497] Justice Kennedy explained that a prisoner satisfies that standard if "reasonable jurists could debate whether ... the petition should have been resolved in a different manner or that the issues presented [are] 'adequate to deserve encouragement to proceed further.'"[498]

The reference to a "constitutional" right raises yet again the question whether non-constitutional claims are precluded by implication. In this context, it would be difficult to read non-constitutional claims out of the picture: Prisoners would be allowed to press non-constitutional claims at the district level, but not higher, thus making district court judgments final.[499] In some cases, moreover, prisoners have non-constitutional claims that could not have been raised and adjudicated at trial or on direct review and can only be determined in collateral proceedings like those authorized by §2254 and §2255.[500] It would be novel and arguably unconstitutional to prohibit appellate review in those cases.[501] Consider that the denial of certificates on non-constitutional claims

---

495. *Hunter v. United States & Bailey v. Nagle*, 101 F.3d 1565 (11th Cir. 1996) (*en banc*). There is an argument that §2253(c)(1) authorizes only an appellate judge to issue a certificate. Yet by all accounts the statutory language is ambiguous. The practical value of assigning the function to district judges in the first instance justifies reading it to allow them to do so.

496. Circuit courts commonly read Fed. R. App. P. 22(b) to require a prisoner to seek a certificate first from a district judge. See *United States v. Youngblood*, 116 F.3d 1113 (5th Cir. 1997).

497. 529 U.S. 473 (2000).

498. Id. at 484, quoting *Barefoot v. Estelle*, 463 U.S. 880, 893 & n.4 (1983).

499. See *United States v. Cepero*, 224 F.3d 256 (3d Cir. 2000) (recognizing the implications but nonetheless reading the adjective "constitutional" to foreclose "non-constitutional" issues). Some circuits have defused the problem by considering certificates issued by district judges to be effective, even when they are arguably erroneous because they identify only substantial non-constitutional claims. The rationale is that the certificate requirement is not jurisdictional, but serves only as an administrative screening device. Once a district judge has identified an issue as appropriate for appellate review, a circuit court can proceed without second-guessing that preliminary action. E.g., *Soto v. United States*, 185 F.3d 48, 52 (2d Cir. 1999) (explaining that it would be a waste of time for a circuit court to act as a "gate keeper for the gate keeper"). Other circuits treat district court decisions to grant certificates as reviewable in the ordinary course. E.g., *Cepero*, 224 F.3d at 261–62.

500. This is especially true in §2255 cases. Prisoners challenging federal convictions and sentences often press federal non-constitutional claims. Prisoners attacking state court judgments are less likely to have non-constitutional theories for habeas relief.

501. Constitutional objections may be defused on the assumption that prisoners might still obtain an adjudication in the Supreme Court by means of an "original" habeas petition or some other

would not be outcome neutral. A respondent needs no certificate in order to seek appellate review of a district court judgment in a prisoner's favor. If paragraph (c)(2) were read to permit government appeals in cases involving non-constitutional claims, but to preclude prisoner-initiated appeals, it would skew the results that appellate courts can reach on federal issues: Errors that favor prisoners could be upset, but errors that favor the government would stand.[502]

Justice Kennedy acknowledged some of these implications in *Slack*. In that case, the prisoner advanced constitutional claims for relief, but the district court declined to consider some of them on the ground that the prisoner's petition was barred by the rules governing multiple federal petitions.[503] The respondent insisted that since that basis for dismissing the claims was non-constitutional, paragraph (c)(2) of §2253 barred the issuance of a certificate of appealability allowing the prisoner to challenge the district court's decision at the circuit level. Justice Kennedy balked at that construction of the statute. If it were adopted, paragraph (c)(2) would prevent circuit courts from overseeing district court determinations of the numerous non-constitutional procedural issues that attend habeas cases: for example, questions regarding filing periods, the exhaustion doctrine, and procedural default. To forestall that untenable result, Justice Kennedy held that in a case in which a district court denies habeas relief on procedural grounds without reaching the merits of a constitutional claim, a prisoner can obtain a certificate of appealability by satisfying the substantiality standard both with respect to the constitutional claim advanced in his petition and with respect to the non-constitutional procedural issue on which the district court decision rests. Kennedy explained that this interpretation of paragraph (c)(2) "gives meaning to Congress' requirement that a prisoner demonstrate substantial underlying constitutional claims."[504] Justice Kennedy did not address the troubling question whether prisoners who advance only non-constitutional claims for habeas relief can obtain a certificate of appealability.[505]

Pursuant to paragraph (c)(3) of §2253, a certificate of appealability "shall indicate which specific issue or issues satisfy [sic] the showing required by paragraph (2)." Initially, that further requirement allows district judges to limit the purview of circuit courts on appeal. If, however, a circuit court thinks that an issue is worth appellate consideration, one of its judges (or the judges on a panel together) can entertain an independent motion for a certificate identifying that issue.[506] If no district or circuit judge issues a certificate, the Supreme Court can exercise appellate jurisdiction to decide whether some issue *does* warrant appellate review.[507]

---

extraordinary procedure. But, of course, that possibility is not a practical answer, only a formal one. Cf. *Felker v. Turpin*, 518 U.S. 651 (1996); see notes 545 and accompanying text.

502. See Chapter IV, notes 77–92 and accompanying text (discussing limits on Congress' ability to manipulate the outcomes that Article III courts can reach).

503. See notes 508–52 and accompanying text.

504. *Slack*, 529 U.S. at 484. In passing, Justice Kennedy said that a federal judge considering an application for a certificate should address the substantiality of a potentially dispositive non-constitutional procedural issue first in order, perhaps, to avoid confronting the substantiality of the prisoner's underlying constitutional claims for relief. Id. at 485.

505. In *Hohn v. United States*, 524 U.S. 236 (1998), the Court initially granted review to determine whether paragraph (c)(2) forecloses certificates of appealability with respect to substantial non-constitutional claims for §2255 relief. The issue ultimately dropped out of that case.

506. But see note 499.

507. *Hohn*, 524 U.S. at 253; see Chapter VII, note 218.

I. Multiple Petitions

Prisoners sometimes attempt to file more than one §2254 petition or §2255 motion.[508] Just as habeas corpus is generally exempt from the Full Faith and Credit Statute, §2254 petitions and §2255 motions are equally exempt (formally speaking) from the federal common law preclusion rules that ordinarily restrict litigants' ability to file multiple federal lawsuits against the same defendant, pressing claims arising from a single transaction.[509] Nevertheless, second or successive federal petitions and motions are restricted by statutes and judicial decisions that typically give preclusive effect to the results of initial proceedings, in fact if not in name.[510]

Under 28 U.S.C. §2244(b)(1), a claim that was presented in a previous §2254 habeas petition "shall be dismissed." This does not mean that *any* claim that was contained in a prior application is barred, irrespective of the disposition. Chief Justice Rehnquist ex-

---

508. Many prisoners are not represented by counsel, either when they file an initial petition or when they file another. Acting for themselves, they may fail to appreciate the value that lawyers and judges place on aggregating claims in a single legal proceeding. Then, too, some prisoners act *pro se* when they file a first petition, but are fortunate enough to obtain counsel later. When an attorney comes into a case, he or she may identify claims or factual allegations that the prisoner overlooked in the prior proceeding. Counsel's only course, then, is to file another petition to do the work that was not done the first time around. This is often the pattern in death penalty cases. The supply of lawyers willing to handle capital cases is extremely limited. Organizations that recruit volunteers must engage in triage, providing lawyers only in the most needy cases at the moment. Those cases typically involve prisoners who have been unsuccessful in court on their own and now face imminent execution—cases, this is to say, in which successive federal petitions offer the only avenue for newly recruited attorneys to follow. See Bryan A. Stevenson, *The Politics of Fear and Death: Successive Problems in Capital Federal Habeas Corpus Cases*, 77 N.Y.U. L. Rev. 699 (2002).

509. *Salinger v. Loisel*, 265 U.S. 224 (1924). For a discussion of the common law backdrop, see Yackle, note 31, at 551–52.

510. The substantive and procedural restrictions placed on second or successive petitions make it essential to determine accurately in each case whether a previous action was genuinely a "first" petition for these purposes and whether a subsequent action is a "second or successive" application. Consider, for example, that a prisoner may have filed a previous habeas corpus petition challenging some aspect of his treatment in prison. See *Preiser v. Rodriguez*, 411 U.S. 475 (1973); notes 558–60 and accompanying text. That kind of action was not an initial collateral attack on the validity of the prisoner's underlying conviction or sentence and should not count as a "first" petition. Cf. *Chambers v. United States*, 106 F.3d 472, 474 (2d Cir. 1997) (holding that a previous habeas petition seeking credit for pre-trial jail time did not invoke §2244(b)). Consider, too, that a prisoner may move to correct the judgment with respect to a previous habeas petition. A motion under Fed. R. Civ. P. 60(b) is part of the proceeding to which it is addressed and should not count as a new and independent "second or successive" habeas petition. *Rodriguez v. Mitchell*, 252 F.3d 191, 198–200 (2d Cir. 2001). Federal courts often attempt to help *pro se* litigants by construing the crude papers they file to be the habeas petitions they presumably want to advance. Cf. *Haines v. Kerner*, 404 U.S. 519, 520–21 (1972) (holding that papers filed *pro se* should be interpreted liberally to avoid unfairness). In this context, however, courts do prisoners no favors by interpreting ambiguous filings to be collateral attacks on convictions or sentences, thus invoking the strict limitations on multiple §2254 petitions and §2255 motions. See *In re Shelton*, 295 F.3d 620 (6th Cir. 2002) (explaining that most circuits decline to recharacterize *pro se* papers in this context without the prisoner's consent). Of course, the label that is placed on a lawsuit is not dispositive. It is essential for a court to determine whether a prisoner is genuinely attempting to challenge a conviction or sentence more than once. See generally Randall S. Jeffrey, *Successive Habeas Corpus Petitions and Section 2255 Motions After the Antiterrorism and Effective Death Penalty Act of 1996: Emerging Procedural and Substantive Issues*, 84 Marquette L. Rev. 43 (2000).

plained in *Stewart v. Martinez-Villareal*[511] that dismissals for "technical procedural reasons" do not trigger §2244(b)(1)'s prohibition on petitions raising the same claim a second time.[512] If, for example, a claim was dismissed on a prior occasion because the prisoner failed to exhaust state opportunities for litigating the claim at that time, the disposition was without prejudice. When the prisoner satisfies the exhaustion doctrine with respect to the claim, §2244(b)(1) permits another petition.[513]

The prisoner in *Martinez-Villareal* filed an initial petition advancing several claims, including a claim that he was incompetent and that his execution would thus violate the eighth amendment as interpreted in *Ford v. Wainwright*.[514] The respondent urged the district court to dismiss the *Ford* claim on the theory that it was premature: The prisoner was not scheduled for immediate execution, and his mental condition might change. The district court agreed, but noted that the dismissal would not affect the prisoner's ability to advance the claim later. Then, when the prisoner revived the *Ford* claim in a subsequent petition, the respondent contended that it was barred by §2244(b)(1). In the Supreme Court, Chief Justice Rehnquist explained that since the district court had dismissed the prisoner's first petition merely because it was premature, the prisoner's renewal of the *Ford* claim did not qualify as a different, successive application for habeas relief on the basis of the same claim.[515]

Under §2244(b)(2), a claim raised for the first time in a second or successive habeas petition may be considered, but only if certain standards are satisfied: (A) the "appli-

---

511. 523 U.S. 637 (1998).

512. Id. at 645.

513. Id. But see note 123 (discussing claims that prisoners deliberately abandon in order to avoid dismissal under the *Lundy* decision).

514. 477 U.S. 399 (1986).

515. Dissenting in *Martinez-Villareal*, Justice Scalia and Justice Thomas insisted that the literal text of §2244(b)(1) barred the prisoner's *Ford* claim and that the Court could not justifiably construe the statute another way merely because it found that result "perverse." 523 U.S. at 651–52. For discussions of instances in which claims are dismissed on procedural grounds and therefore can be presented in subsequent petitions despite §2244(b)(1), see *Benton v. Washington*, 106 F.3d 162 (7th Cir. 1996); Jeffrey, note 510. In *Slack v. McDaniel*, 529 U.S. 473 (2000), the district court dismissed a prisoner's initial §2254 petition on the ground that it included some claims for which state avenues of litigation remained open. See notes 121–23 and accompanying text (discussing the *Lundy* decision). The prisoner exhausted state opportunities for litigating those claims and then filed another federal petition, advancing both the claims he had included in his first petition and additional claims that he had not raised earlier. In the Supreme Court, Justice Kennedy held that the prisoner's second petition was not subject to dismissal as a second or successive application, even though it contained new claims. Since his initial petition was dismissed without prejudice on the basis of the exhaustion doctrine, that petition must be treated in law as though it had never been filed. In the eyes of the law, the prisoner's second petition was actually his first. Justice Kennedy noted, however, that the district court had attached no conditions to its disposition of the prisoner's initial petition and, instead, had simply dismissed it without prejudice. Kennedy thus intimated that a district court might establish conditions that limit a prisoner's options. It seems unlikely that a district court can specify that a prisoner may return to federal court only with the claims contained in his initial application. A condition of that kind would give a dismissal on exhaustion grounds a legal significance that the exhaustion doctrine itself denies. It would have made no sense in *Slack* to confirm that a dismissal for want of exhaustion does not make a subsequent petition successive and then, in the next breath, to invite district courts to defeat that very holding by telling prisoners whose petitions are dismissed that their subsequent applications *will* be successive to the extent they raise new claims. It is more likely that Justice Kennedy meant that district courts can instruct prisoners that, if and when they return to federal court, they must satisfy the exhaustion doctrine with respect to all the claims in a new petition. By that means, district courts might check abusive multiple filings that exploit the Court's decisions in *Martinez-Villareal* and *Slack*.

cant shows" that the claim rests on a "new" rule of "constitutional" law, "made retroactive to cases on collateral review by the Supreme Court, that was previously unavailable;" or (B)(i) the "factual predicate" for the claim could not have been discovered earlier by the exercise of due diligence "and" (ii) the "facts underlying the claim, if proven and viewed in light of the evidence as a whole, would be sufficient to establish by clear and convincing evidence that but for constitutional error, no reasonable factfinder would have found the applicant guilty of the underlying offense."[516]

These standards resemble the standards in §2244(d)(1), establishing filing deadlines,[517] and the standards in §2254(e)(2), governing federal evidentiary hearings.[518] Common interpretive questions thus reappear in this different context. Note, for example, that paragraph (A) and subparagraph (B)(ii) of §2244(b)(2) refer to "constitutional" matters, raising again the question whether non-constitutional claims are precluded by negative implication.[519] In some ways, the standards in §2244(b)(2) are more demanding than the standards in §2254(e)(2). For example, subparagraph (B)(ii) of §2244(b)(2) instructs federal habeas courts to view new factual allegations "in light of the evidence as a whole"—including (presumably) the evidence at trial. Nothing in §2254(e)(2) directs courts to consider the evidence at trial when they are attempting to decide whether to hold a federal evidentiary hearing. A more rigorous test for second or successive petitions may be defensible inasmuch as the prisoners concerned have had one opportunity to be in federal court. In other ways, however, the standards in §2244(b)(2) are *less* demanding than the standards in §2254(e)(2), even though the prisoners affected by §2254(e)(2) have *not* (necessarily) filed previous federal petitions.[520]

In some instances, §2244(b)(2) appears to exclude claims that, by their nature, are likely to be advanced only in second or successive petitions. A *Ford* claim provides an illustration. By hypothesis, a prisoner's claim that he is not competent to be put to death is timely only on the eve of scheduled execution. By that time, a prisoner on death row typically has unsuccessfully sought federal habeas relief on grounds touching his conviction or the imposition of the capital sentence in the first instance. The prisoner is unlikely to have raised a *Ford* claim in that prior habeas petition, either because it would have been premature or because, at that time, his incompetence to suffer execution was not apparent. The prisoner in *Martinez-Villareal* was exceptional in this respect.[521] Recall, moreover, that the filing deadline would not permit an earlier petition to be delayed to allow the prisoner's mental condition to be monitored. As a matter of policy, then, it would seem that a *Ford* claim is quintessentially the kind of claim that should be cognizable in a second or successive petition. Yet under §2244(b)(2), it is far

516. See note 520 (noting the odd grammar in this provision).

517. See note 132 and accompanying text.

518. See note 279 and accompanying text.

519. See notes 151–53, 286–87, 499–505 and accompanying text.

520. See text accompanying note 290. Note, too, that paragraph (A) of §2244(b)(2) expressly places the burden on the prisoner to show that a claim rests on a "new rule," but paragraph (B) makes no express assignment of the burden of proof with respect to newly discovered facts. It is conceivable (if the Court again draws a negative inference) that in cases governed by paragraph (B) federal habeas courts are to proceed without requiring prisoners to bear the burden of persuasion. The text of §2254(e)(2) expressly puts the burden on prisoners to show either new rules or new facts that justify a federal evidentiary hearing. See text accompanying note 279.

521. In *Martinez-Villareal* itself, Chief Justice Rehnquist withheld comment on cases in which prisoners raise *Ford* claims in habeas petitions that follow on earlier applications that were not dismissed on "technical" grounds but rather were adjudicated on the merits. 533 U.S. at 645 n*.

from clear that a *Ford* claim can be advanced in that posture. Paragraph (A) requires a "new" rule, and paragraph (B) demands newly discovered facts that undermine the prisoner's guilt. It is not obvious that a *Ford* claim of incompetence to be executed satisfies either of those requirements.[522]

In any case, the standards in §2244(b)(2) are onerous. Very few "new rule" claims are cognizable, even when they are advanced in an initial application. To be enforceable in habeas corpus proceedings, a new rule must fall within one of the two extremely narrow exceptions to *Teague's* general ban.[523] In this context, moreover, it is insufficient that a new rule exists and that it fits one of those exceptions, so that it *should* be available. In *Tyler v. Cain*,[524] the Court held that paragraph (A) requires a preexisting Supreme Court "holding" that a new rule *is* retroactively applicable as a condition precedent to a prisoner's ability to file a second or successive §2254 petition seeking habeas relief on the basis of that rule. The prisoner in *Tyler* filed one §2254 petition challenging his criminal conviction. After that petition was resolved unfavorably, the Supreme Court held in *Cage v. Louisiana*[525] that a jury instruction is unconstitutional if

---

522. See Stevenson, note 508, at 748; note 291 and accompanying text (noting the same question in cases in which prisoners attacking death sentences seek federal evidentiary hearings). Lawyers who anticipate that their clients will ultimately have *Ford* claims may respond by injecting those claims into first petitions even when it is perfectly clear that they are premature at that time, thus to have the benefit of the Court's decision in *Martinez-Villareal*. Stevenson, at 750 (explaining that this strategy is a good lawyer's only recourse). Then again, many prisoners do not have prescient lawyers, if they have lawyers at all. See note 508 and accompanying text. Other claims are also likely to be advanced only in second or successive petitions and thus raise similar problems for §2244(b)(2)—for example, claims going to the method by which an execution is to be carried out. See *Greenawalt v. Stewart*, 105 F.3d 1287 (9th Cir. 1997) (refusing to consider a challenge to lethal injection in light of a previous petition containing other claims). Cf. *Gomez v. United States District Court*, 503 U.S. 653 (1992) (declining to allow a prisoner to advance a "method of execution" claim in a §1983 action following earlier habeas litigation over the underlying conviction).

523. See notes 335–42 and accompanying text. Paragraph (A) seems plainly to incorporate *Teague's* distinction between new and old rules (though not necessarily the definitions that *Teague* has given to those categories). A rule that is *not* new is applicable in collateral proceedings without any determination of retroactivity; better said, the application of an old rule is not retroactive at all. Notice, then, that paragraph (A) may exclude, by negative implication, claims grounded in rules that were well settled at the time a prisoner's previous petition was filed. If that is what paragraph (A) means, the rationale may be that prisoners should be held responsible for making themselves aware of existing theories and advancing them in an initial petition. That explanation is insufficient, however. In some instances, the content of settled theories is revealed only later. Cf. note 340 (discussing the *Fiore* case). In *Bousley v. United States*, 523 U.S. 614 (1998), for example, the Supreme Court construed the elements of the offense of which a prisoner had been convicted in a way that rendered the prisoner actually innocent. See notes 241–42 and accompanying text. One would have thought that a prisoner in those circumstances would be able to file a second or successive §2254 petition or §2255 motion, so long as he can satisfy the rules governing procedural default. That was the thrust of *Bousley* (where §2244(b)(2) was inapplicable). Yet paragraph (A) makes allowance only for claims that are new. But cf. *United States v. Lloyd*, 188 F.3d 184 (3d Cir. 1999) (finding the reinterpretation of the statute in *Bousley* to be "new" for purposes of the filing deadline established by paragraph (3) of §2255). Consider, too, that if the prisoner did raise his claim the first time around and it was rejected, he may be barred from advancing it again once its validity is demonstrated by a clarifying decision. Under paragraph (1) of §2244(b), a claim that was presented in a prior petition must be dismissed unless it was rejected on some technical procedural ground. See notes 511–15 and accompanying text. In a post–AEDPA case like *Bousley* itself, however, this last possibility may not exist. The prisoner in *Bousley* attacked his federal conviction pursuant to §2255, which contains no analog to §2244(b)(1)). See text accompanying note 547.

524. 533 U.S. 656 (2001).

525. 498 U.S. 39 (1990) (*per curiam*).

it misleads the jury to believe that it can convict a defendant without proof beyond a reasonable doubt. The prisoner then filed a second §2254 petition seeking relief on the basis of *Cage*. In the Supreme Court, Justice Thomas insisted that paragraph (A) refers explicitly to new rules "*made* retroactive... *by the Supreme Court*." Relying on the "plain meaning" of that language, he held that only a formal Supreme Court holding that a rule is retroactive will do.[526]

There was an available alternative interpretation more in keeping with the Court's usual role as the system's ultimate referee.[527] Justice Thomas might have held that the Court itself makes a rule retroactive by announcing the principles for determining the question. Accordingly, in *Tyler*, it was open to say that if *Cage* was retroactively available, the Court had "made" it so by previously establishing that watershed rules of procedure protecting the innocent are excepted from *Teague's* general ban on new rules.[528] If this alternative construction had been placed on paragraph (A), prisoners hoping to have the benefit of new rules once they are announced would be able to file second or successive §2254 petitions or §2255 motions asking the lower courts to decide in the first instance whether a rule fits one of the *Teague* exceptions. If the Supreme Court were dissatisfied with the results in the lower courts, it could grant review in a case presenting the retroactivity issue and give the question an authoritative answer.

The construction that Justice Thomas adopted produces a framework that is awkward by comparison. The Court typically announces new rules in cases on direct review from state court judgments.[529] In that posture, the Court has no occasion to say whether the new rule will be available in habeas corpus proceedings. Even if the Court reaches out to address the retroactivity question, whatever it says will be *dicta*, not holding, and thus presumably will not suffice. The *Tyler* case itself demonstrates that the Court usually cannot decide that a rule is retroactively applicable in a case in which a prisoner raises the question in a second or successive petition. If the Court has not previously rendered a holding on the retroactivity question, by hypothesis the Court has not yet "made" the rule retroactive, and a second or successive application must be dismissed. For that reason, Justice Thomas explained that he was in no position in *Tyler* itself to decide whether *Cage* satisfied one of the *Teague* exceptions.[530] The only viable remaining possibility is that the Court can use some prisoner's first habeas petition as a vehicle for making a new rule retroactively applicable.[531] Even that possibility may be unlikely. Jus-

---

526. In dissent, Justice Breyer argued that the Court had essentially made the necessary retroactivity decision in *Sullivan v. Louisiana*, 508 U.S. 275 (1993), when it held that *Cage* error is "structural" and can never be "harmless." See note 305 and accompanying text (discussing harmless error). Justice O'Connor filed a concurring opinion in *Tyler*, in which she argued that Justice Thomas' opinion did not mean that the Court must expressly hold a new rule retroactively applicable in a "single case" but rather allowed the Court to do so by rendering multiple decisions that "logically dictate the retroactivity of the new rule." 533 U.S. at 668. Justice O'Connor concluded that the *Sullivan* decision lacked that kind of logical power.

527. See Chapter VII, notes 219–45 and accompanying text.

528. See *West v. Vaughn*, 204 F.3d 53, 55 (3d Cir. 2000).

529. See text accompanying note 315.

530. 533 U.S. at 667–68. Actually, the Court might reach a retroactivity issue in the context of a successive petition, notwithstanding *Tyler*. If lower courts allow a petition to go forward because they believe that a prior Supreme Court decision made a rule retroactive, the Court can decide whether its earlier decision counted as a sufficient holding when it reviews the lower courts' application of the new rule to the prisoner's claim.

531. The Court also might make a retroactivity determination on review of a state court judgment regarding a petition for state postconviction relief. But the Court rarely grants review when cases are in that posture. See note 316 and accompanying text.

tice Thomas acknowledged that the Court ordinarily would not grant review in a case to decide a retroactivity issue unless the lower courts are divided on the question.[532] He insisted, however, that the Court is not bound to wait for a division of authority below. And, in any case, he disclaimed any "license to question [the statute] on policy grounds."[533]

Once the Court has decided that a rule is retroactive in the case of one prisoner, then (and only then) other prisoners will be able to file second or successive petitions under the authority of paragraph (A). Yet those would-be petitioners still may be foreclosed if they cannot satisfy the applicable filing deadline. Recall that the filing period for cases of this kind may also turn on actions by the Supreme Court alone.[534] If the Court both announces a new rule and holds it retroactive in one first-petition habeas corpus case, there is little doubt about when the clock begins ticking. It is the date of that decision. If, however, the Court announces a new rule in a direct review case and does not hold it retroactive until some later habeas case, the starting point for the filing period is problematic. If the filing period begins as soon as the Court recognizes the new rule, it may well run out before the Court decides the retroactivity issue and prisoners otherwise eligible to advance second or successive petitions can manage to get those petitions filed in the proper procedural posture.[535]

The procedure that §2254(b) prescribes for multiple §2254 petitions is itself complicated. A prisoner who wishes to file a second or successive petition must be authorized to do so by a circuit court of appeals. Pursuant to paragraphs (A) and (B) of §2244(b)(3), the prisoner must move the circuit court for an order permitting the district court to entertain another petition. Under paragraph (C), a circuit court can authorize a prisoner to proceed in the district court only if it determines that the petition makes a "prima facie showing" that it meets the standards established by §2244(b)(2). Under paragraph (D), the court must act within thirty days after the prisoner files a motion for authorization. Under paragraph (E), the court's decision is neither "appealable" nor "subject to a petition for rehearing or for a writ of certiorari."[536] Finally, under §2244(b)(4), if a circuit court authorizes a prisoner to file another petition in the district court, the district court, in turn, determines whether the application actually satisfies §2244(b)(2)'s standards for second or successive applications.[537]

---

532. See Chapter VII, text accompanying note 223 (explaining that the Court typically accepts cases for review only when there is a difference of lower court opinion to resolve).

533. 533 U.S. at 663 n.5. There was no argument in *Tyler* that *Cage* fit the first *Teague* exception (for substantive rules that place primary behavior beyond the criminal law). Justice Thomas recognized that the only argument was that *Cage* came within the second exception (for watershed rules of procedure), and he may have limited his discussion in *Tyler* to that kind of retroactivity issue. It may be easier for inferior federal courts to deduce that a rule is retroactive if it changes substantive law in the manner of a first-exception rule. Accordingly, the Court may not require a square holding of its own in that kind of case.

534. See notes 154–64 and accompanying text.

535. *Tyler*, 533 U.S. at 667 (Breyer, J., dissenting) ; see note 163 and accompanying text.

536. Justice Thomas cited the thirty-day timetable for circuit court action as another reason for requiring a square Supreme Court holding regarding the retroactivity of a new rule. Circuit panels, he said, have no time actually to make a retroactivity decision and only time to determine whether the Supreme Court itself has already done so. *Tyler*, 533 U.S. at 664. He evidently assumed that the meaning of the Court's decisions is readily apparent.

537. Id. at 661 n.3.

Timetables for federal court action can present constitutional difficulty.[538] Section §2244(b)(3) does not specify what a circuit court is to do if, at the end of thirty days, it is unable either to grant or to deny authorization. Only three possibilities are open. The court might be compelled to grant the prisoner permission to proceed in the district court. That course would have the virtue of ensuring that prisoners are not erroneously denied a judicial forum, but it would sacrifice obvious state interests. Moreover, a compelled disposition (even one favoring the individual) might run afoul of the separation principle and Article III. Congress cannot force an Article III court to reopen a judgment the court considers to be final.[539] It may follow that Congress cannot force an Article III court to make a judgment final when the court has an issue under advisement. Alternatively, the circuit court might be compelled to *deny* the prisoner's request. That response to the timetable would raise even more constitutional problems. The Article III point would be the same, and the court's treatment of the prisoner might violate due process.[540] The only other option is to read the thirty-day timetable to be hortatory only and thus to allow the circuit court to render a proper decision when it can. Mechanically, the court may enter a place-keeping order, but stay that order pending further study. Then, when the court is able to dispose of the applicant's request, it can revisit the matter *sua sponte* and substitute a final judgment. The provision in §2244(b)(3) declaring that a circuit court decision "shall not be the subject of a petition for rehearing" may only bar one of the parties from seeking reconsideration of an order the court considers to be final. The circumstances are different if the court itself has stated that a previous order is *not* final and the court acts unilaterally without receiving a "petition" from one of the parties.[541]

The "gate-keeping" mechanism is presumably meant to promote efficiency by screening unjustified petitions out of the district courts at the door. Yet it also generates a welter of procedural questions and problems. Prisoners typically have no lawyers to explain to them that they must go first to the circuit level before they can proceed at the district level. They thus may file second or successive petitions in the district court and suffer dismissal for want of permission from a circuit panel. Pursuant to 28 U.S.C. §1631, a district court can transfer a premature petition to the circuit court. The circuit court, in turn, can notify the prisoner that circuit permission is necessary and fix a schedule. By the terms of §1631, the one-year statute of limitations established by §2244(d)(1) is met if the petition is timely when filed initially (though erroneously) in the district court.[542] The thirty-day timetable for circuit court action on the motion for authorization begins to run when the prisoner files a proper motion in response to notification of the need to do so.[543]

The Supreme Court held in *Felker v. Turpin*[544] that §2244(b)(3)(E) eliminates the ordinary *certiorari* route to the Court itself, but preserves the Court's independent jurisdiction to entertain habeas applications as an "original" matter. If, then, a circuit court

538. See note 133.

539. *Plaut v. Spendthrift Farm*, 514 U.S. 211 (1995); see Chapter IX, notes 42–44 and accompanying text.

540. See *Logan v. Zimmerman Brush*, 455 U.S. 422, 433 (1982) (holding that a state cannot terminate a party's claim simply because a hearing has not been held within a specified time and that the party is entitled to an "opportunity to present his case and have its merits fairly judged").

541. E.g., *Triestman v. United States*, 124 F.3d 361 (2d Cir. 1997) (following this procedure).

542. See note 191 and accompanying text (discussing filing deadlines in connection with the exhaustion doctrine).

543. See *Liriano v. United States*, 95 F.3d 119 (2d Cir. 1996) (outlining this process).

544. 518 U.S. 651 (1996); see Chapter IV, notes 31–36 and accompanying text.

denies a prisoner's request to file a second or successive petition, the prisoner can seek leave to file a petition for a writ of habeas corpus issued originally from the Court.[545] In passing, Chief Justice Rehnquist said that §2244(b)(2)'s standards for multiple federal petitions "constitute a modified res judicata rule." The "added restrictions" they impose on multiple habeas petitions are "well within the compass" of the "evolutionary process" by which the availability of habeas relief has always been developed.[546]

In the main, second or successive §2255 motions are probably governed by the same general rules. Yet §2255 uses different verbal formulations that might be understood, by negative inference, to establish alternative arrangements for prisoners seeking to file more than one §2255 motion. By contrast to §2244(b)(1), §2255 does not state that a claim that was advanced in a prior §2255 motion must be dismissed.[547] Instead, §2255 (taken literally) contemplates a second or successive §2255 motion irrespective of whether a claim has been presented before, so long as the motion is "certified as provided in §2244 by a panel of the appropriate court of appeals to contain" either "newly discovered evidence that, if proven and viewed in light of the evidence as a whole, would be sufficient to establish by clear and convincing evidence that no reasonable factfinder would have found the movant guilty of the offense" or "a new rule of constitutional law, made retroactive to cases on collateral review by the Supreme Court, that was previously unavailable." By contrast to §2244(b)(3)(C), §2255 does not specify that the circuit court will decide only whether the prisoner can make a "prima facie" showing, but rather appears simply to direct the circuit court to make the judgment whether the prisoner satisfies the stated criteria.[548] And by contrast to §2244(b)(3)(E), §2255 does not state that circuit decisions on whether second or successive applications can go forward are insulated from attack via petitions for rehearing or appellate review.[549]

More importantly, §2255 appears to establish different criteria for successive §2255 motions advancing claims that have not been raised before. A §2254 habeas petitioner who presses a claim based on new allegations of fact must pass two tests. Under paragraph (B)(i) of §2244(b)(2), the prisoner must demonstrate that the "factual predicate" for the claim could not have been discovered previously. And under paragraph (B)(ii),

545. Recall that the Court regards its authority to issue the writ originally as a species of appellate jurisdiction, thus defusing any Article III difficulty. See Chapter IV, note 36. Of course, the Court does not routinely exercise habeas jurisdiction in this way. The Court did it in *Felker*, but has not taken another case since. Cf. *In re Tarver*, 528 U.S. 1152 (2000) (declining to set a case for oral argument even though four members of the Court voted to do so). If the Court were to make "original" habeas cases more routine, it would at the very least have to fashion new means for adjudicating factual issues. See Stevenson, note 508, at 782–87 (suggesting that the Court might accept jurisdiction and transfer cases to district courts).

546. 518 U.S. at 664. Prior to the enactment of §2244(b) as part of AEDPA in 1996, the Court used the doctrine formulated in procedural default cases to determine the circumstances in which prisoners could file second or successive petitions containing claims that might have been, but were not, presented in prior applications. See *McCleskey v. Zant*, 499 U.S. 467 (1991); notes 208–42 and accompanying text. There are differences between those standards and the standards established by §2244(b)(2). In the procedural default cases, prisoners who establish that they were probably convicted erroneously because of violations of their federal rights are excused from default in state court even if they cannot demonstrate cause. See text accompanying note 231. In §2244(b)(2), however, there is a conjunctive "and" between the two elements of paragraph (B). It appears, then, that prisoners must show *both* something akin to cause *and* produce evidence undermining factual guilt—unless they proceed under paragraph (A), which requires a new rule of constitutional law, retroactively applicable.

547. See notes 511–15 and accompanying text.

548. See text accompanying note 536.

549. Id.

the prisoner must show that the newly discovered facts virtually demonstrate his innocence.[550] Under §2255, however, a prisoner advancing a new fact-based claim need satisfy only a version of the second test.[551] The "factual predicate" need not have been undiscoverable earlier.[552]

J. The Ku Klux Klan Act Revisited

There are obvious parallels between habeas corpus proceedings authorized by §2241 and §2254, on the one hand, and lawsuits authorized by §1983, on the other. In both instances, individual litigants can initiate original actions in federal court, contending that state officials have violated their federal rights—typically fourteenth amendment rights. Both §2241 and §1983 establish rights of action. The habeas corpus statute, §2241, also confers jurisdiction on federal courts.[553] The Ku Klux Klan Act, §1983, does not do that independent work. But, of course, the general federal question jurisdictional statute, §1331, invariably fills the void.[554] There are instances, then, in which litigants insist that they are entitled to advance federal claims touching previous state criminal prosecutions in a §1983 lawsuit in addition to (or as a substitute for) a habeas corpus petition filed under the authority of §2241 and §2254.

Ordinarily, §1983 actions offer nothing that habeas corpus does not also deliver, and usually a good deal less. Recall in particular that §1983 suits are *not* exempt from the Full Faith and Credit Statute.[555] In any event, the Supreme Court has construed §1983 not to be available to most litigants who are in a position to seek habeas relief.[556] The ostensible idea is that habeas corpus is the traditional device for contesting unlawful de-

---

550. See text accompanying note 516.

551. The texts of §2244(b)(2)(B)(ii) and §2255 in this respect are a trifle different. Notice, for example, that §2244(b)(2)(B)(ii) refers explicitly to a demonstration that "but for constitutional error" no reasonable finder of fact would have found the prisoner guilty, while §2255 does not employ the "constitutional" modifier with respect to second or successive motions pressing "newly discovered evidence." See note 152 and accompanying text. Read literally, §2255 does not appear to require even a "federal" *claim* as a condition for permission to file a second or successive motion. By its terms, §2255 is satisfied if a prisoner merely advances "newly discovered evidence" that draws his guilt sufficiently into question. This, notwithstanding that a prisoner who is allowed to file another motion must presumably have a meritorious federal claim in order to obtain relief. If a prisoner seeks permission to file a second or successive motion on the basis of a "new" (and retroactively applicable) rule, §2255 *does* demand that the rule be "constitutional" in character. That, notwithstanding that non-constitutional federal claims are cognizable in an initial §2255 motion. See note 297.

552. Some circuits have read §2255 to incorporate anything in §2244(b) that is at all compatible. E.g., *Reyes-Requena v. United States*, 243 F.3d 893, 897–99 (5th Cir. 2001) (holding that the "prima facie" showing standard for circuit panels in §2244(b)(3)(C) applies in §2255 cases); *Triestman*, 124 F.3d at 367 (holding that the ban on petitions for rehearing in §2244(b)(3)(E) also applies in §2255 cases).

553. Federal jurisdiction to entertain habeas corpus petitions is conferred by §2241, which derives from the 1789 and 1867 Acts. See notes 28–31 and accompanying text. The text of §2254 appears to have jurisdictional significance. Yet Congress first enacted that provision in 1948, confirming that habeas is available to prisoners held in custody pursuant to the judgment of a state court. See text accompanying note 46.

554. See Chapter VIII, note 136 and accompanying text.

555. See Chapter VI, note 171 and accompanying text.

556. Prisoners can use §1983 actions to attack the *conditions* under which they are held in confinement. *Wilwording v. Swenson*, 404 U.S. 249 (1971).

privations of liberty. Various features of the habeas process, particularly the exhaustion doctrine, are meant to ensure that prisoners use the habeas corpus mechanism in a proper way at the proper time. It would be inconsistent, then, routinely to allow §1983 lawsuits into the picture—lawsuits that do not entail the same bundle of defining rules and practices.[557]

In *Preiser v. Rodriquez*,[558] state prison inmates claimed that they had been deprived of "good time" credits[559] in prison disciplinary proceedings that failed to meet fourteenth amendment due process standards. They filed a §1983 action in federal court, seeking an injunction ordering prison officials to restore the credits. In the Supreme Court, Justice Stewart regarded the prisoners' suit as a stratagem for eluding the exhaustion doctrine. If the prisoners had advanced their claim in a petition for habeas corpus relief, they would have been required to exhaust state opportunities for litigating that claim before going to federal court. Stewart insisted that they could not avoid that requirement "by the simple expedient of putting a different label on their pleadings." He did not simply hold that, in the circumstances in *Preiser*, the plaintiffs must exhaust state procedures before filing a §1983 action for injunctive relief. Instead, he rested on a narrow construction of §1983. Since the prisoners challenged the "fact or length of their confinement," their suit "fell squarely within [the] traditional scope" of habeas corpus. They were therefore limited to habeas, which occupied the field: The "general" statute (§1983) must give way to the more "specific" statute (§2241).[560]

The prisoners in *Preiser* conceded that they would not have been able to substitute a §1983 suit for a habeas corpus petition if they had sought injunctive relief from the convictions and sentences that sent them to prison in the first place. Justice Stewart insisted that the result must be the same where the prisoners hoped to reduce the duration of their terms by obtaining injunctive relief from the judgment of the prison disciplinary board. Writing for the Court in *Heck v. Humphrey*,[561] Justice Scalia went further. In that case, a state prison inmate filed a §1983 action seeking damages from state police and prosecution officials on the theory that they had violated his federal rights in the course of their investigations and preparation for trial. The prisoner did not seek an injunctive order affecting the "fact or length" of his confinement and thus did not come within *Preiser*. Yet as Justice Scalia understood the complaint, the prisoner did challenge the "legality of his conviction." He premised his claim for monetary relief on allegations of misconduct that, if true, would obligate the state to release him, even if he did not explicitly seek a release order. Viewing the complaint in that way, Justice Scalia said that §1983 would not support it, unless and until the prisoner first established that his conviction was invalid by some other means—for example, by means of a successful habeas corpus action.[562]

---

557. Recall that the Court has also construed §1983 narrowly in other contexts, ostensibly to avoid conflicts with adjacent statutory and doctrinal arrangements. E.g., *Fair Assessment in Real Estate Ass'n v. McNary*, 454 U.S. 100 (1981) (refusing to allow litigants to circumvent the Tax Injunction Act by attacking state taxes in a §1983 action); Chapter XI, notes 44–46 and accompanying text.

558. 411 U.S. 475 (1973).

559. See id. at 477–78 (explaining that "good time" credits are awarded for exemplary behavior in confinement and can substantially reduce the time prisoners must serve).

560. Id. at 487–90.

561. 512 U.S. 477 (1994).

562. Justice Scalia mentioned other possibilities as well. A prisoner may show that the conviction has been reversed on direct review or expunged by executive order. Id. at 486–87. Recall that Scalia interpreted §1983 by analogy to the common law tort of malicious prosecution, which re-

Neither *Preiser* nor *Heck* absolutely bars §1983 actions in all instances in which convicts wish to sue state officials for violating federal rights in connection with state criminal prosecutions. An immediate §1983 suit is barred only if the plaintiff presses a claim that "*necessarily*" implies that a criminal conviction is invalid.[563] If the plaintiff's claim does not do that, §1983 will answer, subject to any other limitations that may apply—for example, abstention[564] or preclusion.[565] In *Heck*, Justice Scalia invited plaintiffs to show that their claims, even if successful, would not draw their convictions into question for any of a number of reasons—including that any violation of federal rights would be ruled harmless.[566]

Between *Preiser* and *Heck*, the Court decided *Wolff v. McDonnell*.[567] In that case, inmates sued prison officials under the authority of §1983 both for damages and for an injunction ordering the defendants to restore "good time" credits. Justice White found §1983 to authorize the suit for compensatory relief, but concluded that *Preiser* barred the injunction. In *Heck*, Justice Scalia set *Wolff* aside because the prisoners there sought damages on the theory that the defendants used "the wrong procedures," not on the theory that they reached the "wrong result," i.e., an erroneous denial of good time credits. Then, in *Edwards v. Balisok*,[568] decided after *Heck*, the Court found a §1983 action for damages not to be authorized where inmates again sued prison officials over prison disciplinary proceedings. With an eye on *Heck*, the prisoners in *Edwards* were careful not to attack the disciplinary committee's judgment, but only its procedures. Nevertheless, Justice Scalia insisted that if the prisoners were right that the procedures violated due process, they "necessarily" implied that the committee's judgment was also invalid. Analogizing the disciplinary committee judgment in *Edwards* to the criminal conviction in *Heck*, Justice Scalia concluded that §1983 did not authorize the *Edwards* suit.

If a plaintiff presses a claim that does necessarily draw a conviction into question, he can maintain a §1983 action only if he first dislodges the conviction by some means. That task can be daunting. There may be no remaining mechanism for asking state courts to revisit the matter, and federal habeas corpus is itself freighted with complexities of heroic proportions.[569] Concurring in *Heck*, Justice Souter argued that a would-be plaintiff who is currently barred from suing for damages must, at the very least, be in custody and thus in a position to apply for federal habeas relief.[570] Justice Scalia explic-

---

quired plaintiffs to prove that the relevant prosecution had been terminated in their favor. See Chapter X, note 406.

563. *Heck*, 512 U.S. at 487 n.7 (emphasis in original).

564. Justice Scalia mentioned this possibility in *Heck*. Id. at 487–88 n.8. He cited *Colorado River Water Conservation Dist. v. United States*, 424 U.S. 800 (1976); see Chapter XI, notes 132–43. Ordinarily, the only form of abstention that is warranted with respect to federal suits for damages is a postponement of federal adjudication, not the relinquishment of jurisdiction associated with *Younger v. Harris*, 401 U.S. 37 (1971); Chapter XI, notes 157–59 and accompanying text. For a discussion, see Chapter XI, notes 60–63 and accompanying text.

565. Justice Scalia noted, but declined to consider, the possibility that the action in *Heck* might have been foreclosed by state preclusion law. 512 U.S. at 480 n.2.

566. See notes 303–14 and accompanying text.

567. 418 U.S. 539 (1974).

568. 520 U.S. 641 (1997).

569. The decision in *Heck* presupposes that litigants who wish ultimately to sue for damages have some near-term access to habeas corpus. If, then, the *Teague* doctrine and §2254(d) are to be reconciled with *Heck*, those features of habeas corpus law cannot desiccate the writ.

570. See notes 75–88 and accompanying text (discussing the custody requirement).

itly rejected that friendly amendment in *Heck* itself.[571] But in *Spencer v. Kemna*,[572] Justice Ginsburg gave Souter another vote for his position.[573] After *Spencer*, it appears that an immediate §1983 lawsuit is not foreclosed if the plaintiff is not in custody and thus has no access to federal habeas corpus as a means of attacking his conviction.

571. 512 U.S. at 490 n. 10.
572. 523 U.S. 1 (1998).
573. Id. at 21 (concurring opinion).

Table of Cases

Index